SEXUALITY NOW

EMBRACING DIVERSITY 4e

JANELL L. CARROLL

University of Hartford

 WADSWORTH
CENGAGE Learning

Australia • Brazil • Japan • Korea • Mexico • Singapore • Spain • United Kingdom • United States

Sexuality Now: Embracing Diversity, **Fourth Edition**

Janell L. Carroll

Executive Editor: Jaime Perkins

Senior Development Editor: Kristin Makarewycz

Development Editor: Mary Falcon

Assistant Editor: Kelly Miller

Editorial Assistant: Jessica Alderman

Senior Media Editor: Lauren Keyes

Marketing Manager: Christine Sosa

Marketing Coordinator: Janay Pryor

Marketing Communications Manager: Laura Localio

Senior Content Project Manager: Pat Waldo

Design Director: Rob Hugel

Senior Art Director: Vernon Boes

Manufacturing Planner: Judy Inouye

Rights Acquisitions Specialist: Thomas McDonough

Production Service: Dan Fitzgerald, Graphic World Inc.

Text Designer: Terri Wright

Photo Researcher: Roman Barnes

Text Researcher: Karyn Morrison

Copy Editor: Graphic World Inc.

Cover Designer: Terri Wright

Cover Images from left to right:

Row 1: © Joel Gordon; © Image Source/Age fotostock RF; © Ebby May/Getty Images RF; © Fancy Photography/Veer

Row 2: both, © Royalty-Free/Masterfile

Row 3: Glowimages/Alamy; jaimaa/Shutterstock; © Royalty-Free/Masterfile; © Radius Images/Corbis RF

Row 4: © Royalty-Free/Masterfile; ©Royalty-Free/Masterfile; © Ebby May/Getty Images RF; © JGI/Blend Images/Corbis RF; © Rodionov/Shutterstock

Row 5: Ocean/Corbis RF; CREATISTA/Shutterstock; © Ron Chapple Stock/Alamy RF; © DreamPictures/Getty Images RF; © Ocean/Corbis RF

Row 6: Royalty-Free/Masterfile; © David Turnley/CORBIS: © Mark Leibowitz/Masterfile; © Supri Suharjoto/Shutterstock; © Poznyakov/Shutterstock

Compositor: Graphic World Inc.

Library of Congress Control Number: 2011936114

Student Edition:
ISBN-13: 978-1-111-83581-1
ISBN-10: 1-111-83581-0

Loose-leaf Edition:
ISBN-13: 978-1-111-84128-7
ISBN-10: 1-111-84128-4

Wadsworth
20 Davis Drive
Belmont, CA 94002-3098
USA

Cengage Learning is a leading provider of customized learning solutions with office locations around the globe, including Singapore, the United Kingdom, Australia, Mexico, Brazil, and Japan. Locate your local office at: **www.cengage.com/global**

Cengage Learning products are represented in Canada by Nelson Education, Ltd.

To learn more about Wadsworth, visit **www.cengage.com/wadsworth**

Purchase any of our products at your local college store or at our preferred online store **www.CengageBrain.com**

Printed in Canada
1 2 3 4 5 6 7 15 14 13 12 11

This book is dedicated to
Greg, Reagan, Kenzie, and Sam,
who have been steadfast in their patience,
support, and encouragement.

ABOUT THE AUTHOR

Dr. Janell L. Carroll received her Ph.D. in human sexuality education from the University of Pennsylvania. A certified sexuality educator with the American Association of Sexuality Educators, Counselors, and Therapists, Dr. Carroll is a dynamic educator, speaker, and author, who has published many articles, authored a syndicated sexuality column, and has appeared on numerous television talk shows. Dr. Carroll has traveled throughout the world exploring sexuality—from Japan's love hotels to Egypt's sex clinics—and has been actively involved in the development of several television pilots exploring sexuality. She has lectured extensively; appeared on and has been quoted in several national publications, Internet news media outlets, and cyber-press articles; and has hosted sexuality-related radio talk shows. She is also the author of a popular press book for young girls about menstruation titled *The Day Aunt Flo Comes to Visit*.

On a personal level, Dr. Carroll feels it is her mission to educate students and the public at large about sexuality—to help people think and feel through the issues for themselves. Dr. Carroll's success as a teacher comes from the fact that she loves her students as much as she loves what she teaches. She sees students' questions about sex as the foundation for her course and has brought that attitude, together with her enthusiasm for helping them find answers, to the fourth edition of *Sexuality Now*.

Dr. Carroll has won several teaching awards, including University of Hartford's Gordon Clark Ramsey Award for Creative Excellence, for sustained excellence and creativity in the classroom, and Planned Parenthood's Sexuality Educator of the Year. Before teaching at University of Hartford, Dr. Carroll was a tenured psychology professor at Baker University, where she was honored with awards for Professor of the Year and Most Outstanding Person on Campus. Dr. Carroll's website (http://www.drjanellcarroll.com) is a popular site for people to learn about sexuality and ask questions.

brief CONTENTS

Contents

▶ **Chapter 1**

Exploring Human Sexuality: Past and Present   1

View in **Video**
1

View in **Video**
12

View in **Video**
20

View in **Video**
22

Chapter 2

Understanding Human Sexuality: Theory and Research   26

View in **Video**
27

View in **Video**
36

Chapter 3

Communication and Sexuality   58

View in **Video**
59

View in **Video**
64

View in **Video**
70

View in **Video**
73

Chapter 4

Gender Development, Gender Roles, and Gender Identity 78

View in Video
79

View in Video
94

View in Video
95

View in Video
100

View in Video
101

Chapter 5

Female Sexual Anatomy and Physiology 106

View in Video
107

View in Video
118

View in Video
121

View in Video
128

▶ **Chapter 6**

Male Sexual Anatomy and Physiology   134

View in **Video**
135

View in **Video**
139

View in **Video**
146

View in **Video**
150

View in **Video**
151

Chapter 7

Love and Intimacy 156

View in **Video**
157

View in **Video**
165

View in **Video**
174

▶ **Chapter 8**

Childhood and Adolescent Sexuality 178

View in **Video**
179

View in **Video**
184

View in **Video**
190

View in **Video**
199

▶ Chapter 9

Adult Sexual Relationships 206

View in **Video**
207

View in **Video**
211

View in **Video**
219

View in **Video**
225

View in **Video**
226

Chapter 10

Sexual Expression 236

View in Video
237

View in Video
240

View in Video
250

View in Video
259

Chapter 11

Sexual Orientation 268

View in Video
269

View in Video
282

View in Video
285

View in Video
290

Chapter 12

Pregnancy and Birth 298

View in Video 299

View in Video 306

View in Video 312

View in Video 320

View in Video 322

Chapter 13

Contraception and Abortion 332

View in **Video** 333

View in **Video** 336

View in **Video** 338

View in **Video** 349

Chapter 14

Challenges to Sexual Functioning 376

View in **Video**
377

View in **Video**
385

View in **Video**
394

View in **Video**
397

Chapter 15

Sexually Transmitted Infections and HIV/AIDS   404

View in Video
405

View in Video
408

View in Video
419

View in Video
424

▶ **Chapter 16**

Varieties of Sexual Expression 434

View in **Video**
435

View in **Video**
443

View in **Video**
444

View in **Video**
448

View in **Video**
450

Chapter 17

Power and Sexual Coercion   460

Chapter 18

Sexual Images and Selling Sex   492

View in **Video**
493

View in **Video**
496

View in **Video**
510

sexuality INDEX

continued

sexuality INDEX

continued

sexuality INDEX

sexuality INDEX

CHAPTER	CULTURE	GENDER	SEXUAL ORIENTATION

9
Adult Sexual Relationships— cont'd
	Hispanic Americans
	    childless marriages, 223
	    divorced, 225
	Intercultural dating, 209
	Interracial marriages
	    illegal, 209
	Marriage, 229
	Marriage customs and practices, 229–231
	Mixed race dating, 209
	Native Americans
	    divorced, 225
	Nonexclusive marriage, 216–217
	Polyamory, 217
	Polyandry, 230
	Polygamy, 229
	Polygyny, 229–230
	Prenuptial agreement, 212
	Sexual behavior, 228–229
			Lesbians
			    emotional closeness in relationships, 218
			    intimate communication in relationships, 218
			    relationships, 218–219
			Mixed race GLB relationships, 209
			Relationship benchmarks in lesbian and gay relationships, 218–219
			Same sex marriage, 221–223

10
Sexual Expression
	African Americans
	    oral sex, 253–254
	Hispanic Americans
	    oral sex, 254
	Love hotel, 258
	Microbicides, 246
	Oral sex, 239
	Sexualized perimeter, 239
		Female anatomy and physiology
		    age-associated changes, 261–263
		Lesbianism, 260–261
		Male anatomy and physiology
		    age-associated changes, 261–263
		Oral sex, 248, 253–254
		Sexual beliefs, 248
		Sexual complaints, 248
		Sexual intercourse, 255–259
			Anal intercourse in gay couples, 260, 263
			High-risk sexual behaviors in gay couples, 260
			Lesbian bed death, 261
			Lesbian erotic role identification, 261
			Lesbians
			    cunnilingus, 253–255
			    oral sex, 260–261
			    sexual behavior, 260–261
			Oral sex in lesbian and gay couples, 254–255
			Sexual positions in lesbian and gay couples, 256
			Sexual behaviors in lesbian and gay couples, 260–261
			Use of sexual fantasy in lesbians and gay men, 248

continued

sexuality INDEX

continued

Preface

Out of all the courses I teach, the human sexuality course is my favorite. Students come to this class with so much interest and enthusiasm—it's hard not to be as excited as they are. My approach to teaching has always been built on the belief that students and teachers have a unique relationship—we teach and learn together. Although it's true that students have much to learn about sexuality, they also are wonderful teachers. I learn a lot in my classes just by listening to my students open up and share their own experiences, beliefs, and attitudes about sexuality. It is through these conversations with students that I've learned to appreciate where students are today and what their experiences in college are like. I've had many conversations about what they want to know and what causes problems in their relationships. All that I have learned throughout my many years of teaching I bring to you in this fourth edition of *Sexuality Now: Embracing Diversity.*

For me, the decision to write this book was an easy one. After teaching this course for more than 20 years, I was aware that many textbooks did not address the experience of today's students. Although I realize that authors include information they think students *need* to know, they often miss teaching what the students *want* to know. I feel strongly that we need to teach students both what they need and what they want to know. For many years, I have kept files of student questions from my classes, travels, and website. These questions are the foundation of the "On Your Mind" feature. This feature enables students to find answers to the common questions they have about human sexuality.

Students who come to this course often have high levels of interest, but their experience and knowledge levels vary tremendously. Teaching a course with such varied student experience and knowledge levels can be tricky at best. But that is why it is important to have a textbook that is inclusive and speaks to every student, regardless of their experiences, family background, knowledge levels, age, race, ethnicity, sexual orientation, or religion. Students have always been the foundation of *Sexuality Now,* and this is even more evident in the fourth edition of the textbook.

▶ NEW to This Edition

This new edition of *Sexuality Now: Embracing Diversity* builds on the successes of prior editions and maintains many of the original features. Large-scale changes include a new design and extensive video program, an increased multicultural and multiethnic focus, and completely updated research with hundreds of new reference citations. There are comprehensive changes in the major areas of sexuality, such as gender, sexual expression, sexual orientation,

contraception, challenges to sexual functioning, sexually transmitted infections, and coercive sexuality. Special attention has also been paid to making this new edition more inclusive of gay, lesbian, bisexual, and transgender students.

This fourth edition also includes increased coverage of cultural, ethnic, gender, and sexual orientation research. This is reflected throughout the textbook in new research studies, figures, features, and photos.

▶▶ CHAPTER OPENING Stories and Videos

One of the biggest changes to this new edition involves a completely new chapter opening story and video package for each chapter. Throughout my travels around the world, I have met many interesting adults, teens, and children who have graciously shared their personal stories about sexuality with me. At the beginning of each chapter, I introduce an individual whose sexual experiences are related to the chapter content. Students will have the opportunity to read each story and also take a "virtual journey" and meet each individual through the medium of video. For example, Chapter 5, "Female Sexual Anatomy and Physiology," begins with the story of Stef, a woman fighting breast cancer; Chapter 9, "Adult Sexual Relationships," begins with the story of Dena and Lenny, a mixed-race couple; Chapter 14, "Challenges to Sexual Functioning," begins with the story of a Dutch physician who shares his thoughts about the importance of regular sexual expression for terminally ill patients; Chapter 15, "Sexually Transmitted Infections and HIV/AIDS," begins with Jessica's story about finding out she was infected with herpes; and Chapter 16, "Varieties of Sexual Expression," begins with Kiki's story about sexual kink. All of these opening stories help to engage students and motivate them to want to learn more. I know you will find these new video segments a valuable part of your classroom activities.

▶▶ VIEW in Video

In addition to the chapter opening videos, videos are placed throughout the chapter to help students gain more knowledge about a variety of key topics. Such "virtual introductions" enable students to more fully understand these issues and take their learning to a higher level. All video segments have been added to encourage student's critical thinking skills and foster classroom dialogue. For example, teens discuss sexting in Chapter 3, "Communication and Sexuality"; college students discuss PMS in Chapter 5, "Female Sexual Anatomy and Physiology"; a man discusses his steroid use in Chapter 6, "Male Sexual Anatomy and Physiology"; two couples discuss the pros and cons of living together in

Chapter 9, "Adult Sexual Relationships"; a woman discusses her preference for nonmonogamy in Chapter 10, "Sexual Expression"; a young father discusses his experiences with an unintended pregnancy in Chapter 12, "Pregnancy and Birth"; a woman who works with a Dutch organization that provides sex for physically challenged people discusses her work in Chapter 14, "Challenges to Sexual Functioning"; and a young woman tells of her experience with an irregular Pap smear in Chapter 15, "Sexually Transmitted Infections and HIV/AIDS."

▶▶ REAL Research

This fourth edition continues to explore cutting-edge research in sexuality by including a "Real Research" feature. This feature developed out of my experiences in the classroom. I noticed that students love to learn "fun facts" about sexuality, and they would share them with their friends outside the classroom. This feature has been consistently rated highly by students. Following are some examples of "Real Research" features:

- Clitoral blood flow in female athletes; voice changes throughout the menstrual cycle; bone density and alcohol consumption (Chapter 5, "Female Sexual Anatomy and Physiology")
- Gender differences in dating versus hooking up; relationship quality in the first year of parenthood; the "seven-year itch" (Chapter 9, "Adult Sexual Relationships")
- Relationship status changes and Facebook; weight and sexual orientation; coming out; gay adoption law (Chapter 11, "Sexual Orientation")
- Morning sickness and breast cancer risk; ultrasounds and childhood cancer; marijuana use and fertility problems; fertility and sexual interest; attachment styles and adjusting to parenting (Chapter 12, "Pregnancy and Birth")
- Motives for contraceptive use; college students and contraception; oral contraceptives and sexual desire; ethnicity and contraceptive use (Chapter 13, "Contraception and Abortion")
- Attitudes and sexually transmitted infection (STI) testing; alcohol use and STIs; female hormones and STI susceptibility; global HIV prevalence (Chapter 15, "Sexually Transmitted Infections and HIV/AIDS")
- Online pornography; porn use by college students; attitudes toward women and porn use; prostitution use (Chapter 18, "Sexual Images and Selling Sex")

▶▶ TIMELINES

Visual representations can often make difficult material easier for students to conceptualize and understand, and for this reason, you will find updated and redesigned timelines. In this edition, there are timelines on the following topics:

- Human Sexuality: Past and Present
- Television
- Important Developments in the History of Sex Research
- Same-Sex Relationships around the Globe
- The History of Assisted Reproduction
- History of Contraceptives in the United States

▶▶ ON YOUR MIND

Throughout my many years of teaching this course, I have collected thousands of questions that students have about sexuality. I have visited colleges and universities all over the world to better understand what today's college students want to know about sexuality and how it differs between the United States and abroad. My search for these student questions has taken me around the United States, as well as to Asia, the Middle East, Latin America, and Europe. I also receive questions about sexuality on my website (http://www.drjanellcarroll.com) and through Twitter (DrJanellCarroll). Student questions are helpful in understanding what information students want. In each "On Your Mind" feature, I answer a student question related to the nearby chapter content. Examples include:

- *Could I get human papillomavirus (HPV) from the HPV vaccine?*
- *Why do men so often wake up with erections?*
- *Can a woman be raped by an ex-boyfriend?*
- *Is it harmful if the sperm do not regularly exit the body?*
- *Is it damaging to children to see their parents naked?*
- *Why do women who live together experience menstruation at the same time?*
- *Can a woman breast-feed if her nipples are pierced?*
- *What are uterine fibroids?*

These types of questions are the backbone of *Sexuality Now* because they reflect what is on students' minds when it comes to sexuality.

▶▶ SEX IN Real Life

In the "Sex in Real Life" features, I present information about sexuality that is relevant to everyday life. These features explore a variety of different topics, such as aphrodisiacs, sex toys, polyamory, social networking, environmental toxins and sperm production, microbicides, Internet sexual addictions, and media use in teens.

▶▶ SEXUAL DIVERSITY in Our World

One way students can challenge their assumptions about sexuality is by understanding how attitudes and practices vary across and among cultures, both within the United States and abroad. In addition to cross-cultural and multicultural information integrated into chapter material, "Sexual Diversity in Our World" features present in-depth accounts of topics such as female genital mutilation, Chinese foot binding, arranged marriage, transsexuality in Iran, AIDS orphans, circumcision, and cultural expressions of sexuality.

▶▶ OTHER Important Features

Throughout each chapter, you will find definitions of important terms in the margin and pronunciation guides that help improve student communication about sexuality. Review Questions conclude each major section so that students can test their retention of the material. In addition, a Chapter Review appears at the end of each chapter to help students review important information.

▶ DISTINCTIVE CONTENT
and Changes by Chapter

CHAPTER 1:
Exploring Human Sexuality: Past and Present

Chapter Opening Video: The first chapter begins with an interview of individuals from three cultures—Japan, Holland, and the United States—and explores the impact of culture on sexual attitudes and behaviors.

Updated and new material includes:

- A new section exploring the importance of **family of origin** in shaping our values, opinions, and attitudes about human sexuality

- Two revised and **updated timelines** on changing attitudes and cultural acceptance of sexuality throughout history and sex on television help students conceptualize difficult materials

- An updated section on **current television shows**—such as *Jersey Shore, 16 & Pregnant, Teen Mom,* and *Gossip Girl*—and the impact of such shows on personal attitudes about sexuality

CHAPTER 2:
Understanding Human Sexuality: Theory and Research

Chapter Opening Video: Valerie, a college student, discusses a unique sexuality research project she designed and implemented on her campus.

Updated and new material includes:

- A review of the recently released **National Survey of Sexual Health and Behavior** (2010), together with major findings from this groundbreaking study

- Detailed review and analysis of privately funded (NHSLS, NCHA, NSSHB) versus government-funded (NSFG, YRBS, ADD Health, NSAM) sexuality research studies

- A new "Sex in Real Life" feature explores **research and skepticism,** critically evaluating various flaws in research studies in an attempt to help students understand how to critically analyze research

- A newly updated and **revised timeline** reviews important developments in the history of sex research to provide students with an overview of major developments; in addition, a summary table of the major theories and a list of questions that each theorist would ask are included to help students conceptualize theoretical differences

- An updated discussion of the use of **Internet-based sexuality research** and the advantages and disadvantages of Internet-based research methods

- A comprehensive exploration of the future of sexuality research, including a review of **problem-driven research** and the importance of collaboration between researchers of various disciplines

CHAPTER 3:
Communication and Sexuality

Chapter Opening Video: Three students, Shadia, Corelle, and Heather, share their thoughts about the importance of communication in intimate relationships.

Updated and new material includes:

- Updated section on the influence of one's **family of origin** on communication

- Updated and streamlined information on communication differences and similarities with respect to **gender, culture, and sexual orientation**

- An expanded section on **computer-mediated communication,** including e-mailing, IMing, texting, and chat rooms, and the impact of this technology on communication patterns; discussion of impact of social networks, such as Facebook, Twitter, and MySpace on communication and the use of avatars

- Revised section on **sexual communication** and the challenges of talking about sexuality; discussion of the importance of a positive self-image, feeling good about oneself, the ability to self-disclose, nonverbal communication, and the importance of trust; discussion of obstacles to sexual communication, such as embarrassment and issues with sexual terminology

CHAPTER 4:
Gender Development, Gender Roles, and Gender Identity

Chapter Opening Video: Sophie, a college student, discusses her experience transitioning gender while at college.

Updated and new material includes:

- A new section on **disorders of sex development** and review of chromosomal and hormonal conditions, together with a revised table outlining the various disorders of sex development

- Updated information on **Bisphenol A (BPA)** and the effect of BPA on the endocrine system

- New section on the **gender spectrum** that explores the **gender binary** and the richness of gender diversity; updated discussion of issues concerning the **transgender community,** including gender dysphoria, gender fluidity, and transprejudice

- Updated information on transsexualism and **medical and surgical gender transitions,** including metoidioplasty; photos of male-to-female and female-to-male reassignment surgery

- Newly updated section on **gender-identity disorder** in childhood

- New section on the impact of the **economy on family systems** and the impact of increased women at work and more stay-at-home fathers

- A review of current debate about the use of **puberty-delaying drugs** in transchildren; exploration of the use of these drugs both in the United States and abroad

CHAPTER 5:
Female Sexual Anatomy and Physiology

Chapter Opening Video: Stef, a woman fighting breast cancer, discusses her experience being diagnosed and treated for breast cancer.

Updated and new material includes:

- A completely revised section on **clitoral anatomy and physiology,** including a new review of all the clitoral structures and research on clitoral magnetic resonance imaging
- Updated research on **female genital mutilation**
- Updated and revised section on **premenstrual syndrome** and **premenstrual dysphoric disorder**
- Updated information about **menstrual suppression** through long-term birth control pills; exploration of safety issues related to menstrual suppression
- Up-to-date information on menopause and the use of **hormone replacement therapy**
- Updated and revised section on **menstrual toxic shock syndrome,** tampon use, and "green" alternatives to tampons and menstrual pads, including the Diva cup
- New research on **breast cancer risk** and various behaviors, including past abortion, antiperspirant use, and bras

CHAPTER 6:
Male Sexual Anatomy and Physiology

Chapter Opening Video: Vic, a 31-year-old man, discusses his thoughts about masculinity and male anxiety about penis size.

Updated and new material includes:

- Updated section on environmental and dietary causes of decreasing sperm counts, and the impact of stress, laptop computer use, biking, smoking, and alcohol use on **sperm production**
- Updated section on **anabolic-androgenic steroid use** and adverse effects associated with its use
- Updated section on **male circumcision**
- Research on **phthalates** and the effects on sperm production and male reproductive health
- Updated information on BRCA genes and **breast cancer** in men

CHAPTER 7:
Love and Intimacy

Chapter Opening Video: Joan and Neil, a happily married couple for 34 years, discuss their relationship and strategies for staying in love.

Updated and new material includes:

- Updated section on the effect of divorce on **childhood attachment styles**
- Expanded information on **neuroscience,** the major histocompatibility complex, pheromones, and brain imaging, and their roles in the development of love
- Revised section on **relationship breakups** and vulnerability to self-blame, loss of self-esteem, and distrust of others

CHAPTER 8:
Childhood and Adolescent Sexuality

Chapter Opening Video: Ruud Winkel, a Dutch biology teacher, discusses his thoughts about sex education and what teens need to know.

Updated and new material includes:

- Current ongoing **governmental research into childhood sexuality,** including the National Survey of Family Growth (NSFG), National Longitudinal Study of Adolescent Males, National Longitudinal Study of Adolescent Health, and the Youth Risk Behavior Surveillance System, with a summary table that shows students the target populations and data methods these four studies used
- New research and figures added from the **National Survey of Sexual Health and Behavior**
- New figures from the NSFG on **teenagers and first sexual experience** and **teenagers and contraceptive use**
- Updated information on **comprehensive and abstinence-only sexuality education programs**
- New figure from Kaiser Family Foundation's nationally representative survey on **media exposure in children and teens**

CHAPTER 9:
Adult Sexual Relationships

Chapter Opening Video: Dena and Lenny, a mixed-race couple, discuss their relationship and their recent engagement.

Updated and new material includes:

- Newly updated and revised section on **interracial and intercultural dating**
- Introduction to the "half-age-plus-seven" rule and exploration of **age differences** in dating couples
- 2010 U.S. Census results on **cohabitation and marriage** and **living arrangements in older adults**
- New section on **mixed marriage,** including prevalence and gender and ethnic differences
- Updated information on **same-sex marriage** and changing patterns of college hookups, buddy sex, and casual dating
- A completely updated section on **same-sex relationships,** together with information on cohabitation, civil unions, domestic partnerships, and same-sex marriage both in the United States and abroad
- A newly updated timeline illustrating **legality of same-sex relationships**
- Updated information on **same-sex divorce**

CHAPTER 10:
Sexual Expression

Chapter Opening Video: A college student discusses her experiences in online sexual chat rooms and the effect these behaviors had on her relationship with her boyfriend.

Updated and new material includes:

- New research and figures added from the most recent **National Survey of Family Growth**

- Completely updated information with data, statistics, and figures from the recently released **National Survey of Sexual Health and Behavior Study**
- Updated information on future directions in **sexual response models,** including research from Leonore Tiefer and Rosemary Basson
- An updated section on **sexual behavior later in life** with data from the National Survey of Sexual Health and Behavior

CHAPTER 11:
Sexual Orientation

Chapter Opening Video: Peter and Stephan, a Dutch married couple, discuss their relationship and struggles along the way.
Updated and new material includes:

- A streamlined section on **sexual orientation theory,** including updated research on biological, developmental, sociological, and interactional theories
- Updated research on the **biological theories of sexual orientation,** including finger length, brain, and hormone research; inclusion of new research on sexual orientation and magnetic resonance brain imaging and spatial ability
- Revised and updated information on the ex-gay movements and **conversion and reparative therapy**
- Updated research on **same-sex parenting and adoption**
- New research on **health problems in lesbian women** and lower levels of preventive care

CHAPTER 12:
Pregnancy and Birth

Chapter Opening Video: Laura and Ozlem, together with their two children, talk about their two-mom family.
Updated and new material includes:

- A newly revised **timeline of assisted reproduction**
- Updated research on **ova cryopreservation** and **preimplantation genetic diagnosis**
- Updated research on **assisted reproductive technologies** for married, unmarried, straight, gay, lesbian, young and old couples
- New figures from the U.S. Department of Health and Human Services on **delayed childbearing**
- New figures from the U.S. Department of Health and Human Services on **ethnicity** and **premature births** and **U.S. cesarean rates**

CHAPTER 13:
Contraception and Abortion

Chapter Opening Video: Joan, a woman who underwent an illegal abortion, discusses her experience and thoughts about abortion today.
Updated and new material includes:

- Updated research and statistics from the recently revised 20th edition of Contraceptive Technology, including a revised

at-a-glance comparison of contraceptive methods table providing students with a quick contraceptive comparison
- Updated research on the relationship between certain progestins in oral contraceptives, including **drospirenone,** and the risk for medical problems
- Updated research on the relationship between **oral contraceptives and breast and cervical cancers**
- New figures from the U.S. Department of Health and Human Services on **contraceptive use** and **contraceptive use by race and Hispanic origin,** from the United Nations Population Division on **worldwide contraceptive prevalence,** from the National Survey of Sexual Health and Behaviors on **condom use,** and from the Alan Guttmacher Institute on **induced abortions**
- Updated research into future directions of contraceptive methods, including oral contraceptives with lower hormone levels, **RISUG,** the **Intra-Vas Device,** and **immunocontraceptives**
- Revised and updated section on emergency contraception, including a discussion about the use of **ella,** a recently FDA-approved nonhormonal form of emergency contraception
- A new section exploring **state laws restricting abortion,** including physician and hospital requirements, gestational limits, public funding restrictions, state-mandated counseling, waiting periods, and parental involvement/notification/consent laws
- Completely updated and revised section on **surgical and medical abortion** procedures
- Updated **timeline of contraceptive methods**

CHAPTER 14:
Challenges to Sexual Functioning

Chapter Opening Video: Interview with Dr. Woet Gianotten, a Dutch oncosexologist who discusses the importance of sexual satisfaction in terminally ill cancer patients.
Updated and new material includes:

- Completely revised sexual response cycle section, including critiques by Leonore Tiefer and alternative female models by Rosemary Basson
- Complete reworking of material with less focus on "dysfunction" and more on "problems"
- A full discussion about the **American Psychiatric Association's proposed** *Diagnostic and Statistical Manual of Mental Disorders,* **Fifth Edition,** including suggested additions such as sexual interest/arousal disorder and ejaculatory disorders, including anejaculation, delayed ejaculation, genito-pelvic pain, and penetration disorders
- Revised figures on **sexual dysfunction prevalence** in the United States based on research by Ed Laumann, Anthony Paik, and Raymond Rosen
- Updated discussion of **vulvodynia** and **vulvar vestibulitis syndrome**
- Recent research on how **breast cancer** and **cancer treatments** affect sexual functioning and satisfaction

CHAPTER 15:
Sexually Transmitted Infections and HIV/AIDS

Chapter Opening Video: Jessica, a college student, discusses her emotional and physical reactions to a recent herpes diagnosis.

Updated and new material includes:

- Completely revised and updated research on sexually transmitted infections and HIV with statistics from the Centers for Disease Control and Prevention's (CDC's) *Sexually Transmitted Disease Surveillance* and the UNAIDS Report on the *Global AIDS Epidemic*

- New figures from the CDC's **Sexually Transmitted Disease Surveillance** (2009), **Sexually Transmitted Disease Treatment** (2010), and the UNAIDS **Global Report on the AIDS Epidemic** (2010)

- Revised sections on **racial and ethnic disparities in sexually transmitted infection (STI)** rates

- Updated information on **STIs in men who have sex with men** and **women who have sex with women**

- Updated recommendations from the CDC for **partners of persons** with syphilis, gonorrhea, chlamydia, human papillomavirus (HPV), herpes simplex virus (HSV), and HIV

- Revised and updated section on the **Gardasil and Cervarix vaccines for HPV,** including new CDC recommendations, negative side effects, and warnings

CHAPTER 16:
Varieties of Sexual Expression

Chapter Opening Video: A young woman discusses her interest in sexual "kink."

Updated and new material includes:

- New information on the proposed move to **depathologize unusual sexual behaviors** in the *Diagnostic and Statistical Manual of Mental Disorders,* Fifth Edition, and consensual versus coercive sexual behavior

- Revised section with updated research on **sexual addiction** and **hypersexual disorder**

CHAPTER 17:
Power and Sexual Coercion

Chapter Opening Video: A college student discusses a recent acquaintance rape experience and some of the reactions of her closest friends.

Updated and new material includes:

- New section on rape and sexual assault legislation on college campuses that explores the Right to Know and Campus Security acts and how various events at schools such as Yale, Harvard, and Princeton universities led to the Obama administration's recommendation for a **national sexual assault awareness campaign** for colleges and K–12 schools in 2011

- Review of new research on child sexual abuse and **eating disorders** in adulthood

- Updated research on **intimate partner violence** and **intimate partner homicide** in both heterosexual and same-sex relationships, stalking, sexual harassment, and cyber-harassment on college campuses

CHAPTER 18:
Sexual Images and Selling Sex

Chapter Opening Video: Two college students discuss the impact of reality shows on sexual attitudes and behaviors in today's college students.

Updated and new material includes:

- Updated information on sex in popular television shows, such as *Jersey Shore, Hung, Gossip Girl,* and *Glee*

- Includes information from Kaiser Family Foundation's nationally representative survey **Generation M2: Media in the Lives of 8- to 18-Year-Olds**

- Revised and updated section on **sex work** that explores the work of prostitutes, escorts, phone sex operators, strippers, and porn stars; exploration of cross-cultural sex work and the difficulties involved in quitting sex work

- New section on **sex trafficking** and **sex slavery** that explores trafficking both within the United States and abroad; review of the work being done to reduce sex trafficking

▶ SUPPLEMENTS TO HELP Teach the Course

▶▶ PSYCHOLOGY COURSEMATE

Cengage Learning's Psychology CourseMate brings course concepts to life with interactive learning, study, and examination preparation tools that support the printed textbook. Watch student comprehension soar as your class works with the printed textbook and the textbook-specific website. Psychology CourseMate goes beyond the book to deliver what you need. Psychology CourseMate includes:

- An interactive eBook
- Interactive teaching and learning tools including:
  - Quizzes
  - Flashcards
  - View in Videos
  - Animations
  - And more
- Engagement Tracker, a first-of-its-kind tool that monitors student engagement in the course

Go to **login.cengage.com** to access these resources.

▶▶ CENGAGENOW™

CengageNOW™ offers all of your teaching and learning resources in one intuitive program organized around the essential activities you perform for class—lecturing, creating assignments, grading, quizzing (Pre-Tests and Post-Tests have been created by Eli Green of Widener University), and tracking student progress and performance. CengageNOW's intuitive "tabbed" design allows you to navigate to all key functions with a single click, and a unique home page tells you just what needs to be done and when. CengageNOW provides students access to an integrated eBook, interactive tutorials, View in Videos, and animations that help them get the most out of your course. Go to **login.cengage.com** to access these resources.

▶▶ WEBTUTOR™

Jump-start your course with customizable, rich, text-specific content within your Course Management System.

- Jump-start—simply load a WebTutor cartridge into your Course Management System
- Customizable—easily blend, add, edit, reorganize, or delete content
- Content—rich, text-specific content, media assets, quizzing, Web links, discussion topics, interactive games and exercises, and more

Whether you want to Web-enable your class or put an entire course online, WebTutor delivers. Visit **webtutor.cengage.com** to learn more.

▶▶ POWERLECTURE™

The fastest and easiest way to build powerful, customized, media-rich lectures, PowerLecture assets include chapter-specific PowerPoint presentations written by Gary Gute of University of Northern Iowa, animations and videos, *Instructor's Manual*, test bank, and more. Included in this edition of the PowerLecture are:

- Images of various types of sex toys
- Centers for Disease Control and Prevention STD Clinical Slides to supplement your lectures on sexually transmitted infections
- Animations of the sexual response cycle for lectures of biological processes

Also included on the PowerLecture is the ability to quickly create customized tests that can be delivered in print or online with ExamView® Computerized Testing. ExamView's simple "what you see is what you get" interface allows you to easily generate tests of up to 250 items. All test bank questions are electronically preloaded.

▶▶ INSTRUCTOR'S MANUAL **with Test Bank**

(ISBN: 9781111841249)

This comprehensive, easy-to-customize, three-ring binder gives you all the support you need to teach an effective course, including the *Instructor's Manual* written by the author along with Lisa Belval of the University of Hartford. This manual contains:

- A detailed outline providing quick access to chapter's content
- A comprehensive video and DVD listing that provides video suggestions for each chapter; a listing of all "View in Videos"

together with three to five suggested discussion questions for each video; inclusion of popular and current television, movie, and YouTube video ideas that relate to chapter content

- Lecture and discussion tie-ins for the "Real Research" features to get students to think critically about sexuality
- Critical thinking questions related to chapter content to help generate classroom discussion
- Suggestions for classroom activities, assessments, and discussions
- Teaching tips for each chapter together with possible pitfalls
- A listing of relevant websites related to chapter content

The Test Bank, written by Amy Popillion of Iowa State University, features multiple-choice questions, true/false items, and short-answer/essay questions for every chapter of the text. Answers, with text references and cognitive level, are provided for all items.

▶ ACKNOWLEDGMENTS

Undertaking a book such as this is a huge task and one that I could never have done without the help of many smart, creative, and fun people. Recognition should first go to all my students who, over the years, have opened themselves up to me and felt comfortable enough to share intimate, and sometimes painful, details of their lives. I know that their voices throughout this book will help students truly understand the complexity of human sexuality.

Second, and of equal importance, a big thank you goes to my family, who helped me pull off this new edition. I couldn't have done it without them. My husband was an endless support, providing around-the-clock statistical and mathematical clarifications. My children have been so patient and helpful and through the process have continued to learn—I am certain they will all grow up with a true understanding of the importance of sexuality in their lives. As in all projects of such magnitude, there are hundreds of others who supported me with friendship, advice, information, laughter, and a focus on the "big picture."

The fourth edition of *Sexuality Now* is the result of a team effort. Jaime Perkins, my senior editor, along with Kristin Makarewycz, my senior developmental editor, had great visions for this new edition of *Sexuality Now,* and both helped support and conceptualize the cutting-edge video package that accompanies this new edition. Mary Falcon, my developmental editor who held down the fort when Kristin was out on maternity leave, was a great support and offered endless help and suggestions. I also thank Dan Fitzgerald, editorial production manager at Graphic World, and Pat Waldo, content project manager at Wadsworth/Cengage Learning, who did a superb job of managing all the production details calmly and creatively. I also appreciate the efforts of Roman Barnes, our photo researcher, who maintained his sanity even through my constant barrage of e-mails, and Sheila Higgins for her detailed eye during copyediting. Vernon Boes, senior art director, and Terri Wright, designer, were instrumental in creating the book's inviting design. I also thank Lauren Keyes, media editor; Kelly Miller, assistant editor; Jessica Alderman, editorial assistant; and Chris Sosa and Janay Pryor in marketing for all their hard work. I look forward to a long and productive relationship with everyone at Wadsworth/ Cengage Learning.

A special thanks to Amy Popillion, Gary Gute, Jason Hans, Joan Garrity, Konnie McCaffree, Eli Green, Laura Saunders, and Lisa Belval for their expert reviews and suggestions to this new edition, and to all the professors using this textbook who shared feedback and offered suggestions.

Also, a big thank you to my videographers, Mark Golembeski, Matthew Sorenson, Johannes Fabery, Jonathan Marks, and Ernie Hiraldo, and to all the men and women who so freely shared their stories with me so that students could more fully understand the reality of many of these issues.

I am so grateful to many others who so willingly gave their time or support (or both), especially students Jessica Morrissey, Shadia Sillman, Kristie Rochette, Danielle Antolini, Rachel Gearhart, Kayleigh Ingraham, and Rachel Eisenberg. Also thank you to my colleagues and friends, including Petra Lambert, Susan "Rietano" Davey, Stef Wood, Carole Mackenzie, Tamara Kanter, Jennifer Siciliani, Kim Acquaviva, Genevieve Ankeny, Barbara Curry, Teo Drake, Kate D'Adamo, Peg Horne, Karen Hicks, Laurie Nassif, Paul Novakowski, Will Hosler, Megan Mahoney, Peterson Toscano, and the Tsacoyeanes family, without whom this would not have been possible.

▶ REVIEWERS

It is important to acknowledge the contributions of the reviewers who have carefully read my manuscript and offered many helpful suggestions. I would like to thank them all for their time and dedication to this project.

▶▶ REVIEWERS

Michael Agopian, Los Angeles Harbor College; Katherine Allen, Virginia Polytechnic Institute and State University; Kristin Anderson, Houston Community College; Veanne Anderson, Indiana State University; Sheryl Attig, University of Arizona; Jim Backlund, Kirtland Community College; Amy Baldwin, Los Angeles City College; Sharon Ballard, East Carolina University; Janice Bass, Plymouth State University; Dorothy Berglund, Mississippi University for Women; Rebecca L. Bosek, University of Alaska, Anchorage; Glenn Carter, Austin Peay State University; Cindi Ceglian, South Dakota State; Jane Cirillo, Houston Community College–Southeast; Kristen Cole, San Diego City College; Lorry Cology, Owens Community College; Sally Conklin, Northern Illinois University; David Corbin, University of Nebraska, Omaha; Randolf Cornelius, Vassar College; Nancy P. Daley, University of Texas at Austin; Christine deNeveu, National Louis University–Chicago; Michael Devoley, Northern Arizona University; Jim Elias, California State University, Northridge; Edith B. Ellis, College of Charleston; Sussie Eshun, East Stroudsburg University; Linda Evinger, University of Southern Indiana; Joe Fanelli, Syracuse University; Jorge Figueroa, University of North Carolina, Wilmington; Anne Fisher, New College of Florida; Randy Fisher, University of Central Florida; Edward Fliss, Saint Louis Community College; Sue Frantz, Highline Community College; Joyce Frey, Pratt Community College; Irene Frieze, University of Pittsburgh; George Gaither, Ball State University; David Gershaw, Arizona Western College; Lois Goldblatt, Arizona State Univer-

sity; Debra L. Golden, Grossmont College; Anne Goshen, California Polytechnic State University, San Luis Obispo; Kevin Gross, East Carolina University; Gary Gute, University of Northern Iowa; Shelley Hamill, Winthrop University; Michelle Haney, Berry College; Robert Hensley, Iowa State University; Roger Herring, University of Arkansas, Little Rock; Karen Hicks, CAPE; Helen Hoch, New Jersey City University; Lisa Hoffman-Konn, The University of Arizona; Susan Horton, Mesa Community College; Jean Hoth, Rochester Community and Technical College; Karen Howard, Endicott College; Jennifer Hughes, Agnes Scott College; Kathleen Hunter, SUNY College at Brockport; Alicia Huntoon, Washington State University; Bobby Hutchison, Modesto Junior College; Ingrid Johnston-Robledo, SUNY at Fredonia; Ethel Jones, South Carolina State University; Shelli Kane, Nassau Community College; Joanne Karpinen, Hope College; Michael Kelly, Henderson State University; Chrystyna Kosarchyn, Longwood College; Gloria Lawrence, Wayne State College; Holly Lewis, University of Houston–Downtown; Kenneth Locke, University of Idaho; Betsy Lucal, Indiana University, South Bend; Laura Madson, New Mexico State University; Jody Martin de Camilo, St. Louis Community College, Meramec; Genevieve Martinez Garcia, George Washington University; Jennifer McDonald, Washington State University; Sue McKenzie, Dawson College; Mikki Meadows, Eastern Illinois University; Corey Miller, Wright State University; Laura Miller, Edinboro University; Robert Morgan, University of Alaska, Fairbanks; Carol Mukhopadhyay, San Jose State University; Jennifer Musick, Long Beach City College; Robin Musselman, Lehigh Carbon Community College; Shirley Ogletree, Texas State University–San Marcos; Missi Patterson, Austin Community College; Julie Penley, El Paso Community College; Robert Pettit, Manchester College; Grace Pokorny, Long Beach City College; Judy Reitan, University of California, Davis; William Robinson, Purdue University Calumet; Jim Santor, College of Southern Nevada; Lisabeth Searing, University of Illinois, Urbana–Champaign; Peggy Skinner, South Plains College; Kandy Stahl, Stephen F. Austin State University; Dana Stone, Virginia Polytechnic Institute and State University; Cassandra George Sturges, Washtenaw Community College; Silvea Thomas, Kingsborough Community College; Karen Vail-Smith, East Carolina University; Jeff Wachsmuth, Napa Valley College; Laurie M. Wagner, Kent State University; Glenda Walden, University of Colorado–Boulder; Michael Walraven, Jackson Community College; Andrew Walters, Northern Arizona University; Mary Ann Watson, Metropolitan State College of Denver; Tanya Whipple, Missouri State University; Julie Wilgen, University of Delaware; Kelly Wilson, Texas A&M University; Midge Wilson, DePaul University; Amanda Woods, Georgia State University; Patty Woodward, Sacramento State University; Lester Wright, Western Michigan University; Susan Wycoff, California State University, Sacramento; Lynn Yankowski, Maui Community College

▶▶ SPECIALIST Reviewers

Talia Ben-Zeev, University of California, San Francisco; Thomas Coates, University of California San Francisco AIDS Research Institute; Eli Green, Widener University; Regan A. R. Gurung, University of Washington; Karen M. Hicks, Lehigh University; Linda

Koenig, Centers for Disease Control and Prevention; Vicki Mays, University of California, Los Angeles; Konstance McCaffree, Widener University; Robin P. McHaelen, University of Connecticut; Leah Millheiser Ettinger, Stanford University; Cheryl Walker, University of California, Davis; Valerie Wiseman, University of Connecticut Medical Center, Department of Obstetrics and Gynecology

▶ NOTE TO the Student

Campus life is different today from what it was when I was in college. For one thing, you have the Internet, cell phones, text messaging, and Facebook. None of these were around when I was in college. We also didn't have DVDs, iPods, iPhones, or iPads, so unlike the majority of students today who tell me they've seen at least one pornographic tape, we never watched any in college. Times were different—we communicated in person or via land-line telephones, and we didn't have emergency contraception, watch reality television, or know what a Brazilian wax was!

College *is* different today, and college textbooks need to reflect these changes. The book you are holding in your hands is contemporary and fun. I think you'll find it easy to keep up with the reading in this class because I've really worked hard to keep the material fresh and thought-provoking. I've included lots of personal stories from students just like you to help in your exploration and understanding of human sexuality. New to this edition are videos containing interviews with various individuals who share their personal stories about sexuality in each chapter. The result is a book that talks to students like yourself, answering questions you have about sexuality.

As you read through the book, if you have any questions, thoughts, or opinions you'd like to share with me, I'd love to hear from you. Many students e-mail me and suggest additions, changes, or just share their thoughts about this book. You can e-mail me at jcarroll@hartford.edu, or contact me through my website: http://www.drjanellcarroll.com or through Twitter (DrJanellCarroll). You can also send snail mail to Dr. Janell L. Carroll, University of Hartford, Department of Psychology, 200 Bloomfield Avenue, West Hartford, CT 06117.

1

Exploring Human Sexuality: Past and Present

View in Video

View in Video

View in Video

View in Video

ABOUT THE CHAPTER OPENING VIDEO – When I went to high school, the health class barely touched on sexuality—it was all about hygiene and diseases. I was excited to take human sexuality in college. It was a great course and it inspired me to pursue sexuality as my graduate specialization. Throughout my studies and work in this field, I have learned that biology is only one component of sexuality. Exactly *how* we express our sexuality and define what is "normal" is shaped by various societal and cultural influences.

To better understand these influences, I've travelled extensively throughout the United States and around the world, consulting with sexuality teachers, experts, and researchers and interviewing ordinary people about their sexuality. What I've gained through these experiences has been invaluable. All my education, training, and research about the interplay of biology, society, and culture gave me *knowledge,* but experiencing other societies and cultures gave me *understanding.* Two important

purposes of this textbook is to help you gain knowledge and an understanding about sexuality. However, to help you gain a true understanding of the varieties of cultural and individual differences in human sexuality, I invite you to take a journey with me, virtually, through the medium of video.

Our virtual exploration into human sexuality begins with a comparison of sexual attitudes, behaviors, and practices in three very different countries: Japan, Holland, and the United States. During one of my visits to Japan, I asked men and women whether they thought Japanese culture was "open" or "closed" when it came to sexuality. Although many people refused to talk to me when they heard the word "sex," those who did stay told me that the Japanese are very "closed" and conservative when it comes to sex. *"It's the culture,"* they said. One man told me that he "loves sex," but then he ran away!

In contrast, during a recent trip to Holland, I was able to talk with several Dutch teens about sexuality. Holland has a reputation

for being one of the most open and liberal countries when it comes to sexuality. Many Dutch parents allow their teenage sons and daughters to have sex at home! For example, one of the teens you will meet in this video told me, *"When my mom calls for dinner and we're late and our hair is all messy then my parents know what has happened. They know and it's okay."*

In my U.S. travels, I've talked to many college students about what their parent's knew about their early sexual behaviors. Many have told me their parents had no clue when they lost their virginity (and they preferred to keep it that way).

I hope this book and its accompanying videos help to broaden your knowledge and understanding of your own sexuality while engaging your interest in the wide spectrum of cultural and individual differences that make human sexuality such a fascinating subject. ‖

Janell Carroll

"Our culture has a powerful influence on our attitudes about sex."
—CHAPTER OPENING VIDEO

View in Video

To watch the entire interview, go to Psychology CourseMate at **login.cengagebrain.com.**

Welcome to the study of human sexuality! Many students come to this class believing they already know everything they need to know about human sexuality. The truth is, everyone comes to this class with differing levels of knowledge. Some students have parents who provided open and honest conversation about **sexuality,** whereas others had parents who never spoke a word about sex. Some students have had comprehensive levels of sex education in school, whereas others have had none and may bring knowledge about sex gained only from years of watching Internet porn. In the end, it doesn't really matter what knowledge level you bring into this class. I guarantee that you will learn plenty more.

Although some people believe that we don't need to be taught about human sexuality, it might surprise you to know that most of sexuality is learned. One of the biggest influences in shaping our values, opinions, and attitudes about human sexuality is our **family of origin.** Our journey begins with our family—which could be our mother and father, step-parents, grandparents, or other caregivers. We learned how to communicate, show affection, deal with emotions, and many more things that contribute to the man or woman we are today. In the end, we learned to be who we are, for better or worse, from our interactions and experiences in our family. We will talk much more about this in the upcoming chapters.

We also learn about sexuality from our friends, romantic partners, religion, culture, society, and many other sources. Our exposure is augmented by the fact that we live in a sex-saturated society that uses sexuality to sell everything from cologne to cars. However, we also live in a time when there is a taboo against honest information about human sexuality. Some people believe that providing sexuality information can cause problems—including increased teenage sexual activity and adolescent pregnancy rates. Others believe that learning about sexuality can empower people to make healthy decisions both today and in the future.

Many recent events have profoundly affected the way we view sexuality. From the ongoing debates about the legality of same-sex marriage to the advent of continuous birth control pills that eliminate menstrual periods, the media is full of stories relating to our sexuality and relationships with others. These stories tell us much about how our culture understands, expresses, and limits our sexuality. The continuing controversy over coed dorm rooms on college campuses, mandatory vaccinations for **sexually transmitted infections (STIs),** or the availability of birth control in middle schools or high schools all influence and shape our sexuality.

In this opening chapter, we define sexuality, examine sexual images in our culture, and explore the effect of the media's preoccupation with sex. A historical exploration of sexuality follows, in which we review the early evolution of human sexuality beginning with the impact of walking erect to ancient civilizations. Following that, we look at religion's role in sexuality and examine

---

REAL RESEARCH 1.1   The National Survey of Sexual Health and Behavior, one of the largest nationally representative studies of sexuality ever done, found enormous variability in the repertoires of U.S. adults (Reece et al., 2010). Most couples engage in several different sexual behaviors when they have "sex."

---

some of the early sexual reform movements. Finally, we take a look at modern developments and influences that continue to shape our sexuality today.

SEXUALITY Today

Human sexuality is grounded in biological functioning, emerging in each of us as we develop, and is expressed by cultures through rules about sexual contact, attitudes about moral and immoral sexuality, habits of sexual behavior, patterns of relations between the sexes, and more. In this section, let's look at how we define sexuality and discuss how our sexuality is affected by the media and changing technologies.

ONLY HUMAN: What Is Sexuality?

The sexual nature of human beings is unique in the animal kingdom. Although many of our fellow creatures also display complex sexual behaviors, only human beings have gone beyond instinctual mating rituals to create ideas, laws, customs, fantasies, and art around the sexual act. In other words, although sexual intercourse is common in the animal kingdom, sexuality is a uniquely human trait.

Sexuality is studied by **sexologists,** who specialize in understanding our sexuality, but also by biologists, psychologists, physi-

Vaccines to protect teens from certain sexually transmitted infections are recommended well before teens become sexually active. Why do you think some parents might not be comfortable getting such vaccines this early?

© Janell Carroll

---

sexuality
A general term for the feelings and behaviors of human beings concerning sex.

family of origin
The family into which one is born and raised.

sexually transmitted infection (STI)
Infection that is transmitted from one person to another through sexual contact. This used to be called sexually transmitted disease (STD) or venereal disease (VD).

sexologist
A person who engages in the scientific study of sexual behavior. Sexologists can be scientists, researchers, or clinicians, and can hold a variety of different graduate degrees.

Sex in Real Life ▶▶ How Do You Decide What Type of Sex You'll Engage in?

All sexually active people make decisions about when, where, and with whom they will engage in sexual activity. For most people, at least part of that decision is based on their views of what behaviors are morally acceptable, which may be derived from their religious beliefs, upbringing, family of origin, or personal decisions about the kind of person they want to be. For example, some people would not have sex with a partner whom they did not love, perhaps because they feel it is meaningless, immoral, or against God's wishes; others find it acceptable if both partners are willing and go into the encounter openly and freely. There are few areas of life in which moral principles are so clearly and commonly debated. Why is it that sexuality evokes so strong a moral response in us?

Human sexual behavior differs from that of all other animals, in part because of our moral, religious, legal, and interpersonal values. How simple it seems for animals, who mate without caring about marriage, pregnancy, or hurting their partner's feelings! Human beings are not (typically) so casual about mating; every culture has developed elaborate rituals, rules, laws, and moral principles that structure sexual relations. The very earliest legal and moral codes archeologists have uncovered discuss sexual behavior at great length, and rules about sexual behavior make up a great part of the legal and ethical codes of the world's great civilizations and religions.

Sexuality is a basic drive, and it is one of the few that involves intimate, one-on-one interaction with another person's basic needs. Conflicts may arise when our own needs, feelings, fears, and concerns are not the same as our partners'. People can be hurt, used, and taken advantage of sexually, or they can be victims of honest miscommunication, especially because sex is so difficult for many people to discuss.

Sexuality is also closely related to the formation of love bonds and to procreation. Every society has a stake in procreation, for without adequate numbers of people, a society can languish, and with too many people, a society can be overwhelmed. Most societies create rules to control the size of their population, such as the outlawing of contraception when childbirth is encouraged or the availability of free contraception during population explosions (Vesperini, 2010).

There are certainly other possible explanations for the moral and ethical standards that have developed around sexual behavior. Why do you think morality and sexuality are so closely bound?

cians, anthropologists, historians, sociologists, political scientists, those concerned with public health, and many other people in scholarly disciplines. For example, political scientists may study how sexuality reflects social power; powerful groups may have more access to sexual partners or use their legislative power to restrict the sexual behaviors of less powerful groups.

Few areas of human life seem as contradictory and confusing as sexuality. The United States is often thought of as a sexually "repressed" society, yet images of sexuality are all around us. We tend to think that everyone else is "doing it"; still, we are often uncomfortable talking about sex. Some feel that we should all be free to explore our sexuality; others believe that there should be strong moral restrictions around sexual behavior. To some, only sex between a man and a woman is natural and acceptable; others believe that all kinds of sexual expression are equally "natural" and valid. Many people find it puzzling that others find sexual excitement by being humiliated or spanked, exposing themselves in public, or wearing rubber. Although parents teach their children about safe driving, fire safety, and safety around strangers, many are profoundly uncomfortable instructing their children on safe sexual practices.

▶▶ SEX SELLS: The Impact of the Media

Modern life is full of visual media. Magazines, newspapers, book covers, CD and DVD packaging, cereal boxes, and other food products are adorned with pictures of people, scenes, or products. Advertisements peer at us from billboards, buses, cell phones, iPods, iPads, and the Internet, and anywhere else that advertisers can buy space. Television, movies, computers, and other moving visual images surround us almost everywhere we go, and we will only depend on them more as information technology continues to develop. We live in a visual culture with images we simply cannot escape.

Many of these images are subtly or explicitly sexual. Barely clothed females and shirtless, athletic males are so common in ads that we scarcely notice them anymore. Although we may not

The target audience for many reality television shows, including *Jersey Shore,* is often teenage girls. What messages do you think such shows give girls about gender, sex, and relationships?

Contour by Getty Images

immediately recognize it, many of the advertisements we are exposed to use Photoshop to digitally alter the models' bodies and faces—raising beauty standards to unattainable levels. Various countries have proposed legislation that would require warning labels on photos that have been retouched (Myslewski, 2009).

Sex is all over television today. The majority of movies, even some of those directed at children, have sexual scenes that would not have been permitted in movie theaters 50 years ago. Popular shows such as *Jersey Shore* and *Gossip Girl* highlight sexual issues, whereas shows such as *16 and Pregnant* and *Teen Mom* explore teenage pregnancy, showcasing the real lives of teen mothers. Critics argue that such shows "glamorize" teen pregnancy and have led to the greater acceptance of teenage pregnancy (Bates, 2010; see Real Research 1.2).

The Internet has also changed patterns of social communication and relationships (Gutkin, 2010; Niedzviecki, 2009; Lever et al., 2008). Social networking sites, such as Facebook or MySpace, together with e-mailing, texting, instant messaging, Skyping, and iChat have changed the way people communicate with one another. Now you can communicate through tweets, blogs, uploads, updates, posts, or chats. You can text a breakup message, let the world know you're dating someone with the click of a button, and get an "app" for just about anything you need. We talk more about these social networks in Chapter 3 (Communication).

Countless websites are also available, offering information and advice and providing visitors with answers to their most personal questions. Vibrators and other sex toys, pornographic pictures and videos, and access to a variety of personal webcam sites can be purchased online, and a variety of blogs cater to just about any conceivable fantasy. The Internet allows for anonymity and provides the freedom to ask questions, seek answers, and talk to others about sexual issues.

All of this information has not been lost on today's teenagers. Today's teens rate the media as one of their leading sources of sex information (Strasburger & The Council on Communications and Media, 2010; Strasburger, 2005). American teens spend more than 7 hours a day with a variety of different media filled with sexual messages and images (Rideout et al., 2010). Yet, the majority of this media information is not educational. Although 70% of teen shows in the United States contain sexual content, less than 10% of these shows contain information on risks associated with sexual activity (Strasburger & The Council on Communications and Media, 2010). Even so, many young people accept these sexual portrayals as realistic, even though the information is often inaccurate and misleading.

We now turn our attention to the history of human sexuality, from prehistoric times to the present. Of course, in the space of one chapter, we cannot begin to cover the variety and richness of human sexual experience. However, this overview will give you an idea of how varied human cultures are, while also showing that human beings throughout history have had to grapple with the same sexual issues that confront us in American society today. As we begin our review of this material, pay attention to the way that at some points in history, attitudes about sexuality were very conservative, whereas at other times, attitudes became more liberal. The pendulum continues to swing back and forth today as our society debates issues related to human sexuality, such as sex education, birth control, and same-sex marriage.

REAL RESEARCH 1.2 In a recent study on sexually active teens, 1 in 5 girls and 1 in 4 boys said they would be pleased if they got pregnant or impregnated someone (ABMA ET AL., 2010).

◀ review QUESTIONS

1 Explain how sexuality can be both contradictory and confusing, and provide one example of how this might be so.

2 Identify some of the ways we learn about sexuality, and give two reasons for questioning the accuracy of these sources.

3 Explain how today's teenagers get messages about sexuality through various media.

timeline Human Sexuality: **Past and Present**

200,000 years ago	**1000** B.C.	**1000** B.C.	**500** B.C.	**400** B.C.	**200** B.C.
First *Homo sapiens* appear.	Early **Hebrews** develop the **Hebrew Bible**—conservative view of sexuality **focuses on marital sexuality and procreation.**	Early **Greek** culture encourages sexual permissiveness—men and **male form is idealized.**	Early **Roman** influence leads to lessening restrictions on sexuality—**focus on "active" male and "passive" female roles** in sexual behavior.	The ***Kamasutra*, an Indian Hindu text,** encourages **sexual liberalism.**	**Chinese philosophy** focuses on the **Tao, views sexual behavior as a natural joining of yin and yang.**

▶ THE EARLY EVOLUTION
of Human Sexuality

Our ancestors began walking upright more than 3 million years ago, according to recent fossil records. Before that, our ancestors were mostly **quadrupeds** (KWA-drew-peds) who stood only for brief moments—as baboons do now—to survey the terrain. The evolution of an upright posture changed forever the way the human species engaged in sexual intercourse.

▶▶ STAND UP AND LOOK AROUND: **Walking Erect**

In an upright posture, the male genitals are rotated to the front of the body, so merely approaching someone involves displaying the genitals. Because male confrontation often involved acts of aggression, the **phallus**—the male symbol of sex and potency—became associated with displays of aggression. In other words, upright posture may have also contributed to a new tie between sexuality and aggression (Rancour-Laferriere, 1985).

The upright posture of the female also emphasized her breasts and hips, and the rotation of the female pelvis forward (the vagina faces the rear in most quadrupeds) also resulted in the possibility of face-to-face intercourse. Because more body area is in contact in face-to-face intercourse than in rear entry, the entire sensual aspect of intercourse was enhanced, manipulation of the breasts became possible (the breasts are sexual organs only in humans), and the female clitoris was much more easily stimulated. Only in human females does orgasm seem to be a common part of sexual contact.

It may seem that ancient civilizations were very different from ours, **yet some societies had surprisingly modern attitudes about sex.**

▶▶ SEXUALITY IN **the Ancient Mediterranean**

It may seem that ancient civilizations were very different from ours, yet some societies had surprisingly modern attitudes about sex. Although the Egyptians condemned adultery, especially among women, it may still have been fairly common. A woman in Egypt had the right to divorce her husband, a privilege, as we will see, that was not allowed to Hebrew women. Egyptians seem to have invented male circumcision, and Egyptian workers left behind thousands of pictures, carvings, and even cartoons of erotic scenes (Doyle, 2005). All told, ancient Egyptians had sexual lives that do not seem all that different from the way humans engage in sex throughout the world today.

ON YOUR MIND **1.1**

Do female primates experience orgasm?

Yes, some do, although it is relatively rare compared with human females. Female primates rarely masturbate, although occasionally they stimulate themselves manually during intercourse. Bonobos (pygmy chimpanzees) do have face-to-face intercourse on occasion and may reach orgasm. However, most chimpanzees engage in rear-entry intercourse, a position that does not favor female orgasm (Margulis & Sagan, 1991).

From writings and art, we know a bit about ancient accounts of STIs (some ancient medical texts discuss cures), menstruation (there were a variety of laws surrounding menstruation), circumcision (which was first performed in Egypt and possibly other parts of Africa), and contraception (heterosexual Egyptian women inserted sponges or other objects in the vagina). Because a great value was put on having as many children as possible—especially sons, for inheritance purposes—abortion was usually forbidden. Prostitution was common, and **temple prostitutes** often greeted worshippers.

It is important to remember that throughout history, men dominated public life and women's voices were effectively silenced; we know far more about what men thought, how men lived, and even how men loved than we do about the lives and thoughts of women. In fact, it was only relatively recently in human history that women's voices have begun to be heard on a par with men's in literature, politics, art, and other parts of public life.

Of all the ancient civilizations, modern Western society owes the most to the interaction of three ancient cultures: Hebraic (Hebrews), Hellenistic (Greek), and Roman. Each made a contribution to our views of sexuality, so it is worthwhile to examine each culture briefly. At the beginning of each section, we give a date as to when these effects began.

quadruped
Any animal that walks on four legs.

phallus
Symbol of power and aggression.

temple prostitutes
Women in ancient cultures who would have sex with worshippers at pagan temples to provide money for the temple or to worship the gods.

50	500	500	1050	1300
Christianity begins, leading to a **condemnation of sexuality,** which is **associated with sin**—attitudes about sexuality become more conservative.	**Early Middle Ages**—church's influence further **strengthens conservative attitudes** about sexuality.	**Islam views sexuality as acceptable only in marriage**—attitudes become more conservative.	**High Middle Ages** brings a **less conservative view** of sexuality.	The **Renaissance brings increasingly liberal attitudes about sexuality** and **more gender equality.**

Greek cups, plates, and other pottery often depicted erotic scenes, such as this one from the fifth century B.C.

ON YOUR MIND 1.2

I've heard that the Greeks believed that sex between men and boys was a "natural" form of human sexuality. Couldn't they see that it was perverted?

One society's perversion may be another society's accepted sexual practice. Every culture sees its own forms of sexuality as natural and obvious—including ours. Not too long ago in our own society, it seemed "obvious" to most people that things such as oral sex and anal sex were perversions (they are still technically illegal in many states), and that masturbation was a serious disease that could lead to mental illness. Today, many people see these acts as part of a healthy sexual life. Sexual beliefs and practices are often very different in other cultures and they can change over time within these cultures.

for centuries thereafter. The Hebrew Bible sees the marital union and its sexual nature as an expression of love and affection, as a man and woman "become one flesh."

The Hebrews (1000–200 B.C.)

The Hebrew Bible, which was put into written form sometime between 800 and 200 B.C., contains explicit rules about sexual behavior, such as forbidding adultery, male homosexual intercourse, and sex with various family members and their spouses. The Bible includes tales of sexual misconduct—ranging from incest, to sexual betrayal, to sex outside of marriage, to sexual jealousy—even by its most admired figures. Yet, the Bible also contains tales of marital love and acknowledges the importance of sexuality in marital relations.

The legacy of the Hebrew attitude toward sexuality has been profound. The focus on marital sexuality and procreation and the prohibition against such things as homosexuality were adopted by Christianity and formed the basis of sexual attitudes in the West

The Greeks (1000–200 B.C.)

The Greeks were more sexually permissive than the Hebrews. Their stories and myths are full of sexual exploits, incest, rape, and even **bestiality** (beest-ee-AL-i-tee; as when Zeus, the chief god, takes the form of a swan to rape Leda). The Greeks clearly distinguished between love and sex in their tales, even giving each a separate god: Aphrodite was the goddess of sexual intercourse; Eros (her son) was the god of love.

Greece was one of the few major civilizations in Western history to institutionalize homosexuality successfully. In Greek **pederasty** (ped-er-AST-ee), an older man would befriend a postpubescent boy who had finished his orthodox education and aid in the boy's continuing intellectual, physical, and sexual development. In return, the boy would have sex with his mentor. The mentor was always the active partner, the penetrator; the student was the passive partner. Socrates, for example, was supposed to have enjoyed the sexual attentions of his students (all male), and his students expressed jealousy when he paid too much physical attention to one or another.

In Greece, men and the male form were idealized. When the ancient Greek philosophers spoke of love, they did so almost exclusively in **homoerotic** terms. Man's nonsexual love for another

bestiality
The act of having intercourse with an animal.

pederasty
Sexual contact between adult men and (usually) postpubescent boys.

homoerotic
The representation of same-sex love or desire.

timeline Human Sexuality: **Past and Present**

1400	1500	1700	1800	1820
A **backlash to growing liberalism** leads to concerns over the practice of witchcraft—**witch hunts reestablish male dominance** and acceptable roles of women.	The **Protestant Reformation continues conservative views of sexuality.**	The **Enlightenment brings a questioning of morals,** and with this a **more liberal attitude about sexuality**—sexual pleasure is viewed as natural and desirable.	The **Victorian Era** begins—sexual attitudes become more conservative and **women are considered delicate and fragile.**	**Free love movement** begins, liberalizing attitudes about sexuality—**love,** rather than marriage, **should lead to sexual behavior.**

man was seen as the ideal love, superior to the sexual love for women. Plato discussed such an ideal love, and so we have come to call friendships without a sexual element **platonic.**

The Romans (500 B.C.–700 A.D.)

Rome had few restrictions about sexuality until late in the history of the empire, so early Romans had very permissive attitudes toward homosexual and bisexual behaviors, which were entirely legal until the sixth century A.D. (Boswell, 1980). Marriage and sexual relations were viewed as a means to improve one's economic and social standing; passionate love almost never appears in the written accounts handed down to us. Bride and groom need not love each other, for that kind of relationship would grow over the life of the marriage; more important was fair treatment, respect, and mutual consideration. Wives even encouraged their husbands to have slaves (of either gender) for the purposes of sexual release.

*Early Romans had **very permissive attitudes** toward homosexual and bisexual behaviors.*

In Rome, as in Greece, adult males who took the passive sexual position in homosexual encounters were viewed with scorn, whereas the same behavior by youths, foreigners, slaves, or women was seen as an acceptable means to try to please a person who could improve one's place in society. Still, long-term homosexual unions did exist.

▶▶ SEXUALITY IN Ancient Asia

Chinese and Indian civilizations also had unique views of sexuality. In Indian culture, Hinduism and rebirth give life direction. In Chinese culture, people work to live in harmony with the Tao, which is made up of **yin and yang.**

India (Beginning About 400 B.C.)

Hinduism, the religion of India for most of its history, concentrates on an individual's cycle of birth and rebirth, or **karma.** Karma involves a belief that a person's unjust deeds in this life are punished by suffering in a future life, and suffering in this life is undoubtedly punishment for wrongs committed in previous incarnations. The goal, then, is to live a just life now to avoid suffering in the future. One of the responsibilities in this life is to marry and procreate, and because sex is an important part of those responsibilities, it was generally viewed as a positive pursuit, and even a source of power and magic.

There are legends about great women rulers early in India's history, and women had important roles in ceremonies and sacrifices. Still, India's social system, like others we have mentioned, was basically **patriarchal** (PAY-tree-arc-al), and Indian writers (again, mostly male) shared many of the negative views of women that were characteristic of other civilizations. Being born a woman was seen as a punishment for sins committed in previous lives. In fact, murdering a woman was not seen as a particularly serious crime, and **female infanticide** (in-FAN-teh-side) was not uncommon (V. L. Bullough, 1973).

By about 400 B.C., the first and most famous of India's sex manuals, the ***Kamasutra*** (CAH-mah-SUH-trah), appeared. India is justifiably famous for this amazing book. The *Kamasutra* discusses not just sex but the nature of love, how to make a good home and family, and moral guidance in sex and love. The *Kamasutra* is obsessive about naming and classifying things. In fact, it categorizes men by the size of their penis (hare, bull, or horse man) and women by the size of their vagina (deer, mare, or cow-elephant woman). A good match in genital size was preferred between heterosexual partners, but barring that, a tight fit was better than a loose one (Tannahill, 1980). The *Kamasutra* recommends that women learn how to please their husbands, and it provides instructions on sexual techniques and illustrations of many sexual positions, some of which are virtually impossible for people who cannot twist their body like a pretzel. The *Kamasutra* proposes that intercourse should be a passionate activity that includes scratching, biting, and blows to the back, accompanied by a variety of animal noises.

platonic
Named after Plato's description, a deep, loving friendship that is devoid of sexual contact or desire.

yin and yang
According to a Chinese belief, the universe is run by the interaction of two fundamental principles: yin, which is negative, passive, weak, yielding, and female; and yang, which is positive, assertive, active, strong, and male.

karma
The belief that a person's actions in this and other lives determines his or her fate in future lives.

patriarchal
A society ruled by the male as the figure of authority, symbolized by the father's absolute authority in the home.

female infanticide
The killing of female infants; practiced in some countries that value males more than females.

Kamasutra
Ancient Indian sex manual.

1873	Late 1800s–early 1900s	1920	1940s and 1950s	Early 1960s
Passage of the Comstock Act prohibiting the mailing of contraceptive information (not struck down until 1965) is indicative of **attitudes about sexuality becoming more conservative.**	**Medical model of sexuality** and **social hygiene movement** lead to **increasingly conservative attitudes.**	**Passage of the 19th Amendment** giving women the right to vote and the beginning of the **first sexual revolution** leads to more liberal attitudes about sexuality.	**Growing liberalism** with the publication of Kinsey's *Sexual Behavior in the Human Male* and *Sexual Behavior in the Human Female.*	**Second sexual revolution** leads to more liberal attitudes. Liberal view of sexuality increases when the **FDA approves the first birth control pill.**

It is often difficult to imagine how sexuality and gender are viewed outside the United States. We become accustomed to norms, practices, and behaviors where we live and may not understand how other cultures view the same practices differently. In this chapter, we've looked at images of beauty in U.S. culture. It may seem strange that some men and women undergo nose jobs, breast implants, liposuction, tattooing, piercing, waxing, or other procedures to look and feel more beautiful. Throughout history, cultures have searched for unique ways to achieve beauty, especially for women. At one point in U.S. history, exceptionally small waists on women were considered beautiful, and many women wore tight-fitting corsets.

Women who did so often underwent tremendous pain and broke ribs or damaged internal organs. More disturbing than corsets, however, was the Chinese practice of foot binding, which began in the 10th century and lasted for 1,000 years (Ko, 2007).

Foot binding originated out of men's desire for women with small, feminine feet. In fact, many men would refuse to marry women with large feet. One 70-year old woman who had her feet bound as a child said:

Men would choose or reject you as a prospective wife based on the size of your feet. There was a well-known saying, "If you don't bind, you don't marry…" When a girl became eligible for marriage, a matchmaker would find a man for whom the young girl might be suitable. Then she would arrange a foot viewing. The man would come to the girl's house just to look at her feet. If he thought they were too large, he would turn her down. This was a very embarrassing affair, should it happen, since the whole village would surely hear about it (Rupp, 2007).

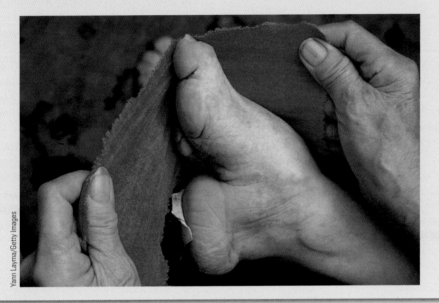

Yann Layma/Getty Images

In India, marriage was an economic and religious obligation; families tried to arrange good marriages by betrothing their children at younger and younger ages, although they did not live with or have sex with their future spouses until after puberty. Because childbearing began so young, Indian women were still in the prime of their lives when their children were grown, and they were often able to assert themselves in the household over elderly husbands.

However, when a husband died, his wife was forbidden to remarry, and she had to live simply, wear plain clothes, and sleep on the ground. She was to devote her days to prayer and rituals that ensured her remarriage to the same husband in a future life. Many women chose (or were forced) to end their lives as widows by the ritual act of *sati*, which consisted of a woman throwing herself on her husband's burning funeral pyre to die (Jamanadas, 2008).

timeline Human Sexuality: **Past and Present**

1965	**1966**	**1969**	**1973**	**2004**
U.S. Supreme Court strikes down Comstock laws, decreasing conservative views of sexuality.	**Liberal view of sexuality increases** with the **publication of Masters & Johnson's** *Human Sexual Response.*	**Liberal view of sexuality increases** with the beginning of the **gay liberation movement** at Stonewall.	**Liberal view of sexuality continues** with the ***Roe v. Wade* decision,** which legalizes abortion and the **removal of homosexuality as a diagnosis** from the *DSM.*	**Massachusetts legalizes same-sex marriage.***

*For more information on the changing legal status of same-sex relationships, see the timeline in Chapter 9.

Foot binding was also sexual in nature—women with bound feet had a sway in their walk that was often viewed as erotic. However, they couldn't walk far, which is why foot binding literally kept women in their place.

The ideal foot length was 3 inches, which was referred to as a *Golden Lotus* (*Golden Lotus* feet were often adorned with beautiful silk shoes). Feet that were 3 to 4 inches long were called *Silver Lotuses*. It is estimated that 40% to 50% of Chinese women had their feet bound in the 19th century, although in the upper classes, the percentages were closer to 100% (W. A. Rossi, 1993).

Foot binding was typically done on girls as young as 4 or 5 years because the bones were still flexible. To bind feet, the mother or grandmother would first soak a girl's feet in warm water. She would then cut the toenails very short, massage the feet, and break the four small toes on each foot. These toes would be folded under, leaving the big toe intact. Silk bandages were wrapped tightly around the toes, and the bandages pulled each broken toe closer to the heel. These bandages were changed and tightened every couple of days so that the foot would not be allowed to grow normally. Typically, this process went on for 10 or more years. It was immensely painful, and most girls could not walk for long distances with their feet bound. Most mothers would start the foot-binding process in the winter months so that the cold would help to numb the pain.

In the beginning, only wealthy families bound their daughters' feet because they could afford not to have their children work in the fields. In the 17th and 18th centuries, peasants and women from the countryside began foot binding when they realized that doing so might attract more wealthy suitors for marriage.

Foot binding had several long-term consequences. Many women had difficulties balancing, walking, standing, and squatting (using the toilet was especially difficult). Muscular atrophy and infections were common, and many girls developed a terrible foot smell from the practice. Older women typically developed severe hip and spinal problems.

The practice of foot binding was outlawed in the latter part of the Qing Dynasty (1644–1911). At that time, women were told to unwrap their feet or face heavy fines. Even so, the practice continued for years, and it wasn't until the formation of the People's Republic of China in 1949 that a strict prohibition was placed on foot binding. This prohibition continues today.

Although it's disturbing to read about this practice, it is interesting to look at how far societies will go for beauty. Foot binding became an integral part of the culture and was much more than a beauty statement. Women whose feet were bound were viewed as more desirable and of a higher social status, making it more likely they would find a husband to provide for them.

SOURCE: The material in this feature was taken from several texts, including *Splendid Slippers: A Thousand Years of an Erotic Tradition* (B. Jackson, 1998), *In Every Step a Lotus: Shoes for Bound Feet* (Ko, 2001), *Cinderella's Sisters: A Revisionist History of Footbinding* (Ko, 2007), *Aching for Beauty: Footbinding in China* (Ping, 2002), and *The Sex Life of the Foot and Shoe* (W. A. Rossi, 1993).

China (Beginning About 200 B.C.)

Chinese civilization emphasizes the interdependence of all things, unified in the Tao, which represents the basic unity of the universe. The Tao itself is made up of two principles, yin and yang, which represent the opposites of the world: yin is feminine, passive, and receptive; yang is masculine, active, and assertive. Sexuality in Chinese thought is not a matter of moral or allowable behavior but, rather, is a natural procreative process, a joining of the yin and yang, the masculine and feminine principles.

Because sex itself was part of the basic process of following the Tao, sexual instruction and sex manuals were common and openly available in early Chinese society. These texts were explicit, with pictures of sexual positions and instructions on how to stimulate partners, and were often given to brides before their weddings.

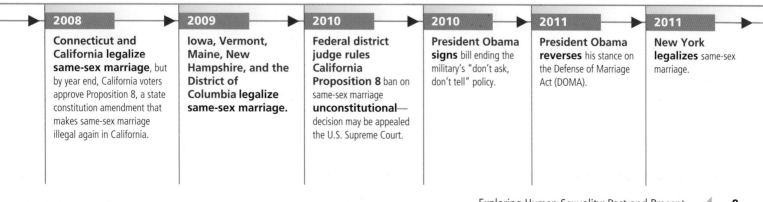

2008	2009	2010	2010	2011	2011
Connecticut and California legalize same-sex marriage, but by year end, California voters approve Proposition 8, a state constitution amendment that makes same-sex marriage illegal again in California.	**Iowa, Vermont, Maine, New Hampshire, and the District of Columbia legalize same-sex marriage.**	**Federal district judge rules California Proposition 8 ban on same-sex marriage unconstitutional**—decision may be appealed the U.S. Supreme Court.	**President Obama signs** bill ending the military's "don't ask, don't tell" policy.	**President Obama reverses** his stance on the Defense of Marriage Act (DOMA).	**New York legalizes** same-sex marriage.

Indian sculptors followed the tradition of tantric art, which is famous for its depictions of eroticism. Of the 85 temples with tantric art originally built, 22 still stand today.

Because women's essence, yin, is inexhaustible, whereas man's essence, yang (embodied in semen), is limited, man should feed his yang through prolonged contact with yin. In other words, heterosexual intercourse should be prolonged as long as possible, without the man ejaculating, to release all the woman's accumulated yin energy. (The man may experience orgasm without ejaculation, however, and techniques were developed to teach men how to do so.) Heterosexual men should try to have sex with many women to prevent the yin energy of any single woman from be-

polygamy
The practice of men or women marrying more than one partner.

coming depleted. It was also important for the man to experience the woman's orgasm, when yin is at its peak, to maximize his contact with yin energy. The Chinese were unique in stressing the importance of female orgasm (Margolis, 2004).

Same-sex relations were not discouraged, but because semen was seen as precious and primarily for impregnation, male homosexuality was viewed as a wasteful use of sperm (we discuss Chinese views of homosexuality more in Chapter 11). Aphrodisiacs were developed, as were drugs for all kinds of sexual problems. Also common were sexual devices to increase pleasure, such as penis rings to maintain erection, balls and bells that were grafted under the skin of the head of the penis to increase its size, and ben-wa balls (usually two or three) containing mercury and other substances that were inserted in the vagina and bounced against each other to bring sexual pleasure.

Taoists believed that yin and yang were equally necessary complements of all existence, so one might guess that men and women were treated more equally in China than in the West. Yet, because yin is the passive, inferior principle, women were seen as subservient to men throughout their lives: first to their fathers, then to their husbands, and finally to their sons when their husbands died. **Polygamy** (pah-LIG-ah-mee) was practiced until late in Chinese history, and the average middle-class male had between three and a dozen wives and concubines, with those in nobility having 30 or more.

REAL RESEARCH 1.3 Research on the practice of Hindu tantric sexual practices has found that there is more to sex than just the act—many sexual practices are performed to provide strength and even magical powers. Consumption of semen, for example, is thought to be one such practice (J. C. GOLD, 2004).

◄ review QUESTIONS

1 How did prehistoric changes in our posture influence human sexuality?

2 What sources provide information on sexuality in early cultures?

3 Explain how the moral standards of past civilizations influence our own judgments about modern events today.

SEXUALITY FROM ST. PAUL to Martin Luther

Religion has influenced views about sexuality throughout history. Perhaps no single system of thought had as much impact on the Western world as Christianity, and nowhere more so than in its views on sexuality (Stark, 1996). We explore early Christianity and the Middle Ages, look at the influence of Islam and Islamic law, and consider the views of sexuality that developed during the Renaissance.

▶▶ EARLY CHRISTIANITY: Chastity Becomes a Virtue (Beginning About 50 A.D.)

Christianity began as a small sect following the teachings of Jesus. It was formalized into a religious philosophy by St. Paul and other early leaders who were influenced by the Roman legal structure. Within a few hundred years, this little sect would become the predominant religion of the Western world, and it has influenced the attitudes of people toward sexuality until the present day.

Jesus himself was mostly silent on sexual issues such as homosexuality and premarital sex. Jesus was born a Jew and was knowledgeable in Jewish tradition, and many of his attitudes were compatible with mainstream Jewish thought of the time. However, he was liberal in his thinking about sexuality; preaching, for example, that men should be held to the same standards as women on issues of adultery, divorce, and remarriage (V. L. Bullough, 1973). The Gospels also show that Jesus was liberal in his recommendations for punishing sexual misadventurers. When confronted with a woman who had committed adultery, a sin for which the Hebrew Bible had mandated stoning, Jesus replied with one of his more famous comments, "Let he who is without sin cast the first stone."

Christianity's view of sex has been one of the harshest of any major religious or cultural traditions.

It was St. Paul and later followers, however, such as St. Jerome and St. Augustine, who established the Christian view of sexuality that was to dominate Western thought for the next 2,000 years. St. Paul condemned sexuality in a way found in neither Hebrew nor Greek thought—nor anywhere in the teachings of Jesus. Paul suggested that the highest love was love of God, and that the ideal was not to allow sexual or human love to compete with that love. Therefore, although sexuality itself was not sinful when performed as part of the marital union, the ideal situation was **celibacy** (SEH-luh-buh-see). **Chastity,** for the first time in history, became a virtue; abstaining from sexual intercourse became a sign of holiness (Bergmann, 1987).

The legacy of early Christianity was a general association of sexuality with sin. All nonprocreative sex was strictly forbidden, as were contraception, masturbation, and sex for pleasure's sake. The result was that the average Christian associated the pleasure of sexuality with guilt (Stark, 1996). Christianity's view of sex has been one of the harshest of any major religious or cultural tradition. You can see how religious views such as these could certainly influence your views on sexuality. It is not uncommon for students to experience **cognitive dissonance** over their disparate views about sexuality and religion.

▶▶ THE MIDDLE AGES: Eve the Temptress and Mary the Virgin (500–1400)

In the early Middle Ages, the church's influence slowly began to increase. Christianity had become the state religion of Rome, and although the church did not have much formal power, its teachings had an influence on law. For example, homosexual relations (even homosexual marriage) had been legal for the first 200 years that Christianity was the state religion of Rome, and the church was very tolerant of homosexuality. Eventually, however, church teachings changed and became much stricter.

Between about 1050 and 1150 (the High Middle Ages), sexuality once again became liberalized. For example, a gay subculture was established in Europe that produced a body of gay literature that had not been seen since the Roman Empire and would not emerge again until the 19th century (Boswell, 1980).

However, the homosexual subculture disappeared in the 13th century when the church cracked down on a variety of groups—including Jews, Muslims, and homosexuals (Boswell, 1980). In 1215, the church instituted **confession,** and soon guides appeared to teach priests about the various sins **penitents** (PENN-it-tents) might have committed. The guides seem preoccupied with sexual transgressions and used sexual sins more than any other kind to illustrate their points (Payer, 1991). All sex outside of marriage was considered sinful, and even certain marital acts were forbidden.

European women in the early Middle Ages were only slightly better off than they had been under the ancient Greeks or Romans. By the late Middle Ages, however, new ideas about women were brought back by the Crusaders from Islamic lands (see the section on Islam that follows). Women were elevated to a place of purity and were considered almost perfect (Tannahill, 1980). Woman was no longer a temptress but a model of virtue. The idea of romantic love was first created at this time, and it spread through popular culture as balladeers and troubadours traveled from place to place, singing songs of pure, spiritual love, untroubled by sex.

At the same time that women were seen to be virtuous, however, they were also said to be the holder of the secrets of sexuality (Thomasset, 1992). Before marriage, men would employ the services of an **entremetteuse** (on-TRAY-meh-toose) to teach them the ways of love. These old women procured young women (prostitutes) for the men and were said to know the secrets of restoring potency, restoring virginity, and concocting potions.

---

celibacy
The state of remaining unmarried; often used today to refer to abstaining from sex.

chastity
The quality of being sexually pure, either through abstaining from intercourse or by adhering to strict rules of sexuality.

cognitive dissonance
Uncomfortable tension that comes from holding two conflicting thoughts at the same time.

confession
A Catholic practice of revealing one's sins to a priest.

penitents
Those who come to confess sins (from the word meaning "to repent").

entremetteuse
Historically, a woman who procures sexual partners for men or one who taught men about lovemaking.

Perhaps no person from the Middle Ages had a stronger impact on subsequent attitudes toward sexuality than Thomas Aquinas (1225–1274). Aquinas established the views of morality and correct sexual behavior that form the basis of the Catholic Church's attitudes toward sexuality even today (Halsall, 1996). Aquinas drew from the idea of "natural law" to suggest that there were "natural" and "unnatural" sex acts. He argued that the sex organs were "naturally" intended for procreation, and other use of them was unnatural and immoral; in fact, he argued that semen and ejaculation were intended only to impregnate, and any other use of them was immoral. Aquinas's strong condemnation of sexuality—and especially homosexuality, which he called the worst of all sexual sins—set the tone for Christian attitudes toward sexuality for many centuries.

▶▶ ISLAM: A New Religion (About 500 A.D.)

In the sixth century, Muhammad began to preach a religion that drew from Jewish and Christian roots and added Arab tribal beliefs. Islam became a powerful force that conquered the entire Middle East and Persian lands; swept across Asia, and so touched China in the East; spread through Northern Africa and, from there, north into Christian Europe, particularly Spain. Between about the 8th and 12th centuries, Islamic society was the most advanced in the world, with a newly developed system of mathematics (Arabic numbers) to replace the clumsy Roman system and having the world's most sophisticated techniques of medicine, warfare, and science (Wuthnow, 1998).

Many Muslim societies have strong rules of *satr al-'awra*, or modesty, that involve covering the private parts of the body (which for women means almost the entire body). Muhammad had tried to preserve the rights of women. There are examples in the **Koran** (koe-RAN), the Muslim bible, of female saints and intellectuals, and powerful women often hold strong informal powers over their husbands and male children. Still, women in many Islamic lands are subjugated to men, segregated and not permitted to venture out of their homes, and forbidden to interact with men who are not family members.

In Islamic law, as in Christian law, sexuality between a man and a woman is legal only when the couple is married (Coulson, 1979). Sexual intercourse in marriage is a good religious deed for the Muslim male, and the Koran likens wives to fields that men should cultivate as frequently as they want. Islam restricts sex to the marital union exclusively (Shafaat, 2004).

In traditional Islamic communities, women who were married to wealthy men usually lived in secluded areas in their husbands' homes, called **harems.** Harems were not the dens of sex and sensu-

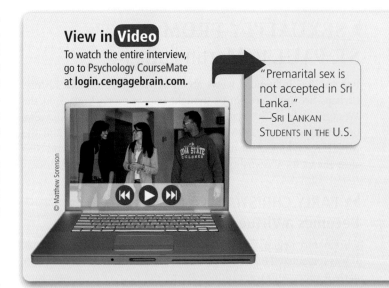

View in Video
To watch the entire interview, go to Psychology CourseMate at **login.cengagebrain.com.**

© Matthew Sorenson

"Premarital sex is not accepted in Sri Lanka."
—Sri Lankan Students in the U.S.

ON YOUR MIND 1.3

I have heard about "honor crimes" in which women are murdered in other countries to maintain family honor. Does this really happen?

The United Nations estimates that about 5,000 honor killings take place every year, although it's impossible to know the exact number (Gill, 2009). Honor crimes occur most frequently in places where female chastity is of utmost importance, including the Middle East and South Asia. These types of crimes target women whose actions—actual or suspected—violate the honor of her family. Crimes might include speaking to someone with whom you should not speak, loss of virginity, wearing inappropriate clothing, extramarital affairs, speaking out about various issues, or even rape. Recent reports suggest that some women in these countries have been raped in an attempt to force them to reclaim their honor by serving as suicide bombers (Mandelbaum, 2010; Navai, 2009; McCracken, 2006). In Chapter 17, we explore other forms of gender-based violence, including domestic violence and sex trafficking.

ality that are sometimes portrayed but were self-contained communities where women learned to become self-sufficient in the absence of men. Among the middle and lower classes, men had less wealth to offer potential wives, which gave women more power.

The sultans of the Ottoman Empire, which ruled most of the Islamic world from the 15th to 20th centuries, had between 300 and 1,200 concubines, mostly captured or bought slaves. The sultan's mother ruled the harem and even sometimes ruled the empire itself if she was strong and her son was weak willed (Tannahill, 1980). Because each woman might sleep with the sultan once or twice a year at most, **eunuchs** (YOU-niks) were employed to guard the women. Eunuchs would not have sex with the women, because they often had their testicles or penises (or both) removed.

Koran
The holy book of Islam. Also spelled Quran or Qur'an.

harem
Abbreviation of the Turkish word *harêmlik* (*harâm* in Arabic), meaning "women's quarters" or "sanctuary."

eunuch
Castrated male (or less often, a man with his penis removed) who guarded a harem. At times, children were also made eunuchs.

21_ MUSÉE DE CLUNY
Ceinture de chasteté _ Commencement du XVII⁰ s.

Chastity belts first appeared in the 15th century and were used primarily by women so that their husbands were assured the children they fathered were their own.

►► THE RENAISSANCE: The Pursuit of Knowledge (Beginning About 1300)

The Renaissance, which began in Italy in the late 1300s, may be summed up as a time when intellectual and artistic thought turned from a focus on God to a focus on human beings and their place in the world; from the sober and serious theology of the Middle Ages to a renewed sense of joy in life; from **asceticism** (ah-SET-ah-siz-um) to sensuality (New, 1969). Part of the cultural shift of the Renaissance was new views of sexuality and, to some degree, the roles of women in society.

During the Renaissance, women made great strides in education and began to become more prominent in political affairs (Bornstein, 1979). Lively debates about the worth and value of women took place, and in 1532, it was argued that each of God's creations in the biblical book of Genesis is superior to the one before. Because the human female is the last thing God created, she

> **asceticism**
> The practice of a lifestyle that rejects sensual pleasures such as drinking alcohol, eating rich food, or engaging in sex.

must be his most perfect creation. In the Bible, a male is the first sinner; men introduce polygamy, drunkenness, and murder into the world; and men are aggressive and tyrannical. Women, on the other hand, are more peaceful, chaste, refined, and faithful.

However, as seems to happen so often in history when women make modest gains, there was a backlash. By the 17th century, witchcraft trials appeared in Europe and the New World, symbols of the fears that men still held of women's sexuality. Thousands of women were killed, and the image of the evil witch became the symbol of man's fear of women for centuries to come.

►► THE REFORMATION: The Protestant Marital Partnership (Beginning About 1500)

In Western Europe in the early 16th century, Martin Luther challenged papal power and founded a movement known as Protestantism. Instead of valuing celibacy, Luther saw in the Bible the obligation to reproduce, saw marital love as blessed, and considered sexuality a natural function. John Calvin, the other great Protestant reformer, suggested that women were not just reproductive vessels but men's partners in all things.

To Luther, marriage was a state blessed by God, and sexual contact was sinful primarily when it occurred out of wedlock, just as any indulgence was sinful (V. L. Bullough, 1973). Because marriage was so important, a bad marriage should not continue, and so Luther broke away from the belief of the Catholic Church and allowed divorce.

Though sexuality was permissible only in the marital union, it had other justifications besides reproduction, such as to reduce stress, avoid cheating, and increase intimacy—a very different perspective on sex than that preached by the Catholic Church. Calvin, in fact, saw the marital union as primarily a social and sexual relationship. Although procreation was important, companionship was the main goal of marriage.

Luther did accept the general subjugation of women to men in household affairs and felt that women were weaker than men and should humble themselves before their fathers and husbands. He excluded women from the clergy because of standards of "decency" and because of women's inferior aptitudes for ministry. Although Calvin and Luther tried to remove from Protestantism the overt disdain of women that they found in some older Christian theologians, they did not firmly establish women's equal place with men.

◄ review QUESTIONS

1 Explain Christianity's impact on our views of human sexuality. Were Islamic views of sexuality more or less conservative than Christianity?

2 Explain how views of sexuality changed from the Reformation through the Renaissance.

3 Explain the changes in the church's view of sexuality from St. Paul to Luther.

4 Explain how religious beliefs can lead to cognitive dissonance in college students.

THE ENLIGHTENMENT
and the Victorian Era

The Enlightenment, an intellectual movement of the 18th century, influenced most of Europe; it prized rational thought over traditional authority and suggested that human nature was to be understood through a study of human psychology. Enlightenment writers argued that human drives and instincts are part of nature's design, so one must realize the basic wisdom of human urges and not fight them (Porter, 1982).

▶▶ THE ENLIGHTENMENT
(Beginning About 1700)

During the Enlightenment, sexual pleasure was considered natural and desirable. In fact, of all the earthly pleasures, enlightenment thinkers praised sexuality as supreme. Sexuality had become so free that there was an unprecedented rise in premarital pregnancy and illegitimate births; up to one fifth of all brides in the late 17th century were pregnant when they got married (Trumbach, 1990).

The Enlightenment influenced most of Europe.

As liberal as the Enlightenment was, many sexual activities, such as homosexuality, were condemned and persecuted. For example, starting in 1730, there was a 2-year "sodomite panic" in the Netherlands; hundreds of men accused of homosexual acts were executed, and hundreds more fled the country. France burned homosexuals long after it stopped burning witches. Yet, there were also times of relative tolerance. Napoleon so eased laws against homosexuality that by 1860 it was tolerated, and male prostitutes were common in France (Tannahill, 1980).

▶▶ THE VICTORIAN ERA (Early 1800s)

The Victorian Era, which refers to Queen Victoria's rule, began in 1837 and lasted until early 1901. It was a time of great prosperity in England. Propriety and public behavior became more important, especially to the upper class, and sexual attitudes became more conservative. Sex was not to be spoken of in polite company and was to be restricted to the marital bed, in the belief that preoccupation with sex interfered with higher achievements. Privately, Victorian England was not as conservative as it has been portrayed, and pornography, extramarital affairs, and prostitution were common. Still, the most important aspect of Victorian society was public propriety, and conservative values were often preached, if not always practiced.

During this period, the idea of male chivalry returned, and women were considered to be virtuous, refined, delicate, fragile, vulnerable, and remote; certainly, no respectable Victorian woman would ever admit to a sexual urge. The prudery of the Victorian era sometimes went to extremes. Victorian women were too embarrassed to talk to a doctor about their "female problems" and so would point out areas of discomfort on dolls (Hellerstein et al., 1981; see Sex in Real Life in this section for more information on women who shared their gynecological concerns with their physicians). Women were supposed to be interested in music but were not supposed to play the flute because pursing the lips was unladylike; the cello was unacceptable because it had to be held between the legs; the brass instruments were too difficult for the delicate wind of the female; the violin forced the woman's neck into an uncomfortable position. Therefore, only keyboard instruments were considered "ladylike" (V. L. Bullough, 1973).

Sexuality was repressed in many ways. Physicians and writers of the time often argued that semen was precious and should be conserved; Sylvester Graham, a Presbyterian minister and founder of the American Vegetarian Society, recommended sex only 12 times a year. He argued that sexual indulgence led to all sorts of ailments and infirmities, such as depression, faintness, headaches, and blindness.

The Victorian era had great influence on sexuality in England and the United States. Many of the conservative attitudes that still exist today are holdovers from Victorian standards.

◀ review QUESTIONS

1 Explain how sexuality was viewed during the Enlightenment.

2 How did the Victorian era influence the view of sexuality?

3 Explain how sexuality was repressed during the Victorian era.

Sex in Real Life ▶▶▶ The History of Vibrators

It might surprise you to know that vibrators have a long history dating back to the late 19th century. At that time, many women began voicing complaints to their physicians (who were mostly male) about miscellaneous gynecological problems. Their symptoms typically included fainting, fluid congestion, insomnia, nervousness, abdominal heaviness, loss of appetite for food or sex, and a tendency to cause trouble for others, especially family members (Maines, 1999). Physicians determined that these gynecological complaints were due to "pelvic hyperemia," otherwise known as genital congestion (Maines, 1999). The condition was diagnosed as "hysteria," a common and chronic complaint in women at the time. In fact, it wasn't until 1952 that the American Psychiatric Association dropped hysteria as a diagnosis (Slavney, 1990).

To relieve the symptoms of hysteria, physicians recommended "intercourse on the marriage bed" or vulvar massage by a physician or midwife (Maines, 1999). Hysteria rates were higher in virgins, unmarried, and widowed women because they did not engage in sexual intercourse. (Notice that there is no mention of lesbian women; physicians believed that hysteria resulted when a woman was not engaging in sexual intercourse with a man.)

Vulvar massage to induce paroxysm (orgasm) was typically painstaking and time-consuming work for a physician, often requiring up to 1 hour of time per woman. It was a strictly medical procedure most commonly prescribed for women diagnosed with hysteria (Maines, 1999). Because religious mandates prohibited self-masturbation, vulvar massage was the only acceptable solution for women without sexual partners.

The vibrator appeared in the late 1800s in response to physician demands for more rapid therapies to treat hysteria. By the early 1900s, several types of vibrators were available, from low-priced foot-powered models to more expensive battery and electric models. Advertisements began to appear in a variety of women's magazines such as *Needlecraft, Woman's Home Companion,* and *Modern Women* (Maines, 1999). Although the advertisements were primarily directed at women, when they were marketed toward men, they claimed that vibrators made good gifts for women because they could give women a healthy glow with "bright eyes" and "pink cheeks" (Maines, 1999).

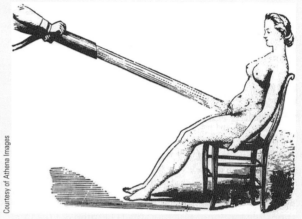

Courtesy of Athena Images

Social awareness of vibrators also began to build in the 1920s when the devices made their way into pornographic films (Maines, 1999). The American Psychiatric Association dropped hysteria as a diagnosis in 1952 and soon afterward vibrators were directly marketed for women (Slavney, 1990). Vibrators were the 15th household appliance to be electrified, after the sewing machine, fan, tea kettle, and toaster (Maines, 1999).

In the 1960s, vibrators were openly marketed as sexual aids to improve sexual functioning and satisfaction. This was because of the changing sexual attitudes and increasingly open atmosphere about sexuality. Today, vibrators are often marketed as "massagers" in most stores, with few, if any, references to sexual health. Have you ever seen vibrator packaging that described how the vibrator might improve your sex life? Give you the best orgasm of your life? Help you learn to orgasm? Although sex stores often sell vibrators with sexual images on the packaging, there is typically no discussion of sexual health. Even so, vibrators have come a long way since the beginning of the century!

© Kurt Rogers/San Francisco Chronicle/Corbis

© Elyse D'Estout

▶ SEX in American History

American society has been influenced most strongly by Europe, particularly England. Yet, it also developed its own unique mix of ideas and attitudes, tempered by the contributions of the many cultures that immigrants brought with them. Let's look at some of these influences, including the colonies, slavery, and the liberalization of sexuality.

▶▶ THE COLONIES: The Puritan Ethic (Beginning About 1600)

The **Puritans** were a religious group who fled England and tried to set up a biblically based society in the New World. They had severe sanctions for sexual transgressions. In New England, for example, the death penalty was applied for sodomy, bestiality, adultery, and rape. In Puritan ideology, the entire community was responsible for upholding morality (D'Emilio & Freedman, 1988). However, the Puritans were not as closed-minded about sex as their reputation suggests, and they believed that sexuality was good and proper within marriage (Escoffier, 2003). In fact, men were obligated to have intercourse with their wives. The Puritans also tolerated most mild sexual transgressions—such as using non-missionary-style sexual positions or engaging in sexual intercourse during menstruation (J. Watkins, 2003).

As the New World began to grow, it suffered from a lack of women, and the speculation in Europe was that any woman seeking a man should come to America, which offered women greater independence than Europe. On the island of Nantucket, for example, whaling kept the men at sea for months. The women took over the island's businesses, and prestige was granted to those who managed to make the money grow while their husbands were away (V. L. Bullough, 1973). Still, women were generally expected to tend to their domain of the home and children.

Sexuality was also a bit freer, and courting youths would wander into barns or look for high crops in the field to obscure their necking and groping. There was also a custom called **bundling,** in which young couples were allowed to share a bed as long as they were clothed, wrapped in sheets or bags, or had a wooden "bundling board" between them. The large number of premarital pregnancies suggests that couples found ways to get around their bundling impediments, but in most such cases, the couple would quickly marry (D'Emilio & Freedman, 1988).

The Wellcome Trust, London

In the late 19th and early 20th centuries, many doctors taught that masturbation was harmful and so devices, such as the two barbed rings and the shock box shown here, were created to keep boys from achieving unwanted erections.

▶▶ THE UNITED STATES: Freedom—and Slavery—in the New World

The pendulum swung back to the liberal side after the Revolutionary War in the late 1700s. This was due mostly to the diminishing power of the church in the United States, leading to more liberal sexual attitudes. This liberalization, together with the continuing slave influx from Africa, had powerful effects on our culture's developing sexuality.

Puritans
Refers to members of a 16th- and 17th-century Protestant group from England who wanted to purge the church of elaborate ceremonies and simplify worship. It has come to mean any person or group that is excessively strict in regard to sexual matters.

bundling
An American practice of placing a wooden board or hanging sheets in the middle of the bed, or wrapping the body in tight clothes, to allow an unmarried couple to spend the night together without having sex.

timeline Television

1927
Philo T. Farnsworth **develops** the first black-and-white television set.

© Bettmann/Corbis

1930
The Association of Motion Pictures devises a rating code to govern events portrayed in motion pictures.

1939
Television makes its debut when the **Radio Corporation of America (RCA)** brings it to the World's Fair in New York City.

1946
First color television set is presented to the Federal Communications Commission (FCC).

1947
Sitcom *Mary Kay and Johnny* shows **first married couple in bed together.**

The Liberalization of Sex (About the 1700s)

With the diminished power of the church came a new period of practical, utilitarian philosophy (as exemplified in Benjamin Franklin's maxims, such as "Early to bed and early to rise…"), which stressed the individual's right to pursue personal happiness. People began to speak more openly about sexuality and romantic love, and women began to pay more attention to appearance and sexual appeal. Children stopped consulting parents about marriage, and some young women simply became pregnant when they wanted to marry. By the late 18th century, as many as one third of all brides in some parts of New England were pregnant (D'Emilio & Freedman, 1988).

This newfound sexual freedom had many implications. In 1720, prostitution was relatively rare, but by the late 18th century, brothels were common in cities and were sometimes attacked by angry mobs (D'Emilio & Freedman, 1988). Contraception, such as early condoms, was readily available (Gamson, 1990), and newspapers and almanacs often advertised contraceptive devices and concoctions to induce abortion. The birth rate dropped, and abortion rates rose through the use of patent medicines, folk remedies, self-induced abortion by inserting objects into the uterus, and medical abortions. Within marriage, sexuality was much celebrated, and in many surviving diaries and letters from that era, couples speak of passion and longing for each other. Extramarital affairs were not uncommon, and some of the diaries quite explicitly record extramarital sexual passion.

Slavery (1600s–1800s)

Before the influx of slaves from Africa, the southern colonies made use of **indentured servants.** Sexual contact with, and even rape of, female indentured servants was fairly common. After 1670, African slaves became common in the South, and many states passed **antimiscegenation** (an-TEE-miss-seg-jen-nay-shun) **laws.** At first the laws were largely ignored. Sexual relations between Whites and Blacks continued, ranging from brutal rape to genuinely affectionate, long-term relationships. By the end of the 18th century, mixed-race children accounted for one fifth of the children born out of wedlock in Virginia (D'Emilio & Freedman, 1988).

The sex lives of slaves were different from those of colonists because of the relative lack of female slaves, the restrictions put on contact with members of the other sex, and the different cultural

traditions of Africa. Whites accused African slaves of having loose morals because women tended to have children by different fathers and children slept in the same rooms as their copulating parents. These sexual habits were used as an excuse to rape them, break up their families, and even, at times, kill them. Of course, slave owners did not consider that they were responsible for forcing slaves to live that way. The fear that freed Black men would rape White women (or accusations that they had) was often used as justification to keep Blacks segregated or to lynch them, even though it was far more common for White men to rape Black slaves and servants.

The slaves themselves developed a social system to protect their few freedoms. Adults formed and tried to maintain stable unions

indentured servants	**antimiscegenation laws**
A person who is bound by requirements to work for another person for a specified time in exchange for payment of travel and living expenses.	Laws forbidding sexuality, marriage, or breeding among members of different races.

1950

Sitcom *I Love Lucy* shows **married couple in separate beds.**

© Bettmann/Corbis

1953

First network children's show, *Captain Kangaroo,* debuts.

© John Springer Collection/Corbis

1953

Color broadcasting on television begins after FCC approves modified version of RCA system.

1956

Elvis Presley appears on the *Ed Sullivan Show* and is **broadcast from the waist up** because his dance moves are thought to be too suggestive.

© Bettmann/Corbis

1957

First remote control for television is introduced.

Exploring Human Sexuality: Past and Present ◀ **17**

when possible, although marriage was officially illegal between slaves. Despite harsh conditions, there was a strong sense of morality within the slave community, and slaves tried to regulate sexual behavior as much as possible, forcing men to take care of the women they impregnated and sanctioning girls who were too promiscuous. The myth of slave sexual looseness is disproved by the lack of prostitution and very low venereal disease (STIs) rates among slaves (D'Emilio & Freedman, 1988). It was difficult, however, to maintain sexual unions when the woman's body was legally owned by the White master or when sexual favors might free one from harsh labor in the cotton fields. Despite the fact that plantation owners often condemned the promiscuity of Blacks (and therefore excused their own sexual exploitation of them), slaves' premarital sexual activity was probably not much different from that of poor Whites (Clinton & Gillespie, 1997).

Settlers throughout early American history used the sexuality of minorities as an excuse to disdain or oppress them. Native Americans had their own cultural system of sexual morality; nonetheless, they were branded as savages for their acceptance of premarital sex and their practice of polygamy, which existed primarily because of the large number of males killed in war. Native Americans were freely raped by White men (D'Emilio & Freedman, 1988). Mexicans, who were religious Catholics with strict sexual rules, were considered promiscuous by the Protestants because they did not consider it wrong to dance or show affection in public. The settlers often criticized others for sexual behaviors, such as homosexuality and premarital sex, that were not uncommon in their own communities.

▶▶ THE 19TH CENTURY: Polygamy, Celibacy, and the Comstock Laws (Beginning in the 1800s)

The pendulum swung back to the liberal side in the 19th century with the rise of a number of controversial social movements focusing on sexuality. The **free love movement,** which began in the

free love movement
A movement of the early 19th century that preached love should be the factor that determines whether one should have sex (not to be confused with the free love movement of the 1960s).

1820s, preached that love, not marriage, should be the prerequisite to sexual relations. Free love advocates criticized the sexual "slavery" of women in marriage, often condemned the sexual exploitation of slaves, and condemned sexuality without love (although their many critics often claimed that they preached promiscuity).

Another controversial group, the Church of Jesus Christ of Latter Day Saints, or Mormons, announced in 1852 that many of its members practiced polygamy, which almost cost Utah its statehood. As with the free love movement, Americans accused the Mormons of loose morals even though, despite their acceptance of polygamy, they were very sexually conservative (Iverson, 1991). A number of small communities that practiced alternative forms of sexual relations also began during this time. The Oneida community preached group marriage, whereas the Shakers, frustrated with all the arguments over sexuality, practiced strict celibacy (Hillebrand, 2008).

By the close of the 19th century, the medical model of sexuality began to emerge. Americans became obsessed with sexual health, and physicians and reformers began to advocate self-restraint, abstention from masturbation, and eating "nonstimulating" foods (those free from additives and easy to digest). Doctors also argued that women were ruled by their wombs, and many had their ovaries surgically removed to "correct" masturbation or sexual passion. An influential group of physicians even argued that women were biologically designed for procreation and destined only for marriage, for they were too delicate to work or undergo the rigors of higher education. These theories completely ignored the fact that lower-class women often worked difficult labor 12 and 15 hours a day. Male sexuality, however, was viewed as normative.

In the 19th century, homosexuality was underground, although there were some open same-sex relationships that may or may not have been sexual. For example, there are a number of recorded cases in which women dressed and passed as men and even "married" other women (we discuss this more in Chapter 4). There were also men who wrote of intimate and loving relationships with other men, without an explicit admission of sexual contact. The great poet Walt Whitman, now recognized as a homosexual, at times confirmed his erotic attraction to men, but at other times denied it. In accordance with the developing medical model of sexuality, physicians began to argue that homosexuality was an illness rather than a sin, a view that lasted until the 1970s (D'Emilio, 1998; see Chapter 11).

*By the close of the 19th century, **Americans** became **obsessed** with sexual health...*

timeline Television

1961	**1962**	**1965**	**1969**	**1975**
***The Dick Van Dyke Show* begins** and airs until 1966. The show is a hit, and unlike most '60s sitcoms, **viewers see a father both in the home and at work.**	**First satellite transmission of a televised program.** Eliminates delays in programming and allows for instant reporting of events around the world.	***I Dream of Jeannie* airs** from 1965 to 1970. Jeannie's harem costume is **controversial for exposing too much flesh.** Her belly button is filled in with flesh-colored putty plug.	***The Brady Bunch* airs.** Show is inspired by the growing statistics of **blended families** with children from previous marriages.	***The Jeffersons* is the first show to include an interracial couple.**

Hulton Archive/Getty Images

CBS-TV/The Kobal Collection

The movements for more open sexual relationships were countered by strong voices arguing for a return to a more religious and chaste morality, an argument that continues more than a century later. In the 1870s, Anthony Comstock, a dry-goods salesman, single-handedly lobbied the legislature to outlaw obscenity. The resulting Comstock Act of 1873 prohibited the mailing of obscene, lewd, lascivious, and indecent writing or advertisements, including articles about contraception or abortion. Comstock himself was the act's most vigorous enforcer, and he reported hundreds of people to the authorities, even for such things as selling reprints of famous artwork containing nudity or famous books that mentioned prostitution (M. A. Blanchard & Semoncho, 2006). Literally thousands of books, sexual objects, and contraceptive devices were destroyed, denying many people sophisticated contraceptive devices or information for almost 60 years (D'Emilio & Freedman, 1988). It wasn't until 1965 that the U.S. Supreme Court struck down Comstock laws.

▶▶ THE 20TH CENTURY: Sexual Crusaders and Sexologists (Beginning in the 1900s)

Even though Comstock laws were in effect at the beginning of the 20th century, one study of 1,000 heterosexual women found that 74% used some form of contraception, most made love at least once a week, and 40% acknowledged masturbating during childhood or adolescence (although others began after marriage; D'Emilio & Freedman, 1988). These statistics reflect the freedom women gradually began to find as they moved to the cities, lived on their own, and began working more outside the home (Irvine, 1990). Yet, the overwhelming majority of heterosexual women still considered reproduction the primary goal of sex.

Moral crusaders were also trying to curb newfound sexual freedoms at this time, and those trying to liberalize sexuality further were in an intense struggle, trying to guide the rapid changes taking place in American sexual behaviors. Crusaders pointed to the spread of prostitution and high rates of STIs. Liberalizers argued that modern industrial society could not sustain the coercive sexual standards of past centuries. In one guise or another, these battles are still being fought today.

REAL RESEARCH 1.4 American parents often believe that while their own teenage children are sexually innocent and uninterested in sex, other teens are hypersexual and predatory (ELLIOTT, 2010).

The Social Hygiene Movement (Beginning in 1905)

In response to high STI rates, a New York physician, Prince Morrow, started a movement in 1905 that was a curious mixture of both liberal and traditional attitudes. The social hygiene movement convinced legislators that scores of virtuous women were catching STIs from husbands who frequented prostitutes, and so laws were passed mandating blood tests before marriage, and a number of highly publicized police actions were brought against prostitutes. Although the movement accepted pleasure as an acceptable motivation for sex, followers were against premarital sex and warned that masturbation harmed one's future sex life. Most important, they were early (if unsuccessful) advocates for sex education in the schools (D'Emilio & Freedman, 1988).

Sexology

Beginning in the early part of the 20th century and increasingly by midcentury, the pioneers of sexual research were beginning to make scientific advances into the understanding of sexuality. Rejecting the religious and moral teachings about how people "should" behave, researchers brought sex out into the open as a subject worthy of medical, scientific, and philosophical debate. We discuss these researchers at length in the following chapter, but here we should note that they had a profound impact on the way people began to talk and think about sexuality.

For example, in the early 1940s, Alfred Kinsey's large-scale surveys of American sexual behavior promised to settle some of the debates and confusion about sexuality by providing scientific answers to questions about how people behaved. Kinsey published his research in two volumes in 1948 and 1953, and both were overnight best sellers. Based on thousands of interviews, Kinsey's findings shocked American culture (Kimmel & Plante, 2007). His findings revealed that sex was much more important to peoples' lives than originally thought. Masturbation, homosexuality, and infidelity were not uncommon, and women had more sexual in-

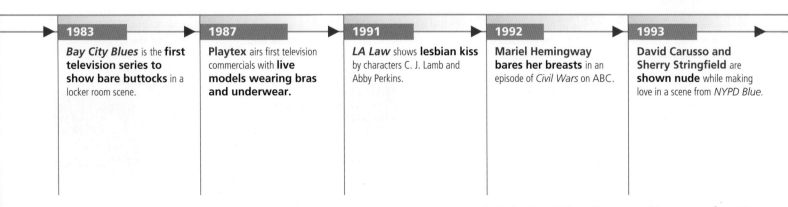

1983
Bay City Blues is the **first television series to show bare buttocks** in a locker room scene.

1987
Playtex airs first television commercials with **live models wearing bras and underwear.**

1991
LA Law shows **lesbian kiss** by characters C. J. Lamb and Abby Perkins.

1992
Mariel Hemingway bares her breasts in an episode of *Civil Wars* on ABC.

1993
David Carusso and Sherry Stringfield are **shown nude** while making love in a scene from *NYPD Blue*.

terest and desire than society had been led to believe (Kimmel & Plante, 2007). The popularity of Kinsey's books showed that the American public was hungry for sexual knowledge.

Other researchers, Dr. William Masters and Virginia Johnson, took Kinsey's research a step further and brought sex into a laboratory to study the physiology of sexual response. Their research yielded two important books (Masters & Johnson, 1966, 1970) that were also overnight best sellers.

The work of these sexologists helped to demystify sex and make it more respectable to publicly discuss the sexual behaviors and problems of real people. Much of this work was condemned by moral crusaders, who criticized its lack of connection to traditional standards of morality (Irvine, 1990).

The Sexual Revolutions (1920s and 1960s)

The phrase **sexual revolution** was coined in the 1920s by Wilhelm Reich, an Austrian psychoanalyst (Allyn, 2000). Reich was one of the leading figures of the sex reform movement in Europe, and he strongly believed in a sexually liberated society. He founded several clinics throughout Europe to educate people about sexuality and disseminate contraceptive information. Unfortunately, Reich's work was cut short by the political turmoil of the 1930s. Even though his dream for liberation never materialized in full, he did set into motion rapid changes in sexual mores throughout Europe and the United States during the first half of the 20th century (Allyn, 2000).

During this time, the values and attitudes about sexuality that were rooted in the Christian tradition slowly began to change as society became more permissive and accepting of sexual freedom. Advertising and other media became more sexualized, and fashion trends changed as the flapper era was ushered in. Flappers were women who typically wore short skirts, had short bob haircuts, and weren't uncomfortable going against societal expectations for women. They wore more makeup than what was generally accepted and had open attitudes about sexuality (Gourley, 2007). The trend toward more liberal ideas and values about sexuality continued in the late 1920s, but it wasn't until the early 1960s when many would say the real sexual revolution took place.

The modern movement that formed the sexual revolution began in San Francisco, where thousands of young people (who were referred to as "hippies") began to proclaim the power of love and sex. There was also an emerging revolt against the moral code of

"Please your partner often and you will please God."
—Muslim Couples and Sexuality

View in Video
To watch the entire interview, go to Psychology CourseMate at **login.cengagebrain.com**.

American society, and movements against the status quo were not uncommon (Lipton, 2003). In fact, the Black Civil Rights movement and the growing student protests against the Vietnam War in the mid-1960s proved that people could organize and stand up for what they believed in.

The 1960s were a time when the pendulum swung back to the liberal side; Americans went from *No Sex Until Marriage* to *If It Feels Good, Do It!* Two of the biggest sexuality challenges at this time were the reformulation of male gender roles and an examination of the double standard of sexuality (Escoffier, 2003). Two important events helped set the stage for the 1960s sexual revolution. One was the discovery of antibiotics in the mid-1930s. This discovery led to decreased fears about STIs, because they were now curable (we discuss STIs in Chapter 15). Another important event was the development of other media. The timeline presented earlier in this chapter showcases the invention of the television and the

sexual revolution
Changes in sexual morality and sexual behavior that occurred throughout the Western world during the 1960s and 1970s.

timeline Television

1994
Rosanne Barr and Mariel Hemingway kiss on *Roseanne*.

1996
Friends **airs episode of lesbian wedding,** even though vows are not sealed with a kiss.

1997
Ellen DeGeneres comes out on the air, making *Ellen* the first openly gay sitcom. Several advertisers withdraw all commercials from this episode.

© Reuters/Corbis

1998
Network and broadcast executives design a rating system to help parents monitor what their children watch on television.

1998
Sex and the City debuts on HBO and covers **sex and relationships with unprecedented candor** from the point of view of the four female lead characters.

© HBO/Courtesy: Everett Collection

events that helped shift our attitudes about sexuality. By the early 1960s, the majority of U.S. homes had a television set (Abramson, 2003). Television, radio, and other mass media began to broadcast more liberal ideas about sexuality to viewers and listeners. Pornography also became more acceptable, and in 1953, Hugh Hefner began publishing *Playboy* magazine.

Nonfiction sex manuals also began to appear, such as Helen Gurley Brown's *Sex and the Single Girl* (1962; Gurley Brown later went on to publish *Cosmopolitan* magazine), Joan Garrity's *The Sensuous Woman* (1969), and David Reuben's *Everything You Always Wanted to Know About Sex (But Were Afraid to Ask)* (1969). There were many others published, and all of them spoke to the changing nature of sexuality. They were all factually written and were best sellers. Mainstream America had been desperate for more information about sexuality. Probably the most important thing these books did was to acknowledge and celebrate one's sexuality.

The introduction of the first contraceptive pill was another important event that liberated female sexuality in the early 1960s. For the first time, heterosexual women were free to engage in sexual intercourse without the fear of becoming pregnant. No longer was sexual intercourse associated solely with procreation. Fashions changed once again in the mid-1960s, emphasizing women's bodies and showing more skin. Women wore miniskirts, plunging necklines, and see-through blouses, further emphasizing women's sexuality. Some women began to burn their bras and "free their breasts" in an act of defiance.

Soon, poets, writers, and songwriters began to embrace both sensuality and sexual experimentation. Sexuality began to come out of the closet as repressive attitudes began to lessen. All of these influences led to a generation that was much more sexually liberal than those preceding it. At the end of the 1960s, the gay and lesbian civil rights movement officially started with the Stonewall riots (we discuss this more later in the chapter).

Feminism (Beginning in Early 1900s)

There have always been women who protested against the patriarchy of their day, argued that women were as capable as men in the realms of work and politics, and defied their culture's stereotypes about women. Yet, the 20th century saw the most successful feminist movement in history. The **women's suffrage** movement of the

> **No longer** *was sexual intercourse* **associated** *solely with procreation.*

early 20th century first put women's agendas on the national scene, but it was Margaret Sanger who most profoundly influenced women's sexuality in the first half of the 20th century.

Sanger, a 30-year-old homemaker, was an early advocate for the rights of women. When her 50-year old mother died after 18 pregnancies, Sanger was determined to help women learn how to protect themselves from pregnancy. In 1917, she met Katharine Dexter McCormick, who had graduated with a degree in biology from the Massachusetts Institute of Technology (McCormick was only the second woman to do so). In the next few years, Sanger worked with McCormick to build the Birth Control League. Sanger brought her drive, passion, and energy, whereas McCormick provided the knowledge and capital necessary for their project. During the Depression, their movement gained momentum because many families were desperate to limit the size of their families. In fact, while there were 55 birth control clinics in the United States in 1930, by 1942, this number grew to more than 800 clinics (Gibbs, 2010). In 1942, Sanger's Birth Control League changed its name to the Planned Parenthood Federation of America.

After Sanger, organized feminism entered a quiet phase, not reemerging until the 1960s. In the middle of the 20th century, women increasingly entered institutions of higher education and entered the labor force in great numbers while men were off fighting World War II. At the same time, divorce rates were rising, many women widowed by war were raising children as single parents, and the postwar baby boom relegated middle-class women to their suburban homes. Social conditions had given women more power just as their roles were being restricted again to wife and mother. A backlash was soon to come, and the pendulum would swing back to the conservative side.

The modern feminist movement can best be summarized by the work of three female authors (Ferree & Hess, 1985). In her 1949 book, *The Second Sex,* Simone de Beauvoir showed that women were not granted an identity of their own but were considered the objects of men's wishes and anxieties. Betty Friedan followed in 1963 with *The Feminine Mystique,* a 10-year follow-up of the lives of her graduating class from Smith College in which she found that these

women's suffrage
The movement to get women the right to vote.

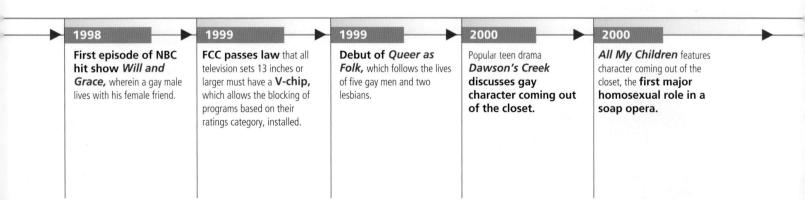

1998

First episode of NBC hit show *Will and Grace,* wherein a gay male lives with his female friend.

1999

FCC passes law that all television sets 13 inches or larger must have a **V-chip,** which allows the blocking of programs based on their ratings category, installed.

1999

Debut of *Queer as Folk,* which follows the lives of five gay men and two lesbians.

2000

Popular teen drama ***Dawson's Creek* discusses gay character coming out of the closet.**

2000

All My Children features character coming out of the closet, the **first major homosexual role in a soap opera.**

educated, bright women felt trapped in the role of housewife and wanted careers to have happier, more fulfilled lives. Finally, at the height of the Vietnam War, Kate Millett's (1969) *Sexual Politics* argued that patriarchy bred violence and forced men to renounce all that is feminine in them. According to Millett, rape was an act of aggression aimed at controlling women, and men saw homosexuality as a "failure" of patriarchy, so it was violently repressed.

Feminists of the 1960s argued that they were entitled to sexual satisfaction, that the existing relations of the sexes were exploitative, and that women had a right to control their lives and their bodies. Some of the more radical feminists advocated lesbianism as the only relationship not based on male power, but most feminists fought for a transformation of the interpersonal relationship of men and women and of the male-dominated political structure. Part of the freedom women wanted was the freedom to choose when to be mothers, and the right to choose abortion became a firm part of the feminist platform.

Feminism has made great cultural and political strides, and has changed the nature of American society and sexual behavior. The pursuit of sexual pleasure is now seen as a woman's legitimate right, and heterosexual men are no longer expected to be the sexual experts relied on by docile, virginal mates. Feminists were at the forefront of the abortion debate and hailed the legalization of abortion as a great step in achieving women's rights over their own bodies. More recently, women have begun entering politics in record num-

"There was a very strong notion that I am a sinner, fundamentally who I am is hated and reviled by God."
—GAY MORMONS

View in Video
To watch the entire interview, go to Psychology CourseMate at **login.cengagebrain.com**.

bers, and the Senate, Congress, and governorships are increasingly counting women among their members. Even so, women still have many struggles. Men are paid more than women for the same work, poverty is increasingly a problem of single mothers, and rape and spousal abuse are still major social problems in the United States (Lips, 2008). Still, feminism as a movement has had a major impact on the way America views sexuality.

Gay Liberation (Beginning in mid-1900s)

The period after World War II was challenging for homosexuals. Senator Joseph McCarthy, who became famous for trying to purge America of communists, also relentlessly hunted homosexuals. Homosexuals were portrayed as perverts, lurking in schools and on street corners ready to pounce on unsuspecting youth, and many were thrown out of work or imprisoned in jails and mental hospitals. The news media participated in this view, as in a 1949 *Newsweek* article that identified all homosexuals as "sex murderers." Doctors tinkered with a variety of "cures," including lobotomies and castration. Churches were either silent or encouraged the persecution, and Hollywood purged itself of positive references to homosexuality. Many laws initiated during this period, such as immigration restrictions for homosexuals and policies banning gays from the military, continued for many years (Adam, 1987).

In 1951, an organization for homosexual rights, the Mattachine Society, was founded in the United States by Harry Hay. The

After homosexuality was removed from the *Diagnostic and Statistical Manual* in 1973, it was no longer considered a psychiatric disorder.

Tim Kitchen/Getty Images

timeline Television

2000	2003	2004	2004	2006
Inquiry into former White House intern Monica Lewinsky's relationship with President Bill Clinton finally concludes.	**Bravo network begins airing** the popular show *Queer Eye for the Straight Guy.*	**Reality shows such as** *The Bachelor, Survivor, Blind Date,* and *Extreme Makeover* flood the market.	**Janet Jackson exposes her breast** during halftime Super Bowl show. The FCC fines CBS more than $500,000.	*Big Love,* **a show about polygamy,** begins airing on HBO.

Getty Images

© Steve Azzara/Corbis

Daughters of Bilitis, the first postwar lesbian organization, was founded by four lesbian couples in San Francisco in 1955. Although these groups began with radical intentions, the vehement antihomosexuality of American authorities forced the groups to lay low throughout the late 1950s.

Although gay activism increased in America with protests and sit-ins throughout the 1960s, modern gay liberation is usually traced to the night in 1969 when New York police raided a Greenwich Village gay bar called Stonewall. For the first time, the gay community erupted in active resistance, and the police were greeted by a hail of debris thrown by the gay patrons of the bar. There had been previous acts of resistance, but the Stonewall riot became a symbol to the gay community and put the police on notice that homosexuals would no longer passively accept arrest and police brutality.

*As of early 2011, **same-sex marriage was legal** in six states.*

Following Stonewall, gay activism began a strong campaign against prejudice and discrimination all over the country. Groups and businesses hostile to gays were picketed, legislators were lobbied, committees and self-help groups were founded, legal agencies were formed, and educational groups tried to change the image of homosexuality in America. For example, in 1973, strong gay lobbying caused the American Psychiatric Association to remove homosexuality from the *Diagnostic and Statistical Manual of Mental Disorders (DSM),* the official reference of psychiatric disorders. The *DSM* change removed the last scientific justification for treating homosexuals any differently from other citizens and demonstrated the new national power of the movement for homosexual rights. Soon the gay movement was a powerful presence in the United States, Canada, Australia, and Western Europe (Adam, 1987).

The 1970s were, in many ways, the golden age of gay life in America. In cities such as San Francisco and New York, gay bathhouses and bars became open centers of gay social life, and gay theater groups, newspapers, and magazines appeared. In 1979, the National March on Washington for Lesbian and Gay Rights was a symbolic step forward for the gay movement (Ghaziani, 2005). The discovery of the AIDS epidemic in the United States and Europe in the beginning of the 1980s doused the excitement of the 1970s, as thousands of gay men began to die of the disease (see Chapter 15). Historically, when such fearsome epidemics arise, people have been quick to find a minority group to blame for the disease, and homosexuals were quickly blamed by a large segment of the public (Perrow & Guillén, 1990; Shilts, 2000).

In 1990, queer theory developed and grew out of lesbian and gay studies (we discuss queer theory in more detail in Chapter 2). The gay rights movement has been at the forefront of trying to change sexual attitudes in the United States not only by pressing for recognition of homosexuality as a legitimate sexual orientation, but also by arguing that all sexual minorities have a right to sexual happiness. Although a handful of states allow gay couples to register as "domestic partners" and allow them certain health and death benefits that married couples have, the issue of same-sex marriage is still controversial in American society. As of 2011, same-sex marriage was legal in six states and the District of Columbia. President Obama signed a bill ending the military's "don't ask, don't tell" policy in 2010, which was one of the first moves toward equality for gays and lesbians. In 2011, he reversed his stance on the Defense of Marriage Act (DOMA), concluding that his administration could no longer defend the federal law that defines marriage as between a man and a woman.

We are the sum total of our history. Our attitudes and beliefs reflect all of our historical influences, from the ancient Hebrews and Greeks to the Christianity of the Middle Ages to the modern feminist and gay liberation movements. Most of us have a hard time recognizing that our own constellation of beliefs, feelings, and moral positions about sex are a product of our particular time and place, and are in a constant state of evolution. It is important to keep this in mind as we explore the sexual behaviors of other people and other cultures throughout this book.

In 2011, President Obama announced that his administration would no longer defend the Defense of Marriage Act (DOMA) that defined marriage as only between a man and a woman.

© Queerstock, Inc./Alamy

2009

Reality series, *Jersey Shore,* whose **cast members openly hook up and discuss sex,** begins airing on MTV.

Contour by Getty Images

2009

Reality series, *16 and Pregnant,* **begins airing** on MTV and spin-off series, *Teen Mom,* soon follows, both of which highlight teenage pregnancy.

2010

Sister Wives, **a reality show about a polygamous family,** begins airing on TLC.

1 Explain how the Puritans viewed sex. Who did they believe was responsible for upholding morality?

2 Explain some of the influences that led to the liberalization of sex in the 1700s.

3 What was the "free love movement," and what did the movement preach?

4 What are the two most important movements to change sexuality in the latter part of the 20th century? What did each contribute?

◄◄ **chapter** REVIEW

SUMMARY **POINTS**

1 Human sexuality is grounded in biological functioning, emerges as we develop, and is expressed by cultures through rules about sexual contact, attitudes about moral and immoral sexuality, habits of sexual behavior, patterns of relations between the sexes, and more.

2 The sexual nature of human beings is unique in the animal kingdom. Humans have created ideas, laws, customs, fantasies, and art around the sexual act. Sexuality is a uniquely human trait.

3 American media are the most sexually suggestive in the Western Hemisphere. However, sexuality is one of the most difficult aspects for us to express and explore.

4 The evolution to an upright posture changed forever the way the human species engage in sexual intercourse.

5 Men dominated public life in early history, and we know far more about men's thoughts than women's. The Hebrew Bible contained explicit rules about sexual behavior. The focus on marital sexuality and procreation formed the basis of sexual attitudes in the West for centuries.

6 The Greeks were more sexually permissive than the Hebrews. In Greek culture, pederasty was considered a natural form of sexuality. Rome had few restrictions about sexuality until late in the history of the empire.

7 Chinese civilization's belief in yin and yang taught people how to maximize their sexuality. A woman's essence, or yin, was viewed as inexhaustible, whereas a man's essence, yang, embodied in semen, was limited. Hinduism concentrates on an individual's cycle of birth

and rebirth, also known as karma. India's most famous sex manual, the *Kamasutra,* appeared sometime during the third or fourth century.

8 Perhaps no single system of thought has had as much impact on the Western world as Christianity. According to early forms of the belief system, sexuality itself was not sinful when performed as part of the marital union, but the ideal situation was celibacy. In fact, with the advent of Christianity, chastity became a virtue for the first time in history.

9 In the early Middle Ages, the influence of the church began to increase. Its teachings began to influence laws, which became much stricter. Perhaps no person from the Middle Ages had a stronger impact on attitudes toward sexuality than the theologian Thomas Aquinas.

10 Muhammad began to preach a religion called Islam in the sixth century. Many Muslim societies have strong rules of modesty for women that involve covering private parts of their bodies. According to the Muslim bible, the Koran, marital sexual intercourse was a good religious deed, and men were encouraged to engage frequently in such behavior. All forms of sexuality were permissible.

11 The Renaissance witnessed a new view of sexuality and of the roles of women in society. Women made great strides in education and became more prominent in political affairs. Pro-female tracts began to circulate, and lively debates about the value of women ensued. However, by the 17th century, witchcraft trials appeared, symbolizing the fear that men held of women's sexuality.

12 In the early 16th century, Martin Luther started Protestantism. Luther saw in the Bible the obligation to reproduce, considered marital

love blessed, and considered sexuality a natural function. Sexuality was permissible only in the marital union, although it had other justifications besides reproduction.

13 Three important movements that influenced modern sexuality were the Reformation, the Renaissance, and the Enlightenment.

14 The Enlightenment (early 1700s) prized rational thought over traditional authority and suggested that human nature was to be understood through a study of human psychology. Sexual pleasure was considered natural and desirable.

15 During the Victorian era (early 1800s), conservative values were often preached, although not always practiced. The idea of male chivalry returned, and women were considered to be virtuous, refined, delicate, fragile, vulnerable, and remote. Sexuality was repressed in many ways for men and women.

16 The Puritans were a religious group who fled England and tried to set up a biblically based society in the New World. Even though they believed that sexuality was good and proper within marriage, they also believed the entire community was responsible for upholding morality.

17 After the Revolutionary War, the church's power began to diminish in the United States. People began to speak more openly about sexuality, and the liberalization of sexual conduct had many results. Prostitution flourished, and contraception became more readily available.

18 Slavery had a profound effect on post-Revolutionary America. Many slaves developed a social system and formed stable unions, although marriage was officially illegal between slaves. There was a strong sense of morality within the slave community, and sexual behavior was regulated as much as possible.

19 During the 19th century, there was an increase in a number of controversial social movements focusing on sexuality. The free love movement preached that only love should be the prerequisite to sexual relations. However, by the end of the 19th century, the medical model of sexuality began to emerge, and physicians and reformers began to advocate self-restraint,

abstention from masturbation, and consumption of "nonstimulating" foods. The Comstock Act of 1873 prohibited the mailing of obscene, lewd, and indecent writings, including articles about contraception or abortion.

20 In 1905, the social hygiene movement convinced legislators to pass laws mandating blood tests before marriage. Premarital sex and masturbation were thought to harm one's future sex life. In the early part of the 20th century, pioneers of sexual research began their work, rejecting the religious and moral teachings about how people "should" behave.

21 The sexual revolution brought changes in values and attitudes about sexuality. Society became more permissive and accepting of sexual freedom. Flappers and hippies helped bring more liberal attitudes about sexuality.

22 Feminism and gay liberation also affected society's attitudes about sexuality. Modern gay liberation is usually traced back to the Stonewall riot of 1969. In 1973, strong gay lobbying caused the American Psychiatric Association to remove homosexuality from the *DSM*.

CRITICAL THINKING QUESTIONS

1 Explain your goals for this class and how you developed each of these goals. Do you think this class will help you in the future? If so, in what ways?

2 Why do you think "sex sells" when our culture traditionally has had a problem openly talking about sexuality?

3 The Bible has had a profound impact on our attitudes toward sexuality. Do you think that it is still influential? In what ways?

4 How different do China's and India's sexual histories seem to you today? Are they different from our Western views of sexuality?

5 Provide two examples of how cultural images of beauty affect how men and women feel about themselves. Explain how the Chinese practice of foot binding became so widespread and lasted for 1,000 years.

6 Explore the many influences that led to the sexual revolution of the 1960s. Explain how these events shaped the cultural view of sexuality.

7 Compare and contrast both the role of women and the views of sexuality in modern society and in Islam. How does the practice of honor crimes tie into gender issues in society?

MEDIA RESOURCES

CourseMate brings course concepts to life with interactive learning, study, and exam preparation tools that support the printed textbook. A textbook-specific website, Psychology CourseMate includes an integrated interactive eBook and other interactive learning tools including quizzes, flashcards, videos, and more. If your textbook does not include an access code card, go to CengageBrain .com to gain access.

CENGAGENOW CengageNOW is an easy-to-use online resource that helps you study in less time to get the grade you want—NOW. Take a pre-test for this chapter and receive a personalized study plan based on your results that will identify the topics you need to review and direct you to online resources to help you master those topics. Then take a post-test to help you determine the concepts you have mastered and what you will need to work on. If your textbook does not include an access code card, go to CengageBrain.com to gain access.

View in Video available in CourseMate and CengageNOW:

Culture and Sexual Attitudes: Author explores sexual attitudes in Japanese, Dutch, and U.S. cultures.

Sri Lankan Students in the U.S.: Two Sri Lankan students who are studying in the U.S. explore differences in sexual attitudes and behavior between Sri Lanka and the U.S.

Muslim Couples and Sexuality: Dr. Heba Kotb, a Muslim sex advice show host in Cairo, addresses the lack of knowledge about sexuality in the Muslim world.

Gay Mormons: Gay men discuss the Mormon viewpoint on homosexuality and grapple with the implications for their lives.

Websites:

The Kinsey Institute ■ This official website for the Kinsey Institute is one of only a handful of centers in the world that conducts interdisciplinary research exclusively on sex and has a large library that includes books, films, video, fine art, artifacts, photography, archives, and more.

The Journal of the History of Sexuality ■ This journal has a cross-cultural and cross-disciplinary focus that brings together

original articles and critical reviews from historians, social scientists, and humanities scholars worldwide. The website offers a look at recently published articles in the journal.

The Sexuality Information and Education Council of the United States (SIECUS) ■ SIECUS is a national organization that promotes comprehensive education about sexuality and advocates the right of individuals to make responsible sexual choices.

2

Understanding Human Sexuality: Theory and Research

View in **Video**

View in **Video**

ABOUT THE CHAPTER OPENING VIDEO – Valerie, a 20-year-old college student, took a human sexuality course her senior year and was excited when her professor assigned a project that required her to develop a research project exploring human sexuality. She needed to design a study, collect the data, and analyze the results. After much thought, she decided to explore the various places where college students have sex. Wanting to be creative and have fun with the assignment, she came up with the "Bikini Sex Project." She would wear a bikini around campus and interview students, asking them where some of the craziest places they had engaged in sex were. Then she asked the students to write the strangest place on her body. She liked the idea of interviews because this would help her establish rapport with students and explain the nature of her project. She hoped her unique approach would entice more students to participate in her study.

"I was really excited as I walked out of my dorm in my bikini. I began to stop students who were walking across campus and explained that I was doing a research study for my human sexuality class. I asked students where the craziest place they ever had sex was and told them they could write their answer anywhere on my body. The males were to write their answers in blue or black markers, while the females were to use

© Masterfile

the red or orange markers. This way I would be able to compare male and female answers, and look for any gender differences. Students who were virgins could write a large V on my body. It was interesting to see their reactions to my research design and even more interesting to see their responses to my question. College students have had sex in some really crazy places! All in all, it was a lot of fun to do. The only downside to my research study was that it took me WEEKS to wash the Sharpie marker off!"

Janell Cauth

"The only downside was that it took me weeks to get all the Sharpie marker off."
—CHAPTER OPENING VIDEO

View in Video

To watch the entire interview, go to Psychology CourseMate at **login.cengagebrain.com.**

© Matthew Sorenson

What would you have done if Valerie had approached you in her bikini, handed you a Sharpie, and asked you to write on her body the craziest place you'd ever had sex? Would you do it? Do you think most students would? Why or why not? In the end, do you think the responses she obtained were representative of all students at her university? These are good questions to ask and they give us a great introduction into the study of human sexuality.

Sex studies seem to appear everywhere today—in magazines, newspapers, and on television. But how do you know whether the research is reliable and has been carried out properly? In this chapter, we explore both the major theories and the research methods that underlie the study of sexuality. We also examine some of the most influential sexuality studies that have been done. Theoretical development and ongoing research combine to provide a foundation on which to build further understanding of sexuality.

Before we start, you might wonder why reviewing theory and research in a sexuality textbook is important. Because theories guide our understanding of sexuality, and research helps answer our many questions, learning how theories are formulated and research is pursued will give you insight into the information that is provided in the chapters to come. Let's examine the various theories of sexuality and some of the important sex researchers.

Sigmund Freud (1856–1939), the father of psychoanalysis, set the stage for all psychological theories that followed.

For example, suppose researchers subscribe to the theory that sexuality is innate and biologically determined; they would probably design studies to examine such things as how the hypothalamus in the brain or the monthly cycle of hormones influences our sexual behavior. It is unlikely they would be interested in studying the societal influences on sexuality. A person who believes sexuality is determined by environmental influences, in contrast, would be more likely to study how the media influences sexuality rather than genetic patterns of sexual behavior.

Several theories—often clashing—guide much of our thinking about sexuality. These include psychological, biological, sociological, and evolutionary theoretical views of human sexuality. In addition, over the last few years, feminist and queer theories have also become important models for exploring and explaining sexual behavior. We first explore each of these and look at how they influence sexuality research. While we do, however, it is important to remember that many theorists borrow from multiple theoretical perspectives, and that these categories often overlap and learn from each other.

▶▶ PSYCHOANALYTIC Theory

Sigmund Freud (1856–1939) was the founder of the psychoanalytic theory. He believed that the sex drive was one of the most important forces in life, and he spent a considerable amount of time studying sexuality. According to Freud, human behavior is motivated by instincts and drives. The two most powerful drives are **libido** (la-BEED-oh), which is sexual motivation, and **thanatos** (THAN-uh-toes), which is aggressiveness motivation. Of these two, the libido is the more powerful. Two of Freud's most controversial concepts include personality formation and psychosexual development.

Freud believed the personality contained the **id, ego,** and **superego.** At birth, a child has only the id portion of the personality, which functions as the pleasure center. If the id were the only part of the personality that developed, we would always be seeking pleasure and fulfillment with little concern for others; in other words, we would operate in the way most animals do. As humans get older, however, the id balances its desires with other parts of the personality.

By the second year of life, the ego develops as the child begins to interact with his or her environment. The ego keeps the id in check by being realistic about what the child can and cannot have.

▶ THEORIES ABOUT Sexuality

The study of sexuality is multidisciplinary. Psychologists, sexologists, biologists, theologians, physicians, sociologists, anthropologists, and philosophers all perform sexuality research. The questions each discipline asks and how its practitioners transform those questions into research projects can differ greatly. However, the insights of these disciplines complement each other, and no single approach to the study of sexuality is better than another.

A **theory** is a set of assumptions, principles, or methods that help a researcher understand the nature of the phenomenon being studied. A theory provides an intellectual structure to help conceptualize, implement, and interpret a topic, such as human sexuality. The majority of researchers begin with theories about human behavior that guide the kind of questions they ask about sexuality.

---

theory
A set of assumptions, principles, or methods that helps a researcher understand the nature of a phenomenon being studied.

libido
According to Freud, the energy generated by the sexual instinct.

thanatos
According to Freud, the self-destructive instinct, often turned outward in the form of aggression.

id
The collection of unconscious urges and desires that continually seek expression.

ego
The part of the personality that mediates between environmental demands (reality), conscience (superego), and instinctual needs (id).

superego
The social and parental standards an individual has internalized; the conscience.

psychoanalysis
System of psychotherapy developed by Freud that focuses on uncovering the unconscious material responsible for a patient's disorder.

psychosexual development
The childhood stages of development during which the id's pleasure-seeking energies focus on distinct erogenous zones.

erogenous zones
Areas of the body that are particularly sensitive to touch and are associated with sexual pleasure.

Because the majority of the id's desires may be socially unacceptable, the ego works to restrain it.

Freud also believed that the last portion of the personality, the superego, develops by the age of 5 years. It contains both societal and parental values, and puts more restrictions on what a person can and cannot do. It acts as our conscience, and its most effective weapon is guilt. For example, let's say that a woman was raised in a very religious family, and she wants to wait until she's married to have sex. One night she starts hooking up with her boyfriend (an id action). It feels good, and the id is being fulfilled. Soon, reality kicks in (the ego), and she realizes that she is about to have sex in the backseat of a car! This causes her to reevaluate the situation, and because she has been taught that premarital sex is wrong, she feels guilty (a superego action). Throughout our lives, the id, ego, and superego are in a constant struggle with each other, but it is the ego, or the realistic portion of our personality, that keeps the other two parts balanced.

Freud's ideas were controversial in the Victorian period in which he lived.

If the ego does not keep things in balance, the superego could take over, and a person could be paralyzed by guilt. The id could also take over, forcing the person to search constantly for pleasure with little concern for others. Freud believed that the only way to bring these conditions into balance was for the person to undergo **psychoanalysis.**

Freud's most controversial idea was his theory of **psychosexual development.** He believed that one's basic personality was formed by events that happened in the first 6 years of life. During each stage of development, Freud identified a different **erogenous** (uh-RAJ-uh-nus) **zone** in which libidinal energy was directed. If the stage was not successfully completed, the libidinal energy was tied up in that zone, and the child could experience a **fixation.** Psychosexual development includes the oral, anal, phallic, and genital stages.

The first stage of psychosexual development, known as the **oral stage,** lasts through the first 18 months of life. According to Freud's theory, problems during this stage could result in an oral fixation, leading to behaviors such as cigarette smoking, overeating, fingernail chewing, or alcohol abuse. The next stage, the **anal stage** begins when a child starts toilet training. Problems during this stage could lead to traits such as stubbornness, orderliness, or cleanliness.

According to Freud, the most important stage is the next one, the **phallic stage,** which occurs between the ages of 3 and 6 years. Freud believed that during the phallic stage, boys go through the **Oedipus** (ED-uh-puss) **complex.** Freud thought girls go through an **Electra complex** and develop penis envy. Freud believed that the Electra stage is never fully resolved, and

because of this, women are less psychologically mature than men. At the end of this stage, boys and girls will typically identify with the same-sex parent and adopt masculine or feminine characteristics. The superego begins to develop during this time as well, and most children adopt their parents' values.

Before puberty (between the ages of 6 and 12), the child passes through the **latency stage,** and sexual interest goes underground. During this stage, little boys often think little girls have "cooties" (and vice versa), and childhood play primarily exists in same-sex groups. Puberty marks the **genital stage,** which is the final stage of psychosexual development. During this stage, sexuality becomes less internally directed and more directed at others as erotic objects.

Freud's ideas were controversial in the Victorian period in which he lived. His claims that children were sexual from birth and lusted for the other-sex parent caused tremendous shock in the conservative community of Vienna. Remember that at the time when Freud came up with his ideas, there was a strong cultural **repression** of sexuality. Doctors and ministers believed that masturbation was physically harmful and conversations about sex were unheard of. Among modern psychologists, Freud and the psychoanalytic theory have received a considerable amount of criticism. The predominant criticism is that his theory is unscientific and does not lend itself to testing (Robinson, 1993). How could a researcher study the existence of the phallic stage? If it is indeed **unconscious,** then it would be impossible to hand out surveys to see when a child was in each stage. Because Freud based his theories on his patients, he has been accused of creating his theories around people who were sick; consequently, they may not apply to healthy people (we discuss this further in the section, "Case Studies," on research methodology). Finally, Freud has also been heavily criticized because of his unflattering psychological portrait of women (Robinson, 1993).

▶▶ BEHAVIORAL Theory

Behaviorists believe that it is necessary to observe and measure behavior to understand it. Psychological states, emotions, the unconscious, and feelings are not measurable and, therefore, are not valid for study. Only overt behavior can be measured, observed, and controlled by scientists. Radical behaviorists (those who believe that we do not actually choose how we behave), such as B. F. Skinner (1953), claim that environmental rewards and punishments determine the types of behaviors in which we engage. This is referred to as **operant conditioning.**

---

fixation
The tying up of psychic energy at a particular psychosexual stage, resulting in adult behaviors characteristic of the stage.

oral stage
A psychosexual stage in which the mouth, lips, and tongue are the primary erogenous zone.

anal stage
A psychosexual stage in which the anal area is the primary erogenous zone.

phallic stage
A psychosexual stage in which the genital region is the primary erogenous zone and in which the Oedipus or Electra complex develops.

Oedipus complex
A male child's sexual attraction for his mother and the consequent conflicts.

Electra complex
The incestuous desire of a daughter for her father.

latency stage
A psychosexual stage in which libido and sexual interest are repressed.

genital stage
Final psychosexual stage in which a person develops the ability to engage in adult sexual behavior.

repression
A coping strategy by which unwanted thoughts or prohibited desires are forced out of consciousness and into the unconscious mind.

unconscious
All the ideas, thoughts, and feelings to which we have no conscious access.

behaviorists
Theorists who believe that behavior is learned and can be altered.

operant conditioning
Learning resulting from the reinforcing response a person receives after a certain behavior.

We learn certain behaviors, including most sexual behaviors, through reinforcement and punishment. Reinforcements encourage a person to engage in a behavior by associating it with pleasurable stimuli, whereas punishments make it less likely that a behavior will be repeated, because the behavior becomes associated with unpleasant stimuli. For instance, if a man decided to engage in extramarital sex with a colleague at work, it may be because of the positive reinforcements he receives, such as the excitement of going to work. If, in contrast, a man experiences an erection problem the first time he has sexual intercourse outside of his marriage, it may make it less likely he will try the behavior again anytime soon. The negative experience reduces the likelihood that he will engage in the behavior again.

To help change unwanted behavior, behaviorists use **behavior modification.** For example, if a man wants to rid himself of sexual fantasies about young boys, a behavioral therapist might use **aversion therapy.** To do so, the therapist might show the man slides of young boys; when he responds with an erection, an electrical shock is administered to his penis. If this is repeated several times, behaviorists believe the man will no longer respond with an erection. The punishment will have changed the behavior. Contrast this form of therapy with that of a psychoanalytic therapist, who would probably want to study what happened to this man in the first 6 years of his life. A behavior therapist would primarily be concerned with changing the behavior and less concerned with its origins. Much of modern sex therapy uses the techniques developed by behaviorists (MacKenzie, 2011).

▶▶ SOCIAL LEARNING Theory

Social learning theory actually grew out of behaviorism. Scientists began to question whether behaviorism was too limited in its explanation of human behavior. Many believed that thoughts and feelings had more influence on behaviors than the behaviorists claimed. A noted social learning theorist, Albert Bandura (1969), argued that both external and internal events influence our behavior. By this, he meant that external events, such as rewards and punishments, influence behavior, but so do internal events, such as feelings, thoughts, and beliefs. Bandura began to bridge the gap between behaviorism and cognitive theory, which we discuss next.

Social learning theorists believe that imitation and identification are also important in the development of sexuality. For example, we identify with our same-sex parent and begin to imitate him or her, which helps us develop our own gender identity. In turn, we are praised and reinforced for these behaviors. Think for a moment about a young boy who identifies with his mother and begins to

We learn certain behaviors through ***reinforcement and punishment.***

ON YOUR MIND 2.1

When scientists come up with new theories, how do they know they are true?

They don't. Theories begin as ideas to explain observed phenomena, but they must undergo testing and evaluation. Many early theories of sexuality were developed out of work with patients, such as Sigmund Freud's work, whereas others base their theories on behaviors they observe or the results of experiments they conduct. However, researchers never really know whether their theories are true. Some scientists become so biased by their own theories that they have trouble seeing explanations other than their own for certain behaviors. This is why scientific findings or ideas should always be tested and confirmed by other scientists.

dress and act like her. He will probably be ridiculed or even punished, which may lead him to turn his attention to a socially acceptable figure, most likely his father. Peer pressure also influences our sexuality. We want to be liked; therefore, we may engage in certain behaviors because our peers encourage it. We also learn what is expected of us from television, our families, and even from music.

▶▶ COGNITIVE Theory

So far, the theories we have discussed emphasize that either internal conflicts or external events control the development of personality. Unlike these, **cognitive theory** holds that people differ in how they process information, and this creates personality differences. We feel what we think we feel, and our thoughts also affect our behavior. Our behavior does not come from early experiences in childhood or from rewards or punishments; rather, it is a result of how we perceive and conceptualize what is happening around us.

As far as sexuality is concerned, cognitive theorists believe that the biggest sexual organ is between the ears (Walen & Roth, 1987). What sexually arouses us is what we think sexually arouses us. We pay attention to our physical sensations and label these reactions. For example, if a woman does not have an orgasm during sex with a partner, she could perceive this in one of two ways: She might think that having an orgasm is not really all that important and maybe next time she will have one; or, she could think that she is a failure because she did not have an orgasm and feel depressed as a result. What has caused the depression, however, is not the lack of an orgasm but her perception of it.

---

behavior modification
Therapy based on operant conditioning and classical conditioning principles used to change behaviors.

aversion therapy
A technique that reduces the frequency of maladaptive behavior by associating it with aversive stimuli.

cognitive theory
A theory proposing that our thoughts are responsible for our behaviors.

self-actualization
Fulfillment of an individual's potentialities, including aptitudes, talents, and the like.

unconditional positive regard
Acceptance of another without restrictions on their behaviors or thoughts.

conditional love
Conditional acceptance of another, with restrictions on their behaviors or thoughts.

evolutionary theory
A theory that incorporates both evolution and sociology, and looks for trends in behaviors.

▶▶ HUMANISTIC Theory

Humanistic (or person-centered) psychologists believe that we all strive to develop ourselves to the best of our abilities and to achieve **self-actualization** (Raskin & Rogers, 1989). This is easier to do if we are raised with **unconditional positive regard,** which involves accepting and caring about another person without any stipulations or conditions. In other words, there are no rules a person must follow to be loved. An example of unconditional positive regard would be a child being caught playing sexual games with her friends and her parents explaining that they loved her but disapproved of her behavior. If, on the other hand, the parents responded by yelling at the child and sending her to her room, she learns that when she does something wrong, her parents will withdraw their love. This is referred to as **conditional love.** The parents make it clear that they will love their child only when she acts properly.

Children who grow up with unconditional positive regard learn to accept their faults and weaknesses, whereas children who have experienced conditional love may try to ignore those traits because they know others would not approve. Accepting our faults and weaknesses leads us toward self-actualization.

Self-actualization occurs as we learn our own potential in life. We want to do things that make us feel good about ourselves. For many of us, casual sex with someone we don't know would not make us feel good; therefore, it does not contribute to our own growth. Sexual intimacy in a loving and committed relationship does feel good and helps contribute to our own self-actualization.

▶▶ BIOLOGICAL Theory

The biological theory of human sexuality emphasizes that sexual behavior is primarily a biological process. Sexual functioning, hormonal release, ovulation, ejaculation, conception, pregnancy, and birth are controlled physiologically. Those who advocate this theory also point out that human sexual behavior, including gender roles and sexual orientation, are primarily due to inborn, genetic patterns and are not functions of social or psychological forces. Sexual problems are believed to be caused by physiological factors, and intervention often includes medications or surgery.

▶▶ EVOLUTIONARY Theory

Unlike biological theory, which focuses on individual physiology, **evolutionary theory** looks more broadly at the physiological changes of an entire species over time. To understand sexual behavior in humans, evolutionary theorists study animal sexual patterns and look for evolutionary trends. They believe that sexuality exists for the purpose of reproducing the species, and individual sexuality is designed to maximize the chances of passing on one's genes. According to evolutionary theorists, the winners in the game of life are those who are most successful at transmitting their genes to the next generation.

Think about the qualities you look for in a partner. Students often tell me that they are looking for someone who is physically attractive, monogamous, has a sense of humor, and is intelligent, honest, extroverted, fun, and sensitive. An evolutionary theorist would argue that these qualities have evolved to ensure that a per-

ON YOUR MIND 2.2

I am a healthy female college student, but lately I've been having trouble reaching orgasm. How would the biological theory explain this?

A person who adopts a biological theory would explain differences in sexuality as resulting from anatomy, hormones, neurochemicals, or other physical explanations. Therefore, a biological theorist would suggest that trouble reaching orgasm would be because of physical reasons, such as hormonal or neurological causes. Treatment might involve a physical workup and blood work to evaluate hormone levels. However, other theoretical approaches would disagree with this assessment and would look at a variety of other issues, such as stress, internal thought processes, or social pressures.

son would be able to provide healthy offspring and care for them well. A physically attractive person is more likely to be fit and healthy. Could this be important to us because of their reproductive capabilities? Evolutionary theorists would say so. They would also argue that qualities such as monogamy, honesty, and sensitivity would help ensure that a partner will be reliable and help raise the offspring.

Some sexual activities have evolved to ensure the survival of the species. For example, evolutionary theorists believe that orgasms have evolved to make sexual intercourse pleasurable; this, in turn, increases the frequency that people engage in it, and the possibility for reproduction is increased. Differences between the sexes in sexual desire and behavior are also thought to have evolved. The double standard, which states that men are free to have casual sex, whereas women are not, exists because men produce millions of sperm per day and women produce only one viable ovum per month. Males try to "spread their seed" to ensure the reproduction of their family line, whereas females need to protect the one ovum they produce each month. When women become pregnant, they have a 9-month

Social influences, such as religion, affect our attitudes about various sexual behaviors, including sex outside of marriage, homosexuality, and abortion.

Colorblind/Getty Images

biological commitment ahead of them (and some would argue a life-long commitment as well).

Evolutionary theory has received a considerable amount of criticism, however, particularly because evolutionary theorists tend to ignore the influence of both prior learning and societal influences on sexuality.

▶▶ SOCIOLOGICAL Theory

Sociologists are interested in how the society in which we live influences sexual behavior. Even though the basic capacity to be sexual might be biologically programmed, how it is expressed varies greatly across societies, as we saw in Chapter 1. For instance, there are differences in what societies tolerate, men's and women's roles, and how sexuality is viewed. A behavior that may be seen as normal in one society may be considered abnormal in another. For instance, on the island of Mangaia in the South Pacific, women are very sexually assertive and often initiate sexual activity (D. S. Marshall, 1971). From an early age, elders teach them how to have multiple orgasms. However, in Inis Beag in Ireland, sexuality is repressed and is considered appropriate only for procreation (Messenger, 1993). Homosexuality is not tolerated, and heterosexual couples engage in sexual intercourse fully clothed, with only the genitals exposed. Each society regulates its sexual behaviors.

Sociologists believe that societal influences, such as the family, religion, economy, medicine, law, and the media, affect a society's rules about sexual expression (DeLamater, 1987). Each of these influences dictates certain beliefs about the place of sexuality in one's life and how the culture determines what is sexually "normal."

The family is the first factor that influences our values about what is sexually right and wrong. As we discussed in Chapter 1, our family provides strong messages about what is acceptable and unacceptable. Religion also influences how a society views sexuality. Some religions provide strong opinions on issues such as premarital sex, homosexuality, and abortion. Many people within society look to religious institutions and leaders for answers to their questions about sexuality.

The economy also influences the societal view of sexuality (DeLamater, 1987). The U.S. economy is based on capitalism, which involves an exchange of services for money. This influences the availability of sex-related services such as prostitution, pornography, and sex shops. These services exist because they are profitable.

In addition to family and the economy, the medical community affects how a society views sexuality. For example, many years ago, physicians taught that masturbation was a disease that could lead to permanent mental illness. This attitude influenced societal opinions of masturbation. Other behaviors in which physicians urged people not to engage included anal intercourse, extramarital sex, homosexuality, and bisexuality. Society's values about these behaviors were guided by the medical community's attitudes and beliefs.

Laws also influence sexual behavior in the United States by establishing social norms and influencing societal attitudes. For example, the availability of certain contraceptive methods, abortion, same-sex marriage, and certain sexual behaviors are regulated by existing laws.

Finally, the media is a strong influence on our attitudes about sexuality. Television, magazines, music, and even YouTube videos provide valuable information about sexuality. Even though the media have been more inclusive over the past few years, a heterosexual bias still exists (the media tell us that heterosexuality is the most acceptable form of sexual behavior). To be homosexual or even **abstinent** is less acceptable. All of these influence the social views of sexuality and what practices we believe are right and wrong.

▶▶ FEMINIST Theory

Feminist theory argues that society has a strong influence on our ideas about sexuality. Many feminists also believe that **sexology** in the United States is dominated by White, middle-class, heterosexist attitudes that permeate sexuality research (Ericksen, 1999; Irvine, 1990). Feminist researchers often claim to have a

---

REAL RESEARCH 2.1 Three-quarters of all 7th to 12th graders in the United States report having a profile on a social networking site (RIDEOUT ET AL., 2010).

---

different view of sexuality that enables them to see things men cannot (Ericksen, 1999; Tiefer, 2004). Several feminist researchers have been leaders in the effort to redefine sexual functioning and remove the medical and biological aspects that permeate sexuality today. Leonore Tiefer, a feminist researcher, has written extensively about the overmedicalization of sexuality. Tiefer argues that there may not be any biological sex drive at all—it may be that our culture is what influences our sexual desire the most (Kaschak & Tiefer, 2001; Tiefer, 2001). We talk more about Tiefer's work in Chapter 14.

Typically, feminism has a number of variations, with some more liberal or radical than others. Overall, however, feminist scholars believe that the social construction of sexuality is based on power, which has been primarily in the hands of men for centuries (Collins, 1998). They believe there is sexual gender inequality that, for the most part, sees women as submissive and subordinate (Collins, 2000). This power over women is maintained through acts of sexual aggression such as rape, sexual abuse, sexual harassment, pornography, and prostitution (M. Jackson, 1984; MacKinnon, 1986). In addition, feminists argue that male sexuality consistently views sex as an act that involves only a penis in a vagina. For "sex" to occur, the erect penis must penetrate the vagina and thrust until the male ejaculates. Catharine MacKinnon (1987) suggests that male-dominated views of sexuality have resulted in a society that believes that "what is sexual gives a man an erection" (p. 75). All of this led to the repression of female sexuality and, as a result, the lack of attention to the female orgasm.

Feminist researchers also believe that there is much to be gained from collaborative or group research, which uses interviews to gain information, because they can provide rich, qualitative data (diMauro, 1995). Controlled laboratory experiments, which have been viewed as more "masculine" in structure (be-

---

abstinent
The state of not engaging in sexual activity.

sexology
The scientific study of sexuality.

Sex in Real Life ▶▶▶ What Questions Would They Ask?

Because theorists from various perspectives are interested in different types of studies, they ask different types of questions. Following are a few questions that theorists from different schools of thought might ask.

Psychoanalytic: How are sexual problems later in life related to early childhood experiences? How do children resolve the Oedipal and Electra complexes? Does an overactive superego cause college students to feel guilt about sexual behavior?

Behavioral: What reinforces a person's attraction to partners of the same sex? What reinforces a heterosexual college student to use contraception? What are the attractions and hesitancies around the decision to lose one's virginity?

Social Learning: How does peer group pressure influence our sexuality? What

effects do the media have on our sexuality? Are children influenced by sexual messages on television?

Cognitive: What is the decision-making process related to contraceptive choice? Do children cognitively understand sexuality? How do men view erectile dysfunction?

Humanist: How do negative parental reactions to first sexual experience affect teenagers? How does self-actualization affect sexuality?

Biological: How does genetics influence sexuality? What are the effects of hormone levels on sexual desire? Does menstruation affect sexual desire in women?

Evolutionary: Why are women the ones who usually control the level of sexual activity? How has monogamy developed?

Sociological: How does religion influence sexuality? How does the threat of HIV/AIDS affect society? Do laws affect sexual behavior?

Feminist: What is the role of rape in repressing female sexuality? How do the media reinforce a male view of sexuality?

Queer: How do homosexual individuals move from a state of identity confusion about their homoerotic feelings to a point at which they accept their lesbian or gay identity? How are same-sex and heterosexual desires interrelated?

As you read through these various questions, which seem of most interest to you? Perhaps these questions can give you insight into which theory makes the most sense to you.

---

cause of the rigid nature of experiments), remove the study from the social context, which affects the outcome of the study (Peplau & Conrad, 1989). We discuss this further later in the chapter.

▶▶ QUEER Theory

Queer theory shares a common political interest with feminist theory—a concern for women's and gay, lesbian, bisexual, and transsexual rights. Growing out of lesbian and gay studies, queer theory developed in the 1990s. Queer theory focuses on mismatches between sex, gender, and desire, and proposes that domination and its related characteristics, such as heterosexism and

homophobia, should be resisted (Isaiah Green, 2007; Schlichter, 2004). Queer theorists believe that studies need to examine how a variety of sexualities are constructed and to abandon various categorizations (homosexual/heterosexual) (Rudy, 2000). Categories are cultural constructions that limit and restrain. Overall, queer theorists and some feminists believe that meaningful societal change can come about only through radical change and cannot be introduced into a society in a piecemeal way (Turner, 2000). (The accompanying Sex in Real Life presents examples of studies that researchers with different theoretical backgrounds might be interested in doing.) Now let's turn our attention to some of the important sexuality studies that have been done.

◀ review QUESTIONS

1 What is a theory?

2 How does a theory help guide research?

3 Describe the influence of Freud's theories on sexuality.

4 Compare and contrast behavioral, social learning, cognitive, humanistic, biological, evolutionary, and sociological theories.

5 Explain how feminist and queer theories have asked a different set of questions about sexuality.

SEXUALITY RESEARCH:
Philosophers, Physicians, and Sexologists

The ancient Greeks, through physicians such as Hippocrates and philosophers such as Aristotle and Plato, may actually be the legitimate forefathers of sex research, because they were the first to develop theories regarding sexual responses and dysfunctions, sex legislation, reproduction and contraception, and sexual ethics. It wasn't until the 18th century, however, that there was increased discussion of sexual ethics, and that the first programs of public and private sex education and classifications of sexual behavior were established.

▶▶ EARLY SEX Research

In the 19th century, researchers (such as Charles Darwin, Heinrich Kaan, Jean-Martin Charcot, and others) from a variety of disciplines laid the foundations of sex research in the modern sense. It was during this time that the study of sex began to concentrate more on the bizarre, dangerous, and unhealthy aspects of sex. In 1843, Kaan, a Russian physician, wrote *Psychopathia Sexualis,* which presented a classification of what he termed *sexual mental diseases.* This system was greatly expanded and refined more than 40 years later by Richard von Krafft-Ebing in another book with the same title. Sex research during this time almost exclusively focused on people believed to be sick (see accompanying Timeline "Important Developments in the History of Sex Research").

During the Victorian period in the 19th century, the majority of sex research was thwarted. Some researchers found that they suddenly lost their professional status, were accused of having the very sexual disorders they studied, or were viewed as motivated solely by lust, greed, or fame. However, as interest in medicine in general grew, researchers began to explore how to improve health and peoples' lives, which included researching various aspects of sexuality.

Physicians were the primary sexuality researchers in the late 19th century (keep in mind that at that time nearly all physicians were male). Because physicians were experts in biology and the body, they were also viewed as the sexuality experts (V. Bullough, 1994). Interestingly, although the majority of physicians had little or no specialized knowledge of sexual topics, most spoke with authority about human sexuality anyway.

The majority of the early sexuality studies were done in Europe, primarily in Germany (V. Bullough, 1994). At the time, sex research was protected because it was considered part of medical research, even though holding a medical degree did not always offer complete protection. Some researchers used pseudonyms to publish their work, some were verbally attacked, and others had their data destroyed.

At the turn of the 20th century, it was the pioneering work of Sigmund Freud, Havelock Ellis, and Iwan Bloch that established the study of sexual problems as a legitimate endeavor in its own right. It is interesting to note that the overwhelming majority of sexology pioneers were Jewish (Haeberle, 1982). The Jewish roots of much of modern sexology have certainly added to its controversial nature in certain countries. As a result of all the negative reactions and problems with sexuality research in Europe, it gradually moved from Germany to the United States, which has led the way in sexuality research ever since.

In 1921, several prominent European doctors attempted to set up an organization called the Committee for Research in Problems of Sex. After much hard work, the organization established itself but experienced problems in low membership rates and a lack of research and publishing support. However, because of strong beliefs and persistence by the founders, the group continued.

Systematic research into sexuality in the United States began in the early 1920s, motivated by pressures from the social hygiene movement, which was concerned about sexually transmitted infections and their impact on marriage and children. American society was generally conservative and viewed the "sex impulse" as a potential threat to societal stability. Funding for sexuality research was minimal. It took philanthropy from the fortunes of men such as John D. Rockefeller and Andrew Carnegie for researchers to afford to implement large-scale, interdisciplinary projects.

> Physicians were the **primary sexuality researchers** in the late 19th century.

timeline Important Developments in the **History of Sex Research**

1843
Russian physician Heinrich Kaan publishes *Psychopathia Sexualis,* a classification system of sexual diseases.

1886
Richard von Krafft-Ebing, a German psychiatrist, expands and refines Kaan's earlier work in *Psychopathia Sexualis.*

1892
American physician Clelia Mosher begins a survey among educated middle-class women concerning sexual attitudes and experiences.

Courtesy of Erwin J. Haeberle, Magnus Hirschfeld Archive for Sexology, Humboldt Universitat du Berlin

1896
English private scholar Havelock Ellis begins *Studies in the Psychology of Sex.* Because they cannot be published in England, they appear in the United States and in Germany.

© Hulton-Deutsch Collection/Corbis

1897
Berlin physician Magnus Hirschfeld founds the Scientific Humanitarian Committee, the world's first "gay rights" organization.

Courtesy of Erwin J. Haeberle, Magnus Hirschfeld Archive for Sexology, Humboldt Universitat du Berlin

1897
Berlin physician Albert Moll publishes *Investigations into Sexuality*.

▶▶ RECENT STUDIES on Sexuality

Early sex research set the stage for sexuality researchers. We talk about their specific contributions later in this chapter, but as we take a look at the whole picture of sexuality research, it's interesting to note that the majority of research into human sexuality has been *problem driven,* meaning that most of the research that has been done has focused on a specific problem. A review of ongoing

---

REAL RESEARCH 2.2   The way a research study is designed and implemented can affect the results of the study (BEGLEY, 2007).

---

research projects at the National Institutes of Health in 2010 revealed several problem-driven areas of research (such as HIV prevention and human papillomavirus [HPV] infection in pregnancy). However, a focus on problems doesn't allow researchers to obtain funds to research topics on healthy sexuality and answer questions such as, "How does sexual development progress in normal children?" or "How is sexuality expressed in loving, long-term relationships?"

Many individuals and groups are opposed to sexuality research today, and some believe that the mystery surrounding sexuality will be taken away by increasing scientific knowledge. Conservative groups believe that research done on topics such as adolescent sexuality encourages young people to have sex. Sex researchers are accustomed to pressure from conservative groups that oppose their work. In fact, after Alfred Kinsey published his two famous studies about male and female sexuality, which were funded by the Rockefeller Foundation, Congress pushed the foundation to withdraw its financial support from Indiana University, which it did (J. H. Jones, 1997). We discuss politics and sexuality research more later in this chapter.

Sexuality research has become very fragmented over the last few decades, with researchers coming from several different disciplines, such as psychology, sociology, medicine, social work, and public health, to name a few. Oftentimes, researchers are unaware of research being published in other disciplines. Journal articles are often inaccessible to a general audience or to researchers outside the discipline from which the research originated (diMauro, 1995). What tends to happen, therefore, is that the popular media

become responsible for disseminating information about sexuality, which is often distorted or sensationalistic.

As you may recall from Chapter 1, sexologists—researchers, educators, and clinicians who specialize in sexuality—are scientists who engage in sophisticated research projects and publish their work in scientific journals. Unfortunately, they are sometimes ridiculed, not viewed as "real" scientists, and accused of studying sexuality because of their own sexual hang-ups or because they are voyeurs. Geer and O'Donohue (1987) claim that, unlike other areas of science, sex research is often evaluated as either moral or immoral. Some groups believe that marital sex for procreation is the only acceptable sexual behavior, and that many sexual practices (such as masturbation, homosexuality, and premarital and extramarital sex) are immoral. Researchers are often encouraged not to invade the privacy of intimate relationships or to study the sexuality of certain age groups (either young or old). People often resist participating in sexuality research because of their own moral or psychological attitudes toward sex. Methodological problems also have made it difficult for the field of sexuality research. We discuss these issues more later in this chapter.

Academic programs that specialize in human sexuality began appearing in the 1970s (for more information about these programs, see the website listings at the end of this chapter). In addition, several groups exist today to promote sexuality research and education, including the Kinsey Institute for Research in Sex, Gender, and Reproduction; the Society for the Scientific Study of Sexuality (SSSS); American Association for Sexuality Educators, Counselors and Therapists (AASECT); Society for Sex Therapy and Research (SSTAR); and the Sexuality Information and Education Council of the United States (SIECUS). Many medical schools and universities now teach sexuality courses as a part of the curriculum.

Although sexuality research is still in its early stages, it has begun to help remove the stigma and ignorance associated with discussing human sexual behavior. Ignorance and fear can contribute to irresponsible behavior. Sexuality research has helped sex become a topic of discussion rather than a taboo subject. Today, understanding sexuality has become increasingly important to the work of psychologists, physicians, educators, theologians, and scientists.

1899	**1903–4**	**1905**	**1907**	**1908**	**1909**
Magnus Hirschfeld begins editing of the *Yearbook for Sexual Intermediate Stages* for the Scientific Humanitarian Committee.	**Magnus Hirschfeld begins** his statistical surveys on homosexuality. They are quickly terminated by legal action.	**Sigmund Freud publishes** *Three Essays on the Theory of Sex,* based on his theory of psychoanalysis. © Hulton-Deutsch Collection/Corbis	**Berlin dermatologist Iwan Bloch coins** the term *Sexualwissenschaft* (sexology) and publishes *The Sexual Life of Our Time.*	**Magnus Hirschfeld publishes** the first issue of *The Journal for Sexology.*	**Albert Moll publishes** *The Sexual Life of the Child,* which challenges Freud's psychoanalytic theory.

▶▶ POLITICS AND Sex Research

In Chapter 1, we discussed how the changing political climate affects attitudes about sexuality. It won't surprise you to learn that the changing political climate also affects sexuality research. When Kinsey's work was published in the 1950s, several politicians claimed that asking people about their sex lives in a nonjudgmental fashion, like Kinsey did, promoted immorality (Bancroft, 2004). Some conservative politicians believed that heterosexual families were threatened by liberal values inherent in sex research. Negative attitudes such as these affected the public's perception of sex research.

Even so, Kinsey's work helped lead to many societal changes associated with sexuality. The changing roles of women and the development of birth control pills, along with Kinsey's work, led to less acceptance for the double standard of sexuality (Bancroft, 2004). In fact, after the publication of Kinsey's second book, the American Law Institute lawyers and judges recommended decriminalizing many forms of sexual behavior (including adultery, cohabitation, and homosexual relationships) (Allyn, 1996). As a result, many states revised their laws about certain sexual practices (Bancroft, 2004).

The HIV/AIDS crisis that began in the 1980s provided a new opportunity for sex research, leading to one large-scale sexuality study titled the National Health and Social Life Survey (NHSLS) by the National Opinion Research Center at the University of Chicago in the early 1990s (Kimmel & Plante, 2007). However, the

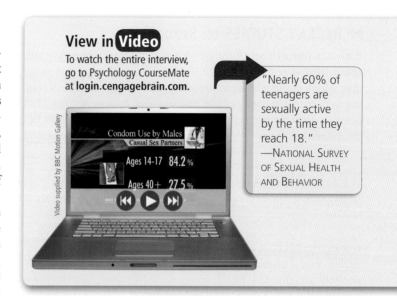

View in Video
To watch the entire interview, go to Psychology CourseMate at **login.cengagebrain.com.**

Video supplied by BBC Motion Gallery

Condom Use by Males
Casual Sex Partners
Ages 14–17 **84.2**%
Ages 40+ **27.5**%

"Nearly 60% of teenagers are sexually active by the time they reach 18."
—National Survey of Sexual Health and Behavior

sexual behavior, the National Survey of Sexual Health and Behavior (NSSHB), was published, the NSSHB was one of the most comprehensive studies on sexual behavior ever done (we further discuss these studies later in this chapter).

Although there is a need for an increased understanding of human sexuality, there are varying levels of political resistance to sex research (Bancroft, 2004). As a result, federal funding for sex research will continue to be problematic, and sex researchers will need to look to private foundations for funding. Many pharmaceutical companies have provided funding for studies on sexual problems and dysfunctions, but this has been controversial because the companies have a vested interest in the studies they fund. In fact, pharmaceutical companies have been accused of creating and promoting certain dysfunctions to "medicalize" the conditions and create a need for medication (Tiefer, 2006). Contraceptive manufacturers have also funded various research studies, and their participation in these studies is often viewed with skepticism.

REAL RESEARCH 2.3 The NSSHB was funded by Church & Dwight, the manufacturer of Trojan condoms. Critics argued that this affiliation influenced the number of questions about condom use throughout the study (CRARY, 2010).

---

original study, which was set to include 20,000 participants, was canceled because of mounting political pressure. Funding was acquired from private sources, reducing the number of participants to 3,500 (Bancroft, 2004). In 2010, another large-scale study of

timeline Important Developments in the **History of Sex Research**

1911
Albert Moll publishes *The Handbook of Sexual Sciences.*

Courtesy of Erwin J. Haeberle, Magnus Hirschfeld Archive for Sexology, Humboldt Universitat du Berlin

1912
Iwan Bloch begins publication of the *Handbook of Sexology.*

1913
Magnus Hirschfeld, Iwan Bloch, and others found *The Society of Sexology* in Berlin.

1913
Albert Moll founds *The International Society of Sex Research* in Berlin.

1914
Magnus Hirschfeld publishes *Homosexuality in Men and Women.*

1919
Magnus Hirschfeld opens the first Institute for Sexology in Berlin.

1 Describe the beginnings of sexuality research, and explain how the focus of sex research has progressed.

2 Explain how sexuality research has been problem driven and give two examples.

3 Explain how politics can influence sexuality research.

▶ SEXUALITY Researchers

All of the researchers discussed in this section and their publications helped give credibility to the area of sexual research. Some of the researchers adopted Freud's psychoanalytic theory, whereas others developed their research without adopting specific theories of sexuality. Although they had introduced scientific principles into the study of sexual behavior, their influence was mostly limited to the field of medicine.

▶▶ EARLY PROMOTERS of Sexology

Several people were responsible for the early promotion of sexology, including Iwan Bloch, Magnus Hirschfeld, Albert Moll, Richard von Krafft-Ebing, Havelock Ellis, Katharine Bement Davis, Clelia Mosher, Alfred Kinsey, Alan Bell, Martin Weinberg, Morton Hunt, William Masters, and Virginia Johnson. All of these researchers made a tremendous contribution to the study of sexology.

Iwan Bloch: *Journal of Sexology*

Iwan Bloch (1872–1922), a Berlin dermatologist, believed that the medical view of sexual behavior was shortsighted, and that both historical and anthropological research could help broaden it. He hoped that sexual science would one day have the same structure and objectivity as other sciences. Along with Magnus Hirschfeld, Bloch and several other physicians formed a medical society for sexology research in Berlin. It was the first sexological society, and it exercised considerable influence (we talk more about this society later). Starting in 1914, Bloch published the *Journal of Sexology,* a scientific journal about sexology. For almost two decades, this journal collected and published many important studies. Bloch planned to write a series of sexological studies, but because of World War I and his untimely death at age 50, he never did.

Magnus Hirschfeld: The Institute for Sexology

Magnus Hirschfeld (1868–1935) was a German physician, whose work with patients inspired him and convinced him that negative attitudes toward homosexuals were inhumane and unfounded. Because Hirschfeld was independently wealthy, all of his work was supported by his own funds (V. Bullough, 1994).

Using a pseudonym, Hirschfeld wrote his first article on sexology in 1896. In this article, he argued that sexuality was the result of certain genetic patterns that could result in a person being homosexual, bisexual, or heterosexual. He fought for a repeal of the laws that made homosexuality and bisexuality punishable by prison terms and heavy fines. In 1899, he began the *Yearbook for Sexual Intermediate Stages,* which was published for the purpose of educating the public about homosexuality and other sexual "deviations."

Thousands of people came to him for his help and advice about sexual problems, and in 1900, Hirschfeld began distributing questionnaires on sexuality. By this time, he had also become an expert in the field of homosexuality and sexual variations, and he testified as an expert witness in court cases of sexual offenders. Hirschfeld used only a small amount of his data in the books he published because he hoped to write a comprehensive study of sexuality at a later date. Unfortunately, his data were destroyed by the Nazis before they could be published.

In 1919, Hirschfeld founded the *Institut für Sexualwissenschaft* (Institute for Sexology), which contained his libraries, laboratory,

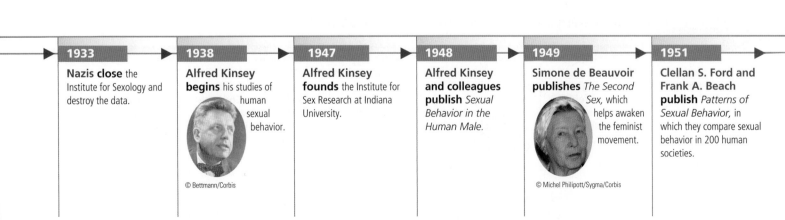

1933	**1938**	**1947**	**1948**	**1949**	**1951**
Nazis close the Institute for Sexology and destroy the data.	**Alfred Kinsey begins** his studies of human sexual behavior. © Bettmann/Corbis	**Alfred Kinsey founds** the Institute for Sex Research at Indiana University.	**Alfred Kinsey and colleagues publish** *Sexual Behavior in the Human Male.*	**Simone de Beauvoir publishes** *The Second Sex,* which helps awaken the feminist movement. © Michel Philipott/Sygma/Corbis	**Clellan S. Ford and Frank A. Beach publish** *Patterns of Sexual Behavior,* in which they compare sexual behavior in 200 human societies.

and lecture halls. The institute grew in size and influence over the next few years, but as the political climate in Berlin heated up, Hirschfeld was forced to flee Germany in 1933. The Nazis publicly burned the institute, and those who were working there were sent to concentration camps. Hirschfeld never returned to Germany and lived in France until his death in 1935.

Albert Moll: *Investigations Concerning the Libido Sexualis*

Albert Moll (1862–1939), a Berlin physician, was another big promoter of sexology. He was a very conservative man who disliked both Freud and Hirschfeld, and tried to counter their research at every opportunity. Moll formed the International Society for Sex Research in 1913 to counter Hirschfeld's Medical Society of Sexology. He also organized an International Congress of Sex Research in Berlin in 1926.

Moll wrote several books on sexology, including *Investigations Concerning the Libido Sexualis* in 1897. Unfortunately, it was probably Moll's disagreements with Freud that caused him to be ignored by the majority of English-speaking sexuality researchers, because Freud's ideas were so dominant during the first half of the 20th century (V. Bullough, 1994).

Richard von Krafft-Ebing: *Psychopathia Sexualis*

Richard von Krafft-Ebing (1840–1902) was one of the most significant medical writers on sexology in the late 19th century (V. Bullough, 1994). His primary interest was what he considered "deviant" sexual behavior. Krafft-Ebing believed that deviant sexual behavior was the result of engaging in nonreproductive sexual practices, including masturbation. In 1886, he published

Magnus Hirschfeld (1868–1935) worked hard to establish sexuality as a legitimate field of study.

Havelock Ellis (1859–1939) was a key figure in the early study of sexuality.

sexual pathology
Sexual disorders.

an update of a book titled *Psychopathia Sexualis,* which explored approximately 200 case histories of individuals who had experienced **sexual pathology,** including homosexuals and people who engaged in sex with children (pedophiles).

Although Krafft-Ebing was sympathetic to those with sexual "deviations" and he worked to help change discriminatory laws, many believed his work was morally offensive (Kennedy, 2002).

Havelock Ellis: *Studies in the Psychology of Sex*

Havelock Ellis (1859–1939) was an English citizen who grew up in Victorian society but rebelled against the secrecy surrounding sexuality. In 1875, when he was 16 years old, he decided to make sexuality his life's work. In fact, it is reported that Ellis sought a medical degree primarily so he could legitimately and safely study sexuality (V. Bullough, 1994). On publication of his famous six-volume *Studies in the Psychology of Sex* (1897–1910; H. Ellis, 1910), Ellis established himself as an objective and nonjudgmental researcher. In his collection of case histories from volunteers, he reported that homosexuality and masturbation were not abnormal and should not be labeled as such (Reiss, 1982). In 1901, *The Lancet,* a prestigious English medical journal, reviewed his early volumes and wrote:

> [Studies in the Psychology of Sex] must not be sold to the public, for the reading and discussion of such topics are dangerous. The young and the weak would not be fortified in their purity by the knowledge that they would gain from these studies, while they certainly might be more open to temptation after the perusal of more than one of the chapters. (Grosskurth, 1980, p. 222)

Unfortunately, Ellis's book was fairly dry and boring; as a result, and much to his dismay, Ellis never found the fame and fortune that Freud did.

---

timeline Important Developments in the **History of Sex Research**

1953	1957	1964	1965	1967	1970
Alfred Kinsey and his colleagues publish *Sexual Behavior in the Human Female.*	**American gynecologist Hans Lehfeldt founds** The Society for the Scientific Study of Sexuality (SSSS).	**An American physician, Mary Calderone, founds** the Sexuality Information and Education Council of the United States (SIECUS).	**SSSS publishes** the first issue of the *Journal of Sex Research.*	**The American Association of Sex Educators, Counselors and Therapists (AASECT) is founded.**	**William Masters and Virginia Johnson publish** *Human Sexual Inadequacy.*

AP/World Wide Photos

© Bettmann/Corbis

The rise of behaviorism in the 1920s added new dimensions to sexuality research. The idea of studying specific sexual behaviors became more acceptable, and the formulation of more sophisticated scientific research techniques provided researchers with more precise methods for sexual research. Many researchers attempted to compile data on sexual behavior, but the results were inconsistent, and the data were poorly organized. This led Alfred Kinsey, an American researcher, to undertake a large-scale study of human sexuality.

▶▶ SEXUALITY RESEARCH MOVES
to the United States

Although Alfred Kinsey was mainly responsible for moving sexuality research to the United States, many other American researchers were laying the foundation for sex research. These include Clelia Mosher, Katharine Bement Davis, and Evelyn Hooker. Other researchers continued to build on the work of these early researchers, including Alan Bell, Martin Weinberg, Morton Hunt, William Masters, and Virginia Johnson. Here we review their work and contributions to the field of sexuality research.

Clelia Mosher:
Important Female Questions

By now you have probably realized that men were doing much of the early research into human sexuality. Male sexuality was viewed as normative, and therefore female sexuality was approached through the lens of male sexuality. Clelia Mosher (1863–1940) was ahead of her time, asking questions about sexuality that were quite different from those of her male predecessors. She was actually the first researcher to ask women about their sexual behavior (Ericksen, 1999).

In 1892, while Mosher was a student at the University of Wisconsin, she began a research project that lasted 28 years. She asked upper-middle-class heterosexual women how often they engaged in sexual intercourse, how often they wanted

Katharine Bement Davis (1861–1935) conducted some of the largest and most comprehensive sexuality studies to date.

Dr. Evelyn Hooker (1907–1996) published the first empirical study to challenge the psychiatric view that homosexuality was a mental illness. Her work ultimately led to the removal of homosexuality from the *Diagnostic and Statistical Manual of Mental Disorders.*

to engage in it, and whether they enjoyed it (Ma-Hood & Wenburg, 1980). Her main motivation was to help married women have more satisfying sex lives. One of the questions that Mosher asked the women in her study was, "What do you believe to be the true purpose of intercourse?" (Ericksen, 1999). Although the majority of women said that intercourse was for both sexual pleasure and procreation, many reported feeling guilty for wanting or needing sexual pleasure. Unfortunately, much of Mosher's work was never published and never became part of the sex knowledge that circulated during her time (Ericksen, 1999).

Katharine Bement Davis:
Defending Homosexuality

Katharine Davis (1861–1935) began her sexuality research along a slightly different path. In 1920, Davis was appointed superintendent of a prison, and she became interested in prostitution and sexually transmitted infections. Her survey and analysis were the largest and most comprehensive of her time (Ellison, 2006; Ericksen, 1999).

Davis defended homosexuality as no different from heterosexuality and believed that lesbianism was not pathological. This idea was considered a threat in the early 1900s because it implied that women did not need men (Ellison, 2006; Faderman, 1981). Her ideas about lesbianism were largely ignored, but the idea that women might have sexual appetites equal to men's worried many male researchers (Ellison, 2006).

Evelyn Hooker:
Comparing Gay and Straight Men

Evelyn Hooker (1907–1996), a psychologist, was another important researcher. Her most notable study was on male homosexuality. Hooker compared two groups of men, one gay and the other straight, who were matched for age, education, and IQ levels. She collected information about their life histories, personality profiles, and psychological evaluations, and asked professionals to try

1971	1973	1974	1974	1974	1976
American psychiatrist Richard Green founds the International Academy of Sex Research. This organization publishes *Archives of Sexual Behavior.*	**Data collection begins** for the *National Survey of Family Growth.*	**The first World Health Organization is convened** in Geneva. Participants include sexologists and public health experts. The following year, it publishes *Education and Treatment in Human Sexuality: The Training of Health Professionals.*	**Hans Lehfeldt organizes** the first World Congress of Sexology.	**The first issue of** *Journal of Homosexuality* **is published.**	**The Institute for Advanced Study of Sexuality is founded** in San Francisco.

to distinguish between the two groups on the basis of their profiles and evaluations. They could not, demonstrating that there was little fundamental psychological difference between gay and straight men. Hooker's research helped challenge the widely held view that homosexuality was a mental illness.

Alfred Kinsey: Large-Scale Sexuality Research Begins in the United States

As we discussed in Chapter 1, Alfred Kinsey (1894–1956) was probably the most influential sex researcher of the 20th century. His work effectively changed many of the existing attitudes about sexuality. In 1938, while he was a professor of zoology at Indiana University, he was asked to coordinate a new course on marriage and the family. Before courses like this appeared on college campuses, human sexuality had been discussed only in hygiene courses, in which the focus was primarily on the dangers of sexually transmitted infections and masturbation (V. L. Bullough, 1998).

Soon after the course began, students came to Kinsey with sexuality questions for which he did not have answers, and the existing literature was of little help. This encouraged him to begin collecting data on his students' sex lives. His study grew and before long included students who were not in his classes, faculty members, friends, and nonfaculty employees. Soon he was able to obtain grant money that enabled him to hire research assistants. By this time, Kinsey's research had become well established in the scientific community.

Alfred Kinsey (1894–1956) implemented the first large-scale survey of adult sexual behavior in the United States.

In his early work, Kinsey claimed to be **atheoretical.** He believed that because sexuality research was so new, it was impossible to construct theories and hypotheses without first having a large body of information on which to base them. Kinsey's procedure involved collecting information on each participant's sexual life history, with an emphasis on specific sexual behaviors. Kinsey chose to interview participants, rather than have them fill out questionnaires, because he believed that questionnaires would not provide accurate responses. He was also unsure about whether participants would lie during an interview, and so he built into the interview many checks to detect false information. Data collected from husbands and wives were compared for consistency, and the interview was done again 2 and 4 years later to see whether the basic answers remained the same.

Kinsey was also worried about **interviewer bias** (interviewer opinions and attitudes that can influence information collected in the interview). To counter interview bias, only Kinsey and three colleagues conducted the interviews. Of the total 18,000 interviews, Kinsey himself conducted 8,000 (Pomeroy, 1972). Participants were asked a minimum of 350 questions, and interviewers memorized each question so that they could more easily build rapport with participants and wouldn't continually have to consult a paper questionnaire. Interviewers used appropriate terminology that participants would understand during the interview. Interviews lasted several hours, and participants were assured that the information they provided would remain confidential.

The sampling procedures Kinsey used were also strengths of his research. He believed that he would have a high refusal rate if he used **probability sampling.** Because of this, he used what he called "quota sampling accompanied by opportunistic collection" (Gebhard & Johnson, 1979, p. 26). In other words, if he saw that a particular group—such as young married women—was not well represented in his sample, he would find organizations with a high percentage of these participants and add them.

Overall, he obtained participants from colleges and universities; hospitals; prisons; mental hospitals; institutions for young delinquents; churches and synagogues; groups of people with sex-

atheoretical
Research that is not influenced by a particular theory.

interviewer bias
The bias of a researcher caused by his or her own opinions, thoughts, and attitudes about the research.

probability sampling
A research strategy that involves acquiring a random sample for inclusion in a study.

volunteer bias
A slanting of research data caused by the characteristics of participants who volunteer to participate.

100% sampling
A research strategy in which all members of a particular group are included in the sample.

generalizable
If findings are generalizable, they can be taken from a particular sample and applied to the general population.

timeline Important Developments in the **History of Sex Research**

1978	**1986**	**1988**	**1989**	**1990**
The World Association for Sexology is founded in Rome.	**The American Board of Sexology organizes** in Washington, D.C.	**The German** *Journal of Sex Research* **is first published.**	**The European Federation of Sexology is founded** in Geneva.	**The Asian Federation for Sexology is founded** in Hong Kong.

table 2.1 ■ What Did Kinsey Find in His Early Research?

Kinsey's groundbreaking research and the publication of his 1948 and 1953 books revealed many new findings about sexuality. Following are a few of these statistics. Keep in mind that these statistics are based on people's lives in the middle of the 20th century. For more information, visit the Kinsey Institute online at http://www.kinseyinstitute.org:

■ Close to 50% of American men reported engaging in both heterosexual and homosexual activities, or having had "reacted to" persons of both sexes in the course of their adult life.

■ Whereas about 25% of males had lost their virginity by the age of 16, only 6% of females had.

■ Married couples reported engaging in sexual intercourse 2.8 times per week in their late teens and only once per week by the age of 50.

■ The majority of couples reported only having sex in the missionary position.

■ By far the majority of men and women reported prefering sex with the lights out (but those who like the lights on were more likely to be men).

■ About 50% of married men reported having sex outside of their marriage, whereas about 25% of married women did.

■ The majority of men and women reported having masturbated.

■ The majority of men and women reached their first orgasm during masturbation.

■ Close to 70% of White heterosexual males reported at least one sexual experience with a prostitute.

SOURCE: Kinsey et al., 1948; Kinsey et al., 1953.

ual problems; settlement houses; homosexual groups throughout the United States; and members of various groups including the YMCA and the YWCA. Within these groups, every member was strongly encouraged to participate in the project to minimize **volunteer bias.** Kinsey referred to this procedure as **100% sampling.**

Kinsey's research found that many practices that had previously been seen as perverse or unacceptable in society (such as homosexuality, masturbation, and oral sex) were found to be widely practiced; as you might guess, such findings were very controversial and created strong reactions from conservative groups and religious organizations. Eventually, continued con-troversy about Kinsey's work resulted in the termination of several research grants. Kinsey's research challenged many of the assumptions about sexuality in the United States, and he stirred up antagonism; in this sense, Kinsey was truly a pioneer in the field of sexuality research (V. L. Bullough, 1998).

Morton Hunt: *Playboy* Updates Dr. Kinsey

Twenty-five years after Kinsey, Morton Hunt (1920–) began a large-scale sexuality study in the 1970s. Hunt gathered his sample through random selection from telephone books in 24 U.S. cities and believed it was comparable with Kinsey's research population. A total of 982 males and 1,044 females were included in the study and were given self-administered questionnaires. In addition, Hunt interviewed an additional 200 males and females for qualitative data.

Although Hunt's sampling technique was thought to be an improvement over Kinsey's techniques, there were also drawbacks. People without listed phone numbers, such as college students or institutionalized persons, were left out of the study. Although each person in Hunt's sample was called and asked to participate in a group discussion about sexuality, only 20% agreed to participate. In addition, because his sample was such a small percentage of those he contacted, volunteer bias (which we discuss in more detail later in this chapter) prevents his results from being **generalizable** to the population as a whole.

Hunt's findings were consistent with Kinsey's—premarital sex was increasing, as was the frequency of other sexual behaviors, such as oral and anal sex. Hunt published his research in a book *Sexual Behavior in the 1970s* (Hunt, 1974). In addition, he reviewed his findings in a series of articles in *Playboy* magazine.

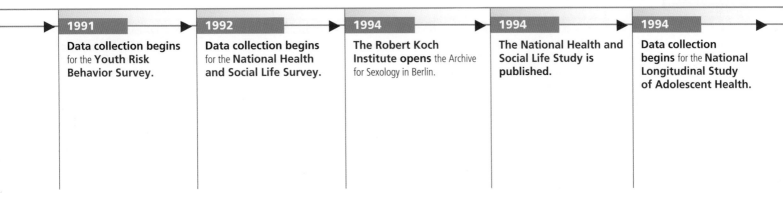

1991
Data collection begins for the **Youth Risk Behavior Survey.**

1992
Data collection begins for the **National Health and Social Life Survey.**

1994
The Robert Koch Institute opens the Archive for Sexology in Berlin.

1994
The National Health and Social Life Study is published.

1994
Data collection begins for the **National Longitudinal Study of Adolescent Health.**

Alan Bell and Martin Weinberg: *Homosexualities*

Continuing the research on sexual orientation, two colleagues from the Kinsey Institute, Alan Bell (1932–2002) and Martin Weinberg (1939–), began a large-scale study in 1968 on the influences of homosexuality. Bell and Weinberg surveyed thousands of gay and straight men and women to evaluate their mental health and social influences that might have influenced their sexual orientation. Their research supported Evelyn Hooker's previous findings—homosexuals were psychologically well-adjusted and satisfied with their intimate relationships. Bell and Weinberg believed their research supported the biological basis for homosexuality, refuting the idea that it was learned or the result of negative experiences (McCoubrey, 2002). Their research was published in two books, *Homosexualites* (1978) and *Sexual Preferences* (1981). Weinberg continued his research and has coauthored several other books based on his research on sexual orientation, including *Dual Attraction* (1994).

William Masters and Virginia Johnson: Measuring Sex in the Laboratory

William Masters (1915–2001), a gynecologist, and Virginia Johnson (1925–), a psychology researcher, began their sex research in 1954. They were the first modern scientists to observe and measure the act of sexual intercourse between heterosexual partners in the laboratory. They were primarily interested in the anatomy and physiology of the sexual response and later also explored sexual dysfunction. Masters and Johnson were a dual sex therapy team, representing both male and female opinions, which reduced the chance for **gender bias.** Much of the work

Martin Weinberg (1939–), a professor of sociology at Indiana University, continues to be active in sexuality research and has been exploring sexual minorities, premarital sex, and sex work in Sweden and New Zealand.

Courtesy of Martin Weinberg

Virginia Johnson (1925–) and William Masters (1915–2001) were the first to bring sexuality research into the laboratory.

© Bettmann/Corbis

done by Masters and Johnson was supported by grants, the income from their books, and individual and couples therapy.

Masters and Johnson's first study, published in 1966, was titled *Human Sexual Response*. In an attempt to understand the physiological process that occurs during sexual activity, the researchers brought 700 heterosexual men and women into the laboratory to have their physiological reactions studied during sexual intercourse. The volunteers participated for financial reasons (participants were paid for participation), personal reasons, and even for the release of sexual tension (Masters and Johnson both stated that they believed some volunteers were looking for legitimate and safe sexual outlets). Because Masters and Johnson were studying behaviors they believed were normative (i.e., they happened to most people), they did not feel they needed to recruit a **random sample.**

When volunteers were accepted as participants in the study, they were first encouraged to engage in sexual activity in the laboratory without the investigators present. It was hoped that this would make them feel more comfortable with the new surroundings. Many of the volunteers reported that after a while they did not notice that they were being monitored. During the study, they were monitored for physiological changes with an electrocardiograph to measure changes in the heart and an electromyograph to measure muscular changes. Measurements were taken of penile erection and vaginal lubrication with **penile strain gauges** and **photoplethysmographs** (FOH-toh-pleth-iss-mo-grafs).

Through their research, Masters and Johnson discovered several interesting aspects of sexual response, including women's potential for multiple orgasms and the fact that sexuality does not disappear in old age. They also pro-

timeline Important Developments in the **History of Sex Research**

2000	**2002**	**2002**	**2007**	**2010**
Data collection begins for the **National College Health Assessment.**	**Pfizer Pharmaceuticals publishes** the *Global Study of Sexual Attitudes and Behaviors.*	**The National Survey of Family Growth begins** including males in the data collection.	**Durex publishes** results from its global sex survey.	**The National Survey of Sexual Health and Behavior is published.**

posed a four-stage model for sexual response, which we discuss in more detail in Chapter 10.

In 1970, Masters and Johnson published another important book, *Human Sexual Inadequacy,* which explored sexual dysfunction. Again they brought couples into the laboratory, but this time only those who were experiencing sexual problems. They evaluated the couples physiologically and psychologically, and taught them exercises to improve their sexual functioning. Frequent follow-ups were done to measure the therapeutic results—some participants were even contacted 5 years after the study was completed.

Masters and Johnson found that there is often dual sexual dysfunction in couples (i.e., males who are experiencing erectile problems often have partners who are also experiencing sexual problems). Their studies also refuted Freud's theory that women are capable of both vaginal and clitoral orgasms, and that only vaginal orgasms result from intercourse. According to Masters and Johnson, all female orgasms result from direct or indirect clitoral stimulation.

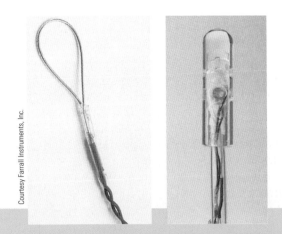

Courtesy Farrall Instruments, Inc.

To measure physiological changes during sexual arousal, researchers rely on strain gauges and photoplethysmographs. A penile strain gauge is placed on the base of the penis to measure erectile changes in the penis, whereas a photoplethysmograph is inserted in the vagina to measure changes in vaginal lubrication.

gender bias
The bias of a researcher caused by his or her gender.

random sample
A number of people taken from the entire population in such a way to ensure that any one person has as much chance of being selected as any other.

penile strain gauge
A device used to measure penile engorgement.

photoplethysmograph
A device used to measure vaginal lubrication.

It is important to point out that Masters and Johnson's books were written from a medical, not a psychological, perspective. They also used clinical language, and many professionals speculate this was a tactic to avoid censorship of the books. However, even with this scientific and medical base, their work was not without controversy. Many people at the time viewed Masters and Johnson's work as both unethical and immoral.

◀ review QUESTIONS

1 Explain the work done by early promoters of sexology.

2 Explore the reasons why there were so few women engaged in the study of human sexuality.

3 Differentiate between Alfred Kinsey's work and that of Masters and Johnson. What did these researchers contribute to our understanding of human sexuality?

▶ LARGE-SCALE Sexuality Research

A variety of large, national sexuality-related studies have contributed to our knowledge about human sexuality and have impacted how we think about various sexual behaviors. Two of the largest nationally representative studies are the NHSLS and the NSSHB. Both of these studies were funded by private organizations. In addition to these privately funded studies, several governmental studies have contributed limited information about sexuality. These ongoing surveys include the National Survey of Family Growth (NSFG) and the Youth Risk Behavior Survey (YRBS). Government studies typically include only a few questions about sexuality and are much broader in scope. For example, the YRBS, which monitors health-risk behaviors in high-

school students, contains 87 questions in total, but only 7 are related to sexual behaviors (Brener et al., 2004). Other studies, such as the National College Health Assessment (NCHA), the National Longitudinal Study of Adolescent Health (ADD Health), and the National Survey of Adolescent Males (NSAM), have also provided research on sexuality. We discuss these surveys in the following section.

▶▶ PRIVATELY FUNDED
Large-Scale Sexuality Studies

In this section, we discuss the NHSLS, the NSSHB, and the NCHA. These privately funded studies made significant contributions to sexuality research.

The National Health and Social Life Study was sponsored by the Robert Wood Johnson Foundation, The Henry J. Kaiser Family Foundation, the Rockefeller Foundation, the Andrew Mellon Foundation, The John D. and Catherine T. MacArthur Foundation, the New York Community Trust, and the American Foundation for AIDS Research. Above (left to right), researchers Robert Michael, John Gagnon, Stuart Michaels, and Edward Laumann.

National Health and Social Life Survey

In 1987, facing a devastating AIDS outbreak, the U.S. Department of Health and Human Services called for researchers to study the sexual attitudes and practices of American adults. A group of researchers from the University of Chicago—Edward Laumann, John Gagnon, Robert Michael, and Stuart Michaels—were selected to coordinate this national study of more than 20,000 people. Originally, the study was to be funded by the government, but as we discussed earlier in this chapter, legislation to eliminate federal funding for studies about sexuality was passed in 1991 and eliminated most of the budget. Eventually, private funding was acquired

The National Survey of Sexual Health and Behavior was conducted by researchers from the Center for Sexual Health Promotion at Indiana University. Below (left to right), researchers Brian Dodge, Debby Herbenick, and Michael Reece (not pictured Vanessa Schick, Stephanie Sanders, and J. Dennis Fortenberry).

from various foundations, but it forced the researchers to significantly reduce the sample size. In the end, a representative sample of 3,432 Americans between the ages of 18 and 59 years was used in the final analysis of data. All respondents were interviewed face-to-face, supplemented with brief questionnaires. The NHSLS was the most comprehensive study of sexual attitudes and behaviors since Kinsey, and because the researchers used better sampling procedures, this study was viewed as the most comprehensive, scientifically accurate sexuality study in the United States.

Overall, the study found that Americans were more sexually conservative than previously thought. The majority of people was found to have sex a few times a month or less. The results also indicated the sexual choices that people make were restricted by their social networks (e.g., friends and family). Among the findings of the NHSLS were the following:

- The median number of sexual partners since age 18 was six for men and two for women.
- 75% of married men and 80% of married women did not engage in extramarital sexuality.
- 2.8% of men and 1.4% of women described themselves as homosexual or bisexual.
- 75% of men claimed to have consistent orgasms with their partners, whereas 29% of women did.
- More than 1 in 5 women said they had been forced by a man to do something sexual.

National Survey of Sexual Health and Behavior

By the time the NSSHB was published in late 2010, it had been 18 years since the last large study of sexual behavior, the NHSLS. Many societal changes occurred during this time—all potentially impacting the sexual lives of Americans (Reece et al., 2010b). For example, policy changes in sexuality education programs and the development of new medications for sexual dysfunctions both affected sexual attitudes and behaviors. The NSSHB research was conducted by a team of sexuality researchers from the Center for Sexual Health Promotion at Indiana University and was funded by the manufacturer of Trojan condoms, which increased participant comfort by allowing them to fill out surveys in the privacy of their own homes and eliminating the presence of an interviewer. One statistician pointed out that online polling "allowed researchers to ask about sex without ever personally asking anyone about sex" (Bialik, 2010a). The NSSHB study included 5,865 adolescents and adults, ages 14 to 94.

Overall, the NSSHB found that people were engaging in a wide variety of sexual behaviors. Young teens were found to be less sexually active than many feared. Whereas prior studies had claimed half of all teens were sexually active, the NSSHB found among 14- to 17-year-olds, fewer than 25% had engaged in vaginal intercourse. Participation in sexual activities was found to

computer-assisted personal interviewing (CAPI)
An interview technique in which an interview takes place in person but a computer is used to input data.

audio computer-assisted self-interviewing
A private method of data collection in which subjects hear the questions and response choices through headphones or read them on a computer screen and can enter responses independently.

table **2.2** ■ **What Did We Learn from the National Survey of Sexual Health and Behavior?**

The National Survey of Sexual Health and Behavior (NSSHB) was a nationally representative study of the sexual health–related behaviors of 5,865 adolescents and adults in the United States. Following are some findings from this study.

■ Although the NSSHB included men, women, and a wide age range, it was not representative of all adults, especially because older adults living in hospitals or long-term care facilities were not included.

■ Results from the NSSHB could not be generalized to gay, lesbian, and bisexual individuals, because a large sample size can blur various data points, such as sexual orientation.

■ Black and Hispanic participants reported higher condom use compared with other racial groups.

■ Vaginal intercourse was more common for men ages 25 to 49 than any other sexual behavior.

■ Since the early 1990s, rates of insertive anal sex have increased in all age groups. More than 40% of men ages 25 to 59 reported having engaged in insertive anal intercourse in their lifetimes (however, the NSSHB did not provide information on the sexual orientation of these participants).

SOURCE: Special Issue: Findings from the National Survey of Sexual Health and Behavior (NSSHB), Center for Sexual Health Promotion, Indiana University. (2010, October). Journal of Sexual Medicine, 7(Suppl. 5).

comprehensive data on the health of U.S. college students. In 2010, a total of 5,233 students completed the NCHA survey. Results from the NCHA are not generalizable to all college students because the schools that participate in the survey are self-selecting (i.e., they ask to be included and pay to participate). Even so, many of the findings are consistent with comparable research studies on college populations. Among the findings from the NCHA are the following:

■ 32% of females and 36% of males reported no sexual partners within the last year.

■ 55% of sexually active heterosexual female students and 48% of sexually active heterosexual male students reported using contraception the last time they engaged in vaginal intercourse.

■ 6% of male students and 3% of female students reported engaging in anal sex within the past 30 days.

■ 13% of sexually active heterosexual college students reported using, or having a partner use, emergency contraception within the last year.

gradually increase as teens matured (Rabin, 2010a). Some of the other notable findings from the NSSHB include the following:

■ 85% of men reported their partner had an orgasm at the most recent sexual interaction, although only 64% of women reported having had an orgasm. (See accompanying Sex in Real Life for more information about this statistic.)

■ Masturbation is common throughout the life span and more common than partnered sexual behavior during adolescence and older age.

■ 30% of women and 5% of men reported pain during sexual intercourse.

■ 23% of men and 13% of women older than 50 years reported their most recent sex was with a "friend" or "new acquaintance."

■ 80% of sexually active boys between the ages of 14 and 17 reported using condoms the last time they engaged in sexual behavior.

National College Health Assessment

The NCHA is an ongoing private study organized by the American College Health Association. Beginning in 2000, the NCHA examined the habits, behaviors, and perceptions of college students' sexual health, alcohol and tobacco use, weight, nutrition, exercise, violence, and mental health. The NCHA is the largest known

REAL RESEARCH 2.4 The NSSHB found condom use was higher among Black and Hispanic Americans than among White Americans (DODGE ET AL., 2010).

▶▶ GOVERNMENT-FUNDED Large-Scale Studies

Several large-scale studies are funded by the U.S. government to collect data on a variety of health-related topics. As we discussed, these studies contain only a limited number of questions about sexuality. In the following sections, we discuss the NSFG, YRBS, National Longitudinal Study of Adolescent Health, and the NSAM.

National Survey of Family Growth

The NSFG is an ongoing government study that gathers data on family life, marriage and divorce, pregnancy, infertility, contraceptive use, and men's and women's health. The study is sponsored by the U.S. National Center for Health Statistics in the Centers for Disease Control, and results from the ongoing surveys are used in planning health education interventions and programs.

Data collection began in 1973, and although originally intended to include only women, the NSFG began studying men in 2002 (interestingly, in the first two rounds of data collection in 1973 and 1976, only married women were included in the sample because it was unacceptable to ask unmarried women questions relating to sexuality). The study is updated every year and will continue to collect data yearly if funding remains available (Lepkowski et al., 2010). The 2006 to 2008 data collection sample included 13,495 men and women between the ages of 15 and 44 years. In-person interviews were conducted by **computer-assisted personal interviewing (CAPI)** and **audio computer-assisted self-interviewing** (Lepkowski et al., 2010; Goodwin et al., 2010). Interviews lasted approximately 80 minutes for women and 60 minutes for men.

REAL RESEARCH 2.5 Because the NSFG uses nationally representative data, in the most recent study, each female participant represented about 8,000 U.S. women, whereas each male participant represented about 12,000 U.S. men (Lepkowski et al., 2010)

Data from the NSFG has been used in more than 600 journal articles and book chapters, and we will review the findings from many of these published studies in the upcoming chapters. Among the findings of the NSFG are the following:

- Nearly 2 of 3 female teens talked to their parents about "how to say no to sex" compared with about 2 of 5 male teens (Martinez et al., 2010).

- The majority of teens receive formal sex education before the age of 18 (Martinez et al., 2010).

- College-educated women are more likely to use birth control pills than noncollege-educated women (Mosher & Jones, 2010).

- Heterosexual couples who lived together were more likely to be a different race or ethnicity than heterosexual couples who were married (Goodwin et al., 2010).

- In 2005, there were 4.1 million live births, 1.2 million abortions, and 1 million miscarriages in the United States (Ventura et al., 2009).

Youth Risk Behavior Survey

The YRBS is an ongoing government study that monitors health-risk behaviors among youths and young adults (grades 9–12), including behaviors that contribute to injuries and violence; tobacco, drug, and alcohol use; sexuality behaviors; and unhealthy dietary behaviors. The survey began in 1991 and is conducted every 2 years by the Centers for Disease Control and Prevention. In 2009, more than 16,000 U.S. high-school students were surveyed, from 42 states and 20 urban school districts (Eaton et al., 2009). This sample is believed to be representative of all students in grades 9 to 12 attending public and private schools in the United States. Questionnaires are used to collect data, and parental permission is required for participation.

Among the findings from the YRBS are the following:

- 34% of students had engaged in sexual intercourse with at least one person.

- Among heterosexual and gay couples, 61% of those who were sexually active reported that they or their partner used a condom the last time they engaged in sexual intercourse.

- 6% of students reported having engaged in sexual intercourse before the age of 13.

- 7.4% of students were physically forced to have sexual intercourse when they did not want to.

- 22% of the sexually active students reported drinking alcohol or using drugs before their last act of sexual intercourse.

- 87% of students reported having been taught about AIDS or HIV in school at some point (Eaton et al., 2009).

National Longitudinal Study of Adolescent Health

ADD Health is the largest, most comprehensive **longitudinal study** of U.S. adolescents ever done. An in-school questionnaire was given to a group of students who were in grades 7 through 12 during the 1994 to 1995 school year. This group of students has been followed into adulthood through the use of four in-home interviews in 1996, 2001 to 2002, and 2007 to 2008. In the most recent update in 2008, the sample was age 24 to 32.

Over the years, data have been collected on each student's family, neighborhood, community, school, friendships, peer groups, romantic relationships, and social, economic, psychological, and physical well-being. ADD Health provides a unique look into adolescent behavior and the health and achievement outcomes in adulthood. The data collected in this study have been used by thousands of researchers and have been analyzed in more than 1,000 research articles. We will discuss these research articles in the upcoming chapters.

National Survey of Adolescent Males

The National Institute for Child Health and Human Development conducted the NSAM, a **longitudinal study** on adolescent males, from 1988 to 1995. The study was designed to collect data on the risk behavior of teen males related to sexually transmitted infections and teen pregnancy. The NSAM included face-to-face interviews and surveys from a nationally representative group of more than 6,500 adolescent males. Parental permission was required for all participants. Interestingly, researchers compared data from two methodologies: questionnaire and computer-assisted self-interviews (see accompanying Sex in Real Life for more information).

Overall, the findings from this study showed that a significant number of heterosexual adolescent males engage in sexual activities beyond vaginal intercourse, such as mutual masturbation and oral and anal sex (Gates & Sonenstein, 2000).

Sexuality research has changed significantly throughout the years, driven mostly by changing societal attitudes and changing data collection method. The use of the Internet for sexuality research made it easier to collect data. However, funding for sexuality studies remains difficult, and many studies are threatened by political pressure, especially if researchers want to study issues beyond fertility and sexual health issues (Bialik, 2010b). As we look ahead to sex research in the future, private funding will continue to be an important avenue for sex research. Next, we take a closer look at some of the contemporary sexuality research methods.

longitudinal study
A study done over a certain period wherein participants are studied at various intervals.

When you read a story in a magazine or newspaper about a research study, do you believe what you read? For example, if the headline in your daily newspaper claimed that eating an orange a day could decrease your risk for sexual dysfunction, would you believe it? Are research studies accurate? Dr. John Ioannidis, an expert on the credibility of research, believes that 90% of the published medical research is flawed (Freedman, 2010). He points out that flaws can be in several areas, such as:

1. The questions asked

2. The methodologies used

3. The participants recruited

4. How the data are analyzed

Although Dr. Ioannidis was referring specifically to medical research, similar issues affect sexuality research. Methodological issues are important, especially because a major problem in sexuality research is getting participants to respond honestly about very personal and sensitive issues. Embarrassment, social pressures, and/or a lack of an ability to discuss such issues can interfere with honest responses. In an attempt to increase honesty, sexuality researchers have used a variety of data collection methodologies. Do you think that you'd be more honest in answering personal questions about sexuality in the privacy of your own home? Researchers thought so.

In the National Survey of Sexual Health and Behavior (NSSHB), online polling was used in hopes that participants would be more comfortable and honest in their responses. The research supports this idea: One study found that when self-administered questionnaire results were compared with online polling results, significant differences were found (see Figure 2.1; Turner et al., 1998).

However, even with the best data collection methods, the numbers in sexuality research don't always add up (Bialik, 2010b). For example:

- Whereas 14- to 17-year-old males reported using condoms 79% of the time during sexual intercourse, 14- to 17-year-old females reported their male partners used condoms 58% of the time.

- Whereas 85% of heterosexual men reported their partners having an orgasm at the most recent sexual event, 64% of heterosexual women reported having had an orgasm at their most recent sexual event.

Another example has to do with the reported number of sexual partners. In one study, males reported a median of seven female sexual partners, whereas females reported a median of four male sexual partners (Kolata, 2007). Another study found males had an average of 12.7 lifetime sexual partners, whereas females reported an average of 6.5 (Johnson et al., 2001). Why the differences? It's too simple to assume that the participants are dishonest or exaggerating. There are a

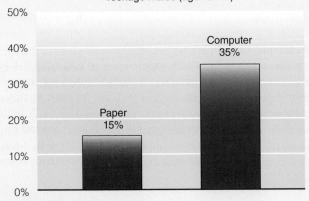

Partner or self was drunk or high at last sex

Teenage males (age 15–19)

FIGURE 2.1 Computer-assisted self-interviews have been found to elicit greater responses on sensitive questions than questionnaire methods. Little difference was found on questions that concerned less sensitive behaviors. Copyright © Cengage Learning 2013

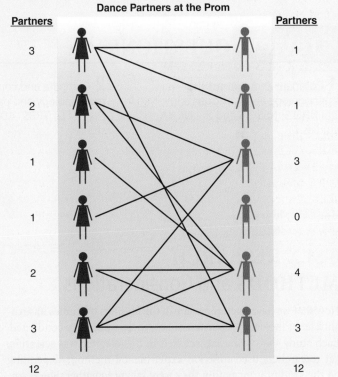

FIGURE 2.2 Let's say we did a study on the average number of partners of the other sex males and females danced with at the prom. Because the prom is a closed event, we would expect there to be consistent answers for both groups. In this example, each male and female danced with an average of two partners. Copyright © Cengage Learning 2013

multitude of reasons for the differences (Kolata, 2007). Some reasons might include:

1. **Sampling differences**—There are inherent group differences within the male participant group that contribute to the differences.

2. **Sexual orientation issues**—Some of the males were engaging in same-sex behavior, which could result in gender differences (however, the difference in number of partners is too large to be accounted for simply by this factor; Bialik, 2010b).

3. **Societal norms and dishonesty**—Societal pressures contributed to male overexaggeratation and female underexaggeration, and/or participants provided false information.

4. **Open populations**—Because participants can have sex with partners outside the study population, this can lead to a "potential mismatch" between sexual encounters (Bialik, 2010b).

5. **Greater number of available females**—More available females would give men more potential partners (Henke, 2010).

Numbers are more likely to add up equally if a study is done on a *closed population*. Think about it this way—If we were to do a study on the average number of partners of the other sex students dance with at the prom, do you think the male and female average would be similar? Probably. Because it is a closed population, they can only dance with each other (see Figure 2.2). However, most large sexuality studies have open populations, which means that participants have sexual partners outside the study population.

The bottom line is that it is important to critically analyze sexuality research. Although great care is taken to ensure that results are valid and generalizable, the sensitive nature of this area of research brings up many issues that could potentially interfere with the questions that are asked, data collection, participant populations, and the interpretation of the data. Sometimes research can raise more questions than it answers.

◀ review QUESTIONS

1 Compare and contrast the methodology and participants involved in the NHSLS, NSSHB, and the NCHA studies.

2 Compare and contrast the methodology and participants involved in the NSFG, YRBS, ADD Health, and NSAM studies.

3 Differentiate between privately and government-funded sexuality research, and explain which studies often yield more comprehensive information about sexuality.

▶ SEX RESEARCH METHODS and Considerations

Now that we have explored some of the findings of studies in sexuality, let us look at the specifics of how these studies are conducted. Each study that we have discussed in this chapter was scientific, yet researchers used different experimental methods depending on the kind of information they were trying to gather. For example, Freud relied on a **case study** methodology, whereas Kinsey used interviews to gather data. There are other ways that researchers collect information, such as questionnaires, laboratory experiments, direct observation, participant observation, correlations, and Internet-based research methods.

Whatever techniques they use, researchers must be certain that their experiment passes standards of validity, reliability, and generalizability. Tests of **validity** determine whether a question or other method actually measures what it is designed to measure.

For example, the people who read the question need to interpret it the same way as the researcher who wrote it. **Reliability** refers to the consistency of the measure. If we ask a question today, we would hope to get a similar answer if we ask it again in 2 months. Finally, generalizability refers to the ability of samples in a study to have wide applicability to the general population. A study can be generalized only if a random sample is used. All of the methods we review here must fit these three criteria.

case study
A research methodology that involves an in-depth examination of one participant or a small number of participants.

validity
The property of a device measuring what it is intended to measure.

reliability
The dependability of a test as reflected in the consistency of its scores on repeated measurements of the same group.

participant observation
A research methodology that involves actual participation in the event being researched.

CASE Studies

When researchers describe a case study, they attempt to explore individual cases to formulate general hypotheses. Freud was famous for his use of this methodology. He would study hysteria in only one patient, because he didn't have several patients with similar complaints. Using this method, however, does not allow researchers to generalize to the wider public because the sample is small. Even so, the case study method may generate hypotheses that can lead to larger, generalizable studies.

INTERVIEWS

We began this chapter with an exploration of Valerie's "Bikini Sex Project," in which she used interviews to collect data about locations for sex. Interviews can be useful research tools because they allow the researcher to establish a rapport with each participant and emphasize the importance of honesty in the study. In addition, the researcher can vary the order of questions and skip questions that are irrelevant. However, they can be time-consuming and expensive.

QUESTIONNAIRES and Surveys

Questionnaire or survey research is generally used to identify the attitudes, knowledge, or behavior of large samples. For instance, Kinsey used this method to obtain information about his many participants, although questions have since been raised about Kinsey's validity and reliability. Kinsey recognized these problems and tried to increase the validity by using interviews to supplement the questionnaires.

Some researchers believe that questionnaires provide more honesty than interviews because the participant may be embarrassed to admit things to another person that he or she would be more likely to share with the anonymity of a questionnaire. Research has revealed that when people answer sexuality questionnaires, they are likely to leave out the questions that cause the most anxiety, especially questions about masturbation (Catania et al., 1986). We discuss using online questionnaires later in this section.

DIRECT Observation

Masters and Johnson used direct observation for their research on sexual response and physiology. This method is the least frequently used because it is difficult to find participants who are willing to come into the laboratory to have sex while researchers monitor their bodily functions. However, if direct observation can be done, it does provide information that cannot be obtained elsewhere.

independent variable
The variable controlled by the experimenter and applied to the participant to determine its effect on the participant's reaction.

dependent variable
The measured results of an experiment that are believed to be a function of the independent variable.

Researchers can monitor behavior as it happens, giving the results more credibility. For example, a man may exaggerate the number of erections per sexual episode in a self-report, but he cannot exaggerate in a laboratory.

Direct observation is expensive and may not be as generalizable, because it would be impossible to gather a random sample. In addition, direct observation focuses on behaviors and, as a result, ignores feelings, attitudes, or personal history.

PARTICIPANT Observation

Participant observation research involves researchers going into an environment and monitoring what is happening naturally. For instance, a researcher who wants to explore the impact of alcohol on male and female flirting patterns might monitor interactions between and among men and women in bars. This would entail several visits and specific note taking on all that occurs. However, it is difficult to generalize from this type of research because the researcher could subtly, or not so subtly, influence the research findings. Also, this method has limited use in the area of sex research because much of sexual behavior occurs in private.

EXPERIMENTAL Methods

Experiments are the only research method that allows us to isolate cause and effect. This is because in an experiment, strict control is maintained over all variables so that one variable can be isolated and examined.

For example, let's say you want to teach high-school students about AIDS, but you don't know which teaching methodology would be most beneficial. You could design an experiment to examine this more closely. First, you choose a high school and randomly assign all the students to one of three groups. You might start by giving them a questionnaire about AIDS to establish baseline data about what they know or believe. Group 1 then listens to a lecture about AIDS, Group 2 is shown a video, and Group 3 listens to people with AIDS talk about their experiences. Strict care is taken to make sure that all of the information that is presented in these classes is identical. The only thing that differs is the teaching method. In scientific terms, the type of teaching method is the **independent variable,** which is manipulated by the researcher. After each class, the students are given a test to determine what knowledge they have gained about AIDS. This measurement is to determine the effect of the independent variable on the **dependent variable,** which in this case is knowledge about AIDS. If one group shows more learning after one particular method was used, we might be able to attribute the learning to the type of methodology that was used.

Experiments can be more costly than any of the other methods discussed, in terms of both finances and time commitment. It is also possible that in an attempt to control the experiments, a researcher may cause the study to become too sterile or artificial (nothing like it would be outside of the laboratory), and the results may be faulty or inapplicable to the real world. Finally, experiments are not always possible in certain areas of research,

Direct observation provides information that cannot be obtained elsewhere.

especially in the field of sexuality. For instance, what if we wanted to examine whether early sexual abuse contributed to adult difficulties with intimate relationships? It would be entirely unethical to abuse children sexually to examine whether they develop these problems later in life.

▶▶ CORRELATIONAL Methods

Correlations are often used when it is not possible to do an experiment. For example, because it is unethical to do a controlled experiment in a sexual abuse study, we would study a given population to see whether there is any correlation between past sexual abuse and later difficulties with intimate relationships. The limitation of a **correlational study** is that it does not provide any information about cause. We would not learn whether past sexual abuse causes intimacy difficulties, even though we may learn that these factors are related. The intimacy difficulties could occur for several other reasons, including factors such as low self-esteem or a personality disorder.

▶▶ INTERNET-BASED Research Methods

Over the last few years, sexuality researchers have been relying on the Internet for data collection in many of their studies. The accessibility and sense of anonymity of the web have given sexuality researchers access to a wider group of diverse participants. Earlier in this chapter, we discussed the use of computer-assisted personal interviewing and audio computer-assisted self-interviewing, both of which are Internet-based research techniques.

There are disadvantages and risks to Internet-based sexuality research (Mustanski, 2001). As in other research methods, participants can lie and sabotage research. Because surveys are anonymous, participants could submit multiple responses. To reduce the possibility of this happening, researchers could collect e-mail addresses to check for multiple submissions, but this would negate participants' anonymity. One study that checked for multiple submissions found that participants rarely submitted more than one response (Reips, 2000).

Although more than 77% of U.S. households used the Internet in 2010 (up from 18% in 1997; Cauley, 2009), these Internet users may not be representative of all Americans—a variety of minorities are not well represented, and neither are those with low socio-

Although there are advantages and disadvantages to Internet-based sexuality research, many researchers believe that subjects who participate online may be more representative of the general population than the typical college student.

economic status or education (National Telecommunications and Information Administration & U.S. Department of Commerce, 1999). Wealthier, White, and better educated individuals are well represented on the Internet, and this can bias research results. However, even though these differences exist, some researchers claim that the participant pool available online may be more representative of the general population than a group of typical college students—who are the most common research participants (Mustanski, 2001; Reips & Bachtiger, 2000). One more concern about Internet-based sexuality research is that minors may have access to the studies. However, researchers must ask for informed consent, and participants must agree that they are older than 18 years before participating.

correlation
A statistical measure of the relationship between two variables.

correlational study
A type of research that examines the relationship between two or more variables.

◀ review QUESTIONS

1 Differentiate between validity and reliability, and give one example of each.

2 What makes a study generalizable?

3 Identify the advantages and disadvantages of using interviews and questionnaires.

4 Explain how direct observation and participant observation are used in research studies.

5 Explain how the Internet can be used in sexuality research. What are some of the benefits and drawbacks of this method?

PROBLEMS AND ISSUES in Sex Research

Many problems in sexuality research are more difficult to contend with than they are in other types of research (see accompanying Sex in Real Life). These include ethical issues, volunteer bias, sampling problems, and reliability.

ETHICAL Issues

Ethical issues affect all social science—and sexuality research in particular. Before people participate in a study of sexuality, researchers must obtain their **informed consent.** This is especially important in an area such as sexuality because it is such a personal subject. Informed consent means that the subjects know what to expect from the questions and procedures, how the information will be used, that their **confidentiality** will be assured, and to whom they can address questions. Some things that people reveal in a study, such as their acknowledgment of an affair or a sexual dysfunction, can cause harm or embarrassment if researchers are careless enough to let others find out. Another ethical question that has generated controversy is whether children should be asked questions about sexuality. Overall, it is standard procedure in sexuality research to maintain confidentiality and obtain informed consent from all participants, regardless of age.

VOLUNTEER Bias

Think back to Valerie's Bikini Sex Project, which we discussed at the beginning of this chapter. Do you think that the students who walked by Valerie and ignored her request for information were different from those who stopped to write on her body? Or, do you believe her results are generalizable to students at all universities? If the volunteers could differ from nonvolunteers, then there is a volunteer bias at work. Volunteer bias prevents the results of her study from being generalizable to the population as a whole.

As early as 1969, Rosenthal and Rosnow (1975) claimed that those who volunteer for psychological studies often have a special interest in the studies in which they participate. Studies that have examined volunteer bias in sexuality research conducted with college students generally support the finding that volunteers differ from nonvolunteers (Catania et al., 1995; Gaither et al., 2003). Volunteers have been found to be more sexually liberal, more sexually experienced, and more interested in sexual variety, and they report less traditional sexual attitudes than nonvolunteers (Bogaert, 1996; Gaither, 2000; Plaud et al., 1999; Wiederman, 1999). Research has also found that, overall, men are more likely than women to volunteer for sexuality studies (Gaither et al., 2003).

ON YOUR MIND 2.3

How do researchers know that what people tell them is true?

The fact is that they don't know, and they hope that people are being honest. Sometimes researchers build into studies little tricks that can catch someone who is lying, such as asking the same questions in different wording again later in a survey. Researchers also anticipate that participants will understand the questions asked and be able to provide the answers. In actuality, researchers may take many things for granted.

You might be wondering how researchers would know whether their volunteer sample is different from the nonvolunteer sample. After all, how can researchers know anything about the nonvolunteers who are not in the study? Researchers have designed ways to overcome this problem. Before asking for volunteers to take part in a sexuality study, researchers ask all participants to fill out a questionnaire that contains personality measures and sexuality questions. Participants are then asked whether they would volunteer for a sexuality study. Because the researchers already have information from both volunteers and nonvolunteers, they simply compare these data.

Because volunteers appear to differ from nonvolunteers, it is impossible to generalize the findings of a study that used a volunteer sample. The Kinsey studies attempted to decrease volunteer bias by obtaining full participation from each member of the groups they studied.

SAMPLING Problems

Sexuality studies routinely involve the use of college-age populations. Brecher and Brecher (1986) refer to these populations as **samples of convenience,** because the participants used are convenient for researchers who tend to work at universities. Kinsey used such samples in his initial research at Indiana University. The question is, can these studies be generalized to the rest of the population? Are college students similar to noncollege students of the same age, or people who are older or younger? Probably not. These samples also underrepresent certain groups, such as minorities and the disabled.

RELIABILITY

How reliable is sex research? Couldn't it be that those who are sexually satisfied overestimate their frequency of sexual behavior, whereas those who are dissatisfied underreport it? Both participant comfort in discussing sexuality and their memory about sexual behaviors have been found to affect the reliability of the study.

Some critics claim that changes in frequency of sexual behavior over time may be due more to changes in the reporting of behavior than to actual changes in frequency (Kaats & Davis, 1971). For instance, if we had done a study in 1995 about the number of college students who engaged in premarital sex and compared this with data collected in 1963, we would undoubtedly find more people reporting having had premarital sex in 1995. However, it could be that these higher numbers are due, in part, to the fact that more

A few global studies have shed some light on cross-cultural sexuality. Global studies are expensive to conduct, and because of this, usually pharmaceutical or contraceptive companies fund them.

The Global Study of Sexual Attitudes and Behaviors (GSSAB) was the first large, multi-country survey to study sexual attitudes, beliefs, and health in middle-age and older adults (Laumann et al., 2005). The study was funded by Pfizer Pharmaceuticals (the maker of Viagra). Interviews and surveys were conducted in 29 countries representing all world regions (Africa/Middle East, Asia, Australasia, Europe, Latin America, and North America). A total of 13,882 women and 13,618 men, aged 40 to 80 years old were included in the study.

Various countries required specific data collection methods. For example, random-digit telephone dialing was used in Europe, Israel, North America, Brazil, Australia, and New Zealand, and interviews were conducted by phone. However, a bias against telephone interviews in certain populations in Mexico required using in-person interviews. Mail surveys were used in Japan, but in other Asian countries, questionnaires were handed out in public locations. Finally, door-to-door methods using questionnaires were used in the Middle East and South Africa (Laumann et al., 2005). Cross-cultural research requires flexibility in the use of data collection methods.

Despite wide cultural variations, there are several predictors of sexual well-being—such as physical and mental health and relationship satisfaction—that are consistent throughout the regions of the world. In addition, ratings of sexual satisfaction throughout the world are correlated with overall happiness in both men and women (Laumann et al., 2006). However, there were some limitations to this study. First of all, there was a relatively low response rate of 19%, which means that those who did agree to participate may have been more interested or comfortable in discussing sexual issues (Laumann et al., 2005). In addition, since a variety of data collection methods were used, the results may not be generalizable in those countries where the data collection didn't enable researchers to collect a random sample, such as the Middle East, South Africa, and certain Asian countries.

Another global study of sexuality, the Durex Sexual Wellbeing Global Survey, was conducted in 2006 and was financed by the Durex Corporation. The study included more than 26,000 adults in 26 countries (Durex Network, 2008). Internet-based research methodologies were used in every country except Nigeria, where face-to-face interviews were done because of low Internet usage. The Durex study found that the frequency of sexual activity varies by country (see Figure 2.3). Although 60% of respondents said that sex is an enjoyable part of their lives, only 44% said they were fully satisfied with their sex lives.

The study also found the average age for engaging in first vaginal intercourse worldwide is 17.3 (Durex.com, 2007). The age at first vaginal intercourse was 15.6 (youngest) in Iceland and 19.8 (oldest) in India. Finally, the study also reported that heterosexual couples in Greece are the most sexually active, whereas heterosexual couples in Japan are the least. Data from the Durex study have been used in a variety of studies, which we will talk about in upcoming chapters.

The London School of Hygiene also conducted a global study and used meta-analysis to analyze 200 studies on demographic sexual behaviors published between 1996 and 2006 from 59 countries (Wellings et al., 2006). This was an interesting idea for a study that compared data on published articles around the world instead of collecting new data. The study found that a shift toward later marriage around the world has led to an increase in premarital sexuality. It also revealed that monogamy is the dominant sexual pattern, and that around the world, men report more sexual partners than women.

There have also been some global studies on specific sexual issues. For example, one study evaluated contraceptive use in adolescents from 24 European and North American countries (Godeau et al., 2008). A total of 34,000 15-year-old students completed self-report questionnaires. The percentages of students reporting engaging in sexual intercourse ranged from 14% in Croatia to 38% in England.

people felt comfortable talking about premarital sex in 1995 than they did in 1963. It is necessary to take into account the time period of the study when evaluating the results, to ensure that we know the increase in numbers is actually due to an increase in behavior.

Another problem that affects reliability involves the participant's memory. Because many sexuality researchers ask questions about behaviors that might have happened in one's adolescence, people may not always remember information accurately. For instance, if we were to ask a 52-year-old man the age at which he first masturbated, chances are good that he would not remember exactly how old he was. He would probably estimate the age at which he first masturbated. Estimates are not always precise enough for scientific study. (See accompanying Sex in Real Life for more information on skepticism in sex research.)

Condom use in Greece was close to 90%, whereas in Sweden it was closer to 53% (Godeau et al., 2008).

The Center for Health Promotion at Indiana University, which authored the National Survey of Sexual Behavior and Health study, has also been actively collecting data on global studies of sexuality, and many of these should be available within the next few years. Global studies can help us learn more about societal and cultural factors that influence sexuality. Unfortunately, these studies are expensive, and funding can be difficult to come by. To reduce cost, many global studies rely on Internet data collection and self-reporting, which also raise several reliability and validity concerns.

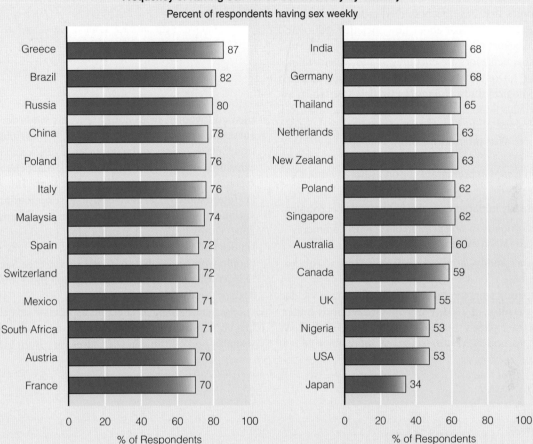

Frequency of Having Sex Varies Considerably by Country

Percent of respondents having sex weekly

Country	% of Respondents
Greece	87
Brazil	82
Russia	80
China	78
Poland	76
Italy	76
Malaysia	74
Spain	72
Switzerland	72
Mexico	71
South Africa	71
Austria	70
France	70

Country	% of Respondents
India	68
Germany	68
Thailand	65
Netherlands	63
New Zealand	63
Poland	62
Singapore	62
Australia	60
Canada	59
UK	55
Nigeria	53
USA	53
Japan	34

FIGURE **2.3** Do you engage in sex at least weekly? SOURCE: Retrieved from http://www.durex.com/EN-US/ SEXUALWELLBEINGSURVEY/FEQUENCY%20OF%20SEX/Pages/default.aspx. All rights reserved. Reproduced by permission.

◀ review QUESTIONS

1 Define informed consent and explain the importance of confidentiality.

2 What differences have been found between those who volunteer and those who don't volunteer for sex research?

3 Define a "sample of convenience" and explain how it is used.

4 How do satisfaction and memory issues potentially affect sex research?

SEXUALITY RESEARCH Across Cultures

Many studies examine sexuality in cultures outside the United States. Some have been general studies that examine knowledge levels and attitudes in different populations; others have evaluated specific areas such as pregnancy, rape, homosexuality, or sex education. Many times these studies are done by researchers in other countries, but some have also been done by American researchers.

Of all the topics that have been studied cross-culturally, we have probably learned the most about how societies' values and culture influence sexuality. Every culture develops its own rules about which sexual behaviors are encouraged and which will not be tolerated. In 1971, Donald Marshall and Robert Suggs published a classic anthropological study, *Human Sexual Behavior,* which examined how sexuality was expressed in several different cultures. This study remains one of the largest cultural studies ever done on sexuality, and some of its interesting findings include:

- Masturbation is rare in preliterate cultures (those without a written language).
- Foreplay is usually initiated by males in heterosexual couples.
- Heterosexuals engage in sexual intercourse most commonly at night before falling asleep.
- Female orgasmic ability varies greatly from culture to culture.

More recent studies on cross-cultural sexuality have yielded other interesting results. In 2002, Pfizer Pharmaceuticals undertook a comprehensive global study of sexuality. The Global Study of Sexual Attitudes and Behaviors surveyed more than 26,000

men and women in 28 countries. This study was the first global survey to assess behaviors, attitudes, beliefs, and sexual satisfaction. Surveys assessed the importance of sex and intimacy in relationships, attitudes and beliefs about sexual health, and treatment-seeking behaviors for sexual dysfunctions. This survey provided an international baseline regarding sexual attitudes to compare various countries and also monitor cultural changes over time. In 2007, Durex undertook another global study to explore sexual attitudes and behaviors in 41 countries. The study included 26,000 people who responded to a web survey (see Sexual Diversity in Our World "Global Sex Research" for more information about both of these studies).

Societal influences affect all aspects of sexuality. Throughout this book, we explore more details from cross-cultural studies on sexuality and examine how cultures vary from each other.

ON YOUR MIND 2.4

How could an entire culture's attitudes about sex differ from those of another culture?

It makes more sense when you think about two very different types of cultures. A collectivist culture (e.g., India, Pakistan, Thailand, or the Philippines) emphasizes the cultural group as a whole and thinks less about the individuals within that society. In contrast, an individualistic culture (e.g., the United States, Australia, or England) stresses the goals of individuals over the cultural group as a whole. This cultural difference can affect the way that sexuality is viewed. For example, a culture such as India may value marriage because it is good for the social standing of members of the society, whereas a marriage in the United States is valued because the two people love each other and want to spend their lives together.

◀ review QUESTIONS

1 Of all the cross-cultural topics that have been studied, what have we learned the most about?

2 Identify two findings from Marshall and Suggs's large-scale cross-cultural study of sexuality.

3 Identify some of the findings from the Pfizer and Durex sex studies.

▶ SEX RESEARCH IN THE FUTURE: Beyond Problem-Driven Research

Many view America as a country "obsessed with sex." As we discussed in Chapter 1, sex is used to sell everything from jeans to iPhones and is oozing from television sitcoms, advertising, music videos, and song lyrics. However, even with this openness and sex all around us, there is a painful lack of solid sexuality research.

Our problem-driven approach has resulted in a lack of information in several key areas in human sexuality. We know little about sexual desire and arousal and what makes couples happy long term or about childhood and adolescent sexuality, which has long been a taboo area of research. Although we are learning more about the development of sexual identity, sexual risk taking, and how the increase in sexual material on the Internet affects people's sexual behaviors, there is still a lack of solid research in this area. Infidelity, sexual trauma, and various sexual variations, including sexual predators and those who sexually abuse children, have also been poorly researched.

In the future, it is hoped that sex research will help us understand the emotional and relational aspects of human sexuality. Instead of focusing primarily on what does not work in sexual relationships, such as problems with erections or orgasms, it will help us understand what does work and what keeps couples happy and satisfied. An increased willingness on the part of the federal government to consider sexuality-related research will also help improve our knowledge about sexuality and will aid in bringing sexuality researchers together. Some collaboration between researchers of various disciplines would help us more fully understand the influences that affect our sexuality and, in turn, help build the field of sexual science.

In the following chapters of this book, keep in mind the importance of theory and how it guides the questions we have about sexuality. The scientific method helps sexologists find answers to the varied questions we have about human sexual behavior. Throughout the upcoming chapters, we will be reviewing the data collected in several of the research studies we have reviewed in this chapter.

◀ review QUESTIONS

1 Explain how our "problem-driven" approach to sex research has limited what we know about sexuality.

2 How do religious institutions often impede sexuality research?

3 What direction does sexuality research need to go in the future and why?

◀◀ chapter REVIEW

SUMMARY POINTS

1 A theory is a set of assumptions, principles, or methods that help a researcher understand the nature of a phenomenon being studied. The psychoanalytic theory was developed by Sigmund Freud. He believed the sex drive was one of the most important forces in life. Two of Freud's most controversial concepts included personality formation (the development of the id, ego, and superego) and psychosexual development (oral, anal, phallic, latency, and genital stages).

2 Behavioral theory argues that only overt behavior can be measured, observed, and controlled by scientists. Behaviorists use rewards and punishments to control behavior. A treatment method called *behavior modification* is used to help change unwanted behaviors.

3 Social learning theory looks at reward and punishment in controlling behavior but also believes that internal events, such as feelings, thoughts, and beliefs, can also influence behavior. Another theory, cognitive theory, holds that people differ in how they process information, and this creates personality differences. Our behavior is a result of how we perceive and conceptualize what is happening around us.

4 Humanistic theory purports that we all strive to develop ourselves to the best of our abilities and to become self-actualized. Biological theory claims that sexual behavior is primarily a biological process, whereas evolutionary theory incorporates both evolution and sociology to understand sexual behavior. Sociological theory is interested in how the society in which we live influences sexual behavior.

5 Feminist theory looks at how the social construction of sexuality is based on power and the view that women are submissive and subordinate to men. Queer theory, another politically charged theory, asserts that domination, such as heterosexism and homophobia, should be resisted.

6 The legitimate forefathers of sexuality research may be Aristotle and Plato, because they were the first to develop theories regarding sexual responses and dysfunctions, sex legislation, reproduction, contraception, and sexual ethics. The majority of the early sex research was done in Europe, primarily in Germany. It wasn't until the 1900s that sexuality research moved to the United States, which has led sexuality research ever since.

7 The majority of sexuality research has been problem driven, and because of this, we know little about what constitutes healthy sexuality. The research has also become fragmented, with researchers coming from several disciplines, many unaware of the work being done by others.

8 The changing political climate affects attitudes about sexuality, as well as sex research. Negative attitudes can affect the public perception of sex research. Politics also can influence what sexuality research gets funded.

9 The most influential early promoters of sexology were Iwan Bloch, Magnus Hirschfeld, Albert Moll, Richard von Krafft-Ebing, and Havelock Ellis. Clelia Mosher did a great deal of sexuality research in the 1800s, but most of her work was never published. Katharine Bement Davis found that homosexuals were no different from heterosexuals, but her work was ignored because it caused fear among male researchers. The focus of sexuality research began to change after her research.

10 Alfred Kinsey was probably the most influential sex researcher of the 20th century. He was the first to take the study of sexuality away from the medical model. Kinsey established the Institute for Sex Research at Indiana University. Morton Hunt updated Kinsey's earlier work on human sexuality.

11 William Masters and Virginia Johnson were the first scientists to observe and measure sexual acts in the laboratory. They discovered several interesting aspects of sexuality, including a model called the *sexual response cycle*.

12 Two of the largest nationally representative studies are the NHSLS and the NSSHB, both of which were funded by private organizations. In addition to these studies, several governmental studies have contributed to our understanding of sexual behavior, including the NSFG, YRBS, the NCHA, ADD Health, and the NSAM.

13 Researchers can use several methods to study sexuality, including case study, questionnaire, interview, participant observation, experimental methods, and correlations.

14 Researchers must be certain that their experiment passes standards of validity, reliability, and generalizability. Several problems can affect sexuality research, such as ethical issues, volunteer bias, sampling, and reliability problems. Of all the topics that have been studied cross-culturally, we have learned the most about how societies' values and culture influence sexuality.

15 Our problem-driven approach to sexuality research has interfered with what we really know and understand about relationships, love, and human development.

CRITICAL THINKING QUESTIONS

1 Is sexuality research as valid and reliable as other areas of research? Explain.

2 Do you think that people would be more honest about their sex lives if they were filling out an anonymous questionnaire or if they were being interviewed by a researcher? Which method of research do you think yields the highest degree of honesty? With which method would you feel most comfortable?

3 Why do you think couples might have volunteered to be in Masters and Johnson's study? Would you have volunteered for this study? Why or why not?

4 If you could do a study on sexuality, what area would you choose? What methods of data collection would you use? Why? How would you avoid the problems that many sex researchers face?

MEDIA RESOURCES

CourseMate brings course concepts to life with interactive learning, study, and exam preparation tools that support the printed textbook. A textbook-specific website, Psychology CourseMate includes an integrated interactive eBook and other interactive learning tools including quizzes, flashcards, videos, and more. If your textbook does not include an access code card, go to CengageBrain.com to gain access.

CENGAGE**NOW**   CengageNOW is an easy-to-use online resource that helps you study in less time to get the grade you want—NOW. Take a pre-test for this chapter and receive a personalized study plan based on your results that will identify the topics you need to review and direct you to online resources to help you master those topics. Then take a post-test to help you determine the concepts you have mastered and what you will need to work on. If your textbook does not include an access code card, go to CengageBrain.com to gain access.

View in Video available in CourseMate and CengageNOW:

Bikini Sex Project: College student describes a unique sex research study she did for her human sexuality course.

National Survey of Sexual Health and Behavior: A review of findings from the National Survey of Sexual Health and Behavior.

Websites:

American Association of Sexuality Educators, Counselors, and Therapists (AASECT) ■ AASECT is devoted to the promotion of sexual health through the development and advancement of the fields of sex therapy, counseling, and education.

Electronic Journal of Human Sexuality ■ Disseminates knowledge to the international community and includes peer-reviewed research articles and dissertations on sexuality.

Sexuality Information and Education Council of the United States (SIECUS) ■ SIECUS is a national, private, nonprofit advocacy organization that promotes comprehensive sexuality education and HIV/AIDS prevention education in the schools.

Society for the Scientific Study of Sexuality (SSSS) ■ SSSS is an interdisciplinary, international organization for sexuality researchers, clinicians, educators, and other professionals in related fields.

3 Communication and Sexuality

View in Video

View in Video

View in Video

View in Video

ABOUT THE CHAPTER OPENING VIDEO – Three of my students, Shadia, Corelle, and Heather, have had some interesting experiences that help illustrate the importance of communication in intimate relationships. Shadia, a self-described "people watcher," tells a story about a couple in the school cafeteria. When she first noticed them she was curious about their relationship. From her standpoint she didn't think they looked like they belonged with each other. But every day they would meet up in the cafeteria and have lunch together. Day after day, Shadia watched them talking, laughing, and interacting. Had they been together a long time? Were they serious? One day she experienced something between the two of them that helped her understand the richness and value of communication.

Another student, Corelle, learned the importance of communication when she painfully realized it was lacking in her relationship. She had been dating her boyfriend for a little over 3 years but they recently broke up—mostly because of communication problems. When Corelle left for school this year, they were forced to rely on the Internet and texting to stay in touch. While it was hard at first, they worked it out. She found the Internet really helped them stay closer, even though they were so far apart. However, one day he just stopped communicating. She knew he had a lot of issues he was dealing with, and she tried to get him to talk to her on the phone or online. Unfortunately, for whatever reason, he couldn't. The more Corelle tried to get him to talk, the more he pulled away. She was exhausted. Finally, she couldn't take it anymore and texted him one final message *"I'm done. Enjoy being single."* Although they talked a few more times after this, the long-term lack of communication had irreparably damaged their relationship. In the end, as sad as she was, she told me that she

Alberto Pomares/Getty Images

learned many things about the importance of communication. *"You need to know your partner and have a sense of how they like to communicate. If they want to meet up and talk in person, text, or Facebook chat, that's all good, but I want to know upfront. Switching it up a bit keeps things interesting!"*

Finally, Heather knows first-hand the difficulties involved in various communication strategies. She goes to school in Connecticut, but her boyfriend lives 2,600 miles away in Las Vegas, Nevada. They have been dating for over 7 months, but most of this time they have been long-distance. They communicate via Skype, e-mail, phone calls, phones, and text messaging. Despite the communication challenges of a long-distance relationship, what has ultimately been the most important factor in making their relationship work has been trust. ▐

Janell Cauch

"We used to text, Skype, and Google but then it just stopped."
—CHAPTER OPENING VIDEO

View in Video

To watch the entire interview, go to Psychology CourseMate at **login.cengagebrain.com.**

© Ernie Hiraldo

Communication has changed drastically over the last few years. In the past, if you wanted to talk to people, you went to see them, picked up the phone, or wrote them a letter. Today's college students rely on texting, e-mail, instant messaging (IMing), Facebook, and Twitter to communicate with friends and family on a daily basis (Christofides et al., 2009; Diamanduros et al., 2007). Although this technology has allowed more communication between friends, lovers, and family members, it has also created many new communication issues, as we saw in the chapter opening stories.

In this chapter, we talk about the importance of communication, how we learn to communicate, how people differ in the ways they communicate, changing communication technologies, and ways to improve interpersonal communication, including the ability to communicate about sexual issues. Improving communication has been found to enrich personal sexuality. We discuss other ways to enrich your personal sexuality by learning to feel good about yourself and about your skills in bed, and by improving your relationships with others. No one is born a good lover; it takes learning and patience. The information in this chapter may be valuable to you throughout your life, as your relationships change and mature.

> *For love and intimacy to grow,* **each partner must know** *how the other feels.*

▶ THE IMPORTANCE
of Communication

Let's say you meet someone new tonight. Your eyes find each other across the room, and slowly you make your way over to talk to each other. What would you say? What wouldn't you say? How do you decide? Most likely you make a comment such as, "Pretty loud in here, huh?" or "I can't believe how crowded it is!" The first unwritten rule about communication early in a relationship is that you talk about something relevant but impersonal. You wouldn't walk up to someone you don't know and say, "Do you get along with your parents?" or "Do you ever get acne?" No, these questions are too personal to discuss with a stranger.

When do you start to talk about personal things in relationships? Social psychologists talk about the "onion" theory of communication. We all are onions with many, many layers, and when we first meet someone, we are careful about what we say—our onion layers stay in place. However, as more and more time goes by (and the amount of time differs from person to person), we begin to peel back our layers. At first we might talk about the weather ("I can't believe it's still so hot in October") and then progress to certain classes or professors ("I really enjoyed my psychology teacher last semester"). These comments are low risk and really don't involve sharing too much personal information. However, the next layer may include information about politics or family relationships, and the information gets more personal. The key to the onion theory is that as you begin to reveal your layers, so, too, does your partner. If you share something personal about yourself, your partner will probably do the same. If your partner tells you something about a bad experience he or she had, you may be more likely to share a negative experience you've been through.

Some people make the mistake of prematurely peeling back their layers. Have you ever met someone who shared really personal information early, maybe within the first few days of meeting you? Some people talk about personal issues very early in the relationship, which may make others feel uncomfortable (Weisel & King, 2007). Yet, there are exceptions to this. For example, have you ever sat next to a stranger on an airplane and shared information that you later realized you've never shared with people you know well? Anxiety may be the culprit here, because you might be a little nervous about flying, and talking might help lessen your anxiety. More important, though, you assume you'll never see this person again, so talk is cheap. There are relatively few risks to sharing so much so soon. When you arrive at your destination, you both go off in different directions and probably won't ever see each other again.

Good communication is one of the most important factors in a satisfying relationship (Eaker et al., 2007; Ledermann et al., 2010; Moore, 2010; Rehman & Holtzworth-Munroe, 2007). Communication skills can be applied to all aspects of life, such as improving family relationships, being more effective in relationships at school or work, developing a love relationship, or discussing relationship issues and sexuality with a partner. Communication fosters mutual understanding, increases emotional intimacy, and helps deepen feelings of love and intimacy. For love and intimacy to grow, each partner must know how the other feels.

Relationships between two people inevitably run into difficulties. It's nearly impossible not to experience difficulties when you are sharing your space with another person. This is precisely why many forms of therapy emphasize learning communication skills and why communication self-help books overflow from bookstore shelves. Communication problems usually occur when partners have poor communication skills, feel unable to self-disclose, or have trouble listening.

Like Corelle pointed out in the chapter opening story, anger and frustration are common reactions to poor communication. Misunderstandings, anger, and frustration can all lead to a downward spiral in which communication becomes less and less effective. Poor communication skills can contribute to many serious

Partners who can talk to each other have a better chance of their relationship working out.

© Rob Bartee/Alamy

The story that follows was written by an international student of mine. We had many interesting discussions about the cultural differences in communication. If you have ever traveled to or lived in a different country, you've probably experienced some communication issues. Not all cultures communicate in the same way, and our cultural background affects our communication strategies and patterns. Wouldn't it be interesting if there were different ways to say "I love you"? Can you imagine using the most intimate way only once, or maybe twice, in your lifetime?

I was born in Regensburg, Germany, and I have lived there all of my life. For the past year, I have been living in the United States, and during this time, I have learned a lot about cross-cultural differences in communication. Americans have a very emotional way of using language. They "love" peanut butter—what does this mean? When someone says, "I love you," does this mean that a person loves you as much as peanut butter? Or is it a different kind of love? This was really confusing for me.

I think that special expressions or words lose their real meaning when you use them all the time. This is especially true when it comes to relationships. Americans say, "I love you," but I'm not sure what that really means. A little boy tells his mother he loves her, good friends say it, you hear it being said in advertisements, and everyone loves everyone! But how can you express real deep feelings if you are using the phrase "I love you" all the time? Does it still mean the same thing? How do you know if Americans really love you, if they also love peanut butter? What does "I love you" really mean?

In Germany, we say something that is between "I love you" and "I like you"; maybe it means more "You are in my heart." You would use the phrase "Ich hab' dich lieb" to tell your mother and father, your friends, or your new boyfriend how you feel about them. But when someone says, "Ich liebe Dich"—the German "I love you"—then your relationship is really serious. This phrase is reserved only for relationships in which you know your partner really well. Saying "Ich liebe Dich" is very hard for some people, because it can make you more vulnerable. When a man would say "Ich liebe Dich" after three months of dating, it would make me wonder whether he could be taken seriously. Germans only use these words when they really mean it, and this gives the phrase much more respect.

I like how Americans are so open about letting someone know that they care about them, but it's hard to tell when it's really serious. Why is there no phrase in the English language that means something between liking and loving someone? Every culture and every country has its own ways of communicating and expressing ideas. What is most important is learning how to accept and learn from the differences.

SOURCE: Author's files.

relationship problems, including physical and emotional abuse (Cornelius et al., 2010).

It is also important to point out, however, that not all relationship problems are caused by a lack of communication or poor communication. Sometimes the problems come from the couple's unwillingness to acknowledge a problem or issue that needs to be worked out. In other cases, issues such as poor health or economic stresses can create problems that hinder communication and intimacy.

Overall, couples who know how to communicate with each other are happier, more satisfied, and have a greater likelihood of making their relationship last (Hahlweg et al., 2000; Moore, 2010; Rehman & Holtzworth-Munroe, 2007). But learning to really communicate with your partner isn't easy. Why is it so hard to talk to your partner? How can you share yourself physically with someone but feel unable to talk about things that are important to you? Why is it difficult to listen to someone when he or she wants to talk about something you don't want to hear?

▶▶ LEARNING to Communicate

Are we born with the ability to communicate with others, or do we learn it as we grow up? If you've ever been around babies, you know that even though they don't have the ability to speak, they certainly know how to communicate with their caregivers. When they are hungry, tired, or just want to be held, they cry. Crying communicates to their caregiver that they need something. As children acquire language, they learn more effective ways of communicating.

Have you ever heard someone use the idiom "out of the mouths of babes"? Typically we use this saying when a child says something that is very intelligent or truthful. My friend Lisanne told me a story about taking her 5-year-old daughter to try on shoes at a store where one of the salespeople had terrible acne. Lisanne's daughter couldn't take her eyes off the salesperson's acne. Finally, her daughter asked, "How did you get all those nipples all over your face?" Lisanne was horrified. But the story illustrates an important point—kids are notorious for saying exactly what they're thinking. We learn various filters as we grow up (well, most of us do—we all have a friend that has a "broken filter" as I like to call it; the friend who blurts out everything without thinking about the consequences of his or her words). The rest of us learn what is socially acceptable in conversation as a host of issues surface and interfere with our ability to talk to others. We begin to worry about what others might think, we feel selfish for asking for things we want and need, and we don't know how to talk about ourselves and our needs. How can we communicate with others but still manage our relationships and our own identity?

▶▶ GOALS of Communication

When we communicate with other people, we have three competing goals (Vanfossen, 1996). The first is to "get the job done"—we have a message for someone, and we want to communicate that message.

Second, we also have a "relational goal"—we want to maintain the relationship and not hurt or offend the person with our message. Finally, we have an "identity management goal"—that is, we want our communication to project a certain image of ourselves.

All of these goals compete with one another (we want to tell someone something, not hurt the relationship, and maintain our image), making the job of communicating our thoughts, needs, or desires even that much tougher. We'll discuss these goals in more detail later in this chapter, but for now, let's explore the impact of our families on our ability to communicate and perhaps we can uncover the mystery of good communication.

▶▶ FAMILIES and Communication

In Chapter 1, we introduced the important influence that our *family of origin* has on our personal development. Our ability to communicate, and the strategies we use to do so, were often learned through our interactions within our families (Schrodt, 2009). Family members use language and communication strategies to negotiate, inform, reinforce values and beliefs, share stories, manage a household, and maintain relationships, among other things (Howe et al., 2010; Tannen et al., 2007). Throughout these processes, interactions and experiences in our families teach us important aspects of communication, such as negotiation, conflict avoidance, arguing, and interpersonal skills in romantic relationships (Ledbetter, 2010; Schrodt et al., 2009). Family communication also helps children develop a social and emotional understanding of the world around them (Howe et al., 2010), and can affect a child's self-esteem, mental well-being (Schrodt & Ledbetter, 2007), and potential for depression (Koerner & Fitzpatrick, 1997).

REAL RESEARCH 3.1 Parents who communicate in ways that encourage an open discussion of ideas and feelings are more likely to have children who learn to cope with stress, solve personal problems, and make healthy decisions (SCHRODT, 2009).

If children learn positive ways of communicating, they will develop healthy strategies of communicating with others. But if they learn negative ways of communicating, they may encounter difficulties later in life. One of my students, Cherie, has always walked away when conflict arose in her intimate relationships. She found that she'd rather leave than have a conversation about what's going on. Her boyfriend was frustrated by this and wanted to talk things out. Cherie has told me that she's "just like her parents" because they always gave each other the *silent treatment*

A male mode of communication uses more report-talk, which imparts knowledge and helps to establish status.

when they disagreed. Could Cherie have learned to walk away from arguments with a partner by watching and interacting with her parents? It's possible.

▶ COMMUNICATION
Differences and Similarities

Many factors, in addition to the family, can influence our communication. Various aspects of who we are, such as our gender, sexual orientation, ethnic and cultural background, and even our mood, health, age, and/or educational background can all affect our communication strategies and skills (Knöfler & Imhof, 2007). Let's review the impact of gender, culture, and sexual orientation on communication.

▶▶ COMMUNICATION and Gender

Do men and women have different styles or ways of communicating? Are your conversations with men different from your conversations with women? Gender differences in communication have long been a topic of scientific interest (Burleson et al., 1996; Lakoff, 1975; Litosseliti, 2006; Tannen, 1990). The research supports the fact that conversations between women and men are often more difficult than conversations that occur in same-sex groups (Athen-

| **genderlect** Coined by Deborah Tannen, this term refers to the fundamental differences between the way men and women communicate. | **tag question** A way of speaking in which speakers renounce or deny the validity of what they are saying by adding a questioning statement at the end of their statement. | **disclaimer** A way of speaking in which speakers renounce or deny the validity of what they are saying by including a negative statement. | **question statement** A way of speaking in which speakers renounce or deny the validity of what they are saying by adding a question at the end of their statement. | **hedge word** A way of speaking in which speakers renounce or deny the validity of what they are saying by using certain words to decrease their perceived assertiveness. |

staedt et al., 2004; Edwards & Hamilton, 2004). Why is this? Is part of the problem a difference in communication styles, so that the content of the communication gets lost in the form it takes?

Research Studies of Gender Differences

Linguist Deborah Tannen (1990) has done a great deal of research in the area of communication and gender differences. She has termed the fundamental differences between the way men and women communicate as **genderlects** (JEN-der-lecks). Women have been found to use more rapport-talk, which establishes relationships and connections, whereas men use more report-talk, which imparts knowledge (Eckstein & Goldman, 2001). Tannen (1990) asserts that women use conversations to establish and maintain intimacy, whereas men use conversations to establish status.

Tannen also found that women use less assertiveness in their communication. For example, when stating an opinion, women often end their statement with **tag questions** (e.g., "It's really cold in here, isn't it?" or "That's an interesting idea, isn't it?") to invite discussion and minimize disagreements. They also use **disclaimers** (e.g., "I may be wrong, but..."), **question statements** ("Am I off base here?") (Vanfossen, 1996), and **hedge words** such as "sort of," "kind of," "aren't you," or "would you mind?" All of these tend to decrease the speaker's perceived assertiveness of speech. Although tag questions are frequently used in English, they are not used as often in other languages. In fact, the French and Swedish languages lack an equivalent feature (Cheng & Warren, 2001).

There have been criticisms of Tannen's genderlect theory. One of the biggest criticisms has been in her unidimensional approach of studying gender differences in communication. To Tannen, gender is based on *biological* sex. Therefore, all women communicate one way and all men another way. However, it could be that differences in communication skills, rather than differences in gender, could contribute to communication differences.

A female mode of communication uses more rapport-talk, which establishes relationships and maintains intimacy.

PhotoDisc./Getty Images

Communication experts have identified two categories of communication skills, affective and instrumental (Burleson, 2003; Burleson et al., 1996). Affectively oriented communication skills are comforting and involve a significant amount of listening, whereas instrumentally oriented communication skills are more persuasive and narrative. Think about friends or lovers who you know and consider for a moment their communication skills. Do you know people who are more comforting and spend a great deal of time listening in your conversations (an affective style)? Or people who always do most of the talking and often try to convince listeners with their ideas or tell long stories (an instrumental style)?

Research has found that we value different types of communication skills in our relationships with others. For example, when we need social support or want to "vent," we are more likely to prefer the company of our friends with affectively oriented skills; but if we want to discuss strategies or learn more about a particular topic, we are more likely to prefer the company of our friends with instrumentally oriented skills (Kunkel & Burleson, 1998). Overall, women are more likely than men to value affectively oriented communication skills, whereas men are more likely to value instrumentally oriented skills (Burleson et al., 1996; Samter & Burleson, 2005).

Another interesting area of research involves speech quantity. The stereotype is that women talk more than men. This stereotype was supported by the research of neuropsychiatrist Louann Brizendine, who reported that women used 20,000 words per day, whereas men used only 7,000 (Brizendine, 2006). Brizendine claimed these differences were due to hormones during fetal development (Brizendine & Allen, 2010). However, when a group of researchers tried to replicate Brizendine's study using electronically activated recorders, they found that men and women both used about 16,000 words a day (Mehl et al., 2007). The subjects in this study were college students, which may limit the results, but the researchers point out that if the differences were biologically based, they would have appeared in this sample regardless.

Keep in mind that numerous studies on gender and communication have found that overall differences in many areas of communication are small (Aries, 1996; Dindia & Canary, 2006). Many other factors contribute to our ability to communicate, such as social philosophies, gender roles, dominance, power, and as we talked about earlier, our family of origin. Many of the studies on gender differences in communication have studied only young, well-educated, middle-class Americans (Mortenson, 2002), and as you remember from our discussion in Chapter 2, we do not know whether these findings are generalizable to different groups and cultures within and outside of the United States.

Theories About Gender Differences

In the preceding section, we discussed gender differences in communication, but what might contribute to some of these differences? Is it biology? Society? Researchers often disagree about whether gender differences exist, but those who agree that there are differences often disagree on the reasons for them. There may be a biological basis—physically innate differences between men and women that cause gender differences in communication. There may be psychological reasons—men and women have experienced different reinforcements for communicating, and these have shaped their patterns of communication. There may also be societal reasons for the differences. Social role theory explains the differences in terms of role expectations about masculinity and femininity in society, whereas societal development theories focus on male dominance in society and its effects on communication patterns.

Although it's true that all of these theories can explain some of the gender differences in communication, gender communication can often be best understood as a form of cross-cultural communication (A. M. Johnson, 2001; Mulvaney, 1994). If you were suddenly in a conversation with a person from another country who had no experience with your culture, you might find this conversation difficult. You wouldn't know the subtleties of that person's communication style, and he or she wouldn't know yours. It's hypothesized that even though men and women grow up in similar environments, they learn different ways of communicating, which resembles a form of cross-cultural communication.

Maltz and Borker (1982) believe that American men and women come from different "sociolinguistic subcultures" and learn different communication rules. They interpret conversations and use language differently. This all begins as children in same-sex play groups, which are often organized very differently. Most young girls play in small groups and have "best friends." Reaching higher levels of intimacy is the goal, and their games, such as playing house, less often have winners and losers. Boys, on the other hand, learn to use speech to express dominance and play in hierarchically organized groups that focus on directing and winning (Maltz & Borker, 1982). Boys often jockey for status by telling jokes, showing off, or claiming they are the best at things.

According to Maltz and Borker (1982), during same-sex conversations, girls and boys learn the rules and assumptions about communication, and these rules follow them through life. As adolescents, they begin to communicate in mixed-sex groups with the

View in Video
To watch the entire interview, go to Psychology CourseMate at **login.cengagebrain.com**.

© Jonathan Marks

"When entering a maid cafe, visitors are greeted with 'Welcome Back Master!'"
—MAID CAFES

rules they learned from same-sex communication, which can cause problems. For example, girls learn to nod their head during conversations with other girls. This lets the talker know that she is being listened to. When a woman nods her head during a conversation with a man, he thinks she agrees with him (when she might not agree or disagree—her head nod may simply be showing him that she is listening). When a man doesn't nod his head when a woman is talking to him, she may think he isn't listening to her. All of this can lead to feeling misunderstood and to poor communication. Understanding the differences in communication styles won't automatically prevent disagreements, but it will help keep the disagreements manageable. We talk more about nonverbal communication techniques later in this chapter.

▶▶ COMMUNICATION and Culture

Cultures differ in many ways, and these differences affect communication patterns. One important dimension that has been extensively studied is the degree to which a culture encourages individual versus group needs (Cai et al., 2000). Individualistic cultures encourage their members to have individual goals and values, and an independent sense of self (Matsumoto, 1996), whereas collectivist cultures encourage members to value group needs over their individual needs. The United States is among the more individualistic countries, together with Canada, Australia, and Great Britain, whereas Asian and Latin cultures tend to be more collectivistic (Adler et al., 2007). This individualistic approach is probably why men and women from the United States are more comfortable disclosing personal information to a variety of people than members of collectivistic cultures (Gudykunst et al., 1996). Persons from collectivistic cultures, such as Japan or Korea, rarely disclose personal information to those outside of their immediate family because it is thought to be inappropriate to do so (Chen & Danish, 2010; Gudykunst et al., 1996; Seki et al., 2002).

In addition, anthropologists have identified two distinct ways in which individuals from various cultures deliver messages to one another (Adler et al., 2007). A "low-context culture," such as the Scandinavian, German, Swiss, and North American countries, use language to express thoughts, feelings, and ideas as directly as pos-

Cultures differ in many ways, and these differences affect communication patterns.

Sex in Real Life ▶▶▶ Gossiping and Complaining

Recently, I asked a group of heterosexual students what it would be like to spend 24 hours with their partner but be able to use only nonverbal communication. Students thought about it, and many didn't know what to make of the question. Would it really be possible for them to be alone with their partner but not (verbally) speak to each other for 24 hours?

Several of the women who were asked this question said that although they'd be willing to try, they didn't think it would work out well. They weren't sure they could be with their partner without verbal communication. The men, on the other hand, enthusiastically responded to my question. "Sure!" many of them said. When pressed for their reasoning, several of the men said, "I wouldn't have to hear her complaining!" This made me think—what exactly is "complaining," and do women do this more than men? The answer depends on your definition. Many women say that it's not really "complaining" but rather "discussing" important issues.

The research indicates that women do more complaining than men and are more likely to commiserate with each other about their complaints (Boxer, 1996; Jaworski & Coupland, 2005). Women report that they enjoy engaging in this type of communication with other women. In fact, it often serves as a bonding tool in women's friendships (Goodwin, 2007; Sotirin, 2000). Women complain to each other in an effort to cope with their disappointments, whereas men address troubles by responding with potential solutions instead of talking at length about the injustice of it all.

Research has found that women's informal talk includes gossip, complaining, "troubles talk," and "bitching" (Sotirin, 2000). Although at first glance these types of talk might seem similar, each appears to have its own structure and function. The focus of gossip is on an absent target and includes contributions from several participants. Gossiping may also have an aggressive component to it, wherein the

gossip is meant to hurt or harm a particular relationship (Conway, 2005; Ferguson, 2004). Complaining is usually brief and to the point. "Bitching," in contrast, relates an in-depth account of events, usually about an injustice or something negative that has happened to the speaker, allowing her to express her dissatisfaction (Sotirin, 2000). In "troubles talk," there is one "troubles teller," and the focus of the conversation stays on the teller the entire length of the conversation. Men have been found to engage in gossip, too, although they are more likely to gossip to a romantic partner, whereas women were equally likely to share gossip with their romantic partners and their same-sex friends (McAndrew et al., 2007).

Next time you stroll through the mall or even your student union, take a look around you. In what kinds of communication are the women around you engaging? What do you think the purpose of the communication is?

---

sible (Hall, 1976; Hall, 1990). Statements are simple, and the meaning of the statement is in the words that are spoken. A "high-context" culture, which is typical of Asian and Arab cultures, relies heavily on subtle and nonverbal cues in its communication (Ambady et al., 1996; Hall, 1990). Communication is not direct, and a listener's understanding depends on the context of the conversation, nonverbal behavior, relationship history, and social rules. Communicators from high-context cultures may often beat around the bush in their conversations and expect listeners to know what they mean.

▶▶ COMMUNICATION and Sexual Orientation

Although the majority of research on communication has used heterosexual couples, we do have limited information about communication patterns and strategies in same-sex couples. As we discussed earlier, many issues are at play when a couple communicates—gender, dominance, gender role, social philosophy, and power. Like heterosexual couples, conversational styles in gay and lesbian relationships have been found to reflect power differences in the relationship more than the biological sex of the communicator (Steen & Schwartz, 1995).

Differences in same-sex communication may also have to do with gender roles. Men who are higher in nurturance engage in more cooperative speech, whereas women who are lower in nurturance engage less in such speech (Edwards & Hamilton, 2004). In addition, stereotypically "feminine" men and women have been

found to use more submissive speech patterns, whereas stereotypically "masculine" men have been found to use more dominance language than stereotypically "feminine" or androgenous men and women (Ellis & McCallister, 1980). It may be that gay men and lesbian women are more flexible in their gender roles, and their communication patterns could reflect this comfort.

When our partner listens to us, we feel worthy and cared about, which, in turn, strengthens our relationship.

Ryan Pierse/Getty Images

When compared with heterosexual men's speech, gay men's speech more commonly includes the use of "qualifying adjectives" (such as "adorable" or "marvelous"), a wider-than-usual pitch range, extended vowel length speech (e.g., "maarvelous"), a tendency to avoid reduced forms of speech (e.g., contractions such as "can't" and "won't"), and a greater likelihood of arm and hand ges-

tures (Salzmann, 2007). We discuss differences in nonverbal behaviors later in this chapter. Lesbian women have been found to use more hedge words and a narrower pitch range than gay men (Salzmann, 2007). Remember that sexual orientation, culture, ethnicity, and communication styles are all interconnected, and it may be impossible to look at one variable without also looking at these other influences.

In the future, more research is needed to examine the speech and communication patterns of gay men and lesbian women. Research addressing communication strengths and weaknesses in gay and lesbian couples would be helpful to further our understanding of these relationships.

Communication patterns begin when children play in same-sex groups.

nonverbal communication
Communication without words (includes eye contact, head nodding, touching, and the like).

computer-mediated communication (CMC)
Communication produced when people interact with one another by transmitting messages via networked computers.

REAL RESEARCH 3.2 In a typical conversation, 80% of each person's gaze is directed at the eyes, nose, and mouth of the other person (WOOD, 2008). Looking over the person's shoulder or to either side of the person implies disinterest and boredom.

▶ TYPES of Communication

There is much more to communication than words alone. We use nonverbal communication to get our message across, and many of us communicate with others online through e-mail, texting, or IMing. All of these methods of communication raise other important issues.

▶▶ NONVERBAL Communication

In the chapter opening story, Shadia (the "people watcher") discussed her fascination observing the **nonverbal communication** of couples around her. The majority of our communication is done nonverbally and nonverbal cues are an important and influential part of our communication (Guffey, 1999; Knapp & Hall, 2005). Although nonverbal communication includes facial expressions, hand and arm gestures, postures, and body positioning, and movements are often used, it can also include many of the specifics of how communication is used, including speech rates, durations, and intensities (Boomer, 1963; Ekman & Friesen, 1969; Mehrabian, 2009; Sauter et al., 2010). Nonverbal communication can also trigger emotional reactions in listeners. While listening to others, we often experience an *emotional contagion,* synchronizing our facial expressions with theirs (Tamiello et al., 2009). For example, watching the nonverbal cues from a friend who looks sad can often make us feel sad.

Although we get better at recognizing nonverbal cues as the intensity of the emotional expressions increases, we also improve our ability to recognize them as we grow up. Young children can identify emotional expressions of anger, fear, happiness, and sadness, but their ability to identify these emotions increases as they age (Montirosso et al., 2010). However, at a certain point, older adults begin to lose the ability to recognize basic emotions in facial, vocal, and bodily expressions (Ruffman et al., 2009). Research has found that approximately 75% of older adults can only identify emotional expressions at a level similar to young teens (Ruffman et al., 2009).

Culture is also important to consider here, because nonverbal communication differs widely from culture to culture. Many of the primarily negative emotions, such as anger or disgust, can be recognized across cultures, but several of the positive emotions, such as joy and happiness, may be communicated with culture-specific signals (Sauter et al., 2010). These signals may include certain vocalizations, facial expressions, and/or posturing.

In most Western cultures, nonverbal communication can completely change the meaning of a verbal expression. When a friend tells you, "You're the best" with a smile on her face and a relaxed body posture, you'll probably believe her. However, the same statement coming from a person who has arms crossed, teeth clenched, and eyebrows furrowed has a completely different message. Most likely, in this second situation, you'd recognize that your friend is being sarcastic. Body language helps fill in the gaps in verbal communication. As humans, we are uniquely designed to read these nonverbal cues and respond accordingly. Interestingly, most children do not learn to identify sarcasm until much later in childhood (Glenwright & Pexman, 2010).

How well can you read the nonverbal cues from the people you interact with? Are you better at reading your partner's nonverbals than those of, say, a friend? Can you ever know exactly what another person is saying nonverbally? The ability to do so is an important ingredient in successful interpersonal relationships. You might be better at reading your best friend's nonverbal behavior than someone you have known only a short time. Overall, women are better at decoding and translating nonverbal communication (DeLange, 1995). Women's nonverbal communication techniques include more eye contact and head nods,

ON YOUR MIND 3.2

My boyfriend spends a lot of time on the Internet. The other night, I discovered that he was obsessed with another girl's Facebook page. He had left her several messages and was checking out her photos from a weekend party. I was heartbroken. Do you think this constitutes cheating? It sure feels that way to me.

This is an interesting question. Many people believe that if their partner is having an intimate relationship with someone on the Internet, this is indeed cheating, but this really depends on how you define "intimate." Online relationships often involve sharing personal information about yourself and learning personal information about the person with whom you are communicating, which can increase emotional connections. Studies have found that emotional online infidelity elicits significant distress in dating and married partners (Guadagno & Sagarin, 2010; Henline et al., 2007; Whitty & Quigley, 2008). Both online and conventional infidelity cause anger, jealousy, and reduce relationship satisfaction (Guadagno & Sagarin, 2010). Another study found that men and women who engage in online infidelity have high levels of narcissism, and are not necessarily unhappy with their present relationships (Aviram, 2005). Communication is key here—see whether he can help you understand why he was drawn to engaging in such conversations on Facebook. We will explore issues related to cybersex and cheating in Chapter 10.

whereas men's has fewer head nods, less eye contact, and minimal "encouragers" (nonverbal cues to let their partner know they are listening; J. C. Pearson et al., 1991). Women have also been found to smile, lean forward, touch, and gaze more often than men in conversation (Wood, 1999).

▶▶ COMPUTER-MEDIATED **Communication**

Computer-mediated communication (CMC) includes communication tools for conveying written text via the Internet. This includes e-mailing, texting, IMing, tweeting, and communicating through Facebook. As we discussed earlier in this chapter, Internet communication has increased in popularity over the last few years, and today's college students use such CMC methods daily in their communication with their friends and family. While these methods of communication can be invaluable for couples in long-distance relationships (recall Heather's story from the chapter opener), there are issues related to their use in many couples. There are questions about these CMC exchanges, however. Is it possible to develop deep and meaningful relationships via online communication? How does it compare with face-to-face communication? Are there differences in how women and men communicate online?

Although we talk about meeting partners online more in Chapter 9, students who like to use the Internet to meet people have told me that they find it easier to meet people online than in a bar or at a party. They like being able to check out a person's website or Facebook page to get some information about them before the first face-to-face meeting (and surprisingly, research

Using the nonverbal cues in this photo, what would you guess is going on with this couple and why?

© Mary Kate Denny/PhotoEdit

has found that information posted on people's Facebook pages can provide fairly accurate information about a person's personality; Back et al., 2010). It seems hard to believe that it would be possible to meet a partner online, given that conversation is reduced to a keyboard or cell phone, yet CMC can be very intimate, and couples can potentially become acquainted faster online than through face-to-face contact. One woman said:

> *I found that our relationship progressed very quickly. We became intimate very early on and told each other things about ourselves that "bonded" us. It seemed that there was less risk, since we weren't face-to-face and didn't have to worry about what each other would think. We could also talk all the time—it wasn't unusual for us to find each other online in the wee hours of the morning.* (Author's files)

Online communication can also reduce the role that physical characteristics play in the development of attraction and enhance rapport and self-disclosure. Couples who communicate online often have higher rates of self-disclosure and direct questioning than those who meet face-to-face (Antheunis et al., 2007; Gibbs et al., 2006). Some studies claim that online communication, such as texting or IMing, is more intimate than face-to-face communication (Horrigan et al., 2001; Ramirez & Zhang, 2007). Online communication can enhance personal communication by making it easier to stay in touch with people. One study found that more than half of Internet users reported increased communication with their families, and close to 70% reported increased communication with friends (Horrigan et al., 2001).

We do know that when couples overindulge in texting, the results can often be destructive. One of my students, Whittney, told

*Women have been found to **have an easier time** making their voices heard online.*

FIGURE **3.1** Avatars, which are often used in online communication, can be used to help users express certain emotions or feelings. What emotions do you think these avatars are expressing?

me that she had dated Bill, a guy she met on MySpace. After a few dates, Bill texted her and asked if she wanted to be his girlfriend. At the time, she was thrilled and texted back a quick "Yes!" However, it soon became apparent to her that texting was the only form of communication that Bill used. He texted her hundreds of messages a day. Whittney soon tired of his texting obsession and stopped responding to them. After a few months, her frustration led to a breakup that happened, not surprisingly, via a text message. As Corelle pointed out in the chapter opening story, it's important to know how your partner prefers to communicate early in the relationship. Relying on one form of communication is never easy.

What about gender differences in online communication? Research indicates there are gender differences in online communication styles (Baron, 2004; Colley et al., 2010). This type of communication has been found to reduce the constraining gender roles that are automatically in place in face-to-face conversation. Because of this, women have been found to have an easier time making their voices heard online than in a face-to-face conversation, and they also use more "smileys" and other **emoticons** (e-MOTE-ick-cons) online than men (B. P. Bailey et al., 2003; Baron, 2004). These often serve to express emotion but may deflect from the seriousness of women's statements (Dresner & Herring, 2010; Riordan & Kreuz, 2010). Emoticons can be compared with tag questions during face-to-face conversations.

Research has also been done on the use of **avatars** in CMC (see Figure 3.1). Avatars have increasingly been used to express emotions or feelings in online communication (Koda et al., 2009; Palomares & Lee, 2010). It would make sense, however, that the online expression of emotion through emoticons or avatars may not be universally understood among all cultures. Studies have found that there are cultural differences in the interpretation of online avatars (Koda et al., 2009). Generally, negative expressions (such as frowns or furrowed brows) have a wider cultural understanding, whereas positive expressions (such as smiling or winking) have more variations in interpretation (Koda et al., 2009).

As an undergraduate student, Mark Zuckerberg created *CourseMatch* in 2003 to help Harvard students find out what courses their friends were taking. Soon afterward he created *Facemash,* which allowed students to rate the attractiveness of two fellow students. In 2004 he launched *Thefacebook*, which eventually become what is known today as *Facebook.* As of 2011, Zuckerberg's personal wealth, mostly from the creation of *Facebook*, was estimated at $13.5 billion.

emoticons	**avatar**
Facial symbols used when sending electronic messages online; an example would be :-).	A computer user's online representation of himself or herself presented in two- or three-dimensional art.

Sex in Real Life ▶▶ Social Networks

Over the past few years, online social networks have become very popular. Social networks are structures made up of individuals who are tied together through institutions, friendship, dating, or special interests. Social relationships are viewed in terms of "nodes" (individuals) and "ties" (the connections between the individuals) forming a map of individual connections between people. Social networks are available for a variety of interests, such as music, cars, sports, clubbing, movies, gaming, business, travel, religion, and books. In addition, there are networks targeted for gay, lesbian, and bisexual members, as well as ethnic and racial groups.

Social network services, such as Facebook, MySpace, Xanga, Yahoo! 360, and Friendster, are great examples of social networks. These sites allow friends to be connected with others and make new friends. On college campuses, Facebook is the most popular networking site, and the majority of students check their Facebook accounts several times a day. Since 2006, Facebook has been open to anyone over age 13. It is the most popular website for uploading photos—14 million photos are uploaded on Facebook each day.

Research into social networks has found that the shape of a network affects its usefulness to the member. Smaller, tighter networks can be less useful because friends in these types of networks tend to have similar knowledge bases and attitudes. Larger networks often allow more creativity and open discussions about new ideas and concepts. Think about it this way: If you only had friends with similar interests to yours, there would be less chance for learning something new. With a larger, looser network, people are often introduced to new ideas and thoughts.

Early work in the field of social networks found that the average person is able to form only a limited number of connections to other people. "Dunbar's number" proposed that the typical size of a social network is 150 members (Bialik, 2007; Dunbar, 1998). This number originated out of cross-cultural and evolutionary research that found there is a limit to how many friends a person can recognize and about whom he or she can track information. The "small-world phenomenon" claims that through social networks, one random person can connect with another random person anywhere in the world.

What are the advantages and disadvantages to using Facebook and other networking sites? Students have told me that although social network sites are great to help them keep in touch and know what's going on, they can also be overwhelming. Once again, balance is the key here—make sure you're not relying on one form of communication, or else you're sure to feel overwhelmed.

It is also important to point out that researchers who study online communication have no sure way of knowing the gender of the people online. In fact, it has been suggested that people create "virtual identities" online (McAdams, 1996; Vaast, 2007). A man can claim to be a woman or a child could claim to be an adult. However, one study found that by using linguistic gender markers, including references to emotion, insults, and compliments, it was possible to identify the gender of anonymous CMCs with 91.4% accuracy (Thomson & Murachver, 2001).

The key to any online relationship is to take it slow and, because you are not meeting the person face-to-face, really get to know your partner as much as you can. Communicate the things that are important to you, and "listen" as your partner talks. Be realistic about the chances the relationship will work out. If you find your partner can't communicate offline, it would be a good idea to find a way to talk about these issues before the relationship progresses.

REAL RESEARCH 3.3 90% of college students log on to Facebook daily, and when they do, they disclose more personal information than they would in any other context (Christofides et al., 2009).

◀ review QUESTIONS

1 Explain why good communication is the hallmark of a healthy relationship, and give three examples of how poor communication could lead to a relationship problem.

2 Identify and describe the three competing goals for good communication.

3 What do we know about the impact of gender, sexual orientation, and culture on communication? Describe the theories that have been proposed to explain gender differences in communication styles.

4 Differentiate between individualistic and collectivistic cultures and high- and low-context cultures. Describe how these issues can affect communication.

5 What is nonverbal communication? What can you learn from your partner's nonverbal behavior? Provide one example.

6 How can the Internet reduce some of the common communication problems that couples experience in face-to-face conversations?

▶ SEXUAL Communication

So far we've been talking about how difficult it can be to communicate with the people in our everyday lives. What about communicating with our intimate partners about sex? This is often more challenging because sexuality tends to magnify all the communication problems that exist in any close relationship. We grow up in a society instilled with a sense of shame about our sexuality and are taught at an early age that talking about sex is "dirty." Approaching the subject of sex for the first time in a relationship implies moving on to a new level of intimacy, which can be scary. It also opens the way for judgment and possible rejection. Because of this, many couples avoid conversations about sex altogether. This is probably why when men and women were asked how they show their consent to engage in sex with a partner, the majority reported they said nothing at all (Hickman & Muehlenhard, 1999). Yet, we know that couples who can communicate with each other about sexual issues report more relationship satisfaction (Faulkner & Lannutti, 2010).

▶▶ IMPORTANT COMPONENTS
in Sexual Communication

Several important components contribute to healthy sexual communication. We will discuss the importance of a positive self-image, self-disclosure, trust, and listening.

Positive Self-Images and Feeling Good About Yourself

Healthy sexuality depends on feeling good about yourself. If you have a negative self-image or do not like certain aspects of your body or personality, how can you demonstrate your attractiveness to an intimate partner? Imagine a man or woman who is overly concerned about his or her body while in bed with a partner. Maybe a woman is worried that her partner will not be attracted to the size or shape of her chest, thighs, or stomach, or to her nipples. Perhaps a man is consumed with anxiety over the size of his penis,

"It's very dangerous and it could come back and harm everyone involved."
—TEENS AND SEXTING

View in Video
To watch the entire interview, go to Psychology CourseMate at **login.cengagebrain.com.**

Video supplied by BBC Motion Gallery

ON YOUR MIND 3.3

Are there any ways that a person can make himself or herself more attractive to a romantic partner?

Although many people might think the answer to this question lies in new perfume or an outfit, researchers at North Carolina State University have found that rewarding partner interactions through communication will make you more physically attractive to your partner (Albada et al., 2002). Couples who communicated with each other in positive ways (such as giving compliments or expressing affection) rated each other more physically attractive than those who didn't communicate in such ways. The bottom line is that good communication can enhance physical attractiveness.

his weight, or his body hair, worrying that his partner won't find it appealing. All of these fears interfere with our ability to let go, relax, open up, and enjoy the sexual experience.

Talking about our anxieties, concerns, or worries with our partners will help them to understand, and it may even be the first step to coming to terms with these issues ourselves. We all have parts of our bodies we wish we could change. In fact, most of us are much more critical of our bodies than our partners would ever be. Self-esteem also has a powerful effect on how we communicate with others (Adler et al., 2007). A person with positive self-esteem will often expect to be accepted by their partners, whereas someone with negative self-esteem will often expect to be rejected by their partners (Hamachek, 1982). It's not difficult to see how negative self-images and fears of rejection can inhibit healthy sexual communication.

In American society, learning to like our bodies is often difficult. We discussed in Chapter 1 the impact that magazines, television, and advertisers all play into our insecurities with their portrayals of the ideal body. The beauty images that the media present to us are often impossible to live up to and leave many of us feeling unattractive by comparison. To sell products, advertisers must first convince us that we are not OK the way we are—that we need to change our looks, our smells, or our habits. In the United States in particular, we put a high value on physical attractiveness throughout the life cycle, and our body image greatly affects how

Good lovers are not mind readers. They learn what turns their partner on through listening and communication.

© ImagesBazaar / Alamy

attractive we feel. It's true that before anyone else can accept us, we need to accept ourselves.

Self-Disclosure and Asking for What You Need

Opening up and talking with your partner and sharing feelings, or **self-disclosure,** helps deepen intimacy and sexual satisfaction (Macneil, 2004; Posey et al., 2010; Schiffrin et al., 2010). It is critical to maintaining healthy and satisfying sexual relationships. Self-disclosure lets your partner know what is wrong and how you feel about it, and it enables you to ask for specific change (Fowers, 1998). When you open up and share, your partner will be more likely to reciprocate by opening up and sharing as well (Posey et al., 2010).

Too often, we assume that being good in bed also means being a mind reader. Somehow, our partner should just know what arouses us. In reality, nothing could be farther from the truth. Good lovers are not mind readers—they are able and willing to listen and communicate with their partners. Doing so helps ensure you are both on the same page when it comes to various sexual activities and behaviors. One man recounts an early sexual experience:

> I'll never forget the first time. She was lying on her parents' bed with the lamplight shining on her, naked and suntanned all over...I climbed on that bed and I lifted her up onto my thighs—she was so light I could always pick her right up—and I opened up her [vagina] with one hand and I rammed my [penis] up there like it was a Polaris missile. Do you know, she screamed out loud, and she dug her nails in my back, and without being too crude about it, I [screwed] her until she didn't know what the hell was happening...She loved it. She screamed out loud every single time. I mean I was an active, aggressive lover. (Masterton, 1987, p. 70)

Yet his partner viewed the sex very differently:

> What did I think about it?...I don't know. I think the only word you could use would be "flabbergasted." He threw me on the bed as if he were Tarzan, and tugged off all of my clothes, and then he took off his own clothes so fast it was almost like he was trying to beat the world record...He took hold of me and virtually lifted me right up in the air as if I were a child, and then he pushed himself right up me, with hardly any foreplay or any preliminaries or anything. (Masterton, 1987, p. 73)

Communication is key here, because whereas the man thinks he is doing exactly what his partner wants, the woman is wondering why he's doing what he's doing! Eventually, this couple's relationship ended, mainly because the couple was unable to open up and talk about what they needed and wanted in the sexual relationship, which left both feeling confused and frustrated. If this couple could have self-disclosed more, they might have been able to work through these issues. Without this, however, the relationship was destined to fail.

Discussing sexual issues within intimate partnerships has been found to increase relationship satisfaction (Moore, 2010; Noland, 2010). But this isn't always easy. Telling your partner what you really

*Sexuality is an area in which **many people feel insecure.***

ON YOUR MIND 3.4

I have been in a relationship with my boyfriend for almost 1 year. We love each other very much, but most of the time I feel that we don't communicate well with each other, mainly because I'm just too afraid to talk about things like sex. I love him very much and want our relationship to last. How can we learn to communicate better?

Communicating our thoughts, needs, wants, hopes, and desires isn't always easy. Usually intimate or personal information is difficult to share. It's natural to worry about what your boyfriend might think or say. It's best to start slowly. Don't try to tell him everything at one time. You might try sharing a few small details about what you're thinking and what you like about your sex life. Remember that asking for what you need involves self-disclosure. If you can open up, share your thoughts, and listen to what your boyfriend is saying, this can help you grow together as a couple.

want and need during sexual activity can be difficult. Sexuality is an area in which many people feel insecure. Many of us wonder whether we are good in bed and worry that our partner(s) might not think so. At the same time, however, we may be hesitant to make suggestions to improve our partner's techniques because we worry our partner will become insulted and think that his or her sexual skills are being criticized. Anxieties like these do not foster a sense of open and mutual communication. Ultimately, not being open about your likes or dislikes is self-defeating because you may end up feeling resentful of your partner or unhappy in your relationship.

Trusting Your Partner

One of the most important ingredients in any happy and satisfying sexual relationship is trust (Simpson, 2007). Trusting your partner means that you have confidence in them and feel secure in the relationship. Earlier we discussed the importance of our family of origin in learning to communicate. Our family also contributes to our ability to trust an intimate partner. Having more trusting relationships early in life lays the foundation for happier and healthier sexual relationships later in life (Campbell et al., 2010). We have been discussing the importance of self-disclosure, and one key factor that is related to the ability to self-disclose in sexual relationships is trust (Ignatius & Kokkonen, 2007). If we trust our partner and feel confident and secure in our relationship, self-disclosure will be much easier.

Building trust takes time, and it is typically a process of *uncertainty reduction* (Holmes & Rempel, 1989). Our prior relationships influence our ability to trust, but the level of trust in any new sexual relationship depends in large part on various aspects of our current partner (Campell et al., 2010). Being hurt by someone in a previous relationship, experiencing a loss, or being fearful about rejection can all interfere with the ability to trust an intimate partner, but over time trust can be improved.

self-disclosure
Opening up, talking with your partner, and sharing feelings.

Men and women who report being more trusting of their partners also tend to be more optimistic about the relationship and think more positive thoughts about their partner's negative behaviors (e.g., trusting partners are less likely to take things personally if their partner is late to meet them; Simpson, 2007). However, nontrusting partners would have many doubts and concerns, and might think their partner doesn't love them anymore.

Nonverbal Communication

Earlier in this chapter we discussed the importance of nonverbal communication. Nonverbal communication can also include facial expressions, hand and arm gestures, postures, body positioning, and movements (Ekman & Friesen, 1969; Mehrabian, 2009; Sauter et al., 2010). This type of communication can be especially important in sexual relationships because many factors may interfere with the ability to communicate verbally.

Although verbal communication about your likes and needs is far more effective than nonverbal communication, through nonverbal communication you can express your sexual desires and also reinforce verbal messages. For example, if you would like your partner to touch your breasts more during foreplay, show this by moving your body more when he or she is doing what you like, or moving his or her hands to your breasts. You can moan, or even move more, to communicate your pleasure to your partner. You might also try performing the behavior on your partner that you wish she or he would do to you. Keep in mind, however, that sometimes exclusive use of nonverbal communication can cause misunderstandings, as demonstrated by this couple:

One woman attempted to communicate her preference for being kissed on the ears by kissing her partner's ears. However, she found that the more she kissed her partner's ears, the less he seemed to kiss hers. Over a period of time her kissing of his ears continued to increase, while his kissing of her ears stopped altogether. Finally she asked him why he never kissed her ears anymore, only to discover that he hated having his ears kissed and was trying to communicate this by not kissing hers. After their discussion, he began to kiss her ears, she stopped kissing his, and both were happier for the exchange. (Barbach, 1982, p. 105)

▶▶ OBSTACLES TO Sexual Communication

Several factors can interfere with our ability to talk about sex with our partners, such as embarrassment and concerns about sexual terminology.

Embarrassment

Earlier we discussed how we live in a society that tends to instill a sense of shame about our sexuality. Many of us have learned that sex is "dirty" or "bad," and we feel uncomfortable talking about it. This is natural and understandable. But how can we learn to reduce our embarrassment and feel more comfortable talking about sex?

The answer: Relax and take it slow.

Research has found that many young adults are embarrassed to talk about sexuality (van Teijlingen et al., 2007). Embarrassment can inhibit our ability to open up and talk with our partners. We may worry that our partner will judge us or think differently about us.

Michael Goldman/Getty Images

Although many couples avoid communication about sex because it can be scary to talk about, learning to communicate your sexual desires and needs can strengthen the relationship.

The good news is that it gets easy over time. The more comfortable you get in a relationship, the less embarrassing it often is. For some, using humor and being able to laugh can help reduce the tension.

Sexual Terminology

Lastly, to have a meaningful conversation about sexuality with your partner, you need to know the correct terminology and have a sexual vocabulary. Throughout this course you will learn the correct terminology for various sexual organs, behaviors, and activities, but you will also need to learn which type of sexual vocabulary you are comfortable using. You can use scientific and anatomical words (such as *vagina, penis,* or *sexual intercourse*), or you can use sexual slang (such as *vajayjay, dick,* or *doin' it*). Sometimes scientific terminology can seem unromantic and awkward, whereas sexual slang may not really let you accurately describe what you want to say. Talking about these language and vocabulary issues with your partner can help lessen the anxiety and make you more comfortable with sexual communication.

▶ LISTENING, EXPRESSING CRITICISM, AND Nonconstructive Communication

The majority of couples spend too much time criticizing each other and not enough time really listening and making affectionate comments (P. Coleman, 2002). One partner often becomes defensive and angry when the other says something that he or she doesn't want to hear. For example, if your partner told you that he felt you weren't giving enough time to your relationship, you could

1 Why is a positive self-image important in sexual relationships, and how can it affect communication?

2 Explain how self-disclosure and trust can increase satisfaction in sexual relationships.

3 How can nonverbal communication be used to help express sexual likes and dislikes?

4 Identify and explain some of the obstacles to sexual communication.

hear this message with an open mind, or you could get angry and think, "What do you know about my time?" Let's now talk about the importance of listening, constructive and nonconstructive communication, and verbal disagreements.

▶▶ THE IMPORTANCE **of Listening**

Listening is one of the most important communication skills (Adler et al., 2007). Adults spend nearly 70% of their waking time communicating and 45% of this time listening (Adler et al., 2007; Rankin, 1952). **Active listening** involves using nonverbal communication to let your partner know that you are attentive and present in the conversation. For example, as your partner talks, you can maintain eye contact to let him or her know you are actively listening.

Another important skill is **nondefensive listening,** which involves focusing your attention on what your partner is saying without being defensive (Gottman, 1994). Nondefensive listening relies on self-restraint, which is often absent in distressed couples, who have a difficult time hearing and listening to each other. It can be difficult to listen fully, but this skill reduces your inclination to interrupt or to defend yourself.

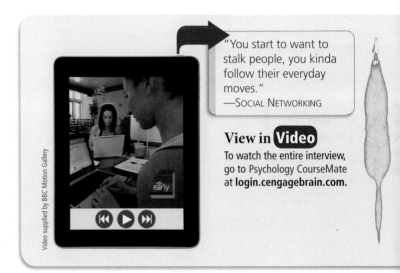

"You start to want to stalk people, you kinda follow their everyday moves."
—SOCIAL NETWORKING

View in Video
To watch the entire interview, go to Psychology CourseMate at **login.cengagebrain.com.**

Poor listeners often think that they understand what their partner is trying to say, but they rarely do. Instead, they try to find a way to circumvent the discussion and talk about something else. It is difficult to really listen to someone when you are angry or defensive. Good listening allows you to understand and retain information while building and maintaining your relationships (Adler et al., 2007).

▶▶ BEING A MORE **Effective Listener**

Many things interfere with our ability to be an effective listener (Golen, 1990; Hulbert, 1989). These include information overload, preoccupation with personal concerns, rapid thoughts, and noise. It is easy to reach information overload today. We hear so much during the course of our day that it can be difficult to listen carefully to everything we hear. As a result, we must choose what information we will listen and pay attention to. A preoccupation with

FIGURE 3.2 The Chinese believe that listening involves much more than simply hearing someone talk. In fact, the Chinese characters that make up the verb "to listen" include the ears, eyes, heart, and undivided attention.

active listening
Communication and listening technique in which the listener uses nonverbal communication, such as nodding or eye contact, to signal that he or she is attentive to the speaker.

nondefensive listening
Listening strategy in which the listener focuses attention on what his or her partner is saying without being defensive.

personal concerns may also interfere with our ability to listen. If we are wrapped up in our own thoughts and issues, it's difficult to listen to someone else. Listening is also affected by our brains actively processing information around us. Consider this: We are capable of understanding speech at rates of up to 600 words per minute (Versfeld & Dreschler, 2002); however, the average person speaks between 100 and 140 words per minute. This gives your brain time to think about other things, such as what you'll say to your professor this afternoon, what you'll have for dinner tonight, or when you'll study for the exam tomorrow. So it may be hard to focus on what is being said. Finally other conversations, music, and even traffic can all interfere with our ability to listen.

Listening and really paying attention can also help you learn important things about your partner. John Gottman, a psychologist known for his research on relationships, gives couples a relationship quiz to determine whether they have been paying attention to each other's likes and dislikes (Gottman, 1999). His questions include the following:

- What is the name of your partner's best friend?
- Who has been irritating your partner lately?
- What are some of your partner's life dreams?
- What are three of your partner's favorite movies?
- What are your partner's major current worries?
- What would your partner want to do if he or she suddenly won the lottery?

We don't ever realize how important it is to have others listen to us until someone we really care about doesn't listen to us (P. Coleman, 2002). When others really listen, we are often able to see more clearly what it is that upsets us. Being listened to can make us feel worthy, protected, and cared about. As we mentioned earlier, encouraging your partner through active listening, such as eye contact, nodding, or saying "um-hum" (Fowers, 1998) shows your partner that you are "tuned in." It also shows that you believe your partner has something worthwhile to say and encourages him or her to continue talking.

When your partner is finished talking, it is important to summarize what your partner has told you as accurately as possible. This lets your partner know that you heard what he or she was saying, and also enables your partner to correct any misunderstandings. Finally, it is also important when listening to validate your partner's statement. Saying "I can understand why you might feel that way" or "I know what you mean" can help you show your partner that you think what he or she is saying is valid. This doesn't necessarily mean that you agree, but that you can accept your partner's point of view.

It is also important when listening *to validate* your partner's statement.

▶▶ MESSAGE Interpretation

When walking across campus one day, you trip and fall. Your partner sees you and says, "Be careful!" How do you interpret that? Does it mean you're moving too fast? You need to slow down? Does it mean that your partner is genuinely worried you might hurt yourself? In all conversations, the recipient of the message must interpret the intended meaning of the message (R.

Edwards, 1998), which is dependent on several factors, such as the nature of the relationship with the person and your mood at the time.

If you are angry or upset, you may perceive more hostility in ambiguous or benign comments than someone who is not angry or upset (Epps & Kendall, 1995). If you are worried about something or preoccupied with an issue, this can also bias how you interpret a message. In one study, women who were preoccupied with their weight were more likely to interpret ambiguous sentences with negative or "fat" meanings, whereas women who were not preoccupied with their weight did not (Jackman et al., 1995). For example, if a woman who was preoccupied with her weight heard someone say, "You look good today!" she might interpret this to mean that she looked fat yesterday. However, couldn't she also interpret the message in other ways? Perhaps she looked tired yesterday or even stressed out.

▶▶ NEGATIVE FEELINGS and Criticism

We all get angry sometimes, and we know that not all conversations have happy, peaceful endings. However, the key is in managing the tension. When we disagree with our partner, the opening minutes of a disagreement can indicate whether the conversation will turn angry or simply be a quiet discussion (P. Coleman, 2002). If harsh words are used, chances are the disagreement will build, and the tension will escalate. However, if softer words are used, there is a better chance the disagreement can be resolved.

Negative feelings may also involve sharing or accepting criticism. Accepting criticism isn't an easy thing to do—we are all defensive at times. Although it would be impossible to eliminate all defensiveness, it's important to reduce defensiveness to resolve disagreements. If you are defensive while listening to your partner's criticism, chances are good that you will not be able to hear his or her message. Common defensive techniques are to deny the criticism (e.g., "That is just NOT TRUE!"), make excuses without taking any responsibility (e.g., "I was just exhausted!"), deflecting responsibility (e.g., "Me? What about your behavior?"), and righteous indignation (e.g., "How could you possibly say such a hurtful thing?") (P. Coleman, 2002). All of these techniques interfere with our ability to really understand what our partner is trying to tell us. Keeping our defensiveness in check is another important aspect of good communication.

John Gottman, the relationship expert we discussed earlier, found that happy couples experienced 20 positive interactions for every negative one (Nelson, 2005). Couples who were in conflict experienced only five positive interactions for every negative one, and those couples soon to be divorced experienced only 0.8 positive interaction for every negative one. This research suggests that positive and negative interactions can shine light on a couple's relationship happiness.

▶▶ NONCONSTRUCTIVE COMMUNICATION: Don't Yell at Me!

Couples often make many mistakes in their communication patterns that can lead to arguments, misunderstandings, and conflicts. **Overgeneralizations,** or making statements such as "Why do you always...?" or "You never...," generally exaggerate an issue. Telling your partner that he or she "always" (or "never") does something can cause defensiveness and will often lead to complete communication shutdown. Try to be specific about your complaints and help your partner to see what it is that is frustrating you. For example, if you find yourself frustrated by the amount of time your partner spends with friends, find a time when you can discuss your concerns. Try not to be defensive or overgeneralizing and share your thoughts (say, "I feel like I would like to spend more time together," rather than "You always seem to want to be with your friends more than me!").

Try to stay away from **name-calling** or stereotyping words, such as calling your partner a "selfish bastard" or a "nag." These derogatory terms will only help escalate anger and frustration, and will not lead to healthy communication. Digging up the past is another nonconstructive communication pattern that accomplishes nothing. It is also important to stay away from old arguments and accusations. The past is just that—the past. So try to leave it there and move forward. Dwelling on past events won't help to resolve them.

Another common mistake that couples make in conversations is to use **overkill.** When you are frustrated with your partner and threaten the worst (e.g., "If you don't do that, I will leave you"), even when you know it is not true, you reduce all communication. Don't make threats if you don't intend to follow through with them. In the same vein, it is important to focus on your frustration in conversation.

Try not to get overwhelmed and throw too many issues in the conversation at once (e.g., the fact that your partner didn't take the trash out last night, forgot to kiss you good-bye, and ignored you when he or she was with friends). This approach makes it really difficult to focus on resolving any one issue because there is just too much happening. Also, avoid yelling or screaming, which can cause your partner to be defensive and angry, and less likely to be rational and understand what you are saying. Even though it's not easy, it's important to stay calm during conversation.

Clinging to any of these communication patterns can interfere with the resolution of problems and concerns. If you recognize any of these patterns in your own relationship, try talking to your partner about it and try to catch yourself before you engage in them.

▶▶ FIGHTING

Verbal disagreements are a common part of intimate relationships and are much more likely during times of stress (Bodenmann et al., 2010). Couples may disagree about public issues, concerns outside of their relationship, or personal issues, concerns related to their relationship (Johnson, 2009). Generally, public issue arguments are engaged in to provide new knowledge or pass the time, whereas personal issue arguments are typically engaged in to help portray oneself in a more positive light (Johnson, 2009). Regardless of the type of argument, however, couples who disagree are usually happier than those who say, "We never, ever fight!" (It's important to point out, however, that verbal disagreements are different from physical disagreements. We will discuss domestic violence in Chapter 17.)

Happy couples have been found to think more positive thoughts about each other during their disagreements, whereas unhappy couples are inundated with negative thoughts about each other (P. Coleman, 2002). Even though a happy couple is disagreeing about an issue, the two partners still feel positively about each

---

REAL RESEARCH 3.4   Although men and women are both likely to apologize for their behavior if they feel they need to, heterosexual men are less likely to perceive the need to apologize; thus, in heterosexual relationships, the women are more likely to apologize than the men (BERNSTEIN, 2010).

---

other, which is important. Forgiveness is another important aspect of healthy couples. Couples who positively rate their relationships are more likely to forgive their partners for transgressions, whereas those who are less invested in a relationship are more likely to withhold forgiveness and believe their partner hurt them intentionally (Guerrero & Bachman, 2010).

Some couples avoid conflict by ignoring problems or avoiding communicating about certain issues (Dillow et al., 2009). Studies have found that although conflict avoidance can cause relationship problems, women are more likely than men to say that conflict avoidance decreases their overall relationship satisfaction (Afifi et al., 2009).

What happens after an argument? Generally, women are more likely to demand a reestablishment of closeness, whereas men are more likely to withdraw (Noller, 1993). Remember that your family of origin also influences your communication strategies. Do you recall what used to happen after your parents had an argument? Do you see any similarities in the way that you behave after arguments in your relationships?

Taking a time-out and finishing a discussion later, learning to compromise, or validating each others' differences in opinions are important ways to resolve a disagreement. Also remember that in every relationship, some issues may simply be unresolvable. It is important to know which issues can be worked out and which cannot. The question is, can you live with the irresolvable issues? How can you work on improving these issues?

Sometimes arguments continue long after both partners have said everything they want to say because neither wants to be the one to call for a truce. Calling for a truce can also be tricky to do. One couple told me that when they want to stop arguing, they have agreed that whoever is ready first holds up a pinky finger. This signals to the other that they are ready to end the fight. The other partner must touch his or her pinky to the partner's pinky to acknowledge that the fight is over. This isn't always easy, but it has helped this couple to end arguments amicably.

Throughout this chapter, we have discussed the importance of communication and its role in the development of healthy, satisfying relationships. When it comes to sexual relationships,

---

overgeneralization
Making statements that tend to exaggerate a particular issue.

name-calling
Using negative or stereotyping words when in disagreement.

overkill
A common mistake that couples make during arguments, in which one person threatens the worst but doesn't mean what he or she says.

good communication skills are vital. By talking to your partner, you can share your sexual needs and desires, and learn what your partner's sexual needs are. In turn, this can strengthen your overall relationship. It's important to be honest and open and ask for what you need. Talking about sex isn't easy. We live in a society that believes sex talk is dirty or bad, but talking about sex is one of the best ways to move a relationship to a new level of intimacy and connection.

REAL RESEARCH 3.5   Men or women who try to "get even" in disagreements with romantic partners do so for three main reasons: to feel better about themselves, to get their partner to change, or in retaliation for being unjustly treated (BOON ET AL., 2009).

◀ **review** QUESTIONS

1 Why is listening one of the most important communication skills? What is nondefensive listening?

2 Explain how information overload, personal concerns, rapid thoughts, and noise interfere with our ability to listen.

3 Describe two nonconstructive communication strategies, and explain why they could lead to a communication shutdown.

◀◀ chapter REVIEW

SUMMARY POINTS

1   Good communication skills are an integral part of all healthy relationships, and couples who know how to communicate with each other are happier, more satisfied, and have a better chance of making their relationship last. Many relationship problems stem from poor communication.

2   Communication fosters mutual understanding, increases emotional intimacy, and helps deepen feelings of love and intimacy. However, a lack of communication skills is a major source of trouble in relationships. Having poor communication skills, an inability to self-disclose, or trouble listening can each lead to communication problems.

3   The three goals of communication include getting the job done, maintaining the relationship, and managing our identity. All of these three goals compete with each other, making communication difficult.

4   Our ability to communicate and the strategies we use to do so were learned in our interactions within our families. We learn many communication skills such as negotiation, conflict avoidance, arguing, and interpersonal communication skills. Children also develop a social and emotional understanding of the world around them. All of this learning can affect a child's self-esteem, mental well-being, and the potential for depression.

5   Deborah Tannen proposed that there are fundamental differences between the way men and women communicate, and she called these differences *genderlects*. She found that women engaged in more rapport-talk, whereas men engaged in more report-talk. Men also tended to use more slang in their communication, whereas women are more supportive and use more words implying feelings.

6   Two categories of communication skills have been proposed, affective and instrumental. Affectively oriented skills involve comforting and listening, whereas instrumentally oriented skills are more narrative and persuasive. Women are more likely to value affectively oriented skills, whereas men are more likely to value instrumentally oriented skills.

7   Many theories have been proposed to explain gender differences in communication. However, gender communication is often best understood as a form of cross-cultural communication. Research suggests that men and women may come from different sociolinguistic subcultures and learn different communication rules.

8   Individualistic cultures encourage their members to have individual goals and values, and an independent sense of self. Collectivist cultures emphasize the needs of their members over individual needs. Communication patterns have been found to vary depending on cultural

orientation. In addition, anthropologists have identified low- and high-context cultures. Low-context cultures use language to express thoughts and feelings directly, whereas high-context cultures rely more on subtle and nonverbal cues.

9   Little research has been conducted on communication in gay and lesbian relationships. We do know that power, gender role, and social philosophies all affect communication patterns. Research has found differences between the speech patterns of gay and heterosexual men.

10   The majority of our communication with others is nonverbal. This form of communication is often done through eye contact, smiling, or touching. Nonverbal communication can trigger an *emotional contagion* in listeners. As we get older, we get better at recognizing nonverbal cues, but at a certain age our abilities to recognize these cues begin to decrease again. Research has found that women are better at decoding and translating nonverbal communication.

11   Computer-mediated communication (CMC) has become more important in the last few years. CMC can reduce the role that physical characteristics play, and can enhance rapport and self-disclosure. It also can reduce the constraining gender roles that exist in face-to-face communication. Overall, women have an easier time making their voices heard during

CMC than in face-to-face communication. They have also been found to use more emoticons online. Avatars can be used to express emotions or feelings in CMC. However, there are cultural differences in the interpretation of online avatars. Negative expressions have a wider cultural understanding, whereas positive expressions have more variations in interpretation.

12 Sexual communication can be challenging because sexuality often magnifies communication that exists in any close relationship. Many of us are taught that talking about sex is "dirty" and, therefore, learn to avoid it. Couples who communicate with each other about sexual issues report more relationship satisfaction. Those with a positive self-esteem often expect their partners to accept them, whereas those with a negative self-esteem often expect rejection. Although verbal communication about sex is preferable, nonverbal communication can also be used.

13 Self-disclosure is critical in maintaining healthy and satisfying sexual relationships. It helps partners know each other's needs and wants. Trust is also important, and self-disclosure is easier if we trust our partner. Those who trust their sexual partners feel more optimistic about their relationships. Both embarrassment and sexual terminology issues can interfere with our ability to communicate about sex.

14 Several things can interfere with our ability to listen, including information overload, personal concerns, rapid thoughts, and noise.

The majority of couples spend too much time criticizing each other and not enough time really listening and making affectionate comments. Active and nondefensive listening are important.

15 When we express negative feelings, it's important not to use harsh words, because tension will escalate. It is also important to learn how to accept criticism without becoming defensive. Mistakes in communication patterns that can get couples into trouble include overgeneralizations, name-calling, and overkill. Verbal disagreements are a common part of intimate relationships and are more common during times of stress. Happy couples think more positive thoughts during disagreements than do unhappy couples.

CRITICAL THINKING QUESTIONS

1 The research shows that couples who know how to communicate have a greater likelihood of making their relationship last. Apply this to a relationship that didn't work out for you, and explain how poor or absent communication may have affected your relationship.

2 Do you think that men and women have different communication styles and may, in fact, have "cross-cultural" styles of communication? Explain why or why not and give examples.

3 Do you agree with findings claiming that women gossip and complain more than men? Why or why not? Give one example.

4 Have you ever communicated with someone online and then met later face-to-face? If so, how did your online communication affect your face-to-face communication? What was your online impression of him or her before you met in person?

5 Identify issues that make it difficult to talk to a sexual partner about your sex life. What can you do to improve the communication?

6 Can you think of any incidence in which a lack of self-esteem on your part negatively affected a relationship? Explain.

7 How have social network services changed communication patterns on today's college campuses? What do you see as the advantages and disadvantages of these services?

MEDIA RESOURCES

CourseMate brings course concepts to life with interactive learning, study, and exam preparation tools that support the printed textbook. A textbook-specific website, Psychology CourseMate includes an integrated interactive eBook and other interactive learning tools including quizzes, flashcards, videos, and more. If your textbook does not include an access code card, go to CengageBrain .com to gain access.

CENGAGENOW   CengageNOW is an easy-to-use online resource that helps you study in less time to get the grade you want—NOW. Take a pre-test for this chapter and receive a personalized study plan based on your results that will identify the topics you need to review and direct you to online resources to help you master those topics. Then take a post-test to help you determine the concepts you have mastered and what you will need to work on. If your textbook does not include an access code card, go to CengageBrain.com to gain access.

View in Video available in CourseMate and CengageNOW:

Perspectives on Communication: Three college students discuss communication issues in intimate relationships.

Maid Cafes: Interview with the owner of Japanese maid café and two maids.

Teens and Sexting: Explores the practice of sexting in teens.

Social Networking: An increasing amount of people are connecting online rather than face-to-face, leading to a decrease in everyday functioning and communication.

Websites:

The American Communication Association ■ The American Communication Association (ACA) has links to the *American Communication Journal* and the Communication Studies Center, which contains a collection of online resources.

Journal of Communication ■ *The Journal of Communication* is an interdisciplinary journal with an extensive online offering that focuses communication research, practice, policy, and theory, and includes the most up-to-date and important findings in the communication field.

4 Gender Development, Gender Roles, and Gender Identity

View in **Video**

View in **Video**

View in **Video**

View in **Video**

View in **Video**

ABOUT THE CHAPTER OPENING VIDEO – If you're like most college students, you probably don't spend a great deal of time thinking about what gender you are. You wake up in the morning and when you catch your reflection in the mirror, you recognize yourself as a man or a woman. But what if when you made that morning trek to the mirror, the face looking back at you wasn't the gender you thought it should be? That's exactly what had been happening to Sophie. I met Sophie a few months before she graduated from the University of Nebraska. She was smart, beautiful, and passionate about life, hoping to one day find a job as a video game journalist. Twenty-two years ago when Sophie was born, she was assigned male, given a male name, and was raised as a boy. Despite her male body, she knew fairly early on that she wasn't a boy. Growing up in a small, Midwestern town, Sophie couldn't easily put a finger on what didn't feel right as a child, but she knew she was different. She didn't fit the idea of what

was expected from boys and men in her hometown. There, boys were respected if they did tough, physical labor and showcased their aggression in sports such as football or wrestling. Sophie didn't play sports and wasn't aggressive. Instead, she loved to act and spent hours writing stories. After graduating from high school, Sophie was excited to begin a new chapter of life in college. During the summer after freshman year, Sophie began to undergo a medical transition so that her body would be in line with her mind.

My parents were very supportive of my decision to explore my gender issues. However, I think they would have preferred it if I waited to do it after college. They were worried about the process and what might happen to me while at college. When I did finally decide I was ready, I came out to the whole campus. I got lots of hate mail, but there was more support overall than antagonism. I'd be lying if I said

© Jupiter Images/Polka Dot/Alamy

there weren't times where I was withdrawn and even clinically depressed. At this point, I'm happy to have had those harder moments because I know they helped me grow. When I look back I can honestly say I'm a better person now because of what I went through.

While many people might look at Sophie and get caught up in gender issues, the bottom line is that she is very much like any other college student—she likes Subway, video games, and drinks Coke. Talking with her made me realize how much many people take gender for granted. I know you'll find our interview intriguing and well worth watching. ▋

Janell Carroll

"A whole new journey began when Sophie returned sophomore year."
—CHAPTER OPENING VIDEO

View in Video

To watch the entire interview, go to Psychology CourseMate at **login.cengagebrain.com.**

© Alesha Crews

As we begin our discussion about gender, imagine that as you are reading this, an alien walks into the room. The alien tells you that "zee" (not he or she) is only on Earth for a short time and would like to learn as much as possible about life here during this visit. One of the things "zee" would like to learn about is **gender,** specifically, "What are a man and woman?" How would you answer such a question? You might try to explain how a man and woman look, act, think, or feel. But what is a man, and what is a woman?

When a baby is born, new parents are eager to hear whether "It's a girl!" or "It's a boy!" but what if it was neither? What if a newborn had ambiguous genitalia, and it was impossible to tell whether it was a boy or a girl? A child with **gonads** (testes or ovaries) of one sex but ambiguous external genitalia has a condition known as a **disorder of sex development (DSD)**. In the past, children with these conditions were often referred to as **intersexuals** or hermaphrodites (Lee et al., 2006; Marino, 2010). Assigning a new term for the condition has helped to improve our understanding about this condition as a congenital disorder (Aaronson & Aaronson, 2010; Davies et al., in press). We discuss DSD further later in this chapter.

Gender raises many issues. For example, if your college or university has on-campus housing, does it allow you to have a roommate who is the other gender? Beginning in 1970, many U.S. colleges began offering coeducational residential halls in addition to single-sex dorms—typically putting males and females on separate floors or wings (Gordon, 2010). Soon afterward, coeducational hallways were available. By 2008, gender-neutral housing, which allows students to share rooms regardless of gender, became available on a few campuses. As of early 2011, over 54 universities offered gender-neutral housing, including Dartmouth, Harvard, Princeton, University of Michigan, University of Pennsylvania, Yale, Stanford, Brown University, and Rutgers University (Branson 2011; National Student GenderBlind, 2010).

Before we go any further, let's talk about how the words *sex* and *gender* are often used synonymously, even though they have different meanings. When you fill out a questionnaire that asks you "What is your *sex*?" how do you answer? When you apply for a driver's license and are asked, "What gender are you?" how do you respond? Although your answers here might be the same, researchers usually use the word *sex* to refer to the biological aspects of being male or female, and *gender* to refer to the behavioral, psychological,

and social characteristics of men and women (Pryzgoda & Chrisler, 2000).

You might wonder why exploring gender is important to our understanding of sexuality. How does gender affect sexuality? Gender stereotypes shape our opinions about how men and women act sexually. For example, if we believe that men are more aggressive than women, we might believe that these gender stereotypes carry over into the bedroom as well. Traditionally, men are viewed as the initiators in sexual activity, and they are the ones who are supposed to make all the "moves." Stereotypes about women, on the other hand, hold that women are more emotional and connected when it comes

---

REAL RESEARCH 4.1 A comparison of television advertisements from Brazil, Canada, China, Germany, South Korea, Thailand, and the United States found that in all these countries women are more likely than men to be portrayed in gender-stereotypical ways (PAEK ET AL., 2010).

---

to sex—more into "making love" than "having sex." Do gender stereotypes really affect how we act and interact sexually? And how do gender stereotypes affect gay and lesbian couples? We explore the relationship between gender and sexuality later in this chapter.

So let's ask again, What is a man? A woman? For many years, scientists have debated whether gender is more genetics and biology ("nature") or social environment and upbringing ("nurture"). Or is it a combination of the two? The story of Bruce and Brenda discussed in the accompanying Sex in Real Life feature illustrates the fact that both nature and nurture are important in the development of gender. In Chapter 2, we discussed evolutionary theory, which argues that many behaviors in men and women have evolved in the survival of the species, and that gender differences between men and women may be at least partially a result of heredity.

In this chapter, we explore the nature versus nurture debate as it relates to gender in hopes of finding answers to the questions "What is a man?" and "What is a woman?" We start by reviewing prenatal development and sexual differentiation. We also look at atypical sexual differentiation and chromosomal and hormonal disorders. Although these disorders are not exceedingly common, their existence and how scientists have dealt with them help us learn more about gender. Our biological exploration of gender will help set the foundation on which we can understand how complex gender really is. We also explore gender roles, theories about gender, and socialization throughout the life cycle.

---

gender
The behavioral, psychological, and social characteristics associated with being biologically male or female.

gonads
The male and female sex glands—ovaries and testes.

disorder of sex development (DSD)
Medical term referring to conditions that can lead to atypical chromosomal, gonadal, or anatomical sexual development.

intersexual
A child with gonads (testes or ovaries) of one sex but ambiguous external genitalia. May also be referred to as a disorder of sexual development.

chromosome
A threadlike structure in the nucleus of a cell that carries genetic information.

sexual reproduction
The production of offspring from the union of two parents.

gamete
A male or female reproductive cell—the spermatozoon or ovum; also referred to as a germ cell.

germ cell
A male or female reproductive cell—the spermatozoon or ovum; also referred to as a gamete.

menopause
The cessation of menstruation.

andropause
A period in a man's life, usually during his 70s or 80s, when testosterone decreases, causing a decrease in spermatogenesis, a thinner ejaculate, a decrease in ejaculatory pressure, decreased muscle strength, increased fatigue, and in some cases, mood disturbances.

autosome
Any chromosome that is not a sex chromosome.

sex chromosomes
Rod-shaped bodies in the nucleus of a cell at the time of cell division that contain information about whether the fetus will become male or female.

In 1967, a young Canadian couple brought their two identical twin boys (Bruce and Brian) to the hospital for routine circumcisions; the boys were 8 months old. A surgical mistake during one of the twin's circumcisions resulted in the destruction of his penis. The couple met with Dr. John Money, a well-known medical psychologist from Johns Hopkins University, who believed that gender was learned and could be changed through child rearing. He did not believe gender was contingent on **chromosomes**, genitals, or even sex hormones (Money, 1975). After meeting with Dr. Money and discussing their options, the couple decided to have their son, Bruce, undergo castration (removal of the testicles) and have surgery to transform his genitals into those of an anatomically correct female. Bruce became Brenda and was put on hormone treatment beginning in adolescence to maintain her feminine appearance. For many years, this Brenda/Bruce case stood as "proof" that children were psychosexually "neutral" at birth, and that gender could be assigned, no matter what the genetics or biology indicated. This case had a profound affect on how children who

were born with ambiguous genitalia or who had experienced genital trauma were raised (Colapinto, 2001).

However, even though Money paraded the Brenda/Bruce story as a success and around the globe intersexed children began sex reassignments, no one paid much attention to the fact that Brenda

© Reuters/Corbis

was struggling with her gender identity. In 1997, a study published by Milton Diamond, a reproductive biologist at the University of Hawaii, exposed the case and discussed how Brenda had struggled against her girlhood from the beginning (Diamond & Sigmundson, 1997). Once

Brenda reached puberty, despite her hormone treatments, her misery increased. She became depressed and suicidal. She never felt that she was a girl, and she was relentlessly teased by peers. Her parents finally told her the truth, and at 15 years old, she stopped hormonal treatments and changed her name to David.

Soon afterward, David Reimer went public with his medical story in hopes of discouraging similar sex reassignment surgeries. In 2001, John Colapinto wrote the details of this real-life story in a book called *As Nature Made Him: The Boy Who Was Raised as a Girl* (Colapinto, 2001). This book, in conjunction with interviews with David, influenced medical understandings about the biology of gender. Today, the Intersex Society of North America opposes the use of sex reassignment surgery for nonconsenting minors.

Although David Reimer eventually married and adopted children, his struggles with depression continued. In 2004, at age 38, Reimer took his own life (Burkeman & Younge, 2005).

▶ PRENATAL DEVELOPMENT:
X and Y Make the Difference

Human beings have a biological urge to reproduce and thus are in some sense "designed" to be sexual beings; any species that does not have good reproductive equipment and a strong desire to use it will not last very long. Simpler organisms, such as amoebas, simply split in two, creating a pair genetically identical to the parent amoeba. More complex organisms, however, reproduce through **sexual reproduction,** in which two parents each donate a **gamete** (GAM-meet), or **germ cell,** the two of which combine to create a new organism.

The tiny germ cells from the male (sperm) and the much larger but also microscopic cell from the female (egg, or ovum) each contain half of the new person's genes and determine his or her sex, hair and eye color, general body shape, the likely age at which he or she will reach puberty, and literally millions of other aspects of the developing fetus's physiology, development,

and emotional nature. The genes direct the development of the genitals and the reproductive organs, and set the biological clock running to trigger puberty and female **menopause** or male **andropause.** We discuss both of these topics in Chapters 5 and 6.

Most cells in the human body contain 46 chromosomes: 23 inherited from the mother and 23 from the father, arranged in 23 pairs. Twenty-two of the pairs look almost identical and are referred to as **autosomes;** the exception is the 23rd pair, the **sex chromosomes.** The two sex chromosomes, which determine whether a person is male or female, are made up of an X chromosome donated by the mother through the ovum and either an X or a Y chromosome donated by the father's sperm. In normal development, if the male contributes an X chromosome, the child will be female (XX); if he contributes a Y chromosome, the child will be male (XY).

All the cells of the body (somatic cells), except gametes, contain all 23 pairs of chromosomes (46 total) and are called *diploid* (meaning "double"). However, if a merging sperm and egg also had 23 pairs each, they would create a child with 46 pairs, which is too many (remember that most cells contain only 23 pairs of chromosomes). So gametes are *haploid,* meaning they contain half the number of chromosomes (23) of a somatic cell (46). During **fertilization,** a haploid sperm and a haploid egg join to produce a diploid **zygote** (ZIE-goat) containing 46 chromosomes, half from each parent. The zygote can now undergo **mitosis,** reproducing its 46 chromosomes as it grows.

The 46 chromosomes are threadlike bodies made up of somewhere between 20,000 and 25,000 genes, each of which contains **deoxyribonucleic** (dee-OCK-see-rye-bow-new-KLEE-ik) **acid** (**DNA;** Human Genome Project, 2003). DNA acts as a blueprint for how every cell in the organism will develop. At first, the zygote reproduces exact copies of itself. Soon, however, the cells begin a process of differentiation. Differentiation is one of the great mysteries of human biology—suddenly, identical cells begin splitting into liver cells, brain cells, skin cells, and all the thousands of different kinds of cells in the body. The DNA determines the order in which cells differentiate, and a cell's position may determine to some degree which type of cell it will become. Researchers in evolutionary developmental biology explore how and when cells differentiate.

Whether the zygote will develop into a male or female is determined at the moment of conception, and part of the process of differentiation includes the development of our sexual characteristics. If sexual differentiation proceeds without a problem, the zygote will develop into a fetus with typically male or typically female sexual characteristics. However, a variety of things can happen during development that can later influence the person's own sense of being either male or female.

▶▶ SEXUAL DIFFERENTIATION in the Womb

A human embryo normally undergoes about 9 months of **gestation.** At about 4 to 6 weeks, the first tissues that will become the embryo's gonads begin to develop. Sexual differentiation begins a week or two later and is initiated by the sex chromosomes, which control at least four important aspects of sexual development: (1) the internal sexual organs (e.g., whether the fetus de-

Since male and female babies look so similar, many American parents dress babies in blue or pink to identify their gender.

velops ovaries or testicles); (2) the external sex organs (such as the penis or clitoris); (3) the hormonal environment of the embryo; and (4) the sexual differentiation of the brain (which includes a cyclic or noncyclic hormonal pattern) (Wilson & Davies, 2007). The timing of all these events varies, however. Although sexual differentiation of the genitals begins within the first 2 months of pregnancy, sexual differentiation of the brain does not occur until sometime after the 5th month of pregnancy (Savic et al., 2010).

Internal Sex Organs

In the first few weeks of development, XX (female) and XY (male) embryos are identical. Around the 5th to 6th week, the primitive gonads form; at this point, they can potentially develop into either **testes** or **ovaries.** Traditional developmental models claim that the "default" development is female; without the specific masculinizing signals sent by the Y chromosome and the SRY (sex-determining region Y) gene, the gonads will develop as female. The SRY is a Y chromosome–specific gene that plays a central role in sexual differentiation and development in males (DiNapoli & Capel, 2008; Ngun et al., 2011). However, it may not be only **testosterone** or the SRY gene that differentiates males from females—it may also be the presence of ovarian hormones (Blecher & Erickson, 2007; Wu & Shah, 2010).

In most males, the testes begin to differentiate from the primitive gonad by the 7th to 8th week after conception. In most females, the development of the primitive gonad begins to differentiate into ovaries by the 10th or 11th week. The primitive duct system, the **Müllerian** (myul-EAR-ee-an) **duct** (female) or the **Wolffian** (WOOL-fee-an) **duct** (male), also appears at this time

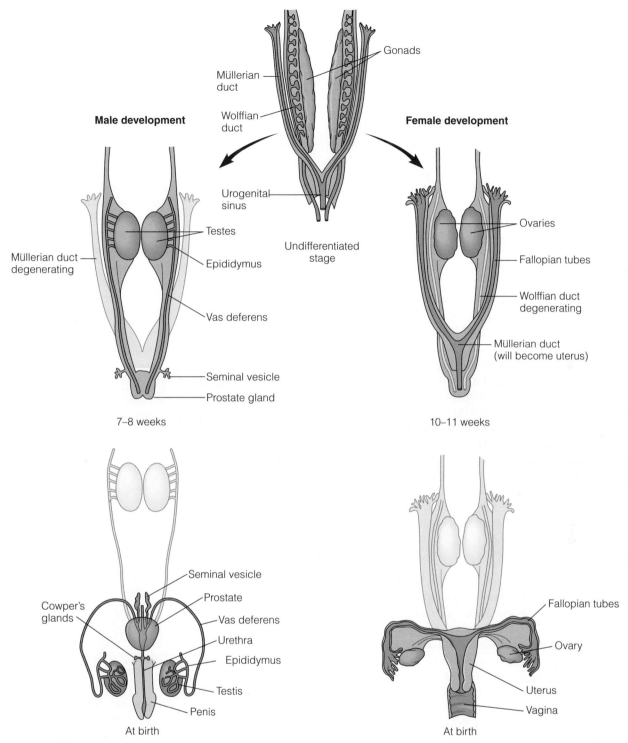

FIGURE **4.1** Development of the male and female internal reproductive systems from the undifferentiated stage. We discuss these specific structures more in Chapters 5 and 6. Copyright © Cengage Learning 2013

fertilization
The union of two gametes, which occurs when a haploid sperm and a haploid egg join to produce a diploid zygote, containing 46 chromosomes.

zygote
The single cell resulting from the union of sperm and egg cells.

mitosis
The division of the nucleus of a cell into two new cells such that each new daughter cell has the same number and kind of chromosomes as the original parent.

deoxyribonucleic acid (DNA)
A nucleic acid in the shape of a double helix in which all genetic information in the organism is encoded.

gestation
The period of intrauterine fetal development.

testes
Male gonads inside the scrotum that produce testosterone.

ovaries
Female gonads that produce ova and sex hormones.

testosterone
A male sex hormone that is secreted by the Leydig cells of mature testes and produces secondary sex characteristics in men.

Müllerian duct
One of a pair of tubes in the embryo that will develop, in female embryos, into the fallopian tubes, uterus, and part of the vagina.

Wolffian duct
One of a pair of structures in the embryo that, when exposed to testosterone, will develop into the male reproductive system.

table 4.1 ■ Homologous Tissue

Male and female organs that began from the same prenatal tissue are called homologous. Below are some of the homologous tissues.

Female	Male
Clitoral glans	Glans penis
Clitoral hood	Foreskin
Labia minora	Penile shaft
Labia majora	Scrotum
Ovaries	Testes

Copyright © Cengage Learning 2013

(Krone et al., 2007). Once the gonads have developed, they then hormonally control the development of the ducts into either the female or male reproductive system (we discuss these specific structures further in Chapters 5 and 6).

In female embryos, the lack of male hormones results in the disappearance of the Wolffian ducts, and the Müllerian duct fuses to form the uterus and inner third of the vagina. The unfused portion of the duct remains and develops into the two oviducts or Fallopian tubes (see Figure 4.1). In the presence of a Y chromosome, the gonads develop into testes, which soon begin producing **Müllerian inhibiting factor** and testosterone. Müllerian inhibiting factor causes the Müllerian ducts to disappear during the 3rd month, and testosterone stimulates the Wolffian duct to develop into the structures surrounding the testicles. The body converts some testosterone into another **androgen,** called *dihydrotestosterone* (DHT), to stimulate the development of the male external sex organs.

External Sex Organs

External genitals follow a pattern similar to that of internal organs, except that male and female genitalia all develop from the same tissue. Male and female organs that began from the same prenatal tissue are called **homologous** (HOE-mol-lig-gus; see Table 4.1 for an overview of homologous tissues). Until the 8th week, the undifferentiated tissue from which the genitalia will develop exists as a mound of skin, or tubercle, beneath the umbilical cord. In females, the external genitalia develop under the influence of female hormones produced by the placenta and by the mother, and also the lack of influence from the Y chromosome. The genital tubercle develops into the clitoris, the labia minora, the vestibule, and the labia majora (see Figure 4.2).

In males, by the 8th or 9th week, the testes begin androgen secretion, which begins to stimulate the development of male genitalia. The genital tubercle elongates to form the penis, in which lies the urethra, culminating in an external opening called the *urethral meatus*. Part of the tubercle also fuses together to form the scrotum, where the testicles will ultimately rest when they descend.

Hormonal Development and Influences

Hormones play an important role in human development. Table 4.2 lists the various sex hormones and the roles they play. **Endocrine glands,** such as the gonads, secrete hormones directly into the bloodstream to be carried to the target organs. The ovaries, for example, produce the two major female hormones, estrogen and progesterone. **Estrogen** is an important influence in the development of female sexual characteristics throughout fetal development and later life, whereas **progesterone** regulates the menstrual cycle and prepares the uterus for pregnancy. The testicles produce androgens, which are quite important to the male, because even a genetically male embryo will develop female characteristics if androgens are not secreted at the right time or if the fetus is insensitive to androgens.

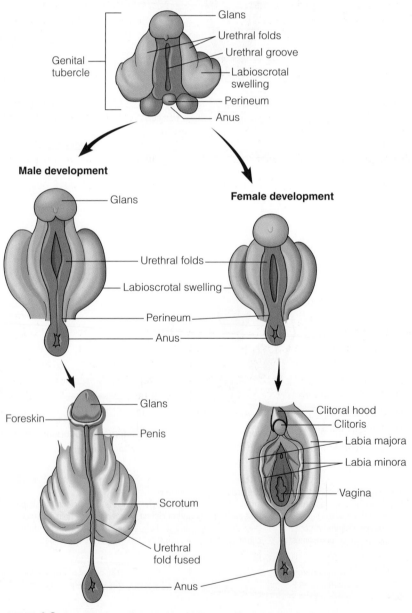

FIGURE 4.2 Development of the male and female external genitalia from the undifferentiated genital tubercle. Copyright © Cengage Learning 2013

table 4.2 ■ The Sex Hormones

Hormone	Purposes
Androgens	A group of hormones that control male sexual development and include testosterone and androsterone. Androgens stimulate the development of male sex organs and secondary sex characteristics such as beard growth and a deepening voice. Testosterone also plays an important part (in both sexes) in stimulating sexual desire. The testes produce androgens in men, although a small amount is also produced by the adrenal glands. Women's ovaries also produce a small amount of androgens, which helps stimulate sexual desire; too much production by the ovaries causes masculinization in women.
Estrogens	A group of hormones that control female sexual development. Estrogen controls development of the female sex organs, the menstrual cycle, parts of pregnancy, and secondary sex characteristics such as breast development. The ovaries produce most of the estrogen in women, although the adrenal glands and the placenta also produce small amounts. Testes also produce a small amount of estrogen in men; if they produce too much, feminization may occur.
Progesterone	A female hormone secreted by the ovaries. Progesterone helps to prepare the lining of the uterus for the implantation of the fertilized ovum, to stimulate milk production in the breasts, and to maintain the placenta. Progesterone works in conjunction with estrogen to prepare the female reproductive system for pregnancy.
Gonadotropin-releasing hormone (GnRH)	A hormone that affects the nervous system. It is produced in the hypothalamus of the brain and is transported through the bloodstream to the pituitary gland. Gonadotropin means "gonad stimulating," and GnRH stimulates the pituitary to release hormones, such as follicle-stimulating hormone and luteinizing hormone, which themselves induce the ovaries and testes (as well as other glands) to secrete their hormones.
Follicle-stimulating hormone (FSH)	A hormone released by the pituitary gland when stimulated by GnRH that stimulates the follicular development in females and the formation of sperm in males.
Luteinizing hormone (LH)	A hormone released by the pituitary gland when stimulated by GnRH that stimulates ovulation and the release of other hormones, notably progesterone in the female and testosterone in the male. It also stimulates the cells in the testes to produce testosterone.
Prolactin	A pituitary hormone that stimulates milk production after childbirth and also the production of progesterone.
Oxytocin	A pituitary hormone that stimulates the ejection of milk from the breasts and causes increased contractions of the uterus during labor.
Inhibin	A hormone produced by the cells of the testes that signals the anterior pituitary to decrease FSH production if the sperm count gets too high.

Brain Differentiation

Most hormonal secretions are regulated by the brain—in particular, by the hypothalamus, which is the body's single most important control center. Yet, hormones also affect the development of the brain itself, both in the uterus and after birth (Savic et al., 2010). Male and female brains have different tasks and thus undergo different development. For example, female brains control menstruation and, therefore, must signal the release of hormones in a monthly cycle, whereas male brains signal release continuously. With the brain, as with sexual organs, the presence of androgens during the appropriate critical stage of development may be the factor that programs the central nervous system to develop male sexual behaviors (Bocklandt & Vilain, 2007; Garcia-Falgueras & Swaab, 2010; Juntti et al., 2010). As we discussed earlier, sexual differentiation of the genitals begins early in a pregnancy, whereas sexual differentiation of the brain occurs much later in pregnancy (Savic et al., 2010).

Müllerian inhibiting factor
A hormone secreted in male embryos that prevents the Müllerian duct from developing into female reproductive organs.

androgen
A hormone that promotes the development of male genitals and secondary sex characteristics. It is produced by the testes in men and by the adrenal glands in both men and women.

homologous
Corresponding in structure, position, or origin but not necessarily in function.

endocrine gland
A gland that secretes hormones into the blood.

estrogen
A hormone that produces female secondary sex characteristics and affects the menstrual cycle.

progesterone
A hormone that is produced by the ovaries and helps to regulate the menstrual cycle.

1 Differentiate between sex and gender, and explain how the Bruce/Brenda case shed light on the nature versus nurture debate.

2 Describe sexual reproduction, and explain what happens after a sperm fertilizes an ovum.

3 Describe sexual differentiation in a developing fetus.

4 Explain the role that hormones and brain differentiation play in human development.

5 Identify the chromosomal conditions that may result in disorders of sexual development.

6 Identify the hormonal conditions that may result in disorders of sexual development.

▶ DISORDERS OF Sex Development

Prenatal development depends on carefully orchestrated developmental stages. At any stage, sex chromosome or hormone conditions can result in disorders of sex development (DSD). The result can be a child born with ambiguous genitals or with the external genitals of one sex and the genetic makeup of the other sex. One of the rarest forms of DSD is **hermaphroditism** (her-MAFF-fro-dit-ism), which is often referred to as *46 XY or XX* today (Krstic et al., 2000). In this condition, a child is born with fully formed ovaries and fully formed testes. Table 4.3 provides an overview of disorders of sex development.

▶▶ CHROMOSOMAL Conditions

Disorders of sex development can be caused by chromosomal conditions. Although medical researchers have identified more than 70 such conditions, we discuss here the three most common.

Klinefelter syndrome occurs when an ovum containing an extra X chromosome is fertilized by a Y sperm (designated XXY), giving a child 47 chromosomes all together (Giltay & Maiburg, 2010). Klinefelter syndrome prevalence rates are roughly 1 in 750 live male births (Forti et al., 2010; Giltay & Maiburg, 2010). In Klinefelter syndrome, the Y chromosome triggers the development of male genitalia, but the extra X prevents them from developing fully. As adults, men with Klinefelter syndrome typically have feminized body contours, small testes, low levels of testosterone, **gynecomastia,** and possible verbal deficits (Forti et al., 2010; Giltay & Maiburg, 2010). **Testosterone therapy,** especially if it is begun during adolescence, can enhance the development of **secondary sexual characteristics.** Although two thirds of men with Klinefelter syndrome are never diagnosed, those who are diagnosed are typically identified during an evaluation for infertility (Forti et al., 2010). Men with Klinefelter syndrome may still be able to father children through sperm retrieval. (We will discuss assisted reproductive techniques in more detail in Chapter 12; Forti et al., 2010).

Turner syndrome is another chromosomal condition; it occurs in 1 of every 2,500 live female births. Turner syndrome results from an ovum without any sex chromosome being fertilized by an X sperm (designated XO), which gives the child only 45 chromosomes altogether (if an ovum without a chromosome is fertilized by a Y sperm, and thus contains no X sex chromosome, it will not

survive). The median age at which a young girl is diagnosed with Turner syndrome is about 6 to 7 years old, although some are not diagnosed until much later (Massa et al., 2005).

Although the external genitalia develop to look like a normal female's, the woman's ovaries do not develop fully, causing **amenorrhea** (aye-men-uh-REE-uh) and probable infertility. In addition, Turner syndrome is characterized by short stature, a relatively high-pitched voice, immature breast development, and abnormalities of certain internal organs (Menke et al., 2010; Moreno-Garcia et al., 2005). Early diagnosis is important because therapeutic administration of estrogen and progesterone during puberty can help enhance secondary sex characteristics and slightly increase height (Sheaffer el al., 2008). Although the majority of girls with Turner syndrome will never undergo puberty, those who do may be capable of pregnancy. However, pregnancies in women with Turner syndrome have a high risk for chromosomal abnormalities and fetal loss (Bouchlariotou et al., 2011). In adulthood, many women with Turner syndrome may experience hypertension, bone thinning, and/or thyroid problems (Conway et al., 2010).

XYY syndrome and **triple X syndrome** are rare conditions. As the names imply, these conditions occur when a normal ovum

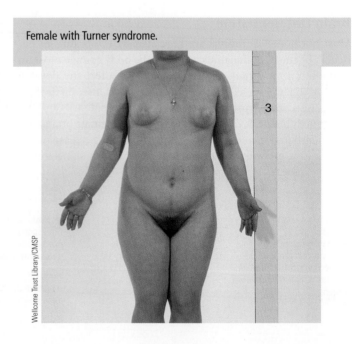

Female with Turner syndrome.

3

Wellcome Trust Library/CMSP

table 4.3 ■ Disorders of Sex Development

Syndrome	Chromosomal Pattern	External Genitals	Internal Structures	Description	Treatment
CHROMOSOMAL					
Klinefelter syndrome	47, XXY	Male	Male	Testes are small; breasts may develop; low testosterone levels, erectile dysfunction, and mental retardation are common; people with this disorder have unusual body proportions and are usually infertile.	Testosterone during adolescence may help improve body shape and sex drive.
Turner syndrome	45, XO	Female	Uterus and oviducts	There is no menstruation or breast development; a broad chest with widely spaced nipples, loose skin around the neck, nonfunctioning ovaries, and infertility.	Androgens during puberty can help increase height, and estrogen and progesterone can help promote breast development and menstruation.
XYY syndrome	47, XYY	Male	Male	There is likelihood of slight mental retardation, some genital irregularities, and decreased fertility or infertility.	None.
Triple X syndrome	47, XXX	Female	Female	There is likelihood of slight mental retardation and decreased fertility or infertility.	None.
HORMONAL					
Congenital adrenal hyperplasia (CAH)	46, XX, XY	Some male and some female traits	Internal organs are consistent with biological gender	Whereas external male genitals are often normal, female infants may have clitoral enlargement and labial fusing.	Surgery can correct external genitals.
Androgen-insensitivity syndrome (AIS)	46, XY	Female	Male gonads in the abdomen	Usually AIS children are raised female. Breasts develop at puberty, but menstruation does not begin. Such a person has a shortened vagina, no internal sexual organs, and is sterile.	Surgery can lengthen vagina to accommodate a penis for intercourse if necessary.

is fertilized by a sperm that has two Y chromosomes or two X chromosomes, or when an ovum with two X chromosomes is fertilized by a normal X sperm. The XYY individual may grow up as a normal male and the XXX as a normal female, and so often their unusual genetic status is not detected. However, many do suffer from some genital abnormalities, fertility problems, and possible learning difficulties later in life. There is no effective treatment for XYY or XXX syndrome.

hermaphroditism
A condition in which a child is born with fully formed ovaries and fully formed testes. May also be referred to as a disorder of sexual development.

Klinefelter syndrome
A genetic disorder in men in which there are three sex chromosomes, XXY, instead of two; characterized by small testes, low sperm production, breast enlargement, and absence of facial and body hair.

gynecomastia
Abnormal breast development in the male.

testosterone therapy
The use of testosterone to replace missing hormones in males with hormone disorders.

secondary sexual characteristics
The physical characteristics, other than the genitalia, that distinguish male from female.

Turner syndrome
A genetic disorder in females in which there is only one X sex chromosome instead of two, characterized by lack of internal female sex organs, infertility, short stature, and mental retardation.

amenorrhea
The absence of menstruation.

XYY syndrome
A genetic abnormality in which a male has an extra Y sex chromosome; characterized by decreased fertility, some genital abnormality, and slight mental retardation.

triple X syndrome
A genetic abnormality in which a female has an extra X sex chromosome; characterized by decreased fertility, some genital abnormality, and slight mental retardation.

▶▶ HORMONAL Conditions

Disorders of sex development can also be caused by hormonal conditions. In this section, we discuss two of the most common hormonal disorders of sex development, **congenital adrenal hyperplasia (CAH)** and **androgen-insensitivity syndrome (AIS).**

Congenital adrenal hyperplasia (CAH) occurs when a child lacks an enzyme in the adrenal gland, forcing the body to produce higher amounts of androgen. It is estimated that approximately 1 in 15,000 infants are born with CAH, and today almost all newborns are screened for it (Johannsen et al., 2010; Roan, 2010). The excess androgens often have little effect on a developing male fetus and may have only a small effect on a developing female fetus, such as an enlarged clitoris (Johannsen et al., 2010; Roan, 2010). Although CAH girls have female internal gonads (uterus and ovaries), in severe cases, these girls may be born with masculinized external genitalia, as well as menstrual irregularities, early body hair, and/or a deepening of the voice (Johannsen et al., 2010). A similar syndrome can also develop if the mother takes androgens or drugs with effects that mimic male hormones (a number of pregnant women were prescribed such drugs in the 1950s, resulting in a group of CAH infants born during that time). Because newborn screening for CAH is common today, most CAH females are diagnosed at birth (Johannsen et al., 2010). Corrective surgery can be done to form female genitalia, and drugs can be prescribed to control adrenal

output (Warne et al., 2005). Because the internal organs are unaffected, even pregnancy is possible in many CAH females.

Early androgen concentrations in CAH girls may also affect childhood play and adult sexual orientation. Research has shown that CAH girls choose more male-typical toys and have higher rates of bisexuality and homosexuality than non-CAH girls (Meyer-Bahlburg et al., 2008; Pasterski et al., 2005, 2007). In 2010, a controversy began over the use of prenatal steroids to decrease the risk for

---

REAL RESEARCH 4.2   Bisphenol A (BPA), an endocrine-interrupting chemical found in certain plastics and resins that line food and beverage containers, has been found to disrupt the endocrine system and affect reproductive and sexual development in mice (POIMENOVA ET AL., 2010; ROY ET AL., 2009). Because BPA has been found in the urine of 93% of the U.S. population (RUBIN & SOTO, 2009), research is now evaluating the effects of BPA exposure in humans.

CAH in female fetuses. Although the use of such hormones was thought to decrease the development of masculinized external genitalia in female fetuses and increase stereotypically feminine behaviors, these drugs also were found to potentially decrease the chances that the fetuses would be lesbian (Begley, 2010; Dreger et al., 2010; Roan, 2010). Critics believed that the use of prenatal steroids for CAH girls was "engineering for sexual orientation" (Roan, 2010).

Androgen-insensitivity syndrome (AIS), another hormonal condition, is often first detected when a seemingly normal teenage girl fails to menstruate and chromosomal analysis discovers that she is XY, a genetic male. Approximately 1 in 20,000 boys are born each year with AIS (Oakes et al., 2008). In this syndrome, although the gonads develop into testes and produce testosterone normally, for some reason, the AIS individual's cells cannot absorb it; in other words, the testosterone is there but has no effect on the body. Because the Wolffian ducts did not respond to testosterone during the sexual differentiation phase, no male genitalia developed; however, because the gonads, which are male, did produce Müllerian inhibiting factor, the Müllerian ducts did not develop into normal female internal organs either. The AIS individual ends up with no internal reproductive organs except two testes, which remain in the abdomen producing testosterone that the body cannot use.

The AIS infant has the "default" female genitals, but because the Müllerian ducts also form the last third of the vagina, the infant has only a very shallow vagina. Usually the syndrome is undetected at birth, and the child is brought up female. Because males do produce a small amount of estrogen, the breasts do develop, so it is only when the teen fails to menstruate that AIS is usually

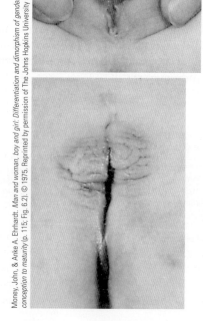

Genitalia of a fetally androgenized female and an androgen-insensitive male with feminized genitals.

Money, John, & Anke A. Ehrhardt. *Man and woman, boy and girl: Differentiation and dimorphism of gender identity from conception to maturity* (p. 115. Fig. 6.2). © 1975. Reprinted by permission of The Johns Hopkins University Press.

congenital adrenal hyperplasia (CAH)
A disorder involving overproduction of androgen in the adrenal glands that can affect males and females. Females born with this condition frequently have masculinized genitals because of excess prenatal androgen exposure, whereas males typically experience early pubertal changes.

androgen-insensitivity syndrome (AIS)
A condition in which a genetic male's cells are insensitive to androgens, resulting in the development of female external genitalia (but no internal reproductive organs).

gender roles
Culturally defined ways of behaving seen as appropriate for males and females.

Over the years, many Americans have reacted with panic and fear to countless real and perceived threats to children. These threats include the fear of bullies, drugs, the Internet, and sexual predators (Radford, 2006). The media has helped to stir more fear in parents by pointing out that sexual predators could be lurking anywhere—near schools, churches, malls, or even movie theaters. By 2008, every state imposed notification laws so that communities would be alerted when a convicted sexual offender moved to town.

Although we talk more about sexual offender registries in Chapter 16, here let's explore how the rising panic in society about sexual predators has led to a fear of men.

Jeff Zaslow, a columnist with the *Wall Street Journal,* wrote an article in 2007 titled "Are We Teaching Our Children to Be

Fearful of Men?" (Zaslow, 2007). In this article, Zaslow points out several ways in which society has contributed to rising fears about men. He discusses how when children get lost in a mall, they are often told to seek out a woman (preferably a "pregnant woman" or a "grandmother"), rather than a man. Or how airlines have changed their policies in seating unaccompanied minor children and now prefer to place them near female passengers. Could this fear of men have led to decreasing rates of male teachers and administrators in the elementary schools? Statistics show that the percentage of male elementary school teachers has declined from 18% to 9% in 2007 (Zaslow, 2007). More fear is instilled by John Walsh, host of *America's Most Wanted,* who advises parents not to hire male baby-sitters. A soccer club in Michigan requires one female parent on the sidelines at all times to protect children from any unwanted behaviors from men.

In Pennsylvania, another soccer coach refrains from hugging his female players after a goal to make sure he's not sending the wrong message (Zaslow, 2007). Many experts today blame this fear of men on the media's image of men as a bad guy, especially when it comes to sexual crimes. John Walsh defended his position by comparing it with how we choose a dog: "What dog is more likely to bite and hurt you? A Doberman, not a poodle" (Zaslow, 2007).

Do you think that panic and fear about sexual predators have changed men's relationships with children? Do you believe that some men may be less likely to coach a female team because they are afraid of their behavior being misinterpreted? These are all valid questions and point to the powerful nature of gender roles and attitudes in society. What do you think needs to be done?

diagnosed. Surgery can then be initiated to lengthen the vagina to accommodate a penis for intercourse, although without any female internal organs, the individual remains infertile. Even though they are genetically male, most AIS individuals seem to be fully feminized and live as females.

Now that we have discussed the various chromosomal and hormonal conditions that may affect gender, the important question becomes, what can a parent do after a child is born with ambiguous genitals or the genitals of one sex and the genetic makeup of the other? For many years, parents of children with DSD have opted for immediate surgery to quickly assign their child's gender when he or she is born (Neergaard, 2005). However, medical experts today recommend waiting until a child is old enough to consent to treatment, unless there is a medical emergency (Wiesemann et al., 2010).

Gender stereotypes are fundamental to our ways of thinking...

▶ GENDER ROLES and Gender Traits

Let's go back for a moment to that alien you met earlier in the chapter. When you describe what is male and female for the alien, chances are you will talk about stereotyped behavior. You might say, "Men are strong, independent, and assertive, and often have a hard time showing emotion," or "Women are sensitive, nurturing, emotional, and soft." Descriptions like these are based on gender stereotypes. Gender stereotypes are fundamental to our ways of thinking, which makes it difficult to realize how thoroughly our conceptions of the world are shaped by gender issues. For example, when a baby is born, the very first question we ask is, "Is it a

boy or a girl?" The parents proudly display a sign in their yard or send a card to friends, proclaiming "It's a girl!" or "It's a boy!" as the sole identifying trait of the child. The card does not state "It's a redhead!" From the moment of birth onward, the child is thought of first as male or female, and all other characteristics—whether the child is tall, bright, an artist, Irish, disabled, gay—are seen in light of the person's gender.

Overall, we expect men to act like men and women to act like women, and we may become confused and uncomfortable when we are denied knowledge of a person's gender. It is very difficult to know how to interact with someone whose gender we do not know because we are so programmed to react to people first according to their gender. If you walked into a party tonight and found yourself face-to-face with someone who you couldn't tell was male or female, how would you feel? Most likely you'd search for gender clues. Often our need to categorize people by gender is taken for granted. But why is it so important?

Even our language is constructed around gender. English has no neutral pronoun (neither do many other languages, including French, Spanish, German, and Italian), meaning that every time you refer to a person, you must write either "he" or "she." Therefore, every sentence you write about a person reveals his or her gender, even if it reveals nothing else about that person.

Many of our basic assumptions about gender are open to dispute. Gender research has been growing explosively since the 1980s, and many of the results challenge long-held beliefs about gender differences. **Gender roles** are culturally defined behaviors that are seen as appropriate for males and females, including the attitudes, personality traits, emotions, and even postures and body language that are considered fundamental to being male or female in a culture. Gender roles also extend into social behaviors, such as the occupations we choose, how we dress and wear our hair, how we talk (as we discussed in Chapter 3), and the ways in which we interact with others.

Note that by saying gender roles are culturally defined, we are suggesting that such differences are not primarily due to biological, physiological, or even psychological differences between men and women but, rather, to the ways in which we are taught to behave. Yet, many people believe that various gender differences in behavior are biologically programmed. Who is correct?

Another way to ask the question is this: Which of our gender-specific behaviors are gender roles (i.e., culturally determined), and which are **gender traits** (innate or biologically determined)? If gender-specific behaviors are biologically determined, then they should remain constant in different societies; if they are social, then we should see very different gender roles in different societies. The majority of gender-specific behaviors, however, differ widely throughout the world and are determined primarily by culture.

▶▶ MASCULINITY and Femininity

What is masculine? What is feminine? Not too long ago, the answers would have seemed quite obvious: Men naturally have masculine traits, meaning they are strong, stable, aggressive, competitive, self-reliant, and emotionally undemonstrative; women are naturally feminine, meaning they are intuitive, loving, nurturing, emotionally expressive, and gentle. Even today, many would agree that such traits describe the differences between the sexes. These gender stereotypes, however, are becoming less acceptable as our culture changes. **Masculinity** and **femininity** refer to the ideal cluster of traits that society attributes to each gender.

Models of masculinity and femininity are changing rapidly in modern American society. It is not uncommon today to see female police officers on crime scenes or apprehending criminals, or

---

REAL RESEARCH 4.3   Gender stereotyping is common on Indian television, where women are portrayed more often in home settings and less often as employed or as authority figures (Das, 2010).

---

women CEOs in the boardroom, nor is it uncommon to find stay-at-home dads at the park with kids or male librarians at the public library shelving books. Yet, gender role change can also result in confusion, fear, and even hostility in society. Gender roles exist, in part, because they allow comfortable interaction between the sexes. If you know exactly how you are supposed to behave and what personality traits you are supposed to assume in relation to the other sex, interactions between the sexes go more smoothly. When things change, determining correct behaviors becomes more difficult.

gender traits
Innate or biologically determined gender-specific behaviors.

masculinity
The ideal cluster of traits that society attributes to males.

femininity
The ideal cluster of traits that society attributes to females.

We also learn about masculinity and femininity from our ethnic group's cultural heritage (M. Crawford, 2006). In the United States, studies have documented less gender role stereotyping among Americans of African descent than among Americans of European descent. Overall, African Americans are less sex-role restricted than European Americans and believe that they possess both masculine and feminine traits (Carter et al., 2009; Dade & Sloan, 2000; Hill, 2002; Leaper, 2000). In fact, African Americans often view others through a lens of age and competency before gender.

▶▶ ARE GENDER ROLES Innate?

As gender stereotypes evolve, a trait may no longer be seen as the exclusive domain of a single gender. For example, many people have been trying to change our current stereotypes of men as "unemotional" and women as "emotional." The constellation of traits that has been traditionally seen as masculine and feminine may be becoming less rigid. For many centuries, these types of gender traits were seen as innate, immutable, and part of the biological makeup of the sexes. Few scientists suggested that the differences between men and women were primarily social; most believed that women and men were fundamentally different.

Not only did scientists believe that the differences in the sexes were innate, but they also believed that men were superior—having developed past the "emotional" nature of women (Gould, 1981). While science has moved forward, these outdated attitudes still exist, both subtly in cultures like our own and overtly in cultures where women are allowed few of the rights granted to men.

How many of our gender behaviors are biological, and how many are socially transmitted? The truth is that the world may not split that cleanly into biological versus social causes of behavior. Behaviors are complex and are almost always interactions between one's innate biological capacities and the environment in which one lives and acts. Behaviors that are considered innately "male" in one culture may be assumed to be innately "female" in another. Even when modern science suggests a certain gender trait that seems to be based on innate differences between the sexes, culture can contradict that trait or even deny it.

For example, most researchers accept the principle that males display more aggression than females; adult males certainly demonstrate this tendency, which is probably the result, in part, of higher levels of testosterone. When female bodybuilders, for example, take steroids, they often find themselves acquiring male traits, including losing breast tissue, growing more body hair, and becoming more aggressive. However, the difference is also demonstrated in early childhood, when boys are more aggressive in play, whereas girls tend to be more compliant and docile.

Yet, Margaret Mead's (1935/1988/2001) famous discussion of the Tchambuli tribe of New Guinea shows that such traits need not determine gender roles. Among the Tchambulis, the women performed the "aggressive" occupations such as fishing, commerce, and politics, whereas the men were more sedentary and artistic, and took more care of domestic life. The women assumed the dress appropriate for their activities—plain clothes and short hair—whereas the men dressed in bright colors. So even if we accept biological gender differences, societies such as the Tchambuli show that human culture can transcend biology.

Some gender differences are considered purely biological. Physically, males tend to be larger and stronger, with more of their body weight in muscle and less in body fat than females (Angier, 1999). Females, however, are born more neurologically advanced than males, and they mature faster. Females are also biologically heartier than males; more male fetuses miscarry, more males are stillborn, the male infant mortality rate is higher, males acquire more hereditary diseases and remain more susceptible to disease throughout life, and men die at younger ages than women (although the gender gap in mortality is smaller among the educated and economically advantaged segments of the U.S. population). Males are also more likely to have developmental problems such as learning disabilities (Martin et al., 2008). It has long been believed that males are better at mathematics and spatial problems, whereas females are better at verbal tasks; for example, female children learn language skills earlier than males (Weatherall, 2002). Yet, many of these differences may be the result of socialization rather than biology (Hyde & Mertz, 2008).

Boys and girls do show some behavioral differences that appear to be universal. For example, in a study of six cultures, Whiting and her colleagues (Whiting & Edwards, 1988; Whiting & Whiting, 1975) discovered that certain traits seemed to characterize masculine and feminine behavior in 3- to 6-year-olds. In almost all countries, boys engaged in more rough-and-tumble play,

and boys "dominated egoistically" (tried to control the situation through commands), whereas girls more often sought or offered physical contact, sought help, and "suggested responsibly" (dominated socially by invoking rules or appealing to greater good).

Interestingly, although their strategies are different, both boys and girls often pursue the same ends; for example, rough-and-tumble play among boys and initiation of physical contact among girls are both strategies for touching and being touched. However, Whiting suggests that even these behaviors might be the result of different kinds of pressures put on boys and girls; for example, in their sample, older girls were expected to take care of young children more often than boys, and younger girls were given more responsibility than younger boys. These different expectations from each gender may explain later differences in their behaviors. So even gender behaviors that are spread across cultures may not prove to be innate differences.

There has always been evidence that men's and women's brains are different; autopsies have shown that men's brains are more asymmetrical than women's, and women seem to recover better from damage to the left hemisphere of the brain (as in strokes), where language is situated. Yet, it has always been unclear what facts such as these mean. Recently, newer techniques in brain imaging have provided evidence that women's and men's brains not only differ in size, but that women and men use their brains differently during certain activities (DeBellis et al., 2001; Hamberg, 2000; Menzler et al., 2011; Sánchez & Vilain, 2010; F. Schneider et al., 2000). Although it is too early to know what these differences mean, future studies may be able to provide clearer pictures of the different ways men and women think, and shed some light on the biological and social influences of these differences.

...almost no differences between the sexes are universally accepted by researchers.

Aside from the behaviors and physical attributes just discussed, almost no differences between the sexes are universally accepted by researchers. This does not mean that there are not other biological gender differences; we simply do not know for sure. We must be careful not to move too far in the other direction and suggest that there are no innate differences between the sexes. Many of these differences remain controversial, such as relative levels of activity, curiosity, and facial recognition skills. These are relatively minor differences, however. Even if it turns out, for example, that female infants recognize faces earlier than males, as has been suggested, or that male children are more active than females, would that really account for the enormous gender role differences that have developed over time? Although biologists and other researchers still study innate differences between the sexes, today more attention is being paid to gender similarities.

◀ **review** QUESTIONS

1 Differentiate between gender roles and gender traits, and explain how cross-cultural research helps us identify each.

2 Compare *masculinity* and *femininity* and explain how our ethnic groups' cultural heritage may affect these concepts.

3 Which gender behaviors/traits are considered to be biologically based?

4 Are any gender differences universal?

GENDER ROLE Theory

In Chapter 2, we reviewed general theories of sexuality, and the debates there centered on how much of human sexuality is programmed through our genes and physiology, and how much is influenced by culture and environment. Gender role theory struggles with the same issues, and different theorists take different positions. Social learning theorists believe that we learn gender roles almost entirely from our environment, whereas cognitive development theorists believe that children go through a set series of stages that correspond to certain beliefs and attitudes about gender. In this section, we talk about evolutionary, social learning, cognitive development, and gender schema theories.

When a baby is born, he or she possesses no knowledge and few instinctual behaviors. However, by the time the child is about age 3 or 4 years, he or she can usually talk, feed himself or herself, interact with adults, describe objects, and use correct facial expressions and body language. The child also typically exhibits a wide range of behaviors that are appropriate to his or her gender. The process whereby this infant who knows nothing becomes a preschooler who has the basic skills for functioning in society is called **socialization.**

Socialization occurs at every age and level of development, and the same is true of gender role socialization. Most boys dress and act like other boys and play with traditionally male toys (guns, trucks), whereas most girls insist on wearing dresses and express a desire to do traditionally "female" things, such as playing with dolls and toy kitchens. Is this behavior innate, or are gender stereotypes still getting through to these children through television and in playing with their peers? The answer depends on which theory of gender role development you accept.

▶▶ EVOLUTIONARY THEORY:
Adapting to Our Environment

Recently, we began to understand more about the biological differences between men and women through the field of evolutionary theory. Gender differences are seen as ways in which we have developed in our adaptation to our environment. For example, later in this book we explore how the double standard in sexual behavior developed, in which a man with several partners was viewed as a "player," whereas a woman with several partners was viewed as a "slut." An evolutionary theorist would explain this gender difference in terms of the biological differences between men and women. A man can impregnate several women at any given time, but a woman, once pregnant, cannot become pregnant again until she gives birth. The time investment of these activities varies tremendously. If evolutionary success is determined by how many offspring we have, the men win hands down.

▶▶ SOCIAL LEARNING THEORY:
Learning from Our Environment

Social learning theory suggests that we learn gender roles from our environment, from the same system of rewards and punishments that we learn our other social roles. For example, research shows that many parents commonly reward gender-appropriate behavior and disapprove of (or even punish) gender-inappropriate behavior. Telling a boy sternly not to cry "like a girl," approving a girl's use of makeup, taking a Barbie away from a boy and handing him Spider-Man, making girls help with cooking and cleaning and boys take out the trash—these little, everyday actions build into powerful messages about gender. Gender stereotypes can also influence our perceptions of a person's abilities. In one study, mothers were asked to guess how steep a slope their 11-month-old sons and daughters could crawl down. Although no gender differences were found in the abilities of the babies to climb the slopes, mothers were significantly more likely to underestimate the ability of their daughters (Eliot, 2009).

Children also learn to model their behavior after the same-gender parent to win parental approval. They may learn about gender-appropriate behavior from parents even if they are too young to perform the actions themselves; for example, they see that Mommy is more likely to make dinner, whereas Daddy is

---

REAL RESEARCH 4.4   College males who play video games that "objectify" women are more likely to view women as sex objects and engage in inappropriate sexual advances toward women (YAO ET AL., 2010).

---

more likely to pay the bills. Children also see models of the "appropriate" ways for their genders to behave in their books, on television, and when interacting with others. Even the structure of our language conveys gender attitudes about things, such as the dominant position of the male; for example, the use of male words to include men and women (using "chairman" or "mankind" to refer to both men and women), or the differentiation between Miss and Mrs. to indicate whether a woman is married. However, people are trying to amend these inequalities today, as evidenced by the growing acceptance of words such as "chairperson" and "humankind," and the title "Ms."

socialization
The process in which an infant is taught the basic skills for functioning in society.

schema
A cognitive mechanism that helps to organize information.

gender schema
A cognitive mechanism that helps us to understand gender roles.

▶▶ COGNITIVE DEVELOPMENT THEORY: Age-Stage Learning

Cognitive development theory assumes that all children go through a universal pattern of development, and there really is not much parents can do to alter it. As children's brains mature and grow, they develop new abilities and concerns; at each stage, their understanding of gender changes in predictable ways. This theory follows the ideas of Piaget (1951), the child development theorist who suggested that social attitudes in children are mediated through their processes of cognitive development. In other words, children can process only a certain kind and amount of information at each developmental stage.

As children begin to be able to recognize the physical differences between girls and boys, and then to categorize themselves as one or the other, they look for information about their genders. Around the ages of 2 to 5, they form strict stereotypes of gender based on their observed differences: Men are bigger and stronger and are seen in aggressive roles such as policeman and superhero; women tend to be associated with motherhood through their physicality (e.g., the child asks what the mother's breasts are and is told they are used to feed children) and through women's social roles of nurturing and emotional expressiveness. These "physicalistic" thought patterns are universal in young children and are organized around ideas of gender.

*As children mature, they become more aware that **gender roles are social and arbitrary.***

As children mature, they become more aware that gender roles are, to some degree, social and arbitrary, and cognitive development theory predicts, therefore, that rigid gender role behavior should decrease after about the age of 7 or 8. So cognitive development theory predicts what set of gender attitudes should appear at different ages; however, the research is still contradictory on whether its predictions are correct (see Albert & Porter, 1988).

Newer theories of gender role development try to combine social learning theory and cognitive development theory to address weaknesses in both. Cognitive development theory neglects social factors and differences in the ways different groups raise children. On the other hand, social learning theory neglects a child's age-related ability to understand and assimilate gender models, and portrays children as too passive; in social learning theory, children seem to accept whatever models of behavior are offered without passing them through their own thought processes.

▶▶ GENDER SCHEMA THEORY: Our Cultural Maps

Sandra Bem's (1974, 1977, 1981) theory is a good example of a theory that tries to overcome the difficulties posed by the other theories. According to Bem, children (and, for that matter, all of us) think according to **schemas** (SKI-muz), which are cognitive mechanisms that organize our world. These schemas develop over time and are universal, like the stages in cognitive development theory; the difference lies in Bem's assertion that the contents of schemas are determined by the culture. Schemas are like maps in our heads that direct our thought processes.

Bem suggests that one schema we all have is a **gender schema,** which organizes our thinking about gender. From the moment we are born, information about gender is continuously presented to us by our parents, relatives, teachers, peers, television, movies, advertising, and the like. We absorb the more obvious information about sexual anatomy, "male" and "female" types of work and activities, and gender-linked personality traits. However, society also attributes gender to things as abstract as shapes (rounded, soft shapes are often described as "feminine," and sharp, angular shapes as "masculine") and even our drinks (champagne is seen as more feminine, whereas beer is seen as more masculine; Crawford et al., 2004).

Gender schemas are powerful in our culture. When we first meet a man, we immediately use our masculine gender schema and begin our relationship with an already established series of beliefs about him. For example, we may believe that men are strong or assertive. Our gender schema is more powerful than other schemas and is used more often, Bem argues, because our culture puts so much emphasis on gender and gender differences. This is where she parts company with cognitive development theorists, who argue that gender is important to children because of their naturally physicalistic ways of thinking.

The gender schema becomes so ingrained that we do not even realize its power. For example, some people so stereotype gender concepts that it would never occur to them to say, "My, how strong you are becoming!" to a little girl, whereas they say it easily to a little boy. Bem argues that "strong" as a feminine trait does not exist in the female schema for many people, so they rarely invoke the term *strong* to refer to women.

◀ review QUESTIONS

1 Explain how gender role socialization occurs in children.

2 Describe the differences among the evolutionary, social learning, and cognitive development theories.

3 Explain how one's development of a "gender schema" influences his or her view of gender. Give examples to support your answer.

► VARIETIES of Gender

Culture and social structure interact to create **sex typing,** a way of thinking that splits the world into two basic categories—male and female—and suggests that most behaviors, thoughts, actions, professions, emotions, and so on fit one gender more than the other (Eliot, 2009; Liben & Bigler, 2002; Maccoby, 2002). Although there are fewer sex-typed assignments and attitudes today than there were years ago, sex typing still exists.

These stereotypes become so basic to our way of thinking that we do not even realize the powerful hold they have over our conceptions of the world. Many cultures build their entire worldviews around masculinity and femininity. Some cultures have taken these ideas and created models of the universe based on masculine and feminine traits, such as the Chinese concept of yin and yang, which we discussed in Chapter 1.

Because gender is socially constructed, societies decide how gender will be defined and what it will mean. J. E. Williams and Best (1994) collected data about masculinity and femininity in 30 countries and found that throughout the world, people largely agree on gender role stereotypes. In a study of 37 countries, Buss (1994) found that women and men value different qualities in each other. Women place a higher value on the qualities of being "good financial prospects" and "ambitious and industrious" for their mates, whereas men place a higher value on physical attractiveness.

In American society, conceptions of "masculinity" and "femininity" have been seen as mutually exclusive; that is, a person who is feminine cannot also be masculine and vice versa (Spence, 1984). However, research has shown that masculinity and femininity are independent traits that can exist in people separately (Bem, 1977; Spence, 1984). Bem (1974) suggests that this can lead to four types of personalities: those high in masculinity and low in femininity, those high in femininity and low in masculinity, those low in both ("undifferentiated"), and those high in both ("androgynous"). Such categories may challenge traditional thinking about gender. In fact, the more one examines the categories of gender that really exist in the social world, the clearer it becomes that gender is more complicated than just splitting the world into male and female.

> *...masculinity and femininity are **independent traits** that can exist in people separately.*

►► MASCULINITY: The Hunter

From the moment of a baby's birth, almost every society has different expectations of its males and females. In many societies, men must go through trials or rights of passage in which they earn their right to be men; few societies have such trials for women. For example, the !Kung bushmen have a "rite of the first kill" that is performed twice for each boy—once after he kills his first large male animal and once after he kills his first large female animal (Collier & Rosaldo, 1981). During the ceremony, a gash is cut in the boy's chest and filled with a magical substance that is supposed to keep the boy from being lazy. Hunting prowess is ritually connected with marriage, and men acquire wives by demonstrating their ability at the hunt (Lewin, 1988). For example, a boy may not marry until he goes through the rite of first kill, and at the wedding, he must present to his bride's parents a large animal he has killed. Even the language of killing and marrying is linked; !Kung myths and games equate marriage with hunting and talk of men "chasing," "killing," and "eating" women just as they do animals.

In American society, men are often judged by their "prowess" in business, with successful men receiving society's admiration. Although in many societies men tend to have privileges that women do not, and despite the fact that male traits in many societies are valued more than female traits (which we discuss in further detail soon), it is not easy for men to live up to the strong social demands of being male in a changing society.

Great contradictions are inherent in the contemporary masculine role: The man is supposed to be the provider and yet is not supposed to live entirely for his work; he is supposed to be a strong, stable force, yet not cut his emotions off from his loved ones; and he is never supposed to be scared, inadequate, sexually inexperienced, or financially dependent on a woman. Men in all societies live with these types of gender role contradictions. In some cases, men simplify their lives by exaggerating the "macho" side of society's expectations and becoming hypermasculine males (Farr et al., 2004). To these macho men, violence is manly, danger is exciting, and sexuality must be pursued callously.

David Gilmore (1990) believes there is an evolutionary purpose behind masculine socialization. In most societies, masculine socialization prepares men to adopt the role of safeguarding the group's survival, to be willing to give their own lives in the hunt or in war to ensure the group's future by protecting the women's ability to reproduce. Gilmore's point is that men are not concerned with being macho as an end in itself, but are concerned with the ultimate welfare of society. In fact, Gilmore argues, men are as much nurturers as women, concerned with society's weaker and more helpless members, willing to give their energy and even their lives for the greater social good.

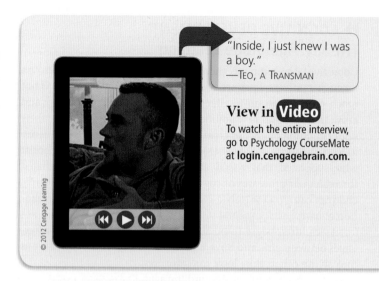

"Inside, I just knew I was a boy."
—Teo, a Transman

View in Video
To watch the entire interview, go to Psychology CourseMate at **login.cengagebrain.com.**

© 2012 Cengage Learning

sex typing
A cognitive thinking pattern that divides the world into male and female categories and suggests the appropriate behaviors, thoughts, actions, professions, and emotions for each.

Although masculinity has its privileges, it has its downside, too. Men do not live as long as women, in part because of the demands of the male role. For example, men are more likely to die of stress-related illnesses, including lung cancer (men smoke more than women), motor vehicle accidents (men drive more than women, often because of work), suicide (women attempt suicide more often, but men are more successful at actually killing themselves), other accidents (men do more dangerous work than women), and cirrhosis of the liver (there are more male alcoholics and drug addicts; Courtenay, 2000; D. R. Nicholas, 2000).

In fact, with all the attention on how gender stereotypes harm women, men are equally the victims of society's expectations. Male stereotypes tend to be narrower than female stereotypes, and men who want to conform to society's ideas of gender have less flexibility in their behavior than women (Lips, 2008). For example, it is still unacceptable for men to cry in public except in the most extreme circumstances. Crying is the body's natural response to being upset. Boys are taught not to cry, but that is difficult when they are emotionally moved; so they stop allowing themselves to be moved emotionally—and then are criticized for not letting their emotions show (Lombardo et al., 2001).

▶▶ FEMININITY: The Nurturer

When someone says, "She is a very feminine woman," what image comes to mind? The president of a corporation? A woman in a frilly pink dress? A soldier carrying her gear? In American culture, we associate femininity with qualities such as beauty, softness, empathy, concern, and modesty. In fact, in almost every culture, femininity is defined by being the opposite of masculinity.

On the other hand, ideas of femininity are not static. Sheila Rothman (1978) has argued that American society has gone through a number of basic conceptions of what "womanhood" (and, by extension, femininity) should be. For example, the 19th century emphasized the value of "virtuous womanhood," whereby women instilled "morality" in society by starting women's clubs

Today men are often judged by how well they do at work, whereas women are often judged by how attractive and thin they are.

"I've come to accept this as an important part of my existence."
—LIZ, A TRANSWOMAN

View in Video
To watch the entire interview, go to Psychology CourseMate at **login.cengagebrain.com**.

that brought women together and eventually led to the battling of perceived social ills. The Women's Christian Temperance Union, for example, started a movement to ban alcohol that eventually succeeded.

By the early part of the 20th century, the concept of the ideal woman shifted to what Rothman calls "educated motherhood," whereby the woman was supposed to learn all the new, sophisticated theories of child rearing and was to shift her attention to the needs of children and family. Over the next few decades, the woman's role was redefined as a "wife–companion," and she was supposed to redirect her energy away from her children and toward being a sexual companion for her husband. Finally, Rothman argues, the 1960s began the era of "woman as person," in which a woman began to be seen as autonomous and competent, and able to decide the nature of her own role in life independent of gender expectations.

Among feminist scholars, ideological battles rage about the meaning of being a woman in today's society. For example, many have faulted feminism for its attitude, at least until recently, that women who choose to stay in the home and raise children are not fulfilling their potential. Yet, women with young children who do work often report feelings of guilt about not being with their children (Crittenden, 2001; Lerner, 1998). Many argue that the idea of femininity itself is an attempt to mold women in ways that are determined by men.

For example, the pressure on women to stay thin, to try to appear younger than they are, and to try to appear as beautiful as possible can be seen as reflections of male power (Wolf, 1991). Sexually, as well, women are supposed to conform to feminine stereotypes and be passive, naïve, and inexperienced. The media reinforce the ideals of feminine beauty, and the pressures on women to conform to these ideals lead to eating disorders and the surge in cosmetic surgery (Wolf, 1991). We further discuss the powerful influences of the media in Chapter 18.

▶▶ ANDROGYNY: Feminine and Masculine

Up until the 1970s, masculinity and femininity were thought to be on the same continuum. The more masculine you were, the less feminine you were, and vice versa. However, in the 1970s, researchers challenged this notion by suggesting that masculinity and femininity were two separate dimensions and a person could be high or low on both dimensions.

The breakdown of traditional stereotypes about gender has refocused attention on the idea of **androgyny.** Bem (1977), as we mentioned earlier, suggested that people have different combinations of masculine and feminine traits. She considers those who have a high score on both masculinity and femininity to be androgynous. Androgyny, according to Bem, allows greater flexibility in behavior because people have a greater repertoire of possible reactions to a situation. Bem (1974, 1977, 1981) has tried to show that androgynous individuals can display "masculine" traits (such as independence) and "feminine" traits (such as gentleness) when situations call for them.

Because of Bem's early research on masculinity, femininity, and androgyny, some have suggested that androgyny was a desirable state and androgynous attitudes were a solution to the tension between the sexes. There has been more research on gender roles and androgyny since, and androgyny may not be the answer to the world's gender problems. Suggesting that people should combine aspects of masculinity and femininity may simply reinforce and retain outdated ideas of gender.

Later research questioned whether the masculine and feminine traits that Bem used were still valid nearly 30 years later. One study found that, although 18 of 20 feminine traits still qualified as feminine, only 8 of 20 masculine traits qualified as strictly masculine (Auster & Ohm, 2000). Traits originally associated with masculinity, such as analytical, individualistic, competitive, self-sufficient, risk taking, and defends own beliefs, were no longer viewed as only masculine traits. These findings reflect recent societal changes that render some masculine traits desirable for both men and women.

*Some have suggested that androgyny was a **desirable state.***

▶▶ THE GENDER Spectrum

In Western culture, the **gender binary** has traditionally divided people into two groups—male and female. When infants are born, the genital anatomy is used to determine biological sex. If there is a penis, the child is a boy; if there is no penis, the child is a girl. If the genitals are ambiguous, the child is intersexed, or has a disorder of sexual development. John Money, whom we discussed earlier in this chapter, suggested that the majority of people are "gender congruent," which means that their biological sex, gender identity, and gender expression all "match" (Money, 1955). An XY male is a man; he acts masculine, and he has sex with a woman.

Today, we know that gender is much more complicated than Money proposed. Our biology, gender identity, and gender expression all intersect, creating a multidimensional **gender spectrum.** One person can be born female (XX), identify as a woman, act feminine, and have sex with a man, whereas another can be born female (XX), identify as a woman, act masculine, and have sex with both men and women.

Typically when people's behaviors fall outside of commonly understood gender norms, they might be referred to as **gender diverse** or **transgender.** The transgender (or simply "trans") community includes a variety of individuals and groups, including **transyouth, transsexuals, transwomen,** and **transmen.** Although the majority of transgender people feel confident and comfortable about their biological sex and gender identity, some experience **gender dysphoria** (dis-FOR-ee-uh), or confusion and/or discomfort. In Chapter 16, we will discuss transvestites, who differ from transmen or transwomen because the cross-dressing behaviors involve a fetish. We will discuss fetishes more in Chapter 16.

The terms **queer** and **genderqueer** have become umbrella terms that refer to a range of different sexual orientations, gender behaviors, or ideologies. Typically, individuals who identify as queer or genderqueer reject traditional gender roles and believe that **gender fluidity** allows them a more flexible range of gender expression. In the past few years there has been more acceptance

---

androgyny
Having high levels of both masculine and feminine characteristics.

gender binary
A gender classification system that divides people into two groups—male and female or masculine and feminine.

gender spectrum
The continuum of possibilities of biological gender, gender identity, gender expression, and sexual orientation.

gender diverse
An individual whose gender identity or gender expression lies outside of the socially accepted gender norms.

transgender or trans
A general term referring to a person or group of people who identify or express their gender in a variety of different ways, typically in opposition to their biological sex.

transyouth
A label often used to describe youths who are experiencing issues related to gender identity or expression.

transsexual
A person who identifies with a gender other than the one he or she was given at birth.

transwomen
A label that may be used by male-to-female transsexuals to signify they are female with a male history.

transmen
A label that may be used by female-to-male transsexuals to signify they are male with a female history.

gender dysphoria
A condition in which a person feels extreme confusion and/or discomfort between his or her biological sex and gender identity.

queer or genderqueer
Umbrella terms in the gender-diverse community that refer to a range of different sexual orientations, gender behaviors, or ideologies.

gender fluidity
A flexible range of gender expression, which can change day-to-day and allows for less restrictive and stereotypical gender expectations.

transprejudice
Negative attitudes, behaviors, or discrimination against those who are transgendered.

transsexualism
A condition in which people identify with a gender other than the one they were given at birth.

sex reassignment surgery (SRS)
A wide range of various surgical options to change genitalia on a transsexual; also referred to as gender reassignment.

For many years, transgendered men and women in Iran were perceived as being homosexual. Because there were strict bans on homosexuality required by the Quran, transsexualism was not accepted. Today, however, Iran has one of the highest rates of sexual reassignment surgeries in the world. But it wasn't always this way. Years before, transsexuals were imprisoned, beaten, and even stoned to death. It took the bravery of one woman to change things around.

For most of Maryann Khatoon Molkara's life, she knew she was a woman, even though she was born male and given a male name. Maryann had experienced years of bullying and harassment, and was fired from her job, injected with male hormones, and institutionalized. Knowing the only way to begin to change attitudes about transsexuals and sexual reassignment surgery was to get the Ayatollah Khomeini to issue a statement, Maryann began writing him letters in 1975. She never received a response. Her luck changed during the mid-1980s when she

was a volunteer helping to care for wounded soldiers during the Iran–Iraq war. One of her patients was a high-ranking government worker who helped her secure a meeting with top officials.

An Iranian male-to-female transsexual.

However, getting to Khomeini required her to break into a heavily guarded compound. She did this wearing a man's suit and carrying a copy of the Quran, but

was quickly surrounded by guards and severely beaten. Hassan Pasandide, Khomeini's brother, intervened and brought her to see the Ayatollah. At first the guards and officers were fearful that Maryann was carrying explosives because they could tell she had tape around her chest. When she removed the tape, she revealed female breasts. After a long talk with the Ayatollah, a *fatwa* (a religious or legal decree) was issued in support of sexual reassignment surgery. The *fatwa* gave her religious authorization to undergo sexual reassignment surgery.

Sexual reassignment surgery has been legal in Iran since 1983. Today, many transsexuals travel to Iran from Eastern European and Arab countries to undergo sexual reassignment. Maryann continues her work fighting for transsexual rights and today runs Iran's leading transsexual campaign group.

[1] The information in this feature was gathered from Barford (2008), Kamali (2010), McDowall and Kahn (2004), and Tait (2005).

for transgender behaviors in the United States, and this may be due, in part, to an increasingly positive depiction of transgender issues in the media. Television shows such as *CSI, Law & Order, The L Word, Family Guy,* and *South Park* have all had transgender characters in their shows. However, many transmen and trans-women experience discrimination or prejudice, known as **transprejudice.**

▶▶ TRANSSEXUALISM AND
Sex Reassignment Surgery

In the chapter opening story, we introduced Sophie, a trans-woman. **Transsexualism** has profound implications for our conceptions of gender categories. Some cases of transsexualism have received great publicity. In 1952, George Jorgensen, a retired Marine, went to Denmark to have his genitals surgically altered to resemble those of a female. George changed his name to Christine, went public, and became the first highly publicized case of a transsexual who underwent **sex reassignment surgery (SRS).** Jorgensen desired to be a girl from an early age, avoided rough sports, and was a small, frail child with underdeveloped male

Billy Tipton, a well-known jazz musician, was discovered to be a female when he died in 1989. He was married to a woman who was aware of his biological gender, and he was also the father of three adopted boys who did not learn of his biological gender until after his death.

genitals (Jorgensen, 1967). Jorgensen's story is typical of other transsexuals, who knew from an early age that they were "born into the wrong body."

Another famous case was that of Richard Raskind, an eye doctor and tennis player who had SRS and then tried to play in a professional women's tennis tournament as Renée Richards. When it was discovered that she was a genetic male, Richards was barred from playing on the women's tennis tour.

Outside the United States, transpeople experience varying degrees of acceptance. Whereas Iran officially recognized transsexualism in the mid-1980s and began allowing transpeople to undergo SRS shortly after (see accompanying Sexual Diversity in Our World; Harrison, 2005), Japan has been more reluctant to deal with transsexual issues. SRS was not approved in Japan until 1996, with the first surgery performed on a transman in 1998 and a transwoman in 1999 (Ako et al., 2001; Matsubara, 2001).

*Outside the U.S., transsexuals experience **varying degrees of acceptance.***

Medical and Surgical Gender Transitions

The World Professional Association for Transgender Health (2001) proposed "Standards of Care" that outline protocols and treatments for those seeking gender reassignment. Around the world, these guidelines have helped men and women who identify as transgender obtain access to safe and legal care.

Female-to-male transsexuals (FtoM or F2M) are biological females, whereas male-to-female transsexuals (MtoF or M2F) are biological males. A variety of medical and surgical options are available, and although some transpeople proceed through all the stages to eventual surgery, many do not. For many, treatment often begins with psychotherapy, which helps explore options, establish realistic life goals, and identify points of conflict that have been interfering with life happiness. They may be encouraged to take on the role of the desired gender, through cross-dressing, hair removal, body padding, vocal training, or various other behaviors. A "real-life test" enables them to live as the desired gender and understand the effects that changing gender will have on their work, home, and personal relationships.

For some transpeople, the next step typically involves cross-sex hormone therapy, in which androgens are given to transmen and estrogens (and possibly testosterone-blockers) are given to transwomen. Taking these drugs significantly changes the physical appearance of a man or woman, typically within about 2 years. However, there are several risks to these drugs, especially for those with chronic health problems or those who are obese or smoke cigarettes.

Transwomen who take estrogens (and possibly testosterone-blockers) will develop breasts, a redistribution of body fat, decreased upper body strength, a softening of the skin, a decrease in body hair, a slowing or stopping of hair loss in the scalp, decreased testicular size, and fewer erections (World Professional Organization for Transgender Health, 2001). However, if the drugs were stopped, most of these effects would be reversible, with the exception of the breast tissue. Transmen who take testosterone will develop several permanent changes, including a deeper voice, clitoral enlargement, increased facial and body hair, and possible baldness (World Professional Organization for Transgender Health, 2001). They may also experience several reversible changes including increased sexual interest, upper body strength, weight gain, and a redistribution of body fat (World Professional Organization for Transgender Health, 2001). For some transpeople, these changes are enough and they do not feel the need to undergo additional surgical interventions.

Although hormonal therapy may produce adequate breast tissue in some transwomen, others may desire additional breast augmentation surgery. Transmen often undergo breast reduction or chest surgery. Although many different genital surgical options are available, it is important to point out that not every transperson desires genital surgery. Some might not be able to afford it, others might not be happy with the options available, and still others might be content with the results of hormonal treatments.

If a person proceeds to genital surgeries, transwoman's genital surgeries include **penectomy, orchiectomy,** urethral rerouting (to allow for urination through the shorter urethra), or **vaginoplasty.** Transmen's genital surgeries include **hysterectomy,** urethral rerouting (to allow for urination through the end of the reconstructed penis), **scrotoplasty, metoidioplasty,** or **phalloplasty.**

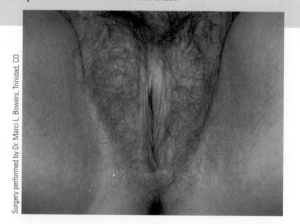

A completed male-to-female transsexual.

Surgery performed by Dr. Marci L. Bowers, Trinidad, CO

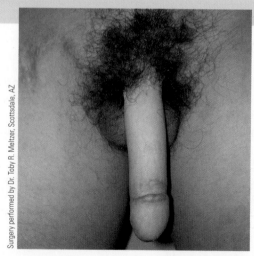

A completed female-to-male transsexual.

Surgery performed by Dr. Toby R. Meltzer, Scottsdale, AZ

For transmen, the most popular option today is a clitoral release procedure called metoidioplasty (Gibson, 2010; Perovic & Djordjevic, 2003). Transmen who undergo testosterone therapy typically experience clitoris elongation anywhere from 1 to 3 inches in length. A metoidioplasty releases the enlarged clitoris, allowing it to hang like a natural penis. Another surgical option, phalloplasty, involves constructing an artificial penis from abdominal skin. Phalloplasty is a difficult procedure and, as a result, is much less popular today. Penises made from phalloplasty cannot achieve a natural erection, so penile implants of some kind are usually used (we will discuss these implants in more detail in Chapter 14). Overall, metoidioplasty is a simpler procedure than phalloplasty, which explains its popularity. It also has fewer complications, takes less time, and is less expensive (e.g., a metoidioplasty takes about 1 to 2 hours and can cost around $15,000 to 20,000, whereas a phalloplasty can take about 8 hours and cost more than $65,000).

Over the years, SRS has been relatively controversial, with some studies showing healthy postoperative functioning (DeCuypere et al., 2005; Johansson et al., 2010; Klein & Gorzalka, 2009; Lawrence, 2006), and other studies showing no alleviation of the psychological suffering (Newfield et al., 2006; Olsson & Möller, 2006). Even so, some people seeking sex reassignment have longed for years to bring their bodies into line with their sense of gender identity, and SRS is their ultimate goal. As surgical techniques improve, some SRS problems may be resolved.

As surgical techniques improve, some SRS problems may be resolved.

▶▶ GENDER DIVERSITY in Other Cultures

Some cultures challenge our notions of gender and even have a gender category that encompasses both aspects of gender. **Two-spirits** (or *berdache*) have been found in many cultures throughout the world, including American Indian, Indian, and Filipino cultures.

A two-spirit was usually (but not always) a biological male who was effeminate or androgynous in behavior and who took on the social role of a female (Blackwood, 1994; Jacobs et al., 1997; W. L. Williams, 1986). Being a two-spirit was considered a vocation, like being a hunter or warrior, which was communicated to certain boys in their first adult vision. In all social functions, the two-spirit was treated as a female. The two-spirit held a respected, sacred position in society and was believed to have special powers.

Biologically female two-spirits also lived in Native American tribes. Female two-spirits began showing interest in boys' activities and games during childhood (Blackwood, 1984; Jacobs et al., 1997). Adults, recognizing this desire, would teach the girls the same skills the boys were learning. (In one tribe, a family with all girl children might select one daughter to be their "son," tying dried bear ovaries to her belt to prevent conception!)

These females were initiated into puberty as men, and thereafter they were essentially considered men. They hunted and trapped, fought in battle, and performed male ceremonial tasks. Among the Alaskan Ingalik, for example, these biological women would even participate in nude, men-only sweat baths, and the men would ignore the female genitalia and treat the two-spirit as a man. The female two-spirit could marry a woman, although the unions remained childless, and the two-spirit would perform the appropriate rituals when her partner menstruated but would ignore her own menses. Female two-spirits became prominent members of some Native American societies.

Other cultures have similar roles. The Persian Gulf country of Oman has a class of biological males called the *xani-th* (Wikan, 1977). The *xani-th* are exempt from the strict Islamic rules that restrict men's interaction with women because they are not considered men. They sit with females at weddings and may see the bride's face; they may not sit with men in public or do tasks reserved for men. Yet, the *xani-th* are not considered females either; for example, they retain men's names.

Another important example is the *hijra* of India. The *hijra* are men who undergo ritual castration in which all or part of their genitals are removed, and they are believed to have special powers to curse or bless male children. *Hijra* dress as women, although they do not really try to "pass" as women; their mannerisms are exaggerated, and some even sport facial hair. In India, the *hijra* are considered neither men nor women but inhabit a unique third social gender (Nanda, 2001).

In Thailand, there is a group of people called the *kathoey*, who are similar to Oman's *xani-th*. Two other examples are the *aikane*

penectomy
Removal of the penis.

orchiectomy
Removal of the testes.

vaginoplasty
Reconstructive surgery procedure used for the construction of the labia and vaginal canal.

hysterectomy
A surgical operation to remove all or part of the uterus.

scrotoplasty
Reconstructive surgery procedure in which a scrotum is made; silicone implants may be placed in the scrotum.

metoidioplasty
A clitoral release procedure used in female-to-male transsexuals in which the enlarged clitoris is released from its position and moved forward to more closely resemble the position of a penis.

phalloplasty
Reconstructive surgery procedure used for the construction of a penis.

two-spirit
A term used in Native American culture and other parts of the world for a male or female who is thought to possess both masculine and feminine spirits. (In Native American culture, also referred to as a *berdache*.)

of native Hawaii, who were attached to the court of the chiefs and served sexual, social, and political functions (Morris, 1990), and the *mahu* of Tahiti (Herdt & Stoller, 1990). The belief in these societies that it is neither obvious nor natural that there are only two genders should make us carefully reconsider our own assumptions about gender.

◀ review QUESTIONS

1 Describe the stereotypic views of masculinity, and identify the risks associated with these stereotypes.

2 Describe the stereotypic views of femininity, and identify the risks associated with these stereotypes.

3 Define androgyny, and give one example of androgynous behavior.

4 Compare and contrast the various trans groups, including transyouth, transsexuals, transmen, and transwomen.

5 Define transsexuality and the medical and surgical options for gender reassignment.

6 Explain how gender diversity can be experienced differently in other cultures.

▶ GENDER ROLE SOCIALIZATION
Throughout the Life Span

Socialization into gender roles begins at birth and nowadays may begin even before. Parents can now know months before birth whether the fetus is a boy or a girl and can begin to prepare accordingly. Parents even speak to the unborn child—a mother simply by talking and the father by putting his mouth close to the mother's belly—and communicate ideas about their "little boy" or "little girl." In a real sense, then, these parents may begin trying to communicate gender-specific messages before the child is even born (whether the child actually is influenced by these sounds diffusing into the womb is, of course, another question). Parents awaiting the birth of a child are filled with gender expectations, stereotypes, and desires.

"Boys are better than girls. . . because boys are stronger than girls, sometimes."
—Perceiving Gender Roles 2–5

View in Video
To watch the entire interview, go to Psychology CourseMate at **login.cengagebrain.com**.

© 2012 Cengage Learning

▶▶ CHILDHOOD: Learning by Playing

From the moment parents find out the sex of their baby, a child's life is largely defined by his or her gender. From the baby's name, to how he or she is dressed, to how his or her room is decorated, gender suffuses the newborn's life. Not only do parents construct different environments for boys and girls from birth, they tend to treat them differently as well.

Parents also serve as gender role models. As early as age 2, children begin to identify with their same-sex parent, and by observing and imitating that parent's behavior, they learn that objects and activities are appropriate to specific genders. The cognitive schema that children develop at this point are not flexible but universal; to the children, only women can wear skirts, and only men can shave their faces. In fact, cross-gender humor is very funny to young children; a television program that shows a man dressed up in a woman's clothes or a woman who appears on TV sporting a mustache will elicit bursts of laughter. As children begin to show more complex behaviors, they realize that there are often societal restrictions on acceptable behaviors. Children watch their parents' behavior and learn what are acceptable behaviors for males and females.

Overall, boys are treated more harshly than girls when they adopt cross-gender characteristics (Sandnabba & Ahlberg, 1999). Children who have a strong and persistent identification with the other sex or the gender role of the other sex and are uncomfortable

gender-identity disorder
A disorder in which a child has a strong and persistent identification with the other sex or the gender role of the other sex and is uncomfortable with his or her own biological sex or gender role. May also be referred to as *gender incongruence*.

homosocial play
Gender-segregated play.

with their own biological sex or gender role may be diagnosed with *gender incongruence* or a **gender-identity disorder.**

Early in childhood, gender segregation in play, also known as **homosocial play,** begins. Children tend to gravitate to same-sex friends, and as early as 2 to 3 years old, children play more actively and more interactively with same-sex playmates (Maccoby & Jacklin, 1987). This tendency is universal. Researchers have tried rewarding children for playing with the other sex, but as soon as the reward is discontinued, play reverts back to same-sex groupings. This gender segregation may be because of the different playing styles of boys and girls, the attraction of children to others like themselves, or to learned social roles; most probably, it involves a combination of all these factors.

During the school years, gender roles become the measure by which children are judged by their peers. Children who violate sex-typed play are usually rejected (and not kindly) by their peers (Blakemore, 2003). This is especially true of boys, who experience more rejection from their peers when they violate gender stereotypes than girls do. In 2008, a 15-year-old boy in California was shot to death in school by a classmate who was not comfortable with the boy's gender-identity disorder (Cathcart, 2008).

The classroom itself can also strongly reinforce gender stereotypes. Even though teachers believe they show equal attention to boys and girls, research shows that teachers spend more time with boys, give them more attention, both praise and criticize boys more, direct more follow-up questions to boys, and tolerate more bad behavior among boys than girls (Duffy et al., 2001). Also, teachers stereotype the tasks they ask boys and girls to do; boys may be asked to help move desks, whereas girls are asked to erase the whiteboard.

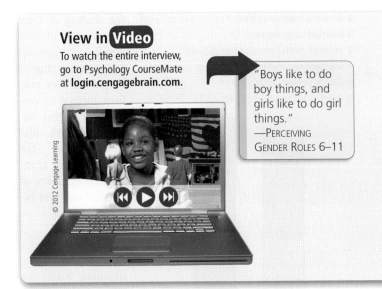

View in Video

To watch the entire interview, go to Psychology CourseMate at **login.cengagebrain.com.**

"Boys like to do boy things, and girls like to do girl things."
—PERCEIVING GENDER ROLES 6–11

© 2012 Cengage Learning

▶▶ ADOLESCENCE: PRACTICE
Being Female or Male

By adolescence, gender roles are firmly established, and they guide adolescents through their exploration of peer relationships and different "love styles" with potential partners. Part of the task of adolescence is to figure out what it means to be a "man" or a "woman" and to try to adopt that role. Boys quickly learn that to be popular, they should be interested in and good at sports, should express interest in sex and women, should not be overly emotional, and should not display interests that are seen as feminine or girlish (recall Sophie's struggle in the chapter opening story). Girls, on the other hand, seem to have more latitude in their behavior but are supposed to express interest in boys and men, show concern with their appearance, and exercise a certain amount of sexual restraint. When boys deviate from gender role behavior, the consequences are more severe than when girls deviate. However, when girls deviate from gender stereotypes of

sexuality (and have multiple sexual partners, for example), they experience more severe consequences.

Adolescence can be a particularly difficult time for those who are transgender, gay, lesbian, or bisexual. There tends to be little tolerance for these behaviors in adolescence because they are viewed as the opposite of what teenagers are "supposed" to do. Teenage boys are supposed to be striving for genuine "masculinity." Although female homosexuality is also seen as deviant and lesbians can be the subject of taunts, females tend to discover their sexual orientation later than males, so fewer "come out" in adolescence.

The life of an emerging gay, lesbian, or bisexual adolescent may be fraught with tension, which contributes to the increased risk for depression among these adolescents. Many gay, bisexual, and transgender youths survive the adolescent years by limiting

Children learn much of their gender role behavior from modeling.

© Tony Freeman/PhotoEdit

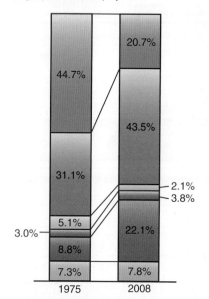

- ▪ Married, traditional (only husband employed)
- ▪ Married, dual earner
- ▫ Married, both parents unemployed
- ▪ Married, nontraditional (only wife employed)
- ▪ Single parent, employed
- ▫ Single parent, unemployed

FIGURE **4.3** Family structure and work in 1975 and 2008. SOURCE: Bureau of Labor Statistics, Economic News Release: Table 4.

the sharing of their sexual orientation or gender identity. Many learn that if they don't, they may be subjected to violence or verbal harassment. We further discuss the physical and emotional harassment of gay, lesbian, and bisexual students in Chapter 11.

Teenage gender roles have been changing since the 1970s. For example, it is more common for heterosexual girls today to assert themselves and text or initiate hanging out with boys than they were 25 years ago, when they may have been considered a "slut." Yet, such changing roles are also confusing; adolescent girls and boys still receive contradictory messages. Traditional male attitudes value sexual achievement, control of the sexual relationship, and suppression of emotions. However, today, as heterosexual teenage boys are being approached by girls, they are not necessarily more sexually experienced than the girls they date, and they are expected to be sensitive to issues of female equality. Heterosexual teenage girls, on the other hand, have often been taught to assert their independence but also must be aware of existing social pressures that contribute to feelings of guilt and shame for girls who seek to fulfill their sexual needs. So even with all the changes that have leveled the playing field between the sexes, it is still not easy for adolescents to negotiate their way into sexual adulthood.

▶▶ ADULTHOOD: Careers and Families

As men and women grow into adulthood, they tend to derive their gender identity primarily from two realms—their careers and their family lives. Although many believe that ideas about gender are firmly established by the time we reach adulthood, recent social changes in sex roles show that adults do have the capacity to revise their thoughts about gender roles. One of the biggest transformations in career and family life in the United States over the last few years involves the movement of women out of the home and into paid employment (Boushey & O'Leary, 2010). These changes have caused a major shift in family gender roles.

Decades ago, the most common family system consisted of a working father and a stay-at-home mother (see Figure 4.3). With high unemployment, more women have been returning to work or working longer hours. In both of these cases, their heterosexual

partners are taking on more of the household duties. As of 2010, U.S. women comprise half of all workers, and 40% are either the family breadwinner or are bringing home as much or more than their partners (Boushey & O'Leary, 2010). Although this has been a significant change across all racial and socioeconomic lines, it is most striking among low-income families—in this group, women are the primary breadwinners in two thirds of their families (Boushey & O'Leary, 2010).

▶▶ THE SENIOR Years

Because American culture values youthfulness and holds many negative stereotypes toward aging, it can often be a difficult time for seniors. There are gender differences, especially because of a double standard of aging in which aging men are viewed as "distinguished," whereas aging women are viewed as "old" (Sontag, 1979; Teuscher & Teuscher, 2006). Because women have historically been valued for their reproductive ability, they may be viewed as old once they lose the ability to reproduce, whereas men are valued for their achievements and are not viewed as old until they are physically incapacitated or unable to work. Overall, although both men and women have been found to value physical appearance, women have been found to be more concerned about the effects of aging on their physical appearance (Slevin, 2010).

American media helps foster negative attitudes toward seniors by pushing advertising for anti-aging products, such as creams, lotions, and cosmetic surgeries to help seniors stay healthy and look

The traditional family structure of a stay-at-home mom and a working dad has been changing over the last few years. During the recent economic recession, many stay-at-home moms took full-time jobs outside the home. These changes have led to shifts in household responsibilities with men taking on more traditionally female household responsibilities, such as child care and preparing dinner. How do you think these became *gendered* jobs?

© imagebroker/Alamy

younger (Gilleard & Higgs, 2000). One study found that the majority of older women equated gray hair with ugliness and poorer health, and because of this, the majority of women in the sample reported dying their hair in later life (Clarke & Korotchenko, 2010).

However, it is important to keep in mind that attitudes about aging vary by race, ethnicity, and sexual orientation. Black and Latina women have less rigid aging stereotypes than White women (Schuler et al., 2008), as do lesbian women, who are more positive about aging and looking old compared with heterosexual women (Slevin, 2010; Wolf, 1991). Gay men, on the other hand, tend to have more negative attitudes about aging, because American gay culture places more emphasis on young and youthful bodies (Slevin, 2010).

The changing economic climate has also contributed to increased stresses in later life. With high levels of unemployment and men and women working at lower paying jobs than they should be, men and women who derive a large sense of their identity from their work may be particularly at risk adjusting to such changes. In families with children, the parents can experience either a great sense of loneliness or a newfound freedom as their children grow and leave the home. A few women, especially those with traditional roles as wife and mother, become depressed about losing their primary roles as caretakers and mothers. The phrase "empty nest syndrome" identifies the feelings of sadness and loss that many women experience when their children leave home or no longer need day-to-day care (McBride, 2007). Significant changes are common in the senior years that may involve difficult adjustments.

Cross-culturally, negative attitudes about seniors and aging persist. In fact, a cross-cultural sample of college students from six countries found negative attitudes about senior citizens and support for the belief that seniors are "incompetent" (Cuddy et al., 2005). Other studies have found significant fears of aging in South Korea (Yun & Lachman, 2006) and Israel (Bodner & Lazar, 2008). It is important to keep in mind how these attitudes and stereotypes affect the aging population.

▶▶ TOWARD GENDER Equality

Can we create a society that avoids gender stereotypes, a society of total gender equality? Would you want to live in such a society? Does a gender-equal society mean that we must have unisex bathrooms and gender-neutral dormitories, or is it something subtler, referring to a sense of equal opportunity and respect? Epstein (1986, 1988) believes that gender distinctions begin with basic, human, dichotomous thinking—the splitting of the world into opposites such as good–bad, dark–light, soft–hard, male–female, and gay–straight. This very basic human process tends to exaggerate differences between things, including the sexes, and society invests a lot of energy in maintaining those distinctions.

Many religious and cultural systems clearly define gender roles. Advocates of such systems deny that differentiating gender roles means that one gender is subordinate to the other. For example, Susan Rogers (1978) has argued that we cannot apply Western notions of gender equality to countries with fundamentally different systems. She argues that inequality can exist in society only when women and men are seen in that society as fundamentally similar.

recover or reactivate.

reactivate with twice the power. regenerist

OLAY
love the skin you're in

Women are surrounded by images of youth and beauty in the media and constantly bombarded by a multitude of products that promise to erase the signs of aging from their faces. These products have been popular because of the double standard of aging in American society, which views aging men as distinguished but aging women as tired and old.

In Oman, for example, women are subject to strict social rules that we in the West would clearly see as subordination. Yet, Rogers argues that women in Oman see themselves as quite different from men and are uninterested in the male role and male definitions of power. Is it appropriate for us to impose our categories on their society and suggest that women in Oman are exploited and subordinate even though they themselves do not think so? Such questions go to the heart of the discussion of power in society.

The goal for many is not a society without gender distinctions; a world without differences is boring. Yet a world that restricts people's ability to express difference because of the color of their

---

REAL RESEARCH 4.5 As of 2010, gender inequalities continue to exist in the division of household labor in the United States. Heterosexual women continue to perform the vast majority of housework (Lachance-Grzela & Bouchard, 2010).

---

skin, their religious beliefs, the type of genitalia they happen to have (or not have!), or their sexual preferences is unjust. It is the content of gender roles, not their existence, that societies can alter to provide each person an opportunity to live without being judged by stereotypes of gender.

1 How are children and teenagers socialized about gender roles throughout childhood and adolescence?

2 How are adults socialized about gender roles throughout adulthood, and how does this socialization affect career choice?

3 Describe the conflicting messages that women receive about career and family life.

4 How has the role of the husband/father in the family changed over the past few decades?

5 Explain how gender roles change as people enter later life.

6 Do you think there could ever be a society without gender distinctions? Why or why not?

⏮ **chapter** REVIEW

SUMMARY **POINTS**

1 Human beings use sexual reproduction to combine 23 chromosomes in the mother's gamete with the 23 in the father's. The zygote then begins to undergo cell differentiation. If the 23rd chromosome pair is XY, the fetus will develop typically female sexual characteristics.

2 Female genitalia develop from the Müllerian duct, whereas male genitalia develop from the Wolffian duct. Both male and female external genitalia develop from the same tubercle, so many male and female genital structures are homologous.

3 Endocrine glands secrete hormones directly into the bloodstream to be carried to the target organs. The ovaries produce estrogen and progesterone, and the testicles produce androgens. The hypothalamus is the body's single most important control center.

4 Disorders of sex development include sex chromosome and hormone disorders. Chromosomal conditions include Klinefelter, Turner, XYY, and triple X syndromes, whereas hormonal conditions include congenital adrenal hyperplasia (CAH) and androgen-insensitivity syndrome (AIS).

5 Gender roles are the culturally determined pattern of behaviors that societies prescribe to the sexes. Gender traits are the biologically determined characteristics of gender. Little agreement exists on which gender characteristics are innate and which are learned.

6 The terms *masculinity* and *femininity* are used in three ways in society: first, a masculine or feminine person is said to exemplify characteristics that differentiate the sexes; second, the terms refer to the extent to which adults adhere to socially prescribed gender roles; and third, masculinity and femininity refer to sexual characteristics.

7 Most people agree that males are larger, stronger, and more aggressive, whereas females are neurologically more advanced than males, mature faster, and are biologically heartier. Some also cite evidence that males have better spatial abilities, whereas females have better verbal abilities.

8 Three types of theories about gender role development have been offered: social learning theories, which postulate that almost all gender knowledge is dependent on what children are taught; cognitive development theories, which suggest that children go through a universal set of stages during which they can learn only certain types of information about gender; and newer theories, such as Bem's gender schema theory, which suggests that children do go through developmental stages, and that the kinds of things they learn at each stage are largely culturally determined.

9 Gender is socially constructed, and societies decide how it will be defined and what it will mean. In American society, masculinity and femininity are seen as mutually exclusive. Masculine traits include being a good provider, strong, stable, unemotional, fearless, sexually experienced, and financially independent.

Feminine traits include being beautiful, soft, empathetic, modest, and emotional. Many traits of femininity are considered to be the opposite of masculinity.

10 Androgyny is high levels of both masculine and feminine characteristics, and some advocate it as a way to transcend gender stereotypes. Transsexuals believe their biological and psychological genders are incompatible, showing us that gender is more complex than simply determining biological gender.

11 The gender binary divides people into two groups—male and female. We are typically put into either of these groups at birth. Societal expectations are that biological sex, gender identity, and gender expression all "match." However, all these variables interact to create a multidimensional gender spectrum. When behaviors fall outside of gender norms, they may be referred to as gender diverse or transgender.

12 Gender dysphoria involves confusion and/or discomfort about gender. Individuals who identify as queer or genderqueer reject traditional gender roles and believe in the fluidity of gender. Many transpeople experience discrimination or prejudice, known as transprejudice.

13 A transsexual is a person who identifies with a gender other than the one he or she was given at birth. Transmen are biological females, whereas transwomen are biological males.

14 There are a variety of medical and surgical options for gender reassignment, and although some transpeople proceed to sex reassignment surgery (SRS), many do not for a variety of reasons. The World Professional Association for Transgender Health has proposed Standards of Care, which outline treatments for those seeking gender reassignment. Treatment usually begins with psychotherapy and then proceeds to medical and/or surgical interventions.

15 Some cultures challenge our notions about gender by proposing categories that are neither male nor female. Native Americans have the two-spirit, whereas other cultures have similar roles, such as the *xani-th* or the *hijra*.

16 Infants are socialized into gender roles early through the way they are dressed and treated, and through the environment in which they are brought up. They are reinforced for appropriate gender activity through ridiculing of children who violate gender boundaries. Adolescents "try on" adult gender roles and attitudes.

17 As men and women grow into adulthood, they tend to derive their gender identity from two realms—careers and family lives. Social changes in sex roles show that adults do have the capacity to revise their thoughts about gender roles. One of the biggest transformations in career and family life in the United States over the last few years involves the movement of women out of the home and into paid employment.

18 Because American culture values youthfulness and holds many negative stereotypes toward aging, it can often be a difficult time for seniors. However, attitudes about aging vary by race, ethnicity, and sexual orientation. With high levels of unemployment and men and women working at lower paying jobs than they should be, men and women who derive a large sense of their identity from their work may be particularly at risk adjusting to such changes. Some parents can experience either a great sense of loneliness or a newfound freedom as their children grow and leave the home.

19 To build a society that avoids gender stereotyping and encourages gender equality, we would need to change our basic, human, dichotomous thinking and the splitting of the world into opposites, such as good and bad. Maintaining this way of thinking only exaggerates differences and invests energy into keeping things separate.

CRITICAL THINKING QUESTIONS

1 What questions does the case study example on Brenda/Bruce raise about the nature of gender? Do you feel that gender is innate, socially learned, or a combination of both?

2 How are definitions of masculinity and femininity changing in society? Are many of the old stereotypes still powerful?

3 Why do you think a woman considers the phrase "She's one of the guys" to be a compliment, whereas a man considers the phrase "He's one of the girls" to be a put-down?

4 Which theory of gender development do you favor? Can you relate this theory to your own gender development? What are the theory's strengths and weaknesses?

5 If you met someone at a party tonight who was transgender, what kind of emotions or thoughts do you think you would have? Would you be interested in pursuing a relationship with him or her? Why or why not?

MEDIA RESOURCES

CourseMate brings course concepts to life with interactive learning, study, and exam preparation tools that support the printed textbook. A textbook-specific website, Psychology CourseMate includes an integrated interactive eBook and other interactive learning tools including quizzes, flashcards, videos, and more. If your textbook does not include an access code card, go to CengageBrain.com to gain access.

CENGAGENOW   CengageNOW is an easy-to-use online resource that helps you study in less time to get the grade you want—NOW. Take a pre-test for this chapter and receive a personalized study plan based on your results that will identify the topics you need to review and direct you to online resources to help you master those topics. Then take a post-test to help you determine the concepts you have mastered and what you will need to work on. If your textbook does not include an access code card, go to CengageBrain.com to gain access.

View in Video available in CourseMate and CengageNOW:

Changing Gender During College: Transgender college student describes beginning college as a male and graduating as a female.

Teo, a Transman: An interview with a transman about his experiences.

Liz, a Transwoman: A transwoman discusses her experiences and challenges.

Early Childhood: Gender Roles: Learn about the actual and perceived gender differences in infancy and early childhood.

Middle Childhood: Gender Roles: Watch boys and girls age 5–11 talk about their conceptions of what it means to be a boy or girl.

Website:

World Professional Association for Transgender Health (WPATH) ■ Formerly known as the Harry Benjamin International Gender Dysphoria Association, WPATH is a professional organization devoted to the understanding and treatment of gender-identity disorders. The mission of WPATH is to promote evidence-based care, education, research, advocacy, public policy, and respect in transgender health.

5

Female Sexual Anatomy and Physiology

View in **Video**

View in **Video**

View in **Video**

View in **Video**

ABOUT THE CHAPTER OPENING VIDEO – Many years ago I lost a good friend, Anne, to breast cancer. Prior to her diagnosis I didn't know too much about breast cancer. Anne was a mom with three young children at home. She fought hard for her life but in the end the cancer won. The main issue that worked against her was the fact that the cancer was not discovered until it was at a very advanced stage. From this painful experience I learned about the importance of breast self-examination (BSE) in the detection of early stage breast cancer. I have always recommended it to my students. It's important to familiarize yourself with your breasts so that you know how things normally look. This will enable you to more readily detect any change, such as a lump, dimpling, or skin irritation. However, the truth is that it wasn't until I met Stef Woods in the fall of 2010 that I realized just how important BSE really is. Stef had been diagnosed with breast cancer only 7 months before I met her and she had already been through countless rounds of chemotherapy.

What makes Stef's story so important for you to hear is that she found the first lump in her breast when she was 25 years old. Stef had always been vigilant about breast self-exams, mostly because her mother had died of cancer 13 years earlier. Thankfully, the lump she found the first time was not cancerous. A few years later she found another lump and once again, it was not cancerous. However, the third time she found a lump she knew her luck might not hold out. Her doctor called to share her test results when she was getting a haircut. As she put the phone to her ear, she was keenly aware of her heart racing:

When I answered the phone, my first thought was that it was weird that my doctor didn't say everything was fine right off the bat. Instead, she asked how I was. Holding the phone was difficult because I was shaking so badly. "Your test is positive. You have breast cancer," she said. I talked to her for a few more moments, got up from the chair, walked

Hill Creek Pictures/Getty Images

to the back room of the salon, and began to cry. In some ways, I had known something was seriously wrong before she told me. Of course I had found the lump, but in addition to that, my dog, Flake, had recently begun sleeping by my right breast. This was strange since she always slept at my feet. They say dogs can sense cancer. Over the next 7 months, I learned many important lessons about life—I was forced to find strength I never knew I had, but I also realized the incredible power of friendship.

When I interviewed Stef for this video, she was receiving her last round of chemotherapy before beginning radiation the following week. I think you will find our conversation both enlightening and encouraging. ▌▌

Janell Caush

"Your test is positive. You have breast cancer."
—CHAPTER OPENING VIDEO

View in Video

To watch the entire interview, go to Psychology CourseMate at **login.cengagebrain.com.**

For many years, only physicians were thought to be privileged enough to know about the human body. Today, we realize how important it is for all of us to understand how our bodies function. Considering the number of sex manuals and guides that line the shelves of American bookstores, it may seem surprising that the majority of questions that students ask about human sexuality are fundamental, biological questions.[1] Yet, it becomes less surprising when we realize that many parents are still uncomfortable discussing sexual biology with their children, and younger people often do not know whom to approach or are embarrassed about the questions they have (we discuss this further in Chapter 8). Questions about sexual biology are natural, however, for the reproductive system is complex, and there are probably more myths and misinformation about sexual biology than any other single part of human functioning.

Children are naturally curious about their genitals and spend a good deal of time touching and exploring them. However, they are often taught that this exploration is something to be ashamed of. Because girls' genitals are more hidden and recessed, and girls are often discouraged from making a thorough self-examination, they tend to be less familiar with their genitals than are boys. This may be reinforced as females mature and are taught that menstruation is "dirty." These attitudes are reflected in ads for "feminine hygiene" products, which suggest that the vagina is unsanitary and has an unpleasant smell.

In this chapter, we explore female anatomy and physiology. Although there are many similarities to male anatomy and physiology, as you will soon learn, female anatomy and physiology are a bit more complicated. Unlike males, females have fluctuating hormone levels, monthly menstruation cycles, and experience menopause. In Chapter 6, we will explore male sexual anatomy and physiology.

▶ THE FEMALE SEXUAL and Reproductive System

It is important for both women and men to understand the structure of the female reproductive system, which is really a marvel of biological engineering. Women who have not done a thorough genital self-examination should do so, not only because it is an important part of the body to learn to appreciate but because any changes in genital appearance should be brought to the attention of a **gynecologist** or other health care provider. See the accompanying Sex in Real Life for instructions on performing a genital self-examination.

▶▶ EXTERNAL Sex Organs

Although many people refer to the female's external sex organs collectively as the "vagina," this is technically incorrect; the more accurate term for the whole region is **vulva.** The vulva, as we will see, is made up of the mons veneris, the labia majora and labia minora, the vestibule, the perineum, and the clitoris (see Figure 5.1). Although the vagina does open into the vulva, it is mainly an internal sex organ and is discussed in the next section.

The Mons Veneris

The fatty cushion resting over the front surface of the pubic bone is called the **mons veneris** or **mons pubis.** The mons veneris becomes covered with pubic hair after puberty, and although it is considered a stimulating place to caress during lovemaking, it serves largely as a protective cushion for the genitals, especially during sexual activity.

All of the women in these photos have "normal" bodies. Individual differences in weight and size and shape of hips, breasts, and thighs, and even pubic hair are normal.

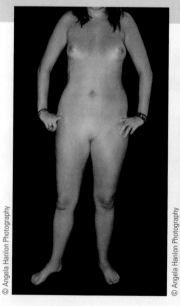 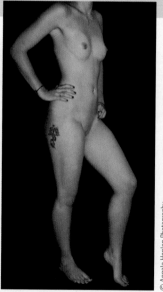 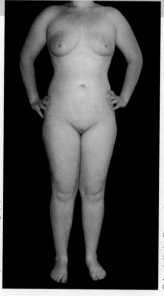 

© Angela Hanlon Photography

[1] Consider the questions two students asked during a lecture on human sexual biology: Can a woman pee with a tampon in? (Yes.) Can a man pee with an erection? (Not that well.) If you didn't know the answers to these questions, this chapter and Chapter 6 can help.

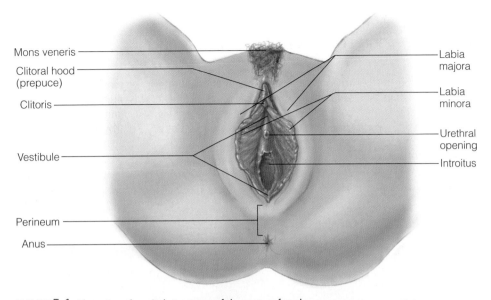

FIGURE **5.1** The external genital structures of the mature female. Copyright © Cengage Learning 2013

Labels on figure:
Mons veneris
Clitoral hood (prepuce)
Clitoris
Vestibule
Perineum
Anus
Labia majora
Labia minora
Urethral opening
Introitus

The Labia Majora

The **labia majora** (LAY-bee-uh muh-JOR-uh) (outer lips) are two longitudinal folds of fatty tissue that extend from the mons, frame the rest of the female genitalia, and meet at the perineum (the tissue between the vagina and the anus). The skin of the outer labia majora is pigmented and covered with hair, whereas the inner surface is hairless and contains sebaceous (oil) glands. During sexual excitement, the labia majora fill with blood and engorge, which makes the entire pubic region seem to swell.

The Labia Minora

The **labia minora** (LAY-bee-uh muh-NOR-uh) (inner lips) are two smaller pink skin folds situated inside the labia majora. They are generally more delicate, shorter, and thinner than the labia majora and join at the clitoris to form the **prepuce** (PREE-peus), the "hood" over the clitoris. The labia minora contain no hair fol-

licles, although they are rich in sebaceous glands. They also contain some erectile tissue and serve to protect the vagina and urethra. During sexual arousal, the labia minora will darken, although the appearance can differ considerably among women.

gynecologist
A physician who specializes in the study and treatment of disorders of the female reproductive system.

vulva
The collective designation for the external genitalia of the female.

mons veneris or mons pubis
The mound of fatty tissue over the female pubic bone, also referred to as mons pubis, meaning "pubic mound."

labia majora
Two longitudinal folds of skin extending downward and backward from the mons pubis of the female.

labia minora
Two small folds of mucous membrane lying within the labia majora of the female.

prepuce
A loose fold of skin that covers the clitoris.

The female vulva comes in various sizes and shapes, and the color and quantity of pubic hair vary as well.

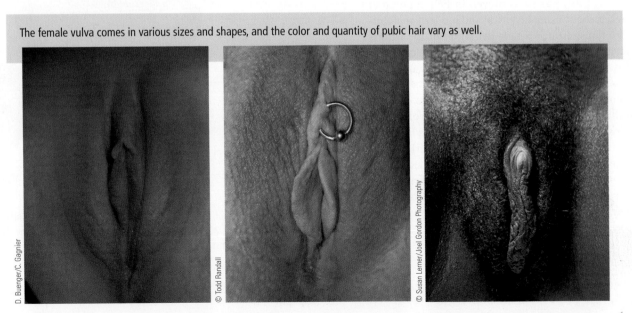

D. Buenger/C. Gagnier

© Todd Randall

© Susan Lerner/Joel Gordon Photography

Female Sexual Anatomy and Physiology

Many female health problems can be identified when changes are detected in the internal or external sexual organs; therefore, self-examination has an important health function as well. If you are female, it will serve you well to follow this simple procedure once a month. If you are male, understanding this procedure will help you better understand why it is so important for females to examine their genitals regularly.

Begin by examining the outside of your genitals; using a hand mirror can help. Using your fingers to spread open the labia majora, try to identify the other external structures—the labia minora, the prepuce, the introitus (opening) of the vagina, and the urethral opening. Look at the way your genitals look while sitting, lying down, standing up, squatting. Feel the different textures of each part of the vagina, and look carefully at the coloration and size of the tissues you can see. Both coloration and size can change with sexual arousal, but such changes are temporary, and the genitals should return

to normal within a couple of hours after sexual activity. Any changes over time in color, firmness, or shape of the genitals should be brought to the attention of a health professional.

Genital self-examination can help a woman become more comfortable with her own body.

If it is not uncomfortable, you may want to move back the prepuce, or hood, over the clitoris and try to see the clitoral glans. Although the clitoris is easier to see when erect, note how it fits beneath the prepuce. Note also whether there is any

whitish material beneath the prepuce; fluids can accumulate and solidify there, and so you should gently clean beneath the prepuce regularly.

If you place a finger inside your vagina, you should be able to feel the pubic bone in the front inside part of your vagina. It is slightly behind the pubic bone that the G-spot is supposed to be, but it is difficult for most women to stimulate the G-spot with their own fingers. Squat and press down with your stomach muscles as you push your fingers deeply in the vagina, and at the top of the vagina you may be able to feel your cervix, which feels a little like the tip of your nose. Note how it feels to touch the cervix (some women have a slightly uncomfortable feeling when their cervix is touched). Feeling comfortable inserting your fingers into your vagina will also help you if you choose a barrier method of birth control, such as the contraceptive sponge or cervical cap, all of which must be inserted deep within the vagina at the cervix (see Chapter 13).

The Clitoris

For a long time, people believed that the **clitoris** (KLIT-uh-rus) was only a small pocket of erectile tissue located under the prepuce. The invisibility of the clitoris led many to believe that this was so. However, in 1991, a group of female researchers, using historical and modern anatomical descriptions, created a new definition of the clitoris that encompasses all of the clitoral structures (see Figure 5.2). This group identified 18 structures of the clitoris—some of which are readily visible, and others that are not (Federation of Feminist Women's Health Centers, 1991). In addition to the glans, the clitoris is composed of a body and paired crura (legs). The bulbs of the clitoris lie under the labia. These bulbs, the glans, the body, and crura form an erectile tissue cluster, which altogether is called the *clitoris*. In 2005, magnetic resonance imaging confirmed this more expansive definition of the clitoris (O'Connell & DeLancey, 2005).

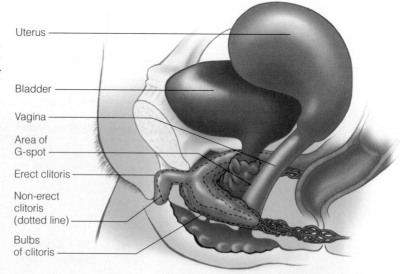

FIGURE **5.2** Side inner view of the erect clitoris. SOURCE: Cass, Vivienne. *The elusive orgasm.* Marlowe & Company, 2007. Copyright © 2007 Marlowe & Company. All rights reserved. Reproduced by permission.

Homologous to the penis, the clitoris is richly supplied with blood vessels, as well as nerve endings. The clitoral glans is a particularly sensitive receptor and transmitter of sexual stimuli. The body, bulbs, and crura enlarge and engorge with blood in much the same way as the penis does during physical arousal. In addition, the clitoris is the only human organ for which the sole function is to bring sexual pleasure (we discuss the clitoris and sexual pleasure in more detail in Chapter 10).

The clitoral glans is difficult to see in many women unless the prepuce is pulled back, although in some women the glans may swell enough during sexual excitement to emerge from under the prepuce (see the accompanying Sex in Real Life). It is easy to feel the clitoral glans, however, by gently grasping the prepuce and rolling it between the fingers. In fact, most women do not enjoy direct stimulation of the glans and prefer stimulation through the prepuce. It is important to clean under the prepuce, for secretions

---

REAL RESEARCH 5.1   The clitoris, although much smaller than the penis, has twice the number of nerve endings (8,000) as the penis (4,000) and has a higher concentration of nerve fibers than anywhere else on the body, including the tongue or fingertips (ANGIER, 1999).

---

can accumulate underneath as a material known as smegma. Smegma can harden and cause pain and, if left uncleaned, can produce an unpleasant odor.

In some cultures, the clitoris is removed surgically in a ritual **circumcision,** often referred to as a **clitorectomy.** Other parts of the vulva can also be removed in a procedure known as **infibulation** (in-fib-you-LAY-shun) (see accompanying Sexual Diversity in Our World).

The Vestibule

The **vestibule** is the name for the entire region between the labia minora and can be clearly seen when the labia are held apart. The vestibule contains the opening of the urethra and the vagina and the ducts of Bartholin's glands.

THE URETHRAL MEATUS   The opening, or meatus (mee-AYE-tuss), to the urethra (yoo-REE-thruh) lies between the vagina and the clitoris. The urethra, which brings urine from the bladder to be excreted, is much shorter in women than in men, in whom it goes through the penis. A shorter urethra allows bacteria greater access into the urinary tract, making women much more susceptible to **urinary tract infections (UTIs)** (Azam, 2000; Kunin, 1997). One

in five women will develop a UTI in her lifetime, and 20% of these women will experience a recurrence of the UTI after treatment (Hooton, 2003). Common symptoms for UTI include pain or burning in the urethra or bladder and an increased urge to urinate. Over-the-counter medication can help decrease pain, but antibiotics are necessary to cure the infection. Consuming cranberry products (i.e., drinks, breads) can be effective in decreasing UTI recurrence (Epp et al., 2010). Scientists are working on a vaccine to prevent UTIs (Serino et al., 2010).

THE INTROITUS AND THE HYMEN   The entrance, or **introitus** (in-TROID-us), of the vagina also lies in the vestibule. The introitus is usually covered at birth by a fold of tissue known as the **hymen** (HIGH-men). The hymen varies in thickness and extent, and is sometimes absent. The center of the hymen is usually perforated, and it is through this perforation that the menstrual flow leaves the vagina and that a tampon is inserted. If the hymen is intact, it will usually rupture easily and tear at several points during the first sexual intercourse, often accompanied by a small amount of blood. If the woman is sexually aroused and well lubricated, the rupture of the hymen usually does not cause more than a brief moment's discomfort. In rare cases, a woman has an **imperforate hymen,** which is usually detected because her menstrual flow is blocked. A simple surgical procedure can open the imperforate hymen.

An intact hymen has been a symbol of "purity" throughout history, a sign that a woman has not engaged in sexual intercourse. In reality, many activities can tear the hymen, including vigorous exercise, horseback or bike riding, masturbation, or the insertion of tampons or other objects into the vagina (Cook & Dickens, 2009). Still, in many cultures during many historical eras, the absence of bloodstained sheets on the wedding night was enough to condemn a woman as "wanton" (promiscuous), and some knowing mothers encouraged their newlywed daughters to have a little vial of blood from a chicken or other animal to pour on the sheet of their bridal bed, just in case. Although virginity "testing" (to check for an intact hymen) is against the law in many parts of the world, including Turkey, Indonesia, and parts of South Africa, illegal virginity tests are still performed. Reconstructive surgery to repair a ruptured hymen, called *hymenoplasty,* is available in many countries, with high demand from Middle Eastern, Korean, and Latina women (Krikorian, 2004). However, many physicians are afraid to perform these surgeries because of fear of repercussions (Essén et al., 2010; O'Connor, 2008).

---

clitoris
An erectile organ of the female located under the prepuce; an organ of sexual pleasure.

circumcision
Surgical removal of the clitoris in women; also referred to as clitorectomy.

clitorectomy
Surgical removal of the clitoris; also referred to as circumcision.

infibulation
The ritual removal of the clitoris, prepuce, and labia, and the sewing together of the vestibule. Although this is practiced in many African societies, today many are working to eliminate the practice.

vestibule
The entire region between the labia minora, including the urethra and introitus.

urinary tract infection (UTI)
Infection of the urinary tract, often resulting in a frequent urge to urinate, painful burning in the bladder or urethra during urination, and fatigue.

introitus
Entrance to the vagina.

hymen
A thin fold of vascularized mucous membrane at the vaginal opening.

imperforate hymen
An abnormally closed hymen that usually does not allow the exit of menstrual fluid.

Female genital mutilation (FGM) involves partial or total removal of the external female genitalia for nonmedical reasons (World Health Organization, 2008). Throughout history, FGM has been performed to distinguish "respectable" women and to ensure and preserve a girl's virginity (Gruenbaum, 2006; O'Connor, 2008). These procedures are also thought to make the female genitals "clean" and "beautiful" by eliminating masculine parts, such as the clitoris (Johansen, 2007). The most common reason given for undergoing such procedures is culture and tradition (Carcopino et al., 2004; Dare et al., 2004).

The World Health Organization has proposed four classifications of FGM:

- Type I: Partial or total removal of the clitoris and/or prepuce (clitorectomy)

- Type II: Partial or total removal of the clitoris and the labia minora with or without excision of the labia majora

- Type III: Narrowing of the vaginal orifice by cutting the labia minora and labia majora with or without excision of clitoris (infibulation)

- Type IV: All other harmful procedures to female genitalia for nonmedical purposes including piercing, pricking, scraping, and cauterization

It is estimated that 130 million women around the world have experienced FGM, and another 2 million girls and young women undergo FGM procedures each year (Dattijo et al., 2010). Although FGM occurs all over the world, it is most prevalent in the eastern, northeastern, and western regions of Africa, some countries in Asia and the Middle East, and among certain immigrant communities in North America and Europe (World Health Organization, 2008).

FGM procedures are usually done on girls between the ages of 4 and 8; although in some cultures, it is performed later (Dare et al., 2004). Procedures are often done without anesthesia or antiseptic, and the majority of procedures are performed by medically untrained personnel (Dare et al., 2004). The most severe type of circumcision involves the complete removal of the clitoris and labia minora, and also the scraping of the labia majora with knives, broken bottles, or razor blades (Carcopino et al., 2004). The remaining tissue is sewn together, leaving a matchstick-sized hole to allow for the passing of urine and menstrual blood. The young girl's legs are then bound together with rope, and she is immobilized for anywhere from 14 to 40 days for the circumcision to heal. The tighter the girl's infibulation, the higher the bride price will be for her.

FGM can cause extreme pain, urinary complications or dysfunction, shock, hemorrhage, infection, scarring, recurrent urinary infections, retention of menses at menarche, vulval cysts, and pelvic inflammatory disease (Nour, 2004; World Health Organization, 2008). Of these symptoms, severe pain and bleeding are most common (Dare et al., 2004).

There is ongoing controversy about what Americans and others should do to try to discourage this practice (Dattijo et al., 2010; O'Connor, 2008). The United States has been strongly opposed to the practice of FGM and has worked hard to help reduce the practice. In 2008, the World Health Organization and other United Nations agencies launched a new Interagency Statement on Eliminating Female Genital Mutilation. They hope to see a worldwide end to the practice of FGM by 2015.

© Ulrike Kotermann/epa/Corbis

Bartholin's glands
A pair of glands on either side of the vaginal opening that open by a duct into the space between the hymen and the labia minora; also referred to as the greater vestibular glands.

perineum
Area between the vagina and the anus.

vagina
A thin-walled muscular tube that leads from the uterus to the vestibule and is used for sexual intercourse and as a passageway for menstrual fluid, sperm, and a newborn baby.

BARTHOLIN'S GLANDS The "greater vestibular glands," or **Bartholin's** (BAR-tha-lenz) **glands,** are bean-shaped glands with ducts that empty into the vestibule in the middle of the labia minora. Historically, Bartholin's glands have been presumed to provide vaginal lubrication during sexual arousal; however, research by Masters and Johnson (see Chapter 2) found that lubrication is a result of vaginal transudation. The Bartholin's glands can become infected and form a cyst or abscess, causing pain and swelling in the labial and vaginal areas. Bartholin gland cysts are most common in women of reproductive age and are typically treated with antibiotics and/or surgery (Bhide et al., 2010).

The Anus and Perineum

The anus is the external opening of the rectum through which feces is expelled. The area of tissue between the vagina and the anus is called the **perineum** (pear-uh-NEE-um), and research has found this area is twice as long in men as in women (McEwen & Renner, 2006). This may be because of fetal hormonal exposure. The perineum is rich with nerve endings, and some men and women like to have this area stroked during sexual behavior. During childbirth, however, care must be taken so that the perineal tissue does not tear, which we will discuss further in Chapter 12.

▶▶ INTERNAL Sex Organs

Now that we've covered the female's external sex organs, let's move inside and explore the internal sex organs. The internal female sex organs include the vagina, uterus, cervix, Fallopian tubes, and ovaries (see Figure 5.3).

The Vagina

The **vagina** is a thin-walled tube extending from the cervix of the uterus to the external genitalia; it serves as the female organ of intercourse, a passageway for the arriving sperm, and a canal through which menstrual fluid and babies can pass from the uterus. It is tilted toward the back in most women and thus forms a 90-degree angle with the uterus, which is commonly tilted forward (see Figure 5.3). The vagina is approximately 4 inches in length when relaxed but contains numerous folds that help it expand somewhat like an accordion. The vagina can expand to accommodate a penis during intercourse and can stretch four to five times its normal size during childbirth.

The vagina does not contain glands but lubricates through small openings on the vaginal walls during engorgement (almost as if the vagina is sweating) and by mucus produced from glands on the cervix. Although the first third of the vaginal tube is well endowed with nerve endings, the inner two thirds are practically without tactile sensation; in fact, minor surgery can be done on the inner part of the vagina without anesthesia.

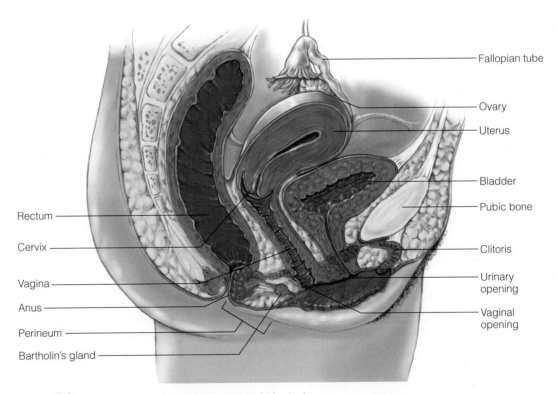

Fallopian tube
Ovary
Uterus
Bladder
Pubic bone
Clitoris
Urinary opening
Vaginal opening
Rectum
Cervix
Vagina
Anus
Perineum
Bartholin's gland

FIGURE **5.3** The female internal reproductive system (side view). Copyright © Cengage Learning 2013

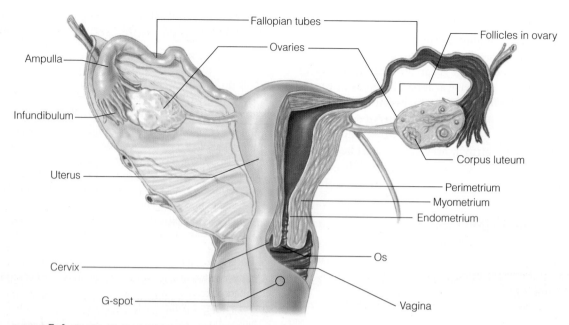

FIGURE 5.4 The female internal reproductive system (front view). Copyright © Cengage Learning 2013

A spot about the size of a dime or quarter in the lower third of the front part of the vagina, the **Gräfenberg spot (G-spot),** was first described by Ernest Gräfenberg in 1950. The G-spot is found about 2 or 3 inches up the anterior (front or stomach) side of the vagina, just past the pubic bone (see Figure 5.4; Whipple, 2000). The existence of the G-spot has been a controversial issue in the field of human sexuality for many years (Buisson et al., 2010). Although some women report pleasurable sensations when this area is stimulated (Foldes & Buisson, 2009; Jannini et al., 2010), there has never been any scientific proof of its existence (Pastor, 2010). Today, growing research on clitoral structures indicates that increased sensitivity in the G-spot area may actually be caused by stimulation of the bulbs of the clitoris (Foldes & Buisson, 2009).

> During childbirth, **the cervix softens to** allow **the baby to pass through.**

The Uterus

The **uterus** is a thick-walled, hollow, muscular organ in the pelvis sandwiched between the bladder in front and the rectum behind. It is approximately the shape of an inverted pear, with a dome-shaped top (fundus), a hollow body, and the doughnut-shaped cervix at the bottom The uterus has several functions: It undergoes a cycle of change every month that leads to menstruation, and it provides a path for sperm to reach the **ovum,** which returns to the uterus after it is fertilized and implants itself in the uterine wall. The uterus also nourishes and protects the developing fetus during gestation and provides the contractions for expulsion of the mature fetus during labor. The uterus is about 3 inches long and flares to about 2 inches wide, but it increases greatly in size and weight during and after a pregnancy, and atrophies after menopause.

The uterine wall is about 1 inch thick and made up of three layers (see Figure 5.4). The outer layer, or **perimetrium,** is part of the tissue that covers most abdominal organs. The muscular layer of the uterus, the **myometrium,** contracts to expel menstrual fluid and to push the fetus out of the womb during delivery. The inner layer of the uterus, the **endometrium,** responds to fluctuating hormone levels, and its outer portion is shed with each menstrual cycle.

The Cervix

The **cervix** (SERV-ix) is the lower portion of the uterus that contains the opening, or **os,** leading into the body of the uterus. It is through the os that menstrual fluid flows out of the uterus and that sperm gain entrance. Glands of the cervix secrete mucus with varying properties during the monthly cycle; during **ovulation,** the mucus helps sperm transport through the os, and during infertile periods, it can block the sperm from entering. During childbirth, the cervix softens and the os dilates to allow the baby to pass through. The cervix can be seen with a mirror during a pelvic examination, and women should not hesitate to ask their gynecologist or other medical professional to show it to them. The cervix can also be felt at the top end of the vagina.

Gräfenberg spot (G-spot)
A structure that is said to lie on the anterior (front) wall of the vagina and is reputed to be a seat of sexual pleasure when stimulated.

uterus
The hollow muscular organ in females that is the site of menstruation, implantation of the fertilized ovum, and labor; also referred to as the womb.

ovum
The female reproductive cell or gamete; plural is ova.

perimetrium
The outer wall of the uterus.

myometrium
The smooth muscle layer of the uterus.

endometrium
The mucous membrane lining the uterus.

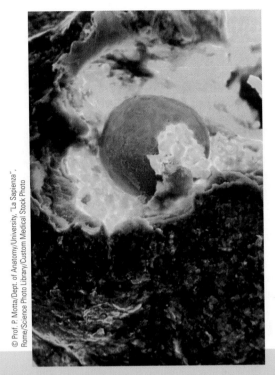

The release of a mature ovum at ovulation is shown. The ovum (red) is surrounded by remnants of cells and liquid from the ruptured ovarian follicle. Mature ova develop in the ovaries from follicles that remained dormant until sexual maturity.

The Fallopian Tubes

Fallopian (fuh-LOH-pee-un) **tubes,** also called **oviducts,** are 4-inch-long, trumpet-shaped tubes that extend laterally from the sides of the uterus. From the side of the uterus, the tube expands into an ampulla, which curves around to a trumpet-shaped end, the **infundibulum** (in-fun-DIB-bue-lum). At the end of the infundibulum are finger-like projections that curl around the ovary, poised to accept **ova** when they are released (see Figure 5.4).

Once a month, an ovary releases an ovum that is swept into the Fallopian tube by the waving action of the **fimbriae** (FIM-bree-ee). The fimbriae sense the chemical messages released from the ovary that signal the release of the ovum and begin a series of muscular contractions to help move the ovum down the tube. If the Fallopian tube is long and flexible, it may even be able to catch the released ovum from the opposite ovary; some women with a single active ovary on one side and a single functioning Fallopian tube on the other have become pregnant (Nilsson, 1990).

The inner surfaces of the Fallopian tubes are covered by cilia (hairlike projections); the constant beating action of the cilia creates a current along which the ovum is moved toward the uterus. The entire transit time from ovulation until arrival inside the uterus is normally about 3 days. Fertilization of the ovum usually takes place in the ampulla because, after the first 12 to 24 hours, postovulation fertilization is no longer possible. Occasionally, the fertilized ovum implants in the Fallopian tube instead of the uterus, causing a potentially dangerous ectopic pregnancy (see Chapter 12).

The Ovaries

The mature ovary is a light gray structure most commonly described as the size and shape of a large almond shell. With age, the ovaries become smaller and firmer, and after menopause, they may become difficult for gynecologists to feel during an examination. The ovaries have dual responsibilities: to produce ova and to secrete hormones.

The ovary is the repository of **oocytes** (OH-oh-sites), also known as ova, or eggs, in the female. A woman is born with approximately 250,000 ova in each ovary, each sitting in its own primary follicle (Rome, 1998). Approximately 300 to 500 of these will develop into mature eggs during a woman's reproductive years (Macklon & Fauser, 2000). The primary follicle contains an immature ovum surrounded by a thin layer of follicular cells. Follicle-stimulating hormone (FSH) and luteinizing hormone (LH) are released in sequence by the pituitary gland during each menstrual cycle, causing about 20 primary follicles at a time to begin maturing. Usually only one follicle finishes maturing each month, which is then termed a *secondary follicle,* containing a secondary oocyte. At ovulation, the secondary follicle bursts, and the ovum begins its journey down the Fallopian tube. The surface of a mature ovary is thus usually pitted and dimpled at sites of previous ovulations.

Ovulation can occur each month from either the right or left ovary. No one knows why one or the other ovary releases an ovum any given month; sometimes they take turns, and sometimes they do not. It seems to be mostly a matter of chance. If one ovary is removed, however, the other ovary will often ovulate every month (Nilsson, 1990). The ovaries are also the female's most important producer of female sex hormones, such as estrogen, which we discuss later in this chapter.

cervix	os	Fallopian tubes	infundibulum	fimbriae
The doughnut-shaped bottom part of the uterus that protrudes into the top of the vagina.	The opening of the cervix that allows passage between the vagina and the uterus.	Two ducts that transport ova from the ovary to the uterus; also referred to as oviducts.	The funnel- or trumpet-shaped open end of the Fallopian tubes.	The branched, fingerlike border at the end of each Fallopian tube.
	ovulation	**oviducts**	**ova**	**oocyte**
	The phase of the menstrual cycle in which an ovum is released.	Another name for the Fallopian tubes.	Two or more ovum; singular is ovum.	A cell from which an ovum develops.

THE BREASTS

Breasts, or mammary glands, are modified sweat glands that produce milk to nourish a newborn child. The breasts contain fatty tissue and milk-producing glands, and are capped by a **nipple** surrounded by a round, pigmented area called the **areola** (ah-REE-oh-luh). Each breast contains between 15 and 20 lobes, made up of a number of compartments that contain alveoli, the milk-secreting glands. Alveoli empty into secondary tubules, which, in turn, pass the milk into the mammary ducts and then into the lactiferous sinuses, where the milk is stored until the lactiferous ducts release it from the nipple (Figure 5.5). When **lactation** begins, infant suckling stimulates the posterior pituitary gland to release **prolactin,** which signals milk synthesis, and **oxytocin,** which allows the milk to be ejected.

Most people see the breasts as an erogenous zone and include stimulation of the breasts in sexual activity. Some women can even experience orgasm from breast and nipple stimulation alone. However, many women in American society are uncomfortable about the size and shape of their breasts. Because breasts are a constant source of attention in our society and are considered an important part of a woman's attractiveness, women may worry that their breasts are unattractive, too small, or too large. As of 2010, breast augmentation was the most commonly performed cosmetic procedure among American women (Pelosi & Pelosi, 2010). In fact, the number of women undergoing breast augmentation more than tripled from 1997 to 2008 (American Society for Aesthetic Plastic Surgery, 2009).

REAL RESEARCH 5.2 Female athletes have been found to have better clitoral blood flow than nonathletes, which has been found to contribute to better sexual health and functioning (Karatas et al., 2010).

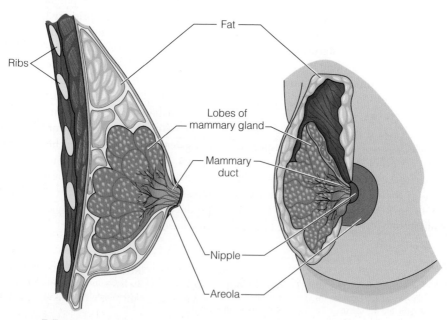

FIGURE **5.5** The female breast. Copyright © Cengage Learning 2013

nipple
A pigmented, wrinkled protuberance on the surface of the breast that contains ducts for the release of milk.

areola
The pigmented ring around the nipple of the breast.

lactation
The collective name for milk creation, secretion, and ejection from the nipple.

prolactin
A hormone secreted by the pituitary gland that initiates and maintains milk secretion.

oxytocin
A hormone secreted by the hypothalamus that stimulates contraction of both the uterus for delivery of the newborn and the mammary gland ducts for lactation.

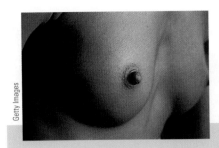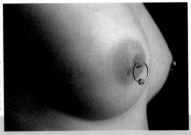

The female breast is mostly fatty tissue and can take various shapes and sizes.

◀ review QUESTIONS

1 Identify and discuss the functions of the external female sexual organs.

2 Identify and discuss the functions of the internal female sexual organs.

3 Explain what breasts are composed of and the various structures contained in them.

4 Discuss female erogenous zones.

▶ THE FEMALE Maturation Cycle

Now that we've discussed the female sexual and reproductive system, let's explore female maturation. The female reproductive system undergoes cyclic hormonal events that lead to pubertal changes, menstruation, and eventually, menopause.

▶▶ FEMALE Puberty

After birth, the female's sexual development progresses slowly until puberty. In the past, the first stirrings of puberty began somewhere between 10 and 14 years old, but research has found that girls are beginning puberty earlier than ever before (Biro et al., 2010). The proportion of girls who experience the physical changes of puberty (such as breast and pubic hair development) at ages 7 and 8 years old is greater today than was reported on girls born 10 to 30 years ago. More research is needed to examine the reasons why girls might be beginning puberty earlier. Experts are looking at a number of factors that may be contributing to this trend, including diet, obesity, and/or exposure to environmental chemicals.

No one really knows how the body senses it is time for puberty to begin. The onset of puberty is often related to weight—a girl typically must have a certain body weight and appropriate fat-to-muscle ratio (Loucks & Nattiv, 2005; Warren et al., 2002). Girls who are overweight typically begin puberty earlier than those who are average or underweight (Blell et al., 2008; Kaplowitz, 2008). The onset of puberty can also vary with race and ethnicity. By the age of 8 years old, 43% of Black, non-Hispanic, 31% of Hispanic, and 18% of White girls have breast development indicating early puberty (Biro et al., 2010). These racial and ethnic differences may be re-

*Estrogen is responsible for the **development and maturation** of female sexual characteristics.*

lated to height and weight differences (Adair & Gordon-Larsen, 2001; Freedman et al., 2002). Other factors, such as genetic mutations (Teles et al., 2008), stressful home environments (Ellis & Essex, 2007; K. Kim & Smith, 1999; Ravert & Martin, 1997), and insecure maternal attachments in early childhood (Belsky et al., 2010) have also been found to contribute to early puberty in girls. More research is needed to explore these possible links.

When puberty begins, a girl's internal clock signals the pituitary gland to begin secreting the hormones FSH and LH, which stimulate the ovaries to produce estrogen while the girl sleeps. As puberty continues, the ovaries, in response to stimulation by the pituitary gland, begin to release more and more estrogen into the circulatory system. Estrogen is responsible for the development and maturation of female primary and secondary sexual characteristics. Under its influence, the Fallopian tubes, uterus, and vagina all mature and increase in size. The breasts also begin to develop, as fat deposits increase and the elaborate duct system develops. The pelvis broadens and changes from a narrow, funnel-like outlet to a broad oval outlet, flaring the hips. The skin remains soft and smooth under estrogen's influence, fat cells increase in number in the buttocks and thighs, and pubic hair develops. Certain bones in the body, which are responsible for height, fuse with the bone shaft, and growth stops. However, if there was a delay or absence of estrogen, females usually grow several inches taller than average.

The changes that accompany puberty prepare the woman for mature sexuality, pregnancy, and childbirth. At some point during puberty, usually at about the age of 11 or 12, the woman will begin to ovulate. Most women are unable to feel any internal signs during ovulation. In a few women, however, a slight pain or sensation, referred to as **mittelschmerz,** accompanies ovulation. The pain may result from a transitory irritation caused by the small amount of blood and fluid released at the site of the ruptured follicle.

For most girls, the beginning of ovulation often closely corresponds to **menarche** (MEN-are-kee), the first menstrual period. However, some may begin menstruating a few months before their first ovulation, whereas others may ovulate a few times before their first full menstrual cycle. In the first year after menarche, 80% of menstrual cycles are anovulatory (do not involve ovulation; Oriel & Schrager, 1999).

With minor variations, the average age of menarche in most developed countries is 12 to 13 years, but the age of menarche has been gradually decreasing. One hundred years ago, the average age of first menstruation was about 16 years (Patton & Viner, 2007; Remsberg et al., 2005). Earlier we discussed racial and ethnic differences in the onset of puberty. The ADD Health (2002) data, which we discussed in Chapter 2, enabled researchers to compare racial and ethnic differences in the onset of menstruation. On average, menarche age is significantly earlier in Black, non-Hispanic girls than White or Hispanic girls (Chumlea et al., 2003; Freedman et al., 2002; Kaplowitz et al., 2001) and significantly later in Asian girls (Adair & Gordon-Larsen, 2001). In less-developed countries, the age of menarche is later. For example, in rural Chile, the average age of menarche is close to 14 years old (Dittmar, 2000). Environmental factors, such as high altitudes and poor nutrition, can delay the age at which a girl begins menstruating. There is also a heritability component to the age at which a woman begins menstruating—many girls reach menarche at approximately the same age as their biological mothers (Towne et al., 2005). An earlier age of menarche in biological mothers has been found to be related to increased risk of obesity in male and female offspring (see Figure 5.6).

"Although I was a little nervous when I saw the blood the first time, I was also excited."
—First Periods

View in Video
To watch the entire interview, go to Psychology CourseMate at **login.cengagebrain.com.**

REAL RESEARCH 5.3   Studies evaluating voice changes in women throughout the menstrual cycle have found that a woman's voice is rated by men as significantly more attractive when she is ovulating (Pipitone & Gallup, 2007). This may be because of the fact that the sound of a woman's voice serves as a subconscious sign of her fitness and fertility. No differences in ratings of voice attractiveness were found for women who were using birth control pills.

In some cultures in the past, as soon as a girl reached menarche, she was considered ready to marry and begin bearing children. In American culture, most people believe that there is a difference between being physiologically capable of bearing children and being psychologically ready for sexual intercourse and childbearing. In Chapter 8, we will discuss the psychological and emotional changes of female puberty.

▶▶ MENSTRUATION

Menstruation (also referred to as a "period") is the name for the monthly bleeding that the majority of healthy women of reproductive age experience. The menstrual cycle lasts from 24 to 35 days, but the average is 28 (meaning there are 28 days from the first day of bleeding to the next first day of bleeding). During the cycle, the lining of the uterus builds up and prepares for a pregnancy. When there is no pregnancy, menstruation occurs, and the lining of the uterus is released in the form of blood and tissue. A cycle of hormones controls the buildup and the release. The biological purpose of menstrual cycles is to enable a woman to become pregnant.

The menstrual cycle can be divided into four general phases: follicular, ovulatory, luteal, and menstrual (see Figure 5.7). The **follicular phase** begins after the last menstruation has been completed and lasts any-

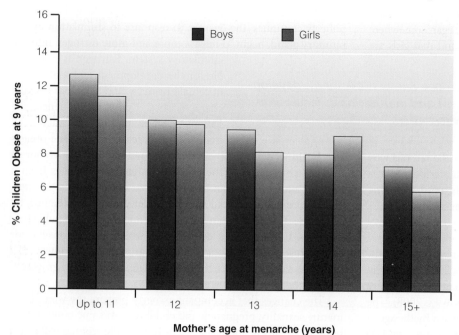

FIGURE **5.6** Prevalence of obesity in children at age 9, by mother's age at menarche (Ong et al., 2007).

Menstrual cycle and hormone cycle

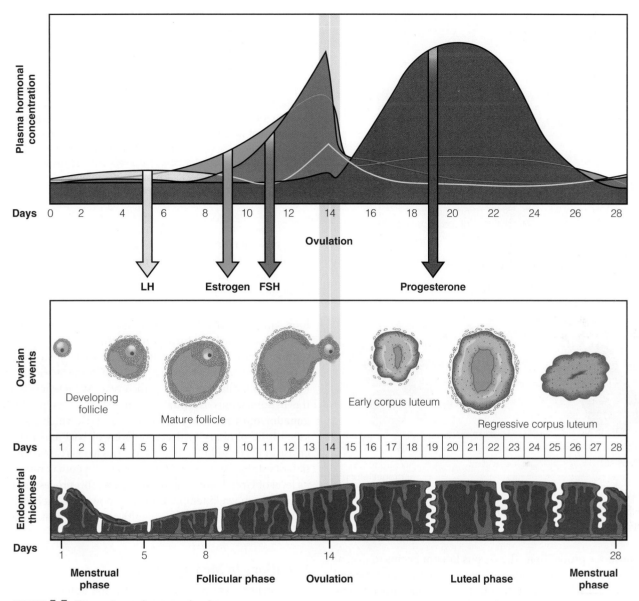

FIGURE **5.7** The ovarian and menstrual cycles. Copyright © Cengage Learning 2013

where from 6 to 13 days. Only a thin layer of endometrial cells remains from the last menstruation. As the follicles in the ovaries begin to ripen with the next cycle's ova, estrogen released by the ovaries stimulates regrowth of the endometrium's outer layer, to about 2 to 5 millimeters thick.

During the **ovulatory phase,** an ovum is released, usually about the 14th day of the cycle. The particulars of ovulation were described in the preceding section on the ovaries and Fallopian tubes. The third phase is the **luteal phase.** Immediately after

ovulation, a small, pouchlike gland, the **corpus luteum,** forms on the ovary. The corpus luteum secretes additional progesterone and estrogen for 10 to 12 days, which causes further growth of the cells in the endometrium and increases the blood supply to the lining of the uterus. The endometrium reaches a thickness of 4 to 6 millimeters during this stage (about a quarter of an inch) in preparation to receive and nourish a fertilized egg. If fertilization does not occur, however, the high levels of progesterone and estrogen signal the hypothalamus to decrease LH and

mittelschmerz
German for "middle pain." A pain in the abdomen or pelvis that some women feel at ovulation.

menarche
The start of menstrual cycling, usually during early puberty.

follicular phase
First phase of the menstrual cycle that begins after the last menstruation has been completed.

ovulatory phase
The second stage of the general menstrual cycle, when the ovum is released.

luteal phase
Third phase of the menstrual cycle, following ovulation, when the corpus luteum forms.

corpus luteum
A yellowish endocrine gland in the ovary formed when a follicle has discharged its secondary oocyte.

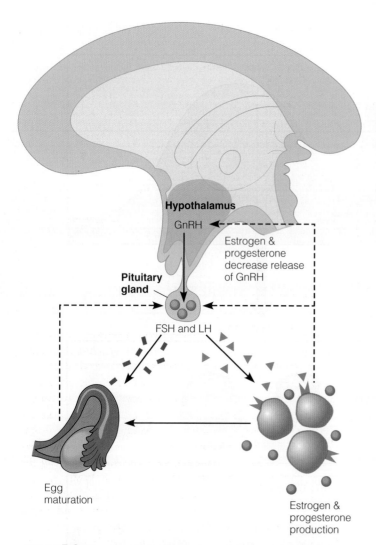

FIGURE 5.8 The cycle of female hormones. Copyright © Cengage Learning 2013

nificantly smaller; see Chapter 13.) Some women lose too much blood during their menstruation and may develop **anemia.** For most women, menstrual flow stops about 3 to 7 days after the onset of menstruation.

This monthly cyclical process involves a **negative feedback loop,** in which one set of hormones controls the production of another set, which, in turn, controls the first (see Figure 5.8). In the menstrual cycle, the negative feedback loop works like this: Estrogen and progesterone are produced by the ovaries at different levels during different parts of the cycle. As these levels increase, the hypothalamus is stimulated to decrease its production of **gonadotropin-releasing hormone (GnRH),** which sends a message to the pituitary to decrease levels of FSH and LH. The decrease in FSH and LH signals the ovaries to decrease their production of estrogen and progesterone, so the hypothalamus increases its level of GnRH, and it all begins again. This process is similar to a thermostat; when temperature goes down, the thermostat kicks on and raises the temperature, until the rising heat turns off the thermostat and the heat begins slowly to fall.

Variations in Menstruation

Amenorrhea (Aye-men-oh-REE-uh), the absence of menstruation, can take two forms. In **primary amenorrhea,** a woman never even begins menstruation, whereas in **secondary amenorrhea,** previously normal menses stop before the woman has gone through menopause. Primary amenorrhea may result from malformed or underdeveloped female reproductive organs, glandular disorders, general poor health, emotional factors, or excessive exercise. The most common cause of secondary amenorrhea is pregnancy, although it can also occur with emotional factors, certain diseases, surgical removal of the ovaries or uterus, hormonal imbalance caused naturally or through the ingestion of steroids, excessive exercise, or eating disorders. For example, almost all women with anorexia nervosa will experience amenor-

other hormone production. The corpus luteum begins to degenerate as LH levels decline. Approximately 2 days before the end of the normal cycle, the secretion of estrogen and progesterone decreases sharply as the corpus luteum becomes inactive, and the menstrual phase begins.

In the **menstrual phase,** the endometrial cells shrink and slough off (this flow is referred to as **menses** [MEN-seez]). The uterus begins to contract in an effort to expel the dead tissue along with a small quantity of blood. (It is these contractions that cause menstrual cramps, which can be painful in some women). During menstruation, approximately 35 milliliters of blood, 35 milliliters of fluid, some mucus, and the lining of the uterus (about 2 to 4 tablespoons of fluid in all) are expelled from the uterine cavity through the cervical os and ultimately the vagina. (If a woman is using oral contraceptives, the amount may be sig-

menstrual phase	**menses**	**anemia**	**negative feedback loop**	**gonadotropin-releasing hormone (GnRH)**
Final stage of the general menstrual cycle, when the endometrial cells shrink and slough off.	The blood and tissue discharged from the uterus during menstruation.	A deficiency in the oxygen-carrying material of the blood, often causing symptoms of fatigue, irritability, dizziness, memory problems, shortness of breath, and headaches.	When one set of hormones controls the production of another set, which, in turn, controls the first, thus regulating the monthly cycle of hormones.	A hormone produced in the hypothalamus that triggers the onset of puberty and sexual development, and is responsible for the release of FSH and LH from the pituitary.

rhea (Pinheiro et al., 2007). When they regain weight, they often will not begin ovulating and menstruating, and may need drugs to induce ovulation and start their periods again (Ayala, 2009). If amenorrhea persists, a physician should be consulted.

Menstrual cramps are caused by prostaglandins, which stimulate the uterus to contract and expel the endometrial lining during menstruation. The uterine muscles are powerful (remember that the muscles help push an infant out at birth), and the menstrual contractions can be strong and sometimes quite painful. Although the majority of women experience mild-to-moderate cramping during menstruation, some experience **dysmenorrhea** (dis-men-uh-REE-uh), or extremely painful menstruation. Dysmenorrhea may be caused by a variety of inflammations, constipation, or even psychological stress. Poor eating habits, an increase in stress, alcohol use, insufficient sleep, and a lack of exercise can aggravate the problem. Reducing salt, sugar, and caffeine intake; moderate exercise; relaxation; warm baths; yoga; and gentle massage of the lower back sometimes help, as do antiprostaglandin pain relievers, such as ibuprofen. Newer research has also found that acupressure may also be effective in reducing dysmenorrhea (Liu et al., 2011; Mirbagher-Ajorpaz et al., 2010).

Dysfunctional uterine bleeding includes irregular periods or unusually heavy periods and is a common complaint among women (Maness et al., 2010). Dysfunctional uterine bleeding is most common in women at both ends of the age spectrum (younger and older women) and typically occurs when the body does not respond to key hormones, such as estrogen and progesterone, resulting in anovulatory cycles. Causes include stress, excessive exercise, significant weight loss, vaginal injury, hormonal imbalances, and/or chronic illness (Estephan & Sinert, 2010).

There are no overall ethnic differences in the prevalence of premenstrual symptoms.

Dysfunctional uterine bleeding can affect a woman's quality of life and can lead to both medical and social complications (Frick et al., 2009). Some women suffer from excessive menstrual flow, known as **menorrhagia** (men-or-RAY-gee-uh). Oral contraceptives may be prescribed to make menses lighter and more regular (Read, 2010). Later in this chapter, we discuss some newer options that women have to avoid menstruation altogether.

Premenstrual Syndrome and Premenstrual Dysphoric Disorder

The term **premenstrual syndrome (PMS)** refers to physical or emotional symptoms that appear in some women during the latter half of the menstrual cycle. Estimates of the numbers of women who experience PMS vary widely depending on how it is defined, but only a small number of women find it debilitating. Research has found that the majority of women experience emotional, behavioral, or physical premenstrual symptoms (Boyle et al., 1987;

View in Video
To watch the entire interview, go to Psychology CourseMate at **login.cengagebrain.com**.

"The week before my period I just feel so out of control."
—PMS: REAL OR IMAGINED?

Shulman, 2010). Common complaints include feelings of sadness, irritability, restlessness, and sleep problems (including trouble falling asleep and also excessive sleepiness; Strine et al., 2005).

Interestingly, although there are no overall ethnic differences in the prevalence of premenstrual symptoms, research has found some differences in the types of symptoms that women experience. For example, Black women have been found to experience more food cravings during the premenstrual week than White women (Stout et al., 1986), whereas White women are more likely to report premenstrual mood changes and weight gain (Woods et al., 1982). Hispanic women report more severe symptoms associated with premenstrual times, whereas Asian women report less (Sternfeld et al., 2002). Keep in mind, however, that we don't know if these data are more reflective of variations in subjects' comfort in reporting symptoms or symptom severity.

The existence of PMS has been controversial (Knaapen & Weisz, 2008). The term became well-known in the early 1980s when two separate British courts reduced the sentences of women who had killed their husbands on the grounds that severe PMS reduced their capacity to control their behavior (Rittenhouse, 1991). Although this defense never succeeded in a U.S. trial, publicity over the British trials led to much discussion about this syndrome. Some women objected to the idea of PMS, suggesting that it would reinforce the idea that women were "out of control" once a month and were slaves to their biology, whereas others supported it as an important biological justification of the symptoms they were experiencing each month. The extreme views of PMS have been tempered somewhat, and women who suffer from it can now find sympathetic physicians and a number of suggestions for coping strategies.

---

primary amenorrhea
The lifelong absence of menstruation.

secondary amenorrhea
The absence of menstruation after a period of normal menses.

dysmenorrhea
Painful menstruation.

dysfunctional uterine bleeding
Menstrual bleeding for long periods of time or intermittent bleeding throughout a cycle.

menorrhagia
Excessive menstrual flow.

premenstrual syndrome (PMS)
A group of physiological and psychological symptoms related to the postovulation phase of the menstrual cycle.

In 1994, the American Psychiatric Association introduced the diagnosis of **premenstrual dysphoric disorder (PMDD),** used to identify the most debilitating cases of PMS (Rapkin & Winer, 2008). PMDD will be listed in the *DSM*-5, the latest guide to accepted disorders of the American Psychiatric Association. It is estimated that approximately 3% to 8% of women meet the criteria for PMDD (Breech & Braverman, 2010; Rapkin et al., 2011). Overall, the research shows that Black women are less likely than White women to experience PMDD (Pilver et al., 2010).

There are four main groups of PMDD symptoms—mood, behavioral, somatic, and cognitive. Mood symptoms include depression, irritability, mood swings, sadness, and hostility. Behavioral symptoms include becoming argumentative, increased eating, and a decreased interest in activities. Somatic symptoms include abdominal bloating, fatigue, headaches, **hot flashes,** insomnia, backache, constipation, breast tenderness, and a craving for carbohydrates (Yen et al., 2010). Cognitive symptoms include confusion and poor concentration. PMDD symptoms seem to have both biological and lifestyle components, and so both medication and lifestyle changes can help.

Although the exact causes for PMDD remain unclear, it is often blamed on physiological factors, such as hormones, neurotransmitters, and brain mechanisms (Shulman, 2010). Hormonal fluctuations are related to mood disorders associated with PMDD, such as depression and hopelessness (Zukov et al., 2010), whereas neurotransmitters, such as serotonin, have been found to be involved in the expression of irritability, anger, depression, and specific food cravings (Rapkin & Winer, 2008). Brain imaging has revealed that increased activity in certain areas of the brain may also contribute to PMDD (Rapkin et al., 2011).

Once documented, the first treatment for PMS or PMDD usually involves lifestyle changes. Dietary and vitamin/nutritional changes such as decreasing caffeine, salt, and alcohol intake; maintaining a low-fat diet; increasing calcium, magnesium, and vitamin E (to decrease negative mood and fluid retention); and various herbal remedies (such as *vitex agnus castus* [Chasteberry]; Dante & Facchinetti, 2011) have been found to be helpful. Stress management, increased regular exercise, improved coping strategies, and drug therapy can also help (Shulman, 2010).

Women who have a history of major depression, **posttraumatic stress disorder,** or sexual abuse, or those who smoke cigarettes tend to be more at risk for development of PMS or PMDD (L. S. Cohen et al., 2002; Koci, 2004; Wittchen et al., 2002). One of the most promising pharmacological treatments has been the selective serotonin reuptake inhibitors, such as fluoxetine (Prozac) (Clayton, 2008; Rendas-Baum et al., 2010). Fluoxetine has yielded some promising results in the treatment of PMDD, although it can

While regular exercise is a good thing, it's important for female athletes to maintain a healthy weight. Females who significantly reduce their body fat may stop menstruating.

cause adverse effects, such as headaches and sexual dysfunction (Carr & Ensom, 2002). Overall, the majority of women who suffer from PMS and PMDD do respond well to treatment.

Menstrual Manipulation and Suppression

Many years ago, women had fewer periods than they do today. Because of poorer health and nutrition, shorter life spans, more pregnancies, and longer periods spent breast-feeding, women had 50 to 150 periods during their lifetime (Ginty, 2005; Thomas & Ellertson, 2000), whereas today they have up to 450. Many women today wish they could schedule their periods around certain events in their lives (e.g., athletic events, dates, or vacations).

Over the last few years, **menstrual manipulation** has become more popular, and in the future it is likely that **menstrual suppression** will make periods optional (Hicks & Rome, 2010). Birth control pills have been used to reduce menstrual bleeding and to delay the onset of menstruation. Some physicians prescribe continuous birth control pills (in which a woman takes birth control pills with no break), progesterone **intrauterine devices,** and injections to suppress menstrual periods.

---

premenstrual dysphoric disorder (PMDD)
The most debilitating and severe cases of premenstrual syndrome.

hot flashes
A symptom of menopause in which a woman feels sudden heat, often accompanied by a flush.

posttraumatic stress disorder
A stress disorder that follows a traumatic event, causing flashbacks, heightened anxiety, and sleeplessness.

menstrual manipulation
The ability to plan and schedule the arrival of menstruation.

menstrual suppression
The elimination of menstrual periods.

intrauterine devices
Devices that are inserted into the uterus for contraception. Progesterone IUDs often inhibit menstruation.

endometriosis
The growth of endometrial tissue outside the uterus.

climacteric
The combination of physiological and psychological changes that develop at the end of a woman's reproductive life; usually includes menopause.

perimenopause
Transition period in a woman's life, just before menopause.

Seasonale, an extended-use oral contraceptive, has been available since 2003. It is taken for 84 consecutive days instead of the usual 21-day birth control regimen. Another similar extended-use pill, Seasonique, was approved by the FDA in 2006. Users of Seasonale and Seasonique experience only 4 periods a year, compared with the usual 13. Many women are excited about the option of reducing the number of menstrual periods; one study found that given a choice of having a period or not, 90% of women would choose not to have periods (Sulak et al., 2002). In 2007, Lybrel, the first continuous-use birth control pill, was available to women. Lybrel is taken for 365 days without placebos, allowing a woman to stop menstruating altogether. We will discuss these forms of birth control in more detail in Chapter 13.

Methods such as taking Seasonale, Seasonique, and Lybrel suppress the growth of the uterine lining, leaving little or nothing to be expelled during menstruation. Actually, this treatment has been used for years to treat a menstrual condition known as **endometriosis** (en-doe-mee-tree-OH-sus), which can cause severe menstrual cramping and irregular periods. Overall, there is no medical evidence that women need to have a monthly menstrual period, and studies conclude that continuous use of FDA-approved pills to stop periods is a safe and effective option for preventing pregnancy and reducing menstrual-related symptoms (Anderson et al., 2006; Merki-Feld et al., 2008; A. L. Nelson, 2007; Stacey, 2008).

Women with painful periods, intense cramps, heavy menses, migraines, PMS, epilepsy, asthma, rheumatoid arthritis, irritable bowel syndrome, and diabetes all can benefit from menstrual suppression (F. D. Anderson et al., 2006; Freeman, 2008; Merki-Feld et al., 2008; A. L. Nelson, 2007; Stacey, 2008). In addition, menstrual disorders are the number one cause of gynecological disease and affect millions of American women yearly (Clayton, 2008). Some experts suggest that amenorrhea may be healthier than monthly periods because menstrual suppression also avoids the sharp hormonal changes that occur throughout the menstrual cycle.

REAL RESEARCH 5.4 In women who are not on hormonal contraception, cravings for foods high in carbohydrates and fat are common 2 weeks before their period starts, during the luteal phase of the menstrual cycle (DAVIDSEN ET AL., 2007).

Originally, birth control pills were designed to mimic the normal menstrual cycle, which is why they allowed a period of time for a woman to bleed. This bleeding, called *withdrawal bleeding*, is a result of stopping birth control pills or taking placebo pills for 1 week each month (Stacey, 2008). Withdrawal bleeding itself bears little biological resemblance to a menstrual period because there is little built-up endometrium to be shed (Thomas & Ellertson, 2000). Even so, most women link having their period with health and fertility. Bleeding has "psychological importance" to many women; many report it lets them know that their bodies are working the way they should. In fact, abnormal bleeding (spotting or clotting) or an absence of bleeding is an important event that should be reported to a health care provider promptly.

Menstruation and Sexual Behavior

Many cultures have taboos about engaging in sexual intercourse, or any sexual behaviors, during menstruation. Orthodox Jewish women are required to abstain from sexual intercourse for 1 week after their menstrual period. After this time, they engage in a mikvah bath, after which sexual activity can be resumed.

Although many heterosexual couples report avoiding sexual intercourse during menstruation (Hensel et al., 2004), research has found that this might have to do more with personal comfort than anything else. Heterosexual couples who are more comfortable with their sexuality report higher levels of sexual intercourse during menstruation than couples who are less comfortable (Rempel & Baumgartner, 2003).

Heterosexual and lesbian couples should discuss these issues and decide what they are comfortable with. As mentioned earlier, however, menstrual suppression might make this question obsolete.

▶▶ MENOPAUSE

The term menopause refers to a woman's final menstrual period but is often (incorrectly) used as a synonym for the **climacteric.** This term refers to the time in a woman's life in which the ovaries become less responsive to hormonal stimulation from the anterior pituitary, resulting in decreased hormone production. Decreased hormone production can lead to irregular cycles or a lack of menstruation. Amenorrhea may occur for 2 or 3 months, followed by a menstrual flow. Women may begin to experience these symptoms during **perimenopause** (pear-ee-MEN-oh-pawz), which occurs anywhere from 2 to 8 years before menopause (Huang, 2007; Twiss et al., 2007). In most cases, menstruation does not stop suddenly. Periods become irregular and intervals between periods become longer. Once menopause has occurred and a woman has not had a period in 1 year, she is considered *postmenopausal* and is no longer considered at risk for pregnancy. Menopause typically occurs sometime between the ages of 40 and 58, although women whose mother gave birth after the age of 35 tend to experience menopause at a later age (Steiner et al., 2010).

The Diva Cup is a silicone menstrual cup that can be used as an alternative to disposable menstrual products such as tampons.

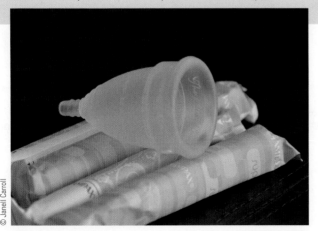

© Janell Carroll

Decreasing estrogen can lead to several possible adverse effects, including hot flashes, forgetfulness, mood swings, sleep disorders, bone loss, menstrual irregularities, vaginal dryness, decreased sexual interest, and joint aches (H. D. Nelson, 2008; Pinkerton & Stovall, 2010; Soares, 2010; Timur & Sahin, 2010; Tom et al., 2010). Changes in estrogen can also lead to atrophy of the primary sexual glands. The clitoris and labia become smaller, and degenerative changes occur in the vaginal wall. At the same time, the ovaries and uterus also begin to shrink. Other possible changes include thinning of head hair, growth of hair on the upper lip and chin, drooping of the breasts and wrinkling of skin because of loss of elasticity, and **osteoporosis** (ah-stee-oh-po-ROW-sus), resulting in brittle bones.

It is estimated that 70% of women over age 80 will experience osteoporosis (Pinkerton & Stovall, 2010; Stanford, 2002). Incidentally, osteopenia (a thinning of the bones) also can occur in younger women and is a precursor to osteoporosis. If you smoke, use Depo Provera, or have an eating disorder or a family history of osteoporosis, consider asking your doctor for a bone density test. Beginning in their 20s, women are advised to ingest at least 1,000 milligrams of calcium each day and to engage in frequent exercise to maintain bone strength (Lloyd et al., 2004; Manson, 2004).

Women who have undergone certain surgeries, such as removal of the ovaries, may experience a surgically induced meno-

women are not the classic complaints but rather the lack of tenderness and sexual contact with a partner (von Sydow, 2000). In fact, for many menopausal women, life satisfaction is more closely related to relationship with a partner, stress, and lifestyle than menopause status, hormone levels, or **hormone replacement therapy (HRT)** (Dennerstein et al., 2000). Keep in mind, however, that a woman's experience of menopause is also shaped by the culture in which she lives (Pitkin 2010). In Chapter 4, we discussed how American media help foster negative attitudes toward aging, especially in women. Cultural issues have an enormous impact on our attitudes about aging, fertility, health, and sexuality.

Hormone Replacement Therapy

In the past, HRT was used to help maintain vaginal elasticity and lubrication, restore regular sleep patterns, and reduce hot flashes and depression. It was also helpful in decreasing the risks for development of osteoporosis, cardiovascular disease, and colorectal and lung cancers (Brinton & Schairer, 1997; Mahabir et al., 2008; Parry, 2008). However, in 2002, after the publication of results from the Women's Health Initiative that linked HRT to an increased rate of breast cancer, the use of HRT declined significantly.

Today, the use of HRT remains controversial (Pluchino et al., 2011; Yang & Reckelhoff, 2011). Although some health care providers continue to prescribe it for some patients, others have stopped prescribing it altogether; and some prescribe hormone replacement only for those women with severe menopausal symptoms (Mueck & Seeger, 2008; Tsai et al., 2011; Zanetti-Dallenbach et al., 2008). Newer therapies containing lower levels of hormones have recently become available, and an increasing number of physicians and health care providers are prescribing these newer options to their menopausal patients (Gardiner et al., 2011; Leite et al., 2010; Nappi et al., 2010; Tsai et al.,2011). Some women use nutritional or vitamin therapy or use herbal remedies that contain natural estrogens, such as black cohosh, ginseng, or soy products, instead of hormones to help lessen symptoms (although the use of these products is controversial and may lead to a variety of adverse effects).

Menopausal women need to weigh the risks and benefits of menopausal treatments and HRT. It is important to discuss these issues with a trusted health care provider. No single treatment option is best for all women.

REAL RESEARCH 5.5 Female beer drinkers have been found to have greater bone density compared with non-beer and/or wine drinkers (PEDRERA-ZAMARANO ET AL., 2009). Researchers believe this may be a result of the *phytoestrogen* content (chemicals that are structurally similar to estrogen) in beer, which can contribute to increased bone density.

---

pause because of estrogen deprivation (Francucci et al., 2010). For this reason, estrogen treatment may be suggested for these women to decrease the potential menopausal symptoms.

Most American women go through menopause with few problems and many find it to be a liberating time, signaling the end of their childbearing years and a newfound freedom from contraception. In fact, the most prevalent sexual problems of older

osteoporosis
An age-related disorder characterized by decreased bone mass and increased susceptibility to fractures as a result of decreased levels of estrogens.

◀ review QUESTIONS

1 Identify and explain the physiological changes that signal the onset of puberty.

2 Identify and explain the four phases of the menstrual cycle.

3 Explain what is known about the existence of PMS/PMDD. What treatments are available?

4 Differentiate between menstrual manipulation and menstrual suppression.

5 Explain what causes the physical and emotional changes of perimenopause and menopause.

6 Explain the benefits and risks of HRT.

▶ FEMALE REPRODUCTIVE
and Sexual Health

It is a good idea for every woman to examine and explore her own sexual anatomy. A genital self-examination (see the accompanying Sex in Real Life) can help increase a woman's comfort with her genitals. In addition, to maintain reproductive health, all women should undergo routine gynecological examinations with Papanicolaou (Pap) smears beginning within 3 years after first sexual intercourse or at age 21 (E. R. Tuller, 2010).

Routine gynecological examinations include a general medical history and a general checkup, a pelvic examination, and a breast examination. During the pelvic examination, the health care provider inspects the genitals, both internally and externally, and manually examines the internal organs.

In a pelvic exam, the health professional will often use a **speculum** to hold open the vagina to examine the cervix (although there is a sense of stretching, this is not generally painful). Many women report discomfort with speculums, and research is currently being done to find alternatives that would allow health care providers access to the cervix. During a pelvic exam, a **Papanicolaou (Pap) smear** is taken from the cervix (see the discussion on cervical cancer that follows). The practitioner will then insert two fingers in the vagina and press down on the lower abdomen to feel the ovaries and uterus for abnormal lumps or pain. A rectovaginal exam may also be performed, in which the practitioner inserts one finger into the rectum and one into the vagina to feel the membranes in between.

It is important to choose a gynecologist or nurse practitioner with care, for this person should be a resource for sexual and birth control information as well. Referrals from friends or family members, college health services, women's health centers, and Planned Parenthood centers can direct you to competent professionals. Do not be afraid to change practitioners if you are not completely comfortable.

▶▶ GYNECOLOGICAL Health Concerns

Several conditions can interfere with gynecological health. We discuss some of the most prevalent, including endometriosis, toxic shock syndrome, polycystic ovarian syndrome (PCOS), uterine fibroids, vulvodynia, and vaginal infections.

Endometriosis

Endometriosis is a common gynecological condition that occurs when endometrial cells begin to migrate to places other than the uterus (Brown et al., 2010). Endometrial cells may implant on any

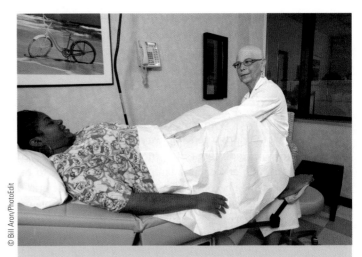

During a pelvic examination, a woman lies on her back with her feet in stirrups. A speculum is used during the pelvic exam to view the cervix.

of the reproductive organs or other abdominal organs and then engorge and atrophy every month with the menstrual cycle, just like the endometrium does in the uterus. The disease ranges from mild to severe, and women may experience a range of symptoms or none at all.

Endometriosis is most common in women aged between 25 and 40 years who have never had children; it has been called the "career woman's disease" because it is more common in professional women (Simsir et al., 2001). Women who have not had children and those who experience short and heavy menstrual cycles have also been found to be more at risk for endometriosis (Vigano et al., 2004). Among women of childbearing age, the estimated prevalence rate of endometriosis is as high as 10%; among infertile women, between 20% and 40% (Frackiewicz, 2000; Vigano et al., 2004). If you or someone you know has had symptoms of endometriosis, it is important that complaints are taken seriously.

The cause of endometriosis is still unknown, although some have suggested that it is due to retrograde menstrual flow (a process in which parts of the uterine lining are carried backward during the menstrual period into the Fallopian tubes and abdomen; Frackiewicz, 2000; Leyendecker et al., 2004). The symptoms of endometriosis depend on where the endometrial tissue has invaded but commonly include painful menstrual periods, pelvic or lower back pain, and pain during penetrative sex; some women also experience pain on defecation (Prentice, 2001). Symptoms often wax and wane with the menstrual cycle, starting a day or two before menstruation, becoming worse during the period, and gradually decreasing for a day or two afterward. The pain is often sharp and can be mistaken for menstrual cramping. Many women discover their endometriosis when they have trouble becoming pregnant. The endometrial cells can affect fertility by infiltrating the ovaries or Fallopian tubes and interfering with ovulation or ovum transport through the Fallopian tubes.

Traditionally, endometriosis is diagnosed through biopsy or the use of a **laparoscope.** Researchers are working on a urine test to aid in diagnosing endometriosis (Tokushige et al., 2011). Treatment

---

speculum
An instrument for dilating the vagina to examine the cervix and other internal structures.

Papanicolaou (Pap) smear
A microscopic examination of cells scraped from the cervix. Named after its inventor.

laparoscope
A small instrument through which structures within the abdomen and pelvis can be viewed.

hormone replacement therapy (HRT)
Medication containing one or more female hormones, often used to treat symptoms of menopause.

consists of hormone therapy, surgery, or laser therapy to try to remove endometrial patches from the organs (Brown et al., 2010). Endometriosis declines during pregnancy and disappears after menopause.

Menstrual Toxic Shock Syndrome

Menstrual toxic shock syndrome (mTSS) is an acute inflammatory disease that develops when *Staphylococcus aureus* bacteria are allowed to grow in the vagina. It is most commonly associated with the use of high-absorbency tampons and forgetting to remove a tampon, which becomes a breeding ground for bacteria.

mTSS is a fast-developing disease that can cause multiple organ failure. Symptoms of mTSS usually include fever, sore throat, diarrhea, vomiting, muscle aches, and a scarlet-colored rash. It may progress rapidly from dizziness or fainting to respiratory distress, kidney failure, shock, and heart failure, and can be fatal if medical attention is not received immediately.

Despite the risks, it is estimated that more than 70% of women in the United States, Canada, and much of Western Europe use tampons during their periods (Parsonnet et al., 2005). Although any woman who uses tampons is at risk for development of mTSS, Black women have been found to be more susceptible than White women (Parsonnet et al., 2005). Regularly removing tampons and using less absorbent tampons or using only pads reduces the risk for development of mTSS. Research is evaluating whether adding various fibers to tampons can decrease the risk for development of mTSS (Strandberg et al., 2009).

Polycystic Ovarian Syndrome

Polycystic ovarian syndrome (PCOS) is an endocrine disorder that affects approximately 7% of premenopausal women worldwide (Diamanti-Kandarakis, 2007). PCOS causes cyst formation on the ovaries during puberty, which causes estrogen levels to decrease and androgen levels (including testosterone) to increase. A girl with PCOS typically experiences irregular or absent menstruation; a lack of ovulation; excessive body and facial hair or hair loss; obesity; acne, oily skin, or dandruff; infertility; or any combination of these. Many women with PCOS experience fertility issues, and research is ongoing to find ways to help them achieve successful pregnancies (Nader, 2010).

Because many of the symptoms, including increased body and facial hair, acne, and weight gain, affect a woman's sense of self, many young women with PCOS experience emotional side effects, including mild depression or self-esteem issues. Getting adequate medical care, education, and support are crucial factors in managing PCOS. There are many possible long-term health concerns associated with PCOS, such as an increased risk for diabetes, high

> It is estimated that **more than 70%** of women in the U.S. **use tampons** during their periods.

ON YOUR MIND 5.4

My gynecologist told me I have uterine fibroids and I'm scared to death. Could fibroids turn into cancer? Will I ever be able to have a baby?

The majority of fibroids are benign. It is rare for a uterine fibroid to turn into a cancer. Cancerous growths in the uterus called uterine *leiomyosarcomas* are rare and are not caused by the presence of uterine fibroids. The majority of women who have uterine fibroids have normal pregnancies and deliveries. However, in some cases, there may be some issues related to delivery, especially if the fibroids are large when it is time to deliver. If so, a cesarean section may be indicated. Finding a health care provider you trust and educating yourself about uterine fibroids will lessen your fears.

blood pressure, and increased cholesterol levels (Chen & Shi, 2010). A variety of treatment options are available, including oral contraception to regulate the menstrual period and inhibit testosterone production. Many women find that some of the symptoms associated with PCOS decrease with weight loss (A. M. Clark et al., 1995).

Although the actual cause of PCOS is unknown, researchers continue to explore possible causes. In Chapter 4, we discussed bisphenol A (BPA), a chemical used in various plastics that can disrupt the endocrine system. Recent research has found greater levels of BPA in women with PCOS, which indicates that BPA may play a role in the development of PCOS (Kandaraki et al., 2011; see Chapter 4 for more information about BPA).

Uterine Fibroids

Uterine fibroids are noncancerous growths that occur in the myometrium layer of the uterus (see Figure 5.3). It is estimated that three of four women have uterine fibroids, but because of the lack of symptoms, many women are unaware of them. If there are symptoms, a woman might experience pelvic pain and pressure, constipation, abdominal tenderness or bloating, frequent urination, heavy cramping, prolonged or heavy bleeding, and/or painful penetrative sex. Of all of these symptoms, excessive menstrual bleeding is the most common complaint. It is important to point out that the majority of uterine fibroids are not cancerous and do not cause any problems.

Overall, Black women are at greater risk for the development of fibroids and typically experience them earlier in life than White women (Wise et al., 2005). Women who are overweight are at greater risk for development of uterine fibroids (Pandey & Bhattacharyta, 2010), as are women who have a genetic risk in their

---

menstrual toxic shock syndrome (mTSS)
A bacteria-caused illness, associated with tampon use, that can lead to high fever, vomiting, diarrhea, sore throat and shock, loss of limbs, and death if left untreated.

polycystic ovarian syndrome (PCOS)
An endocrine disorder in women that can affect the menstrual cycle, fertility, hormones, a woman's appearance, and long-term health.

uterine fibroid
A (usually noncancerous) tumor of muscle and connective tissue that develops within, or is attached to, the uterine wall.

vulvodynia
Chronic vulvar pain and soreness.

douching
A method of vaginal rinsing or cleaning that involves squirting water or other solutions into the vagina.

family (i.e., a mother or sister with fibroids). Research has found that an early life hormonal exposure (such as being fed soy formula during infancy), having a mother with pre-pregnancy diabetes, or being born at least 1 month early may be related to the development of uterine fibroids later in life (D'Aloisio et al., 2010). More research is needed to explore these links.

Various treatments are used to treat uterine fibroids, including hormone or drug therapy to decrease endometrial buildup (Nieman et al., 2011), laser therapy, and/or surgery (Rabinovici et al., 2010). For many years, hysterectomy, the surgical removal of the uterus, was the leading treatment for uterine fibroids, although this is no longer the case today (Laughlin et al., 2010). Today, hysterectomy is used only in extreme cases in which the fibroids are very large; other treatment options include the use of intrauterine devices (Maruo et al., 2010) and various herbs, such as *curcumin* (a component of turmeric), which have been found to decrease uterine fibroids (Tsuiji et al., 2011).

Vulvodynia

At the beginning of the 21st century, many physicians were unaware that a condition known as **vulvodynia** (vull-voe-DY-nia) existed. Vulvodynia refers to chronic vulval pain and soreness, and it is estimated that 16% of women experience such pain (Danby & Margesson, 2010). Although a burning sensation is the most common symptom, women also report itching, burning, rawness, stinging, or stabbing vaginal/vulval pain (Danby & Margesson, 2010; Goldstein & Burrows, 2008). Pain can be either intermittent or constant and can range from mildly disturbing to completely disabling. Over the years, many women with vulvodynia were undiagnosed and left untreated because of a lack of understanding about the condition (Groysman, 2010). Because of this, women who suffer from vulvodynia experienced high levels of psychological distress and depression (Danby & Margesson, 2010; Jelovsek et al., 2008; Plante & Kamm, 2008).

No one really knows what causes vulvodynia, but there have been several speculations, including injury or irritation of the vulval nerves, hypersensitivity to vaginal yeast, allergic reaction to environmental irritants, or pelvic floor muscle spasms (Bohm-Starke, 2010; Murina et al., 2008, 2010; Tommola et al., 2010). Treatment options include biofeedback, diet modification, drug therapy, oral and topical medications, nerve blocks, vulvar injections, surgery, and pelvic floor muscle strengthening (Groysman, 2010; Murina et al., 2010; Tommola et al., 2010). Treatment plans for women experiencing vulvodynia should be individualized, and care should be taken to address each individual woman's symptoms and functioning (Groysman, 2010).

Infections

Numerous kinds of infections can afflict the female genital system. Some are sexually transmitted; these are discussed in Chapter 15. However, some infections of the female reproductive tract are not necessarily sexually transmitted. For example, as we discussed earlier in this chapter, the Bartholin's glands and the urinary tract can become infected, just as any area of the body can become infected when bacteria get inside and multiply. These infections may happen because of certain hygiene practices and are more frequent in those who engage in frequent sexual intercourse. When infected, the glands can swell and cause pressure and discomfort,

and can interfere with walking, sitting, or sexual intercourse. Usually a physician will need to drain the infected glands with a catheter and will prescribe a course of antibiotics (H. Blumstein, 2001).

Concern about vaginal odor and cleanliness is typically what drives women to use a variety of feminine hygiene products. However, not all of these products are safe. For example, **douching** may put a woman at risk for vaginal infections because it changes the vagina's pH levels and can destroy healthy bacteria necessary to maintain proper balance.

▶▶ CANCER OF THE
Female Reproductive Organs

Cancer is a disease in which certain cells in the body do not function properly—they divide too quickly or produce excessive tissue that forms a tumor (or both). A number of cancers can affect the female reproductive organs. In this section, we discuss breast, uterine, cervical, endometrial, and ovarian cancers. We will also review preventive measures for detecting or avoiding common female health problems. In Chapter 14, we will discuss how these illnesses affect women's lives and sexuality.

Breast Cancer

We opened this chapter with a story about Stef, who has been battling breast cancer. Breast cancer is one of the most common cancers among American women and the second leading cause of cancer death in women (after lung cancer; American Cancer Society, 2010). The American Cancer Society estimated that approximately 207,100 new cases of invasive breast cancer occurred in America in

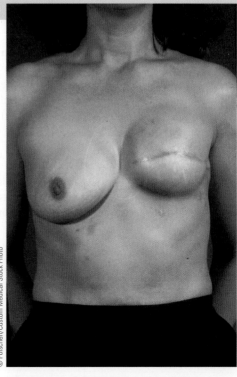

Partial or modified mastectomies are more common today than radical mastectomies.

© Polschen/Custom Medical Stock Photo

2010. There is no known way to prevent breast cancer; however, as Stef's story shows, early detection improves the chances that it can be treated successfully. So it is extremely important to detect it as early as possible. Every woman should regularly perform breast self-examinations (see the accompanying Sex in Real Life). Women should also have their breasts examined during routine gynecological checkups, which is a good time to ask for instruction on self-examination if you have any questions about the technique.

Another important preventive measure is **mammography,** which can detect, on average, 80% to 90% of breast cancer in women without symptoms (American Cancer Society, 2010). Mammography can detect cancer at early stages when treatment is more effective and cures are more likely (Narod, in press). The American Cancer Society advises women to have regular mammograms taken, beginning at the age of 40. However, you should discuss with your health care provider whether mammography is appropriate for you, and if so, how often.

The earliest sign of breast cancer is often an abnormality seen on a mammogram before a woman or her health care provider can feel it. However, sometimes there are symptoms, including nipple discharge, changes in nipple shape, and skin dimpling. It should be noted here that the discovery of a lump or mass in your breast does not mean you have cancer; most masses are **benign,** and many do not even need treatment. If it is **malignant** and left untreated, however, breast cancer usually spreads throughout the body, which is why it is important that any lump be immediately brought to the attention of your physician or other medical practitioner.

TREATMENT   In the past, women with breast cancer usually had a **radical mastectomy.** Today, few women need such drastic surgery. More often, if necessary, a partial or modified mastectomy is performed, which leaves many of the underlying muscles and lymph nodes in place (see photo accompanying this section). If the breast must be removed, many women choose to undergo breast reconstruction, in which a new breast is formed from existing skin and fat or breast implants (Bellino et al., 2010).

If it appears that the tumor has not spread, a **lumpectomy** may be considered. A lumpectomy involves the removal of the tumor, together with some surrounding tissue, but the breast is left intact. Survival rates from lumpectomies are similar to the rates for mastectomies (American Cancer Society, 2010). **Radiation, chemotherapy,** or both are often used in conjunction with these surgeries.

RISK FACTORS   Several factors may put a woman at greater risk for development of breast cancer. A woman's chance of acquiring breast cancer increases significantly as she ages. In fact, 77% of breast can-

*A woman's chance of acquiring breast cancer **increases significantly as she ages.***

View in Video
To watch the entire interview, go to Psychology CourseMate at **login.cengagebrain.com.**

Video supplied by BBC Motion Gallery

"Some people take out car loans. I took out a boob loan."
—Breast Implants

cers appear in women who are 50 years or older, whereas less than 5% appear in women younger than 40 years (Jemal et al., 2005). Racial and ethnic factors are also important—although White women are at greater risk for development of breast cancer, Black women are more likely to die of it, mainly because of the fact that Black women have more aggressive tumors. Asian, Hispanic, and Native American women have lower risks for development of breast cancer. An early onset of puberty and menarche may increase the chances of developing breast cancer, probably because of prolonged estrogen exposure (American Cancer Society, 2010). However, obesity, low levels of physical activity, and consuming one or more alcoholic drinks per day may have more to do with the development of breast cancer than do early onset of puberty or menarche (American Cancer Society, 2010; Li et al., 2010a; Verkasalo et al., 2001). Decreased risks have been found in women who exercise. In fact, in women with breast cancer, those who are physically active are less likely to die than those who are inactive (American Cancer Society, 2010). Breast-feeding has also been found to reduce a woman's lifetime risk for development of breast cancer (Eisinger & Burke, 2002).

Family history also may be a risk factor in breast cancer; however, about 90% of women who experience development of breast cancer do not have any family history of the disease (American Cancer Society, 2010). No study has been large enough to reliably show how the risk for breast cancer is influenced by familial patterns of breast cancer. Although women who have a first-degree relative with breast cancer may have an increased risk for the disease, most of these women will never experience the development of breast cancer (Collaborative Group on Hormonal Factors in Breast Cancer, 2001).

---

mammography
A procedure for internal imaging of the breasts to evaluate breast disease or screen for breast cancer.

benign
A nonmalignant, mild case of a disease that is favorable for recovery.

malignant
A cancerous growth that tends to spread into nearby normal tissue and travel to other parts of the body.

radical mastectomy
A surgical procedure that involves removal of the breast, its surrounding tissue, the muscles supporting the breast, and underarm lymph nodes.

lumpectomy
A modern surgical procedure for breast cancer in which only the tumorous lump and a small amount of surrounding tissue are removed.

radiation
A procedure that uses high-energy radiation to kill cancer cells by damaging their DNA.

chemotherapy
A procedure that uses chemicals to kill rapidly dividing cancer cells.

A breast self-examination (BSE), together with mammography and a clinical breast examination from a health care provider, can help reduce breast cancer in women. Recall that in the chapter opening story, Stef found a lump through a routine breast self-examination she was doing. Beginning in their 20s, women should become familiar with the shape and feel of their breasts so they can report any breast changes to a health care provider. If a woman does detect a thickening or a lump, however, she should make sure to inform her health care provider. After age 40, mammography, clinical breast exams, and even magnetic resonance imaging become more useful, although a monthly BSE may still be recommended (Saslow et al., 2007). Women with breast implants are also encouraged to perform BSEs (Tang & Gui, in press).

Because the breasts are often less tender after menstruation, it is best to perform a BSE about a week after your period ends (see the photo below for more information about a BSE).

Thinkstock/Getty Images

In the Mirror

The first step of a BSE is inspection. Look at your breasts in a mirror to learn their natural contours. With arms relaxed, note any elevation of the level of the nipple, dimpling, bulging, or dimpling. Compare the size and shape of the breasts, remembering that one (usually the left) is normally slightly larger. Next, press your hands down firmly on your hips to tense the pectoral muscles, then raise your arms over your head looking for a shift in relative position of the two nipples. These maneuvers also bring out any dimpling or bulging. After doing BSEs over time, any changes will become obvious, which is why it is best to begin BSEs earlier rather than later in life.

In the Shower

The shower is a good place to do a breast palpation (pressing)—fingers glide well over wet or soapy skin. Press the breast against the chest wall with the flat of the hand, testing the surface for warmth and moving the hand to test mobility. Pay close attention to increased heat or redness of the overlying skin, tenderness, dilated superficial veins, and retraction (dimpling, asymmetry, decreased mobility). Feel the tissue carefully in all four quadrants of the breast, being sure to include the tissue that extends up toward the armpit, and examine the armpit itself for any lymph node enlargement (see accompanying photo). Finally, gently squeeze the nipple inward and upward to determine whether there is any discharge.

Lying Down

Finally, lie down and put a folded towel or a pillow under your left shoulder. Placing your left hand behind your head, use your right hand to press firmly in small, circular motions all around the left breast, much as you did in the shower. As the figure below illustrates, there are a variety of techniques used in BSE, including the circle, line, and wedge methods. In the circle method, a woman moves her fingers in a circular pattern around the breast to feel for abnormal breast tissue. In the line method, a woman begins in the underarm area and uses an up-and-down motion to explore the breast. Finally, in the wedge method, a woman works her way toward the nipple, exploring one wedge section at a time. It is also important to check the nipples for any sign of discharge. Irregularities, lumps, or discharge should be reported to your health care provider immediately.

SOURCE: American Cancer Society, 2007a.

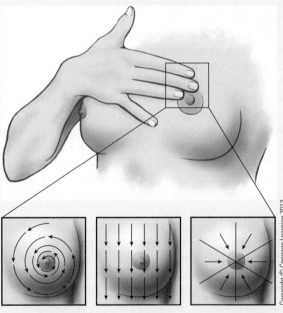

Copyright © Cengage Learning 2013

Genetic mutations (BRCA1 and BRCA2) associated with breast cancer have been found to lead to high risk for both breast and ovarian cancer. Although these mutations are rare, they are more common in women with relatives who have been diagnosed with breast or ovarian cancer or who have ethnicity or racial factors. The prevalence of pathogenic genetic mutations was found to be highest in women over age 35 who were of Ashkenazi Jewish ancestry (8.3%) and lowest in Asian Americans (0.5%) (John et al., 2007); other ethnicity findings included Hispanics (3.5%), non-Hispanic Whites (2.2%), and African Americans (1.3%). However, in patients diagnosed before age 35 years, the prevalence rate was particularly high in African American women (17%). Some women who have been found to have a high risk for development of breast cancer choose to undergo prophylactic (preventive) mastectomies before breast cancer can develop (American Cancer Society, 2010; Harmon, 2007; D. A. Levine & Gemignani, 2003; Sakorafas, 2005).

There has been some controversy over the effect of oral contraceptives on breast cancer rates, with many contradictory studies; some studies found an increased risk, and others found no increased risk (American Cancer Society, 2010; Cabaret et al., 2003; Narod et al., 2002). Although there have been slightly more breast cancers found in women who use oral contraceptives, these cancers have been less advanced and less aggressive (Fraser, 2000). A comprehensive study conducted by the U.S. Food and Drug Administration (FDA) concluded that there is no concrete evidence that the pill causes or influences the development of breast cancer; however, the long-term effects of using oral contraception are not yet certain, and those with a family history of breast cancer might want to consider using other forms of contraception.

Ovarian cancer causes more deaths than any other cancer of the female reproductive system.

Finally, many rumors and myths about things that cause breast cancer circulate from time to time such as the idea that using antiperspirant, wearing bras, undergoing elective abortion, having breast implants, or engaging in night work increases a woman's risk for breast cancer. Currently, none of these factors has been associated with an increased risk for breast cancer (American Cancer Society, 2010).

Uterine Cancer

Different types of cancer can affect the uterus. In this section, we discuss cervical, endometrial, and ovarian cancers.

CERVICAL CANCER The American Cancer Society estimated that there were approximately 12,200 new cases of cervical cancer in the United States in 2010. The rates of cervical cancer have decreased over the past several decades. A Pap smear, taken during routine pelvic exams, can detect early changes in the cervical cells, which may indicate cervical cancer. Early diagnosis can lead to more effective treatment and higher cure rates. During a Pap smear, a few cells are painlessly scraped from the cervix and are examined under a microscope for abnormalities. The majority of cervical cancers develop slowly, so if a woman has regular Pap tests, nearly all cases can be successfully treated (American Cancer Society, 2010).

The main cause of cervical cancer is an infection with certain types of human papillomavirus (HPV), which we will discuss further in Chapter 15. Women who begin having sex at a young age or who have multiple sex partners are at an increased risk for HPV infection and cervical cancer (American Cancer Society, 2010). Long-term use of birth control pills and cigarette smoking are also associated with an increased risk for cervical cancer (American Cancer Society, 2010).

Unfortunately, few symptoms are associated with cervical cancer until the later stages of the disease. When the cervical cells become cancerous and invade nearby cells, a woman may experience abnormal bleeding during the month or after penetrative sex or a pelvic exam.

Cervical cancer has high cure rates because it starts as an easily identifiable lesion, called a **cervical intraepithelial neoplasia,** which usually progresses slowly into cervical cancer. Better early detection of cervical cancer has led to a sharp decrease in the numbers of serious cervical cancer cases. For some poor or uninsured women in the United States and for many women abroad, routine pelvic examinations and Pap smears are not available. It is for this reason that approximately 80% of the 500,000 new cases of cervical cancer diagnosed every year are in poor countries such as sub-Saharan Africa and Latin America (Nebehay, 2004).

Cervical lesions can be treated with surgery, radiation, chemotherapy, or a combination of these treatments, which has resulted in cure rates up to 90% in early stage disease and a dramatic decline in mortality rate for cervical cancer. If the disease has progressed, treatment commonly includes a **hysterectomy** followed by radiation and chemotherapy. The FDA has approved two vaccines for the prevention of most types of HPV that cause cervical cancer: Gardasil and Cervarix. We discuss these vaccines more in Chapter 15.

ENDOMETRIAL CANCER The American Cancer Society estimated that there were approximately 43,500 new cases of uterine cancer in 2010, most of which involved the endometrial lining. Incidence rates have been decreasing over the last few years. Symptoms include abnormal uterine bleeding or spotting and pain during urination or penetrative sex. Because a Pap smear is rarely effective in detecting early endometrial cancer, a **D&C (dilation and curettage)** is more reliable. Endometrial cancer is typically treated with surgery, radiation, hormones, and chemotherapy, depending on the stage of the disease.

Estrogen is a risk factor for endometrial cancer. Women who have been exposed to high levels of estrogen for hormone replacement therapies, and those who are overweight, experienced late menopause, never had children, or who have a history of PCOS are at increased risk for endometrial cancer (American Cancer Society, 2010). Because unexpected and heavy bleeding are possible indications of endometrial cancer, women who experience changes in menstrual bleeding should report this to their health care providers. If detected at an early stage, endometrial cancer has high survival rates (American Cancer Society, 2010).

cervical intraepithelial neoplasia	hysterectomy	dilation and curettage (D&C)	ovarian cysts	false negatives
A change in the cells on the surface of the cervix that may signal early beginnings of cervical cancer; sometimes referred to as cervical dysplasia.	The surgical removal of the uterus.	The surgical scraping of the uterine wall with a spoon-shaped instrument.	Small, fluid-filled sacs, which can form on the ovary, that do not pose a health threat under most conditions.	Incorrect result of a medical test that wrongly shows the lack of a finding, condition, or disease.

OVARIAN CANCER The American Cancer Society estimated there were approximately 22,000 new cases of ovarian cancer in 2010. Ovarian cancer is more common in northern European and North American countries than in Asia or developing countries. Overall rates of ovarian cancer have been decreasing over the last few years. Although not as common as uterine or breast cancer, ovarian cancer causes more deaths than any other cancer of the female reproductive system, because it invades the body silently, with few warning signs or symptoms until it reaches an advanced stage (American Cancer Society, 2010). Because the ovary floats freely in the pelvic cavity, a tumor can grow undetected without producing many noticeable symptoms (i.e., there is little pressure on other organs; see Figure 5.4).

*Understanding anatomy and physiology **is an important piece** in learning about human sexual behavior.*

Although there are few symptoms of ovarian cancer, some women experience abdominal bloating, pelvic pain, difficulty eating or feeling full quickly, and an increased need to urinate (American Cancer Society, 2010). Because these symptoms are similar to other conditions (such as irritable bowel syndrome), it is important for a woman to check with her health care provider should she experience such symptoms for more than a week or two. The most important factor in the survival rate from ovarian cancer is early detection and diagnosis. It is estimated that two thirds of cases of ovarian cancer are diagnosed late (Mantica, 2005). A woman in whom an ovarian lump is detected need not panic, however, for most lumps turn out to be relatively harmless **ovarian cysts;** about 70% of all ovarian tumors are benign.

The cause of ovarian cancer is unknown. Like other cancers, an increased incidence is found in women who are childless, undergo early menopause, or eat a high-fat diet. Women who are lactose-intolerant or who use talc powder (especially on the vulva) have also been found to have higher rates of ovarian cancer. Women who take birth control pills, who were pregnant at an early age, or who had several pregnancies have particularly low rates of ovarian cancer. One study demonstrated that women who undergo tubal ligation (have their tubes tied to prevent pregnancy) also reduce the risk for ovarian cancer (Narod et al., 2001).

Although there is no 100% accurate test for ovarian cancer, health care providers can use blood tests, pelvic examinations, and ultrasound to screen for the cancer. Women who are at high risk for ovarian cancer may be given an ultrasound and pelvic exam, together with a CA-125 blood test. However, there is some controversy over the usefulness of these tests, because they have fairly high **false negatives** (Mantica, 2005; Rettenmaier et al., 2010; U.S. Preventive Services Task Force, 2005). This is why many women with ovarian cancer are diagnosed after the cancer has spread beyond the ovary.

Treatment for ovarian cancer is removal of the ovaries and possibly the Fallopian tubes and uterus. Chemotherapy may also be used. In women who have not yet had children, the uterus may be spared, although chemotherapy is more successful after these have been removed (American Cancer Society, 2010).

As you have learned throughout this chapter, understanding anatomy and physiology is an important piece in learning about human sexual behavior. It is important to understand all of the physiological and hormonal influences and how they affect the female body before we can move on to the emotional and psychological issues involved in human sexuality. Anatomy and physiology, therefore, are really the foundations of any human sexuality class. We continue to lay this foundation in Chapter 6, "Male Sexual Anatomy and Physiology."

◀ review QUESTIONS

1 Explain what is done in a yearly pelvic exam and why.

2 Name and explain three gynecological health concerns.

3 Identify and explain the risk factors that have been identified for breast cancer.

4 Explain how a vaccine for HPV can decrease the incidence of cervical cancer.

5 Identify and describe the two most common forms of uterine cancer.

6 Explain why ovarian cancer is the most deadly gynecologic cancer.

SUMMARY POINTS

1 Endocrine glands produce hormones. Female reproductive hormones include estrogen and progesterone, whereas the primary male reproductive hormone is testosterone.

2 The women's external sex organs, collectively called the vulva, include a number of separate structures, including the mons veneris, labia majora, and labia minora. The clitoris is composed of a glans, body, and paired crura (legs). It is richly supplied with both blood vessels and nerve endings and becomes erect during sexual excitement. The opening of the vagina is also referred to as the introitus.

3 The female's internal sexual organs include the vagina, uterus, Fallopian tubes, and ovaries. The vagina serves as the female organ of intercourse and the passageway to and from the uterus.

4 The uterus is a thick-walled, hollow, muscular organ that provides a path for sperm to reach the ovum and provides a home for the developing fetus. On the sides of the uterus lie two Fallopian tubes, and their job is to bring the ovum from the ovary into the uterus. The mature ovaries contain a woman's oocytes and are the major producers of female reproductive hormones.

5 The breasts are modified sweat glands that contain fatty tissue and produce milk to nourish a newborn. Milk creation, secretion, and ejection from the nipple are referred to as breast-feeding, or lactation.

6 Female puberty occurs when the ovaries begin to release estrogen, which stimulates growth of the woman's sexual organs and menstruation. Menstruation can be divided into four general phases: the follicular phase, the ovulatory phase, the luteal phase, and the menstrual phase.

7 A number of menstrual problems are possible, including amenorrhea, which involves a lack of menstruation; menorrhagia, which involves excessive menstrual flow; and dysmenorrhea, which is painful menstruation. The physical and emotional symptoms that may occur late in the menstrual cycle are called premenstrual syndrome (PMS). The most debilitating and severe cases of PMS are referred to as premenstrual dysphoric disorder (PMDD).

8 Menstrual manipulation, the ability to schedule menstrual periods, and menstrual suppression, the ability to completely eliminate menses, are becoming more popular. There are cultural taboos against sexual intercourse during menstruation. However, engaging in sexual intercourse during menstruation is a personal decision; although there is no medical reason to avoid intimacy during this time, couples need to talk about what they are comfortable doing.

9 As women age, hormone or estrogen production wanes, leading to perimenopause and then menopause, or the cessation of menstruation. Some women use nutritional therapy to help lessen menopausal symptoms, whereas others use hormone replacement therapy (HRT), which has its advantages and disadvantages.

10 Regular gynecological examination is recommended for all women to help detect uterine, ovarian, and cervical cancers. Genital self-examination is also an important part of women's health behavior.

11 There are several gynecological health concerns. Endometriosis is a condition in which the uterine cells begin to migrate to places other than the uterus. Menstrual toxic shock syndrome (mTSS) is an infection, usually caused by the use of tampons. Symptoms of mTSS include high fever, vomiting, diarrhea, and sore throat. If left untreated, it can result in death.

12 Uterine fibroids are hard tissue masses in the uterus, and symptoms include pelvic pain, heavy cramping, and prolonged bleeding.

13 The most prevalent cancer in the world is breast cancer. Breast self-examination and mammography can help detect breast cancer early. The most common forms of uterine cancer are cervical and endometrial. The most deadly of all gynecologic cancers is ovarian.

CRITICAL THINKING QUESTIONS

1 What were the early messages that you received (as a man or a woman) about menstruation? Did you receive any information about it when you were growing up? What do you wish would have been done differently?

2 Do you think that PMS really exists? Provide a rationale for your answer.

3 If you are heterosexual or a lesbian, how would you feel about engaging in sex during menstruation? Why do you think you feel this way? Trace how these feelings may have developed.

4 If you are a woman, have you ever practiced a breast self-exam? If so, what made you decide to perform one? If you have never performed one, why not? If you are a man, do you encourage the women in your life to perform breast self-exams? Why or why not?

MEDIA RESOURCES

CourseMate brings course concepts to life with interactive learning, study, and exam preparation tools that support the printed textbook. A textbook-specific website, Psychology CourseMate includes an integrated interactive eBook and other interactive learning tools including quizzes, flashcards, videos, and more. If your textbook does not include an access code card, go to CengageBrain.com to gain access.

CENGAGENOW   CengageNOW is an easy-to-use online resource that helps you study in less time to get the grade you want—NOW. Take a pre-test for this chapter and receive a personalized study plan based on your results that will identify the topics you need to review and direct you to online resources to help you master those topics. Then take a post-test to help you determine the concepts you have mastered and what you will need to work on. If your textbook does not include an access code card, go to CengageBrain.com to gain access.

View in Video available in CourseMate and CengageNOW:

Beating Breast Cancer: Stef's Story: Meet Stef Woods, a breast cancer survivor, as she discusses her journey through the discovery and treatments for breast cancer.

First Periods: Young teens discuss their experiences with first menstrual periods.

PMS: Real or Imagined?: Young women and men discuss their experiences with PMS and explore their thoughts about whether it is real or imagined.

Breast Implants: An eighteen-year-old describes the reasons she opted to get breast implants after high school graduation.

Websites:

Museum of Menstruation & Women's Health (MUM) ■ An online museum that illustrates the rich history of menstruation and women's health. It contains information on menstruation's history and various aspects of menstruation.

The American College of Obstetricians and Gynecologists (ACOG) ■ ACOG is the nation's leading group of professionals providing health care for women. This site contains information on recent news releases relevant to women's health, educational materials, and links to various other health-related websites.

National Women's Health Information Center (NWHIC) ■ This website, operated by the Department of Health and Human Services, provides a gateway to women's health information services.

Information is available on pregnancy, cancers, nutrition, menopause, and HRT, as well as many other health-related areas.

National Vulvodynia Association (NVA) ■ The National Vulvodynia Association (NVA) is a nonprofit organization created to educate and provide support. NVA coordinates a central source of information and encourages further research.

Cancer.net ■ This site contains material for health professionals, including cancer treatments, prevention, and CANCERLIT, a bibliographic database.

Forward USA ■ Forward USA is a nonprofit organization that works to eliminate female genital mutilation (FGM) and provide support services for those young girls and women who are victims of FGM.

6 Male Sexual Anatomy and Physiology

View in **Video**

View in **Video**

View in **Video**

View in **Video**

View in **Video**

ABOUT THE CHAPTER OPENING VIDEO – Over the years, I've given many lectures on sexual anatomy and physiology. Students are always interested in learning more about both male and female reproductive anatomy. I usually ask students to submit anonymous questions about anatomy and then have a class discussion about these issues. One particular topic always gets a lot of questions: *penises.* Students are often very curious about them—how big are they, how men feel about them, do guys check out other guys' penises, and whether guys are intimidated by the size of men's penises in pornography. While I've had lots of conversations with groups of students about how men feel about penises in general, I have not had many opportunities to sit down with one man and talk about how he came to know his penis. What did he remember thinking about it when he was young? How did he feel he compared to other boys and men? Was there pressure to compare oneself with others? Lucky for me, I met Vic, a very funny and interesting man who just so happened to want to talk about his penis. He grew up in a neighborhood surrounded by older kids, which is why he knew more about sex and anatomy than most kids his age. But being the youngest also had its problems. One early memory involved being *pantsed* at the age of 4.

The kids who pantsed me were a good 10 years older than me. We had been hanging out with a big group of older kids, both girls and guys. I don't know why they did it. I bet the boys just wanted to make the girls laugh. All in all, I learned a ton from hanging out with older kids. I remember looking at Playboy *magazines all the time at one kid's house. I was really active in sports and I also learned a lot in the locker room. It's funny because in high school, locker rooms were pretty reserved. No one showered and everyone tried to hide his junk. But, then came college and there were naked swinging penises everywhere! While most guys were fairly modest and*

didn't just throw it around, some felt the need to show their penis to everyone! And it wasn't always the biggest guys, either. I often shied away from this because I felt I was kind of on the smaller side, but at some point it's inevitable that everyone sees it. I don't care what anyone says, but EVERY guy checks out each other's junk. The funny thing is that I always imagined that the huge soft penises in the locker room got enormous when they were hard. But since I didn't ever see them hard, I didn't know. Then one night I had an interesting experience that proved to me if a guy is huge when he's soft, he probably doesn't get much bigger when he's hard.

My conversation with Vic was refreshing, honest, and a lot of fun. I know you'll find his interview thought provoking and extremely interesting. ❙❙

Janell Carroll

"I don't care what anyone says, but every guy checks out each other's junk."
—CHAPTER OPENING VIDEO

View in Video

To watch the entire interview, go to Psychology CourseMate at **login.cengagebrain.com.**

In this chapter, we take a closer look at being male, and explore male anatomy and physiology. In the previous chapter, we discussed female anatomy and physiology, and although there are many similarities between the two, there are also many important differences. One obvious difference is the fact that the male gonads (the testes) lie outside of the body, whereas the female gonads (ovaries) are located deep within the abdomen. Because of the location of the male genitalia, boys are often more comfortable and familiar with their genitalia compared with girls. In this chapter, we explore the male reproductive system, maturation, and sexual health issues.

▶ MALE SEXUAL
and Reproductive System

Most men are fairly familiar with their penis and scrotum. Boys learn to hold their penises while urinating, certainly notice them when they become erect, and generally talk more freely about their genitals among themselves than girls do. Yet, the male reproductive system is a complex series of glands and ducts, and few men have a full understanding of how the system operates physiologically.

REAL RESEARCH 6.1 The penis has evolved into a shape that allows it to remove another lover's sperm from the reproductive tract of a woman (SHACKELFORD & GOETZ, 2007). Researchers used two dildos shaped like penises, one with a coronal ridge and one without. The coronal ridge penis removed 56% more of the (other man's) semen with only one thrust. Sperm competition occurs when the sperm of two or more men is present in the female reproductive tract, and the coronal ridge of the penis helps to push existing sperm out of the way.

▶▶ EXTERNAL Sex Organs

The external sex organs of the male include the penis (which consists of the glans and root) and the scrotum. In this section, we discuss these organs and the process of penile erection.

The Penis

The **penis** is the male sexual organ. It contains the urethra, which carries urine and semen to the outside of the body. The penis has the ability to engorge with blood and stiffen, which evolutionary theorists would tell us allows for easier penetration of the vagina to deposit sperm near the cervical os for its journey toward the ovum. Although there is no bone and little muscle in the human penis, the root of the penis is attached to a number of muscles that help eject **semen** and allow men to move the penis slightly when erect. Throughout history, men have experienced anxiety

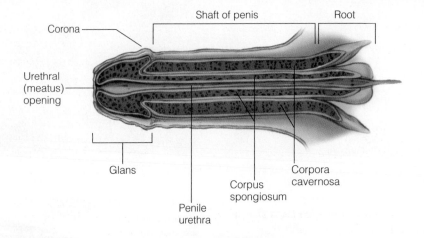

(a)

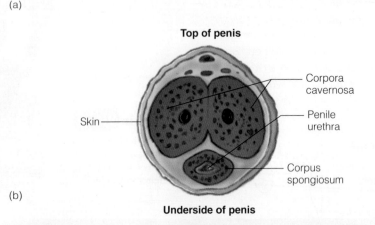

(b)

FIGURE **6.1** The internal structure of the penis. Copyright © Cengage Learning 2013

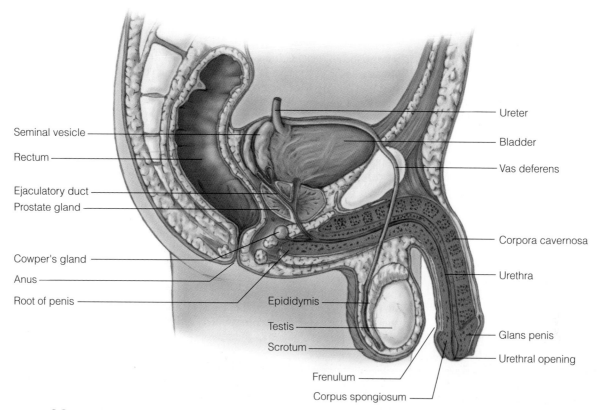

Seminal vesicle

Rectum

Ejaculatory duct

Prostate gland

Cowper's gland

Anus

Root of penis

Epididymis

Testis

Scrotum

Frenulum

Corpus spongiosum

Ureter

Bladder

Vas deferens

Corpora cavernosa

Urethra

Glans penis

Urethral opening

FIGURE 6.2 The male reproductive organs. Copyright © Cengage Learning 2013

about penis size. In the accompanying Sex in Real Life, we discuss this anxiety.

The penis is composed of three cylinders, each containing erectile tissue—spongelike tissue that fills with blood to cause **erection.** Two lateral **corpora cavernosa** (CORE-purr-uh cav-er-NO-suh) lie on the upper sides of the penis, and the central **corpus spongiosum** (CORE-pus spon-gee-OH-sum) lies on the bottom and contains the urethra. The three are bound together with connective tissue to give the outward appearance of a single cylinder and are permeated by blood vessels and spongy tissues that fill with blood when the penis is erect.

THE GLANS PENIS The corpus spongiosum ends in a conelike expansion called the **glans penis.** The glans penis is made up of the **corona,** the **frenulum** (FREN-yu-lum), and the **urethral opening,** or **meatus** (mee-ATE-us; see Figures 6.1 and 6.2). The

glans is very sensitive to stimulation, and some males find direct or continuous stimulation of the glans irritating.

The prepuce of the glans penis is a circular fold of skin usually called the **foreskin.** The foreskin is a continuation of the loose skin that covers the penis as a whole to allow it to grow during erection. The foreskin can cover part or all of the glans and retracts back over the corona when the penis is erect. In many cultures, the foreskin is removed surgically through a procedure called a circumcision (sir-kum-SI-zhun; see the Sexual Diversity in Our World feature in this chapter for more information about circumcision).

THE ROOT The root of the penis enters the body just below the pubic bone and is attached to internal pelvic muscles (see Figure 6.2). The root of the penis goes farther into the body than most men realize; it can be felt in the perineum (between the scrotum and anus), particularly when the penis is erect.

penis
The male copulatory and urinary organ, used both to urinate and move spermatozoa out of the urethra through ejaculation; it is the major organ of male sexual pleasure and is homologous to the female clitoris.

semen
A thick, whitish secretion of the male reproductive organs, containing spermatozoa and secretions from the seminal vesicles, prostate, and bulbourethral glands.

erection
The hardening of the penis caused by blood engorging the erectile tissue.

corpora cavernosa
Plural of corpus cavernosum (cavernous body); areas in the penis that fill with blood during erection.

corpus spongiosum
Meaning "spongy body," the erectile tissue in the penis that contains the urethra.

glans penis
The flaring, enlarged region at the end of the penis.

corona
The ridge of the glans penis.

frenulum
Fold of skin on the underside of the penis.

urethral opening or meatus
The opening of the penis through which urine and semen are expelled.

foreskin
The fold of skin that covers the glans penis; also called the *prepuce.*

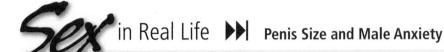

The penis has been defined as the symbol of male sexuality throughout history. Men have often been plagued by concerns about penis function and size. As Vic discussed in the chapter opening story, many men worry about the size of their penis. Some men assume there is a correlation between penis size and masculinity, or sexual prowess, and many men assume that their partners prefer a large penis. Others worry about their size and fear that they are not "normal." Although there may be a psychological preference for large penises among some partners (just as some partners desire women with large breasts), penis size has no correlation with the ability to excite a partner sexually during sex.

The average flaccid penis is between 3 and 4 inches long, and the average erect penis is 6 inches. Gary Griffen, author of *Penis Size and Enlargement* (1995), has found that only 15% of men have an erect penis measuring more than 7 inches, and fewer than 5,000 erect penises worldwide measure 12 inches. In the end, penis size has been found to be largely dependent on heredity—fathers' penis sizes correlate well with their sons' (T. Hamilton, 2002).

The opinion most men have that the average penis size is greater than it really is comes from pornographic films (which tend to use the largest men they can find), from men's perspective on their own penis (which, from the top, looks smaller than from the sides), and from overestimates of actual penis size (researchers consistently find that people's estimation of the size of penises they have just seen is exaggerated; Shamloul, 2005).

It is erroneous beliefs such as these that cause some men to be anxious about their penis size. Some succumb to the advertisements for devices promising to enlarge their penises. Men who purchase these devices are bound to be disappointed, for there is no nonsurgical way to enlarge the penis, and many of these techniques (most of which use suction) can do significant damage to the delicate penile tissue (D. Bagley, 2005). Other men with size anxiety refrain from sex altogether, fearing they cannot please a partner or will be laughed at when their partner sees them naked. Yet, the vast majority of women and men report that penis size is not a significant factor in the quality of a sex partner.

ERECTION Erections can occur with any form of stimulation the individual perceives as sexual—visual, tactile, auditory, olfactory, or cognitive. In addition, involuntary sleep-related erections occur several times each night in healthy men (Hirshkowitz & Schmidt, 2005). During an erection, nerve fibers swell the arteries of the penis, allowing blood to rush into the corpora cavernosa and corpus spongiosum, while veins are compressed to prevent the blood from escaping. The erectile tissues thus will fill with blood, causing the penis to become erect (Japanese folk wisdom claims that men's erection angles change as they age; see Figure 6.3 for more information). The penis returns to its flaccid state when the arteries constrict, the pressure closing off the veins is released, and the sequestered blood is allowed to drain. Drugs for erectile dysfunction, such as Viagra, work in a similar way by regulating blood flow in the penis and inhibiting blood loss (Eardley, 2010).

Erection is basically a spinal reflex, and men who have spinal injuries can sometimes achieve reflex erections, in which their penis becomes erect even though they can feel no sensation there.

All of the men in these photos have "normal" bodies. Individual differences in weight, the size and the shape of the torso, and fullness of pubic hair are normal.

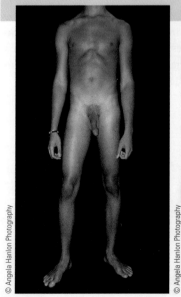
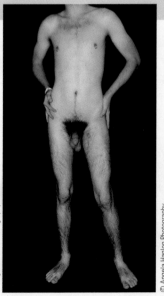
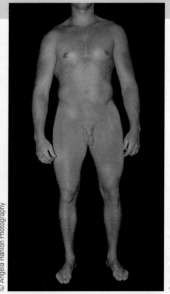

© Angela Hanlon Photography

FIGURE **6.3** When a man jumps into a cold swimming pool, muscles in the scrotum pull the testicles up closer to the body in an attempt to maintain the correct temperature.

These erections generally occur without cognitive or emotional excitement.

The Scrotum

The **scrotum** (SKROH-tum) is a loose, wrinkled pouch beneath the penis, covered with sparse pubic hair. The scrotum contains the testicles, each in a sac, separated by a thin layer of tissue. In Chapter 5, we discussed how a woman's gonads (the ovaries) are located in her abdomen. This is different from the male gonads (the testicles), which sit outside the body. This is because the production and survival of sperm require a temperature that is a few degrees lower than the body's temperature, so the scrotum is actually a kind of cooling tank for the testicles.

When the testicles become too hot, sperm production is halted; in fact, soaking the testicles in hot water has been used as a form of birth control. (Of course, such a technique is highly unreliable, and it takes only a few hardy sperm to undo an hour of uncomfortable soaking. I do not recommend you try it!) Likewise, after a prolonged fever, sperm production may be reduced for as long as 2 months. It has also been suggested that men who are trying to impregnate their partner wear loose-fitting underwear, because tight jockstraps or briefs have been shown to reduce sperm counts somewhat, although the effects are reversible (Shafik, 1991). In the accompanying Sex in Real Life feature, we explore factors that have been found to decrease sperm concentrations and quality.

The scrotum is designed to regulate testicular temperature using two mechanisms. First, the skin overlying the scrotum contains many sweat glands and sweats freely, which cools the testicles when they become too warm. Second, the **cremaster muscle** of

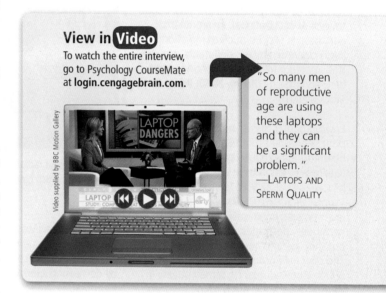

View in Video
To watch the entire interview, go to Psychology CourseMate at **login.cengagebrain.com.**

"So many men of reproductive age are using these laptops and they can be a significant problem." —LAPTOPS AND SPERM QUALITY

the scrotum contracts and expands: When the testicles become too cool, they are drawn closer to the body to increase their temperature; when they become too warm, they are lowered away from the body to reduce their temperature. Men often experience the phenomenon of having the scrotum relax and hang low when taking a warm shower, only to tighten up when cold air hits it after exiting the shower. The scrotum also contracts and elevates the testicles in response to sexual arousal, which may be to protect the testicles from injury during sexual behavior.

▶▶ INTERNAL Sex Organs

The internal sex organs of the male include the testes, epididymis, vas deferens, seminal vesicles, prostate gland, and Cowper's glands. All of these organs play important roles in spermatogenesis, testosterone production, and the process of ejaculation.

The Testicles

The testicles (also referred to as the testes [TEST-eez]) are egg-shaped glands that rest in the scrotum, each about 2 inches long and 1 inch in diameter. The left testicle usually hangs lower than the

---

scrotum
External pouch of skin that contains the testicles.

cremaster muscle
The "suspender" muscle that raises and lowers the scrotum to control scrotal temperature.

Spermatogenesis occurs throughout a man's life, although sperm morphology (sperm form and structure) and motility (sperm's ability to swim), together with semen volume, have been found to decline continuously between the ages of 22 and 80 years (Eskenazi et al., 2003). Researchers have been evaluating changes in total sperm counts, quality, morphology, and motility, and have found that sperm counts have been declining in men throughout the world (Dindyal, 2004; Huang et al., 2010; Muratori et al., 2011; Povey & Stocks, 2010). Although declines in sperm counts and quality are a normal function of aging, researchers have begun to look at occupational, environmental, and lifestyle factors, such as radiation, heat, cigarette smoke, pollutants, sexually transmitted infections, cell phone usage, diet, and obesity (Pacey, 2010; Povey & Stocks, 2010).

Environmental toxins, such as dioxins, bisphenol A, and phthalates, have also been found to reduce sperm quality (Galloway et al., 2010; Li et al., 2011; Mocarelli et al., 2008; Taioli et al., 2005; Toppari et al., 2010). Dioxins are petroleum-derived chemicals that are in herbicides, pesticides, and industrial waste, but they are also commonly found in fish and cow milk products (Taioli et al., 2005). A U.S. study comparing semen quality in various geographic areas found reduced semen quality in areas where pesticides are commonly used (Swan, 2006). Phthalates have also been found to decrease sperm counts and quality (Stahlhut et al., 2007; Voiland, 2008).

Cell phones have also been identified as a possible factor in the decreasing quality of sperm. Cell phones emit radiofrequency

© Anthony Hatley/Alamy

Cell phones emit radiofrequency electromagnetic waves, which have been found to affect sperm quality.

electromagnetic waves, which have been found to affect sperm quality. High cell phone usage reduces semen quality in men by decreasing sperm counts, motility, and morphology (Agarwal et al., 2008). A strong association was found between the length of cell phone use and sperm count: Those who talked more than 4 hours a day had lower sperm quality. Other studies claim that cell phone usage may not be harmful to sperm (Deepinder et al., 2007; Erogul et al., 2006; Wdowiak et al., 2007).

Several other factors have been found to affect sperm production, such as stress (see the Real Research on page 143; Lampiao, 2009), laptop computer use (Sheynkin et al., 2005), biking 5 or more hours a week (Wise et al., 2011), and smoking cigarettes and drinking alcohol (Kalyani et al., 2007). Researchers have also explored soy food intake and sperm concentrations, and have found conflicting results (Cederroth et al., 2010; Chavarro et al., 2008; Messina, 2010). Soy products contain high levels of isoflavones, which mimic estrogen in the body, causing hormonal changes in a man's body. Research in all these areas will continue to explore the effects of these behaviors on sperm production and quality.

Decreasing sperm counts and quality may contribute to male infertility—in fact, 7% of infertility cases are due to defects in the quality, concentration, and/or motility of sperm (Muratori et al., 2011). There are no known treatments to help a man produce more or higher quality sperm (Barratt et al., 2011). We will discuss male infertility in more detail in Chapter 12.

---

right in most men (T. Hamilton, 2002), although this can be reversed in left-handed men. Having one testicle lower than the other helps one slide over the other instead of crushing together when compressed. The testicles serve two main functions: **spermatogenesis** and testosterone production (see Figures 6.4 and 6.5).

SPERMATOGENESIS Sperm are produced and stored in some 300 microscopic tubes located in the testes, known as **seminiferous** (sem-uh-NIF-uh-rus) **tubules.** Uncoiled, this network of tubes would extend over a mile! Figure 6.5 shows the development of the **spermatozoon** in the seminiferous tubules. First, a **spermatogonium** (sper-MAT-oh-go-nee-um) develops in the cells

lining the outer wall of the seminiferous tubules and progressively moves toward the center of the tubules. Sertoli cells located in the seminiferous tubules secrete nutritional substances for the developing sperm.

As the spermatogonium grows, it becomes a primary **spermatocyte** (sper-MAT-oh-site) and then divides to form two secondary spermatocytes. As the developing sperm approach the center of the seminiferous tubules, the secondary spermatocytes

---

REAL RESEARCH 6.2 The word *testify* originates from the word *testes,* the Latin word for "testicles." The practice of holding one's testicles while testifying in a court of law was based on the belief that unborn generations would seek revenge if the truth wasn't told (T. HAMILTON, 2002). This is why during Greek and Roman times, eunuchs (men whose testicles were removed) were not allowed to testify in court.

---

spermatogenesis
The production of sperm in the testes.

seminiferous tubules
The tightly coiled ducts located in the testes where spermatozoa are produced.

spermatozoon
A mature sperm cell.

spermatogonium
An immature sperm cell that will develop into a spermatocyte.

divide into two **spermatids**. The spermatid then reorganizes its nucleus to form a compact head, topped by an acrosome, which contains enzymes to help the sperm penetrate the ovum. The sperm also develops a midpiece, which generates energy, and a **flagellum** (flah-GEL-lum), which propels the mature spermatozoon. Human sperm formation requires approximately 72 days; yet because sperm is in constant production, the human male produces about 300 million sperm per day (for more information on sperm production, see the accompanying Sex in Real Life feature).

TESTOSTERONE PRODUCTION   Testosterone is produced in the testicles in **interstitial** (in-ter-STIH-shul) or **Leydig** (LIE-dig) **cells** and is synthesized from cholesterol. Testosterone is the most important male hormone; we discuss its role when we examine male puberty later in this chapter.

The Epididymis

Once formed, immature sperm enter the seminiferous tubule and migrate to the **epididymis** (ep-uh-DID-uh-mus; see Figure 6.4), where they mature for about 10 to 14 days and where some faulty or old sperm are reabsorbed. The epididymis is a comma-shaped organ that sits atop the testicle and can be easily felt if the testicle is gently rolled between the fingers. If uncoiled, the epididymis

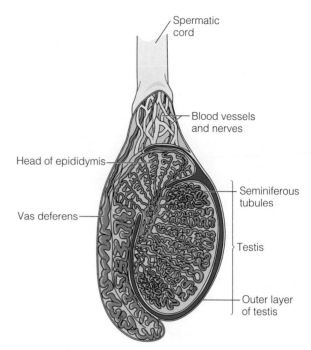

FIGURE 6.4 The internal structure of the testicle. Copyright © Cengage Learning 2013

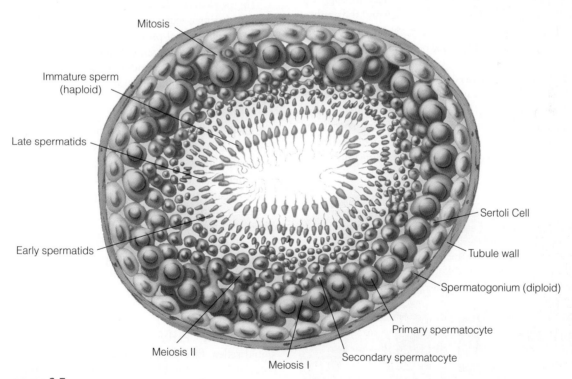

FIGURE 6.5 Spermatogenesis is continually taking place with various levels of sperm development throughout the testis.
Copyright © Cengage Learning 2013

| **spermatocyte** The intermediate stage in the growth of a spermatozoon. | **flagellum** The tail-like end of a spermatozoon that propels it forward. | **interstitial cells** Cells responsible for the production of testosterone; also referred to as Leydig cells. | **Leydig cells** The cells in the testes that produce testosterone; also referred to as interstitial cells. | **epididymis** A comma-shaped organ that sits atop the testicle and holds sperm during maturation. |
| **spermatids** The cells that make up the final intermediate stage in the production of sperm. | | | | |

Colored scan of seminiferous tubules, each containing a swirl of forming sperm cells (in blue).

ON YOUR MIND 6.2

I've heard people say that what a man eats can influence the taste of his semen. Is this really true?

Yes. The flavor and taste of the ejaculate varies from man to man and is strongly influenced by what a man eats (T. Hamilton, 2002). For example, the ejaculate of a man who smokes cigarettes or marijuana and drinks coffee or alcohol is often bitter. A man who eats red meat, certain vegetables (such as spinach, asparagus, or broccoli), chocolate, garlic, or greasy foods often has a very sharp flavor to his ejaculate. And a mild to sweet ejaculate is often due to a vegetarian diet or one high in fruits (especially pineapple) and herbs such as peppermint, parsley, or spearmint.

would be about 20 feet in length. After sperm have matured, the epididymis pushes them into the vas deferens, where they can be stored for several months.

The Ejaculatory Pathway

The **vas deferens** (vass DEH-fuh-renz), or ductus deferens, is an 18-inch tube that carries the sperm from the testicles, mixes it with fluids from other glands, and propels the sperm toward the urethra during ejaculation (see Figure 6.2). **Ejaculation** is the physiological process whereby the seminal fluid is forcefully ejected from the penis. During ejaculation, sperm pass successively through the epididymis, the vas deferens, the ejaculatory duct, and the urethra, picking up fluid along the way from three glands—the seminal vesicles, the prostate gland, and the Cowper's glands.

THE SEMINAL VESICLES The vas deferens hooks up over the ureter of the bladder and ends in an **ampulla.** Adjacent to the ampulla are the **seminal vesicles.** The seminal vesicles contribute rich secretions, which provide nutrition for the traveling sperm and make up about 60% to 70% of the volume of the ejaculate. The vas deferens and the duct from the seminal vesicles merge into a com-

At some point in their lives men will be offered a prostate exam to help detect prostate cancer in its early stages. A man may be asked to either lean over or lie on his side while the health care provider inserts a gloved finger into a man's rectum to check the size of the prostate gland.

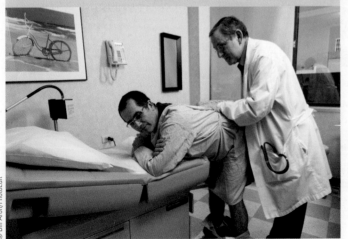

mon **ejaculatory duct,** a short straight tube that passes into the prostate gland and opens into the urethra.

THE PROSTATE GLAND The **prostate** (PROSS-tayt) **gland,** a walnut-sized gland at the base of the bladder, produces several substances that are thought to aid sperm in their attempt to fertilize an ovum. The vagina maintains an acidic pH to protect against bacteria, yet an acidic environment slows down and eventually kills sperm. Prostatic secretions, which comprise about 25% to 30% of the ejaculate, effectively neutralize vaginal acidity almost immediately after ejaculation.

The prostate is close to the rectum, so a doctor can feel the prostate during a rectal examination. The prostate gland can cause a number of physical problems in men, especially older men, including prostate enlargement and the development of prostate cancer (see the Male Reproductive and Sexual Health section later in this chapter). Annual prostate examinations are recommended for men older than 35 years.

THE COWPER'S GLANDS The **Cowper's** or **bulbourethral** (bulbow-you-REE-thral) **glands** are two pea-sized glands that flank the urethra just beneath the prostate gland. The glands have ducts that open right into the urethra and produce a fluid that cleans and lubricates the urethra for the passage of sperm, neutralizing any acidic urine that may remain in the urethra. The drop or more of pre-ejaculatory fluid that many men experience during arousal is the fluid from the Cowper's glands. Although in the past researchers believed there was no sperm in the pre-ejaculatory fluid, newer research has found that the fluid may contain live sperm, so heterosexual men should use condoms if pregnancy is not desired (Killick et al., 2010).

EJACULATION Earlier in this chapter, we discussed erection as a spinal reflex. Ejaculation, like erection, also begins in the spinal column; however, unlike erection, there is seldom a "partial" ejaculation. Once the stimulation builds to the threshold, ejaculation usually continues until its conclusion. When the threshold is reached, the first stage of ejaculation begins: the epididymis, seminal vesicles, and prostate all empty their contents into the urethral bulb, which swells up to accommodate the semen. The bladder is closed off by an internal sphincter so that no urine is expelled with the semen. Once these stages begin, some men report feeling that ejaculation is imminent, that they are going to ejaculate and nothing can stop it; however, others report that this feeling of inevitability can be stopped by immediately ceasing all sensation.

If stimulation continues, strong, rhythmic contractions of the muscles at the base of the penis squeeze the urethral bulb, and the ejaculate is propelled from the body, usually accompanied by the pleasurable sensation of orgasm. Most men have between 5 and 15 contractions during orgasm, and many report enjoying strong pressure at the base of the penis during orgasm. From an evolutionary standpoint, this may be a way of encouraging deep thrusting at the moment of ejaculation to deposit semen as deeply as possible within the woman's vagina.

Once orgasm subsides, the arteries supplying the blood to the penis narrow, the veins taking the blood out enlarge, and the penis usually becomes limp. Depending on the level of excitement, the person's age, the length of time since the previous ejaculation, and his individual physiology, a new erection can occur anywhere from immediately to an hour or so later. In older men, however, a second erection can take hours or even a day or so (we will discuss aging and sexual function further in Chapter 10).

EJACULATE The male ejaculate, or semen, averages about 2 to 5 milliliters—about 1 or 2 teaspoons. Semen normally contains secretions from the seminal vesicles and the prostate gland and about 50 to 150 million sperm per milliliter. If there are fewer than 20 million sperm per milliliter, the male is likely to be infertile—even though the ejaculate can have up to 500 million sperm altogether! Sperm is required in such large numbers because during procreation only a small fraction ever reach the ovum. Also, the sperm work together to achieve fertilization; for example, many die to plug up the os of the cervix for the other sperm, and the combined enzyme production of all sperm is necessary for a single spermatozoon to fertilize the ovum.

Directly after ejaculation, the semen initially coagulates into a thick, mucous-like liquid, probably an evolutionary development to aid in procreation by decreasing the chances it would leak back out of the vagina. After 5 to 20 minutes, the prostatic enzymes contained in the semen cause it to thin out and liquefy. If it does not liquefy normally, coagulated semen in heterosexual men may be unable to complete its movement through the cervix and into the uterus.

▶▶ OTHER Sex Organs

Like women, men have other erogenous zones, or areas of the body that may be responsive to sexual touch. This is often an individual preference, but it can include the breasts and other erogenous zones, including the scrotum, testicles, and anus.

The Breasts

Men's breasts are mostly muscle, and although they do have nipples and areolae, they seem to serve no functional purpose. Transsexual males, who want to change their sex (see Chapter 4), can

---

REAL RESEARCH 6.3 Stress can affect sperm production—semen samples from male college students during exam periods found lower concentrations of sperm than samples collected at the beginning of the semester (LAMPIAO, 2009).

---

enlarge their breasts to mimic the female breast by taking estrogen. Some men experience sexual pleasure from having their nipples stimulated, especially during periods of high excitement, whereas others do not.

Breast cancer does affect men, although it is rare and accounts for less than 1% of all cases (Reis et al., in press). We will discuss breast cancer further later in this chapter. Another breast disorder that occurs in men is gynecomastia, or breast enlargement. Gynecomastia is common in all stages of a man's life; in fact, the prevalence rate is 60% to 90% in newborns, 50% to 60% in adolescents, and up to 70% in men aged 50 to 69 years old (Carlson, 2011; Johnson & Murad, 2009). It is usually caused by hormonal issues, such as increased estrogen or decreased testosterone, the use of various medications, excessive weight, marijuana use, and/or certain diseases (Johnson & Murad, 2009). Certain environmental toxins have also been found to be related to the development of gynecomastia (Durmaz et al., 2010).

---

vas deferens
One of two long tubes that convey the sperm from the testes and in which other fluids are mixed to create semen.

ejaculation
The reflex ejection or expulsion of semen from the penis.

ampulla
Base of the vas deferens, where the vas hooks up over the ureter of the bladder.

seminal vesicles
The pair of pouchlike structures lying next to the urinary bladder that secrete a component of semen into the ejaculatory ducts.

ejaculatory duct
A tube that transports spermatozoa from the vas deferens to the urethra.

prostate gland
A doughnut-shaped gland that wraps around the urethra as it comes out of the bladder, contributing fluid to the semen.

Cowper's or bulbourethral gland
One of a pair of glands located under the prostate gland on either side of the urethra that secretes a fluid into the urethra.

nocturnal emissions
Involuntary ejaculation during sleep, also referred to as wet dreams.

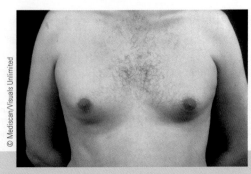

Gynecomastia is common in puberty and old age and can be caused by a variety of factors.

Although gynecomastia can make men feel self-conscious, most cases resolve without treatment within about 1 year (Johnson & Murad, 2009). It is typically a benign condition, but if there is pain or psychological distress, treatment options include pharmacological intervention and surgery, including liposuction (Cigna et al., in press).

Other Erogenous Zones

Besides the penis, many men experience pleasure from stimulation of the scrotum, testicles (usually through gentle squeezing), and anus. As with women's erogenous zones, there is no part of the male body that is not erogenous if caressed in the right way and at the right time during sex. When the body is sexually stimulated, almost all moderate sensation can enhance excitement.

◀ review QUESTIONS

1 Identify the external male sex organs and discuss the functions of each.

2 Explain why the male gonads are located outside of the body.

3 Identify and discuss the functions of the internal male sexual organs.

4 Identify the internal male sex organs and discuss the functions of each.

5 Describe the path taken by a sperm from the moment it is a spermatogonium until it is ejaculated. What other internal male organs contribute to semen along the way?

▶ MALE Maturation Cycle

Now that we've discussed the male sexual and reproductive system, let's explore male maturation. In the following section, we discuss the physical changes that accompany male puberty. Many of these changes are controlled by hormonal changes that occur and contribute to physical changes in a young boy's body. In Chapter 8, we discuss the psychosexual changes of male puberty.

▶▶ MALE Puberty

During a boy's early life, the two major functions of the testes—to produce male sex hormones and to produce sperm—remain dormant. No one knows exactly what triggers the onset of puberty or how a boy's internal clock knows that he is reaching the age at which these functions of the testes will be needed. Still, at an average of 10 years of age, the hypothalamus begins releasing gonadotropin-releasing hormone (GnRH), which stimulates the anterior pituitary gland to send out follicle-stimulating hormone (FSH) and luteinizing hormone (LH; see Table 4.2).

These hormones flow through the circulatory system to the testes, where LH stimulates the production of the male sex hormone, testosterone, which, together with LH, stimulates sperm production. A negative feedback system regulates hormone production; when the concentration of testosterone in the blood increases to a certain level, GnRH release from the hypothalamus

*No one knows exactly what triggers the **onset of puberty**...*

is inhibited, causing inhibition of LH production and resulting in decreased testosterone production (see Figure 6.6 for more information about the negative-feedback loop). Alternately, when testosterone levels decrease below a certain level, this stimulates GnRH production by the hypothalamus, which increases the pituitary's LH production and testosterone production goes up.

As puberty progresses, the testicles grow, and the penis begins to grow about a year later. The epididymis, prostate, seminal vesicles, and Cowper's glands also grow over the next several years. Increased testosterone stimulates an overall growth spurt in puberty, as bones and muscles rapidly develop. This spurt can be dramatic; teenage boys can grow 3 or 4 inches within a few months.

The elevation of testosterone affects a number of male traits: The boy develops longer and heavier bones, larger muscles, thicker and tougher skin, a deepening voice because of growth of the voice box, pubic hair, facial and chest hair, increased sex drive, and increased metabolism.

Spermatogenesis begins at about 12 years of age, but ejaculation of mature sperm usually does not occur for about another 1 to 1.5 years. At puberty, FSH begins to stimulate sperm production in the seminiferous tubules, and the increased testosterone induces the testes to mature fully. The development of spermatogenesis and the sexual fluid glands allows the boy to begin to experience his first nocturnal emissions, although at the beginning, they tend to contain a very low live sperm count.

Male circumcision is practiced in many parts of the world. The World Health Organization estimates that more than 664 million males—or 30%—are circumcised (Malone & Steinbrecher, 2007). Reasons for circumcision vary around the world but include religious, cultural, social, and/or medical reasons. Nonreligious circumcision became popular in the 1870s because it was thought to promote hygiene, reduce "unnatural" sexual behaviors, prevent syphilis and gonorrhea, and reduce masturbation (G. Kaplan, 1977; Wallerstein, 1980). An article published in 1947 supporting circumcision reported that cancer was more common in laboratory mice who were not circumcised (Plaut & Kohn-Speyer, 1947). All of these medical reports and social considerations have influenced the incidence of male circumcision.

Circumcision can be done at any age, but it is most commonly done at birth up until the mid-20s. Infant circumcision is commonly done in the United States, Canada, Australia, New Zealand, the Middle East, Central Asia, and West Africa. Many parents cite hygiene and health reasons for circumcising their infants at birth. In other areas of the world, such as East and southern Africa, male circumcisions are done in the mid-teens to early 20s and are viewed as rites of passage for boys and a transition from child to man (Crowley & Kesner, 1990). Other cultures believe that circumcision makes a boy a man because the foreskin is viewed as feminine (Silverman, 2004).

Various ethnic groups have different preferences concerning circumcising their male children. If circumcision is common in a particular ethnic group, parents may be inclined to circumcise their male children so their sons will look like other boys (Centers for Disease Control and Prevention, 2008h). In addition, fathers who are circumcised often have their sons circumcised (Goldman, 1999). These social considerations have been found to outweigh the medical facts when parents are deciding whether to circumcise their sons (M. S. Brown & Brown, 1987). Medical reasons for circumcision are rare, and it is mainly practiced for religious and cultural reasons today (Malone & Steinbrecher, 2007).

The practice of male circumcision has elicited more controversy than any other surgical procedure in history (Alanis & Lucidi, 2004; Fox & Thomson, 2010; Hinchley, 2007; Patrick, 2007). Most of the controversy revolves around the risks and potential benefits of circumcision. A wide-scale study done in Africa found that male circumcision offered protection from HIV infection (M. S. Cohen et al., 2008d; Drain et al., 2006; Morris, 2007; Thomson et al., 2007; Weiss et al., 2000). Male circumcision has been found to reduce the risk for HIV in men by 60% (Smith et al., 2010; Weiss et al., 2010). Circumcision offered protection to both men who had sex with women and men who had sex with men (Dinh et al., 2011; Fox & Thomson, 2010).

Circumcised men have also been found to have lower rates of infant urinary tract infections (Simforoosh et al., in press) and sexually transmitted infections, such as herpes and human papillomavirus (see

Chapter 15; Weiss et al., 2010). Female partners of circumcised men also have lower rates of certain types of vaginal infections and cervical cancer (Alanis & Lucidi, 2004; Drain et al., 2006; Morris, 2007; Weiss et al., 2010).

Even though there may be some medical benefits to circumcision, experts believe these benefits are not strong enough for health care providers to recommend routine circumcision (Kinkade & Meadows, 2005; Tobian et al., 2010). In 1999, the American Academy of Pediatrics stopped recommending routine male circumcision and suggested that parents make the decision to circumcise based on their own experiences, their family, and religious beliefs (American Academy of Pediatrics, 1999).

© John Warburton-Lee Photography/PhotoLibrary

A Samburu youth is circumcised in Kenya while his sponsors attend to him—one holding his leg, while the other turns his face away from the circumciser. Boys are not allowed to show any signs of fear or pain during the procedure. Even the blink of an eyelid is frowned upon.

▶▶ ANDROPAUSE

As men age, their blood testosterone concentrations decrease. Hormone levels in men have been found to decrease by about 1% each year after age 40 (Daw, 2002). Men do not go through an obvious set of stages, as menopausal women do, but some experience a less well-defined set of symptoms in their 70s or 80s called andropause (Makrantonaki et al., 2010). It is estimated that 2% of elderly men experience symptoms related to andropause (Pines, 2011). Although men's ability to ejaculate viable

REAL RESEARCH 6.4 Men whose mothers smoked more than 19 cigarettes while they were in the womb have 19% lower semen volume and 38% lower total sperm count compared with men with nonsmoking mothers (RAMLAU-HANSEN ET AL., 2007).

sperm is often retained past age 80 or 90, spermatogenesis does decrease, the ejaculate becomes thinner, and ejaculatory pressure decreases. The reduction in testosterone production results in decreased muscle strength, decreased libido, easy fatigue, and mood fluctuations (Bassil & Morley, 2010; Seidman, 2007). Men can also experience osteoporosis and anemia from the decreasing hormone levels (Bain, 2001). Benefits to androgen replacement therapy include increased sexual interest and functioning, increased bone density and muscle mass, and improved mood (Bassil & Morley, 2010).

The use of androgen replacement therapy is controversial due to possible risks and limited long-term studies of its use (Basaria et al., 2010; Cunningham & Toma, 2011; Morales, 2004; Pines, 2011; Wu et al., 2010). One of the largest controversies revolves around the risks involved in taking testosterone, especially the possibility of an increased risk for prostate cancer, although there has been no evidence to support this risk (Bassil & Morley, 2010). Even so, the use of androgen replacement therapy is commonly used in the U.S. today (Bassil & Morley, 2010; Cunningham & Toma, 2011).

"As we age, our hormone levels decline, along with our energy, alertness, libido, and much else that makes life fun."
—FIGHTING AGAINST AGING

View in Video
To watch the entire interview, go to Psychology CourseMate at **login.cengagebrain.com**.

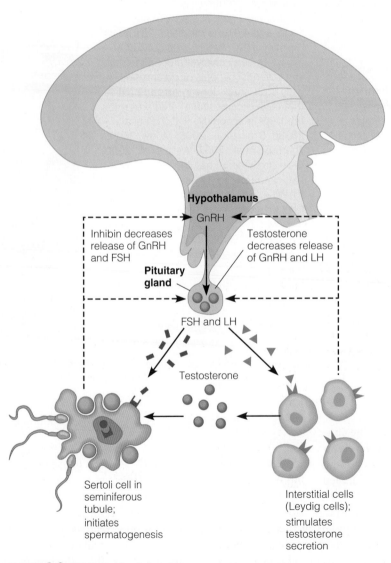

FIGURE **6.6** The cycle of male hormones. Copyright © Cengage Learning 2013

1 Describe the two major functions of the testes, and explain the negative feedback loop in males.

2 Identify the age at which spermatogenesis typically begins. At what age does the ejaculate contain mature sperm?

3 What effect do decreasing levels of testosterone have on men? How has androgen replacement therapy been found to help?

▶ MALE REPRODUCTIVE and Sexual Health

It is a good idea for every man to examine and explore his own sexual anatomy. A regular genital self-examination can help increase a man's comfort with his genitals (see the accompanying Sex in Real Life feature). It can also help a man know what his testicles feel like just in case something were to change. We will first discuss various disorders that may affect the male reproductive organs; then we turn to cancer of the male reproductive organs, its diagnosis, and its treatment.

▶▶ DISORDERS OF THE MALE Reproductive Organs

Several conditions can affect the male reproductive organs, including cryptorchidism, testicular torsion, priapism, and Peyronie's disease. It is important for both men and women to have a good understanding of what these conditions are and what symptoms they might cause.

Cryptorchidism

Cryptorchidism (krip-TOR-kuh-diz-um), or undescended testes, is the most common genital disorder in boys (Mathers et al., 2011). One third of male infants who are born prematurely have cryptorchidism, whereas 2% to 5% of full-term male infants have at least one undescended testicle (Mathers et al., 2011). The testicles of a male fetus begin high in the abdomen near the kidneys and, during fetal development, descend into the scrotum through the inguinal canal (Hutson et al., 1994).

There are no clear reasons why cryptorchidism occurs, although research has explored several risks including genetics, hormones (Massert & Saggese, 2010; Robin et al., 2010), placental abnormalities (Thorup et al., 2010), and maternal smoking during pregnancy (Lacerda et al., 2010). Recent research has found geographic variations and increasing trends in several countries, which may indicate environmental effects and exposure to certain chemicals (Robin et al., 2010; Sharpe & Skakkebaek, 2008; Toppari et al., 2010). Research in these areas is ongoing (see the accompanying Sex in Real Life feature).

Newborn boys with cryptorchidism may be given testosterone to help with testicular descent. However, if the testes have not descended by 6 months of age, surgery is often required to relocate the undescended testis to the scrotum (Hack et al., 2003; Hutson & Hasthorpe, 2005). It is estimated that 90% of untreated men

ON YOUR MIND 6.4

Can a male have an orgasm without an ejaculation?
Yes. Before puberty, boys are capable of orgasm without ejaculation. In adulthood, some men report feeling several small orgasms before a larger one that includes ejaculation, whereas other men report that if they have sex a second or third time, there is orgasm without ejaculatory fluid. There are also some Eastern sexual disciplines, such as Tantra, that try to teach men to achieve orgasm without ejaculation because they believe that retaining semen is important for men.

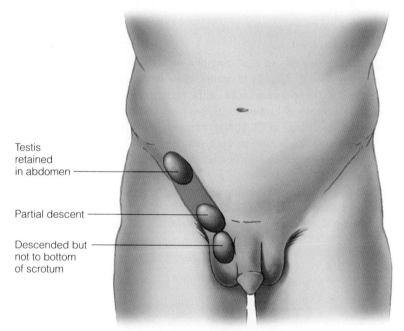

Testis retained in abdomen

Partial descent

Descended but not to bottom of scrotum

FIGURE 6.7 Although the testicles of a fetus begin high in the abdomen, they must descend into the scrotum during fetal development. If they do not, the male may become infertile. Copyright © Cengage Learning 2013

with cryptorchidism will be infertile, because excessive heat in the abdomen impairs the ability to produce viable sperm (AbouZeid et al., 2011; Mathers et al., 2011; see Figure 6.7 for more information on cryptorchid testes). Men with a history of cryptorchid testes also have an increased risk for testicular cancer (Robin et al., 2010; Thorup et al., 2010; Toppari et al., 2010).

cryptorchidism
A condition in which the testes fail to descend into the scrotum.

Although there are no obvious symptoms of testicular cancer, when detected early, it is treatable. The only early detection system for testicular cancer is testicular

self-examination. However, a nationally representative sample of American men found that only 2% to 10% of men perform monthly testicular self-examinations, and that various factors, such as gender roles and norms, may inhibit a man from performing a testicular self-examination (Reece et al., 2010a). Just like breast self-examinations in women, men should examine their testicles at least monthly. This will enable them to have an understanding of what things feel like

under normal conditions, which will help them to find any lumps or abnormal growths, should they appear.

To do a testicular examination, compare both testicles simultaneously by grasping one with each hand, using thumb and forefinger. This may be best done while taking a warm shower, which causes the scrotum to relax and the testicles to hang lower. Determine their size, shape, and sensitivity to pressure.

As you get to know the exact shape and feel of the testicles, you will be able to notice any swelling, lumps, or unusual pain. Report any such occurrence to your physician without delay, but do not panic; most lumps are benign and nothing to worry about.

Testicular Torsion

Testicular torsion refers to a twisting of a testis on its spermatic cord (see Figure 6.8). Usually it occurs when there is abnormal development of the spermatic cord or the membrane that covers the testicle (Wampler & Llanes, 2010). It is most common in men from puberty to the age of 25, and approximately 1 in 4,000 men are affected by testicular torsion each year (Ringdahl & Teague, 2006). Testicular torsion can occur after exercise, sexual behavior, or even while sleeping.

Acute scrotal pain and swelling are two of the most common symptoms, although there can also be abdominal pain, nausea, and vomiting (Kapoor, 2008). Testicular torsion should be consid-

ered a medical emergency, and any man who experiences a rapid onset of scrotal pain should have this pain checked by a health care provider immediately. An ultrasound is often used to help diagnose this condition, but because the twisted cord can cut off blood supply to the testicle, the condition must be diagnosed very quickly (Cokkinos et al., 2010; Kapoor 2008; Ringdahl & Teague, 2006). Restoration of blood flow to the testicle, through manipulation of the spermatic cord or surgery, must be made within 6 hours of the onset of symptoms or the testicle may be lost (Kapoor, 2008; Mongiat-Artus, 2004; Ringdahl & Teague, 2006). Although we don't know exactly what causes testicular torsion, research indicates there may be a genetic risk. One study found testicular tor-

sion was more common in men with a family history of the condition (Shteynshlyuger & Freyle, 2011).

Priapism

Priapism (PRY-uh-pizm) is an abnormally prolonged and painful erection that is not associated with sexual desire or excitement (Cakin-Memik et al., 2010; Mi et al., 2008; Van der Horst et al., 2003). It is primarily a vascular condition that causes blood to become trapped in the erectile tissue of the penis. Although researchers don't know exactly what causes priapism, men with certain conditions, such as sickle cell disease, leukemia, and/or spinal cord injuries, are at greater

Normal anatomy

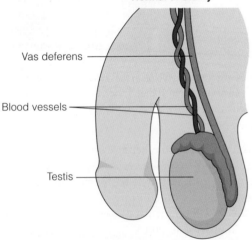

Vas deferens

Blood vessels

Testis

Testicular torsion

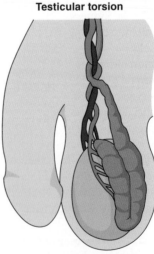

FIGURE 6.8 Testicular torsion can occur after exercise or sexual intercourse, or even while sleeping. Copyright © Cengage Learning 2013

risk for development of priapism (Mi et al., 2008). In some cases, drug use (erection drugs, cocaine, marijuana, or anticoagulants) is to blame. Researchers have been using penile tissue from various animals, such as dogs, cats, rabbits, and mice, to study priapism, which has enhanced researchers understanding of this condition (Dong et al., 2011).

Like testicular torsion, priapism is considered a medical emergency because it can damage erectile tissue if left untreated (Mi et al., 2008). Treatment may involve pharmaceutical agents to reduce blood flow or stents to remove the built-up blood. If there is a neurological or other physiological cause for the priapism, anesthesia and surgery may be necessary (Shrewsberry et al., 2010).

Peyronie's Disease

Every male has individual curves to his penis when it becomes erect. These curves and angles are quite normal. However, in approximately 1% of men, painful curvature makes penetration impossible, leading to a diagnosis of a condition known as **Peyronie's** (pay-row-NEEZ) **disease** (C. J. Smith et al., 2005; Perovic & Djinovic, 2010). Typically, this happens between the ages of 45 and 60, although younger and older men can also experience Peyronie's disease.

Peyronie's disease occurs in the connective tissue of the penis, and although some cases are asymptomatic, others experience development of plaques or areas of hardened tissue, which can cause severe erectile pain (Gelbard, 1988). In extreme cases, penetrative sex is impossible due to the curvature.

No one knows what causes Peyronie's disease. It is possible that fibrous tissue buildup, excessive calcium, or trauma may contribute to this disorder (Gelbard, 1988). Usually this disease lasts approximately 2 years and may go away just as suddenly as it appears. It is treated in a variety of ways, including medication, surgery, or both (Austoni et al., 2005; Heidari et al., 2010; Perovic & Djinovic, 2010; Seveso et al., 2010). Research has found that penile curvature can be successfully reduced with treatment, and many

men find they are able to engage in penetrative sex again after treatment (Heidari et al., 2010).

▶▶ INGUINAL Hernia

An **inguinal hernia** (ING-gwuh-nul HER-nee-uh) is caused when the intestine pushes through the opening in the abdominal wall into the **inguinal canal** (the inguinal canal was originally used by the testes when they descended into the scrotum shortly before birth). This can happen during heavy lifting or straining. When it does, the intestine pushes down onto the testicles and causes a bulge or lump in the scrotum. The bulge may change shape and size depending on what the man is doing, because it can slide back and forth within the testicle. Other symptoms include pain and possible blockage of the intestine. Depending on the size and the pain associated with the bulge, surgery may be necessary to push the protruding intestines back into the abdomen (Hussain et al., 2010).

▶▶ HYDROCELE

A **hydrocele** (HI-druh-seal) is a condition in which there is an excessive accumulation of fluid within the tissue surrounding the testicle, which causes a scrotal mass (making the scrotum look and feel like a water balloon). This accumulation could be caused by an overproduction of fluid or poor reabsorption of the fluid, and it can also be caused by a leak through the inguinal canal. Hydroceles are common in newborn males and typically go away on their own after a few months. Although they are relatively painless, some men experience pain and swelling within the testicle. Health care providers often use ultrasound to diagnose a hydrocele, and treatment involves removing the built-up fluid through needle aspiration.

testicular torsion	Peyronie's disease	inguinal hernia	inguinal canal	hydrocele
The twisting of a testis on its spermatic cord, which can cause severe pain and swelling.	Abnormal calcifications or fibrous tissue buildup in the penis, which may cause painful curvature, often making sexual intercourse impossible.	A condition in which the intestines bulge through a hole in the abdominal muscles of the groin.	Canal through which the testes descend into the scrotum.	A condition in which there is an excessive accumulation of fluid within the tissue surrounding the testicle, which causes a scrotal mass.
priapism				
A condition in which erections are long-lasting and often painful.				

Accusations of steroid use in Major League Baseball circulated in 2005. Photos of before and after supported these claims. Here is Barry Bonds in 1989 (left) and in 2003 (right).

View in Video

To watch the entire interview, go to Psychology CourseMate at **login.cengagebrain.com.**

"I was like a female that time of the month."
—STEROID USE

ANABOLIC-ANDROGENIC Steroid Abuse

Since the early 2000s, steroids have become a controversial topic as more and more male athletes disclose past steroid use. In 2005, congressional hearings began to evaluate steroid abuse in Major League Baseball. Anabolic-androgenic steroids (AAS), also known as synthetic testosterone, have been used by elite athletes since the 1950s, but it wasn't until the 1980s that these types of drugs were abused by nonathletes as well (Kanayama et al., 2010).

There are steroids that occur naturally in the body, and they are known as androgens. During puberty in males, the release of androgens increases weight and muscle size, and can also increase endurance and aggressiveness. We know that millions of boys and men, primarily in Western countries, use AAS to enhance their appearance or athletic performance (Brennan et al., 2011; Kanayama et al., 2010). Women have also been found to abuse these drugs, although at lower levels than men (Gruber & Pope, 2000). However, the actual number of people who abuse AAS is unknown.

AAS use comes at a high price. It has been associated with many damaging changes in the physiological characteristics of organs and body systems. The best documented effects are to the liver, serum lipids, and the reproductive system, including shrinkage of the testicles (and menstrual cycle changes in women; Bonetti et al., 2007; Kanayama et al., 2010; Sato et al., 2008). Other areas of concern include cerebrovascular accidents (strokes), prostate gland changes, and impaired immune function (Wysoczanski et al., 2008). In younger athletes, steroids can cause early fusion of the bone-growth plates, resulting in permanently shortened stature. Use of AAS has also been associated with changes in mood and behavior. Schizophrenia and increases in irritability, hostility, anger, aggression, depression, hypomania, psychotic episodes, and guilt have all been reported among AAS users (Kanayama et al., 2010; Venâncio et al., 2008). AAS users have also been found to be at greater risk for illicit drug use, particularly opioid use (Kanayama et al., 2010).

*Even though breast cancer is rare in men, it has a **higher mortality rate** in men than in women.*

CANCERS OF THE Male Reproductive Organs

As we discussed in Chapter 4, cancer is a disease in which certain cells in the body do not function properly—they divide too fast or produce excessive tissue that forms a tumor, or both. A number of cancers can affect the male reproductive organs. Let's now look at breast, penile, testicular, and prostatic cancers. In this section, we also review preventive measures for detecting or avoiding common male health problems. In Chapter 14, we will discuss how these illnesses affect men's lives and sexuality.

Male Breast Cancer

The American Cancer Society (2011) estimated there were approximately 2,000 cases of breast cancer diagnosed in men in 2010. Even though breast cancer is rare in men, it has a higher mortality rate in men than in women, mainly because it is often diagnosed at a more advanced stage in men compared with women (Al-Saleh, 2011; Rosa & Masood, in press).

Risk factors for breast cancer in men are similar to some of the risk factors for women, including heredity, obesity, hormonal issues, and physical inactivity. Newer research has found that a history of a bone fracture is a risk for breast cancer in men probably because of the association with osteoporosis (Brinton et al., 2008). Exposure to environmental toxins may also increase a man's risk for breast cancer (Maffini et al., 2006).

In Chapter 4, we reviewed the research on cancer and the *BRCA* genes. The presence of these genes in men can also lead to a higher risk for the development of both breast and prostate cancer (Stromsvik et al., 2010). In fact, the presence of these genes doubles the normal risk for prostate cancer and increases the risk for breast cancer by seven times (Tai et al., 2007). Today, some men opt for genetic testing to learn whether they have a *BRCA* mutation. Research has found that, like women, men experience strong emotional reactions to positive test results for the *BRCA* genes. However, few disclose this information to others (Stromsvik et al., 2010). If they do talk to friends about it, most men report females as their main source of support and find it difficult to talk to other men about their diagnosis.

Treatment for breast cancer for men involves radiation or chemotherapy, and if the cancer has spread to other parts of the body, surgical removal of the breasts may be necessary to eliminate the hormones that could support the growth of the cancer.

Penile Cancer

A wide variety of cancers involving the skin and soft tissues of the penis can occur, although cancer of the penis is rare (Mosconi et al., 2005). Any lesion on the penis must be examined by a physician, for benign and malignant conditions can be very similar in appearance, and sexually transmitted infections can appear as lesions. Even though most men handle and observe their penis daily, there is often significant delay between a person's recognition of a lesion and seeking medical attention. Fear and embarrassment may contribute most to this problem, yet almost all of these lesions are treatable if caught early.

Testicular Cancer

The American Cancer Society (2011) estimated there were 8,500 cases of testicular cancer diagnosed in 2010. Testicular cancer is the most common malignancy in men aged 25 to 34 (Garner et al., 2008). There are few symptoms until the cancer is advanced, which is why early detection is so important. Most men first develop testicular cancer as a painless testicular mass or a harder consistency of the testes. If there is pain or a sudden increase in testicular size, it is usually due to bleeding into the tumor. Sometimes lower back pain, gynecomastia, shortness of breath, or urethral obstruction may also be found.

Risk factors for testicular cancer include a family history, cryptorchidism, increased height, body size, age at puberty, and

Lance Armstrong, who has won the Tour de France a record number of times, was diagnosed with testicular cancer when he was 25, by which time the cancer had spread to his lungs and brain. Had he known about the importance of early detection, he would have never ignored the swelling and pain in his testicle. Armstrong underwent aggressive surgery and chemotherapy. One year later, he began racing again and he was still able to have five children through in vitro fertilization (see Chapter 12).

Al Bello/Getty Images

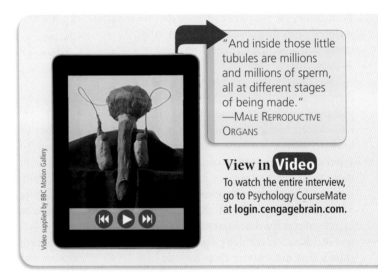

Video supplied by BBC Motion Gallery

"And inside those little tubules are millions and millions of sperm, all at different stages of being made."
—MALE REPRODUCTIVE ORGANS

View in Video
To watch the entire interview, go to Psychology CourseMate at **login.cengagebrain.com.**

dairy consumption (McGlynn et al., 2007). In addition, newer research has found that frequent marijuana use (daily or greater) increases a man's risk for testicular cancer (Trabert et al., 2011).

Although the incidence of testicular cancer has continuously increased during the last few decades, cure rates have significantly improved. In fact, testicular cancer is one of the most curable forms of the disease (American Cancer Society, 2005). Treatment may involve radiation, chemotherapy, or the removal of the testicle (although radiation and chemotherapy can affect future fertility, the removal of a testicle does not). If removal of the testicle is necessary, many men opt to get a prosthetic testicle implanted, which gives the appearance of having two normal testicles. Early diagnosis is very important, because the treatment is less severe early on, and one's chance of being cured is greater.

Prostate Cancer

As men age, their prostate glands enlarge. In most cases, this natural occurrence, **benign prostatic hypertrophy (BPH),** causes few problems. Because of its anatomical position surrounding the urethra, BPH may block urination, and surgeons may need to remove the prostate if the condition becomes bad enough. Of far more con-

benign prostatic hypertrophy (BPH)
The common enlargement of the prostate that occurs in most men after about age 50.

cern than BPH is prostate cancer, which is the most frequently diagnosed cancer in men besides skin cancer (American Cancer Society, 2007b). The American Cancer Society estimates that 1 in 6 men will be diagnosed with prostate cancer in their lifetime, and 1 in 36 will die of this cancer (American Cancer Society, 2011). Approximately 218,000 new cases of prostate cancer were diagnosed in 2010.

Although men of all ages can experience development of prostate cancer, it is found most often in men older than 50 years. In fact, risk for prostate cancer increases in men up until the age of 70 and then begins to decline (American Cancer Society, 2011). For reasons not clearly understood, prostate cancer is about twice as common among Black men as it is among White men (American Cancer Society, 2011). In addition, Black men are more likely to die of it than are White men. Other ethnic and racial groups have lower rates of prostate cancer than either White or Black men. Worldwide, the incidence of prostate cancer varies, with the majority of cases diagnosed in economically developed countries (American Cancer Society, 2011).

*Prostate cancer is the **most frequently diagnosed** cancer in men besides skin cancer.*

We don't know exactly what causes prostate cancer, but we do know that several risk factors have been linked to prostate cancer. Men with a first-degree relative, such as a father or brother, with prostate cancer are two to three times more likely to experience development of prostate cancer, whereas men with more than one first-degree relative are three to five times more likely to experience development of the cancer (American Cancer Society, 2011). In addition, men with the *BRCA* gene are also at increased risk for development of prostate cancer. Other risk factors include race/ethnicity, age, and a diet high in fat. Studies have shown that men whose diets include high levels of calcium and consumption of red and processed meats have higher risks (American Cancer Society, 2011).

Early signs of prostate cancer may include lower back, pelvic, or upper thigh pain; inability to urinate; loss of force in the urinary stream; urinary dribbling; pain or burning during urination; and frequent urination, especially at night. Many deaths from prostate cancer are preventable, because a simple 5- or 10-second rectal examination by a physician, to detect hard lumps on the prostate, detects more than 50% of cases at a curable stage. Digital rectal examinations are recommended for men each year beginning at the age of 50 (or 45 for men with a history of prostate cancer).

In 1986, the U.S. Food and Drug Administration approved the **prostate-specific antigen (PSA)** blood test that measures levels of molecules that are overproduced by prostate cancer cells. This enables physicians to identify prostate cancer and is recommended yearly for men older than 50 (although Black men and those with a first-degree relative with prostate cancer are often advised to begin screening at 45 years old; American Cancer Society, 2011). The PSA test has been one of the most important advances in the area of prostate cancer (Lakhey et al., 2010; Madan & Gulley, 2010). Although not all tumors will show up on a PSA test, a high reading does indicate that something (such as a tumor) is releasing prostatic material into the blood, and a biopsy or further examination is warranted.

There are many treatments for prostate cancer, and almost all of them are controversial. Some argue that, in older men especially, the best thing is "watchful waiting" in which the cancer is simply left alone, because this type of cancer is slow growing and most men will die of other causes before the prostate cancer becomes life-threatening. Men who have a history of poor health, are older than 80 years, or are living in a geographically undesirable location for medical treatment often opt for watchful waiting (Harlan et al., 2001).

Others choose **radical prostatectomy** or radiation treatment, or **cryosurgery,** which uses a probe to freeze parts of the prostate and has had good success in reducing the occurrence of postsurgical erectile disorder and incontinence (J. K. Cohen et al., 2008c). Two of the most common surgical adverse effects of prostate cancer treatment include erectile dysfunction and the inability to hold one's urine. However, the likelihood of these problems depends on several things, including the extent and severity of the cancer and a man's age at the time of surgery (H. Stewart et al., 2005). Although younger men who experienced satisfactory erections before any prostate cancer treatments have fewer erectile problems after surgery, for most men, erections will improve over time. Difficulty holding urine or urinary leakage may also occur; however, treatments are available to lessen these symptoms.

Newer treatments include drugs that attack only cells with cancer, unlike radiation and chemotherapy, which both kill healthy cells in addition to cells with cancer. Research has found that these drugs hold much promise in the treatment of prostate cancer (Plosker, 2011; C. J. Ryan & Small, 2005). Research into vaccines for prostate cancer also continues. In 2010, the U.S. Food and Drug Administration approved Provenge, the first vaccine for prostate cancer (Madan & Gulley, 2011). This vaccine uses a patient's own white blood cells to attack cancer cells. Research will continue to explore the use of vaccines for prostate cancer.

As you have learned throughout this chapter and Chapter 5 on female anatomy, understanding anatomy and physiology is an important part of learning about human sexual behavior. We must understand all of the physiological and hormonal influences, and how they affect both the female and male body, before we can move on to the emotional and psychological issues involved in human sexuality. Anatomy and physiology, therefore, are really the foundations of any human sexuality class. Now we can turn our attention to other important aspects of human sexuality. In Chapter 7, we discuss love and intimacy.

prostate-specific antigen (PSA)
Blood test that measures levels of molecules that are overproduced by prostate cancer cells, enabling physicians to identify prostate cancer early.

radical prostatectomy
The surgical removal of the prostate.

cryosurgery
Surgery that uses freezing techniques to destroy part of an organ.

1 Differentiate between cryptorchidism, testicular torsion, priapism, and Peyronie's disease. Explain what these conditions are and what symptoms they might cause. What are some treatments for these conditions?

2 Explain the adverse effects of anabolic-androgenic steroid use.

3 Identify the most common cancer in men between the ages of 25 and 34, and describe early symptoms and treatment.

4 Identify which cancer is most frequently diagnosed in men overall, and describe early symptoms and treatment.

◂◂ **chapter** REVIEW

SUMMARY POINTS

1 Because the male genitalia sit outside the body, unlike female gonads, boys are often more comfortable with their genitalia. The external male sex organs include the penis and the scrotum.

2 The penis has the ability to fill with blood during sexual arousal. It contains the urethra and three cylinders—two corpora cavernosa and one corpus spongiosum. These cylinders are bound together with connective tissue.

3 In many cultures, the foreskin of the penis is removed during circumcision. Although it is the single most common surgical procedure performed on male patients in the United States, medical professionals have questioned the health value of circumcision.

4 An erection is a spinal reflex, and many types of sexual stimulation can lead to this response. When stimulation stops, the penis returns to its unaroused state. Most men have regular erections during their sleeping cycle and often wake up with an erection.

5 The scrotum sits outside the man's body and contains the testicles. Sperm survival requires a temperature that is a few degrees lower than the body's temperature. The cremaster muscle is responsible for the scrotum's positioning. When it is too hot, the muscle allows the scrotum to hang farther away from the body. When it is too cold, the muscle elevates the scrotum so that it is closer to the body.

6 The internal male sex organs include the testes, epididymis, vas deferens, seminal vesicles, prostate gland, and Cowper's glands. All of these organs play important roles in spermatogenesis, testosterone production, and the process of ejaculation.

7 The testicles have two main functions: spermatogenesis and testosterone production. One testicle usually hangs lower (or higher) than the other so that they do not hit each other when compressed. Testosterone is produced in the Leydig cells.

8 Ejaculation is the physiological process whereby the seminal fluid is ejected from the penis. The vas deferens, seminal vesicles, prostate, and Cowper's glands all work together during ejaculation. Most men experience between 5 and 15 contractions during orgasm. After orgasm, the blood that has been trapped in the penis is released, and the penis becomes flaccid.

9 Gynecomastia, or abnormal breast development, is common during male puberty and again in older age. It can be caused by drug therapy, drug abuse, hormonal imbalance, and certain diseases. It will often disappear on its own without surgical intervention. Some men do get breast cancer, and because it is rare, men who are diagnosed are often in advanced stages before their diagnoses.

10 At about the age of 10, a boy enters the first stages of puberty. A negative feedback system regulates hormone production. As puberty progresses, the testicles increase in size, and the penis begins to grow. Increased testosterone stimulates an overall growth spurt in puberty, and the bones and muscles grow rapidly.

Spermatogenesis usually begins about the age of 12, but it takes another year or so for an ejaculation to contain mature sperm.

11 Blood testosterone levels decrease as a man ages, and although it is not as defined as menopause, men experience a condition known as andropause. During this time, sperm production slows down, the ejaculate becomes thinner, and ejaculatory pressure decreases.

12 There are several diseases of the male reproductive organs, including cryptorchidism, testicular torsion, priapism, Peyronie's disease, inguinal hernia, and hydrocele. Fortunately, all of these are treatable conditions.

13 Athletes' use of steroids has increased notably since the late 1980s, even though it had been associated with several damaging changes in the body. Steroid use can cause liver and prostate gland changes, testicular shrinkage, and impaired immune function. Research has also found an increased risk for cerebrovascular accidents and, for young people, early fusion of bone growth plates.

14 Men who are diagnosed with breast cancer often do not tell anyone. Penile cancer is relatively uncommon, but it usually appears as a lesion on the penis. Testicular cancer is difficult to catch early because there are few symptoms. It is one of the most curable forms of the disease. Prostate cancer is more common in men older than 50 and is the most common cause of cancer deaths among men older than 60. For unknown reasons, this type of cancer is twice as common in African-American as it is among European American men.

CRITICAL THINKING QUESTIONS

1 We don't seem to need to know how the digestive system works to eat. Why is detailed knowledge of the sexual functioning of men important in human sexuality?

2 If you have a baby boy in the future, would you have him circumcised? Why or why not?

3 Why do you think men are uncomfortable talking about their own body image issues? Why aren't men encouraged to explore these issues?

MEDIA RESOURCES

CourseMate brings course concepts to life with interactive learning, study, and exam preparation tools that support the printed textbook. A textbook-specific website, Psychology CourseMate includes an integrated interactive eBook and other interactive learning tools including quizzes, flashcards, videos, and more. If your textbook does not include an access code card, go to CengageBrain.com to gain access.

CENGAGENOW CengageNOW is an easy-to-use online resource that helps you study in less time to get the grade you want—NOW. Take a pre-test for this chapter and receive a personalized study plan based on your results that will identify the topics you need to review and direct you to online resources to help you master those topics. Then take a post-test to help you determine the concepts you have mastered and what you will need to work on. If your textbook does not include an access code card, go to CengageBrain.com to gain access.

View in Video available in CourseMate and CengageNOW:

Growing Up Male: Conversation with a young man about masculinity and pressures related to penis size.

Laptops and Sperm Quality: Learn about research that has found that heat from laptops can affect sperm quality in men.

Fighting Against Aging: See how one group uses hormones to combat the effects of aging.

Steroid Use: Male discusses using steroids and male role pressures.

Male Reproductive Organs: An up-close look at the male reproductive system and its functioning.

Websites:

Testicular Cancer Resource Center ■ The Testicular Cancer Resource Center provides accurate information about testicular self-examination and the diagnosis and treatment of testicular cancer. Links are also provided for other cancers and additional websites.

Medical Education Information Center (MEdICTM) ■ The Medical Education Information Center contains information about men's health issues. The site has information on cancer screening, PSA testing, prostate concerns, and other health issues.

MedlinePlus Health Information: Men's Health Topics ■ MedlinePlus contains information on issues such as prostate cancer, circumcision, reproductive health concerns, gay and bisexual health, and male genital disorders.

Lance Armstrong Foundation ■ The Lance Armstrong Foundation focuses on cancer information and education. It provides services, support, and strives to help cancer patients through diagnosis and treatment, encouraging each to adopt the same positive attitude that Lance Armstrong adopted in his own battle with cancer.

National Organization of Circumcision Information Resource Centers (NOCIRC) ■ NOCIRC is the first national clearinghouse for information about circumcision. It claims that it owns one of the largest collections of information about circumcision in the world.

7

Love and Intimacy

View in **Video**

View in **Video**

View in **Video**

ABOUT THE CHAPTER OPENING VIDEO – Neil and Joan met for the first time many years ago when Joan's mother invited him over for dinner. She had invited him so he could meet Joan's older sister, Jeanne. Neil was 21-years-old and he was looking forward to meeting her. However, when he arrived at their house, he couldn't help but notice Jeanne's younger sister, Joan. Since Joan was only 16-years-old, her family wasn't thrilled about Neil's interest. But it was "love at first sight" for Neil and he actively pursued her. Three years later they married. Today, they are getting ready to celebrate their 34th wedding anniversary and they have three grown children. I was able to sit and talk with them recently about their relationship, thoughts about love, and how their marriage has survived the test of time.

I think what helps makes love last is being nice to each other, respecting each other, and treating each other the way you want to be treated. Relationships really take a lot of work and compromise to work. Neil and I have worked hard to find common interests. A good example is camping—I had never been camping before but it was something Neil really loved. Although I hesitated at first, I agreed to go with him and over time I realized that I enjoyed it as well. We took the family camping and it was a lot of fun.

Yes, it's important to have common interests. We have the same political interests and feel the same way about religion—well, neither of us has strong religious backgrounds, so we agree on that. After our kids were born, Joan and I were interested in going back to college, so we began taking classes together and eventually got our degrees together.

PhotoAlto/Michele Constantini

At the beginning of our marriage it was tough to keep the focus on us since most of our time was spent on our children. We worked hard to find time for ourselves as a couple. Sometimes one of our parents would come stay with the kids so that we could have a weekend together. Our relationship has never been perfect, but we never have had a problem working things out. The key to staying in love is being willing to work at it.

One of the first things I noticed about Joan and Neil was their genuine affection for each other. As they sat together on the couch for our talk they smiled at each other, laughed, and often finished each other's sentences. I know you'll enjoy hearing their story. ❚❚

Janell Cauih

"The key to staying in love is to be willing to work at it."
—CHAPTER OPENING VIDEO

View in Video
To watch the entire interview, go to Psychology CourseMate at **login.cengagebrain.com**.

© 2012 Cengage Learning

Love and the ability to form loving, caring, and intimate relationships with others are important for both our physical and emotional health. In his 1999 best-selling book *Love and Survival: The Scientific Basis for the Healing Power of Intimacy*, Dean Ornish (1999) discusses the importance of love and intimacy. He points to a variety of research studies that support the fact that physical health is strengthened when people feel loved and can open up and talk to each other. Many studies support Ornish's findings and have found that social support and love are related to stronger immune systems and lower levels of illnesses (Dodd, 2010; Goldman-Mellor et al., 2010; Maunder & Hunter, 2008). Following are some other interesting findings from Ornish's (1999) longitudinal research:

- College students who had distant and nonemotional relationships with their parents had significantly higher rates of high blood pressure and heart disease years later than did students who reported close and emotionally connected relationships.

- Heart patients who felt "loved" had 50% less arterial damage than those who said they did not feel "loved."

In this chapter, we talk about the forms and measures of love, where love comes from, love throughout the life cycle, and building intimate relationships. Before we begin, try answering this question: What is love?

WHAT IS LOVE?

One of the great mysteries of humankind is the capacity to love, to make attachments with others that involve deep feeling, selflessness, and commitment. Throughout history, literature and art have portrayed the saving powers of love. How many songs have been written about its passion, and how many films have depicted its power to change people's lives? Yet after centuries of writers discussing love, philosophers musing over its hold on men and women, and religious leaders teaching of the neces-

---

REAL RESEARCH 7.1 Romantic love has been found to be a natural analgesic—one study found college students who reported being "in love" were less likely to feel physical pain than those who said they were not in love (YOUNGER ET AL., 2010).

---

sity to love one another, how much do we really know about love? Are there different, separate kinds of love—friendship, passion, love of parents—or are they all simply variations on one fundamental emotion? Does love really "grow"? Is love different at age 15 than at 50? What is the relationship between love and sexuality?

We go through life trying to come to terms with loving, trying to figure out why we are attracted to certain types or why we fall in love with the people we do. The mystery of love is part of its attraction. We are surrounded with images of love in the media and are taught from the time we first listen to fairy tales that love is the answer to most of life's problems. Movies, music, and television inundate us with stories of what love is, and these stories have a powerful impact on us (Griffin, 2006).

▶▶ LOVE IN OTHER Times and Places

The desire for love is as old as humanity. Each new generation somehow imagines that it is the first, the inventor of "true love," but look at this poem from the late Egyptian empire, written more than 3,000 years ago:

> *I found my lover on his bed, and my heart was sweet to excess.*
> *I shall never be far away (from) you while my hand is in your hand,*
> *and I shall stroll with you in every favorite place.*
> *How pleasant is this hour, may it extend for me to eternity;*
> *since I have lain with you, you have lifted high my heart.*
> *In mourning or in rejoicing be not far from me.*
> (Quoted in Bergmann, 1987, p. 5)

The Hebrew Bible speaks of God's love of Israel, and the metaphorical imagery in the Song of Solomon, usually interpreted as depicting God and Israel as lovers, is highly erotic and sexual. The Middle Ages glorified the modern idea of **romantic love,** including loving from afar, or loving those one could not have (**unrequited** [un-ree-KWI-ted] **love**).

Not until the 19th century did people begin to believe that romantic love was the most desirable form of loving relations. Through most of Western history, marriage was an economic union, arranged by the parents. Once wed, husbands and wives were encouraged to learn love for one another, to develop love. How different that is from the modern romantic ideal of love preceding marriage.

When people love each other, they experience less stress in their lives, stronger immune systems, and better overall health.

© Jupiter Images/Creatas/Alamy

1 Discuss the research on the effects of love and intimacy on physical health.

2 Explain how images of love in the media influence our concept of what love is.

3 Explain how love today may be different from love that was experienced through most of Western history.

▶ FORMS AND MEASURES of Love

We must admire those researchers who are willing to tackle a difficult subject such as the origins of love or the different forms of love. We all love, and one of the characteristics of love is that we often believe that the intensity of the emotion is unique to us, that no one else has ever loved as we have loved. We also feel many different kinds of love, such as love of a friend, love of a parent, love of a child, love of a celebrity, or love of a pet. Philosophers, historians, social scientists, and other scholars have made attempts to untangle these types of love.

▶▶ ROMANTIC VERSUS Companionate Love

Romantic love is the all-encompassing, passionate love of romantic songs and poetry, of tearjerker movies and romance novels, and has become the prevailing model of sexual relationships and marriage in the Western world. Romantic love is also sometimes called passionate love, infatuation, obsessive love, and even lovesickness, and with it comes a sense of ecstasy and anxiety, physical attraction, and sexual desire. We tend to idealize the partner, ignoring faults in the newfound joy of the attachment. Passionate love blooms in the initial euphoria of a new attachment to a sexual partner, and it often seems as if we're swept away by it; that is why we say we "fall" in love, or even fall "head over heels" in love.

Companionate love involves deep affection, trust, loyalty, attachment, and intimacy; although passion is often present, companionate love lacks the high and low swings of romantic love.

© David Young-Wolff/Alamy

Few feelings are as joyous or exciting as romantic love. The explosion of emotion is often so intense that people talk about being unable to contain it; it feels as if it spills out of us onto everything we see. Some people joke that there is nothing quite as intolerable as those in love; they are just so annoyingly happy all the time! It is not surprising that such a powerful emotion is celebrated in poetry, story, and song. It is also not surprising that such a powerful emotion seems as though it will last forever. After all, isn't that what we learn when the couples in fairy tales "live happily ever after" and when the couples in movies ride off into the sunset?

Unfortunately, perhaps, passion of that intensity fades after a time. If the relationship is to continue, romantic love usually develops into **companionate love,** or **conjugal** (CONN-jew-gull) **love.** Companionate love involves feelings of deep affection, attachment, intimacy, and ease with the partner, as well as the development of trust, loyalty, acceptance, and a willingness to sacrifice for the partner (Critelli et al., 1986; Regan, 2006; Shaver & Hazan, 1987). Although companionate love does not have the passionate high and low swings of romantic love, passion is certainly present for many companionate lovers. Companionate love may even be a deeper, more intimate love than romantic love.

romantic love
Idealized love, based on romance and perfection.

unrequited love
Loving another when the love will never be returned.

companionate love
An intimate form of love that involves friendly affection and deep attachment based on a familiarity with the loved one. Also referred to as conjugal love.

conjugal love
An intimate form of love that involves friendly affection and deep attachment based on familiarity with the loved one. Also referred to as companionate love.

table 7.1 ■ Lee's Colors of Love

1. Eros: The Romantic Lover	Eros is like romantic love. Erotic lovers speak of their immediate attraction to their lover, to his or her eyes, skin, fragrance, or body. Most have the picture of an ideal partner in their mind, which a real partner cannot fulfill; that is why purely erotic love does not last. In childhood, erotic lovers often had a secure attachment style with their caregivers.
2. Ludus (LOO-diss): The Game-Playing Lover	Ludic lovers play the "game" of love, enjoying the act of seduction. Commitment, dependency, and intimacy are not valued, and ludic lovers will often juggle several relationships at the same time. In childhood, ludic lovers often had an avoidant attachment style with their caregivers.
3. Storge (STOR-gay): The Quiet, Calm Lover	Storgic love is a quiet, calm love that builds over time, similar to companionate love. Storgic lovers don't suddenly "fall in love" and do not dream of some idealized, romantic lover; marriage, stability, and comfort within love are the goal. Should the relationship break up, the storgic partners would probably remain friends, a status unthinkable to erotic lovers who have split.
4. Mania: The Crazy Lover	Manic lovers are possessive and dependent, consumed by thoughts of the beloved, and are often on a roller-coaster of highs and lows. Each encouraging sign from the lover brings joy; each little slight brings heartache, which makes their lives dramatic and painful. Manic lovers fear separation; they may sit by the phone waiting for the beloved to call, or they may call their beloved incessantly. They tend to wonder why all their relationships ultimately fail. In childhood, manic lovers often had an anxious/ambivalent attachment style with their caregivers.
5. Pragma: The Practical Lover	Pragmatic lovers have a "shopping list" of qualities they are looking for in a relationship. They are very practical about their relationship and lovers. Pragmatic lovers want a deep, lasting love but believe the best way to get it is to assess their own qualities and make the best "deal" in the romantic marketplace. They tend to be planners—planning the best time to get married, have children, and even when to divorce ("Well, in two years the house will be paid for and Billy will be in high school, so that would be a good time to get divorced.").
6. Agape (AH-ga-pay): The Selfless Lover	Altruistic, selfless, never demanding, patient, and true is agapic love. Never jealous, not needing reciprocity, agapic love tends to happen in brief episodes. Lee found very few long-term agapic lovers. Lee gives the example of a man whose lover was faced with a distressing choice between him and another man, and so he gracefully bowed out.

As you read through these descriptions, where do you think your love style fits in? Are you a pragmatic lover, planning all the details of your love affair? Do you feel stir-crazy in a relationship and end up juggling lovers and playing games? Or do you have a romantic and sensitive love style? It is possible that more than one style will fit you, and also that your love style may change throughout your lifetime. What influences in your life do you think contributed to your love style today?

SOURCE: John Alan Lee, "The Styles of Loving," Psychology Today, 8, 43–51. Reprinted by permission of Psychology Today. Copyright © 1974 by Sussex Publishers, Inc.

It can be difficult for couples to switch from passionate love to the deeper, more mature companionate love (Peck, 1978). Because the model of love we see on television and in movies is the highly sexual, swept-off-your-feet passion of romantic love, some may see the mellowing of that passion as a loss of love rather than a development of a different kind of love. Yet the mutual commitment to develop a new, more mature kind of love is, in fact, what we should mean by "true love."

▶▶ THE COLORS OF LOVE: John Alan Lee

Psychologist John Alan Lee (1974, 1988, 1998) suggests that in romantic relationships, there are more forms of love than just romantic and companionate love. Lee collected statements about love from hundreds of works of fiction and nonfiction, starting with the Bible and including both ancient and modern authors. He gathered a panel of professionals in literature, philosophy, and the social sciences, and had them sort into categories the thousands of statements he found. Lee's research identified six basic ways to love, which he calls "colors" of love, to which he gave Greek and Latin names. Lee's categories are described in Table 7.1.

Lee's colors of love have generated a substantial body of research, much of which shows that his love styles are independent from one another, and that each can be measured to some degree (Hendrick & Hendrick, 1989). Lee points out that two lovers with compatible styles are probably going to be happier and more content with each other than two with incompatible styles. Couples

table 7.2 ■ Sternberg's Triangular Theory of Love

Robert Sternberg, a professor of psychology at Yale University, believes that love is made up of three elements: passion, intimacy, and commitment, each of which may be present or absent in a relationship. The presence or absence of these components produces eight triangles (seven of these involve at least one component; the eighth represents the absence of any components, referred to as nonlove). Problems can occur in a relationship if one person's triangle differs significantly from the other's. This can happen when one person has more or less of one of the three elements of love. Following are the various types of love proposed by Sternberg.

	Nonlove	In most of our casual daily relationships, there is no sense of intimacy, passion, or commitment.
	Liking	When there is intimacy without (sexual) passion and without strong personal commitment, we are friends. Friends can separate for long periods of time and resume the relationship as if it had never ended.
	Infatuation	Passion alone leads to infatuation. Infatuation refers to physiological arousal and a sexual desire for another person. Casual hookups and one-night stands would fall into this category. Typically, infatuation quickly fades, often to be replaced with infatuation for someone else!
	Empty love	Empty love involves only commitment, as in a couple who stays together even though their relationship long ago lost its passion and intimacy. However, relationships can begin with commitment alone and develop intimacy and passion.
	Romantic love	Passion and intimacy lead to romantic love, which is often the first phase of a relationship. Romantic love is often an intense, joyful experience.
	Companionate love	Companionate love ranges from long-term, deeply committed friendships to married or long-term couples who have experienced a decrease in the passionate aspect of their love.
	Fatuous (FAT-you-us) love	Love is fatuous (which means silly or foolish) when one does not really know the person to whom one is making a commitment. Hollywood often portrays two people who meet, become infatuated, and make a commitment by the end of the movie. However, a committed relationship continues even after passion fades, so it makes sense to know one's partner before making a commitment.
	Consummate love	Consummate, or complete, love has all three elements in balance. Even after achieving consummate love, we can lose it: passion can fade, intimacy can stagnate, and commitment can be undermined by attraction to another. But it is consummate love we all strive for.

SOURCE: Sternberg, Robert J. (1986). "A Triangle Theory of Love," Psychological Review, 93, 119–135. Reprinted by permission of the author.

who approach loving differently often cannot understand why their partners react the way they do or how they can hurt their partners unintentionally. Imagine how bored an erotic lover would be with a pragmatic lover, or how much a ludic lover would hurt a manic lover. Each would consider the other callous or even cruel, suggests Lee, when people simply tend to love differently. Higher levels of manic and ludic love styles are associated with poorer psychological health, whereas higher levels of storge and eros love styles are associated with higher levels of psychological health (Blair, 2000).

▶▶ LOVE TRIANGLES: Robert Sternberg

Robert Sternberg (1998, 1999) has suggested that different strategies of loving are really different ways of combining the basic building blocks of love. He has proposed that love is made up of three elements—passion, intimacy, and commitment—that can be combined in different ways. Sternberg refers to a total absence of all three components as nonlove.

Passion is sparked by physical attraction and sexual desire, and drives a person to pursue a romantic relationship. Passion instills a deep desire for union, and although it is often expressed sexually, self-esteem, nurturing, domination, submission, and self-actualization may also contribute to the experience. Passion is the element that identifies romantic forms of love; it is absent in the love of a parent for a child. Passion fires up quickly in a romantic relationship but is also the first element to fade (Ahmetoglu et al., 2010).

Intimacy involves feelings of closeness, connectedness, and bondedness in a loving relationship. It is the emotional investment one has in the relationship and includes such things as the desire to support and help the other, happiness, mutual understanding, emotional support, and communication. The intimacy component of love is experienced in many loving relationships, such as parent–child, sibling, and friendship relationships.

Commitment, in the short term, is the decision to love someone; in the long term, it is the determination to maintain that love. This element can sustain a relationship that is temporarily (or even permanently) going through a period without passion or intimacy. The marriage ceremony, for example, is a public display of a couple's commitment to each other. Unlike passion, which is quick to fire up and die out, commitment builds slowly and is often related to relationship length (Ahmetoglu et al., 2010).

Sternberg combines these elements into seven forms of love, which are described in Table 7.2. A person may experience different forms of love at different times; romantic love may give way to companionate love, or the infatuated lover may find a person to whom he or she is willing to commit and settle down. In the emotionally healthy person, as we shall see, love evolves and changes as we mature (Sternberg, 1998).

▶▶ CAN WE **Measure Love?**

Based on these types of theories, theorists have tried to come up with scales that measure love. However, you can't just ask people, "How deeply do you love [your partner]?" Participants will interpret love in their own way. One strategy is to create a scale that measures love by measuring something strongly associated with love. Zick Rubin (1970, 1973) was one of the first to try to scientifically measure love. Rubin thought of love as a form of attachment

---

REAL RESEARCH 7.2 Birth-order research has found that love styles may be related to where a child is born into a family (McGuirk & Pettijohn, 2008). Middle children have higher rates of ludic love styles, whereas the youngest children are more likely to have pragma, storge, or agape love styles. Finally, only children have higher rates of eros and mania love styles.

---

to another person, and created a "love scale" that measured what he believed to be the three components of attachment: degrees of needing ("If I could never be with _____, I would feel miserable."), caring ("I would do almost anything for _____."), and trust-

ON YOUR MIND **7.2**

What is the difference between love and lust? How do I know if it's love or just physical attraction?

Each individual must struggle with these questions as he or she matures, particularly in the teenage and early adulthood years, before gaining much experience with romantic love. There is no easy answer, but there are some indications that a relationship may be infatuation rather than love when it involves a compulsion (rather than a desire) to be with the person, a feeling of lack of trust (such as a need to check up on the partner), extremes of emotions (ecstatic highs followed by depressing lows), and a willingness to take abuse or behave in destructive ways that one would not have before the relationship. Some questions to ask yourself about your love relationship are: Would I want this person as a friend if he or she were not my partner? Do my friends and family dislike this person or think he or she is not right for me? (Friends and family are often more level-headed judges of character than the infatuated individual.) Do I really know this person, or am I fantasizing about how he or she is with little confirmation by his or her actual behavior? It's not always easy to tell the difference between infatuation and love—many couples have a hard time differentiating between the two (Aloni & Bernieri, 2004)!

ing ("I feel very possessive about _____."). Rubin's scale proved to be an extraordinarily powerful tool to measure love. For example, how a couple scores on the "love scale" is correlated not only with their rating of the probability that they will get married, but their score even predicts how often they will gaze at each other!

Others have since tried to create their own scales. Keith Davis and his colleagues (K. E. Davis & Latty-Mann, 1987; K. E. Davis & Todd, 1982) created the Relationship Rating Scale (RRS), which measures various aspects of relationships, such as intimacy, passion, and conflict. Hatfield and Sprecher (1986) created the Passionate Love Scale (PLS), which tries to measure the degree of intense passion or "longing for union."

Will measures of love eventually tell us what love is made of? Well, as you can imagine, many problems are inherent in trying to measure love. Most love scales really focus on romantic love and are not as good at trying to measure the degree of companionate love (Sternberg, 1987). Also, measuring degrees of love, or types of love, is different from saying what love actually is. Finally, when you ask people questions about love, they can answer only with their conscious attitudes toward love. Many theorists suggest that we don't consciously know why we love, how we love, or even how much we love. Other theorists argue that people do not realize to what degree love is physiological (see the section on physiological arousal theories later in this chapter). So we may be measuring only how people think they love.

1 What is the difference between romantic and companionate, or conjugal, love?

2 Identify and describe John Alan Lee's six colors of love.

3 Identify and describe the three elements of love according to Robert Sternberg. Explain how these elements combine to make seven different forms of love.

4 Is it possible to measure love? What problems have researchers run into when attempting to do so?

▶ ORIGINS OF LOVE

Why do we love in the first place? What purpose does love serve? After all, most animals mate successfully without experiencing "love." Researchers' theories on why we form emotional bonds in the first place can be grouped into five general categories: behavioral reinforcement, cognitive, evolutionary, physiological arousal, and biological.

▶▶ BEHAVIORAL Reinforcement Theories

One group of theories suggests that we love because another person reinforces positive feelings in ourselves. Lott and Lott (1961) suggested that a rewarding or positive feeling in the presence of another person makes us like them, even when the reward has nothing to do with the other person. For example, they found that children who were rewarded continually by their teachers came to like their classmates more than children who were not equally rewarded. The opposite is also true. Griffitt and Veitch (1971) found that people tend to dislike people they meet in a hot, crowded room, no matter what those people's personalities are

Love develops through a series of mutually reinforcing activities.

like. Behavioral reinforcement theory suggests that we like people we associate with feeling good and love people if the association is very good. Love develops through a series of mutually reinforcing activities.

▶▶ COGNITIVE Theories

Cognitive theories of liking and loving are based on an interesting paradox: The less people are paid for a task, the more they tend to like it. In other words, a person tends to think, "Here I am washing this car, and I'm not even getting paid for it. Why am I doing this? I must like to wash cars!" The same goes for relationships. If we are with a person often and find ourselves doing things for them, we ask, "Why am I with her so often? Why am I doing her laundry? I must like her—I must even love her!" This theory suggests the action comes first and the interpretation comes later (Tzeng, 1992). Studies have also found that when we think certain people like us, we're more likely to be attracted to them (Ridge & Reber, 2002).

▶▶ EVOLUTIONARY Theory

Evolutionary theorists try to understand the evolutionary advantages of human behaviors. Love, they believe, developed as the human form of three basic instincts: the need to be protected from outside threats, the instinct of the parent to protect the child, and the sexual drive. Love is an evolutionary strategy that helps us form the bonds we need to reproduce and pass our genes on to the next generation (Gonzaga & Haselton, 2008). We love to propagate the species.

To evolutionary theorists, that would explain why we tend to fall in love with people whom we think have positive traits; we want to pass those traits along to our children. In fact, evolutionary theorists argue that their perspective can explain why heterosexual men look for attractive women, and heterosexual women look for successful men, the world over (see the section on cultural influences on attraction later in this chapter). Heterosexual men want a fit, healthy woman to carry their offspring, and heterosexual women want a man with the resources to protect them and help care for the infant in the long period they devote to reproduction. For most of history, this included 9 months of pregnancy and more than a year of breast-feeding. Love creates the union that maximizes each partner's chance of passing on their genes to the next generation.

The behavioral reinforcement theory suggests that we love people we associate with feeling good. Our love for them grows out of doing things together that are mutually reinforcing.

© Image Source/Alamy

▶▶ PHYSIOLOGICAL AROUSAL Theory

How does love feel? Most people describe physiological sensations: "I felt so excited I couldn't breathe"; "My throat choked up"; "I felt tingling all over." If you look at those descriptions, couldn't they also be descriptions of fear, anger, or excitement? Is there a difference between being in love and being on a roller-coaster?

Perhaps not. In a famous experiment, Schachter and Singer (1962) gave students a shot of epinephrine (adrenaline), which causes general arousal, including sweaty palms, increased heart rate, increased breathing, and so on. They split the students into four groups: one was told exactly what was happening and what to expect; another was told the wrong set of symptoms to expect (itching, numbness, a slight headache); a third group was told nothing; and a fourth group got an injection of saline solution (saltwater) rather than epinephrine.

Each group was put into a waiting room with a student who was actually part of the study. In half the cases, the confederate acted happy, and in half, angry. The interesting result was that the students in the informed group, when they felt aroused, assumed they were feeling the effects of the epinephrine. However, the uninformed groups tended to believe they were experiencing the same emotion as the other person in the room. They thought they were happy, or they thought they were angry. Schachter and Singer (2001) concluded that an emotion happens when there is general physiological arousal for whatever reason and a label is attached to it—and that label might be any emotion. In other words, people tend to be vulnerable to experiencing love (or another emotion) when they are physiologically aroused for whatever reason. More recent studies confirm the physiological arousal theory (Aron et al., 2005; H. Fisher, 2004). For example, couples who met during a crisis (such as during an emergency plane landing) were found to be more likely to feel strongly about one another (Aron et al., 2005; Kluger, 2008). They often incorrectly attributed their high levels of arousal to feelings for the other person.

So, is love just a label we give to a racing heart? The idea may explain why we tend to associate love and sex so closely; sexual excitement is a state of intense physiological arousal. Certainly arousal of some sort is a necessary component of love. Would you want to be in love with someone who wasn't the least bit excited when you entered the room? Love, however, is almost certainly more than arousal alone. Perhaps arousal has a stronger connection to initial attraction than to love. Maybe that is why lust is so often confused with love.

> *Pheromones* have been found to influence **attraction, mating, and bonding.**

▶▶ OTHER BIOLOGICAL Factors

Finally, research has shown that other biological factors can also influence whom we fall in love with (Garver-Apgar et al., 2006; Rodriguez, 2004; Santos et al., 2005; Savic et al., 2005; Thorne & Amrein, 2003). We register the "smells" of people through their **pheromones** (FAIR-oh-moans)—odorless chemicals secreted by both humans and animals (Rodriguez, 2004; Thorne & Amrein, 2003). These pheromones are processed in the hypothalamus, and they influence our choice of sexual partner (Savic et al., 2005). Both men and women respond to pheromones. One study found that women report their male partners are more loving (and jealous) when they were ovulating (Hasleton et al., 2007).

In fact, pheromones have been found to influence attraction, mating, and bonding (Crawford et al., 2011; Wright, 1994), and have also been found to promote the love bond between a mother and her infant (Kohl & Francoeur, 2002). Research on pheromones and sexual orientation has found that homosexual and heterosexual men respond differently to odors that are involved in sexual attraction, with homosexual men responding in similar ways as heterosexual women (Savic et al., 2005).

Our odor preferences are influenced by our *major histocompatibility complex* (MHC), a group of genes that helps the body recognize invaders such as bacteria and viruses (Garver-Apgar et al., 2006; Herz, 2007; Santos et al., 2005). To pass a more complete MHC along to our offspring and protect them with the broadest array of disease resistance, heterosexual men and women may be programmed to mate with a partner whose MHC differs from their own (Crawford et al., 2011; Roberts & Roiser, 2010). We are more likely to be attracted and fall in love with someone whose MHC is different from our own (Garver-Apgar et al., 2006). Newer research has been exploring how the use of hormonal contraceptives, such as birth control pills, may alter MHC and odor preferences in women (Crawford et al., 2011; Ferdenzi et al., 2009; Roberts & Roiser, 2010; Roberts et al., 2008).

Finally, researchers have also been looking for love in neurotransmitters and various areas of the brain. Using magnetic resonance imaging, researchers have found that certain areas of the brain are stimulated when couples are in love (Aron et al., 2005; Fisher et al., 2010; H. Fisher, 2004; Ortigue et al., 2010). In addition, when these areas of the brain are stimulated, neurotransmitters, such as dopamine, create motivation and cravings to be with a particular partner (see Sex in Real Life, "Love—It's All in Your Head," later in the chapter; Fisher et al., 2010). So it appears there may be more to love and attraction than we thought. Certainly more research is needed in these areas.

◀ review QUESTIONS

1 How does the behavioral reinforcement theory explain love?

2 How do cognitive theories explain love?

3 How does evolutionary theory explain love?

4 How does the physiological arousal theory explain love?

5 What other biological factors influence love?

▶ LOVE FROM CHILDHOOD to Maturity

Throughout our lives, we love others. First, we love our parents or caretakers, and then siblings, friends, and romantic partners. At each stage of life, we learn lessons about love that help us mature into the next stage. Love gets more complex as we get older. Let us walk through the different stages of individual development and look at the various ways love manifests itself as we grow.

▶▶ CHILDHOOD

In infancy, the nature and quality of the bond with the caregiver can have profound effects on the ability of a person to form attachments throughout life (we will discuss this further in Chapter 8). Our parents, or the adults who raised us, are our first teachers of love and intimacy. Loving, attentive caregivers tend to produce secure, happy children (Rauer & Volling, 2007). Children are keenly aware of parental love, and those who feel loved report feeling safe and protected (D'Cruz & Stagnitti, 2010).

When babies or young children feel sad, scared, or threatened, they often seek out their mother. From an evolutionary perspective, the desire for closeness with the mother increases the infant's chances of survival (Mofrad et al., 2010). Bowlby (1969) proposed that infants develop an attachment, or an emotional bond, with their mother. (Although Bowlby wrote about attachment as a mother–child bond, we know today that children can develop this bond with a mother, father, nanny, grandparent, or primary caregiver. However, it was the mother's response to her child that Bowlby [1969] believed was most important.) If the mother responded in a sensitive, patient, and kind manner, the child was more likely to form a secure attachment (Prior & Glaser, 2006). However, if the mother responded in an inconsistent, angry, or dismissive manner, the child would form an insecure attachment. Throughout this time, an infant's brain responds to facial expressions, the touch, and the scent of the primary caregiver (Hall, 2005). Consistent and sensitive caregiving makes a child feel pro-

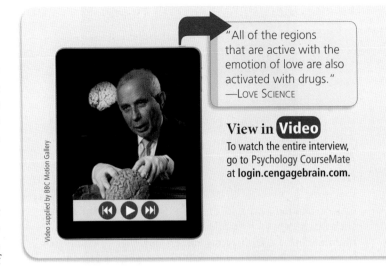

"All of the regions that are active with the emotion of love are also activated with drugs."
—LOVE SCIENCE

View in Video
To watch the entire interview, go to Psychology CourseMate at **login.cengagebrain.com.**

Video supplied by BBC Motion Gallery

tected and safe, which sets the foundation for regulating emotions later in life (Wellisch, 2010).

Ainsworth and her colleagues (Ainsworth et al., 1978) built on Bowlby's research and suggested that infants form one of three types of attachment behaviors that follow them throughout life. Secure infants tolerate caregivers being out of their sight because they believe the caregiver will respond if they cry out or need care. Inconsistent caregiving results in anxious/ambivalent babies, who cry more than secure babies and panic when the caregiver leaves them. Avoidant babies often have caregivers who are uncomfortable with hugging and holding them, and tend to force separation on the child at an early age. Research has found that a child's attachment style is established by the age of 9 months (Prior & Glaser, 2006).

Our childhood attachment styles stay with us as we grow up and may influence the type of intimate relationships we form as adults (K. Burton, 2005; Mikulincer & Shaver, 2005). In fact, we tend to relate to others in our love relationships much as we did with our primary caregiver when we were young. Adults who had a secure attachment in childhood report more positive childhood experiences, higher levels of self-esteem (Feeney & Noller, 1990), better health (Maunder & Hunter, 2008), and even more advanced language development (Prior & Glaser, 2006). They have less anxiety (Diamond & Fagundes, 2010; Gentzler et al., 2010), shame, guilt, and loneliness (Akbag & Imamoglu, 2010). They also have positive views of themselves and others, and have a fairly easy time trusting and establishing intimate relationships (Bartholomew & Horowitz, 1991; Neal & Frick-Horbury, 2001).

Adults who had anxious/ambivalent attachments with their caregivers often have a negative view of others as adults and tend to have a difficult time with trust. They may worry that their partner doesn't really love them or will leave them. Finally, those with an avoidant attachment often have a negative view of others and are uncomfortable with intimacy. If you grew up in a family in

A strong and secure bond with a caregiver can have profound effects on the ability of the person to form attachments throughout life.

© Chris Rout/Alamy

pheromones
Chemical substances that are secreted by humans and animals and facilitate communication.

Young love lays the groundwork for adult intimacy.

with at least one of their parents, the negative effects from the divorce may be reduced (Ensign et al., 1998).

▶▶ ADOLESCENCE

There is something attractive about young love, which is why it is celebrated so prominently in novels and movies. The love relationship seems so important, so earnest, and so passionate at the time, and yet so innocent in retrospect. Why are the dips and rises of our loves so important to us in adolescence? Adolescent love teaches us how to react to love, to manage our emotions, and to handle the pain of love. It also lays the groundwork for adult intimacy. Adolescents must learn to establish a strong personal identity separate from their family. Experimentation with different approaches to others is natural, and during adolescence, we develop the **role repertoire** that follows us into adulthood. Similarly, we experiment with different intimacy styles (J. Johnson & Alford, 1987) and develop an **intimacy repertoire,** a set of behaviors that we use to forge close relationships throughout our lives.

The process of establishing our repertoires can be a difficult task. This helps explain why adolescent relationships can be so intense and fraught with jealousy, and why adolescents often are unable to see beyond the relationship (J. Johnson & Alford, 1987). Our first relationships often take the form of a "crush" or infatuation and are often directed toward unattainable partners such as teachers or movie stars. Male and female movie stars provide adolescents with safe outlets for developing romantic love before dating and sexual activity begin (Karniol, 2001).

Sometimes the first lessons of love are painful, as we learn that love may not be returned or that feelings of passion fade. Yet managing such feelings helps us develop a mature love style. Many factors have been found to be associated with the ability to find romantic love in adolescence, such as marital status of the parents, the quality of the parental relationship, and comfort with one's body (Cecchetti, 2007; Coordt, 2005; Seiffge-Krenke et al., 2001). In fact, as we discussed earlier, difficulties with college students' intimate relationships may be related to the attachment styles created in childhood.

The emotions of adolescent love are so powerful that adolescents may think that they are the only ones to have gone through such joy, pain, and confusion. They may gain some comfort in knowing that almost everyone goes through the same process to some degree. Confusion about love certainly does not end with adolescence.

which your caregiver was inconsistent or distant, you learn that love is emotionally risky. In fact, those who do not experience intimacy growing up may have a harder time establishing intimate relationships as adults (Brumbaugh & Fraley, 2010; Dorr, 2001). This doesn't mean it's not possible to love someone if you didn't experience intimacy as a child, but it can be more challenging to allow yourself to love and be loved.

Attachment styles can also be affected by parental divorce. Research has found that children with divorced parents have decreased psychological, social, and physical well-being after their parents divorce (Hetherington, 2003), are less trusting of their partners in intimate relationships (Coordt, 2005; Ensign et al., 1998; Jacquet & Surra, 2001), and are more likely to experience a divorce in their own lives (Amato & De-Boer, 2001). Interestingly, men whose parents have divorced are less likely to experience problems in their intimate relationships unless their female partner has divorced parents (Jacquet & Surra, 2001). But keep in mind that having divorced parents does not put children at an overall disadvantage in the development of love relationships (Coordt, 2005; Sprecher et al., 1998). The most important factor is the quality of the relationships with the parents after the divorce. If children have a good relationship

*Adolescents must learn to establish **a strong personal identity** separate from their family.*

◀ review QUESTIONS

1 Explain how the nature and quality of our bond with caregivers can affect our ability to form relationships later in life.

2 Identify the various attachment styles. Which of these styles is most like yours?

3 What makes love relationships so difficult and unstable for many adolescents? Why do you think those highs and lows even out as we get older?

▶ ADULT LOVE and Intimacy

Love relationships can last many years. As time goes by, love and relationships grow and change, and trying to maintain a sense of stability and continuity while still allowing for change and growth is probably the single greatest challenge of long-term love relationships.

Attaining intimacy is different from loving. We can love our cat, our favorite musician, or a great leader, but intimacy requires reciprocity—it takes two. Intimacy is a dance of two souls, each of whom must reveal a little, risk a little, and try a lot. In some ways, therefore, true intimacy is more difficult to achieve than true love because the emotion of love may be effortless, whereas the establishment of intimacy always requires effort.

Does fate determine whom you will fall in love with, or are there other factors at work? We now talk about some of the factors that contribute to adult love and intimacy.

▶▶ ATTRACTION

Why are we attracted to certain people but not others? We've already discussed the role of pheromones and you'll probably agree that smell is an important component of attraction. But researchers also talk about the **field of eligibles** (Kerckhoff, 1964). Although we are surrounded by hundreds of people, we are only attracted to a handful of them. Our culture helps determine who is in our field of eligibles through social rules about acceptable and unacceptable partners. Because of these rules, we are more likely to be attracted to those who are similar to us in race, ethnicity, religion, socioeconomic group, and even age. Think about an older man who dates a much younger woman. Many people might criticize him and laugh at the relationship. In this way, society teaches us to whom we should, and shouldn't, be attracted.

One of the most reliable predictors of attraction is proximity. Although we might want to believe that we could meet a complete stranger at a bar and fall madly in love, the research tells us this scenario is rare. People are most likely to find lovers among the people they know or meet through the people they know. We are much more likely to meet our romantic partners at a party, religious institution, or friend's house, where the people are likely to come from backgrounds very similar to our own. Typically, we are first attracted to another person based on physical factors. It might be their hair, eyes, physique, or another physical feature. However, physical appearance tends to fade in importance over the life of the relationship.

We also tend to be attracted to partners who are similar to ourselves—in ethnicity, race, social class, religion, education, and even in attitudes and personality (Byrne & Murnen, 1988; Hitsch et al., 2010). Although folklore tells us both that "birds of a feather flock together" and that "opposites attract," the research supports only the first saying. We are also more likely to be attracted to someone who has a similar family history and political views (Michael et al., 1994; Z. Rubin, 1973). The "matching hypothesis" claims that people are drawn to others with similar levels of attractiveness. When considering a romantic partner, both men and women may be willing to compromise on some qualities they are looking for in a partner, but not on physical attractiveness (Sprecher & Regan, 2002). As we discussed in Chapter 4, the media have put such a premium on physical appearance that the majority of people in the United States report they are unhappy with their appearance and would change it if they could. Physically attractive people are assumed by others to have more socially desirable personalities and to be happier and more successful (Little et al., 2006; Swami & Furnham, 2008).

We like people who are open, receptive, social, emotionally stable, and who have a good sense of humor. We also are attracted to partners who are financially stable. In the past, research on gender and attraction found that heterosexual women were more likely to rate financial stability in a partner as more important than heterosexual men did (Buss, 1989). This was consistent across cultures. However, these gender differences have decreased, and both heterosexual men and women report being attracted to partners with financial resources (Buss et al., 2001; Sheldon, 2007).

What is it, finally, that we really look for in a partner? Although physical attractiveness is important, men and women around the world also report that mutual attraction, kindness, and reciprocal love are important factors (Buss et al., 2001; Pearce et al., 2010). In addition to this, people are in surprising agreement on what factors they want in an ideal partner. A study of homosexual, heterosexual, and bisexual men and women showed that, no matter what their sexual orientation, gender, or cultural background, all really wanted the same thing. They wanted partners who had similar interests, values, and religious beliefs, who were physically attractive, honest, trustworthy, intelligent, affectionate, warm, kind, funny, financially independent, and dependable (Amador et al., 2005; Toro-Morn & Sprecher, 2003). Now that doesn't seem to be too much to ask, does it?

*We tend to be attracted to partners who are **similar to ourselves.***

▶▶ ATTRACTION IN Different Cultures

Do men and women in every culture look for the same traits? For example, are more males than females looking for physically attractive mates in Nigeria? Is earning potential more important in males than females in China? David Buss (1989) did an ambitious study comparing the importance of, among other things, physical attractiveness, earning potential, and age difference to men and women in 37 cultures. His results confirmed the nature of mate attraction (although Buss assumed all his respondents were heterosexual and, therefore, assumed they were all talking about the other sex). He found that across all 37 cultures, men valued "good looks" in a partner more than women did, and in all 37 cultures, women valued "good financial prospect" in a partner more than men did. Also interesting is that in all 37 cultures, men preferred mates who were younger than they were, whereas women preferred mates who were older. Selected results of Buss's study appear in the accompanying Human Sexuality in a Diverse World feature.

---

role repertoire
A set of behaviors that we use in our interactions with others. Once we find what works, we develop patterns of interacting with others.

intimacy repertoire
A set of behaviors that we use to forge intimate relationships throughout our lives.

field of eligibles
The group of people from which it is socially acceptable to choose an intimate partner.

This young girl is from a Longneck tribe in Mae Hong Son, Thailand. In this culture, an elongated neck is viewed as physically attractive.

▶▶ INTIMATE Relationships

What exactly is intimacy? Think about the word; what does it imply to you? The word *intimacy* is derived from the Latin word *intimus,* meaning "inner" or "innermost" (Hatfield, 1988). Keeping our innermost selves hidden is easy; revealing our deepest desires, longings, and insecurities can be scary. As we discussed in Chapter 3, intimate partners reveal beliefs and ideas to each other, disclose personal facts, share opinions, and admit to their fears and hopes. In fact, self-disclosure is so important to intimacy that early researchers thought that willingness to self-disclose was itself the definition of intimacy (M. S. Clark & Reis, 1988). True self-disclosure is a two-way street, and it involves both partners sharing feelings, fears, and dreams, not just facts and opinions. Individuals who can self-disclose have been found to have higher levels of self-esteem and confidence in their relationships, and rate their relationships as more satisfying (Macneil, 2004; Posey et al., 2010; Schiffrin et al., 2010; Sprecher & Hendrick, 2004).

Intimacy involves a sense of closeness, bondedness, and connectedness (Popovic, 2005; R. J. Sternberg, 1987). People who value intimacy tend to express greater trust in their friends; are more concerned for them; tend to disclose more emotional, personal, and relational content; and have more positive thoughts about others. They also tend to be seen as more likable and noncompetitive by peers; to smile, laugh, and make eye contact more often; and to report better marital enjoyment (M. S. Clark & Reis, 1988).

However, all types of disclosures are risky; the other person may not understand or accept the information offered or may not reciprocate. Thus, risk taking and trust are crucial to the development of intimacy. Because intimacy makes us vulnerable and be-

cause we invest so much in the other person, intimacy can also lead to betrayal and disappointment, anger, and jealousy. We explore the dark side of intimacy later in this chapter.

Male and Female Styles of Intimacy

If any area of research in love and intimacy has yielded conflicting findings, it is the question of gender differences. Overall, the research has found that heterosexual women tend to give more importance to the hope of having an intimate relationship in their future than heterosexual men do (Oner, 2001). However, M. S. Clark and Reis (1988) suggest that the subject remains murky because many other variables are at work, such as culturally determined gender roles.

For example, men and women report equally desiring and valuing intimacy, but many men grow up with behavioral inhibitions to expressing intimacy. We are taught how to be male and female in society, and from a very young age, boys are discouraged from displaying vulnerability or doubt about intimacy. As one man's experience reveals in the accompanying Sex in Real Life, it is acceptable for men to talk about sex, but talk of intimacy is often taboo. Although this man's experience may have been extreme, exaggerated by the all-male atmosphere of the athletic team, such attitudes are communicated in subtle ways to most men. Therefore, men may remain unexpressive about intimacy, however strongly they may desire it. It could also be that men simply express intimacy differently—perhaps more through action than words (Gilmore, 1990).

One study measured male and female participants on scales of masculinity and femininity and compared those who scored higher on one scale than the other with those who scored high on

---

REAL RESEARCH 7.3   Research has found that because of the difficulties involved in managing close relationships, men and women who begin a new romance are at risk for losing two close friends (SAMPLE, 2010).

---

both scales (androgyny; Coleman & Ganong, 1985). In Chapter 4, we discussed androgyny. Androgynous people have been found to be more aware of their love feelings, more expressive, and more tolerant of their partner's faults than those who scored high only on the masculinity scale; they were also more cognitively aware, willing to express faults, and tolerant than those who scored high only on the femininity scale.

However, some evidence indicates that the differences in attitudes between the genders may be changing. Although in the past women were more comfortable with intimate encounters and men were more comfortable taking independent action, now a new, more androgynous breed of men and women may be emerging who are more comfortable in both roles (Choi, 2004). If so, maybe we can expect greater ease in intimacy between and among the sexes in the upcoming generations of men and women.

The importance of accepting traditional gender roles is also reflected in comparisons of homosexual and heterosexual men. Although homosexual and heterosexual men agree on the ideal characteristics of love partners and express the same amounts and kinds of love, gay men are more likely to believe that "you should share your most intimate thoughts and feelings with the person

Sexual Diversity in Our World ▶▶

Good Looks or a Good Prospect? What Do You Want in a Partner?

In a classic study on cultural differences in what men and women look for in a mate, David Buss (1989) found that, almost universally, men value good looks more in a mate, and women value good financial prospects. More recent research has found that in the United States, good looks and financial stability are important partner qualities for both men and women (Amador et al., 2005; Lacey et al., 2004). As for age, almost universally, men want their mates to be a few years younger than they are, and women want their mates to be a few years older. After taking a look at these graphs, if you were a young, poor, handsome male, what country would you want to live in?

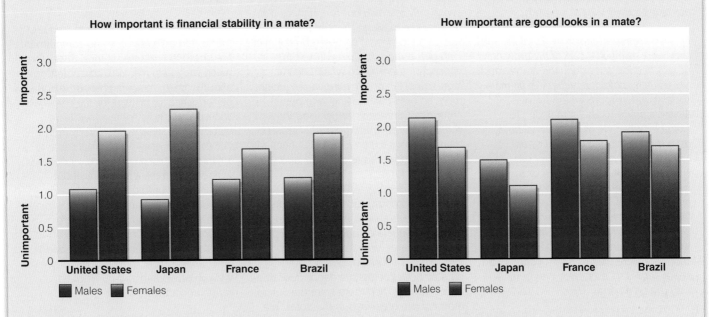

How important is financial stability in a mate?

How important are good looks in a mate?

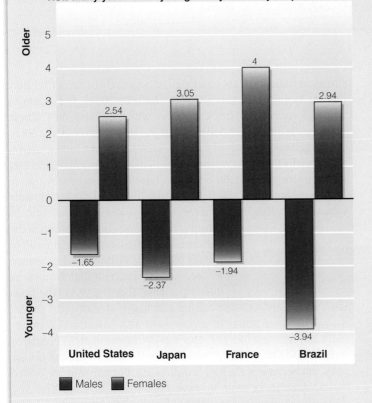

How many years older/younger do you want your partner to be?

In the accompanying graphs, males and females from different countries rate the importance of a mate's looks and financial prospects and their ideal age difference. In the "Good Looks" and "Good Financial Prospects" graphs, participants rated importance from 0 (unimportant) to 3 (very important). In the "Age Difference" graph, participants rated the importance of age difference in potential mates. A negative number refers to a desire for a mate who is younger by a certain number of years, whereas a higher number refers to a desire for a mate who is older by a certain number of years.

SOURCE: Adapted from Buss (1989). Reprinted by permission of Cambridge University Press.

Following is a story written by a heterosexual man who was reflecting about his experiences growing up as a young boy. As you read through it, consider the impact of gender roles on our expressions of love and intimacy today. Do you think most men are comfortable expressing their emotions today? Why or why not?

I played organized sports for 15 years, and they were as much a part of my growing up as Cheerios, television, and homework. My sexuality unfolded within this all-male social world of sport, where sex was always a major focus. I remember, for example, when we as prepubertal boys used the old "buying baseball cards" routine as a cover to sneak peeks at Playboy *and* Swank *magazines at the newsstand. We would talk endlessly after practices about "boobs" and what it must feel like to kiss and neck. Later, in junior high, we teased one another in the locker room about "jerking off" or being virgins, and there were endless interrogations about "how far" everybody was getting with their girlfriends.*

Eventually, boyish anticipation spilled into real sexual relationships with girls, which, to my delight and confusion, turned out to *be a lot more complex than I ever imagined. While sex (kissing, necking, and petting) got more exciting, it also got more difficult to figure out and talk about. Inside, most of the boys, like myself, needed to love and be loved. We were awkwardly reaching out for intimacy. Yet publicly, the message that got imparted was to "catch feels," be cool, and connect with girls but don't allow yourself to depend on them. Once when I was a high-school junior, the gang in the weight room accused me of being wrapped around my girlfriend's finger. Nothing could be further from the truth, I assured them; to prove it, I broke up with her. I felt miserable about this at the time, and I still feel bad about it.*

Within the college jock subculture, men's public protests against intimacy sometimes became exaggerated and ugly. I remember two teammates, drunk and rowdy, ripping girls' blouses off at a mixer and crawling on their bellies across the dance floor to look up skirts. Then there were the Sunday morning late breakfasts in the dorm. We jocks would usually all sit at one table and be forced to listen to one braggart or another describe his sexual exploits of the *night before. Although a lot of us were turned off by such kiss-and-tell, ego-boosting tactics, we never openly criticized them. Real or fabricated, displays of raunchy sex were also assumed to "win points."*

When sexual relationships were "serious," that is, tempered by love and commitment, the unspoken rule was silence. It was rare when we young men shared our feelings about women, misgivings about sexual performance, or disdain for the crudeness and insensitivity of some of our teammates. I now see the tragic irony in this: We could talk about superficial sex and anything that used, trivialized, or debased women, but frank discussions about sexuality that unfolded within a loving relationship were taboo. Within the locker room subculture, sex and love were seldom allowed to mix. There was a terrible split between inner needs and outer appearances, between our desire for the love of women and our feigned indifference toward them.

SOURCE: Adapted from Sabo and Runfola (1980).

---

you love" (Engel & Saracino, 1986, p. 242). This may be because gay men tend to adopt fewer stereotyped beliefs about gender roles than heterosexual men.

Intimacy in Different Cultures

Love seems to be a basic human emotion. Aren't "basic human emotions" the same everywhere? Isn't anger the same in Chicago and Timbuktu, and sadness the same in Paris and Bombay? Although there is evidence that the majority of worldwide cultures experience romantic love (see the accompanying Sexual Diversity in Our World feature), we do know that one's culture has been found to have a more powerful impact on love beliefs than one's gender (Sprecher & Toro-Morn, 2002). Culture affects how a person defines love, how easily he or she falls in love, whom he or she falls in love with, and how the relationship proceeds (Kim & Hatfield, 2004).

    As we discussed in Chapter 3, cultural differences in individual versus group needs can affect communication patterns (Cai et al., 2000). It should come as no surprise that these cultural differences can also affect patterns of intimacy. Passionate love is typically emphasized in individualistic cultures, but in collectivist cultures, pas-

Love seems to be a *basic human emotion.*

sionate relationships are often viewed negatively because they may disrupt family traditions (Kim & Hatfield, 2004). For example, although Americans often equate love with happiness, the Chinese have equated love with sadness and jealousy (Shaver et al., 1992). This is because collectivist cultures, such as that of China or Japan, traditionally marry for reasons other than love. Passionate love dies and is not viewed as stable enough to base a marriage on. In a study of France, Japan, and the United States, intimacy style was directly related to whether the culture was individualistic, collectivistic, or mixed (France), and also to how much the culture had adopted stereotypical views of gender roles (that is, how much it tended to see men as assertive and women as nurturing; Ting-Toomey, 1991). The Japanese, with a collectivistic culture and highly stereotypical gender roles, had lower scores in measures of attachment and commitment and were less likely to value self-disclosure than the French or Americans (Kito, 2005). Americans also have stereotypical gender roles, but because of the highly individualistic culture in the United States, Americans tend to have high levels of confusion and ambivalence about relationships. Interestingly, the French, who have a culture with high individual motivation yet with a strong group orientation, and who also have a more balanced view of

What does our brain have to do with our feelings of love and romance? New research into brain physiology has found that our brain is more involved than you might think. Magnetic resonance imaging of brain functioning revealed that certain areas of the brain experience increases in blood flow when a newly in love person looks at a photograph of his or her romantic partner (Aron et al., 2005; Ortigue et al., 2010). More than 2,500 brain images from 17 men and women who rated themselves as "intensely in love" were analyzed using magnetic resonance imaging technology (which monitors increases in blood flow indicating neural activity). Strong activity was noted in the motivation areas of the brain, where an overabundance of cells produces or receives the neurotransmitter dopamine (Aron et al., 2005). Other studies have found that when a person falls in love, 12 areas of the brain are stimulated to release neurotransmitters, including dopamine, oxytocin, adrenaline, and vasopressin (Ortigue et al., 2010). All of these neurotransmitters contribute to feelings of euphoria and happiness.

Dopamine has also been found to be critical for motivation. In fact, neuroscien-tists have found that men and women who gamble have increased dopamine when they are winning (Carey, 2005). The researchers concluded that romantic love serves as a motivation for a person to reach a goal. In this case, the goal is to spend time with the love interest.

The area of our brain responsible for sexual arousal was also found to be stimulated in these newly in love participants, but it was the motivation area that received the most stimulation. There is a biological urge that comes from sexual arousal, but also from new love (Carey, 2005). The researchers hypothesized that when the motivation area is stimulated, a person is motivated to get rewards with his or her love interest above all else. Think about it for a minute. When we are hungry, thirsty, or tired, the motivation area of our brain is stimulated, motivating us to find food, water, or a place to sleep. When we are romantically in love, this same area motivates us to make the connection and seek out the person we wish to be with.

This may also explain why new love often feels so crazy. Feelings of euphoria, sleeplessness, a preoccupation of thoughts of the partner, and an inability to concen-trate are all common when a person is newly in love. Some men and women describe new love as a "drug," one that often leads them to do things they wouldn't normally do. Perhaps it is a result of the increased blood flow to our motivation center—and the increases in dopamine—that motivate us to get more of what we desire.

Although more research is needed on neuroscience, brain activity, and emotions, it has been suggested that this research might help us understand why people with autism often are indifferent to romantic relationships (Carey, 2005). It could be because of the atypical brain development in the motivation areas of brain that is typical in those with autism. In addition, this research may also help us understand why love changes as the years go by. The strength of activity in the motivation section of the brain has been found to weaken as the length of the relationship increases (Carey, 2005). In the future, research into brain physiology will continue to teach us more about the physiology of romantic love.

SOURCE: Aron et al., 2005.

---

masculine and feminine gender roles, had the lowest degree of conflict in intimate relationships.

Culture also affects one's sense of self. For example, in China, people's sense of self is entirely translated through their relationships with others. "A Chinese man would consider his roles as a son, brother, husband, or a father, before he would think of himself as an individual" (Dion and Dion, 2010). In China, love is thought of in terms of how a mate would be received by family and community, not in terms of one's own sense of romance. Because of this, the Chinese have a more practical approach to love than do Americans (Sprecher & Toro-Morn, 2002).

Finally, a cross-cultural study of college students from Brazil, India, Philippines, Japan, Mexico, Australia, the United States, England, Hong Kong, Thailand, and Pakistan studied the perceived significance of love for the building of a marriage (we further discuss marriage in Chapter 9). Researchers found that love is given highest importance in Westernized nations and the lowest importance in the less developed Asian nations (R. Levine et al., 1995). Thus, culture plays a role in how we experience and express both love and intimacy.

*Many people regard love as **something that happens to them.***

▶▶ LONG-TERM LOVE and Commitment

The ability to maintain love over time is the hallmark of maturity. Many people regard love as something that happens to them, almost like catching the flu. As we learned in the chapter opening story, it takes effort and commitment to maintain love—not only commitment to the other person but commitment to continually build on and improve the quality of the relationship. Most long-term relationships that end do so not because the couple "fell out of love" but because, somewhere down the line, they stopped working together on their relationship. In this sense, the old saying is true: The opposite of love is not hate, but indifference.

R. J. Sternberg (1985), you may recall, claimed that passion, intimacy, and commitment are the three elements of love; in consummate love, he says, all three are present. Research has found that age and relationship length are both positively related to intimacy and commitment; that is, the older the couple and the longer the relationship, typically the stronger the intimacy and commitment in the relationship (Ahmetoglu et al., 2010). Yet, one tends to hear very little talk of commitment in our culture, with its great

The ability to maintain love over time is the hallmark of maturity. Couples who have been together a long time often have a sense of ease with each other.

ON YOUR MIND 7.3

I've always wondered, how can a person stay with only one person his or her whole life and not get bored?

Although it might be hard to believe you could do this, it's also important to remember that love grows and changes when two people commit themselves to work on a relationship. Are you the person you were 10 years ago? What makes you think you'll be the same 10 years from now? When two people allow each other to grow and develop, they find new experiences and new forms of love all the time. People get bored primarily when they lose interest, not because the other person has no mysteries left.

emphasis on passionate love. Couples going through hard times can persevere and build even stronger and more intimate relationships when their commitment reflects such a deep sense of trust.

If you watched the chapter opening interview, you saw Joan and Neil, who have been together for many years. You probably noticed their strong sense of ease with each other. Couples who continue to communicate with each other, remain committed to each other and the relationship, and remain interested in and intimate with each other build a lasting bond of trust. Those who don't may feel isolated and lonely in relationships that nevertheless endure for many years. Although passionate love may fade over time, love itself does not necessarily diminish. The decline of passion can allow the other components of love to flourish in the relationship (Ahmetoglu et al., 2010).

*Couples going through hard times **can persevere and build** even stronger relationships.*

▶▶ LOSS of Love

Popular songs are often about the loss of love; the blues is a whole genre of music built on the experience of losing love, and country-western music is well-known for its songs of lost love. For most people, a breakup can cause deep sadness and a profound sense of loss (Locker et al., 2010). Research on social rejection has found that when people think another has rejected them, they experience physiological changes, including a skip in their heartbeat (Moor et al., 2010).

After a relationship breakup, many men and women are vulnerable to self-blame, loss of self-esteem, and distrust of others, and they may rush into another relationship to replace the lost partner (Locker et al., 2010; Timmreck, 1990). Research on brain physiology has found that a relationship breakup stimulates areas of the brain that are related to motivation, reward, and addiction, which sheds some light on the excessive alcohol consumption or drug abuse of those who have been rejected (Fisher et al., 2010).

As difficult as a breakup can be, several factors may lower the level of distress. One of these is high self-esteem, which can help a person continue to feel hopeful and think more positive thoughts about themselves after a breakup (Svoboda, 2011). Those with low self-esteem tend to blame themselves and worry that no one will ever love them. Earlier, we discussed the importance of attachment styles, and it probably won't surprise you to learn that those with secure attachment styles often have the easiest time with breakups, whereas those with anxious attachment styles have the most difficulties (Locker et al., 2010; Svoboda, 2011). They may desperately try to get the relationship back or refuse to let go.

There is no easy way to decrease the pain of a breakup. Time can help a rejected partner feel better, mostly because as time goes by there is less activity in the area of the brain related to attachment (Fisher et al., 2010). When this activity slows down, a person is better able to reappraise the breakup and assess what was learned in the relationship (Fisher et al., 2010). We will discuss relationship breakups more in Chapter 9.

◀ review QUESTIONS

1 What do we know about why we are attracted to certain people? Explain what factors might be involved.

2 Explain what we know about cross-cultural attraction and identify some of the qualities that men and women may find attractive in other cultures.

3 Explain the importance of self-disclosure on the development of intimacy.

4 Explain what the research has found with respect to gender differences in intimacy styles.

5 Provide three ways in which cultural differences may affect patterns of intimacy.

6 Explain how the ability to maintain love over time is the hallmark of maturity.

▶ LOVE, SEX, AND How We Build Intimate Relationships

One way to express deep love and intimacy is through sexual behavior, but sexual behavior itself is not necessarily an expression of love or intimacy. How do we make the decision to have sex? There are many levels of relationships that can lead to sex. Casual sex and "hooking up" can happen between people who barely know each other, generated by excitement, novelty, and/or pure physical pleasure.

▶▶ LOVE and Sex

Sex can be an expression of affection and intimacy without including passionate love; sex can also be engaged in purely for sexual pleasure or for procreation; or sex can be an expression of love within a loving relationship. Problems can develop when one partner has one view of the developing sexual relationship and the other partner takes a different perspective.

Because the decision to engage in sexual contact involves the feelings and desires of two people, examining your own motivations, as well as your partner's, is important. When making the decision to initiate a sexual relationship with another person, consider the following:

1. Clarify your values. At some point, each of us needs to make value decisions regarding intimacy, sex, and love. What role does love play in your sexual decisions? How will you reconcile these values with those you have learned from your family, friends, and religion?

2. Be honest with yourself—which is often more difficult than being honest with others. Entering a relationship with another person takes close self-examination. What do you really want out of this encounter? Out of this person? Are you hoping the sexual contact will lead to something deeper, or are you in it simply for the sex? What will you do if you find that you (or your partner) have a sexually transmitted infection? Are you in this because you want to be or because you feel some kind of pressure to be sexual—from yourself or from your partner? Could you say "no" comfortably? Are you ready for a sexual relationship with this person?

3. Be honest with your partner. Another person's feelings and needs are always at issue in any relationship, and part of our responsibility as caring human beings is not to hurt or exploit others. Why is your partner interested in sex with you? Do his or her expectations differ from yours? Will she or he be hurt if your relationship does not develop further? Have you discussed your feelings?

The decision to engage in a sexual relationship may or may not be related to feelings of love. Casual sex has become much more common and accepted than it was before the 1970s, when young people (especially women) were strongly advised to save their "greatest asset," their virginity, for marriage. Overall, the impor-

ON YOUR MIND 7.4

How can I tell the difference between being in love and just deeply liking someone?

Unfortunately, no one has come up with a foolproof way of making that distinction. Being "in love" can feel a lot like being "in deep like." One would hope we deeply like those whom we love, and in fact, we probably love those we deeply like. The element that may be missing from those we deeply like is sexual passion, but sometimes we don't realize that we are not in love with them until after we develop a sexual relationship. The discovery can be painful to both parties, which is why it is advisable to think it through before initiating a sexual relationship with a friend.

tance of love as an essential condition for sexual relations has diminished. Yet, casual sex has become more physically risky with the spread of sexually transmitted infections (we will discuss this more in Chapter 15).

When we begin to feel attracted to someone, we begin to act intimate; we gaze longer at each other, lean on each other, and touch more (Hatfield, 1988). People meeting each other for the first time tend to reveal their levels of attraction by their body language. Perper (1985) observed heterosexual strangers approaching each other in bars. The first stage he called the initial contact and conversation (which, by the way, Perper found to be commonly initiated by the female). If the couple is mutually attracted, they will begin to turn their bodies more and more toward each other, until they are facing one another. The first tentative touches begin, a hand briefly on a hand or a forearm, for example, and an increase in duration and intimacy as the evening progresses (again, also often initiated by the female). Finally, the couple shows "full body

REAL RESEARCH 7.4 Although similar numbers of men and women report "hooking up" on college campuses, women were less likely to report the hook up experience was a positive emotional experience than men (OWEN AND FINCHAM, 2011).

synchronization"; their facial expressions, posture, and even breathing begin to mirror their partner's. As we discussed in Chapter 3, women smile, gaze, lean forward, and touch more often than men do in conversation. Women also "flirt" with their nonverbal cues (such as hair flipping and head nodding) to encourage their partner to reveal more about themselves, which would, in turn, allow the women to formulate an impression of the person (W. E. Martin, 2001).

▶▶ DEVELOPING Intimacy Skills

There are many ways to improve our intimacy skills. Developing intimacy often begins with understanding and liking ourselves—self-love. Other important skills we can develop to enhance our ability to form relationships include receptivity, listening, showing affection, trust, and respect.

Self-Love

Self-love is different from conceit or **narcissism;** it is not a process of promoting ourselves but of being at ease with our positive qualities and forgiving ourselves for our faults. If you are not willing to get to know yourself and to accept your own faults, why would others think you are any more interested in them or that you would judge them any less harshly? Many people look to others for indications of their own self-worth. We must first take responsibility to know ourselves (self-intimacy) and then to accept ourselves as we are. Once we like ourselves, we can reach out to others.

Receptivity

Many of us think we are receptive to others when actually we are sending subtle signals that we do not want to be bothered. Receptivity can be communicated through eye contact and smiling. This allows the other person to feel comfortable and makes us approachable. Taking 5 minutes a day to sit and reconnect with your partner may improve your relationship and help preserve intimacy and passion.

Listening

We discussed in Chapter 3 how true communication begins with listening. Nothing shows you care about another person quite as much as your full attention. It can be very difficult to listen to people talk only of themselves or to people who see any comment made by another person primarily in terms of how it relates to them. Learning to truly listen enhances intimacy.

Affection

How do we show affection to another person? If you watch loving parents with their child, it is easy to see how affection is displayed. Parents attend to their children, smile at them, touch them in affectionate ways, look in their eyes, and hug and kiss them. Most people want the same things from their intimate friends and lovers. Affection shows that you feel a sense of warmth and security with your partner.

Trust

To trust another is an act of courage because it grants that person the power to hurt or disappoint you. However, intimacy requires trust. Usually trust develops slowly. You trust your partner a little bit at the beginning of your relationship and begin to trust him or her more and more as he or she proves to be dependable and predictable. Having trust in our partner leads to more confidence that the relationship will last. When a couple trusts each other, each expects the partner to care and respond to the other's needs, now and in the future (Zak et al., 1998).

Remember earlier we talked about women from divorced families being less able to trust in intimate relationships? Perhaps it is because these women have seen firsthand what happens in unsuccessful marriages, and they fear intimate relationships

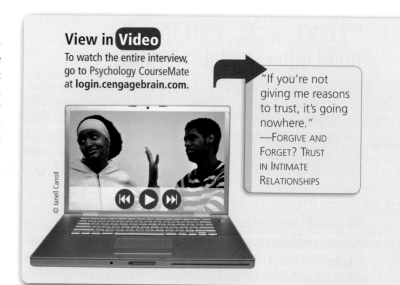

View in Video

To watch the entire interview, go to Psychology CourseMate at **login.cengagebrain.com.**

© Janell Carroll

"If you're not giving me reasons to trust, it's going nowhere." —FORGIVE AND FORGET? TRUST IN INTIMATE RELATIONSHIPS

just don't work. Men, too, may feel less able to trust when their partner is ambivalent or cautious about trust. The important thing to remember is that often the longer a relationship lasts, the more trust builds between the partners (Jacquet & Surra, 2001).

Respect

We enter into relationships with our own needs and desires, which sometimes cloud the fact that the other person is different from us and has his or her own special needs. Respect is the process of acknowledging and understanding that person's needs, even if you don't share them.

▶▶ THE DARK SIDE of Love

Love evokes powerful emotions; this is both its strength and its weakness. Many of the emotions that can come from strong feelings about another person can also be destructive to a relationship and may require great maturity or a strong act of will to overcome. Let's now examine three of the dark sides of love: jealousy, compulsiveness, and possessiveness.

We are often jealous when we think, fantasize, or imagine that another person has traits we ourselves want.

Michael Krasowitz/Getty Images

---

self-love
Love for oneself; the instinct or desire to promote one's own well-being.

narcissism
Excessive admiration of oneself.

Jealousy: The Green-Eyed Monster

Jealousy is a common experience in intimate relationships (Knox et al., 2007). Imagine you are at a party with a person with whom you are in an exclusive sexual relationship. You notice that person standing close to someone else, talking and laughing, and occasionally putting his or her hand on the other person's arm. At one point, you notice your partner whispering in the other person's ear, and they both laugh.

How does that make you feel? Are you jealous? But wait, I forgot to tell you: The person your partner was talking to was of the same sex as your partner (if you are heterosexual) or the other sex (if you are homosexual). Are you still jealous? Oh yes, one more thing. The other person was your partner's younger sibling. Now are you jealous?

Jealousy is an emotional reaction to a relationship that is being threatened (Knox et al., 1999, 2007; Sharpsteen & Kirkpatrick, 1997). A threat is a matter of interpretation; people who deeply trust their partners may not be able to imagine a situation in which the relationship is really threatened. We are most jealous in the situation just described when the person flirting with our partner has traits we ourselves want (or we fantasize that they do; see the accompanying Real Research feature). Maybe we imagine our partner will find the other person more desirable than us, sexier, or funnier. We imagine that the partner sees in the other person all those traits we believe that we lack.

Men and women experience similar levels of jealousy in intimate relationships, yet there is controversy over what triggers jealousy (Fleischmann et al., 2005). Some research supports the fact that heterosexual men are more jealous when they believe that their partner has had a sexual encounter with another man, whereas heterosexual women are often more focused on the emotional or relationship aspects of infidelity (Buss, 2003; Schützwohl, 2008). However, it may have to do with whether the relationship is short or long term (Penke & Asendorpf, 2008). In short-term relationships, both men and women are more threatened by sexual infidelity, whereas emotional infidelity is often more threatening in a long-term relationship (Mathes, 2005). Other studies have found physiological responses (e.g., increased blood pressure) in both men and women when they imagined scenarios of their partner committing either emotional or sexual infidelity (DeSteno et al., 2002; C. R. Harris, 2003; Turner, 2000). Cheating, either emotional or sexual, can lead to jealousy in both men and women.

Past research on heterosexual couples has found that men report that female–female sexual infidelity was rated the least jealousy-producing—perhaps because a man can fantasize about being with the two women (Sagarin et al., 2003). Unfortunately, we know little about infidelity in same-sex relationships and marriages because the majority of the research has been done on heterosexual relationships (Blow & Hartnett, 2005). Overall, we know that people who do not experience jealousy have been found to be more secure, and this security in intimate relationships tends to increase as the couple's relationship grows (Knox et al., 1999, 2007). That is, the longer we are in a relationship with someone, the more our vulnerability to jealousy decreases.

Although many people think that jealousy shows that they really care for a person, in fact, it shows a lack of trust in the partner. One study on levels of distrust of men among women of different ethnicities found that heterosexual Hispanic women had more distrust of men with whom they had intimate relationships than either African-American or White women (levels were highest in Dominican women, followed by Puerto Rican and Mexican; Estacion & Cherlin, 2010). Overall, jealousy is a demonstration of lack of trust and low self-esteem (Knox et al., 2007; Puente & Cohen, 2003). It can also be a self-fulfilling prophecy; jealous individuals can drive their mates away, which convinces them that they were right to be jealous in the first place. Jealousy can be contained by trying to improve one's own self-image, by turning it around into a compliment (not "she's flirting with other guys" but "look at how lucky I am—other guys also find her attractive"), and by trust of one's partner. Communicating with your partner about your jealous feelings can often help to maintain your relationship (Guerrero & Afifi, 1999). Opening up and talking about your uncertainty about the relationship or reassessing the relationship can help restore and strengthen the relationship.

Compulsiveness: Addicted to Love

Being in love can produce a sense of ecstasy, euphoria, and a feeling of well-being, much like a powerful drug (see accompanying Sex in Real Life feature for more information). In fact, when a person is in love, his or her body releases the drug phenylethylamine, which produces these feelings (Sabelli et al., 1996). (Phenylethylamine is also an ingredient in chocolate, which may be why we love it so much, especially during a breakup!) Some people do move from relationship to relationship as if they were

---

REAL RESEARCH 7.5 Heterosexual men and women systematically overestimate the attractiveness of members of their own sex, and these overestimations may be because of biological programming to view others as potential threats to their love relationships (HILL, 2007).

---

love addicted, trying to continually recreate that feeling, or else they obsessively hang on to a love partner long after his or her interest has waned (see Table 7.1).

Love addiction is reinforced by the popular media's portrayals (even as far back as Shakespeare's *Romeo and Juliet*) of passionate love as all-consuming. It fosters the belief that only one person is fated to be your "soul mate," that love is always mutual, and that you'll live "happily ever after." Some people feel the need to be in love because society teaches that only then are they really whole, happy, and fulfilled in their role as a woman or a man. Yet love based solely on need can never be truly fulfilling. In Peele and Brodsky's (1991) book *Love and Addiction,* they argue that love addiction is more common than most believe, and that it is based on a continuation of an adolescent view of love that is never replaced as the person matures. Counseling or psychotherapy may help people come to terms with their addiction to love.

Possessiveness: Every Move You Make, I'll Be Watching You

Because love also entails risk, dependency to some degree, and a strong connection between people, there is always the danger that the strength of the bond can be used by one partner to manipulate the other. Abusive love relationships exist when one partner tries to increase his or her own sense of self-worth or to control the other's behavior by withdrawing or manipulating love.

For intimacy to grow, partners must nurture each other. Controlling behavior may have short-term benefits (you might get the person to do what you want for a while), but long term, it smothers the relationship. No one likes the feeling of being manipulated, whether it is subtle, through the use of guilt, or overt, through physical force. Part of love is the joy of seeing the partner free to pursue his or her desires and appreciating the differences between partners. Although every relationship has its boundaries, freedom within those agreed-on constraints is what encourages the growth and maturation of both partners.

Possessiveness indicates a problem of self-esteem and personal boundaries, and can eventually lead to **stalking.** Most states have passed stalking laws, which enable the police to arrest a person who constantly shadows someone (usually, but not always, a woman) or makes threatening gestures or claims. Thinking about another person with that level of obsession is a sign of a serious psychological problem, one that should be brought to the attention of a mental health professional.

We started this chapter talking about the importance of love in our lives. The ability to form loving, caring, and intimate relationships with others is important for our emotional health and also our physical health. Love and intimacy are two of the most powerful factors in well-being. Love might not always be easy to understand, but it is a powerful force in our lives, and intimacy is an important component of mature love in our culture.

stalking
Relentlessly pursuing someone, shadowing him or her, or making threatening gestures or claims toward the person when the relationship is unwanted.

◀ **review** QUESTIONS

1 What factors might a couple consider when making the decision to initiate a sexual relationship?

2 Why do people feel jealous, and how are jealousy and self-esteem related?

3 Compare and contrast compulsiveness and possessiveness.

⏮ **chapter** REVIEW

SUMMARY **POINTS**

1 We go through life trying to come to terms with loving, trying to figure out why we are attracted to certain types or why we fall in love with all the wrong people. The mystery of love is part of its attraction.

2 Not until the 19th century did people begin to believe that romantic love was the most desirable form of loving relationships. Through most of Western history, marriage was an economic union arranged by the parents. Once wed, husbands and wives were encouraged to learn to love one another, to develop love.

3 Romantic love comes with a sense of ecstasy and anxiety, physical attraction, and sexual desire. We tend to idealize the partner, ignoring faults in the newfound joy of the attachment. Passionate love blooms in the initial euphoria of a new attachment to a sexual partner. If a relationship is to continue, romantic love must develop into companionate love.

4 Romantic love is the passionate, highly sexual part of loving. Companionate love involves feelings of affection, intimacy, and attachment to another person. In many cultures, marriages are based on companionate love, assuming that passion will grow as the couple does.

5 John Alan Lee suggests that there are six basic types of love, and Robert Sternberg suggests that love is made up of three elements: passion, intimacy, and decision/commitment, which can combine in different ways in relationships, creating seven basic ways to love and an eighth state, called *nonlove,* which is an absence of all three elements.

6 The behavioral reinforcement theories suggest that we love because the other person reinforces positive feelings in ourselves. Positive feelings in the presence of another person make us like him or her, even when the reward has nothing to do with the other person.

7 The cognitive theories propose that we love because we think we love. This theory suggests that the action comes first and the interpretation comes later.

8 In the physiological arousal theory, people are vulnerable to experiencing love (or another emotion) when they are physiologically aroused for whatever reason. An emotion happens when there is general physiological arousal for whatever reason and a label is attached to it—and that label might be any emotion.

9 Evolutionary perspectives of love believe that love developed out of our need to be protected from outside threats, to protect children, and from our sexual drive. Love is an evolutionary strategy that helps us form the bonds we need to reproduce and pass our genes on to the next generation.

10 Biological theories believe that pheromones may contribute to feelings of love. Our odor preferences are influenced by our major histocompatibility complex (MHC). Neurotransmitters and the brain also have been found to affect our feelings of love.

11 Love develops over the life cycle. In infancy, we develop attachments to our caregivers; receiving love in return has an influence on our capacity to love later in life. In adolescence, we deal with issues of separation from our parents and begin to explore adult ways of loving. Adolescents tend to experience romantic love. Attachment styles we learn in infancy, such as secure, avoidant, and ambivalent styles, may last through life and influence how we begin to form adult attachments in adolescence.

12 As we mature and enter adulthood, forming intimate relationships becomes important. Developing intimacy is risky, and men and women have different styles of intimacy, but intimacy is seen as an important component of mature love in our culture. As we grow older, commitment in love becomes more important, and passion may decrease in importance.

13 Relationships take effort, and when a couple stops working on the relationship, both partners can become very lonely, love can fade, and intimacy can evaporate. When love is lost, for whatever reason, it is a time of pain and mourning. The support of family and friends can help us let go of the lost love and try to form new attachments.

14 Men and women may have different intimacy styles. For example, men may learn to suppress communication about intimacy as they grow, or they may learn to express it in different ways.

15 The decision to be sexual is often confused with the decision to love. Values need to be clarified before a sexual relationship is begun.

16 Developing intimacy begins with understanding ourselves and liking ourselves.

Receptivity, listening, showing affection, trusting in your partner, and respecting him or her are important in the development of intimacy.

17 Love also has its negative side. Jealousy plagues many people in their love relationships, whereas others seem addicted to love, going in and out of love relationships. Some people also use love as a means to manipulate and control others.

18 Possessiveness indicates a problem of self-esteem and personal boundaries and can eventually lead to stalking. Most states have passed stalking laws, which enable the police to arrest a person who constantly shadows someone or makes threatening gestures or claims.

CRITICAL THINKING QUESTIONS

1 Using John Alan Lee's colors of love, examine a relationship that you are in (or were in) and analyze the styles of love that you and your partner use(d). Which love style do you think would be hardest for you to deal with in a partner and why?

2 Think of a love relationship that you have been in. Describe how each of the theories proposed in this chapter would explain why

you loved your partner. Which theory do you think does the best job? Why?

3 Do you think the research on pheromones fits with your own experiences? Are you attracted (or not attracted) to people by their smell?

4 Explain what gender differences have been found in love and tie this research to an example from one of your past relationships.

5 How long do you think is appropriate to wait in a relationship before engaging in sex? Why?

6 Have you ever been involved with a partner who was jealous? What was the hardest part of this relationship? How did you handle the jealousy?

MEDIA RESOURCES

CourseMate brings course concepts to life with interactive learning, study, and exam preparation tools that support the printed textbook. A textbook-specific website, Psychology CourseMate includes an integrated interactive eBook and other interactive learning tools including quizzes, flashcards, videos, and more. If your textbook does not include an access code card, go to CengageBrain.com to gain access.

CENGAGENOW   CengageNOW is an easy-to-use online resource that helps you study in less time to get the grade you want—NOW. Take a pre-test for this chapter and receive a personalized study plan based on your results that will identify the topics you need to review and direct you to online resources to help you master those topics. Then take a post-test to help you determine the concepts you have mastered and what you will need to work on. If your textbook does not include an access code card, go to CengageBrain.com to gain access.

View in Video available in CourseMate and CengageNOW:

The Secret to Staying in Love: Couple who has been married for 38 years will discuss strategies for staying in love.

Love Science: American high school students discuss the feelings they get when they think about their significant others. Discussion

of research using teenagers to analyze what happens in the brain during feelings of love.

Forgive and Forget? Trust in Intimate Relationships: Student discusses the importance of trust in intimate relationships.

Websites:

Love Is Great ■ This website is all about love, dating, romance, and relationships. The website contains information and links to single/dating websites.

Loving You ■ This website contains advice, love poems, and free romantic love notes and quotes. There are also links to dating services, love libraries, and gift shops.

Love Test ■ A nonscientific but fun website that offers a multitude of different "love" tests. Compatibility analysis, astrology reports, fortune tellers, and relationship rating tests are available.

Queendom ■ This site offers the largest online battery of professionally developed and validated psychological assessments. This website is a fun place to find a variety of different quizzes.

8 Childhood and Adolescent Sexuality

View in **Video**

View in **Video**

View in **Video**

View in **Video**

ABOUT THE CHAPTER OPENING VIDEO – The Sexuality Information and Education Council of the U.S. proposes the primary goals of sex education should be to help teens develop a positive view of sexuality, provide them with adequate information to protect their sexual health, and help them to make good decisions. However, there is an ongoing debate about the form that sexuality education should take in the U.S. Around the world, the majority of teens do not get the information they need about sex to protect themselves. One place where this is definitely not the case is in the Netherlands, where comprehensive sex education is mandatory. I decided to take a trip to the Netherlands to learn more about their approach to sex education. I met with Ruud Winkel, a well-known biology/sex education teacher at Amsterdam Lyceum, a Dutch secondary school. Ruud teaches human sexuality to 13- to 18-year-olds. Each child is required to take his class and no one is allowed to opt out. Ruud also told me many interesting facts about his class:

I spend the first 5 minutes of every class letting students ask me questions about sex. I've had the strangest questions but I'm glad they can ask me. Common questions are "How much sperm have you got?" "What does an orgasm feel like?" "What's a wet dream?" or "How long does it take to get a baby out?" I answer their questions and we have great discussions about them. Throughout the class, I teach them about sexually transmitted infections, orgasms, birth control, and masturbation. I think it's important for them to know that masturbation is normal and that everyone does it. We also talk about sexual intercourse. In fact, we show students a video with a man and woman making love. We think it's

important that they understand what making love is all about. How can we teach about making babies if we didn't teach them about making love? In the end, I want students to understand that sex is good and that they should enjoy it.

The Netherlands has the world's lowest rates of teenage pregnancy, birth, and abortion. While we can't say that comprehensive programs are directly responsible for these lower rates, we do know that the Dutch have a unique approach. My work in the Netherlands has helped me to understand the complexity of sexuality education. Dutch sex education focuses on responsibility, respect, and pleasure, and doesn't shy away from the tough questions. You may find this interview somewhat shocking, but at the same time, refreshing. ▌

"Children should know that sex is good and that you should enjoy it."
—CHAPTER OPENING VIDEO

View in Video

To watch the entire interview, go to Psychology CourseMate at **login.cengagebrain.com.**

Today's adolescents have grown up with conflicting messages about sexuality. Although they have grown up during a time of relative political and social conservatism with school health programs concentrating on abstinence and the risks of sexual behavior (such as sexually transmitted infections [STIs] or unintended pregnancy), they have also had unlimited exposure to sexual information and images through the Internet (Hennessy et al., 2009). Nightly news stories focus on a variety of issues related to sexuality, including same-sex marriage, erectile drugs, vaccines for STIs, and increasing rates of HIV and AIDS around the world (Fortenberry et al., 2010; Kelly et al., 2009; Romer et al., 2009). Popular reality television shows. such as *16 and Pregnant* and *Teen Mom* tell stories about teen pregnancy. All of these events and influences have shaped this generation of adolescents.

We think of children today as undergoing their own, exclusive stage of development. Children are not just "little adults," and though they can be sexual, children's sexuality is not adult sexuality (Gordon & Schroeder, 1995). Children want love, appreciate sensuality, and engage in behaviors that set the stage for the adult sexuality to come. Nonetheless, we must be careful not to attribute adult motives to childhood behaviors. When a 5-year-old boy and a 5-year-old girl sharing a bath reach out to touch each others' genitals, the meaning that they ascribe to that action cannot be considered "sexual" as adults use the term. As

Plummer (1991) notes, a little boy having an erection shows simply that his physiology functions normally; seeing the erection as "sexual" is to overlay an adult social meaning onto the physiology. The child is probably not even aware of the "sexual" nature of his erection and, indeed, may not even be aware that his penis is erect.

Every society distinguishes between young and old; every society also creates rules around the sexuality of the young. Sexual growth involves a host of factors—physical maturation of the sexual organs, psychological dynamics, familial relations, and peer relations, all within the social and cultural beliefs about gender roles and sexuality. In this chapter, we'll begin with the special challenges faced by researchers who study childhood and adolescent sexuality. Then we'll take a look at sexuality from infancy through adolescence. Finally, we'll discuss the importance of sexuality education and the controversies surrounding it.

▶ STUDYING CHILDHOOD
and Adolescent Sexuality

Many people oppose questioning children about sexuality, often believing that research on child sexuality will somehow encourage promiscuity. Others seem to believe that if we do not talk about children's sexuality, it will just go away.

Despite the opposition, many researchers have been forging ahead in their study of children's sexual behavior despite the opposition. We will discuss the research on child and adolescent sexuality throughout this chapter. We will also discuss findings from the National Survey of Sexual Health, as well as findings from several of the ongoing, large-scale governmental studies, including the National Longitudinal Study of Adolescent Health, the National Survey of Family Growth, the National Longitudinal Study of Adolescent Males, and the Youth Risk Behavior Surveillance System (see Chapter 2 for more information about these studies).

Although methodologies and populations varied for each of the aforementioned governmental studies, adolescents between the ages of 14 and 17 were a common subpopulation. As we discussed in Chapter 2, sexuality research has always been problem driven—that is, many studies are aimed at decreasing "problems," such as STI rates or teenage pregnancy—and nowhere is this more apparent than the research on adolescent sexuality. In the future, more research is needed on a variety of aspects of adolescent sexuality, including frequency of sexual behaviors; differences in gender, ethnicity, race, religion, and social class; same-sex attraction and behavior; cross-cultural research; and the meaning of eroticism and sexuality in young people's lives.

Throughout most of history, children were treated as miniature adults, and concepts such as "childhood" and "adolescence" did not exist (Aries, 1962). Most children worked, dressed, and were expected to behave (as much as they were capable) like adults.

Oscar Gustav Rejlander/Getty Images

gender constancy
The realization in the young child that one's gender does not normally change over the life span.

1 Explain how today's adolescents are being exposed to sexuality in different ways than the generations before them.

2 Explain why there has been opposition to childhood sexuality research.

3 Identify the large-scale studies on adolescent sexual behavior and explain their study populations.

4 Give one example of how research into childhood sexuality has been problem driven.

▶ BEGINNINGS: Birth to Age 2

Let's first take a look at physical and psychosexual changes from birth to age 2. We would not label behavior as "sexual" during this time; however, many behaviors arise out of curiosity.

▶▶ PHYSICAL DEVELOPMENT:
Fully Equipped at Birth

Our sexual anatomy becomes functional even before we are born; ultrasound has shown male fetuses with erections in the uterus, and some infants develop erections shortly after birth—even before the umbilical cord is cut (Masters et al., 1982). Female infants are capable of vaginal lubrication from birth (Martinson, 1981). Infant girls produce some estrogen from the adrenal glands before puberty, whereas infant boys have small testes that produce very small amounts of testosterone. Young children are even capable of orgasm!

*Most children develop **gender constancy** by about age 6.*

Kinsey and his colleagues (1948, 1953) established that half of boys between the ages of 3 and 4 could achieve the urogenital muscle spasms of orgasm (although no fluid is ejaculated), and almost all boys could do it 3 to 5 years before puberty. Kinsey did not collect systematic data on the abilities of young girls to reach orgasm, although he did include some anecdotal stories on the subject. Still, there is no reason to think that girls should be any less able than boys to orgasm.

▶▶ PSYCHOSEXUAL DEVELOPMENT:
Bonding and Gender

Throughout this textbook we have discussed the importance of early relationships and the development of an attachment to a primary caregiver. Infants can develop many attachment styles, including secure, anxious/ambivalent, or avoidant (see Chapter 7).

Infants are helpless creatures, incapable of obtaining nourishment or warmth or relieving pain or distress. In fact, the bond between a mother and child is more than psychological; a baby's crying actually helps stimulate the secretion of the hormone *oxytocin* in the mother, which releases her milk for breast-feeding (Rossi, 1978; we'll discuss this further in Chapter 12).

In Chapter 7, we also discussed the importance of pheromones, which promote the bond between a mother and her infant (Kohl & Francoeur, 2002). Equally important as the infant's need for nourishment is the need for holding, cuddling, and close contact with caregivers. An infant's need for warmth and contact was demonstrated in Harlow's (1959) famous experiment, in which rhesus monkeys were separated at birth from their mothers. When offered two surrogate mothers, one a wire figure of a monkey equipped with milk bottles and one a terry-cloth–covered figure, the monkeys clung to the terry-cloth figure for warmth and security, and ventured over to the wire figure only when desperate for nourishment. The need for a sense of warmth and security in infancy overwhelms even the desire to eat.

In Chapter 4, we discussed how infants between 1 and 2 years of age begin to develop their gender identity (M. Lewis, 1987). After about age 2, it becomes increasingly difficult to change the child's gender identity (which is occasionally done when, for example, a female with an enlarged clitoris is mistakenly identified at birth as a boy). It takes a little longer to achieve gender constancy, whereby young children come to understand that they will not become a member of the other sex sometime in the future. Most children develop **gender constancy** by about age 6, and a strong identification with one gender typically develops that becomes a fundamental part of a child's self-concept (Warin, 2000).

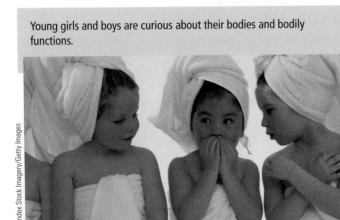

Young girls and boys are curious about their bodies and bodily functions.

Fabrizio Cacciatore/Index Stock Imagery/Getty Images

▶▶ SEXUAL BEHAVIOR: Curiosity

In infancy, children's bodies are busy making sure all of their organs work and learning to control them. The sexual system is no exception. Male infants sometimes have erections during breast-feeding (which can be very disconcerting to the mother), whereas girls have clitoral erections and lubrication (although this is less likely to be noticed). The baby's body (and mind) has not yet differentiated sexual functions from other functions, and the pleasure of breast-feeding, as well as the stimulation from the lips, mouth, and tongue, create a generalized neurological response that stimulates the genital response.

Genital touching is common in infancy, and many infants touch their genitals as soon as their hands are coordinated enough to do so (Casteels et al., 2004). Some babies only occasionally or rarely touch themselves, whereas others do it more regularly. Although babies clearly derive pleasure from this activity; it is not orgasm based. In fact, it is soothing to the baby and may serve as a means of tension reduction and distraction. Overall, genital touching is normal at this age, and parents should not be concerned about it.

◀ review QUESTIONS

1 Explain how infants have functional sexual anatomy, perhaps even before birth.

2 Identify the single most important aspect of infant development, and explain the importance of pheromones, warmth, and contact with caregivers.

3 Differentiate between gender identity and gender constancy.

4 Discuss genital touching in infancy and possible parental concerns about this behavior.

▶ EARLY CHILDHOOD: Ages 2 to 5

Children continue to develop physically, and in early childhood they begin to understand what it means to be a boy or girl. Curiosity is still the basis for their sexuality during this time. Children also learn that their genitals are private during these years, and they often begin to associate sexuality with secrecy.

▶▶ PHYSICAL DEVELOPMENT:
Mastering Coordination

Early childhood is a crucial period for physical development. Children of this age must learn to master the basic physical actions, such as eye–hand coordination, walking, talking, and generally learning to control their bodies. Think of all the new things a child must learn—all the rules of speaking and communicating; extremely complex physical skills such as self-feeding, walking, and running; how to interact with other children and adults; control of bodily wastes through toilet training; and handling all the frustrations of not being able to do most of the things they want to do when they want to do them. Although this period of childhood is not a particularly active one in terms of physical sexual development, children may learn more in the first few years of childhood about the nature of their bodies than they learn in the entire remainder of their lives. It is truly a time of profound change and growth.

▶▶ PSYCHOSEXUAL DEVELOPMENT:
What It Means to Be a Girl or a Boy

In early childhood, children begin serious exploration of their bodies. It is usually during this period that children are toilet trained, and they go through a period of intense interest in their genitals and bodily wastes. They begin to ask the first, basic questions about sex, usually about why boys and girls have different genitals and what they are for. They begin to explore what it means to be "boys" or "girls" and turn to their parents, siblings, or television for models of gender behavior. Sometimes children at this age will appear flirtatious or engage in sexual behaviors such as kissing in an attempt to understand gender roles.

▶▶ SEXUAL BEHAVIOR:
Curiosity and Responsibility

Toddlers are not yet aware of the idea of sexuality or genital sexual relations. Like infants, toddlers and young children engage in

REAL RESEARCH 8.1 First-born children get approximately 3,000 more hours of quality time with their parents than their later-born siblings, which may help explain why first-borns score higher on intelligence tests (PRICE, 2008).

many behaviors that involve exploring their bodies and doing things that feel good. Both girls and boys at this age continue to engage in genital touching. More than 70% of mothers in one study reported that their children younger than 6 touched themselves (Okami et al., 1997).

Young boys develop strong relationships with same-sex and other-sex friends and relatives, and these relationships set the stage for adult intimate relationships.

ON YOUR MIND 8.1

Is it damaging to children to see their parents naked? What about accidentally seeing them having sex?

For many years in Western society, it has been thought that children would be somehow traumatized by seeing their parents naked. In fact, nudity is natural and common in many cultures, such as European countries, which have a reputation for physical health and beauty. Parents' casual nudity, openness to sexual questions, and willingness to let their children sleep at times in their beds has been found to be correlated with generally positive overall effects on the well-being of children (Lewis & Janda, 1988; Okami et al., 1998). If children walk in on their parents having sex, the parents' best tactic is not to be upset, but to tell the children calmly that the parents are showing each other how much they love each other. Most children are scared when they walk in on their parents having sex and talking about it can help the children understand. More significant trauma can come from the parents' overreaction than from the sight of parents having sex.

Genital touching is actually more common in early childhood than later childhood, although it picks up again after puberty (Friedrich et al., 1991). The act may be deliberate and obvious, and may even become a preoccupation. Boys at this age are capable of erection, and some proudly show it off to visitors. Parental reaction at this stage is important; strong disapproval may teach their children to hide the behavior and to be secretive and even ashamed of their bodies, whereas parents who are tolerant of their children's emerging sexuality can teach them to respect and take pride in their bodies. It is perfectly appropriate to make rules about the times and places that such behavior is acceptable, just as one makes rules about other childhood actions, such as the correct time and place to eat or to urinate.

Child sex play often begins with games exposing the genitals ("I'll show you mine if you show me yours...."), and by the age of 4, may move on to undressing and touching, followed by asking questions about sex around age 5. Sometimes young children will rub their bodies against each other, often with members of the same sex, which seems to provide general tactile pleasure.

▶▶ SEXUAL KNOWLEDGE and Attitudes

During this period of early childhood, children learn that the genitals are different from the rest of the body. They remain covered up, at least in public, and touching or playing with them is either discouraged or to be done only in private. This is the beginning of the sense of secrecy surrounding sexuality.

As we discussed in Chapters 5 and 6, children this age, especially girls, rarely learn the anatomically correct names for their genitals. Why is it that some parents teach their children the correct names for all the body parts except their genitalia? What message do you think it might send children when we use cute play words such as "weiner" or "piddlewiddle" for their genital organs?

In our culture, boys are often taught about the penis, but girls rarely are taught about the vagina or clitoris. This tends to discourage girls from learning more about their sexuality (Ogletree & Ginsburg, 2000). Although girls are quite interested in boys' genitalia, boys tend to be relatively uninterested in girls' genitalia (Gundersen et al., 1981).

◀ review QUESTIONS

1 Explain how curiosity is still the basis for sexuality in early childhood.

2 What does the research show about genital touching during this age range?

3 Explain how a lack of knowledge about proper anatomical terms for the genitals may affect girls.

4 What is the impact of learning in childhood that the genitals are different from the rest of the body? Explain.

MIDDLE CHILDHOOD TO PRETEEN: Ages 6 to 12

Between ages 6 and 12, the first outward signs of puberty often occur, and both boys and girls become more private about their bodies. Children begin building a larger knowledge base about sexual information—and acquire information from many sources, including their parents/caregivers, peers, and siblings. During the middle childhood to preteen years, children often play in same-sex groups and may begin masturbating and/or engaging in sexual fantasy and/or sexual contact.

▶▶ PHYSICAL DEVELOPMENT: Puberty

Puberty is one of the three major stages of physiological sexual development, together with prenatal sexual differentiation and menopause. Puberty marks the transition from sexual immaturity to maturity and the start of reproductive ability. In Chapters 5 and 6, we discussed the physiological and hormonal changes that accompany puberty, so in this chapter we review only those physical changes that have an effect on the nature of adolescent sexuality.

Until a child's body starts the enormous changes involved in puberty, the sexual organs grow in size only to keep up with general body growth and change very little in their physiological activity. Although the body begins internal changes to prepare for puberty as early as age 6 or 7, the first outward signs of puberty begin at 9 or 10. The physiological changes of puberty begin anywhere between the ages of 8 and 13 in most girls and 9 and 14 in most boys. As we discussed in Chapter 5, research has found that girls are beginning puberty earlier than ever before (Biro et al., 2010). See Figure 8.1 for more information about signs of puberty in boys and girls. Overall, girls' maturation is about 1.5 to 2 years ahead of boys' (Gemelli, 1996).

In girls, **breast buds** appear, and pubic hair growth may begin. In boys, pubic hair growth generally starts a couple of years later than in girls, and on average, girls experience menarche (which we discussed in Chapter 5) before boys experience their first ejaculation (often referred to as **semenarche**; SEM-min-ark). Preadolescent boys experience frequent erections, even to nonerotic stimuli. Common reactions to semenarche include surprise, curiosity, confusion, and pleasure—and typically most boys don't tell anyone about this event (Frankel, 2002; J. H. Stein & Reiser, 1994). Pubertal changes can be frightening for both boys and girls if they are not prepared for them, and even if prepared, the onset of puberty can be emotionally, psychologically, and physically difficult for some children.

The physiological changes of puberty almost seem cruel. At the time when attractiveness to others begins to become important, the body starts growing in disproportionate ways; fat can accumulate before muscles mature, feet can grow before the legs catch up, the nose may be the first part of the face to begin its growth spurt, and one side of the body may grow faster than the other (M.

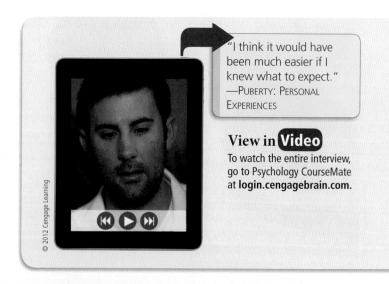

"I think it would have been much easier if I knew what to expect."
—PUBERTY: PERSONAL EXPERIENCES

View in Video
To watch the entire interview, go to Psychology CourseMate at **login.cengagebrain.com.**

© 2012 Cengage Learning

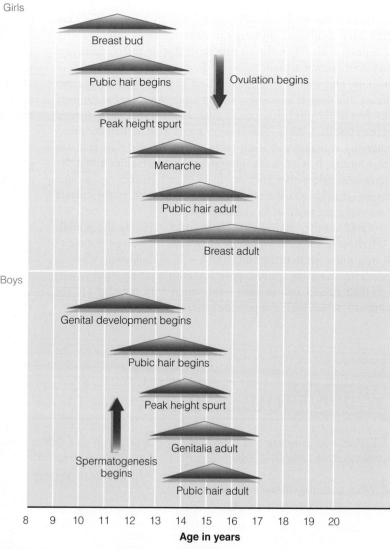

The Age Sequence of Pubertal Maturation in Boys and Girls

Girls
- Breast bud
- Pubic hair begins
- Ovulation begins
- Peak height spurt
- Menarche
- Public hair adult
- Breast adult

Boys
- Genital development begins
- Pubic hair begins
- Peak height spurt
- Genitalia adult
- Spermatogenesis begins
- Pubic hair adult

Age in years: 8 9 10 11 12 13 14 15 16 17 18 19 20

FIGURE 8.1 This graph illustrates the average ages when boys and girls go through the major bodily changes of puberty. SOURCE: From Lancaster, J. B., & B. A. Hamburg (Eds.), *School-age pregnancy and parenthood: Biosocial dimensions* (p. 20). New York: Aldine DeGruyter. Reprinted by permission.

Diamond & Diamond, 1986). Add acne, a voice that squeaks at unexpected moments, and unfamiliarity with limbs that have suddenly grown much longer than one is accustomed to, and it is no wonder that adolescence is often a time of awkwardness and discomfort. Fortunately, the rest of the body soon catches up, so the awkward phase does not last too long.

▶▶ PSYCHOSEXUAL DEVELOPMENT:
Becoming More Private

As children mature, sexual behaviors, such as public genital touching or sex games, decrease. However, this may be because such behaviors are less tolerated by parents and adults as the child grows older. For example, although it may be acceptable for a 3-year-old to put his hand down his pants, such behavior would not be as acceptable for a 9-year-old.

Typically, children engage in more sexual exploration behavior up until age 5; then this behavior decreases. One study found that 2-year-old children of both sexes engaged in more natural sexual exploration than did children in the 10- to 12-year-old range (Friedrich, 1998). This may simply be because children get better at hiding such behaviors.

▶▶ SEXUAL BEHAVIOR:
Learning About the Birds and Bees

Children through the middle and late childhood years continue to engage in genital touching and may explore both same- and other-sex contact. Curiosity drives some to display their genitals and seek out the genitals of other children. Prepubescence is the age of sexual discovery; most children learn about adult sexual behaviors such as sexual intercourse at this age and assimilate cultural taboos and prejudices concerning unconventional sexual behavior. For example, it is at this age that children (especially boys) first begin to use sexual insults with each other (using taunts like "You're so gay!" or "You're a fag!"), questioning their friends' desirability and/or sexual orientation. In 2010, a new campaign was launched in the United States called "Think B4 You Speak" to help children and adolescents understand the negativity of such phrases and the potential consequences of the words they use.

Masturbation

Generally, by the end of this period, most children are capable of stimulating themselves to orgasm. Although orgasm is possible, not all children in this age range engage in genital touching for the purpose of orgasm. Boys often learn masturbation from peers, and as they get older, they may masturbate in groups. Girls, on the other hand, typically discover masturbation by accident. When masturbation does begin, both boys and girls may stimulate themselves by rubbing their penis or vulva against soft objects like blankets, pillows, or stuffed animals. Many girls experience pleasure and even orgasm by rhythmically rubbing their legs together.

breast buds
The first swelling of the area around the nipple that indicates the beginning of breast development.

semenarche
The experience of first ejaculation.

Sexual Contact

Children from age 6 to puberty engage in a variety of same- and other-sex play. Sex games, such as "spin the bottle" (spinning a bottle in a circle while asking a question such as, "Who is going to kiss Marie?" then the person whom the bottle points to must perform the task), are common and allow children to make sexual contact under the guise of a game. Play, in a sense, is the "work" of childhood, teaching interpersonal and physical skills that will be developed as we mature. Children at this age have some knowledge about sex and are curious about it, but they often have incomplete or erroneous ideas. Both boys and girls exhibit a range of same-sex sexual behaviors as they move through childhood, from casual rubbing and contact during horseplay to more focused attention on the genitals.

Rates of sexual contact among school-age children are difficult to come by, and most experts still cite Kinsey's data of 1948 and 1953. Kinsey found that 57% of men and 46% of women remembered engaging in some kind of sex play in the preadolescent years. However, the problems with research in this area is that many studies are retrospective (i.e., they asked older adults to remember what they did when they were young), and there are many reasons to think people's recollections of childhood sexuality may not be entirely accurate.

Negative language about GLBT people is common in schools today, although most of it may not be meant to be hurtful. The "Think B4 You Speak" campaign encourages people to understand what they are saying and to think about the consequences of the words they use.

Sex in Real Life ▶▶▶ Parents and Anxiety: Where Does It Come From?

When parents think about talking to their children about sex, many report feeling very anxious and insecure about their ability to talk about it. Anxiety comes from many places, including the following:

■ **Fear:** Many parents worry that something bad will happen to their children if they start talking to them about sex. Parents worry that they will wait too long, start too early, say the wrong thing, or give misinformation. They also may worry that talking about sexuality will take away their children's innocence, by making them grow up too fast or become overly interested in sexuality.

■ **Lack of comfort:** Because most parents did not talk to their parents about sex, many feel uncomfortable in presenting it themselves. Those who did talk about it usually talked with their mothers. This causes many fathers to feel especially uncomfortable facing the prospect of educating their sons and daughters.

■ **Lack of skills:** Parents often do not know how to say what they want to say. Some resort to a lecture about the "birds and bees," whereas others simply ask their children, "Do you have any questions?"

■ **Misinformation:** Many parents do not have the necessary facts about sexuality. Having received little sex education themselves, many might not have information and be unsure about where to go to get it.

SOURCE: Adapted from P. Wilson (1994, pp. 1–2).

▶▶ SEXUALITY AND RELATIONSHIPS: What We Learn

As we grow up, all of our experiences influence our sexuality in one way or another. We learn different aspects of sexuality from these varied influences; for example, we may learn values and taboos from our parents, information from our siblings, and techniques and behavior from our peers, television, and the Internet. All of these influences contribute to our developing sexuality.

Relationships with Parents and Caretakers

In Chapter 7, we discussed how our parents, or the adults who raised us, are the very first teachers of love and intimacy. As we grow and find relationships of our own, we tend to relate to others in our love relationships much as we did when we were young.

When it comes to childhood sexual behaviors, many American parents feel conflicted. They may want their children to have a positive attitude toward sexuality, but many do not know how to go about fostering this attitude. Children have a natural curiosity

In their relationships with each other, boys and girls in middle childhood often imitate adults.

© Creatas/Picturequest

about sex, and when parents avoid children's questions, they reinforce children's ideas that sex is secret, mysterious, and bad. As adolescents' bodies continue to change, they may feel anxious about these changes or their relationships with other people. Accurate knowledge about sex may lead to a more positive self-image and self-acceptance. We discuss the importance of sexuality education later in this chapter.

Parents may get upset and confused when they discover that their child engages in sexual play. Sex play in children is perfectly normal, and parents should probably be more concerned if their children show no interest in their own or other children's bodies than if they want to find out what other children have "down there."

Relationships with Peers

As children age and try to determine how they will fare in the world outside the family, their peer groups increase in importance. Friendships are an essential part of adolescent social development (Ojanen et al., 2010). Learning acceptable peer-group sexual standards is as important as learning all the other attitudes and behaviors. Children learn acceptable attitudes and behaviors for common games, sports, and even the latest media trends.

SAME-SEX PEERS During middle childhood, adolescents overwhelmingly prefer same-sex to other-sex friends (Hendrick & Hendrick, 2000; Mehta & Strough, 2010). Although other-sex friendships do develop, the majority of early play is done in same-sex groupings (Fabes et al., 2003). Early on these friendships tend to be activity based (friends are made because of shared interests or proximity), but by early adolescence, affective qualities (such as trust, loyalty, honesty) replace the activity-based interests (Bigelow, 1977; Ojanen et al., 2010). With these qualities in place, friendships can tolerate differences in interests or activities and reasonable distance separations (such as not being in the same classroom). As a result, friendships in adolescence become more stable, supportive, and intimate than they were before this time.

Many cultures have rituals of passage that signify the entry of the child into adulthood. Here a young Jewish boy reads from the Torah at his Bar Mitzvah.

Peers are a major catalyst in the decision to partake in voluntary sexual experimentation with others. Often initial sexual experimentation takes place among preadolescents of the same sex.

Same-sex experimentation is quite common in childhood, even among people who grow up to be predominantly heterosexual.

OTHER-SEX PEERS For most American children, preadolescence is when they begin to recognize their sexual nature and to see peers as potential boyfriends or girlfriends. Although this does not happen until the very end of this period, children as young as 11 begin to develop interest in others and may begin pairing off within larger groups of friends or at parties. Preadolescence has traditionally been a time of early sexual contact, such as kissing and petting, but for many this does not occur until later.

SIBLINGS Another fairly common childhood experience is sexual contact with siblings or close relatives, such as cousins. Most of the time, this occurs in sex games or fondling, but it can also occur as abuse, with an older sibling or relative coercing a younger one into unwanted sexual activity. Greenwald and Leitenberg (1989) found that among a sample of college students, 17% reported having sibling sexual contact before age 13. Only a small percentage involved force or threat, and penetration was rare. Research on sexual contact between siblings suggests that it can be psychological damaging when there is a large difference between the ages of siblings or coercive force is used (Finkelhor, 1980; Rudd & Herzberger, 1999).

◀ review QUESTIONS

1 Explain physical and psychosexual development in middle childhood through the preteen years.

2 Identify and discuss the types of sexual behaviors that are common in middle childhood through the preteen years.

3 Discuss the importance of relationships with parents, peers, and siblings in childhood through preadolescence.

▶ ADOLESCENCE: Ages 12 to 18

Adolescence begins after the onset of puberty and is, in part, our emotional and cognitive reactions to puberty. Adolescence ends when the person achieves "adulthood," signified by a sense of individual identity and an ability to cope independently with internal and external problems (Lovejoy & Estridge, 1987). People reach adulthood at different times; adolescence can end at around age 17 or 18, or it can stretch into a person's 20s. It is recognized the world over as a time of transition, as the entrance into the responsibilities and privileges of adulthood. Most societies throughout history have developed rites of passage around puberty; the Jewish Bar or Bat Mitzvah, Christian confirmation, and the Hispanic Quinceañera come to mind, and other cultures have other rites. The Quinceañera—a 15th birthday celebration for Latina girls—has traditionally been used as an opportunity to discuss female adolescent developmental tasks and challenges, including teenage pregnancy and sexuality (H. Stewart, 2005).

We know the most about this developmental period because of ongoing research studies on adolescent sexual behavior. Overall, we know there is no other time in the life cycle that so many things happen at once: the body undergoes rapid change; the individual begins a psychological separation from the parents; peer relationships, dating, and sexuality increase in importance; and attention turns to job, career, or college choices.

Many young people have their first experience with partnered sex during this time. It is no wonder that many adults look back on their adolescence as both a time of confusion and difficulty, and a time of fond memories.

▶▶ PHYSICAL DEVELOPMENT: Big Changes

During early adolescence, parents are often shocked at the extreme changes that occur in their children; children can add 5 or 6 inches in height and gain 10 to 20 pounds in less than a year. Boys may develop a lower voice and a more decidedly adult physique, whereas girls develop breasts and a more female physique.

Biological changes take place in virtually every system of the body and include changes in cardiovascular status, energy levels, sexual desire, mood, and personality characteristics (Hamburg, 1986).

Maturing early or late can also be awkward for boys or girls. Because girls' growth spurts happen earlier than boys', there is a period when girls will be at least equal in height and often taller than boys; this reversal of the cultural expectation of male height often causes both sexes to be embarrassed at dances. Girls who consider themselves to be "on time" in developing feel more attractive and positive about their bodies than those who consider themselves "early" or "late" (Hamburg, 1986).

Being the last boy (or the first) in the locker room to develop pubic hair and have the penis develop can be a humiliating experience that many remember well into adulthood. Similarly, girls who are the first or last to develop breasts often suffer the cruel taunts of classmates, although the messages can be mixed. It may be this combination of beginning of sexual exploration, changing bodies, and peer pressure that results in the average adolescent having a negative **body image** (Brumberg, 1997).

Females

Menarche is the hallmark of female puberty and is often viewed as one of the most important events in a woman's life (Ersoy et al., 2005; we discussed the physiology of menarche in Chapter 5). Menarche can be a scary time for a girl who is uninformed about what to expect and an embarrassing time if she is not taught how to use tampons or pads correctly.

The beginning of menstruation can mean different things to an adolescent girl depending on how her family or her culture explains it to her. It can signify the exciting beginning of adulthood, sexuality, and the ability to have babies—but with all the potential problems that brings as well. Girls who are prepared for menstrua-

tion and who are recognized for their intellectual or creative capabilities are more likely to describe pleasurable reactions to the onset of menstruation, whereas girls who are not recognized for other abilities often experience more fear and embarrassment associated with first menstruation (Teitelman, 2004).

Although boys' first sign of sexual maturity—ejaculation—is generally a pleasurable experience that is overtly associated with sexuality, girls' sign of maturity is not associated with sexual pleasure and may be accompanied by cramps and discomfort, as well as embarrassment if the onset is at an inopportune time (such as in the middle of school). Some girls begin menstruation with little idea of what is happening or with myths about it being bad to bathe, swim, exercise, or engage in sexual activities. Many are unfamiliar with their genital anatomy, making tasks such as inserting tampons difficult and frustrating (Carroll, 2009; M. Diamond & Diamond, 1986).

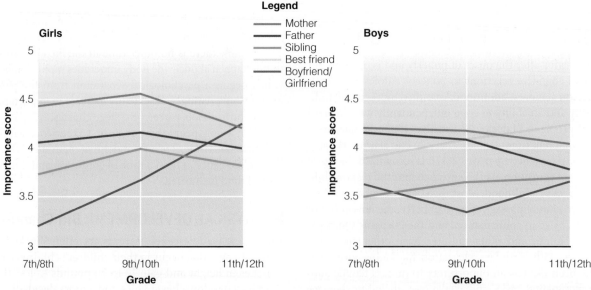

FIGURE **8.2** This graph shows the age differences in mean ratings of the importance of each type of relationship to one's life during adolescence (1 = not at all important; 5 = extremely important). SOURCE: Brown et al. (1997). Reprinted by permission of Cambridge University Press.

Males

Adolescent development in males differs in many ways from the development in girls. Boys' voices change more drastically than girls', and their growth spurts tend to be more extreme and dramatic, usually accompanied by an increase in appetite. Because boys' adolescent growth tends to be more uneven and sporadic than girls', the adolescent boy will often appear gangly or awkward. As boys continue to develop, the larynx enlarges, bones grow, and the frame takes on a more adult appearance.

For the most part, early development in boys is usually not as embarrassing as it is in girls; beginning to shave may be seen as a sign of maturity and adulthood. However, adolescent boys do experience frequent spontaneous erections, which may have no association with sexuality but are nonetheless quite embarrassing. Their increased sexual desire is often released through nocturnal emissions and increased masturbation.

▶▶ PSYCHOSEXUAL DEVELOPMENT: Emotional Self-Awareness

Adolescence is, by far, the most psychologically and socially difficult of the life cycle changes. Adolescents struggle with a number of tasks: achieving comfort with their bodies, developing an iden-

In early and middle adolescence, teens try on different looks, from trendy to rebellious, as they develop an identity separate from their parents.

DreamPictures/Getty Images

tity separate from their parents', trying to prove their capacity to establish meaningful intimate and sexual relationships, beginning to think abstractly and futuristically, and establishing emotional self-awareness (Gemelli, 1996). We now examine these life cycle changes.

Adolescence (Ages 12 to 18)

In early adolescence, preteens begin to shift their role from child to adolescent, trying to forge an identity separate from their family by establishing stronger relationships with peers. Same-sex friendships are common by the eighth grade and may develop into first same-sex sexual contacts as well (L. M. Diamond, 2000). The importance of a best friend grows as an adolescent matures. In fact, by the end of high school, both girls and boys rated their relationship with their best friend as their most important relationship (B. B. Brown et al., 1997; see Figure 8.2).

Early adolescence, as most of us remember, is often filled with "cliques," as people look to peers for validation and standards of behavior. Dating also often begins at this age, which drives many adolescents to become preoccupied with their bodily appearance and to experiment with different "looks." Young adolescents are often very concerned with body image at this time. Many young girls, in an attempt to achieve the perfect "model" figure, will endlessly diet, sometimes to the point of serious eating disorders. The Youth Risk Behavior Survey (YRBS) found that many young boys and girls are developing eating disorders and may turn to drugs such as steroids to achieve the perfect body (Pisetsky et al., 2008) (see Chapter 2 for more information about the YRBS).

By about age 14, most adolescents experience an increasing interest in intimate relationships. The social environment also helps build this interest through school-sponsored dances and private parties (B. B. Brown et al., 1997). Adolescents who have not yet reached puberty or those who feel they might be gay or lesbian often feel intense pressure to express interest in other-sex relationships at this time (K. M. Cohen & Savin-Williams, 1996). Many adolescents increase the frequency of dating as they try to integrate sexuality into their growing capacity for adult-to-adult intimacy.

For the average middle adolescent, dating consists of going to movies or spending time together after school or on weekends. Early dating is often quite informal, and going out in mixed groups is very popular. During this period, couples develop longer term and more exclusive relationships, and early sexual experimentation (deep kissing, fondling) may also begin.

Oftentimes, the pattern for gay, lesbian, bisexual, or unsure/questioning adolescents may be quite different from that of their heterosexual counterparts. They might not fit into the heterosexual dating scene and may try to hide their disinterest in the discussions of the other sex (Faulkner & Cranston, 1998). Rates of depression, loneliness, drug and alcohol abuse, and suicide are significantly higher for gay, lesbian, bisexual, unsure/questioning youth (Cochran et al., 2007; King et al., 2008; Marshal et al., 2009; McCabe et al., 2010; Needham & Austin, 2010; Zhao et al., 2010).

body image
A person's feelings and mental picture of his or her own body's beauty.

Because developing the adolescent sense of self is a delicate process, adolescents may be very sensitive to perceived threats to their emerging ideas of "manhood" or "womanhood." There is an unfortunate tendency among adolescents to portray certain partners as "desirable" and others as undesirable or outcast, which as you can imagine (or remember) can be extremely painful if you are on the wrong side of that judgment. The development of a gay identity may challenge long-held or socially taught images of the acceptable way to be a man or a woman. Family reactions to a gay, lesbian, or bisexual identity and self-expectations may result in depression or confusion. Studies have found that gay, lesbian, and bisexual youths who have supportive families and high levels of family connectedness have better health outcomes than those without this family support (Doty et al., 2010; Needham & Austin, 2010; Ryan et al., 2009; we discuss this further in Chapter 11).

There is no clear line between adolescence and adulthood. Almost all cultures allow marriage and other adult privileges in late adolescence, although there still may be certain restrictions (such as needing parental permission to marry). Late adolescence was, until recently, the stage during which people in Western cultures were expected to begin their search for marital partners through serious dating. As we discuss in Chapter 9, many of today's adults wait longer to establish permanent relationships and perhaps marry (see Figure 8.3 for more information on important sexual and reproductive events for men and women).

▶▶ SEXUAL BEHAVIOR:
Experimentation and Abstinence

Although many television reports and news headlines about adolescent sexual behavior seem to imply that adolescents are reckless and becoming sexually active at young ages, the National Survey of Sexual Health and Behavior (NSSHB) found that today's adolescents are more likely to abstain or act responsibly about sexual behavior (Fortenberry et al., 2010). By studying a variety of teenage sexual behaviors, including masturbation, oral sex, penile-vaginal intercourse, anal intercourse, and the use of condoms, the NSSHB was able to explore changes in adolescent sex behaviors since the other national surveys (National Survey of Family Growth and the Youth Risk Behavior Survey) had been done (see Chapter 2 for more information about these studies).

REAL RESEARCH 8.2 Whereas 31% of teens say their parents most influence their decisions about sex, 43% of parents say friends most influence their teens' decisions about sex (ALBERT, 2009).

Masturbation

As boys and girls enter adolescence, masturbation sharply increases, and the activity is more directed toward achieving orgasm than simply producing pleasurable sensations. The NSSHB found that masturbation is common throughout the life span, increases during adolescence, and then decreases as partnered sex increases later in life (Herbenick et al., 2010a). Kinsey and his

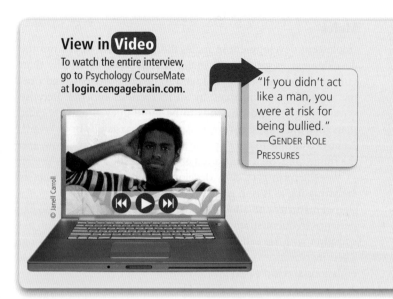

View in Video
To watch the entire interview, go to Psychology CourseMate at **login.cengagebrain.com.**

© Janell Carroll

"If you didn't act like a man, you were at risk for being bullied."
—GENDER ROLE PRESSURES

ON YOUR MIND 8.3

I am 19 years old, and I masturbate at least twice a week, but not as much if I am having good sex with my girlfriend. But she tells me that she doesn't masturbate as much as I do. Why do teenage men masturbate so much more than teenage women?

While research has found that many adolescents and young adults in the United States masturbate, masturbation rates in males are generally higher than in females (Herbenick et al., 2010a). This could be because of several things. First of all, women may underreport their masturbation in surveys because they are less comfortable discussing it. Boys tend to reinforce the social acceptability of masturbation by talking about it more freely among themselves. There may also be biophysical reasons for more frequent male masturbation, such as the obvious nature of the male erection and higher levels of testosterone.

colleagues (1953) also found a sharp increase between the ages of 13 and 15 in boys, with 82% of boys having masturbated by age 15. The girls' pattern was more gradual, with 20% having masturbated by age 15 and no sharp increase at any point.

Abstinence

The Sexuality Information and Education Council of the United States promotes **abstinence** and encourages adolescents to delay sex until they are physically, cognitively, and emotionally ready for mature sexual relationships and their consequences. However, there is some confusion about what sexual behaviors might be included in a

---

abstinence
Refraining from intercourse and often other forms of sexual contact.

fellatio
The act of sexually stimulating the male genitals with the mouth.

cunnilingus
The act of sexually stimulating the female genitals with the mouth.

definition of "abstinence." One study found that college students were more likely to believe a sexual behavior could fit into the definition of abstinence if an orgasm did not occur (Byers et al., 2009).

Adolescents often think about many factors when deciding to be sexual. Perceived family and peer attitudes about sexuality are key factors in the decision to become sexual (Akers et al., 2011). Heterosexual teens who delay sexual intercourse are more likely to live with both biological parents (Upchurch et al., 2001), feel a personal connection to their family (Meschke et al., 2000; Resnick et al., 1997), have discussed sex and abstinence with their parents (Sprecher & Regan, 1996), believe that their mother disapproves of premarital sex, and have higher intelligence levels (C. J. Halpern et al., 2000). Some teens decide they are not ready because they haven't met the "right" person, whereas others delay sex because of STI or pregnancy fears (Morrison-Beedy et al., 2008). Other heterosexual teens decide to delay sexual activity, or at least sexual intercourse, until marriage.

MASTURBATION

AGE	MALE	FEMALE
14–15	67.5%	43%
16–17	79%	52%
18–19	86%	66%
20–24	92%	77%

(a)

VAGINAL INTERCOURSE

AGE	MALE	FEMALE
14–15	10%	12%
16–17	30%	32%
18–19	62.5%	64%
20–24	70%	86%

(b)

ANAL SEX

AGE	MALE		FEMALE
	GAVE	RECEIVED	
14–15	4%	1%	4%
16–17	6%	1%	7%
18–19	10%	4%	20%
20–24	24%	11%	40%

(c)

REAL RESEARCH 8.3 Sexually active teens who were in serious relationships did not differ from abstinent teens in terms of grade point average (GPA), school work, or future goals (McCarthy & Casey, 2008). However, teens engaging in casual sex were found to have lower GPAs, care less about school, and experience more school problems.

Sexual Contact

Adolescents may engage in a variety of sexual behaviors, including kissing, oral sex, sexual intercourse, and anal sex. See Figure 8.3 for more information on selected sexual behaviors in adolescence.

KISSING AND PETTING Kissing and touching are the first sexual contact that most adolescents have with potential sexual partners. Coles and Stokes (1985) reported that 73% of 13-year-old girls and 60% of 13-year-old boys had kissed at least once. Because younger heterosexual girls tend to date older boys, they have higher rates of these kinds of activities at earlier ages than heterosexual boys do, but the differences diminish over time. For example, 20% of 13-year-old boys reported touching a girl's breast, whereas 35% of 13-year-old girls reported having had their breasts touched, a difference that disappears within a year or two.

ORAL SEX Acceptance of oral sex has increased among young people. Kinsey and his colleagues (1948, 1953) reported that 17% of adolescents reported engaging in **fellatio** (fil-LAY-she-oh) and 11% in **cunnilingus** (kun-nah-LING-gus). The National Survey of Family Growth found that among teenagers between the ages of 15 and 19, 54% of girls and 55% of boys reported having engaged in oral sex (Flanigan et al., 2005; Lindberg et al., 2008). The more recent NSSHB found that oral sex has increased in all age groups (Herbenick et al., 2010a; see Figure 8.3).

For many years, there has been a popular perception in the media that heterosexual teens engage in oral sex instead of sexual intercourse because it allows them to preserve their virginity and eliminates pregnancy risk (Stein, 2008; Wind, 2008). However, research challenges this idea (Lindberg et al., 2008). An analysis of the sexual practices of 2,271 15- to 19-year-olds found that oral sex was more common in adolescent couples who had already initiated sexual intercourse—87% of nonvirgin teens reported engaging in oral sex, whereas only 27% of virgins reported engaging in oral sex (Lindberg et al., 2008). In fact, 6

ORAL SEX

AGE	MALE				FEMALE			
	WITH A MALE		WITH A FEMALE		WITH A FEMALE		WITH A MALE	
	GAVE	RECEIVED	GAVE	RECEIVED	GAVE	RECEIVED	GAVE	RECEIVED
14–15	2%	2%	8.5%	13%	5%	4%	13%	10%
16–17	3%	3%	20%	34%	9%	7%	29%	26%
18–19	10%	9%	61%	60%	8%	8%	61%	62%
20–24	9%	9%	71%	73.5%	14%	17%	78%	77%

(d)

FIGURE **8.3** Average percentage of men and women by age who have engaged in specific sexual behaviors. SOURCE: National Survey of Sexual Health and Behavior (NSSHB) results in Herbenick et al. (2010a).

months after first engaging in sexual intercourse, 82% of heterosexual teens have engaged in oral sex. The majority of heterosexual teens engage in oral sex after they have already engaged in sexual intercourse.

Other research on adolescent oral sex has found that heterosexual female adolescents are significantly more likely than heterosexual males to indicate they have given oral sex (Lindberg et al., 2008). As for ethnic differences, White heterosexual females were significantly more likely than their male counterparts to indicate they had given oral sex and significantly more likely than their Hispanic/African American counterparts to have done so (Lindberg et al., 2008). However, these differences were most notable in African American adolescent girls, who were twice as likely to report receiving oral sex rather than giving oral sex (Lindberg et al., 2008). Socioeconomic differences have been found. Heterosexual teens from lower socioeconomic classes and those with more conservative attitudes about sexuality were significantly less likely to report engaging in oral sex, whereas heterosexual adolescents from higher socioeconomic classes and those with more liberal attitudes were more likely to report engaging in oral sex.

ANAL SEX The NSSHB also collected information on prevalence of anal sex in adolescence (see Figure 8.3). Adolescents who had already engaged in penile-vaginal intercourse were more likely to have engaged in anal sex (Lindberg et al., 2008). Although the overall likelihood of engaging in heterosexual anal sex was not found to differ significantly by ethnic or racial group, Hispanic males were more likely than non-Hispanic White males to report ever having engaged in anal intercourse (Lindberg et al., 2008).

The NSSHB found that same-sex receptive anal sex was the least common sexual behavior reported in men (Herbenick et al., 2010a). For some gay adolescents, engaging in anal sex is their defining moment of "losing their virginity." One study of college students found that 80% of respondents believed that a man or woman could lose his or her virginity with a same-sex

*The majority of heterosexual teens experience first sexual intercourse **with someone they are in a relationship with.***

partner, whereas 10% believed that only a man could do so (Trotter & Alderson, 2007). More research is needed in this area.

HETEROSEXUAL INTERCOURSE Close to half of American students in grades 9 to 12 have engaged in sexual intercourse, and the prevalence rate of having ever had sexual intercourse is higher among Black (65%) and Hispanic (49%) students than among White students (42%) (Centers for Disease Control and Prevention, 2010g; Eaton et al., 2006; Herbenick et al., 2010a). Although the number of sexually active teens hasn't changed much since 2002, there has been a steady decline in the number of teens engaging in sexual intercourse since 1988 (Abma et al., 2010; see Figure 8.4).

Although 6% of students experience sexual intercourse before the age of 13, the average age for first engaging in sexual intercourse is approximately 17.2 years (Centers for Disease Control and Prevention, 2010g). However, there are some ethnic differences; on average, Black males are younger, and Asian American males are older. Most studies find that females have sex later than males throughout the teen years in all racial groups (Centers for Disease Control and Prevention, 2010g; Eaton et al., 2006). In most of the developed world, the majority of heterosexual men and women engage in sexual intercourse during their teen years (Alan Guttmacher Institute, 2002). In fact, the age at which heterosexual teenagers become sexually active is similar across comparable developed countries, such as Canada, France, Sweden, and the United States. Contrast this with Japan, where the majority of heterosexual men and women wait until they are in their 20s (Althaus, 1997).

The majority of heterosexual teens experience first sexual intercourse with someone they are in a relationship with, rather than someone they just met (Abma et al., 2010; see Figure 8.5). However, males and females tend to react differently to their first sexual intercourse. The National Health and Social Life Survey found that more than 90% of men said they wanted to have sexual intercourse the first time they did it; more than half were motivated by curiosity, whereas only a quarter said they had sexual intercourse out of affection for their partner. About 70% of women reported wanting to have sexual intercourse. Nearly half of women said they had sex the first time out of affection for their partner, whereas a quarter cited curiosity as their primary motivation. Twenty-four percent said they just went along with it (less than 8% of men said that); 4% of women reported being forced to have sex the first time, whereas only about 3 men in 1,000 (0.3%) reported being forced (see Figure 8.6 for more information about gender differences in feelings about first sexual intercourse). For many, the first sexual intercourse is a monumental occasion. For many teens, this experience contributes to the redefining of self and the reconfiguration of relationships with friends, family members, and sexual partners (Upchurch et al., 1998).

Although the majority of female teens have first sex partners who are 1 to 3 years older, 25% of female teens have first sex partners who are 4 or more years older than themselves (Abma et al., 2010). Other research has found that age differences between sex partners are more common in Latinas' relationships than among non-Latinas (Frost & Driscoll, 2006). In fact, these age differences

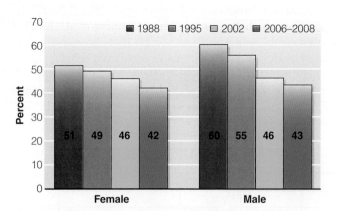

FIGURE 8.4 Never-Married Females and Males Aged 15–19 Years Who Have Ever Had Sexual Intercourse*—National Survey of Family Growth, United States, 1988–2008. SOURCE: Abma et al., 2010

*Based on responses by females to the question "At any time in your life have you ever had sexual intercourse with a man, that is, made love, had sex, or gone all the way?" and by males to the question "Have you ever had sexual intercourse with a female (sometimes called making love, having sex, or going all the way)?"

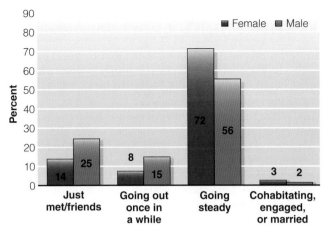

FIGURE **8.5** Relationship with partner at first intercourse among males and females aged 15–19: United States, 2006–2008. SOURCE: Abma et al., 2010.

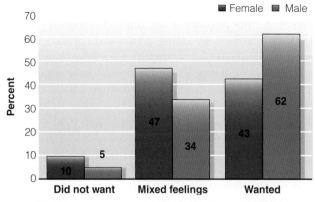

FIGURE **8.6** How much first sex was wanted when it happened among females and males aged 18–24 who had their first sex before age 20: United States, 2006–2008. SOURCE: Abma et al., 2010.

can put younger heterosexual Latinas at an increased risk for early initiation into sexual behavior, unprotected sex, pregnancy, and STIs. First sex with a partner who is older has been found to be associated with higher percentages of females saying they didn't want the sex to happen (Abma et al., 2010).

SAME-SEX SEXUAL BEHAVIOR We know that same-sex sexual behavior is common in adolescence, both for those who will go on to have predominantly heterosexual relationships and those who will have predominantly homosexual relationships. Some gay and lesbian adolescents experience sexual intercourse during their teenage years, before they identify themselves as lesbian or gay (Saewyc et al., 1998).

It is difficult to determine actual figures for adolescent same-sex sexual behavior. Studies of high-school students find that about 10% to 13% report being "unsure" about their sexual orientation, whereas 1% to 6% consider themselves homosexual or bisexual; still, anywhere from 8% to 12% report sexual contact with same-sex partners (Faulkner & Cranston, 1998). Such research, however, relies on self-reports; people may define homosexual differently, or they may not be comfortable being open about their experiences because of homosexual stigma. The NSSHB found that same-sex sexual activity was relatively uncommon in adolescence, but increased in older age groups (Herbenick et al., 2010a). See Figure 8.3 for more information about specific same-sex sexual behaviors.

*Same-sex sexual behavior **is common in adolescence.***

OTHER SEXUAL SITUATIONS There are many other types of sexual situations that adolescents can experience. Some teenagers, especially runaways—both male and female—engage in prostitution. Others make money by becoming involved in child pornography, posing nude for pictures, or performing sexual acts. Although there are few comprehensive studies of the results of engaging in prostitution or pornography as an adolescent (or younger), there is every clinical indication that it results in many sexual and psychological difficulties later on (we discuss this more in Chapter 18).

Many of the sexual variations seen in adults, such as transvestism, exhibitionism, and voyeurism, may begin in adolescence, although it is more common for these desires to be expressed in early adulthood. We discuss these sexual variations in depth in Chapter 16.

Ethnic and Racial Differences in Sexual Activity

An adolescent's ethnicity, race, and culture affect his or her sexual attitudes, which sexual behaviors he or she engages in, and the frequency of these behaviors (Centers for Disease Control and Prevention, 2010g; Fortenberry et al., 2010; Zimmer-Gembeck & Helfand, 2008).

Several ethnic and racial differences have been found in participation of certain sexual behaviors, such as oral and anal sex, age of first sexual intercourse, and age differences between sexual partners (Eaton et al., 2006; Fortenberry et al., 2010; Frost & Driscoll, 2006; Herbenick et al., 2010a; Lindberg et al., 2008). As you will soon see, ethnic and racial differences have also been found in contraceptive use, teen pregnancy, birth rates, abortion, and rates of STIs (Buffardi et al., 2008; Forhan, 2008; Martin et al., 2007; Martinez et al., 2006; Mosher et al., 2004; Reece et al., 2010c; Ventura et al., 2007). We explore these issues in more detail in upcoming chapters.

▶▶ INFLUENCES: Peers, Family, and Religion

The decision to engage in sexual contact with another person is a personal one, yet it is influenced by many social factors, including peers, family, and religion. A number of other social factors influence sexual behavior as well, and we discuss here a few of the more important ones.

Peer Influences

Peer pressure is often cited as the most important influence on teen sexual behavior, and adolescence is certainly a time when the influence of one's friends and peers is at a peak (Busse et al., 2010).

Many adolescents base their own self-worth on peer approval (Akers et al., 2011; Rudolph et al., 2005). Even among preadolescents, peer influences are strong; among sixth graders who have engaged in sexual intercourse, students were more likely to initiate sexual intercourse if they thought that peers were engaging in it and that it would bring them some kind of social gain. Those who did not initiate sexual intercourse were more likely to believe that their behavior would be stigmatized or disapproved of by their peers (Grunbaum et al., 2002).

Remember, though, that a person's perceptions of what his or her peers are doing has a greater influence than peers' actual behavior. Among those subject to and applying peer pressure, many heterosexual adolescent males feel the need to "prove" their masculinity, leading to early sexual activity. Peer pressure is often rated as one of the top reasons that adolescents give for engaging in sexual intercourse.

Relationship with Parents

Good parental communication, an atmosphere of honesty and openness in the home, a two-parent home, and reasonable rules about dating and relationships are among the most important factors associated with adolescents delaying their first sexual intercourse (Akers et al., 2011; Hahm et al., 2008; Lam et al., 2008; Regnerus & Luckies, 2006). This may be attributed to the fact that

---

REAL RESEARCH 8.4 Lesbian, gay, and bisexual men and women report lower levels of parental support than heterosexual men and women (NEEDHAM & AUSTIN, 2010). Unfortunately, lower levels of parental support are related to higher levels of depression, drug and alcohol use, and suicidal thoughts.

---

close families are more likely to transmit their sexual values and integrate their children into their religious and moral views. Heterosexual children from these homes are also more likely to use contraception when they do engage in sexual intercourse (Halpern-Felsher et al., 2004; Zimmer-Gembeck & Helfand, 2008). This is the case among almost all races and ethnic groups (L. M. Baumeister et al., 1995; Brooks-Gunn & Furstenberg, 1989; Kotchick et al., 1999).

Research has found that many American parents do not discuss sex before an adolescent's first sexual experience (Beckett et al., 2010). If a parent does talk about sex, it is generally the mother who tends to be the primary communicator about sexuality to children; in one study of Latino youths, mothers did the majority of all communication about sexuality to their teenagers (L. M. Baumeister et al., 1995; Raffaelli & Green, 2003). Typically mothers talk more to daughters about sexuality than sons (Martin & Luke, 2010).

The ADD Health study (2002) has also found that there is a maternal influence on the timing of first sexual intercourse for heterosexual adolescents, especially for females. A mother's satisfaction with her relationship with her daughter, disapproval of her daughter having sex, and frequent communication about sex is related to a delay of first sexual intercourse (Lam et al., 2008; Tsui-Sui et al., 2010). Fathers are also important—in fact, girls who have a close relationship with their father are more likely to delay sex (Day & Padilla-Walker, 2009; Regnerus & Luchies, 2006; Wilson et al., 2010).

ON YOUR MIND 8.4

Sometimes I feel I should have sex just to get it over with—being a virgin is embarrassing! It's pretty hard to resist when everybody else seems to be doing it.

The decision to have sex is an important one. Too often this step is taken without consideration of its consequences—for example, whether we feel psychologically or emotionally ready and whether our partner does. Sex should never be the result of pressure (by our partner, our friends, or ourselves). There may be many reasons that we want to delay sexual experimentation—including moral or religious reasons. Teens also often overestimate the numbers of their friends who are sexually active.

Religion

Although the relationship between religiosity and sexual activity is complex, in general, more religious heterosexual youths tend to delay first sexual intercourse, have fewer incidents of premarital sexual activity, and have fewer sexual partners (S. Hardy & Raffaelli, 2003; Hull et al., 2010; Nonnemaker et al., 2003). This correlation may be because young people who attend church frequently and who value religion in their lives are less sexually experienced overall (P. King & Boyatzis, 2004; S. D. White & DeBlassie, 1992). Not only do major Western religions and many other world religions discourage premarital sex, but religious adolescents also tend to develop friendships and relationships within their religious institutions, and thus have strong ties to people who are more likely to disapprove of early sexual activity. However, once teens begin engaging in sexual behaviors, religious affiliation and frequency of religious attendance have been found to have little impact on frequency of sexual behaviors (R. Jones et al., 2005).

▶▶ CONTRACEPTION, PREGNANCY, AND ABORTION: Complex Issues

Although we discuss pregnancy, contraception, and abortion more in Chapters 12 and 13, we introduce these concepts here. Approximately 80% of U.S. teens use a contraceptive method the first time they engage in sexual intercourse and condoms are the most popular method (Abma et al., 2010; see Figure 8.7). In fact, condoms are the most frequently used contraceptive method among sexually active adolescents (Abma et al., 2010; Reece et al., 2010c; see Figure 8.8). Adolescents who are able to talk to their mothers about sexuality are more likely to use contraception than adolescents who cannot talk to their mothers (Jaccard et al., 2000; Lam et al., 2008; Meschke et al., 2000).

Of all the areas of adolescent sexual behavior, we probably know the most about teenage pregnancy because of its many impacts on the life of the teenager, the teenager's family, and society as a whole. The U.S. birth rate for female teens was 42.5 births per 1,000 females in 2007, which was higher than many other countries around the world (Abma et al., 2010; Brugman et al., 2010). For comparison, the teen birth rate in Canada was 13, Germany was 10, and Italy was 7.

Teen birth rates in the United States decreased steadily from 1991 to 2005, rose again until 2007, and then decreased in 2008 (Abma et al., 2010). Interestingly, although the majority of U.S. teens want to avoid a pregnancy, 70% of females and 50% of males say they would be accepting of a pregnancy outside of marriage (Abma et al., 2010).

The long-term consequences of teenage pregnancy may be difficult for the mother, child, and extended family. Teenage mothers are more likely to drop out of school, have poorer physical and mental health, and be on welfare than their non-childbearing peers, and their children often have lower birth weights, poorer health and cognitive abilities, more behavioral problems, and fewer educational opportunities (Meschke et al., 2000). Teen parenting also has an impact on others, such as the parents of the teens (who may end up having to take care of their children's children), and on society in general, because these parents are more likely to need government assistance.

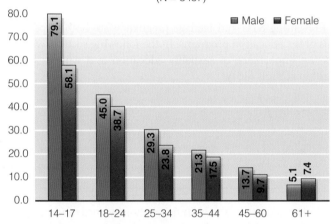

Condom Use Rates by Age & Gender
(% of past 10 vaginal intercourse acts that included condom use)
(N = 3457)

FIGURE **8.7** Condom Use Rates by Age and Gender. SOURCE: National Survey of Sexual Health and Behavior (2010).

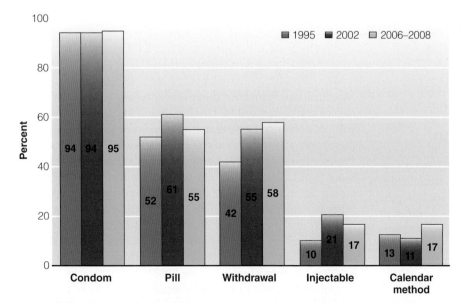

FIGURE **8.8** Ever-use of contraception among sexually experienced females aged 15–19, by method of contraception: United States, 1995, 2002, and 2006–2008. SOURCE: Abma et al., 2010.

REAL RESEARCH 8.5 A study of 24 industrialized countries found that the 3 most popular contraceptive methods used by teens were condoms, condoms along with birth control pills, and birth control pills alone (GODEAU ET AL., 2008).

However, teen pregnancies do not always preclude teen mothers from living healthy, fulfilling lives. In fact, there are examples of teenagers who become pregnant and raise healthy babies while pursuing their own interests. However, the problems a teenage mother faces are many, especially if there is no partner participating in the child's care. A teen who has support from her partner, family, and friends, and who is able to stay in school, has a better chance of living a fulfilling life.

In studies of teen pregnancy and birth, most of the focus has been on the mothers, who often bear the brunt of the emotional, personal, and financial costs of childbearing (Wei, 2000). Adolescent fathers are more difficult to study. Teenage fathers may not support their partners and become uninvolved soon after, and thus the problem of single mothers raising children can be traced, in part, to the lack of responsibility of teen fathers. Society asks little of the teenage male, and there are few social pressures on him to take responsibility for his offspring.

However, some adolescent fathers do accept their role in both pregnancy and parenthood, and realistically assess their responsibilities toward the mother and child. Ideally, teenage fathers should be integrated into the lives of their children and should be expected to take equal responsibility for them.

Adolescent parenthood affects every race, every income group, and every part of American society; it is not just a problem of the inner-city poor. Historically, White teenagers have had lower birth rates than African American or Latino adolescents, a trend that continued in the 1990s. Although through much of the 1990s, African American teenagers had the highest rates of pregnancy, birth, and abortion, all three rates declined by about 20% between 1990 and 1996. Because the birth rate declined more steeply among African American than White teenagers, the gap between these two groups narrowed. Unmarried mothers and their children of all races are more likely to live in poverty than any other segment of the population.

What is it about American society that seems to foster such high rates of teenage pregnancy? A complex series of factors is at work. American society is extremely conflicted about the issue of sexuality in general. Our teens are exposed to sexual scenes in movies and television, yet we hesitate to discuss sex frankly with them. We allow advertising to use blatantly sexual messages and half-dressed models, yet we will not permit advertising for birth control; there is also significant resistance to sex education in the schools.

Today, when teenagers do become pregnant, opportunities may be limited; it is difficult to have a baby and attend high school all day or work at a job. The United States is far behind most other Western countries in providing day-care services that would help single or young parents care for their children. Better counseling, birth control, day-care services, and hope for the future can help ensure that the teenagers who are at risk for unwanted pregnancies and the children of those unwanted pregnancies are cared for by our society.

▶▶ SEXUALLY TRANSMITTED INFECTIONS: Education and Prevention

Although we discuss STIs in great detail in Chapter 15, here we briefly talk about adolescent STI rates. Sexually active teens are at greater risk for acquiring some STIs for behavioral, cultural, and biological reasons (Abma et al., 2010). Rates of chlamydia and gonorrhea are higher in 15- to 19-year-old females than any other age group (Abma et al., 2010). Although rates of other STIs are lower, they have been steadily increasing every year. Even though 15- to 24-year-olds account for only 25% of the sexually active population, they acquire approximately 50% of all new STIs (Weinstock et al., 2004).

Although gay, lesbian, and bisexual youths may not need contraception for birth control purposes, they do need it for protection from STIs. Research has found that gay men are less likely to use condoms than their straight counterparts (S. M. Blake et al., 2001; Saewyc et al., 1998). Increasing condom use in all teens, regardless of sexual orientation, is imperative in decreasing STIs.

© David J. Green - Lifestyle/Alamy

The United States has one of the highest rates of teen pregnancy in the developed world. It's estimated that 10% of all U.S. births are to girls aged 19 or younger (Hamilton et al., 2010).

Preventing STIs and teenage pregnancy are both important goals of sex education programs. In the following section, we discuss the importance of sexuality education and what is being taught in schools today.

◀ review QUESTIONS

1 Explain physical and psychosexual development in adolescence.

2 Explain what we know about the specific sexual behaviors that often occur during adolescence.

3 Identify and explain the influences on adolescent sexuality.

4 Identify and discuss the reasons that adolescents may be erratic users of contraception.

5 Explain how ethnicity, race, and culture are all important influences on adolescent sexual behavior.

▶ WHAT CHILDREN NEED TO KNOW: Sexuality Education

We opened this chapter with an interview with a Dutch sex educator. As we discussed, sexuality education inspires powerful emotions and a considerable amount of controversy. In fact, it may be one of the most heated topics in the field of sexuality, as different sides debate whether and how sexuality education programs should be implemented in the schools.

▶▶ WHY SEXUALITY Education Is Important

Although many people claim that knowledge about sexuality may be harmful, studies have found that it is the lack of sexual-

ity education, ignorance about sexual issues, or unresolved curiosity that is harmful (S. Gordon, 1986). Students who participate in comprehensive sexuality education programs are less permissive about premarital sex than students who do not take these courses. Accurate knowledge about sex may also lead to a more positive self-image and self-acceptance. Sexuality affects almost all aspects of human behavior and relationships with other persons. Therefore, if we understand and accept our own sexuality and the sexuality of others, we will have more satisfying relationships. Some experts believe that not talking to children about sex before adolescence is a primary cause of sexual problems later in life (Calderone, 1983).

Another reason to support sexuality education in the U.S. is that children receive a lot of information about sex through the media, and much of it is not based on fact (Rideout et al., 2010; see

Figure 8.9 for more information about media exposure by age, race/ethnicity, gender, and parents' education). The media and peers are often primary sources of information about sexuality. Sex is present in the songs children listen to, the magazines they read, and the shows they watch on television and on the Internet.

REAL RESEARCH 8.6 Research on parent–adolescent communication has found that many adolescent boys receive little or no parental communication about sex (M. Epstein & Ward, 2008). Instead, boys learn about sex mostly from their peers and the media.

Although it is true that there is a growing number of educational sites on the Internet dedicated to sexuality, there are also many poor sources of information on the Web.

Proponents of sexuality education believe that sexual learning occurs even when there are no formalized sexuality education programs. When teachers or parents avoid children's questions or appear embarrassed or evasive, they reinforce children's ideas that sex is secret, mysterious, and bad (Walker & Milton, 2006). As adolescents approach puberty, they may feel anxious about their bodily changes or their relationships with other people. Many teenagers feel uncomfortable asking questions and may be pressured by their peers to engage in sexual activity when they do not feel ready. Giving teenagers information about sex can help them to deal with these changes. The majority of parents, teachers, and students want sexuality education to be taught in secondary schools and high schools and favor comprehensive sex education (Bleakley et al., 2006).

▶▶ HISTORY OF SEXUALITY
Education in the United States

People have always been curious about sex. However, it was only in the 20th century that the movement to develop formal and effective sexuality education programs began. Public discussion of sexuality was due, in part, to the moral purity movement of the late 19th century and the medicalization of the sex movement in the early 20th century.

Several developments in the United States set the stage for sexuality education. Concern over skyrocketing rates of venereal diseases (what we now refer to as STIs) in the early 1900s resulted in the formation of two groups, the American Society of Sanitary and Moral Prophylaxis and the American Federation for Sex Hygiene. Although these groups helped to further the cause of sexuality education, they concentrated their attention on STIs. Their approach was to use sexuality education to explain biology and anatomy, and to address adolescents' natural sexual curiosity. School sexuality education was very scientific and avoided all discussions of interpersonal sexuality.

Starting in the early 1900s, sexuality education was implemented by various national youth groups, including the YMCA, YWCA, Girl Scouts, Boy Scouts, and 4-H Clubs. These programs were developed mainly to demonstrate to young people the re-

sponsibilities required in parenting and to discourage early childbearing. More controversial, however, has been whether to include sexuality education as part of the public school curriculum.

In the United States, for example, the opposition to sexuality education has often been due to two attitudes: first, that sexuality is private, should be discouraged in children, and is best discussed in the context of a person's moral and religious beliefs; and second, that public schools are by their nature public, cannot discuss sex without giving children implicit permission to be sexual, and should not promote the moral or religious beliefs of any particular group. The result of these conflicting attitudes was the belief that sexuality education was best performed by parents in the home.

Attitudes toward sexuality, however, began to change, and sexuality education was seen as more important, not only because of the high teenage pregnancy rate (which shatters the illusion that kids are not actually having sex) but also because of STIs and AIDS. Television and other media contributed by being so sex-saturated that sexuality was no longer a private topic. Yet even with all these changes, many still believe that public educational institutions will present a view of sexuality that they object to, and so they still oppose sexuality education in the United States.

▶▶ SEXUALITY Education Today

Today, the majority of states either recommend or require sexuality education in public schools. Most place requirements on how abstinence or contraception information should be included, and overall, curriculums are heavily weighted toward stressing abstinence. As of 2010, 27 states require that abstinence be stressed in school sexuality education, whereas 9 states require it be covered (Alan Guttmacher Institute, 2011).

Sexuality education can have different goals. Knowledge acquisition, improving personal psychological adjustment, and improving relationships between partners are popular goals. Early sexuality education programs focused primarily on increasing

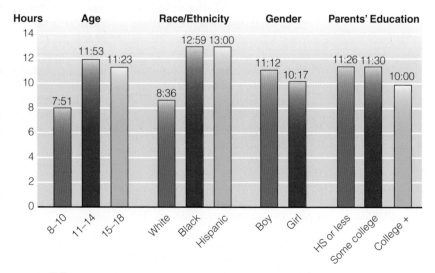

Average amount of total media exposure by:

FIGURE **8.9** Total Media Exposure by Demographics, Kaiser Family Foundation, 2010.
SOURCE: Rideout et al., 2010.

Sex in Real Life ▶▶▎ **What Do Children Want to Know and What Are They Ready For?**

Because developmental differences influence children's ability to comprehend sexuality education, educators often evaluate what types of questions students ask to develop programs that can meet the needs of different age levels. Many proponents of sexuality education programs believe that these programs should be sequential (i.e., there should be a logical order in the curriculum) and comprehensive (i.e., they should include information on biological, psychological, social, and spiritual components). Following are some typical questions students ask at various ages and suggestions for what to include in sexuality education programs at these levels.

Age Range	Developmental Issues	Questions Children Might Ask	Focus of Sexuality Education
3 to 5 years	Shorter attention spans	*What is that?* (referring to specific body parts) *What do mommies do? What do daddies do? Where do babies come from?*	At this level, sexuality education can focus on the roles of family members, the development of a positive self-image, and an understanding that living things grow, reproduce, and die.
6 to 8 years	Very curious about how the body works	*Where was I before I was born? How does my mommy get a baby? Did I come from an egg?*	Sexuality education can include information on plant and animal reproduction, gender similarities and differences, growth and development, and self-esteem.
9 to 12 years	Curiosity about their bodies continues, and heterosexual children are often interested in the other sex and reproduction; gay, lesbian, and bisexual children may experience same-sex interests at this time	*How does the reproductive system work? Why do some girls have larger breasts than others? Do boys menstruate? Why don't some women have babies?*	Sexuality education can include focus on biological topics such as the endocrine system, menstruation, masturbation and wet dreams, sexual intercourse, birth control, abortion, self-esteem, and interpersonal relationships.
12 to 14 years	Preteens may be concerned or confused about the physical changes of puberty, including changes in body shape, body control, reproductive ability, menstruation, breast and penis development, and voice changes	*How can you keep yourself looking attractive? Should your parents know if you're going steady? Why are some people homosexual? Does a girl ever have a wet dream? Does sexual intercourse hurt? Why do people get married?*	Sexuality education can focus on increasing knowledge of contraception, intimate sexual behavior (why people do what they do), dating, and variations in sexual behaviors (homosexuality, transvestism, transsexualism).
15 to 17 years	Increased interest in sexual topics and curiosity about relationships with others, families, reproduction, and various sexual activity patterns; many teenagers begin dating at this time	*What is prostitution? What do girls really want in a good date? How far should you go on a date? Is it good to have sexual intercourse before marriage? Why is sex considered a dirty word?*	Sexuality education can include more information on birth control, abortion, dating, premarital sexual behavior, communication, marriage patterns, sexual myths, moral decisions, parenthood, sexuality research, sexual dysfunction, and the history of sexuality.

SOURCE: Based on Breuss & Greenberg (1981, pp. 223–231).

knowledge levels and educating students about the risks of pregnancy (Kirby, 1992), believing that if knowledge levels were increased, then students would understand why it was important for them to avoid unprotected sexual intercourse. Soon sexuality education programs added values clarification and skills, including communication and decision-making skills. These second-generation sexuality education programs were based on the idea that if knowledge levels were increased and if students became more aware of their own values and had better decision-making skills, they would have an easier time talking to their partners and evaluating their own behavior.

In the United States, each state is responsible for developing its own sexuality education programs. Therefore, the programs vary greatly. Overall, programs are typically either comprehensive or abstinence based. **Comprehensive sexuality education programs** are those that begin in kindergarten and continue through 12th grade; they include a wide variety of topics and help students to develop their own skills and learn factual information. **Abstinence-only programs** emphasize abstinence from all sexual behaviors, and they typically do not provide information about contraception or disease prevention.

Comprehensive Sexuality Education Programs

Today, comprehensive sexuality education programs try to help students develop a positive view of sexuality. The Guidelines for Comprehensive Sexuality Education (Sexuality Information and Education Council of the United States, 2004) are a framework designed to help promote the development of comprehensive sexuality education programs nationwide. Originally developed in 1990, the guidelines were revised again in 2004 and include four main goals for sexuality education:

1. To provide accurate information about human sexuality

2. To provide an opportunity for young people to question, explore, and assess their sexual attitudes

3. To help young people develop interpersonal skills, including communication, decision making, peer refusal, and assertiveness skills that will allow them to create satisfying relationships

4. To help young people develop the ability to exercise responsibility regarding sexual relationships

The guidelines have also been adapted for use outside the United States and are being used in many countries to help design and implement a variety of sexuality education programs.

Abstinence-Only Sexuality Education Programs

Abstinence-only programs began in the early 1990s when there was a proliferation of sexuality education programs that used fear to discourage students from engaging in sexual behavior. These programs include mottos such as "Do the right thing—wait for the ring," or "Pet your dog—not your date." Important information about topics such as anatomy or STIs is often omitted from these programs, and there is an overreliance on the negative consequences of sexual behavior. These negative consequences are often exaggerated, portraying sexual behavior as dangerous and harmful. In 1996, the federal government also

View in Video
To watch the entire interview, go to Psychology CourseMate at **login.cengagebrain.com.**

"You need to know where the penis goes, or else you might not get a baby."
—CROSS CULTURAL SEX TALK

© Kenzie Henke

passed a law outlining the federal definition of abstinence education. These programs teach:

- Abstinence from sexual activity outside marriage as the expected standard for all school-age children

- That sexual activity outside of the context of marriage is likely to have harmful psychological and physical effects

- That bearing children out of wedlock is likely to have harmful consequences for the child, the child's parents, and society

From 1996 to 2010, federal funding for abstinence-based sexuality education grew significantly. In fact, during this time, the federal government spent more than $1.5 billion promoting abstinence-based programs, which prohibited the discussion of contraception (Alan Guttmacher Institute, 2010; Waxman, 2004). Federal funds could be used for sexuality education only if programs taught abstinence only until marriage, which often excluded information about contraception and sexually transmitted infections.

The majority of Americans believe that sexuality education should emphasize abstinence but also include contraception and STI information (Bleakley et al., 2006). Some of the abstinence-only programs use scare tactics to encourage abstinence, by claiming the consequences of premarital sexual behavior to include:

> [L]oss of reputation; limitations in dating/marriage choices; negative effects on sexual adjustment; negative effects on happiness (premarital sex, especially with more than one person, has been linked to the development of emotional illness [and the] loss of self-esteem); family conflict and possible

comprehensive sexuality education programs
Programs that often begin in kindergarten and continue through 12th grade, presenting a wide variety of topics to help students develop their own skills while learning factual information.

abstinence-only programs
Sexuality education programs that emphasize abstinence from all sexual behaviors.

In 2010, the World Health Organization (WHO) published the first detailed European guidelines to help develop curricula for sexuality education programs, entitled the *Standards for Sexuality Education in Europe: A Framework for Policy Makers, Educational and Health Authorities and Specialists* (World Health Organization, 2010). The guidelines were developed by a group of 20 experts from nine European countries, along with the WHO and the Federal Centre for Health Education in Germany. The focus of sexuality education in Europe has shifted from the risks associated with sex to a more holistic approach that asserts that children and teens need unbiased, scientifically correct information about sexuality in order to develop the skills necessary to protect themselves in the future (World Health Organization, 2010).

Around the world, the European countries have the longest history of sexuality education. Sweden made sexuality education a mandatory subject in schools in 1955. From there, it became mandatory in Germany (1968), Austria (1970), the Netherlands (1970), France, the United Kingdom, Portugal, Spain (2001), and Ireland (2003; World Health Organization, 2010). Today, Swedish children receive a portion of sexuality education in youth health centers in addition to schools, since this helps them to learn where to seek

out services should they need them. As we discussed in the chapter opening story, the Netherlands has the world's lowest rates of teenage pregnancy, abortion, and childbearing (see Figure 8.10). It is the best example of the value of high-quality sex education. The Dutch government supports a variety of sexuality organizations and finances mass-media campaigns aimed at educating the public about sexuality.

The majority of European sexuality education programs are "personal-growth" oriented, unlike the United States, which tends to be "prevention" oriented or "problem-solving" oriented (World Health Organization, 2010). In fact, educators point out that:

In Western Europe, sexuality, as it emerges and develops during adolescence, is not primarily perceived as a problem and a threat, but as a valuable source of personal enrichment (World Health Organization, 2010:15).

In many other countries around the world, the focus of sex education has also been "prevention" oriented, focusing specifically on HIV and AIDS education, especially in those countries that are significantly affected by HIV and AIDS (United Nations Scientific and Cultural Organization [UNESCO], 2008). In Japan, the Japanese Association for

Sexuality Education was established in 1974 to help design comprehensive sexuality education in the schools, although abstinence education has always been very popular in Japan. In 1986, a new sexuality education curriculum was distributed to all middle and high schools in Japan (Kitazawa, 1994). This was again revised in 1992, and the Japanese Ministry of Education approved the discussion of secondary sex characteristics in coeducational fifth-grade classes and also mandated that sexuality education be taught in schools. Before this time, there was no discussion of sexuality in elementary schools (Hatano & Shimazaki, 2004).

We know that around the world, few young adults receive adequate sex education and, as a result, are at risk for negative consequences (UNESCO, 2009). Today, there is overwhelming evidence to support the need for sex education. Sex education can increase knowledge levels and reduce the risk for teen pregnancy and STIs. Yet, debates and controversies will continue throughout the world about the necessity of these programs; how best to implement the programs; who should teach them; and how success should be measured (UNESCO, 2009). Experts are hopeful that continued research on global sex education will increase support for global sex education.

Dr. Carroll visits with students from Amsterdam's Lyceum, a Dutch secondary school.

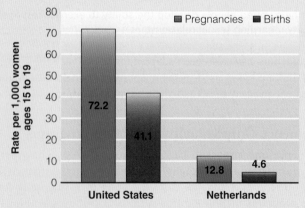

FIGURE **8.10** Pregnancy and Birth Rates per 1,000 women ages 15 to 19, United States and the Netherlands. SOURCE: Advocates for Youth, Feijoo, (2008).

premature separation from the family; confusion regarding personal value (e.g., "Am I loved because I am me, because of my personality and looks, or because I am a sex object?"); and loss of goals. (Kantor, 1992, p. 4)

In 2010, in a sharp departure from the abstinence-only model of sex education, the federal government approved a new health law that put $375 million into grants to the states over a 5-year period (Rabin, 2010b). These funds were available to schools that provide teens with comprehensive sexuality education programs. However, each year, $50 million was available to schools who teach abstinence-only education, although these funds were to be matched by each individual state, unlike funding for comprehensive programs.

Do abstinence-only programs work? This is the important question, and the responses will differ depending on whom you ask. Supporters of abstinence-only programs often have very strong feelings about comprehensive sexuality education programs and claim that talking only about abstinence lets children and young adults know that this is the only choice. Those who believe in these programs would say that they are effective. However, a major study done by the National Campaign to Prevent Teen and Unplanned Pregnancy in 2007 found that abstinence-only programs failed to delay sexual behavior and decrease the number of sex partners (Kirby, 2007). In addition, when students who had abstinence-based sexuality programs do become sexually active, they often fail to use condoms or any type of contraception (Brückner & Bearman, 2005; Walters, 2005). Comprehensive sexuality education programs that included abstinence education together with contraceptive education were found to delay sexual behavior and to reduce the frequency of sexual behaviors and unprotected sex (Kirby, 2007).

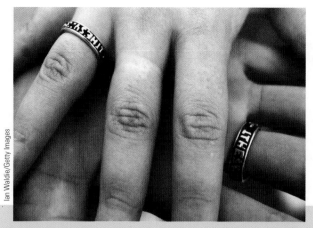

Celibacy rings are often worn by those who pledge not to engage in sexual intercourse until marriage.

►► EFFECTS AND RESULTS of Sexuality Education Programs

*Comprehensive sexuality programs have been found to be the **most successful.***

The main way that researchers determine whether a sexuality program is successful is by measuring behavioral changes after a program has been presented. The standard measures include sexual behavior, pregnancy, and contraceptive use (Remez, 2000). If the rates of sexual behavior increase after sexuality education, a program is judged to be ineffective. If these rates decrease, a program is successful. So what are the effects of sex education programs? Do sexuality education courses change people's actual sexual behavior? It is difficult to measure and evaluate these behavioral changes after a sexuality education program, but it appears that there are some limited changes.

Comprehensive sexuality programs have been found to be the most successful at helping adolescents delay their involvement in sexual intercourse and help protect adolescents from STIs and unintended pregnancies (Kirby, 2001, 2007; Kohler et al., 2008; Starkman & Rajani, 2002). In addition, sexuality education programs that teach contraception and communication skills have been found to delay the onset of sexual intercourse or reduce the frequency of sexual intercourse, reduce the number of sexual partners, and increase the use of contraception (Kirby, 2007; Kohler et al., 2008). Abstinence-only programs, in contrast, have not yielded successful results in delaying the onset of intercourse

(Kirby, 2007; Weed, 2008). In 2007, a federally funded study of abstinence-only programs, conducted by Mathematica Policy Research, found these programs had no effects on sexual abstinence (Trenholm et al., 2007). Overall, there have been no published reports of abstinence-based programs providing significant effects on delaying sexual intercourse. Although many who teach abstinence-only classes claim that these programs are successful, outside experts have found the programs to be ineffective and methodologically unsound (Kirby, 2007; Kohler et al., 2008; Weed, 2008).

Recently, some students have begun taking "virginity pledges" in which they sign pledge cards and promise to remain a virgin until marriage. The ADD Health study, which we discussed earlier in this chapter, found that teenagers who took a virginity pledge were less likely to become sexually active in the months that follow the pledge than students who did not take a pledge (Bearman & Bruckner, 2001). However, these types of programs have also been found to put teenagers at higher risk for pregnancy and STIs (Brückner & Bearman, 2005).

Why do you think this might be? Researchers believe that it is because signing the pledge may make a teenager unable to accept the responsibilities of using contraception when he or she decides to engage in sexual intercourse. One study found that 88% of students who pledged virginity engaged in premarital sex, and when they did they were less likely to use contraception (Brückner & Bearman, 2005; Planned Parenthood Federation of America, 2005).

Measuring attitudes or changes in attitudes and values is difficult at best. Overall, we do know that comprehensive sex education programs can increase knowledge levels, affect attitudes, and change behaviors (Kirby, 2007; Kohler et al., 2008). The most successful programs were those in which schools and parents worked together to develop the program. However, many effects of sexuality education programs may not be quantifiable. Programs may help students to feel more confident, be more responsible, improve their mental health, and increase their communication skills. We rarely measure for these changes.

In summary, childhood sexuality is an evolving phenomenon. Sexual knowledge and sexual behavior are common among children in today's society, in which sexuality is so much a part of our culture. However, knowledge does not necessarily mean that children must act on it; there are still very good reasons to encourage children and teenagers to think carefully about sexuality and to advise them to refrain from expressing their sexual feelings physically until the time is right for them.

What we do know is that a close and respectful parent–adolescent relationship that allows for open communication

> **Sexual knowledge and sexual behavior are common** among children in today's society.

about sexuality has been found to decrease adolescent sexual behaviors and reduce the influence of peers with regard to sexual issues (Meschke et al., 2000). This is an important finding and is partially responsible for delaying first intercourse, fewer teenage pregnancies, and fewer numbers of sexual partners. Open communication about sexuality, along with good, solid sexuality education, encourages this kind of responsible sexual behavior.

◀ review QUESTIONS

1 Explain both sides of the sexuality education debate.

2 Identify and discuss the various types of sexuality education programs.

3 Discuss research findings on the effects of sexuality education.

⏮ chapter REVIEW

SUMMARY POINTS

1 Throughout most of history, children were treated as miniature adults, and concepts such as childhood did not exist. Children were considered presexual. Four large-scale longitudinal studies have been conducted on adolescent sexuality: the National Survey of Family Growth, the National Longitudinal Study of Adolescent Males, the National Longitudinal Study of Adolescent Health, and the Youth Risk Behavior Survey.

2 Sexual anatomy is functional even before we are born. Male infants are capable of erection, and female infants are capable of vaginal lubrication. The single most important aspect of infant development is children's relationship with their caretakers. Gender identity develops between the ages of 1 and 2 years. It takes a little longer to develop gender constancy, which is the realization that their gender will not change during their lifetime. Genital touching is common at this age.

3 In early childhood, physical development continues. In fact, children may learn more in the first few years of childhood about the nature of their bodies than they learn in the entire

remainder of their lives. Child sex play is common at this age, and many parents or caregivers need to teach that this behavior is private. Children learn that their genitals are private and must be covered up in public. Boys are often taught about the penis, yet it is rare for girls to be taught about the clitoris.

4 Sometime between the ages of 6 and 12, a child experiences the first outward signs of puberty. In girls, the first sign of puberty is the appearance of breast buds, and soon they will experience menarche. Preadolescent boys experience frequent erections, and soon they will experience semenarche. Typically boys do not tell anyone about this event. Prepubescence is the age of sexual discovery.

5 During preadolescence, genital touching continues, and both sexual fantasies and sex games may begin. A sexual script is the sum total of a person's internalized knowledge about sexuality, and it can have different themes. All of our intimate relationships influence our sexuality. We learn from our parents and our peers. Sexual contact with siblings is common at this age and has been found to be harmful

only when there is coercive force used or a large age difference between siblings.

6 Puberty prepares the body for adult sexuality and reproduction. Adolescence often includes our emotional and cognitive reactions to puberty. There are many physical, emotional, and cognitive changes during this time. The three major stages of physiological sexual development include prenatal sexual differentiation, puberty, and menopause. Some of the first signs of female puberty include the development of breast buds, the appearance of pubic hair, a widening of the hips, a rounding of the physique, and the onset of menstruation.

7 Unlike ovulation, which occurs late in female puberty, spermatogenesis and ejaculation occur early in male puberty. Some of the first signs of male puberty include body changes, increased body hair, a growth spurt, and voice deepening. For the most part, early development in boys is usually not as embarrassing as it is in girls.

8 Adolescents tend to fantasize about sex, and masturbation increases, especially for boys.

Mature sexual experimentation begins, often with kissing. Girls' body image tends to improve as they progress through adolescence, whereas boys' tends to worsen. However, girls' general self-image tends to worsen as they grow older, whereas boys' tends to improve.

9 The National Survey of Sexual Health and Behavior (NSSHB) explored several sexual behaviors in teens. Masturbation was found to increase during adolescence and then decrease as partnered sex increases later in life. Oral sex has increased in all age groups and is usually engaged in after sexual intercourse. Rates of anal sex were low for young teens, but for some gay teens anal sex may be the defining moment of losing their virginity.

10 Approximately half of all American students in grades 9 through 12 have engaged in sexual intercourse; this prevalence is higher in Black and Hispanic students and lower in White students. First intercourse is usually unplanned but rarely spontaneous. Today's adolescents have high contraceptive use. However, the United States has the highest rates of teen pregnancy, abortion, and childbearing of any Western country.

11 Opposition to sexuality education has often been due to two attitudes: One says that sexuality is private, and the second says that public schools cannot discuss sex without giving children implicit permission to be sexual and should not promote certain values. Individual states can mandate that schools provide sexuality education.

12 Comprehensive sexuality education programs include a wide variety of topics and help students to develop their own skills and learn factual information. Abstinence-only programs emphasize abstinence from all sexual behaviors, and they typically do not provide information about contraception or disease prevention.

13 Although many Americans believe that contraception should be included in sexuality education, they also believe that information on contraception and STIs should be included.

14 To find out if sex education programs are successful, researchers often measure behavioral changes after the program. The standard measures include sexual behavior, pregnancy, and contraceptive use. Comprehensive sexuality programs have been found to be the most successful at helping adolescents delay their involvement in sexual intercourse, help protect adolescents from STIs and unintended pregnancies, delay the onset of sexual intercourse or reduce the frequency of sexual intercourse, reduce the number of sexual partners, and increase the use of contraception. Abstinence-only programs have not yielded successful results in delaying the onset of intercourse. In 2007, a federally funded study of abstinence-only programs found these programs had no effects on sexual abstinence. There have not been any published reports showing that abstinence-based programs can delay sexual intercourse.

CRITICAL THINKING QUESTIONS

1 Should genital touching in young children be encouraged, ignored, or discouraged? What message do you think it sends to a child when parents encourage their child to discover and play with toes, ears, and fingers but pull the child's hands away when he or she discovers his or her genitals?

2 Young children often play sex games, such as "doctor," with each other. What age differences do you think pose the biggest problems? Are sex games acceptable? Why or why not? How should a parent respond?

3 Where should children get their sexual knowledge? Should children learn everything from their parents, school, or church? Is it better to learn about some things from a particular place? Explain.

4 Why do you think adolescence is a difficult time for many people? What can be done to make the transition through adolescence easier?

5 People today are engaging in sex relatively early in life, often in their middle or early teens. Do you think this is a good time to experiment with sex, or do you think it is too early? What do you think is the "ideal" age to begin experimenting with sex?

MEDIA RESOURCES

CourseMate brings course concepts to life with interactive learning, study, and exam preparation tools that support the printed textbook. A textbook-specific website, Psychology CourseMate includes an integrated interactive eBook and other interactive learning tools including quizzes, flashcards, videos, and more. If your textbook does not include an access code card, go to CengageBrain.com to gain access.

CENGAGENOW   CengageNOW is an easy-to-use online resource that helps you study in less time to get the grade you want—NOW. Take a pre-test for this chapter and receive a personalized study plan based on your results that will identify the topics you need to review and direct you to online resources to help you master those topics. Then take a post-test to help you determine the concepts you have mastered and what you will need to work on. If your textbook does not include an access code card, go to CengageBrain.com to gain access.

View in Video available in CourseMate and CengageNOW:

Sex Education: The Dutch Approach: Dutch sex educator discusses sex education in the Netherlands.

Puberty: Personal Experiences: Personal experiences of puberty from various men and women.

Gender Role Pressures: A Male's Perspective: Male student discusses pressures during childhood to be masculine.

Cross Cultural Sex Talk: Children and Teens: Explore sex talks with various children and teens from around the world.

Websites:

Sexuality Information and Education Council of the United States ■ The Sexuality Information and Education Council of the United States (SIECUS) is a national nonprofit organization that develops, collects, and disseminates information; promotes comprehensive education about sexuality; and advocates the right of individuals to make responsible sexual choices.

National Survey of Sexual Health and Behavior ■ Findings from the largest nationally representative study of sexual and sexual health behaviors ever fielded, conducted by Indiana University sexual health researchers, provide an updated and much needed snapshot of contemporary Americans' sexual behaviors, including adolescent and teen sexual behaviors.

Alan Guttmacher Institute ■ The mission of the Alan Guttmacher Institute (AGI) is to provide information and services about issues of sexuality. The institute conducts important research on adolescent and child sexual issues.

Society for Research on Adolescence ■ The Society for Research on Adolescence's goal is to promote the understanding of adolescence through research and dissemination. Members conduct theoretical studies, basic and applied research, and policy analyses to understand and enhance adolescent development.

9 Adult Sexual Relationships

View in **Video**

View in **Video**

View in **Video**

View in **Video**

View in **Video**

▶ **ABOUT THE CHAPTER OPENING VIDEO** – Our first relationship is with our primary caregiver—our mother, father, or whomever was responsible for our care. The attachment bond we formed with that person profoundly influenced our ability to develop and maintain successful relationships in the future. As we grow up, we learn many things about relationships from watching those around us. Many of us learn what type of partners our parents have in mind for us. Some parents want their children to have partners of the same race, ethnicity, religion, or even age, while others have no preferences. I recently met an engaged couple, Dena and Lenny, who have been dating for over two years. Dena said:

I remember walking into the party on campus and seeing Lenny across the room. When our eyes met, I felt like everyone else at the party disappeared. We started talking

and the next thing I knew, the sun had come up. We both had strong feelings about each other, but the timing wasn't right for us to pursue a relationship. Seven years later, we finally admitted that we couldn't live without each other.

Although Dena and Lenny are different races, they told me that this has never been an issue in their relationship. They have both been raised in very open-minded families that stressed the importance of hard work, dedication, and education. Lenny's father told him that as long as he got a good education and was a good man, he could date whomever he wanted to. In fact, Lenny remembered his father telling him *"You can date an alien or a purple person—I don't care."*

Both Dena and Lenny told me that their families were incredibly supportive of their relationship. Lenny said:

© Steve Prezant/Corbis

There are absolutely no issues about race with my parents or even my grandparents. I love Dena for who she is—she's beautiful, honest, loving, and we are very similar in how we view the world. These are the important things that drew us to each other. While some people do react to the fact that we are different races, that is just not important to us. However, when we have kids it will be an issue. We both worry about whether our children have trouble because they are mixed-race. We have spent a lot of time talking about this and we're both in agreement that we will raise our children to be strong and self-confident, just like our parents raised us.

I know you'll enjoy watching the interview I did with Dena and Lenny. They are a wonderful example of a relationship that is based on honesty, communication, and trust. ‖

Janell Carroll

"You can date an alien or a purple person—I don't care!"
—Chapter Opening Video

View in Video

To watch the entire interview, go to Psychology CourseMate at **login.cengagebrain.com**.

Throughout this book, we've talked about the importance of family and the impact that your family has on your feelings about love, intimacy, and relationships. We also know that other factors, such as society, culture, ethnicity, race, religion, and age, also influence our connections with others. By late adolescence, the majority of adolescents have attained the ability to become involved in an intimate sexual relationship (Shulman et al., 2010). However, every society has rules to control the ways that people develop sexual bonds with other people. Until recently, in many parts of the world, parents or other family members arranged for their children to meet members of the other sex, marry them, and begin their sexual lives together. The expectation was that couples would remain sexually faithful and that marital unions would end only in death. In such societies, adult sexual relationships were clearly defined, and deviating from the norm was frowned upon.

In our society today, people openly engage in a variety of adult sexual relationships, including same-sex, other-sex, premarital, marital, extramarital, and polyamorous relationships. (Note that a term such as "premarital sex" assumes eventual marriage; for people who never marry, or same-sex couples who are not allowed to marry in most states, their sexual relationships for their entire lives are considered "premarital"!) These relationships can change and evolve over the course of a lifetime, and at different times, a person might live alone and date, cohabit with a partner or partners, marry, divorce, or remarry. In this chapter, we look at adults' intimate sexual relationships with others.

▶ DATING

In traditional heterosexual dating, before the 1970s, the boy would pick up the girl at her house, the father and mother would meet or chat with the boy, and then the boy and girl would go to a well-defined event (e.g., a "mixer"—a chaperoned, school-sponsored dance—or a movie), and she would be brought home by the curfew her parents imposed (Benokraitis, 1993). Today, however, for-

In the 1950s, traditional heterosexual dating involved going out together to share a fountain drink.

The dating years usually begin in high school in the United States.

REAL RESEARCH 9.1 Research on the costs and benefits of dating versus hooking up has found that while college women prefer dating, college men prefer hooking up (BRADSHAW ET AL., 2010).

---

mal dating has given way to more casual dating, in part because of teenagers' almost universal access to cars and parents' more permissive attitudes toward exploring romantic relationships. Teenagers still go to movies and dances, but just as often they will get together at someone's house. Because of the risk of rejection, today's adolescents often use friend networks to find out if someone might be interested in them before asking them out. This way they can assess whether a partner might be interested in them before asking them out. It can be more difficult to meet potential partners as a person gets older. Socializing and going out to bars and clubs may work for some, but others are uncomfortable with this approach. Perhaps the best way to meet others as one gets older is through friends, to get involved in community, religious, and singles groups, and to find events and programs where other single people go. The Internet has provided a new way to meet people, through websites, chat rooms, and online dating services.

In Chapter 7, we discussed the physical benefits of love and intimacy. Dating has been found to provide similar benefits. Relationships provide companionship, emotional support, and even, at times, economic support. Of course, the key may be the kind of people who are in the relationship. For example, people with a strong sense of self have been found to be more satisfied and happy with their dating relationships (Fruth, 2007; Fuller-Fricke, 2007). Not surprisingly, those without a strong sense of self have been found to experience more relationship conflict (Longua, 2010).

"Dating" has changed on college campuses; today, it is much more common for groups of students to "hang out" rather than go out on a date. Typically, men and women go out with friends and plan on meeting up at a party on campus and going home together, rather than prearranging a date. One study found that 50% of heterosexual female seniors reported being asked out by a man on six or more dates while at college; and one third of respondents said they had been on only two or fewer dates (Glenn & Marquardt, 2001).

Why might there be less "dating" today? The sexual revolution has changed society's attitudes about sexuality, making hooking up, casual sex, and "friends with benefits" more acceptable. Today, hooking up has become more common on college campuses than dating (Bradshaw et al., 2010; Littleton et al., 2009b). This may be a result of the decreasing number of males on college campuses. A report by the American Council on Education found that since 2000, women represent close to 57% of enrollments at American colleges (Williams, 2010). When there are fewer men on campus, women report more negative appraisals of campus men, go on fewer traditional dates, and are less likely to have a college boyfriend (Uecker & Regnerus, 2010).

The problem with discussing the intimate sexual relationships of single people is that there are no agreed-on words for different levels of commitment. "Hanging out," "dating," "going out," or "seeing each other"—these terms mean different things to different people.

Although mixed-race dating was not always acceptable, today many college students are open to the idea of dating someone of a different race or ethnicity.

▶▶ INTERRACIAL AND **Intercultural Dating**

A rapidly growing minority population in the United States has led to increases in interracial and intercultural (usually grouped

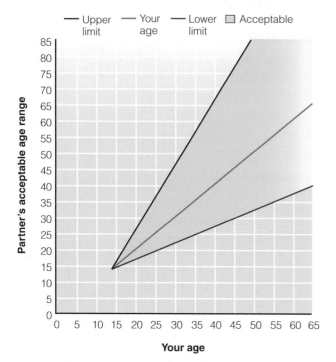

Half-Age-Plus-Seven Relationship Rule

FIGURE **9.1** The "half-age-plus-seven" rule is a mathematical guide to judge the socially acceptable age differences in an intimate couple. A person takes his or her age, divides it in half, and adds seven to arrive at the lowest socially acceptable age of a person he or she should date (for example, a 20-year-old man divides his age in half = 10, plus 7 = 17, which means he should date someone 17 or older). A large age difference is less socially acceptable when individuals are younger but becomes more acceptable as a person ages (for example, it would be socially acceptable for a 70-year-old man to date a 42-year-old. But a 28-year age difference wouldn't be acceptable for someone younger). SOURCE: http://en.wikipedia.org/wiki/File:Half-age-plus-seven-relationship-rule.svg.

together as "mixed race") dating (Lewis & Ford-Robertson, 2010). In fact, today's college students include the largest group of mixed-race students in the history of the United States (Saulny, 2010). By mid-century, multiracial Americans will represent a majority of the U.S. population (Yen, 2011). These changing demographics have led to an increase in dating a person of a different race, religion, or culture. However, it wasn't until 1967 that the Supreme Court struck down state antimiscegenation laws, which enforced racial segregation at the level of interracial relationships and criminalized interracial marriage (we discussed these laws in Chapter 1).

Overall, those who are more open to dating someone from a different race or ethnic group are from a younger generation (Generation X or later; Tsunokai et al., 2009) and they are often more politically liberal and less religious than those who would not date such partners (Yancey, 2007). Blacks are twice as likely as Whites to report being open to the possibility of a mixed-race relationship (Knox et al., 2000; Rosenblatt et al., 1995), possibly because there are more Whites to choose from. Non-White women with higher educations are more likely to be involved in mixed-race relationships, as are White women with lower educations (Fu, 2010). Research has found that although college students may be more likely to engage in uncommitted sexual interactions (i.e., hookups) or go on dates with men and women from other ethnic and racial groups, they prefer someone from the same race or ethnic group for a long-term relationship (McClintock, 2010). Gays and lesbians are more open to mixed-race relationships. In fact, research has found gays and lesbians are twice as likely to be in a mixed-race relationship compared with straight men and women (Oswald & Clausell, 2005).

Race and ethnicity are not the only criterions on which a couple's suitability is judged; there are also issues of different religions, social classes, disabilities, and ages. Couples with these issues may also face some of the same challenges that interracial couples do. In Figure 9.1, we explore the "half-age-plus-seven rule," which claims you should never date anyone less than half your age plus 7.

▶▶ SEXUALITY IN Dating Relationships

Although we discuss specific sexual behaviors in Chapter 10, in this chapter, we introduce sexuality in dating relationships. A study on the timing of sex in a relationship found that couples who wait to have sex in a relationship experience better relationship outcomes (Busby et al., 2010). Researchers suggest that waiting allows a couple to develop other aspects of their relationship. However, every couple has to determine what works best for them as individuals. We do know that sexual satisfaction in long-term intimate relationships is a strong predictor of how happy a couple is in the relationship (Holmberg & Blair, 2009). This is true in gay, lesbian, and heterosexual relationships.

On college campuses, sexual practices have been changing and today "hooking up" or having a "friend with benefits" is common. It is estimated that 79% to 85% of college students have engaged in at least one hookup (Littleton et al., 2009b). Research has explored how sexual behaviors like hooking up reinforce traditional gender roles and male dominance on college campuses (Hamilton & Armstrong, 2009). Although both men and women report these behaviors are often engaged in purely for the physical pleasures they provide, the research isn't so clear-cut (Eshbaugh & Gute, 2008).

I once had two heterosexual students in my class who I thought were strangers because they never talked or sat next to each other. However, in reading papers they had handed in, I learned they had been "hooking up" almost every weekend for more than 8 months. What was interesting to me, however, was how they each described their relationship in a class assignment. Blye wrote that she was sure Laizon was looking for a commitment because he had sex with her every weekend, whereas Laizon wrote that he was relieved that Blye understood their relationship was purely sexual because he never talked to her during the week. Both Blye and

---

REAL RESEARCH 9.2 When choosing someone to date, a person's race has been found to be more important than his or her religion (STILLWELL, 2010). This may be because a person from a different religion would be more culturally and physically similar to themselves, creating less societal stigma.

Laizon were evaluating the same behavior differently. Among heterosexuals, it might be easy to assume that it's always the female who is looking for more commitment in these "hookups," but that wouldn't be entirely true. Many men hope for more out of a "hookup" but settle for what they can get (see On Your Mind 9.1).

Sexuality is also an important component in older adult dating relationships. However, when we picture people engaging in sex, we rarely think of two people older than 60 years. In fact, when I show a film on older adult sexuality, many of my students cover their eyes and feel repulsed. Why is this? Why are we so averse to the idea that older people have healthy and satisfying sex lives? It is probably because we live in a society that equates sexuality with youth. Even so, the majority of older adults maintain an interest in sex and sexual activity, and many engage in sexual activity (Arena & Wallace, 2008; de Vries, 2009; Waite et al., 2009). There are many similarities in aging among gay, lesbian, and heterosexual populations. In fact, the physical changes of aging affect all men and women, regardless of sexual orientation (Woolf, 2002).

ON YOUR MIND 9.1

I have a "sex buddy" whom I hook up with at least once a week, sometimes more. We don't ever talk about our "relationship," but the sex is great. I'd like to take this to the next level and become a "couple," but I just don't know how.

Overall, couples report less relationship satisfaction in hookups compared with long-term dating relationships (Paik, 2010). Moving from a hookup into a more serious dating situation can be difficult primarily because of this dissatisfaction, but also because there is often a significant lack of communication between the partners. Although it is possible for a serious relationship to develop out of a hookup, many do not make it past the hookup stage. Your best bet would be to find a time when the two of you can talk about your feelings and hope for a more committed relationship. Students have different motivations for hooking up and engaging in casual sex, and you won't know your partner's motivations unless you ask.

A positive correlation was found between good health and sexual activity, with healthier people reporting higher levels of sexual activity (Holmberg & Blair, 2009; Trudel et al., 2010). A healthy sex life in the later years may keep aging adults happy and vibrant. We discuss sexuality and the physical and psychological changes of aging in Chapter 10.

▶▶ BREAKING UP

How a person reacts to a breakup really depends on several factors, including who initiated the breakup, the amount of contact with the ex-partner after the breakup, and how much social support a person has. Typically, the person who initiated the breakup feels less distress but is more at risk for guilt (Locker et al., 2010). Those who were broken up with often feel rejection and experience more depression and a loss of self-esteem (Perilloux & Buss, 2008). Some rejected partners become obsessive about the lost relationship and engage in stalking behaviors such as repeated texting and/or calling (Fisher et al., 2010). Having continued contact with an ex-partner can make it more difficult to recover from the breakup. One of the most important factors in recovering from a breakup is social support. Those who have friends to lean on and talk to have an easier time moving on after a breakup.

▶ COHABITATION

Until fairly recently there was little research on nonmarital **cohabitation**, or living together. In fact, researchers documented no increase in cohabitation rates between 1880 and 1970. This was probably because researchers had no labels for such relationships. In the mid-1990s, the Census and the Current Population Survey started allowing couples to identify themselves as "unmarried partner" of the homeowner (instead of a roommate), which allowed researchers to get more accurate statistics about cohabitation (Stevenson & Wolfers, 2007). Even so, researchers today believe that statistical data on cohabitation is skewed because of inadequate relationship labels. Some cohabiting heterosexual couples might not think of themselves as "unmarried partners" but rather "boyfriend and girlfriend"; gay and lesbian couples might describe themselves as "roommates." You can see how this terminology can get a little tricky.

▶▶ STATISTICS AND **Current Trends**

The number of cohabiting couples has increased significantly over the last few years and as of 2008–2009, more than 70% of U.S. heterosexual couples live together before marriage (Rhoades et al., 2009). Although there were 3.2 million unmarried couples living together in 1990, this number grew to 7.5 million couples in 2010 (Bumpass & Lu, 2000; Pew Research Center, 2010). Over the next few years, it is anticipated that the number of cohabiting couples will continue to increase.

The main reason for the increase in cohabitation is financial (Pew Research Center, 2010). The U.S. Census found a connection between partners' employment status and cohabitation. Since the late 2000s, the percentage of couples who moved in together in which one was unemployed increased, whereas the percentage of couples who moved in together who were both employed decreased (Pew Research Center, 2010).

Although the increases in cohabitation have led to decreases in marriage (which we will discuss further later in this chapter), heterosexual couples who live together have been found to transition to marriage within 3 years (Goodwin et al., 2010). Not all couples marry, however; some couples live together, break up, and live with someone else, referred to as **serial cohabitation**. Overall, longer cohabitation has been found to be associated with higher likelihood of divorce in heterosexual couples (Cohan & Kleinbaum, 2002; Seltzer, 2000; Stevenson & Wolfers, 2007).

> *The main reason* for the increase in cohabitation *is financial.*

▶▶ ADVANTAGES AND
Disadvantages of Cohabitation

There are advantages and disadvantages to cohabitation. Cohabitation allows couples to learn more about each other's habits and idiosyncrasies, share finances, and mature in their relationship. Yet, there are also problems. Parents and relatives may not support the union, and society as a whole tends not to recognize people who live together for purposes of health care or taxes. Also, the partners may want different things out of living together: One partner may view it as a stronger commitment to the relationship, whereas the other sees it as a way to have a more accessible sexual partner.

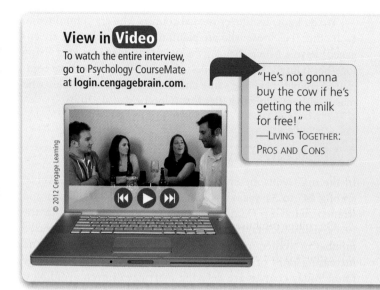

View in Video
To watch the entire interview, go to Psychology CourseMate at **login.cengagebrain.com.**

"He's not gonna buy the cow if he's getting the milk for free!"
—Living Together: Pros and Cons

© 2012 Cengage Learning

Some couples believe that living together can help them smooth out the rough spots in their relationship and see whether they would be able to take their relationship to the next level. Research indicates, however, that this might not be exactly true. Couples who live together before marriage are more likely to get divorced than those who do not live together (Guzzo, 2009; Rhoades et al., 2009). However, there are several possible shortcomings of the foregoing findings. It may not be that living together itself increases the chance of divorce, but that heterosexual couples who choose to live together may have been more likely to divorce even if they didn't live together first (Stevenson & Wolfers, 2007). They may feel that they would not be happy in a marriage; they may be more accepting of divorce; they may be less religious and less traditional in the first place; or they may be less committed in the beginning of the relationship. Because we do not know about the samples in the studies on cohabiting couples, it is difficult to generalize their findings. A recent study found that 60% of couples moved in together to spend more time together; 19% did so for financial reasons; and 14% did so to "test" the relationship (Rhoades et al., 2009).

cohabitation
Living together in a sexual relationship when not legally married.

serial cohabitation
A series of cohabitating relationships with a person living with one partner, breaking up, and living with a new partner.

◀ review QUESTIONS

1 Explain how dating has changed on college campuses today.

2 Identify some of the reasons why there have been increases in mixed-race dating on college campuses.

3 How has sexuality changed on college campuses today? In older dating relationships?

4 What factors are associated with an easier breakup?

5 What is responsible for current increases in cohabitation?

6 Explain the relationship between cohabitation and divorce.

We do know that heterosexual couples who are committed to each other (i.e., those who are planning to get married or are engaged) have a better chance of a successful marriage after living together (Guzzo, 2009; Rhoades et al., 2009). In fact, these committed couples have the same chance of divorce as couples who marry without living together first (Goodwin et al., 2010).

▶ MARRIAGE

In the mid-1960s, heterosexual marriage was nearly universal among 24- to 34-year olds, with more than 80% of men and women marrying (Mather & Lavery, 2010). However, in the 1970s, many societal issues, such as the economy, an increased number of women in higher education and the labor force, and increasing rates of cohabitation, led to decreases in marriage rates. Today couples are delaying marriage or even avoiding it altogether (Dougherty, 2010; Mather & Lavery, 2010). In this section, we discuss marriage statistics and trends, mixed marriages, marriages in later life, marital satisfaction, sex within marriage, and sex outside of marriage. Although we discuss same-sex marriage later in this chapter, here we focus on heterosexual marriage.

▶▶ STATISTICS AND Current Trends

The average age at which a heterosexual man and woman marry today in the United States is the highest in recorded history. Although the median age for first marriage in the United States for men and women was 23 and 21, respectively, in 1970, theses ages increased to 28 for men and 26 for women by 2010 (Mather & Lavery, 2010).

Overall, the proportion of married people older than 18 years decreased from 57% in 2000 to 52% in 2009, which was the lowest percentage recorded since the U.S. Census Bureau began collecting data more than 100 years ago (Ruggles et al., 2009; see Figure 9.2). In fact, the number of unmarried women (single, separated, divorced, widowed) in 2009 outnumbered the number of married women for the first time in U.S. history (Mather & Lavery, 2010). Even so, it is important to point out that most young adults will get married at some point in their lives (Cherlin, 2009; Mather & Lavery, 2010).

ON YOUR MIND 9.2

What is a "prenuptial" agreement?

If a couple divorces, their marriage contract is governed by state law, which determines how assets are divided. However, some couples decide to implement nuptial agreements, or financial plans that couples agree on in marriage, that supersede state laws (Kaslow, 2000). These agreements can be either prenuptial (drawn up before a marriage) or postnuptial (drawn up after a couple has wed). Since 2005, there has been an increase in prenuptial agreements (Strickler, 2010). An increase in prenuptials is mainly because of societal changes, including a delay in the age at which couples marry, as well as an increase in divorce and remarriages.

Proponents of prenuptial agreements believe that because many couples have a hard time talking about financial issues, a prenuptial agreement can help them to sort through these important issues before marriage (Daragahi & Dubin, 2001). However, these types of agreements can also cause problems because they are often initiated by the financially stronger partner and may involve issues of power (Margulies, 2003).

Research has found that many factors, such as education, ethnicity, and race, affect marital rates. Although before 1990 marriage rates for those with a high-school education were higher than for those with a college degree; today, college graduates are more likely to marry than those with less education (Mather & Lavery, 2010). From 1980 to 2008, female high-school dropouts went from "most likely to marry" to "least likely to marry" (Stevenson & Isen, 2010). Racial differences have also been found, with Blacks less likely to marry than Whites (Pew Research Center, 2010). In 2010, 37% to 44% of Blacks, 65% of Asians, 56% to 58% of Hispanics, and 58% to 62% of Whites were married (Bryant, 2010).

▶▶ MIXED Marriages

Less than 1 in 1,000 new marriages were between a Black and a White spouse in 1961, but this number increased to 1 in 150 in 1980, and in 2010, 1 in 7 new marriages was between spouses of different races or ethnicities (Fincham & Beach, 2010; Lewis & Ford-Robertson, 2010; Saulny, 2010; Shibusawa, 2009; Figure 9.3). Of the almost 4 million U.S. couples who married in 2008, 31% of Asians, 26% of Hispanics, 16% of Blacks, and 9% of Whites married someone whose race or ethnicity was different from their own (Passel et al., 2010).

Among Blacks and Asians, there are significant gender differences in marrying outside of one's race or ethnicity. Although 22% of Black male newlyweds in 2008 married outside their race, only 9% of Black females did (Passel et al., 2010). Gender differences were found in the opposite direction for Asians. Whereas 40% of Asian female newlyweds married outside their race, only 20% of Asian males did (see Fig. 9.3c).

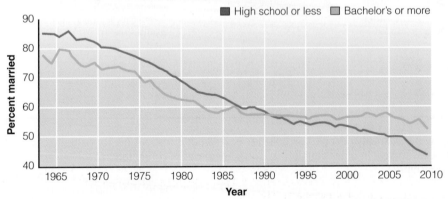

Marriage Rates Among Young Adults Ages 25–34, 1965–2010 (Percent)

■ High school or less ■ Bachelor's or more

FIGURE **9.2** Since 1965, the proportion of young adults who marry has continued to decrease.
SOURCE: U.S. Census Bureau, 2000 Census and American Community Survey.

Geographically, mixed marriages are more common in Western states, where 1 in 5 newlyweds married someone of a different race or ethnicity in 2008 (Passel et al., 2010). The U.S. Census Bureau reported that Hawaii had the highest percentage of mixed-race marriages (48%), followed by Nevada, Oregon, Oklahoma, and California. Whereas 22% of all newlyweds in the West were from different races or ethnicities, 13% of couples in the South and 11% of couples in the Midwest were (Passel et al., 2010).

The loosening up of relationship conventions has also led to mixed-age marriages as well. Historically, the majority of heterosexual men married younger women, which was probably related to the fact that a younger woman could produce more offspring (Biello, 2007; Kershaw, 2009). But the older women–younger man marriage has received more attention recently (Proulx et al., 2006). Think about Demi Moore's marriage to Ashton Kutcher, who is 15 years her junior. Courteney Cox popularized the concept of the predator–seductress, older woman in her television series *Cougar Town*.

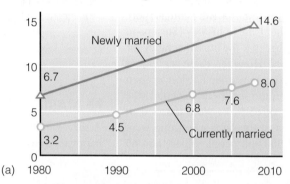

(a)

Percent of people that married someone of a different race/ethnicity. Source: Passel et al., 2010.

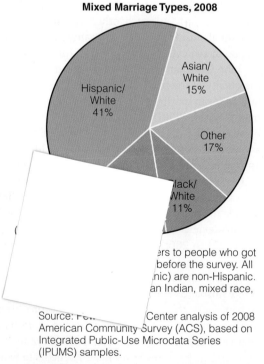

...ers to people who got ...before the survey. All ...nic) are non-Hispanic. ...an Indian, mixed race,

Source: Pew ... Center analysis of 2008 American Community Survey (ACS), based on Integrated Public-Use Microdata Series (IPUMS) samples.

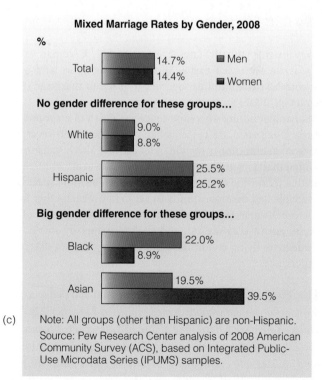

(c)

Note: All groups (other than Hispanic) are non-Hispanic.

Source: Pew Research Center analysis of 2008 American Community Survey (ACS), based on Integrated Public-Use Microdata Series (IPUMS) samples.

FIGURE **9.3** (a) Percent of men and women in the U.S. who married someone of a different race or ethnicity. (b) Percentage of each type of newly married, mixed-race or -ethnicity couples in the U.S., 2008. (c) Percentage of mixed marriages among newlyweds by gender in the U.S. SOURCE: Passel, S. Wang, W., Taylor, P. (2010). Marrying Out: One-in-Seven New U.S. Marriages Is Interracial or Interethnic. http://pewresearch.org/pubs/1616/american-marriage-interracial-interethnic.

▶▶ MARRIAGES in Later Life

Marriage has a positive impact on the lives of both aging men and women. Older adults who are married are happier and have lower rates of disease than their nonmarried counterparts (Dupre & Meadows, 2007). In fact, married older adults who have been diagnosed with cancer are less likely to die than widowed older adults diagnosed with cancer (Ortiz et al., 2007).

Most married older adults report that their marriages have improved over time and that the later years are some of the happiest. Older adults usually have few nonspousal places to turn for emotional assistance. Married children are less likely to stay in touch and give emotional, financial, and practical help to their parents, compared with single or divorced children (Sarkisian & Gerstel, 2008).

In 2007, men and women older than 65 were much more likely to be married than at any other time in history (Stevenson & Wolfers, 2007). This is probably because the life expectancy for both men and women has improved. However, there is a higher percentage of married men than women; women live longer than men and widowhood is more common for them. Seventy-nine percent of men between the ages of 65 to 74 were married in 2004, whereas only 57% of women in the same age group were married. Although an estimated 500,000 people older than 65

Most older married couples say their marriages have improved over time and that the later years are some of their happiest.

REAL RESEARCH 9.3   UCLA researchers collected more than 1,500 hours of videotape from 30 dual-earner, multiple-child, middle-class American households and found that husbands and wives were together alone in the home only 10% of their waking time (CAMPOS ET AL., 2009).

---

remarry in the United States every year (M. Coleman et al., 2000), as we discussed earlier in this chapter, more and more older couples decide to live together in place of marriage (S. L. Brown et al., 2006).

Many older adults who experience the death of a spouse will remarry. Older men are twice as likely to remarry, however, because women outnumber men in older age and also because older men often marry younger women (M. Coleman et al., 2000). Marriages that follow the death of a spouse tend to be more successful if the couple had the opportunity to get to know each other fairly well before the marriage, if their children and peers approve of the marriage, and if they are in good health, financially stable, and have adequate living conditions. One 73-year-old man describes his experience:

I can't begin to tell you how happy I am. I am married to a wonderful woman who loves me as much as I love her. My children gave me a hard time of it at first, especially because she is a bit younger than me, but they finally accepted the relationship and came to our wedding. In fact, they gave me away at the ceremony. That's a switch, isn't it?
(Janus & Janus, 1993, p. 8)

▶▶ MARITAL Satisfaction

A survey in 2000 found that marriages in the United States are as happy today as they were 20 years ago (Amato et al., 2003). Marital satisfaction for men is related to the frequency of pleasurable activities that involve doing fun things together in the relationship, whereas for women is related to the frequency of pleasurable activities that focus on emotional closeness. Other important variables, including being able to talk to each other and self-disclose, physical and emotional intimacy, and personality similarities, are all instrumental in achieving greater relationship quality.

John Gottman, whom we discussed in Chapter 3, found that the quality of the friendship with one's spouse is the most important factor in marital satisfaction for both men and women (Gottman & Silver, 2000). Gottman also found that a couple's ability to resolve conflict added to their marital stability. High rewards, such as emotional support and a satisfying sex life, and low costs, such as arguing, conflicts, and financial burdens, are also important in marital satisfaction (Impett et al., 2001). If a marriage has high costs but low rewards, a person might end the relationship or look outside the marriage for alternative rewards.

In a review of trends in marital happiness by gender and race from 1973 to 2006, researchers found that White husbands report the highest levels of marital happiness, whereas Black wives report the lowest (Corra et al., 2009). Even though over time White husbands consistently reported the highest levels of marital happiness, there has been a steady decline in the gap between these groups, and Black wives reported more marital happiness relative to the other groups over time (Corra et al., 2009). Overall, marriage provides fewer health benefits to women than men. For instance, although married men have better physical and mental health, more self-reported happiness, and experience fewer psychological problems than either divorced, single, or widowed men (Joung et al., 1995), married women do not receive these same health benefits (Hemstrom, 1996). This may be because women have multiple role responsibilities; for example, married women still tend to do the bulk of the housework and disproportionately take care of the children (Baxter & Hewitt, 2010). Women, regardless of race, report their marriages are more unfair to them than their husbands (Forry et al., 2007). The good news is that since the early 2000s there has been a trend in the mental health benefits of marriage applying equally to men and women (R. W. Simon, 2002; K. Williams & Umberson, 2004), which may be a result of an increased equality in heterosexual marriage (W. B. Wilcox & Nock, 2006).

People who are married tend to be happier and healthier and have longer lives than either widowed or divorced persons of the same age (Dush & Amato, 2005; Waldinger & Schulz, 2010). In fact, in a study of heterosexual couples, married couples had the highest level of well-being, followed by (in order) cohabitating couples, steady dating relationships, casual dating relationships, and individuals who dated infrequently or not at all (Dush & Amato, 2005). Marriage has also been found to reduce the impact of several potentially traumatic events, including job loss, retirement, and illness (Waldinger & Schulz, 2010). In Black men and women, remaining single was found to be related to increased risk for health problems (Schwandt et al., 2010).

Although traditional marriages may have involved one partner staying home with children whereas the other worked outside the home, today more and more couples are both in the workforce, which has increased equality (Stevenson & Isen, 2010). These marriages have been found to be happier and more fulfilling than traditional marriages (Stevenson & Wolfers, 2008). Partners with more education report more happiness in their marriages (Stevenson & Isen, 2010).

Sexuality remains an essential part of many marriages, even though many couples experience changes in their sex lives over time.

▶▶ SEX WITHIN Marriage

Sexuality is an essential part of most marriages. Married men and women both report that sex is integral to a good marriage, although men often report higher sexual needs than women (Elliott & Umberson, 2008). However, there is a great deal of variation in who initiates sex, what behaviors a couple engages in, and how often they engage in it (Figure 9.4). Overall, the majority of married couples report satisfaction with their marital sex (Sprecher, 2002).

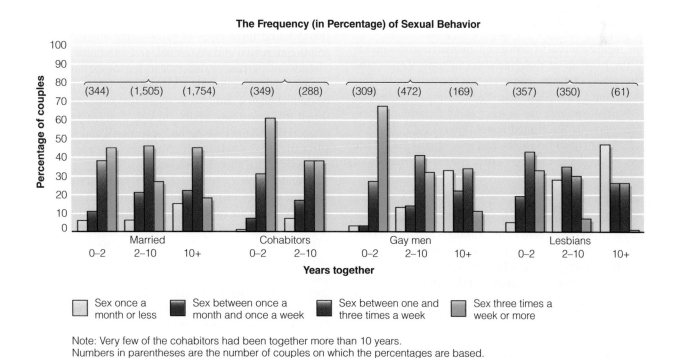

FIGURE **9.4** Frequency of sexual behavior in various types of relationships by years. The numbers above each category represent the total number of respondents. SOURCE: Blumstein, P., & Schwartz, P. (1983). *Frequency of sex in marriage from American couples* (p. 196). New York: HarperCollins Publishers. © 1983 by Philip B. Blumstein and Pepper S. Schwartz. Reprinted by permission of HarperCollins Publishers, Inc. and International Creative Management, Inc.

The National Survey of Sexual Health and Behavior found that the majority of married couples have sex weekly or a few times per month, and that younger married couples engage in more frequent sex (Herbenick et al., 2010a). Laumann and colleagues (1994) found that 40% of married couples have sexual intercourse two or more times a week, whereas 50% engage in it a few times each month. The frequency of sexual activity and satisfaction with a couple's sex life have been found to be positively correlated (Blumstein & Schwartz, 1983); that is, the more frequent the sexual behavior, the greater the relationship satisfaction. However, it is not known whether increased sexual frequency causes more satisfaction or whether increased relationship satisfaction causes increased sexual behavior.

As we discussed in Chapter 7, most long-term relationships often start out high on passion, but this decreases over time (Brewis & Meyer, 2005; Starling, 1999). Many couples report engaging in less sex as a marriage progresses. This is consistent with cross-cultural studies that have found that a declining frequency of sexual behavior over time is a common feature of human populations (Brewis & Meyer, 2005). Typically, the reason sex decreases in long-term relationships has less to do with getting bored with one's partner than it has to do with the pressures of children, jobs, commuting, housework, and finances.

*Most long-term relationships often **start out high on passion,** but this **decreases over time.***

Some marriages are **asexual relationships,** which means that the partners do not engage in sexual behavior. This may be because one partner does not have sexual desire anymore, or it may be a mutual decision not to have sex (Donnelly & Burgess, 2008). In either case, most asexual married couples are in stable relationships and feel reluctant to leave (Donnelly & Burgess, 2008).

▶▶ SEX OUTSIDE of Marriage

All societies regulate sexual behavior and use marriage as a means to control the behavior of their members to some degree. The United States is one of the few countries that has traditionally forbidden sexual contact outside of marriage; research estimates that less than 5% of all societies are as strict about forbidding extramarital intercourse as the United States (Lance, 2007; Leslie & Korman, 1989). Half of all U.S. states have laws against sex outside of marriage, although these laws are rarely enforced.

Extramarital Sex

Almost all couples, whether dating, living together, or married, expect sexual exclusivity from each other. Although extramarital sex refers to sex outside of marriage, we are also referring here to extra-relationship sex, or dating couples who have sex with someone other than their partner. Not surprisingly, adults in the United States are more likely to cheat while living together than while married (Treas & Giesen, 2000). Those who cheat in intimate relationships have been found to have stronger sexual interests, more permissive sexual values, less satisfaction in their intimate relationship, and more opportunities for sex outside the relationship (Treas & Giesen, 2000). Studies on same-sex couples have found that gay men are more likely to cheat than lesbian women (Roisman et al., 2008).

Laumann and colleagues (1994) found that 20% of women and 15% to 35% of men of all ages reported that they had engaged in extramarital sex while they were married. Even for those couples who never consider sex outside of marriage, the possibility looms, and people wonder about it—what it would be like or whether their partners are indulging in it. Typically, religiosity and church attendance are associated with lower odds of extramarital affairs (Burdette et al., 2007).

How does an extramarital affair typically begin? In the first stage, a person might become emotionally close to someone at school, work, a party, or even on the Internet. As they get to know each other, there is chemistry and a powerful attraction. This moves into the second stage, in which the couple decides to keep the relationship secret. They don't tell their closest friends about their attraction. This secret, in turn, adds fuel to the passion. In the third stage, the couple starts doing things together, even though they would not refer to it as "dating." Each still believes that the relationship is all about friendship. Finally, in the fourth stage, the relationship becomes sexual, leading to an intense emotional and sexual affair (Layton-Tholl, 1998).

Although many people think that sexual desire drives an extramarital affair, research has found that more than 90% of extramarital affairs occur because of unmet emotional needs within the marital relationship (Previti & Amato, 2004). Laumann and colleagues (1994) found that, overall, couples are faithful to each other as long as the marriage is intact and satisfying. A. P. Thompson (1984) found three types of extramarital affairs: sexual but not emotional, sexual and emotional, and emotional but not sexual. Twenty-one percent of respondents having extramarital sex were involved in predominantly sexual affairs; 19% in both sexual and emotional affairs; and 18% in affairs that were emotional but not sexual (the remaining affairs did not fit clearly into any of these categories). Affairs that are both emotional and sexual appear to affect the marital relationship the most, whereas affairs that are primarily sexual affect it the least.

Gender plays a role in both the type of extramarital affairs in which a person engages and a partner's acceptance of these affairs. Women are more likely than men to have emotional but not sexual affairs, whereas men are more likely to have sexual affairs. When it comes to accepting a partner's extramarital affair, women experience more emotional distress about affairs than men do, but they rate emotional affairs as more harmful than sexual affairs (Guerrero et al., 2004). Men, on the other hand, rate sexual affairs as more harmful than emotional affairs (see Chapter 7 for more information about gender differences in jealousy). Extramarital affairs lower marital happiness and increase the risk for divorce (Previti & Amato, 2004).

Nonexclusive Marriages

Some married couples open up their relationships and encourage their partners to have sexual activity outside of the marriage,

asexual relationship
A type of intimate relationship in which the partners do not engage in sexual behavior.

comarital sex
The consenting of married couples to exchange partners sexually.

swinger
A man, woman, or couple who openly exchanges sexual partners.

polyamorist
A man, woman, or couple who openly exchanges sexual partners.

Sex in Real Life ▶▶ What Is Polyamory?

If you are in a relationship, do you insist on monogamy from your partner? Most of us would answer this question with a resounding "Yes!" But have you talked to your partner about it? Studies have found that while many gay couples make agreements about whether to be monogamous, many heterosexual couples neither discuss it nor come to an agreement about it (Hoff et al., 2010; Warren et al., in press). However, we live in a society that expects monogamy from our sexual partners. Serial monogamy, a form of monogamy in which partners have only one sexual partner at any one time, is common on college campuses today. Although the majority of men and women have more than one sexual partner in their lifetime, they are monogamous while in these relationships. Researchers are just beginning to explore the concept of polyamory—"ethically

nonmonogamous" relationships in which partners engage in loving, sexual relationships with more than one person at a time (Bennett, 2009). A "polyamorous" man or woman has a consensual and agreed-on context to these intimate relationships outside of his or her primary partnership (Weitzman, 1999). Polyamorous couples can be old, young, gay, or straight, and the key to the relationship is honesty. Polyamorous men and women openly discuss sexual behavior outside their primary relationship. Unlike "swingers," the emphasis is on the relationships, rather than simply the sex. Research estimates that as of 2009, there were more than half a million openly polyamorous families living in many major cities in the United States (Bennett, 2009). Polyamorous relationships can take many forms, including:

1. Primary-Plus: One person in a primary relationship agrees to pursue outside relationships. New lovers are "secondary lovers," and the primary relationship remains the most important.

2. Triad: Three people involved in a committed intimate relationship. All three relationships are equal, and there is no primary relationship.

3. Individual with Multiple Primaries: This relationship resembles a "V," in which one person has separate but equal relationships with two other people who have no relationship with one another" (Davidson, 2002).

believing that sexual variety and experience enhance their own sexual life. Couples engage in **comarital sex** (the consenting of married couples to sexually exchange partners), and the partners are often referred to as **swingers** or **polyamorists** (pah-lee-AM-more-rists). Nonmarried couples can also be polyamorists and can have relationships outside of their primary relationship.

In 1972, George and Nena O'Neill published a book titled *Open Marriage* (O'Neill & O'Neill, 1972). In this book, they explained that "sexual adventuring" was fine, as long as both spouses knew about it. In open marriages, each partner is free to seek out sexual partners outside of the marriage. Many swingers engage in "safe-sex circles" in which they have sex only with people who have tested negative for sexually transmitted infections.

The majority of swingers are White, middle class, middle-aged, and churchgoing (Bergstrand & Williams, 2000). Swinging appears to be increasing in popularity among mainstream married couples in the United States. The North American Swing Club Association

claims there are organized swing clubs in almost every U.S. state, as well as in Japan, Canada, England, Germany, and France (Bergstrand & Williams, 2000). In addition, SwingFest, an annual U.S. swinger lifestyle convention, brings in thousands of swingers from around the world (Swingfest.com). Not surprisingly, the Internet is the main source of contact for swingers (R. H. Rubin, 2001).

Most swingers have strict rules meant to protect the marriage; sex in those cases is seen as separate from the loving relations of marriage. The marriage is always viewed as the primary relationship, and sex outside this relationship is thought only to strengthen the marriage (deVisser & McDonald, 2007). In fact, swingers report happier marriages and a higher life satisfaction than nonswingers (Bergstrand & Williams, 2000). Research has found that jealousy increased sexual excitement and arousal in swinging couples, particularly in men (deVisser & McDonald, 2007). However, for some couples, jealousy can be detrimental to the relationship (Bergstrand & Williams, 2000).

◀ review QUESTIONS

1 Explain current trends in heterosexual marriage.

2 Define "mixed marriage" and explain how it has changed over the years.

3 Explain what we know about marital happiness, gender, and race.

4 Explore the importance of sexuality in marriage.

5 What do we know about sex outside of marriage? Explain extramarital affairs, polyamory, and nonexclusive marriages.

▶ SAME-SEX Relationships

In many ways, gay and lesbian relationships have changed more than heterosexual relationships over the last few decades. First, these relationships came "out of the closet" in the 1960s and 1970s, when there was a blossoming and acceptance of a gay subculture. Then the advent of AIDS resulted in fewer sexual partners and more long-term, monogamous relationships, especially in the gay community.

Heterosexual, gay, and lesbian men and women all hold similarly positive views of their intimate relationships (Roisman et al., 2008). Even so, there has been considerable debate throughout the years about what type of intimate relationships promote the healthiest psychological adjustment. One study by Blumstein and Schwartz (1983) compared same- and other-sex couples using interviews and questionnaires. Although this study is dated, it remains a classic, because no other studies have undertaken such a large sample population comparing couples in a variety of different relationships.

*Gay and lesbian couples **have higher levels of relationship satisfaction.***

Although accurate statistics can be difficult to come by, because some couples might not report being in a same-sex relationship, we know that in 2008 there were 565,000 same-sex couples—415,000 were unmarried and 150,000 were married (30,000–35,000 were legally married and 80,000 were in nonmarital forms of legal recognition; Gates, 2008). We will talk more about same-sex marriage later in this chapter.

▶▶ DIFFERENCES AND SIMILARITIES in Gay and Straight Relationships

For many years, researchers suggested that same-sex relationships were less stable in adulthood because of negative early life experiences and the challenges of accepting one's sexual orientation (Savin-Williams, 2001). Others claim that societal pressures on same-sex couples, such as the struggle to manage a gay or lesbian identity in a heterosexist culture, lead to weaker intimate relationships (Pachankis & Goldfried, 2004). However, although it may be true that same-sex couples face more relationship challenges than do heterosexual couples, these theories have not been supported by research (Herek, 2006; Roisman et al., 2008). The majority of gay men and lesbian women were found to be secure in both their

sexual orientation and childhood experiences, and able to connect fully in intimate relationships (Roisman et al., 2008). Partnered gay and lesbian men and women reported more happiness than singles (Wienke & Hill, 2008).

Same-sex couples are more likely to have freedom from gender roles, equal sharing of household responsibilities, less emphasis on attractiveness, increased intimacy, and better communication than other-sex couples (Balsam et al., 2008; Boon & Alderson, 2009; Cohen et al., 2008; R. J. Green, 2008; Mock & Cornelius, 2007; Soloman et al., 2005; Wienke & Hill, 2009). Gay and lesbian couples have higher levels of relationship satisfaction; share more affection, humor, and joy in their relationships; have less conflict; and have less fear and negative feelings about their relationship than other-sex couples (Gottman et al., 2003; Herek, 2006; Pachankis & Goldfried, 2004; Roisman et al., 2008). Like heterosexual relationships, partners in gay relationships with more resources or power have been found to perform fewer household chores (Sutphin, 2010). Many same-sex couples also report that they have more challenges dealing with societal discrimination and negative attitudes about homosexuality (we discuss this further in Chapter 11).

Overall, same-sex couples may be more satisfied with their intimate relationships because they are forced to work harder at them (R. J. Green et al., 1996). Same-sex couples may not have as much family or societal support as heterosexual couples do, which tends to put more focus on their intimate relationships. In addition, more similar communication styles may contribute to higher relationship satisfaction (Kurdek, 2004).

Lesbian relationships are emotionally closer than gay male couples, who, in turn, have been found to be emotionally closer than heterosexual married couples (R. J. Green, 2008; Mock & Cornelius, 2007). Women in lesbian relationships have also been found to have higher levels of intimate communication in their relationships compared with other couple types (Henderson et al., 2009).

Another interesting area of research has explored "benchmarks," or events that mark important dates, in a couple's relationship (such as first date, engagement, or wedding). For many same-sex couples, the lack of a unified definition for defining the beginning of a gay or lesbian relationship can be difficult. They may celebrate first meeting, first date, first sex, or a commitment ceremony. One lesbian couple said, "We celebrate our anniversary

timeline Same-Sex Relationships around the Globe

1989
Denmark becomes the first country to legally recognize same-sex unions with the Danish Registered Partnership Act.

Doug Menuez/Getty Images

1993
Norway legalizes registered partnerships.

1994
Sweden legalizes registered partnerships.

© Rob Chapple/Thinkstock/Picturequest

1996
Iceland legalizes registered partnerships.

1996
U.S. President Clinton signs the Defense of Marriage Act into law, which upholds states rights to ban same-sex marriage and not recognize marriages performed elsewhere.

from that day that we acknowledged that we were attracted to each other," whereas a gay couple said, "We use the day we exchanged rings" (Degges-White & Marszalek, 2008). Commitment ceremonies, civil unions, and domestic partnerships have become important celebrations for many same-sex couples because they help establish a couple's relationship (R. J. Green & Mitchell, 2002). Without the availability of formal relationship status, many same-sex couples experience boundary and commitment ambiguity (R. J. Green & Mitchell, 2002). Because there are few same-sex couple role models, many same-sex couples do not know what their relationships should look like and must work together to form relationships that work for them. Although this gives them increased flexibility in defining roles, it also may present additional challenges to their relationships (Degges-White & Marszalek, 2008). We discuss many more aspects of same-sex relationships in Chapter 11, but in this chapter we explore sexuality in these relationships and the advent of civil unions, domestic partnerships, and same-sex marriages.

"We're seen as married in the eyes of our family and our church."
—SAME-SEX MARRIAGE

View in Video
To watch the entire interview, go to Psychology CourseMate at **login.cengagebrain.com.**

© 2012 Cengage Learning

▶▶ SEXUALITY IN **Same-Sex Relationships**

Like heterosexual couples, gay men and lesbian women report many positive aspects of sex in their relationships. Some of the most important benefits cited by gay men and lesbian women are emotional and physical intimacy, feeling accepted and supported, increased communication, and a positive view of self (Cohen et al., 2008). Yet, to gain these benefits, they report it is necessary to be vulnerable and take risks. The stigma of social and cultural attitudes about same-sex relationships can interfere with healthy sexual functioning (Cohen et al., 2008).

Earlier in this chapter, we discussed gender differences in initiating sexual activity in heterosexual relationships: Men often do more of the initiating. Does this mean that lesbians may be uncomfortable initiating sex or that gay men never have problems doing so? According to a classic study done by Blumstein and Schwartz (1983), this may be the case. They found that some lesbians do have difficulty initiating or balancing sex in their relationships. Problems with initiating sex in lesbian relationships may be because of the social pressures women have while growing up. In lesbian couples, it is often the

Gay men engage in sexual behavior more often than both lesbian and heterosexual couples.

more emotionally expressive partner who is responsible for maintaining the couple's sex life.

Similarly, in relationships between gay men, the more emotionally expressive partner is usually the one who initiates sexual activity. However, gay men are much less bothered by their role of initiator. Again, this may lead to other problems, with one partner feeling he is always the initiator.

Gay men engage in sexual behavior more often than both lesbian and heterosexual couples (Kurdek, 2006). Lower rates of sexual behavior in lesbian couples have been explained in many ways. It could be that the biological nature of the sex drive is lower in women, that females typically do not initiate sexual activity and may not be comfortable doing so, or that women are less likely than men to express their feelings through sex. Finally, it also must be pointed out that perhaps lesbian lovemaking lasts longer than heterosexual lovemaking (focusing more on foreplay), and a longer duration of lovemaking could lead to a decrease in the actual number of occurrences. We discuss same-sex sexual behavior more in Chapter 10.

1997
Netherlands legalizes registered partnerships.

© Don Mason/Corbis

1999
Belgium legalizes registered partnerships.

1999
France legalizes civil unions for both same- and other-sex couples with the *Pacte civil de solidarité.*

2000
Netherlands becomes first country to legalize same-sex marriage.

© Lorne Harris

2001
Finland legalizes registered partnership.

2001
Germany legalizes civil unions.

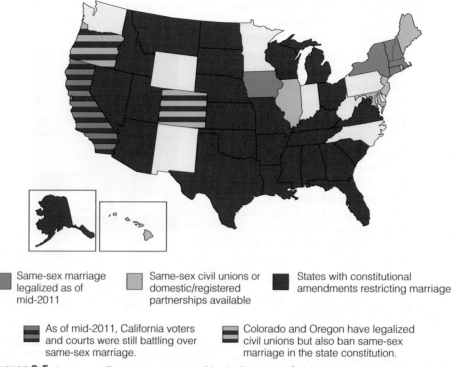

FIGURE **9.5** Laws regarding same-sex partnerships in the U.S. as of mid-2011. Copyright © Cengage Learning 2013.

Legend:
- Same-sex marriage legalized as of mid-2011
- Same-sex civil unions or domestic/registered partnerships available
- States with constitutional amendments restricting marriage
- As of mid-2011, California voters and courts were still battling over same-sex marriage.
- Colorado and Oregon have legalized civil unions but also ban same-sex marriage in the state constitution.

▶▶ CIVIL UNIONS and Domestic Partnerships

Many same-sex couples cohabit, whereas others choose **civil unions** and **domestic partnerships** (also referred to as civil partnerships or registered partnerships). These are legally recognized unions that come with varying rights and benefits. The rights and benefits awarded couples vary and depend on the laws of each individual state. Typically, domestic partnerships offer fewer rights than do civil unions.

The terms for same-sex relationships vary around the globe. In Australia, same-sex relationships are referred to as "significant relationships"; in the Netherlands, they are *geregistreerd partnerschap* ("registered partnerships"); in Germany, they are *lebenspartnerschaft* ("life partnerships"); and in Iceland, they are *staðfesta samvist* ("confirmed cohabitation"). Not only do the terms for same-sex relationship vary, their legal status does as well. Some

countries legalize relationships, whereas others "approve" or "allow" them. See the accompanying timeline of major events in the changing legal status of same-sex relationships.

Legalized relationships are unavailable to the majority of same-sex couples in the United States today. In 2000, Vermont was the first state to legalize civil unions, and by 2010, civil unions and domestic partnerships were available in several states, including California, Colorado, Connecticut, Hawaii, Illinois, Maine, Maryland, Nevada, New Jersey, Oregon, Vermont, Washington, Wisconsin, and the District of Columbia. Several other states are considering legislation for legal status of same-sex relationships.

civil union
A legal union of a same-sex couple, sanctioned by a civil authority.

domestic partnership
Persons other than spouses who cohabit. Domestic partners can be either same or other sex.

timeline Same-Sex Relationships around the Globe

2003

Belgium becomes the second country in the world to legalize same-sex marriage.

Ryan Pierse/Getty Images

2004

New Zealand approves Civil Union Bill, giving same-sex couples the same rights as married couples in child custody, taxes, and welfare.

2005

Spain and Canada legalize same-sex marriage.

AP Photo/CP, Jonathan Hayward

2006

South Africa legalizes same-sex marriage.

2007

Switzerland legalizes registered partnerships.

See Figure 9.5 for more information. Typically, civil unions and domestic partnerships that are performed in one state are not recognized in other states, even if they have a civil union or domestic partnership law (Vestal, 2008).

Since 2010, there has been an increase in public support of legal recognition for same-sex couples. A 2010 CBS News Poll found that the majority of Americans think there should be some legal recognition of gay and lesbian couples—40% of respondents reported same-sex couples should be allowed to marry, whereas 30% thought they should be able to get civil unions (CBS, 2010). However, one fourth of respondents reported same-sex couples should not have any legal recognition. Many same-sex couples across the United States are challenging existing laws that regulate issues such as civil unions, domestic partnerships, same-sex marriage, separation, child custody, and gay adoption. These court cases will continue, some say, until same-sex couples are given the same marital rights as their heterosexual counterparts. The changing legal status of same-sex relationships is especially important to lesbian women, who are more likely than gay men to marry or enter into domestic partnerships and have children (we discuss these issues further in Chapter 11).

Same-sex marriages performed in states with legal same-sex marriage are typically not recognized outside of these states.

Same-sex couples who are able to have their relationships legally recognized are more likely to be out about their sexual orientation, have children and joint back accounts with their partner, and have more connections with their families compared with those who did not have civil unions (Balsam et al., 2008). Some researchers suggest that civil unions may increase the stability of same-sex relationships, improve the physical and mental health of the individuals in the relationship, and reduce outside discrimination (M. King & Bartlett, 2005; Lubbers et al., 2009).

▶▶ SAME-SEX Marriage

In 1996, the U.S. Congress enacted the Defense of Marriage Act, which prohibits federal recognition of civil unions, domestic partnerships, and same-sex marriages. As discussed earlier, even though individual U.S. states may offer these legal options, the federal government will not recognize these unions. In addition, based on the Defense of Marriage Act, each state can recognize or deny any relationship between same-sex couples, recognizing marriage as a "legal union of one man and one woman as husband and wife," by referring to a "spouse" only as a person of the other sex. The Defense of Marriage Act also removes any federal spousal rights of civil unions, domestic partnerships, and same-sex marriage, including social security, federal tax law, and immigration rights for foreign same-sex spouses of American citizens (Mason et al., 2001). In 2010, President Barack Obama mandated that U.S. hospitals extend visitation rights to partners of gay and lesbians, and also respect patients' choices about health-care decisions (Shear, 2010).

Even though the U.S. Census Bureau began collecting data on same-sex marriage in 2010, it is estimated that 1 in 7 same-sex couples were not identified as such in the Census data collection. Some couples neglected to identify themselves or their partners as spouse or unmarried partner because they didn't view the relationship in this way, because of confidentiality concerns, or because they were offended by the Census options that were presented (Gates & Renna, 2010). Same-sex couples who were married and lived in a state that legally recognized their marriage were more likely to report being married.

Same-sex marriage was available in the states of Massachusetts, Connecticut, Iowa, Vermont, New Hampshire, New York, and the District of Columbia as of mid-2011. Same-sex marriages performed in states with legal same-sex marriage are typically not recognized outside of these states. Think about it this way: A het-

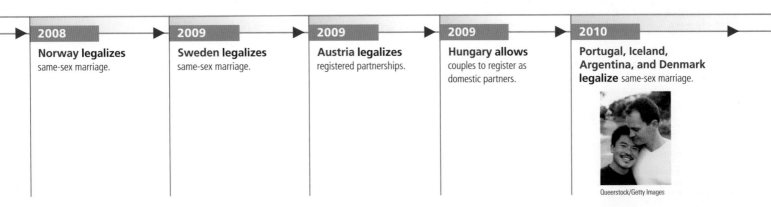

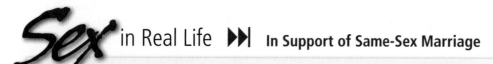

Sex in Real Life ▶▶ In Support of Same-Sex Marriage

Following is a letter written by a 39-year-old gay man who lost his long-term partner, Ken. This letter was read to Connecticut lawmakers in support of same-sex marriage.

I define my marital status as widowed, principally as the result of the death of my lover, Ken; his death brought to a close a relationship which had spanned close to seven years. The cause of death was heart failure, the result of a congenital lung condition. Soon after we started dating, he told me of his health condition and of its eventually fatal consequences. He did so not to scare me away, but to prepare me for what lay ahead.

One of my greatest regrets was my inability to place my lover on my health care plan. He was self-employed and found premiums prohibitively expensive. When his health declined to the point that he required around-the-clock care, I lost my job. My employer informed me that a leave of absence would not be granted as care for a dying lover failed to meet guidelines for such consideration. Survival necessitated liquidating, one after another, all of my assets. Upon his death, the estate being insolvent, household items were sold to cover just debts. For those who've experienced the death of a legally defined spouse, if you feel that my relationship with my lover does not equate to the loss that you've sustained, let me tell

you this. I remember every restless night, waking up screaming, trembling, and crying; I've lived with the overwhelming loneliness associated with birthdays, anniversaries, and the countless private rituals now remembered only by one; and I can state, unequivocally, that the worst part of widowhood is sleeping alone again—and it has nothing to do with sex—it is literally just sleeping alone again.

The one thing that no one can take away are the last words that Ken spoke, some 20 minutes before he breathed his last, addressed to me, "My beautiful boy, I love you very much."

SOURCE: Author's files.

---

erosexual couple who gets married in Kansas and moves to Connecticut is still legally married, and their marriage license from Kansas proves it. However, a same-sex couple who gets married in Massachusetts will not be legally recognized when they move to Kansas, even though they have a valid marriage license from the state of Massachusetts.

Why should marriage be allowed only for heterosexual couples and not for gay and lesbian couples? Shouldn't same-sex marriages (or an equivalent marriage-like status) be legalized? The answers to these questions go back many years. Aristotle discussed the importance of legislators to establish rules regulating marriage (Dixit & Pindyck, 1994).

Societies have always given preference to heterosexual couples, presumably because of the benefits that heterosexual marriages provide to society. Wardle (2001) discusses eight social interests for marriage, including:

1. Safe sexual relations
2. Responsible procreation
3. Optimal child rearing
4. Healthy human development
5. Protecting those who undertake the most vulnerable parenting roles (i.e., mothers/wives)
6. Securing the stability and integrity of the basic unit of society
7. Fostering civic virtue and social order
8. Facilitating interjurisdictional compatibility

As you can see, heterosexual marriage is strongly linked to procreation, childbirth, and child rearing (Wardle, 2001). The United States has long regulated marriage in an attempt to protect procreative health. This is precisely why marriages between relatives are illegal (birth defects are more prevalent in couples who are related), and marriages between "unfit" or mentally challenged partners are regulated.

Even with all this controversy, many gay and lesbian couples "marry" their partners in ceremonies that are not recognized by the states in which they live. As we discussed earlier, approxi-

---

timeline Same-Sex Relationships around the Globe

2011

U.S. President Barack Obama declares the Defense of Marriage Act unconstitutional and directs the Justice Department to stop defending the law in court.

Melanie Stetson Freeman/The Christian Science Monitor via Getty Images

2011

Legislation legalizing same-sex marriage is proposed in the following countries: Australia, Chile, Colombia, Finland, Luxembourg, Nepal, Paraguay, and Uruguay.

mately 1 of 4 same-sex couples (150,000 couples) refer to one another as "husband" or "wife," even though researchers estimate that approximately 32,000 of the couples have been legally married (Gates, 2008). Same-sex couples who are married, or who identify as married, are similar to heterosexual couples in terms of age, income, and parenting (Gates, 2008). These relationships, whether legally recognized or not, often suffer from the same jealousies, power struggles, and "divorces" as heterosexual marriages (P. H. Collins, 1988). A study comparing same-sex couples who were married in Massachusetts, had domestic partnerships in California, and civil unions in Vermont found males were older and waited longer to legalize their relationships than women did, and males were less likely to have children (Rothblum et al., 2008).

© Lorne Harris

The families of same-sex couples often include children and grandchildren.

◄ review QUESTIONS

1 Explain why same-sex relationships may experience less power imbalances and greater equality and satisfaction than heterosexual relationships.

2 Differentiate between civil unions, domestic partnerships, and same-sex marriage.

3 Explain how and why societies have given preference to heterosexual marriage over same-sex marriage.

▶ HAVING CHILDREN
or Remaining Childless

Although we discuss pregnancy and childbirth in Chapter 12, here we'll examine the impact of parenting on adult relationships. We know that in heterosexual relationships, children can be conceived and born at any time—while a couple are hooking up, dating, living together, or married. Some couples decide to have children without a formal commitment to each other, some get married to have children, and others get married because the woman is pregnant. Although pregnancies can be experienced as unplanned events, ambivalence and uncertainty are common in couples mak-

---

REAL RESEARCH 9.4   All new parents, regardless of sexual orientation, experience declines in their relationship quality after the first year of parenthood, with women reporting larger declines in love for their partners (GOLDBERG ET AL., 2010).

---

ing decisions about parenthood (Pinquart et al., 2008). Unlike heterosexual couples, same-sex couples can't get pregnant by accident, but many do decide to become parents in a variety of ways, including surrogacy, adoption, foster care, arrangements with friends and family, or through a partner's biological children. Like heterosexual couples, same-sex couples may decide to have children while dating, living together, or married. In any case, the decision to have or raise children is one that most people face at one

time or another, and research shows that the timing of parenthood can affect a couple's relationship quality. Although some gay and lesbian couples expect to raise their own biological children, others said they would adopt or become foster parents.

▶▶ STATISTICS AND **Current Trends**

Today's parents are more likely to be older, more educated, ethnically diverse, and less likely to be married (Koropeckyj-Cox et al., 2007; Livingston & Cohn, 2010). While there were more teenage births in 1990, teenage births decreased and there were more births among older women by 2008. In fact, between 1990 and 2008, births to women older than 35 years increased 64%, increasing in all ethnic and racial groups (Livingston & Cohn, 2010). In addition to this, births among unmarried women increased. Whereas 28% of births were to unmarried women in 1990, 41% of births were to unmarried women in 2008 (Livingston & Cohn, 2010). Unmarried births were highest in Black women (72%) and lowest in Asians (18%; Livingston & Cohn, 2010). Although rates were lower in Hispanics (53%) and Whites (29%) than Blacks, the increases in unmarried births among White women increased 69% since the 1990s (Livingston & Cohn, 2010). All of these changing trends are because of demographic and behavioral changes, such as population changes, delays in marriage, increases in education, and changing attitudes about marriage, pregnancy, and birth. Whereas several years ago having a child outside of wedlock might have seemed odd, today most Americans know at least one woman who has had a baby without being married and at least one man who fathered a baby without being married (Livingston & Cohn, 2010).

Studies of lesbian and gay youths have found that two thirds of females and more than 50% of males are interested in raising children at some point in their lives (D'Augelli et al., 2006/2007). Many gay men and lesbian women also express a desire to have and raise children, even though same-sex couples are less likely than heterosexual couples to have children (Balsam et al., 2008; Riskind & Patterson, 2010). The 2008 Community Survey found that 31% of same-sex couples were raising children, compared with 43% of heterosexual couples (Gates & Renna, 2010).

▶▶ PARENTING AND Relationship Satisfaction

Longitudinal research on heterosexual, gay, and lesbian couples has found the quality of intimate relationships declines when couples become parents (Campos et al., 2009; Claxton & Perry-Jenkins, 2008; Goldberg et al., 2010). Parents with children often experience decreases in leisure time and time to work on their relationship, which is why they often report lower relationship satisfaction than those without children. Relationship satisfaction continues to decline as the number of children increases. In fact, relationship happiness is higher before the children come, declines steadily until it hits a low when the children are in their teens, and then begins to increase once the children leave the house (Papalia et al., 2002). This may be because of several factors, including reduced time for the relationship or disagreements about child-care responsibilities.

Having children decreases a couple's quality time together, which can lower relationship satisfaction.

REAL RESEARCH 9.5 In one study, 60% of African American couples entered into marriage with children, whereas 22% of White couples did (BRYANT, 2010).

Many gay and lesbian parents also have to contend with societal attitudes about same-sex couple parenting. Couples who live in areas where there is little acceptance of gay families have higher levels of depression and negativity after becoming parents (Goldberg et al., 2010). Living in a gay-friendly area can make the transition to parenthood easier for gay and lesbian couples.

◀ review QUESTIONS

1 Identify one way in which having children impacts adult relationships.

2 Explore similarities and differences in having children in heterosexual and homosexual couples.

3 Identify a current trend in parenting and give one reason for this trend.

4 Give two examples of how an intimate relationship might decline when a couple becomes parents.

▶ DIVORCE

There have been substantial changes in the institution of marriage since the early 1980s. During most of U.S. history, a married couple was viewed as a single, legal entity (M. A. Mason et al., 2001). Today, however, marriage is viewed more as a partnership between a couple. This shift in perception of marriage brought with it a shift in how marriage was dissolved. The liberalization of divorce laws made it easier to obtain a divorce and made it a less expensive process.

Since 2010, **no-fault divorce,** which means neither partner needs to be found guilty of a transgression (such as having sex outside marriage) to dissolve the marriage has been legal in all 50 states and the District of Columbia. Before this, most states required a partner to produce evidence of partner wrongdoing (such as extramarital sex or abuse) to be granted a divorce. The avail-

no-fault divorce
A divorce law that allows for the dissolution of a marriage without placing blame on either of the partners.

covenant marriage
A marriage that is preceded by premarital counseling and has strict rules about divorce.

ability of no-fault divorce contributed to skyrocketing divorce rates (Stevenson & Wolfers, 2007). In an attempt to reduce divorce rates, some states instituted **covenant marriages,** which revolve around restrictive agreed-on rules and regulations for ending a marriage and also involve premarital counseling and an agreement to pursue additional counseling if marital problems develop. Covenant marriages also extend the wait time for a divorce, in some cases to 2 years or more, unless there is domestic violence involved. We will talk more about covenant marriages later in this chapter.

▶▶ STATISTICS AND Current Trends

Divorce rates for married heterosexuals increased sharply between 1970 and 1975, in part because of the liberalization of divorce laws (Kreider, 2005). Rates stabilized after this and began to decrease. By 2005, divorce rates were at the lowest level since 1970 (Stevenson & Wolfers, 2007). It is estimated that roughly 1 in 5 adults has divorced, and the U.S. Census Bureau reports that 50% of U.S. marriages end in divorce (Kreider, 2005; U.S. Census Bureau, 2007). However, research has found that marital stability has increased each decade. Whereas 23% of couples who married in the 1970s split within 10 years, only 16% of those who wed in the 1990s divorced (Parker-Pope, 2010). In 2008, the median duration of a marriage between a man and woman in the United States was 18 years (Cohn, 2009).

Divorce rates are also highest in women in their teens and decline with increasing age. Generally, divorce occurs early in the marriage; on average, first marriages that end in divorce last about 8 years (U.S. Census Bureau, 2007). Second marriages that end in divorce last about 8.6 years for men and 7.2 years for women (U.S. Census Bureau, 2007).

Koreans, Asian Indians, and Chinese couples have the lowest separation rates and divorce rates in the United States, whereas African Americans, Native Americans, and Puerto Ricans show the highest separation and divorce rates in the United States (Kreider, 2005; Skolnick, 1992). Mexican Americans, Cubans, and Whites lie somewhere in between (Skolnick, 1992). A study using data from the National Survey of Family Growth found that married mixed-race couples have higher rates of divorce compared with same-race couples (Bratter & King, 2008). White female–Black male and White female–Asian male couples were more prone to divorce than White–White couples.

The changing economic conditions in the United States have led to some couples staying together for financial reasons (Paul, 2010). For example, legal fees and health insurance costs may make it necessary for couples to stay together, either in the same home or different homes. However, these couples are still legally and economically married and responsible for joint finances and expenses. In 2010, divorce "insurance" became available, called WedLock (Schultz, 2010). WedLock is sold in units of protection, each costing $15.99 per month for $1,250 in coverage. If a couple bought 10 units, they would have $12,500 in coverage in case of a divorce. Although it is unlikely such insurance will become popular, it is certainly a sign of changing times.

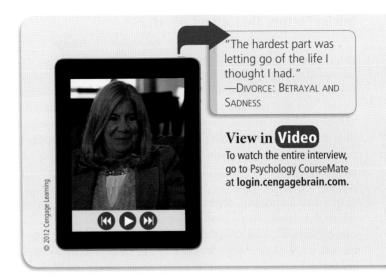

"The hardest part was letting go of the life I thought I had." —DIVORCE: BETRAYAL AND SADNESS

View in Video
To watch the entire interview, go to Psychology CourseMate at **login.cengagebrain.com.**

© 2012 Cengage Learning

▶▶ REASONS FOR Divorce

What causes a couple to end their marriage? The question is complicated because not all unstable or unhappy marriages end in divorce. Couples stay together for many reasons—for the children, because of lack of initiative, because of religious prohibitions against divorce, or financial reasons—even though they have problems in their marriages. Similarly, couples with seemingly happy marriages separate and divorce, sometimes to the surprise of one of the partners who did not even know the marriage was in trouble.

A mutually shared decision to divorce is actually uncommon. Usually, one partner wants to terminate a relationship more than the other partner, who is still strongly attached to the marriage and who is more distraught at its termination. In fact, the declara-

---

REAL RESEARCH 9.6 Researchers often point out that divorces are more common in the seventh year of marriage because of a "seven-year itch" (FEILER, 2010). Interestingly, the "seven-year itch" originally referred to an infection with scabies, an untreatable skin condition at the time that took seven years to go away.

---

tion that a partner wants a divorce often comes as a shock to his or her spouse. When one partner is the initiator, it is usually the female. One study found that women initiated two thirds of all divorces (Brinig & Allen, 2000). The individual who wants his or her marriage to end is likely to view the marriage totally differently from the individual who wants the marriage to continue (H. Wang & Amato, 2000). In addition, the partner who initiated the divorce has often completed the mourning of the relationship by the time the divorce is complete, unlike the partner whose mourning begins once the divorce is finalized.

Why do people get divorced? It is difficult to determine why some marriages fail; every couple has their own story. Sometimes the spouses themselves are at a loss to understand why their marriage failed. We now explore some of the social, predisposing, and relationship factors that may contribute to divorce.

Social Factors That Affect Divorce

Divorce rates in the United States are influenced by changes in legal, political, religious, and familial patterns. For example, as we discussed earlier, no-fault divorce laws have made divorce easier for couples to dissolve a marriage. The growth of low-cost legal clinics and the overabundance of lawyers have made divorce cheaper and thus more accessible. In addition, the more equitable distribution of marital assets has made some people less apprehensive about losing everything to their spouses. Changing social issues, such as more women entering the workforce and earning advanced degrees, have also had an impact on divorce rates. Research has found that divorce is more common in couples in which the woman has a professional degree (Wilson, 2008). Another interesting finding in the research is that male college graduates are more likely to have married by age 45 than those without college degrees, whereas female college graduates are less likely to have married than women without college degrees (Stevenson & Wolfers, 2007).

As we discussed earlier in this chapter, a few states have passed laws allowing people to choose a covenant marriage. Because a covenant marriage involves premarital counseling and makes

"A divorce ceremony will cast aside our doubts, and will be a new start for us."
—DIVORCE IN JAPAN

View in Video
To watch the entire interview, go to Psychology CourseMate at **login.cengagebrain.com.**

Video supplied by BBC Motion Gallery

In the much publicized divorce between Sandra Bullock and Jesse James, infidelity by James was cited as the main cause of the divorce.

Steve Granitz/WireImage/Getty Images

divorce more difficult even if the couple decides later they want one (Wardle, 1999), couples who choose them tend to be more conservative and religious and have stronger gender-role ideologies than those who choose a traditional marriage (Baker et al., 2009; Hawkins et al., 2002).

Predisposing Factors for Divorce

Certain situations may predispose a couple to divorce. People who have been divorced before or whose parents have divorced have more accepting attitudes toward divorce than those who grew up in happy, intact families (Amato & Hohmann-Marriott, 2007; El-dar-Avidan et al., 2009; Sassler et al., 2009; Wolfinger, 2000). In addition, people who have divorced parents are significantly more likely to report marital problems in their own relationships than people from intact families, and they also tend to be more skeptical about marriage, feeling insecure about the permanence of these relationships (Gähler et al., 2009; Jacquet & Surra, 2001; Weigel, 2007; Wolfinger, 2000).

Other factors that may contribute to divorce are marrying at a young age (S. P. Morgan & Rindfuss, 1985), marrying because of an unplanned pregnancy (G. Becker et al., 1977), alcohol or drug abuse (R. L. Collins et al., 2007), and having children quickly after getting married (S. P. Morgan & Rindfuss, 1985). The interval between marriage and the arrival of children is an important factor; waiting longer promotes marital stability by giving couples time to get accustomed to being a married couple before the arrival of children and may also allow them to become more financially secure (S. P. Morgan & Rindfuss, 1985). Religion is also important: Catholics and Jews are less likely to divorce than Protestants, and divorce rates tend to be higher for marriages of mixed religions. However, overall, the more religious a person is, the more conservative views they hold about divorce (Stokes & Ellison, 2010).

Relationship Factors in Divorce

In general, couples who divorce have known for a long time that there were difficulties in their marriage, although they may not have contemplated divorce. These problems are made worse, in most cases, by communication problems. Some warning signs are communication avoidance (not talking about problems in the relationship); demand and withdrawal patterns of communication, whereby one partner demands that they address the problem and the other partner pulls away; and little mutually constructive communication (Thompson, 2008).

Some couples make poor assessments of their partner or believe that the little annoyances or character traits that they dislike in their potential spouses will disappear or change after marriage (Neff & Karney, 2005). Marrying a person with the intention to change his or her personality or bad habits is a recipe for disaster.

▶▶ SAME-SEX Divorce

Because same-sex marriage has been legalized for a short time in the United States, there is not a great deal of research on same-sex divorce. We do know that many long-term same-sex couples typically dissolve their relationships privately, married or not. However, without divorce laws, these breakups can be difficult or unfair to one or both partners. A few same-sex married couples began seeking out divorce approximately 7 months after the legalization of same-sex marriage (Gallagher & Baker, 2004). One of the issues in same-sex divorce is whether a state that does not allow same-sex marriage can legally dissolve a same-sex marriage (Chen, 2010). If a same-sex couple cannot get a divorce, they will likely experience problems with the division of property, children's visitation rights, and the ability to enter into other relationships (Chen, 2010). Without legal intervention, the Human Rights Campaign, a national nonprofit organization, advocates for equal marital and divorce rights for same-sex couples.

*The majority of divorced men and women **remarry**.*

▶▶ ADJUSTING TO Divorce

How a person will adjust to a divorce depends on several factors, including who initiated the divorce, attitudes toward divorce, income levels, and the onset of a new relationship (Wang & Amato, 2000). Social connectedness is also an important factor in a person's adjustment (Moller et al., 2003). Although most divorces are emotionally painful for both partners, after 10 years, 80% of the women and 50% of the men said that their divorce was the right decision (Faludi, 1991).

Depression and sadness can surface when divorced men and women find that they have less in common with married friends as many friends separate into "hers" and "his." Older individuals experience more psychological problems because there are fewer options for forming new relationships in older age (H. Wang & Amato, 2000). Older divorced women are more likely to feel anger and loneliness than are younger divorced women.

Another area that is affected after divorce are finances. Financial adjustment is often harder for women, because after a divorce a woman's standard of living declines more than a man's (H. Wang & Amato, 2000). Research has found that after a divorce, a man's income increases by around one third, whereas a woman's income falls more than a fifth and remains low for years after the divorce (Jenkins, 2009). Many women who previously lived in a middle-class family find themselves slipping below the poverty line after divorce.

Dating after a divorce can be difficult for some. People may have been involved in committed relationships for many years; consequently, they may find that the dating environment has changed drastically since they were younger. It is not uncommon for newly single people to feel frustrated or confused about this unfamiliar environment. The majority of divorced men and women remarry, and some remarry, divorce, and remarry again (often referred to as **serial divorce**). In fact, the median time between a divorce and a second marriage is about 3.5 years (U.S. Census Bureau, 2007). Overall, 13% to 14% of heterosexuals marry twice, 3% marry three or more times, and less than 1% marry four or more times (Kreider, 2005). Men remarry at higher rates than women, and Hispanics and African Americans remarry at lower rates than Whites (M. Coleman et al., 2000). Couples in second marriages report higher relationship satisfaction in their marriages than do couples in first marriages (McCarthy & Ginsberg, 2007).

serial divorce
The practice of divorce and remarriage, followed by divorce and remarriage.

◀ review QUESTIONS

1 Explain what makes a no-fault marriage different from a covenant marriage.

2 Identify some of the factors that research has found might predispose a couple to divorce.

3 Explain how men and women adjust to divorce.

▶ ADULT SEXUAL
Relationships in Other Cultures

Dating, cohabitation, marriage, divorce, and same-sex relationships are often viewed differently outside the United States. Let's now take a look at some of these institutions, customs, and practices outside the United States.

▶▶ DATING AND Marriages in Other Cultures

In most industrialized countries, partner selection through dating is the norm. However, some countries have no dating systems. For example, in Sweden, there is no Swedish term for what Americans call "dating"—couples meet at dance clubs, bars, schools, or through friends (Trost, 2004).

There are still a few industrialized cultures in which **arranged marriages** take place. In Iran, all marriages are arranged, even those that are based on love (Drew, 2004). A young man will visit the home of the woman he wishes to marry accompanied by three members of his family. The woman is not allowed to speak unless directly questioned. A contract is signed, and although the couple is not formally married, this contract is legally binding. A formal marriage ceremony usually takes place a year later. (For more information about arranged marriage, see the accompanying Sexual Diversity in Our World.)

In some cultures, courtship is a highly ritualized process in which every step is defined by one's kin group or tribe (Hutter,

In India, where arranged marriage is common, divorce rates are amongst the lowest in the world.

© Plush Studios/PhotoLibrary

1981). For example, the marriages of the Yaruros of Venezuela are arranged and highly specified; a man must marry his "cross-cousin"—that is, the daughter of either his father's sister or his mother's brother. The marriages are arranged by the shaman or religious leader in consultation with one of the boy's uncles.

The Hottentots of South Africa also marry their cross-cousins, but here the boy can choose which cousin he wants to marry; once he does, he informs his parents, who send someone to seek permission from the girl's parents. Tradition dictates that they must refuse. The youth then approaches the girl, going to her house late at night once everyone is asleep and lying down next to her. She then gets up and moves to the other side of the house. The next night he returns, and if he finds her back on the side where he first lay next to her, he lies down again with her, and the marriage is consummated (Hutter, 1981).

For 2,000 years, marriages in China were arranged by parents and elders, and emotional involvement between prospective marriage partners was frowned upon; if a couple appeared to like having their marriage arranged, the marriage was called off! In China, the primary responsibility of each person was supposed to be to his or her extended family. If there was a marriage bond that was very strong outside of that extended family, it could jeopardize the cohesiveness of the group.

This all began to change with the Communist Revolution of 1949. Through contact with the West, these customs began to erode. Only 8 months after coming to power, the Communist leaders established the Marriage Law of the People's Republic of China, in which, among other things, they tried to end arranged marriages and establish people's right to choose their spouse freely. Today in China, although arranged marriages still take place in the rural areas, people date and meet each other in public places—a condition that was virtually unknown a few generations before.

In many parts of Africa, too, parents used to be involved in mate selection (Kayongo-Male & Onyango, 1984). Marriages were arranged between families, not really individuals, and each family had a set of expectations about the other's role. Courtship was highly ritualized, with the groom's family paying a "bride wealth" to the bride's family. The rituals that preceded marriage were intended to teach the couple what their particular tribe or culture believed married couples needed to know to keep their marriage successful. However, young people did have some say in whom they were to marry; in many cases, young people would reject their parents' choices or meet someone they liked and ask their parents to arrange a marriage. One Egyptian boy commented:

> We all know the girls of our village. After all, we played together as kids, and we see them going back and forth on errands as they get older. One favorite place for us to get a glimpse of girls is at the village water source. The girls know that and like to linger there. If we see one we like and think she might be suitable, we ask our parents to try to arrange a marriage, but usually not before we have some sign from the girl that she might be interested. (Rugh, 1984, p. 137)

arranged marriage
Marriage that is arranged by parents or relatives and is often not based on love.

Today, however, mate selection in most places is a much more individual affair. However much we in the West believe in the right of individuals to choose their own mates, there were some advantages to parental participation in mate selection, and the transition to individual mate selection in traditional societies is often difficult.

Forced marriages, where families force their daughters into early marriage or sell them to make money, have been on the rise in countries such as Afghanistan and Bangladesh (Hinshelwood, 2002). Girls between the ages of 8 to 12 years old are sold for between $300 to $800. These young girls can stay with their families until their future husband comes to claim them, usually around their first menstrual period. Worldwide, forced marriages of girls younger than 18 years are common, and in 2002, 52 million girls younger than 18 years were forced into marriage (Nour, 2006).

Girls who are forced to marry early are less educated, experience more domestic violence, have partners who are significantly older, and have more children (United National Children's Fund, 2005). Another practice, sex trafficking, in which young girls are sold for prostitution, is discussed in Chapter 18. Today, many women's groups in the West are working to stop these practices.

▶▶ COHABITATION IN Other Cultures

There has been a delay of entry into marriage in all countries around the world, which is mainly the result of an earlier entry into cohabitation. Instead of viewing these changes as shifts in moral attitudes, however, they are often viewed as simply cultural changes.

The most acceptance comes from Western European nations where there have been substantial increases in unmarried cohabitation among heterosexual partners. Couples who live together in Norway for a minimum of 2 years are given similar rights as married couples, including obligations to social security, pensions, and joint taxation. Cohabitation is also common in Sweden, where the majority of heterosexual couples live together before marriage (Trost, 2004). In France, cohabitating couples (other and same sex) can apply for legal recognition of their relationship. We will discuss the legal recognition of these relationships later in this chapter.

However, cohabitation among heterosexual couples in Spain and Italy is not as popular as it is in most other European countries, mainly because many young adults remain in their family home at least until their 30s (Lanz & Tagliabue, 2007). Cohabitation is also rarer in more traditional societies where, even if a couple has sex before or outside of marriage, social customs would never tolerate an unmarried heterosexual couple living together openly. For example, Asian societies still frown on it, although it is sometimes allowed, and it is severely discouraged in Islamic societies.

▶▶ MARITAL CUSTOMS
and Practices in Other Cultures

Marriage ceremonies take place in every society, but marriage customs vary widely from culture to culture. In some cultures, girls can be married very young, whereas other cultures mandate marriages between certain relatives, and still others allow multiple spouses.

Most cultures celebrate marriage as a time of rejoicing and have rituals or ceremonies that accompany the wedding process. Among various Berber tribes in Morocco, for example, wedding rituals can include performing a sacrifice, painting the heels of the couple's feet with goat's blood, having a feast, having fish cast at the feet of the bride, or feeding bread to the family dog (Westermarck, 1972). In Iranian culture, a "temporary marriage" allows a Muslim man an opportunity for female companionship outside of legal marriage when he travels or is employed by the military (Drew, 2004). Temporary marriages were formally approved by the Iranian government in 1990.

Most cultures celebrate marriage as a time of rejoicing and have rituals that accompany the wedding process.

In many preliterate cultures (and in some literate ones, too), there is a tendency to believe that the main purpose of being female is to get married and have babies. Among the Tiwi, a group of Australian aborigines, this was taken to its logical conclusion; a woman was to get married, and there was no word in their language for a single woman, for there was, in fact, no female—of any age—without at least a nominal husband. The Tiwi believed that pregnancy happens because a spirit entered the body of a female, but one could never be sure exactly when that happened; so the best thing to do was to make sure that the woman was married at all times. Therefore, all Tiwi babies were betrothed before or as soon as they were born, and widows were required to remarry at the gravesides of their husbands, no matter how old they were (Hart & Pilling, 1960).

Earlier in this chapter we discussed arranged marriages. For some, the concept of "loving" one's partner is not a relevant aspect of marriage. In Japan, for example, "love" marriages are often frowned upon because a couple can fall out of love and split up (N. D. Kristof, 1996). Some would argue that Japanese men and women actually love each other less than American couples do. Yet the secret to a strong family, claim the Japanese, is low expectations and patience (Kristof, 1996). These factors lead to couples staying together through thick or thin, rather than splitting up when the going gets rough. When one Japanese man, married for 33 years, was asked whether he loved his wife, he replied, "Yeah, so-so, I guess. She's like air or water. You couldn't live without it, but most of the time, you're not conscious of its existence" (Kristof, 1996). This is probably why Japanese couples scored the lowest on what they have in common with each other, compared with couples in 37 other countries (Figure 9.6).

Some countries allow the practice of polygamy (pah-LIGG-uh-mee). Usually, this takes the form of **polygyny** (pah-LIDGE-uh-nee), or having more than one wife, which is a common practice in many areas of Africa and the Middle East, among other places. Although it is rarely practiced in the United States, some small Mormon fundamentalist groups do practice polygyny. Most commonly, a polygynous marriage involves two or three wives, although in Islam a man is allowed up to four.

Some have suggested that polygyny began as a strategy to increase fertility, but the suggestion is controversial. In fact, the majority of studies have found that polygyny is associated with lower

polygyny
The condition or practice of having more than one wife at one time.

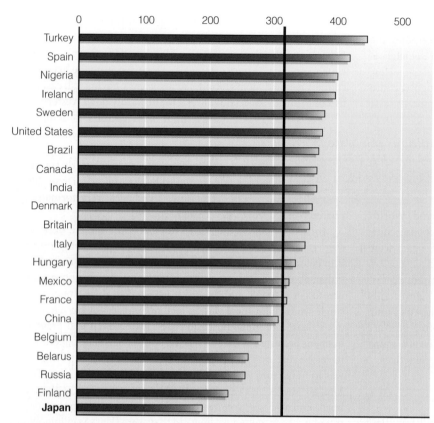

Compatibility of Spouses Index (Average = 316)

| | 0 | 100 | 200 | 300 | 400 | 500 |

Turkey
Spain
Nigeria
Ireland
Sweden
United States
Brazil
Canada
India
Denmark
Britain
Italy
Hungary
Mexico
France
China
Belgium
Belarus
Russia
Finland
Japan

FIGURE 9.6 In a survey by the Dentsu Research Institutes and Leisure Development Center in Japan, spouses answered questions about politics, sex, social issues, religion, and ethics. A score of 500 would indicate perfect compatibility. SOURCE: Who needs love! In Japan, many couples don't. *New York Times*, February 11, 1996, p. A1. Copyright © 1996 by New York Times Co. Reprinted by permission.

Big Love, a television show produced by HBO, explores the life of Bill Hendrickson, a modern polygamist and his three wives.

fertility among wives (Anderton & Emigh, 1989), although a few studies have found no differences and a few have even found higher rates of fertility (Ahmed, 1986). This is because husbands in polygynous marriages must divide their time between each of their wives, which decreases the chance of impregnation for each individual wife. Therefore, it may be more likely that polygyny developed as a strategy for men to gain prestige and power by having many wives, whereas women could gain the protection of a man in countries where there was a scarcity of men (Barber, 2008).

In Islam, a woman may have sex with only one man, but a man may marry up to four wives. Al-Ghazali, the great Islamic thinker and writer of the 11th century, believed that polygyny was permitted because of the desires of men. What determines whether a Muslim man has multiple wives in most Islamic countries today is his wealth more than anything else, for he usually sets up a different household for each wife. Another reason for polygyny in many Muslim countries is the desire for a male child; if one wife does not deliver a male heir, the man may choose a second and third wife in hopes of having a male child (Donnan, 1988).

One woman commented on the negative aspects of polygamy:

You hear everything, your husband and the other wives. You hear how he behaves with his favorite, usually the new one. The women end up hating the man. Everyone feels bad inside. (M. Simons, 1996, p. A1).

However, polygamous husbands have a different view. One polygamous husband says:

My father did it, my grandfather did, so why shouldn't I? When my wife is sick and I don't have another, who will care for me? Besides, one wife on her own is trouble. When there are several, they are forced to be polite and well behaved. If they misbehave, you threaten that you'll take another wife. (M. Simons, 1996, p. A1)

Polyandry (PAH-lee-ann-dree), in which a woman has more than one husband, is much less common than polygyny, and it is usually used to consolidate inheritance. For example, in Tibet, a woman may marry several brothers to avoid dividing up the inherited property. The same rationale is used in many **consanguineous** (con-san-GWIN-ee-us) **marriages,** in which a woman marries her own relative to maintain the integrity of family property.

Marriage between certain blood relatives is illegal in all U.S.

polyandry
The condition or practice of having more than one husband at one time.

consanguineous marriage
A type of marriage between blood relatives, usually to maintain the integrity of family property.

Ron Batzdorff/© HBO/Courtesy: Everett Collection

How would you feel about your mother or father choosing a partner for you to marry? Don't they know you better than anyone else? Although arranged marriages aren't common in the United States today, in large parts of Africa, Asia, and the Middle East, a significant proportion of all marriages are arranged (M. Moore, 1994). Arranged marriages are more common in countries where dating is less prevalent.

Marriage partners are chosen by parents, relatives, friends, and matchmakers based on the prospective partner's finances, family values, status, and perceived compatibility (Batabyal, 2001). Parents or relatives are thought to know their children the best and not be blinded by emotion in choosing a partner for their sons and daughters. Although the relationship does not begin with "love," couples in arranged marriages are thought to fall more in love with their partners because they are from similar families, religions, cultures, and socioeconomic groups (Xiaohe & Whyte, 1990).

Some of the women who are offered as brides come with a dowry (cash or gifts for the groom or the groom's family at the time of the marriage). Although giving and accepting a dowry is illegal in many countries, it is still widely practiced. In fact, despite the changing roles of women in many countries that have a dowry system, the practice and value of the dowry has increased over the years (Srinivasan & Lee, 2004).

The Manhattan-based *India Abroad*, which can be accessed online, runs about 125 classified ads every week for families or others searching for Indian brides and grooms. The ads are very specific about what qualities the potential bride or groom has to offer. For example, a recent search yielded the following results:

[bride] Hindu physician family seeks match for son, 31/6'1", very handsome, fair, athletic, pursuing surgical fellowship at Washington University, St. Louis.

[groom] Hindu Punjabi family invites alliance from tall, handsome and successful professionals (MDs/investment bankers/entrepreneurs) for their very beautiful, vivacious and charming daughter—35/170 (never married); physician at Ivy League hospital in Boston.

[groom] Correspondence invited by Sindhi parents for strikingly attractive accomplished U.S. born MD daughter 33/5'2"/slim working in California. Will relocate.

[bride] Lady companion needed: Handsome, Senior (who lost his wife) from North India, who has just about everything one can think of; seeks wife for travel & to share good things in life.

[groom] Punjabi Khatri parents invite alliance for U.S. Citizen daughter, IT educated, working for City of New York, earning six-figures. Looking for Hindu/Sikh, never-married groom, late 20s up to 33, at least 5'8", willing to relocate.

[groom] Seeking accomplished professional for U.S. born Sikh girl. 29/5'5", beautiful & bright. Ivy League grad. Earning 6 figures & pursuing MBA.

SOURCE: Retrieved February 1, 2011 from http://www.indiaabroad.com/CLASSIFIED/current-listing/2920.shtml.

---

states and has been since the late 19th century. However, in many Muslim countries in northern Africa; western and southern Asia; north, east, and central India; and the middle Asian republics of the former Soviet Union, marriages take place between relatives between 20% and 55% of the time (Bittles et al., 1991). In Islamic societies, marriages between first cousins are most common, whereas in Hindu states of south India, uncle–niece and first cousin marriages are equally common. Incidentally, marriages between certain cousins are legal in many U.S. states.

▶▶ EXTRAMARITAL SEX in Other Cultures

Extramarital sex is forbidden in many cultures but often tolerated—even in cultures in which it is technically not allowed. For example, it is considered a grave transgression in Islam and, according to the Koran, is punishable by 100 lashes for both partners (Farah, 1984). However, there are a number of Muslim societies in areas such as Africa and Pakistan where adultery is tacitly accepted as a fact of life (Donnan, 1988; Kayongo-Male & Onyango, 1984).

Those countries that tolerate extramarital sex often find it more acceptable for men than for women. In Zimbabwe, for example, women were asked what they would do if they found out

their partners were engaging in extramarital sex: 80% reported they would confront their partners, 15% said they would caution their husbands, and 5% were indifferent. However, when men were asked the same question, 60% replied they would divorce their wives, 20% would severely beat their wives, 18% would severely caution her, and 2% would express disappointment and ask their partner to change (Mhloyi, 1990). In China, elderly neighborhood women keep watch in "neighborhood committees" and report suspicious extramarital activities (Ruan & Lau, 2004).

▶▶ DIVORCE IN Other Cultures

Divorce is common in almost all societies, but cultural views are changing as societies develop. In societies such as the United States, Sweden, Russia, and most European countries, divorce is relatively simple and has little stigma. The exceptions are countries that are largely Roman Catholic; because Catholicism does not allow divorce, it can be difficult to obtain in Catholic countries. Ireland legalized divorce in 1995; before this, it was the only country in the Western world to constitutionally ban divorce (Pogatchnik, 1995). In South America, a heavily Roman Catholic continent, Chile was the last country to legalize divorce in late 2004.

Traditional laws about divorce can still be enforced, especially in more patriarchal cultures. Islamic law, like traditional Jewish law, allows a man to divorce his wife simply by repudiating her publicly three times. A wife, on the other hand, must go to court to dissolve a marriage (Rugh, 1984). In Egypt, it is far easier for men to divorce than for women, and because of this only about 33% of divorces in Egypt are initiated by females. In Israel, women need their husband's permission for a divorce, and councils have been set up to try to convince men to let their wives have a divorce.

In 2001, China's government revised its 20-year-old marriage law and included the concept of fault in marriage (Dorgan, 2001; Ruan & Lau, 2004). Before this law was implemented, Chinese couples had an equal division of family property regardless of the reasons for the divorce. Under this new law, however, if a partner is caught engaging in extramarital sex, he can lose everything (research has found that it is mostly men who cheat in China).

The reasons that people get divorced are numerous, although different patterns emerge in different societies. In Egypt, the most common reason given for divorce is infidelity by the husband, whereas among the Hindus of India, the most common reason is cruelty (either physical or mental) from their partner (Pothen, 1989). Arab women's main reasons for divorce include the husband's physical, sexual, or verbal abuse; alcoholism; mental illness; and in-law interference (Savaya & Cohen, 2003). In China, more than 70% of divorces are initiated by women, and the main reason given is an extramarital affair of the husband (Ruan & Lau, 2004). This is also the main reason for divorce in Brazil and many other countries (de Freitas, 2004).

Overall, divorce rates seem to be increasing worldwide as countries modernize and as traditional forms of control over the family lose their power. Only time will tell, however, whether a backlash will stabilize marriage rates, as they seem to be doing in the United States.

*When people are asked what makes them happy, most say **their close relationships** and **feeling loved and needed.***

▶▶ SAME-SEX RELATIONSHIPS in Other Cultures

Same-sex relationships outside the United States are supported in some countries and ignored in others. The Netherlands was the first country to legalize same-sex marriage in 2000, and since then many developed countries have established civil unions or similar legal status to provide same-sex couples with benefits and rights similar to marriage (see the accompanying Timeline of Same-Sex Relationships for more information).

As of 2010, same-sex marriage was legal in Belgium, Canada, Denmark, the Netherlands, South Africa, Spain, Norway, Sweden, Portugal, Iceland, and Argentina. In addition, many other countries have proposed same-sex marriage legislation. Civil unions and domestic or registered partnerships have also be legalized in several countries.

Strongly religious countries, such as Italy, are not supportive of same-sex relationships. Even so, in the city of Padua, Italy, same-sex couples were allowed to have their relationships legally recognized, which met with strong criticism from the Vatican (Shoffman, 2006). Although homosexuality is outlawed in many countries in Africa, legal marriage rights were nonetheless extended to same-sex couples in 2006.

Finally, it is also interesting to note that there are more than 35,000 U.S. citizens living with same-sex foreign partners (Titshaw, 2010). However, because they are not able marry in the majority of U.S. states, many are forced to choose between their foreign partners and their country.

Throughout this chapter, we have explored various aspects of adult sexual relationships. Relationships hold a central place in our lives. When people are asked what makes them happy, most say their close relationships and feeling loved and needed (Perlman, 2007). In the next chapter, we turn our attention to adult sexual behaviors.

◀ review QUESTIONS

1 Explain how marital quality typically changes throughout the life cycle.

2 How does marriage affect a person's health?

3 Explain how sexuality changes throughout marriage and the reasons this might be so.

4 Explain what we know about marital satisfaction in older couples.

5 Explain what is known about dating, marriage, cohabitation, divorce, and same-sex relationships outside the United States.

SUMMARY POINTS

1 Intimate relationships are a fundamental part of human development. Overall, married men and women, gay men, and lesbian women all feel positive about their intimate relationships. Although same-sex couples face more relationship challenges than heterosexual couples, the majority of couples are secure and happy in their relationships.

2 By examining the customs and rules a culture sets up for choosing a mate, we can learn about the level of patriarchy in that particular society, ideals about masculinity and femininity, roles of women and men, the value placed on conformity, the importance of childbearing, the authority of the family, and attitudes toward childhood, pleasure, and responsibility.

3 On college campuses, there have been many recent changes in dating practices. Some researchers argue that college dating doesn't exist. In traditional dating, the boy would pick up the girl at her house, giving her father and mother time to meet with the boy, and then they would go to a well-defined event. The most difficult part of dating is the initial invitation.

4 We are living in a multicultural world. As a result, it is not uncommon to date someone of a different race, religion, or culture. There are still strong social forces that keep the races separate and make it difficult for people to meet. It can be difficult to begin dating again after the end of a marriage or the death of a spouse. Oftentimes this has to do with the fact that the dating environment has changed.

5 Sexual practices have changed on college campuses today. Hooking up, or having a friend with benefits, has become more common. Lesbian women are more likely to self-identify as lesbian before pursuing a sexual relationship with other women, whereas gay men are more likely to pursue sex with men before self-identifying as gay. As people age, their sexual functioning changes, and this can affect their relationships. Sexual inactivity has been found to be a major cause of decreases in sexual functioning.

6 In recent years, cohabitation, or living together outside of marriage, has increased dramatically. In the United States, the typical pattern is to live together before marriage and not in place of marriage. Advantages of cohabitation are that it allows couples to learn more about each other, share finances, and mature in their relationship. Cohabitating couples tend to either marry or separate after just a few years. About 50% of all couples who live together break up within a year or less, and those who marry are at increased risk for divorce. Longer cohabitation has been found to be associated with higher likelihood of divorce.

7 The majority of young people say they are planning and expecting to marry at some point in their lives. The median age for first marriage has been increasing, and in 2010, the age at first marriage was 28.2 for men and 26.1 for women. Marital satisfaction has been found to be related to the quality of the friendship, frequency of pleasurable activities, being able to talk to each other and offer self-disclosure, physical and emotional intimacy, and personality similarities. High rewards–low costs are also important.

8 Marital quality tends to peak in the first few years of a marriage and then declines until midlife, when it rises again. However, the majority of married couples report that their marriages are happy and satisfying. People who are married tend to be happier, healthier, and have longer lives than either widowed or divorced persons of the same age. Marriage has also been found to reduce the impact of several potentially traumatic events including job loss, retirement, and illness. Overall, marriage provides more health benefits to men than women.

9 Marital happiness is higher before having children, declines steadily until it hits a low when the children are in their teens, and then begins to increase once the children leave the house. Many couples do not realize how time-consuming children are, and they find themselves with little leisure time or time to work on their relationship.

10 The higher the frequency of sexual behavior in marriage, the greater the sexual satisfaction. During the early years, sex is more frequent and generally satisfying. During the next 15 or so years, other aspects of life take precedence over sex, and the couple may experience difficulty in maintaining sexual interest in each other. In the later years, men often report more satisfaction with marriage than do women.

11 Almost all couples, whether dating, living together, or married, expect sexual exclusivity from each other. Those who cheat have stronger sexual interests, more permissive sexual values, less satisfaction in their intimate relationship, and more opportunities for sex outside the relationship. Studies on same-sex couples have found that gay men are more likely to cheat than lesbian women.

12 Women experience more emotional distress about infidelity than men do. A woman is also more likely to be upset about emotional infidelity, whereas a man is more likely to be upset about his partner's sexual infidelity. Some couples engage in comarital sex, but the sex is viewed as separate from the marriage.

13 In many ways, same-sex relationships have changed more than heterosexual relationships over the past few decades. Compared with heterosexual couples, gay and lesbian couples have higher levels of relationship satisfaction; share more affection, humor, and joy; and have less fear and negative feelings about the relationship. These relationships often have more equality as well.

14 Many same-sex couples cohabit, whereas others choose civil unions, domestic partnerships, or same-sex marriage. These are legally recognized unions that come with varying rights and benefits determined by the state in which they live.

15 As of mid-2011, same-sex marriage was legal in Massachusetts, Connecticut, Iowa, New Hampshire, Vermont, New York, and the District of Columbia. Societies have always given preference to heterosexual couples, presumably because of the benefits that heterosexual marriages provide to society. Even with all this controversy, many same-sex couples "marry" their partners in ceremonies that are not recognized by the states in which they live.

16 Today, marriage is seen as a partnership between a man and a woman. This shift in perception of marriage has brought with it a shift in divorce. The liberalization of divorce laws has made it easier and less expensive to obtain a divorce. The current U.S. divorce rate remains high compared with earlier times and with other countries. African Americans, Native Americans, and Puerto Ricans show the highest separation and divorce rates in the United States; Korean, Asian Indian, and Chinese Americans have the lowest rates.

17 Certain factors increase the likelihood of divorce. These include marrying at a young age, marrying because of an unplanned pregnancy, having no religious affiliation, being Protestant or a mixed-religion couple, having many communication problems, having divorced before, or having parents who have divorced. Women often have an increase in depression after a divorce, whereas men experience poorer physical and mental health. Men remarry at higher rates than women, and Hispanics and African Americans remarry at lower rates than Whites.

18 In most industrialized countries, dating is the norm. There are still a few industrialized cultures in which arranged marriages take place. Mate selection in most places is a much more individual affair. However, although many in the West believe in the right of individuals to choose their own mates, there were some advantages to parental participation in mate selection, and the transition to individual mate selection in traditional societies is often difficult.

19 Cohabitation is rarer in more traditional societies in which, even if a couple has sex before or instead of marriage, social customs would never tolerate an unmarried heterosexual couple living together openly. In some countries, cohabitation is often a step toward marriage or is seen as a "lower form" of marriage.

20 Marriage ceremonies take place in every society on Earth, but marriage customs vary widely from culture to culture. Some cultures mandate marriages between certain relatives, whereas other cultures allow multiple spouses.

Usually, this takes the form of polygyny, or having more than one wife, which is a common practice in many areas of Africa and the Middle East. Attitudes toward marriage vary in different cultures in different times. Same-sex marriages are legal in some countries outside of the United States. The Netherlands was the first country to allow same-sex marriages. Extramarital sex is forbidden in many cultures, but it is often tolerated even in cultures in which it is technically not allowed.

21 Divorce is common in almost all societies, but cultural views about it are changing as societies develop. In societies such as the United States, Japan, Sweden, Russia, and most European countries, divorce is relatively simple and has little stigma. The exceptions are countries that are largely Roman Catholic, because Catholicism has negative attitudes toward divorce.

CRITICAL THINKING QUESTIONS

1   What are the qualities you look for in a partner? Why do you think these qualities are important to you? Which could you live without? Which are nonnegotiable?

2   Do you ever want to settle down in a lifelong, committed relationship? Why or why not? If so, how long do you think you would want to date someone before settling down for life?

3   How would you feel if your partner cheated on you and engaged in sex outside of your relationship without your knowledge? What would you say to him or her? Have you ever had a conversation about monogamy?

4   Suppose this morning when you woke up, you realized your roommate had another "hookup" last night. How do you feel about his or her frequent hooking up activity? What do you think encourages or discourages hookups on your campus?

5   Pretend you live in a country that practices arranged marriage, and write an informational paragraph about yourself to give to a matchmaker. What would you want the matchmaker to look for in your marriage partner?

6   Jeff and Steve have been dating for 3 years and are ready to commit to each other for life. Do you think their "marriage" should be formally recognized by the law? Why or why not?

7   There have been many changes in the liberalization of divorce laws. Do you think that divorce has become too easy today? Do couples give up on their marriages too soon because of this?

8   Do you think the expansion of marriage rights to same-sex couples erodes or damages heterosexual marriage? Why or why not?

MEDIA **RESOURCES**

CourseMate brings course concepts to life with interactive learning, study, and exam preparation tools that support the printed textbook. A textbook-specific website, Psychology CourseMate includes an integrated interactive eBook and other interactive learning tools including quizzes, flashcards, videos, and more. If your textbook does not include an access code card, go to CengageBrain.com to gain access.

CENGAGENOW   CengageNOW is an easy-to-use online resource that helps you study in less time to get the grade you want—NOW. Take a pre-test for this chapter and receive a personalized study plan based on your results that will identify the topics you need to review and direct you to online resources to help you master those topics. Then take a post-test to help you determine the concepts you have mastered and what you will need to work on. If your textbook does not include an access code card, go to CengageBrain.com to gain access.

View in Video available in CourseMate and CengageNOW:

Dena and Lenny Are Getting Married: An interracial couple discusses their relationship.

Living Together: Pros and Cons: Two heterosexual couples discuss the pros/cons of living together.

Same Sex Marriage: A lesbian woman discusses her commitment ceremony and personal views on same-sex marriage.

Divorce: Betrayal and Sadness: A personal story about the dissolution of a marriage from a woman whose husband left the marriage and children.

Divorce in Japan: A new phenomenon in Japanese culture is the divorce ceremony, marking a fresh start in life for the former bride and groom.

Websites:

The Gottman Institute ■ This website provides information on the work of John Gottman and Julie Schwartz Gottman. They have conducted research on all facets of married life, including parenting issues. The Gottman Institute provides information and training workshops for both gay and straight couples.

Divorce Service Center ■ CompleteCase.com is an online uncontested divorce service center. This site offers assistance with divorce documents without the expenses of a personal lawyer. This is an interesting website that illustrates the changing attitudes about divorce today.

Queendom Tests ■ This Internet magazine includes interactive tests to explore personality, relationships, intelligence, and health. Tests appear in four formats—for lesbians, gay men, heterosexual women, and heterosexual men. Although these tests allow you to explore important issues related to relationships, they are not scholarly or scientific.

Romance 101 ■ Hosted by womensforum.com, this website contains humorous information about relationships, including information about men's and women's views on dating, romance, and the "dating bill of rights." This is a fun place to visit for a lighthearted look at romance.

10 Sexual Expression

View in Video

View in Video

View in Video

View in Video

▶ **ABOUT THE CHAPTER OPENING VIDEO** – The popularity of the Internet has raised some interesting issues related to sexual behaviors and intimate relationships. Endless sex-related websites, online pornography, and sexual chat rooms lure many of us, often causing problems in our personal relationships. Students often ask me whether or not "virtual sex" constitutes cheating—if you have "sex" with someone online are you cheating on your partner? Heidi's story really made me think about this question. Prior to starting college she had been dating her high school sweetheart for two years. They were inseparable and as a result, neither of them had many friends. When Heidi left for college their relationship became long-distance. They would see each other once or twice a month, but since Jason didn't have access to the Internet, their only communication was done by phone. Heidi had a single room her freshman year, but without Jason around she was very lonely. One night she decided to look online for people to talk to and her searches led her to a site with several sexual chat rooms. She figured it wouldn't hurt anything just to talk to some of the people in the chat room.

When I first went into the chat room I noticed that most of the people there were men. I was worried about being there so I just blocked my video and only talked with some of them. I could see that some of the people were naked and doing sexual things, such as masturbating or using sex toys. Some rooms had couples having sex or doing other sexual things. The guys kept telling me to turn on my video. They'd tell me I was so beautiful and that I needed to share my body. They were very persistent. Soon I decided there would be no harm in turning my video on because I was fully dressed. I would spend so much time in these chat rooms. Over the next couple of weeks, I can't really explain what happened. I found myself actually looking forward to my

Hola Images/Getty Images

online chat sessions. I would spend time on my hair and makeup and I began to feel really pretty. The men online would all tell me how beautiful and sexy I was and I began to believe them. One day I found myself riding on the bus thinking how PUMPED I was because everyone looking at me must have thought I was so young and innocent, but inside I knew I was really naughty. After awhile, though, I started thinking that I needed to tell Jason about my sexual chats. When I gathered enough courage to tell him, I was totally unprepared for his reaction.

Heidi's experience in sexual chat rooms was really interesting and my interview with her really illustrates the effects that "virtual sex" can have on an intimate relationship. ▐▐

Janell Caush

"Everyone thought I was so young and innocent, but I knew I was really naughty." —CHAPTER OPENING VIDEO

View in **Video**

To watch the entire interview, go to Psychology CourseMate at **login.cengagebrain.com.**

© Matthew Sorenson

Human sexuality is a complex part of life, with cultural, psychological, and biological influences shaping how people choose to express their sexuality. Some adults choose not to engage in sexual behavior, whereas others may choose to experiment with various sexual behaviors. Celibacy, or abstinence, occurs when a person chooses not to engage in sexual behavior (most notably penetrative intercourse, such as vaginal or anal sex). People may choose abstinence for many reasons (e.g., religious values, fear of physical consequences, past negative experiences, or wanting to "save" themselves for the right person; Raspberry, 2007). Some people remain abstinent their whole lives and have no sexual partners (may also be referred to as asexuality), whereas others may go through life with just one partner, and still others have multiple partners. The National Survey of Sexual Health and Behavior (NSSHB) found that our sexual repertoire varies with age, health, and ethnicity (Herbenick et al., 2010).

In this chapter, we explore the various influences on sexuality, review the human sexual response cycle, and explore various ways that adults express their sexuality.

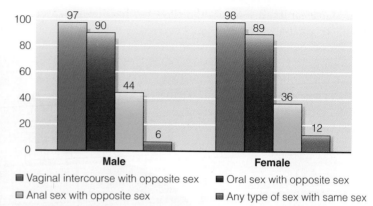

FIGURE **10.1** Lifetime sexual behavior among men and women aged 25–44 years in the U.S., 2006–2008. SOURCE: Chandra et al., 2011.

INFLUENCES on Sexuality

Our sexual attitudes and behaviors are shaped by many factors, including hormones, culture, ethnicity, religion, and the media. As we grow, we learn strong messages about acceptable and unacceptable sexual behaviors from the culture at large, our family, social classes, and even our language. In this section, we discuss four of the biggest influences: hormones and neurotransmitters, family background, ethnicity, and religion.

HORMONES and Neurotransmitters

Hormones and **neurotransmitters** both have powerful effects on our bodies. In most animals, the brain controls and regulates sexual behavior chiefly through hormones and neurotransmitters, and these both have an enormous effect on sexual behavior in humans as well (Krüger et al., 2006). We discussed hormones in Chapters 5 and 6 and reviewed the various endocrine glands that secrete hormones into the bloodstream, carrying them throughout the body. Sexologists believe that testosterone is the most influential hormone in the sexual behavior of both men and women. Estrogen also plays a role in regulating the sexual behavior of both sexes. Both men and women produce these hormones, although in differing quantities. For example, in men, testosterone is produced in the testes and adrenal glands, and in women, testosterone is produced in the adrenal glands and ovaries. Even so, men produce much more testosterone than women: Men produce 260 to 1,000 nanograms per deciliter (ng/dL) of blood plasma (a nanogram is one billionth of a gram), whereas women produce about 15 to 70 ng/dL. The amount also varies and decreases with age.

Women's estrogen levels decline during menopause, which can lead to slower growth in the vaginal cells, resulting in thinner vaginal walls, vaginal dryness, and decreased vaginal sensitivity.

neurotransmitters
Specialized chemical messengers in the body that transmit messages from one nerve cell to another.

Despite this decrease in estrogen, testosterone levels often remain constant, which may result in an increase in sexual desire even though the physical changes of menopause can negatively affect sexual functioning. In men, decreases in testosterone can lead to lessening sexual desire and decreases in the quality and quantity of erections. We discuss aging and sexuality in more detail later in this chapter.

Neurotransmitters, chemical messengers in the body that transmit messages from one nerve cell to another, also have a powerful effect on our bodies. Various neurotransmitters, including oxytocin, serotonin, dopamine, and vasopressin, have been found to affect sexual desire, arousal, orgasm, and our desire to couple with certain partners (Ishak et al., 2008; Kosfeld et al., 2005; Lim & Young, 2006; Walch et al., 2001; K. A. Young et al., 2008; L. J. Young & Wang, 2004). Directly after orgasm, levels of serotonin, oxytocin, and vasopressin increase, which can lead to feelings of pleasure, relaxation, and attachment (Fisher, 2004). Researchers have also explored using various neurotransmitters to eliminate sexual urges and desires in sexual offenders (Saleh & Berlin, 2003).

Although hormones and neurotransmitters are important, our social experiences are as well. Unlike animals, humans are strongly influenced by learned experiences and their social, cultural, and ethnic environment.

FAMILY Background

Our family of origin is our first reference group and we internalize norms about sexual attitudes and behaviors from our interactions with our family (Davidson et al., 2008). Although the influence of our family is tied into our culture and religion, there have been some interesting studies about many aspects of the influences of family, including family composition. Students who come from households with married parents and traditional family backgrounds have been found to have more conservative attitudes about sexual behavior (Davidson et al., 2008). They are more likely to have witnessed displays of affection between their parents and to have talked to one or both parents about sex. Overall, men and women from such homes have fewer lifetime sexual partners.

Ethnic differences in family composition reveal that Black college students are more likely than students of other ethnicities to have divorced, separated, or never-married parents (Davidson et al., 2008). Research has found that Black teens engage in vaginal intercourse earlier than other ethnicities and have lower rates of contraceptive use, higher pregnancy and birth rates, and the highest rates of adult sexual behavior (Buffardi et al., 2008; Davidson et al., 2008; Eaton et al., 2006; Eisenberg, 2001; Forhan, 2008; Herbenick et al., 2010a; Sharp & Ispa, 2009; Ventura et al., 2007). Although experts in family systems would say that these events are closely tied to family background, there are several other potential issues to consider, such as poverty, discrimination, and racism (Sharp & Ispa, 2009). We will talk more about ethnicity and family influences later in this section.

▶▶ ETHNICITY

Our ethnicity forms a barrier, a "sexualized perimeter," that helps us decide who we let in for sex and who we keep out (Nagel, 2003). It also affects our sexual attitudes, our ability to communicate about sex, which sexual behaviors we engage in, and the frequency of these behaviors (Quadagno et al., 1998). Many studies have explored sexual behavior in racial and ethnic minorities (Davidson

et al., 2008; Dodge et al., 2010; Eisenman & Dantzker, 2006; Laumann et al., 1994). Race has been found to be one of the most influential variables that affect both sexual attitudes and behaviors (Davidson et al., 2008).

We will explore ethnic and racial differences throughout this chapter, but as we discussed, the highest levels of sexual behavior are among Blacks, followed by Whites, Hispanic Americans, and Asian Americans (Davidson et al., 2008; Eisenberg, 2001; Fryar et al., 2007; see Figure 10.2 for more information about ethnicity/race, gender, and sexual behavior). However, the rates of sexual behavior have increased the most among White women (Dodge et al., 2010).

Keep in mind that many racial and ethnic identities are closely tied to religious affiliation. For example, although studies have found that Hispanic college students are more conservative and less permissive about sexual behaviors than many other students, this may also be because a large number of Hispanics are Catholic (Davidson et al., 2008). Let's discuss the impact of religion on sexual behavior.

▶▶ RELIGION

Religiosity and strength of religious beliefs also influence sexual attitudes and behavior (Daniluk & Browne, 2008; Eisenman & Dantzker, 2006; Laumann et al., 1994; Murray et al., 2007; Njus & Bane, 2009). The more religious people are, the more conservative their sexual behavior tends to be. For example, men and women with high levels of religiosity are more likely to have conservative attitudes about sex and engage in less premarital sexual intercourse; are less likely to engage in risky sexual behavior; are less approving of certain types of sexual behaviors, such as oral sex; and experience more guilt about sexual behavior (Daniluk &

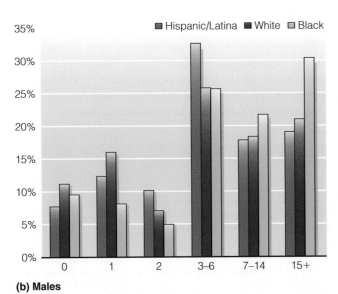

(a) Females

(b) Males

FIGURE **10.2** Number of other-sex partners in lifetime for females (a) and males (b) 15 to 44 years old in the United States by ethnicity/race, 2006–2008. SOURCE: Chandra et al., 2011.

In early 2011, Brandon Davies, a Brigham Young University starting basketball player, was suspended from the team for engaging in consensual sex with his girlfriend. The school's honor code prohibits premarital sex.

© Craig Bennett/Icon SMI/Corbis

Browne, 2008; Eisenman & Dantzker, 2006; Njus & Bane, 2009). In addition, religious men and women have fewer partners (Davidson et al., 2008; Murray et al., 2007). A meta-analysis of 40 studies found a negative correlation between religiosity and premarital sex—those with higher levels of religiosity engaged in less premarital sexual activity.

1 Identify the most influential hormones and neurotransmitters in sexual behavior and explain their roles in sexual behavior.

2 Explain how our family background can affect sexual behavior.

3 Explain how ethnicity and culture can affect sexual behavior.

4 Explain how religion may influence sexual behavior.

▶ STUDYING Sexual Response

A series of physiological and psychological changes occur in the body during sexual behavior, referred to collectively as our **sexual response.** Over the years, several models of these changes have been proposed to explain the exact progression and nature of the human sexual response. These models are beneficial in helping physicians and therapists identify how dysfunction, disease, illness, and disability affect sexual functioning. The most well-known model has been Masters and Johnson's sexual response cycle. Many other sex therapists and sexologists have criticized and suggested changes to this model throughout the years.

▶▶ MASTERS AND JOHNSON'S
Sexual Response Cycle

Based on their laboratory work (see Chapter 2), William Masters and Virginia Johnson proposed a four-phase model of physiological arousal known as the **sexual response cycle** (see Figure 10.3). This cycle occurs during all sexual behaviors in which a person progresses from excitement to orgasm, whether it is through oral or anal sex, masturbation, or vaginal intercourse. These physiological processes are similar for all sexual relationships, whether they are between heterosexual or homosexual partners.

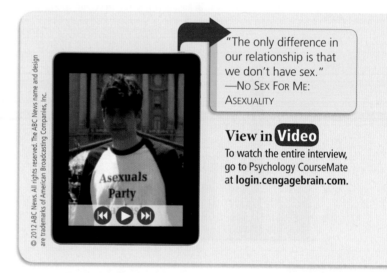

"The only difference in our relationship is that we don't have sex."
—NO SEX FOR ME: ASEXUALITY

View in Video
To watch the entire interview, go to Psychology CourseMate at **login.cengagebrain.com.**

The four phases of the sexual response cycle are **excitement, plateau, orgasm,** and **resolution.** The two primary physical changes that occur during the sexual response cycle are **vasocongestion** (VAZ-oh-conn-jest-shun) and **myotonia** (my-uh-TONE-ee-uh), which we will discuss in greater detail shortly.

sexual response
Series of physiological and psychological changes that occur in the body during sexual behavior.

sexual response cycle
Four-stage model of sexual arousal proposed by Masters and Johnson.

excitement
The first stage of the sexual response cycle, in which an erection occurs in males and vaginal lubrication occurs in females.

plateau
The second stage of the sexual response cycle, occurring before orgasm, in which vasocongestion builds up.

orgasm
The third stage of the sexual response cycle, which involves an intense sensation during the peak of sexual arousal and results in a release of sexual tension.

resolution
The fourth stage of the sexual response cycle, in which the body returns to the prearoused state.

vasocongestion
An increase in the blood concentrated in the male and female genitals, as well as in the female breasts, during sexual activity.

myotonia
Involuntary contractions of the muscles.

transudation
The lubrication of the vagina during sexual arousal.

tenting effect
During sexual arousal in females, the cervix and uterus pull up, and the upper third of the vagina balloons open, making a larger opening in the cervix.

Sexual Response Cycle in Women

Sexual response patterns vary among women (and in the same woman depending on her menstrual cycle). These variations can be attributed to the amount of time spent in each phase. For example, more time spent during arousal in foreplay may result in a greater orgasmic response. The intensity of the response may also be affected by factors such as menstrual cycle and previous child-bearing. However, even with these differences, the basic physical response is always the same.

EXCITEMENT PHASE The first phase, excitement, begins with vasocongestion, an increase in the blood concentrated in the genitals, breasts, or both. Vasocongestion is the principal physical component of sexual arousal (Frohlich & Meston, 2000). Many circumstances can induce excitement, including hearing your partner's voice, seeing an erotic picture, having a fantasy, or being touched a certain way. Within 30 seconds, vasocongestion causes the vaginal walls to begin lubricating, a process called **transudation** (trans-SUE-day-shun). If a woman is lying down (which is common during foreplay), the process of lubricating the vaginal walls may take a little longer than if she is standing up. This may help explain why it takes most women longer than men to feel physically ready to have sexual intercourse. During the excitement phase, the walls of the vagina, which usually lie flat together, expand. This has also been called the **tenting effect** (see Figure 10.4).

During sexual arousal in women who have not had children, the labia majora thin out and become flattened, and may pull slightly away from the introitus. The labia minora often turn bright pink and begin to increase in size. The increase in size of the vaginal lips adds an average of 0.5 to 1 inch of length to the vaginal canal.

The breasts also experience changes during this phase. Nipple erections may occur in one or both breasts, and the areolas enlarge (Figure 10.5). The breasts enlarge, which may cause an increased definition of the veins in the breasts, especially if a woman has large breasts and is fair skinned.

Because of the increased vascularity (blood flow) to the genitals during pregnancy and childbirth, women who have had children have a more rapid increase in vasocongestion and enlargement of both the labia majora and minora, which may become

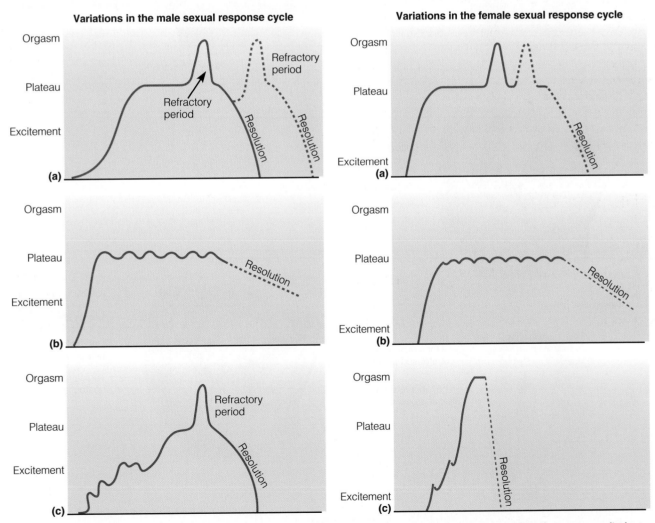

FIGURE 10.3 Variations within male and female response cycles. SOURCE: Masters, W., Johnson, V., & Kolodny, R. (1994). *Heterosexuality* (pp. 51–52). New York: HarperCollins Publishers. Copyright © 1994 by William H. Masters, Virginia E. Johnson, and Robert C. Kolodny. Reprinted by permission of HarperCollins Publishers, Inc.

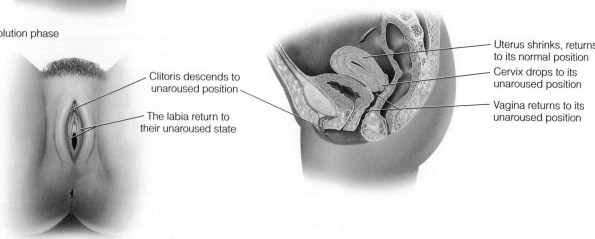

Excitement phase

The clitoral glans and the labia swell resulting from vasocongestion

Vagina begins to lubricate

Clitoris

Labia majora

Labia minora

Plateau phase

Clitoris retracts under hood

Labia minora increase in size and turn reddish purple

Bartholin's glands secrete fluid

Uterus elevates and increases in size

Inner two-thirds of vagina expands and lengthens

Outer thrid of vagina forms orgasmic platform

Orgasmic phase

Uterus contracts

Orgasmic platform contracts

Rectal sphincter contracts

Resolution phase

Clitoris descends to unaroused position

The labia return to their unaroused state

Uterus shrinks, returns to its normal position

Cervix drops to its unaroused position

Vagina returns to its unaroused position

FIGURE 10.4 Internal and external changes in the female sexual response cycle. SOURCE: Masters, W., Johnson, V., & Kolodny, R. (1994). *Heterosexuality.* New York: HarperCollins Publishers. Copyright © 1994 by William H. Masters, Virginia E. Johnson, and Robert C. Kolodny. Reprinted by permission of Harper-Collins Publishers, Inc.

two to three times larger by the end of the excitement phase. Vasocongestion may also cause the clitoral glans to become erect, depending on the type and intensity of stimulation. Generally, the more direct the stimulation, the more engorged the entire clitoral organ will become. Sexual arousal may also be facilitated by the neurotransmitter serotonin, which we discussed earlier in this chapter (Frohlich & Meston, 2000).

The excitement phase can last anywhere from a few minutes to hours. Toward the end of the excitement phase, a woman may experience a **sex flush,** which resembles a rash. This usually begins on the chest and, during the plateau stage, spreads from the breasts to the neck and face, shoulders, arms, abdomen, thighs, buttocks, and back. Women report varied sensations during the excitement phase, which are often felt all over the body, rather than being concentrated in one area.

PLATEAU PHASE Women often need more time than men to reach the plateau phase, because they have a larger and more vascular pelvic area, requiring more intense vasocongestion. Once they reach this stage, breast size continues to increase, and the nipples may remain erect. The clitoral glans retracts behind the clitoral hood anywhere from 1 to 3 minutes before orgasm, and just before orgasm, the clitoris may not be visible at all. Masters and Johnson claim that it is the clitoral hood rubbing and pulling over the clitoris that is responsible for the orgasm during sexual intercourse.

During sexual arousal in women who have not had children, the labia majora are difficult to detect, because of the flattened-out appearance. The labia minora, in contrast, often turn a brilliant red. In women who have had children, the labia majora become very engorged with blood and turn a darker red, almost burgundy. At this point, if sexual stimulation were to stop, the swelling of the clitoris and labia, which can continue for anywhere from a few minutes to hours, can be very uncomfortable. Orgasm helps to relieve this pressure, whether through masturbation or sexual activity with another person. Overall, the plateau stage may last anywhere from 30 seconds to 3 minutes.

REAL RESEARCH 10.1 Although orgasms experienced during masturbation are more physiologically intense than orgasms during partner sex, orgasms during masturbation provide less overall sexual satisfaction than orgasms experienced during partner sex (LEVIN, 2007; MAH & BINIK, 2005).

ORGASM PHASE At the end of the plateau phase, vasocongestion in the pelvis creates an **orgasmic platform** in the lower third of the vagina, labia minora (and labia majora in women who have had children), and uterus (see Figure 10.4). When this pressure reaches a certain point, a reflex in the surrounding muscles is set off, causing vigorous contractions. These contractions expel the blood that is trapped in the surrounding tissues and, in doing so, cause pleasurable orgasmic sensations. Myotonia of the pelvic muscles is primarily responsible for these contractions; without these muscles (as in the case of a woman who has had a hysterec-

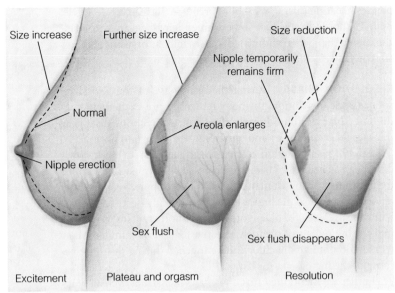

FIGURE **10.5** Breast changes in the female sexual response cycle. SOURCE: Masters, W., Johnson, V., & Kolodny, R. (1994). *Heterosexuality* (p. 59). New York: HarperCollins Publishers. Copyright © 1994 by William H. Masters, Virginia E. Johnson, and Robert C. Kolodny. Reprinted by permission of HarperCollins Publishers, Inc.

tomy, the surgical removal of the uterus), the orgasmic response may be significantly reduced.

Muscular contractions occur about every 0.8 second during orgasm. In total, there are about 8 to 15 contractions, and the first 5 or 6 are felt most strongly. In women, contractions last longer than in men. A possible explanation for this is that vasocongestion occurs in the entire pelvic region in women (the internal clitoral organ fills the pelvic region), whereas it is very localized in men (mainly in the penis and testicles). Because of this, women need more muscle contractions to remove the built-up blood supply. In Chapter 2, we discussed Freud's two types of orgasms, the clitoral and the vaginal. Today, we know that all orgasms in women are thought to be the result of direct or indirect clitoral stimulation, even though orgasms might feel different.

During orgasm, there is a release of vasocongestion and muscle tension. The body may shudder, jerk uncontrollably, or spasm. In addition, orgasms may involve facial grimacing, groans, spasms in the hands and feet, contractions of the gluteal and abdominal muscles, and contractions of the orgasmic platform. Peaks in blood pressure and respiration patterns have been found during both male and female orgasms.

Kinsey reported that 14% of women regularly experienced **multiple orgasms,** and although Masters and Johnson believed all women were capable of such orgasms, the majority of women they studied did not experience them. Multiple orgasms are more likely to occur from direct stimulation of the clitoris, rather than from

sex flush
A temporary reddish color change of the skin that sometimes develops during sexual excitement.

orgasmic platform
The thickening of the walls of the lower third of the vagina.

multiple orgasms
More than one orgasm experienced within a short period.

penile thrusting during vaginal intercourse. Research into the female G-spot indicates that some women may have an area inside the vagina that, when stimulated, causes intense orgasms and possibly female ejaculation of fluid (see Chapter 5).

RESOLUTION PHASE During the last phase of the sexual response cycle, resolution, the body returns to pre-excitement conditions. The extra blood leaves the genitals, erections disappear, muscles relax, and heart and breathing rates return to normal.

After orgasm, the skin is often sweaty, and the sex flush slowly disappears. The breasts begin to decrease in size, usually within 5 to 10 minutes. Many women appear to have nipple erections after an orgasm because the breast as a whole quickly decreases in size while the areolae are still engorged. The clitoris returns to its original size but remains extremely sensitive for several minutes. Many women do not like the clitoris to be touched during this time because of the increased sensitivity.

Earlier we mentioned that a woman's menstrual cycle may influence her sexual responsiveness. Research has found that sexual excitement occurs more frequently during the last 14 days of a woman's menstrual cycle (Sherfey, 1972). During this time, more lubrication is produced during the excitement phase, which may be because of the increased vasocongestion. Orgasms can be very helpful in reducing cramps during menstruation, presumably because they help to relieve the buildup of pelvic vasocongestion that may occur as a side effect of menstruation (Ellison, 2000).

Sexual Response Cycle in Men

The sexual response cycle in males is similar to that of females, with vasocongestion and myotonia leading to physiological changes in the body (see Figure 10.6). However, in men, the four phases are less well defined.

REAL RESEARCH 10.2 Male ejaculation has been found to have physiological benefits for women, as well as for men. In men, regular ejaculations help keep sperm morphology (form and structure) and semen volume within normal ranges, and the deposit of sperm in the vaginal canal has been found to regulate ovulatory cycles, enhance mood, and reduce vaginal atrophy (a decrease in tissue firmness) in aging women (LEVIN, 2007).

EXCITEMENT PHASE During the excitement phase, the penis, like the clitoris in women, begins to fill with blood and become erect. Erection, or **tumescence** (too-MESS-cents), begins quickly during excitement, generally within 3 to 5 seconds (although the speed of this response lengthens with age). The excitement phase of the sexual response cycle in men is often very short, unless a man uses deliberate attempts to lengthen it. Often this causes **detumescence** (dee-too-MESS-cents), a gradual loss of tumescence. Distractions during the excitement phase (such as a roommate walking into the room) may also cause detumescence. However, once the plateau stage is reached, an erection is often more stable and less sensitive to outside influences.

ON YOUR MIND 10.1

I've heard that many women fake orgasm. Why would they do that?

It might surprise you, but both men and women report having faked orgasms at some point in their lives (Knox et al., 2008; Muehlenhard & Shippee, 2010). As for female faking, the National Survey on Sexual Health and Behavior found that although 85% of men said their female partner reached orgasm the last time they had sex, only 64% of women said they did (Herbenick et al., 2010). Although there are several potential reasons for this difference (see the Sex in Real Life feature on "Research and Skepticism" in Chapter 2), it is possible that some of the partners of the men who responded to the survey were faking. Women fake orgasm for several reasons, including not knowing what type of physical stimulation would lead to orgasm, wanting to end a sexual encounter, or to avoid hurting a partner's feelings (because we live in a culture that often expects men to provide women's orgasms, a woman might fake to minimize any negative feelings in her partner; Muehlenhard & Shippee, 2010). Men have also been known to fake orgasms, and although the majority report doing so during vaginal intercourse, some men report faking orgasm during oral sex, manual stimulation, and/or phone sex (Muehlenhard & Shippee, 2010). Men's reasons for faking are similar to women's, but common reasons are because they are tired or don't feel that orgasm is possible. In all of these instances, partners are giving false information, and even though they are probably doing it under the guise of good intentions, open, honest communication about sexual needs and feelings is a far better strategy.

During the excitement phase, the testicles also increase in size, becoming up to 50% larger. This is both a vasocongestive and myotonic response. The cremaster muscle pulls the testicles closer to the body to avoid injury during thrusting (see Chapter 6 for more information about this muscle). If sexual stimulation were to stop at this point, the swelling in the testicles may be uncomfortable.

PLATEAU PHASE All of these physical changes continue during the plateau phase. Some men may experience a sex flush, which is identical to the sex flush women experience. In addition, it is not uncommon for men to have nipple erections. Just before orgasm, the glans penis becomes engorged (this is comparable with the engorgement of the clitoral glans in women). At this point, a few drops of pre-ejaculatory fluid from the Cowper's gland may appear on the glans of the penis.

ORGASM PHASE Orgasm and ejaculation do not always occur together (see Figure 10.6). In fact, there are men who are able to have orgasms without ejaculating and can have several orgasms

---

tumescence
The swelling of the penis because of vasocongestion, causing an erection.

detumescence
The return of an erect penis to the flaccid state.

ejaculatory inevitability
A feeling that ejaculation can no longer be controlled.

before ejaculating. Although it is rare, some men are capable of anywhere from 2 to 16 orgasms before ejaculation, although the ability to have them decreases with age (Chia & Abrams, 1997; J. Johnson, 2001).

If orgasm and ejaculation occur at the same time, ejaculation can occur in two stages. During the first stage, which lasts only a few seconds, there are contractions in the vas deferens, seminal vesicles, and prostate gland. These contractions lead to **ejaculatory inevitability,** whereby just before orgasm there is a feeling that ejaculation can no longer be controlled. In the second stage, the semen is forced out of the urethra by muscle contractions (the same set of muscles that contract in female orgasm).

The first three or four contractions are the most pleasurable and tend to be the most forceful (various herbal and drug products have recently appeared on the market claiming to increase male orgasmic contractions; see the accompanying Sex in Real Life). The force of the ejaculation can propel semen up to 24 inches, although this distance is considerably shorter in older men. After these major contractions, minor ones usually follow, even if stimulation stops. As with women, the muscular contractions during orgasm occur about every 0.8 second.

Some men are able to experience multiple orgasms, whereby the orgasm phase leads directly into another orgasm without a refractory period. Research has found that some men are able to

teach themselves how to have multiple orgasms (Chia & Abrams, 1997; J. Johnson, 2001). The Chinese were the first to learn how to achieve multiple orgasm by delaying and withholding ejaculation. Some men learn to separate orgasm and ejaculation, thereby allowing themselves to learn to become multiorgasmic. The average number of orgasms a multiorgasmic man can have varies between two and nine orgasms per sexual interaction (Chia & Abrams, 1997; Dunn & Trost, 1989).

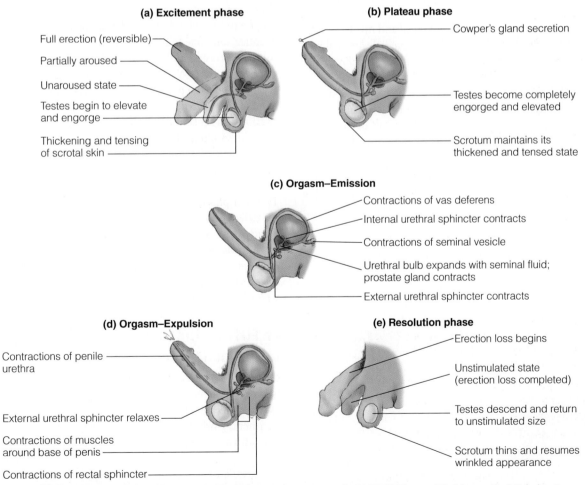

(a) Excitement phase
- Full erection (reversible)
- Partially aroused
- Unaroused state
- Testes begin to elevate and engorge
- Thickening and tensing of scrotal skin

(b) Plateau phase
- Cowper's gland secretion
- Testes become completely engorged and elevated
- Scrotum maintains its thickened and tensed state

(c) Orgasm–Emission
- Contractions of vas deferens
- Internal urethral sphincter contracts
- Contractions of seminal vesicle
- Urethral bulb expands with seminal fluid; prostate gland contracts
- External urethral sphincter contracts

(d) Orgasm–Expulsion
- Contractions of penile urethra
- External urethral sphincter relaxes
- Contractions of muscles around base of penis
- Contractions of rectal sphincter

(e) Resolution phase
- Erection loss begins
- Unstimulated state (erection loss completed)
- Testes descend and return to unstimulated size
- Scrotum thins and resumes wrinkled appearance

FIGURE **10.6** External and internal changes in the male sexual response cycle. SOURCE: Masters, W., Johnson, V., & Kolodny, R. (1994). *Heterosexuality* (p. 60). New York: HarperCollins Publishers. Copyright © 1994 by William H. Masters, Virginia E. Johnson, and Robert C. Kolodny. Reprinted by permission of HarperCollins Publishers, Inc.

RESOLUTION PHASE   Directly after ejaculation, the glans of the penis decreases in size, even before general penile detumescence. During the resolution phase of sexual response, when the body is returning to its prearousal state, men go into a **refractory stage,** during which they cannot be restimulated to orgasm for a certain time period. The refractory period gets longer as men get older (we discuss this further later in this chapter). Younger men, in contrast, may experience another erection soon after an ejaculation.

Masters and Johnson's model of sexual response is the most comprehensive model sexologists use. It has not been without controversy, however. Many feminist therapists believe that Masters and Johnson's sexual response cycle should not be used universally for classification and diagnosis of sexual dysfunctions (we will discuss this more later in this chapter). What has happened is that the definition of healthy sexuality has been focused on orgasm and has given less importance to emotions and relationships (Tiefer, 2001). Other researchers would say that the model of sexuality that values performance, penetration, and orgasm is a male model of sexuality (Burch, 1998). Often this belief leads to a view of female sexuality that is passive and even nonexistent.

▶▶ HELEN SINGER KAPLAN'S **Triphasic Model**

Unlike Masters and Johnson's model, Kaplan believes sexual response starts with a psychological component. Kaplan's model of sexual response is called the **triphasic model,** and it includes sexual desire, excitement, and orgasm (Figure 10.7). Although Kaplan's second and third stages are physiological and involve genital vasocongestion and muscular contractions, sexual desire is of paramount importance, because without sexual desire, the physiological functions cannot occur.

Kaplan believes that many factors may block sexual desire, such as depression, pain, fear, medications, or past sexual abuse. We discuss the importance of the desire phase and disorders associated with it in Chapter 14. An advantage to Kaplan's model is that it is easier to conceptualize than Masters and Johnson's model. For example, most of us can recognize and differentiate desire, excitement, and orgasm but may have a difficult time recognizing when we are in Masters and Johnson's plateau phase.

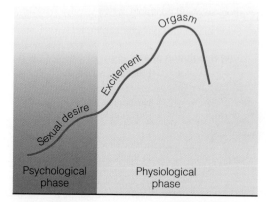

FIGURE **10.7** Helen Singer Kaplan's three-stage model of sexual response includes the psychological phase of sexual desire and two physiological stages of excitement and orgasm. Copyright © Cengage Learning 2013

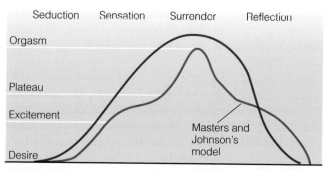

FIGURE **10.8** David Reed's Erotic Stimulus Pathway (ESP) model blends features of Masters and Johnson's and Kaplan's models using four phases: seduction, sensation, surrender, and reflection. Copyright © Cengage Learning 2013

However, Beverly Whipple, who researched and reported on the G-spot in women, criticized the Kaplan model for being based on the male linear model of sexual function (Sugrue & Whipple, 2001). She contends that women can experience sexual arousal, orgasm, and satisfaction without sexual desire, and can experience desire, arousal, and satisfaction without orgasm.

▶▶ DAVID REED'S **Erotic Stimulus Pathway**

David Reed's Erotic Stimulus Pathway (ESP) model blends features of Masters and Johnson's and Kaplan's models and uses four phases, including seduction, sensation, surrender, and reflection (Figure 10.8). Seduction includes all those things that we might do to entice someone to have sex with us—what we wear, perfume or cologne, flowers, and so on. In the next stage of sensation, our senses take over. What we hear, smell, taste, touch, and fantasize about all have the potential to turn us on and enhance our excitement. This, in turn, moves us into the plateau phase. Both the seduction and sensation phase are psychosocial, and they contribute to our physiological response.

In the third phase, surrender—orgasm—occurs. Reed believes that we need to be able to let go and let ourselves reach orgasm. Too much control or not enough may interfere with this response. The final phase of Reed's model is the reflection phase, in which we reflect on the sexual experience. Whether the experience was positive or negative will affect future sexual functioning.

Beverly Whipple expanded Reed's Erotic Stimulus Pathway to demonstrate that if the sexual experience was pleasant and produced satisfaction, then it could lead to the seduction phase of the next sexual experience (Whipple & Brash-McGreer, 1997).

▶▶ FUTURE DIRECTIONS
in Sexual Response Models

One of the chief critics of medically based sexual response models is Leonore Tiefer, a noted feminist sexologist. Tiefer has practiced as a sex therapist for many years in a hospital-based urology department, working with couples in whom the male partner presents with a sexual problem. Tiefer suggests that Masters and John-

---

refractory stage
The period after an ejaculation in which men cannot be stimulated to another orgasm.

triphasic model
A model of sexual response, proposed by Helen Singer Kaplan, which includes three phases.

Sex in Real Life ▶▶ Sexual Performance Scams

Is it possible to take an over-the-counter drug to improve your sex drive, erections, or orgasms? Will $59.95 buy you a 1-month supply of awesome orgasms? How much would you pay to find out? Although we discuss the use of aphrodisiacs in Chapter 14, here we consider those advertisements that clog our email accounts and appear in many magazines, promoting better sex.

Over the years, I've had many male students ask me about a drug called

Mioplex. This "male orgasm intensifier" has intrigued many college students, a group the company tends to target. Produced in Europe, Mioplex claims that it can increase a man's "ropes," or number of physical ejaculatory contractions during orgasm. It also claims that increasing a man's ejaculatory contractions will help female partners to have better and longer orgasms. Mioplex is a flower seed extract, which has been unavailable in the United States but can be ordered online.

These vitamins or health food supplements are considered "food" items and not drugs—as such, they don't have to be approved by the U.S. Food and Drug Administration. There is no guarantee that they work, and they may cause adverse effects. The bottom line on products like this is that many are ineffective. But an interesting question remains: Why would so many people be so willing to pay for such products?

son's model leaves out important aspects of sexual functioning because it focuses exclusively on adequate genital functioning—vasocongestion, myotonia, physical excitement, and orgasm (Tiefer, 2001). As Tiefer characterizes the perspective of the medical model, "If it's wet and hard and works, it's normal; if it's not, it's not" (Tiefer, 2001).

Tiefer believes that pleasure, emotionality, sensuality, cultural differences, power issues, and communication are important components of sexual response. Women's sexual experiences do not fit neatly into Masters and Johnson's four stages, according to Tiefer, and as a result, women complain of desire and arousal issues and other difficulties in emotionality, sensitivity, or connectedness (Tiefer, 2001).

Rosemary Basson (2000) agreed with Tiefer and believes women's motivations for sex are more complex than men's motivations. Although many men experience sexual arousal with a genital response (i.e., erection), sexual arousal in women is often dependent on various thoughts and feelings (Basson, 2005). She believes that the decision to have sex for many women is driven by the desire for intimacy. A woman might agree to sex for a variety of reasons: to express feelings for her partner, to feel emotionally closer to her partner, to feel wanted and needed, or to receive and share pleasure (Basson, 2005). These motivations lead to a conscious decision to focus on sexual stimuli, which can lead to sexual arousal. Like Tiefer, Basson believes that nonsexual distractions of everyday life (i.e., work and home responsibilities) in addition to sexual distractions (i.e., worries about arousal or the ability to orgasm) interfere

with a woman's ability to feel sexual arousal. If a woman can overcome these distractions, Basson suggests that continued sexual stimulation could lead to sexual pleasure, which will eventually trigger desire for sex itself (Figure 10.9).

Tiefer's and Basson's work have begun a much-needed dialogue about the importance of gender and sexual functioning.

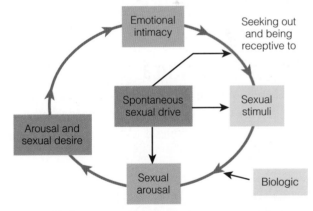

Basson's Non-Linear Model

FIGURE **10.9** Basson believes that many women do not feel spontaneous sexual desire. Instead, a desire for intimacy may lead a woman to seek out, and being receptive to, sexual stimuli which then may lead to sexual arousal. SOURCE: Basson, R. 2001.

◀ review QUESTIONS

1 Identify and describe the four stages of Masters and Johnson's female sexual response cycle and explain what happens in women.

2 Identify and describe the four stages of Masters and Johnson's male sexual response cycle, noting any differences between the male and female cycles.

3 Compare and contrast the various models of sexual response that have been proposed.

▶ SOLITARY Sexual Behavior

We began this chapter with a story about a woman who engaged in solitary sexual behavior while she was online. Would you consider her behavior to be solitary or partnered? Below we will discuss typical solitary sexual behavior, sexual fantasy, and masturbation. Solitary sexual behaviors can also be engaged in with a partner.

▶▶ SEXUAL Fantasy

Sexual fantasy is a common form of sexual expression (Frostino, 2007; Hicks & Leitenberg, 2001). Whereas Sigmund Freud believed that only sexually unsatisfied people fantasized about sex, today many researchers believe that not only are sexual fantasies normal and healthy, but they may be a driving force behind human sexuality.

Overall, men have been found to have more **sexual cognitions,** or thoughts about sex, than women (Renaud & Byers, 1999). In fact, the National Health and Social Life Survey (NHSLS) found that 54% of men and 19% of women thought about sex at least once a day (Laumann et al., 1994). However, both men and women have been found to use sexual fantasies, either during masturbation, partnered sexual behavior, or both (Kahr, 2008; Leitenberg & Henning, 1995).

Liberal attitudes and more sexual experience have been found to be associated with longer and more explicit sexual fantasies (Kahr, 2008). Those who do not have sexual fantasies have been found to experience a greater likelihood of sexual dissatisfaction and sexual dysfunction (Cado & Leitenberg, 1990). The sexual fantasies of homosexuals and heterosexuals have also been found to be more similar than different, except for the sex of the fantasized partner (Leitenberg & Henning, 1995).

REAL RESEARCH 10.3 Significant gender differences have been found in sexual beliefs. Men are more likely to believe that oral sex is not sex, cybersex is not cheating, and sex frequency decreases in marriage, whereas women are more likely to believe that oral sex is sex, cybersex is cheating, and sex frequency in marriage stays high (KNOX ET AL., 2008).

Overall, research on men's and women's sexual fantasies has shown that fantasies are becoming more similar (Block, 1999; Shulman & Horne, 2006). In fact, women have been reporting more graphic and sexually aggressive fantasies than they have reported in the past (Shulman & Horne, 2006). The majority of men and women have a select few fantasies that are used to arouse them over and over again. Sexual fantasies are used for a variety of reasons, including to help enhance masturbation, increase sexual arousal, help a person reach orgasm, and allow a person to explore various sexual activities that he or she might find taboo or too threatening to actually engage in.

Women's Sexual Fantasies

Many women report using sexual fantasy on a regular basis, and they use it to increase their arousal, self-esteem, and sexual interest, or to relieve stress (Maltz & Boss, 2001; Shulman & Horne,

2006). Overall, women's sexual fantasies tend to be more emotional than men's and include more touching, feeling, partner response, and ambiance (Zurbriggen & Yost, 2004). The five most common sexual fantasies for women include sex with their current partner, reliving a past sexual experience, engaging in different sexual positions, having sex in rooms other than the bedroom, and sex on a carpeted floor (Maltz & Boss, 2001). Female sexual fantasies tend to be more romantic than male fantasies, as illustrated by this 21-year-old woman's fantasy:

> My ultimate fantasy would be with a tall, strong man. We would spend a whole day together—going to a beach on a motorcycle, riding horses in the sand, and making love on the beach. Then we'd ride the motorcycle back to town, get dressed up, and go out to dinner. After dinner we'd come home and make love by the fire. Or we could make love in a big field of tall grass while it is raining softly. (Author's files)

Lesbian and bisexual women also use sexual fantasy. Research has found that relationship quality affects the content of sexual fantasy (J. D. Robinson & Parks, 2003). One 20-year-old lesbian shares her favorite sexual fantasy:

> She has black hair and I stop the car and motion her to get in. She walks quickly, with a slight attitude. She gets in with silence—her hands and eyes speak for her. I take her home, and she pulls me in. I undress her, and she is ready for me. Down on the bed she goes, and down on her I go. With legs spread, her clitoris is swollen and erect, hungry for my touch. I give her what she wants. She moans as orgasm courses through her body. (Author's files)

Sexual fantasies are commonly used by older women as well. In fact, using fantasies later in life may help women experience arousal and orgasm (Maltz & Boss, 2001). Studies have shown that age is unrelated to what types of sexual fantasies a person has (Block, 1999). One 50-year-old woman reveals her fantasies at this point in her life:

> One big change in my imaginary sex life since I was a young woman: I no longer have those fluffy romantic fantasies where most of the story is about pursuit and the sex at the end is NG, no genitals, in view. Now I picture the genitals, mine and his, and I watch them connect in full juicy color. I see a big penis, always a big penis, and every detail, including the little drops of pre-ejaculate like dew on the head. (Block, 1999, p. 100)

Fantasies about forced sex are common in women (Zurbriggen & Yost, 2004). In one study, more than 50% of participants reported using force fantasies at some point during sex (Strassberg & Lockerd, 1998). Force fantasies are also found in lesbian

sexual cognitions
Thoughts about sex.

couples (J. D. Robinson, 2001). Why would a woman incorporate force into her sexual fantasies? Researchers claim it is a way to reduce the guilt women feel for having sexual desires, a way for women to show their "openness" to a variety of sexual experiences, or a result of past sexual abuse (Barner, 2003; Strassberg & Lockerd, 1998).

Women who incorporate force in their sexual fantasies have been found to be less sexually guilty and open to more variety of sexual experiences than those who do not (Shulman & Horne, 2006). There has also been a connection found between force in sexual fantasies and childhood sexual abuse (Shulman & Horne, 2006). It is important to keep in mind that fantasizing about certain sexual behaviors does not mean a person wants to engage in them. In a fantasy, the woman is in control. In her fantasy, she is able to transform something fearful into something pleasurable (Maltz & Boss, 2001).

Men's Sexual Fantasies

Overall, men's sexual fantasies tend to be more active and aggressive than women's (Zurbriggen & Yost, 2004). They are often more frequent and impersonal, dominated by visual images. These fantasies move quickly to explicit sexual acts and often focus on the imagined partner as a sex object. They generally include visualizing body parts, specific sexual acts, group sex, a great deal of partner variety, and less romance.

Compared with women, men's sexual fantasies more often include someone other than their current partner (Hicks & Leitenberg, 2001). The five most common sexual fantasies for men include engaging in different sexual positions, having an aggressive partner, getting oral sex, having sex with a new partner, and having sex on the beach (Maltz & Boss, 2001). Following is a sexual fantasy from a 20-year-old man:

Sexual fantasies play a role in many people's lives, and may or may not be shared with a partner.

Ben Edwards/Getty Images

ON YOUR MIND 10.3

I've always had a fantasy about having sex in a very public place, with lots of people watching. I don't really want to try this, but the thought turns me on. Am I weird?

Fantasies are private mental experiences that involve sexually arousing thoughts or images. They are used for many reasons, but primarily to heighten sexual arousal. Having sexual fantasies does not mean you want certain events to happen. It can be a turn-on to think about having sex with a lot of people watching, even though you would never do it in real life. Researchers today have found that sexual fantasies are a concern only if they interfere with healthy sexual expression or the development of partner intimacy (Block, 1999).

My sexual fantasy is to be stranded on an island with beautiful women from different countries (all of them horny, of course). I'm the only male. I would make all of them have multiple orgasms, and I would like to have an everlasting erection so I could please them all nonstop. (Author's files)

Sexual fantasy is used by heterosexual, homosexual, and bisexual men. For gay and bisexual men, common sexual fantasies are receiving oral sex from another man, being manually stimulated by another man, engaging in anal intercourse, and kissing another man's lips (Kahr, 2008). When asked about his favorite sexual fantasy, one 21-year-old gay man reports:

My favorite sexual fantasy consists of a purely coincidental meeting between myself and an old friend from high school, Jason. We would eventually end up at my house and talk for hours about what each of us had been up to for the last few years. Eventually, the conversation would become one of his talking about trouble with a girlfriend or something of that nature. Jason tells me that he was always aware that I was gay and that he had been thinking about that a lot lately. He tells me that he has always wondered what it would be like to have sex with another man. I offer to have sex with him. He agrees and we engage in passionate, loving sex. (Author's files)

Are there gender differences in sexual fantasy? On the surface, it appears so. But we have to be careful in interpreting these findings. It could be that men have an easier time discussing their sexual fantasies than women do.

▶▶ MASTURBATION

For a period in the 19th and early 20th centuries in the United States and Europe, there was a fear that masturbation caused terrible things to happen, such as insanity, death, or even sterility. Parents would go to extremes to protect their children from the sins of masturbation. In fact, aluminum gloves were sold to parents for the purpose of covering children's hands at bedtime so that children wouldn't be able to masturbate (Laqueur, 2003; Stengers & Van Neck, 2001).

FIGURE **10.10** Female masturbation.

Today, experts view masturbation as a strategy to improve sexual health, reduce unwanted pregnancy, and avoid sexually transmitted infections (STIs; Kaestle & Allen, 2011). Masturbation fulfills a variety of needs for people at different ages, and it can decrease sexual tension and anxiety and provide an outlet for sexual fantasy. It allows people the opportunity to experiment with their bodies to see what feels good and where they like to be touched. It can provide information on what kind of pressure and manipulation give a person the greatest pleasure and orgasmic response.

For some, masturbation complements an active sex life, whereas for others, it compensates for a lack of partnered sex or satisfaction with sex (Das, 2007). The majority of American boys experience their first ejaculation through masturbation, and it is often the main sexual outlet for both boys and girls during adolescence (see Chapter 8). Interestingly, the majority of men and women report learning about masturbation from the media and peers, not from their parents or teachers (Kaestle & Allen, 2011). The NSSHB found that unlike other sexual behaviors, masturbation is unrelated to a person's health or relationship status (Herbenick et al., 2010).

Masturbation is common throughout the life span for both men and women (Herbenick et al., 2010). However, although the majority of men in all age groups reported masturbating during the past year, only 40% of women reported doing so. Experts believe this may be because women are more likely to feel a stigma against masturbation, which can decrease masturbatory behavior or the ability to talk about it (Kaestle & Allen, 2011).

The NSSHB found that more than half of women age 18 to 49

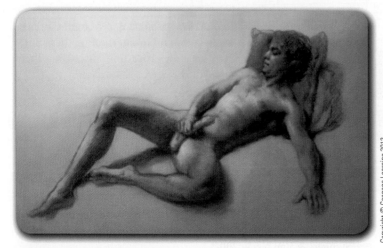

FIGURE **10.11** Male masturbation.

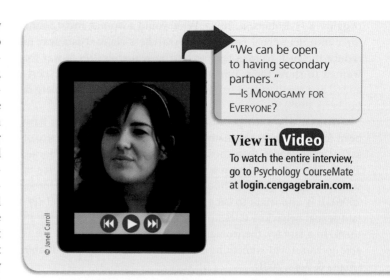

"We can be open to having secondary partners."
—IS MONOGAMY FOR EVERYONE?

View in Video
To watch the entire interview, go to Psychology CourseMate at **login.cengagebrain.com.**

years masturbate (Herbenick et al., 2010a). Although rates are highest in the 25- to 29-year age group, rates begin to decrease after this. At age 50, 40% of women report masturbating, 33% at age 60, and 16% at age 70 (Dodge et al., 2010; Herbenick et al., 2010a).

REAL RESEARCH 10.4 Masturbation is not unique to humans; it is common in most primates, as well as other mammals including dogs, cats, horses, rats, hamsters, deer, and whales (LEVIN, 2007).

As men and women age, the frequency of masturbation decreases. Women who masturbate report engaging in this behavior a few times a month or more.

Masturbation is a common and frequent component of male sexual behaviors, regardless of age or relationship status. Rates of masturbation were greatest in those who were 25 to 39 years old and lowest among married men older than 70 (Dodge et al., 2010; Reece et al., 2010d). Whereas men who were in a relationship reported less masturbation than men who were not in a relationship, 60% of men in a relationship reported masturbating (Reece et al., 2010d). Men report masturbating more than twice a week on average, up until the age of 50, when frequency decreases (Reece et al., 2010d).

Although the NSSHB did not ask about the use of vibrators or dildos, we know that some women and men use vibrators or dildos during masturbation and/or partnered sex (Herbenick et al., 2009; Reece et al., 2009). A vibrator uses batteries and can vibrate at different speeds. Vibrators may be used directly on the genitals, or a woman may insert the vibrator into her vagina. A dildo, which can be made of silicone, rubber, or jelly, and comes in a variety of shapes and sizes, can also be inserted into the vagina or anus but does not use batteries.

Cultural and religious taboos against masturbation can lead to increased guilt. These cultural taboos are related to whether masturbation is perceived to be "normal" in a particular culture. In addition, conservative cultures have less approval for masturbation, which may decrease masturbation. For example,

Asian American women have been found to masturbate significantly less than non-Asian women (Meston et al., 1996). A study on masturbation in 20- to 59-year-old Chinese men and women found that 35% of men and 13% of women engaged in masturbation (Das et al., 2009). However, Chinese culture proposes that frequent masturbation is heavily influenced by early sexualization in childhood and often begins with a "gateway event," such as early puberty or early sexual contact (Das et al., 2009).

◀ review QUESTIONS

1 Describe the research on sexual fantasy, noting any gender differences.

2 How has masturbation been viewed throughout history? Are there cultural differences in masturbation attitudes?

3 Explain the differences in frequency of male versus female masturbation.

▶ PARTNERED Sexual Behavior

The NSSHB found that sexual behaviors peak in a person's 20s and decrease with age (Herbenick et al., 2010; Table 10.1). Although some men and women experiment with different techniques, others engage in only certain behaviors. Below we will discuss various sexual behaviors including foreplay, manual sex, oral sex, vaginal intercourse, anal intercourse, and same-sex sexual behaviors (for more information about the practice of certain sexual behaviors see Figure 10.13).

▶▶ FOREPLAY

It is interesting to consider how people define "foreplay." Is foreplay all of the sexual behaviors that take place before penetration? What if penetration does not occur? For the majority of heterosexuals, foreplay is often defined as everything that happens before sexual intercourse (touching, kissing, massage, oral sex, etc.). It has been viewed as something a man has to do to get a woman ready for sexual intercourse.

For many, caressing, fondling, and snuggling are common pieces of foreplay. Hugging can also be an important aspect in caring relationships but also one that is often neglected. In fact, research has shown that married couples have deeper, more relaxed hugs with their young children than they do with each other (Schnarch, 1997).

▶▶ MANUAL SEX

Manual sex (also referred to as a "hand job") refers to the physical caressing of the genitals and it can be done individually or during **mutual masturbation** (also called *partnered masturbation*). Generally, people think of manual sex as something that happens before penetrative sex, but it has become more popular over the years as a form of safer sex. This is because during manual sex, there is no exchange of body fluids (we will discuss safer sex later in this chapter).

Although the NHSLS did not collect data on mutual masturbation, the NSSHB found that mutual masturbation is less common than solo masturbation (Dodge et al., 2010; Reece et al., 2010d). Overall, men and women in the 25- to 39-year-old age group are most likely to engage in mutual masturbation (Herbenick et al., 2010, 2010a). Among Black men and women, mutual masturbation was much less common than solo masturbation, with 24% of men and 28% of women reporting engaging in this behavior (Dodge et al., 2010). Decreased rates of mutual masturbation were also found in Hispanic men and women, with 41% of men and 34% of women reporting engaging in this behavior (Dodge et al., 2010).

Manual Sex on Women

Many men (and women, too) may not know exactly what to do with the female genitals. What feels good? Rubbing? Can rubbing hurt? When does a woman like to have her clitoris touched? Where do women like to be touched? Men and women who worry

Caressing and snuggling are common during foreplay.

© Exactostock/SuperStock

---

manual sex
The physical caressing of the genitals during solo or partner masturbation.

mutual masturbation
Simultaneous masturbation of sexual partners by each other.

table **10.1** ■
Percentage of Americans Performing Certain Sexual Behaviors in the Past Year Based on the 2010 National Survey of Sexual Health and Behavior (N = 5,865)

	Age Groups							
	14–15		16–17		18–19		20–24	
Sexual Behaviors	Men	Women	Men	Women	Men	Women	Men	Women
Masturbated Alone	62%	40%	75%	45%	81%	60%	83%	64%
Masturbated with Partner	5%	8%	16%	19%	42%	36%	44%	36%
Received Oral Sex from Women	12%	1%	31%	5%	54%	4%	63%	9%
Received Oral Sex from Men	1%	10%	3%	24%	6%	58%	6%	70%
Gave Oral Sex to Women	8%	2%	18%	7%	51%	2%	55%	9%
Gave Oral Sex to Men	1%	12%	2%	22%	4%	59%	7%	74%
Vaginal Intercourse	9%	11%	30%	30%	53%	62%	63%	80%
Received Penis in Anus	1%	4%	1%	5%	4%	18%	5%	23%
Inserted Penis into Anus	3%		6%		6%		11%	

about these questions may become overly cautious or eager in touching a woman's clitoris and vulva.

Because each woman differs in how she likes her clitoris stroked or rubbed, it is important that partners communicate their preferences. A water-based lubricant, such as K-Y Jelly, can make manual sex more comfortable. The majority of women enjoy a light caressing of the shaft of the clitoris, together with an occasional circling of the clitoris, and maybe digital (finger) penetration of the vagina. Other women dislike direct stimulation and prefer to have the clitoris rolled between the lips of the labia. Some women like to have the entire area of the vulva caressed, whereas others like the caressing to be focused on the clitoris. As a woman gets more aroused, she may breathe more deeply or moan, and her muscles may become tense. Stopping stimulation when a partner is close to orgasm can cause frustration.

Manual Sex on Men

Many women (and some men) may not know exactly what to do with the penis. Does rubbing feel good? How do men like to have their penis stroked? When do men like to have their penis touched? To reach orgasm, many men like to have the penis stimulated with strong and consistent strokes.

However, at the beginning of sexual stimulation, most men like soft, light stroking of the penis and testicles. The testicles can be very responsive to sexual touch, although out of fear of hurting them, oftentimes partners avoid touching them at all. It is true that the testicles can be badly hurt by rough handling, but a light stroking can be pleasurable. A good rule to follow is that most men do not like to have their testicles squeezed any harder than a woman would like to have her breasts squeezed. Remember, also, that the friction of a dry hand can cause irritation, so hand lotion, baby oil,

ON YOUR MIND 10.4

I'm happily involved in a very serious relationship with a wonderful woman. We have both had other partners, but I have found that my girlfriend is reluctant to talk to me about the things she has done with other men. What can I do to get her to talk more?

Your girlfriend's reluctance to share her sexual history with you probably has to do with the fact that she worries about your reactions to her past behaviors. It can be difficult for some men and women to talk about their past, and this is complicated by the fact that hearing about your lover's past can often stir up jealousy and strong emotions. Talk to your girlfriend about your thoughts and ask her what holds her back. Do remember, though, that sometimes the past is best left in the past.

or a lubricant can be used while manually stimulating the penis. However, if manual stimulation leads to vaginal or anal penetration, any lotion or oil should be washed off, because these products may cause vaginal problems in women and can weaken the strength of latex condoms or diaphragms.

The most sensitive parts of the male penis are the glans and tip, which are very responsive to touch. In fact, some men can masturbate by rubbing only the glans of the penis. For others, stimulation at the base may help bring on orgasm because it mimics deep thrusting. Switching positions, pressures, and techniques often can be frustrating for a man who feels almost at the brink of an orgasm.

All men have their own individual preferences for what feels good during manual sex. However, the most common techniques involve a quick up-and-down motion that is applied without a

Age Groups											
25–29		30–39		40–49		50–59		60–69		70+	
Men	Women	Men	Women	Men	Women	Men	Women	Men	Women	Men	Women
84%	72%	80%	63%	76%	65%	72%	54%	61%	47%	46%	33%
49%	48%	45%	43%	38%	35%	28%	18%	17%	13%	13%	5%
77%	3%	78%	5%	62%	2%	49%	1%	38%	1%	19%	2%
5%	72%	6%	59%	6%	52%	8%	34%	3%	25%	2%	8%
74%	3%	69%	4%	57%	3%	44%	1%	34%	1%	24%	2%
5%	76%	5%	59%	7%	53%	8%	36%	3%	23%	3%	7%
86%	87%	85%	74%	74%	70%	58%	51%	54%	42%	43%	22%
4%	21%	3%	22%	4%	12%	5%	6%	1%	4%	2%	1%
27%		24%		21%		11%		6%		2%	

great deal of pressure. To enhance the effectiveness of this motion, partners should try varying the pressure every once in awhile (harder and then softer). At the point of orgasm, firm stroking on the top and sides of the penis can continue but not on the underside. Firm pressure on the underside (the underside is the part of the penis that is "under" when the penis is not erect) of the penis during orgasm can restrict the urethra, which can be uncomfortable during ejaculation.

▶▶ ORAL SEX

Oral sex, also called cunnilingus (oral sex on a woman) and fellatio (oral sex on a man), has been practiced throughout history. Ancient Greek vases, 10th-century temples in India, and even 19th-century playing cards, all portrayed couples engaging in different types of oral sex. Over the years, however, there have been many taboos associated with oral sex. For some people, oral sex is not an option. It may be against their religion or beliefs, or they may simply find it disgusting. However, for many people, oral sex is an important part of sexual behavior.

Compared with the 1992 NHSLS, the NSSHB found that more men and women are engaging in oral sex (Herbenick et al., 2010). Most adults in all age groups have engaged in oral sex at some point, and rates of oral sex tend to decrease with age. Although only 7% of women older than 70 years report giving oral sex to a man in the last year, 43% said they had done so at some point in their lives (Herbenick et al., 2010a). Men and women in better health engage in more oral sex than those in poor or failing health (Herbenick et al., 2010).

Overall, men and women of all ages report recent oral sex with the other sex, both giving and receiving (Herbenick et al., 2010a;

ON YOUR MIND 10.5

ON YOUR MIND 10.5

I have heard that you can get genital herpes if your partner performs oral sex on you and has a cold sore on his or her lip. Is this true?

It appears that even though oral herpes (a cold sore) is caused by a different strain of the herpes virus than genital herpes, this strain can be passed on during oral sex and lead to a herpes infection on the genitals. It is best to avoid oral sex when either partner has a cold sore. We discuss herpes in more depth in Chapter 15.

Reece et al., 2010d). More than half of all women younger than 50 have received from or given oral sex to a male partner in the previous year, as have 34% of 50- to 59-year-old women and 25% of 60- to 69-year-old women (Herbenick et al., 2010). Among men, oral sex rates with women are highest in the 20-to 30-year-old group and lowest among those older than 70.

Among Black men and women, rates of receiving oral sex from the other sex are greater than rates of giving oral sex (Dodge et al., 2010). Although 44% of Black women have received oral sex from a man, only 37% have given oral sex. Among Black men, 53% have received oral sex from a woman, but 43% have given oral sex.

REAL RESEARCH 10.5 When college students were asked what sexual behaviors constitute "having sex," 98% said vaginal intercourse, 78% said anal intercourse, but only 20% said oral-genital sex constituted "having sex" (HANS ET AL., 2010).

FIGURE **10.12** The sixty-nine position.

Rates of same-sex oral sex in Black men and women are lower than other-sex oral sex. Approximately 7% of Black men have given oral sex to or received oral sex from a man, and between 12% and 13% of Black women have given oral sex to or received oral sex from a woman (Dodge et al., 2010).

Among Hispanics, 62% of men have given oral sex to a woman, whereas 65% have received it from a woman. Half of Hispanic women have given or received oral sex from a man. Rates of same-sex oral sex in Hispanic men and women are lower than other-sex oral sex. Whereas 12% of Hispanic women have given oral sex to a woman, 10% have received oral sex from a woman (Dodge et al., 2010). Among Hispanic men, 11% have given oral sex to a man and 13% have received it (Dodge et al., 2010).

Although same-sex oral sex was not commonly reported by women, it was most prevalent among 18- to 24-year-olds (Herbenick et al., 2010a). In men, same-sex oral sex was less common than oral sex with women: 5% to 8% of 18- to 59-year-old men have received oral sex from a man in the past year (Herbenick et al., 2010). However, 14% of 40- to 49-year-old men and 15% of 50- to 59-year-old men have received oral sex from a man in their lifetimes. Between 4% and 8% of men have performed oral sex on a man in the previous year, whereas more than 10% in the 40- to 59-year-old age group have.

Some couples use oral sex as a form of foreplay, whereas others engage in oral sex as their main form of sexual behavior. Couples may also engage in **sixty-nine** (Figure 10.12). This position, however, can be challenging for some couples and may not provide the best stimulation for either of them. **Anilingus** (ain-uh-LING-gus; also called *rimming*), another form of oral sex, involves oral stimulation of the anus. However, hygiene is extremely important to avoid the spread of intestinal infections, hepatitis, and various STIs by an infected partner.

Some heterosexual couples may feel that engaging in oral sex is less intimate than sexual intercourse and may not like it for this reason. Because there is little face-to-face contact during cunnilingus or fellatio, it may make partners feel emotionally distant. Other people report that engaging in oral sex is one of the most intimate behaviors that a couple can engage in because it requires total trust and vulnerability. Not surprisingly, the majority of men and women are more interested in receiving oral sex rather than giving it (Brewster & Tillman, 2008; Laumann et al., 1994).

*The majority of men and women are more interested **in receiving** oral sex **rather than giving** it.*

Cunnilingus

In the United States, women have historically been inundated with negative messages about their vaginas. Many makers of feminine powders, douches, creams, jellies, and other scented items try to persuade women that their products will make the vagina smell "better." For this reason, many women express concern about the cleanliness of their vaginas during cunnilingus. When their partners try to have oral sex with them, fears and anxieties often prevent women from enjoying the sexual experience. This, coupled with many women's lack of familiarity with their own genitals, contributes to many women's strong discomfort with oral sex.

Many heterosexual men and lesbian women find cunnilingus to be erotic. They report that the taste of the vaginal secretions is arousing to them, and they find the female vulva beautiful and sexy, including its smell and taste. Generally, when we are highly aroused, we are less alert to sensory impressions than when we are not stimulated. This means that when we are aroused, the flavor of the vagina or of semen may be more appealing than it would be if we were not aroused. However, for those who do not find the scent and taste of the vagina arousing, taking a bath or shower together before engaging in oral sex is recommended.

Women report that they like oral sex to begin in a slow and gradual way. They dislike an immediate concentration on the clitoris. Before cunnilingus, many women like to be kissed and have their neck and shoulders, breasts, stomach, and finally their vulva massaged. A persistent rhythmic caressing of the tongue on the clitoris will cause many women to reach orgasm. During cunnilingus, some women enjoy a finger being inserted into their vagina or anus for extra stimulation. Because pregnant women have an increased vascularity of the vagina and uterus, care should be taken to never blow air into a woman's vagina during cunnilingus. This can force air into her uterine veins, which can cause a fatal condition known as an air embolism, in which an air bubble travels through the bloodstream and can obstruct the vessel (Hill & Jones, 1993; Kaufman et al., 1987; Nicoll & Skupski, 2008; Sánchez et al., 2008).

Cunnilingus is the most popular sexual behavior for lesbian and bisexual women. In fact, Blumstein and Schwartz's classic study (1983) found that the more oral sex a woman-to-woman couple has, the more sexually satisfied the couple is. Although women in heterosexual relationships often worry that their partners may find the

sixty-nine
Oral sex that is performed simultaneously between two partners.

anilingus
Oral stimulation of the anus.

vagina unappealing, this is not so in woman-to-woman relationships. As one woman said, "Gay women are very much into each other's genitals....Not only accepting, but truly appreciative of women's genitals and bodies....Lesbians are really into women's bodies, all parts" (Blumstein & Schwartz, 1983, p. 238).

Fellatio

The majority of men enjoy oral sex and many are displeased if their partners do not like to perform fellatio (Blumstein & Schwartz, 1983). Like lesbian couples, the more oral sex that occurs in gay couples, the more sexually satisfied the couple is (Blumstein & Schwartz, 1983).

Before fellatio, many men enjoy having their partners stroke and kiss various parts of their bodies, gradually getting closer to their penis and testicles. Some men like to have their testicles orally stimulated as well. They may also like to have the head of the penis gently sucked while their partner's hand is slowly moving up and down the shaft. When performing fellatio, partners must be sure to keep their teeth covered with their lips, because exposed teeth can cause pain. Some men like the sensation of being gently scratched with teeth during oral sex, but this must be done very carefully.

Pornographic movies tend to show a sex partner who takes the entire penis into his or her mouth, but this is often uncomfortable for many people because of the gagging response. It is often helpful to place a hand around the base of the penis while performing fellatio to avoid a gagging response. By placing a hand there, the penis will be kept from entering the back of the mouth, thus reducing the urge to gag. In addition, the hand can be used to provide more stimulation to the penis.

Some partners are concerned about having their partners' ejaculate in their mouths after fellatio. If your partner is free from all STIs, swallowing the ejaculate is harmless. Some people enjoy the taste, feel, and idea of tasting and swallowing ejaculate, but others do not. If swallowing is unacceptable, another option may be to spit out the ejaculate after orgasm or not allow your partner to ejaculate in your mouth. Holding a partner's head during orgasm can make it impossible for the partner to remove the penis and not swallow the ejaculate.

How much semen a man ejaculates often depends on how long it has been since his last ejaculation. If a long period has gone by, generally the ejaculate will be larger. An average ejaculation is approximately 1 to 2 teaspoons; consists mainly of fructose, enzymes, and different vitamins; and contains approximately 5 calories. The taste of the ejaculate can vary, depending on a man's use of drugs or alcohol, stress level, and diet (Tarkovsky, 2006). Coffee and alcohol can cause the semen to have a bitter taste, whereas fruits (pineapple in particular) can result in sweet-tasting semen. Men who eat lots of red meat often have very acid-tasting semen. The taste of semen also varies from day to day.

Some men and women dislike performing fellatio. There have been some ethnic differences found as well. For example, in Gail Wyatt's study of African American female sexuality, more than 50% of the hundreds of women in her sample had never engaged in fellatio and had no desire to do so (Wyatt, 1998). If you dislike performing fellatio on your partner, try talking about it. Find out if there are things that you can do differently (using your hands more) or that your partner can vary (ejaculating outside of your mouth).

*Most heterosexual couples engage in vaginal intercourse **almost every time they have sex.***

ON YOUR MIND 10.7

Do men want their partners to swallow the ejaculate after their orgasms?

Some men do; some don't care. Men who like their partners to swallow after fellatio say that it increases the stimulation, leading to a better orgasm. Others say that swallowing shows their partner is totally into them (they believe that spitting the ejaculate is a rejection). Some men differentiated between casual and long-term partners, and believe that partners should "swallow when dining, but spit when sampling." It's important to remember that communication is key here. Partners should talk about their desires and decide what would work best for them. Some men and women avoid swallowing because of a gag reflex when a man ejaculates into their mouth.

▶▶ VAGINAL Intercourse

Most heterosexual couples engage in vaginal intercourse almost every time they have sex, and when most people think about "sex," they think of vaginal intercourse (Sanders & Reinisch, 1999). Vaginal intercourse involves inserting the penis into the vagina. However, there are a variety of ways in which couples perform this behavior. We will discuss the various positions for sexual intercourse shortly.

The 1992 NHSLS found that Americans fell into three groups: those who engaged in vaginal intercourse at least twice a week (one third), those who engaged in vaginal intercourse a few times a month (one third), and those who engaged in vaginal intercourse a few times a year or have no sexual partners (one third; Laumann et al., 1994). Age makes a difference—18- to 29-year-olds engage in vaginal intercourse 112 times per year on average, whereas 30- to 39-year-olds engage in vaginal intercourse 86 times per year, and 40- to 49-year-olds engage in vaginal intercourse 69 times per year (Piccinino & Mosher, 1998).

The more recent NSSHB found that vaginal intercourse is the most prevalent sexual behavior among men and women of all ages and ethnicities (Herbenick et al., 2010a). The majority of 18- to 49-year-old men and women reported engaging in vaginal intercourse in the past 90 days. Like other partnered sexual behaviors, men and women in better health were more likely to report engaging in vaginal intercourse.

As men and women age, the frequency of vaginal intercourse decreases (Figure 10.13). In women, 25% of 30- to 39-year-olds, 33% of 40- to 49-year-olds, 50% of 50- to 59-year-olds, and 80% of 70+-year-olds reported not engaging in vaginal intercourse in the last year (Herbenick et al., 2010). Among men, 15% of 20- to 30-year-olds, 26% of 40-year-olds, and 42% of 50-year-olds reported not engaging in vaginal intercourse during the past year (Herbenick et al., 2010; see Figure 10.13 for more information about the frequency of sexual behavior and age).

We discussed the sexual response cycle earlier in this chapter, and how, during arousal, the vagina becomes lubricated, making penetration easier and providing more pleasure for both partners. It is important for couples to delay vaginal penetration until after lubrication has begun. Penetrating a dry vagina, forcefully or not, can be very uncomfortable for both partners. If the woman is

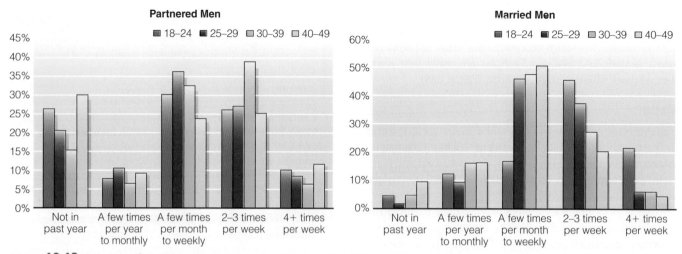

FIGURE **10.13** Frequency of vaginal intercourse by age for (a) partnered and (b) married men in the United States based on findings from the 2010 National Survey of Sexual Health and Behavior.

aroused but more lubrication is needed, a water-based lubricant should be used.

Pornography helps reinforce the idea that women like thrusting to be fast and rough during vaginal intercourse. Video after video shows men engaged in hard and fast thrusting—and women asking

---

REAL RESEARCH 10.6 A survey by the America College Health Association found that college students believe their peers have more sexual partners than themselves (AMERICAN COLLEGE HEALTH ASSOCIATION, 2009).

---

for more (we discuss pornography in more detail in Chapter 18). In reality, many women like a slower pace for intercourse. It can be intimate and erotic to make love very slowly, circling the hips, varying pressure and sensations, while maintaining eye contact. Both nonverbal and verbal communication can help ensure that both partners are happy with the timing and pace of intercourse.

Although many men try to delay ejaculation until their partners are satisfied with the length of thrusting, longer thrusting does not always ensure female orgasm. If intercourse lasts for too long, the vagina may become dry, and this can be uncomfortable.

Couples use a variety of positions to engage in vaginal intercourse.

Sex therapists report that heterosexual intercourse typically lasts anywhere from 3 to 13 minutes (Corty & Guardiani, 2008). Intercourse that lasts only 1 to 2 minutes was viewed as "too short," whereas intercourse that lasts more than 13 minutes was "too long." "Adequate" vaginal intercourse lasts 3 to 7 minutes, and "desirable" intercourse lasts 7 to 13 minutes (Corty & Guardiani, 2008).

The majority of couples do not have eye contact during sexual behavior, regardless of their positions (Schnarch, 1997). Schnarch proposes that eye contact during sexual behavior intensifies intimacy, and this is difficult for most couples. In addition, over time, we have learned to close our eyes during sexual behavior. To increase the intensity of sexual behavior, try keeping your eyes open (it's not as easy as you might think).

Positions for Vaginal Intercourse

According to the *Complete Manual of Sexual Positions* (J. Stewart, 1990), there are 116 vaginal entry positions, and in *The New Joy of Sex* (Comfort & Rubenstein, 1992), 112 positions are illustrated. Of course, we don't have enough room to describe all of these positions, so we will limit this discussion to the four main positions for vaginal intercourse: male-on-top, female-on-top, rear entry, and side by side. There are advantages and disadvantages to each of these positions, and couples must choose the sexual positions that are best for them. Keep in mind that although we are discussing positions for heterosexual vaginal intercourse here, many gay and lesbian couples use similar positions in their sexual activity.

MALE-ON-TOP The male-on-top (also called the "missionary" or "male superior") position is one of the most common positions for vaginal intercourse. In this position, the woman lies on her back and spreads her legs, often bending her knees to make penetration easier. The man positions himself on top of the woman, between her legs (Figure 10.14). Because his full weight is usually uncomfortable and perhaps even painful for the woman, he should support himself on his arms or elbows and knees.

The male-on-top position allows the male to control the thrusting and permits deep penetration for the man during inter-

FIGURE **10.14** The male-on-top position.

FIGURE **10.15** The female-on-top position.

course. It enables the partners to look at each other, kiss, and hug during vaginal intercourse. The woman can move her legs up around her partner or even put them on his shoulders. She can also use a pillow under her hips to increase clitoral stimulation. For some couples, this position is the most comfortable because the male is more active than the female. This position may also be the most effective for procreation, because the penis can be thrust deep into the vagina, which allows the semen to be deposited as deeply as possible; furthermore, because the woman is lying on her back, the semen does not leak out as easily.

*The **male-on-top position** may also be the **most effective** for procreation.*

However, there are also some disadvantages to the male-on-top position. If either partner is overweight, or if the female is in the advanced stages of pregnancy, this position can be very uncomfortable. Also, the deep penetration that is possible in this position may be uncomfortable for the woman, especially if her partner has a large penis, which can bump the cervix. This position also makes it difficult to provide clitoral stimulation for the female and may prevent the woman from moving her hips or controlling the strength or frequency of thrusting. Finally, in the male-on-top position, it may be difficult for the man to support his weight, because his arms and knees may get tired.

FEMALE-ON-TOP In the female-on-top position (also called "female superior"), the man lies on his back while his partner positions herself above him (Figure 10.15). She can either put her knees on either side of him or lie between his legs. By leaning forward, she has greater control over the angle and degree of thrusting and can get more clitoral stimulation. Other variations of this position include the woman sitting astride the man facing his feet or the woman sitting on top of her partner while he sits in a chair.

In the female-on-top position, the female can control clitoral stimulation either by manual stimulation or through friction on her partner's body. She can also control the depth and rhythm of thrusting. Her partner's hands are also free so that he can caress her body during

sexual intercourse. Because this position is face-to-face, the partners are able to see each other, kiss, and have eye contact.

Sex therapists often recommend this position for couples who are experiencing difficulties with premature ejaculation or a lack of orgasms, because the female-on-top position can extend the length of erection for men and facilitates female orgasm. It also doesn't require a man to support his weight. For women who are in the advanced stages of pregnancy, the female-on-top position may be a very good position.

There are, however, some drawbacks to the female-on-top position. This position puts the primary responsibility on the female, and some women may not feel comfortable taking an active role in vaginal intercourse. Some men may feel uncomfortable letting their partners be on top and may not receive enough penile stimulation in this position to maintain an erection.

SIDE BY SIDE The side-by-side position takes the primary responsibility off both partners and allows them to relax during vaginal intercourse. In this position, the partners lie on their sides, and the woman lifts one leg to facilitate penile penetration (Figure 10.16). This is a good position for couples who want to take it slow

FIGURE **10.16** The side-by-side position.

Sexual Diversity in Our World ▶▶▶ Meet Me in the Love Hotel

A "love hotel" is a short-stay hotel room that is commonly found in many Asian countries, such as Japan, Hong Kong, or South Korea. Typically rooms are rented for several hours (a "rest") or for the night (a "stay"). Reservations are not accepted; a "rest" typically costs anywhere from 3,000 to 7,000 yen ($30–$70), whereas a "stay" costs approximately 10,000 yen ($100). It is estimated that 1.4 million couples visit a love hotel every day in Japan (Chaplin, 2007). I had the opportunity to explore love hotels on my recent trip to Shibuya, a district of Tokyo, Japan.

Because Japanese homes and apartments are very small and often have paper-thin walls, they offer little privacy to couples wanting to have sex. Many Japanese couples say they have a hard time getting "in the mood" in their traditional homes (Keasler, 2006). A love hotel offers couples privacy, and the sexual décor can often help increase sexual interest and desire. Entrances to love hotels are discreet, and there is limited contact with hotel staff. Rooms are selected from an electronic display board posted in the entrance way—if the room is lit up, it is available. Payment is often automated or done through pneumatic tubes, but some hotels offer small windows through which payment can be made discreetly without exposing a customer's face. Identification is not required, and there are no age limits to enter a love hotel. Some love hotels offer specific themes, such as samurai, jungle, pirate, S&M, or even cartoon character themes ("Hello Kitty" is popular).

The rooms in most love hotels are small; in fact, the room I saw was slightly bigger than the double-sized bed. Many rooms

© Janell Carroll

come with various amenities, including large flat screen televisions with DVD players, slot or karaoke machines, video consoles, refrigerators, or microwaves. The room I saw even came with a costume rental option offering maid, nurse, stewardess, schoolgirl, or cheerleader costumes (I found it interesting there were only costumes for women). There was also a large electric vibrator attached to the head of the bed, with a sign that said "disinfected." Many rooms also have vending machines that offer a full line of skin care and sex-related products (condoms, lubricants, and sex toys). Couples often talk for a while, play games, have sex, and take a bath (love hotel bathrooms are often fully stocked—the room I saw even offered peppermint bath crystals; Keasler, 2006).

Starting in 2008, Japan began to consider laws that would regulate these hotels. One main issue revolves around collecting personal information from customers. Although Japanese inns and hotels are required to collect personal information from guests, including name and address, love hotels are not (Shimanaka, 2008). As you could guess, many love hotel guests are reluctant to share such information. Lawmakers are also trying to reduce the amount of sexual content both outside and within the love hotels, in an attempt to improve the overall concept of the hotels. Interestingly, many Japanese believe that American motels are like Japanese love hotels—illustrating how commonly we believe our cultural traditions and values are shared (Keasler, 2006).

---

and extend vaginal intercourse. Both partners have their hands free and can caress each other's bodies. In addition, they can see each other, kiss, and talk during intercourse.

Disadvantages include the fact that sometimes couples in this position have difficulties with penetration. It can also be difficult to get a momentum going, and even more difficult to achieve deep penetration. Women may also have a difficult time maintaining contact with the male's pubic bone during intercourse, which often increases the chances of orgasm.

REAR ENTRY There are many variations to the rear-entry position of vaginal intercourse. Intercourse can be fast or slow depending on the variation chosen. One variation involves a woman on her hands and knees (often referred to as "doggie style"), while her partner is on his knees behind her. The female can also be lying on her stomach with a pillow under her hips while the male enters her from behind. Another variation is to use the side-by-side position, in which the male lies behind his partner and introduces his penis from behind (Figure 10.17).

FIGURE **10.17** The side rear-entry position.

View in Video

To watch the entire interview, go to Psychology CourseMate at **login.cengagebrain.com.**

"Love hotels really cater to a couple's privacy."
—JAPANESE LOVE HOTELS

The rear-entry positions provide an opportunity for clitoral stimulation, either by the male or the female. It may also provide direct stimulation of the G-spot. The rear-entry position also can be good for women who are in the later stages of pregnancy or who are overweight.

▶▶ ANAL Intercourse

During anal intercourse, the man's penis enters his partner's anus (Figure 10.18). There are many nerve endings in the anus, and it is frequently involved in sexual response, even if it is not directly stimulated. Some men and women experience orgasm during anal intercourse, especially with simultaneous penile or clitoral stimulation (Maynard et al., 2009). The landmark University of Chicago study found that only 1 in 10 heterosexual couples had engaged in anal sex (Laumann et al., 1994); however, the more recent NSSHB found that a significantly greater proportion of men and women had engaged in anal sex (Herbenick et al., 2010).

Although fewer women reported engaging in anal intercourse than other partnered sex behaviors, it was not an uncommon behavior. Approximately 10% to 14% of women aged 18 to 39 years reported engaging in anal sex in the past 90 days (Herbenick et al., 2010a). The majority of women who engage in anal sex report doing it once a month to a few times per year.

Insertive anal intercourse among men was less common than vaginal intercourse (Reece et al., 2010d). However, 13% to 15% of men age 25 to 49 years have engaged in insertive anal intercourse. Among men, receptive anal intercourse is infrequent: an estimated 7% of men age 14 to 94 years reported being a receptive partner during anal intercourse (Reece et al., 2010d).

Because the anus is not capable of producing lubrication and the tissue is so fragile, it is important that additional water-based lubricants (such as K-Y Jelly) be used. An oil-based lubricant (such as Vaseline) may cause problems later because the body cannot easily get rid of it, and it can damage latex condoms. Without

anal sphincter
A ringlike muscle that surrounds the anus; it usually relaxes during normal physiological functioning.

ON YOUR MIND **10.8**

My girlfriend told me that my penis is too large for her vagina and that it causes her pain during intercourse. How far can the vagina expand?

Although it is true that the vagina expands and lengthens during sexual arousal, not every vagina expands to the same degree. If a man's penis is very large, it can bump against the woman's cervix during thrusting, which can cause discomfort. In such cases it is particularly important to make sure the woman is fully aroused before attempting penetration and to try a variety of positions to find which is most comfortable for her. The female-superior position or the rear-entry position may help her control the depth of penetration. Either partner's hand around the base of the penis (depending on the position) may also prevent full penetration, as will some devices such as "cock rings," which are sold through adult catalogs or in adult stores. If the woman's pain continues, she should consult with her gynecologist to rule out a physiological problem and to get more advice and information.

lubrication, there may be pain, discomfort, and possibly tearing of the tissue in the anus.

During anal intercourse, the **anal sphincter** muscle must be relaxed or intercourse can be painful. If a couple decides to engage in anal intercourse, it is important to take it slowly. A condom is a must (unless partners are absolutely sure that both are free of STIs and are HIV-negative). Anal intercourse is one of the riskiest of all sexual behaviors and has been implicated in the transmission of HIV. Research has shown that the risk for contracting HIV through unprotected anal intercourse is greater than the risk for contracting HIV through unprotected vaginal intercourse (Mumba, 2010; Silverman & Gross, 1997; we discuss this further in Chapter 15).

In addition, any couple who decides to engage in anal intercourse should never transfer the penis from the anus to the vagina or mouth without changing the condom or washing the penis (sex toys should also be washed with antibacterial soap). The bacteria in the anus can cause vaginal infections in women.

FIGURE **10.18** Anal intercourse.

▶▶ SAME-SEX
Sexual Behaviors

There are many similarities in the sexual behaviors of heterosexuals, gays, and lesbians. Like heterosexual couples, gays and lesbians report engaging in sexual behavior to increase emotional and physical intimacy, feel accepted and supported, and increase the positive view of self (Cohen et al., 2008). In the following sections we discuss sexual behaviors in same-sex couples.

Gay Men

Gay men use a variety of sexual techniques, including hugging, kissing, oral sex, mutual masturbation, and anal intercourse. Overall, gay and bisexual men engage in oral sex more often than heterosexual or lesbian couples (Figure 10.19). This is not surprising, given the fact that research has shown that men

FIGURE **10.19** Gay men use a variety of sexual techniques in their lovemaking.

are more likely than women to have received oral sex (Brewster & Tillman, 2008).

Although many gay men report engaging in anal intercourse, not all gay men do. The NHSLS study found that although 80% of gay men reported engaging in anal intercourse, 20% did not (Laumann et al., 1994). Some gay couples (and other couples, too) engage in **fisting** (also called "hand-balling"), which involves the insertion of the fist and even part of the forearm into the anus or vagina. The use of rubber gloves during fisting has become more common since the early 2000s (Richters et al., 2003).

Like many other couples, gay men enjoy hugging, kissing, and body caressing; **interfemoral** (in-ter-fem-OR-ull) **intercourse** (thrusting the penis between the thighs of a partner); and **buttockry** (BUT-ock-ree; rubbing of the penis in the cleft of the buttocks).

Gay male sexual behavior changed significantly in the 1980s after the arrival of AIDS. Undoubtedly because of the massive education efforts initiated in the gay community, in the early 1990s, safe sex practices increased (at least in the major cities) among gay men (Catania et al., 1989). However, researchers believe that STI increases among sexually active gay men since the mid-2000s are due to a decreased fear of acquiring HIV, an increase in high-risk sexual behaviors (e.g., oral sex without a condom), a lack of knowledge about diseases, and increased Internet access to sexual partners (Hughes, 2006). We discuss this further in Chapter 15.

Lesbians

Lesbians enjoy a wide range of sexual behaviors, including kissing, hugging, body rubbing, manual stimulation, oral sex, and the use of sex toys such as dildos or vibrators (Figure 10.20). Manual stimulation of the genitals is the most common sexual practice among lesbians, although lesbians tend to use a variety of techniques in their lovemaking. Two-woman couples kiss more than man–woman couples, and two-man couples kiss least of all. After manual stimulation, the next most common practice is cunnilingus, which many lesbians report is their favorite sexual activity. Another common practice is **tribadism** (TRY-bad-iz-um), also called *scissoring*,[1] in which the women rub their genitals together. As we noted earlier, some lesbians engage in fisting and also may use dildos or vibrators, often accompanied by manual or oral stimulation.

Although it is rather dated, a nonscientific survey was conducted of more than 100 members of a lesbian social organization in Colorado (Munson, 1987). When asked what sexual techniques they had used in their last 10 lovemaking sessions, 100% reported kissing, sucking on breasts, and manual stimulation of

---

[1] In a popular *South Park* episode, one character yells, "Scissor me timbers!" during her first sexual experience after a sex change from man to woman.

---

fisting Sexual technique that involves inserting the fist and even part of the forearm into the anus or vagina.	**interfemoral intercourse** Thrusting the penis between the thighs of a partner.	**buttockry** Rubbing of the penis in the cleft of the buttocks.	**tribadism** Rubbing genitals together with another person for sexual pleasure.	**lesbian erotic role identification** The roles of "butch" and "femme" in lesbian relationships.

the clitoris; more than 90% reported French kissing, oral sex, and fingers inserted into the vagina; and 80% reported scissoring. Lesbians in their 30s were twice as likely as other age groups to engage in anal stimulation (with a finger or dildo). Approximately a third of women used vibrators, and there were a small number who reported using a variety of other sex toys, such as dildo harnesses, leather restraints, and handcuffs. Sexual play and orgasm are important aspects of lesbian sexuality (Bolso, 2005; Tomassilli et al., 2009).

Lesbian women also report frequently thinking about sex and the use of sexual fantasy. One woman said:

I think about sex during the day, staring at my computer screen, while I'm supposed to be writing. Sometimes I call Dana up at work, she picks up the phone, I say, "I'll meet you at home in fifteen minutes, and I'm going to rip off your clothes and throw you down on the couch, and I'm going to eat your pussy. That's what I'm having for lunch." (S. E. Johnson, 1996, p. i)

There has been some preliminary research done on the existence of **lesbian erotic role identification** (or the roles of "butch" [masculine] and "femme" [feminine] in lesbian relationships). Some scholars believe that such roles are simply social contracts, whereas others believe they are natural expressions of lesbian sexuality (D. Singh et al., 1999; Vidaurri et al., 1999). One study examined physiological and behavioral differences of women in these self-identified roles. Butch lesbians were found to have higher saliva testosterone levels, higher waist-to-hip ratios, and recalled more childhood behavior atypical for their gender (D. Singh et al., 1999). It is important to remember that there is no "typical" lesbian couple. Some lesbian couples may engage in role identification, but many others do not.

FIGURE **10.20** Lesbians have been found to be more sexually responsive and more satisfied in their sexual relationships than are heterosexual women.

Copyright © Cengage Learning 2013

Overall, lesbians have been found to be more sexually responsive, more satisfied with their sexual relationships, and to have lower rates of sexual problems than heterosexual women (Henderson et al., 2009; Kurdek, 2008). Some studies have suggested that the frequency of sexual contact among lesbians declines dramatically in their long-term, committed relationships (Blumstein & Schwartz, 1983; Nichols, 1990). By the beginning of the 1990s, the decreasing sexual interest among lesbian women had become well established and was referred to as "lesbian bed death" (Nichols, 2004). Although some studies have found decreased sexual activity among lesbian couples over time (Rosmalen-Noojjens et al., 2008), other studies have found no differences in sexual frequency between heterosexual and lesbian couples (Henderson et al., 2009; Matthews et al., 2003).

◄ **review** QUESTIONS

1 Explain why manual sex can be a form of safer sex.

2 Describe the differences that have been found in how men and women view oral sex.

3 Identify any gender differences that have been found in the experience of sexual intercourse.

4 Identify various positions for sexual intercourse. Name some advantages and disadvantages of each.

5 Identify the risks of engaging in anal sex.

6 Compare and contrast gay and lesbian sexual behavior.

▶ **SEXUAL BEHAVIOR** Later in Life

Today, older men and women are healthier and more active than previous generations (Bancroft, 2007). Many remain interested in sex and engage in several sexual behaviors, including masturbation, oral sex, and vaginal and anal intercourse (Figure 10.21). The

NSSHB found that 20% to 30% of men and women remain sexually active well into their 80s (Schick et al., 2010). However, as men and women age, a variety of physical changes affect sexual functioning and behavior. We now discuss these physical changes and their effect on sexual behavior (we discuss more of the challenges of aging and health concerns in Chapter 14).

table 10.2 ■ Physical Changes in Older Men and Women

In men:

- Delayed and less firm erection
- More direct stimulation needed for erection
- Extended refractory period (12–24 hours before rearousal can occur)
- Reduced elevation of the testicles
- Reduced vasocongestive response to the testicles and scrotum
- Fewer expulsive contractions during orgasm
- Less forceful expulsion of seminal fluid and a reduced volume of ejaculate
- Rapid loss of erection after ejaculation
- Ability to maintain an erection for a longer period
- Less ejaculatory urgency
- Decrease in size and firmness of the testes, changes in testicle elevation, less sex flush, and decreased swelling and erection of the nipples

In women:

- Reduced or increased sexual interest
- Possible painful intercourse because of menopausal changes
- Decreased volume of vaginal lubrication
- Decreased expansive ability of the vagina
- Possible pain during orgasm because of less flexibility
- Thinning of the vaginal walls
- Shortening of vaginal width and length
- Decreased sex flush, reduced increase in breast volume, and longer postorgasmic nipple erection

Copyright © Cengage Learning 2013

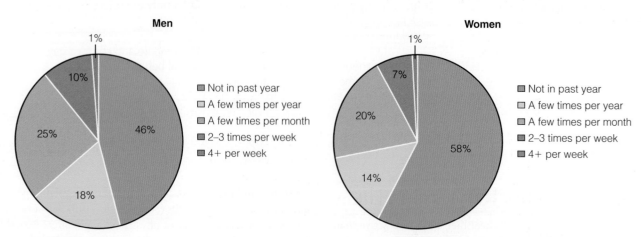

FIGURE **10.21** Percentage of men and women 50 to 80 years old who reported engaging in vaginal intercourse within the past year.
SOURCE: National Survey of Sexual Health and Behavior, 2010.

▶▶ PHYSICAL Changes

As people age, they inevitably experience changes in their physical health, some of which can affect normal sexual functioning (Table 10.2). Many of these changes in sexual functioning are exacerbated by sexual inactivity. In fact, research clearly indicates that older adults who have remained sexually active throughout their aging years have a greater potential for a more satisfying sex life later in life (Dimah & Dimah, 2004; Lindau & Gavrilova, 2010). Better knowledge of these changes would help older adults anticipate changes in their sexual activity.

▶▶ CHANGES IN
Sexual Behavior

Frequent complaints among older adult women are decreases in sexual desire and pain during vaginal intercourse (Schick et al., 2010). Older men are more likely to report problems with erectile functioning, and many turn to erectile drugs to enhance sexual functioning (we will discuss these drugs in more detail in Chapter 14).

The majority of older men and women report continued masturbation (63% of men and 47% of women; Schick et al., 2010). Masturbation may fulfill a variety of needs. If older adults find that their partners are no longer interested in sexual activity, masturbation often becomes an important outlet (Schick et al., 2010). This can also be an important activity for older people who have lost their sexual partners, because it offers a sexual release that may help decrease depression, hostility, or frustration. Many older couples continue to engage in vaginal intercourse (67% of men and 68% of women; Schick et al., 2010). Research on older gay men has found that they continue to be sexually active; however,

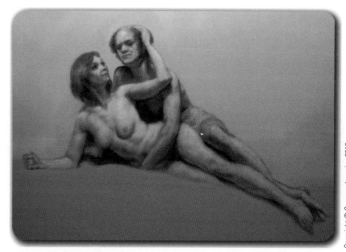

FIGURE **10.22** The majority of older adults maintain an interest in sex and sexual activity.

they tend to engage in less anal intercourse than younger gay men (Van de Ven et al., 1997). Physical problems, such as arthritis, diabetes, and osteoporosis, can interfere with sexual functioning. We discuss many other physical problems, such as illness, surgery, and injuries, that can affect sexual functioning in Chapter 14.

The stereotype that sex worsens with age is not inevitably true. Many older adults are very interested in maintaining an active sex life (Dimah & Dimah, 2004; Ginsberg et al., 2005; Schick et al., 2010). A key to sexual enjoyment later in life is for partners to be patient and understanding with each other. Physical fitness, good nutrition, adequate rest and sleep, a reduction in alcohol intake, and positive self-esteem can all enhance sexuality throughout the life span (Figure 10.22).

◀ review QUESTIONS

1 Identify the two most frequent sexual complaints in older men and explain how they affect aging men.

2 Identify and explain some of the physiological changes that occur with aging.

3 Explain how the physical changes of aging might affect the sexual response cycle.

▶ SAFER SEX Behaviors

What exactly is **safe sex**? Does it mean wearing a condom? Limiting the number of sex partners? Not engaging in oral, anal, vaginal, or casual sex? Although safe sex does include condom use, it also refers to specific sexual behaviors that are "safe" to engage in because they protect against the risk for acquiring STIs. However, no sexual behaviors protect a person 100% of the time (with the exception of abstinence, solo masturbation, and sexual fantasy). Therefore, maybe the real question is, "Is there really any such thing as safe sex?" In response to that question, it may be more appropriate to refer to **safer sex** behaviors, because we do know

that some sexual behaviors are safer than others (see accompanying Sex in Real Life). In Chapter 15, we discuss high-risk sexual behaviors.

All sexually active people should be aware of the risks associated with various sexual behaviors. Not only should people decrease the number of sexual partners, they must learn more about the sexual history of their partners, avoid unprotected vaginal and

safe sex
Sexual behaviors that do not pose a risk for the transmission of sexually transmitted infections.

safer sex
Sexual behaviors that reduce the risk for sexually transmitted infections.

Sex in Real Life ▶▶| Safer Sex Behavior Guidelines

Following are some sexual activities that are rated for safety. Remember that engaging in "hookups" (casual sex) and alcohol use are two activities that can increase your risk for acquiring a sexually transmitted infection. Typically, unsafe behaviors involve contact with semen, blood, or other body fluids. Those behaviors that are considered safe include activities that involve no exchange of bodily fluids.

Contact your local health clinic or AIDS organization for more information.

Safe
■ Massage
■ Hugging
■ Kissing without sharing saliva
■ Body rubbing, dry humping
■ Sexual fantasy

■ Masturbation (self only)
■ Watching porn or erotica
■ Phone/Internet sex
■ Sex toys (provided condoms are used if toys are shared)
■ Taking a bath together

Possibly Safe
■ French kissing
■ Anal intercourse with condom
■ Vaginal intercourse with condom
■ Fisting with glove
■ Cunnilingus with dental dam
■ Fellatio with condom
■ Anal rimming or anilingus with dental dam
■ Vaginal or anal stimulation with fingers using latex glove

Possibly Unsafe
■ Cunnilingus without a dental dam
■ Vaginal or anal stimulation with fingers without latex glove
■ Fellatio without a condom
■ Sharing sex toys without cleaning or changing condoms in between uses
■ Fisting without a glove
■ Anal rimming or anilingus without a dental dam

Unsafe
■ Anal intercourse without condom
■ Vaginal intercourse without condom
■ Blood contact
■ Cunnilingus without a dental dam during menstruation

SOURCE: Adapted from "Safer Sex Basics" (2005).

---

anal intercourse and other risky activities, and use barrier methods of contraception.

Even though most people feel anxious about the possibility of acquiring an STI, casual sexual activity has increased in recent years (Uecker & Regnerus, 2010). Although many people are familiar with condoms, the dental dam, which is a square piece of thin latex, similar to the latex used in condoms, is lesser known and can be used to prevent the transmission of STIs. It is stretched across the vulva or anus to prevent the exchange of bodily fluids. It is available without a prescription in many drugstores and women's health clinics across the United States and now comes in a variety of flavors and colors.

Although condom use in adolescents has become more commonplace in the late 2000s (Fortenberry et al., 2010), one behavior that has been clearly linked to unsafe sexual behaviors is drinking alcohol, which can impair judgment. In one study, 75% of college students had made decisions that they later regretted while under the influence of alcohol (Poulson et al., 1998). In fact, alcohol use is one of the most important factors repeatedly linked to unsafe sexual behavior (Griffin et al., 2010; Scott-Sheldon et al., 2010).

In Chapter 3, we talked about the importance of communication. Communication is key to safer sex relationships. When there is talk about safe sex, women are more likely than men to bring up the topic (M. Allen et al., 2002). However, it is important for all couples to talk about each other's past sexual relationships (such as number of partners and history of STIs) before engaging in sexual activity. Such openness will result not only in safer sex, but also a healthier relationship.

Throughout this chapter you have learned that human sexuality is shaped by a multitude of factors, including cultural, ethnic, religious, psychological, and biological. All of these factors influence our attitudes about sexuality and our decisions to engage in certain sexual behaviors.

> *Alcohol use* is one of the *most important factors* repeatedly linked to *unsafe sexual behavior.*

◀ review QUESTIONS

1 Define "safe sex" and differentiate it from "safer sex."

2 Give some guidelines for safer sex behaviors.

3 Explain how drinking may be linked to engaging in unsafe sexual behaviors.

SUMMARY POINTS

1 Our hormones have a powerful effect on our bodies. The endocrine glands secrete hormones into the bloodstream. The most influential hormones in sexual behavior are estrogen and testosterone. In most animals, the brain controls and regulates sexual behavior chiefly through hormones, although in humans, learned experiences and social, cultural, and ethnic influences are also important. Hormone levels decrease as we age, and this can cause a variety of problems, such as vaginal dryness and decreased vaginal sensitivity in women, and slower and less frequent erections in men.

2 Our ethnic group affects the types of sexual behaviors we engage in, our sexual attitudes, and our ability to communicate about sexuality. Differences have been found between African Americans, Hispanics, Whites, and Asian Americans. Religiosity also influences sexual behavior. The more religious people are, the more conservative their sexual behavior tends to be.

3 A series of physiological and psychological changes occur during sexual behavior. Masters and Johnson's sexual response cycle involves four physiological phases, including excitement, plateau, orgasm, and resolution. During these phases, there are changes in both vasocongestion and myotonia. In men, there is a refractory period during resolution, and generally the stages are less well defined. In women, the menstrual cycle may affect the sexual response cycle.

4 Kaplan's model of sexual response has three stages: desire, excitement, and orgasm. It is easier to recognize when a person is going through Kaplan's stages. Reed's Erotic Stimulus Pathway (ESP) model encompasses features of both Kaplan's and Masters and Johnson's models. Phases include seduction, sensation, surrender, and reflection. Tiefer argues that these models are all based on the medical model, and because of this, they leave out important aspects of sexual functioning.

5 The majority of heterosexuals define foreplay as "anything that happens before penetration" or something a man does to get a woman in the mood. Many people use fantasies to help increase their sexual excitement, and people use them during periods of sexual activity and inactivity. Female sexual fantasies often reflect personal sexual experiences, whereas male fantasies are more dependent on erotica and images.

6 Adult sexual behavior includes a range of sexual activities. Some adults choose to be celibate, or abstinent. Overall, research on men's and women's sexual fantasies has shown that fantasies are becoming more similar. Men masturbate more than women, and women feel more guilt about their masturbatory activity than do men. Masturbation fulfills a variety of needs for different people at different ages. In manual sex, no exchange of bodily fluids occurs. Men and women both have concerns about how best to stimulate their partners manually. Fellatio and cunnilingus are becoming more popular as forms of sexual behavior. Both heterosexual and homosexual couples engage in oral sex.

7 Most heterosexual couples engage in sexual intercourse almost every time they have sex, and when most people think of sex, they think of sexual intercourse. It is important to delay intercourse until after a woman's vaginal lubrication has begun. If a woman needs more lubrication, a water-based lubricant can be used. There are a variety of positions for sexual intercourse.

8 Same-sex couples engage in many of the same sexual behaviors as heterosexual couples do. There are more similarities than differences in the sexual behavior of homosexuals and heterosexuals. Lesbians tend to be more sexually satisfied than heterosexual women and have lower rates of sexual problems. Both heterosexual and homosexual couples engage in anal sex, and some experience orgasm from this technique. After anal intercourse, the penis should never be transferred from the anus to the vagina because of the risk for infection.

9 The majority of elderly persons maintain an interest in sex and sexual activity, even though society often views them as asexual. A lack of education about the physiological effects of aging on sexual functioning may cause elderly adults to think their sex lives are over when a sexual dysfunction is experienced.

10 There may be no such thing as safe sex; instead, we refer to "safer" sex. Other than abstinence, solo masturbation, and sexual fantasies, there are no 100% safe sexual behaviors. Few changes in the heterosexual behavior of male and female college students have occurred as a result of the AIDS crisis. Men and women should learn the sexual histories of all their sexual partners and consistently use condoms and dental dams.

CRITICAL THINKING QUESTIONS

1 Why do you think so many people are hesitant to talk about sexual pleasure? There is no doubt that you talk about sex with friends, but why has it become so taboo and so difficult to talk about what brings you sexual pleasure?

2 Do you think your ethnicity affects your sexuality? In what ways? Why do you think this is?

3 Suppose that your sexual partner shares with you that he or she has been engaging in sexual fantasies during sexual activity with you. How would this make you feel? Would you want to talk to your partner about these fantasies? Why or why not?

4 Susan has been masturbating regularly since age 15, although she feels very guilty about it. She realizes that she is unable to reach orgasm with her partner. After reading this chapter, explain to Susan what you've learned about masturbation, and offer her some advice.

5 Flash forward 30 years and imagine what your life will be like in a committed, long-term relationship. How do you hope your sex life will be? What factors might contribute to any problems you might experience?

6 Suppose you are in a new relationship and have just begun engaging in sexual activity. How can you communicate your desires to keep the sex safe? What problems might come up in this discussion?

MEDIA RESOURCES

CourseMate brings course concepts to life with interactive learning, study, and exam preparation tools that support the printed textbook. A textbook-specific website, Psychology CourseMate includes an integrated interactive eBook and other interactive learning tools including quizzes, flashcards, videos, and more. If your textbook does not include an access code card, go to CengageBrain.com to gain access.

CENGAGENOW CengageNOW is an easy-to-use online resource that helps you study in less time to get the grade you want—NOW. Take a pre-test for this chapter and receive a personalized study plan based on your results that will identify the topics you need to review and direct you to online resources to help you master those topics. Then take a post-test to help you determine the concepts you have mastered and what you will need to work on. If your textbook does not include an access code card, go to CengageBrain.com to gain access.

View in Video available in CourseMate and CengageNOW:

Is Virtual Sex Cheating?: A college student talks about her experience in online sexual chat rooms and the effect these behaviors had on her relationship with her boyfriend.

No Sex for Me: Asexuality: Hear from people who claim they are asexual, and listen to them explain their feelings about sexuality.

Is Monogamy for Everyone?: A woman discusses her non-monogamous relationship and explains the differences between cheating and experiencing sex outside of her relationship.

Japanese Love Hotels: Author takes a personal tour of a Japanese Love Hotel.

Websites:

Electronic Journal of Human Sexuality ■ This online publication of the Institute for Advanced Study of Human Sexuality in San Francisco disseminates information about all aspects of human sexuality. The site offers a database of research articles, book reviews, and posters from various conference presentations.

San Francisco Sex Information Organization ■ San Francisco Sex Information (SFSI) is a free information and referral switchboard that provides anonymous, accurate, nonjudgmental information about sex. If you have a question about sex, they will answer it or refer you to someone who can.

Healthy Sex ■ HealthySex.com is an educational site, designed by Wendy Maltz, to promote healthy sexuality based on caring, respect, and safety. The site contains information on sexual health, intimacy, communication, sexual abuse and addiction, sexual fantasies, and midlife sex, and links to a variety of sexuality sites.

Go Ask Alice! ■ Go Ask Alice! is a question-and-answer format website produced by Columbia University's Health Education Program. It provides factual, in-depth, straightforward, and nonjudgmental information to improve sexual health. You can visit recently asked questions or search the database.

11 Sexual Orientation

View in **Video**

View in **Video**

View in **Video**

View in **Video**

ABOUT THE CHAPTER OPENING VIDEO – In 2001, the Netherlands became the first country in the world to legalize same-sex marriage. Couples who had been together for many years were finally given the right to marry, which gave them the ability to make a legal commitment to each other. Legal marriage also provided them with all the rights and benefits associated with marriage. Prior to this legalization, couples lived together in registered partnerships that did not provide the same benefits as marriage. Peter and Stephan had been together for 22 years when they wed in 2001. They had a big wedding and invited friends and family from around the world to celebrate their marriage. When I met them in 2010, they had been together for 31 years. In fact, they had been together for so long that they had recently ordered new wedding rings (the original ones had worn out). I spoke with them about how they met, why they married, and same-sex relationships in the Netherlands.

"I was 20 years old when I saw Stephan across the room. It was definitely love at first sight for me. I had a hard time believing that he could be interested in me because he was just so handsome!" Peter said. *"I was seeking a relationship with a guy who had the same ideas and values about life. I found that in Peter,"* Stephan said. *"We have been together since 1979,"* Peter said. *"We have a big group of gay and straight friends, but we were never really into the 'gay scene.' Over the years we have seen many changes in the Netherlands. During the 1980s we lost many good friends to AIDS. We both felt so lucky to be in a committed relationship. It was a sad time. In the mid-1990s, the Netherlands became more accepting of same-sex relationships, but it wasn't until 2001 that same-sex marriage was legalized. We got married as soon as it was legalized. We wanted to make sure that we were protected in case anything happened to either of us. We had a friend whose partner died in the*

hospital, but she wasn't allowed to go in and be with her. When she got back home her partner's belongings were all gone—the family had taken them, and she had nothing to remember her girlfriend. We wanted to make sure this didn't happen to us. We have been with each other longer than either of us was with our parents! When I think back at the hard times in my life, I am still happy to be gay. In fact, if I were ever born again I'd want to be gay again!"

My interview with Peter and Stephan was interesting, funny, and at times heartbreaking. Peter and Stephan's story will help you to understand the depth of love, respect, and commitment inherent in many same-sex relationships. ❚

Janell Caur

"If I were ever born again, I'd want to be gay again."
—CHAPTER OPENING VIDEO

View in Video
To watch the entire interview, go to Psychology CourseMate at **login.cengagebrain.com.**

Sexual orientation refers to the gender(s) that a person is attracted to emotionally, physically, sexually, and romantically. Heterosexuals are predominantly attracted to members of the other sex; homosexuals to members of the same sex; and bisexuals are attracted to both sexes (the word *gay* is often used to refer to a male homosexual, whereas *lesbian* is often used to refer to a female homosexual).

Although such distinctions may seem simple, human sexual behavior does not always fit easily into such neat boxes. Today, many people use the acronym **GLBTQ** to refer to people whose identity is gay, lesbian, bisexual, transgender, or questioning (or queer). Because we discussed transgender issues in Chapter 4 and we focus on gay, lesbian, and bisexual (GLB) issues in this discussion, we will use the acronym *GLB* throughout this chapter.

Before the 1980s, most of published research on homosexuality focused on the causes or on associated mental disorders (because homosexuality was classified as such until 1973; see Chapter 1), whereas in the 1990s, HIV and AIDS dominated the research studies (Boehmer, 2002). Today, we are learning more about the development of GLB identities, coming-out issues, aging, and health care, to name a few areas. We discuss this research throughout this chapter.

▶ WHAT DETERMINES
Sexual Orientation?

How should we categorize a person's **sexual orientation**? The simplest way to categorize a person's sexual orientation seems to be through sexual behavior; that is, with whom does the person have sex? However, there are many other factors to consider. What about a person's sexual fantasies? If a man sometimes fantasizes about sex with men, even though he considers himself **straight** and has sex only with women, what is his sexual orientation?

© Angela Hanlon

People can show enormous variety in their sexual behavior, sexual fantasies, emotional attachments, and sexual self-concept, and each contributes to a person's sexual orientation.

REAL RESEARCH 11.1   In early 2011, Facebook added two new relationship status options. Users can now choose *in a civil union* and *in a domestic partnership* in addition to several other options, including *single, in a relationship, engaged, married, it's complicated, in an open relationship, widowed, separated,* and *divorced* (KELLER, 2011).

Perhaps we should consider romantic love instead of sex to determine a person's sexual orientation. Whom does the person love, or whom could the person love? If a married man has sex

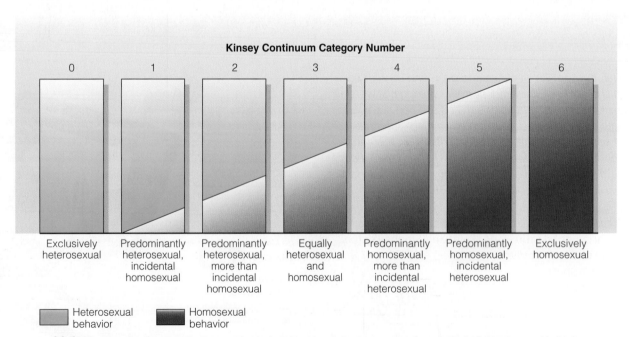

Kinsey Continuum Category Number

| 0 | 1 | 2 | 3 | 4 | 5 | 6 |

| Exclusively heterosexual | Predominantly heterosexual, incidental homosexual | Predominantly heterosexual, more than incidental homosexual | Equally heterosexual and homosexual | Predominantly homosexual, more than incidental heterosexual | Predominantly homosexual, incidental heterosexual | Exclusively homosexual |

Heterosexual behavior   Homosexual behavior

FIGURE **11.1**   The Kinsey continuum. The seven-point scale is based on behaviors ranging from exclusively heterosexual behavior to exclusively homosexual behavior. SOURCE: From Kinsey, A., Pomeroy, W. B., & Martin, C. E. (1948). *Sexual Behavior in the Human Male.* Philadelphia: Saunders. Reprinted by permission of The Kinsey Institute for Research in Sex, Gender, and Reproduction, Inc.

with men but loves his wife romantically and would never consider an emotional attachment to the men he has sex with, would you consider him **heterosexual** just because he loves only his wife? Maybe we should just let people decide for themselves; if they believe they are heterosexual, they are, no matter how they behave. Yet when people's behavior and beliefs about themselves are in conflict, social scientists usually define them by their behavior.

The problem may be that we tend to think of sexual orientation in discrete categories: People are either **homosexual** or heterosexual (or, occasionally, **bisexual**). The full variety and richness of human sexual experience, however, cannot be easily captured in such restrictive categories. People can show enormous variety in their sexual behavior, sexual fantasies, emotional attachments, and sexual self-concept, and each contributes to a person's sexual orientation.

In this chapter, we explore the nature of sexual orientation and the ways researchers and scholars think about it. Heterosexuality is a sexual orientation, and the question "Why is a person heterosexual?" is no less valid than "Why is a person homosexual?" or "Why is a person bisexual?" In this chapter, however, we focus our attention primarily on the research and writing about homosexuality and bisexuality.

ON YOUR MIND 11.1

If I played sex games with a friend of the same sex when I was 15, am I gay?

Sexual experimentation and sexual orientation are two different things. It is very common, especially in the teenage years and before, to experiment with same-sex contact (and for people who are predominantly gay or lesbian to experiment with the other sex). Yet only a fairly small percentage of people who experiment are gay, lesbian, or bisexual (Fay et al., 1989).

MODELS OF SEXUAL ORIENTATION: Who Is Homosexual?

Kinsey and his colleagues (1948) believed that relying on the categories "homosexual" and "heterosexual" to describe sexual orientation was inadequate. They also suggested that using a category such as "homosexual" was not as helpful as talking about homosexual behavior. Trying to decide who is a homosexual is difficult; trying to compare amounts or types of homosexual behavior (including fantasies and emotions) is easier.

So Kinsey introduced a 7-point scale (Figure 11.1) ranging from exclusively heterosexual behavior (0) to exclusively homosexual behavior (6). The Kinsey continuum was the first scale to suggest that people engage in complex sexual behaviors that cannot be reduced simply to "homosexual" and "heterosexual." Many theorists agree that sexual orientation is a continuous variable rather than a categorical variable; that is, there are no natural cutoff points that would easily separate people into categories such as "heterosexual" or "homosexual" (Berkey et al., 1990; L. Ellis et al., 1987).

The Kinsey scale is not without its problems, however. First, Kinsey emphasized people's behavior (although he did consider other factors such as fantasies and emotions), but some researchers suggest that people's emotions and fantasies are the most important determinants of sexual orientation (Bell et al., 1981; F. Klein, 1993; Storms, 1980, 1981). Second, the scale is static in time; how recently must one have had homosexual contact to qualify for "incidents" of homosexual behavior? If a man slept with six men over the last year and had sex with his wife once a week, is he in category 5 (because he had sex with six men and only one woman) or category 2 (because he had 52 experiences with a woman, but only 6 with men; F. Klein, 1990)?

Other models, such as the Klein Sexual Orientation Grid (KSOG; Figure 11.2), try to take the Kinsey continuum further by including seven dimensions—attraction, behavior, fantasy, emotional preference, social preference, self-identification, and

The Klein Sexual Orientation Grid

	Past	Present	Ideal
A. Sexual attraction			
B. Sexual behavior			
C. Sexual fantasies			
D. Emotional preference			
E. Social preference			
F. Self-identification			
G. Heterosexual/homosexual lifestyle			

0 = other sex only
1 = mostly other sex, incidental same sex
2 = mostly other sex, more than incidental same sex
3 = both sexes equally
4 = mostly same sex, more than incidental other sex
5 = mostly same sex, incidental other sex
6 = same sex only

FIGURE 11.2 The Klein Sexual Orientation Grid (KSOG) was designed to examine seven dimensions of an individual's sexual orientation to determine whether these dimensions have changed over time and to look at a person's fantasy of his or her "ideal" sexual orientation. The KSOG gives a set of numbers that can be compared to determine rates of different sexual orientations. Use the Kinsey categories in this grid to rate yourself. SOURCE: From Klein, F. (1990). The need to view sexual orientation as a multivariable dynamic process: A theoretical perspective. In D. P. McWhirter, S. A. Sanders, & J. M. Reinisch (Eds.), *Homosexuality/heterosexuality: Concepts of sexual orientation* (p. 280). New York: Oxford University Press. Reprinted by permission of The Kinsey Institute for Research in Sex, Gender, and Reproduction, Inc.

GLBTQ
Acronym for gay, lesbian, bisexual, transgendered, or questioning (or queer) adults or youths.

sexual orientation
The gender(s) that a person is attracted to emotionally, physically, sexually, and romantically.

straight
Slang for heterosexual.

heterosexual
Man or woman who is erotically attracted to members of the other sex.

homosexual
Man or woman who is erotically attracted to members of the same sex.

bisexual
Person who is erotically attracted to members of either sex.

lifestyle (Horowitz et al., 2001). Each of these dimensions is measured for the past, the present, and the ideal. Take the KSOG to create a profile of your sexual orientation.

▶▶ MEASURING SEXUAL ORIENTATION: **How Prevalent?**

How prevalent are homosexuality, heterosexuality, and bisexuality in society? Kinsey and his colleagues (1948) found that 37% of men and 13% of women reported that they had had at least one adult sexual experience with a member of the same sex that resulted in orgasm, and that about 4% of men and 3% of women were lifelong homosexuals. He also reported that 10% of White men had been mostly gay for at least 3 years between the ages of 16 and 55, and this statistic became the one most people cited when estimating the prevalence of homosexuality in the United States. However, because of the problems with Kinsey's sampling (see Chapter 2), these figures may be unreliable.

There continues to be controversy about how many gays, lesbians, or bisexuals there are today.

There continues to be controversy about how many gays, lesbians, or bisexuals there are today. Estimates for homosexuality range from 2% to 4% to more than 10% in males and 1% to 3% in females, whereas estimates for bisexuality are approximately 3% (M. Diamond, 1993; Hughes, 2006; Seidman & Rieder, 1994; Whitam et al., 1999). Laumann and colleagues (1994) found that although 5.5% of women said they found the thought of having sex with another woman appealing, only about 4% said they had had sex with another woman after the age of 18, and fewer than 2% had had sex with another woman in the past year. Similarly, although 9% of men said they had had sex with another male since puberty, a little more than 5% had had sex with a man since turning 18, and only 2% had had sex with a man in the past year. National studies in France, Britain, Norway, Denmark, and Canada all found same-sex behavior in 1% to 3% of men and a slightly lower percentage in women (Muir, 1993). Overall, surveys indicate that the frequency of same-sex behavior in the United States has remained fairly constant over the years despite changes in the social status of homosexuality (Pillard & Bailey, 1998).

However, there are problems with some of the studies just discussed. For example, many concentrate on same-sex behavior, not attraction, fantasies, or desires. One national population-based study measured both same-sex attraction and behavior, and found that 16% to 20% of the adult population of the United States, United Kingdom, and France reported some same-sex attraction or behavior since age 15 (Sell et al., 1995). Researchers claim these statistics were higher than past percentages because they included same-sex attraction. In addition, these researchers also included men and women who were not currently sexually active but reported a history of same-sex behavior in the past (many studies often do not count nonsexually active men and women as being gay or lesbian, even with a history of same-sex behavior; Sell et al., 1995). Although there is much work to be done in determining the prevalence of homosexuality, scholars generally agree that between 3% and 4% of males are predominantly gay, 1.5% to 2% of women are predominantly lesbian, and about 2% to 5% of people are bisexual (Jenkins, 2010; Laumann et al., 1994).

Although the National Survey of Sexual Health and Behavior provided the most recent statistics on U.S. sexual behaviors, it showed us little about GLB sexual behaviors. Same-sex sexual behavior was relatively uncommon in the National Survey of Sexual Health and Behavior (Herbenick et al., 2010). However, a major limitation of nationally representative survey data is that minority groups, such as gays, lesbians, and bisexuals, are often not well represented (Herbenick et al., 2010).

◀ review QUESTIONS

1 Describe the difficulties involved in our attempts to categorize sexual behavior.

2 Outline the Kinsey model of sexual orientation, and compare and contrast it with the KSOG.

3 Describe the research on the prevalence of GLB orientations. Explain why this research is difficult and may be controversial.

▶ WHY ARE THERE DIFFERENT Sexual Orientations?

In the 1930s and 1940s, a group of scientists tried to explain homosexuality by looking for "masculine" traits in lesbians and "feminine" traits in homosexual men. They claimed that gay men had broad shoulders and narrow hips (indicating "immature skeletal development"), and lesbians had abnormal genitalia, including larger-than-average vulvas, longer labia minora, a larger glans on the clitoris, a smaller uterus, and higher eroticism, shown by their tendency to become sexually aroused when being examined (Terry, 1990)! Modern research has failed to find any significant physiological differences between homosexuals and heterosexuals, although attempts to examine physical differences continue.

Today's theories can be divided into five basic types: biological, developmental, behavioral, sociological, and interactional theories. Biological theories suggest that homosexuals are physically different from heterosexuals. Developmental theories, in contrast, suggest that homosexuality develops in response to a person's upbringing and personal history, and therefore nothing is physically different between the two. Behavioral theory explores how homosexuality is a learned behavior, whereas sociological theories look at how social forces produce homosexuality in a society. Finally, interactional theories look at the interaction between biology, development, and societal factors.

Scholars in different fields tend to take different approaches to explain why some people are gay, lesbian, or bisexual. Note, however, that almost all the researchers we will discuss assume there are two exclusive, nonoverlapping categories: homosexual and heterosexual. Most theories on sexual orientation ignore bisexuality or do not offer enough research to explain why bisexuality exists. We discuss bisexuality throughout this chapter.

▶▶ BIOLOGICAL Theories

Early biological theories implied that homosexuality was an abnormality in development, which contributed to the argument that homosexuality is a sickness. More recently, gay and lesbian scholars, in an attempt to prove that homosexuality is not a "lifestyle choice" as antihomosexual forces have argued, have themselves been arguing that homosexuality is a biologically based sexual variation. Biological theories claim that differing sexual orientations are due to differences in physiology. These differences can be due to genetics, hormones, birth order, or physiology.

Genetics

In 1952, Franz Kallman tried to show that there was a genetic component to homosexuality. Kallman compared identical twins (who come from one zygote and have the same genes; we talk more about twins in Chapter 12) with fraternal twins (who come from two zygotes). Although Kallman found a strong genetic component to homosexuality, his study had a number of problems and is unreliable.

Bailey and his colleagues have performed a number of studies of twins to determine the genetic basis of homosexuality. They report that in homosexual males, 52% of identical twins, 22% of fraternal twins, and 11% of adoptive brothers were also gay, showing that the more closely genetically related two siblings were, the more likely they were to share a sexual orientation (J. M. Bailey & Pillard, 1995). Among females, 48% of identical twins, 16% of fraternal twins, and 6% of adoptive siblings of lesbians were also lesbians (J. M. Bailey et al., 1995). However, identical twins share much more than genetics. They also share many more experiences than do other kinds of siblings. So the studies cannot tell how much of the concordance is due to genetic factors and how much is due to the identical twins having grown up under similar environmental influences.

Some studies have found that sexual orientation is familial (runs in the family; Francis, 2008; Schwartz et al., 2010). Hamer and colleagues (1993) found that gay males tended to have more

ON YOUR MIND 11.2

Why are men often turned on by watching two females having sex but turned off by watching two males?

Heterosexual men's magazines often feature two women together in sexual positions but almost never two men. In the United States, watching women interact sexually is much more socially acceptable. These pictorials always imply that the women are still attracted to men, waiting for them, just biding their time until a man arrives. An internalized fear of homosexuality in men also makes it difficult for many men to see two men being sexual with each other. It is much less threatening to watch two women. In Chapter 18, we discuss gender and the use of pornography.

gay relatives on their mother's side, and he traced that to the existence of a gene that he found in 33 of 40 gay brothers. This gene is inherited from the mother's, but not the father's, side (Keller, 2005). Gay men also have more gay brothers than lesbian sisters, whereas lesbians have more lesbian sisters than gay brothers (Bogaert, 2005; Pattatucci, 1998). Other studies support the familial link but have found that male sexual orientation is inherited from the father's, and not the mother's, side (Schwartz et al., 2010). In this study, gay men were found to have more homosexual male relatives than heterosexual men, and sisters of gay men were more likely to be lesbians than sisters of heterosexual men (Schwartz et al., 2010).

If homosexuality were solely a genetic trait, it should have disappeared long ago. Because homosexuals have been less likely than heterosexuals to have children, each successive generation of homosexuals should have become smaller, until genes for homosexuality disappeared from the gene pool. Yet rates of homosexuality have remained constant. Concordance rates for siblings, twins, and adoptees reveal that genes account for at least half of the variance in sexual orientation (Pillard & Bailey, 1998). Even so, Bailey and his colleagues agree that environmental factors are also important.

Hormones

Hormonal theories can concentrate either on hormonal imbalances before birth or on hormone levels in adults. In this section, we examine both prenatal and adult hormonal levels.

PRENATAL FACTORS When certain hormones are injected into pregnant animals, such as rats or guinea pigs, at critical periods of fetal development, the offspring can be made to exhibit homosexual behavior (for more information about hormones, see Chapter 4; Dorner, 1983). Some researchers have found evidence that sexual orientation may be influenced by levels of prenatal hormones in human beings as well (Berenbaum & Snyder, 1995; Cohen-Bendahan et al., 2005; Jenkins, 2010; Rahman, 2005; Swaab, 2004). Hormonal levels can be affected by stress during pregnancy, and research has explored how this stress can influence the sexual orientation of a fetus (L. Ellis, 1988; Hall & Schaeff, 2008).

Although many of the hormonal studies have focused on deficiencies in certain hormones, there is also research indicating that excess hormonal exposure during prenatal development may be related to sexual orientation. For example, females who were exposed to diethylstilbestrol (DES; synthetic estrogen) in the womb are more likely to identify as bisexual or lesbian compared with those females not exposed to DES (Meyer-Bahlburg et al., 1985).

Overall, the evidence for the effect of prenatal hormones on both male and female homosexuality is weak (Gooren, 2006; Hall & Schaeff, 2008; Whalen et al., 1990). In other words, even if prenatal hormones are a factor in sexual orientation, environmental factors may be equally important. The one area of research in prenatal hormones that has yielded the most interesting research has

---

REAL RESEARCH 11.2 Studies have found that gay men are better at recognizing faces than both lesbians and straight men (BREWSTER ET AL., 2010).

---

been on finger lengths, which we will discuss in the upcoming physiology section. Finger-length ratios have been found to be related to prenatal hormonal levels (Hall & Schaeff, 2008).

ADULT HORMONE LEVELS Many studies have compared blood androgen levels in adult male homosexuals with those in adult male heterosexuals, and most have found no significant differences (Green, 1988; Mbügua, 2006). Of five studies comparing hormone levels in lesbians and straight women, three found no differences between the two groups in testosterone, estrogen, or other hormones, and the other two found higher levels of testosterone in lesbians (and one found lower levels of estrogen; Dancey, 1990). Thus, studies so far do not support the idea of adult hormone involvement.

Birth Order

Gay men have more older brothers than heterosexual men (Blanchard, 2008; McConaghy et al., 2006). This is often explained by the **maternal immune hypothesis,** which proposes there is a progressive immunization to male-specific antigens after the birth of successive sons in some mothers, which increases the effects of anti-male antibodies on the sexual differentiation of the brain in the developing fetus (this has also been referred to as the fraternal birth order effect; R. Blanchard, 2008; Bogaert & Skorska, 2011; Schwartz et al., 2010; Valenzuela, 2010). Research has found that in families with multiple brothers, later born brothers from the same mother are more likely to be homosexual (R. Blanchard, 2004; Bogaert and Skorska, 2011; Camperio-Ciani et al., 2004; Francis, 2008). Each older brother increase's a man's chance of being gay by about 33% (Blanchard, 2008; Francis, 2010). However, the presence of older sisters from the same biological mom decreases the likelihood of homosexuality (Francis, 2008). Siblings from different mothers do not have an effect on sexual orientation (Blanchard, 1997).

Although most of the research on birth order has been done on men, limited research on women has found that having an older brother or any sisters decreases the likelihood of homosexuality in women (Francis, 2008). This research is controversial, but nonetheless research in this direction continues to look for possible interactions.

Physiology

Two articles in the early 1990s reported differences between the brains of homosexual and heterosexual men (S. LeVay, 1991; Swaab & Hofman, 1990). Both studies found that certain areas of the hypothalamus, known to play a strong role in sexual urges, were either larger or smaller in gay men than in straight men. More recent studies have also found brain differences—specifically in the cerebral hemispheres—of heterosexual and homosexual men and women (Hu et al., 2008; Ponseti et al., 2006, 2009; Savic & Lindström, 2008). Another study found that straight men and lesbian women have similar brain structures, as do gay men and straight women (Savic & Lindström, 2008). Brain research has found that gay men use both sides of their brain, a pattern similar to heterosexual women (Brewster et al., 2010). However, it has not yet been determined whether brain differences were there from birth or developed later in life, and the research cannot prove that the differences were primarily due to sexual orientation (Kinnunen et al., 2004; Swaab, 2004).

Physiology studies have also looked at differences between heterosexuals and homosexuals for a variety of factors, such as the amount of facial hair, size of external genitalia, ear structure, hair whorls (a cowlick in the back of a hair part), hearing, body shape, eye-blink startle responses, and spatial ability (A. Bailey & Hurd, 2005; Beaton & Mellor, 2007; Hall & Schaeff, 2008; Johnson et al., 2007; McFadden, 2011; Rahman et al., 2010; Rahman & Koerting, 2008). Gay men and heterosexual women have similar spatial learning and memory abilities that differ from heterosexual men (Rahman & Koerting, 2008). Research on handedness has found that gay men are more likely than straight men to be left-handed (R. Blanchard et al., 2006, 2008; Brewster et al., 2010; Martin et al., 2008; Schwartz et al., 2010; Valenzuela, 2008).

However, the most physiological research has been done on finger lengths. The typical male-type finger pattern is a longer ring finger than index finger, whereas the typical female-type pattern is similar index and ring finger lengths, or a longer index finger. Lesbian women are more commonly found to have a typical male-type finger length pattern, whereas gay men are more likely to have a typical female-type finger length pattern (Galis et al., 2010; Grimbos et al., 2010; Hall & Schaeff, 2008; Martin et al., 2008; Schwartz et al., 2010). In addition, men with typical female-type finger length patterns have been found to be more emotional than men with a typical male-type finger length (Rizman et al., 2007). Researchers have found that finger length is affected by prenatal testosterone and estrogen levels, especially in the right hand (McFadden et al., 2005; Rizwan et al., 2007; Schwartz et al., 2010).

In summary, although there have been some biological differences found among homosexuals, heterosexuals, and bisexuals, the findings are inconsistent, and in many cases, the evidence is weak. Given the complexity of biological factors, it is impossible to

---

maternal immune hypothesis
Theory of sexual orientation that proposes that the fraternal birth order effect of gay brothers reflects the progressive immunization of some mothers to male-specific antigens by each succeeding male fetus.

gender-role nonconformity
Theory that looks at the role of early childhood in the development of homosexuality and explores cross-gendered traits in childhood.

make accurate individual predications because of the randomness of neural connections during development (Pillard, 1998). Because of this, it appears that sexual orientation is the result of an interaction of genetic, biological, and social influences (Schüklenk et al., 1997). We now examine some of the developmental, behaviorist, sociological, and interactional theories of sexual orientation.

►► DEVELOPMENTAL Theories

Developmental theories focus on a person's upbringing and personal history to find the origins of homosexuality. First, we discuss the most influential development theory, psychoanalytic theory; then we examine gender-role nonconformity and peer-interaction theories of homosexuality.

Freud and the Psychoanalytic School

Sigmund Freud (1953) seemed to be of two minds about homosexuality. On the one hand, he believed that the infant was "polymorphous perverse"—that is, the infant sees all kinds of things as potentially sexual. Because both males and females are potentially attractive to the infant, thought Freud, all of us are inherently bisexual. He therefore did not see homosexuals as being sick.

On the other hand, Freud saw male heterosexuality as the result of normal maturation and male homosexuality as the result of an unresolved Oedipal complex (see Chapter 2 for a more complete discussion of this topic). An intense attachment to the mother coupled with a distant father could lead the boy to fear revenge by the father through castration. Female genitalia, lacking a penis, could then represent this castration and evoke fear throughout his life. After puberty, the child might shift from desire for the mother to identification with her and begin to look for the love objects she would look for—men.

Like Freud's view of female sexuality in general, his theories on lesbianism were less coherent, but he basically argued that the young girl becomes angry when she discovers she lacks a penis and blames her mother (we discussed the Electra complex in Chapter 2). Unable to have her father, she defensively rejects him and all men, and minimizes her anger at her mother by eliminating the competition between them for male affection.

Freud viewed homosexuality as partly narcissistic; by making love to a body like one's own, one is really making love to a mirror of oneself. Freud's generally tolerant attitude toward homosexuality was rejected by some later psychoanalysts, especially Sandor Rado (1949). Rado claimed that humans were not innately bisexual and that homosexuality was a mental illness. This view (not Freud's) became standard for the psychiatric profession until at least the 1970s.

Another influential researcher who followed Rado's perspective was Irving Bieber. Bieber and colleagues (1962) studied 106 homosexual men and 100 heterosexual men who were in psychoanalysis. He claimed that all boys had a normal, erotic attraction to women. However, some had overly close and possessive mothers who were also overintimate and sexually seductive. Their fathers, in contrast, were hostile or absent, and this drove the boy to the arms of his mother, who inhibited his normal masculine develop-

ment. Bieber thus blamed homosexuality on a seductive mother who puts the fear of heterosexuality in her son. However, Bieber's participants were all in psychoanalysis and thus might have had other issues. Also, fewer than two thirds of the homosexual par-

ticipants fit his model, and almost a third of heterosexual participants came from the same type of family and yet did not engage in homosexual behavior.

The psychoanalytic views of homosexuality dominated for many years. Evelyn Hooker, a clinical psychologist, was a pioneer in gay studies who tried to combat the psychoanalytic view that homosexuality was an illness (see Chapter 2). Hooker (1957) used psychological tests, personal histories, and psychological evaluations to show that homosexuals were as well-adjusted as heterosexuals, and that no real evidence existed that homosexuality was a psychological disorder. Although it took many years for her ideas to take hold, many modern psychoanalysts eventually shifted away from the pathological view of homosexuality. Lewes (1988) demonstrated that psychoanalytic theory itself could easily portray homosexuality as a result of healthy development, and that previous psychoanalytic interpretations of homosexuality were based more on prejudice than on science.

Gender-Role Nonconformity

One group of studies that has begun to fuel debate about the role of early childhood in the development of homosexuality is **gender-role nonconformity** research. The studies are based on the observation that boys who exhibit cross-gender traits—that is, who behave in ways more characteristic of girls of that age—are more likely to grow up to be gay, whereas girls who behave in typically male ways are more likely to grow up to be lesbian. As

---

REAL RESEARCH 11.3 Studies on physical development have found significant differences in the heights and weights of gay/bisexual and straight men (BOGAERT, 2010). Gay/bisexual men were significantly shorter and lighter than heterosexual men.

---

children, gay men, on average, have been found to be more feminine than straight men, whereas lesbians have been found to be more masculine (Alanko et al., 2010; Bailey & Pillard, 1995; Pillard, 1991). In childhood, both gays and lesbians recall more gender-atypical behavior than heterosexual men and women (Alanko et al., 2010), and similar findings have been found in different cultural groups (Lippa & Tan, 2001). Remember, though, that these findings are correlational, meaning that cross-gender traits and later homosexuality appear to be related but do not have a cause-and-effect relationship.

Overall, in U.S. society, cross-gender boys are viewed more negatively than cross-gender girls (Sandnabba & Ahlberg, 1999). In addition, cross-gender boys are more often thought to be gay than cross-gender girls are thought to be lesbian. One therapist who works with gay men reports that they saw themselves as:

> …more sensitive than other boys; they cried more easily, had their feelings more readily hurt, had more aesthetic interests, enjoyed nature, art, and music, and were drawn to other "sensitive" boys, girls and adults. Most of these men also felt they were less aggressive as children than others of their age, and most did not enjoy participating in competitive activities. They report that they experienced themselves as being outsiders since these early childhood years. (Isay, 1989, p. 23)

R. Green (1987) did a prospective study by comparing 66 pervasively feminine boys with 56 conventionally masculine boys as they matured. Green calls the feminine boys "sissy-boys," an unfortunate term. However, he found that these boys cross-dressed, were interested in female fashions, played with dolls, avoided rough play, wished to be girls, and did not desire to be like their fathers from a young age. Three fourths of them grew up to be homosexual or bisexual, whereas only one of the masculine boys became bisexual. The "sissy-boys," however, also tended to be harassed, rejected, and ignored more by their peers, and they had higher rates of physical and psychological disorders (Zucker, 1990).

One cannot tell from these types of studies whether these boys are physiologically or developmentally different, or whether society's reaction to their unconventional play encouraged them to develop a particular sexual orientation. Whether right or wrong, gender-role nonconformity theory cannot be the sole explanation of homosexuality, for many, if not most, gay men were not effeminate as children; not all effeminate boys grow up to be gay, and not all "tomboy" girls grow up to be lesbians.

Peer Group Interaction

Storms (1981) suggests a purely developmental theory of homosexuality. Noting that a person's sex drive begins to develop in adolescence, Storms suggests that those who develop early begin to become sexually aroused before they have significant contact with the other sex. Because dating usually begins around age 15, boys who mature at age 12 still play and interact in predominantly same-sex groupings, and thus their emerging erotic feelings are more likely to focus on boys.

Storms's theory is supported by the fact that homosexuals do tend to report earlier sexual contacts than heterosexuals. Also,

men's sex drive may emerge at a younger age than women's, if such things as frequency of masturbation are any measure, which may explain why there are fewer lesbians than gay men.

Yet Storms's theory also has its problems. Later in this chapter, we will discuss the example of Sambian boys who live communally and have sex with other boys from an early age until they are ready to marry. If Storms is right and a male becomes homosexual because only males are available at the time of sexual awakening, then all male Sambians should be gay. However, almost all go on to lead heterosexual lives.

▶▶ BEHAVIORIST Theories

Behaviorists consider homosexuality a learned behavior, brought about by the reinforcement of homosexual behaviors or the punishing of heterosexual behavior (Masters & Johnson, 1979). For example, a person may have a same-sex encounter that is pleasurable, coupled with an encounter with the other sex that is frightening; in his or her fantasies, that person may focus on the same-sex encounter, reinforcing its pleasure with masturbation. Masters and Johnson (1979) believed that even in adulthood, some men and women move toward same-sex behaviors if they have bad heterosexual encounters and pleasant same-sex ones.

It is interesting to point out, however, that in a society like ours that tends to view heterosexuality as the norm, it would seem that few men and women would be societally reinforced for homosexual behavior. Yet homosexuality exists even without this positive reinforcement from society.

reparative therapy
Therapy to change sexual orientation; also called *sexual reorientation* or *conversion therapy.*

▶▶ SOCIOLOGICAL Theories

Sociological theories look at how social forces produce homosexuality in a society. They suggest that concepts such as homosexuality, bisexuality, and heterosexuality are products of our social fabric and are dependent on how we as a society decide to define things. In other words, we learn our culture's way of thinking about sexuality, and then we apply it to ourselves.

The idea of "homosexuality" is a product of a particular culture at a particular time; the idea did not even exist before the 19th century (although the behavior did). Some have argued that the use of the term *homosexuality* as a way to think about same-sex behavior arose only after the Industrial Revolution freed people economically from the family unit and urbanization allowed them to choose new lifestyles in the cities (Adam, 1987). Thus, the idea that people are either "heterosexual" or "homosexual" is not a biological fact but simply a way of thinking that evolves as social conditions change. In other countries, as we note later, these terms are not used, and a person's sexuality is not defined by the gender of his or her partners.

Sociologists are interested in the models of sexuality that society offers its members and how individuals come to identify with one model or another. For example, maybe effeminate young boys begin to behave as homosexuals because they are labeled homosexual, are called "faggot" by their peers, are ridiculed by their siblings, and even witness the worry and fear on the faces of their parents. They begin to doubt themselves, search for homosexuality in their own behavior, and eventually find it. If American society did not split the sexual world into "homosexual" and "heterosexual" categories, perhaps these boys would move fluidly through same-sex and other-sex contacts without having to choose between the "gay" and "straight" communities.

Many gay and lesbian children report **playmates of both the same sex and the other sex** *while growing up.*

▶▶ INTERACTIONAL Theory

Finally, interactional theory proposes that homosexuality results from a complex interaction of biological, psychological, and social factors. Perhaps a child is born after being exposed to prenatal hormones that could predispose him or her toward a particular sexual orientation, but this predisposition, in conjunction with social experiences, either facilitates or inhibits a particular sexual orientation.

Social psychologist Daryl Bem (2000) has proposed an interactional theory that combines both biology and sociological issues. Bem suggests that biological variables, such as genetics, hormones, and brain neuroanatomy, do not cause certain sexual orientations, but rather they contribute to childhood temperaments that influence a child's preferences for sex-typical or sex-atypical activities and peers.

Bem believes that males who engage in "male-typical activities," such as rough-and-tumble play or competitive team sports, prefer to be with other boys who also like these activities. Girls, in contrast, who prefer "female-typical activities," such as socializing quietly or playing jacks, prefer the company of other girls who like to do the same activities. Gender-conforming children (those who engage in activities typical for their gender) prefer the other gender for romantic interests, whereas nonconforming children prefer the same gender. Bem's "exotic-becomes-erotic" theory suggests that sexual feelings evolve from experiencing heightened arousal in situations in which one gender is viewed as more exotic, or different from oneself (Bem, 2000). Bem asserts that gay and lesbian children had playmates of the other sex while growing up, and this led them to see the same sex as more "exotic" and appealing. However, his research has been contradictory and hasn't been supported by other research (Peplau et al., 1998). Many gay and lesbian children report playmates of both the same sex and the other sex while growing up.

◀ review QUESTIONS

1 Identify and describe the various areas of research within the biological theory of homosexuality.

2 Identify and describe the various developmental theories of homosexuality.

3 Explain the behavioral theory of homosexuality.

4 Explain the sociological theory of homosexuality.

5 Explain the interactional theory of homosexuality.

6 Differentiate the various theories that have been proposed to explain homosexuality.

HOMOSEXUALITY IN OTHER Times and Places

When the APA decided in 1973 to remove homosexuality from its list of official mental diseases, many psychiatrists were outraged. They demanded a vote of the full APA membership (Bayer, 1981). For 100 years or so, homosexuality was considered a sickness. Only when scientists dropped that assumption did they make real progress in understanding homosexuality. The enormous complexity of the human brain allows highly flexible human behavior patterns in almost every aspect of life, and human sexuality is not an exception to that rule.

Homosexuality remains controversial in the United States. Some people see homosexuality as a sin. Others argue that homosexuals are a "bad influence" on society and children (and, for example, believe they should not be allowed to fight in the military, or become parents and/or teachers). Still others defend homosexual rights and attack America's whole view of sexuality.

Many other countries are much more tolerant of homosexuality than the United States. Western history has included many periods when homosexuality was generally accepted. In fact, Gilbert Herdt (1988), a prominent scholar of homosexuality, states that the modern American attitude is much harsher toward homosexuality than most other countries throughout most of history. The history of social attitudes toward homosexuality can teach us something about our own attitudes today.

HOMOSEXUALITY in History

Homosexuality has been viewed differently throughout history. Although there have been times when homosexuality has been accepted, there have also been times it has been scorned. The influence of the Church has greatly affected societal tolerance and acceptance of homosexuality.

Ancient societies left evidence to show that same-sex behavior was not uncommon.

© Mimmo Jodice/Corbis

The Classical Era

Before the 19th century, men who engaged in homosexual acts were accused of **sodomy** (SA-duh-mee), or **buggery,** which were simply seen as crimes and not considered part of a person's fundamental nature. Homosexual activity was common, homosexual prostitution was taxed by the state, and the writers of the time seemed to consider men loving men as natural as men loving women. Even after Rome became Christian, there was no antihomosexual legislation for more than 200 years.

Lesbian love seems to have puzzled ancient writers (who were almost all men). The word *lesbian* itself comes from the island of Lesbos, in Greece, where the poet Sappho lived about 600 B.C. Lesbianism was rarely explicitly against the law in most ancient societies (in fact, two or more unmarried women living together has usually been seen as proper, whereas a woman living alone was viewed with suspicion; Bullough, 1979).

Contrary to popular belief, homosexuality was not treated with concern or much interest by early Christians (Boswell, 1980). Neither ancient Greek nor Hebrew had a word for homosexual; it was rarely mentioned in the Bible; Saint Paul never explicitly condemned homosexuality; and Jesus made few pronouncements on proper or improper sexuality (except fidelity) and never mentioned homosexuality. Why, then, did Christianity become so antihomosexual?

The Middle Ages

By the ninth century, almost every part of Europe had some sort of local law code based on Church teachings, and although these codes included strong sanctions for sexual transgressions, including rape, adultery, incest, and fornication, homosexual relations were not forbidden in any of them (Boswell, 1980). Church indifference to homosexuality lasted well through the 13th century; in other words, for the first 1,000 years of Christianity, the Church showed little interest in homosexuality and did not generally condemn the behavior (Boswell, 1980; Kuefler, 2006; Siker, 1994). Male brothels appeared, defenses of homosexual relations began to appear in print, and homosexuality became a fairly accepted part of the general culture until the late Middle Ages.

Homosexuality was completely legal in most countries in Europe in the year 1250 (Boswell, 1980). By 1300, however, there was a new intolerance of differences, and homosexuality was punishable by death almost everywhere (Boswell, 1980; Kuefler, 2006). This view from the late Middle Ages has influenced the Western world's view of homosexuality for the last 700 years.

The Modern Era

From the 16th century on, homosexuals were subject to periods of tolerance and periods of severe repression. In the American colonies, for example, homosexuality was a serious offense. In 1656, the New Haven Colony prescribed death for both males and females who engaged in homosexual acts (Boswell, 1980). The severe attitude toward homosexuality in America reflects its Puritan origins, and America remains, even today, more disapproving of homosexuality than Europe is.

Even in times when homosexual acts were condemned, however, homoerotic poems, writings, and art were created. Openly homosexual communities appeared now and then. Other cultures

It is important to remember that although we have been exploring the gay, lesbian, and bisexual (GLB) experiences in the United States, in different parts of the world, GLB adolescents may have very different experiences. Here we take a look at adolescents in a variety of places around the globe.

English (male): Between the ages of 13 and 15 I closed myself off from the outside world. I would rarely go out and would never dare to go places where other people of my own age would be. The only thing I knew was that homosexuality was bad. (Plummer, 1989, p. 204)

East Indian (female): My family holds Western culture somehow responsible for offbeat youth. They think my being a lesbian is my being young, and confused, and rebellious. They feel it has something to do with trying to fit into white culture....They're waiting for me to stop rebelling and go heterosexual, go out on dates, and come home early. (Tremble et al., 1989, p. 260)

Mexican (male): I thought myself very bad, and many times I was at the point of suicide. I don't know if I really might have killed myself, but many times I thought about it and believed it was the only alternative. That caused me many problems with my friends. I felt they thought me to be different, homosexual, and really sick. It made me separate from them. I felt myself inferior and thought I was the only one these things happened to. (Carrier, 1989, p. 238)

Chinese (male): I am longing to love others and to be loved. I have met some other homosexuals, but I have doubt about this type of love. With all the pressure I was afraid to reveal myself and ruined everything. As a result, we departed without showing each other homosexual love. As I am growing older my homosexual desire increases. This is too troubling and depressing for anyone. I thought about death many times. When you are young you cannot fall in love and when you are old you will be alone. Thinking of this makes the future absolutely hopeless. (Ruan & Tsai, 1988, p. 194)

Canadian (female): I feel like I am the terrific person I am today because I'm a lesbian. I decided I was gay when I was very young. After making that decision, which was the hardest thing I could ever face, I feel like I can do anything. (Schneider, 1989, p. 123)

Scottish (male): I don't like being gay. I wouldn't choose to be gay, and I don't like the gay scene. It's too superficial. I've got high moral standards. Lust is a sin but love isn't. In the gay scene people use other people and throw them away again. (Burbidge & Walters, 1981, p. 41)

Asian American (gender not identified): I wish I could tell my parents—they are the only ones who do not know about my gay identity, but I am sure they would reject me. There is no frame of reference to understand homosexuality in Asian American culture. (Chan, 1989, p. 19)

also had periods of relative tolerance of homosexuality. In Japan, for example, the Edo period (1600–1868) saw a flourishing homosexual subculture, with openly gay clubs, geisha houses, and a substantial gay literature (Hirayama & Hirayama, 1986).

During the 19th and early 20th centuries in the United States, it was not uncommon for single, upper-middle-class women to live together in committed, lifelong relationships, although they may not all have engaged in genital sexuality (Nichols, 1990). At the same time, **passing women** disguised themselves as men, entered the workforce, and even married women—who sometimes never knew their husbands were female. In most cases, of course, the wife knew, and the couple probably lived as lesbians in a disguised heterosexual marriage. Some of these passing women held offices of great power, and their biological sex was not discovered until their death (Nichols, 1990).

In the 19th and early 20th centuries, physicians and scientists began to suggest that homosexuality was not a sin but an illness, which, if left "untreated," would spread like a contagious disease (Hansen, 1989). The dangers of this perspective were realized in Nazi Germany, where homosexuals were imprisoned and murdered along with Jews, Gypsies, epileptics, and others as part of the program to purify the "Aryan race" (Adam, 1987). In America, psychiatry continued to view homosexuality as a mental disorder into the 1970s—and some psychiatrists still do today.

Ironically, the medical model's view of homosexuality, which influenced modern ideas of sexual orientation, changed the politics of homosexuality. Because physicians saw homosexuality not as just a behavior but as a built-in trait, it became a primary part of the way people looked at each other (Risman & Schwartz, 1988). Homosexuals began to argue: "If homosexuality is something I am, not just something I do, then I should have a right to be 'who I am' just as Blacks, women, and other groups have a right to be who they are." The new view of homosexuality encouraged homosexuals to band together and press for recognition of their civil rights as a minority group, which led to the modern gay and lesbian liberation movement we discussed in Chapter 1.

sodomy
Any of various forms of sexual intercourse held to be unnatural or abnormal, especially anal intercourse or bestiality (also called *buggery*).

buggery
Any of various forms of sexual intercourse held to be unnatural or abnormal, especially anal intercourse or bestiality (also called *sodomy*).

lesbian
Woman who is sexually attracted to women.

passing woman
Woman who disguises herself as a man.

▶▶ HOMOSEXUALITY IN **Other Cultures**

We all have a natural tendency to believe that others see the world the way we do. Yet what we call "homosexuality" is viewed so differently in other cultures that the word itself might not apply. In many societies, individuals have same-sex sexual relations as a normal part of their lives. This can be minor, as in Cairo, Egypt, where heterosexual men casually kiss and hold hands, or it can be fully sexual, as in the sequential homosexuality of Papua New Guinea, where young males have sexual contact exclusively with other males until getting married at age 18, after which they have sexual contact only with women (see the subsequent discussion on the Sambian tribe).

Cultural factors play an important role in acceptance of homosexuality.

Same-sex behavior is found in every culture, and its prevalence remains about the same no matter how permissive or repressive that culture's attitude is toward it (Mihalik, 1988). A classic study by Broude and Greene (1976) examined 42 societies for which there were good data on attitudes toward homosexuality. They found that a substantial number of the cultures in the sample have an accepting or only mildly disapproving view of homosexual behavior, and less than half punished homosexuals for their sexual activities.

The International Gay and Lesbian Human Rights Commission works to protect the rights of gays, lesbians, and bisexuals around the world. In many parts of the world, GLB men and women experience discrimination, harassment, physical and emotional abuse, and violence. Many are forbidden to live with a same-sex partner, and some are forced into heterosexual marriages, raped, imprisoned, beaten, or killed because of their sexual orientation. In this section, we explore some country-specific information on how GLB men and women are treated around the world.

Cultural factors play an important role in acceptance of homosexuality. Following we explore a variety of cultures.

Latin American Countries

Several Latin American countries have decriminalized consensual intimacy between same-sex couples, including Brazil, Colombia, Ecuador, Mexico, Chile, Puerto Rico, and Nicaragua (International Gay and Lesbian Human Rights Commission, 2010). Although many other Latin American countries may be open to same-sex relationships, political and public support for these relationships may not be as strong. For example, many older and younger Costa Ricans support same-sex relationships and the legal recognition of these relationships, but the country has been controlled by the Catholic church, which does not support these relationships (Mayer, 2011).

In Brazil, same-sex behavior has been legal since 1830, although there are less legal rights for same-sex couples. Over the last few years, there have been several legal amendments to legalize same-sex relationships, but as of 2010, no laws had been passed (Moreira, 2007). There are many GLB organizations in Brazil, and every year the São Paulo Gay Pride Parade, one of the world's largest gay, lesbian, bisexual, and transgender (GLBT) celebrations, takes place. Beginning in 2010, the Brazilian census collected information on same-sex relationships.

In many Central and South American countries, people do not tend to think in terms of homosexuality and heterosexuality, but rather in terms of masculinity and femininity. Male gender roles, for example, are defined by one's **machismo,** which, in terms of sexual behavior, is determined by being the active partner, or penetrator. Therefore, a man is not considered homosexual for taking the active, penetrating role in intercourse, even if he is penetrating other men. As long as he is penetrating, he is masculine.

In Nicaragua, for example, penetrating another man does not make you homosexual; a man who is the active partner in same-sex anal intercourse is called *machista* or *hombre-hombre* ("manly man"), a term used for any masculine male (Murray & Dynes, 1999). In fact, penetrating other men is seen as a sign of manliness and prestige, whereas feminine men allow themselves to be penetrated and are generally scorned.

Note that the implicit message of such cultures is that to mimic female behavior is disgraceful and shameful in a male. This attitude reflects the general nature of these societies, which tend to be patriarchal, with women lacking political and social power. Because women are, in general, considered inferior to men, men who mimic women are to be ridiculed.

Arabic Cultures

Although classic works of Arabic poetry use homoerotic imagery, and young boys were often used as the standard of beauty and sexuality in Arabic writing (Boswell, 1980), homosexuality in Arab countries, like sexuality in general, is usually not discussed. It is not uncommon to see men holding hands or walking down the street arm in arm, but for the most part, male homosexuality is taboo. Sexual relations in the Middle East are often about power and are based on dominant and subordinate positions. Because of this, similar to some Latin American countries, being the penetrating partner with another man does not make a man gay (Sati, 1998).

In many Middle Eastern countries, homosexuality is a crime punishable by death. Although the same-sex behavior in Iraq is not prohibited, there are high levels of persecution of gays and lesbians made worse by constant war (International Gay and Lesbian Human Rights Commission, 2010). Although attitudes about homosexuality are slowly changing in Arabic cultures, many countries still view homosexuality as aberrant (Sherif, 2004).

Asian and Pacific Countries

Several Asian countries, including Bangladesh, India, Malaysia, Pakistan, Singapore, and Sri Lanka have laws against same-sex behavior (International Gay and Lesbian Human Rights Commission, 2010; Misra, 2009). In 2001, the Chinese Psychiatric As-

---

machismo
Characterized or motivated by stereotypical masculine behavior or actions.

sequential homosexuality
Situation in which heterosexual or bisexual men and women go through a period of homosexuality for a variety of reasons, including cultural and societal.

sociation removed homosexuality from its list of mental disorders (Gallagher, 2001). This is a significant change for China, which as recently as 1994 openly opposed homosexuality. Homosexuality was seen as a result of Western influences, and it was considered a "Western social disease" (Ruan & Lau, 2004). In India, although homosexual sex is punishable by up to 10 years in jail, several gay couples have made headlines by publicly declaring themselves married in an attempt to overturn an existing law from 1861 (Predrag, 2005). Not much is known about lesbians in Indian culture, but we do know that lesbians are less accepted than gay men overall (Biswas, 2005). Indian culture has long been patriarchal, and it is not uncommon for some families who fear their daughters might be gay to quickly marry them off (Biswas, 2005).

Other Asian societies have different views of homosexuality. Buddhism does not condemn homosexuality, and so Buddhist countries generally accept it. In Thailand, for example, there are no laws against homosexuality, and men may live sexually with boys over 13, who are considered old enough to make their own decisions (W. L. Williams, 1990). In Hong Kong, although the age of consent for heterosexual sex and sex between women is 16, the age of consent for sex between two men is 21 years old (Leonard, 2006). Men who have sex with a man before age 21 risk a life in prison, whereas heterosexuals and lesbians face a maximum of 5 years in jail if they have sex before age 16. Experts claim that the age of consent differences are based on the fact that gay men engage in anal sex, which is more likely to spread sexually transmitted infections (Leonard, 2006).

Argentina was the first country in Latin America to allow gay couples to wed. However, the battle to legalize same-sex marriage was very bitter between the government and the Roman Catholic Church. Here a man holds a sign reading "Yes, I want equality" during a 2010 demonstration in support of gay marriage in Argentina.

African Countries

More than two thirds of African countries have laws against homosexual behavior (International Gay and Lesbian Human Rights Commission, 2010). Homosexuality is illegal and punishable by death in countries such as Nigeria, Sudan, and Saudi Arabia, and punishable by up to 10 years of jail in Egypt, Tanzania, Algeria, Morocco, and Ethiopia. In many of countries, those who challenge existing laws are arrested, punished, jailed, and/or discriminated against in work, education, and/or health care.

In 2010, news about "corrective rape" of South African lesbians began circulating on the Internet (Huff-Hannon, 2011). To call attention to the practice, a group in Capetown, South Africa, named *Luleki Sizwe* (named after two South African women who died after "corrective rape") began posting photographs of women who had been beaten and raped, along with a petition to stop the practice. Within a few weeks, the group had more than 130,000 signatures on their petition from countries all over the world (Huff-Hannon, 2011). This got the attention of politicians and the national media, which supporters believe will be helpful in ending the practice.

Sambia

A famous and much discussed example of a very different cultural form of sexual relations, called **sequential homosexuality,** is found in a number of cultures in the Pacific islands. The Sambia

tribe of Papua New Guinea has been described in depth by Gilbert Herdt (Herdt, 1981; Stoller & Herdt, 1985). Life in Sambia is difficult because food is scarce and war is common; warriors, hunters, and many children are needed to survive. Sambians believe that mother's milk must be replaced by man's milk (semen) for a boy to reach puberty, and so, at age 7, all Sambian boys move to a central hut where they must fellate the postpubescent Sambian boys and drink their semen. After a boy reaches puberty, he no longer fellates others but is himself sucked by the prepubescent boys until he reaches the age of marriage at about 18. Despite his long period of same-sex activity, he will live as a heterosexual for the rest of his life.

The Lesson of Cross-Cultural Studies of Homosexuality

With all these very different cultural forms of sexuality, trying to pigeonhole people or ways of life into our restrictive, Western "homosexuality–heterosexuality–bisexuality" model seems inadequate. This is a good time to think about your personal theory about homosexuality and to ask yourself: What theory do I believe, and how can it account for the cross-cultural differences in sexual orientation that exist around the world today?

1 Explain how our views on homosexuality have changed from ancient times through the Middle Ages.

2 Discuss how the medical model's view of homosexuality during the modern era influenced modern ideas of sexual orientation.

3 Explain how homosexuality has been viewed in other cultures, citing as many examples as possible.

▶ GAYS, LESBIANS, AND BISEXUALS throughout the Life Cycle

Gays, lesbians, and bisexuals in America face particular problems that are not faced by most heterosexuals. Many struggle with families and friends who reject them, discrimination, prejudice, laws that do not recognize same-sex unions, and/or lack of benefits for their partners. Even so, many gay and lesbian couples live together in stable, happy unions, leading lives not really that much different from the heterosexual couple next door. GLB lifestyles are as varied and different as those of the rest of society. In this section, we examine the special challenges and circumstances that face gays, lesbians, and bisexuals.

▶▶ GROWING UP GAY, LESBIAN, or Bisexual

Imagine what it must be like to be an adolescent and either to believe or know that you are gay, lesbian, or bisexual (a number of you reading this book do not have to imagine it). All your life, from the time you were a toddler, you were presented with a single

"Society was telling me I needed to be a straight, White man."
—TRYING NOT TO BE GAY

View in Video
To watch the entire interview, go to Psychology CourseMate at **login.cengagebrain.com.**

Positive portrayals of same-sex couples in advertising, such as this ad by Kenneth Cole, can help improve the image of gays and lesbians in society.

PRNewsFoto/Kenneth Cole Productions, Inc.

WE ALL WALK IN DIFFERENT SHOES.

model of sexual life: You were expected to be attracted to the other sex, to go on dates, and eventually to marry. No other scenario was seriously considered; if you are heterosexual, you probably have never even reflected on how powerfully this "presumption of heterosexuality" (Herdt, 1989) was transmitted by your parents, your friends, television and movies, newspapers and magazines, even the government. Advertisements on TV and in magazines always show heterosexual couples; your friends probably played house, doctor, or spin the bottle, assuming everyone was attracted to the other sex; your grade school, parties, and social activities were organized around this presumption of heterosexuality. There were open questions about many things in your life—what career you would pursue, where you might live, what college you would attend. However, one thing was considered certain: You were going to marry (or at least date) someone of the other sex.

Imagine that while all your friends were talking about the other sex, dating, and sex, you were experiencing a completely different set of emotions. Why, you wondered, can't I join in on these conversations? Why can't I feel the attractions that all my friends feel? Then, at some point in your early teens, you began to realize why you felt differently from your friends. All of a sudden you understood that all the models you had taken for granted your whole life did not apply to you. You began to look for other models that described your life and your feelings—and they simply were not there. In fact, in hundreds of subtle and not-so-subtle ways, society taught you that you were different—and

A number of authors have created models of the process of coming out. For example, Vivienne Cass (1979, 1984) has proposed one of the leading models, which encompasses six stages of gay and lesbian identity formation. Not all gays and lesbians reach the sixth stage; it depends how comfortable one is at each stage with one's sexual orientation.

Stage 1: Identity confusion. The individual begins to believe that his or her behavior may be defined as gay or lesbian. There may be a need to redefine one's own concept of gay and lesbian behavior, with all the biases and misinformation that most people have. The person may accept that role and seek information, may repress it and inhibit all gay and lesbian behaviors (and even perhaps become an antihomosexual crusader), or may deny its relevance at all to his or her identity (like the man who has same-sex behavior in prison but doesn't believe he is "really" gay).

Stage 2: Identity comparison. The individual accepts potential gay and lesbian identity; he or she rejects the heterosexual model but has no substitute. The person may feel different and even lost. If willing to even consider a gay and lesbian self-definition, he or she may begin to look for appropriate models.

Stage 3: Identity tolerance. Here the person shifts to the belief that he or she is probably gay or lesbian and begins to seek out the homosexual community for social, sexual, and emotional needs. Confusion declines, but self-identity is still more tolerated than truly accepted. Usually, the person still does not reveal new identity to the heterosexual world but maintains a double lifestyle.

Stage 4: Identity acceptance. A positive view of self-identity is forged, and a network of gay and lesbian friends is developed. Selective disclosure to friends and family is made, and the person often

immerses himself or herself in homosexual culture.

Stage 5: Identity pride. Homosexual pride is developed, and anger over treatment may lead to rejecting heterosexuality as bad. One feels validated in one's new lifestyle.

Stage 6: Identity synthesis. As the individual truly becomes comfortable with his or her lifestyle and as nonhomosexual contacts increase, the person realizes the inaccuracy of dividing the world into "good gays and lesbians" and "bad heterosexuals." No longer is sexual orientation seen as the sole identity by which an individual can be characterized. The person lives an open, gay lifestyle so that disclosure is no longer an issue and realizes that there are many sides and aspects to personality, of which sexual orientation is only one. The process of identity formation is complete.

SOURCE: From Cass (1979, 1984).

---

possibly perverted, sinful, illegal, or disgusting. Now what are you supposed to do? Whom do you turn to? How can you possibly tell anyone your deep, painful secret?

The experiences of many lesbians, gays, and bisexuals, at least until recently, followed this scenario, although the timing and intensity varied with individual cases. For example, many gay men grew up with close male friends, enjoyed sports, and differed only in their secret attraction to other boys, whereas others remember feeling and acting differently from their friends as early as 4 or 5 years old (H. P. Martin, 1991).

▶▶ COMING OUT to Self and Others

One of the most important tasks of adolescence is to develop and integrate a positive adult identity. This task is an even greater challenge for gay and lesbian youths because they learn from a very young age the stigma of being different from the heterosexual norm (C. Ryan & Futterman, 2001). Special challenges confront the person who believes he or she is gay, lesbian, or bisexual, including the need to establish a personal self-identity and communicate it to others, known as **coming out** (see the accompanying Sex in Real Life feature). A number of models have been offered to explain how this process proceeds (see, for example, Cass, 1979, 1984; E. Coleman, 1982; H. P. Martin, 1991; M. Schneider, 1989; Troiden, 1989).

Coming out refers, first, to acknowledging one's sexual identity to oneself, and many GLB persons have their own negative feelings about homosexuality to overcome. The often difficult and

anxiety-ridden process of disclosing the truth to family, friends, and eventually the public at large comes later. Disclosure of identity plays an important role in identity development and psychological adjustment for GLB men and women.

Although first awareness of sexual orientation typically occurs between the ages of 8 and 9, men and women vary in when they share this information with others. Some may come out early in their lives, whereas others remain closeted into adulthood (Savin-Williams & Diamond, 2000; H. E. Taylor, 2000). Coming out does not happen overnight; being homosexual for some may mean a lifetime of disclosing different amounts of information to family, friends, and strangers in different contexts (Hofman, 2005). Deciding whether and how to tell friends and family are difficult decisions. To minimize the risk for rejection, gay and lesbian adolescents choose whom they come out to very carefully (Vincke & van Heeringen, 2002).

Today's teens are coming out earlier than any other time in history. Although in the 1970s many teens waited until adulthood to come out, in the 1980s and 1990s, they began coming out in their teens (Ryan et al., 2009). By 2007, teens began coming out as early as middle school (Denizet-Lewis, 2009; Elias, 2007). A more accepting social climate and increased acceptance of homosexuality are responsible for these changes. In addition, increases in gay support groups in middle and high school and a more positive

coming out
The process of establishing a personal self-identity and communicating it to others.

portrayal of gay role models in the popular media have also contributed to early ages in coming out (Elias, 2007). Years ago, many GLB men and women worked hard to hide their sexual orientation for fear of discrimination, harassment, and violence (Hudson, 2010). However, the changing social climate has also lessened the pressure to "fit in." Today, many more GLB men and women live openly as gay, lesbian, or bisexual.

In Chapter 7, we discussed attachment styles that form in our childhood and stay with us as we grow up. These attachment styles can influence many aspects of our adult development, including the coming-out process for GLB men and women. Research has found a strong relationship between anxious/ambivalent and avoidant attachment styles, shame, and negativity about being gay (Brown & Trevethan, 2010).

Family Reactions to Coming Out

Some parents of GLB youths initially react with disappointment, shame, and shock when they learn about a son's or daughter's sexual orientation (D'Augelli, 2005; LaSala, 2000). They may feel responsible and believe they did something to "cause" their child's sexual orientation. In one study, more than 50% of gay and lesbian teens experienced a negative reaction from their parents when they came out (Martin et al., 2010; Ray, 2007). The family must go

---

REAL RESEARCH 11.4 Most gays and lesbians disclose their sexual orientation to a friend first and then their mother (Rossi, 2010). Mothers were often told through direct methods (i.e., in a conversation), whereas if fathers were told at all, it was often through indirect methods (i.e., notes, sarcasm, innuendo).

---

through its own "coming out," as parents and siblings slowly try to accept the idea and then tell their own friends. The importance of positive resolution in the family has prompted the formation of a national organization, Parents, Families, & Friends of Lesbians and Gays (PFLAG), which helps parents learn to accept their children's sexual orientation and gain support from other families experiencing similar events.

Gay and lesbian youths who have a positive coming-out experience have higher self-confidence, lower rates of depression, and better psychological adjustment than those who have negative coming-out experiences (Needham & Austin, 2010; Ryan & Futterman, 2001). The following story was written by a student of mine who had a positive coming-out experience:

I was worried about coming out to my mom since we were so close. I wondered what she would think of me and if she would still love me. One day she picked me up from school early, and asked me if everything was OK. I assured her it was, but she knew something was up. She stopped the car and told me I needed to talk to her. I looked at her concerned face and started to give in. "It is something about me…" I said slowly. "What is it?" she said, looking as if she was about to cry. "It's something that you may not like about me…" I said as I started to get teary eyed. "I'm…I'm…" and tears began rolling down my face. "You're…gay…?" I nodded my head and started to cry. My mother unbuckled her seatbelt and hugged me. "Did you think

that would change our relationship? You're still my son and I still love you," she said as she wiped the tears away from my eyes. (Author's Files)

Parental rejection during the coming-out process is a major health risk for GLB youth. Children who are rejected by their parents have been found to have increased levels of isolation, loneliness, depression, thoughts of suicide, sexually transmitted infections, and homelessness (Calzavara et al., 2011; D'Augelli, 2005; Needham & Austin, 2010; Ray, 2007; Ryan et al., 2009; Savin-Williams & Dube, 1998). Compared with GLB teens with no or low levels of family rejection, GLB teens who reported high levels of family rejection were:

- 8.4 times more likely to attempt suicide
- 6 times more likely to report high levels of depression
- 3.4 times more likely to use illegal drugs
- 3.4 times more likely to report engaging in unprotected sexual behavior (Ryan et al., 2009)

At least half of gay teens experienced negative reactions from their parents when they came out and 26% were kicked out of their homes (Brown & Trevethan, 2010; Remafedi, 1987). In fact, the number one cause for homelessness for GLB teens is family conflict (Ray, 2006). It is estimated that between 20% and 40% of homeless youths are gay, lesbian, or bisexual (Lockwood, 2008; Ray, 2006). Homeless GLB youths are also more at risk than homeless heterosexual youths to abuse drugs and alcohol and experience physical and sexual abuse (Chakraborty et al., 2011; Cochran et al., 2002; Gaetz, 2004; Needham & Austin, 2010; Ray, 2006). Today, homeless shelters that cater specifically to GLB youths have been set up across the United States.

▶▶ EFFECTS OF **Stigma**

Many gay and male bisexual youths report a history of feeling unattached and alienated—most probably because heterosexual dating was often a focal point in peer group bonds (Bauermeister et al., 2010; Herdt, 1989). The same is true of young lesbians and female bisexuals, although the pressure and alienation may be felt slightly later in life because same-sex affection and touching are more accepted for girls and because lesbians tend to determine their sexual orientation later than gay men. GLB youths have been found to experience high levels of stigmatization and discrimination (Bauermeister et al., 2010; Chakraborty et al., 2011; Cox et al., 2010).

For many years, psychiatrists and other therapists argued that homosexual and bisexual groups had greater psychopathology than heterosexuals. Research has found they are more likely than heterosexuals to experience stress and tension, and are more at risk for the development of chronic diseases and mental health issues (Conron et al., 2010). GLB youths have higher levels of depression and are more likely than heterosexual youths to think about and to commit suicide (Bauermeister et al., 2010; Chakraborty et al., 2011; Cox et al., 2010; A. R. D'Augelli et al., 2005b; Doty et al., 2010; Espelage et al., 2008; Hegna & Rossow,

2007; Newcomb & Mustanski, 2010). They also have higher rates of substance abuse and alcohol-related problems (Conron et al., 2010; Rivers & Noret, 2008; D. F. Roberts et al., 2005), together with more widespread use of marijuana and cocaine (Rosario et al., 2004; Ryan & Futterman, 2001), and higher rates of truancy, homelessness, and sexual abuse (D'Augelli et al., 2006; H. E. Taylor, 2000) compared with heterosexual youths and adults. Overall, bisexuals are more likely than heterosexuals, gays, and lesbians to experience sadness, have thoughts of suicide, engage in binge drinking, and have experienced intimate partner violence (Conron et al., 2010; S. T. Russell et al., 2002).

In fact, the problems of GLB life may not be because of psychopathology but rather the enormous pressures of living in a society that discriminates against them (Kertzner et al., 2009; Lock & Steiner, 1999; Roberts et al., 2010). Vulnerable and stigmatized groups in general have higher rates of these types of behaviors, and these problems often result from coping with stigma-related stress. In addition, homosexuals and bisexuals are particularly vulnerable to harassment and other forms of risk, further compounding their stress (Mishna et al., 2008).

Workplace discrimination also adds stress to the lives of GLB individuals. Gay men have been found to earn 23% less than married heterosexual men and 9% less than single heterosexual men who are living with a woman (Elmslie & Tebaldi, 2007). However, lesbians were not discriminated against when compared with heterosexual women. Lesbian workers earn more than their heterosexual female peers, perhaps because employers may believe lesbian women are more career-oriented and less likely to leave the workforce to raise children (Elmslie & Tebaldi, 2007; Peplau & Fingerhut, 2004).

As of 2011, 21 states[1] and the District of Columbia have laws that prohibit workplace discrimination based on sexual orientation. Although there is no federal law that protects GLB persons from employment discrimination, the Employment Non-Discrimination Act, which would provide protections to all GLB

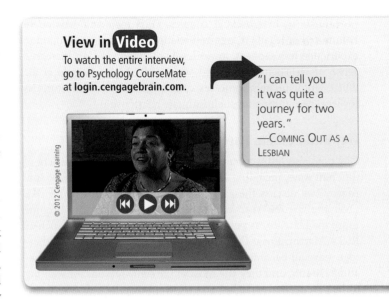

View in Video
To watch the entire interview, go to Psychology CourseMate at **login.cengagebrain.com.**

"I can tell you it was quite a journey for two years."
—COMING OUT AS A LESBIAN

© 2012 Cengage Learning

employees throughout the United States, has been included in every session of the U.S. Congress since 1994 (Human Rights Campaign, 2011). As of 2011, however, it had not been passed. Around the world, many countries, such as France, Canada, and the Netherlands, offer such protections to their employees.

▶▶ LIFE ISSUES: PARTNERING, SEXUALITY, Parenthood, and Aging

Although growing up and coming out can be difficult for many GLB youths, the next step is establishing intimate relationships. Let's now explore same-sex coupling, sexuality, parenting, and aging.

Looking for Partners

In Chapter 9, we discussed some of the difficulties gay men and lesbian women face in meeting others. Meeting other same-sex partners in the heterosexual world can be difficult, so the gay community has developed its own social institutions to help people meet one another and socialize. Today, many schools and universities have clubs, support groups, and meeting areas for GLB students. Whereas in the mid-1990s, there were only a handful of gay–straight alliance clubs in U.S. high schools, as of 2008, there were more than 4,000 such clubs and a handful of clubs in middle schools (Eckholm, 2011).

Today, adults can meet others at gay bars or clubs that cater primarily to GLB couples, at mainstream bars that offer gay or lesbian nights, through GLB support or discussion groups, at churches, and through GLB organizations. Gay magazines such as *The Advocate* carry personal ads and ads for dating services, travel clubs, resorts, bed and breakfasts, theaters, businesses, pay phone lines, sexual products, and other services to help gays and lesbians find partners. And of course, gay individuals are introduced through gay and straight friends.

Sexuality in gay and lesbian couples can be an expression of deep love, affection, or lust.

© Uwe Krejci/zefa/Corbis

[1] California, Colorado, Connecticut, Delaware, Hawaii, Illinois, Iowa, Maine, Maryland, Massachusetts, Minnesota, Nevada, New Hampshire, New Jersey, New Mexico, New York, Oregon, Rhode Island, Vermont, Washington, and Wisconsin.

Similar to heterosexual couples, GLB men and women in committed or legally recognized relationships have been found to experience less sadness, lower levels of stress, and an increased sense of well-being compared with GLB singles (Riggle et al., 2010). Unfortunately, same-sex couples have fewer opportunities for legal recognition for their intimate relationships.

Gay and Lesbian Parenting

Gay men and lesbian women can become parents in a variety of different ways, including artificial insemination, adoption, or surrogacy (we discuss these options in more detail in Chapter 12). Over the last few years, gay and lesbian parenting has become more mainstream, as popular gay and lesbian celebrities, such as Ricky Martin, Rosie O'Donnell, Elton John, and Melissa Etheridge, have all become parents. Many gay and lesbian couples become parents, and they cite most of the same reasons for wanting to be parents that straight parents do (D'Augelli et al., 2006). Although fewer lesbian women have children than heterosexual women (18% vs. 50%; Elmslie & Tebaldi, 2007), it is estimated that more than one in three lesbians has given birth and one in six gay men has fathered or adopted a child (Gates et al., 2007).

Gay and lesbian couples who wish to be parents may encounter many problems that heterosexual couples do not face. Parenting is seldom an individual or couple decision for them and often involves several negotiations with others (Berkowitz & Marsiglio, 2007). In addition, because same-sex marriages are not yet legally recognized nationally in the United States, gay couples may have trouble gaining joint custody of a child, and employers may not grant nonbiological parents parental leave or benefits for the child. For the most part, our society assumes a heterosexist view of parenting. However, it has slowly been changing over the last couple

Each state has specific rules about who can legally adopt children. It wasn't until late 2010 that same-sex couples in Florida could legally adopt children.

of years. The majority of Americans today say that their definition of a family includes same-sex couples with children (Roberts, 2010).

Many gay and lesbian couples adopt children. However, adoption is regulated by state law, and each state has specific rules about who can adopt. Although many states allow same-sex couples to adopt, others do not specifically mention gay or lesbian adoption and decisions about legality are done on a case-by-case basis or by court rulings. For many years, Florida had laws against same-sex couple adoption, even though a single gay man or lesbian woman in Florida could legally adopt (or foster a child). However, laws against same-sex adoption were struck down in Florida in 2010. Throughout the United States, organizations, such as PFLAG and Lambda (a national organization committed to the civil rights of gays, lesbians, and bisexuals), support gay and lesbian parents and are helping to make it easier for them to adopt.

REAL RESEARCH 11.5 In late 2010, a Florida state appeals court struck down the state's 30-year ban on gay adoptions (KOPPEL, 2010). The law forbidding adoptions by same-sex couples in Florida was the only law of its kind in the nation.

No significant differences have been found in the psychological adjustment and social relationships between the children of same-sex and heterosexual couples (Bos & Gartrell, 2010; Farr et al., 2010; Gartrell & Bos, 2010; Greenfeld, 2005; Hicks, 2005). All of the scientific evidence suggests that children who grow up with one or two gay and/or lesbian parents do as well emotionally, cog-

In 2010, pop singer Ricky Martin came out of the closet, announcing that he was a "fortunate homosexual man." He is the proud father of two sons who were born via a surrogate mother.

nitively, socially, and sexually as children from heterosexual parents (American Psychological Association, 2005; Bos & Gartrell, 2010; Greenfeld, 2005; Perrin, 2002). Even so, some gay and lesbian couples find minimal support to parent children, and a social stigmatization of children that they do have (Pawelski et al., 2006).

Overall, the research has not found any significant differences between the children raised by same- or other-sex couples (Bos & Gartrell, 2010; Farr et al., 2010; Greenfeld, 2005; Hicks, 2005). One study claimed that gay and lesbian parents are more likely to have GLB sons and daughters (Cameron, 2006; Morrison, 2007). A statistical review of these data confirmed that social and parental factors influenced the expression of nonheterosexual sexual orientations, especially in females (Schumm, 2010). Controversy surrounds these studies for many reasons, including researcher bias (one researcher works at a conservative family institute) and statistical errors in analysis.

Gay and Lesbian Seniors

Coming out before the senior years often helps a gay or lesbian senior to feel more comfortable with his or her life and sexuality. Gay and lesbian seniors who have not come out or come to terms with their sexual orientation may feel depressed or alone as they continue to age. In addition, they may experience depression and isolation from the years of internalized homophobia (Altman, 2000; Gross, 2007). For some, hiding their sexual orientation when they are ready for a nursing home is their only choice. One gay man who had been in a relationship with his partner for more than 20 years said, "When I'm at the gate of the nursing home, the closet door is going to slam shut behind me" (Gross, 2007).

Many issues confront aging gay and lesbian seniors. Studies have found that nursing home staff often report intolerant or condemning attitudes toward GLB residents (Cahill et al., 2000; Gross, 2007; Röndahl et al., 2004). Because of this, many retirement homes for aging gay, lesbian, bisexual, and transgendered individuals have been established. In 2010, the National Resource Center on GLBT Aging was launched by Services and Advocacy for GLBT Elders (SAGE) with the help of a federal grant from the U.S. Department of Health and Human Services. This organization will help connect aging providers and GLB organizations around the country to provide better services to aging GLB members.

▶▶ GAY, LESBIAN, and Bisexual Organizations

Because many organizations misunderstand the needs of homosexuals and bisexuals, gay and lesbian social services, medical, political, entertainment, and even religious organizations have formed. For example, the National Gay and Lesbian Task Force (NGLTF) and its associated Policy Institute advocate for gay civil rights lobby Congress for such things as a Federal Gay and Lesbian Civil Rights Act, health care reform, AIDS policy reform, and hate-crime laws. In 1987, they helped establish the Hate Crimes Statistics Act, which identifies and records hate crimes. Also well-known are the Lambda Legal Defense and Education Fund (for more information, see the Media Resources at the end of this chapter), which pursues litigation issues for the gay and lesbian community, and the Human Rights Campaign Fund, which lobbies Capitol Hill on gay and lesbian rights, AIDS, and privacy issues.

Since the advent of the AIDS epidemic, many organizations have formed to help GLB men and women obtain medical, social, and legal services. Local GLB organizations, including counseling centers, hotlines, legal aid, and AIDS information, have been established in almost every reasonably sized city in the United States.

The Harvey Milk School in New York City is the first and largest accredited public school in the world devoted to the educational needs of lesbian, gay, bisexual, transgendered, and questioning youth. The school was named after a gay elected official from San Francisco who was murdered in 1978. Fourteen- to 18-year-old students from across the country come to the Harvey Milk School to study in an environment in which their sexual orientation is accepted and where they will not be ridiculed, ostracized, or assaulted, as many were in the schools they came from. Universities and colleges have also begun to offer gay and lesbian students separate housing, and as we discussed earlier, many high schools provide gay–straight alliances that help encourage tolerance and provide a place for students to meet.

Since the early 1980s, gay and lesbian media, including countless magazines and newspapers across the country, have been published. The largest and best-known magazine, *The Advocate,* is a national publication that covers news of interest, entertainment reviews, commentaries, gay- and lesbian-oriented products and services, and hundreds of personal ads. Many other specialty magazines are available for GLB men and women, including parenting magazines (such as *Gay Parent* and *Proud Parenting*), travel magazines (such as *Out and About*), and religious magazines (such as *Whosoever*).

Most major cities now have their own gay newspaper, some of which get national exposure; some noteworthy examples are New York's *Next*, Philadelphia's *Gay News,* Chicago's *Free Press,* and the *Seattle Gay News.* These newspapers are often the best first sources for young gay men and lesbians who are looking for the resources available in their community.

> The research **has not found any significant differences** between the children raised by same- or other-sex couples.

◀ review QUESTIONS

1 Identify the need for GLB youths to establish a personal self-identity, and describe the task of coming out.

2 Explain some of the tasks involved in living a GLB life, including looking for partners, sexuality, parenting, aging, and specific problems encountered by GLB individuals.

3 Explain why many GLB groups have set up their own organizations, and give one example of such an organization.

HOMOPHOBIA and Heterosexism

GLBs have long been stigmatized. When homosexuality as an illness was removed from the *Diagnostic and Statistical Manual of Mental Disorders* in 1973, negative attitudes toward homosexuality persisted. It was at this time that researchers began to study these negative attitudes and behaviors.

WHAT IS Homophobia?

Many terms have been proposed to describe the negative, often violent, reactions of many people toward homosexuality—antihomosexualism, homoerotophobia, homosexism, homonegativism, and **homophobia.** The popularity of the term *homophobia* is unfortunate, for *phobia* is a medical term describing an extreme, anxiety-provoking, uncontrollable fear accompanied by obsessive avoidance. We use this term here to refer to strongly negative attitudes toward homosexuals and homosexuality.

Are people really homophobic? Some might accept homosexuality intellectually and yet still dislike being in the presence of homosexuals, whereas others might object to homosexuality as a practice and yet have personal relationships with individual homosexuals whom they accept (Forstein, 1988). When compared with people who hold positive views of gays, lesbians, and bisexuals, people with negative views are less likely to have had contact with homosexuals and bisexuals, and they are more likely to be older and less well educated; be religious and to subscribe to a conservative religious ideology; have more traditional attitudes toward sex roles and less support for equality of the sexes; be less permissive sexually; and be authoritarian (Herek, 1984). Overall, heterosexual men, compared with heterosexual women, have been found to have significantly more negative attitudes toward gay men (Davies, 2004; Verweij et al., 2008).

It is important to point out that heterosexuals aren't the only people to experience homophobia. Homosexuals who harbor negative feelings about homosexuality experience internalized homophobia. This is especially true in older generations in which there has been less overall acceptance of homosexuality. Overall, older gay men have been found to experience more internalized homophobia (or negative feelings based on sexual orientation directed at oneself) than lesbian women (D'Augelli et al., 2001). Homosexuals with internalized homophobia have been found to have decreased levels of self-esteem and increased levels of shame and psychological distress (D. J. Allen & Oleson, 1999; Szymanski et al., 2001).

An even bigger problem for most gay men and lesbians is **heterosexism.** Heterosexism describes the "presumption of heterosexuality" discussed earlier and the social power used to promote it (Neisen, 1990). Because heterosexual relationships are seen as

homophobia
Irrational fear of homosexuals and homosexuality.

heterosexism
The "presumption of heterosexuality" that has sociological implications.

hate crime
A criminal offense, usually involving violence, intimidation, or vandalism, in which the victim is targeted because of his or her affiliation with a particular group.

"normal," a heterosexist person feels justified in suppressing or ignoring those who do not follow that model.

For example, even those with no ill feelings toward homosexuality are often unaware that businesses will not provide health care and other benefits to the partners of homosexuals. In other words, heterosexism can be passive rather than active, involving a lack of awareness rather than active discrimination. One woman said:

I remember there was a really cute guy in my psychology class. It took me all semester to walk up to him and talk. I was hoping to ask him out for coffee or something. As I walked up behind him to say hello I became aware of a button pinned to the back of his backpack. I was horrified when I read what it said, "How dare you assume I'm heterosexual!!" I nearly tripped and fell over backwards. (Author's files)

The gay rights movement has been successful at changing some of these assumptions, especially in larger cities, but today heterosexism still dictates a large part of the way the average American considers his or her world. Heterosexism can lead to a lack of awareness of issues that can harm GLB individuals today. Let's now turn our attention to hate crimes against GLB individuals.

HATE CRIMES AGAINST GAY, LESBIAN, and Bisexual Individuals

Throughout history, persecution of minorities has been based on philosophies that portrayed those minorities as illegitimate, subhuman, or evil. Likewise, homophobia is not just a set of attitudes; it creates an atmosphere in which people feel they are permitted to harass, assault, and even kill homosexuals. **Hate crimes** are those motivated by hatred of someone's religion, sex, race, sexual orientation, disability, gender identity, or ethnic group. They are known as "message crimes" because they send a message to the victim's affiliated group (American Psychiatric Association, 1998). Typically, hate crimes involve strong feelings of anger (Parrott & Peterson, 2008).

The number of victims of hate crimes based on sexual orientation continues to increase. In 2009, there were nearly 8,000 hate crimes reported by the Federal Bureau of Investigation, and 18% of these were motivated by the victims' sexual orientation (U.S. Department of Justice, 2009). In 2009, hate crimes based on sexual orientation were the second most common type of hate crime (race was the first; Human Rights Campaign, 2009). The APA reports that hate crimes against homosexuals are the most socially acceptable form of hate crimes.

Approximately 80% of GLB youths report verbal victimization, whereas 11% report physical and 9% report sexual victimization (D'Augelli et al., 2006). Victimization begins, on average, at age 13, although some verbal attacks began as early as age 6, physical attacks as early as age 8, and sexual attacks as early as age 9 (D'Augelli et al., 2006). Overall, rates of victimization are higher overall for boys.

▶▶ WHY ARE PEOPLE Homophobic?

What motivates people to be homophobic? A number of theories have been suggested. Because rigid, authoritarian personalities are more likely to be homophobic, it may be a function of personality type; for such people, anything that deviates from their view of "correct" behavior elicits disdain (K. T. Smith, 1971). Another common suggestion is that heterosexual people fear their own suppressed homosexual desires or are insecure in their own masculinity or femininity (H. E. Adams et al., 1996). Others believe that this explanation is too simplistic (Rosser, 1999). Perhaps people are simply ignorant about homosexuality and would change their attitudes with education. Most likely, all of these are true to some degree in different people.

▶▶ HOW CAN WE COMBAT
Homophobia and Heterosexism?

Heterosexism is widespread and subtle, and therefore difficult to combat. Adrienne Rich (1983), a prominent scholar of lesbian studies, uses the term *heterocentrism* to describe the neglect of homosexual existence, even among feminists. Perhaps we can learn from the history of a similar term: *ethnocentrism*. Ethnocentrism refers to the belief that all standards of correct behavior are determined by one's own cultural background, leading to racism, ethnic bigotry, and even sexism and heterosexism. Although ethnocentrism is still rampant in American society, it is slowly being eroded by the passage of new laws, the media's spotlight on abuses, and improved education. Perhaps a similar strategy can be used to combat heterosexism.

Legislating against Hate Crimes

Hate crimes legislation targets violence that is committed in response to a victim's identity, including sexual orientation. The Hate Crimes Statistics Act was enacted by Congress in 1990. This law requires the compilation of data on hate crimes so that there is a comprehensive picture of these crimes. In 1997, the Hate Crimes Right to Know Act was passed, which requires college campuses to report all hate crimes. In 2009, the Matthew Shepard and James Byrd, Jr Hate Crimes Prevention Act was signed into law, which provided the Justice Department with jurisdiction over hate crimes and enabled the department to help in the investigation of such crimes (Human Rights Campaign, 2009).

In 2011, Lady Gaga, a prominent and long-time supporter of GLB rights, pulled the plug on a lucrative marketing deal with Target because of the company's inadequate support of GLB rights.

Promoting Positive Change through the Media

The representation of the GLB community is increasing in the media today (Draganowski, 2004; Freymiller, 2005). Shows such as *The L Word, Ellen, Gossip Girl,* and *Brothers and Sisters* have helped pave the way for GLBs on television, resulting in vastly different programming from just a few years ago. Before this, homosexuality was portrayed negatively, with images of GLBs as psychopaths or murderers.

Another important development in the media is the explosion of music, fiction, nonfiction, plays, and movies that portray gay and lesbian life in America more realistically. Whereas once these types of media were shocking and hidden, now they appear on radio stations and in mainstream bookstores and movie theaters.

Promoting Positive Change through Education

Another important step to stopping heterosexism is education. Homosexuality remains a taboo subject in many schools, and most proposals to teach sexuality in general—never mind homosexuality in particular—encounter strong opposition by certain parent groups. When sexuality education is taught in schools, there is often very little information included about sexual orientation. Educating today's students about homophobia and heterosexism can help reduce negative attitudes, gay bashing, and hate crimes.

1 Define homophobia and explain what factors have been found to be related to its development. Explain how homosexuals can be homophobic.

2 Define heterosexism and heterocentrism, and give one example of each.

3 Explain how hate crimes are known as "message crimes" and give one example.

4 Explain how laws, the media, and education have all helped to reduce homophobia and hate crimes.

▶ DIFFERENCES AMONG
Homosexual Groups

Because homosexuality exists in almost every ethnic, racial, and religious group, many gays, lesbians, and bisexuals also belong to other minority groups. We now discuss the unique situations of some of these groups.

▶▶ LESBIANISM

Many women do not fall neatly into homosexual–heterosexual categories. Maybe this is because society is less threatened by lesbian sexuality than by gay sexuality. The research on lesbianism suggests that women's sexual identity is more fluid than men's (see the accompanying Sex in Real Life feature; Diamond, 2005; Gallo, 2000; Notman, 2002). For some women, an early lesbian relationship is temporarily or permanently replaced by a heterosexual one, or a heterosexual relationship may be replaced by a lesbian relationship later in life (Notman, 2002). Women have also been found to experience more bisexual attractions and experiences than men (Hoburg et al., 2004). Overall, lesbian relationships have been found to be more satisfying, egalitarian, empathic, and have more effective conflict resolution than heterosexual relationships (Ussher & Perz, 2008).

The lesbian community is a vibrant one. Bars, coffeehouses, bookstores, sports teams, political organizations, living cooperatives, media, and lesbian-run and -owned businesses often represent a political statement about the ways in which women can live and work together. A number of lesbian musicians—including k.d. lang, Melissa Etheridge, and Tracy Chapman—sing of issues important to the lesbian community and yet have strong crossover appeal to the heterosexual community. Many lesbian magazines are dedicated to lesbian fiction, erotica, current events, and photography.

Society is less threatened by lesbian sexuality than by gay sexuality.

However, lesbian women are more at risk for health problems. They report higher levels of depression and antidepressant use than heterosexuals, are more likely to be overweight, smoke cigarettes, and have high rates of alcohol consumption (Case et al., 2004; Struble et al., 2010). Some research suggests that much of this hinges on the amount of personal acceptance from their parents. Lesbians who felt that their mothers were accepting of their sexual orientation had higher self-esteem and lower rates of smok-

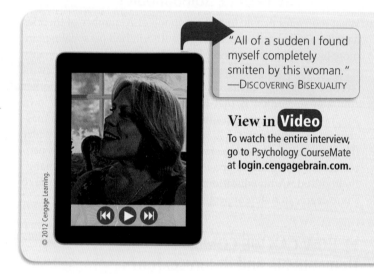

"All of a sudden I found myself completely smitten by this woman."
—DISCOVERING BISEXUALITY

View in Video
To watch the entire interview, go to Psychology CourseMate at **login.cengagebrain.com**.

© 2012 Cengage Learning.

ing and alcohol consumption than those whose mothers were not accepting (LaSala, 2001). In addition, lesbians who feel supported and accepted have higher levels of self-esteem and well-being overall (Beals & Peplau, 2005). Lesbians have also been found to have lower rates of preventive care (yearly physical examinations) than heterosexual women (Herrick et al., 2010; Mays et al., 2002; Moegelin et al., 2010), yet they report high levels of optimism and excitement related to menopause (J. M. Kelly, 2005).

A recent study by the Zuna Institute found that Black lesbians are one of the most vulnerable groups, with an increased risk for physical and emotional health issues, shorter life expectancies, and poverty rates of 21% (compared with poverty rates of 4% for White lesbians and 14% for gay Black men; Ramsey et al., 2010). As adults, they are more likely than White gay and lesbian couples to be parenting. Unfortunately, Black lesbians are less likely than other groups to seek out mental or physical health services (Ramsey et al., 2010).

▶▶ BISEXUALITY

Although we have been discussing bisexuality throughout this chapter, bisexuality has really emerged more recently as a separate identity from lesbian, gay, or heterosexual identities, and we are

Let's imagine you go to a party on campus tonight and while you are there, two heterosexual girls kiss each other deeply. Why do they do it? What would the reaction of the other partygoers be? What if two straight men kissed in the same way? Chances are there would be less support for the two men, but why? Overall, sexual behavior between women is more acceptable than sexual behavior between men (Turner et al., 2005). Girl–girl sexual contact does occur between heterosexual women on college campuses, and it typically occurs in front of friends in public places where the men and women have been drinking alcohol (Hegna & Rossow, 2007). The women might kiss to see what it feels like, to show off to the boys, or to feel more attractive and sexy.

Attitudes about girl–girl sexual behavior have become more liberal in the past few decades. The percentage of women

responding that sexual behavior between two women is "not wrong at all" increased from 5.6% (for women born before 1920) to 45% (for women born

Paula Eureka

after 1970; men showed a similar increase from 7.5% to 32%; Turner et al., 2005). The actual prevalence of girl–girl sexual contact has also increased substantially across the 20th century, rising from 1.6%

for those U.S. women born before 1920 to 7% for women born in or after 1970 (Turner et al., 2005). The reported prevalence of girl-girl sexual contact has almost tripled since 1996, although much of this increase may be due to the fact that women are more likely to report engaging in these behaviors (Turner et al., 2005).

Researchers believe that there is more stigmatization of sexual contact between males (Otis & Skinner, 1996), and perhaps this is one reason why young heterosexual women who engage in sexual contact with other women experience fewer negative reactions from others (Hegna & Rossow, 2007). An interesting question is what would the partygoers responses be if the two girls who were kissing in front of the crowd were lesbians and not straight? Would it still garner attention and be socially accepted?

still learning more each year. Social and political bisexual groups began forming in the 1970s, but it wasn't until the late 1980s that an organized bisexual movement achieved visibility in the United States (Herek, 2002).

We do know that people who identify as bisexual often first identified as heterosexuals, and their self-labeling generally occurs later in life than either gay or lesbian self-labeling (Weinberg et al., 1994). Notably, for many years, few people noticed the absence of research on bisexuality. This absence stemmed from the fact that researchers believed that sexuality was composed of only two opposing forms of sexuality: heterosexuality and homosexuality (Herek, 2002; Rust, 2000).

Homosexuals have tended to see bisexuals either as on their way to becoming homosexual or as people who want to be able to "play both sides of the fence" by being homosexual in the gay community and heterosexual in straight society. Heterosexuals have tended to lump bisexuals in with homosexuals. Sexuality scholars have suggested that bisexuality is a myth, or an attempt to deny one's homosexuality; identity confusion; or an attempt to be "chic" or "trendy" (Rust, 2000). Some studies claim that bisexuals are men and women who are ambivalent about their homosexual behavior (Carey, 2005; Rieger et al., 2005). Bisexuals themselves have begun to speak of **biphobia,** which they suggest exists in both the straight and gay and lesbian commu-

*Heterosexuals have tended **to lump bisexuals in with homosexuals.***

nities (Eliason, 1997; Galupo, 2006; Mulick & Wright, 2002; L. Wright et al., 2006). Like gays and lesbians, bisexuals experience hostility, discrimination, and violence in response to their sexual orientation (Herek, 2002). Some researchers suggest that bisexuals experience "double discrimination," because they may experience discrimination from both the heterosexual and homosexual communities (Mulick & Wright, 2002). Compared with gays and lesbians, bisexuals have been found to have decreased social well-being, more barriers to health care, and increased sadness and suicidal thoughts (Conron et al., 2010; Kertzner et al., 2009).

Many bisexuals see themselves as having the best of both worlds. As one bisexual put it, "The more I talk and think about it, and listen to people, I realize that there are no fences, no walls, no heterosexuality or homosexuality. There are just people and the electricity between them" (quoted in Spolan, 1991). In our society, fear of intimacy is expressed through either homophobia if you are heterosexual or **heterophobia** if you are gay or lesbian; no matter what your sexual orientation, one gender or another is

biphobia
Strongly negative attitudes toward bisexuals and bisexuality.

heterophobia
Strongly negative attitudes toward heterosexuals and heterosexuality.

always taboo—your sexual intimacy is always restricted (F. Klein, 1978). From that perspective, bisexuality is simply lack of prejudice and full acceptance of both sexes.

More people in American society exhibit bisexual behavior than exclusively homosexual behavior (F. Klein, 1990). In **sequential bisexuality,** the person has sex exclusively with one gender, followed by sex exclusively with the other; **contemporaneous bisexuality** refers to having male and female sexual partners during the same period (J. P. Paul, 1984). Numbers are hard to come by because bisexuality itself is so hard to define. How many encounters with both sexes are needed for a person to be considered bisexual? One? Fifty? And what of fantasies? It is difficult to determine what percentage of people is bisexual because many who engage in bisexual behavior do not self-identify as bisexual (Weinberg et al., 1994).

Some people experience bisexuality through intimate involvement with a close friend of the same sex, even if they have not had same-sex attractions before. Others come to it through group sex or swinging, in which in the heat of passion, a body is a body and distinctions between men and women easily blur. The new bisexual movement may succeed in breaking through the artificial split of the sexual world into homosexuals and heterosexuals. Perhaps we fear the fluid model of sexuality offered by bisexuals because we fear our own cross-preference encounter fantasies and do not want to admit that most of us, even if hidden deep in our fantasies, are to some degree attracted to both sexes.

▶▶ MINORITY Homosexuality

Special problems confront homosexuals who are members of racial or ethnic minorities in the United States. Homosexuality is less accepted by many ethnic groups, and yet the gay community does not easily accommodate expressions of ethnic identity. Minority homosexual youths have been found to experience greater psychological distress than nonminority homosexual youths (Diaz et al., 2001; McCabe et al., 2010). Many end up feeling torn between the two communities (Nagel, 2003). As one gay Asian American put it, "While the Asian-American community supports my Asian identity, the gay community only supports my being a gay man; as a result I find it difficult to identify with either" (Chan, 1989).

Gay African Americans can find their situation particularly troubling because they often have to deal with the heterosexism of the African American community and the racism of the homosexual and straight communities (Tye, 2006). Some progress is being made, however. Books such as *Brother to Brother: New Writings by Black Gay Men* (Hemphill, 1991) have raised the issue in public. Many feminist and lesbian anthologies and most lesbian and feminist journals include writings explicitly by minority lesbians.

It is also worth pointing out that research has found that although many African American lesbians report positive relationships and pleasant feelings about their sexual relationships, more than half also report feeling guilty about these relationships (Wyatt, 1998). This is consistent with the aforementioned research noting the prevalence of psychological distress in homosexual minorities.

▶▶ SAME-SEX SEXUAL BEHAVIOR in Prison

Homosexual behavior varies greatly in prisons. Sexual contact between inmates, although prohibited, still occurs in prisons today (L. G. Hensley, 2002). Researchers who study prison rape have had difficulties defining it (L. G. Hensley, 2002). If a man is scared for his life and provides sex to a more powerful man for protection, is this rape (see Chapter 17)?

Sexual behaviors in prison are governed by a hierarchy of roles and relationships that define an inmate's position within the prison system (L. G. Hensley, 2002). Although forced sex does occur in prisons, overall it is less common in women's prisons than in men's (Girshick, 1999).

Many men and women who engage in same-sex sexual behavior in prison claim that they are not gay or lesbian and that their sexual behavior is an adaptation to their all-male or all-female environments (Girshick, 1999). Many claim they plan to return to heterosexual relationships exclusively once they are released. One female prisoner said:

> I think a lot of [the motivation for gay relationships] is loneliness, despair, and in some cases I know for a fact that it's for financial purposes. I have seen women have relationships with women, leave this dorm hugging and kissing this woman, then go out to visitation and hug and kiss their husband. (Girshick, 1999, p. 87)

This **situational homosexuality** is also found in other places where men and women must spend long periods of time together, such as on ships at sea.

Same-sex relationships in prison can be strong and jealously guarded (Girshick, 1999; Nacci & Kane, 1983). Inmates speak of loving their inmate partners, and relations can become extremely intimate, even among those who return to a heterosexual life on release.

sequential bisexuality
Having sex exclusively with one gender followed by sex exclusively with the other.

contemporaneous bisexuality
Having sexual partners of both sexes during the same period.

situational homosexuality
Homosexuality that occurs because of a lack of heterosexual partners.

1 Explain how women's sexual identity may be more fluid than men's sexual identity and give one example.

2 Some researchers claim that bisexuality is a "trend," but what does the research tell us about bisexuality? Differentiate between sequential and contemporaneous bisexuality.

3 Describe some of the problems that confront GLB minority youths.

4 Explain what is known about same-sex sexual behavior in prisons.

▶ HOMOSEXUALITY
in Religion and the Law

Religion has generally been considered a bastion of antihomosexual teachings and beliefs, and these beliefs have often helped shape laws that prohibit homosexual behaviors. We now discuss both of these powerful influences.

▶▶ HOMOSEXUALITY and Religion

There has been a great deal of negativity surrounding homosexuality in religion, and changes in social attitudes toward homosexuality beginning in the early 1980s have provoked conflict over homosexual policies in many religious denominations. Traditionally, both Judaism and Christianity have strongly opposed homosexual behavior.

Some Christian religions are more tolerant, such as the United Church of Christ. This church and its members have welcomed GLB members, worked for equal rights, and ordained GLB clergy. They generally view homosexuality as neither a sin nor a choice, and they believe that it is unchangeable. One of the most accepting churches, the Metropolitan Community Churches, promotes itself as the world's largest organization with a primary, affirming ministry to GLBT persons (Metropolitan Community Churches, 2005).

Some Christian religions, such as Presbyterian, Methodist, Lutheran, and Episcopalian, have more conflict over the issue of sexual orientation, resulting in both liberal and conservative views. In recent years, a number of Christian denominations have voted to allow noncelibate gays to serve as clergy if they are in a committed relationship (Condon, 2010). This includes the Evangelical Lutheran Church in America, the U.S. Episcopal Church, and the United Church of Christ.

In many churches and synagogues, most of the more conservative views, including the idea that homosexuality can be changed through prayer and counseling, come from older members and those living in the southern part of the United States. The conservative Christian faiths, such as Catholics, Southern Baptists, and the Assemblies of God, view homosexuality as a sin and work to restrict GLB rights.

There is also controversy over sexual orientation in Jewish synagogues throughout the United States. Although Orthodox Jews believe that homosexuality is an abomination forbidden by the Torah, reform congregations are more likely to welcome all sexual orientations. A Reform movement in 1990 allowed the ordaining of gay rabbis (Albert et al., 2001). In 2010, a Statement of Principles was signed and released by a group of Orthodox rabbis that supports the acceptance of homosexual members (Nahshoni, 2010).

There is also no real consensus about gay and lesbian relationships among the various Buddhist sects in the United States. Buddhism differs from Christianity in that it views behaviors as helpful or nonhelpful (whereas Christianity views behaviors as good/evil) and looks at whether there was intent to help. As a result of this, Buddhism encourages relationships that are mutually loving and supportive.

Recently, religious scholars, both homosexual and heterosexual, have begun to promote arguments based on religious law and even scripture for a more liberal attitude toward homosexuality. For example, some Jewish scholars have argued that because homosexual orientation is not a free choice but an unalterable feature of the personality, it is immoral to punish someone for it (Kahn, 1989–90).

▶▶ HOMOSEXUALITY and the Law

Throughout history, laws have existed in the Western world that prohibited same-sex sexual behavior, even on pain of death. In the United States, sodomy has been illegal since Colonial days, and it was punishable by death until the late 18th century (Boswell, 1980). Fellatio was technically legal until the early 20th century, although it was considered to be "loathsome and revolting" (Murphy, 1990). All 50 states outlawed homosexual acts until 1961.

Although there is still hostility toward homosexuality within many major religions, religious scholars have begun to promote a more liberal attitude, including ordination of gay and lesbian clergy and marriage or commitment ceremonies.

AP/Wide World Photos

Lesbians, gay men, and bisexual people who also belong to other minority groups must deal with the prejudices of society toward both groups, as well as each group's prejudices toward the other.

The Supreme Court overturned the Texas antisodomy law—which made consensual sex between same-sex couples illegal—in 2003. Before 2003, under Texas homosexual conduct law, for example, individuals who engaged in "deviate sexual intercourse" with a person of the same sex (even if the partner was consenting) could be charged with a misdemeanor punishable by up to $500 in fines (Lambda, 2001).

Homosexuals are often denied equal housing rights through exclusionary zoning, rent control, and rent stabilization laws. Even in long-term, committed, same-sex couples, partners are routinely denied the worker's compensation and health care benefits normally extended to a spouse or dependents. In addition, without legal marriage, gay and lesbian couples are denied tax breaks, Social Security benefits, and rights of inheritance, all of which are available to married heterosexual couples.

Over the last few years, the legal landscape for gay rights has been changing in the United States. In 2010, President Obama signed a bill ending the military's "don't ask, don't tell" policy, which was one of the first moves toward equality for gays and lesbians. In 2011, he reversed his stance on the Defense of Marriage Act (DOMA), concluding that his administration could no longer defend the federal law that defines marriage as between a man and a woman. DOMA was enacted in 1996 and was supported by the Clinton, Bush, and most of Obama's administration. Dismantling DOMA was a major victory for gay rights advocates and one of the first steps toward a federal legal recognition of same-sex marriage in the United States. As a variety of legal cases that challenge the federal government's denial of same-sex marriage and marriage-related benefits make their way to the Supreme Court, it is likely support for these issues will continue to grow. We are hopeful that this momentum for support of gay rights will continue in the future.

◀ review QUESTIONS

1 Explain how changes in social attitudes toward homosexuality have provoked conflict over GLB policies in many religious denominations.

2 Identify some of the more liberal and conservative religions and explain how each religion views homosexuality.

3 Explain how the legal landscape has been changing for gay rights in the United States.

◀◀ chapter REVIEW

SUMMARY POINTS

1 Sexual orientation refers to the sex(es) that a person is attracted to emotionally, physically, sexually, and romantically. Heterosexuals are predominantly attracted to members of the other sex, homosexuals to members of the same sex, and bisexuals are attracted to both men and women.

2 Alfred Kinsey introduced a seven-point sexual orientation scale based mostly on people's sexual behaviors, whereas other researchers suggest that people's emotions and fantasies, more than their behaviors, are the most important determinants of sexual orientation. The Klein Sexual Orientation Grid (KSOG) includes the elements of time, fantasy, social and lifestyle behavior, and self-identification.

3 The frequency of gay, lesbian, and bisexual (GLB) behavior in the United States has remained constant over the years. Scholars generally agree that between 3% and 4% of males are predominantly gay, 1.5% to 2% of women are predominantly lesbian, and about 2% to 5% of people are bisexual. However,

many of these studies have methodological flaws and have not taken into account feelings of attraction or fantasies.

4 Several theories have been proposed to explain homosexuality. These include the biological, developmental, behavioral, sociological, and interactional theories.

5 Biological theories claim that differences in sexual orientation are caused by genetics, hormones, birth order, or simple physical traits. Developmental theories focus on a person's upbringing and personal history to find the origins of homosexuality. Developmental theories include psychoanalytic, gender-role nonconformity, and peer-group interaction. Behaviorist theories view homosexuality as a learned behavior, whereas the sociological theories explain how social forces produce homosexuality in a society. The interactional theories explore the combined impact of biology and sociology.

6 Same-sex activity was common before the 19th century, and homosexual prostitution was taxed by the state. Homosexuality was not treated with concern or much interest by either early Jews or early Christians. The church's indifference to homosexuality lasted well through the 13th century. By 1300, however, the new intolerance of differences resulted in homosexuality being punishable by death almost everywhere. This view, from the late Middle Ages, has influenced the Western world's view of homosexuality for the past 700 years. In the 19th and early 20th centuries, physicians and scientists began to suggest that homosexuality was not a sin but an illness.

7 Same-sex sexual behavior is found in every culture, and its prevalence remains about the same no matter how permissive or repressive that culture's attitude is toward it. Many homosexuals and bisexuals struggle with discrimination, prejudice, laws that do not recognize their same-sex unions, lack of benefits for their partners, and families who may reject them.

8 Someone who is gay or lesbian must first acknowledge his or her sexual identity to himself or herself, and undergo a process known as coming out. Today's teens are coming out earlier than at any other time in history. A changing social climate has lessened the pressure to "fit in." However, there are still some youths who remain closeted into late adolescence and even adulthood. Parental rejection during the coming-out process is a major health risk for GLB youths.

9 GLB youths are more likely than heterosexuals to experience stress and tension and are at greater risk for the development of chronic diseases and mental health issues. They have higher rates of substance abuse, more widespread use of marijuana and cocaine, and higher rates of truancy, homelessness, and sexual abuse compared with heterosexual youth and adults. These issues may all be related to the pressures of living in a society that discriminates against GLB men and women.

10 Children who grow up with one or two gay and/or lesbian parents do as well emotionally, cognitively, socially, and sexually as children from heterosexual parents. Although many states allow same-sex couples to adopt, in some states, decisions about the legality of same-sex adoption are done on a case-by-case basis or by court ruling. In 2010, laws against same-sex adoption were struck down in Florida.

11 Homophobia is an irrational fear of homosexuals and homosexuality, and heterosexism is the presumption of heterosexuality and the social power used to promote it. Hate crimes, also known as "message crimes," are motivated by hatred of someone's religion, sex, race, sexual orientation, disability, or ethnic group. Many states punish perpetrators of hate crimes, but the way they are punished varies from state to state. One of the best ways to stop heterosexism is through education.

12 Society is less threatened by lesbian sexuality, and perhaps this is the reason that women's sexual identity is more fluid than men's. Overall, lesbian and bisexual women have been found to have lower rates of preventive care than heterosexual women.

13 Bisexuals often identify first as heterosexuals, and their self-labeling generally occurs later in life than either gay or lesbian self-labeling. Biphobia is a fear of bisexuals.

14 Minority homosexual youths have been found to experience greater psychological distress than nonminority homosexual youths.

15 Some religions have become more accepting of homosexuals. Laws that prohibited homosexual behavior have existed throughout history in the Western world, even on pain of death. In the United States before new legislation, sodomy had been illegal since Colonial days.

16 Over the last few years the legal landscape for gay rights has been changing. The military's "don't ask, don't tell" policy ended in 2010, and in 2011, the Defense of Marriage Act (DOMA) was challenged.

CRITICAL THINKING QUESTIONS

1 If you are not gay, lesbian, or bisexual, imagine for a moment discovering that you are. Whom do you think you would approach first to talk about the issues surrounding this discovery? Would you feel comfortable talking with your friends? Parents? Siblings? Teachers? Why or why not?

2 Suppose that one of your good friends, Tim, comes to you tomorrow and tells you that he thinks he is bisexual. You have seen Tim date only women and had no idea he was interested in men. What kinds of questions do you ask him? After reading this chapter, what can you tell him about the current research on bisexuality?

3 If a person only fantasizes about engaging in same-sex behavior but never has actually done so, would he or she be homosexual? Why or why not?

4 Where do you fall on Kinsey's continuum? What experiences in your life contribute to your Kinsey ranking? Why?

5 What theory do you think best explains the development of sexual orientation? What features do you feel add to the theory's credibility?

6 Do you think same-sex couples should be allowed to marry each other? Why or why not? Should they be allowed to have children? Why or why not?

MEDIA RESOURCES

CourseMate brings course concepts to life with interactive learning, study, and exam preparation tools that support the printed textbook. A textbook-specific website, Psychology CourseMate includes an integrated interactive eBook and other interactive learning tools including quizzes, flashcards, videos, and more. If your textbook does not include an access code card, go to CengageBrain.com to gain access.

CENGAGENOW   CengageNOW is an easy-to-use online resource that helps you study in less time to get the grade you want—NOW. Take a pre-test for this chapter and receive a personalized study plan based on your results that will identify the topics you need to review and direct you to online resources to help you master those topics. Then take a post-test to help you determine the concepts you have mastered and what you will need to work on. If your textbook does not include an access code card, go to CengageBrain.com to gain access.

View in Video available in CourseMate and CengageNOW:

Peter and Stephan: A Dutch Couple: Dutch gay couple discusses their relationship and struggles along the way.

Trying Not To Be Gay: Hear a gay man describe his struggle to come to terms with his attraction to men.

Coming Out as a Lesbian: Listen to one woman describe coming out as a lesbian at age 38 and how it affected her family and children.

Discovering Bisexuality: Hear a woman describe how she gradually realized that she was bisexual.

Websites:

GLBTQ ■ An encyclopedia of gay, lesbian, bisexual, transgender, and queer culture. Contains information about GLBTQ culture, history, and current rulings on same-sex marriage, civic unions, and domestic partnerships.

National Gay and Lesbian Task Force ■ The National Gay and Lesbian Task Force (NGLTF) is a national organization that works for the civil rights of GLBT people. The website contains press releases and information on many GLBT issues, including affirmative action, domestic partnerships, and same-sex marriage.

Gay and Lesbian Association of Retiring Persons ■ The Gay and Lesbian Association of Retiring Persons (GLARP) is an international, nonprofit membership organization that was launched to enhance the aging experience of gays and lesbians. This website provides retirement-related information and services and also works to establish retirement communities for gays and lesbians in the United States and abroad.

Healthy Lesbian, Gay, and Bisexual Students Project ■ This site strives to strengthen the ability of the nation's schools to prevent risk to GLBTQ students. The site contains information about workshops, training, and issues that affect GLBTQ students today.

Lambda Legal Defense and Education Fund ■ The Lambda Legal Defense and Education Fund is a national organization that works for recognition of the civil rights of lesbians, gay men, bisexuals, the transgendered, and people with HIV and AIDS. Their website contains information on a variety of issues related to GLBT individuals.

Parents, Families, & Friends of Lesbians and Gays ■ Parents, Families, & Friends of Lesbians and Gays (PFLAG) is a national organization that works to promote the health and well-being of GLB persons, as well as their families and friends. Through education, support, and dialogue, PFLAG provides opportunities to learn more about sexual orientation and helps to create a society that is respectful of human diversity.

12 Pregnancy and Birth

View in Video

View in Video

View in Video

View in Video

View in Video

ABOUT THE CHAPTER OPENING VIDEO – Laura and Ozlem, a lesbian couple, have been together for almost 18 years, but from the very beginning of their relationship they knew they wanted to have children. Unlike fertile heterosexual couples, they were faced with the decision of *how* to have children. After years of discussions about their options, they finally decided on a "known" donor because they wanted their children to know who their father was and have a relationship with him. Since Ozlem was a few years older, she was artificially inseminated first, and in 2001, Deniz was born. Laura was artificially inseminated a few years later, and in 2005 Isabelle was born.

Besides our love, shared values, common interests, and commitment to each other, the fact that we wanted children to be in our lives has always been a part of our relationship. The specifics on how to make that happen were long discussed and well planned. We are fortunate to have a large circle of lesbian couples and friends who were also making similar decisions, and we all shared our experiences with each other. We decided to use sperm from a friend who agreed to relinquish all parental decision-making and responsibility to us. Our donor is a carpenter by trade with tremendous visual-spatial skills, athletic ability, and intelligence. He is kind and thoughtful and understood that we would be the parents but that he would get to have the experience of knowing these children and having a relationship with them. He has no other children, so this would be his first and perhaps only opportunity to be a father. He also needed to make a commitment to help us have more than one child. Our children, aged 10 and 6 years old, know their dad and call him

by his first name. They see him about once a month, and he is thrilled that they are in his life.

Deniz and Isabelle were both excited to tell me about their two-mom family. They talked about what they do for fun, other two-mom families, and what they do when someone at school asks them about their family. Laura put it best: *"We're just like any other family. In fact, our similarities are far greater than our differences."* ❙❙

Janell Carroll

"We're just like any other family."
—CHAPTER OPENING VIDEO

View in Video

To watch the entire interview, go to Psychology CourseMate at **login.cengagebrain.com.**

© Janell Carroll

Traditionally, a family consisted of a father, mother, and their biological children. However, increasing divorce, adoption, teenage pregnancy, and single and same-sex parenting, together with advances in assisted reproductive technologies (ARTs), have led to a new view of the family. Whereas at one time vaginal intercourse was required for pregnancy, this is no longer true—donor sperm, ova, embryos, and surrogate uterus' can be used today. In this chapter, we begin to explore issues related to fertility, pregnancy, and childbearing.

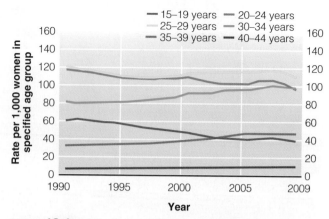

FIGURE **12.1** Birth rates by selected age of mother: final 1990–2008 and preliminary 2009. SOURCE: Martin et al., 2010.

FERTILITY

Most parents, sooner or later, must confront the moment when their child asks, "Where did I come from?" The answer they give depends on the parent, the child, the situation, and the culture. Every culture has its own traditional explanations for where babies come from. The Australian Aborigines, for instance, believe that babies are created by the mother earth and, therefore, are products of the land. The spirits of children rest in certain areas of the land, and these spirits enter a young woman as she passes by (Dunham et al., 1992). Women who do not want to become pregnant either avoid these areas or dress up like old women to fool the spirits. In Malaysia, the Malay people believe that because man is the more rational of the two sexes, babies come from men. Babies are formulated in the man's brain for 40 days before moving down to his penis for eventual ejaculation into a woman's womb.

In American culture, we take a more scientific view of where babies come from, and so it is important to understand the biological processes involved in conceiving a child, being pregnant, and giving birth. The biological answer to the question, "Where did I come from?" is that we are created from the union of an ovum and a spermatozoon. You may recall from the sexual anatomy and physiology chapters that fertilization and conception are dynamic processes that result in the creation of new life, a process so complex it is often referred to as "the incredible journey."

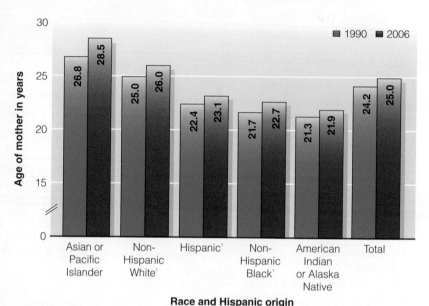

Race and Hispanic origin

[1]For 1990, excludes data for New Hampshire and Oklahoma, which did not report Hispanic origin.

FIGURE **12.2** Average age of mother at first birth, by race and Hispanic origin of mother, in United States in 1990 and 2006. SOURCES: National Center for Health Statistics, Matthews & Hamilton, 2009.

STATISTICS AND **Current Trends**

In 2009, there were 4,131,019 registered births in the United States, which was 3% lower than the number of registered births in 2008 (Hamilton et al., 2010a). The number of U.S. births declined for almost all ages, races, and ethnicities from 2008 to 2009 (Hamilton et al., 2010b). Births to teenagers (15–19 years old) were at the

---

mucus plug
A collection of thick mucus in the cervix that prevents bacteria from entering the uterus.

spontaneous abortion
A natural process through which the body expels a developing embryo.

blastocyst
The hollow ball of embryonic cells that enters the uterus from the Fallopian tube and eventually implants.

---

lowest level since 1940. Increases were found in women older than 30 years, as well as unmarried women (Hamilton et al., 2010; Figure 12.1). However, this is not surprising because more women are delaying and/or foregoing marriage today (see Chapter 9).

From 1970 to 2006, the average age of the first-time mother in the United States increased by almost 4 years—from 21.4 to 25 years old (Matthews & Hamilton, 2009; Figure 12.2). The average age of first-time birth was 26 years old for non-Hispanic White women (which was above the U.S. average of 25), 22.7 years old for non-Hispanic Black women, and 23.1 years old for Hispanic women (Matthews & Hamilton, 2009). Of particular interest to researchers was the proportion of first births to women 35 and older during this period. Whereas in 1970, 1 in 100 births was to a woman older than 35, in 2006, 1 in 12 births was to a woman older than 35 (Matthews & Hamilton, 2009). Around the world, women's ages at first birth have been increasing. In 2006, average ages ranged from 25 (United States) to 29.4 (Switzerland; Figure 12.3).

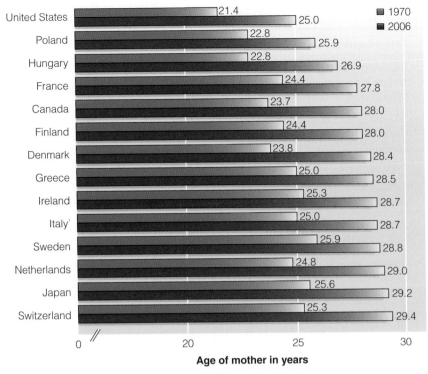

United States 21.4 / 25.0
Poland 22.8 / 25.9
Hungary 22.8 / 26.9
France 24.4 / 27.8
Canada 23.7 / 28.0
Finland 24.4 / 28.0
Denmark 23.8 / 28.4
Greece 25.0 / 28.5
Ireland 25.3 / 28.7
Italy[1] 25.0 / 28.7
Sweden 25.9 / 28.8
Netherlands 24.8 / 29.0
Japan 25.6 / 29.2
Switzerland 25.3 / 29.4

■ 1970
■ 2006

0   20   25   30

Age of mother in years

[1] Latest data are for 2005.

FIGURE **12.3** Average age of mother at first birth in selected countries, 1970–2006.
SOURCES: CDC/NCHS, National Vital Statistics System, Council of Europe, Vienna Institute of Demography, Statistics Canada, and Japanese Ministry of Health, Labour and Welfare, Matthews and Hamilton, 2009.

▶▶ CONCEPTION

Our bodies are biologically programmed in many ways to help pregnancy occur. For instance, a woman's sexual desire is usually at its peak during her ovulation until just before her menstruation (Bullivant et al., 2004). During ovulation, a **mucus plug** in the cervix disappears, making it easier for sperm to enter the uterus, and the cervical mucus changes in consistency (becoming thinner and stretchy), making it easier for sperm to move through the cervix. The consistency of this mucus also creates wide gaps, which vibrate in rhythm with the tail motion of normal sperm, helping to move the healthy sperm quickly and detain abnormal sperm. The cervical mucus also helps filter out any bacteria in the semen. Finally, the female orgasm may help pull semen into the uterus; once there, continuing muscular contractions of the vagina and uterus help push sperm up toward the Fallopian tubes (pregnancy can certainly still occur, however, without the woman having an orgasm). The consistency of the ejaculated semen also helps. Almost immediately after ejaculation, semen thickens to help it stay in the vagina. Twenty minutes later, when the sperm has had a chance to move up into the uterus, it begins to liquefy again.

With all the help our bodies are programmed to give, the process of getting pregnant may appear rather easy; however, this is not always the case. The process of becoming pregnant is complex, and there are several potential problems. For example, the female's immune system itself begins to attack the semen immediately after ejaculation, thinking it is unwanted bacteria. Yet although many sperm are killed by the woman's immune system, this process is usually not a threat to conception. When a fertile woman engages in unprotected vaginal intercourse, 30% of the time she becomes pregnant, although a significant number of these pregnancies end in **spontaneous abortion** (Zinaman et al., 1996).

Because the ovum can live for up to 24 hours and the majority of sperm can live up to 72 hours in the female reproductive tract, pregnancy may occur if intercourse takes place either a few days before or after ovulation (A. J. Wilcox et al., 1995). Although most sperm die within 72 hours, a small number, less than 1%, can survive up to 7 days in the female reproductive tract (Ferreira-Poblete, 1997). Throughout their trip into the Fallopian tubes, the sperm haphazardly swim around, bumping into various structures and each other. When (and if) they reach the jelly-like substance that surrounds the ovum, they begin wriggling violently. Although it is not clear how the sperm locate the ovum, research indicates that the ovum releases chemical signals that indicate its location (Palca, 1991).

Several sperm may reach the ovum, but only one will fertilize it. The sperm secretes a chemical that bores a hole through the outer layer of the ovum and allows the sperm to penetrate for fertilization. The outer layer of the ovum immediately undergoes a physical change, making it impossible for any other sperm to enter. This entire process takes about 24 hours. Fertilization usually occurs in the ampulla (the funnel-shaped open end of the Fallopian tube; Figure 12.4); after fertilization, the fertilized ovum is referred to as a zygote.

The sperm carry the genetic material from the male. Each sperm contains 23 chromosomes, including the X or Y sex chromosome, which will determine whether the fetus is male or female. Other information is determined by both the male and female genes, including eye and hair color, skin color, height, and weight.

Approximately 12 hours after the genetic material from the sperm and ovum join together, the first cell division begins. At this point, the collection of cells is referred to as a **blastocyst.** The blastocyst will divide in two every 12 to 15 hours, doubling in size. As

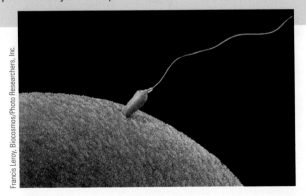

As the head of the spermatozoon enters the ovum, the ovum prevents penetration by another spermatozoon.

table 12.1 ■ Pregnancy Signs

Physical Sign	Time of Appearance	Other Possible Reasons
Period late/absent	Entire pregnancy	Excessive weight gain or loss, fatigue, hormonal problems, stress, breast-feeding, going off birth control pills
Breast tenderness	1–2 weeks after conception	Use of birth control pills, hormonal imbalance, period onset
Increased fatigue	1–6 weeks after conception	Stress, depression, thyroid disorder, cold or flu
Morning sickness	2–8 weeks after conception	Stress, stomach disorders, food poisoning
Increased urination	6–8 weeks after conception	Urinary tract infection, excessive use of diuretics, diabetes
Fetal heartbeat	10–20 weeks and then throughout entire pregnancy	None
Backaches	Entire pregnancy	Back problems
Frequent headaches	May be entire pregnancy	Caffeine withdrawal, dehydration, eyestrain, birth control pills
Food cravings	Entire pregnancy	Poor diet, stress, depression, period onset
Darkening of nipples	Entire pregnancy	Hormonal imbalance
Fetal movement	16–22 weeks after conception	Bowel contractions, gas

Copyright © Cengage Learning 2013

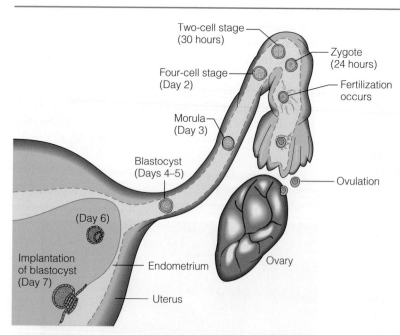

FIGURE **12.4** After ovulation, the follicle moves through the Fallopian tube until it meets the spermatozoon. Fertilization takes place in the wide outer part of the tube. Approximately 24 hours later, the first cell division begins. For some 3 or 4 days, the fertilized ovum remains in the Fallopian tube, dividing again and again. When the fertilized ovum enters the uterus, it sheds its outer covering to be able to implant in the wall of the uterus. Copyright © Cengage Learning 2013

this goes on, the cilia in the Fallopian tube gently push the blastocyst toward the uterus. Fallopian tube muscles also help to move the blastocyst by occasionally contracting.

Approximately 3 to 4 days after conception, the blastocyst enters the uterus. For 2 to 3 days, it remains in the uterus and absorbs nutrients secreted by the endometrial glands. On about the sixth day after fertilization, the uterus secretes a chemical that dissolves the hard covering around the blastocyst, allowing it to implant in the uterine wall (R. Jones, 1984). Implantation involves a series of complex interactions between the lining of the uterus and the developing embryo, and this usually occurs 5 to 8 days after fertilization. The endometrium must have been exposed to the appropriate levels of estrogen and progesterone to facilitate implantation. Most of the time, implantation takes place in the upper portion of the uterus, and after this occurs, the woman's body and the developing embryo begin to exchange chemical information. Hormones are released into the woman's bloodstream (these can be detected through pregnancy tests). If implantation does not occur, the blastocyst will degenerate and the potential pregnancy will be terminated.

It is fascinating that a woman's body allows the blastocyst to implant when so many of her body's defenses are designed to eliminate foreign substances. Apparently there is some weakening of the immune system that allows for an acceptance of the fertilized ovum (Nilsson, 1990). Some women do continually reject the fertilized ovum and experience repeat **miscarriages.** We will discuss this in greater detail later in this chapter.

After implantation, the blastocyst divides into two layers of cells, the ectoderm and endoderm. A middle layer, the mesoderm, soon follows. These three layers will develop into all the bodily tissues. From the second through the eighth weeks, the developing human is referred to as an **embryo** (EMM-bree-oh). Soon a membrane called the **amnion** begins to grow over the developing embryo, and the amniotic cavity begins to fill with amniotic fluid. This fluid supports the fetus, protects it from shock, and also assists in fetal lung development. The **placenta,** which is the portion that is attached to the uterine wall, supplies nutrients to the developing fetus, aids in respiratory and excretory functions, and secretes hormones necessary for the continuation of the pregnancy. The **umbilical cord** connects the fetus to the placenta. By the fourth week of pregnancy, the placenta covers 20% of the wall of the uterus, and at 5 months, the placenta covers half of the uterine wall (R. Jones, 1984).

Toward the end of pregnancy, approximately 75 gallons of blood will pass through the placenta daily.

The majority of women deliver a single fetus. However, in approximately 2 of every 100 pregnancies there is a multiple birth. This can happen in two ways. Sometimes two ova are released by the ovaries, and if both are fertilized by sperm, **fraternal twins** (nonidentical) result. These twins are **dizygotic,** and they can be either of the same or different sexes. Two thirds of all twins are fraternal and are no more closely genetically related than any two siblings. The tendency to have fraternal twins may be inherited from the mother, and older women (over the age of 30) seem to have fraternal twins more often than younger women (because of erratic ovulation and an increased possibility of releasing more than one ovum).

Identical twins occur when a single zygote completely divides into two separate zygotes. This process produces twins who are genetically identical and are referred to as **monozygotic** twins. They often look alike and are always of the same sex. In rare cases, the zygote fails to divide completely, and two babies may be joined together at some point in their bodies; these are known as **conjoined twins,** once referred to as Siamese twins. In some instances, many ova are released and fertilized, and triplets (three offspring) or quadruplets (four offspring) may result. Recently, the number of multiple births has been increasing as more older women become pregnant and fertility drug use, which can stimulate the release of ova, becomes widespread (Brandes et al., 2010; V. C. Wright et al., 2008).

▶▶ EARLY SIGNS of Pregnancy

If the zygote does implant, most women experience physical signs very early that alert them to their pregnancy. The most common early indicator is missing a period, although some women notice some "spotting" that occurs during the pregnancy (anything more than this is often referred to as irregular bleeding and may indicate a possible miscarriage). Other physical signs include breast tenderness, frequent urination, and **morning sickness** (see Table 12.1).

It is estimated that between 50% and 80% of all pregnant women experience some form of nausea, vomiting, or both, during pregnancy (Atanackovic et al., 2001; Matthews et al., 2010). This sickness is due to the increase in estrogen and progesterone during pregnancy, which may irritate the stomach lining. It is often worse in the morning because there is no food in the stomach

to counter its effects, although it can happen at any point during the day. Researchers believe that morning sickness may protect the fetus from food-borne illness and chemicals in certain foods during the first trimester, which is the most critical time in development (Boyd, 2000). The lowest rates of morning sickness are found in cultures without animal products as a food staple. Some women also develop food aversions, the most common of which are to meat, fish, poultry, and eggs—all foods that can carry harmful bacteria.

In rare cases, **pseudocyesis** (sue-doe-sigh-EE-sis), or false pregnancy, occurs. This is a condition in which a woman believes she is pregnant when she is not. Her belief is so strong that she begins to experience several of the signs of pregnancy (Svoboda, 2006). She may miss her period, experience morning sickness, and gain weight.

Although the majority of cases of pseudocyesis have a psychological basis, some have physical causes. For instance, a tumor on the pituitary gland may cause an oversecretion of prolactin, which, in turn, can cause symptoms such as breast fullness and morning sickness. Pseudocyesis has been found to be more common in women who believe childbearing is central to their identity, have a history of infertility or depression (or both), or have had a miscarriage (Whelan & Stewart, 1990). Although rare, there have been a few cases in which men experienced pseudocyesis, although this is typically due to psychological impairment (Shutty & Leadbetter, 1993). Male and female partners of pregnant women may experience a related condition called **couvade** (coo-VAHD). Partners with this condition experience the symptoms of their pregnant

---

miscarriage
A pregnancy that terminates on its own; also referred to as a spontaneous abortion.

embryo
The developing organism from the second to the eighth week of gestation.

amnion
A thin, tough, membranous sac that encloses the embryo or fetus.

placenta
The structure through which the exchange of materials between fetal and maternal circulations occurs.

umbilical cord
The long, ropelike structure that connects the fetus to the placenta.

fraternal twins
Two offspring developed from two separate ova fertilized by different spermatozoa.

dizygotic
Pertaining to or derived from two separate zygotes.

identical twins
Two offspring developed from a single zygote that completely divides into two separate, genetically identical zygotes.

monozygotic
Pertaining to or derived from one zygote.

conjoined twins
Twins who are born physically joined together.

morning sickness
The nausea and vomiting that some women have when they become pregnant; typically caused by the increase in hormones. Can occur at any point in the day.

cesarean section (C-section)
A surgical procedure in which the woman's abdomen and uterus are surgically opened and a child is removed.

pseudocyesis
A condition in which a woman experiences signs of pregnancy, even though she is not pregnant.

couvade
A condition in which the male or female partner experiences the symptoms of the pregnant woman.

Throughout the world, people have relied on folk wisdom to predict the sex of their baby. Here are some examples:

It's a Girl!

- Baby sits on the left side of the womb (Nyinba, Nepal)
- Mother puts her left foot first crossing the threshold (Bihar, India)
- Baby sits low in the belly (Lepchas, Himalayas, and Bedouin tribes)
- Mother is grumpy with women (Dinka, Africa)
- Fetus moves slowly and gently (Dustin, North Borneo, and Egypt)
- Mother first feels the baby when she is outside (Serbia)

- Mother dreams of human skulls (Maori, New Zealand)
- Mother dreams of a head kerchief (Egypt)
- Mother craves spicy foods (Nyinba, Nepal)
- Mother's face has yellow spots (Poland)
- Baby "plays in stomach" before sixth month (Nyinba, Nepal)

It's a Boy!

- Baby sits on the right side of the womb (Nyinba, Nepal)
- Mother puts her right foot first crossing the threshold (Bihar, India)
- Baby sits high in the belly (Lepchas, Himalayas, and Bedouin tribes)

- Mother is grumpy with men (Dinka, Africa)
- Fetus moves fast and roughly (Dustin, North Borneo, and Egypt)
- Mother first feels baby move when at home (Serbia)
- Mother dreams of huia feathers (Maori, New Zealand)
- Mother dreams of a handkerchief (Egypt)
- Mother craves bland foods (Nyinba, Nepal)
- Mother looks well (Poland)
- Baby first "plays in stomach" after sixth month (Nyinba, Nepal)

SOURCE: Dunham et al. (1992).

---

partners, including nausea, vomiting, increased or decreased appetite, diarrhea, or abdominal bloating (Brennan et al., 2007).

▶▶ PREGNANCY Testing

If you have had vaginal intercourse without using birth control or have experienced any of the signs of pregnancy, it is a good idea to take a pregnancy test. Over-the-counter pregnancy tests can be purchased in drugstores, but sometimes tests are less expensive or even free in university health centers.

Pregnancy tests measure for a hormone in the blood called **human chorionic gonadotropin (hCG;** corr-ee-ON-ick go-nadoh-TRO-pin), which is produced during pregnancy. The hormone hCG is manufactured by the cells in the developing placenta and can be identified in the blood or urine 8 to 9 days after ovulation. The presence of hCG helps build and maintain a thick endometrial layer, and thus prevents menstruation. Peak levels of hCG are reached in the second and third months of pregnancy and then drop off.

Home pregnancy tests can be inaccurate if taken too soon after conception, and some women who postpone pregnancy tests until after the 12th week may have a false-negative pregnancy test because the hCG levels are too low to be detected by the test. If you are using an at-home test, be sure you know how soon after ovulation it can be used. Many tests today can detect hCG levels before a period is late. **False-positive** test results may occur in the presence of a kidney disease or infection, an overactive thyroid gland, or large doses of aspirin, tranquilizers, antidepressants, or anticonvulsant medications (Hatcher et al., 2007).

Of all pregnancy tests, **radioimmunoassay** (**RIA;** ray-dee-ohim-mue-noh-ASS-say) **blood tests** are the most accurate. RIA tests can detect hCG within a few days after conception and are also useful for monitoring the progress of a pregnancy that may be in jeopardy. The levels of hCG increase early in pregnancy, and if a woman's hormones do not follow this pattern, a spontaneous abortion or an **ectopic pregnancy** may have occurred. We will discuss both of these later in this chapter.

---

human chorionic gonadotropin (hCG)
The hormone that stimulates production of estrogen and progesterone to maintain pregnancy.

false positive
Incorrect result of a medical test or procedure that wrongly shows the presence of a finding.

radioimmunoassay (RIA) blood test
Blood pregnancy test.

ectopic pregnancy
The implantation of the fertilized egg outside the uterus, such as in the Fallopian tubes or abdomen.

due date
The projected birth date of a baby.

Naegele's rule
A means of figuring the due date by subtracting 3 months from the first day of the last menstrual period and adding 7 days.

amniocentesis
A procedure in which a small sample of amniotic fluid is analyzed to detect chromosomal abnormalities in the fetus or to determine the sex of the fetus.

If a woman plans on continuing the pregnancy, her health care provider helps her to calculate a **due date**. Most physicians date the pregnancy from the first day of the last menstrual period rather than the day of ovulation or fertilization. The standard for due date calculation is called the **Naegele's** (nay-GEL-lays) **rule**—subtract 3 months from the first day of the last period and add 7 days for a single birth (Mittendorf et al., 1990; for example, if the last period began on August 1, subtract 3 months and add 7 days, which means that the due date would be May 8). This rule works most effectively with women who have standard 28-day menstrual cycles.

▶▶ SEX SELECTION: **Myth and Modern Methods**

Throughout time, many couples have searched for ways to choose the sex of their child. A variety of techniques have been proposed by different cultures at different times. Aristotle believed that if a couple had sexual intercourse in the north wind, they would have a male child, and if intercourse took place in the south wind, they would have a female child. Hippocrates believed that males formed on the right side of the uterus and females on the left; so, to conceive a daughter, a woman was advised to lie on her left side directly after intercourse. The ancient Greeks thought that if a man cut or tied his left testicle, a couple would not have girls because male sperm were thought to be produced in the right testicle (Dunham et al., 1992). Although some of these suggestions sound absurd today, people in many cultures still hold on to myths of how to choose and how to know the gender of their child (see accompanying Sexual Diversity in Our World).

Reasons for wanting to choose a child's sex vary; although some couples simply prefer a male or female child, others desire to choose the sex of their children for medical reasons. For example, certain inherited diseases are more likely to affect one sex (such as hemophilia, which affects more males).

Modern-day methods of gender selection were popularized by Shettles and Rorvik (1970) in their groundbreaking book *Your Baby's Sex: Now You Can Choose*. According to these authors, by taking into account the characteristics of the female (X) and male (Y) sperm, couples can use timing and pH-level adjustments to the vaginal environment (douches) to increase the concentration of X or Y sperm.

Because Y sperm swim faster and thrive in an alkaline environment, Shettles and Rorvik recommend that to have a boy, a couple should have intercourse close to ovulation (to allow the faster-swimming Y sperm to get there first) and douche with a mixture of baking soda and water. Because X sperm tend to live longer and thrive in an acidic environment, for a girl, a couple should time intercourse 2 to 3 days before ovulation and douche with a mixture of vinegar and water.

Medical procedures for sex selection include "microsorting" (also known as "spinning"—separating the X and Y sperm followed by artificial insemination). Other tests that can be used to identify sex include genetic embryo testing and amniocentesis. When using these methods, the reported likelihood of conceiving

ON YOUR MIND 12.2

I have missed my period now for 2 months in a row. Does this mean that I am pregnant? What should I do?

If you have been engaging in vaginal intercourse, there is certainly a chance that you are pregnant. However, there are several other reasons for missing your period, including stress, losing weight, active participation in sports, or changes in eating patterns, as well as certain diseases. In any case, it is a good idea to see a gynecologist or your school nurse for an evaluation.

a male is between 50% and 70% and a female is between 50% and 90% (Pozniak, 2002). Preimplantation genetic diagnosis (PGD) is a procedure typically used during assisted reproduction to determine where there are chromosomal or genetic abnormalities in an embryo. Some couples who prefer a child of a certain sex may also use PGD for this preference. As you can imagine, the use of PGD has become controversial because it has also been used for sex selection (Ehrich et al., 2007; Gleicher et al., 2008; Kuliev & Verlinsky, 2008). Finally, an **amniocentesis** (am-nee-oh-sent-TEE-sis) can also determine, among other things, the chromosomal sex of the fetus. These tests raise many moral, sociological, and ethical issues about sex selection. For example, controversy surrounds whether parents should be able to selectively abort a fetus on the basis of sex.

In several countries around the world, such as India, China, South Korea, and Taiwan, parents go to extremes to ensure the birth of a male baby. In some Indian states, for example, males are valued more than females because of their ability to care for and financially support aging parents. Female offspring, in contrast, move into a husband's home after marriage and are unavailable to help care for their parents. An old Indian saying claims that having a girl is like "watering your neighbor's lawn" (Sharma & Haub, 2008). The increasing availability of prenatal testing in India has been linked to an increase in the ratio of male to female births (Dubuc & Coleman, 2007; Jha et al., 2006; Sharma & Haub, 2008). Since 2001, however, male/female ratios have stabilized in India (Sharma & Haub, 2008).

REAL RESEARCH 12.1 Research on morning sickness has found that it may offer protection from breast cancer. One study found that women who experienced morning sickness during pregnancy had a 30% lower chance of development of breast cancer later in life, compared with women who did not experience morning sickness (and women who experienced severe morning sickness had an even lower risk; JAWOROWICZ, 2007). Researchers suggest that changing levels of hCG may be responsible for the nausea, and that these levels seem to offer protection from breast cancer later on.

1 Explain the process of conception, and describe how the human body is programmed to help pregnancy occur.

2 Identify four signs of pregnancy and explain why they occur.

3 Explain how pregnancy tests work.

4 Explain the methods for sex selection, and define and discuss infanticide.

▶ INFERTILITY

Infertility is defined as the inability to conceive (or impregnate) after 1 year of regular vaginal intercourse without the use of any form of birth control (if a woman is older than 35, usually infertility is diagnosed after 6 months of not being able to conceive). In 2010, there were an estimated 7.3 million infertile couples in the United States (Chavarro et al., 2007b).

We know that fertility rates naturally decline in men and women with increasing age, beginning as early as 30 and then decreasing more quickly after age 40—fewer than 10% of women in their early 20s have infertility issues, whereas 30% of women in their 40s do (Chavarro et al., 2007b). Sperm quality in men is also affected by aging (Girsh et al., 2008). In Chapter 6, we discussed the worldwide declines in sperm counts and quality because of occupational, environmental, and lifestyle factors. Studies have found that male infertility can be caused by exposure to many environmental toxins, including bisphenol A (BPA), mercury, paint solvents, lead, video display terminals, and computers (El-Helaly et al., 2010; Wong & Cheng, 2011). In addition, shift work and work-related stress can significantly increase the risk for male infertility (El-Helaly et al., 2010).

Infertility has a strong impact on a couple's well-being (Forti & Krausz, 1998). Emotional reactions to infertility can include depression, anxiety, anger, self-blame, guilt, frustration, and fear. Because the majority of people have no experience dealing with infertility, many of those who find out they are infertile isolate themselves and try not to think about it. Overall, women tend to have more emotional reactions to infertility and are more willing

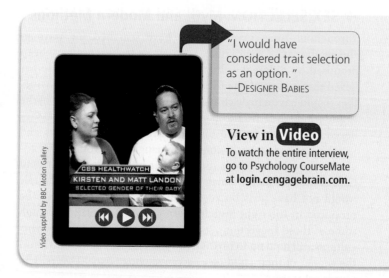

Video supplied by BBC Motion Gallery

"I would have considered trait selection as an option."
—DESIGNER BABIES

View in Video
To watch the entire interview, go to Psychology CourseMate at **login.cengagebrain.com**.

to confide in someone about their infertility than are men (Hjelmstedt et al., 1999). Childbearing in the United States is part of what defines being female, and so women who are infertile often feel less valued than fertile women. The term **motherhood mandate** refers to the idea that something is wrong with a woman if she does not play a central role in caregiving and child care (Riggs, 2005).

The most common causes of female infertility include ovulation disorders, blocked Fallopian tubes, endometriosis (see Chapter 5), structural uterine problems, or excessive uterine fi-

timeline The History of Assisted Reproduction

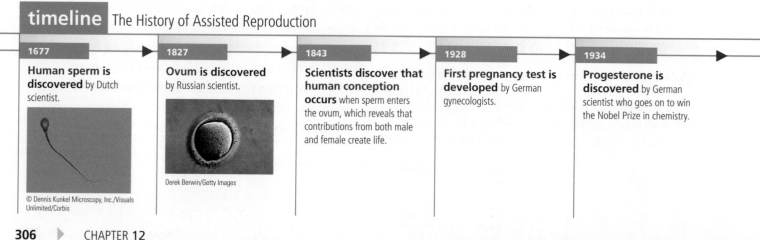

1677
Human sperm is discovered by Dutch scientist.

© Dennis Kunkel Microscopy, Inc./Visuals Unlimited/Corbis

1827
Ovum is discovered by Russian scientist.

Derek Berwin/Getty Images

1843
Scientists discover that human conception occurs when sperm enters the ovum, which reveals that contributions from both male and female create life.

1928
First pregnancy test is developed by German gynecologists.

1934
Progesterone is discovered by German scientist who goes on to win the Nobel Prize in chemistry.

broids. The most common causes for male infertility include problems with sperm production (Lewis et al., 2008). Traditional semen analysis may not accurately identify fertility issues, and as a result, newer sperm tests are used today (Natali & Turek, 2011). Infertility can also be caused by past infections with gonorrhea, chlamydia, or pelvic inflammatory disease (Centers for Disease Control and Prevention, 2010a; Chavarro et al., 2007b; Eley & Pacey, 2010), which is one of the reasons college students are encouraged to have regular medical checkups and women are encouraged to have regular Pap smears. If a sexually transmitted infection is treated early, there is less chance that it will interfere with fertility. Infertility is also affected by age. Women and men who delay pregnancy may experience infertility because of the decreasing quality of their ova and sperm (Coccia & Rizzello, 2008; Girsh et al., 2008). For some men and women who experience reproductive problems, changing lifestyle patterns, reducing stress, avoiding rigorous exercise, and maintaining a recommended weight may restore fertility (Chavarro et al., 2007b). For other couples, new medical interventions offer new possibilities.

> *The most common causes for male infertility include **problems with sperm production.***

Fertility problems can be traced 61% of the time to one of the partners (43% of the time to the female, and 18% of the time to the male). In 18% of cases, there is a combined problem, and in 20% the reason is unknown (Centers for Disease Control and Prevention, 2010a). Historically, women have been blamed for infertility problems, and until recently, men were not even considered a possible part of the problem.

▶▶ ASSISTED REPRODUCTIVE Technologies

Today, many couples—married, unmarried, straight, gay, lesbian, young, and old—use ARTs. Some couples use these techniques because they have infertility issues, whereas others use them to get pregnant without a partner or with a same-sex partner. Although in the past single women and gay, lesbian, and bisexual couples were denied access to ARTs, this has been changing (Greenfeld, 2005; McManus et al., 2006; L. E. Ross et al., 2006b). In 2006, the Ethics Committee of the American Society for Reproductive Medicine released a statement supporting access to fertility treatment by unmarried, gay, and lesbian persons (Ethics Committee Report, 2006). Unique issues face gays, lesbians, and bisexuals who want to be pregnant. Lesbian and bisexual women who use infertility services often find that because these centers primarily cater to infertile heterosexual women, they are required to undergo significant infertility workups (even though they are not "infertile") before any reproductive procedures (Mulligan & Heath, 2007; L. E. Ross et al., 2006a, 2006b). Gay men also face unique issues, as assisted reproduction is often more complicated and expensive because they need a surrogate to carry the pregnancy (C. Friedman, 2007). Although in the past, gay men sought out coparenting arrangements with female friends, today many gay men use adoption and surrogacy (C. Friedman, 2007). Surrogacy raises additional issues for gay couples because they must choose whose sperm will be used. Some gay men mix their sperm so they don't know which one of them is the biological father.

In 2008, the average age of a woman using ART was 36 years, although 21% were older than 40 (Centers for Disease Control and Prevention, 2010a). Although many technologies are available to men and women today, deciding which treatment to use depends on factors such as cost, a woman's age, duration of infertility, and chances of conceiving without treatment. Many of these options are very time-consuming and expensive, and they do not guarantee success. The Centers for Disease Control and Prevention reported that in 2008, 37% of ART cycles led to a pregnancy, but only 30% resulted in a live birth—in other words, 19% of these procedures did not result in a live birth (Centers for Disease Control and Prevention, 2010a). Now we'll discuss several of the available ARTs.

In 2007, the Centers for Disease Control and Prevention released a national summary of ART success rates (Centers for Disease Control and Prevention, 2007a). This report showed that of the 134,260 ART cycles performed in United States, 38,910 resulted in a live birth (and 52,041 infants).

infertility
The inability to conceive (or impregnate).

motherhood mandate
The belief that something is wrong with a woman if she is not involved in caregiving or child care.

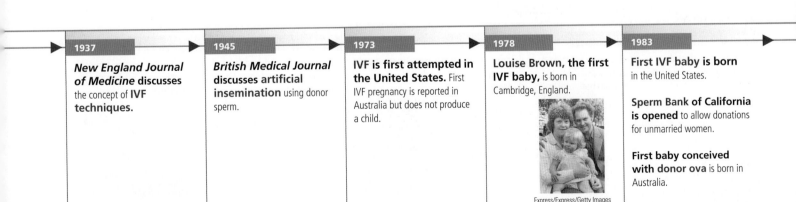

1937	1945	1973	1978	1983
***New England Journal of Medicine* discusses** the concept of **IVF techniques.**	***British Medical Journal* discusses artificial insemination** using donor sperm.	**IVF is first attempted in the United States.** First IVF pregnancy is reported in Australia but does not produce a child.	**Louise Brown, the first IVF baby,** is born in Cambridge, England.	**First IVF baby is born** in the United States. **Sperm Bank of California is opened** to allow donations for unmarried women. **First baby conceived with donor ova** is born in Australia.

Express/Express/Getty Images

Fertility Drugs

Some couples may use fertility drugs to help achieve a pregnancy. As we discussed in Chapters 5 and 6, ovulation and sperm production are a result of a well-balanced endocrine system (pituitary, hypothalamus, and gonads). Some women and men have hormonal irregularities that may interfere with the process of ovulation or sperm production. Although we do not always know why these hormonal problems develop, many problems can be treated with fertility drugs.

A major risk of the use of fertility drugs has been the development of **ovarian hyperstimulation syndrome** because the drugs stimulate the ovaries to produce more ova (Jakimiuk et al., 2007; Kwan et al., 2008; Van Voorhis, 2006; V. C. Wright et al., 2008). This has raised concern about the possible correlation between the use of fertility drugs and the development of breast or ovarian cancer. Whereas some studies have found a possible increased risk in women who have never been pregnant, older women, those with extensive fertility workups, and those with a history of cancer (Brinton, 2007; Pappo et al., 2008), other studies have found no increased risk (Hollander, 2000; Lerner-Geva et al., 2006). Fertility drugs also increase the likelihood of multiple births. Infants born through these techniques have been found to have lower birth rates, increased prematurity, and higher rates of birth defects and infant death (we will discuss birth defects more later in this chapter; see also Allen et al., 2008;

Buckett et al., 2007; Centers for Disease Control and Prevention, 2007a; Kelly-Vance et al., 2004; Van Voorhis, 2006). Newer fertility drugs are less likely to overstimulate the ovaries and have led to fewer multiple births (Check, 2010).

Surgery

Cervical, vaginal, or endometrial abnormalities that prevent conception may be corrected surgically. Scar tissue, cysts, tumors, or adhesions, as well as blockages inside the Fallopian tubes, may be surgically removed. The use of diagnostic techniques such as **laparoscopy** (la-puh-RAH-ske-pee) and **hysteroscopy** (hissstare-oh-OSK-coe-pee) are also common (Coccia et al., 2008). In men, surgery may be required to remove any blockage in the vas deferens or epididymis, or repair a **varicocele** (VA-ruh-coe-seal).

Artificial Insemination

Artificial insemination is the process of introducing sperm into a woman's reproductive tract without vaginal intercourse. This is a popular option for both heterosexual and same-sex couples. Ejaculated sperm, collected through masturbation, can come from a partner or from a sperm donor. Several samples may be collected from men with a low sperm count to increase the number of healthy sperm. Once medically washed, sperm can be deposited in the vagina, cervix, uterus (intrauterine), or Fallopian tubes (intratubal).

---

ovarian hyperstimulation syndrome
Adverse effects of excessive hormonal stimulation of the ovaries through fertility drugs, including abdominal bloating, nausea, diarrhea, weight gain, and abdominal, chest, and leg pain.

laparoscopy
A procedure that allows a direct view of all the pelvic organs, including the uterus, Fallopian tubes, and ovaries; also refers to a number of important surgeries (such as tubal ligation or gall bladder removal) involving a laparoscope.

hysteroscopy
Visual inspection of the uterine cavity with an endoscope.

varicocele
An unnatural swelling of the veins in the scrotum.

artificial insemination
Artificially introducing sperm into a woman's reproductive tract.

sperm bank
A storage facility that holds supplies of sperm for future use.

in vitro fertilization (IVF)
A procedure in which a woman's ova are removed from her body, fertilized with sperm in a laboratory, and then surgically implanted back into her uterus.

test-tube baby
A slang term for any zygote created by mixing sperm and egg outside a woman's body.

gamete intra–Fallopian tube transfer (GIFT)
A reproductive technique in which the sperm and ova are collected and injected into the Fallopian tube before fertilization.

zygote intra–Fallopian tube transfer (ZIFT)
A reproductive technique in which the sperm and ova are collected and fertilized outside the body, and the fertilized zygote is then placed into the Fallopian tube.

---

timeline   The History of Assisted Reproduction

1984
First baby developed from a frozen embryo is born in Australia.

1987
Embryo transfer procedure is patented.

1988
After a **surrogate mother refuses to give up custody** of baby she carried, the New Jersey Supreme Court gives custody of "Baby M" to the genetic father and his wife, and the surrogate is given visitation rights.

AP Photo

1991
A 42-year-old woman becomes a **surrogate mother** for her daughter after becoming pregnant with the daughter's embryo.

1992
Intracytoplasmic sperm injection (ICSI) for male infertility is introduced.

© ISM/Phototake

Men who decide to undergo sterilization or who may become sterile because of surgery or chemotherapy can collect sperm before the procedure. Sperm can be frozen for up to 10 years in a **sperm bank.** Although the cost of donor sperm varies among sperm banks, typically donor sperm costs between $200 and $600 per insemination. Many sperm banks charge more for more information about the donor, such as a handwriting sample, photographs, or a video. Some couples buy several vials from the same donor so that offspring can have the same donor father. Recall that in the chapter opening story, Laura and Ozlem's children were conceived with sperm from the same known donor so they are genetically related to each other.

A donor may be found through one of the many sperm banks throughout the United States and abroad, usually from an online donor catalog (see Web Resources at the end of this chapter for more information). After a donor is chosen, the sperm bank will typically send sperm to the physician who will be performing the insemination procedure, but in some cases, the sperm is sent directly to the buyer. Fertility drugs are often used in conjunction with artificial insemination to increase the chances that there will be healthy ova present when the sperm is introduced.

In Vitro Fertilization

Another reproductive technology is **in vitro fertilization (IVF),** or the creation of a test-tube baby. In 1978, Louise Brown, the first **test-tube baby,** was born in England. Since that time, thousands of babies have been conceived in this fashion. The name is a bit deceiving, however, because these babies are not born in a test tube; rather, they are *conceived* in a petri dish, which is a shallow circular dish with a loose-fitting cover. In 2010, Robert Edwards, a British scientist who developed IVF, won the Nobel Prize in medicine (Jha, 2010).

Heterosexual and lesbian women with infertility problems may use IVF because of blocked or damaged Fallopian tubes or endometriosis (see Chapter 5). Like other artificial reproductive technologies, fertility drugs are typically used before IVF to help stimulate the ovaries. When the ova have matured, four to six are retrieved with the use of microscopic needles inserted into the abdominal cavity. The ova are put into a petri dish and mixed with washed sperm. Once fertilization has occurred (usually anywhere from 3 to 6 days), the zygotes are either transferred to the woman's uterus or frozen for use at another time (we will discuss this further later in the chapter). Improved understanding of human reproduction has led to many improvements in IVF, such as increased success rates and decreased multiple births (Fechner & McGovern, 2011).

Earlier we discussed how PGD can be used on embryos to determine gender. However, this test is more commonly used to screen for chromosomal and genetic abnormalities. A PGD screening costs between $3,000 and $5,000.

Gamete and Zygote Intra–Fallopian Tube Transfer

Gamete intra–Fallopian tube transfer (GIFT) is similar to IVF in that ova and sperm are mixed in an artificial environment. However, after this occurs, both the ova and sperm are placed in the Fallopian tube, via a small incision, before fertilization. Fertilization is allowed to occur naturally rather than in an artificial environment. **Zygote intra–Fallopian tube transfer (ZIFT)** differs slightly from GIFT in that it allows ova and sperm to fertilize outside the body (similar to IVF). However, directly after fertilization, the embryo is placed in the woman's Fallopian tube (and not the uterus, like in IVF), which allows it to travel to the uterus and implant naturally. Although higher success rates were initially reported with these two procedures, they are more invasive than IVF, and today only a small percentage of couples use these procedures (Centers for Disease Control and Prevention, 2007a).

In this enlarged image, a single sperm is injected into the center of an ovum during an intracellular sperm injection procedure.

© ISM/Phototake

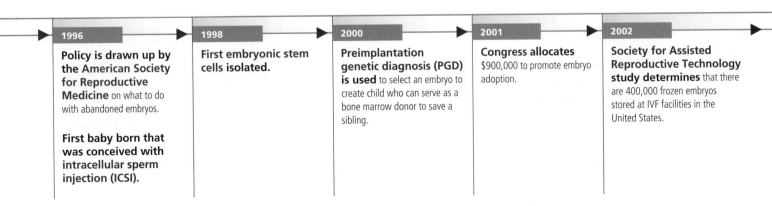

1996	1998	2000	2001	2002
Policy is drawn up by the American Society for Reproductive Medicine on what to do with abandoned embryos. **First baby born that was conceived with intracellular sperm injection (ICSI).**	**First embryonic stem cells isolated.**	**Preimplantation genetic diagnosis (PGD) is used** to select an embryo to create child who can serve as a bone marrow donor to save a sibling.	**Congress allocates** $900,000 to promote embryo adoption.	**Society for Assisted Reproductive Technology study determines** that there are 400,000 frozen embryos stored at IVF facilities in the United States.

Intracellular Sperm Injections

Couples who experience sperm problems or ova that are resistant to fertilization may use **intracytoplasmic sperm injection (ICSI).** ICSI involves injecting a single sperm into the center of an ovum under a microscope. Usually, fresh, ejaculated sperm are used, but sperm can also be removed from the epididymis or the testes, or frozen sperm can be used (Balaban et al., in press; Kalsi et al., 2011; Yanagimachi, 2011).

Overall, ICSI results have been controversial—with some studies showing no adverse outcomes compared with natural conception (Knoester et al., 2008; Nauru et al., 2008) and other studies showing increased risks (J. L. Simpson & Lamb, 2001). Research indicates that ICSI may lead to an increased risk for genetic defect, which may be because ICSI eliminates many of the natural barriers to conception, increasing the transmission of abnormal genes (Al-Shawaf et al., 2005; Chemes & Rawe, 2010; Neri et al., 2008; Stanger et al., 2010; Terada et al., 2010). Scientists do not know how nature chooses one sperm for fertilization, and choosing one randomly may not be appropriate, although physicians usually try to pick one that appears vigorous and healthy.

Oocyte and Embryo Transplants

Women who are not able to produce healthy ova because of ovarian failure or age-related infertility and same-sex couples may use oocyte (egg) and embryo donation. Oocyte donation involves using a donor ova, whereas embryo donation can involve using frozen embryos donated by a couple or the creation of an embryo with a donated ova and sperm. Younger women are more likely to use their own ova, whereas 38% of 43- to 44-year-old women and 71% of 44-year-old and older women use donor ova (Centers for Disease Control and Prevention, 2010a). This is because women older than 40 have a higher chance of achieving pregnancy by using a donated ova than by using their own aged ova.

Surrogate Parenting

Surrogate parenting is a popular option for both heterosexual couples who cannot carry a pregnancy to term and same-sex couples. In this procedure, sperm and ovum are combined, and the zygote is implanted in another woman, called a **surrogate mother** or gestational carrier.

In the United States, laws regulating surrogacy vary state by state. However, many states have ambiguous laws or do not directly address surrogacy issues. States also vary with respect to

---

REAL RESEARCH 12.2 Researchers found that women who had a clown visit them while they were recovering from an IVF procedure were 16% more likely to become pregnant than women who did not have such a visit (FRIEDLER ET AL., 2011). Experts believe that humor can have a beneficial effect on pregnancy.

---

whether the surrogacy is traditional (mother is the biological contributor of the ova) or gestational (mother is not the biological contributor of the ova) and issues related to the sexual orientation of the couple (Human Rights Campaign, 2010). Some states, such as New York and Michigan, refuse to recognize surrogacy contracts, whereas others, such as California, have legalized it and fully support it (Human Rights Campaign, 2010; Klimkiewicz, 2008). Outside the United States, surrogacy continues to grow. For example, commercial surrogacy is growing in western India, where one clinic matches infertile U.S. couples with local women who are willing to serve as surrogates (Dolnick, 2007). These women are impregnated with embryos of couples who are unable to carry a pregnancy to term. These practices are available in many countries, although they raise many moral, ethical, and legal issues.

---

intracytoplasmic sperm injection (ICSI)
Fertility procedure that involves mechanically injecting a sperm into the center of an ovum.

surrogate parenting
Use of a woman who, through artificial insemination or in vitro fertilization, gestates a fetus for another woman or man.

surrogate mother
A woman who is hired to carry a pregnancy for a couple who may not be able to do so.

sperm cryopreservation
The freezing of sperm for later use.

embryo cryopreservation
The freezing of embryos for later use.

ova cryopreservation
The freezing of ova for later use.

---

timeline The History of Assisted Reproduction

2004

U.S. government bans surrogate contracts and the sale of human eggs and sperm in the most comprehensive attempt to regulate assisted human reproduction.

2006

American Society for Reproductive Medicine publicly supports access to fertility treatment by unmarried, gay, and lesbian persons.

© Lester Lefkowitz/Corbis

2007

U.S. researcher announces the first birth of a baby from eggs matured in a laboratory, frozen, thawed, and then fertilized.

2007

Scientists exploring the creation of female sperm and male ova from the cells of adult men and women. Such cells would allow offspring of same-sex couple to have equal genetic contributions from both partners.

2010

Researchers at Brown University develop the first artificial human ovary that can produce mature human ova in the laboratory.

Other Options

Other options involve the freezing of embryos and sperm for later fertilization. It is estimated that 30% to 40% of all births from IVF were from frozen embryos (Borini et al., 2008). This can be beneficial for men and women who are diagnosed with illnesses (such as cancer) whose treatment might interfere with their ability to manufacture healthy sperm or ova. The sperm can be collected from the testis, the epididymis, or an ejaculate, and can be frozen and stored in liquid nitrogen for many years through a process called **sperm cryopreservation.**

The effectiveness of the sperm, once thawed, is variable, and sometimes the sperm do not survive the thawing process. **Embryo cryopreservation** is also possible; but like sperm, not all embryos can survive the freezing and thawing process (Borini et al., 2008; Leibo, 2008; Youssry et al., 2008).

A growing number of women have been undergoing **ova cryopreservation** (also called *vitrification*), although this is still considered an experimental procedure (Scaravelli et al., 2010; Shufaro & Schenker, 2010; see the Extend Fertility website detailed in Media Resources later in this chapter). Typically, a woman uses fertility drugs to stimulate the ovulation of several ova, which are surgically extracted, frozen, and stored (Shellenbarger, 2008). However, unlike sperm and embryos, human eggs have a higher water concentration, which makes chromosomal damage more likely during the freezing and thawing processes (Martínez-Burgos et al., 2011).

Ova cryopreservation can give women the opportunity to preserve their eggs for use later in life. It can also give women undergoing cancer radiation or chemotherapy an option to save ova for a later pregnancy (J. E. Roberts & Oktay, 2005; This, 2008). Newer research has evaluated the use of ovarian stimulation drugs and partial removal of ovarian tissue for cryobanking before cancer treatment (Huober-Zeeb et al., 2011). Ovarian tissue and ova cryopreservation are both areas of research that will continue to grow in the future.

◀ review QUESTIONS

1 Define infertility, and identify some of the most common causes of both male and female infertility.

2 Explain how same-sex couples, older women, and single women who seek assisted reproduction have been treated unfairly and identify some of the unique issues that confront these groups.

3 Identify and describe the various assisted reproductive options.

4 Differentiate between sperm, ova, and embryo cryopreservation. What are the risks associated with each?

▶ A HEALTHY Pregnancy

Pregnancy is divided into three periods called **trimesters.** Throughout these trimesters, important fetal development occurs as a pregnant woman's body changes and adjusts to these developments. We now explore these changes.

▶▶ PRENATAL Period

Although you would think a trimester would be a 3-month period, because pregnancies are dated from the woman's last menstrual period, a full-term pregnancy is actually 40 weeks; therefore, each trimester is approximately 12 to 15 weeks long. Throughout the pregnancy, physicians can use electronic monitoring and **sonography,** or **ultrasound,** to check on the status of the fetus. We now discuss the physical development of the typical, healthy mother and child in each of these trimesters.

REAL RESEARCH 12.3   Although the use of ultrasound during pregnancy has become more popular over the last few years, research has found ultrasound scans of the fetus may increase the risks for childhood cancer (RAJARAMAN ET AL., 2011). Researchers suggest cautious use of diagnostic radiation imaging of a woman's abdomen and pelvis during pregnancy.

trimester
Three periods of 12–15 weeks each; typically refers to the division of the nine months of pregnancy.

sonography
Electronic monitoring; also called *ultrasound.*

ultrasound
The use of ultrasonic waves to monitor a developing fetus; also called *sonography.*

First Trimester

The first trimester includes the first 13 weeks of pregnancy (weeks 1–13). It is the trimester in which the most important embryonic development takes place. When a woman becomes pregnant, her entire system adjusts. Her heart pumps more blood, her weight increases, her lungs and digestive system work harder, and her thyroid gland grows. All of these changes occur to encourage the growth of the developing fetus.

PRENATAL DEVELOPMENT By the end of the first month of pregnancy, the fetal heart is formed and begins to pump blood. In fact, the circulatory system is the first organ system to function in the embryo (Rischer & Easton, 1992). In addition, many of the other major systems develop, including the digestive system, beginnings of the brain, spinal cord, nervous system, muscles, arms, legs, eyes, fingers, and toes. By 14 weeks, the liver, kidneys, intestines, and lungs have begun to develop. In addition, the circulatory and urinary systems are operating, and the reproductive organs have developed. By the end of the first trimester, the fetus weighs 0.5 ounce and is approximately 3 inches long.

CHANGES IN THE PREGNANT MOTHER During the first few weeks of pregnancy, a woman's body adjusts to increased levels of estrogen and progesterone. This can cause fatigue, breast tenderness, constipation, increased urination, and nausea or vomiting (see Table 12.1). Some women experience nausea and vomiting so severe during pregnancy that they must be hospitalized because of weight loss and malnutrition (Sheehan, 2007). This study found that ginger decreased severe nausea associated with pregnancy (Sheehan, 2007). Specific food cravings are normal, as is an increased sensitivity to smells and odors.

Although some women feel physically uncomfortable because of all these changes, many also feel excited and happy about the life growing within them. The final, confirming sign of pregnancy—a fetal heartbeat—can be a joyous moment that offsets all the discomforts of pregnancy. The fetal heartbeat can usually be heard through ultrasound by the end of the first trimester.

Since its introduction in 1950, ultrasound has become a useful tool in obstetrics. It can capture images of the embryo for measurement as early as 5.5 weeks into the pregnancy, and a heartbeat can be seen by 6 weeks. Fetal heartbeat can also be heard through a stethoscope at approximately 9 to 10 weeks, and after a heartbeat is either seen or heard, the probability of miscarriage declines significantly. Ultrasounds help to confirm a pregnancy, rule out abnormalities, indicate gestational age, and confirm multiple

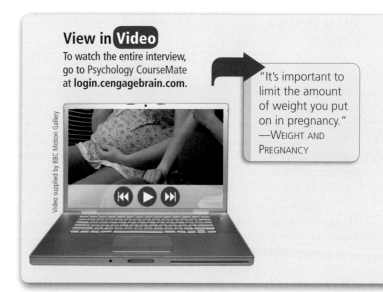

View in Video
To watch the entire interview, go to Psychology CourseMate at **login.cengagebrain.com**.

"It's important to limit the amount of weight you put on in pregnancy."
—WEIGHT AND PREGNANCY

Video supplied by BBC Motion Gallery

pregnancies (we further discuss its use as a prenatal screening device later in this chapter). Newer three-dimensional and even four-dimensional ultrasounds allow parents to view almost lifelike fetal images, including yawns and facial expressions (see the nearby photo). However, the standard two-dimensional images may still offer better diagnostic information than either three- or four-dimensional ultrasounds because they allow physicians to see inside of structures (Handwerk, 2005).

Second Trimester

The second trimester includes the second 15 weeks of pregnancy (weeks 14–28). The fetus looks noticeably more human.

PRENATAL DEVELOPMENT The fetus grows dramatically during the second trimester and is 13 inches long by the end of the trimester. The fetus has developed tooth buds and reflexes, such as sucking and swallowing. Although the sex of the fetus is determined at conception, it is not immediately apparent during development. If

Newer ultrasounds can produce both three- and four-dimensional ultrasounds like the one below.

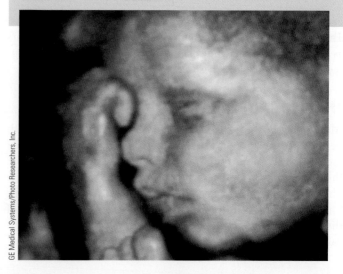

GE Medical Systems/Photo Researchers, Inc.

An embryo at 7 to 8 weeks. This embryo is approximately 1 inch long.

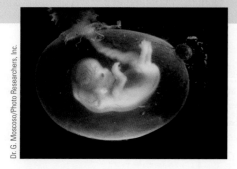

Dr. G. Moscoso/Photo Researchers, Inc.

At 5 months, the fetus is becoming more and more lively. It can turn its head, move its face, and make breathing movements. This 5-month fetus is approximately 9 inches long.

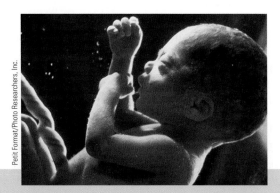

The fetus at 9 months, ready for birth.

the fetus is positioned correctly during ultrasound, the sex may be determined as early as 16 weeks, although most of the time it is not possible until 20 to 22 weeks.

During the second trimester, soft hair, called **lanugo** (lan-NEW-go), and a waxy substance, known as **vernix,** cover the fetus's body. These may develop to protect the fetus from the constant exposure to the amniotic fluid. By the end of the second trimester, the fetus will weigh about 1.75 pounds. If birth takes place at the end of the second trimester, the baby may be able to survive with intensive medical care. We discuss premature birth later in this chapter.

CHANGES IN THE PREGNANT MOTHER During the second trimester, nausea begins to subside as the body adjusts to the increased hormonal levels. Breast sensitivity also tends to decrease. However, fatigue may continue, as well as an increase in appetite, heartburn, edema (ankle or leg swelling), and a noticeable vaginal discharge. Skin pigmentation changes can occur on the face. As the uterus grows larger and the blood circulation slows down, constipation and muscle cramps bother some women. Internally, the cervix turns a deep red, almost violet color because of increased blood supply.

As the pregnancy progresses, the increasing size of the uterus and the restriction of the pelvic veins can cause more swelling of the ankles. Increased problems with varicose veins and hemorrhoids may also occur. Fetal movement is often felt in the second

trimester, sometimes as early as the 16th week. Usually women can feel movement earlier in their second or subsequent pregnancies because they know what fetal movement feels like.

The second trimester of pregnancy is usually the most positive time for the mother. The early physiological signs of pregnancy such as morning sickness and fatigue lessen, and the mother-to-be finally feels better physically. Feeling better physically often leads to positive psychological feelings including excitement, happiness, and a sense of well-being. Many women report an increased sex drive during the second trimester, and for many couples, it is a period of high sexual satisfaction.

As the developing fetus begins to move around, many women feel reassured after anxiously wondering whether the fetus was developing at all. In fact, many women report that the kicking and moving about of the developing fetus are very comforting. Finally, many women are happy to finally make the transition to maternity clothes because they are more comfortable and enable women to publicly share their pregnancies.

Third Trimester

The third trimester includes the final weeks of pregnancy (weeks 28–40) and ends with the birth of a child. The fetus gains both fat deposits and muscle mass during this period.

PRENATAL DEVELOPMENT By the end of the seventh month, the fetus begins to develop fat deposits. The fetus can react to pain, light, and sounds. Some fetuses develop occasional hiccups or begin to suck their thumb. If a baby is born at the end of the seventh month, there is a good chance of survival. In the eighth month, the majority of the organ systems are well developed, although the brain continues to grow. By the end of the eighth month, the fetus is 15 inches long and weighs about 3 pounds. During the third trimester, there is often stronger and more frequent fetal movement, which will slow down toward the ninth month (because the fetus has less room to move around). At birth, an infant, on average, weighs 7.5 pounds and is 20 inches long.

CHANGES IN THE PREGNANT MOTHER Many of the symptoms from the second trimester continue, with constipation and heartburn increasing in frequency. Backaches, leg cramps, increases in varicose veins, hemorrhoids, sleep problems, shortness of breath, and **Braxton–Hicks contractions** often occur. At first these contractions are scattered and relatively painless (the uterus hardens for a moment and then returns to normal). In the eighth and ninth

lanugo
The downy covering of hair over a fetus.

vernix
Cheeselike substance that coats the fetus in the uterus.

Braxton–Hicks contractions
Intermittent contractions of the uterus after the third month of pregnancy.

months, the Braxton–Hicks contractions become stronger. A thin, yellowish liquid called **colostrum** (kuh-LAHS-trum) may be secreted from the nipples as the breasts prepare to produce milk for breast-feeding. Toward the end of the third trimester, many women feel an increase in apprehension about labor and delivery; impatience and restlessness are common.

The Partner's Experience

In the United States today, partners are allowed and encouraged to participate in the birth. However, this was not always the case. For many years, fathers were told to go to the waiting room and sit until the baby was born. In some other cultures, such as in Bang Chan, Thailand, the father aids in the actual birth of his child (Dunham et al., 1992). The role of the father in pregnancy varies among cultures. Some fathers are required to remain on a strict diet during the course of the pregnancy or to cater to their partner's food cravings at all times.

Pregnancy can be a time of joy and anticipation for the partner of a pregnant woman, but it can also be a time of stress and anxiety. Feelings about parenting in combination with the many changes their partners are undergoing can all add to increased vulnerability.

◀ review QUESTIONS

1 How many weeks is a typical pregnancy, and how are trimesters determined?

2 Trace prenatal development and changes in the pregnant mother throughout the three trimesters of pregnancy.

3 Explain the changes in a pregnant mother, and identify the trimester in which a woman generally feels the most positive and explain why.

▶ HEALTH CARE during Pregnancy

A pregnant woman can do many things to be healthy during her pregnancy, including participating in physical exercise, getting good nutrition, and avoiding drugs and alcohol. Women often maintain sexual interest during pregnancy, although it may begin to decrease during the third trimester.

▶▶ EXERCISE and Nutrition

How much exercise should a woman get during pregnancy? Many physicians strongly advise light exercise during pregnancy; it has been found to result in a greater sense of well-being, enhanced mood, shorter labor, and fewer obstetric problems (Gavard & Artal, 2008; Polman et al., 2007). However, although participation in ongoing exercise throughout pregnancy can enhance birth weight, severe exercise can result in a low-birth-weight baby (Pivarnik, 1998). Most health care providers agree that a woman's exercise routine should not exceed pre-pregnancy levels. Although a woman should always discuss exercise with her health care provider, if she exercised before her pregnancy, keeping up with a moderate amount of exercise during the pregnancy is usually fine.

Although it is true that pregnant women are "cardiovascularly challenged" early in pregnancy, it is a myth that too much exercise may cause a miscarriage or harm the developing fetus. Hundreds of pregnant women learned this before the legalization of abortion when they tried to exercise excessively or punch their abdomens in an unsuccessful attempt to dislodge the fertilized ovum. The implanted embryo is difficult to dislodge.

However, certain sports should be avoided during pregnancy, such as waterskiing, scuba diving, vigorous racquet sports, contact sports, and horseback riding, because these may cause injuries in both the mother and her fetus. Aquatic exercise may be the best choice for a pregnant woman because it is non–weight bearing, low impact, and reduces the risk for injury. In addition, aquatic exercise has been found to decrease maternal discomfort and improve body image (S. A. Smith & Michel, 2006). Physical stresses, such as prolonged standing, long work hours, and heavy lifting, can also affect a pregnancy. These stresses can reduce blood flow to the uterus, resulting in lower birth weights and prematurity (Clapp, 1996). It is also important to drink lots of water during pregnancy because water is an essential nutrient and is important for all bodily functions.

Nutritional requirements during pregnancy call for extra protein, iron, calcium, folic acid, and vitamin B6 (found in foods such as milk, yogurt, beef, vegetables, beans, and dried fruits). In addition, it is important for a woman to increase her caloric intake during pregnancy. Pregnant women who do not follow nutritional requirements may have low-birth-weight babies or an increased risk for miscarriage.

*Most health care providers agree that **a woman's exercise routine should not exceed** pre-pregnancy levels.*

Research indicates that poor nutrition during pregnancy may also have long-term consequences for the infant's risk for cardiovascular disease, hypertension, and diabetes (Clapp & Lopez, 2007; Godfrey et al., 1996). Fetuses who are forced to adapt to a limited supply of nutrients may permanently "reprogram" their physiology and metabolism (Barker, 1997).

During the second trimester, an average-weight woman is advised to increase her caloric intake by 300 calories per day, and protein requirements increase. For vegetarians and vegans, it is necessary to increase consumption of vegetables, whole grains, nuts, and seeds, and also to include a protein supplement to ensure adequate protein intake. An increase in calcium is also necessary to help with bone calcification of the growing fetus. Because a woman's blood volume increases as much as 50% during pregnancy, iron may be diluted in the blood; thus, many pregnant women are advised to take prenatal vitamins, which include iron supplements.

▶▶ DRUGS and Alcohol

Physicians recommend avoiding several substances during pregnancy, including caffeine, nicotine, alcohol, marijuana, and other drugs. All of these substances are teratogens that can cross the placenta, enter into the developing fetus's bloodstream, and cause physical or mental deficiencies. **Fetal alcohol syndrome (FAS),** a condition associated with alcohol intake, occurs when a woman drinks heavily during pregnancy, producing an infant with irreversible physical and mental disabilities. Experts agree that there is no safe level of alcohol use during pregnancy (Sayal et al., 2007).

In one study of more than 12,000 U.S. women, 8% of the women reported consuming alcohol during the last 3 months of their pregnancy (Cheng et al., 2011). Another study found that 10% of women smoked cigarettes throughout their pregnancy (Weaver et al., 2008). Smoking during pregnancy has been associated with spontaneous abortion, low birth weight, prematurity, and low iron levels (R. P. Martin et al., 2005; Pandey et al., 2005).

REAL RESEARCH 12.4 Research has found that marijuana use can negatively affect sperm development and production, leading to potential fertility problems (BADAWY ET AL., 2008; ROSSATO ET AL., 2008). In addition, marijuana use in both men and women can negatively affect assisted reproduction procedures and contributes to lower infant birth rates (KLONOFF-COHEN ET AL., 2006).

It has also been found to increase the risk for vascular damage to the developing fetus's brain and potentially interfere with a male's future ability to manufacture sperm (Storgaard et al., 2003). Children whose mothers smoked during pregnancy have been found to experience an increased aging of the lungs and a higher risk for lung damage later in life (Maritz, 2008). Secondhand smoke has negative effects, too, and partners, fathers, friends, relatives, and strangers who smoke around a pregnant woman jeopardize the future health of a developing baby.

▶▶ PREGNANCY in Women Older Than 30

Earlier in this chapter, we discussed how fertility decreases with age—both ova and sperm quality are affected by age (Coccia & Rizzello, 2008; Girsh et al., 2008; Lazarou & Morgentaler, 2008). Declines in fertility make it more difficult for older women to become pregnant. As we discussed earlier, today it is common for women to postpone their first pregnancies (see Figures 12.1 and 12.2; Coccia & Rizzello, 2008). In the United States, from 1996 to 2006, birth rates for women 37 to 39 and 40 to 44 years old increased 70% and 50%, respectively (Caplan & Patrizio, 2010). In fact, the birth rate for women 40 to 44 years old was the highest since 1967 (Hamilton et al., 2010).

Success rates for ARTs in older women are low (Marinakis & Nikolaou, 2011). Although older women who do get pregnant are

ON YOUR MIND 12.4

I've heard women say that if the average baby weighs about 7 pounds, then they will gain no more than 10 pounds during pregnancy. Is that safe? How small a weight gain is considered healthy? What about anorexics and bulimics?

It is estimated that a pregnant woman of average size should gain between 15 and 40 pounds throughout a pregnancy, and weight loss or weight maintenance is not recommended (Bish et al., 2008). Pregnancy weight gain accounts for the fetus, amniotic fluid, placenta, and breast, muscle, and fat increases. Gaining less than this is not healthy for either the developing fetus or the mother—and may actually predispose a baby to obesity later in life (because fetuses learn to restrict calories in the womb, but when nutrition is readily available, overeating is likely; Barker, 1997). In addition, too little weight gain during pregnancy has also been found to be related to a higher blood pressure in offspring once they reach early childhood (P. M. Clark et al., 1998). Although women with eating disorders often experience an improvement in symptoms during a pregnancy (Crow et al., 2008), it's important that anyone with an eating disorder consult with her health care provider before getting pregnant to determine an appropriate weight gain.

more likely to take better care of themselves and eat healthier than younger women, there are increased risks to the pregnancies, including spontaneous abortion, first-trimester bleeding, low birth weight, increased labor time and rate of C-section, and chromosomal abnormalities (see Table 12.2; Loke & Poon, 2011; Shelton et al., 2010).

▶▶ SEX during Pregnancy

In some cultures, sex during pregnancy is strongly recommended because it is believed that a father's semen is necessary for proper development of the fetus (Dunham et al., 1992). In an uncomplicated pregnancy, sexual behavior during pregnancy is safe for most mothers and the developing fetus up until the last several weeks of pregnancy. During a woman's first trimester, sexual interest is often decreased because of physical changes, including nausea and fatigue.

Orgasm during pregnancy is also safe in an uncomplicated pregnancy, but occasionally it may cause painful uterine contractions, especially toward the end of pregnancy. Cunnilingus can also be safely engaged in during pregnancy; however, as we discussed in Chapter 10, air should never be blown into the vagina of a pregnant woman because it could cause an air embolism, which could be fatal to both the mother and baby (Hill & Jones, 1993; Kaufman et al., 1987; Nicoll & Skupski, 2008; Sánchez et al., 2008).

Sexual interest and satisfaction usually begin to subside as the woman and fetus grow during the third trimester (Gokyildiz &

colostrum
A thin, yellowish fluid, high in protein and antibodies, secreted from the nipples at the end of pregnancy and during the first few days after delivery.

fetal alcohol syndrome (FAS)
A disorder involving physical and mental deficiencies, nervous system damage, and facial abnormalities found in the offspring of mothers who consumed large quantities of alcohol during pregnancy.

Beji, 2005). The increasing size of the abdomen puts pressure on many of the internal organs and also makes certain sexual positions for vaginal intercourse difficult. During the first and part of the second trimester, heterosexual women use the male-on-top position most often during vaginal intercourse. However, later in pregnancy, the side-by-side, rear-entry, and female-on-top positions are used more frequently because they take the weight and pressure off the uterus.

REAL RESEARCH 12.5 Women with declining fertility think more about sex and have higher levels of sexual interest than younger women (Easton et al., 2010). Researchers claim the "biological clock" ticking may be responsible for these shifts in sexual interest.

 in Real Life ▶▶ **"I Want to Have a Baby!"**

Throughout this chapter we have been discussing trends in pregnancy and birth. Although birth rates have been decreasing in every ethnicity, race, and age group, birth rates in single women older than 40 are increasing. Following is a story written by a woman who had a child on her own.

My life is not according to plan. I expected that after college, I would get a good job, find a great guy, fall in love, get married, and have three kids while establishing a rewarding career—all before the age of 30. In the real world, I have a successful career that I truly enjoy; I've been in love more than once but never married and never had children. At 43 years old, I was faced with the biggest decision of my life—having a child on my own. This is something I have discussed with friends and family over the years as a possibility but always hoped it wouldn't be necessary. Although I felt nervous, I also was really excited about my decision.

Anonymous sperm donation did not appeal to me. I really wanted to know the father: his personality, sense of humor, looks, intelligence, athleticism, and medical history. I did some research into sperm banks and sperm donation, and was actually pleasantly surprised at the amount of information each sperm bank provides (such as height, weight, hair color, eye color, ethnicity, education, occupation, family medical history). In many ways, it felt like an online dating service—but still wasn't the route I wanted to take.

Over the years, I have floated the idea of fathering a child for me to numerous male friends of mine. The man I chose has been a friend for a long time (we

dated briefly many years ago); he is married with children of his own and is a good father. We have agreed to keep his identity secret, and that he will not play a role in the child's life—emotionally or financially. We will remain good long-distance friends, and I will always be thankful for his generosity.

© Janell Carroll

I went through a battery of fertility tests, and the test results were favorable for a woman my age. The entire process took about a year, and the year was full of excitement, as well as anguish and disappointment. I estimate that the treatments cost about $30,000 altogether, and my insurance company covered about half these costs, which is pretty good.

After a comprehensive workup, I started fertility drugs in preparation for in vitro fertilization (IVF). I was put on a series of drugs that produced several ova, and when the time was right, I was scheduled for ova retrieval. The doctor used a needle through my vagina to retrieve the four ova that were available. The lab took the ova and immediately attempted to fertilize them. Four embryos resulted, but only three survived to be frozen. I was unable to complete the transfer on that cycle, so we decided to do a

new full IVF cycle the following month.

The next month, everything seemed to be going perfectly—the ova retrieval and fertilization resulted in three embryos, and all three were transferred to my uterus (the transfer happened 3 days after the ova retrieval). I was sure I was pregnant, and when my period started again I was devastated. Afterward the doctor counseled me that it was highly unlikely my eggs would work and that I should consider egg donation or adoption unless I had unlimited funds and the stamina to keep trying. I said I would look into both options but wanted to transfer my frozen embryos as soon as possible.

The transfer took place that cycle. This time my optimism took a negative turn. In fact, I was so certain it failed that I didn't even bother with a home pregnancy test before going to the doctor for testing on the 12th day. To my surprise, while the nurse was drawing my blood, the urine test showed positive. My doctor said I was his oldest patient to get pregnant with her own eggs. As happy and relieved as I was, I tried to keep my joy in check—knowing that miscarriage and genetic abnormalities were not uncommon for someone my age. So I viewed each checkup and test as clearing a hurdle. Even so, the smile didn't leave my face for 9 months.

After a 22-hour labor, I delivered a healthy baby girl. All in all, I feel like I hit the jackpot. Even though life is very different for me today, it is better than I could have ever imagined.

SOURCE: Author's files.

table 12.2 ■ Risk for Down Syndrome in Live Birth Infants Based on Maternal Age

Age of Mother	Risk for Down Syndrome
20	1 in 1527
25	1 in 1352
30	1 in 895
35	1 in 356
40	1 in 97
45	1 in 23

SOURCE: Hook, E. B. (1981). Rate of chromosome abnormalities at different maternal ages. Obstetrics and Gynecology, 58(3), 282–285.

◀ review QUESTIONS

1 Explain the benefits of exercise in pregnancy, and describe some of the issues that must be considered when exercising during pregnancy.

2 Explain the importance of avoiding drugs and alcohol during pregnancy.

3 Discuss the reasons women are delaying pregnancy more often these days. What are the risks of delayed pregnancy?

4 Discuss the changes in women's sexual interest during pregnancy.

▶ PROBLEMS during Pregnancy

The majority of women go through their pregnancy without any problems. However, understanding how complex the process of pregnancy is, it should not come as a surprise that occasionally things go wrong.

▶▶ ECTOPIC Pregnancy

Most zygotes travel through the Fallopian tubes and end up in the uterus. In an ectopic pregnancy, the zygote implants outside of the uterus (Figure 12.5). Ninety-five percent of ectopic pregnancies occur when the fertilized ovum implants in the Fallopian tube (Hankins, 1995). These are called *tubal pregnancies.* The remaining 3% occur in the abdomen, cervix, or ovaries. Approximately 2% (1 in 50) of all U.S. pregnancies are ectopic, and this number has been steadily increasing primarily because of increases in the incidence of pelvic inflammatory disease caused by chlamydia infections (Tay et al., 2000).

The effects of ectopic pregnancy can be serious. Because the Fallopian tubes, cervix, and abdomen are not designed to support a growing fetus, when one is implanted in these places, they can rupture, causing internal hemorrhaging and possibly death. Possible symptoms include abdominal pain (usually on the side of the body that has the tubal pregnancy), cramping, pelvic pain, vaginal

bleeding, nausea, dizziness, and fainting (Levine, 2007; Seeber & Barnhart, 2006; Tay et al., 2000). Future reproductive potential may also be affected by ectopic pregnancy. A woman who has experienced an ectopic pregnancy is at greater risk for development of another in future pregnancies (Sepilian & Wood, 2004). Today, physicians can monitor pregnancies through ultrasound and hCG levels, and many ectopic pregnancies can be treated without surgery (Seeber & Barnhart, 2006).

Before the 19th century, half of all women with an ectopic pregnancy died. Doctors began surgical intervention, and as a result, only 5% of women with ectopic pregnancy died by the end of the 20th century (Sepilian & Wood, 2004). Survival rates are improving, even though ectopic pregnancy remains the leading cause of maternal mortality in the first trimester, accounting for 10% to 15% of all maternal deaths (Tenore, 2000).

What contributes to the likelihood of an ectopic pregnancy? Although many women without risk factors can experience an ectopic pregnancy (Seeber & Barnhart, 2006), there are some factors that may put a woman at greater risk. Women who smoke and those who have had a sexually transmitted infection are at greater risk for an ectopic pregnancy (Ankum et al., 1996). Smoking cigarettes has been found to change the tubal contractions and muscular tone of the Fallopian tubes, which may lead to tubal inactivity, delayed ovum entry into the uterus, and changes in the tubes' ability to transport the ovum (Albers, 2007; Handler et al., 1989; Seeber & Barnhart, 2006).

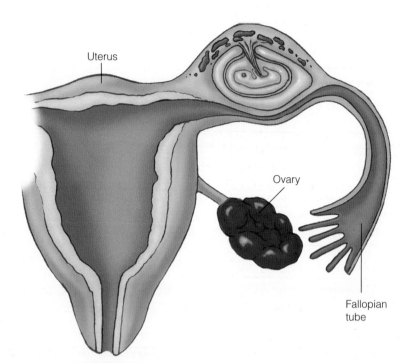

Uterus

Ovary

Fallopian tube

FIGURE 12.5 In an ectopic pregnancy, the fertilized ovum implants outside the uterus. In most cases, it remains in the Fallopian tube. Copyright © Cengage Learning 2013

▶▶ SPONTANEOUS Abortion

A spontaneous abortion, or miscarriage, is a natural termination of a pregnancy before the time that the fetus can live on its own. Approximately 15% to 20% of all diagnosed pregnancies end in miscarriage (Friebe & Arck, 2008). Miscarriages can occur anytime during a pregnancy, although the percentage declines dramatically after the first trimester.

In a significant number of miscarriages, there is some chromosomal abnormality (Christiansen, 1996; Vorsanova et al., 2010). In other cases, in which there are no chromosomal problems, the uterus may be too small, too weak, or abnormally shaped, or the miscarriage may be caused by maternal stress, nutritional deficiencies, drug exposure, or pelvic infection.

Common symptoms of miscarriage include vaginal bleeding, cramps, and lower back pain. Usually a normal menstrual period returns within 3 months after a miscarriage, and future pregnancies may be perfectly normal. However, some women experience repeated miscarriages, often caused by anatomic, endocrine, hormonal, genetic, or chromosomal abnormalities (Bick et al., 1998), as well as problems with defective sperm (Carrell et al., 2003). Tests are being developed to try to predict when a miscarriage will occur.

A miscarriage can be emotionally difficult for both a woman and her partner, although research has found that male partners experience less intense emotional symptoms for a shorter period (Abboud & Liamputtong, 2003; Musters et al., 2011). Lesbian couples have been found to have an especially difficult time with miscarriage, probably because the complexity of planning and achieving a pregnancy are often much more difficult for lesbian couples (Wojnar, 2007).

Although historically health care providers have recommended women wait between 6 and 24 months before trying to get pregnant again after a miscarriage, newer research has found that shorter delays are associated with lower complication rates (Love et al., 2010). In addition, research on miscarriages after IVF has found that those who experience an early miscarriage have a greater likelihood of achieving a pregnancy that results in a live birth in their next IVF attempt (Kalu et al., in press).

▶▶ BIRTH Defects

It is estimated that 1 of every 33 babies is born with a birth defect (MMWR, 2008). There are many different types of birth defects that may be present at birth, and they range from minor to serious. Although many can be treated or cured, they are also the number one cause of death in the first year of life (Klausen, 2007). Prenatal diagnostic testing can be used to determine whether there are chromosomal or genetic abnormalities in the fetus. The most common tests include blood work, ultrasound, **chorionic villus sampling (CVS), maternal-serum alpha-fetoprotein screening (MSAFP),** amniocentesis, and cord blood sampling. Most of these tests are used by couples who have an increased risk for birth defects, although some couples may also use them to determine fetal sex. Because older women are more at risk for chromosomal and genetic abnormalities, these tests are often recommended for women older than 35. As we've already discussed, women who have undergone artificial reproductive technologies may choose to use PGD to identify any abnormalities in an embryo before implantation in the uterus (Kuliev & Verlinsky, 2008; Wang, 2007).

Genetic abnormalities include **spina bifida** (SPY-na BIF-id-uh), **anencephaly** (an-en-SEH-fuh-lee), sex chromosome abnormalities (such as Turner and Klinefelter syndromes; see Chapter 4), and many other diseases, such as cystic fibrosis or sickle cell disease. The most common chromosomal abnormality appears on the 21st chromosome and is known as **Down syndrome.**

---

chorionic villus sampling (CVS)
The sampling and testing of the chorion for fetal abnormalities.

maternal-serum alpha-fetoprotein screening (MSAFP)
A blood test used during early pregnancy to determine neural tube defects such as spina bifida or anencephaly.

spina bifida
A congenital defect of the vertebral column in which the halves of the neural arch of a vertebra fail to fuse in the midline.

anencephaly
Congenital absence of most of the brain and spinal cord.

Down syndrome
A problem occurring on the 21st chromosome of the developing fetus that can cause mental retardation and physical challenges.

amniotic fluid
The fluid in the amniotic cavity.

RhoGAM
Drug given to mothers whose Rh is incompatible with the fetus; prevents the formation of antibodies that can imperil future pregnancies.

toxemia
A form of blood poisoning caused by kidney disturbances.

preeclampsia
A condition of hypertension during pregnancy, typically accompanied by leg swelling and other symptoms.

eclampsia
A progression of toxemia with similar, but worsening, conditions.

Down syndrome, a chromosomal defect, can cause delayed mental and social development and the characteristics of slanted eyes and a flat face.

Down syndrome occurs in 1 of every 691 live births (Parker et al., 2010; Irving et al., 2008). In Down syndrome, an extra chromosome has been added to the 21st chromosome; although most of us have 46 chromosomes (23 from each parent), a person with Down syndrome has 47. A child with Down syndrome often exhibits low muscle tone, a flat facial profile, slanted eyes, delayed mental and social development, and an enlarged tongue. Although screening for Down syndrome used to be recommended primarily for women older than 35, in 2007, the American College of Obstetricians and Gynecologists recommended Down syndrome screening for all women, regardless of age (American College of Obstetricians and Gynecologists, 2007). Screening can help determine whether a woman is at risk for having a child with Down syndrome.

If testing is necessary, first-trimester screening typically involves a simple blood test combined with an ultrasound (Malone et al., 2005; Nicolaides et al., 2005; Orlandi et al., 2005). An ultrasound can evaluate the fetal neck thickness, which may indicate an increased risk for Down syndrome. In addition, ultrasound is often used to evaluate structural abnormalities in the fetus and to locate the fetus during other tests (Watson et al., 2008). Another more invasive test, a chorionic villus sampling (CVS), is available between the 10th and 12th weeks of pregnancy. In this procedure, a sliver of tissue from the chorion (the tissue that develops into the placenta) is removed and checked for abnormalities. CVS testing has more risks than ultrasound, including increased risk for miscarriage and potential limb reduction and deformities (Caughey et al., 2006).

Between the 15th and 20th week an amniocentesis may be used to detect either genetic or chromosomal abnormalities. In this procedure, **amniotic fluid** is extracted from the womb using a needle and is evaluated for genetic and chromosomal abnormalities. Amniocentesis increases the risk of miscarriage, cramping and vaginal bleeding, leaking amniotic fluid, and infection.

Another second trimester test, MSAFP, can be performed between the 16th and the 19th week. MSAFP is a simple blood test that evaluates levels of protein in the blood. High levels may indicate the presence of potential birth defects, including spinal bifida or anencephaly (Reynolds et al., 2008). The MSAFP can provide useful information that can help a woman decide whether she wants to undergo further testing. There are no risks to the MSAFP test besides the discomfort of drawing blood.

Screening can help determine whether a woman is at risk for having a child with Down syndrome.

Finally, cordocentesis, or cord blood sampling, involves collecting blood from the umbilical cord anytime after the 18th week of pregnancy for a chromosome analysis (Berkow et al., 2000). Cordocentesis is an invasive test, and although it can slightly increase the risk for miscarriage, it is considered a safe and reliable procedure for prenatal diagnosis (Ghidini & Bocchi, 2007; Liao et al., 2006).

A diagnostic blood test for Down syndrome is currently in production and can be performed earlier in a pregnancy (Edwards, 2010). Keep in mind that if a woman does decide to undergo such testing, she and her partner must decide what to do with the information these tests provide.

▶▶ Rh Incompatibility

The Rh factor naturally exists on some people's red blood cells. If your blood type is followed by "+," you are "Rh positive," and if not, you are "Rh negative." This is important when you are having a blood transfusion or when pregnant.

A father or donor who is Rh positive often passes on his blood type to the baby. If the baby's mother is Rh negative, any of the fetal blood that comes into contact with hers (which happens during delivery, not pregnancy) will cause her to begin to manufacture antibodies against the fetal blood. This may be very dangerous for any future pregnancies. Because the mother has made antibodies to Rh-positive blood, she will reject the fetal Rh-positive blood, which can lead to fetal death. After an Rh-negative woman has delivered, she is given **RhoGAM** (row-GAM), which prevents antibodies from forming and ensures that her future pregnancies will be healthy. RhoGAM is also given if an Rh-negative pregnant woman has an amniocentesis, miscarriage, or abortion.

▶▶ TOXEMIA

In the last 2 to 3 months of pregnancy, 6% to 7% of women experience **toxemia** (tock-SEE-mee-uh), or **preeclampsia** (pre-ee-CLAMP-see-uh). Symptoms include rapid weight gain, fluid retention, an increase in blood pressure, and protein in the urine. If toxemia is allowed to progress, it can result in **eclampsia,** which involves convulsions, coma, and in approximately 15% of cases, death. Even though preeclampsia typically occurs at the end of pregnancy, research indicates that it may actually be caused by defective implantation or placental problems at the beginning of pregnancy (Urato & Norwitz, 2011).

Preeclampsia is a complication that occurs in approximately 3% of pregnancies (Hutcheon et al., 2011). Overall, Black women are at greater risk for eclampsia than White or Hispanic women (Mbah et al., 2011). In addition, women whose mothers experienced preeclampsia are more likely to experience preeclampsia in their own pregnancies, and male offspring from mothers with preeclampsia are twice as likely to father children through a preeclampsia pregnancy as are men who were born from a normal pregnancy (Seppa, 2001; Urato & Norwitz, 2010). Screening tests for preeclampsia are being evaluated to identify women who might be at risk (Huppertz, 2011; Urato & Norwitz, 2010).

1 Define ectopic pregnancy and spontaneous abortion, and discuss what we know about these conditions.

2 Define prenatal diagnostic testing, identify some of the tests, and explain how they can be used to determine whether there are fetal abnormalities.

3 What is Down syndrome and what testing is available to detect it?

4 What is RhoGAM and why would a woman use it?

▶ CHILDBIRTH

The average length of a pregnancy is 9 months, but a normal birth can occur 3 weeks before or 2 weeks after the due date. It is estimated that only 4% of American babies are born exactly on the due date predicted (Dunham et al., 1992). Early delivery may occur in cases in which the mother has exercised throughout the pregnancy, the fetus is female, or the mother has shorter menstrual cycles (R. Jones, 1984).

No one knows why, but there is also a seasonal variation in human birth. More babies are conceived in the summer months and in late December (Macdowall et al., 2008). There are also more babies born between the hours of 1 and 7 A.M., and again this is thought to have evolved because of the increased protection and decreased chances of predator attacks (R. Jones, 1984).

We do not know exactly what starts the birth process. It appears that in fetal sheep, a chemical in the brain signals that it is time for birth (Palca, 1991). Perhaps this may also be true in humans, but the research remains incomplete.

▶▶ PREPARING for Birth

As the birth day comes closer, many women (and their partners!) become anxious, nervous, and excited about what is to come. This is probably why the tradition of baby showers started. These gatherings enable women (and more recently, men) to gather and discuss the impending birth. People often share their personal experiences and helpful hints. This ritual may help couples to prepare themselves emotionally and to feel more comfortable.

Increasing knowledge and alleviating anxiety about the birth process are the main concepts behind childbirth classes. In these classes, women and their partners are taught what to expect during labor and delivery, and how to control the pain through breathing and massage. Tension and anxiety during labor have been found to increase pain, discomfort, and fatigue. Many couples feel more prepared and focused after taking these courses. However, some same-sex couples report feeling uncomfortable with childbirth classes that cater primarily to heterosexual couples (L. E. Ross et al., 2006a). Having other same-sex couples in the class often makes it a more positive experience.

A few weeks before delivery, the fetus usually moves into a "head-down" position in the uterus (Figure 12.6). This is referred to as **engagement.** Ninety-seven percent of fetuses are in this position at birth (Nilsson, 1990). If a baby's feet or buttocks are first (**breech position**), the physician may try either to rotate the baby before birth or recommend a C-section. We discuss this later in the chapter.

View in Video

To watch the entire interview, go to Psychology CourseMate at **login.cengagebrain.com.**

© Lisa Belval

"It's scary to realize that you're responsible for someone else."
—UNINTENDED PREGNANCY: A MAN'S PERSPECTIVE

▶▶ BIRTHPLACE Choices

In nonindustrialized countries, nearly all babies are born at home; worldwide, approximately 80% of babies are (Dunham et al., 1992). For low-risk pregnancies, home birth has been found to be as safe as a hospital delivery (K. C. Johnson & Daviss, 2005). Although the American College of Obstetricians and Gynecologists

ON YOUR MIND 12.5

What determines how long a woman will be in labor? Why do they say a woman's first baby is hardest? A friend of mine was in labor for 36 hours!

Usually, first labors are the most difficult. Second and subsequent labors are usually easier and shorter because there is less resistance from the birth canal and the surrounding muscles. Overall, the biggest differences are in the amount of time it takes for the cervix to fully dilate and the amount of pushing necessary to move the baby from the birth canal. Typically, first labors are longer than subsequent labors. We do not know why some women have easier labors than others. It could be the result of diet or exercise during the pregnancy. Ethnic, racial, and maternal age differences have been found in the length of labor. Black women have been found to experience shorter second-stage labors than White, Asian, and Latina women (Greenberg et al., 2006). In addition, increasing maternal age is related to prolonged labor (Greenberg et al., 2007).

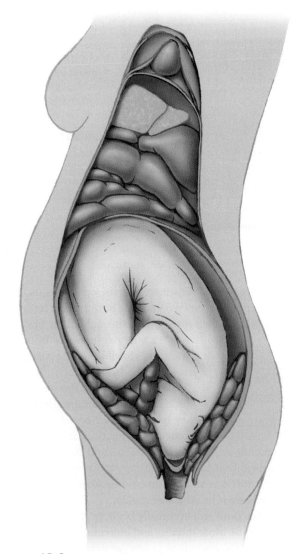

FIGURE **12.6** A full-term fetus in the head-down position in the uterus. Copyright © Cengage Learning 2013

include comfortable rooms with a bed for a woman's partner, music, a television, a shower, and perhaps even a Jacuzzi (to help ease labor pains). Interestingly, from 1990 to 2006, home births increased for non-Hispanic White women but decreased for all other races and ethnicities (Macdorman et al., 2011). In fact, non-Hispanic White women were three to four times more likely than women of other races and ethnicities to have a home birth.

▶▶ INDUCING the Birth

Inducing birth involves using techniques to start the birth process artificially. Usually this is in the form of drugs given in increasing doses to mimic the natural contractions of labor, although induced contractions can be more painful and prolonged than natural labor. Birth can occur anywhere from a few hours to several days after induction begins, depending on a woman's prior birth history. Since the early 2000s, there has been a tremendous increase in childbirth induction. In fact, labor induction is one of the fastest growing medical procedures in the United States (Mac-Dorman et al., 2002). In the United States, labor induction rates reached a high of 21.2% of births in 2003–2004 (Durham et al., 2008).

Labor induction may be done in cases in which labor is slow to progress, pregnancy has lasted beyond 42 weeks, the baby is large, preeclampsia exists, or in cases of fetal death. Unless there is a medical reason, most women are advised to avoid labor induction (Amis, 2007; Durham et al., 2008). Some women elect to have inductions for nonmedical reasons, including anything from wanting to avoid birth on a certain day (such as a holiday) or to accommodate a woman's or her partner's work schedule.

believes the risks associated with home births are low, women need to make medically informed decisions about birthplace choices.

The majority of home births are done with the help of a **midwife** (Macdorman et al., 2011). Same-sex couples are more likely to use midwives in their birthing experience, even if they deliver in a hospital setting. This is primarily because many same-sex couples feel that midwives are more accepting of nontraditional families (L. E. Ross et al., 2006b).

The majority of babies today are born in hospitals in the United States. Most hospitals now offer the use of birthing centers, which

▶▶ BIRTHING Positions

Although women can assume a variety of positions during childbirth, the dominant position in Westernized countries is the semi-reclined position with a woman's feet up in stirrups (DeJonge et al., 2008). Some feminist health professionals claim that this position is

engagement
When the fetus moves down toward the birth canal before delivery.

breech position
An abnormal and often dangerous birthing position in which the baby's feet, knees, or buttocks emerge before the head.

midwife
A person who assists women during childbirth.

easier for the doctor than for the pregnant woman, and that it is the most ineffective and dangerous position for labor. Recently, women have been given more freedom in deciding how to position themselves for childbirth in the United States. A woman on her hands and knees or in the squatting position allows her pelvis and cervix to be at their widest. In addition, the force of gravity can be used to help in the birth process. Health care providers today recommend that women use whatever birthing position feels most comfortable for them (DeJonge et al., 2008; Gupta & Nikodem, 2000).

Positions for birth vary in different parts of the world. Rope midwives in rural areas of the Sudan hang a rope from the ceiling and have the mother grasp the rope and bear down in a squatting position. In Bang Chan, Thailand, a husband cradles his pregnant wife between his legs and digs his toes into her thighs. This toe pressure is thought to provide relief from her pain (Dunham et al., 1992).

"The appearance of a newborn does not fit most people's definition of a cute baby."
—Birth and APGAR Assessment

View in Video
To watch the entire interview, go to Psychology CourseMate at **login.cengagebrain.com.**

▶▶ STAGES of Childbirth

Birth itself begins with **cervical effacement** and **dilation,** which leads to expulsion of the fetus and, soon afterward, expulsion of the placenta. The beginning of birth is usually marked by an expulsion of the mucus plug from the cervix. This plug protects the fetus from any harmful bacteria that might enter the vagina during pregnancy. Sometimes women experience false labor, in which contractions are irregular and do not dilate the cervix. In real labor, contractions will be regular and get closer together over time. In a typical birth process, the process is divided into three stages.

In real labor, **contractions will be regular and get closer** *together over time.*

Stage One

In the United States, if the birth process is taking too long, physicians may administer the drug Pitocin to speed up labor. In Bolivia, however, certain groups of people believe that nipple stimulation helps the birth move quicker. So if a birth is moving too slowly, a woman's nipples may be massaged. Biologically, nipple stimulation leads to a release of oxytocin, which is a natural form of Pitocin. This is why many midwives in the United States also practice nipple stimulation during childbirth.

In some Guatemalan societies, long and difficult labors are believed to be due to a woman's sins, and so she is asked to confess her sins. If this does not help speed up labor, her husband is asked to confess. If neither of these confessions helps, the father's loincloth is wrapped around the woman's stomach to assure her that he will not leave her once the baby is born (Dunham et al., 1992).

The first stage of labor can last anywhere from 20 minutes to 24 hours and is longer in first births. When true labor begins, the Braxton–Hicks contractions increase. The cervix begins dilation (opening up) and effacement (thinning out) to allow for fetal passage (this phase is called *early labor*). Throughout the first stage of labor, the entrance to the cervix (the os) increases from 0 to 10 centimeters to allow for the passage of the fetus.

Toward the end of this stage, the amniotic sac usually ruptures (however, this may happen earlier or not at all in some women). Contractions may last for about 30 to 60 seconds at intervals of between 5 and 20 minutes, and the cervix usually dilates to 4 to 5 centimeters. Couples are advised to time the contractions and the interval between contractions and report these to their health care provider.

The contractions will eventually begin to last longer (1 minute or more), become more intense, and increase in frequency (every 1 to 3 minutes). Dilation of the cervix continues from 4 to 8 centimeters (this phase is called *active labor*). The contractions that open the os can be very painful, and health care providers will usually monitor the progress of cervical dilation.

The last phase in stage one is called **transition,** which for most women is the most difficult part of the birth process. Contractions are very intense and long and have shorter periods in between, and the cervix dilates from 8 to 10 centimeters. The fetus moves into the base of the pelvis, creating an urge to push; however, the woman is advised not to push until her cervix is fully dilated. Many women feel exhausted by this point.

The woman's body produces pain-reducing hormones called **endorphins,** which may dull the intensity of the contractions. Should a woman feel the need for more pain relief, she can also be given various pain medications. The most commonly used pain

cervical effacement
The stretching and thinning of the cervix in preparation for birth.

dilation
The expansion of the opening of the cervix in preparation for birth.

transition
The last period in labor, in which contractions are strongest and the periods in between contractions are the shortest.

endorphins
Neurotransmitters, concentrated in the pituitary gland and parts of the brain, that inhibit physical pain.

episiotomy
A cut made with surgical scissors to avoid tearing of the perineum at the end of the second stage of labor.

crowning
The emergence of a baby's head at the opening of the vagina at birth.

Apgar test
Developed by Virginia Apgar, M.D., this system assesses the general physical condition of a newborn infant for five criteria: (A) activity/muscle tone, (P) pulse rate, (G) grimace and reflex irritability, (A) appearance/skin color, and (R) respiration.

medications include analgesics (pain relievers) and anesthetics (which produce a loss of sensation). Which drug is used depends on the mother's preference, health history, and present condition and the baby's condition. An epidural block (an anesthetic) is very popular for the relief of severe labor pain. Although there has been an increased use of drugs to reduce the pain of labor in recent years, advances in medical technology today allow physicians to customize pain-relieving drugs for each woman (Leo & Sia, 2008; Moen & Irestedt, 2008).

The fetus is monitored for signs of distress, such as slowed heart rate or lack of oxygen. This is done either through the woman's abdomen with a sensor or by accessing the fetus's scalp through the cervix. Fetal monitoring can determine whether the fetus is in any danger that would require a quicker delivery or a C-section.

Stage Two

After the cervix has fully dilated, the second stage of birth, the expulsion of the fetus, begins. Contractions are somewhat less intense, lasting about 60 seconds and spaced at 1- to 3-minute intervals.

Toward the end of this stage of labor, the doctor may perform an **episiotomy** (ee-pee-zee-AH-tuh-mee) to reduce the risk for a tearing of the tissue between the vaginal opening and anus as the fetus emerges. Currently, episiotomies are controversial, and the debate centers around several issues (Dahlen et al., in press). Those who support the practice argue that it can speed up labor, prevent tearing during a delivery, protect against future incontinence, and promote quicker healing. Those who argue against the practice claim that it increases infection, pain, and healing times, and may increase discomfort when penetrative sex is resumed (Chang et al., 2011; Hartmann et al., 2005; Radestad et al., 2008). In 2006, the American College of Obstetricians and Gynecologists recommended against routine use of episiotomy and suggested its use only in limited cases.

As the woman pushes during contractions, the top of the head of the baby soon appears at the vagina, which is known as **crowning.** Once the face emerges, the mucus and fluid in the mouth and nostrils are removed by suction. The baby emerges and, after the first breath, usually lets out a cry. After the baby's first breath, the umbilical cord, which supplies the fetus with oxygen, is cut; this is painless for the mother and child. Eye drops are put into the baby's eyes to prevent bacterial infection.

Directly after birth, many physicians and midwives place the newborn directly on the mother's chest to begin the bonding process. However, sometimes the woman's partner may be the first to hold the child, or the nurses will perform an **Apgar test** (Finster &

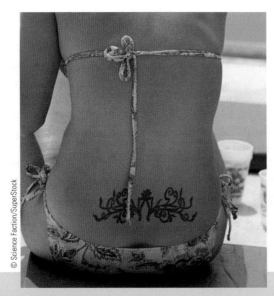

© Science Faction/SuperStock

There is some controversy over whether lumbar tattoos can interfere with an epidural during labor. Whereas some studies claim they pose no risks (Douglas & Swenerton, 2002), others cite possible risks such as the potential for the epidural to push pigmented tissue into the spinal canal (Kuczkowski, 2006). If the tattoo is large, an anesthesiologist either needs to find a pigment-free area or make a small incision into the tattoo before administering the epidural.

Wood, 2005). A newborn with a low Apgar score may require intensive care after delivery.

Stage Three

During the third stage of labor, the placenta (sometimes referred to as the "afterbirth") is expelled from the uterus. Strong contractions continue after the baby is born to push the placenta out of the uterus and through the vagina. Most women are not aware of this process because of the excitement of giving birth. The placenta must be checked to make sure all of it has been expelled. If there was any tearing or an episiotomy was performed, this will need to be sewn up after the placenta is removed. Usually this stage lasts about 30 minutes or so.

In parts of Kenya, the placenta of a female baby is buried under the fireplace, and the placenta of a male baby is buried by the stalls of baby camels. This practice is thought to forever connect the children's future to these locations. Some cultures bury their placentas, whereas others hang the placentas outside the home to show that a baby indeed arrived!

◄ review QUESTIONS

1 Describe the emotional and physical preparation necessary for the birth of a child, childbirth induction, and the various birthing positions.

2 Identify the three stages of birth and explain what happens at each stage. Generally, how long does each stage last?

3 Which phase of the birthing process is the most difficult for most women and why?

4 What is an episiotomy and why might it be used?

PROBLEMS during Birthing

For most women, the birth of a newborn baby proceeds without problems. However, a number of problems can arise, including premature birth, breech birth, C-section delivery, and stillbirth. Earlier we discuss seasonal variations in birth, and research has found there are also seasonal variations in birthing problems around the world (Strand et al., 2011). Low birth weights, premature births, and stillbirths peak in the winter and summer. Experts believe this may be because of extreme temperature changes.

PREMATURE Birth

The majority of babies are born late rather than early. Birth that takes place before the 37th week of pregnancy is considered **premature birth.** The incidence of premature birth has been rising, mostly due to the increased use of assisted reproductive technologies (Arpino et al., 2010). From 1990 to 2006 the U.S. premature birth rate rose 20% (Martin et al., 2009). Racial and ethnic differences have been found in the rates of prematurity, with Black women having more premature births than White women (Burris et al., 2011; Maugh, 2006).

Prematurity increases the risk for birth-related defects and infant mortality. In fact, prematurity accounts for 28% of infant deaths worldwide (Menon, 2008). Research into pediatrics has led to tremendous improvements in the survival rates of premature infants. Infants born at 24 weeks' gestation have a greater than 50% chance of survival (Welty, 2005). Unfortunately, more than half of these infants who survive experience development of complications and long-term effects of prematurity.

Birth may occur prematurely for several reasons, including early labor or early rupture of the amniotic membranes or because of a maternal or fetal problem. It is common for women who have had one premature birth to have subsequent premature births. Approximately 50% of all twin births are premature, and delivery of multiple fetuses occurs about 3 weeks earlier, on average, than single births (Croft et al., 2010). In 2004, the world's smallest surviving premature baby was born, weighing in at 8.6 ounces (her twin sister weighed 1 pound, 4 ounces; Huffstutter, 2004). These twins were delivered via C-section in the 26th week of pregnancy because of medical problems experienced by their mother. Other factors that may be related to premature birth include smoking during pregnancy, alcohol or drug use, inadequate weight gain or nutrition, heavy physical labor during the pregnancy, infections, and teenage pregnancy. Eating or drinking artificial sweeteners may also increase a woman's risk for premature birth. Pregnant women who drank one or more artificially sweetened soft drinks a day had higher rates of premature birth than women who either drank sugar-sweetened soft drinks or didn't drink soft drinks at all (Halldorsson et al., 2010).

premature birth	**fetal distress**
Any infant born before the 37th week of pregnancy.	Condition in which a fetus has an abnormal heart rate or rhythm.
placenta previa	**stillbirth**
A condition in which the placenta is abnormally positioned in the uterus so that it partially or completely covers the opening of the cervix.	An infant who is born dead.

BREECH Birth

In 97% of all births, the fetus emerges in the head-down position. However, in 3% to 4% of cases, the fetus is in the breech position, with the feet and buttocks against the cervix (Figure 12.7). Interestingly, about half of all fetuses are in this position before the seventh month of pregnancy, but most rotate before birth (R. Jones, 1984). Sometimes doctors are aware of the position of the fetus before delivery and can try to change the fetus's position for normal vaginal delivery. However, if this is not possible, or if it is discovered too late into delivery, labor may take an unusually long time. A skilled midwife or physician often can flip the baby or deliver it safely even in the breech position. However, in the United States today, a C-section will often be performed to ensure the health and well-being of both the mother and her child (Ghosh, 2005).

Although no one knows why some fetuses are born in the breech position, there have been some interesting studies done. One study found that there is an intergenerational recurrence of breech births: Fathers and mothers who were born breech have more than twice the risk for a breech delivery in their first births

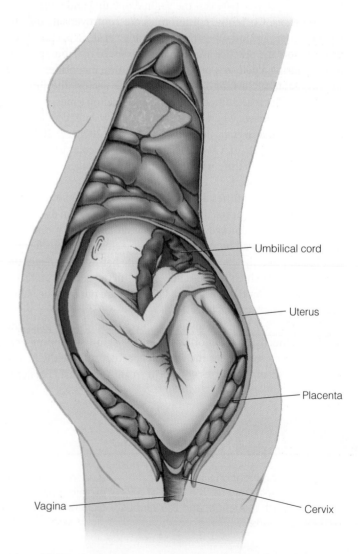

FIGURE **12.7** A full-term fetus in the breech position, with feet and buttocks against the cervix. Copyright © Cengage Learning 2013

(Nordtveit et al., 2008). Another study found that breech births were twice as high in women who had a past C-section delivery (Vendittelli et al., 2008).

▶▶ CESAREAN-SECTION Delivery

The rate of C-section delivery continues to climb in the United States. From 1996 to 2007, C-section rates grew 53%, and in 2009 reached 32%, which was the highest rate ever reported in the United States (Figure 12.8; Hamilton et al., 2010b; Menacker & Hamilton, 2010; Rubin, 2008). Some researchers believe these increases are due to an increased number of women requesting C-sections or needing them for medical reasons (Addo, 2010). However, the reasons for the increases are not clear-cut; whereas older women are more likely to have a C-section birth, we also know that some physicians recommend C-section births to minimize the risk for lawsuits or to decrease the amount of time doctors have to be present for the birth. Some critics have suggested that C-section births have increased because they are more lucrative for hospitals. One study found that from 2005 to 2007, women in California were 17% more likely to have had a C-section at a for-profit hospital than at a not-for-profit or public hospital (Johnson, 2010).

A C-section involves the delivery of the fetus through an incision in the abdominal wall. Since the late 1990s, rates of C-sections have increased for many reasons, including improvements in the procedure and to reduce the risks associated with vaginal deliveries. In addition, some women choose a C-section birth to reduce possible pelvic floor trauma that can occur during vaginal delivery (Dietz, 2006; Herbruck, 2008).

C-sections are medically necessary when the baby is too large for a woman to deliver vaginally, the woman is unable to push the baby out the birth canal, the placenta blocks the cervix (**placenta** previa), the cervix does not dilate to 10 centimeters, or the baby is in **fetal distress.** If a health care provider decides that a C-section is necessary, the woman is moved to an operating room and given either a general anesthetic or an epidural. The operation usually lasts between 20 and 90 minutes from start to finish (although the baby can be out within minutes if necessary). Women who have C-sections usually stay in the hospital longer than those who have vaginal deliveries.

In a subsequent pregnancies, women who have had a C-section may be at greater risk for small fetal size, placental separation from the uterine wall, and uterine rupture (Daltveit et al., 2008). Even so, some women deliver their next babies vaginally after a C-section (referred to as a VBAC, or vaginal birth after C-section), whereas others choose another C-section for a variety of reasons, including to avoid the pain or the increased risks of vaginal labor.

▶▶ STILLBIRTH

A fetus that dies after 20 weeks of pregnancy is called a **stillbirth** (before 20 weeks, it is called a *miscarriage*). There are many possible causes for a stillbirth, including umbilical cord accidents, problems with the placenta, birth defects, infections, and maternal diabetes or high blood pressure (Incerpi et al., 1998). Oftentimes the fetal loss is completely unexpected, because half of all stillbirths occur in pregnancies that appeared to be without problems (Pasupathy & Smith, 2005). Approximately 86% of fetal deaths occur before labor even begins, whereas 14% occur during labor and delivery (Fretts et al., 1992). In most cases, a woman goes into labor approximately 2 weeks after the fetus has died; if not, her labor will be induced. Some ethnic differences have been noted: Higher rates of stillbirth have been found in Black and mixed-race couples (Getahun et al., 2005).

Improved treatments of certain maternal medical conditions have decreased the frequency of stillbirths in the U.S. Many women are advised to do "kick checks" beginning in the 26th week of pregnancy. If a woman notices that her fetus is kicking fewer than 6 times in an hour or has stopped moving or kicking, fetal monitoring can be performed to check on the status of the fetus. Research has shown that women who have experienced a stillbirth often have a live birth in their next pregnancy, even though they are often viewed as high-risk patients (Black et al., 2008).

In the 1970s, a perinatal bereavement movement began in the United States, which offered parents a way to deal with the death of a newborn (Banerjee, 2007). Since the late 1990s, at least 40 perinatal hospice programs have started in the United States. These groups help families deal with issues related to stillbirth and infant death.

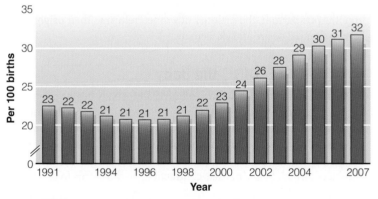

FIGURE **12.8** U.S. Cesarean rates 1991–2007. SOURCES: CDC/NCHS, National Vital Statistics System, Menacker and Hamilton, 2010.

◀ review QUESTIONS

1 Define premature birth, and discuss some of the causes and risks associated with premature birth.

2 Define breech birth and identify some of the factors that have been associated with breech birth.

3 Explain some of the reasons for a C-section birth.

4 Differentiate between a miscarriage and a stillbirth.

▶ POSTPARTUM Parenthood

The majority of women and men are excited about being parents. However, many couples are not prepared for the many physical and emotional changes that occur after the child is born. They may also find changes in their sex lives because of the responsibility and exhaustion that often accompany parenthood.

▶▶ MORE PHYSICAL CHANGES for the Mother

Many women report painful contractions for a few days after birth. These contractions are caused by the secretion of oxytocin, which is produced when a woman breast-feeds and is responsible for the shrinking of the uterus. The uterus returns to its original size about 6 weeks postpartum; in breast-feeding women, the uterus returns to its original size quicker than in non–breast-feeding women. A bloody discharge can persist for anywhere from a week to several weeks after delivery. After the bleeding stops, the discharge is often yellow–white and can lasts for a couple of weeks in mothers who breast-feed and up to a month or so in women who do not.

Women may experience an increase in frequency of urination, which can be painful if an episiotomy was performed or natural tearing occurred. Women may be advised to take sitz baths, in which the vagina and perineum are soaked in warm water to reduce the pain and to quicken the healing process. Until the cervix returns to its closed position, full baths are generally not advised.

REAL RESEARCH 12.6 Attachment styles of new mothers and fathers have been found to affect adjustments to parenting (TALBOT ET AL., 2009). Mothers and fathers with insecure attachments experienced the most difficult transitions.

▶▶ POSTPARTUM Psychological Changes

Many women experience an onset of intense emotions after the birth of a baby. One study found that 52% of new mothers felt excited and elated, 48% reported feeling like they did not need sleep, 37% reported feeling energetic, and 31% reported being more chatty (Heron et al., 2008). At the same time, many women report feeling overwhelmed and exhausted. Minor sadness is a common emotion after the birth of a baby (Howard et al., 2005). However, for some, it is a difficult time with endless crying spells and anxiety.

Research has found that 1 in 8 women experience **postpartum depression** (Storm, 2011). Physical exhaustion, physiological changes, and an increased responsibility of child rearing all contribute to these feelings, coupled with postpartum hormonal changes (including a sudden decline in progesterone). Women with premature infants are at greater risk for postpartum depression because of the increased stress involved in these births (Storm, 2011).

Some ethnic and racial differences have been found in the rates of postpartum depression, with Black and Hispanic mothers reporting more postpartum depression than White mothers (Howell et al., 2005). Limited research on postpartum depression among lesbian and bisexual women has found that it may be more common than in heterosexual women, but more research is needed in this area (L. E. Ross et al., 2007). Postpartum depression may also be higher among lesbian and bisexual women than in heterosexual women (L. E. Ross et al., 2007). A lack of social support and relationship problems can contribute to stress and depression after the birth of a baby in any couple (L.E. Ross et al., 2005). Male partners may also experience postpartum depression after the birth of a baby (Davé et al., 2010).

Partner violence has also been found to be related to postpartum depression (Ludermir et al., 2010). We discuss intimate partner violence in more detail in Chapter 17.

Partner support has been found to decrease postpartum depression in both heterosexual and same-sex couples (Misri et al., 2000; L. E. Ross, 2005; Storm, 2011). In the most severe cases, mental disturbances, called **postpartum psychosis,** occur; in rare cases, women have killed or neglected their babies after delivery (Rammouz et al., 2008).

▶▶ SEXUALITY for New Parents

Although most physicians advise their heterosexual patients to wait 6 weeks postpartum before resuming intercourse, in an uncomplicated vaginal delivery (with no tears or episiotomy), intercourse can safely be engaged in 2 weeks after delivery. This period is usually necessary to ensure that no infection occurs and that the cervix has returned to its original position. If an episiotomy was performed, it may take up to 3 weeks for the stitches to dissolve. Health care providers generally advise women who have had a C-section birth to wait 4 to 6 weeks to resume sexual activity. In an uncomplicated delivery, 90% of women report resuming sexual activity by 6 months after the baby is born, although those with a complicated labor often wait longer to resume sexual activity (Brubaker et al., 2008). Immediately after delivery, many women report slower and less intense excitement stages of the sexual response cycle and a decrease in vaginal lubrication (Masters & Johnson, 1966). However, at 3 months postpartum, the majority of women return to their original levels of sexual desire and excitement.

▶▶ BREAST-FEEDING the Baby

Within an hour after birth, the newborn baby usually begins a rooting reflex, which signals hunger. The baby's sucking triggers the flow of milk from the breast. This is done through receptors in the nipples, which signal the pituitary to produce prolactin, a chemical necessary for milk production. Another chemical, oxytocin, is also produced, which helps increase contractions in the uterus to shrink

---

postpartum depression
A woman's clinical depression that occurs after childbirth.

postpartum psychosis
The rare occurrence of severe, debilitating depression or psychotic symptoms in the mother after childbirth.

weaned
To accustom a baby to take nourishment other than nursing from the breast.

it to its original size. In the first few days of breast-feeding, the breasts release a fluid called *colostrum,* which is very important in strengthening the baby's immune system. This is one of the reasons that breast-feeding is recommended to new mothers.

Breast-feeding rates in the United States increased significantly between 1993 and 2006. Whereas 60% of newborn babies were breast-fed in 1993–1994, 77% were breast-fed in 2005–2006 (McDowell et al., 2008). In 2010, three of every four new mothers in the United States started out breast-feeding; however, rates of breast-feeding decreased significantly by time the infants were 6 months old (Centers for Disease Control and Prevention, 2010b).

Benefits of breast-feeding include strengthening of the infant's immune system and cognitive development, and a reduction in infant allergies, asthma, diarrhea, tooth decay, and ear, urinary tract, and respiratory infections (Daniels & Adair, 2005; Duijts et al., 2010; Khadivzadeh & Parsai, 2005). One study found that breast-fed children attain higher IQ scores than non–breast-fed children (Caspi et al., 2007). Benefits to the mother include an earlier return to prepregnancy weight and a lower risk for breast cancer and osteoporosis (Stuebe et al., 2009). In addition, the body-to-body contact during breast-feeding has been found to decrease stress and improve mood for both mother and child (Groer, 2005).

For some women, however, breast-feeding is not physically possible. Time constraints and work pressures may also prevent breast-feeding. It is estimated that a baby's primary caregiver loses between 450 and 700 hours of sleep in the first year of the baby's life, and overall, breast-feeding mothers lose the most sleep (Brizendine, 2006; Maas, 1998).

Some women who want to breast-feed but who also wish to return to work use a breast pump. This allows a woman to express milk from her breasts that can be given to her child through a bottle while she is away. Breast milk can be kept in the refrigerator or freezer, but it must be heated before feeding. In early 2011, the Internal Revenue Service (IRS) announced that breast pumps and other breast-feeding supplies were tax deductible (Belkin, 2011). This reversed an earlier decision by the IRS that stated that breast-feeding did not contribute sufficient medical benefits to qualify for such a deduction. In 2010 President Obama signed a law

Research has found that body contact during breast-feeding can decrease stress and improve mood for both the mother and her infant.

Benefits of breast-feeding include **strengthening of the infant's immune system and cognitive development.**

that requires employers to provide reasonable break time, as well as a comfortable space other than a bathroom, to express breast milk for a nursing child up to 1 year after a child's birth (NCSL, 2010).

There have been some heated debates about when a child should be **weaned** from breast-feeding. The American Academy of Pediatrics recommends exclusive breast-feeding (no other fluids or food) for 6 months and then continued breast-feeding for a minimum of 1 year, whereas the World Health Organization recommends exclusive breast-feeding for the first 4 to 6 months of life and continued breast-feeding until at least age 2.

Throughout this chapter, we have explored many issues related to fertility, infertility, pregnancy, and childbearing. In the next chapter, we begin to look at limiting fertility through contraception and abortion.

◀ **review** QUESTIONS

1 Describe the physical and emotional changes that women experience after the birth of a child.

2 Differentiate between postpartum depression and postpartum psychosis.

3 How might a woman's sexuality change after the birth of a baby?

4 Identify and explain some of the benefits of breast-feeding.

SUMMARY POINTS

1 The number of U.S. births has been declining for all ages, races, and ethnicities in the United States. The only two groups to have increases in births were unmarried women and women between the ages of 40 and 44. Births to women 35 and older increased 8 times from 1970 to 2006.

2 Our bodies are biologically programmed to help pregnancy occur: A woman's sexual desire peaks at ovulation, female orgasm helps push semen into the uterus, and semen thickens after ejaculation.

3 Pregnancy can happen when intercourse takes place a few days before or after ovulation, and the entire process of fertilization takes about 24 hours. The fertilized ovum is referred to as a *zygote*. After the first cell division, it is referred to as a *blastocyst*. From the second to the eighth week, the developing human is called an *embryo*.

4 Early signs of pregnancy include missing a period, breast tenderness, frequent urination, and morning sickness. Pregnancy tests measure for a hormone in the blood known as human chorionic gonadotropin (hCG). Pseudocyesis and couvade are rare conditions that can occur in both women and men.

5 Some couples try to choose the sex of their children by using sex-selection methods. During the 16th or 17th week of pregnancy, an amniocentesis can be performed to evaluate the fetus for chromosomal abnormalities, and it can also identify the sex of the fetus.

6 Increased pregnancy terminations have been noted in areas where females are less valued in society and where there are governmental regulations on family size.

7 Many couples, including married, unmarried, straight, gay, lesbian, young, and older men and women, use assisted reproductive technologies. Although all couples use ARTs in hopes of achieving a pregnancy, same-sex couples and single women often use these methods to create a pregnancy. Infertility is the inability to conceive (or impregnate) after 1 year of regular vaginal intercourse without the use of any form of birth control. Although unmarried individuals, gay men, and lesbian women have historically been denied access to ARTs, this has been changing. An increasing

number of singles and same-sex couples are using assisted reproduction today.

8 Couples interested in assisted reproduction have many options: fertility drugs; surgery to correct cervical, vaginal, or endometrial abnormalities and blockage in the vas deferens or epididymis; artificial insemination; in vitro fertilization (IVF); gamete intra–Fallopian tube transfer (GIFT); zygote intra–Fallopian tube transfer (ZIFT); zonal dissection; intracellular sperm injections; oocyte or embryo transplants; surrogate parenting; and cryopreservation.

9 Pregnancy is divided into three 3-month periods called *trimesters*. In the first trimester, the most important embryonic development takes place. At this time, the fetus grows dramatically and is 3 inches long by the end of this trimester.

10 The mother often feels the fetus moving around inside her uterus during the second trimester. By the end of this period, the fetus is approximately 13 inches long and weighs about 2 pounds. The second trimester of pregnancy is usually the most positive time for the mother.

11 By the end of the eighth month, the fetus is 15 inches long and weighs about 3 pounds. Braxton–Hicks contractions begin, and colostrum may be secreted from the nipples.

12 A woman's exercise routine should not exceed pre-pregnancy levels. Exercise has been found to result in a greater sense of well-being, shorter labor, and fewer obstetric problems. Certain sports should be avoided during pregnancy, such as waterskiing, scuba diving, vigorous racquet sports, contact sports, and horseback riding.

13 Underweight and overweight women are at greater risk for impaired pregnancy outcome, and they are advised to gain or lose weight before pregnancy.

14 Drugs and alcohol can cross the placenta, enter into the developing fetus's bloodstream, and cause physical or mental deficiencies. FAS occurs when a woman drinks heavily during pregnancy, producing an infant with irreversible physical and mental disabilities.

15 Delaying pregnancy has some risks, including an increase in spontaneous abortion,

first-trimester bleeding, low birth weight, increased labor time, increased rate of C-sections, and chromosomal abnormalities.

16 Sexual behavior during pregnancy is safe for most mothers and the developing child up until the last several weeks of pregnancy, and maybe up to delivery; orgasm is safe but occasionally may cause painful uterine contractions.

17 In an ectopic pregnancy, the zygote implants outside the uterus, usually in the Fallopian tube. Although many women without risk factors can develop an ectopic pregnancy, some factors may put a woman at increased risk. These include smoking and a history of sexually transmitted infections.

18 The majority of miscarriages occur during the first trimester of pregnancy. The most common reason for miscarriage is a fetal chromosomal abnormality. Prenatal diagnostic testing can be used to determine whether there are chromosomal or genetic abnormalities in the fetus.

19 One of every 33 babies is born with a birth defect. Prenatal diagnostic testing can be used to determine whether there are chromosomal or genetic abnormalities in the fetus. The risk for chromosomal abnormality increases as maternal age increases. The most common chromosomal abnormality is Down syndrome.

20 An Rh-negative woman must be given RhoGAM immediately after childbirth, abortion, or miscarriage so that she will not produce antibodies and to ensure that her future pregnancies are healthy. Toxemia is a form of blood poisoning that can develop in pregnant women; symptoms include weight gain, fluid retention, an increase in blood pressure, and protein in the urine.

21 Increasing knowledge and alleviating anxiety about the birth process are the main concepts behind childbirth classes. Worldwide, the majority of babies are born at home, although most U.S. babies are born in hospitals.

22 Birth itself takes place in three stages: cervical effacement and dilation, expulsion of the fetus, and expulsion of the placenta. The first stage of labor can last anywhere from 20 minutes to 24 hours and is longer in first births.

Transition, the last part of stage one, is the most difficult part of the birth process. The second stage of birth involves the expulsion of the fetus. In the third stage of labor, strong contractions continue and push the placenta out of the uterus and through the vagina.

23 The majority of babies are born late, but if birth takes place before the 37th week of pregnancy, it is considered premature. Premature birth may occur early for several reasons, including early labor, early rupture of the amniotic membranes, or a maternal or fetal problem.

24 Problems during birthing include premature birth, breech birth, and stillbirth. A birth that takes place before the 37th week of pregnancy is considered premature and may occur for various reasons. The amniotic membranes may have ruptured, or there may be a maternal or fetal problem. Multiple births also occur earlier than single births. In a breech birth, the fetus has his or her feet and buttocks against the cervix, and either the baby is rotated or a C-section must be performed.

25 A C-section involves the delivery of the fetus through an incision in the abdominal wall. C-sections are necessary when the baby is too large for a woman to deliver vaginally, the woman is unable to push the baby out the birth canal, there is placenta previa or placental separation from the baby before birth, or the baby is in fetal distress. Some women also choose to have an elective C-section for a variety of reasons.

26 A fetus that dies after 20 weeks of pregnancy is called a *stillbirth*. The most common cause of stillbirth is a failure in the baby's oxygen supply, heart, or lungs.

27 After delivery, the uterus returns to its original size in about 6 weeks. Many women report painful contractions, caused by the hormone oxytocin, for a few days after birth. Uteruses of breast-feeding women return to the original size quicker than those of non–breast-feeding women.

28 The majority of women feel both excitement and exhaustion after the birth of a child. However, for some, it is a very difficult

time of depression, crying spells, and anxiety. In severe cases, a woman might experience postpartum depression or postpartum psychosis.

29 Although most physicians advise their heterosexual patients to wait 6 weeks postpartum before resuming sexual intercourse, in an uncomplicated vaginal delivery (with no tears or episiotomy), intercourse can safely be engaged in 2 weeks after delivery. Many women report slower and less intense excitement stages of the sexual response cycle and a decrease in vaginal lubrication immediately after delivery; however, at 3 months' postpartum, most women return to their original levels of desire and excitement.

30 In the first few days of breast-feeding, the breasts release a fluid called *colostrum,* which is very important in strengthening the baby's immune system. The American Academy of Pediatrics recommends breast-feeding for at least 1 year, whereas the World Health Organization recommends breast-feeding for up to 2 years or longer.

CRITICAL THINKING QUESTIONS

1 If sex preselection were possible, would you want to determine the sex of your children? Why or why not? If you did choose, what order would you choose? Why?

2 Do you think assisted reproductive techniques should be used in women older than 50? Older than 60? Do you think older moms can make good mothers? What about older dads?

3 If women can safely deliver at home, should they be encouraged to do so with the help of a midwife, or should they be encouraged to have children in the hospital? If you have children, where do you think you would want them to be born?

4 At what age do you think a child should be weaned? Should a woman breast-feed a child until he or she is 6 months old? Two years old? Four years old? How old?

5 In 2001, a woman ran an ad in a school newspaper at Stanford University offering $15,000 for a sperm donation from the right guy. She required the guy be intelligent, physically attractive, and over 6 feet tall. The year before, an ad ran in the same newspaper from a couple who offered $100,000 for eggs from an athletically gifted female student. Would you have answered either of these ads? Why or why not?

MEDIA RESOURCES

CourseMate brings course concepts to life with interactive learning, study, and exam preparation tools that support the printed textbook. A textbook-specific website, Psychology CourseMate includes an integrated interactive eBook and other interactive learning tools including quizzes, flashcards, videos, and more. If your textbook does not include an access code card, go to CengageBrain.com to gain access.

CENGAGENOW   CengageNOW is an easy-to-use online resource that helps you study in less time to get the grade you want—NOW. Take a pre-test for this chapter and receive a personalized study plan based on your results that will identify the topics you need to review and direct you to online resources to help you master those topics. Then take a post-test to help you determine the concepts you have mastered and what you will need to work on. If your textbook does not include an access code card, go to CengageBrain.com to gain access.

View in Video available in CourseMate and CengageNOW:

Love Makes a Family: Lesbian couple discusses their decision to have children and the process of doing so. The children will also share their thoughts about having two moms.

IVF and Multiple Births: An explanation of the IVF process and families' reaction to multiple births.

Weight and Pregnancy: A look at the benefits of exercise during pregnancy and the importance of weight control.

Unintended Pregnancy: A Man's Perspective: A young father discusses his feelings and experience with an unintended pregnancy.

Designer Babies: A fertility doctor offers parents the ability to select their offspring's genetic traits.

Websites:

American Society for Reproductive Medicine (ASRM) ■ The ASRM is an organization devoted to advancing knowledge and expertise in reproductive medicine, infertility, and ARTs. Links to a variety of helpful websites are available.

BirthStories ■ This interesting website contains true birth stories from a variety of women, including first-time moms, veteran moms, and births after a pregnancy loss. It also has information on birthing, breast-feeding, and newborns.

International Council on Infertility Information Dissemination (INCIID) ■ This website provides detailed information on the diagnosis and treatment of infertility, pregnancy loss, family-building options, and helpful fact sheets on various types of fertility treatments and assisted reproductive techniques. Information on adoption and child-free lifestyles is also included.

Extend Fertility ■ Extend Fertility is the nation's first firm devoted solely to getting the word out about egg freezing. This website, started by a woman who froze her eggs, provides a guide for women and the names of clinics offering such services.

Resolve ■ The National Infertility Association was established in 1974. It works to promote reproductive health, ensure equal access to fertility options for men and women experiencing infertility or other reproductive disorders, and provide support services and physician referral and education.

Sperm Bank Directory ■ A national directory of sperm cryobanks. Provides information on cryopreservation, sperm donation, and donor sperm. There are also links to sperm banks throughout the country, some of which include online donor catalogs.

Storknet ■ This website provides a week-by-week guide to a woman's pregnancy. For each of the 40 weeks of pregnancy, there is information about fetal development, what types of changes occur within the pregnant body, and suggested readings and links for more information.

13 Contraception and Abortion

View in **Video**

View in **Video**

View in **Video**

View in **Video**

ABOUT THE CHAPTER OPENING VIDEO –
Contraception exists to help women and men control their fertility. However, unintended pregnancy can be a reality for all women who are sexually active. In this chapter, we'll explore various issues related to contraception and abortion. We begin with the story of Joan who experienced an unintended pregnancy in 1967 at the age of 18.

I knew I wasn't ready to have a baby. But I was terrified about my lack of options. I somehow found a doctor that would do illegal abortions in his office after hours. He told me that I needed to bring him $500 cash, come by myself, and not tell ANYONE where I was going. I took the bus by myself to get to his office. I can still remember how blue the sky was that morning. I remember looking at it and thinking that today might be the day I die. But I still knew that I

needed to go through with it. When I arrived at his office, no one was there except him. He told me to go to the examination room and take off all my clothes. When he came in the room, he sternly told me not to scream or make any noise during the procedure. Screaming would cause attention and no one could know what was going on. He said he gave me a drug to reduce the pain of the procedure but looking back now, I think it was a different drug because I felt everything. The procedure was incredibly painful. I just laid on the table and cried the whole time. When he finished he told me not to move. I was extremely uncomfortable because I was completely naked. He began telling me that I had a beautiful body and that he wanted to touch my breasts. I was shocked and feeling totally out of it. Thinking back now, I'm amazed that I did what he told me to but I honestly didn't know any better. A few years later,

© Michelle D. Bridwell/PhotoEdit

abortion was legalized in the United States and I underwent a second abortion. It was a totally different experience for me.

Today Joan works in women's health and is a firm supporter of woman's rights. No matter what your position on abortion, I hope you find her firsthand account as moving and powerful as I did. ▌

"He sternly told me not to scream."
—CHAPTER OPENING VIDEO

View in Video

To watch the entire interview, go to Psychology CourseMate at **login.cengagebrain.com.**

© Kari Mutscheller

The typical American woman spends about 30 years trying *not* to get pregnant and only a couple of years trying to become pregnant (Figure 13.1; Boonstra et al., 2006). Contraceptive use has increased in the United States over the last few years, and today more than 99% of sexually active women aged 15 to 44 years old have used at least one contraceptive method (Mosher & Jones, 2010). Condom use continues to increase, which has helped decrease sexually transmitted infections (STIs). Overall, the most popular contraceptive methods in the United States are birth control pills (used by close to 11 million women) and female sterilization (used by approximately 10 million women; Mosher & Jones, 2010). Although contraceptive use has increased in the mid-2000s, many user characteristics interact with contraceptive use, such as age, ethnicity, race, marital status, past pregnancies, education, and income. Although unintended pregnancy can affect all women, research has found that several issues put women at greater risk for unintended pregnancies, such as being young, unmarried, or poor (see Figure 13.2).

College students take risks when it comes to **contraception,** even though they are intelligent and educated about birth control. Many factors increase one's motivation to use contraception, including the ability to communicate with a partner, cost of the method, effectiveness rates, frequency of vaginal intercourse, motivation to avoid pregnancy, the contraceptive method's side effects, and one's openness about sexuality (Frost et al., 2008; Hatcher et al., 2011). Contraceptive use is further complicated by the fact that an ideal method for one person may not be an ideal method for another, and an ideal method for one person at one time in his or her life may not be an ideal method as that person enters into different life stages. Having a wide variety of choices available is important to allow couples to choose and change methods as their contraceptive needs change.

As we begin our exploration into contraception and abortion, consider this: Have you thought about whether you ever want to have a child? Maybe you have an exact plan about when you'd like to experience a pregnancy in your life. Or perhaps you have already decided you won't have any children. For many couples, deciding how to plan, and also how to avoid, pregnancies are important issues in their lives. In this chapter, we explore the array of contraceptive methods available today, investigate their advantages and disadvantages, and also discuss emergency contraception and abortion.

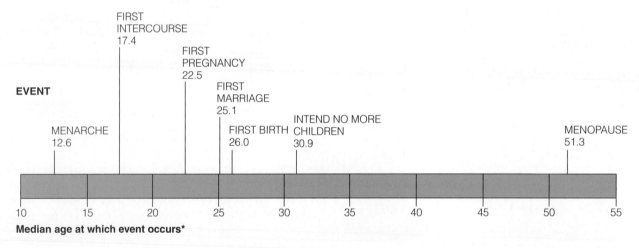

EVENT

MENARCHE 12.6
FIRST INTERCOURSE 17.4
FIRST PREGNANCY 22.5
FIRST MARRIAGE 25.1
FIRST BIRTH 26.0
INTEND NO MORE CHILDREN 30.9
MENOPAUSE 51.3

10 15 20 25 30 35 40 45 50 55

Median age at which event occurs*

Note *Age by which half of women have experienced event.

FIGURE **13.1** The Alan Guttmacher Institute has found that the average woman spends 5 years pregnant, postpartum, or trying to get pregnant, and 30 years avoiding pregnancy. Above is a timeline of reproductive events for the typical American woman. SOURCE: Boonstra, H. D., Gold, R. B., Richards, C. L., & Finer, L. B. (2006). *Abortion in women's lives* (Figure 1.1, p. 7). New York: Guttmacher Institute. Reprinted by permission.

timeline History of Contraceptives in the United States

1839
Goodyear manufactures rubber condoms.
© Joel Gordon

1873
Comstock laws prohibit dissemination of contraceptive information through the U.S. mail.

1882
A German physician, Wilhelm Mensinga, invents the diaphragm.

1914
Margaret Sanger coins the term *birth control.*

1921
Margaret Sanger founds the American Birth Control League, which eventually becomes the **Planned Parenthood Federation of America.**

1925
First diaphragms available in the United States.
© Kenzie Henke

CONTRACEPTION:
History and Method Considerations

Although many people believe that contraception is a modern invention, its origins actually extend back to ancient times. We now explore contraception throughout history, both within and outside of the United States.

▶▶ CONTRACEPTION in Ancient Times

People have always tried to invent ways to control fertility. The ancient Greeks used magic, superstition, herbs, and drugs to try and control their fertility. The Egyptians tried fumigating the female genitalia with certain mixtures, inserting a tampon into the vagina that had been soaked in herbal liquid and honey, and inserting a mixture of crocodile feces, sour milk, and honey (Dunham et al., 1992). Another strategy was to insert objects into the vagina that could entrap or block the sperm. Such objects include vegetable seed pods (South Africa), a cervical plug of grass (Africa), sponges soaked with alcohol (Persia), and empty pomegranate halves (Greece). These methods may sound far-fetched to us today, but they worked on many of the same principles as modern methods. In the accompanying Sexual Diversity in Our World feature, we discuss some of these methods.

▶▶ CONTRACEPTION IN THE UNITED STATES: 1800s and Early 1900s

In the early 1800s, several groups in the United States wanted to control fertility to reduce poverty. However, contraception was considered a private affair, to be discussed only between partners in a relationship. As we learned in Chapter 1, Anthony Comstock worked with Congress in 1873 to pass the Comstock Laws, which

---

REAL RESEARCH 13.1 There is often a disconnect between which partner college students *think* should be responsible for birth control and which one is actually responsible (BRUNNER HUBER & ERSEK, 2011). Although close to 90% of college students report that the responsibility should be shared, it is shared in only about half of relationships.

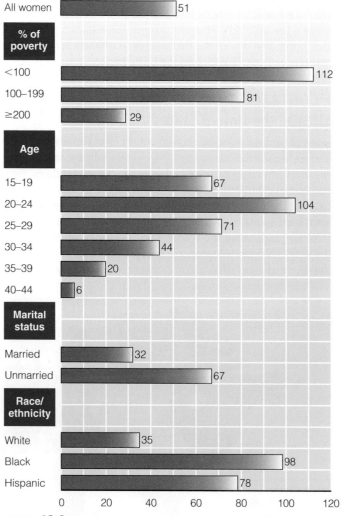

Unintended Pregnancies per 1,000 Women Aged 15–44

All women	51
% of poverty	
<100	112
100–199	81
≥200	29
Age	
15–19	67
20–24	104
25–29	71
30–34	44
35–39	20
40–44	6
Marital status	
Married	32
Unmarried	67
Race/ethnicity	
White	35
Black	98
Hispanic	78

FIGURE **13.2** Unintended pregnancy rates vary dramatically based on income, age, marital status, and race/ethnicity. *Note: Poverty levels are defined by government standards of income. Groupings are <100 (making less income than the poverty level), 100–199 (earning more than poverty but below 2× the poverty level), and >200 (earning more than 2× the poverty level).* SOURCE: Alan Guttmacher Institute (2006). Abortion in Women's Lives, http://www.guttmacher.org/pubs/2006/05/04/AiWL.pdf.

contraception
The deliberate use of artificial methods or other techniques to prevent pregnancy as a consequence of vaginal intercourse.

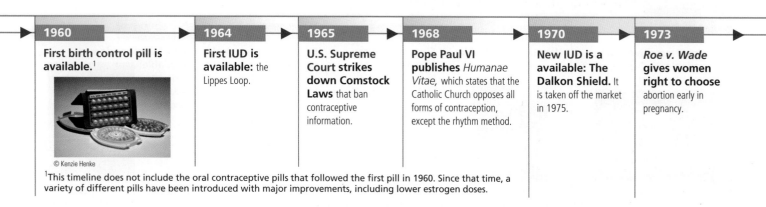

1960 — **First birth control pill is available.**[1]

© Kenzie Henke

1964 — **First IUD is available:** the Lippes Loop.

1965 — **U.S. Supreme Court strikes down Comstock Laws** that ban contraceptive information.

1968 — **Pope Paul VI publishes** *Humanae Vitae,* which states that the Catholic Church opposes all forms of contraception, except the rhythm method.

1970 — **New IUD is available: The Dalkon Shield. It** is taken off the market in 1975.

1973 — *Roe v. Wade* **gives women right to choose** abortion early in pregnancy.

[1]This timeline does not include the oral contraceptive pills that followed the first pill in 1960. Since that time, a variety of different pills have been introduced with major improvements, including lower estrogen doses.

prohibited the distribution of all obscene material; this included contraceptive information and devices. Even medical doctors were not allowed to provide information about contraception (although a few still did). Margaret Sanger, the founder of Planned Parenthood, was one of the first people to publicly advocate the importance of contraception in the United States.

▶▶ CONTRACEPTION OUTSIDE the United States

Studies of contraceptive use throughout the world have found that social and economic issues, knowledge levels, religion, and gender roles affect contraceptive use (see Figure 13.3 for more information about unmet contraceptive needs throughout the world). A woman might not use contraception because she is uneducated about it or doesn't have access to methods; she may also worry about adverse effects, not understand she is at risk for pregnancy, or believe that she needs to be married to use contraception (Sedgh et al., 2007a). A country's religious views can also affect contraceptive use. In fact,

View in **Video**

To watch the entire interview, go to Psychology CourseMate at **login.cengagebrain.com**.

"In the end, when I thought of my health and being there for my two girls, it was an easy decision."
—PERMANENT CONTRACEPTION

Video supplied by BBC Motion Gallery

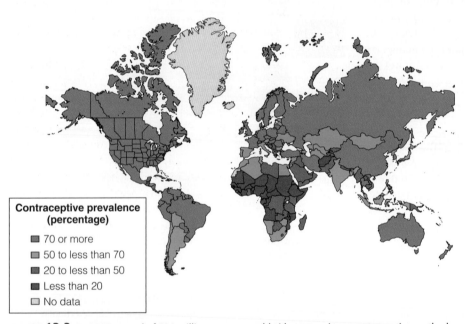

Contraceptive prevalence (percentage)

- 70 or more
- 50 to less than 70
- 20 to less than 50
- Less than 20
- No data

FIGURE **13.3** In 2007, a total of 721 million women worldwide were using a contraceptive method. Contraceptive use ranges from 3% in Chad to 88% in Norway, for a worldwide average of 63%. SOURCE: United Nations http://www.un.org/esa/population/publications/contraceptive2009/contracept2009_wallchart_front.pdf.

many predominantly Catholic regions and countries, such as Ireland, Italy, Poland, and the Philippines, have limited contraceptive devices available. These countries often promote natural methods of contraception, such as withdrawal or natural family planning. In 2010, Catholic bishops in the Philippines led a massive national protest against the president of the Philippines, who supported artificial birth control (such as pills or other hormonal methods; France-Presse, 2010). In 2008, many Filipino bishops refused to give Holy Communion to politicians who approved of artificial birth control (Burke, 2008; Hoffman, 2008). Despite opposition from the Catholic Church, the Philippine government began providing family planning services in 2010.

It is also important to point out, however, that not all residents of Catholic countries agree with the Church's contraceptive views (de Freitas, 2004; Tomaso, 2008). In the Philippines, although more than 80% of the Philippine population is Catholic, the

timeline History of Contraceptives in the United States

1983
First contraceptive sponge is available: The Today sponge. It is taken off the market in 1995.
© Janell Carroll

1984
New IUD is available: The ParaGard Copper T.
© Joel Gordon

1988
First cervical cap is available: The Prentif cap. It is taken off the market in 2005.

1990
First 6-rod hormonal contraceptive implant is available: Norplant. Approved for use for up to 5 years. It is taken off the market in 2002.

1993
First femal condom is available: the Instead female condom.
© Joel Gordon

majority of people believe that couples should have legal assess to family planning (France-Presse, 2010). One study in Brazil, which contains one of the highest concentrations of Catholics, found that 88% of participants did not follow the Church's contraceptive teachings (in the United States, 75% of Catholics do the same; de Freitas, 2004; Tomaso, 2008). In 2008, 40 years after Pope Paul VI released *Humanae Vitae* (the document that prohibits Catholics from using artificial contraception), more than 50 Catholic groups from around the world joined forces to urge Pope Benedict XVI to lift the Catholic Church's ban on birth control (Tomaso, 2008).

Gender roles and power differentials also contribute to a country's contraceptive use. Outside the United States, many women may not be involved in contraceptive decision making, and contraceptive use is thought to reduce a man's masculinity. For example, in Israel, while Jewish law often opposes family planning, religious law often teaches that men should not "spill their seed." Contraceptive methods that can cause direct damage to sperm, such as vasectomy, withdrawal, condoms, or spermicides, are often not acceptable (Shtarkshall & Zemach, 2004). Contraceptive methods that do not harm sperm, such as oral contraceptives, are more acceptable.

Men are primarily responsible for birth control decisions in Japan, where Japanese women express shock over the liberal views that many American woman hold about birth control pill usage (Hatano & Shimazaki, 2004). In Kenya, married couples report low condom usage because condoms in marriage signify unfaithfulness on the part of the husband (Brockman, 2004).

Scandinavian countries are regarded as some of the most progressive with respect to contraceptive usage. In fact, Finland has been rated as a "model country" because a variety of contraceptive methods are easily available and students can obtain contraception from school health services (Kontula & Haavio-Mannila, 2004). In the Netherlands and Norway, oral contraceptive use is high, and many couples begin taking it before becoming sexually active. In many of these countries, birth control is free and easily accessible.

▶▶ CONTRACEPTION in the United States Today

Several methods of contraception, or **birth control,** are currently available. Before the availability of any contraceptive method in the United States, the **U.S. Food and Drug Administration (FDA)** must formally approve the method. Let's explore the FDA approval process and individual lifestyle issues that may affect contraceptive method choice.

REAL RESEARCH 13.2 Motivations for contraceptive use are often influenced by cultural factors. In some areas of eastern Africa, condom use is extremely low because of the cultural significance of semen (Coast, 2007). Strongly held beliefs about wasting semen have led to low condom use, even when knowledge levels about contraception and STIs are high.

▶▶ FDA APPROVAL Process

The FDA is responsible for approving all prescription medications and medical devices in the United States. To get approval for a new drug, a pharmaceutical company must first submit a new drug application to the FDA showing that the drug is safe in animal tests and that it is reasonably safe to proceed with human trials of the drug. After this, there are a total of three phases to evaluate the safety of the medication. In Phase 1, the drug is introduced to approximately 20 to 80 healthy volunteers to collect information on the drug's effectiveness. In Phase 2, several hundred people take the drug to evaluate how it works and determine adverse effects and risks. In Phase 3 trials, the study is expanded, and hundreds to thousands of people are enrolled in the study. Like drugs, medical devices, such as intrauterine devices (IUDs) and diaphragms, are also subject to strict evaluation and regulation. It is estimated that it takes 10 to 14 years to develop a new contraceptive method (Hatcher et al., 2007; F. H. Stewart & Gabelnick, 2004).

---

birth control
Another term for contraception.

U.S. Food and Drug Administration (FDA)
The agency in the U.S. federal government that has the power to approve and disapprove new drugs.

1994	1996	1999	2000
First polyurethane condoms become available.	**First two-rod hormonal contraceptive implant is** available: Norplant-2 or Jadelle. Although originally approved for up to 3 years, in 2002, FDA approves for up to 5 years. However, not marketed in the United States.	**First emergency contraception is available** by prescription only: Plan B.	First contraceptive injectable is available: Lunelle. It is taken off the Market in 2002. Mifepristone (also known as RU-486, or the abortion pill) is available by prescription only. **New hormone-releasing IUD is available:** Mirena. Reduces menstrual flow and cramping, and can be used for up to 5 years.

© Joel Gordon

CHOOSING A METHOD of Contraception

As we discussed earlier, no single method of birth control is best for everyone; the best one for you is one that you and your partner will use correctly every time you have vaginal intercourse.

Lifestyle Issues

Choosing a contraceptive method is an important decision and one that must be made with your lifestyle in mind. Important issues include your own personal health and health risks, the number of sexual partners you have, frequency of vaginal intercourse, your risk for acquiring an STI, how responsible you are, the cost of the method, and the method's advantages and disadvantages.

The majority of women in the United States use some form of contraception (Figure 13.4 and Table 13.2). However, there are racial and ethnic differences in contraceptive use in the United States. Although female sterilization, oral contraceptives, and condoms are the most widely used methods, White women are more likely to use birth control pills, and Black and Hispanic women are more likely to rely on female sterilization (Mosher &

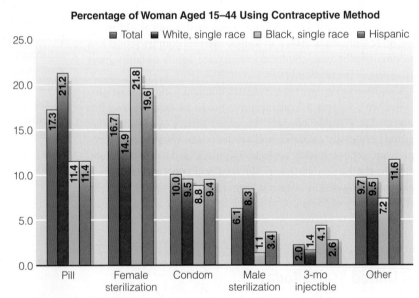

"This array of contraceptive methods can help you make better decisions."
—VIRTUAL CONTRACEPTIVE KIT

View in Video
To watch the entire interview, go to Psychology CourseMate at **login.cengagebrain.com**.

Jones, 2010). See Figure 13.5 for more information about race/ethnicity and contraceptive use.

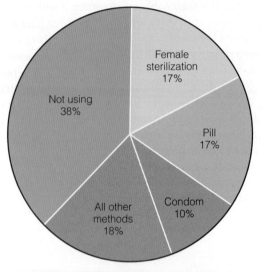

FIGURE **13.4** Distribution of women aged 15 to 44 years by contraceptive status in the United States, 2006–2008. SOURCE: Jones J. (2010). Use of contraception in the United States: 1982-2008. National Center for Health Statistics. Vital Health Stat 23(29). http://www.cdc.gov/nchs/data/series/sr_23/sr23_029.pdf.

FIGURE **13.5** Contraceptive method use by race and ethnicity in the United States, 2006–2008. SOURCE: Centers for Disease Control http://www.cdc.gov/nchs/data/series/sr_23/sr23_029.pdf (see Table 6).

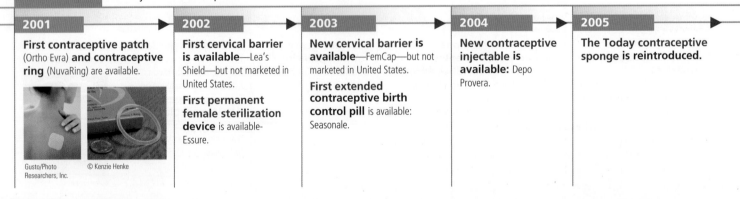

timeline History of Contraceptives in the United States

2001
First contraceptive patch (Ortho Evra) **and contraceptive ring** (NuvaRing) are available.

Gusto/Photo Researchers, Inc.   © Kenzie Henke

2002
First cervical barrier is available—Lea's Shield—but not marketed in United States.

First permanent female sterilization device is available-Essure.

2003
New cervical barrier is available—FemCap—but not marketed in United States.

First extended contraceptive birth control pill is available: Seasonale.

2004
New contraceptive injectable is available: Depo Provera.

2005
The Today contraceptive sponge is reintroduced.

In many places around the world, herbs are used as contraception. For example, American women in Appalachia drink tea made from Queen Anne's lace directly after sexual intercourse to prevent pregnancy (Rensberger, 1994). They are not alone. Many women from South Africa, Guatemala, Costa Rica, Haiti, China, and India rely on herbal contraceptives (L. Newman & Nyce, 1985). Newer hormonal methods of birth control have reduced fertility around the world, but nonhormonal methods such as natural family planning and herbal methods continue to be used. Some of the tested herbs have been found to have high success rates for contraceptive ability (Chaudhury, 1985).

A common herbal contraceptive in Paraguay is known as yuyos. Many types of yuyos are taken for fertility regulation (Bull & Melian, 1998). The herbs are usually soaked in water and drunk as tea. Older women teach younger women how to use these herbs, but problems sometimes occur when herbal methods are used improperly. Remember that this method works only when using a mix of herbs that have been found to offer contraceptive protection. Drinking herbal tea from the grocery store isn't going to protect you in the same way.

Failure rates from herbal contraceptives are higher than from more modern methods, but many do work better than using nothing at all. What is it that makes the herbal methods effective? We don't know, but perhaps some future contraceptive drugs may come from research into plant pharmaceuticals.

Unreliable Birth Control

Unfortunately, many men and women rely on myths and false information when it comes to contraception. They may keep their fingers crossed in hopes of not getting pregnant, have sex standing up to try and invoke gravity, or even jump up and down after sex in an attempt to dislodge sperm from swimming up the vagina. We know these techniques won't work, but for many years people thought they would. In the mid-1800s, physicians recommended douching as a contraceptive. Douching involves using a syringe-type instrument to inject a stream of water (which may be mixed with other chemicals) into the vagina (see Chapter 5 for more information about douching). Today, health care providers strongly recommend against douching because it can increase the risk for pelvic infections and STIs. It is not an effective contraceptive method.

Another ineffective method is the **lactational amenorrhea method (LAM),** which is based on the postpartum infertility that many women experience when they are breast-feeding (Hatcher et al., 2007). During breast-feeding, the cyclic ovarian hormones are typically suspended, which may inhibit ovulation. However, this is an ineffective contraceptive method because ovulation may still occur (Hatcher et al., 2011; see Chapter 12 for more information about breast-feeding).

In the following sections, we will discuss effective methods of contraception, including barrier, hormonal, chemical, intrauterine, natural, permanent, and emergency contraception. For each of these methods, we will cover how they work, **effectiveness rates,** cost, advantages and disadvantages, and cross-cultural patterns of usage. Table 13.1 provides an overview of available contraceptive methods with their effectiveness in **typical use** (which includes user error) and **perfect use** (when a method is used without error).

lactational amenorrhea method (LAM)
A method of avoiding pregnancies based on the postpartum infertility that many women experience when they are breast-feeding.

effectiveness rates
Estimated rates of the number of women who do not become pregnant each year using each method of contraception.

typical use
Refers to the probability of contraceptive failure for less than perfect use of the method.

perfect use
Refers to the probability of contraceptive failure for use of the method without error.

2006	2008	2009	2010
First single-rod hormonal contraceptive implant is available: Implanon.	**New female condom that uses polyurethane sponge** to aid insertion is available: the Reddy condom for women.	**Generic form of emergency contraception is available:** Next Choice. Available without a prescription if older than 17 years.	**New emergency contraception method** is available: ella.
New extended contraceptive birth control pill is available: Seasonique.	**New nonsurgical, permanent female sterilization** procedure is available: Adiana.	**Plan B One-Step is available** without a prescription to those older than 17.	
Plan B is available without a prescription over age 17. Prescription required if 16 or younger.	**Catholic groups attempt to reverse** Catholic Church's contraceptive ban (*Humanae Vitae*).	**New female condom is available:** the FC2.	

table 13.1 ■ Overview of Contraceptive Methods

Following is an overview of contraceptive methods, including effectiveness rates, prescription requirements, cost, and noncontraceptive benefits. Even though both typical and perfect effectiveness rates are provided here, remember that a method's effectiveness depends on the user's ability to use the method correctly and to continue using it. For many methods, user failures are more common than method failures. Also keep in mind that the cost for each method depends on where it is purchased. Typically, health care clinics are less expensive than pharmacies or private physicians.

| Method | Effectiveness | | | |
	Typical Use	Perfect Use	MD Visit?	Cost
Male sterilization	99%	99.9%	Yes	$300–1,000
Female sterilization	99%	99.9%	Yes	$2,000–5,000
Implanon	99%	99%	Yes	$400–800 but medical examination extra; removal ranges from $75–150
Mirena IUD	99.2%	99.9%	Yes	$500–1,000; but medical examination extra
ParaGard IUD	99.2%	99.9%	Yes	$500–1,000; but medical examination extra
Depo-Provera	97%	99.7%	Yes	$35–70 but medical examination extra
NuvaRing	92%	99.7%	Yes	$15–70 per month
Ortho Evra Patch	92%	99.7%	Yes	$15–75 per month
Combination birth control pill	92%	99.7%	Yes	$15–60 per month; less at health clinics
Progestin-only birth control pill	92%	99.7%	Yes	$15–60 per month
Extended-use birth control pill	98%	99.9%	Yes	$90–100 per pack
Male condom	85%	98%	No	$10–15 per dozen (latex); $20 per dozen (polyurethane)
Female condom	79%	95%	No	Approximately $3–4 each
Cervical barrier	84%	94%	Yes	$60–75, but medical examination and spermicide extra
Contraceptive sponge	84%	91%	No	$13–17 for three sponges
Fertility awareness methods	88%	97%	No	Not applicable (n/a)
Withdrawal	73%	96%	No	n/a
Spermicide	71%	82%	No	$5–15
No method	15%	15%	No	n/a

SOURCE: Hatcher et al., 2011.

◄ review QUESTIONS

1 Explain what we know about contraception in ancient times.

2 How was contraception viewed in the United States in the early 1900s?

3 What factors have been found to be related to contraceptive nonuse outside the United States?

4 Identify two important lifestyle issues to consider when choosing a contraceptive method.

5 Identify and discuss ineffective contraceptive methods.

Noncontraceptive Benefits	Male Involved?
Possible reduction in prostate cancer risk	Yes
Reduces risk for ovarian cancer	No
Reduced menstrual flow and cramping; can be used while breast-feeding	Yes
Decreases menstrual flow and cramping; reduced risk for endometrial cancer	No
Reduced risk for endometrial cancer	No
Reduced menstrual flow and cramping; decreased risk for pelvic inflammatory disease (PID) and ovarian and endometrial cancers; can be used while breast-feeding	No
Decreases menstrual flow and cramping, premenstrual syndrome (PMS), acne, ovarian and endometrial cancers, the development of ovarian cysts, uterine and breast fibroids, and PID	No
Decreases menstrual flow and cramping, PMS, acne, ovarian and endometrial cancers, the development of ovarian cysts, uterine and breast fibroids, and PID	No
Decreases menstrual flow and cramping, PMS, acne, ovarian and endometrial cancers, the development of ovarian cysts, uterine and breast fibroids, and pelvic inflammatory disease	No
May have similar contraceptive benefits as combination pills	No
Four periods or less per year and fewer menstrual-related problems; may reduce uterine fibroids and endometriosis symptoms	No
Protects against sexually transmitted infections (STIs); delays premature ejaculation	Yes
Protects against STIs	Possibly
Diaphragm may protect from cervical dysplasia	Possibly
None	Possibly
Can help a woman learn her cycle and eventually help in getting pregnant	Possibly
None	Yes
Provides lubrication	Possibly
n/a	n/a

▶ BARRIER Methods

Barrier methods of contraception work by preventing the sperm from entering the uterus. These methods include condoms, cervical barriers, and the contraceptive sponge.

▶▶ MALE Condoms

Penile coverings have been used as a method of contraception since the beginning of recorded history. In 1350 B.C., Egyptian men wore decorative sheaths over their penises. Eventually, sheaths of linen and animal intestines were developed. In 1844, the Goodyear Company improved the strength and resiliency of rubber, and by 1850, rubber (latex) **condoms** were available in the United States (McLaren, 1990). Polyurethane (paul-lee-YUR-ith-ain; nonlatex) condoms were launched in the United States in 1994 and can be used by those with latex allergies. However, if a person does not have a latex allergy, health care providers generally recommend using latex condoms because they have lower rates of slippage and breakage.

Male condoms are one of the most inexpensive and cost-effective contraceptive methods, providing not only high effectiveness rates but also added protection from STIs and HIV (Hatcher et al., 2011). They are the most widely available and commonly used barrier contraceptive method in the United States today (see Figure 13.6 for more information on condom use by age and gender). Male condoms are made of either latex or plastic and typically cost about $1 each but may be free at health clinics.

condom
A latex, animal membrane, or polyurethane sheath that fits over the penis and is used for protection against pregnancy and sexually transmitted infections; female condoms made of either polyurethane or polymer, which protect the vaginal walls, are also available.

table 13.2 ■ Contraceptive Method Use among U.S. Women Who Practice Contraception, 2006–2008

Method	No. of Users (in 000s)	Users (%)
Pill*	10,700	28.0
Tubal sterilization*	10,400	27.1
Male condom	6,200	16.1
Vasectomy	3,800	9.9
Intrauterine device	2,100	5.5
Withdrawal	2,000	5.2
Three-month injectable (Depo-Provera)	1,200	3.2
Vaginal ring (NuvaRing)	900	2.4
Implant (Implanon or Norplant), 1-month injectable (Lunelle) or patch (Evra)	400	1.1
Periodic abstinence (calendar)	300	0.9
Other†	200	0.4
Periodic abstinence (natural family planning)	100	0.2
Diaphragm	‡	‡
Total	38,214	100.0

*The pill and female sterilization have been the two leading contraceptive methods in the United States since 1982. However, sterilization is the most common method among Black and Hispanic women, whereas White women most commonly choose the pill.

†Includes emergency contraception, female condom or vaginal pouch, foam, cervical cap, Today sponge, suppository or insert, jelly or cream (without diaphragm), and other methods.

‡Figure does not meet standards of reliability or precision.

SOURCE: Alan Guttmacher Institute. (2010, June). Facts on Contraceptive Use in the United States. New York: Alan Guttmacher Institute. Retrieved from http://www.guttmacher.org/pubs/fb_contr_use.html.

doms come prelubricated, if extra lubrication is needed, water, contraceptive jelly or cream, or a water-based lubricant such as K-Y Jelly should be used. Oil-based lubricants such as hand or body lotion, petroleum jelly (e.g., Vaseline), baby oil, massage oil, or creams for vaginal infections (e.g., Monistat and Vagisil) should not be used because they may damage the latex and cause the condom to break (polyurethane condoms are not damaged by these products; see Table 13.3).

To avoid the possibility of semen leaking out of the condom, withdrawal must take place immediately after ejaculation, while the penis is still erect, and the condom should be grasped firmly at the base to prevent its slipping off into the vagina during withdrawal. Condom users should always remember to check expiration dates before using condoms.

There are many types of male condoms on the market, including dry, lubricated, colored, spermicidal, reservoir-tip, and ribbed-texture condoms. For protection from STIs, the most effective condoms are latex and polyurethane condoms. Spermicidal condoms are lubricated with a small amount of **nonoxynol-9,** but there are risks to using this **spermicide** (Hatcher et al., 2011; see the accompanying Sex in Real Life).

Effectiveness

Effectiveness rates for male condoms range from 85% to 98%. Studies have demonstrated that when used correctly, the overall risk for condom breakage is very low (Hatcher et al., 2011). Using a condom after the expiration date is the leading cause of breakage.

How They Work

The male condom ("rubber" or "prophylactic") is placed on an erect penis before vaginal penetration. Condoms must be put on before there is any vaginal contact by the penis because sperm may be present in the urethra. Some condom manufacturers recommend leaving space at the tip of the condom to allow room for the ejaculation, but others do not. To prevent tearing the condom, the vagina should be well lubricated. Although some con-

Consistent and correct use of condoms has been widely recommended to reduce the risk of sexually transmitted infections. A condom should be placed on an erect penis prior to any penetration.

A female condom is inserted deep into the vagina prior to vaginal intercourse. The ring at the closed end holds the condom in the vagina, while the ring at the open end stays outside the vaginal opening during intercourse. The female condom can also be used during anal intercourse. It is inserted into the anus.

© Joel Gordon

© Joel Gordon

table 13.3 ■ What to Use with Condoms

Male condoms can be made out of latex or polyurethane. All types of lubricants, including oil-based lubricants, can be safely used with polyurethane condoms. However, latex condoms should be used with only a water-based lubricant. Following is a listing of products that can be used with all condoms and products that should never be used with latex condoms.

Use with All Condoms

- Water-based lubricants (including products such as AquaLube, AstroGlide, or K-Y Jelly)
- Glycerine
- Spermicides
- Saliva
- Water
- Silicone lubricant

Do Not Use with Latex Condoms

- Baby oil
- Cold creams
- Edible oils (such as olive, peanut, or canola oil)
- Massage oil
- Petroleum jelly
- Rubbing alcohol
- Suntan oil and lotions
- Vegetable or mineral oil
- Vaginal infection medications in cream or suppository form

SOURCE: Hatcher et al. (2011).

Advantages

Male condoms allow men to help prevent pregnancy, can be discreetly carried in a pocket or purse, offer some protection from many STIs, can be purchased without a prescription, are relatively inexpensive, have minimal adverse effects, may reduce the incidence of premature ejaculation, reduce **postcoital drip,** can be used in conjunction with other contraceptive methods, and can be used during oral or anal sex to reduce the risk for STIs (we discuss this further in Chapter 15). Polyurethane condoms are more resistant to damage than latex condoms, have a longer shelf life, and can be used with both oil- and water-based lubricants (Hatcher et al., 2011).

Disadvantages

The male condom decreases spontaneity, may pose sizing and erection problems, and may reduce male sensation. In one study, more than 75% of men and nearly 40% of women reported decreased sexual sensation with condom use (Crosby et al., 2008b). Condoms may not be comfortable for all men, and some who use polyurethane condoms report slipping or bunching up during use (Hollander, 2001). Finally, some men may feel uncomfortable interrupting foreplay to put one on.

Cross-Cultural Use

Worldwide, male condoms are the fourth most popular contraceptive method (behind female sterilization, IUDs, and birth control pills), with 6% of couples reporting relying on this method ("World Contraceptive Use 2009," 2009). Condoms are popular in more developed regions of the world, such as Europe and North America (Figure 13.7). Usage rates of between 20% and 40% have been reported in Argentina, Demark, Finland, Greece, Ireland, Jamaica, Singapore, Spain, Ukraine, the United Kingdom, and Uruguay.

In many other countries, however, male condoms are not widely used. This may be because of embarrassment, lack of availability, or religious prohibition. In Botswana, for example, many couples are embarrassed to purchase condoms (Mookodi et al., 2004), and a similar attitude is found in Brazil, especially among women (de Freitas, 2004). However, these attitudes are slowly changing because of increased condom availability. In Costa Rica, where religious prohibitions discourage condom use, men report not wanting to use condoms and prohibit their partners from using protection as well (Arroba, 2004).

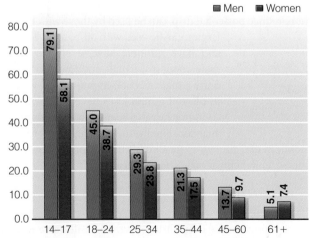

Condom Use Rates by Age and Gender in the U.S.
(% of past ten vaginal intercourse acts that included condom use)
(N = 3,457)

■ Men ■ Women

Age	Men	Women
14–17	79.1	58.1
18–24	45.0	38.7
25–34	29.3	23.8
35–44	21.3	17.5
45–60	13.7	9.7
61+	5.1	7.4

FIGURE **13.6** Condom Use Rates by Age and Gender. SOURCE: National Survey of Sexual Health and Behavior. Reece et al., 2010b.

nonoxynol-9
A spermicide that has been used to prevent pregnancy and protect against sexually transmitted infections.

spermicide
Chemical method of contraception, including creams, gels, foams, suppositories, and films, that works to reduce the survival of sperm in the vagina.

postcoital drip
A vaginal discharge (dripping) that occurs after sexual intercourse.

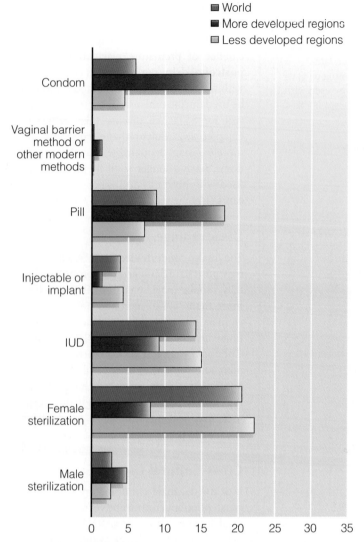

World
More developed regions
Less developed regions

Condom

Vaginal barrier
method or
other modern
methods

Pill

Injectable or
implant

IUD

Female
sterilization

Male
sterilization

0   5   10   15   20   25   30   35

FIGURE 13.7 Comparisons of worldwide contraceptive prevalence (by percentage) by level of economic development. SOURCE: http://www.un.org/esa/population/publications/contraceptive2009/contracept2009_wallchart_back.pdf.

▶▶ FEMALE Condoms

The first female condom, the Reality Vaginal Pouch (often referred to as "FC"), became available in the United States in 1993. It is made of polyurethane and is about 7 inches long with two flexible

---

REAL RESEARCH 13.3   College students view condoms primarily as a means of preventing pregnancy, but few describe disease prevention as a main motivation for their use (O'SULLIVAN ET AL., 2010).

---

polyurethane rings. The inner ring serves as an insertion device, and the outer ring stays on the outside of the vagina. In 2005, a newer female condom (the "FC2") made of a softer and more flexible material was available in the United States. A third female condom made of latex with an inner sponge to hold the condom in place (called the "Reddy") is pending FDA approval. Female condoms are more expensive than male condoms and cost approximately $3.50 each. Women in many countries in Africa have

---

been known to wash and reuse FCs because of the high cost, although they are not made to be used this way (Potter et al., 2003).

How They Work

A female condom is inserted into the vagina before penile penetration. The inner ring (or sponge, depending on which type of female condom used) is squeezed between the thumb and middle finger, making it long and thin, and then inserted into the vagina. Once this is done, an index finger inside the condom can push the inner ring/sponge up close to the cervix. The outer ring sits on the outside of the vulva (Figure 13.8). During intercourse, the penis is placed within the female condom, and care should be taken to make sure it does not slip between the condom and the vaginal wall. It is important that the vagina is well lubricated so that the female condom stays in place. Female and male condoms should never be used together, because they can adhere to each other and slip or break.

Effectiveness

Effectiveness rates for female condoms range from 79% to 95%.

Advantages

Like male condoms, female condoms can be discreetly carried in a purse, offer some STI protection, can be purchased without a prescription, reduce postcoital drip, can be used by those with latex allergies, can be used with oil-based lubricants, and have minimal adverse effects. Unlike male condoms, female condoms do not require a male erection to put on and will stay in place if a man loses his erection. Female condoms can also be used in the anus during anal sex. Finally, the external ring of the female condom may provide extra clitoral stimulation during vaginal intercourse, enhancing female sexual pleasure.

Disadvantages

Female condoms can be difficult to insert, uncomfortable to wear and expensive, and they may decrease sensations, and slip during vaginal intercourse (Kerrigan et al., 2000; Lie, 2000). One study

Over the years, public health experts have recommended using condoms that contain the spermicide nonoxynol-9 (N-9) to decrease the possibility of pregnancy. Although N-9 is an effective spermicide, several studies have raised concerns about its safety and protection effects for sexually transmitted infections (STIs). Frequent use of N-9 may increase HIV risk by creating rectal and vaginal ulceration. In addition to this, N-9 does not offer protection from gonorrhea, chlamydia, or HIV. In 2007, the U.S. Food and Drug Administration (FDA) released a statement requiring all over-the-counter spermicidal products that contained N-9 to include a warning that N-9 does not protect against STIs and HIV (U.S.

Food and Drug Administration, 2007). In addition, the revised labeling included the warning that spermicides can cause vaginal and anal irritation, which may increase STI transmission. The required label on vaginal contraceptives and spermicidal products now states:

For vaginal use only.

Sexually Transmitted Infection Alert: This product does not protect against HIV/AIDS or other STIs and may increase your risk of getting HIV from an infected partner.

Do not use if you or your partner has HIV/AIDS.

Stop using and seek medical attention if you develop burning, itching, a rash, or vaginal or anal irritation.

Concern over the use of N-9 has spurred development of new products, **microbicides**, which can reduce the risk for STIs. Ongoing trials are evaluating a variety of safer spermicides and/or microbicides (Baptista & Ramalho-Santos, 2009; Burke et al., 2010; Hughes et al., 2007; Ramjee et al., 2010; Saha et al., 2010). We discuss microbicides further in Chapter 15.

found that 57% of women and 30% of men reported difficulties with insertion, discomfort during sex, and/or excess lubrication with use (Kerrigan et al., 2000). Although some users reported that female condoms were "noisy" to use and uncomfortable because they hung outside the vagina during use, newer generation female condoms are made of more flexible materials, making them less "noisy." The addition of a stabilizing sponge in the newer "Reddy" female condoms has decreased slippage problems. Finally, some women may feel uncomfortable interrupting foreplay to put one in.

Cross-Cultural Use

Female condoms have not been popular in developing countries. Several issues may contribute to this, including the fact that they are expensive and difficult to insert. Many women in other cultures are not comfortable touching the vagina or inserting anything into it (in fact, tampon use is also much lower in countries outside the United States). However, there are signs that female condom use is increasing in some countries. For example, in Zimbabwe, although acceptance of the female condom was low when the female condom was first introduced in 1997, after a creative media campaign using billboards, television, and radio commercials about female condoms, use increased six-fold (Helmore, 2010). The media campaign helped increase knowledge levels and broke down the stigma associated with female condoms.

▶▶ CERVICAL BARRIERS:
Diaphragms and Cervical Caps

Cervical barriers include **diaphragms** (DIE-uh-fram) and **cervical caps.** These devices are inserted into the vagina before intercourse and fit over the cervix, creating a barrier so that sperm and ova can-

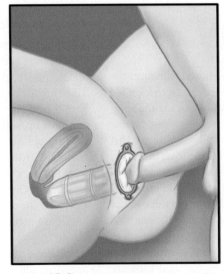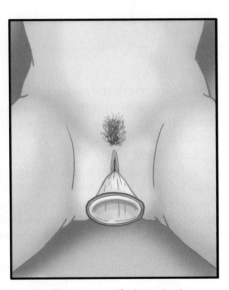

FIGURE **13.8** Female condoms are inserted into the vagina like a tampon. The inner ring is pushed up inside the vagina until it reaches the cervix, while the outer ring hangs about an inch outside of the vagina. Copyright © Cengage Learning 2013

not meet. We will discuss traditional diaphragms, Lea's Shield, and the FemCap. Although these methods work in similar ways, they are designed and function a bit differently from each other.

The diaphragm is a dome-shaped cup, made of either latex or silicone, with a flexible rim. It comes in several sizes and shapes, and must be fitted by a health care provider. Like latex condoms,

microbicide
Chemical that works by inhibiting sperm function; effective against HIV and other STIs, and not harmful to the vaginal or cervical cells.

cervical barrier
A plastic or rubber cover for the cervix that provides a contraceptive barrier to sperm.

diaphragm
A birth control device consisting of a latex dome on a flexible spring rim; used with spermicidal cream or jelly.

cervical cap
A birth control device similar to a diaphragm, but smaller.

PRNewsFoto/Population Services International/AP Images/AP Images

Debra Messing, an ambassador with Population Services International (PSI), visits a beauty salon outside of Zimbabwe. PSI trains hairdressers as peer educators to talk to their clients about female condoms and HIV prevention. The hairdressers have helped to stop the rise of HIV and AIDS.

ON YOUR MIND 13.2

Is it okay to borrow someone else's diaphragm if I can't find mine?

Absolutely not. The diaphragm prevents sperm from entering the uterus by adhering to the cervix through suction. A health care provider must measure the cervix and prescribe the right size diaphragm for each individual woman to get this suction. If you use someone else's diaphragm, it may be the wrong size and thus ineffective. Also, because of the risk for acquiring an STI, it is not a good idea to share diaphragms.

latex diaphragms should not be used with oil-based lubricants because these can damage the latex (see Table 13.3). In the United States, diaphragms range in cost from $15 to $75 and require spermicidal cream or jelly.

Lea's Shield is a silicone, one-size-fits-all diaphragm that works like a regular diaphragm. The biggest difference is that it has a one-way valve that allows the flow of cervical fluids and air. Although Lea's Shield is often available without a prescription around the world, it must be prescribed by a health care provider in the United States. In the near future, however, it may be available without a prescription.

FemCap, the only cervical cap available in the United States today, works like the other cervical barriers. Cervical caps are much smaller than diaphragms and are designed to sit more

snugly on the cervix. They are made of silicone and come in three sizes—small for women who have never been pregnant, medium for women who have been pregnant but have not had a vaginal delivery, and large for women who have had a vaginal delivery of a full-term baby.

Diaphragms and cervical caps cost approximately $60 to $75, a medical examination may cost anywhere from $50 to $200, and spermicidal cream or jelly costs about $8 to $10.

How They Work

Cervical barriers work by blocking the entrance to the uterus and deactivating sperm through the use of spermicidal cream or jelly. Before insertion, spermicidal cream or jelly should be placed inside the device and rubbed on the rim. They are folded and inserted into the vagina while a woman is standing with one leg propped up, squatting, or lying on her back (Figure 13.9). The device should be pushed downward toward the back of the vagina, while the front rim or lip is tucked under the pubic bone. After insertion, a woman must check to see that the device is covering her cervix. Once in place, a woman should not be able to feel the device; if she does, it is improperly inserted.

These methods can be inserted before intercourse but should be left in place for at least 8 hours after intercourse. Users of the Lea's Shield and FemCap can have repeated intercourse without applying additional spermicidal cream or jelly, although health care providers recommend diaphragm users insert additional spermicide into the vagina without removing the device. The diaphragm should not be left in place for longer than 24 hours, whereas Lea's Shield and the FemCap can be left in for up to 48 hours. After use, all the devices should be washed with soap and water and allowed to air-dry.

With proper care, these devices can be used for approximately 1 year, depending on usage. If a woman loses or gains more than 10 pounds or experiences a pregnancy (regardless of how the pregnancy was resolved-through birth, miscarriage, or **abortion**), the

Diaphragms come in a variety of different shapes and sizes and must be fitted by a health care practitioner.

© Kenzie Henke

Lea's Shield
Reusable silicone barrier vaginal contraceptive that contains a one-way valve.

FemCap
Reusable silicone barrier vaginal contraceptive that comes in three sizes.

abortion
Induced termination of a pregnancy before fetal viability.

contraceptive sponge
Polyurethane sponge impregnated with spermicide, inserted into the vagina for contraception.

diaphragm or FemCap must be refitted by her health care provider.

Effectiveness

Effectiveness rates for these devices range from 84% to 94%. Women who have not had children have higher effectiveness rates than women who have given birth.

Advantages

Cervical barriers can be discreetly carried in a purse, are immediately effective, do not affect spontaneity or hormonal levels, and allow couples to engage in intercourse multiple times. Research has also found that diaphragm use may reduce the risk for cervical dysplasia and cancer (Hatcher et al., 2007).

Disadvantages

Cervical barriers require a prescription, do not offer protection from STIs, may be difficult to insert and/or remove, require genital touching, increase postcoital drip, may shift during vaginal intercourse, cannot be used during menstruation, and may develop a foul odor if left in place too long. In addition, some women experience allergic reactions to the spermicidal cream or jelly.

Cross-Cultural Use

Cervical barriers are widely used in England, and in some countries—including Germany, Austria, Switzerland, and Canada—Lea's Shield has been available without a prescription since 1993 (Long, 2003). However, similar to cervical barriers, they are used infrequently in less-developed countries (see Figure 13.7). This is possibly related to a shortage of health care providers, limited availability of spermicidal cream or jelly, high cost, and required genital touching.

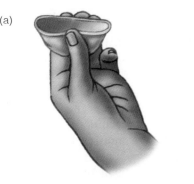
(a)

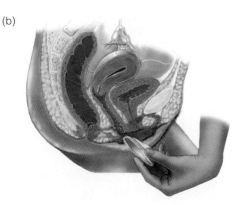
(b)

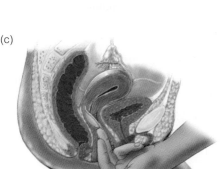
(c)

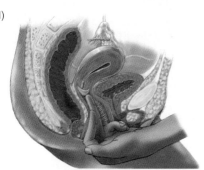
(d)

FIGURE **13.9** Insertion of diaphragm (and other cervical barriers): (a) after placing the spermicide, the diaphragm is folded in half, rim to rim and (b) inserted into the vagina (c) as far as it will go, (d) check to feel the cervix is covered by the diaphragm. Copyright © Cengage Learning 2013

▶▶ CONTRACEPTIVE Sponge

The Today **contraceptive sponge** was approved by the FDA in 1983; however, it was withdrawn from the market in 1995 because of stringent new government safety rules that had to do with the manufacturing plant. In late 2005, the sponge was reintroduced and is available without a prescription in the United States. The one-size-fits-all sponge is a combination of a cervical barrier and spermicide. A box of three sponges can cost approximately $16 to $20, depending on where it is purchased.

How It Works

A contraceptive sponge works in three ways: as a barrier, blocking the entrance to the uterus; absorbing sperm; and deactivat-

(a) The FemCap is a silicone cup shaped like a sailor's hat that fits securely over the cervix. (b) Lea's Shield is a silicone cup with a one-way valve and a loop for easier removal.

© Kenzie Henke (a)

© Kenzie Henke (b)

The contraceptive sponge is an FDA-approved contraceptive device that prevents sperm from entering the uterus. It is made of polyurethane foam. Before sex, the contraceptive sponge is inserted deep into the vagina and held in place by vaginal muscles. The strap is used to remove the sponge.

ing sperm. Before vaginal insertion, the sponge is moistened with water, which activates the spermicide. It is then folded in half and inserted deep into the vagina (Figure 13.10). Like the diaphragm and cervical cap, the sponge must be checked to make sure it is covering the cervix. Intercourse can take place immediately after insertion or at any time during the next 24 hours and can occur as many times as desired without adding additional spermicidal jelly or cream. However, the sponge must be left in place for 6 hours after intercourse. For removal, a cloth loop on the outside of the sponge is grasped to gently pull the sponge out of the vagina. Like the diaphragm, the sponge must be removed within 24 hours to reduce the risk for toxic shock syndrome.

Effectiveness

Effectiveness rates for the contraceptive sponge range from 84% to 91%. Women who have not had children have higher effectiveness rates than women who have given birth.

Advantages

Like cervical barriers, a contraceptive sponge can be discreetly carried in a purse, is immediately effective, does not affect spontaneity or hormonal levels, and allows couples to engage in intercourse multiple times during a 24-hour period. Unlike the cervical barriers, the contraceptive sponge can be purchased without a prescription.

Disadvantages

The contraceptive sponge does not offer protection from STIs, may be difficult to insert and/or remove, requires genital touching, increases postcoital drip, cannot be used during menstruation, may cause a foul odor if left in place too long, and may increase the risk for toxic shock syndrome and urinary tract infections (Hatcher et al., 2011). In addition, some women experience allergic reactions to the spermicidal cream or jelly.

Cross-Cultural Use

Contraceptive sponges have been fairly popular in European countries. In fact, women in France have used vaginal sponges dipped in various chemicals to avoid pregnancy for years. These sponges are washed and used over and over. This practice is not recommended, however, because of the risk for infection and toxic shock syndrome.

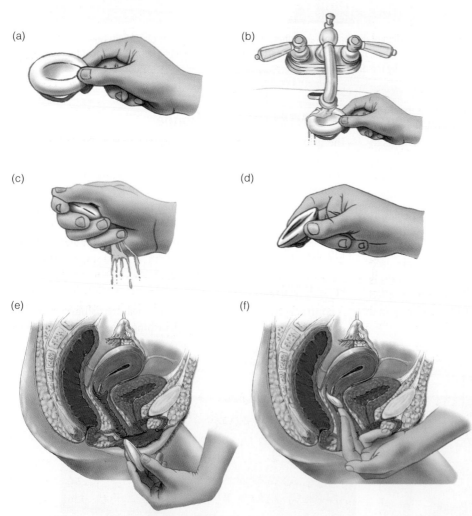

FIGURE **13.10** Insertion of a contraceptive sponge: (a) take it out of the packaging, (b) moisten with water, (c) wring out extra water, (d) fold in half, (e) insert the sponge into the vagina as far as it will go, (f) check to feel the cervix is covered by the sponge. Copyright © Cengage Learning 2013

1 Explain how barrier methods of contraception work, and identify four barrier contraceptive methods in order of their effectiveness rates.

2 How do male and female condoms work, and what are some of the advantages and disadvantages of these barrier methods?

3 Differentiate between the various cervical barriers. How do these methods work, and what are some of the advantages and disadvantages of these methods?

4 How does the contraceptive sponge work, and what are some of the advantages and disadvantages of this method?

▶ COMBINED HORMONE
Methods for Women

Combined hormone methods use a blend of hormones to suppress ovulation and thicken the cervical mucus to prevent sperm from joining the ovum. We will discuss birth control pills, vaginal rings, and patches. Combined hormone methods have been found to be effective, safe, reversible, and acceptable to most women. However, for protection against STIs, condoms must also be used.

▶▶ BIRTH CONTROL Pills

Margaret Sanger was the first to envision **oral contraceptives** (the birth control pill, or simply "the pill"). Many researchers had been working with chemical methods to inhibit pregnancy in animals, but they were reluctant to try these methods on humans because they feared that increasing hormones could cause cancer. The complexity of a woman's body chemistry and the expense involved in developing the pill inhibited its progress. The birth control pill was approved as a contraceptive method in the United States in 1960.

At first, the pill was much stronger than it needed to be. In the search for the most effective contraception, researchers believed that more estrogen was more effective. Today's birth control pills have less than half the dose of estrogen the first pills had. After more than 50 years on the market, oral contraceptives still remain the most popular contraceptive method not only in the United

"It would probably be a bit intimidating going into a pharmacy to buy it."
—MORNING AFTER PILL

Video supplied by BBC Motion Gallery

View in Video
To watch the entire interview, go to Psychology CourseMate at **login.cengagebrain.com**.

States, but around the world as well (Frost et al., 2008; Hatcher et al., 2011).

Combination birth control pills, which contain synthetic estrogen and progestin (a type of progesterone), are the most commonly used contraceptive method in the United States. They require a prescription and a medical office visit, and typically cost between $30 and $60 per month. Typical birth control pills have been designed to mimic an average menstrual cycle, which is why a woman takes them for 21 days and then has 1 week off,

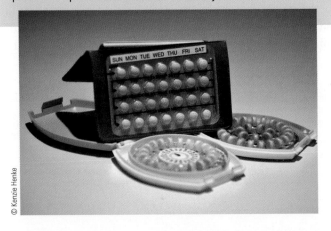

Many types of birth control pills are available, and a health care provider can prescribe the one that's best for you.

© Kenzie Henke

REAL RESEARCH 13.4 Some brands of birth control pills may decrease sexual desire and vaginal lubrication, and these effects may last after a woman has stopped taking the pill (GRAHAM ET AL., 2007; HATCHER ET AL., 2011). However, if a woman is less sensitive to hormonal changes, she may not notice these adverse effects. If she does, changing birth control pill brands may restore sexual desire.

---

oral contraceptive
The "pill"; a preparation of synthetic female hormones that blocks ovulation.

combination birth control pill
An oral contraceptive that contains synthetic estrogen and progesterone.

table 13.4 ■ What To Do If You Forget

Many women who take birth control pills forget to take one at some time. As we've discussed throughout this chapter, the pill is most effective if taken every day at approximately the same time. If you miss a pill, it's a good idea to talk to your health care provider about what would be best to do. In many cases, it depends on several factors, including what kind of pill you are on, the dosage of the pill, how many pills you missed, and how soon into the pack you missed them. A 7-day backup method or emergency contraception may be needed. The following information is for women using a 21- or 28-day combination birth control pill.

Number of Pills Missed	When Pills Were Missed	What to Do	Use a Back-up Method?
First 1–2 pills	Beginning of pack	Take a pill as soon as you remember. Take the next pill at usual time.	Yes
1–2 pills	Days 3–21	Take the pill as soon as you remember. Take the next pill at the usual time.	No
3 or more pills	First 2 weeks	Take the pill as soon as you remember. Take the next pill at the usual time.	Yes
3 or more pills	Third week	Do not finish pack. Start new pack.	Yes

SOURCE: Planned Parenthood Federation of America. (2007). What to do if you forget to take the pill. Retrieved June 5, 2011 from, http://www.plannedparenthood.org/health-topics/birth-control/if-forget-take-pill-19269.htm.

when she usually starts her period (these pills are often referred to as 21/7 pills). Originally, this 3-week-on/1-week-off regimen was developed to convince women that the pill was "natural," which pill makers believed would make the product more acceptable to potential users and reassure them that they were not pregnant every month (Clarke & Miller, 2001; Thomas & Ellertson, 2000). As we discussed in Chapter 5, the bleeding that women experience while on the pill is medically induced and has no physiological benefit.

Extended-cycle birth control pills became available in 2003 with the FDA approval of Seasonale, which uses a continuous 84-day active pill with a 7-day placebo pill (an 84/7 pill). Seasonale enabled women to have only four periods per year. In 2006, Seasonique, a similar extended-cycle pill, was approved by the FDA. The difference between Seasonale and Seasonique is in the placebo pills—although they are inactive in Seasonale, Seasonique placebo pills contain a low dose of estrogen that has been found to cause less spotting during the active pills. Another continuous birth control pill that completely stops menstrual periods, Lybrel, was approved by the FDA in 2007. Lybrel contains lower levels of estrogen than other pills but is taken daily for 365 days a year.

Continuous-use birth control pills are not new. In fact, before FDA approval of these methods, some health care providers were known to "bicycle" birth control pills (back-to-back use of two packs of active pills with placebo pills at the end of the second pack) or "tricycle" (back-to-back-back use of three packs of active pills with placebo pills at the end of the third pack; Hatcher et al., 2011). In addition, some health care providers have used short-term, continuous-use birth control pills for scheduling convenience (i.e., to eliminate the chance of having a period during an athletic event, vacation, or honeymoon; Hatcher et al., 2011). Birth control pills are also prescribed for noncontraceptive reasons, such as heavy or dysfunctional menstrual bleeding, irregular periods, recurrent ovarian cysts, polycystic ovary syndrome, or acne (see Chapter 5; Hatcher et al., 2011).

Today, more than 70 brands of birth control pills are on the market in the United States. They vary with the amount of estrogen (low, regular, high, or varied levels) and the type of progestin (there are eight different types of progestin hormones). Recent studies have found that one type of progestin, *drospirenone*, may increase the risk for cardiovascular problems (Jick & Hernandez, 2011; Reid, 2010; Sehovic & Smith, 2010; Shapiro & Dinger, 2010). It is important to talk to a health care provider to determine which pills are right for you.

How They Work

The hormones estrogen, progesterone, luteinizing hormone (LH), and follicle-stimulating hormone (FSH) fluctuate during a woman's menstrual cycle. These fluctuations control the maturation of an ovum, ovulation, the development of the endometrium, and menstruation. The synthetic hormones replace a woman's own natural hormones but in different amounts. The increase in estrogen and progesterone prevent the pituitary gland from sending hormones to cause the ovaries to begin maturation of an ovum. Hormone levels while taking the pill are similar to when a woman is pregnant, and this is what interferes with ovulation. Birth control pills also work by thickening the cervical mucus (which inhibits the mobility of sperm) and by reducing the build-up of the endometrium.

Combination birth control pills can either be **monophasic, biphasic,** or **triphasic** (try-FAY-sic). Monophasic pills contain the same amount of hormones in each pill, whereas biphasic and tri-

monophasic pill
A type of oral contraceptive that contains one level of hormones in all the active pills.

biphasic pill
A type of oral contraceptive that contains two different doses of hormones in the active pills.

triphasic pill
A type of oral contraceptive that contains three different doses of hormones in the active pills.

breakthrough bleeding
Slight blood loss from the uterus that may occur when a woman is taking oral contraceptives.

start day
The actual day that the first pill is taken in a pack of oral contraceptives.

placebo pills
In a pack of 28-day oral contraceptives, the seven pills at the end; these pills are sugar pills and do not contain any hormones; they are used to help a woman remember to take a pill every day.

phasic pills vary the hormonal amount. Biphasic pills change the level of hormones once during the menstrual cycle, whereas triphasic pills contain three sets of pills for each week during the cycle. Each week, the hormonal dosage is increased, rather than keeping the hormonal level consistent, as with monophasic pills. **Breakthrough bleeding** is more common in triphasic pills because of the fluctuating hormone levels.

Traditionally, birth control pills have been used on a monthly cycling plan that involved either a 21- or 28-day regimen and started on the first or fifth day of menstruation or on the first Sunday after menstruation. **Start days** vary depending on the pill manufacturer. The majority of manufacturers recommend a Sunday start day, which enables a woman to avoid menstruating during a weekend. Each pill must be taken every day at approximately the same time. This is important because they work by maintaining a certain hormonal level in the bloodstream. If this level drops, ovulation may occur (see the accompanying Table 13.4 for more information).

In most 28-day birth control pill packs, the last seven pills are **placebo pills.** The placebo pills do not contain hormones, and because of this, a woman usually starts menstruating while taking them. In fact, some low-dose pill brands extended usage to 24 days with a reduced 2- or 4-day placebo pill regimen (a 24/2 or 24/4 pill; Hatcher et al., 2011). Women on these extended cycle regimens report higher levels of satisfaction than women on traditional 21/7 regimens (Caruso et al., 2011; Cremer et al., 2010; Davis et al., 2010; Dinger et al., 2011). Women who take birth control pills usually have lighter menstrual periods and decreased cramping because the pills decrease the buildup of the endometrium. Menstrual discomfort, such as cramping, is also reduced.

Before starting on birth control pills, a woman must have a full medical examination. Women with a history of circulatory problems, strokes, heart disease, breast or uterine cancer, hypertension, diabetes, and undiagnosed vaginal bleeding are generally advised not to take oral contraceptives (Hatcher et al., 2011). Although migraine headaches have typically been a reason for not using birth control pills, some women may experience fewer migraines while taking birth control pills, especially if used continuously without placebo pills (Hatcher et al., 2011). If a woman can use birth control pills, health care providers usually begin by prescribing a low-dose estrogen pill, and they increase the dosage if breakthrough bleeding or other symptoms occur.

There are several potential adverse effects to the use of birth control pills. Because the hormones in birth control pills are similar to those during pregnancy, many women experience signs of pregnancy. These may include nausea, increase in breast size, breast tenderness, water retention, increased appetite, fatigue, and high blood pressure (Hatcher et al., 2011; see Chapter 12). Symptoms usually disappear within a couple of months, after a woman's body becomes used to the hormonal levels. Other possible adverse effects include migraines, weight gain, depression, and decreases in sexual desire and bone density (Hatcher et al., 2011; Pitts & Emans, 2008). Possible serious adverse effects include blood clots, strokes, or heart attacks.

If a woman taking the pill experiences abdominal pain, chest pain, severe headaches, vision or eye problems, and severe leg or calf pain, she should contact her health care provider immediately. In addition, a woman who takes birth control pills should always inform her health care provider of her oral contraceptive use, especially if she is prescribed other medications or undergoes any type of surgery. Certain drugs may have negative interactions with oral contraceptives (see the accompanying Sex in Real Life feature). Women are advised not to smoke cigarettes while taking birth control pills, because smoking may increase the risk for cardiovascular disease (Bounhoure et al., 2008; Hatcher et al., 2011; Raval et al., 2011).

Finally, as we discussed in Chapter 5, there has been a very vocal debate in recent years about the relationship between oral contraceptive use and cancer. Although research has found that birth control pill use offers possible protection from breast and cervical cancers (Althuis et al., 2003; Deligeoroglou et al., 2003; Franceschi, 2005; Gaffield et al., 2009; Hatcher et al., 2007; Marchbanks et al., 2002; Moreno et al., 2002; Vessey et al., 2010), the research on other cancers has been less clear-cut. According to some studies, birth control pill use *increases* the risks for endometrial and ovarian cancers (Burkman et al., 2004; Emons et al., 2000; Greer et al., 2005; Modan et al., 2001; Schildkraut et al., 2002); however, more recent studies have found that use *decreases* the risks (Grimbizis & Tarlatzis, 2010; Ness et al., 2011; Schindler, 2010; Vessey et al., 2010). In fact, recent studies have found that the use of birth control pills may provide a significant protective effect from both ovarian and endometrial cancer, and protection may increase the longer birth control pills are taken (Cibula et al., 2010; Grimbizis & Tarlatzis, 2010; Mueck et al., 2010; Schindler, 2010). The risk for ovarian cancer decreased 20% for each 5 years of birth control use (Cibula et al., 2010). Experts believe that risks for cancer were higher in women who took oral contraceptives before 1975 because hormonal levels were much higher than the oral contraceptives available today (Gaffield et al., 2009). Women who have used oral contraceptives have a significantly lower rate of death from all cancers, compared with nonusers (Geraghty, 2009; Hannaford et al., 2010).

> Before starting on birth control pills, **a woman must have a full medical examination.**

ON YOUR MIND 13.3

I usually take my birth control pill at 7:00 a.m. each morning. When we switch to daylight savings time, what should I do? Should I continue to take my pill at 7:00 a.m. (the normal time I take it), or should I take it at 8:00 a.m. (what would have been 7:00 a.m.) now?

It is important to take birth control pills at about the same time each day. Making sure you pick a time that works for you and allows you to regularly remember is the most important thing. Typically, most pills have about a 1- to 2-hour window in which effectiveness is not compromised. Although an hour in each direction probably wouldn't matter, it's probably better to take it 1 hour earlier than later (especially if you are taking a low-dose pill). So, take the pill at your normal time when the clock springs forward (and you'll probably be fine taking it at the same time in the fall when the time changes back, but check with your health care provider to be sure).

Many over-the-counter (nonprescription) drugs, prescription medications, and herbal supplements may reduce the effectiveness of the pill. Birth control pills may also increase or decrease another drug's effectiveness. When you take medications, you should always let your health care provider know that you are taking birth control pills.

Drugs that interact with oral contraceptives include the following:

Drug	Effect of Birth Control Pills on Drug
Acetaminophen (Tylenol)	Decreases effect of pain relief
Alcohol (beer, wine, mixed drinks, etc.)	Increases effect of alcohol
Anticoagulants	Decreases anticoagulant effect (aspirin may be less effective when used with oral contraceptives)
Antibiotics (amoxicillin, tetracycline, ampicillin)	May decrease effectiveness of oral contraceptives
Antidepressants (Prozac, Paxil)	Increases blood levels of antidepressant
Antifungal medications (Grisactin)	Can cause breakthrough bleeding and spotting
Barbiturates (Seconal, Nembutal)	Decreases effectiveness of oral contraceptives
Vitamin C	May increase estrogen side effects in daily doses of 1,000 mg or more
St. John's wort (Hypericum)	Decreases effectiveness of oral contraceptives

SOURCE: Hatcher et al. (2007).

Effectiveness

Effectiveness rates for oral contraceptives range from 92% to 99.7% (Hatcher et al., 2011). However, women who are significantly overweight may experience lower effectiveness rates using oral contraceptives (Brunner-Huber & Toth, 2007; Gardner, 2004; Hatcher et al., 2011).

Advantages

Oral contraceptives offer one of the highest effectiveness rates; do not interfere with spontaneity; increase menstrual regularity; and reduce the flow of menstruation, menstrual cramps, premenstrual syndrome, and facial acne (Hatcher et al., 2011). They also provide important degrees of protection against ovarian cysts, uterine and breast fibroids, certain cancers, and **pelvic inflammatory disease.** They may increase sexual enjoyment because fear of pregnancy is reduced, and they have rapid reversibility (the majority of women who stop taking the pill return to ovulation within 2 weeks; Hatcher et al., 2011).

REAL RESEARCH 13.5 Studies have found that the majority of adverse effects from birth control pill use, such as headaches, breast tenderness, or bloating, occur during the week when women take their placebo pills and not when they are taking their hormone pills (HATCHER ET AL., 2007; SULAK ET AL., 2000). This is one of the reasons pharmaceutical companies developed continuous-use birth control pills that reduce or eliminate menstrual periods.

The NuvaRing is inserted deep into the vagina; moisture and heat cause it to time release hormones that inhibit ovulation.

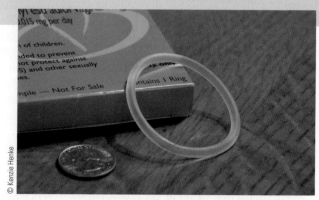

© Kenzie Henke

Disadvantages

Oral contraception require a prescription, provide no protection from STIs, and have several potential adverse effects, including nausea, increase in breast size, headaches, and decreased sexual desire. In addition, oral contraceptives can be expensive, and a woman must remember to take them every day.

Cross-Cultural Use

Worldwide, birth control pills are the third most popular contraceptive method (behind female sterilization and IUDs), with 9% of women relying on this method ("World Contraceptive Use 2009," 2009). However, usage is higher in more developed countries (see Figure 13.7). Contraceptive pill use is high in Europe but lower in Asian countries. For example, 60% of women use birth control pills in France (Schuberg, 2009), whereas approximately 1% of women in Japan use them (Hayashi, 2004). By comparison, approximately 31% of women in the United States use birth control pills (Alan Guttmacher Institute, 2008a).

Birth control pill use is high in Latin America, Belgium, France, Germany, Morocco, the Netherlands, Portugal, and Zimbabwe ("World Contraceptive Use 2009," 2009). In some countries, birth control pills are available without a prescription (Arroba, 2004; Ng & Ma, 2004).

Fears about safety and reliability issues in countries such as Japan and Russia reduce birth control pill use (Hayashi, 2004; Kon, 2004). Birth control pills were not approved for use in Japan until 1999. However, they have remained unpopular because of safety concerns, negative side effects, required daily pill taking, countrywide conservatism, and lack of advertising (Hayashi, 2004).

▶▶ HORMONAL Ring

NuvaRing is a hormonal method of birth control that was approved by the FDA in 2001. It is a one-size-fits-all plastic ring that is inserted into the vagina once a month and releases a constant dose of estrogen and progestin. The amount of hormones released into the bloodstream with the NuvaRing is lower than in both oral contraceptives and the patch (we will talk more about the patch later in this chapter; Hatcher et al., 2011; van den Heuvel et al., 2005). The hormonal ring costs approximately $15 to $70 per month to use.

How It Works

Like birth control pills, NuvaRing works chiefly by inhibiting ovulation, but it is also likely to increase cervical mucus and changes the uterine lining (Hatcher et al., 2007). The ring is inserted deep inside the vagina, where the vaginal muscles hold it in place, and moisture and body heat activate the release of hormones. Each ring is left in place for 3 weeks and then taken out for 1 week, during which a woman typically has her period. The used ring is disposed of and a new ring is put back in after the week break.

Although rare, the NuvaRing may fall out of the vagina during a bowel movement, tampon use, or vaginal intercourse. If this happens and the ring has been out less than 3 hours, it should be washed and immediately be reinserted. If the ring falls out for more than 3 hours, a backup method of contraception should be used, because contraceptive effectiveness may be reduced.

Researchers continue to evaluate whether the NuvaRing can be used as continuous-use method, although it is not approved for this type of use at present (Hatcher et al., 2011; Mulders & Dieben, 2001). A longer-use vaginal ring that is continuously inserted after being removed for 1 week every month (unlike the shorter-use one that is disposed of after the 1-week break) is currently available outside the United States (Hatcher et al., 2011).

Effectiveness

Effectiveness rates for the NuvaRing range from 92% to 99.7% (Hatcher et al., 2011). Effectiveness rates may be lower when other medications are taken, when the unopened package is exposed to high temperatures or direct sunlight, or when the ring is left in the vagina for more than 3 weeks.

Advantages

The NuvaRing is highly effective, does not interfere with spontaneity, increases menstrual regularity, and reduces the flow of menstruation, menstrual cramps, and premenstrual syndrome (Hatcher et al., 2011). It is easy to use and provides lower levels of hormones than some of the other combined hormone methods. In addition, NuvaRing may also offer some protection from pelvic inflammatory disease and various cancers.

Disadvantages

A prescription is necessary to use NuvaRing, and it offers no protection against STIs. In addition, it requires genital touching and may cause a variety of adverse effects, including breakthrough bleeding, weight gain or loss, breast tenderness, nausea, mood changes, headaches, decreased sexual desire, increased vaginal irritation and discharge, and a risk for toxic shock syndrome (Hatcher et al., 2011; Lopez et al., 2008). It may also take up to 1 to 2 months for a woman's period to return after she stops using the vaginal ring, and periods may not be regular for up to 6 months.

Cross-Cultural Use

NuvaRing was first approved in the Netherlands in 2001 and has since been approved by many other European countries. Australia approved the NuvaRing in 2007, which brought the total number of countries using NuvaRing to 32 ("NuvaRing Now Available for Australian Women," 2007). In some countries, usage levels may be low because the NuvaRing requires genital touching. Even so, cross-cultural research has found that the NuvaRing is highly effective, and users report high levels of satisfaction with this method (Brucker et al., 2008; Bruni et al., 2008; Merki-Feld & Hund, 2007; Novák et al., 2003).

---

pelvic inflammatory disease
Widespread infection of the female pelvic organs.

NuvaRing
A small plastic contraceptive ring that is inserted into the vagina once a month and releases a constant dose of estrogen and progestin.

▶▶ HORMONAL Patch

The **Ortho Evra patch** is a hormonal method of birth control that was approved by the FDA in 2001. It is a thin, peach-colored patch that sticks to the skin and time-releases hormones into the bloodstream. The hormonal patch costs approximately $15 to $75 per month to use.

How It Works

Like other hormonal methods, the Ortho Evra patch uses synthetic estrogen and progestin to inhibit ovulation, increase cervical mucus, and render the uterus inhospitable to implantation. The patch is placed on the buttock, stomach, upper arm, or torso (excluding the breast area) once a week for 3 weeks, followed by a patch-free week (break week), which usually causes a woman to have her period. A woman can maintain an active lifestyle with the patch in place—she can swim, shower, use saunas, and exercise without the patch falling off (Burkman, 2002; Zacur et al., 2002).

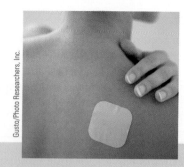

The Ortho Evra contraceptive patch can be placed on the upper outer arm, abdomen, buttock, or back. It should not be placed on the breasts, on cut or irritated skin, or in the same location as the last patch.

REAL RESEARCH 13.6 A study on the knowledge and beliefs about contraception in Latina women found that less than 50% of Latinas perceived birth control pills to be safe, and they had high levels of uncertainty and negative beliefs about the patch, IUDs, and hormonal injectables (VENKAT ET AL., 2008). Compared with other ethnic groups, Latina women are more likely to overrate the risks associated with contraceptive use.

Effectiveness

Effectiveness rates for the Ortho Evra patch range from 92% to 99.7% (Hatcher et al., 2011). It may be less effective in women who are significantly overweight (Hatcher et al., 2011; Zieman et al., 2002), and as with other hormonal methods, certain medications can decrease effectiveness.

Advantages

The Ortho Evra patch is highly effective, does not interfere with spontaneity, increases menstrual regularity, and reduces menstrual flow, menstrual cramps, and premenstrual syndrome (Hatcher et al., 2011). Unlike other hormonal methods, the patch has a more than 90% perfect dosing level because it is applied directly to the skin (Burkman, 2002).

Disadvantages

The Ortho Evra patch has been found to expose women to higher levels of estrogen than typical birth control pills (Hitti, 2008; U.S. Food and Drug Administration, 2008), offers no protection from STIs, and may cause a variety of adverse effects, including breakthrough bleeding, breast tenderness, nausea, mood changes, changes in sexual desire, skin reactions, or headaches (Hatcher et al., 2011). Users of the hormonal patch may also be more at risk for the development of blood clots (Hitti, 2008; U.S. Food and Drug Administration, 2008). Beginning in 2005, lawsuits were filed against the patch's manufacturer, Ortho McNeil, claiming the device caused strokes and blood clots. In 2008, the FDA approved revised labeling to include information about these risks (U.S. Food and Drug Administration, 2008). Any woman with a history of or risk for blood clots should fully discuss her medical history with health care providers before using the Ortho Evra patch. Finally, because the patch is worn on the skin, it is nearly impossible to conceal, and it can collect fuzz and lint from the user's clothing. Because it is peach-colored, it is also readily apparent on darker skin.

Cross-Cultural Use

We do not know a lot about Ortho Evra's use outside the United States because it is fairly new. However, early estimates have found that approximately 2 million women worldwide use the contraceptive patch (Bestic, 2005).

◀ review QUESTIONS

1 Explain how combination hormonal methods of contraception work.

2 Identify three combined hormonal contraceptive methods in order of their effectiveness rates.

3 What are extended-cycle birth control pills? How do they work?

4 How have health care providers been using regular birth control pills for extended-cycle use?

5 Identify the advantages and disadvantages of combined-hormonal contraceptive methods.

6 What do we know about the cross-cultural usage of combined-hormone contraceptive methods?

PROGESTIN-ONLY HORMONE Methods for Women

Progestin-only birth control methods are hormonal methods that do not contain estrogen. The methods can be used by women who cannot take estrogen or by women who are breast-feeding, because the hormones do not affect the production of breast milk. Progestin-only birth control works by changing a woman's menstrual cycle, which may result in changes in menstrual flow and frequency of periods, as well as an increase in breakthrough bleeding. Over time, many users of progestin-only methods report having no periods at all.

▶▶ PROGESTIN-ONLY Pills

Progestin-only pills (**minipills**) are similar to combination birth control pills, except they contain a progestin hormone and no estrogen. Minipills are taken every day with no hormone-free days (Hatcher et al., 2011).

How They Work

Similar to combination birth control pills, minipills work by inhibiting ovulation, thickening cervical mucus, and decreasing Fallopian tube cilia movement and the buildup of the endometrial lining.

Effectiveness

Effectiveness rates for minipills range from 92% to 99.7% (Hatcher et al., 2011).

Advantages

Minipills contain a lower overall hormone level than combination birth control pills and can be safely used by almost all women, including those who are older than 35, are overweight, smoke, have high blood pressure, have a history of blood clots, or women who are breast-feeding (Hatcher et al., 2011). They also reduce menstrual symptoms and may eliminate periods altogether. Once discontinued, fertility is quickly restored.

Disadvantages

Because minipills contain lower hormone levels, they require obsessive regularity in pill taking (Hatcher et al., 2011). They offer no protection from STIs and may cause several adverse effects, including menstrual cycle disturbances (such as breakthrough bleeding or spotting), headaches, nausea, weight gain or loss, breast tenderness,

decreased sexual desire, and an increased risk for ovarian cysts (Hatcher et al., 2011). Because progestin affects cilia movement in the Fallopian tubes, women who get pregnant while taking minipills have a higher rate of ectopic pregnancy compared with women taking combination birth control pills (see Chapter 12 for more information about ectopic pregnancy). Finally, many pharmacies do not stock minipills, so they may be more difficult to find.

▶▶ SUBDERMAL Implants

Subdermal contraceptive implants involve surgically inserting under the skin a matchstick-sized rod that time-releases progestin. **Norplant** was the first such method introduced in the United States in 1990. However, because of multiple lawsuits and court battles, Norplant was withdrawn from the U.S. market in 2002. As of 2010, the only implant available in the United States is a system called Implanon, which was approved by the FDA in 2006. Several other versions are currently in development both within and outside the United States. The cost of Implanon and the insertion ranges from $400 to $800. Removal ranges from $75 to $150.

How They Work

A subdermal contraceptive implant is inserted during the first 5 days of a woman's menstrual cycle (to ensure she is not pregnant). The implant time-releases progestin, and like other hormonal methods, it works by suppressing ovulation, thickening cervical mucus, and changing the endometrial lining. The Implanon implant can be left in place for 3 years. Once removed, ovulation usually returns within approximately 6 weeks (Makarainen et al., 1998).

Effectiveness

Effectiveness rates for Implanon are approximately 99%. Like other hormonal methods, effectiveness rates may be lower in women who are significantly overweight.

Advantages

Implanon is a highly effective, long-lasting, easily reversible contraceptive method with a rapid onset of protection (Hatcher et al., 2007). It can decrease menstrual flow, cramping, and risk for endometrial cancer, and can be used by women who are unable to take estrogen. In addition, Implanon can be left in place for up to 3 years and can be removed anytime before this.

Disadvantages

Implanon requires a prescription and medical office visit, which may be expensive depending on where it is done. Possible adverse

---

Ortho Evra patch
A thin, peach-colored patch that sticks to the skin and time-releases synthetic estrogen and progestin into the bloodstream to inhibit ovulation, increase cervical mucus, and render the uterus inhospitable; also referred to as the "patch."

progestin-only birth control method
Contraceptive hormonal method that does not contain estrogen and works by changing a woman's menstrual cycle.

minipills
A type of birth control pill that contains only synthetic progesterone and no estrogen.

subdermal contraceptive implant
Contraceptive implant that time-releases a constant dose of progestin to inhibit ovulation.

Norplant
A hormonal method of birth control using doses that are implanted in a woman's arm and that can remain in place for up to 5 years.

effects include irregular or heavy bleeding, especially within the first 6 to 12 months of usage. Other possible adverse effects include headaches, dizziness, nausea, weight gain, development of ovarian cysts, decreases in sexual desire, vaginal dryness, arm pain, and bleeding from the injection site (Hatcher et al., 2011). Removal may be difficult and generally takes longer than insertion. Researchers are working on a system that involves self-dissolving cylinders so that removal is unnecessary.

Cross-Cultural

Subdermal implants are more commonly used in less-developed regions of the world (see Figure 13.7). They are approved in more than 60 countries and have been used by more than 11 million women worldwide (Hatcher et al., 2011; Meirik et al., 2003). Prior to U.S. FDA approval, Norplant and Implanon had been used throughout Europe, Latin America, Australia, and Asia.

In the United Kingdom, health care providers have switched from Implanon to a new contraceptive implant, Nexplanon (Mansour, 2010; Rowlands et al., 2010). Nexplanon is easier to insert than Implanon, is good for 3 years, and has a rapid return to fertility after use.

▶▶ HORMONAL Injectables

The most commonly used hormonal injectable is depo-medroxyprogesterone acetate (DMPA, or **Depo-Provera;** DEP-poe PRO-vair-uh), which was approved by the FDA for contraceptive use in 2004 (Hatcher et al., 2007). Depo-Provera is injected once every 3 months, and each injection costs anywhere from $35 to $70 (an initial examination/visit may cost anywhere from $35 to $250, although subsequent visits will be less).

How It Works

Depo-Provera is a progestin injected into the muscle of a woman's arm or buttock. It begins working within 24 hours. Like other hormonal methods, it works by suppressing ovulation, thickening cervical mucus, and changing the endometrial lining.

Effectiveness

Effectiveness rates for Depo-Provera range from 97% to 99.7% (Hatcher et al., 2011).

Advantages

Depo-Provera is highly effective; does not interfere with spontaneity; reduces menstrual flow, cramping, and premenstrual syndrome; does not contain estrogen; lasts for 3 months; is only moderately expensive; and is reversible (Hatcher et al., 2011). In addition, users need only four shots per year.

Disadvantages

Women who use Depo-Provera must schedule office visits every 3 months for their injections, and they experience a range of adverse effects, including irregular bleeding and spotting, fatigue, dizzy spells, weakness, headaches or migraines, weight gain (it is estimated that a woman will gain an average of 5.4 pounds in the first year of Depo use), and a decrease in bone density (Hatcher et al., 2011; Pitts & Emans, 2008). More recent studies have found that bone loss is reversible after a woman stops using Depo-Provera (Kaunitz et al., 2008; Pitts & Emans, 2008). In addition, it may take a couple months to restore fertility after the last injection (Hatcher et al., 2011; Kaunitz, 2002).

Cross-Cultural Use

Like implants, injectable contraception is more commonly used in less-developed countries (see Figure 13.7). In some regions, such as Eastern and Southern Africa, injectable contraception is the most popular method, accounting for almost half of all contraceptive use. Depo-Provera has been approved for use in more than 80 countries, including Botswana, Denmark, Finland, Great Britain, France, Sweden, Mexico, Norway, Germany, New Zealand, South Africa, and Belgium (Francoeur & Noonan, 2004; Hatcher et al., 2004). In addition, another combination injectable, Lunelle, is popular cross-culturally but is not available within the United States.

> **Depo-Provera**
> Depo-medroxyprogesterone, an injectable contraceptive that prevents ovulation and thickens cervical mucus.

◀ review QUESTIONS

1 Explain how minipills differ from combined hormone birth control pills.

2 Explain how minipills, subdermal implants, and hormonal injectables work to prevent pregnancy.

3 Identify the advantages and disadvantages of each of the progestin-only hormone methods.

4 What do we know about the cross-cultural usage of progestin-only hormone methods?

▶ CHEMICAL METHODS for Women

Spermicides come in a variety of forms, including creams, suppositories, gels, foams, foaming tablets, capsules, and films. Nonoxynol-9 is a spermicide that has been used for many years. It is available over the counter in many forms (creams, gels, suppositories, film, and condoms with spermicide) and can be used alone or in conjunction with another contraceptive method. However, as you saw from the earlier Sex in Real Life feature, there has been some controversy surrounding the use of nonoxynol-9. Today in the United States, the cost for most spermicides ranges from $5 to $10. They are generally less expensive in clinics.

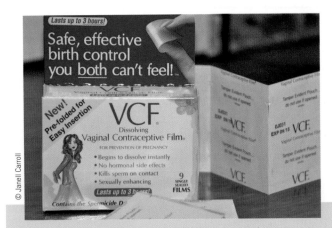

Vaginal contraceptive film is a paper-thin translucent film that dissolves in the vagina and releases spermicide.

How They Work

Spermicides contain two components: One is an inert base such as jelly, cream, foam, or film that holds the spermicide close to the cervix; the second is the spermicide itself. Foam, jelly, cream, and film are usually inserted into the vagina with either an applicator or a finger. **Vaginal contraceptive film** contains nonoxynol-9 and comes in a variety of package sizes. The film is wrapped around the index finger and inserted into the vagina.

Suppositories are inserted in the vagina 10 to 30 minutes before intercourse to allow time for the outer covering to melt. It is important to read manufacturer's directions for spermicide use carefully. Douching and tampon use should be avoided for 6 to 8 hours after the use of spermicides because they interfere with effectiveness rates.

Effectiveness

Effectiveness rates for spermicides range from 71% to 82%. However, effectiveness depends on the type of spermicide and how consistently it is used. Overall, foam is more effective than jelly, cream, film, or suppositories.

Advantages

Spermicides do not require a prescription and can be easily purchased in drug stores, can be discreetly carried in a pocket or purse, do not interfere with a woman's hormones, can be inserted during foreplay, provide lubrication during intercourse, have minimal adverse effects, and can be used by a woman who is breast-feeding.

Disadvantages

Spermicides must be used each time a couple engages in vaginal intercourse, which may be expensive depending on frequency of intercourse. In addition, there is an increase in postcoital drip and some couples may be allergic or have adverse reactions. Spermicides often have an unpleasant taste, and they may cause vaginal skin irritations or an increase in urinary tract infections (Hatcher et al., 2011).

Cross-Cultural Use

Spermicides are widely used in some countries, including Argentina, Australia, Colombia, Costa Rica, Cuba, and many European and Scandinavian countries (Francoeur & Noonan, 2004). However, in many other countries, including Botswana, Brazil, Canada, China, Hong Kong, Japan, Kenya, and Puerto Rico, spermicides are not widely used, probably because of the relatively high cost or required genital touching.

vaginal contraceptive film
Spermicidal contraceptive film that is placed in the vagina.

◀ review QUESTIONS

1 Identify the various forms of spermicidal contraception.

2 What are some of the risks and controversies surrounding the use of nonoxynol-9 spermicide?

3 Explain how spermicides work and discuss effectiveness rates.

4 Identify the advantages and disadvantages of spermicidal contraceptive use.

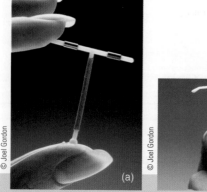
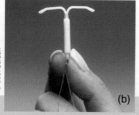

(a) The ParaGard is a T-shaped intrauterine device (IUD) made of flexible plastic; it contains copper and can be left in place for up to 12 years. (b) The Mirena is a T-shaped IUD made of flexible plastic; it continuously releases a small amount of progestin and can be left in place for up to 5 years.

▶ INTRAUTERINE METHODS for Women

An IUD is a small device made of flexible plastic that is placed in the uterus to prevent pregnancy (Figure 13.11). The Dalkon Shield was a popular type of IUD up until 1975, when the A. H. Robins Company recommended that it be removed from all women who were using them. Users experienced severe pain, bleeding, and pelvic inflammatory disease, which led to sterility in some cases. The problems with the Dalkon Shield were primarily caused by the multifilament string that allowed bacteria to enter into the uterus through the cervix. As of 2010, only two IUDs are available in the United States, the ParaGard and Mirena.

Data from the 2006 to 2008 National Survey of Family Growth (NSFG) found that more than 2 million U.S. women (or 5.5% of women who use contraception) use an IUD, which is the highest level of use since the early 1980s (Mosher & Jones, 2010). Increases in use are due to many factors, including higher safety standards, more physicians and health care providers being trained in inser-

tion and removal techniques, immigration from areas where IUDs are popular (e.g., Mexico), increased advertising, and positive word of mouth from other users (Hubacher et al., 2010).

The cost for an IUD, a medical examination, IUD insertion, and follow-up visits can range from $500 to $1,000. Typically, the Mirena IUD costs more than the ParaGard.

How They Work

The ParaGard IUD is placed in the uterus and causes an increase in copper ions and enzymes, which impairs sperm function and prevents fertilization (Hatcher et al., 2011). It can be left in place for up to 12 years. The Mirena IUD time-releases progestin, which thickens the cervical mucus, inhibits sperm survival, and suppresses the endometrium (Hatcher et al., 2011). It can be left in place for up to 5 years. The IUD string hangs down from the cervix, and a woman can check the string to make sure the IUD is still properly in place. Both IUDs may also interfere with the implantation of a fertilized ova.

Effectiveness

Effectiveness rates for IUDs range from 99.2% to 99.9% (Hatcher et al., 2011).

Advantages

IUDs are the least expensive method of contraception over time, and they do not interfere with spontaneity. In addition, they have long-lasting contraceptive effects. In addition, the Mirena IUD reduces or eliminates menstrual flow and cramping. IUDs can also be used as emergency contraception (we discuss emergency contraception later in this chapter). Once the IUD is removed, fertility is quickly restored. IUDs can be used during breast-feeding.

Disadvantages

IUDs require moderately painful insertion and removal procedures, may cause irregular bleeding patterns and spotting (and heavier periods if using the ParaGard IUD), offer no protection from STIs, and carry a small risk for uterine perforation. The IUD may also be felt by a sexual partner.

Cross-Cultural Use

Worldwide, IUDs are the second most popular contraceptive method (behind female sterilization), with 14% of women relying on this method ("World Contraceptive Use 2009," 2009). However, they are more popular in less developed regions of the world (see Figure 13.7). Whereas 5.5% of women in the United States use IUDs, 15% of women in Western Europe, 12% in Northern Europe, and 9% in Southern Europe use IUDs (Hubacher et al., 2010). The IUD has high usage rates in many Asian countries, Israel, Cuba, Egypt, and Estonia ("World Contraceptive Use 2009," 2009). The newer Mirena IUD has been available in Europe for more than 10 years, and it is estimated that millions of women have used it throughout the world. Overall, IUD usage rates vary depending on how much the devices are marketed and advertised, as we discussed earlier.

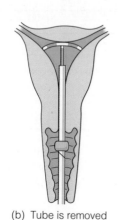
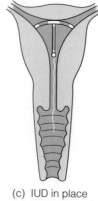

Uterus

Cervix

Vagina

(a) IUD is inserted through tube into uterus

(b) Tube is removed

(c) IUD in place

FIGURE **13.11** Insertion of an intrauterine device: (a) IUD is inserted through tube into the uterus, (b) tube is removed, (c) IUD is in place. Copyright © Cengage Learning 2013

GyneFix, an IUD containing a flexible row of copper beads instead of a rigid plastic frame like other IUDs, has been used for many years in countries such as Asia, Latin America, and Africa (Wildemeersch & Andrade, 2010). It is currently awaiting FDA approval in the United States.

◀ **review** QUESTIONS

1 What is an IUD? How does it work to prevent pregnancy?

2 How effective is the IUD, and what factors are important in determining effectiveness rates?

3 Identify some of the advantages and disadvantages of IUD use.

4 Are IUDs popular outside the United States? Explain.

▶ NATURAL METHODS
for Women and Men

Natural methods of contraception do not alter any physiological function. They include natural family planning and **fertility awareness,** withdrawal, and abstinence.

▶▶ FERTILITY AWARENESS–BASED **Methods**

Fertility awareness–based methods involve identifying a woman's fertile period and either abstaining from vaginal intercourse or using another contraceptive method during this time. With the **rhythm method,** a couple simply keeps track of a woman's cycle; other, more intensive methods involve charting and recording physical fertility signs (such as monitoring daily **basal body temperature [BBT]** and checking cervical mucus; Hatcher et al., 2011). Typically, these intensive methods are referred to as **natural family planning,** or the **symptothermal method.**

How They Work

With the symptothermal method, a woman takes her BBT every morning before she gets out of bed and records it on a BBT chart. Changes in hormonal levels cause body temperature to increase 0.4° to 0.8°F (0.2°-0.4°C) immediately before ovulation, and it re-

Cyclebeads can be used with fertility awareness–based methods to help determine fertile days. A ring is moved over a series of color-coded beads that represent low- and high-fertility days.

© Kenzie Henke

mains elevated until menstruation begins. A woman using this method monitors her cervical mucus, which becomes thin and stretchy during ovulation to help transport sperm. At other times of the month, cervical mucus is thicker. After 6 months of consistent charting, a woman will be able to estimate the approximate time of ovulation, and she can then either abstain from vaginal intercourse or use contraception during her high-risk times (usually this period is between 1 and 2 weeks).

---

fertility awareness
Basal body temperature charting used in conjunction with another method of contraception.

fertility awareness–based methods
Contraceptive or family planning method that involves identifying a fertile period in a woman's cycle and either avoiding intercourse or using contraception during this time.

rhythm method
A contraceptive method that involves calculating the period of ovulation and avoiding sexual intercourse around this time.

basal body temperature (BBT)
The body's resting temperature used to calculate ovulation in the symptothermal method of contraception.

natural family planning
A contraceptive method that involves calculating ovulation and avoiding sexual intercourse during ovulation and at other unsafe times.

symptothermal method
A contraceptive method that involves monitoring both cervical mucus and basal body temperature to determine ovulation.

Effectiveness

Effectiveness rates for fertility awareness–based methods range from 88% to 97% (Hatcher et al., 2011). However, effectiveness rates depend on the accuracy of identifying a fertile period and a couple's ability to avoid intercourse (or use another contraceptive method) during this time.

Advantages

Fertility awareness–based methods are an acceptable form of birth control for those who cannot use another method for religious reasons. They can teach couples about the menstrual cycle, are inexpensive, may encourage couples to communicate more about contraception, can involve the male partner, and have no medical side effects. This method can also be helpful when a woman is ready to get pregnant because she may be familiar with when she is ovulating. Couples who use these methods often use a variety of sexual expressions when they avoid intercourse during the fertile period.

Disadvantages

Fertility awareness–based methods restrict spontaneity and provide no protection from STIs. In addition, they take time and commitment to learn, and require several cycles of records before they can be used reliably. The majority of failures with this method are due to couples engaging in intercourse too close to ovulation. A woman may ovulate earlier or later than usual because of diet, stress, or alcohol use. These methods are often best suited for those needing to space pregnancies, rather than for those who want to avoid pregnancy.

Cross-Cultural Use

Fertility awareness–based contraceptive methods are popular around the world. Mostly this is because they are inexpensive and do not require much assistance from health care providers. These methods are commonly used in parts of Africa, Western Asia, and Eastern Europe. These methods may be the only form of acceptable contraception in predominantly Catholic countries such as Ireland, Brazil, and the Philippines. In the Philippines, natural family planning and the rhythm method are thought to improve a couple's relationship because they need to work together to use the method (remember our earlier discussion about pressure from the Church against using modern methods of contraception in the Philippines; Leyson, 2004). Societal issues and marketing may also affect the use of this method. For example, cultural resistance to condom use has increased the popularity of these fertility awareness–based methods in Kenya, where they are the most commonly used contraceptive method (Brockman, 2004). Today, many women's groups from the United States travel to developing countries to teach fertility awareness–based methods.

▶▶ WITHDRAWAL

Withdrawal, or **coitus interruptus,** involves withdrawing the penis from the vagina before ejaculation. Although withdrawal is a popular contraceptive method, many couples use it because of convenience and dissatisfaction with other methods (Whittaker et al., 2010). When women in the NSFG (see Chapter 2) study were asked about using withdrawal, 56% reported they had used it as a contraceptive method (Hatcher et al., 2007). However, many couples express anxiety about using it because it relies on the male to pull out in time. Withdrawal can be used alone or in conjunction with another contraceptive method.

How It Works

Withdrawal does not require any advance preparation. A couple engages in vaginal intercourse; before ejaculation, the male withdraws his penis away from the vaginal opening of the woman. The ejaculate does not enter the vagina.

Effectiveness

Effectiveness rates for withdrawal range from 73% to 96% (Hatcher et al., 2011).

Advantages

Withdrawal is an acceptable method of birth control for those who cannot use another method for religious reasons. It is free, does not require any devices or chemicals, and is better than using no method at all (Hatcher et al., 2011). In addition, it may be a good method for couples who don't have another method available.

Disadvantages

Withdrawal provides no protection from STIs, may contribute to ejaculatory problems, and can be difficult and stressful to use. Many men experience a mild to extreme "clouding of consciousness" just before orgasm when physical movements become involuntary (Hatcher et al., 2011). This method also requires trust from the female partner.

Cross-Cultural Use

Withdrawal is a popular contraceptive method throughout the world. It is one of the most frequently used methods in Austria, the Czech Republic, Greece, Ireland, and Italy (Francoeur & Noonan, 2004). In Azerbaijan, 64% of contraceptive users rely on withdrawal ("World Contraceptive Use 2009," 2009). Overall, it is a popular contraceptive method for couples with limited contraceptive choices or for those who are reluctant to use modern methods of contraception. In many countries, such as Iran, a lack of education and misconceptions about withdrawal has led to low usage rates (Rahnama et al., 2010). Many Iranian men and women believe that withdrawal does not work and will lead to multiple health problems, which it does not.

▶▶ ABSTINENCE

Abstinence (or not engaging in vaginal intercourse at all) is the only 100% effective contraceptive method (Hatcher et al., 2011). It has probably been the most important factor in controlling fertility throughout history. Abstinence may be primary (never having engaged in vaginal intercourse) or secondary (not currently engaging in vaginal intercourse). Couples may choose abstinence to prevent pregnancy, to protect against STIs, or for many other reasons.

1 Differentiate between the various types of fertility awareness–based methods. What factors influence the effectiveness rates of these methods?

2 Explain how changes in cervical mucus and body temperature provide information about ovulation.

3 Explain the use and effectiveness of withdrawal as a contraceptive method.

4 Identify the advantages and disadvantages of natural contraceptive methods.

5 Explain the cross-cultural use of natural contraceptive methods.

▶ PERMANENT CONTRACEPTIVE Methods

Male and female **sterilization** methods are the most commonly used contraceptive methods in the United States (Hatcher et al., 2011). The NSFG (see Chapter 2) reported that 28% of all women aged 15 to 44 years who were using contraception relied on tubal sterilization, whereas 9% relied on a partner's vasectomy (Hatcher et al., 2007).

The primary difference between sterilization and other methods of contraception is that sterilization is typically considered irreversible. Although some people have been able to have their sterilizations reversed, this can be expensive and time-consuming (Peterson, 2008). The majority of people who request sterilization reversals do so because they have remarried and desire children with their new partners.

▶▶ FEMALE Sterilization

Female sterilization, or **tubal sterilization,** is the most widely used method of birth control in the world (Hatcher et al., 2011). In a tubal sterilization, a health care provider may close or block both Fallopian tubes so that the ovum and sperm cannot meet. Block-ing the tubes can be done with **cauterization;** a ring, band, or clamp (which pinches the tube together); or **ligation** or nonsurgical procedures that involve placing inserts to block the Fallopian tubes. In the United States, female sterilization procedures are generally done with the use of a laparoscope through a small incision either under the navel or lower in the abdomen. After the procedure, a woman continues to ovulate, but the ovum does not enter the uterus. The costs for female sterilization vary but generally range from $2,000 to $5,000.

Another nonsurgical sterilization method for women includes Essure, which was approved in 2002. Essure is a tiny, spring-like device that is threaded into the Fallopian tubes (Figure 13.12). Within 3 months, the body's own tissue grows around the device, blocking fertilization. A woman using this method must undergo testing to make sure that the Fallopian tubes are fully blocked. Essure is considered an irreversible method of female sterilization (Hatcher et al., 2011; Ledger, 2004). Another nonsurgical sterilization method, Adiana, was approved by the FDA in 2009. This sterilization method involves placing small, silicone inserts in the Fallopian tubes that stimulate the body's own tissue to grow around the inserts, blocking the tubes. Both of these methods require follow-up visits with a health care provider to ensure the tubes are blocked.

Overall, the majority of women who choose permanent sterilization are content with their decision to do so (although the risk for regret is highest in women who undergo these procedures before age 30; Jamieson et al., 2002; Peterson, 2008). There are no hormonal changes, and ovaries continue to work and produce estrogen. Women maintain their levels of sexual interest and desire after permanent sterilization and report more positive than negative sexual side effects (Costello et al., 2002).

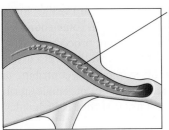

Essure is inserted into the Fallopian tube

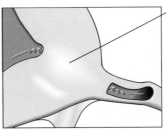

Body tissue grows into the Essure micro-insert, blocking the Fallopian tube

FIGURE **13.12** Essure, a permanent contraceptive method, is inserted into the Fallopian tubes in order to block the sperm from meeting the ovum. Copyright © Cengage Learning 2013

---

coitus interruptus
A contraceptive method that involves withdrawal of the penis from the vagina before ejaculation.

sterilization
Surgical contraceptive method that causes permanent infertility.

tubal sterilization
A surgical procedure in which the Fallopian tubes are cut, tied, or cauterized for permanent contraception.

cauterization
A sterilization procedure that involves burning or searing the Fallopian tubes or vas deferens for permanent sterilization.

ligation
A sterilization procedure that involves the tying or binding of the Fallopian tubes or vas deferens.

▶▶ MALE Sterilization

Male sterilization, or **vasectomy,** blocks the flow of sperm through the vas deferens (see Chapter 6). Typically, this procedure is simpler, less expensive, and has lower rates of complications than female sterilization (Shih et al., 2011). Even so, vasectomies are performed at less than half the rate of female sterilizations (Shih et al., 2011). It is also the least used in Black and Latino populations, which have the highest rates of female sterilization.

After a vasectomy, the testes continue to produce viable sperm cells, but with nowhere to go, they die and are absorbed by the body. Semen normally contains approximately 98% fluid and 2% sperm, and after a vasectomy, the man still ejaculates semen, but the semen contains no sperm (there is no overall change in volume or texture of the semen after a vasectomy). All other functions, such as the manufacturing of testosterone, erections, and urination, are unaffected by a vasectomy procedure.

The surgery for a vasectomy is performed as **outpatient surgery** with local anesthesia. Two small incisions about a one-fourth to one-half inch long are made in the scrotum, and the vas deferens is clipped or cauterized, which usually takes approximately 20 minutes (Figure 13.13). Men are advised to use another form of contraception for 12 weeks after a vasectomy to ensure that there is no sperm left in the ejaculate (Hatcher et al., 2011). Typically, one or two repeat semen analyses are required to evaluate whether there is viable sperm in the sample. Semen samples can be collected during masturbation or through the use of a special condom during vaginal intercourse. In 2008, the FDA approved a postvasectomy home sperm test called SpermCheck, which allows a man to test his semen sample at home rather than returning to a medical facility (Coppola et al., 2010).

After a vasectomy, a man may experience swelling, bleeding, bruising, or pain, but generally these subside within 2 weeks (Hatcher et al., 2011). The cost for the procedure varies widely, depending on where it is done. Overall, the cost for a vasectomy ranges from $300 to $1,000.

Effectiveness

Effectiveness for both male and female sterilization procedures ranges from 99% to 99.9% (Hatcher et al., 2011). Tubal sterilizations are effective immediately, whereas vasectomies require semen analysis for 12 weeks after the procedure to ensure no viable sperm remains.

Advantages

Sterilization is a highly effective permanent method of contraception. It offers a quick recovery, few long-term adverse effects, and once completed, does not interfere with spontaneity (Shih et al., 2011).

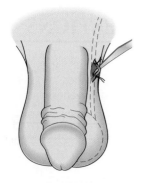
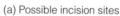

(a) Possible incision sites   (b) Incision on one side of the testicle and right and left vas are cut   (c) Incision closed

FIGURE 13.13 In a vasectomy, each vas deferens is clipped, cut, or cauterized. Copyright © Cengage Learning 2013

Disadvantages

Sterilization requires medical intervention and/or surgery, can be expensive, provides no protection from STIs, and is considered irreversible.

Cross-Cultural Use

Worldwide, female sterilization is used by more women than any other contraceptive method (see Figure 13.7). However, this procedure is more popular in less-developed regions of the world. Overall, female sterilizations are more popular than male, even though these procedures are often expensive and have more potential risks. In China, whereas 32% of women undergo sterilization, only 6% of men do (Wu, 2010).

In Brazil and India, nearly two fifths of women elect sterilizations, and most women do this early in their reproductive life (Brazilian women have the surgery at about 30 years old, whereas Indian women have it at about 26 years old; Leone & Padmadas, 2007). The Essure method has been used outside the United States in many countries in Europe, as well as Mexico, Brazil, Venezuela, Chile, and Uruguay.

In countries where family planning clinics are sparse, many women travel long distances to be sterilized. In some countries, female sterilization procedures are outpatient procedures using local anesthesia (Hatcher et al., 2007). As we have discussed, access to and promotion of a certain method also contribute to its popularity. In addition, cultural acceptance of female sterilization has also led to higher rates of usage (Leone & Padmadas, 2007).

vasectomy	**outpatient surgery**
A surgical procedure in which each vas deferens is cut, tied, or cauterized for permanent contraception.	Surgery performed in the hospital or doctor's office, after which a patient is allowed to return home; inpatient surgery requires hospitalization.

1 Identify the two main differences between sterilization and other contraceptive methods.

2 Explain some of the procedures used for female sterilization.

3 Explain some of the procedures used for male sterilization.

4 What are the advantages and disadvantages of sterilization as a contraceptive method?

5 Is sterilization a popular contraceptive method outside the United States? Explain.

▶ EMERGENCY Contraception

Many couples use ineffective methods in an attempt to avoid pregnancy, and some experience unintended pregnancies. Emergency contraception can be used when a couple fails to use contraception or uses ineffective methods.

Emergency contraception (EC; also referred to as "morning after" contraception, or emergency contraceptive pills) can prevent pregnancy when taken shortly after unprotected vaginal intercourse. It is designed to be used in cases in which no contraception was used, contraception was used improperly (such as missed or delayed birth control pills, hormonal injections, replacement vaginal rings or patches), a male condom slipped or broke, a female condom or barrier device was improperly inserted or dislodged during intercourse, an IUD was expelled, or a sexual assault occurred (Hatcher et al., 2011). There are some misconceptions about emergency contraception. Although it is referred to as the "morning after pill," this is misleading because the pill can be used up to 5 days after unprotected intercourse and not just the morning after. In addition, it is important to point out that emergency contraception does *not* cause an abortion. Emergency contraception is birth control in that it works to *prevent* pregnancy (we will talk more about abortion later in this chapter).

*Emergency contraception is birth control in that **it works to prevent pregnancy.***

There are several methods of emergency contraception, but only Plan B is approved by the FDA as an emergency contraceptive. Plan B was approved in 1999; it is a progestin-only method that works by inhibiting ovulation, thickening cervical mucus, and reducing endometrial buildup. Originally, Plan B involved taking two pills, 12 hours apart, but recently, Plan B One-Step became available, which requires taking only one pill. Plan B One-Step is gradually replacing the original Plan B. Another progestin-only emergency contraceptive method, Next Choice, is the generic equivalent to Plan B. All of these methods of emergency contraception must be taken within 3 days (72 hours) of vaginal intercourse and can reduce the likelihood of pregnancy by 81% to 90%. These methods are available without a prescription to men and women who are older than 17 years (Food and Drug Administration, 2006; Kavanaugh & Schwarz, 2008). A prescription is required for teens younger than 17. Emergency hormonal contraception costs vary anywhere from $35 to $60, depending on where it is purchased.

Concerns about emergency contraception being available without a prescription have raised fears about increased sexual risk taking in women. However, research has shown this is not the case—having available emergency contraception has not been found to increase sexual risk taking (M. Gold et al., 2004; Hu et al., 2005; Raymond et al., 2006).

In mid-2010, the FDA approved ella, a new, nonhormonal form of emergency contraception. Ella is a single-dose pill that can prevent pregnancy up to 5 days after unprotected intercourse. However, as of early 2011, ella was available only by prescription. The benefit of ella over Plan B is that it has a higher effectiveness rate (98%) and a longer window in which it can be used (5 versus 3 days).

Other options for emergency contraception include the use of ordinary combination and progestin-only birth control pills or the insertion of a copper-releasing IUD (Hatcher et al., 2011; Jensen, 2008). Birth control pills that contain estrogen and progestin work by inhibiting or delaying ovulation, making the endometrium less hospitable for implantation of an embryo, thickening the cervical mucus, altering the transportability of the Fallopian tubes, and inhibiting fertilization (Hatcher et al., 2011). Birth control pills that contain only progestin impair the ovulatory process but may also interfere with sperm functioning in the female reproductive tract

Emergency contraception, such as Next Choice, must be taken within 72 hours to prevent pregnancy.

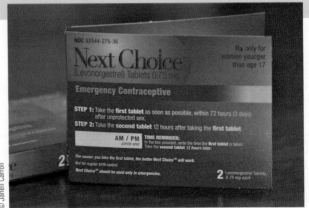

© Janell Carroll

emergency contraception
Contraception that is designed to prevent pregnancy after unprotected vaginal intercourse.

(Hatcher et al., 2007). The IUD insertion method is used much less frequently than other methods of emergency contraception. Adverse effects for emergency insertion of a copper-releasing IUD include abdominal discomfort and vaginal bleeding or spotting (Hatcher et al., 2007).

Using birth control pills as emergency contraception can lead to nausea, vomiting, cramping, breast tenderness, headaches, abdominal pain, fatigue, and dizziness (Hatcher et al., 2011). The incidence of nausea and vomiting is significantly lower in women who use progestin-only pills, such as Plan B One-Step or Next Choice (Hatcher et al., 2007). Women who take emergency contraception may be advised to take antinausea medicine, such as dimenhydrinate (Dramamine), before taking their pills.

Studies have found that 10% (or 5.1 million) of U.S. women aged 15 to 44 years have used emergency contraception at least once between 2006 and 2008 (Mosher & Jones, 2010). The typical user of emergency contraception in the United States is single, educated, without children, and between the ages of 15 and 25 (Phipps et al., 2008). Outside the United States, emergency contraception has been available in many countries throughout the world, including Australia, Belgium, Canada, China, Denmark, Finland, France, Greece, Iceland, India, Israel, Jamaica, Libya, New Zealand, the Netherlands, Norway, Portugal, Senegal, South Africa, Sri Lanka, Sweden, Switzerland, Tunisia, the United Kingdom, and many other countries. Emergency contraception is registered in 134 countries around the world, and in 63 of these countries, women have access to emergency contraception without a prescription (Wanja, 2010). It can be purchased without a prescription in countries such as France (since 1999), Norway (since 2000), Sweden (since 2001), the Netherlands (since 2004), and India (since 2005). In France, emergency contraception is free of charge.

Research on global users of emergency contraception found that 24- to 25-year-old Kenyan women are the major users of emergency contraception (Wanja, 2010). High usage was noted during weekends and holidays. In 2009, Europe approved ella, and today it is available in many countries around the world, including Austria, Belgium, Bulgaria, Czech Republic, Denmark, Finland, France, Germany, Greece, Guadeloupe, Hungary, Iceland, Lithuania, Monaco, Netherlands, Norway, Poland, Portugal, Romania, Spain, Sweden, and the United Kingdom.

◀ review QUESTIONS

1 Identify the various types of emergency contraception available today.

2 Identify some of the reasons why a woman might use emergency contraception and explain how it works.

3 How soon does a woman need to take emergency contraception to have it be effective?

4 Identify some of the adverse effects of emergency contraception.

5 Who is the typical user of emergency contraception in the United States?

▶ CONTRACEPTION in the Future

Although many pregnancies occur because couples used no contraception, it is estimated that half of all unintended pregnancies occur because of contraceptive failures (Hatcher et al., 2011). Researchers and scientists today continue to look for effective contraceptive methods that are easy to use and have few or no side effects. A consistent concern has been finding a method that can offer high effectiveness rates along with STI protection (Hatcher et al., 2011).

▶▶ WHAT'S AHEAD for Men?

Historically, birth control has been considered a female's responsibility, and that may be why the condom and vasectomy are the only birth control methods available to men. Many feminists claim that the lack of research into male methods of birth control has to do with the fact that birth control research is done primarily by men. As a result, women are responsible for using birth control and must suffer through the potential adverse effects. Others claim that there are few male methods because it is easier to block the one ovum women produce each month than the millions of sperm in each ejaculation. Other arguments cite the fact that chemical contraception may decrease testosterone production, reduce the male sex drive, and harm future sperm production. We do know that many men express a willingness to share the burden of family planning (Mruk, 2008).

As of 2011, research into male contraception continued to explore chemical and hormonal contraception, reversible vasectomies, vas deferens plugs, herbal contraceptives, and vaccines. One of the most promising areas of research in male contraception is in the use of hormonal implants and injections for men. Subdermal implants are placed under the skin, and testosterone injections are used to suppress pituitary hormones responsible for spermatogenesis. The first large, placebo-controlled study using these methods found successful reductions in sperm production (Mommers et al., 2008). This method was well tolerated by the men in the study,

gossypol
An ingredient in cottonseed oil that, when injected or implanted, may inhibit sperm production.

immunocontraceptives
Vaccines designed to suppress testicular function and eliminate sperm and testosterone production.

and sperm production was back to normal levels within 15 weeks of discontinuing the method.

Research continues to explore another injectable implant, RISUG (reversible inhibition of sperm under guidance). RISUG is currently in advanced Phase III clinical trials in India (Jha et al., 2009; Kumar et al., 2008; Lohiya et al., 2010). It is injected into the vas deferens where it blocks the passage of sperm. Ongoing research will determine whether this will be a viable contraceptive option for men. Other implants, such as the Intra-Vas Device, are also being studied (Crawford, 2008; Sun et al., 2011).

Gossypol, a nonhormonal agent derived from cottonseed oil, has been used for years in China and reduces sperm production without changing testosterone levels (Chang et al., 2010; Hatcher et al., 2007; Li et al., 2010b; Song et al., 2006). Anticancer drugs, such as Lonidamine, are also being studied for their ability to reduce sperm production (Maranghi et al., 2005). Researchers continue to explore the development of a male pill that inhibits male ejaculation, causing an orgasm without ejaculation, or "dry orgasm" (Dawar, 2006; Hisasue et al., 2006).

*Researchers continue to explore the development of **a male pill that inhibits male ejaculation.***

Finally, scientists are evaluating contraceptive vaccines (called **immunocontraceptives**) that would suppress testicular function causing infertility until pregnancy is desired (Naz, 2009; Samuel & Naz, 2008; Wang et al., 2009). Antisperm contraceptive vaccines and genetically produced human antibodies inhibit sperm functions. Although there continues to be ongoing research into new contraception options for men, it is likely that no options will be available until perhaps 2015 at the earliest (Hatcher et al., 2007).

▶▶ WHAT'S AHEAD for Women?

Women report that they want contraceptives that are simpler to use, have fewer adverse effects, and offer additional noncontra-ceptive benefits, such as STI protection, clearer skin, or less weight gain (Hatcher et al., 2007). Research is ongoing in an attempt to find a contraceptive method that addresses all these concerns.

Research continues to explore immunocontraceptives for women that would inhibit the function of human chorionic gonadotropin (see Chapter 12) and interrupt a woman's ability to become pregnant (Talwar et al., 2009). Other researchers are looking at vaccines that target sex hormones or gamete production (An et al., 2009; Naz, 2005; Wang et al., 2009). Unfortunately, vaccines often negatively affect other functions and do not offer adequate effectiveness yet. New IUDs, implants, injections, and permanent sterilization procedures are also being evaluated. Other research is evaluating longer-acting versions of existing methods, such as the contraceptive patch and hormonal ring. Extended-use patches or rings may be options in the next few years. Finally, natural methods of contraception are also being studied. Saliva and urine tests can help natural planning by allowing a woman to determine whether she is ovulating. Fertility computers, which allow a woman to identify fertile periods, are currently undergoing clinical trials for FDA approval. Although we still have a long way to go in making better methods available for controlling whether pregnancy occurs, many improvements are in the works and may be available in the near future.

Financial factors, political pressure, and legal concerns hold back most of the contraceptive research today. Private funding is often difficult because such large amounts are necessary for most research. Unfortunately, the threat of lawsuits (such as the Dalkon Shield situation discussed earlier in the chapter) has effectively scared most big pharmaceutical companies away from contraceptive research (Hatcher et al., 2007; J. L. Schwartz & Gabelnick, 2002).

◀ review QUESTIONS

1 What do couples look for in new contraceptive methods?

2 Describe why there have been fewer birth control options for men and what the future holds for new male contraception.

3 Describe what the future holds for new female contraceptive methods.

▶ ABORTION

Because family planning involves controlling conception and birth, there are two main methods to achieve these goals—contraception and abortion (Leonard, 2006). Many believe that the ability to determine whether and when to have a child is a necessity today (Boonstra et al., 2006). At the beginning of this chapter we pointed out that the typical American woman spends at least 30 years trying *not* to get pregnant. Although the majority of women have used contraception, we know that many methods are difficult to use consistently and/or effectively, and no method is 100% effective. Unintended pregnancies do occur when a woman is using effective contraception, even though they are much more likely to occur when a woman uses no contraception. In fact, 52% of unintended pregnancies occur in the 11% of the women who use no contraception (Boonstra et al., 2006).

As we discussed earlier in this chapter, certain groups of women have higher rates of unintended pregnancies, including those who are young, unmarried, poor, and/or members of racial/ethnic minorities (see Figure 13.2). Unintended pregnancy is a stressful event for most women. It has also been found to be related to high levels of intimate partner violence (Saftlas et al., 2010).

For women with stable relationships or the resources to raise a child, or both, an unintended pregnancy might not present much of a hardship. However, for many women, an unintended pregnancy can lead to serious consequences. In this section, we discuss the abortion debate, historical perspectives, legal versus illegal abortions, statistics, abortion procedures, reactions to abortion, and cross-cultural research on abortion.

▶▶ THE ABORTION Debate

Today, abortion is the moral issue of the times in the United States. It is an issue that leads many people to question the role that the government should play in their lives. Disagreements about this issue have been very emotional and, at times, even violent. In 2009, Dr. George Tiller, one of only a few doctors who provided abortions late in a pregnancy, was murdered (Stumpe & Davey, 2009). He had several death threats before his murder and was even shot in both arms in 1993 in an attempt to get him to stop performing abortions.

Although some men and women are unsure about how they feel about abortion or feel somewhat in the middle, the majority of us fall on one side or the other of the abortion debate. **Pro-life supporters** believe that human life begins at conception, and thus an embryo, at any stage of development, is a person. Although

---

REAL RESEARCH 13.7   Abortion is one of the most common medical interventions in women of reproductive age, and it is estimated that 1 in 3 women have an abortion by the age 45 (JONES ET AL., 2010).

---

some pro-life supporters believe that aborting a fetus is murder and that the government should make all abortions illegal, others believe that abortion should be available only for specific cases (such as rape or danger to a mother's life).

On the other side of the issue, **pro-choice supporters** believe that a woman should have control over her fertility. Many people who are pro-choice believe there are a number of situations in which a woman may view abortion as a necessary option. Because not everyone agrees that life begins at conception, pro-choice supporters believe that it is a woman's choice whether to have an abortion, and they strongly believe that the government should not interfere with her decision.

The abortion debate often polarizes people into pro-life and pro-choice camps. College students have generally been viewed as fairly liberal in their attitudes about abortion, but studies have

ON YOUR MIND 13.4

In the future, is abortion going to be illegal?

The Supreme Court may eventually overturn the *Roe v. Wade* decision. Should this happen, each state will be responsible for regulating abortion. As of 2011, only seven states—California, Connecticut, Hawaii, Maine, Maryland, Nevada, and Washington— had laws that protected the right to choose abortion before fetal viability or when necessary to protect the life or health of the woman if *Roe v. Wade* was overturned (Alan Guttmacher Institute, 2011). Four states—Louisiana, Mississippi, North Dakota, and South Dakota—would automatically ban abortion, 13 states would enforce their existing abortion bans, and 7 states would restrict the right to a legal abortion to the maximum degree possible (Alan Guttmacher Institute, 2011).

found the same distribution of abortion attitudes as in other age groups (Carlton et al., 2000).

▶▶ HISTORICAL Perspectives

Abortion has been practiced in many societies throughout history; in fact, there are few large-scale societies in which it has not been practiced. Aristotle argued that abortion was necessary as a backup to contraception. He believed that a fetus was not alive until certain organs had been formed; for males, this occurred 40 days after conception, and for females, 90 days. In early Roman society, abortions were also allowed, but husbands had the power to determine whether their wives would undergo abortion.

Throughout most of Western history, religion determined general attitudes toward abortion, and both Judaism and Christianity have generally condemned abortion and punished those who used it. Still, throughout recorded history, abortions were performed. Many women died or were severely injured by illegal surgical abortions performed by semiskilled practitioners. Although it was little discussed publicly, abortion was apparently quite common; the Michigan Board of Health estimated in 1878 that one third of all pregnancies in that state ended in abortion (D'Emilio & Freedman, 1988).

In 1965, all 50 states banned abortion, although there were exceptions that varied by state (for instance, to save the mother's life, or in cases of rape or incest or fetal deformity). Those who could not have a legal abortion had the baby or underwent an illegal abortion (others may have used *self-induced abortion* methods, such as inserting sticks in the vagina, applying pressure to the abdomen, or drinking bleach). Illegal abortions, known as **back-alley abortions,** were very dangerous because they were often performed under unsanitary conditions and resulted in multiple complications, sometimes ending in death (re-

---

pro-life supporter
Individual who believes that abortion should be illegal or strictly regulated by the government.

pro-choice supporter
Individual who believes that the abortion decision should be left up to the woman and not regulated by the government.

back-alley abortion
Illegal abortion, which was all that was available before the legalization of abortion in the 1970s.

parental notification
Abortion legislation that requires the notification of the parents of a minor before an abortion procedure.

parental consent
Abortion legislation that requires the consent of the parents of a minor before an abortion procedure.

call the chapter opening story about a woman who underwent an illegal abortion). In 1967, abortion laws in England were liberalized, and many American women traveled to England for an abortion. By 1970, "package deals" appeared in the popular media advertising roundtrip airfare, airport transfers, passport assistance, lodging, meals, and the procedure itself (R. B. Gold, 2003).

In 1973, the Supreme Court ruled in the *Roe v. Wade* decision that a woman's right to an abortion is constitutionally protected, but not absolute (Boonstra et al., 2006). After the point of fetal viability (when a fetus can live on its own outside of the womb), a state could restrict or prohibit abortion unless it was necessary to protect the life and health of the woman. Since the Supreme Court handed down its decision in *Roe v. Wade* in 1973, individual states have regulated and limited whether, and under what circumstances, a woman can obtain an abortion ("An Overview of Abortion Laws," 2011). Following are some of the provisions of some of these state laws:

- *Physician and hospital requirements:* Some states require abortions to be performed by licensed physicians, whereas others require procedures to be done in hospitals.

- *Gestational limits:* Prohibit abortion after a specified time period.

- *Public funding restrictions:* Limit the use of state funds for women who cannot afford abortion.

- *State-mandated counseling:* Require women who choose abortion to undergo counseling that informs her of certain risks, including the development of breast cancer, the ability of the fetus to feel pain, long-term mental health consequences, and long-term fertility risks; women are also to be informed about the availability of ultrasound to view the fetus.

- *Waiting periods:* Require women who want to have an abortion to wait a specified period (usually 24 hours) between when she receives counseling and when the procedure is done. In early 2011, South Dakota signed a 3-day waiting period into law, the longest waiting period in the nation.

- *Parental involvement:* **Parental notification** and **parental consent** regulations require minors to involve their parents and get their consent before undergoing an abortion.

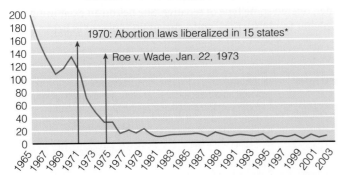

Number of Abortion-Related Deaths

FIGURE **13.14** Since abortion was legalized in 1973, the number of deaths from abortion has declined dramatically. SOURCE: Alan Guttmacher Institute (2008b); Strauss et al. (2006).

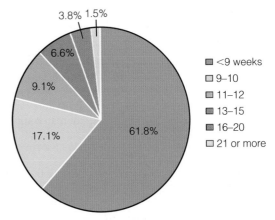

FIGURE **13.15** The majority of abortions are done within the first 12 weeks of pregnancy. Copyright © Cengage Learning 2013

As of 2011, these laws were all in effect, although some were not always enforced. Although these restrictions have made it more difficult for women to choose abortion, they have not reduced the number of women who seek abortion (Gold, 2009).

Since John Roberts was confirmed as Chief Justice in 2005, the U.S. Supreme Court has undergone several changes in membership, and some experts believe there is a possibility that *Roe v. Wade* could be overturned, giving full regulation of abortion back to the individual states ("Abortion Policy in the Absence of Roe," 2011). If *Roe v. Wade* were overturned today, several states would likely ban abortion, including Louisiana, Mississippi, North Dakota, and South Dakota, whereas others would likely protect a woman's right to choose, including California, Connecticut, Hawaii, Maine, Maryland, Nevada, and Washington. Still other states would either retain their pre-*Roe v. Wade* abortion bans or restrict the right to legal abortion in the absence of *Roe v. Wade.*

▶▶ LEGAL VERSUS Illegal Abortions

Although legalization of abortion in the United States gave women the right to choose abortion, it also led to the development of safer abortion procedures. As a result, fewer women were hospitalized for abortion-related complications and fewer died. Abortion-related deaths dropped significantly after Roe v. Wade was passed in 1973 (see Figure 13.14).

Many experts believe that making abortion illegal does not affect the underlying cause for abortion—unintended pregnancies (Boonstra et al., 2006). Legal or illegal, unintended pregnancies still occur and women will seek out options.

▶▶ ABORTION Statistics

Worldwide, of the 208 million pregnancies that occurred in 2008, 64% were planned, 16% resulted in unplanned births, and 20% (41 million) ended in abortion (Singh et al., 2009). In the United States, 40% of unintended pregnancies end in abortion (Boonstra et al., 2006). The majority of these abortions are done in the first 12 weeks of pregnancy (see Figure 13.15). But what is the typical profile of a woman in the United States who has an abortion?

table 13.5 ■ Early Abortion Options

Surgical Abortion	Medication Abortion
Highly effective	Highly effective
Relatively brief procedure	Procedure can take up to several days or more to complete
Involves invasive procedure	No invasive procedure (unless incomplete)
Allows local or general anesthesia	No anesthesia
Usually requires only one clinic or medical visit	Involves at least two clinic or medical visits
Bleeding is typically lighter after procedure	Bleeding is typically heavier after procedure
Occurs in medical setting	Can occur in privacy of own home

SOURCE: Hatcher et al. (2007).

Who Has Abortions?

In the United States, women who have abortions are most likely to be in their 20s, poor or low-income, unmarried, and from ethnic or racial minorities (Cohen, 2008; Jones et al., 2010). In 2008, 36% of women having abortions were non-Hispanic White women, 30% were non-Hispanic Black women, 25% were Hispanic women, and 9% were non-Hispanic women of other races (Jones et al., 2010). Higher abortion rates are directly related to rates of unintended pregnancy, which is typically a result of the lack of access to high-quality contraception, as well as a lack of consistency in using certain methods (see Figure 13.2; Cohen, 2008).

Although many believe that young teenagers are the ones most likely to have abortions, the largest group of women having abortions are in their 20s, followed by women in their 30s (Jones et al., 2010). Although most of these women were unmarried and not living with their partners at the time of the abortion, the majority were in relationships (Jones et al., 2010). However, approximately 12% are not in a relationship with the man who got them pregnant.

Why Do Women Have Abortions?

Women choose abortion for many different reasons—an inability to care for a child, financial reasons, partner or relationship issues, as well as work, school, or family issues (Boonstra et al., 2006; Jones et al., 2010). There is no simple answer to the question of why a woman decides to have an abortion.

The majority of women—regardless of age, marital status, income, ethnicity, education, or number of children—cite a concern for others as a main factor in their decision to have an abortion (Boonstra et al., 2006). Many women consult with others when they are deciding what to do about an unintended pregnancy. In fact, 60% report talking to someone, most often their partner, when they make their decision (Finer et al., 2006).

▶▶ ABORTION Procedures

Since 1973, abortion has been one of the most common surgical procedures in the United States, and the majority of abortion procedures are performed in specialized abortion clinics. However, this has not always been the case. After *Roe v. Wade*, the majority of abortions were performed in hospitals. The move away from hospitals and into clinics has reduced the cost of an abortion. In 2000, the availability of the "abortion pill" in the United States enabled women to terminate their pregnancies in the privacy of their own homes.

Today, a woman can choose between a surgical abortion and a medication abortion (see Table 13.5 for more information about early abortion options). The most important factor in determining which procedure a woman should choose is the duration of a woman's pregnancy. A surgical abortion can be used in both the first and second trimester, whereas a medication abortion can be done up to 63 days after the first day of a woman's last period (before 9 weeks).

Surgical Abortion Procedures

A **first-trimester surgical abortion** (also called **vacuum aspiration**) is performed up to 16 weeks after a woman's last period. It is simpler and safer than abortions performed after this time. The procedure can be done in a private clinic, physician's office, or hospital.

In a first-trimester surgical abortion procedure, a woman is often offered some type of sedative. She lies on an examining table with her feet in stirrups, and a speculum is placed in her vagina to

first-trimester surgical abortion
Termination of pregnancy within the first 14 weeks of pregnancy.

vacuum aspiration
The termination of a pregnancy by using suction to empty the contents of the uterus.

dilation rods
A series of graduated metal rods that are used to dilate the cervical opening during an abortion procedure.

cannula
A tube, used in an abortion procedure, through which the uterine contents are emptied.

vacuum aspirator
A vacuum pump that is used during abortion procedures.

second-trimester surgical abortion
Termination of pregnancy between the 14th and 21st weeks of pregnancy.

dilation and evacuation (D&E)
A second-trimester abortion procedure that involves cervical dilation and vacuum aspiration of the uterus.

laminaria
Seaweed used in second-trimester abortion procedures to dilate the cervix. Used dried, it can swell three to five times its original diameter.

mifepristone
Drug used in medication abortion procedures; it blocks the development of progesterone, which causes a breakdown in the uterine lining. Referred to as RU-486 when it was in development.

misoprostol
A synthetic prostaglandin drug used for early abortion.

prostaglandin
Oral or injected drug taken to cause uterine contractions.

view the cervix. Local anesthesia is injected into the cervix, which numbs it slightly. **Dilation rods** are used to open the cervix and usually cause mild cramping of the uterus. After dilation, a **cannula** is inserted into the cervix and is attached to a **vacuum aspirator,** which empties the contents of the uterus. A first-trimester procedure usually takes between 4 and 6 minutes.

Second-trimester surgical abortions are those performed later than 16 weeks after a woman's last period. These procedures can be done in a private clinic, physician's office, or hospital. A woman may undergo a second-trimester procedure for several reasons, such as medical complications, fetal deformities that were not revealed earlier, divorce or marital problems, miscalculation of date of last menstrual period, financial or geographic problems (such as not living near a clinic that offers the procedure), or a denial of the pregnancy until the second trimester.

A **dilation and evacuation (D&E)** is often used in second-trimester procedures. The procedure is similar to a vacuum aspiration, but dilation may be done differently. Because the fetal tissue is larger, the cervix must be dilated more than it is in a first-trimester procedure. Dilators such as **laminaria** (lam-in-AIR-ree-uh) may be inserted into the cervix 12 to 24 hours before the procedure to help begin the dilation process. These dilators absorb fluid and slowly dilate the cervix. When a woman returns to the clinic or hospital, she will be given pain medication and numbing medication will be injected into the cervix. The dilators are removed, and the uterus is then emptied with suction and various instruments. A D&E usually takes about 15 to 20 minutes.

After a surgical abortion procedure, most women experience bleeding and cramping. Over-the-counter pain relievers, such as ibuprofen, will adequately reduce the pain and cramping. Although the heaviest bleeding might last only a few days, spotting can last for up to 6 weeks. Because these are medical procedures, potential risks are associated with these procedures, and these risks increase the longer a woman has been pregnant. Possible risks include an allergic reaction to medications, excessive bleeding, infection, injury to the cervix, uterine perforation, and/or an incomplete abortion. Health care providers advise women who are considering abortion to have an earlier procedure because the risks are lower in first-trimester procedures.

Most clinics and medical offices require a woman to stay a few hours after the procedure so that she can be monitored. If a woman is Rh-negative, she will be given RhoGAM after these procedures (see Chapter 12). Once home, she is advised to rest, not to lift heavy objects, to avoid vaginal intercourse, and not to use tampons for at least 1 week; all of these activities may increase the risk for infection. Typically, a woman's period will return within 4 to 8 weeks. Most clinics advise a follow-up visit 2 to 4 weeks after the procedure.

Medication Abortion

A medication abortion involves the use of an "abortion pill" to end an early pregnancy. The abortion pill is actually a drug known as **mifepristone** (MYFE-priss-tone). Mifepristone was first approved for use in pregnancy termination in France in 1988, during which time it was referred to as RU-486. It was approved for use in the United States by the FDA in 2000. In a medication abortion, mife-

pristone is used in conjunction with a second pill containing another drug, **misoprostol.**

Many clinics require a physical examination, blood work, and an ultrasound to determine the length of the pregnancy before prescribing the abortion pill. During this visit, medication abortion is explained and a woman is given antibiotics to reduce the possibility of infection. The actual medication abortion involves three steps.

The first step involves taking the abortion pill. A woman will usually begin bleeding within 4 to 5 hours after taking the pill. Mifepristone works by blocking the hormone progesterone, which is responsible for maintaining the buildup of the endometrium (see Chapter 5). Without it, however, the endometrial lining will break down and a pregnancy can no longer continue.

The second step of a medication abortion involves taking another medication, misoprostol. This is usually taken within 3 days of the abortion pill. Misoprostol is a **prostaglandin,** and it causes the uterus to contract and expel the uterine contents. Many women experience heavy bleeding, cramping, nausea, diarrhea, abdominal pain, dizziness, or a minor fever and chills. This process may take 4 to 5 hours or more, and during this time a woman will experience an abortion. The bleeding will continue for up to 4 weeks after the medications are taken, and women can use pads or tampons during this time.

The third, and final, step involves a follow-up visit to the health care provider to make sure that the abortion is complete. A blood test, ultrasound, or both may be performed. Women who undergo a medication abortion must be prepared to have a surgical abortion if they experience an incomplete abortion. Because the drugs for medication abortion are known to cause birth defects, women are not advised to continue a pregnancy after using these drugs.

Medication abortion is a safe and effective procedure, and research indicates that it may be safer than surgical abortion procedures (Gan et al., 2008; M. Singh et al., 2008). Some women choose medication abortion over surgical abortion because it feels more "natural," offers privacy, can be done earlier, does not use anesthesia, and provides more control (see Table 13.5; F. H. Stewart et al., 2004). However, medication abortions often cause heavier bleed-

*Medication abortion is a safe and effective procedure; it **may be safer than surgical abortion procedures.***

ing and cramping than surgical abortions, and some women worry about being away from a medical facility (Lie et al., 2008). Finally, the length of time to expulsion (days compared with minutes) often makes medication abortion less appealing than a surgical abortion.

In 2008, close to 60% of abortion providers offered medication abortion and approximately 17% of nonhospital abortions were medication abortions (Jones & Kooistra, 2011).

▶▶ REACTIONS to Abortion

Although the decision to have an abortion is a difficult one, the physiological and psychological effects vary from person to person, and they depend on many factors. Here we'll explore the reactions of women, men, and teens.

Women's Reactions

The majority of evidence from research studies has found that legal abortion is safe and has few long-term physiological, psychological, or fertility-related problems later in life (Boonstra et al., 2006; Munk-Olsen et al., 2011; Warren et al., 2010). Although we know less about reactions to medication abortion, preliminary research has found that women are pleased with this type of procedure because it allows them more control and privacy (Cameron et al., 2010).

After a first-trimester abortion, the most common physiological symptoms include cramping, heavy bleeding with possible clots, and nausea. These symptoms may persist for several days, but if any of these are severe, a health care provider should be seen for an evaluation. Severe complications are much more frequent in second-trimester procedures, as we discussed earlier. They include hemorrhaging, **cervical laceration, uterine perforation,** and infection (F. H. Stewart et al., 2004). Of these complications, uterine perforation is the most serious, although the risk for occurrence is small. Earlier, we mentioned a state provision that involved informing women about the risks for breast cancer and impaired future fertility after an abortion. Reviews of scientific literature have found that women who have abortions do not have an increased risk for breast cancer or long-term risks to future fertility (Finer & Henshaw, 2006; Hatcher et al., 2007; Richardson & Nash, 2006).

Although women experience a range of emotions after an abortion, the most prominent response is relief (Fergusson et al., 2009). Even though relief may be the immediate feeling, there are three categories of psychological reactions to abortion. Positive emotions include relief and happiness; socially based emotions include shame, guilt, and fear of disapproval; and internally based emotions include regret, anxiety, depression, doubt, and anger,

The most prominent response a woman experiences after an abortion *is relief.*

which are based on the woman's feelings about the pregnancy (Thorp et al., 2003). A woman may cycle through each of these reactions—feeling relief one minute, depression or guilt the next. Other possible negative psychological symptoms include self-reproach, increased sadness, and a sense of loss.

Certain conditions may put a woman more at risk for development of severe psychological symptoms. These include being young, not having family or partner support, being persuaded to have an abortion when she does not want one, having a difficult time making the decision to have an abortion, blaming the pregnancy on another person or on oneself, having a strong religious and moral background, having an abortion for medical or genetic reasons, having a history of psychiatric problems before the abortion, and having a late abortion procedure (Rue et al., 2004; Zolese & Blacker, 1992).

In most cases, although discovering an unintended pregnancy and deciding to abort are very stressful decisions, in the majority of cases, the emotional aftermath does not appear to be severe (Munk-Olsen et al., 2011; Warren et al., 2010). Still, it is very beneficial for a woman (and her partner) who is contemplating an abortion to discuss this with a counselor or health care provider.

Men's Reactions

A woman's choice to have an abortion forces many couples to reevaluate their relationship and ask themselves some difficult questions (Naziri, 2007). Do they both feel the same about each other? Is the relationship serious? Where is the relationship going? Keeping the lines of communication open during this time is very important. The male partner's involvement makes the abortion experience less traumatic for the woman; in fact, women whose partners support them and help them through the procedure show more positive responses after the abortion (Jones et al., 2011). Women who have no support from their partners or who make the decision themselves often experience greater emotional distress. In some cases, women have been found to conceal abortion decisions from their partners (Coker, 2007; Woo et al., 2005).

Although we know that an unintended pregnancy is difficult for many woman, we often fail to acknowledge that men can also

cervical laceration
Cuts or tears on the cervix.

uterine perforation
Tearing a hole in the uterus.

judicial bypass option
Abortion legislation that allows for a judge to bypass parental consent or notification for a minor to acquire an abortion.

have a difficult time and may experience sadness, a sense of loss, and fear for their partner's well-being (Holmes, 2004). What makes it even more difficult for most men is that they often do not discuss the pregnancy with anyone other than their partner (Naziri, 2007).

Finally, earlier we mentioned the increased rate of intimate partner violence in couples with unintended pregnancies. Research has found that some men try to control their partner's abortion-related decisions (Hathaway et al., 2005; Miller et al., 2007). These behaviors are part of a larger pattern of behaviors involving forced sex, condom refusal, and contraceptive control. Abusive men have been found to be more involved in pregnancies ending in abortion than their nonabusive counterparts, especially in cases where there are repeat abortions (Silverman et al., 2010). This is an area of research that will continue to be explored in the future.

▶▶ TEENS and Abortion

Overall, 18% of U.S. women who have abortions are teenagers—11% of 18- to 19-year-olds, 6% of 15- to 17-year-olds, and 0.4% of teens younger than 15 have had an abortion (Jones et al., 2010). Teenagers may be more vulnerable to postabortion anxiety, depression, sleep problems, and substance use/abuse, mostly because of developmental limitations and a lack of emotional support from those around them (Coleman, 2006; Ely et al., 2010). As we discussed earlier, women who have no support often experience increased emotional distress after an abortion. However, most teens with adequate support do not experience negative postabortion emotional reactions (Warren et al., 2010).

*Countries with liberal abortion laws have been found **to have lower rates of abortion.***

Earlier we discussed the laws and regulations that individual states impose on access to abortion. Many of these are designed to control teenagers' access to abortion. The majority of states require parental involvement in a teen's decision to have an abortion. Typically, consent is required by one or both parents, usually 24 to 48 hours before the abortion procedure ("Parental Involvement in Minors' Abortions," 2011). Some states offer a medical emergency exception or a **judicial bypass option,** in which a minor can obtain consent from a judge rather than from her parents. Laws and regulations that restrict a teenager's access to abortion disproportionately affect ethnic and racial minority teens, leading to higher rates of unintended births (Coles et al., 2010).

▶▶ CROSS-CULTURAL ASPECTS of Abortion

Worldwide, approximately 42 million abortions occur each year, and half of these involve illegal abortion procedures (Cohen, 2009). Abortion is legal throughout most of Europe, with the exception of Ireland and Poland, and it is widely available and safe (Cohen, 2009). Ironically, countries with liberal abortion laws

have been found to have lower rates of abortion. For example, in the Netherlands, abortion is legal, free, and widely available, yet abortion rates are among the world's lowest (and the rate of abortion in the Netherlands is less than half the U.S. rate; Boonstra et al., 2006). The Netherlands also has comprehensive sexuality education programs and liberal access to contraception, both of which contribute to low abortion rates (see Chapter 8 for more information about comprehensive sexuality education).

Many other countries have legalized abortion, including China (1957), Cuba (1965), Singapore (1970), India (1972), Zambia (1972), Vietnam (1975), Turkey (1983), Taiwan (1985), and South Africa (1996; Cohen, 2009). Since 1997, many more countries have legalized abortion, including Colombia, Ethiopia, Iran, Nepal, Portugal, and Thailand. During this same time, three countries, Poland, Nicaragua, and El Salvador, have decreased the availability of abortion by increasing various restrictions (Cohen, 2009). As of 2009, 60% of women live in countries where abortion is legal.

However, 40% of women live in areas where abortion is illegal or highly restricted. In countries where abortion is illegal, many women undergo dangerous procedures with no access to hospitals or medical care when complications occur (Boonstra et al., 2006). Illegal abortions are high in countries where abortion is prohibited, such as Bangladesh, Brazil, Colombia, the Dominican Republic, Nigeria, and Peru, where rates of illegal abortion are twice as high as the rates of legal abortion in the United States (Boonstra et al., 2006). Worldwide, an estimated 70,000 women die of unsafe abortion procedures each year (or 7 women each hour; Cohen, 2009). In addition to this, more than 8 million women experience complications from unsafe abortions and are at risk for infertility (Cohen, 2009).

Researchers and experts are working to help legalize abortion around the world to help reduce the incidence of illegal abortions and postabortion complications. However, this is only the first step to ensuring that women have adequate access to abortion services. In some countries where abortion is legal, safe services are unavailable to many women because of prohibitive prices or certain restrictions, such as the necessity of getting the consent of multiple physicians (as is the case in Zambia, where abortion has been legal since 1994; Cohen, 2009).

Abortion remains a controversial procedure in the United States, as well as in the rest of the world. In the United States, both sides of the issue battle from what they believe are basic principles: one side from a fetus's right to be born and the other from a woman's right to control her own body. The pendulum of this debate continues to swing back and forth. Current politics may influence whether *Roe v. Wade* is one day overturned. Although new developments like medication abortion may take the fight out of the abortion clinics and into women's homes, the only real certainty about the future of abortion is that it will remain one of the most controversial areas of American public life.

1 Trace the status of abortion throughout history and differentiate between legal and illegal abortion.

2 Differentiate between first- and second-trimester surgical abortion procedures.

3 Differentiate between surgical and medication abortion, and explain how a woman might decide which procedure would be best for her.

4 Identify some physiological and psychological reactions to abortion, and discuss the research on men and abortion.

5 Discuss the laws that have been imposed in an attempt to decrease abortion in adolescent populations.

6 Describe what we know about abortion outside the United States.

▸▸ chapter REVIEW

SUMMARY POINTS

1 Contraception is not a modern invention. The ancient Greeks and Egyptians used a variety of techniques to try to control their fertility. Several groups began to explore controlling fertility in the early 1800s, and Margaret Sanger was one of the first people to advocate the importance of birth control.

2 Contraception throughout the world has always been affected by social and economic issues, knowledge levels, religion, and gender roles. Outside the United States, many women are not involved in contraceptive decision making, and contraceptive use is thought to reduce a man's masculinity. Scandinavian countries are regarded as some of the most progressive with respect to contraceptive usage. Finland has been rated as a model country in contraceptive use.

3 The FDA has approved several methods of contraception, but no method is best for everyone. The FDA is responsible for approving all prescription medicine in the United States. A pharmaceutical company must submit proof that the drug is safe for human use. It is estimated that it takes 10 to 14 years to develop a new contraceptive method.

4 Issues that must be considered when choosing a contraceptive method include personal health, number of sexual partners, frequency of vaginal intercourse, risk for acquiring a sexually transmitted infection, responsibility of partners, method cost, and method advantages and disadvantages.

5 Barrier methods of birth control work by preventing the sperm from entering the uterus. Barrier methods include the male and female condoms, cervical barriers, and the contraceptive sponge. Male condoms can be made of latex, polyurethane, or lambskin. Female condoms are made of polyurethane.

6 Hormonal methods work by changing hormone levels to interrupt ovulation. Combined hormone methods include birth control pills, injections, vaginal rings, and patches. Combination birth control pills contain synthetic estrogen and a type of progestin. The increase in estrogen and progesterone prevents the pituitary gland from sending hormones to cause the ovaries to begin maturation of an ovum.

7 Other hormonal contraceptive options include a monthly injection of synthetic hormones, including estrogen and progestin; NuvaRing, a small plastic ring that releases a constant dose of estrogen and progestin, and is changed once a month; the Ortho Evra patch, which sticks to the skin and time-releases synthetic estrogen and progestin into the bloodstream. All of these work by inhibiting ovulation, increasing cervical mucus, and/or rendering the uterus inhospitable to implantation.

8 Progestin-based methods include subdermal implants, injectables, and minipills. Progestin-only methods include minipills, Implanon, and Depo-Provera. Implanon is a subdermal contraceptive implant, whereas Depo-Provera is a progestin-only injectable

contraceptive that works by preventing ovulation and thickening cervical mucus.

9 Chemical methods of contraception include spermicides such as creams, jellies, foams, suppositories, and films. Spermicides work by reducing the survival of sperm in the vagina.

10 IUDs are placed in the uterus and inhibit ovulation, whereas causing an increase in cervical mucus and endometrial buildup. The ParaGard IUD can be left in place for up to 12 years. The Mirena IUD also time-releases progestin into the lining of the uterus and can be left in place for up to 5 years.

11 Fertility awareness–based methods identify a woman's fertile period so she can abstain from vaginal intercourse or use another method of contraception. A more intensive method involves charting and recording physical fertility signs, such as monitoring daily body temperature.

12 Withdrawal, or coitus interruptus, is a method of contraception in which the man withdraws his penis from the vagina before ejaculation. This method can be used in conjunction with other contraceptive methods.

13 Tubal sterilization is the most widely used method of birth control in the world. In this procedure, a health care provider may sever or block both Fallopian tubes so that the ovum and sperm cannot meet. A vasectomy blocks the flow of sperm through the vas deferens, and although the testes will continue to produce viable sperm cells, the cells die and are reabsorbed by the body.

14 Emergency contraception prevents pregnancy when taken after unprotected vaginal intercourse. As of 2010, three brands have FDA approval, including Plan B One-Step, Next Choice, and ella. All are progestin-only methods and work by inhibiting ovulation. Emergency contraception should be started within 72 hours of unprotected intercourse to be effective. Birth control pills or an IUD may also be used as emergency contraception.

15 Contraception has long been thought to be a female's responsibility, and that may be why the condom and vasectomy are the only birth control methods available to men. Many feminists claim the lack of male methods is because most of those doing the contraceptive research are men, whereas others claim that most methods are for women because it is easier to interfere with one ovum a month than thousands of sperm a day.

16 Many new contraceptive methods are on the horizon, and many will be easier to use, longer acting, and have higher effectiveness rates. Immunocontraceptives are also being studied.

17 There are two methods of controlling conception: contraception and abortion. Although the majority of women use contraception, many methods are difficult to use effectively and/or consistently, and no method is 100% effective.

18 Certain groups of women are at greater risk for an unintended pregnancy, including those who are young, unmarried, poor or low-income, and/or from racial/ethnic minorities.

19 In the United States, disagreements about abortion have been emotional and, at times, violent. Whereas some are pro-life supporters, others are pro-choice supporters.

20 Abortion has been practiced in many societies throughout history; in fact, there are few large-scale societies where it has not been practiced. Before abortion was legalized, illegal abortions were common. Throughout most of Western history, religion determined general attitudes toward abortion.

21 In 1973, the court case *Roe v. Wade* gave women a constitutionally protected right to have an abortion in the early stages of pregnancy. In the first trimester of pregnancy, a woman has a right to choose abortion without the state interfering. In the second trimester, a state can regulate abortion to protect a woman's health. Since 1973, individual states have regulated and limited whether, and when, a woman can obtain an abortion. Provisions include physician and hospital requirements, gestational limits, public funding restrictions, state-mandated counseling, waiting periods, and parental involvement.

22 Legalization of abortion in the United States gave women the right to choose abortion, but also increased the safety of abortion. Experts believe the legality of abortion does not affect the incidence of unintended pregnancy, the real underlying cause of abortion.

23 The typical woman who has an abortion in the United States is most likely to be in her 20s, poor or low-income, unmarried, and from an ethnic or racial minority. Although women choose abortion for many different reasons, some of the most common include an inability to care for a child, financial reasons, partner or relationship issues, or work, school, or family commitments.

24 Today a woman can choose between a surgical abortion and a medication abortion. The most important factor in determining which procedure a woman should have is the duration of her pregnancy.

25 The decision to have an abortion is a difficult one, and physiological and psychological effects vary from person to person and depend on many factors. The most prominent reaction after an abortion is relief. Men may also experience difficulties, but the male partner's involvement makes the abortion experience less traumatic for the woman.

26 Intimate partner violence is higher in couples with unintended pregnancies. There are men who try and control their partner's abortion-related decisions. Abusive men are more involved in pregnancies ending in abortion, especially in cases where there are repeat abortions.

27 Teens may be more vulnerable to postabortion anxiety, depression, sleep problems, and substance use and abuse, especially if there is a lack of emotional support from those around them. Many state laws have been enacted to limit teenagers' access to abortion.

28 Worldwide, 42 million abortions occur each year, and half of these involve illegal abortion procedures. Countries that have liberal abortion laws have been found to have lower rates of abortion.

CRITICAL THINKING QUESTIONS

1 If you found out tomorrow that you (or your partner) were 6 weeks' pregnant, what would your options be? Where would you go for help, and whom would you talk to? What would your biggest concerns be?

2 Suppose a good friend of yours, Sylvia, tells you that she is 10 weeks' pregnant, and she and her boyfriend have decided that she will have an abortion. She knows that you are taking the sexuality course and asks you about her abortion options. What can you tell her?

3 What method of contraception do you think would work best for you at this time in your life? In 5 years? In 10 years? Why?

4 Do you think women who use herbal contraceptives should be taught about newer, more modern methods of birth control? What if the methods they are using are working for them?

MEDIA RESOURCES

CourseMate brings course concepts to life with interactive learning, study, and exam preparation tools that support the printed textbook. A textbook-specific website, Psychology CourseMate includes an integrated interactive eBook and other interactive learning tools including quizzes, flashcards, videos, and more. If your textbook does not include an access code card, go to CengageBrain.com to gain access.

CENGAGENOW CengageNOW is an easy-to-use online resource that helps you study in less time to get the grade you want—NOW. Take a pre-test for this chapter and receive a personalized study plan based on your results that will identify the topics you need to review and direct you to online resources to help you master those topics. Then take a post-test to help you determine the concepts you have mastered and what you will need to work on. If your textbook does not include an access code card, go to CengageBrain.com to gain access.

View in Video available in CourseMate and CengageNOW:

Abortion Before Roe v. Wade: A woman discusses her views on abortion and her experience undergoing an illegal abortion in 1967.

Permanent Contraception: A new permanent contraceptive procedure involves the injection of an insert into each Fallopian tube.

Virtual Contraceptive Kit: Collection of various birth control methods.

Morning After Pill: Should the availability of the morning after pill lead to a decrease in abortion? This program explores the possible impact of the pill on sexual health and abortion rates.

Websites:

Planned Parenthood Federation of America ▪ Founded by Margaret Sanger in 1916 as America's first birth control clinic, Planned Parenthood Federation of America is the world's largest voluntary reproductive health care organization. This website offers information on birth control, emergency contraception, STIs, safer sex, pregnancy, abortion, and other health-related concerns.

Alan Guttmacher Institute ▪ The Alan Guttmacher Institute (AGI) is a nonprofit organization that focuses on sexual and reproductive health research, policy analysis, and public education. The institute's mission is to protect the reproductive choices of all women and men in the United States and throughout the world.

Birthcontrol.com ▪ This Canadian website sells innovative contraceptive products from around the world. Sponges, condoms, spermicides, and barrier methods of contraception can be found, all at relatively inexpensive prices.

National Abortion Federation ▪ The National Abortion Federation (NAF) is the professional association of abortion providers in the United States and Canada. NAF members provide the broadest spectrum of abortion expertise in North America.

National Abortion Rights Action League ▪ National Abortion Rights Action League (NARAL) is a pro-choice league that strives to help find workable answers to ultimately reduce the need for abortions. NARAL believes that ignoring limited access to contraception, reproductive health care, and sex education while taking away a woman's right to choose will only result in more unintended pregnancies and more abortions.

National Right to Life ▪ The National Right to Life Committee was founded in response to the U.S. Supreme Court's 1973 decision in *Roe v. Wade.* Since its official beginning, the National Right to Life Committee has grown to more than 3,000 chapters in all 50 states and the District of Columbia. The goal of the National Right to Life Committee is to restore legal protection to human life.

14 Challenges to Sexual Functioning

View in **Video**

View in **Video**

View in **Video**

View in **Video**

ABOUT THE CHAPTER OPENING VIDEO – Dr. Woet Gianotten, cofounder of the International Society in Sexuality and Cancer, is an expert in oncosexology, an area of medicine that focuses on the sexual and relational needs of patients with cancer, as well as their partners. As a physician and sexologist, he has spent many years exploring how disease, cancer, physical impairments, and medical interventions affect sexual functioning. Intrigued by the benefits of a satisfying sexual relationship, he began asking, *"How can a good sex life affect physical health?"* He strongly believes that an active and satisfying sex life can lead to better health and a greatly improved quality of life. I caught up with Dr. Gianotten in Utrecht, Holland, to learn more about his work.

Many doctors are hesitant to talk to patients about sex, and when they don't ask about it, many cancer patients feel anxious or embarrassed and think they shouldn't have sexual needs. I have learned that patients are often afraid to talk to their doctors about sex, and that doctors are afraid to talk to their patients about sex. The funny thing is, I have also found that sex therapists are often afraid to talk to patients about cancer! When I ask patients if they would like it if their doctor asked them about their sex lives, all my patients say "Yes!" It would help them to feel recognized as a sexual being and would let them know they are still a member of the living tribe. Maintaining a regular and satisfying sex life helps them feel loved, secure, and more like a man or woman. In addition to this, orgasms release endorphins and can decrease pain and suffering. Even those in the end stages of their lives desire sex and orgasms. One woman told me that she had more sex during the last days of her husband's life because they were so afraid that each day would be his last.

© Masterfile

Sexual expression and orgasm are important aspects of many people's lives. One 65-year-old woman I met was prescribed medication to help alleviate her depression after her husband died. Sometime later, she entered into a new relationship but found that she was unable to reach orgasm. She was one of those women who always enjoyed an active sex life—even when her husband was dying. But she was a plain woman, and when she went to her physician to talk about her problems reaching orgasm, he asked her if an orgasm was really that important to her. She told him, "If I can't get an orgasm, please give me pills to die."

I know you'll find my interview with Dr. Gianotten very thought-provoking. ❙❙

Janell Carroll

"If I can't have an orgasm, give me pills to die."
—CHAPTER OPENING VIDEO

View in Video

To watch the entire interview, go to Psychology CourseMate at **login.cengagebrain.com.**

© 2012 Cengage Learning

377

Sexual health is important to our overall health and quality of life. Although many people might believe that satisfactory sexual functioning comes naturally, we know that many men and women experience challenges to their sexual functioning. In this chapter, we explore how physiological and psychological issues, together with chronic illnesses and disabilities, can create problems in sexual functioning, and we explore current treatments for these problems.

CHALLENGES
TO Sexual Functioning

As we begin our exploration of challenges to sexual functioning, it is important to point out that sexual problems are quite common. Many of us experience times when we do not feel sufficiently aroused, have a lower level of enthusiasm, or have trouble relaxing during sex. In fact, the majority of couples report periodic sexual problems (E. Frank et al., 1978). Most of the time these problems do not interfere with overall sexual functioning and they go away on their own. However, for some people, the problems continue and may even get worse over time.

Defining a sexual problem can be difficult. If a woman can't reach orgasm during intercourse or a man can't get an erection one night, would you say they have a sexual problem? To help clarify definitions, some sex therapists in the United States use the *Diagnostic and Statistical Manual of Mental Disorders* (DSM), which provides diagnostic criteria for the most common sexual problems. It is occasionally updated, with the last text revision of the fourth edition in 2000 (referred to as the DSM-IV-TR; American Psychiatric Association, 2000). A revised, fifth edition of the DSM (DSM-5) is due to be released in 2013. In this chapter we will discuss diagnostic changes in the criteria for various sexual problems that have been proposed by the DSM Task Force along with the American Psychiatric Association. As of mid-2011 these criteria were still being evaluated for inclusion in the DSM-5.

Although the DSM has been an important tool in helping to diagnose and classify sexual problems, it has some potential problems. First, the DSM has used a physiological framing of sexual problems, which fails to acknowledge the relational aspects of

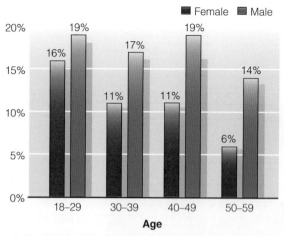

Anxiety About Sexual Performance

FIGURE **14.1** Percentage of self-reported anxiousness about performance during sex, by gender and age. SOURCE: Laumann et al., 1999

sexual behavior (Basson, 2000; Tiefer, 1991). Although physiological functions, such as erection and lubrication, may be important aspects of sexual functioning, so too are relationship and gender issues. The DSM has also had a heterosexist focus (Jern et al., 2009). The criteria for diagnosis often revolved around the ability to engage in vaginal intercourse—which only heterosexual couples experience. Does this mean that gays and lesbians don't experience sexual problems? No. Anyone who engages in sexual behavior is at risk for sexual problems. They can happen to anyone—gay, lesbian, straight, or bisexual. In this chapter, we refer to an inclusive definition of sexual problems.

It is also important to point out that, although some men and women who experience sexual problems are not distressed by them, others do feel distressed and seek out therapy. When a man or woman does seek out sex therapy, it typically begins with a medical evaluation to explore any physiological issues that might be contributing to the sexual problem. This is not always an easy task because psychological and physiological factors can overlap. Let's take a look at some of these factors.

▶▶ PSYCHOLOGICAL CHALLENGES
to Sexual Functioning

A variety of psychological factors can challenge sexual functioning, including unconscious fears, ongoing stress, anxiety, depression, guilt, anger, fear of intimacy, dependency, abandonment, and concern over loss of control (Reynaert et al., 2010). Anxiety plays an important role in developing and maintaining sexual problems (Figure 14.1). **Performance fears,** distractions, shifts in attention, or preoccupation during sexual arousal may interfere with the ability to respond sexually (Bancroft et al., 2005; Kaplan, 1974; Masters & Johnson, 1970). When anxiety levels are high, physiological arousal may be impossible. A lack of privacy or feeling rushed can also contribute to sexual problems.

Throughout this textbook we have discussed various components of healthy and successful relationships, including trust, respect, and the ability to communicate one's needs. Because sexual problems often occur within the context of intimate relationships,

Although our sexual response changes as we age, many older couples still enjoy an active, satisfying sex life.

© Roy McMahon/Corbis

Sex in Real Life ▶▶ Beyond the Medical Model

Masters and Johnson's sexual response cycle (see Chapter 10) and the *Diagnostic and Statistical Manual of Mental Disorders* medical classification for sexual dysfunction have long been used as the foundation for treating sexual disorders. However, critics challenge how these models apply to female sexuality and contend that they are incomplete by not encompassing psychosocial dimensions of sexual expression (see Figure 10.9). In 2000, Leonore Tiefer, a leading sex therapist and feminist sexologist, and a group of colleagues proposed the New View of Women's Sexual Problems that included a revision in the classification system for female sexual dysfunction (Kaschak & Tiefer, 2001).

According to Tiefer and colleagues, most sexual problems occur when there is emotional, physical, or relational dissatisfaction with some aspect of a sexual experience (Tiefer, 2001). The New View of Sexual Problems includes four categories that account for most of the limitations in women's sexual functioning:

I. Sexual problems caused by socio-cultural, political, economic factors: Some contributing factors may include ignorance and anxiety because of lack of sex education, lack of access to reproductive health services, or other social constraints and pressures; perceived inability to meet cultural norms for ideal sexuality; and conflict between the sexual norms of culture of origin and another culture.

II. Sexual problems relating to partner and relationship factors: May include inhibition, avoidance, or distress arising from betrayal, dislike, or fear of partner; partner's abuse or unequal power; partner's negative patterns of communication; or discrepancies in desire for various sexual activities.

III. Sexual problems caused by psychological factors: These factors include sexual aversion, mistrust, or inhibition of sexual pleasure because of past experiences of physical, sexual, or emotional abuse; depression and anxiety; or general personality problems.

IV. Sexual problems caused by medical factors: Such problems can arise from a wide variety of factors, including numerous local or systemic medical conditions affecting neurological, neurovascular, circulatory, endocrine or other systems of the body; pregnancy, sexually transmitted diseases, or other sex-related conditions; and adverse effects of many drugs, medications, or medical treatments.

New View proponents believe that an overmedicalization of female sexuality has resulted in an obsessive focus on the physical (genital) aspect of sexuality, leaving psychological and social aspects trivialized or ignored (Tiefer, 1996, 2002). The medical approaches to women's sexual problems have evolved into an increasing emphasis on pills, creams, gels, and other pharmaceutical agents, to the dismay of those who believe sexual behavior is multidimensional, complex, and context dependent (see websites at the end of the chapter for more information on the New View Campaign).

---

all of these issues can affect sexual functioning. Feeling unappreciated, anger, insecurity, resentment, conflict, or a lack of trust can lead to problems with sexual functioning. In addition, worrying about whether a partner is being faithful can also cause stress and anxiety, increasing the chances of sexual problems.

▶▶ PHYSIOLOGICAL CHALLENGES to Sexual Functioning

Healthy sexuality depends on a fine interplay of vascular, hormonal, and neurological functioning. However, a variety of physiological factors can interfere with these functions including various injuries, disabilities, illnesses, and diseases. Treatments for various diseases, such as chemotherapy and radiation, can also contribute to sexual problems (Bessede et al., in press; Ho et al., 2011; Ochsenkühn et al., 2011; Smith, 2010).

We also know that prescription drugs, such as **psychotropic medications** and birth control pills, can affect certain aspects of sexual functioning (see Chapter 13 for more information about birth control usage; Fava et al., 2011; Strohmaier et al., 2011; Yee, 2010). Nonprescription drugs such as tobacco, alcohol, marijuana, LSD, and cocaine may also affect sexual functioning.

Finally, the common physical changes of aging can affect sexual functioning. In Chapter 10, we discussed the effects of aging on sexual functioning (see Table 10.1). As men and women age, these physical changes contribute to an increased prevalence of sexual problems (Beaudreau et al., 2011; Camacho & Reyes-Ortiz, 2005; Yassin & Saad, 2008; Yee, 2010). We will discuss treatment for various physiological factors later in this chapter.

▶▶ EVALUATING Sexual Problems

For a sex therapist to formulate a treatment plan for a sexual problem, it is important that the therapist understand more about how the patient experiences the problem. For example, how long has it been going on? Has it always happened or is it fairly new? A **primary sexual problem** is one that has always existed, whereas a **secondary sexual problem** is one that develops after a period of adequate functioning.

Therapists also need to know the context of the sexual problem: Does it occur all the time or just some of the time? A

---

performance fears
The fear of not being able to perform during sexual behavior.

psychotropic medications
Medications prescribed for psychological disorders, such as depression.

primary sexual problem
A sexual problem that has always existed.

secondary sexual problem
A sexual problem that occurs after a period of normal sexual functioning.

situational sexual problem is a problem that occurs during certain sexual activities or with certain partners (for instance, a man who can get an erection with his girlfriend but not his wife, or a woman who can have orgasms during masturbation but not during oral sex). A **global sexual problem** is a problem that occurs in every situation, during every type of sexual activity, and with every sexual partner. It is important to clarify these differences, for they may affect treatment strategies. For instance, primary problems tend to have more biological or physiological causes, whereas secondary problems tend to have more psychological causes.

▶▶ TREATING Sexual Problems

In the United States, treatment of most sexual problems begins with a medical history and workup to identify any physiological causes. In addition to a medical history and examination, it is also important to evaluate any past sexual trauma or abuse that may cause or contribute to the problem. After identifying potential causes, the next step is to determine a plan of treatment. Such treatment may be **multimodal,** involving more than one type of therapy.

Much of the current clinical research today focuses on developing new drugs to treat sexual problems (even though a number of problems may be caused by or worsened by other medications). As we discussed in Chapter 13, the U.S. Food and Drug Administration (FDA) plays a major role in the approval of all new drugs in the United States. Many drug therapies used today for sexual problems, such as Viagra, were originally approved by the FDA to treat other diseases. There is also a brisk business in health supplements to aid in sexual functioning, including aphrodisiacs (see Sex in Real Life feature later in the chapter).

We will discuss illness, disability, and sexual functioning later in this chapter, but now let's turn to specific sexual problems and treatment options. Problems commonly occur with sexual desire or arousal, orgasm, or pain during sexual behavior.

REAL RESEARCH 14.1 Many men and women who experience sexual problems do not talk about their concerns with their health care providers, mostly because they feel embarrassed and/or lack the communication skills to do so (KINGSBERG & KNUDSON, 2011).

◀ review QUESTIONS

1 Identify and describe some of the psychological factors that have been found to interfere with sexual functioning.

2 Identify and describe some of the physiological factors that have been found to interfere with sexual functioning.

3 Explain how sexual problems are evaluated and how this might affect treatment strategies.

4 Explain the approach to treatment of sexual problems.

▶ PROBLEMS WITH Sexual Desire

Problems with sexual desire involve a deficient or absent desire for sexual activity. There may be a lack of sexual fantasies, a reduction of or absence in initiating sexual activity, or a decrease in self-stimulation.

The DSM-IV-TR had two categories of sexual desire disorders, **hypoactive sexual desire disorder (HSDD)** and **sexual aversion.** However, experts believe that since women often have fewer sexual fantasies, are less likely to initiate sexual activity, and have lower levels of self-stimulation, these criteria didn't adequately access the female experience. Because of this, experts have recommended adding **sexual interest/arousal disorder** for women and using HSDD only for men in the DSM-5. They have also recommended that sexual aversion be dropped from the desire disorders since symptoms are more similar to phobias rather than sexual desire. HSDD and sexual interest/arousal disorder both involve a lack of sexual desire or interest.

▶▶ HYPOACTIVE SEXUAL DESIRE DISORDER and Sexual Interest/Arousal Disorder

In the DSM-IV-TR, HSDD was defined as a persistent or recurrent deficiency or absence of sexual fantasies and desire for sexual activity. Sexual interest/arousal disorder in women involves a lack of sexual interest and arousal of at least 6 months with absent or reduced sexual thoughts or fantasies; no initiation of sexual activity and little receptiveness to partner's sexual initiation; absent or reduced sexual excitement or pleasure during sexual activity; desire rarely triggered by internal or external sexual or erotic stimuli; and absent or reduced genital and/or nongenital sensations during sexual activity. These conditions cause a significant level of distress (Leiblum et al., 2006).

situational sexual problem
A sexual problem that occurs only in specific situations.

global sexual problem
A sexual problem that occurs in every sexual situation.

multimodal
Using a variety of techniques.

hypoactive sexual desire disorder (HSDD)
Diminished or absent sexual interest or desire.

sexual aversion
Extreme aversion to, and avoidance of, all genital sexual contact with a sexual partner.

sexual interest/arousal disorder
A category of sexual problems that involves a lack of sexual interest or arousal in women.

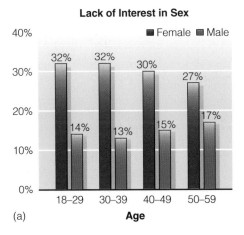

Lack of Interest in Sex

■ Female ■ Male

(a) **Age**

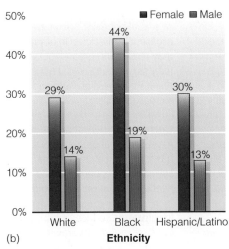

■ Female ■ Male

(b) **Ethnicity**

FIGURE **14.2** Percentage of self-reported lack of interest in sex, by gender, ethnicity, and age.
SOURCE: Laumann et al., 1999

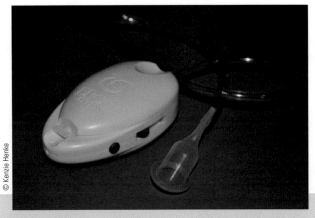

© Kenzie Henke

The EROS-CTD is a handheld device that increases blood flow to the clitoris. The plastic cup is placed directly over the clitoris during use.

For many years, sexual interest and arousal disorders were thought to be the most common sexual problem in women (see Figure 14.2; Palacios, 2011). A nationally representative sample of U.S. women found that 27% of premenopausal women and 52% of naturally menopausal women experienced such problems (West et al., 2008).

Psychological factors that may contribute to either of these disorders include a lack of attraction to one's partner, fear of intimacy or pregnancy, marital or relationship conflicts, religious concerns, depression, and other psychological disorders (Lai, 2011). Desire disorders can also result from negative messages about sexuality while growing up, treating sex as a chore, a concern over loss of control, or a negative body image (Heiman & LoPiccolo, 1992). In addition, eating disorders, sexual coercion, and sexual abuse have also been found to be associated with problems of desire (Carter et al., 2007; Gilmore et al., 2010; Pinheiro et al., 2010; Rellini et al., 2011). In one study of survivors of sexual assault, more than half had long-lasting problems with sexual desire (Campbell et al., 2006).

Physiological factors, such as hormonal problems, medication side effects, chronic use of alcohol, chronic illness, and treatment for various illnesses may also contribute to decreased sexual desire

*For many years, **sexual interest and arousal disorders** were thought to be the **most common sexual problem in women.***

(Basson et al., 2010; Bessede et al., in press; Graziottin, 2007; Ho et al., 2011; Leiblum et al., 2006; Lutfey et al., 2008; Ochsenkühn et al., 2011; Smith, 2010).

Treating Desire and Sexual Interest Disorders

Many therapists consider problems with sexual desire to be one of the most complicated sexual problems to treat. As we discussed previously, treatment first involves a medical workup to identify any physiological causes. A psychological evaluation will explore any past sexual trauma or abuse that may interfere with sexual desire or interest.

A variety of different treatment options are available. Cognitive–behavioral therapy, a form of psychotherapy that emphasizes the importance of how a person thinks and the effect these thoughts have on a person's feelings and behaviors, has offered promising results. These types of therapy are brief, highly instructional, and structured. The client may also be assigned homework exercises to help identify these motivations.

In 2000, the EROS clitoral therapy device was approved by the FDA as a prescription device for the treatment of female sexual arousal and desire problems (see nearby photo; Wilson et al., 2001). The small, battery-powered device is designed to be used in the privacy of a woman's own home. It creates a gentle suction on the clitoris and genital area, which increases blood flow and leads to clitoral engorgement. The clitoral engorgement triggers responses in the vaginal nerves, which increases sexual stimulation and sensations and causes vaginal lubrication. Studies have found that the EROS device can help increase vaginal lubrication and vasocongestion.

Since the release of Viagra for men in 1998, there has been a rush of research trying to find the magic pill for women (Berman et al., 2003; Caruso et al., 2006; Feldhaus-Dahir, 2010). Although some studies have evaluated the use of Viagra in women, overall, it has been found to provide little benefit in the treatment of female sexual arousal and desire problems (Alexander et al., 2011; Basson et al., 2002).

In the mid-2000s, there was growing interest in a nasal spray inhaler dubbed PT-141 (bremelanotide) for treatment of female

Throughout history, people from primitive—and not so primitive—cultures have searched for the "ultimate" aphrodisiac to enhance sexual interest and performance. Oysters, for example, have been reported to increase sexual desire, although this has never been proved. The idea that oysters are an aphrodisiac may have originated from their resemblance to male testicles, or even to female ovaries. Ancient people believed that food with the shape or

In Bangkok, Thailand, a vendor is pushing cobra blood to improve sexual drive. Customers choose their own snake; then the snake is split open with a razor blade. An incision is made in the major artery of the snake, and all the blood is drained into a wineglass. The blood is then mixed with warm whiskey and a dash of honey. Users believe it helps their sex drive.

qualities of the genitals possessed aphrodisiac qualities; seeds of all kinds were associated with fertility and desire. Scientists have also reported that watermelon can increase sexual desire and interest (Santa Ana, 2008).

In various cultures, carrots, cucumbers, chili peppers, rhino horns, and various seafood, as well as eggs and poppy seeds, were thought to increase sexual desire. The market for so-called aphrodisiacs in some countries has added to the decline of some endangered species, such as the rhinoceros, valued for its horn.

There are no proven aphrodisiacs, but it is possible that if a person thinks something will increase his or her sexual desire, it just might do so (Shamloul, 2010). Simply believing something will increase desire may cause it to work. Overall, to increase sexual desire, rely on regular exercise, a healthy diet, candlelight, the use of scents, romantic music, and whatever else enhances your personal sexual arousal. Following are some of the most popular substances that have been thought to increase sexual desire.

Alcohol: Although some people believe that alcohol increases their sexual desire, in actuality, it merely decreases anxiety and inhibitions, and then only in low doses. In large amounts, alcohol can impair sexual functioning.

Amyl nitrate: Amyl nitrate (also called "snappers" or "poppers") is thought to increase orgasmic sensations. It is inhaled from capsules that are "popped" open for quick use. Amyl nitrate causes a rapid

dilation of arteries that supply the heart and other organs with blood, which may cause warmth in the genitals. Amyl nitrate may dilate arteries in the brain, causing euphoria or giddiness, and relax the sphincter muscle to ease penetration during anal sex. Adverse effects include severe dizziness, migraine headaches, and fainting. (Amyl nitrate is used by cardiac patients to reduce heart pain.)

Cocaine: Thought to increase frequency of sexual behavior, sexual desire, and orgasmic sensations. In actuality, cocaine may reduce inhibitions, possibly leading to risky sexual behaviors. Long-term use can result in depression, addiction, and increased anxiety.

Ginseng: An herb that has been thought to increase sexual desire. Preliminary research has found it may have some positive aphrodisiac properties, but more research is needed to confirm (Shamloul, 2010).

Marijuana: Reduces inhibitions and may improve mood. No proven effect on sexual desire.

Spanish fly: Consists of ground-up beetle wings (cantharides) from Europe and causes inflammation of the urinary tract and dilation of the blood vessels. Although some people find the burning sensation arousing, Spanish fly may cause death from its toxic side effects.

Yohimbine: From the African Yohimbe tree. Preliminary research has found it may have some mild aphrodisiac properties, but this does not support its widespread use (Shamloul, 2010).

---

sexual arousal and desire problems, which showed some promise in increasing sexual interest and behaviors in women by stimulating the central nervous system (Diamond et al., 2006; Pfaus et al., 2007; Safarinejad, 2008; Shadiack et al., 2007). However, in 2008, the FDA reduced clinical trials of PT-141 because of safety con-

cerns (Diamond et al., 2006; Perelman, 2007; Pfaus et al., 2007; Safarinejad, 2008; Shadiack et al., 2007). Limited ongoing trials continue to evaluate this drug and variations of the drug. Studies have also been conducted on a variety of **vasoactive agents** to reduce female sexual arousal and desire problems, including Vasomax, or phentolamine. Although testosterone has been used in women, this has been controversial (Hubayter & Simon, 2008; Talakoub et al., 2002). Because of safety concerns, the FDA has delayed approval of products for women that contain testosterone (Fabre et al., 2011). As of mid-2011, the FDA had not approved any medications for arousal and desire disorders in women, although a variety of medications have been proposed (Fabre et al., 2011; Feldhaus-Dahir, 2010).

vasoactive agent
Medication that causes dilation of the blood vessels.

yohimbine
Produced from the bark of the African yohimbe tree; often used as an aphrodisiac.

discrepancy in desire
Differences in levels of sexual desire in a couple.

Sexual Diversity in Our World ▶▶▶ Treating Sexual Problems in Other Cultures

Sex therapy in the United States has been criticized for its adherence to Western sexual attitudes and values, with an almost total ignorance of cultural differences in sexual problems and therapy. Our view of sex tends to emphasize that activity is pleasurable (or at least natural), both partners are equally involved, couples need and want to be educated about sex, and communication is important to have good sexual relationships (Lavee, 1991; So & Cheung, 2005). It is important to recognize, however, that these ideas might not be shared outside the United States or within different ethnic groups; therefore, Masters and Johnson's classic therapy model is much less acceptable to these groups. Sexual goals are different among cultural groups with an egalitarian ideology than among those without (Lau et al., 2005). An egalitarian ideology views mutual sexual pleasure and communication as important, whereas nonegalitarian ideologies view heterosexual intercourse as the goal and men's sexual pleasure as more important than women's (Reiss, 1986). Double standards of sexual pleasure are common, for example, in many Portuguese, Mexican, Puerto Rican, and Latino groups. Some

Asian groups also often have strong cultural prohibitions about discussing sexuality. So U.S. values such as open communication, mutual satisfaction, and accommodation to a partner's sexuality may not be appropriate in working with people from these cultures.

In cultures in which low female sexual desire is not viewed as a problem, hypoactive sexual desire wouldn't be viewed as a sexual problem; it would be an acceptable part of female sexuality. In some Muslim groups, for example, the only problems that exist are those that interfere with men's sexual behavior (Lavee, 1991).

Approaches to sexual problems also differ outside the United States. Some cultures believe in supernatural causes of sexual disorders (such as the man being cursed by a powerful woman or being given the evil eye; So & Cheung, 2005). Malay and Chinese men who experience erectile disorders tend to blame their wives for the problem, whereas Indian men attribute their problem to fate (Low et al., 2002). However, Asian culture has also produced the Tantric ceremonial sexual ritual, which might be viewed as therapy for sexual disorders.

Tantric sex involves five exercises (Voigt, 1991). First, a couple begins by developing a private ritual to prepare them to share sexual expression: the lighting of candles; using perfume, lotions, music, a special bed or room; certain lighting patterns; massage; reciting poetry together; or meditating. Then they synchronize their breathing by lying together and "getting in touch" with each other. Direct eye contact is sustained throughout the ritual. (Couples often say that they feel uncomfortable using eye contact, but with practice it becomes very powerful.)

Next, "motionless intercourse" begins, in which the couple remains motionless at the peak of the sensual experience. For many couples, this may be during the time of initial penetration. Initially, this motionlessness may last only a few minutes, building up to increasingly longer periods. The final aspect of the Tantric ritual is to expand the sexual exchange without orgasm, resulting in an intensification of the sexual–spiritual energy (this is similar to Masters and Johnson's technique of delaying orgasm to enjoy the physical sensations of touching and caressing).

A variety of herbal products are available for female sexual arousal and desire problems, including Avlimil, a nonprescription daily supplement, and Zestra, a botanical massage oil formulated to increase female arousal and pleasure. Studies have found that Zestra can increase sexual desire, arousal, and sexual satisfaction, although there are side effects (Ferguson et al., 2003, 2010). Viacreme, an amino acid–based cream that contains menthol, has also been used for problems with sexual desire in women. The makers of Viacreme claim that when it is applied to the clitoris, blood flow increases through dilation of clitoral blood vessels. Studies are also testing other agents to increase female sexual arousal, including the aphrodisiac **yohimbine** (yo-HIM-bean; Meston & Worcel, 2002). Yohimbine is a substance produced in the bark of the African yohimbe tree, which has been found to improve sexual functioning. Although these products do not require FDA approval, more research is needed to assess their possible adverse effects and complications (Islam et al., 2001). Despite a great deal of research, few of these hormonal and vasoactive agents have withstood scientific scrutiny (Perelman, 2007). In ad-

dition, safety issues have not been addressed for many of these products, adding to concerns of potential harm that these products may produce. As of mid-2011, no FDA-approved medications were available for the treatment of low sexual desire in women. Even so, research continues to explore a variety of pharmacological treatments for women, including the drug Gepirone, other methods of testosterone administration, and medications that act on the central nervous system (Fabre et al., 2011; Palacios, 2011).

Pharmacological treatment has also been used in men with low sexual desire. Because testosterone is largely responsible for male sexual desire, men with low testosterone levels have historically been treated with testosterone injections. However, research has been unable to show a consistent and beneficial role of testosterone in increasing sexual desire in men (Allan et al., 2008; Isidori et al., 2005). Overall, the majority of men who experience low sexual desire have normal levels of testosterone (Wespes & Schulman, 2002).

Sometimes it is not one partner's level of desire that is the problem but the **discrepancy in desire** between the partners.

Challenges to Sexual Functioning ◀ **383**

Many couples experience differences in their levels of desire—one partner may desire sex more often than the other. If Lisa wants to have sex once a week, but her partner wants sex every day, which partner do you think would be identified as having a problem? If you guessed Lisa, you're right. Often the partner with a lower level of desire will show up at a therapist's office and not the partner with higher desire (R. C. Rosen & Leiblum, 1987). But if Lisa had a partner with a similar level of desire, there would be no sexual problems. Men and women experiencing low levels of sexual de-

sire may turn to **aphrodisiacs** for help (see the accompanying Sex in Real Life feature).

REAL RESEARCH 14.2   Sexual problems are common in men and women who experience posttraumatic stress disorder, which can affect overall sexual activity, desire, arousal, orgasm, and satisfaction (CHUDAKOV ET AL., 2008).

◀ review QUESTIONS

1 Differentiate the problems of desire that men and women may experience.

2 Explore some of the possible causes for the problems of sexual desire and interest.

3 Identify the strategies for treating desire and sexual interest problems.

▶ PROBLEMS WITH Sexual Arousal

In the past, a woman experiencing problems with sexual arousal may have been diagnosed with female **sexual arousal disorder**, but as we just discussed, experts have proposed that these problems are part of sexual interest/arousal disorders. In men, sexual arousal disorders can lead to **erectile disorder (ED).** These problems can occur even when a person reports adequate focus, intensity, and duration of sexual stimulation. Disorders can be primary or, more commonly, secondary, in that they only occur with a certain partner or specific sexual behavior.

▶▶ ERECTILE Disorder

Normal erectile functioning involves neurological, endocrine, vascular, and muscular factors. Psychological factors including fear of failure and performance anxiety may also affect erectile functioning. Anxiety has been found to have a cyclical effect on erectile functioning: If a man experiences a problem getting an

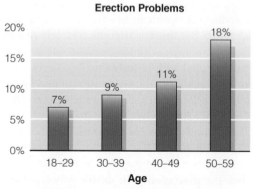

FIGURE 14.3 The prevalence of erection problems in men increases with age. SOURCE: Laumann et al., 1999

Erection Problems

Age	
18–29	7%
30–39	9%
40–49	11%
50–59	18%

ON YOUR MIND 14.1

Is erectile disorder hereditary?

No, erectile disorder itself is not hereditary. However, certain diseases, such as diabetes, may be inherited and can lead to an erectile disorder or other sexual problems. It is important to catch these diseases early so that medical intervention can decrease any possible sexual adverse effects.

---

erection one night, the next time he engages in sexual behavior he remembers the failure and becomes anxious. This anxiety, in turn, interferes with his ability to have an erection.

ED is defined as the persistent inability to obtain or maintain an erection sufficient for satisfactory sexual behavior. ED affects millions of men, and the incidence increases with age (Figure 14.3). Whereas 12% of men younger than 59 experience ED, 22% of men aged 60 to 69, and 30% of men older than 69 experience ED (Bacon et al., 2003; Costabile et al., 2008; Liu et al., 2010; Lue, 2000).

Approximately 70% of ED cases have a physical basis, with the major risk factors being diabetes, high cholesterol levels, or chronic medical illnesses (Fink et al., 2002; Yassin & Saad, 2008). In many cases, ED is due to a combination of factors. Unfortunately, when health care providers identify a physical problem (such as hypertension) in a patient suffering from ED, they might not continue to explore the psychological factors. Or if a psycho-

---

REAL RESEARCH 14.3   A Finnish study found that regular vaginal intercourse in heterosexual men protects against the development of erectile disorders among men aged 55 to 75 years (KOSKIMÄKI ET AL., 2008).

---

logical problem is found first (such as a recent divorce), health care providers might not perform a medical evaluation. Overall, EDs in younger men (20–35 years old) are more likely to be psychologically based, whereas EDs in older men (60 and older), they are more likely to be due to physical factors (Lue, 2000).

To diagnose the causes of ED, health care providers and sex therapists may use tests such as the **nocturnal penile tumescence test** (Elhanbly et al., 2009). Men normally experience two or three erections a night during stages of rapid eye movement (REM) sleep. If these erections do not occur, it is a good indication that there is a physiological problem; if they do occur, erectile problems are more likely to have psychological causes. The nocturnal penile tumescence test requires a man to spend the night in a sleep laboratory hooked up to several machines, but newer devices allow him to monitor his sleep erections in the privacy of his own home. RigiScan, a portable diagnostic monitor, measures both rigidity and tumescence at the base and tip of the penis. Stamp tests and other at-home devices are also used (Elhanbly et al., 2009). A stamp test uses perforated bands resembling postage stamps, which are placed on the base of the penis before retiring for the night. In the morning, if the perforations have ripped, this indicates that the man had normal physiological functioning while sleeping.

"In the process of becoming aroused, all of a sudden it would be over."
—ERECTILE DISORDER

View in Video
To watch the entire interview, go to Psychology CourseMate at **login.cengagebrain.com.**

© 2012 Cengage Learning

Treating Male Erectile Disorder

Of all the sexual disorders, there are more treatment options for male ED than for any other disorder. A tremendous amount of research has been dedicated to finding causes and treatment options for ED. Depending on the cause, treatment for ED includes

---

REAL RESEARCH 14.4   Research has found that a heterosexual woman's sexual functioning may be affected by a partner's sexual problems. Seventy-eight percent of women whose partners had premature ejaculation had at least one sexual disorder themselves, compared with only 43% of women in a control group (HOBBS ET AL., 2008).

---

psychological treatment, pharmacological treatment (drugs), hormonal and intracavernous injections, vascular surgery, vacuum constriction devices, and prosthesis implantation. The success rate for treating male ED ranges from 50% to 80% (Lue, 2000).

PSYCHOLOGICAL TREATMENT   The primary psychological treatments for ED include **systematic desensitization** and sex therapy that includes education, **sensate focus,** and communication training (Heiman, 2002). These treatments can help reduce feelings of anxiety and can evaluate issues that are interfering with erectile

response. Relationship therapy can also help explore issues in a relationship that might contribute to ED, such as unresolved anger, bitterness, or guilt.

PHARMACOLOGICAL TREATMENT   The first oral medication for ED, Viagra (sildenafil citrate), was approved by the FDA in 1998, and in 2003, Cialis (tadalafil) and Levitra (vardenafil) were approved. Several additional drugs are being tested for the treatment of ED (Limin et al., 2010) These drugs can be used in a variety of ED cases—those that are **psychogenic** (sike-oh-JEN-nick), illness related, or have physical causes. Today, more than 50 million men with ED worldwide have used one of these drugs, and they are considered the first line of treatment for ED (Eardley, 2010; Palit & Eardley, 2010).

All of these drugs produce muscle relaxation in the penis, dilation of the arteries supplying the penis, and an inflow of blood, which can lead to penile erection. They do not increase a man's sexual desire and will not produce an erection without adequate sexual stimulation. Typically, a man must take Viagra about 1 hour before he desires an erection, and Cialis and Levitra often work within 15 to 30 minutes. Erections can last up to 4 hours, although Cialis can aid in erections for up to 36 hours (which is why French media referred to it as "le weekend," because it can be taken on a Friday night and last until early Sunday; Japsen, 2003). Overall, studies have found that patients prefer Cialis over Viagra and Levitra, mainly because of its longer duration (Morales et al., 2011).

---

aphrodisiac
A substance that increases, or is believed to increase, a person's sexual desire.

sexual arousal disorder
Diminished or absent lubrication response of sexual excitation.

erectile disorder (ED)
Diminished or absent ability to attain or maintain, until completion of the sexual activity, an adequate erection.

nocturnal penile tumescence test
A study performed to evaluate erections during sleep that helps clarify the causes of erectile disorder.

systematic desensitization
A treatment method for sexual disorders that involves neutralizing the anxiety-producing aspects of sexual situations and behavior by a process of gradual exposure.

sensate focus
A series of touching experiences that are assigned to couples in sex therapy to teach nonverbal communication and reduce anxiety.

psychogenic
Relating to psychological causes.

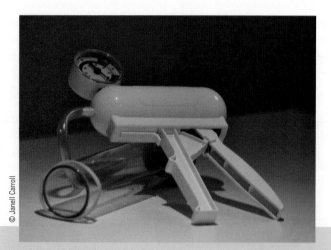

Vacuum constriction devices, such as the ErecAid, are often used in the treatment of erectile dysfunction. A man places his penis in the cylinder and vacuum suction increases blood flow to the penis, creating an erection.

ON YOUR MIND 14.2

A couple of guys I know have some Viagra, and they have been trying to get me to take it. Is it safe to use this drug if you don't have ED?

Although recreational use of Viagra and other erectile drugs is not uncommon, it does not always live up to expectations (Crosby & Diclemente, 2004; Eloi-Stiven et al., 2007; Fisher et al., 2006; Musacchio et al., 2006). Men who use these drugs are often disappointed because it doesn't always lead to longer and firmer erections, and can often contribute to physical adverse effects, such as harmful changes in blood pressure (Crosby & Diclemente, 2004; D. Fisher et al., 2006). In addition, men who use these drugs recreationally are more likely to engage in unsafe sex compared with those not using these drugs, which puts them at greater risk for sexually transmitted infections (Swearingen & Klausner, 2005).

These medications have several adverse effects, including headaches, a flushing in the cheeks and neck, nasal congestion, and indigestion. Less common adverse effects include an increased risk for vision problems, including changes in color vision and possible total vision loss, and ringing in the ears or total hearing loss (Mukherjee & Shivakumar, 2007; Wooltorton, 2006). In fact, the FDA called for revised labeling of all erectile drugs outlining possible vision adverse effects in 2005 (Kaufman, 2005) and hearing loss in 2007 (Mukherjee & Shivakumar, 2007). Critics of pharmacological treatment for ED point out that drug use focuses solely on an erection and fails to take into account the multidimensional nature of male sexuality (B. W. McCarthy & Fucito, 2005).

Yohimbine, which we discussed earlier in this chapter, has been found to improve erections and can be successfully used with various erectile medications (Tanweer et al., 2010; Zhang et al., 2010). It works by stimulating the parasympathetic nervous system, which is linked to erectile functioning. Adverse effects include dizziness, nervousness, irritability, and an increased heart rate and blood pressure. Nitroglycerin and nitrates have also been used to treat ED in men (Wimalawansa, 2008).

HORMONAL TREATMENTS   Hormonal treatments may help improve erections in men who have hormonal irregularities (such as too much prolactin or too little gonadal hormones; Lue, 2000).

Excessive prolactin can interfere with adequate secretion of testosterone and can cause ED. A man with low testosterone levels can be prescribed testosterone therapy through injections, patches, gels, or creams. However, as we discussed earlier, research has been unable to show a consistent and beneficial role of testosterone in increasing sexual functioning in men (Allan et al., 2008; Isidori et al., 2005). Even so, these drugs are commonly used to treat ED.

A testosterone patch is applied directly to the scrotum, whereas gels and creams can be applied to other parts of the body such as the arms or stomach. AndroGel, a clear, colorless, odorless gel, was approved by the FDA in 2000 for the treatment of low testosterone (Morley & Perry, 2000). It is applied daily and is absorbed into the skin. Some men prefer this type of application over a painful injection or patch. Adverse effects are rare but include headaches, acne, depression, gynecomastia, and hypertension. None of these testosterone preparations should be used by men with prostate cancer because they can exacerbate this condition.

INTRACAVERNOUS INJECTIONS   Also used to treat ED are **intracavernous** (in-truh-CAV-er-nuss) **injections** (Alexandre et al., 2007; Lue, 2000). Men and their partners are taught to self-inject these preparations directly into the corpora cavernosa (see Chapter 6) while the penis is gently stretched out. The injections cause the blood vessels to relax, which increases blood flow to the penis. The majority of patients report very minor pain from these injections. However, each time a man desires an erection, he must use

---

intracavernous injection
A treatment method for erectile disorder in which vasodilating drugs are injected into the penis for the purpose of creating an erection.

vacuum constriction device
Treatment device for erectile disorder used to pull blood into the penis.

revascularization
A procedure used in the treatment of vascular erectile disorder in which the vascular system is rerouted to ensure better blood flow to the penis.

prosthesis implantation
A treatment method for erectile disorder in which a prosthesis is surgically implanted into the penis.

semirigid rod
A flexible rod that is implanted into the penis during prosthetic surgery.

hypersexual disorder
Recurrent and intense sexual fantasies, sexual urges, and sexual behavior.

persistent sexual arousal syndrome
An excessive and unremitting level of sexual arousal. May also be referred to as persistent genital arousal disorder.

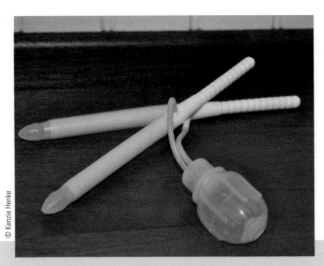

Semirigid prostheses are surgically implanted in the penis and can enable a man with erectile dysfunction to have an erection suitable for penetrative sexual behavior.

© Kenzie Henke

SURGICAL TREATMENTS Surgical intervention has increased as a treatment for ED. In some cases, physicians perform **revascularization** to improve erectile functioning; in other cases, **prosthesis** (pross-THEE-sis) **implantation** may be recommended. Acrylic implants for ED were first used in 1952, but they were replaced by silicone rubber in the 1960s and then by a variety of synthetic materials in the 1970s. Today there are two main types of implants: **semirigid rods,** which provide a permanent state of erection but can be bent up and down; and inflatable devices that become firm when the man pumps them up (Simmons & Montague, 2008). Penetrative sexual behaviors may safely be engaged in 4 to 8 weeks after surgery. After prosthesis implantation, a man is still able to orgasm, ejaculate, and impregnate (Simmons & Montague, 2008).

Sexual satisfaction after a prosthesis implantation has been found to be related to several factors, such as a man's relationship with his partner and feelings about his own masculinity (Kempeneers et al., 2004). While many couples report increased sexual satisfaction after surgery (Bettocchi et al., 2010), between 10% and 20% of patients remain dissatisfied, dysfunctional, or sexually inactive (Minervini et al., 2006). If a man has psychological factors that contribute to his erectile difficulties, these issues are likely to resurface after a prosthesis is implanted.

Some studies have found greater success rates when using a combination of various therapies, such as a vacuum erectile device together with medications or injections, or various other combinations (Dhir et al., in press).

▶▶ OTHER PROBLEMS with Sexual Arousal

The DSM-5 has recommended adding a new sexual disorder category called **hypersexual disorder.** This disorder involves recurrent and intense sexual fantasies, sexual urges, and sexual behavior. This disorder causes personal distress and can impair social, occupational, or other areas of functioning. Another disorder that has been explored in the research, **persistent sexual arousal syndrome,** is not listed in either version of the DSM (Leiblum & Goldmeier, 2008; Leiblum & Seehuus, 2009; Levin &

this injection. The higher the dosage of medication, the longer the erection will last.

One possible adverse effect of treatment using intracavernous injections is priapism. Other side effects are more related to the injection than to the drug itself and may include pain, bleeding, or bruising (Alexandre et al., 2007; Israilov et al., 2002). Prostaglandin pellets have also been used to increase blood flow to the penis. The pellets are inserted directly into the urethra, where they are absorbed. Erections with these methods will typically occur within 20 minutes and can last for an hour and a half.

VACUUM CONSTRICTION DEVICES In the past several years, **vacuum constriction devices,** which use suction to induce erections, have become more popular, in part because they are less invasive and safer than injections. One such device, the ErecAid System, involves putting the flaccid penis into a vacuum cylinder and pumping it to draw blood into the corpora cavernosa (similar to the one Austin Powers was caught with in *Austin Powers: International Man of Mystery*). A constriction ring is rolled onto the base of the penis after it is removed from the vacuum device to keep the blood in the penis. This ring is left on the penis until the erection is no longer desired. When it is removed, the man will lose his erection. Negative side effects include possible bruising and, in rare cases, testicular entrapment in the vacuum chamber (Lue, 2000). Overall, these devices can be expensive, bulky, and noisy, and they reduce spontaneity, which some couples find unappealing.

REAL RESEARCH 14.5 Hair loss treatments, including Propecia and Minoxidil, have been found to cause various adverse sexual effects in men, such as reduced sexual interest and erection and orgasm problems, and these effects were found to last for up to 40 months after discontinuing the treatment (IRWIG & KOLUKULA, 2011).

Wylie, 2010; Waldinger & Schweitzer, 2009). The opposite of an arousal problem, a woman's complaint is usually an excessive and unremitting arousal. Genital arousal can last for hours or days despite a lack of sexual desire or stimulation and can be distressing and worrisome to women, although many may be reluctant to discuss it with health care providers. More research is needed to shed more light on this disorder.

1 Identify and explain the problems with sexual arousal.

2 Identify possible treatment strategies for female sexual arousal disorder.

3 Define erectile disorder (ED) and identify some of the tests used to diagnose male ED.

4 Identify some of the pharmacological and hormonal treatments for ED.

5 Identify how intracavernous injections, vacuum constriction devices, and surgery are used in the treatment of ED.

▶ PROBLEMS with Orgasm

Every individual reaches orgasm differently, and has different wants and needs to build sexual excitement. Some men and women need very little stimulation, others need a great deal of stimulation, and some never reach orgasm. The DSM-IV-TR had three categories of orgasmic disorders, including female **orgasmic disorder,** male orgasmic disorder, and **premature ejaculation.** Experts have recommended changing male orgasmic disorder to **delayed ejaculation** and premature ejaculation to **early ejaculation** in the DSM-5. Following, we will discuss these disorders.

▶▶ FEMALE ORGASMIC Disorder

Historically, this disorder was referred to as "frigidity," which had negative implications about the woman. The DSM defines female orgasmic disorder as a delay or absence of orgasm after a normal phase of sexual excitement. This is a common complaint among women, and studies have found that approximately one quarter of women report orgasmic disorder (Ishak et al., 2010; Laumann et al., 1994; Meston et al., 2004). Research has found that educational levels are related to orgasmic problems. Those with higher levels of education report lower levels of orgasmic problems (Figure 14.4). Re-

member, though, that the DSM definition does not indicate that orgasm must occur during vaginal intercourse. In fact, the majority of heterosexual women are unable to orgasm during vaginal intercourse. If a woman is unable to orgasm during all sexual activities after a normal phase of sexual excitement, she may be experiencing orgasmic disorder. Some women who take certain psychotropic drugs, including many types of antidepressants, experience delayed or absent orgasms (Labbate, 2008).

Primary orgasmic disorder describes a condition in which a woman has never had an orgasm. Secondary orgasmic disorder refers to a condition in which a woman was able to have orgasms previously but later has trouble reaching orgasm. Situational orgasmic disorder refers to a condition in which a woman can have orgasms only with one type of stimulation.

Women with orgasmic disorders, compared with orgasmic women, often report less relationship satisfaction and lower levels

---

REAL RESEARCH 14.6 A nationally representative study of U.S. women found that although 40% of women reported experiencing low sexual desire, decreased sexual arousal, and/or problems reaching orgasm, only 12% indicated these issues were a source of personal distress (SHIFREN ET AL., 2008).

---

of emotional closeness (González et al., 2006). They also have more difficulties in asking their partners for direct clitoral stimulation, discussing how slow or fast they want to go, or how hard or soft stimulation should be. Some women worry about what their partners might think if they make sexual suggestions or feel uncomfortable receiving stimulation (such as cunnilingus or manual stimulation) without stimulating their partners at the same time. Distracting thoughts, such as "his hand must be falling asleep" or "he can't be enjoying this" can increase existing anxiety and interfere with orgasm (Birnbaum et al., 2001; M. P. Kelly et al., 1990).

Physical factors can also cause female orgasmic disorder. Severe chronic illness and disorders such as diabetes, neurological problems, hormonal deficiencies, and alcoholism can all interfere with orgasmic response. Certain prescription drugs can also impair this response.

Treating Female Orgasmic Disorder

Today, the majority of treatment programs for orgasmic disorder involve a combination of different treatment approaches, such as homework assignments, sex education, communication skills training, cognitive restructuring, desensitization, and other tech-

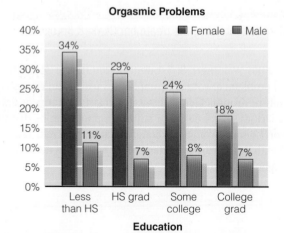

Orgasmic Problems

■ Female ■ Male

- Less than HS: 34% / 11%
- HS grad: 29% / 7%
- Some college: 24% / 8%
- College grad: 18% / 7%

Education

FIGURE **14.4** Higher educational levels are negatively associated with sexual problems for both men and women. SOURCE: Laumann et al., 1999

niques (Meston et al., 2004). The most effective treatment for female orgasmic disorder was developed by LoPiccolo and Lobitz (1972) and involves teaching a woman to masturbate to orgasm.

On a psychological level, masturbation also helps increase the pleasurable anticipation of sex. Education, self-exploration, communication training, and body awareness are also included in masturbation training for orgasmic problems. Masturbation exercises begin with a woman examining her body and vulva with mirrors. Then she is instructed to find which areas of her body feel the most pleasurable when touched and to stroke them. If this does not result in orgasm, a vibrator is used. As a woman progresses through these stages, she may involve her sexual partner so that the partner is able to learn which areas are more sensitive than others.

Although masturbation training is the most effective treatment for female orgasmic disorder, some therapists do not incorporate it into their treatment for a variety of reasons (including patient or therapist discomfort). Interestingly, improving orgasmic responses does not always increase sexual satisfaction. Heterosexual women may report increased pleasure with vaginal intercourse over masturbation because it provides more intimacy and closeness (Jayne, 1981), even though masturbation may be a better means of reaching orgasm (Dodson, 1993).

Two additional treatments involve systematic desensitization and **bibliotherapy.** Both of these have been found to be helpful in cases in which there is a great deal of sexual anxiety. In systematic desensitization, events that cause anxiety are recalled into imagination; then a relaxation technique is used to decrease the anxiety. With enough repetition and practice, eventually the anxiety-producing events lose the ability to create anxiety. Both masturbation training and systematic desensitization have been found to be effective; however, masturbation training has higher effectiveness rates (Heiman & Meston, 1997).

Bibliotherapy, which uses written works as therapy, has also been found to be helpful for not only orgasmic disorders but other disorders as well. It can help a person regain some control and understand the problems she is experiencing. Although the results may be short-lived, bibliotherapy has been found to improve sexual functioning (van Lankveld et al., 2001).

▶▶ EJACULATORY Disorders

The ejaculatory process is controlled by various endocrine factors, including testosterone, oxytocin, prolactin, and thyroid hormones (Corona et al., 2011). There is a wide spectrum of ejaculatory disorders, ranging from early to a delayed or absent ejaculation (Bettocchi et al., 2008). In the following subsections, we discuss early ejaculation, delayed ejaculation, and various other ejaculatory problems.

Early Ejaculation

Early ejaculation is difficult to define. Does it depend on how many penile thrusts take place before orgasm, how many minutes elapse between actual penetration and orgasm, or whether a man reaches orgasm before his partner does? All of these definitions are problematic because they involve individual differences in sexual functioning. Although the time it takes to ejaculate may vary based on a man's age, sexual experience, health, and stress level, early ejaculation refers to a persistent or recurrent pattern of ejaculation occurring during partnered sexual activity within approximately 1 minute of beginning of sexual activity and before a man wishes it (Althof et al., 2010; Feige et al., 2011).

Early ejaculation is the most common sexual problem affecting men.

Early ejaculation is the most common sexual problem affecting men and it can affect men of all ages (Figure 14.5; Linton & Wylie, 2010; Renshaw, 2005; Rowland et al., 2010; Serefoglu et al., 2011; Vardi et al., 2008). In the United States, estimates are that close to 30% of men report experiencing early ejaculation in the previous year (Laumann et al., 1994). Early ejaculation can lead to decreases in sexual satisfaction and quality of life for both men and their partners.

Historically, early ejaculation has been considered a psychological disorder (Benson et al., 2009). Psychological factors that have been found to contribute include stress, anxiety, unresolved conflict, guilt, shame, and performance pressures (i.e., wanting to satisfy a partner). Some evolutionary theorists claim that early ejaculation may provide a biological advantage in that a man who ejaculates quickly would be more likely to impregnate a partner than a man who requires prolonged stimulation. Masters and Johnson (1970) originally proposed that early ejaculation

orgasmic disorder
A delay or absence of orgasm after a normal phase of sexual excitement.

premature ejaculation (PE)
(also referred to as early ejaculation)

delayed ejaculation
An orgasm disorder characterized by a delay, an infrequency, or the absence of ejaculation.

early ejaculation
Pattern of ejaculating with minimal sexual stimulation before, on, or shortly after penetration and before the person wishes it. (also referred to as premature ejaculation).

bibliotherapy
Using books and educational material for the treatment of sexual disorders or other problems.

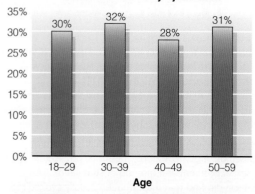

FIGURE **14.5** Although early ejaculation is often associated with younger males, studies have found it can occur at any age. SOURCE: Laumann et al., 1999

develops when a man's early sexual experiences are rushed because of the fear of being caught or discovered. These fears, they believed, could condition a man to ejaculate rapidly. Others have pointed out that early ejaculation occurs in men who are unable to accurately judge their own levels of sexual arousal, which would enable them to use self-control and avoid rapid ejaculation (H. S. Kaplan, 1974).

Potential physiological factors also might contribute to early ejaculation. Research has found that some men might have "hyperexcitability" or an "oversensitivity" of their penis, which prevents them from delaying orgasm. Nerves in the lumbar spine are related to ejaculation, and research continues to explore medications to decrease the increased sensitivity (Benson et al., 2009). Other physiological factors that may contribute to early ejaculation include hormones, infections, as well as prescription and nonprescription drug use. Interestingly, there is also evidence that early ejaculation may have a genetic component, wherein a male has a higher chance of experiencing it if his father did (Jern et al., 2009).

Delayed Ejaculation

Delayed ejaculation involves a delayed, infrequent, or absent ejaculation that has occurred for 6 months or more and occurs on most occasions of sexual activity. Delayed ejaculation is relatively rare—less than 3% of men report experiencing it (Perelman & Rowland, 2006). However, those who do experience it often experience considerable anxiety and distress, and may also experience relationship problems related to the problem. Studies have found that many men with delayed ejaculation have a history of high masturbatory activity, lower levels of sexual satisfaction, and higher levels of anxiety and depression (Abdel-Hamid & Saleh, 2011).

Delayed ejaculation can be the result of both psychological and physiological factors. Psychological factors include stress, a lack of attraction to one's partner, a strict religious background, atypical masturbation patterns, or past traumatic events such as sexual abuse. Physiological factors include the use of certain drugs and various illnesses, nerve damage, and spinal cord injury (SCI).

Other Ejaculatory Disorders

A relatively uncommon ejaculatory disorder involves **retrograde ejaculation,** in which the ejaculate empties into the bladder instead of being ejaculated outside the body through the urethra. A man with retrograde ejaculation typically experiences orgasm with little or no ejaculation (also called a "dry orgasm"; Ohl et al., 2008; Rowland et al., 2010). Some experts refer to this condition as **anejaculation.** Although both of these conditions are not harmful, they can cause infertility (Aust & Lewis-Jones, 2004; Zhao et al., 2004). Although it is not considered a sexual problem, some men may experience painful ejaculation, which can be the result of infections or other medical issues (Lee et al., 2008; Schultheiss, 2008). Common causes for these conditions include chronic illnesses, surgeries, SCI, or prescription drug use (Bettocchi et al., 2008; Kaplan, 2009; Mufti et al., 2008; Nagai et al., 2008; Tsivian et al., 2009).

▶▶ TREATING Ejaculatory Disorders

Treatment for ejaculatory disorders often depends on the duration, context, and causes of the disorder. Lifelong ejaculatory problems are often treated with medications or topical anesthetics, whereas other cases might be treated with behavioral therapy, with or without medications (Rowland et al., 2010; Shindel et al., 2008).

Treating Early Ejaculation

A variety of psychological, topical, and oral therapies have been used to treat early ejaculation, with varying levels of success (Hellstrom, 2006; Owen, 2009). A common treatment for early ejaculation has been the use of selective serotonin reuptake inhibitors (SSRIs), because a common side effect of these drugs is delayed ejaculation (Linton & Wylie, 2010; Rowland et al., 2010; Shindel et al., 2008). However, these medications need to be taken daily and have a slow onset of action (Owen, 2009). Although research continues to explore a variety of other drugs for the treatment of early ejaculation, one promising drug, *Dapoxetine,* has undergone several large Phase III trials (Corona et al., 2011; Owen, 2009).

Treatment may also include the use of behavioral techniques known as the **squeeze** or **stop–start techniques** (Shindel et al., 2008). Both involve stimulating the penis to the point just before ejaculation. With the squeeze technique, sexual stimulation or masturbation is engaged in just short of orgasm; then stimulation is stopped. The man or his partner puts a thumb on the frenulum and the first and second fingers on the dorsal side of the penis (Figure 14.6). Pressure is applied for 3 to 4 seconds, until the urge to ejaculate subsides. With the stop–start technique, stimulation is simply stopped until the ejaculatory urge subsides. Stimulation is then repeated up until that point, and this process is repeated over and over. Using these methods, a man can usually gain some control over his erection within 2 to 10 weeks and can have excellent control within several months. It is believed that these techniques

retrograde ejaculation
A condition in which the male ejaculate is released into the bladder instead of being ejaculated outside the body through the urethra.

anejaculation
A sexual disorder that involves an absence of ejaculation.

squeeze technique
A technique in which the ejaculatory reflex is reconditioned using a firm grasp on the penis.

stop–start technique
A technique in which the ejaculatory reflex is reconditioned using intermittent pressure on the glans of the penis.

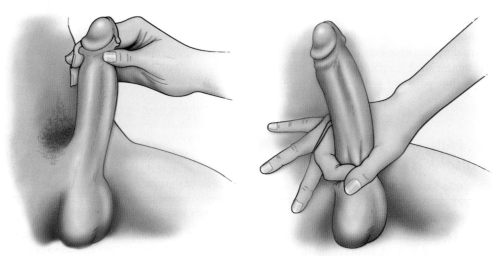

FIGURE **14.6** The squeeze technique is often recommended in the treatment of premature ejaculation. Pressure is applied either at the top or to the base of the penis for several seconds until the urge to ejaculate subsides. Copyright © Cengage Learning 2013

may help a man get in touch with his arousal levels and sensations. Suggested effectiveness rates have been as high as 98%, although it is unclear how this effectiveness is being measured (Masters & Johnson, 1970). In addition, many studies fail to mention whether the treatment permanently solves the problem or if periodic repetition of the techniques is necessary.

Treating Delayed Ejaculation

Treatment for delayed ejaculation can include changing prescription medications, discontinuing the use of nonprescription drugs or alcohol, or sex therapy. Delayed ejaculation is often difficult to treat, and no evidence-based treatments have been proved to eliminate this disorder (Nelson et al., 2007; Richardson et al., 2006). A novel treatment uses penile vibratory stimulation, which involves increasing penile sensations during sexual activity with a small vibrator (Nelson et al., 2007). It has been found to be an effective treatment, although more research is needed. A variety of

medications, including *Bupropion,* are being evaluated for the treatment of delayed ejaculation (Abdel-Hamid & Saleh, 2011; Chan et al., 2008; Waldinger, 2005).

It can be challenging to treat delayed ejaculation caused by psychological factors. One 43-year-old man shared with me his lifelong problem in reaching orgasm with his partner. He had been sexually abused as a child for many years by an uncle who was a few years older than he. During this abuse, the uncle tried to make him reach orgasm. However, as a boy, he had learned to withhold the orgasmic response. Later on in life, this pattern continued even though he was not consciously trying to do so.

One psychological treatment involves instructing a man to use situations in which he is able to achieve ejaculation to help him during those in which he is not. For example, if a man can ejaculate during masturbation while fantasizing about being watched during sexual activity, he is told to use this fantasy while he is with his partner. Gradually, the man is asked to incorporate his partner into the sexual fantasy and to masturbate while with the partner.

◀ review QUESTIONS

1 Define female orgasmic disorder, and explain possible psychological and physical factors that might contribute to it.

2 Identify the various treatments for female orgasmic disorder.

3 Identify and differentiate the various ejaculatory disorders.

4 Identify the various psychological and physiological causes for the ejaculatory disorders.

5 Identify the various treatments for the ejaculatory disorders.

▶ PROBLEMS WITH Sexual Pain

Sexual pain disorders can occur at any stage of the sexual response cycle, and they occur primarily in women of all ages (Figure 14.7). The DSM-IV-TR had two categories of pain disorders—**vaginismus** (vadg-ih-NISS-muss) and **dyspareunia** (diss-par-ROON-ee-uh). Because of problems differentiating between these two disorders, experts have recommended combining them into one diagnosis called **genito-pelvic pain** and **penetration disorder** in the DSM-5.

▶▶ GENITO-PELVIC PAIN and Penetration Disorders

Women who have a genito-pelvic pain and penetration disorder often experience persistent or recurrent difficulties for at least 6 months with one of the following symptoms: an inability to engage in vaginal penetration; significant vaginal or pelvic pain during vaginal penetration; marked fear or anxiety about vaginal/pelvic pain or vaginal penetration; and marked tensing of the pelvic floor muscles during vaginal penetration (Binik 2010a, 2010b). These problems cause significant distress in their lives.

The **pubococcygeus** (pub-oh-cock-SIGH-gee-us) **muscle** surrounds the entrance to the vagina and controls the vaginal opening. Involuntary spasms of this muscle can make penetration painful and virtually impossible (Lahaie et al., 2010; Ozdemir et al., 2008; Rosenbaum, 2011). Many women tolerate the sexual pain in order to meet their partners' needs or expectations (Boardman & Stockdale, 2009). These conditions may be

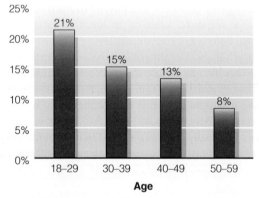

Women's Experience of Pain During Sex

FIGURE **14.7** Although fewer women may be sexually active as they age, fewer older women self-report pain during sex. SOURCE: Laumann et al., 1999

situation-specific, meaning that a woman may be able to allow penetration under certain circumstances but not in others (e.g., during a pelvic examination but not during intercourse; LoPiccolo & Stock, 1986). It is estimated that between 4% and 42% of women have experienced involuntary spasms of the vaginal muscles (Hope et al., 2010), whereas approximately 15% of heterosexual women report experiencing pain during penetration (Laumann et al., 1999).

Sexual pain can occur before, during, or after sexual behavior and may range from slight pain to severe. When severe, it can make sexual behavior and penetration difficult, if not impossible. One woman had been in a relationship with her partner for more than 3 years, but they had never been able to engage in penile–vaginal intercourse because she felt as if her vagina "*was closed up*" (Author's files). Penetration of her vagina with her partner's fingers was possible and enjoyable, but once penile penetration was attempted, her vagina was impenetrable. She also shared that she had been forced to engage in sex with her stepfather for several years of her early life.

Unfortunately, few well-controlled studies exist on causes of sexual pain (Lahaie et al., 2010; van Lankveld et al., 2010). However, we know that a number of factors may contribute to sexual pain and fear of penetration, from physical problems to allergies or infections. Vulvodynia and **vulvar vestibulitis** (vess-tib-u-LITE-is) **syndrome,** a type of vulvodynia, are considered common causes of sexual pain today (Perrigouard et al., 2008; see Chapter 5 for more information about vulvodynia).

---

vaginismus
Involuntary spasms of the muscles around the vagina in response to attempts at penetration.

dyspareunia
Genital pain associated with sexual behavior.

genito-pelvic pain/ penetration disorders
A category of sexual problems that involve persistent or recurrent difficulties with penetrative sex, pelvic pain, and/or fear or anxiety about pelvic pain, which causes significant distress.

pubococcygeus muscle
A muscle that surrounds and supports the vagina.

vulvar vestibulitis syndrome
Syndrome that causes pain and burning in the vaginal vestibule and often occurs during sexual intercourse, tampon insertion, gynecological examinations, bicycle riding, and wearing tight pants.

dilators
A graduated series of metal rods used in the treatment of vaginismus.

Psychological problems can also contribute. Sexual pain and fear of penetration is more common in women who have been sexually abused or raped, and these problems often occur together with other sexual problems, such as desire or arousal problems (Weaver, 2009). In addition, women with conservative values and relatively strict sex-related moral standards have been found to be at greater risk for these disorders (Borg et al., 2011), as are women who report feelings of disgust when they think of sex (Borg et al., 2010).

▶▶ TREATING GENITO-PELVIC PAIN
and Penetration Disorders

Although many women who experience sexual pain and fear of penetration do not seek treatment, medical evaluations and counseling can help isolate possible causes and solutions. It is important to consult with a health care provider. A physical examination can check for physiological problems that may be contributing to these disorders. It is also helpful for couples to become educated about these disorders to reduce their anxiety or tension. If a history of sexual abuse or rape exists, it is important to work through the trauma before beginning treatment specifically aimed at reducing the pain or fear associated with sexual behavior.

Treatments can include physical therapy, prescription medications, and various therapies. Cognitive–behavioral therapy has been found to reduce pain and increase comfort with penetration (Engman et al., 2010). After undergoing cognitive–behavioral therapy, 81% of women reported they were able to engage in penetrative sex and had experienced increases in self-esteem and self-worth as a sexual partner (Engman et al., 2010).

Other treatment options include biofeedback, surgery, and the use of Botox to reduce vaginal and pelvic pain (Butrick, 2009; Gunter, 2007; Pacik, 2009; Park & Paraiso, 2009). Some health care workers teach women experiencing pain and penetration disorders to use **dilators,** which can help to open and relax the vaginal muscles. If this is successful, penetration can be attempted. In some cases, however, it may be necessary to use a dilator on a regular basis just before penetration. It is estimated that between 75% and 100% of women who use this technique are able to experience penetrative sex by the end of treatment (Heiman, 2002). Although sex surrogates are not commonly used in the United States today, one study from Israel found that incorporating surrogate sex partners into the treatment of single women with sexual pain yielded successful treatment rates (Ben-Zion et al., 2007).

◀ review QUESTIONS

1 Identify and differentiate among the various sexual pain disorders.

2 Explain how genito-pelvic pain and penetration disorders are treated.

▶ ILLNESS, DISABILITY,
and Sexual Functioning

We all need love, and we all need touching and contact with others. Yet, somehow we have grown to think that sexuality is the privilege of the healthy. Health care providers often rely on the International Classification of Diseases (ICD), an official system of identifying various illnesses. Several of these illnesses and their treatments can interfere with a person's sexual desire, physiological functioning, or both. Sexual functioning involves a complex physiological process, which can be impaired by pain, immobility, changes in bodily functions, or medications. Often problems involve psychological issues as well. Sudden illness causes shock, anger, resentment, anxiety, and depression, all of which can adversely affect sexual desire and functioning. Many illnesses cause disfiguration and force a person to deal with radical changes in body image; after removal of a limb, breast, testicle, or the need to wear an external bag to collect bodily waste, many people wonder: How could anyone possibly find me sexually attractive?

Serious illness often puts strains on loving relationships. A partner may be forced to become nurse, cook, maid, and caretaker, as well as lover. The caretaker of an ill person may worry that the sick partner is too weak or fragile for sex or be too concerned with his or her illness to want sexual contact. Still, many couples do enjoy loving, full relationships. Recall the chapter opening interview with Dr. Woet Gianotten, who discussed that even terminally ill men and women desire sexual intimacy. Maintaining a healthy and satisfying sex life can increase personal happiness and satisfaction for those who are chronically ill or suffering from a variety of medical conditions.

As Dr. Gianotten discussed, the real questions that sick people and their partners have about their sexuality are too often ignored by medical professionals (Ivarsson et al., 2010). They may be questions of mechanics: *"What positions can I get into now that I have lost a leg?"*; questions of function: *"Will my genitals still work now that I have a spinal cord injury?"*; questions of attractiveness: *"Will my husband still want me now that I have lost a breast?"* The nearby View in Video explores the importance of sexual behavior in the lives of many disabled men and women in the Netherlands. Regular sexual expression is so important that if a handicapped man or woman is unable to find a sexual partner, the government may cover the expenses of providing one for them. Let's review a sample of physical and mental challenges that confront people, and also some of the sexual questions and problems that can arise.

▶▶ CARDIOVASCULAR Illnesses

Heart disease, including **hypertension, angina,** and **myocardial infarction,** is the number one cause of death in the United States. A person with heart disease—even a person who has had a heart transplant—can return to a normal sex life shortly after recovery. Most cardiologists allow sexual behavior as soon as the patient feels up to it, although they usually recommend that heart transplant patients wait from 4 to 8 weeks to give the incision time to heal. However, researchers have found that the frequency of sexual behavior after myocardial infarctions does decrease. In fact, only 1 in 4 couples returns to their previous levels of sexual behavior (Ben-Zion & Shiber, 2006). Why does this occur?

One reason is fear. Many patients (or their partners) fear that their damaged (or new) heart is not up to the strain of sexual behavior or orgasm (Eyada & Atwa, 2007; Kazemi-Saleh et al., 2007; McCall-Hosenfeld et al., 2008; Masoomi et al., 2010). This fear can be triggered by the fact that, when men and women become sexually excited, their heartbeat and respiration increases, and they may break out into a sweat (these are also signs of a heart attack). Some people with heart disease actually do experience some angina during sexual activity. Although not usually serious, these incidents may be frightening. Although sexual activity can trigger a myocardial infarction, this risk is extremely low (Baylin et al., 2007; Muller et al., 1996). In fact, except for patients with very serious heart conditions, sex puts no more strain on the heart than walking up a flight or two of stairs.

Some problems also involve physical factors. Because penile erection is a vascular process, involving the flow of blood into the penis, it is not surprising that ED is a common problem in male patients with cardiovascular problems (Hebert et al., 2008). Some heart medications also can dampen desire or cause erectile problems, or, less often, women may experience a decrease in lubrication. Sometimes adjusting medications can help couples who are experiencing such problems.

After a heart attack or other heart problems, it is not uncommon to have feelings of depression, inadequacy (especially among men), or loss of attractiveness (especially among women; Almeida et al., in press; Duarte Freitas et al., 2011; Eyada & Atwa, 2007). In addition, in older patients, a partner often assumes the responsibility of enforcing the doctor's orders: *"Watch what you eat!" "Don't drink alcohol!" "Don't put so much salt on that!" "Get some exercise!"* This is hardly a

*A person with heart disease **can return to a normal sex life** shortly after recovery.*

role that leads to sexual desire. Any combination of these factors may lead one or both partners to avoid sex.

Strokes, also called cerebrovascular accidents, happen when blood is cut off from part of the brain, usually because a small blood vessel bursts. Although every stroke is different depending on what areas of the brain are damaged, some common results are **hemiplegia** (he-mi-PLEE-jee-uh), **aphasia** (uh-FAY-zhee-uh), and other cognitive, perceptual, and memory problems. As with other types of brain injury (such as those caused by automobile accidents), damage to the brain can affect sexuality in a number of ways.

In most cases of stroke, sexual functioning itself is not damaged, and many stroke victims do go on to resume sexual activity. After a stroke, the problems that confront a couple with normal functioning are similar to those with cardiovascular disease: fear of causing another stroke, worries about sexual attractiveness, and the stresses and anxieties of having to cope with a major illness.

However, a stroke can also cause physiological changes that affect sexuality. Some men may experience priapism after a stroke, because the nerves controlling the erectile tissue on one side of the penis are affected. Hemiplegia can result in spasticity (jerking motions) and reduced sensation on one side of the body. Paralysis can also contribute to a feeling of awkwardness or

---

hypertension
Abnormally high blood pressure.

angina
Chest pains that accompany heart disease.

myocardial infarction
A cutoff of blood to the heart muscle, causing damage to the heart; also referred to as a heart attack.

stroke
Occurs when blood is cut off from part of the brain, usually because a small blood vessel bursts.

hemiplegia
Paralysis of one side of the body.

aphasia
Defects in the ability to express and/or understand speech, signs, or written communication, caused by damage to the speech centers of the brain.

disinhibition
The loss of normal control over behaviors such as expressing sexuality or taking one's clothes off in public.

hyposexuality
Abnormal suppression of sexual desire and behavior; the term usually refers to behavior caused by some disturbance of the brain.

ostomies
Operations to remove part of the small or large intestine or the bladder, resulting in the need to create an artificial opening in the body for the elimination of bodily wastes.

stoma
Surgical opening made in the abdomen to allow waste products to exit the body.

mastectomy
Surgical removal of a breast.

simple mastectomy
Surgical removal of the breast tissue.

unattractiveness. In addition, aphasia can affect a person's ability to communicate or understand sexual cues.

Some stroke victims also go through periods of **disinhibition,** in which they exhibit behavior that, before the stroke, they would have been able to suppress. Often this includes hypersexuality, in which the patient may make lewd comments, masturbate in public, disrobe publicly, or make inappropriate sexual advances (Larkin, 1992). Others may experience **hyposexuality,** in which they show decreased sexual desire, or they may experience ED. Sexual intervention programs have been designed for use in rehabilitation hospitals, and they can be of great help in teaching couples how to deal with the difficulties of adjusting to life after a stroke.

▶▶ CANCER

Cancer can involve almost any organ of the body and has a reputation of being invariably fatal. In fact, cure rates have increased dramatically, and some cancers are now more than 90% curable. Still, cancer can kill, and a diagnosis of cancer is usually accompanied by shock, numbness, and gripping fear. Also, as in other illnesses, partners may need to become caretakers, and roles can change. Cancer treatments are likely to disrupt a patients' sexual functioning (Burns et al., 2007; Carpentier & Fortenberry, 2010; Li & Rew, 2010; Ofman, 2004; Reese, 2011). These disruptions may be temporary or long lasting.

For example, surgery is required for a number of cancers of the digestive system, and it can lead to **ostomies** (OST-stome-mees).

An advertising campaign by the Breast Cancer Fund parodied the fact that society routinely represents women's breasts as only sexual in nature, whereas breast cancer is treated with secrecy.

Courtesy of www.breastcancerfund.org/Heward Jue

People with cancer of the colon often need to have part or all of the large intestine removed; the rectum may be removed as well. A surgical opening, called a **stoma** (STOW-mah), is made in the abdomen to allow waste products to exit the body. This is collected in a bag, which, for many patients, must be worn at all times (others can take it off periodically). Ostomy bags are visually unpleasant and may emit an odor, and the adjustment to their presence can be difficult for some couples. Having a new opening in the body to eliminate bodily wastes is itself a hard thing to accept for many people, but most eventually adjust to it and, barring other problems related to their disease, go on to live healthy and sexually active lives.

Cancer can affect sexual functioning in other ways as well. Physical scars, the loss of limbs or body parts, changes in skin texture when radiation therapy is used, the loss of hair, nausea, bloating, weight gain or loss, and acne are just some of the ways that cancer and its treatment can affect the body and one's body image. In addition, the psychological trauma and the fear of death can lead to depression, which can inhibit sexual relations. Perhaps the most drastic situations, however, occur when cancer affects the sexual organs themselves.

Breast Cancer

In American society, breasts are a focal part of female sexual attractiveness, and women often invest much of their feminine self-image in their breasts. For many years, a diagnosis of breast cancer usually meant that a woman lost that breast; **mastectomy** was the preferred treatment. **Simple mastectomies** meant that the breast tissue alone was removed, whereas radical mastectomies involved the removal of the breast together with other tissues and lymph nodes. As we discussed in Chapter 5, the numbers of mastectomies have decreased today, and many women are opting for lumpectomies. These are often coupled with chemotherapy, radiation therapy, or both.

Breast cancer and cancer treatments can negatively affect several physiological, psychological, and interpersonal aspects of sexual functioning and satisfaction (Biglia et al., 2010; Davis et al., 2010b; Emilee et al., 2010; Manganiello et al., 2011; Melisko et al., 2010; Reese et al., 2010; Sadovsky et al., 2010). Chemotherapy and endocrine treatments have been found to create abrupt menopause in young women, leading to vaginal dryness, pain, discomfort, and significantly reduced levels of sexual desire (Carter et al., 2011; Ochsenkühn et al., 2011). Mastectomies have also been found to have a negative impact on women's sexuality and body images (Brandberg et al., 2008; Manganiello et al., 2011). A woman who loses a breast may worry that her partner will no longer find her attractive or desirable.

One study found that although 80% of women reported a satisfying sex life before breast cancer, 70% reported sexual problems after their treatment for breast cancer (Panjari et al., 2011). Sexual problems included decreased arousal and desire, problems with body image, as well as an increase in menopausal symptoms (i.e., hot flashes and night sweats). Educating women about these changes and providing them with information on how to cope with them can improve sexual functioning (Carter et al., 2011).

Pelvic Cancer and Hysterectomies

Cancer can also strike a woman's vagina, uterus, cervix, or ovaries. Although women with vaginal and cervical cancers often experience more sexual problems than women without these cancers, rates of sexual activity and partnering are similar (Lindau et al., 2007). Negative changes in sexual functioning have been found in some studies, but not in others (Donovan et al., 2007; Gamel et al., 2000; Greenwald & McCorkle, 2008). Common sexual issues include insufficient vaginal lubrication, shortened vaginas, reduced vaginal elasticity, and sexual pain (Bergmark et al., 1999). Overall, a woman's feelings about her cancer treatment and her social support network are both important in sexual recovery from these treatments. As we mentioned earlier, educating women about the sexual effects of cancer can help improve sexual functioning (Lindau et al., 2007).

Cancer of the reproductive organs may result in a hysterectomy. In a total hysterectomy, the uterus and cervix (which is part of the uterus) are removed; in a radical hysterectomy, the ovaries are also removed (**oophorectomy;** oh-uh-for-RECT-toe-mee), together with the Fallopian tubes and surrounding tissue. Hysterectomies are also performed for conditions other than cancer, such as fibroids, endometriosis, and uterine prolapse. In fact, the Centers for Disease Control and Prevention report that hysterectomy is the second most frequently performed surgical procedure on women in the United States (Whiteman et al., 2008).

A hysterectomy may or may not affect sexual functioning, but many health care providers neglect to discuss the sexual implications of hysterectomy (Jongpipan & Charoenkwan, 2007). If the ovaries are removed with the uterus, a woman will experience hormonal imbalances that can lead to reduced vaginal lubrication, hot flashes, night sweats, insomnia, mood swings, and other bodily changes. In Chapter 10, we discussed myotonia and the importance of the uterine muscles during sexual response. When the uterus is removed, some women may experience fewer uterine contractions during orgasm. Whether removal of the uterus decreases physical sexual response is controversial, with some studies finding that it does and others finding that it does not (Jongpipan & Charoenkwan, 2007; Maas et al., 2004; Srivastava et al., 2008). Women with a history of depression or sexual problems are often at increased risk for development of more of these symptoms after a hysterectomy (Shifren & Avis, 2007).

Prostate Cancer

As we discussed in Chapter 6, almost all men will experience a normal enlargement of the prostate gland if they live long enough. Prostate cancer is one of the most common cancers in men older than 50. In the past, when a man experienced an en-

larged prostate or was diagnosed with prostate cancer, a **prostatectomy** (pross-tuh-TECK-toe-mee) may have been performed, sometimes along with a **cystectomy.** These procedures often involved cutting the nerves necessary for erection, resulting in ED. A possible adverse effect of prostatectomy may be **incontinence,** sometimes necessitating an **indwelling catheter.** Many couples fear that this means the end of their sex life because removing and reinserting the catheter can lead to infection. However, the catheter can be folded alongside the penis during sexual behavior or held in place with a condom (Sandowski, 1989). For men who experience ED from the surgery, penile prostheses or intracavernous injections are possible.

Today, newer surgical techniques have resulted in less EDs. Although improved prostate cancer screening has led to higher survival rates, the development of androgen deprivation therapy to decrease the development of prostate cancer has been found to contribute to sexual problems (Elliott et al., 2010). Because men begin this therapy earlier and stay on it longer, many experience decreases in sexual performance and satisfaction (Elliott et al., 2010). As in all surgeries of this kind, the man must also cope with the fear of disease, concern about his masculinity and body image, concern about the reactions of his sexual partner, and the new sensations or sexual functioning that can accompany prostate surgery.

*When men are diagnosed with prostate cancer, **many worry about sexual functioning after treatment.***

When men are diagnosed with prostate cancer, many worry about sexual functioning after treatment (Knight & Latini, 2009). Overall, many men do experience declines in sexual functioning after prostate cancer treatment (Droupy, 2010; Howlett et al., 2010; Huyghe et al., 2009; Savareux & Droupy, 2009; Wittmann et al., 2011).

Testicular Cancer

Cancer of the penis or scrotum is rare, and cancer of the testes is only slightly more common. Still, the sexual problems that result from these diseases are similar to those from prostate cancer. Testicular cancer is most common in men who are in their most productive years. Research has found that although sexual issues, including ejaculatory problems, are common after treatment for testicular cancer (Dahl et al., 2007), there is considerable improvement 1 year after diagnosis (van Basten et al., 1999).

In Chapter 6, we discussed testicular cancer, and although the surgical removal of a testicle (orchiectomy) because of cancer usually does not affect the ability to reproduce (sperm can be banked, and the remaining testicle may produce enough sperm and adequate testosterone), some men do experience psychological difficulties. This is mainly because of feelings that they have lost part of their manhood or fears about the appearance of their scrotum. The appearance of the scrotum can be helped by inserting a tes-

---

oophorectomy
Surgical removal of the ovaries.

prostatectomy
The surgical removal of the prostate gland.

cystectomy
Surgical removal of the bladder.

incontinence
Lack of normal voluntary control of urinary functions.

indwelling catheter
A permanent catheter, inserted in the bladder, to allow the removal of urine in those who are unable to urinate or are incontinent.

hyperestrogenemia
Having an excessive amount of estrogen in the blood.

ticular prosthesis that takes the place of the missing testicle. In some rare cases, cancer of the penis may necessitate a partial or total penectomy (pee-NECK-toe-mee). In a total penectomy, the man's urethra is redirected downward to a new opening that is created between the scrotum and anus. Even with a penectomy, some men can have orgasms by stimulating whatever tissue is left where the penis was, and the ejaculate leaves the body through the urethra (Schover & Jensen, 1988).

It is well documented that sexual problems can occur as a result of any type of cancer or cancer treatment (Ofman, 2004; Sheppard & Wylie, 2001). However, they may only be a temporary result of the stress associated with the situation (Ofman, 2004).

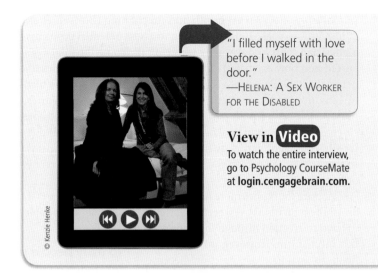

"I filled myself with love before I walked in the door."
—HELENA: A SEX WORKER FOR THE DISABLED

View in Video
To watch the entire interview, go to Psychology CourseMate at **login.cengagebrain.com**.

© Kenzie Henke

▶▶ DIABETES

Diabetes is caused by the inability of the pancreas to produce insulin, which is used to process blood sugar into energy, or by the inability of the body to use the insulin produced. Diabetes may affect children (Type I diabetes), who must then depend on insulin injections for the rest of their lives, or it may appear later (Type II diabetes) and may then be controlled through diet or oral medication. Diabetes is a serious condition that can ultimately lead to blindness, renal failure, and other problems.

People with diabetes often experience multiple and complex sexual difficulties. In fact, sexual problems (especially difficulty in getting an erection for men) may be one of the first signs of diabetes. A large number of men in the later stages of diabetes have penile prostheses implanted. Although women with Type I diabetes may experience some problems with vaginal lubrication, the majority do not seem to have significantly more problems than nondiabetic women. However, women with Type II diabetes often experience loss of desire, difficulties in lubrication, decreased sexual satisfaction, and problems with orgasm (Esposito et al., 2010; Giraldi & Kristensen, 2010; Schover & Jensen, 1988).

Differentiating between how much of a person's sexual difficulty is due to underlying physiological problems and how much is due to psychological issues is often difficult. Depression, fear of ED, lack of sexual response, anxiety about the future, and the life changes that diabetes can bring can all dampen sexual desire. Sex therapy is often an important part of diabetes treatment.

▶▶ MULTIPLE Sclerosis

Multiple sclerosis (MS) involves a breakdown of the myelin sheath that protects all nerve fibers, and it can be manifested in a variety of symptoms, such as dizziness, weakness, blurred or double vision, muscle spasms, spasticity, and loss of control of limbs and muscles. Symptoms can come and go without warning, but MS is progressive and may worsen over time. MS often strikes people between the ages of 20 and 50, at a time when they are establishing sexual relationships and families (M. P. McCabe, 2002).

MS can affect sexual functioning in many ways. Most commonly, men with MS experience ED (M. P. McCabe, 2002), whereas women with MS experience difficulties reaching orgasm (Tepavcevic et al., 2008; Tzortzis et al., 2008). Both men and

women may become hypersensitive to touch, experiencing even light caresses as painful or unpleasant. Fatigue, muscle spasms, and loss of bladder and bowel function can also inhibit sexual contact. Sexual counseling, penile prostheses in men, and artificial lubrication in women can help overcome some of these difficulties.

▶▶ ALCOHOLISM

Alcohol dependence and alcohol abuse can both contribute to sexual problems. Ethyl alcohol is a general nervous system depressant that has both long- and short-term effects on sexual functioning. It can impair spinal reflexes and decrease serum testosterone levels, which can lead to ED. **Hyperestrogenemia** (high-per-ess-troh-jen-EE-mee-uh) can result from the liver damage caused by alcoholism, which, combined with lower testosterone levels, may cause gynecomastia (which we discussed in Chapter 6), testicular atrophy, sterility, ED, and desire problems. In women, liver disease can lead to decreased or absent menstrual flow, ovarian atrophy, loss of vaginal membranes, infertility, and miscarriages. Alcohol can affect almost every bodily system; after a while, the damage it causes, including the damage to sexual functioning, can be irreversible, even if the person stops drinking alcohol.

Alcoholism also has a dramatic impact on relationships. It often coexists with anger, resentment, depression, and other familial and relationship problems. Some people become abusive when drunk, whereas others may withdraw and become noncommunicative. Problem drinking may lead a person into a spiral of guilt, lowered self-esteem, and even thoughts of suicide. Recovery is a long, often difficult process, and one's body and sexuality need time to recover from periods of abuse.

▶▶ SPINAL CORD Injuries

The spinal cord brings impulses from the brain to the various parts of the body; damage to the cord can cut off those impulses in any areas served by nerves below the damaged section. SCIs can significantly affect sexual health and functioning (Borisoff et al., 2010; Cardoso et al., 2009). However, to assess potential problems, a physician must know exactly where on the spine the injury occurred and how extensively the cord has been damaged (Alexander et al., 2009; Benevento & Sipski, 2002). Although some return of sensation and movement can be achieved in many injuries, most people are left with permanent disabilities. In more extreme cases, SCI can result in total or partial **paraplegia** (pah-ruh-PLEE-jee-uh) or total or partial **quadriplegia** (kwa-druh-PLEE-jee-uh). In these cases, the person is rendered extremely dependent on his or her partner or caretaker.

Men are four times more likely than women to experience SCI, and if the injury is above a certain vertebra, a man may still be able to have an erection through the body's reflex mechanism. However, it may be difficult to maintain an erection because there are reduced skin sensations in the penis. Injuries to the lower part of the spine are more likely to result in erectile difficulties in men, but they are also more likely to preserve some sensation in the genitals. Men without disabilities maintain erections, in part, through psychic arousal, such as sexual thoughts, feelings, and fantasies; however, with SCI, psychic arousal cannot provide continuing stimulation. Most men with SCIs who are capable of having erections are not able to climax or ejaculate, which involves a more complex mechanism than an erection (Benevento & Sipski, 2002). A number of men report experiencing orgasm without ejaculation (Sipski et al., 2006).

Women with SCI can lose sensation in the genitals, and with it the ability to lubricate during sexual activity, making penetrative sex difficult (Lombardi et al., 2009, 2010). However, many men and women with SCIs maintain orgasmic ability (M. Alexander & Rosen, 2008; Kreuter et al., 2011). "Phantom orgasm," a psychic sensation of having an orgasm without the corresponding physical reactions, is also common. Skin sensation in the areas unaffected by the injury can become greater, and new erogenous zones can appear (D. J. Brown et al., 2005; Ferreiro-Velasco et al., 2005).

Sexual problems develop over time as the full impact of their situation takes effect. Although men with SCI can resume sexual activity within a year of their injury, their frequency of sexual activity decreases after the injury (C. J. Alexander et al., 1993). Many men and women enjoy a variety of sexual activities after SCI, including kissing, hugging, and touching. A healthy sex life after SCI is possible if a man or woman can learn to overcome the physical and psychological obstacles of their injuries (Kreuter et al., 2008).

Rehabilitation from SCI can be a long, difficult process. Still, with a caring partner, meaningful sexual contact can be achieved. Men incapable of having an erection can still use their mouths and sometimes their hands. If penetrative sex is desired, couples can use "stuffing" techniques, in which the flaccid penis is pushed into the vagina or anus. Possible treatment methods include prosthesis implantation, vacuum erection devices, and the injection of vasoactive drugs. Prosthesis implantation in men with SCIs have shown high satisfaction and low complication rates (Kim et al., 2008). Research has found that various erectile drugs, including Viagra, can significantly improve erections in men with SCI (Fink et al., 2002; Lombardi et al., 2009, 2010).

▶▶ MENTAL Illness

People with psychological disorders have sexual fantasies, needs, and feelings, and they have the same right to a fulfilling sexual expression as others do. However, historically they have either been treated as asexual, or their sexuality has been viewed as illegitimate, warped, or needing external control (Apfel & Handel, 1993). Yet a sudden or drastic change in sexual habits may be a sign of mental illness or a sign that a mentally ill person is getting worse (or better, depending on the change).

To deny people with psychiatric problems the pleasure of a sexual life is cruel and unnecessary.

People with **schizophrenia,** for example, can be among the most impaired and difficult psychiatric patients. **Neuroleptics,** antipsychotic drugs such as Thorazine and Haldol, can cause increased or decreased desire for sex; painful enlargement of the breasts, reproductive organs, or testicles; difficulty in achieving or maintaining an erection; delayed or retrograde ejaculation; and changes, including pain, in orgasm.

Outside of the effects of neuroleptics, people with schizophrenia have been found to grapple with the same sexual questions and problems as other people. The same is true of people with **major depression** and other **affective disorders.** They may experience hyposexuality when depressed or hypersexuality in periods of mania. Both can also occur as a result of antidepressant medications. Otherwise, their sexual problems do not differ significantly from those of people without major psychiatric problems (Schover & Jensen, 1988).

Sexual issues among those with intellectual disabilities are often neglected in psychiatric training, and health care providers who treat these patients have often spent more time trying to control and limit patients' sexual behavior than they have in treating sexual problems. For years, those with intellectual disabilities have been kept from learning about sexuality and having sexual relationships. It is as if an otherwise healthy adult is supposed to display no sexual interest or activity at all. Educators have designed special sexuality education programs for the intellectually and developmentally disabled to make sure that they express their sexuality in a socially approved manner (Monat-Haller, 1992). However, to deny people with psychiatric problems or disabilities the pleasure of a sexual life is cruel and unnecessary.

---

paraplegia
Paralysis of the legs and lower part of the body, affecting both sensation and motor response.

quadriplegia
Paralysis of all four limbs.

schizophrenia
Any of a group of mental disorders that affect the individual's ability to think, behave, or perceive things normally.

neuroleptics
A class of antipsychotic drugs.

major depression
A persistent, chronic state in which the person feels he or she has no worth, cannot function normally, and entertains thoughts of or attempts suicide.

affective disorders
A class of mental disorders that affect mood.

chronic obstructive pulmonary disease (COPD)
A disease of the lung that affects breathing.

Many people with intellectual disabilities (and physical disabilities) must spend long periods of their lives—sometimes their entire lives—in institutions, which makes developing a sex life difficult. Institutions differ greatly in the amount of sexual contact they allow; some allow none whatsoever, whereas others allow mutually consenting sexual contact, with the staff carefully overseeing the patients' contraceptive and hygienic needs (Trudel & Desjardins, 1992).

Another aspect of institutional life involves the sexual exploitation of patients with mental illness or intellectual disabilities. This is well-known but seldom discussed by those who work in such institutions. About half of all women in psychiatric hospitals report having been abused as children or adolescents, and many are then abused in a hospital or other institutional setting. Children who grow up with developmental disabilities are between 4 and 10 times more likely to be abused than children without those difficulties (Baladerian, 1991). Therefore, it is difficult to separate the sexual problems of mental illness, developmental disability, and psychiatric illness from histories of sexual abuse (Apfel & Handel, 1993; Monat-Haller, 1992).

▶▶ OTHER Conditions

Many other conditions, such as chronic pain from illnesses such as arthritis, migraine headaches, and back pain, can make sex behavior difficult or impossible at times. Respiratory illnesses, such as **chronic obstructive pulmonary disease (COPD)** and asthma, can also have a significant negative effect on sexual functioning. Not only do these diseases make physical exertion difficult, but they can also impair perceptual and motor skills. Millions of people who have COPD learn to take medicine before sexual activity and slow down their pace of sexual activity; their partners learn to use positions that allow the person with COPD to breathe comfortably.

◀ review QUESTIONS

1 Explain how physical illness and its treatment can interfere with sexual desire, physiological functioning, or both.

2 Explain why it is important for health care workers to ask patients about their sex lives.

3 Explain how cardiovascular illnesses can affect sexual functioning.

4 Explain how various cancers can affect sexual functioning.

5 Explain how diabetes, MS, alcoholism, SCIs, HIV and AIDS, and mental illness can affect sexual functioning.

▶ GETTING Help

People who are ill or disabled have the same sexual needs and desires as everyone else. In the past, these needs have too often been neglected not because the disabled individuals themselves were not interested in sexuality, but because health care providers and other health care professionals were uncomfortable learning about their sexual needs and discussing them with their patients. Fortunately, this has been changing, and now sexuality counseling is a normal part of the recuperation from many diseases and injuries in many hospitals. It is important for all of us to learn that those with disabilities are just like everybody else and simply desire to be treated as such.

If you are experiencing problems with sexual functioning, it is important to seek help as soon as possible. Often, when the problems are ignored, they lead to bigger problems down the road. If you are in college and have a student counseling center available to you, this may be a good place to start looking for help. Request a counselor who has received training in sexuality or ask to be referred to one who has.

Today, many therapists receive specific training in sexuality. One of the best training organizations in the United States is the American Association of Sexuality Educators, Counselors, and Therapists (AASECT). This organization offers certification programs in human sexuality for counselors, educators, and therapists, and can also provide information on those who are certified as therapists or counselors.

◀ review QUESTIONS

1 Explain how the sexual needs of people who are ill or disabled have been neglected over the years.

2 Explain why sexuality counseling is an important part of the recovery process.

3 Why might it be beneficial to seek help and not ignore a sexual problem?

SUMMARY POINTS

1 Healthy sexuality depends on good mental and physical functioning. Sexual problems are common and may occur when we don't feel sufficiently aroused, have a lower level of enthusiasm, or have trouble relaxing during sex. The majority of couples report periodic sexual problems, but most of the time these problems do not interfere with overall sexual functioning and they go away on their own.

2 Defining a sexual problem can be difficult. To help clarify definitions, some sex therapists in the United States use the *Diagnostic and Statistical Manual of Mental Disorders* (DSM), which provides diagnostic criteria for the most common sexual problems. The DSM-5 is due to be released in 2013. There are problems with the use of the DSM, including the fact that it uses a physiological framing of sexual problems and fails to acknowledge relational aspects of sexual behavior. It also has an inherent heterosexist focus.

3 Psychological factors that can challenge sexual functioning include unconscious fears, stress, anxiety, depression, guilt, anger, fear of intimacy, dependency, abandonment, concern over loss of control, and performance fears. In addition, relationship issues can also contribute to sexual problems, such as feeling unappreciated, anger, insecurity, resentment, conflict, or a lack of trust.

4 Physiological factors that can challenge sexual functioning include various injuries, disabilities, illnesses, diseases, medications, street drugs, and aging. Treatments for various diseases, such as chemotherapy and radiation, can also contribute to sexual problems.

5 Sexual problems can be primary or secondary and situational or global. Research has found that primary problems have more biological or physiological causes, whereas secondary problems tend to have more psychological causes. Situational problems occur during certain sexual activities or with certain partners, whereas global problems occur in every situation, during every type of sexual activity, and with every sexual partner.

6 The DSM-IV-TR had two categories of sexual desire disorders, hypoactive sexual desire disorder and sexual aversion. However, experts believe that since women often have fewer sexual fantasies, are less likely to initiate sexual activity, and have lower levels of self-

stimulation, these criteria didn't adequately access the female experience. Experts have recommended adding sexual interest/arousal disorder for women and using HSDD only for men in the DSM-5. They have also recommended that sexual aversion be dropped from the desire disorders since symptoms are more similar to phobias rather than sexual desire. Many therapists consider problems with sexual desire to be one of the most complicated sexual problems to treat. A variety of different treatment options are available. Cognitive–behavioral therapy, a form of psychotherapy that emphasizes the importance of how a person thinks and the effect these thoughts have on a person's feelings and behaviors, has offered promising results. Pharmacological and herbal treatments have also been used.

7 In the past, a woman experiencing problems with sexual arousal may have been diagnosed with female sexual arousal disorder, but experts have proposed that these problems become a part of sexual interest/arousal disorders. In men, sexual arousal disorders can lead to *erectile disorder (ED)*. Approximately 70% of EDs have a physical basis, with the major risk factors being diabetes, high cholesterol levels, or chronic medical illnesses. EDs in younger men are more likely to be psychologically based, whereas EDs in older men are more likely to be due to physical factors. Of all the sexual disorders, there are more treatment options for male ED than for any other sexual disorder.

8 Treatment options include psychological treatment (including systematic desensitization and sex therapy); psychopharmacological, hormonal, and intracavernous injections; transurethral therapy; vascular surgery; vacuum constriction devices; and prosthesis implantation. The treatment of ED has changed considerably since erectile drugs became available.

9 The DSM-IV-TR had three categories of orgasmic disorders, including female orgasmic disorder, male orgasmic disorder, and premature ejaculation. Experts have recommended changing male orgasmic disorder to delayed ejaculation and premature ejaculation to early ejaculation in the DSM-5. There are both physiological factors (such as chronic illness, diabetes, neurological problems, hormonal deficiencies, or alcoholism) and psychological factors (such as a lack of sex education, fear or anxiety, or psychological

disorders) that may interfere with a woman's ability to reach orgasm. The majority of treatment programs for orgasmic disorder involve a combination of different treatment approaches, such as homework assignments, sex education, communication skills training, cognitive restructuring, desensitization, and other techniques.

10 The ejaculatory process is controlled by various endocrine factors, including testosterone, oxytocin, prolactin, and thyroid hormones. There is a wide spectrum of ejaculatory disorders, ranging from early ejaculation to a delay or absence of ejaculation. Early ejaculation refers to a condition in which a man reaches orgasm just before, or immediately following, penetration. Early ejaculation is the most common sexual problem affecting men. Treatment methods include behavioral cognitive therapy and pharmaceutical treatments. Two popular behavioral techniques include the stop–start and the squeeze techniques.

11 Delayed ejaculation involves a delayed, infrequent, or absent ejaculation that has occurred for 6 months or more and occurs on most occasions of sexual activity. Delayed ejaculation is relatively rare—less than 3% of men report experiencing it.

12 Other ejaculatory disorders include retrograde ejaculation, in which the ejaculate empties into the bladder instead of being ejaculated outside the body through the urethra. A man with retrograde ejaculation typically experiences orgasm with little or no ejaculation (also called a "dry orgasm" or anejaculation). Treatment for ejaculatory disorders often depends on the duration, context, and causes of the disorder. Lifelong ejaculatory problems are often treated with medications or topical anesthetics, whereas other cases might be treated with behavioral therapy, with or without medications.

13 The DSM-IV-TR had two categories of pain disorders—vaginismus and dyspareunia. Because of problems differentiating between these two disorders, experts have recommended combining them into one diagnosis called genito-pelvic pain and penetration disorder in the DSM-5.

14 Treatment for genito-pelvic pain and penetration disorders can include physical therapy, prescription medications, and various therapies. Cognitive–behavioral therapy has been found to reduce pain and increase comfort with penetration. After treatment, many women report being able to engage in penetrative sex, as well as increases in self-esteem and self-worth. Other treatment options include biofeedback, surgery, and the use of Botox to reduce vaginal and pelvic pain.

15 Physical illness and its treatment can interfere with a person's sexual desire, physiological functioning, or both. Cardiovascular problems, including

hypertension, myocardial infarctions, strokes, and cancer, can all affect sexual functioning. There can be physical problems that interfere with physiological functioning, or there can be psychological problems or fear of sexual activity that can interfere with sexual functioning. Breast cancer and cancer treatments can negatively affect several physiological, psychological, and interpersonal aspects of sexual functioning and satisfaction.

16 Chronic illnesses, such as diabetes, multiple sclerosis (MS), muscular dystrophy, and alcoholism can also negatively affect sexual

functioning. Spinal cord injuries (SCIs), mental illness and intellectual disabilities, and infection with HIV and AIDS all present specific challenges to sexual functioning. People who are ill or disabled have the same sexual needs and desires that healthy people do.

17 People who are experiencing sexual problems, illness, disease, or disability should seek treatment as soon as possible to avoid the development of further problems. When problems are ignored, they tend to lead to bigger problems down the road.

CRITICAL THINKING QUESTIONS

1 Suppose that one night you discover that you are having trouble reaching orgasm with your partner. What do you do about it? When it happens several times, what do you do? Who would you feel comfortable talking to about this problem?

2 If you were suddenly disabled or developed a chronic illness, would you lose your desire to love and be loved, to touch and be touched, to be regarded by another as sexy and desirable?

3 Do you think insurance plans should cover erectile drugs? Do you think college students without ED should recreationally take erectile drugs? Why or why not?

4 Do you think that drug companies could convince us that a sexual problem exists when there is none? Should researchers be doing more work to uncover the causes of female sexual problems, even if the pharmaceutical

companies are paying for this research? Why or why not?

5 Although women may be diagnosed with persistent sexual arousal syndrome, there is no companion diagnosis for men. Why do you think this is? Do you think there should be such a diagnosis for men? Why or why not?

MEDIA RESOURCES

CourseMate brings course concepts to life with interactive learning, study, and exam preparation tools that support the printed textbook. A textbook-specific website, Psychology CourseMate includes an integrated interactive eBook and other interactive learning tools including quizzes, flashcards, videos, and more. If your textbook does not include an access code card, go to CengageBrain.com to gain access.

CENGAGENOW CengageNOW is an easy-to-use online resource that helps you study in less time to get the grade you want—NOW. Take a pre-test for this chapter and receive a personalized study plan based on your results that will identify the topics you need to review and direct you to online resources to help you master those topics. Then take a post-test to help you determine the concepts you have mastered and what you will need to work on. If your textbook does not include an access code card, go to CengageBrain.com to gain access.

View in Video available in CourseMate and CengageNOW:

Oncosexology: Sex and Illness: Interview with European Oncosexologist—Dr. Woet Gianotten.

Erectile Disorder: Listen to an interview with an older patient who has experienced changes in his sexual functioning.

The Importance of Sexual Expression in People with Disabilities: Interview with director of *de schildpad,* a Dutch organization that provides sex to the handicapped.

Helena: A Sex Worker for the Disabled: Interview with woman who works as a sex worker for *de schildpad.*

Websites:

International Society for the Study of Women's Sexual Health (ISSWSH) ■ The ISSWSH is a multidisciplinary, academic, and scientific organization that works to provide opportunities for communication among scholars, researchers, and practitioners about women's sexual functioning, as well as to provide the public with accurate information about women's sexual health.

Disability Resources ■ This website offers information on sexuality for people with disabilities and for parents of children with disabilities. General disability information can be found, as well as disability-specific information.

New View Campaign ■ Formed in 2000, this campaign challenges the medicalization of sex by the pharmaceutical companies. The website contains information, contacts, and media interviews.

Female Sexual Dysfunction—ALERT ■ This website, founded by Leonore Tiefer, a sex therapist and activist whose research we discussed in this chapter, challenges the myths promoted by the pharmaceutical industry and calls for research on the many causes of women's sexual problems. A variety of links to sexual health organizations are available.

Masters and Johnson's Therapy Program ■ Masters and Johnson's website provides information on relational and sex therapy, trauma-based disorders, eating disorders, sexual compulsivity, and dissociative disorders. A question-and-answer section of the site answers the most frequently asked questions about sex therapy and the treatment of various disorders.

Dr. Carne's Resources for Sex Addiction & Recovery ■ Dr. Patrick Carne is a pioneer in the field of sexual addiction. This website offers information, research, and assistance for sex addiction and recovery. Several online tests are available for sexual addiction (gay and straight), Internet sexual addiction, and betrayal bonds.

The Sexual Health Network ■ The Sexual Health Network is dedicated to providing easy access to sexuality information, education, mutual support, counseling, therapy, health care, products, and other resources for people with disabilities, illness, or natural changes throughout the life cycle and those who love them or care for them.

15 Sexually Transmitted Infections and HIV/AIDS

View in **Video**

View in **Video**

View in **Video**

View in **Video**

▶ **ABOUT THE CHAPTER OPENING VIDEO –**
Throughout this chapter we'll discuss sexually transmitted infections (STIs) and behaviors that can put a person at risk for acquiring an STI. Being able to talk with your partner about any infections or sexual experiences that might put you at risk is an important piece of avoiding STIs. However, these are not easy issues to talk about and that's why it's important for you to hear Jessica's story. Jessica and Ryan had an "on and off" relationship throughout their junior year of college. Like many couples, they didn't have great communication skills. When they left school for the summer they both had different ideas about the status of their relationship. Jessica thought they were a couple and they'd be monogamous over the summer. However, Ryan thought they were both free to explore sex outside of their relationship during the time they were apart. When they both returned to campus in the fall, their sexual relationship resumed. However, a few weeks later Jessica began experiencing a variety of symptoms, including severe pain. A visit to the health center on campus confirmed that she had been infected with herpes.

I was in class the day I was diagnosed. The doctor called me and told me on the phone. I had to go back to class because I was in the middle of a test. Afterwards I went back to my room and ran upstairs and locked myself in the bathroom because I just didn't know what to do. It was like the worst time of my whole entire life. My boyfriend had become infected over the summer when he cheated on me with my ex-best friend. He did not tell me he had been with someone or that he was infected until it was too late. I ended up

getting a medical leave from school and my mom came and picked me up. As time went by I opened up to a couple friends—but only those I knew I could trust.

Although Jessica is taking care of herself and slowly mending, her story is heartbreaking and illustrates the importance of communication and safe sex. Her situation is one to which a lot of people can relate, and though difficult to listen to, probably one of the most important stories for you to hear.

Janell Carroll

"It was the worst time of my whole life."
—CHAPTER OPENING VIDEO

View in Video

To watch the entire interview, go to Psychology CourseMate at **login.cengagebrain.com.**

In the United States, more than 19 million cases of sexually transmitted infections (STIs) are reported each year, and almost half of these are in young people aged 15 to 24 (Centers for Disease Control and Prevention [CDC], 2009d). However, because many STIs are either unreported or undiagnosed, the actual number of STIs is much higher. We live in a society that is often reluctant to openly discuss issues related to sexuality and, as a result, communication about STIs is difficult for many of us. STIs often create fear and judgment, and because of this, many college students are apprehensive about getting tested for STIs even when they are worried they might have one. Some students say they would feel "embarrassed" to get tested and would just "rather not know" if they were infected (Barth et al., 2002). Many people are unaware of the risk and consequences of many of the STIs, and it is clear that these infections are a global public health challenge today.

SEXUALLY TRANSMITTED Infections

Although the CDC collects and analyzes data on many STIs in the United States, only cases of syphilis, gonorrhea, chlamydia, and HIV have mandatory reporting rules. These rules have led to the development of federally funded programs to track the prevalence of these infections in the United States (Workowski & Berman, 2010).

REAL RESEARCH 15.1 Adolescents who hold negative attitudes about sexually transmitted infections (STIs) are less likely to get tested for STIs (CUNNINGHAM ET AL., 2009).

STIs can be caused by several agents, some of which are bacterial, others viral. The causal agents are important in treating STIs. The most effective way to avoid STI transmission is to abstain from oral, vaginal, and anal sex or to be in a long-term, mutually monogamous relationship with someone who is free from STIs.

▶▶ ATTITUDES ABOUT
Sexually Transmitted Infections

The sudden appearance of a new disease has always elicited fear about the nature of its **contagion.** Cultural fears about disease and sexuality in the early 20th century gave way to many theories about casual transmission (Brandt, 1985). At the turn of the 20th century, physicians believed that STIs could be transmitted on pens, pencils, toothbrushes, towels, and bedding. In fact, during World War I, the U.S. Navy removed doorknobs from its battleships, claiming that they were responsible for spreading sexual infections (Brandt, 1985).

STIs have historically been viewed as symbols of corrupt sexuality (P. L. Allen, 2000). When compared with other illnesses, such as cancer or diabetes, attitudes about STIs have been considerably more negative, and many people believe that people so afflicted "got what they deserved." This has been referred to as the **punishment concept** of disease. It was generally believed that to acquire an STI, one must break the silent moral code of sexual responsibil-

ity. Those who become infected therefore have done something bad, for which they are being punished.

Kopelman (1988) suggested that this conceptualization has endured because it serves as a defense mechanism. By believing that a person's behavior is responsible for acquiring an STI, we believe ourselves to be safe by not engaging in whatever that behavior is. For example, if we believe that herpes happens only to people who have more than 10 sexual partners, we may feel safe if we limit our sexual partners. Whether we are safe, of course, depends on whether our beliefs about the causes of transmission are true. Negative beliefs and stigma about STIs persist. One study found that many people who are diagnosed with STIs experience "self-stigmatization," which is an acceptance of the negative aspects of stigma (feeling inadequate and ashamed; Fortenberry, 2002). These negative feelings can also interfere with the act of getting tested at all.

▶▶ HIGH-RISK GROUPS and
Sexually Transmitted Infections

Since 1946, the CDC has been monitoring public health issues, including sexually transmitted diseases, with an eye on gaps and vulnerabilities in certain U.S. residents (Frieden, 2011). Large discrepancies have been found in STI prevalence, with higher rates in young people, certain racial/ethnic groups and minority populations, and men who have sex with men (MSM). Young adults are disproportionately affected by STIs, and the incidence of these infections continues to grow in this population, primarily because many engage in high-risk sexual behaviors, such as multiple partners or inconsistent condom use, or both. Studies have found that close to half of the nearly 19 million STIs that occur in the United States each year occur in people 15 to 24 years old (Casey et al., 2008; Crosby & Danner, 2008; T. Hall et al., 2008; Weinstock et al., 2004; see the accompanying Sex in Real Life feature for more information.)

Overall, women are at greater risk for long-term complications from STIs because the tissue of the vagina is much more fragile than penile skin. Heterosexual women have another additional risk because semen often remains in the female reproductive tract (Bolton et al., 2008; CDC, Division of STD Prevention, 2007). Heterosexual women are more susceptible than men if they engage in vaginal intercourse with an infected male partner. Women are also more likely to be **asymptomatic;** therefore, they do not know that they are infected. Some infections, such as herpes and HIV, also have properties of **latency.** A person can have the virus that causes the infection but not have symptoms, and tests may even show up negative. As a result, the person may be unaware that he or she is infecting others. This is

---

contagion
Disease transmission by direct or indirect contact.

punishment concept
The idea that people who had become infected with certain diseases, especially sexually transmitted infections, did something wrong and are being punished.

asymptomatic
Without recognizable symptoms.

latency
A period in which a person is infected with a sexually transmitted infection but does not test positive for it.

There are several things you can do to decrease your risk for acquiring a sexually transmitted infection (STI), such as making sure you know your partner's STI history, maintaining a monogamous sexual relationship, and using condoms and barriers for all sexual activity. It is also important to understand that certain sexual behaviors—called *high-risk sexual behaviors*—increase your risk for acquiring an STI. Alcohol use can also increase your risk because people are often more likely to engage in high-risk sexual behaviors when they have been drinking alcohol.

Following are some of these high-risk behaviors:

- Engaging in unprotected vaginal or anal intercourse without the use of a male or female condom unless this occurs in a long-term, single-partner, monogamous relationship in which both partners have been tested for STIs

- Engaging in oral sex with a male or female partner without using a condom or dental dam unless this occurs in a long-term, single-partner, monogamous relationship in which both partners have been tested for STIs

- Engaging in vaginal or anal intercourse before age 18

- Having multiple sex partners

- Engaging in vaginal or anal intercourse with a partner who has multiple sex partners

- Engaging in oral sex with a partner who has multiple sex partners

- Engaging in any sexual behaviors with a partner who has ever injected drugs

- Engaging in sex work or sexual activity with a partner who has ever engaged in sex work

- Engaging in sexual activity with a partner who has a history of STIs

- Engaging in sexual activity with a partner with an unknown STI history

why it is important to inform past sexual partners if you find yourself infected. In 2008, the CDC formally recommended testing for men and women whose partners have been infected with HIV, syphilis, chlamydia, or gonorrhea (Dooley, 2008).

Racial and ethnic disparities in STI rates also exist. African American communities have higher rates of many STIs than any other group in the United States (Barrow et al., 2008). Although

---

REAL RESEARCH 15.2   Black teenage women whose male partner was intoxicated during sex were significantly more likely to test positive for a sexually transmitted infection than were teens whose partners were not intoxicated (CROSBY ET AL., 2008a).

Blacks make up a minority of the total population, national STI surveillance data found that Blacks accounted for 69% of gonorrhea, 47% of chlamydia, and 43% of syphilis cases in 2006 (Barrow et al., 2008). These differences may be partially because Blacks are more likely to be treated in public clinics, which are more likely to report STIs (Arrington-Sanders et al., 2007). Even so, this cannot explain all of the ethnic and racial differences in STI rates. Other factors, such as access to health care, the ability to seek help, poverty, and sexual practices are also responsible for some of the rate disparities (CDC, 2010c).

Over the past several decades, the rates of STIs in MSM have been increasing. Researchers believe this is due to several factors, including a lack of knowledge about STIs, increased Internet access to sexual partners, a decreased fear of acquiring HIV, the increased use of alcohol and other drugs, and an increase in high-risk sexual behaviors, including oral sex and a lack of condom use in this population (Brooks et al., 2008; Mackesy-Amiti et al., 2008; Ogilvie et al., 2008; Workowski & Berman, 2010). Compared with heterosexual men and women, MSM report significantly more sexual risk taking (i.e., inconsistent condom use and

multiple sexual partners; Workowski & Berman, 2010). MSM are also at greater risk for anal cancer from engaging in anal sex with infected partners (Workowski & Berman, 2010).

Although some health care providers believe that women who have sex with women (WSW) are at low, or no, risk for STIs, WSW can, in fact, acquire bacterial and viral STIs (Workowski & Berman, 2010). Transmission can occur with skin-to-skin contact, oral sex, and vaginal or anal sex using hands, fingers, or sex toys, especially when toys are shared. WSW are also at risk for various vaginal infections, which can be transmitted during vulva-to-vulva sexual practices. Because WSW often have fewer sexual partners than heterosexual women and they engage in less penetrative sex, their overall risk for STI is reduced (VanderLaan & Vasey, 2008). However, WSW are less likely than heterosexual women to obtain yearly pelvic examinations, putting them at greater risk for adverse complications of STIs (Bauer & Welles, 2001; Marrazzo, 2004; Tjepkema, 2008). Overall, the incidence of STIs is significantly greater in bisexual women than among lesbians (Koh et al., 2005; Morrow & Allsworth, 2000; Tao, 2008).

▶▶ BIRTH CONTROL, PREGNANCY,
and Sexually Transmitted Infections

In Chapter 13, we discussed how birth control methods offer varying levels of protection from STIs. In 1993, the U.S. Food and Drug Administration (FDA) approved labeling contraceptives for STI protection. Barrier methods, such as condoms, diaphragms, or contraceptive sponges, can decrease the risk for acquiring an STI, although the FDA recommended revised labeling on condom packaging in 2005 to indicate that condoms must be used "consistently and correctly" to decrease STI risk (Alonso-Zaldivar & Neuman, 2005).

Although nonoxynol-9 (N-9) is an effective spermicide, frequent use can cause vaginal and anal irritation, which may increase the rate of genital ulceration, causing a higher risk for STI infection (Boonstra, 2005; Jain et al., 2005; B. A. Richardson, 2002; Wilkinson et al., 2002).

Overall, condoms are the most effective contraceptive method for reducing STI risk. The degree of protection, however, depends on correct and consistent use (Mindel & Sawleshwarkar, 2008). The role of oral contraceptives in preventing STIs is complicated. The increased hormones change the cervical mucus and the lining of the uterus, which can help prevent any infectious substance from moving up into the genital tract. In addition, the reduced buildup of the endometrium decreases the possibility of an infectious substance growing (because there is less nutritive material for bacteria to survive). However, oral contraceptives may also cause the cervix to be more susceptible to infections because of changes in the vaginal discharge.

When a woman does become pregnant, untreated STIs can adversely affect her pregnancy. Syphilis, gonorrhea, chlamydia, herpes, hepatitis B, and HIV can cause miscarriage, stillbirth, early onset of labor, premature rupture of the amniotic sac, mental retardation, and fetal or uterine infection (Kimberlin, 2007; Su et al., 2010). Syphilis can cross the placenta and infect a developing fetus, whereas other STIs, such as gonorrhea, chlamydia, and herpes, can infect a newborn as he or she moves through the vagina during delivery. HIV can cross the placenta, infect a newborn at birth, or unlike other STIs, be transmitted during breastfeeding (Salazar-Gonzalez et al., 2011).

Bacterial STIs can be treated during pregnancy with antibiotics, and if treatment is begun immediately, there is less chance the newborn will become infected. Antiviral medications can be given to pregnant women to lessen the symptoms of viral infections (Bardeguez et al., 2008; Kriebs, 2008). If there are active vaginal lesions or sores from an STI at the time of delivery, a health care provider may recommend a cesarean section. Women who do not know their partner's STI history should always use latex condoms during pregnancy.

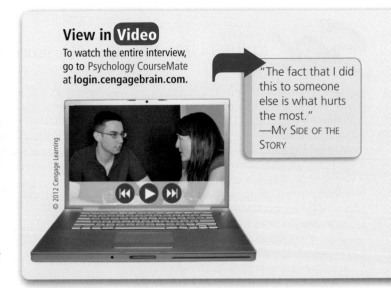

View in Video

To watch the entire interview, go to Psychology CourseMate at **login.cengagebrain.com.**

© 2012 Cengage Learning

"The fact that I did this to someone else is what hurts the most."
—MY SIDE OF THE STORY

ON YOUR MIND 15.1

Can sexually transmitted infections (STIs) be transmitted through oral sex?

It's often difficult to study the exact risk for acquiring an STI from oral sex, because many couples engage in other sexual behaviors, such as vaginal or anal intercourse. But studies have shown that oral sex can transmit STIs, such as herpes, syphilis, gonorrhea, **human papillomavirus (HPV),** HIV, and hepatitis A (CDC, 2010c). Although the risks for acquiring a STI from oral sex may be slightly smaller than the risk during other sexual behaviors, there is still a risk. To decrease your risk for acquiring an STI from oral sex, condoms or other barriers should be used.

In the following section, we will explore several categories of STIs, including ectoparasitic, bacterial, and viral, and then examine cross-cultural aspects of STIs.

◀ review QUESTIONS

1 Define the punishment concept of disease, and explain how the punishment concept might make a person neglect protecting themselves from STIs.

2 Identify specific populations that are at higher risk for STIs, and explain the reasons they are high risk.

3 Define the "asymptomatic" and "latent" aspects of STIs, and explain how these may affect a man or woman.

4 Discuss the role of birth control in decreasing STI risk.

5 Explain how untreated STIs can affect pregnancy.

ECTOPARASITIC INFECTIONS:
Pubic Lice and Scabies

Ectoparasitic infections are those that are caused by parasites that live on the skin's surface. The two ectoparasitic infections that are sexually transmitted are pubic lice and scabies.

▶▶ PUBIC Lice

Pubic lice (or "crabs") are a parasitic STI; the lice are very small, wingless insects that can attach themselves to pubic hair with their claws. They feed off the tiny blood vessels just beneath the skin and are often difficult to detect on light-skinned people. They may also attach themselves to other hairy parts of the body, although they tend to prefer pubic hair. When not attached to the human body, pubic lice cannot survive more than 24 hours. However, they reproduce rapidly, and the female cements her eggs to the sides of pubic hair. The eggs hatch in 7 to 9 days, and the newly hatched nits (baby pubic lice) reproduce within 17 days.

Incidence

Pubic lice are common and regularly seen by health clinics and various health care providers. Although there are no mandated reporting laws, pubic lice affect millions of people worldwide.

Symptoms

The most common symptom is a mild to unbearable itching, which often increases during the evening hours. This itching is thought to be a result of an allergic reaction to the saliva that the lice secrete during their feeding. The itching usually forces a person to seek treatment, although some people detect the lice visually first. People who are not allergic to this saliva may not experience any itching.

Diagnosis

A pubic lice infection is diagnosed by finding the parasites or eggs in the pubic hair. Although they can typically be seen with the naked eye, a magnifying lens may also be used.

Pubic lice attach to pubic hair and feed off the tiny blood vessels beneath the skin.

The Wellcome Medical Photo Library, London

Treatment

It is necessary to kill both the parasites and their eggs to treat pubic lice. In addition, the eggs must be destroyed on sheets and clothing. Over-the-counter creams or shampoos can be used to treat pubic lice. If necessary, prescription creams and shampoos can be prescribed if the over-the-counter methods do not work. Sheets and any articles of clothing that have been worn 2 to 3 days prior to treatment should be machine washed and dried. Hot water and dryer cycles should be used. Items that cannot be washed can be dry-cleaned or stored in a sealed plastic bag for 2 weeks. As with the other STIs, it is important to inform all sexual partners within the previous month that they are at risk for pubic lice.

▶▶ SCABIES

Scabies is an ectoparasitic infection of the skin with the mite *Sarcoptes scabiei*. It is spread during skin-to-skin contact, both during sexual and nonsexual contact. The mites can live for up to 48 hours on bed sheets and clothing, and are impossible to see with the naked eye.

Incidence

Infection with scabies occurs worldwide and among all races, ethnic groups, and social classes. Like pubic lice, there are no mandated reporting laws, but scabies affects millions of people worldwide.

Symptoms

Usually the first symptoms include a rash and intense itching. The first time a person is infected, the symptoms may take between 4 and 6 weeks to develop. If a person has been infected with scabies before, the symptoms usually develop more quickly.

human papillomavirus (HPV)
A sexually transmitted viral infection that can infect the genitals, anus, mouth, and throat, causing genital warts, cervical, anal, oral, and penile cancer.

pubic lice
A parasitic sexually transmitted infection that infests the pubic hair and can be transmitted through sexual contact; also called *crabs*.

scabies
A parasitic sexually transmitted infection that affects the skin and is spread during skin-to-skin contact, both during sexual and nonsexual contact.

Diagnosis

A diagnosis can usually be made on examination of the skin rash. A skin scraping can be done to confirm the diagnosis. A delay in diagnosis can lead to a rapid spread of scabies, so immediate diagnosis and treatment are necessary (Tjioe & Vissers, 2008).

Treatment

Prescription creams are available to treat scabies. All bed sheets, clothing, and towels must be washed in hot water, and all sexual partners should be treated. Usually itching continues for 2 to 3 weeks after infection, even after treatment.

◀ review QUESTIONS

1 Identify the two ectoparasitic STIs and describe how common they are.

2 Identify the most common symptoms associated with ectoparasitic STIs and explain what a person should do if he or she experiences any of these symptoms.

3 Identify the treatment for ectoparasitic STIs.

▶ BACTERIAL INFECTIONS:
Gonorrhea, Syphilis, Chlamydia, and More

Some STIs are caused by bacteria, including gonorrhea, syphilis, chlamydia, chancroid, and a variety of vaginal infections. In this section, we explore the incidence, symptoms, diagnosis, and treatment for these bacterial infections.

▶▶ GONORRHEA

Gonorrhea (the "clap" or "drip") is caused by the bacterium *Neisseria gonorrhoeae,* which can survive only in the mucous membranes of the body. These areas, such as the cervix, urethra, mouth, throat, rectum, and even the eyes, provide moisture and warmth that help the bacterium survive. *N. gonorrhoeae* is actually fragile and can be destroyed by exposure to light, air, soap, water, or a change in temperature, and so it is nearly impossible to transmit gonorrhea nonsexually. The only exception to this is the transmission of gonorrhea from a mother to her baby as the baby passes through the vagina during delivery. Transmission of gonorrhea occurs when mucous membranes come into contact with each other; this can occur during vaginal intercourse, oral sex, vulva-to-vulva sex, and anal sex.

Incidence

Gonorrhea rates declined significantly from 1975 to 1996, leveled off for 10 years, and then began decreasing again (CDC, 2010c). In 2009, there were 301,174 reported cases of gonorrhea in the United States (although the CDC estimates the actual number of cases was probably closer to 700,000; CDC, 2010c). Four main factors are related to gonorrhea prevalence in the United States: age, gender, race/ethnicity, and geographical area. Gonorrhea rates are highest in those age 15 to 24 years. Although the rates of gonorrhea have been similar in men and women since about 1996, in 2009, rates were higher in women (see Figure 15.1). Research has also found differences in certain racial and/or ethnic groups. For example, the rate of gonorrhea in Black men was 26 times higher than in White men in 2009, whereas the rate in Black women was 17 times higher than in White women (see Figure 15.2; CDC, 2010c). Geographically, even though rates in all areas of the country have continued to decrease since the early 2000s, rates in the Southern and Midwestern states are higher than rates in the West and Northeast.

Symptoms

Most men who are infected with gonorrhea experience symptoms alerting them of the infection, although they can infect others before the onset of symptoms (Workowski & Berman, 2010). If a man does experience symptoms, he may notice a urethral discharge, painful urination, and/or an increase in the frequency and urgency of urination, as well as **epididymitis** (epp-pih-did-ee-MITE-us). Symptoms usually appear between 2 and 6 days after infection.

The majority of men infected with gonorrhea experience symptoms and will seek out treatment. However, this may not happen until they have already infected others.

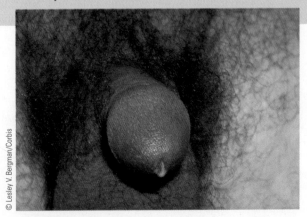

© Lesley V. Bergman/Corbis

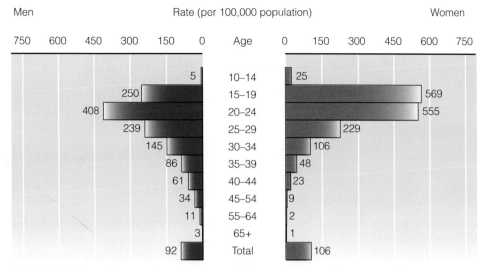

FIGURE 15.1 Gonorrhea rates by age and sex, United States, 2009. SOURCE: Centers for Disease Control and Prevention, http://www.cdc.gov/std/stats09/figures/19.htm.

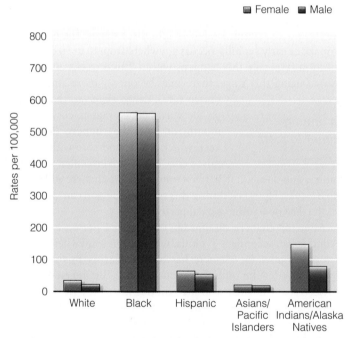

FIGURE 15.2 Gonorrhea rates by race, ethnicity, and sex: United States, 2009. SOURCE: Centers for Disease Control and Prevention, http://www.cdc.gov/std/stats09/tables/21b.htm.

Unlike men, the majority of women do not experience symptoms until complications develop, such as pelvic inflammatory disease (PID; we will discuss PID more later in this chapter). If symptoms do develop, they typically begin within 3 to 5 days and include an increase in urinary frequency, abnormal uterine bleeding, and bleeding after vaginal penetration, which results from an irritation of the cervix. The cervical discharge can irritate the vaginal lining,

causing pain and discomfort. Urination can be difficult and painful. Gonorrhea is a major cause of PID in women.

Rectal gonorrhea, which can be transmitted to men and women during anal intercourse, may cause bloody stools and a puslike discharge. If left untreated, gonorrhea can move throughout the body and settle in various areas, including the joints, causing swelling, pain, and pus-filled infections.

Diagnosis

Testing for gonorrhea involves collecting a sample of the discharge from the cervix, urethra, or another infected area with a cotton swab. The discharge is incubated to allow the bacteria to multiply. It is then put on a slide and examined under a microscope for the presence of the **gonococcus bacterium.** Although the CDC does not recommend widespread screening for gonorrhea, certain high-risk groups should be tested (i.e., those with prior infections or other STIs, multiple sex partners, or inconsistent condom use).

Treatment

The recommended treatment for gonorrhea infection is antibiotics, typically an injection of Ceftriaxone (one dose) or a variety of other antibiotic combinations (Workowski & Berman, 2010). In 2007, drug-resistant strains of gonorrhea forced the CDC to recommended the use of only one class of antibiotics (Workowski & Berman, 2010). Because patients with gonorrhea are often co-infected with other STIs, such as chlamydia, dual treatment is possible (Workowski & Berman, 2010). All sexual partners should also be tested for gonorrhea, regardless of whether they are experiencing symptoms. If a sexual partner is unlikely to seek treatment, some health care providers will provide patients with antibiotics or a prescription for them. Patients should be retested 3 months after treatment. Typically, becoming infected again after treatment is most likely caused by the failure of sex partners to get tested or receive treatment.

---

gonorrhea
A bacterial sexually transmitted infection that causes a puslike discharge and frequent urination in men; many women are asymptomatic.

epididymitis
An inflammation of the epididymis in men, usually resulting from sexually transmitted infections.

gonococcus bacterium
The bacterium that causes gonorrhea (*Neisseria gonorrhoeae*).

ON YOUR MIND **15.3**

Which sexually transmitted infections (STIs) do gynecologists check for during a regular examination?

During a woman's yearly visit, health care providers perform a Pap smear, which is designed to evaluate the cervical cells. Close to half of women believe that a Pap test can identify STIs (Hawkins et al., 2011). Although it is possible that some STIs, such as genital warts and herpes, *may* show up during Pap testing, many will not. If you think that you may have been exposed to any STIs, it is important for you to ask your health care provider to perform specific tests to screen for these. Specific tests can be run for syphilis, gonorrhea, chlamydia, herpes, genital warts, or HIV. The CDC recommends routine chlamydia tests for women younger than 25, as well as older women with risk factors, such as multiple partners.

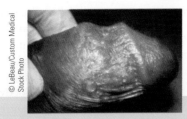

The chancre, which appears on the underside of the penis in this photo, is the classic painless ulcer of syphilis.

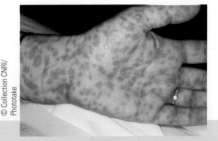

A secondary syphilis infection produces rashes on the palms or soles, as well as a generalized body rash.

▶▶ SYPHILIS

Syphilis is caused by an infection with the bacterium *Treponema pallidum*. The bacteria enter the body through small tears in the skin and live in the mucous membranes. Syphilis is transmitted during sexual contact, and it usually first infects the cervix, penis, anus, lips, or other area of the body. **Congenital syphilis** may also be transmitted through the placenta during the first or second trimester of pregnancy.

Incidence

Syphilis rates decreased in the 1990s, and in 2000, the syphilis rate in the United States was the lowest it had ever been since reporting began in 1941 (CDC, 2010c). As a result of these decreases, in 1999, the Surgeon General announced a plan to eliminate syphilis from the United States (which was updated in 2006). However, since 2000, syphilis rates have slowly been increasing. In 2009, there were a total of 13,997 reported cases of primary and secondary syphilis, which was the highest rate reported since 1995 (CDC, 2010c). There were also 427 cases of congenital syphilis reported in 2009, the first increase in congenital syphilis in 14 years (CDC, 2010c).

Like gonorrhea rates, four main factors are related to syphilis prevalence in the United States: age, gender, race/ethnicity, and geographical area. Syphilis rates are highest among younger people, and higher in men, which is due, in part, to increased numbers of men having sex with men (see Figures 15.3 and 15.4). Syphilis rates have also increased in WSM. Overall, racial and ethnic differences in syphilis rates have decreased since the early 2000s: in 2009, syphilis rates were 9 times higher in Blacks than Whites, which was a significant decrease from 1999 rates, when the rate was 24 times higher in Blacks (see Figure 15.5; CDC, 2010c). One major concern has to do with a trend found in 20- to 24-year-old Black men. There was a 212% increase in syphilis rates in Black men from 2005 to 2009. This was the largest increase

*Syphilis rates are **highest among younger people** and **higher in men.***

found in any age, sex, or racial/ethnic group. Because of this, plans to eliminate syphilis have focused on racial and/or ethnic minorities, as well as MSM (see Figure 15.5). Since the mid-1990s, higher rates of unsafe sexual behaviors have been documented among MWM in the United States (Workowski & Berman, 2010). Geographically, syphilis rates are highest in the Southern states.

Symptoms

Infection with syphilis is divided into three stages. The first stage, primary or early syphilis, occurs anywhere from 10 to 90 days after infection (typically this happens within 2 to 6 weeks after infection). During this stage, there may be one or more small, red–brown sores, called *chancres,* that appear on the vulva, penis, vagina, cervix, anus, mouth, or lips. The **chancre** (SHANK-ker), which is a round sore with a hard, raised edge and a sunken center, is usually painless and does not itch. If left untreated, the chancre will heal in 3 to 8 weeks. However, during this time, the person can still transmit the disease to other sexual partners.

After the chancre disappears, the infected person enters the second stage, secondary syphilis, which begins anywhere from 3 to 6 weeks after the chancre has healed. During this stage, the syphilis invades the central nervous system. The infected person develops reddish patches on the skin that look like a rash or hives. There may also be wartlike growths in the area of infection (D. L. Brown & Frank, 2003). If the rash develops on the scalp, hair loss can also occur. The lymph glands in the groin, armpit, neck, or other areas enlarge and become tender. Additional symptoms at this stage include headaches, fevers, anorexia, flulike symptoms, and fatigue.

In the third and final stage of the disease, tertiary or late syphilis, the disease goes into remission. The rash, fever, and other symptoms go away, and the person usually feels fine. The infected individual is still able to transmit the disease for about

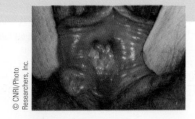

Typical syphilis chancre on a woman's labia.

syphilis
A bacterial sexually transmitted infection that is divided into primary, secondary, and tertiary stages.

congenital syphilis
A syphilis infection acquired by an infant from the mother during pregnancy.

chancre
A small, red–brown sore that results from syphilis infection; the sore is actually the site at which the bacteria entered the body.

chlamydia
A bacterial sexually transmitted infection (STI); although often asymptomatic, it is thought to be one of the most damaging of all the STIs.

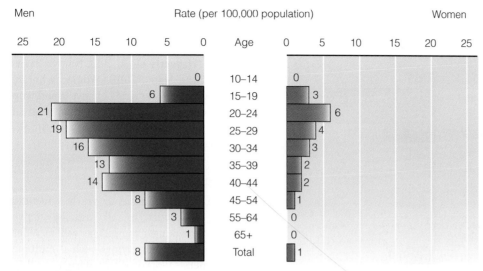

| Men | Rate (per 100,000 population) | | Women |

FIGURE **15.3** Primary and secondary syphilis—rates by age and sex, United States in 2009. SOURCE: Centers for Disease Control and Prevention, http://www.cdc.gov/std/stats09/figures/38.htm.

sexual partners should also be tested for syphilis, regardless of whether they are experiencing symptoms. If a person thinks that he or she may have been exposed to syphilis but tests negative, the person should consult with a health care provider immediately.

Treatment

In its early stages, syphilis is relatively easy to treat. If a person has been infected for less than a year, treatment typically involves a single injection of an antibiotic. Additional doses may be required if a person has been infected longer than a year (Workowski & Berman, 2010). However, if syphilis is allowed to progress to the later stages, it is no longer treatable and is often fatal.

1 year, but after this time, the individual is no longer infectious. Left untreated, however, tertiary or late syphilis can cause neurological, sensory, muscular, and psychological difficulties, and is eventually fatal.

Diagnosis

Anyone who develops a chancre should immediately go to a health care provider to be tested for the presence of the syphilis-causing bacteria. A diagnosis can be made by culturing and evaluating the lesion or through a blood test. Blood tests check for the presence of antibodies, which develop after a person is infected with the bacteria. During late syphilis, blood tests may be negative or weakly positive even if the infection exists (Singh et al., 2008). All

►► CHLAMYDIA

Chlamydia is the common name for infections caused by a bacterium called *Chlamydia trachomatis*. Chlamydia can be transmitted during various sexual behaviors that include genital contact, such as vaginal intercourse, oral sex, and/or anal sex. Oral sex with an infected partner can lead to pharyngeal (throat) chlamydia infections (Karlsson et al., 2011). An infected woman can also pass the infection to her newborn during childbirth.

Incidence

Chlamydia infections are the most common bacterial STI in the United States today (Cooksey et al., 2010). Rates have been in-

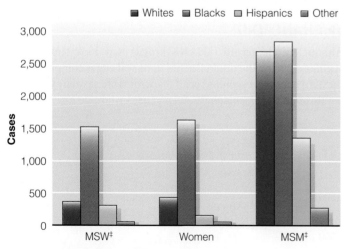

*Of the reported male cases of primary and secondary syphilis, 20% were missing sex of sex partner information; 1.7% of reported male cases with sex of sex partner data were missing race/ethnicity data.

†No imputation was done for race/ethnicity.

‡MSW = men who have sex with women only; MSM = men who have sex with men.

FIGURE **15.4** Primary and secondary syphilis, reported cases by sex, sexual behavior, race/ethnicity, United States, 2009. SOURCE: Centers for Disease Control and Prevention, http://www.cdc.gov/std/stats09/figures/43.htm.

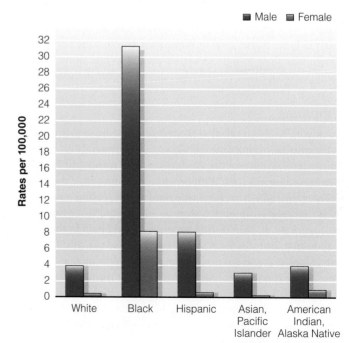

FIGURE **15.5** Primary and secondary syphilis—reported cases by race/ethnicity, age group, and sex, United States, 2009. SOURCE: Centers for Disease Control and Prevention, http://www.cdc.gov/std/stats09/tables/34.htm.

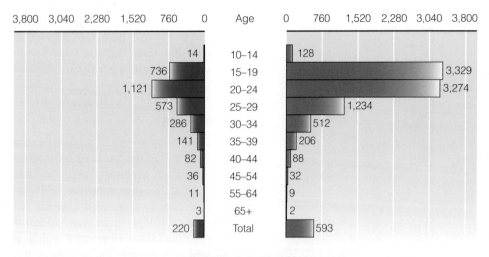

Men					Rate (per 100,000 population)			Women				
3,800	3,040	2,280	1,520	760	0	Age	0	760	1,520	2,280	3,040	3,800
					14	10–14	128					
			736			15–19			3,329			
	1,121					20–24			3,274			
			573			25–29		1,234				
				286		30–34	512					
				141		35–39	206					
				82		40–44	88					
				36		45–54	32					
				11		55–64	9					
				3		65+	2					
				220		Total	593					

FIGURE **15.6** Chlamydia rates by age and sex, United States, 2009. SOURCE: Centers for Disease Control and Prevention, http://www.cdc.gov/std/stats09/figures/5.htm.

creasing since the late 1980s when the first screening programs were established. However, in 2009, there were 1,244,180 cases of chlamydia in the United States, which was the largest number of STI cases ever reported (CDC, 2010c). Increased numbers may be because of more active screening for chlamydia, but experts believe they represent a true increase in the infection. Like other STIs, there are age, gender, race/ethnicity, and geographical differences in the prevalence of chlamydia.

Chlamydia rates are highest in men and women younger than 25 years (Workowski & Berman, 2010). Rates were three times higher in women than men in 2009, which was probably due to the fact that more women were being screened for the infection (see Figure 15.6). Since the availability of urine tests for men, significant increases in chlamydia rates have been reported in men as well. Research has also found differences in certain racial and/or ethnic groups (see Figure 15.7). The chlamydia rate in Black men was nearly 12 times higher than in White men, whereas the rate in Black women was close to 8 times higher than in White women (CDC, 2010c). Geographically, chlamydia rates are higher in the South.

Symptoms

Chlamydia has been called a "silent disease" because many women and men are asymptomatic (Workowski & Berman, 2010). Those who do have symptoms usually develop them within 1 to 3 weeks after becoming infected. With or without symptoms, chlamydia is contagious, which explains why rates are increasing.

If there are symptoms, a woman might experience burning during urination, pain during penetration, and pain in the lower abdomen. In most women, the cervix is the site of infection with chlamydia, and so cervical bleeding or spotting may occur. Men may experience a penile discharge, burning sensations during urination, burning and itching around the opening of the urethra, and a pain or swelling in the testicles. The bacterium that causes chlamydia can also cause epididymitis and **nongonococcal urethritis** in men.

In women, the bacteria can move up from the uterus to the Fallopian tubes and ovaries, leading to PID, and increasing the risk for infertility and ectopic pregnancies (Workowski & Ber-

man, 2010). In fact, infection with chlamydia is thought to be one of the agents most responsible for the development of PID (Haggerty et al., 2010; Nair & Baguley, 2010; Soper, 2010). Women who are infected with cervical chlamydia and who undergo a surgical abortion or vaginal birth are also at increased risk for the development of PID (Boeke et al., 2005).

Diagnosis

The CDC recommends yearly screening for chlamydia in all sexually active women younger than 25, as well as older women with risk factors, such as multiple partners (Workowski & Berman, 2010). Chlamydia is most often diagnosed through urine testing, but it can also be diagnosed from cultures of the vagina, cervix, urethra, rectum, or mouth.

Treatment

The recommended treatment for chlamydia is antibiotics, typically azithromycin (one oral dose) or doxycycline (twice a day for 7 days; Workowski & Berman, 2010). Patients are advised to abstain from vaginal intercourse for 7 days after beginning antibiotic treatment. All sexual partners should also be tested, even if they are not experiencing symptoms. As we discussed earlier, some health care providers may provide antibiotics for partners who are unwilling to get treated (Schembri & Schober, 2011). Rapid reinfection is usually due to the failure of sex partners to get tested or receive treatment. All men and women diagnosed with chlamydia should be retested within 3 months of treatment.

▶▶ CHANCROID

Although a **chancroid** (SHANK-kroyd) may look similar to a syphilis chancre, the difference lies in its soft edges compared with the hard edges of a syphilis sore. Chancroids are sexually transmitted through the *Haemophilus ducreyi* bacterium.

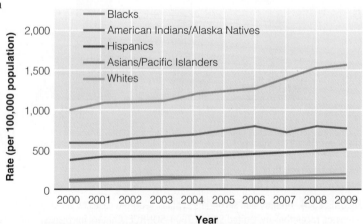

FIGURE **15.7** Chlamydia rates by race/ethnicity, United States, 2000–2009. SOURCE: Centers for Disease Control and Prevention, http://www.cdc.gov/std/stats09/figures/6.htm.

Incidence

The CDC reports that the prevalence of chancroid has declined in the United States (CDC, 2010c). Whereas approximately 5,000 cases of chancroid were reported in 1987, only 28 were reported in 2009 (CDC, 2010c). The majority of cases diagnosed in the United States involve a person who has traveled to a country where the disease is more common, such as countries in Africa, Asia, and the Caribbean.

Symptoms

Both women and men infected with chancroid experience development of a small lesion or several lesions at the point of entry. Four to 7 days after infection, a small lump appears and ruptures within 2 or 3 days, forming a shallow ulcer. These ulcers are painful, with ragged edges, and may persist for weeks and even months (D. A. Lewis, 2000). The infection may spread to the lymph nodes of the groin, which can cause swelling and pain.

Diagnosis

Diagnosis can be difficult, mainly because of problems culturing *H. ducreyi*, the responsible bacteria. A fluid sample from the ulcers is collected to examine for the presence of the bacteria.

Treatment

Chancroids are treated with antibiotics. HIV testing is often recommended, as are regular follow-ups. Ulcers typically improve between 3 and 7 days after treatment is begun. All recent sexual contacts should be told to seek testing and treatment.

▶▶ VAGINAL Infections

Vaginal infections, characterized by a discharge, itching, and/or odor are most frequently associated with **bacterial vaginosis (BV)**, trichomoniasis, and candidiasis (Workowski & Berman, 2010).

BV is caused by an overgrowth of various types of bacteria in the vagina, which replace normal healthy bacteria. BV is the most common cause of vaginal discharge, although many women might be asymptomatic (Workowski & Berman, 2010). If there are symptoms, they may include an increase in vaginal discharge (usually a thin, white discharge), accompanied by a strong "fishy" odor. Risk factors include multiple sex partners, inconsistent condom use, and/or douching (see Chapter 13; Workowski & Berman, 2010). Women who have sex with women may be at increased risk for BV because they have more exposure to vaginal secretions (Evans et al., 2007; Marrazzo et al., 2008, 2010).

Treatment involves the use antibiotics, most commonly metronidazole (twice a day for 7 days) or clindamycin cream (one full applicator intravaginally at bedtime for 7 days; Workowski & Ber-

*Bacterial vaginosis is the **most common cause** of vaginal discharge.*

ON YOUR MIND 15.4

I have a vaginal discharge that is yellowish white, but there is no odor. I think it's a yeast infection because it's kind of itchy. Should I use an over-the-counter cream?

Remember that having a discharge doesn't mean that you definitely have a vaginal infection. Normal vaginal discharge can range from white to slightly yellow, and it varies throughout the menstrual cycle. A yeast infection often causes vaginal itching and burning, pain during sex and urination, and a thick, white discharge. Keep in mind, however, that research has found only one in four women who seek treatment for a yeast infection actually has one (Hoffstetter et al., 2008). Vaginal itching can also include inflammation, dry skin, and other STIs, including BV. Like a yeast infection, BV can sometimes be triggered by the use of antibiotics or the use of feminine hygiene products. However, over-the-counter medications for yeast infections, which fight fungus, are ineffective against BV.

man, 2010). Although female sex partners are advised to get tested, the CDC does not recommend treating male sex partners, because it has not been found to be beneficial in the treatment of BV. Research is evaluating the use of probiotics in the treatment of BV (Bolton et al., 2008; Marrazzo et al., 2007). Probiotics are dietary supplements, such as the bacterium ***Lactobacillus***, that help regulate bacteria and yeast in the body.

Trichomoniasis (trick-oh-mun-NYE-iss-sis; also called *trich*) is caused by *Trichomonas vaginalis* bacteria. Women can get trichomoniasis from an infected man or woman, whereas a man usually contracts it only from an infected woman. This is because the bacteria is acquired through heterosexual or lesbian sexual behavior and is rarely transmitted through gay male sexual behavior; symptoms usually appear anywhere from 3 to 28 days after infection.

The most common symptom for women is an increase in vaginal discharge, which may be yellowish or green–yellow, frothy, and foul smelling; it may cause a burning or itching sensation in the vagina. Some women are asymptomatic or have minimal symptoms (Workowski & Berman, 2010). In men, the most common site of infection is the urethra, although trichomoniasis infection is often asymptomatic. If there are symptoms, there may be a slight increase in burning on the tip of the penis, mild discharge, or slight burning after urination or ejaculation.

Treatment for trichomoniasis is similar to treatment for BV, with the most common medication being a large, single dose of metronidazole, which can cause adverse effects such as nausea, headaches, loss of appetite, diarrhea, cramping, and a metallic taste in the mouth. It is recommended that all partners should be treated, and sex should be avoided until after treatment.

Vulvovaginal candidiasis (can-DID-i-ass-sis; yeast infections, also called *moniliasis* or *candidiasis*) is usually caused by

---

nongonococcal urethritis
Urethral infection in men that is usually caused by an infection with chlamydia.

chancroid
A bacterial sexually transmitted infection characterized by small bumps that eventually rupture and form painful ulcers.

bacterial vaginosis (BV)
Bacterial infection that can cause vaginal discharge and odor but is often asymptomatic.

Lactobacillus
Bacteria in the vagina that helps maintain appropriate pH levels.

trichomoniasis
A vaginal infection that may result in discomfort, discharge, and inflammation.

vulvovaginal candidiasis
An infection of the vagina that involves an overgrowth of yeast, known as candida; also called a yeast infection.

C. albicans, but it can also be caused by other *Candida* (or yeast). Seventy-five percent of women will experience a **yeast infection** in their lifetime, and about 40% to 45% will have two or more episodes in their lifetime (C. Wilson, 2005; Workowski & Berman, 2010). Typically, the organism multiplies when the pH balance of the vagina is disturbed because of antibiotics, douching, pregnancy, oral contraceptive use, diabetes, or careless wiping after defecation (yeast is present in fecal material, and so it is important to make sure it does not come into contact with the vulva). Although yeast infections are usually not sexually transmitted during heterosexual sex, if a woman experiences multiple infections, her partner should be evaluated and treated with topical antifungal creams (C. Wilson, 2005). Although male partners are less likely to transmit yeast because the penis does not provide the right environment for the growth of the yeast, female partners can transmit yeast infections during sexual activity (R. Bailey et al., 2008).

Symptoms of a yeast infection include burning, itching, and an increase in vaginal discharge. The discharge may be white, thin, and watery and may include thick white chunks. Treatment includes either an antifungal prescription or over-the-counter drugs (such as Monistat, Gyne-Lotrimin), which are applied topically on the vulva and can be inserted into the vagina. Misuse of over-the-counter drugs can contribute to medication-resistant strains of yeast (Hoffstetter et al., 2008).

Like BV, probiotics have also been used in the treatment of yeast infections (Falagas et al., 2006; Watson & Calabretto, 2007). Earlier we discussed the use of *Lactobacillus* in the treatment of BV. It is a type of "good" bacteria found in the vagina of healthy women and also in yogurt. Eating one cup of yogurt daily may help reduce yeast infection recurrences (Falagas et al., 2006; Watson & Calabretto, 2007).

▶▶ PELVIC Inflammatory Disease

PID is an infection of the female genital tract, including the endometrium, Fallopian tubes, and the lining of the pelvic area. Although the exact rates of PID are unknown, the CDC estimates that 750,000 women experience acute cases of PID each year. In Chapter 12, we discussed the role that PID plays in infertility. Although PID can be caused by many agents, two of the most common are chlamydia and gonorrhea (Workowski & Berman, 2010). Long-term complications of PID include ectopic and tubal pregnancies, chronic pelvic pain, and infertility. Between 10% and 15% of women with PID become infertile each year (CDC, 2011a).

Symptoms of PID vary from none to severe. The most common symptom is lower abdominal pain. Severe symptoms may include acute pelvic pain, fever, painful urination, and abnormal vaginal bleeding or discharge. There are a variety of treatment approaches to PID, and treatment is usually dependent on how progressed the infection is. For women with mildly to moderately severe PID, treatment is typically done with antibiotics. Women with acute cases may be required to undergo injections or intravenous treatments. Sexual partners should be treated if they have had sexual contact with the woman during the 60 days before the onset of her symptoms.

REAL RESEARCH 15.3   Research has found that female sex hormones, including estrogen and progesterone, may increase a woman's susceptibility and immune responses to STIs (KAUSHIC ET AL., 2011).

◀ review QUESTIONS

1 Identify the bacterial STIs and describe those that are most common today.

2 Explain how age, gender, race, ethnicity, geographic area, and sexual orientation have been found to affect incidence rates.

3 Explain the asymptomatic nature of the bacterial STIs and identify possible symptoms. How many people who are infected with a bacterial STI are typically asymptomatic?

4 Identify the common treatments for bacterial STIs.

5 Compare the common vaginal infections, including trichomoniasis, BV, and vulvovaginal candidiasis.

6 Define pelvic inflammatory disease (PID), and identify causes, symptoms, and long-term risks.

▶ VIRAL INFECTIONS: Herpes, Human Papillomavirus, and Hepatitis

STIs can also be caused by viruses. Once a virus invades a body cell, it is able to reproduce itself, so most of the time people will have the virus for the rest of their lives. Viruses can live in the body, and although people may not experience symptoms, they still have the virus. We now discuss herpes, HPV, and viral hepatitis; later in this chapter we will explore HIV and AIDS.

Herpes simplex 2 blisters appear on the penis.

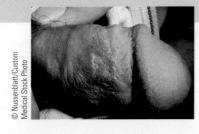

© Nussenblatt/Custom Medical Stock Photo

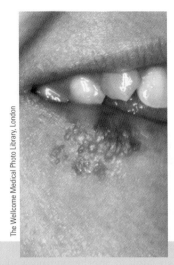

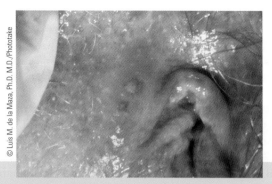

Herpes simplex 2 infection in women can cause blisters on the vulva, vagina, or anyplace the virus entered the body.

This is a typical patch of herpes simplex 1 blisters, which often appear on the lips or mouth.

▶▶ HERPES

Herpes simplex 1 (HSV-1) and **herpes simplex 2 (HSV-2)** are members of the **herpes** virus family. HSV-1 is often transmitted through kissing or sharing eating or drinking utensils and causes cold sores or blisters. Although HSV-1 can lead to genital herpes—if an infected person performs oral sex on someone—the majority of cases of genital herpes are caused by an infection with HSV-2 (Workowski & Berman, 2010). When the virus infects a nonpreferred site (i.e., HSV-1 infects the genitals or HSV-2 infects the mouth or lips), symptoms are often less severe.

HSV is highly contagious, and the virus may be released between outbreaks from the infected skin (often referred to as **viral shedding**). Because of this, it is possible to transmit the virus even when the infected partner does not have any active symptoms (Mertz, 2008; Wald et al., 2000). Viral shedding is more common in genital HSV-2 infection than genital HSV-1 infection, especially during the first year after infection (Workowski & Berman, 2010). Infected people can also **autoinoculate** themselves by touching a cold sore or blister and then rubbing another part of their body.

Although HSV-2 is almost always sexually transmitted, HSV-1 is usually transmitted during childhood through nonsexual contact (Usatine & Tinitigan, 2010; Xu et al., 2006). In fact, studies suggest that by adolescence, 62% of people have been infected with HSV-1, and by the age of 60, 85% have been infected. Pregnant mothers can pass HSV-2 on to their infants while the baby is in the uterus, during delivery from exposure to active sores in the birth canal, or directly after birth (Corey & Handsfield, 2000).

*The majority of people who become infected with genital herpes **are infected by someone that doesn't even know they have it.***

Incidence

There are no federal mandatory reporting regulations for HSV in the United States, but it is known to be a common virus. It is also estimated that one of every five Americans is infected with HSV-2 (Tirabassi et al., 2011). However, because many men and women might have mild or unrecognized infections, the majority of people with HSV-2 infections have never been diagnosed, mainly because many infected men and women do not experience blisters or ulcers (Workowski & Berman, 2010). In fact, the majority of people who become infected with genital herpes are infected by someone that doesn't even know they have it (Workowski & Berman, 2010).

Symptoms

Although many people infected with herpes do not experience the classic blisters associated with herpes, if they do have symptoms, the symptoms usually appear within 2 to 12 days after infection. If blisters are present, the first episode is generally the most painful (Workowski & Berman, 2010).

At the onset, there is usually a tingling or burning feeling in the affected area, which can grow into an itching and a red, swollen appearance of the genitals (this period is often referred to as the **prodromal phase**). The sores usually last anywhere from 8 to 10 days, and the amount of pain they cause can range from mild to severe. Pain is usually most severe at the onset of the infection and improves thereafter. Depending on the amount of pain, urination may be difficult. Small blisters may appear externally on the vagina or penis. The blisters, which are usually red and sometimes have a grayish center, will eventually burst and ooze a yellowish discharge. As they begin to heal, a scab will form over them. Other symptoms of HSV include a fever, headaches, pain, itching, vaginal or urethral discharge, and general fatigue. These symptoms

yeast infection
An infection of the vagina that involves an overgrowth of yeast, known as *candida*; also called vulvovaginal candidiasis.

herpes simplex 1 (HSV-1)
A viral infection that is usually transmitted through kissing or sharing eating or drinking utensils and can cause cold sores or blisters on the face and mouth.

herpes simplex 2 (HSV-2)
A viral infection that is often sexually transmitted and is responsible for genital ulcerations and blisters.

herpes
A highly contagious viral infection that causes eruptions of the skin or mucous membranes.

viral shedding
The release of viral infections between outbreaks from infected skin.

autoinoculate
To cause a secondary infection in the body from an already existing infection.

prodromal phase
The tingling or burning feeling that precedes the development of herpes blisters.

peak within 4 days of the appearance of the blisters. A few patients with severe symptoms require hospitalization.

The frequency and severity of recurrent episodes of herpes depend on several things, including the amount of infectious agent (how much of the virus was contained in the original infecting fluids), the type of herpes, and the timing of treatment (Mark et al., 2008). Men and women who experience symptoms during their first outbreak of genital HSV-2 infection will most likely experience recurrent episodes of blisters, but those infected with genital HSV-1 infections may not have recurrences (Workowski & Berman, 2010). Over time the frequency of recurrent outbreaks diminishes. Certain triggers may increase the likelihood of an HSV outbreak, including exposure to sunlight (natural or tanning beds), lip trauma or chapping, sickness, menstruation, fatigue, and persistent anxiety and stress (F. Cohen et al., 1999). After several years, a person may no longer experience outbreaks, although he or she may still be contagious and able to infect others.

Psychological reactions to herpes outbreaks can include anxiety, guilt, anger, frustration, helplessness, a decrease in self-esteem, and depression (Dibble & Swanson, 2000). Persons with supportive partners and social relationships tend to do better psychologically. In addition, those who receive psychological support services experience a greater reduction in recurrent episodes of herpes and an improvement in their emotional health (Swanson et al., 1999).

Diagnosis

During the first several weeks after infection, antibodies to HSV develop and will remain in the body indefinitely. Blood tests are often used to diagnose HSV infection and also to distinguish between HSV-1 and HSV-2. The presence of blisters caused by the herpes virus is often enough to diagnose the disease. Oftentimes, however, health care providers will take a scraping of the blisters to evaluate for the presence of HSV (Whitley & Roizman, 2001). No tests for the detection of HSV-1 or HSV-2 are 100% accurate because tests depend on the amount of infectious agent and the stage of the disease. Success rates for detecting HSV-2 antibodies vary from 80% to 98%, and there are high false-negative results, mainly because the tests are performed too early.

Treatment

The standard treatments for HSV infection today are oral antiviral drugs, such as acyclovir (Zovirax or an available generic), valacyclovir (Valtrex), and famciclovir (Famvir). These drugs can be taken as needed to reduce an outbreak, or they can be taken as suppressive therapy to reduce recurrences (Workowski & Berman, 2010). These drugs also shorten the duration of outbreaks, prevent complications (such as itching or scarring), and reduce viral shedding. Suppressive therapy has been found to reduce the risk for infecting sexual partners with genital HSV-2. Once a person stops taking these drugs, however, HSV symptoms will return.

Natural remedies for herpes outbreaks include applying an ice pack to the affected area during the prodromal phase and ap-

plying cooling or drying agents such as witch hazel. Increasing intake of foods rich in certain amino acids, such as L-lysine, which includes fish or yogurt, and decreasing the intake of sugar and nuts (which are high in another amino acid, arginine) may also help reduce recurrences (Griffith et al., 1987; Vukovic, 1992). Lysine can also be purchased from the vitamin section of any drugstore. Herbal treatments have also been used, including lemon balm (to dry cold sores), aloe (to decrease healing time of blisters), and peppermint oil (to inhibit the virus from replicating). However, the use of herbs can trigger outbreaks in some people, so it is recommended that they be used under medical supervision.

Support groups, relaxation training, hypnosis, and individual therapy have also been found to reduce the stress associated with HSV infections. Reducing stress can also reduce the frequency and severity of outbreaks. Research continues to explore the development of a vaccine for HSV, although it may a few more years before an effective vaccine is available (Brans & Yao, 2010; Hu et al., 2011; Kask et al., 2010; Morello et al., 2011; Pouriayevali et al., 2011; Tirabassi et al., 2011). Several studies have also been exploring antiviral therapy to decrease viral shedding, but as of early 2011, no medications have been found to effectively reduce viral shedding (Bernstein et al., 2011; Schiffer et al., 2010; Tan et al., 2011).

Warts that appear on the penis are usually flesh colored and may have a bumpy appearance.

© Science VU/Visuals Unlimited

genital wart
Wartlike growth on the genitals; also called venereal wart, condylomata, or papilloma.

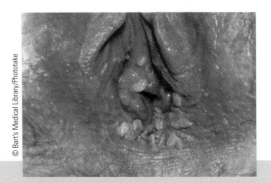

Genital warts appear on the outside of the vulva.

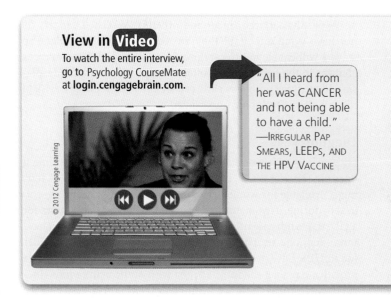

View in Video
To watch the entire interview, go to Psychology CourseMate at **login.cengagebrain.com.**

"All I heard from her was CANCER and not being able to have a child." —Irregular Pap Smears, LEEPs, and the HPV Vaccine

▶▶ HUMAN Papillomavirus

There are more than 40 types of HPVs, which can infect the genitals, anus, mouth, and throat during various sexual behaviors, including vaginal and anal intercourse, oral sex, and vulva-to-vulva contact. The majority of people who are infected do not know they have it. "Low-risk" HPV (types 6 and 11) can cause **genital warts** (condyloma acuminata, venereal warts), which are different from warts that appear on other parts of the body. "High-risk" HPV (types 16 and 18) can cause abnormal Pap tests and increase cancer risk, especially cervical cancer in women (Grce & Davies, 2008; Tovar et al., 2008). Almost all cervical cancers can be attributed to HPV infection (Smith & Travis, 2011; Wattleworth, 2011). HPV is also a risk factor for several other types of cancer, including oral, penile, and anal cancer (Dietz & Nyberg, 2011). In fact, the incidence of anal cancer in MSM is greater than the incidence of cervical cancer among women (Chin-Hong et al., 2008; Dietz & Nyberg, 2011; Goodman et al., 2008; Palefsky, 2008).

One important aspect of HPV infection that sets it apart from other viruses is the fact that research has found that in more than 90% of cases, a person's immune system can clear HPV within 2 years (CDC, 2009c).

Incidence

HPV is the most common viral STI in the United States today. Approximately 20 million men and women in the United States are currently infected with HPV, and 6 million more become infected each year (CDC, 2009c). In Figure 15.8 the prevalence of HPV types by age is illustrated. It is estimated that at least half of all sexually active men and women will get HPV at some point in their lives. Because of the contagious nature of genital warts, approximately 65% of sexual partners of people with cervical warts experience development of warts within 3 to 4 months of contact (Krilov, 1991).

Studies have found that many lesbians believe that HPV cannot be spread by female-to-female sex and/or do not identify HPV as a cancer risk (Polek & Hardie, 2010). However, HPV is prevalent in both WSW and MSM (Dunne et al., 2006; Marrazzo et al., 2001). Whereas one study found a 53% prevalence rate in U.S. men (Giuliano et al., 2008a), another study evaluating HPV prevalence in men in the United States, Mexico, and Brazil found an overall prevalence rate of 65%, which was higher in Brazil (72%) than in the United States (61%) and Mexico (62%; Giuliano et al., 2008b). In gay men, HPV infections have been found to co-occur with HIV infection (Pierangeli et al., 2008).

Symptoms

Symptoms for HPV are dependent on the type of HPV infection. Although several types may cause genital warts, the two most common types associated with genital warts are types 6 and 11 (Workowski & Berman, 2010). These types are also related to the development of warts in the throat, nose, and mouth. Warts are usually flesh colored, with a bumpy surface. In some areas, warts may grow together and have a cauliflower-like appearance. Warts develop in women on the vagina, vulva, introitus, or cervix, and in men on the penile shaft or under the foreskin in an uncircumcised penis (Workowski & Berman, 2010). Warts can also appear on the anus in both men and women. Warts are generally asymptomatic, and unless they are large, many people do not notice them and unknowingly infect other sexual partners. If warts grow in the throat (referred to as *recurrent respiratory papillomatosis*), they can potentially block the airway, causing breathing difficulties and/or a hoarse voice.

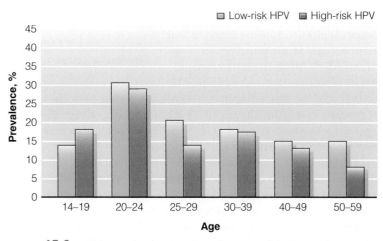

FIGURE **15.8** Prevalence of high-risk and low-risk types of human papillomavirus in females 14 to 59 years old, 2003–2004. SOURCE: National Health and Nutrition Examination Survey, 2007.

Typically, cervical cancer and other HPV-related cancers do not have symptoms until they are very advanced. Regular Pap smears will enable health care providers to monitor precancerous changes in the cervical cells (often referred to as **cervical dysplasia**). Identifying problems early can significantly reduce the risk of the infection developing into cancer.

Diagnosis

HPV may show up on Pap testing, but 80% to 90% of the time it does not (Kassler & Cates, 1992). Today, high-risk HPV DNA testing is available for women (Huang et al., in press). Cells are collected during a woman's Pap test and sent to a laboratory for analysis. Health care providers recommend that women who have more than one sexual partner should ask their medical provider for an HPV DNA test. If genital warts are suspected, a health care provider can soak the infected area with acetic acid (white vinegar), which turns the warts white and makes them easier to see under magnification. An examination of the cervix under magnification (called *colposcopy*) can also be used. Biopsies are also performed to check for HPV.

Treatment

As we've discussed, HPV infection can cause genital warts or abnormal changes in the cervical cells. It is important to seek treatment immediately if a person notices the development of genital warts because they can quickly grow and multiply. Genital warts can be treated in several ways, and no treatment method is superior to another or best for all patients with HPV. Important factors for a health care provider to consider when deciding treatment options include the number and size of the warts, patient preference, treatment costs, convenience, and adverse effects.

Treatment alternatives include chemical topical solutions (to destroy external warts), cryotherapy (freezing the warts with liquid nitrogen), electrosurgical interventions (removal of warts using a mild electrical current, often referred to as a LEEP, or "loop electrosurgical excision procedure"), or laser surgery (high-intensity lasers to destroy the warts). It may be necessary to try several treatment methods, and repeat applications are common.

Although the majority of sexual partners of those infected with HPV are already infected, if they are not, an infected person should use condoms during sexual behavior for at least 6 months after treatment (Lilley & Schaffer, 1990). Some couples decide to use condoms long term because of the possibility of transmitting the virus when no warts are present. It is possible that a low-risk type infection may be cleared up by the immune system over time (Corneanu et al., 2011; Dunne, 2007). Women who have been diagnosed with a high-risk type of HPV may be encouraged to have pelvic examinations and Pap tests more frequently.

Currently, two vaccines are available in the United States, Gardasil and Cervarix. Gardasil is a "quadrivalent" vaccine, which means that it protects from four HPV types—types 6 and 11 (which cause 90% of genital warts) and types 16 and 18 (which cause 70% of cervical cancer and many anal, vaginal, and penile cancers)—whereas Cervarix is a "bivalent" vaccine, which means it protects from two HPV types—16 and 18. Both vaccines are given as shots

Ideally, the HPV vaccine should be given **before a person is sexually active.**

ON YOUR MIND 15.6

Could I get human papillomavirus (HPV) from the HPV vaccine? Can I get the vaccine if I've already had sex?
Both Gardasil and Cervarix contain inactivated virus-like particles from the HPV. Unlike most vaccines, they do not contain live viruses. The particles in the vaccine stimulate a woman's body to produce antibodies against HPV (Food and Drug Administration, 2006; Schlegel, 2007). Current recommendations are for women to have the vaccine before age 26, and ideally before becoming sexually active. However, if you are already sexually active but have not been exposed to HPV types 6, 11, 16, and 18, the vaccine will protect you from the types you have not already been exposed to (Schlegel, 2007). It is important to discuss these issues with your health care provider, but keep in mind that providers' opinions and attitudes about the vaccine influence whether they offer or promote the vaccine (Ishibashi et al., 2008).

and require three injections. They are approved for use in women age 9 to 26. Gardasil can also protect boys and men against most genital warts, although no formal recommendations have been made by the FDA (Giuliano et al., 2011; Workowski & Berman, 2010). Research also indicates that MSM can benefit from HPV vaccination (Dietz & Nyberg, 2011).

Ideally, the HPV vaccine should be given before an individual is sexually active, although there is evidence that sexually active individuals may also benefit from the vaccine (National Cancer Institute, 2009). The vaccines can protect sexually active individuals from HPV types they have not been exposed to and may offer some protection from types they have already been exposed to (National Cancer Institute, 2009). In addition to the reduced risk for cervical cancer in women and genital warts in both men and women, these vaccines may also reduce the risk for anal and mouth/throat cancers, as well as cancer of the penis in men.

Because the vaccines are relatively new, the actual duration of immunity is unknown. Research continues to evaluate immunity duration, but it appears the vaccines are effective for at least 4 years (National Cancer Institute, 2009). At some point, it is possible that booster vaccinations (additional doses of a vaccine) will be necessary. Because the HPV vaccine does not protect against all types of HPV that can cause cancer, it is important that women continue to have regular Pap tests (Tovar et al., 2008).

In women, vaccine negative side effects include arm soreness, possible joint and muscle pain, fatigue, and general weakness. In men, the most common negative side effect has been soreness at the site of the injection (Garnock-Jones & Giuliano, 2011). Some women have reported feeling light-headed after the injection, and health care providers recommend waiting 15 minutes after the vaccine is given before leaving a health care provider's office (National Cancer Institute, 2009).

As of early 2011, the HPV vaccine was still fraught with controversy, mostly surrounding the safety and long-term adverse effects of the vaccine, as well as issues surrounding who should get the vaccine (Lechuga et al., in press).

▶▶ VIRAL Hepatitis

Viral hepatitis is an infection that causes impaired liver function. The three main types of viral hepatitis include hepatitis A virus (HAV), hepatitis B virus (HBV), and hepatitis C virus (HCV). HAV is transmitted through fecal–oral contact and is often spread by food handlers but can also be spread through anal–oral contact. HBV is predominantly spread during high-risk sexual behaviors (see earlier Sex in Real Life feature). Although HCV can be spread through sexual behavior, it is mostly caused by illegal intravenous drug use or unscreened blood transfusions.

Incidence

In 2008, there were approximately 2,500 acute, symptomatic cases of HAV reported in the United States, which was the lowest rate ever recorded (CDC, 2010a). This is probably a result of the HAV vaccine, which became available in 1995. However, after adjusting for asymptomatic cases and underreporting, the total number of HAV cases was probably closer to 22,000 (CDC, 2010a). Rates are highest in males, among American Indian/Alaska Natives, and in Western regions of the United States.

Rates of HBV have also been declining; in 2008, there were approximately 4,000 acute, symptomatic cases of HBV reported in the United States, which was the lowest ever recorded (CDC, 2010a). However, after adjusting for asymptomatic cases and underreporting, the total number of HBV cases was probably closer to 38,000. Rates are highest in males, among non-Hispanic Blacks, and in Western and Southern regions of the United States.

Finally, in 2008, there were only 878 confirmed cases of acute, symptomatic HCV reported in the United States. However, after adjusting for asymptomatic cases and underreporting, the total number of HCV cases was probably closer to 18,000 in 2008 (CDC, 2010c). However, HCV is the most common chronic blood-borne infection in the United States, with an estimated 3.2 million people chronically infected (CDC, 2010d).

Symptoms

Symptoms of HAV usually occur within 4 weeks and include fatigue, abdominal pain, loss of appetite, and diarrhea. Symptoms of HBV usually occur anywhere from 6 weeks to 6 months after infection, although infection with HBV is usually asymptomatic. Possible symptoms may include nausea, vomiting, jaundice, headaches, fever, a darkening of the urine, moderate liver enlargement, and fatigue. Finally, most people infected with HCV are asymptomatic or have a mild illness, and this illness develops within 8 to 9 weeks. The CDC estimates that between 60% and 70% of those infected with HCV will experience development of a chronic liver infection (Workowski & Berman, 2010).

Diagnosis

Blood tests are used to identify viral hepatitis infections.

Treatment

Antiviral therapies are available for the treatment and management of hepatitis. These therapies have been designed to reduce viral load by interfering with the life cycle of the virus and also causing the body to generate an immune response against the virus (Guha et al., 2003). Health care providers generally recommend bed rest and adequate fluid intake so that a person does not experience dehydration. Usually after a few weeks, an infected person feels better, although this can take longer in persons with severe and chronic infections.

Vaccines are available for the prevention of both HAV and HBV, and persons at high risk for contracting either of these should have the vaccine. Young children are often routinely vaccinated against both HAV and HBV (CDC, 2010a). High-risk individuals include health care workers who may be exposed to blood products, intravenous drug users and their sex partners, people with multiple sexual partners, people with chronic liver disease, MSM, and housemates of anyone with hepatitis (CDC, 2010a). Research continues to explore a vaccine for HCV (Hwu et al., 2011; Ruhl et al., 2011).

cervical dysplasia	**viral hepatitis**
Disordered growth of cells in the cervix, typically diagnosed with Pap testing.	A viral infection; three main types of viral hepatitis include hepatitis A, B, and C.

◀ review QUESTIONS

1 Identify the viral STIs and describe those that are most common today.

2 Explain how age, gender, race, ethnicity, geographic area, and sexual orientation have been found to affect the incidence of viral STIs.

3 Differentiate between "high-risk" and "low-risk" HPV, and explain long-term consequences of these risk types.

4 Explain how the Gardasil vaccine works. What are current recommendations for its use?

5 Differentiate between HAV, HBV, and HCV. What hepatitis vaccines are available, and what are the current recommendations for their use?

▶ HIV and AIDS

Although the **human immunodeficiency virus (HIV)** is a viral infection, several factors set it apart from other STIs and also shed some light on why the **acquired immune deficiency syndrome (AIDS)** debate became so politically charged. HIV/AIDS appeared in the early 1980s, a time when modern medicine was believed to be well on its way to reducing epidemic disease (D. Altman, 1986). In addition, AIDS was first identified among gay and bisexual men and intravenous drug users. Because of this early identification, the disease was linked with "socially marginal" groups in the population (D. Altman, 1986; Kain, 1987). The media gave particular attention to the lifestyle of "victims" and implied that social deviance has a price. One study found that one in five people believed that people who got AIDS through sex or drugs got what they deserved (Valdiserri, 2002). Although the stigma of HIV/AIDS decreased in the 1990s, in 1999, nearly one in five American adults said they "fear" a person with AIDS (Herek et al., 2002). We will talk more about public attitudes about AIDS later in this chapter.

AIDS is caused by a viral infection with HIV, a virus primarily transmitted through body fluids, including semen, vaginal fluid, breast milk, and blood. During vaginal or anal intercourse, this virus can enter the body through the vagina, penis, or rectum. Intravenous drug users can also transmit the virus by sharing needles. Oral sex may also transmit the virus, although the research has shown that the risk for HIV transmission from unprotected oral sex is lower than that of unprotected vaginal or anal sex (Kohn et al., 2002; E. D. Robinson & Evans, 1999). Kissing has been found to be low risk for transmitting HIV, especially when there are no cuts in the mouth or on the lips.

Like the herpes virus, HIV never goes away; it remains in the body for the rest of a person's life. However, unlike the herpes virus, an untreated HIV infection is often fatal. After a person is infected, the virus may remain dormant and cause no symptoms.

This is why some people who are infected may not realize that they are infected. However, a blood test can be taken to reveal whether a person is HIV-positive. Even individuals who do not know that they have been infected can transmit the virus to other people immediately after infection.

HIV attacks the **T lymphocytes** (tee-LIM-foe-sites; **T helper cells**) in the blood, leaving fewer of them to fight off infection. When there is a foreign invader in the bloodstream, antibodies develop

---

REAL RESEARCH 15.4 Of the 33.3 million people living with HIV in the world, 22.5 million live in sub-Saharan Africa (UNAIDS, 2010).

---

that are able to recognize the invader and destroy it. However, if the antibodies cannot do this or if there are too many viruses, a person will become ill. These antibodies can be detected in the bloodstream anywhere from 2 weeks to 6 months after infection, which is how the screening test for HIV works. The immune system also releases many white blood cells to help destroy invaders.

HIV attaches itself to the T helper cells and injects its infectious RNA into the fluid of the helper cell. The RNA contains an enzyme known as **reverse transcriptase** (trans-SCRIPT-ace), which is capable of changing the RNA into DNA. The new DNA takes over the T helper cell and begins to manufacture more HIV.

The attack on the T helper cells causes the immune system to be less effective in its ability to fight disease, and so many **opportunistic diseases** infect people with AIDS that a healthy person could easily fight off. No one knows exactly why some people acquire the virus from one sexual encounter, whereas others may not be infected even after repeated exposures. We do know that a person who has an STI is at greater risk for acquiring HIV (Gilson & Mindel, 2001; Hader et al., 2001; Pialoux et al., 2008).

It is unknown exactly where HIV came from, although scientists have many different theories. None of these theories has been proven, however. In the early 1980s, a number of gay men, mostly in Los Angeles and New York City, began coming down with rare

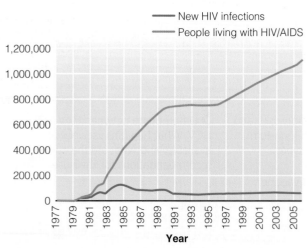

FIGURE **15.9** HIV and AIDS in the United States, 1977–2005. SOURCE: Hall et al., 2008; Centers for Disease Control, 2006.

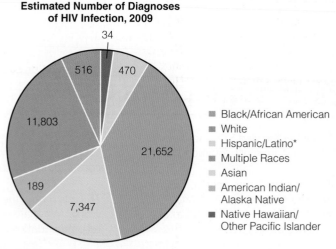

FIGURE **15.10** Estimated number of HIV diagnoses by race/ethnicity, 2009. SOURCE: Centers for Disease Control and Prevention, http://www.cdc.gov/hiv/surveillance/resources/reports/2009report/pdf/2009SurveillanceReport.pdf.

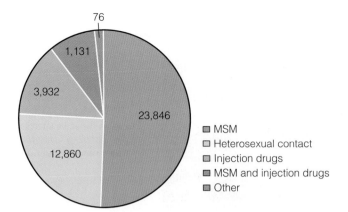

FIGURE **15.11** Estimated diagnoses of HIV infection by transmission category, 2009. SOURCE: Centers for Disease Control and Prevention, http://www.cdc.gov/hiv/surveillance/resources/reports/2009report/pdf/2009SurveillanceReport.pdf.

forms of pneumonia and skin cancer. At first, the disease was called GRID, for "gay-related immunodeficiency syndrome." Three hypotheses were offered: that there was a new infectious agent causing the disease, that the immune system was being suppressed by a drug that the infected persons were using, and that perhaps a sexual lubricant was involved. Many medical experts believed that this infectious agent would quickly be isolated and wiped out.

REAL RESEARCH 15.5 Infrequent condom use, low rates of male circumcision, and multiple sexual partners are major drivers of the AIDS epidemic in southern Africa today (EPSTEIN & MORRIS, 2011).

▶▶ INCIDENCE

As mentioned earlier in this chapter, all U.S. states and the District of Columbia require that HIV and AIDS cases be reported to local or state health departments. To help encourage testing, some states use confidential codes to keep HIV-positive people anonymous. These statistics help to track the spread of the virus.

The CDC estimates that there are approximately 1.1 million adults and teens living with HIV in the United States, with an additional 50,000 to 60,000 more Americans becoming infected each year (Hall et al., 2011). However, one in five people living with HIV in the United States is unaware of their infection (see Figure 15.9). Like other STIs, there are age, gender, race/ethnicity, and geographical differences in the prevalence of

HIV. From 2006 to 2009, the highest rate of HIV—15% of diagnoses—was in persons 20 to 24 years old (CDC, 2010b). Although the rate of HIV in females decreased from 2006 to 2009, rates in males remained stable—males accounted for 76% of all HIV diagnoses (CDC, 2010b). Racial and ethnicity factors were also important during this period. In 2009, Blacks accounted for 52% of all HIV diagnoses, and the rates were 66.6 per 100,000 population in Blacks, 23 in Hispanic/Latinos, 21 in Native Hawaiian or other Pacific Islanders, 17 in those reporting multiple races, 10 in American Indian or Alaskan Natives, 7 in Whites, and 6.4 in Asians (see Figure 15.10; CDC, 2010b).

Overall, the majority of people infected with HIV in 2009 were MSM (57%), followed by heterosexuals (31%; see Figure 15.11; CDC, 2010b). In 2008, MSM were 64 times more likely than heterosexual men to become infected with HIV (Hall et al., 2011). This was the largest relative difference among groups and represented a 1,218% increase from 2005 to 2008 (Hall et al., 2011).

Although **perinatal HIV infections** have declined in the United States since 2000, it is estimated that 8,700 HIV-infected women gave birth in 2006 (Whitmore et al., in press). Worldwide, it is estimated there are 2.1 million children younger than 15 living with HIV, and every year 430,000 new HIV infections occur in newborns, mostly in Africa (Fowler et al., 2010). Fortunately, because of improvements in obstetric care, rates of maternal–infant transmission have decreased. Today, HIV tests are routinely offered to pregnant women, and if a test is positive, medications can be used to reduce **viral load;** also, a planned cesarean section can be done to reduce the risk for transmission to the infant during delivery.

▶▶ KNOWLEDGE and Attitudes About AIDS

High-risk behaviors in college students, including multiple sexual partners, inconsistent condom use, high rates of sexual activity, and the use of alcohol during sexual activity, increases risks for HIV infection (Aicken et al., 2011; Bersamin et al., 2011; Shapiro et al., 1999). Knowledge levels about HIV/AIDS among U.S. college students are generally high, although higher knowledge levels do not consistently correlate with behavior changes or the practice of safer sex (Bruce & Walker, 2001; Shapiro et al., 1999).

Although fewer people hold negative attitudes about people with AIDS today, AIDS remains a stigmatized condition in the United States (Herek et al., 2002). We've discussed that many Americans hold negative opinions of those infected with STIs; today we find that many people are also afraid and uncomfortable around someone with HIV and AIDS, and have many mistaken beliefs about how it is transmitted.

---

human immunodeficiency virus (HIV)
The retrovirus responsible for the development of AIDS; can be transmitted during vaginal or anal intercourse.

acquired immune deficiency syndrome (AIDS)
A condition of increased susceptibility to opportunistic diseases; results from an infection with HIV, which destroys the body's immune system.

T lymphocyte (T helper cell)
Type of white blood cell that helps to destroy harmful bacteria in the body.

reverse transcriptase
A chemical that is contained in the RNA of HIV; it helps to change the virus's DNA.

opportunistic disease
Disease that occurs when the immune system is weakened.

perinatal HIV infections
HIV transmission from mother to child during pregnancy, labor and delivery, or breast-feeding.

viral load
The measure of the severity of a viral infection calculated by estimating the amount of virus in body fluid.

▶▶ SYMPTOMS

HIV infection results in a gradual deterioration of the immune system through the destruction of T helper lymphocytes (Friedman-Kien & Farthing, 1990). For those who are not being treated, this decline in T helper lymphocytes takes an average of 3 years in those who are emotionally depressed and more than 5 years in those who are nondepressed (B. Bower, 1992).

The average person who is HIV-positive and is not on any type of treatment will experience development of AIDS within 8 to 10 years. Flulike symptoms such as fever, sore throat, chronic swollen lymph nodes in the neck or armpits, headaches, and fatigue may appear. After this period, an infected person will seem to recover, and all symptoms will disappear. Later symptoms may include significant weight loss, severe diarrhea that persists for more than 1 month, night sweats, **oral candidiasis,** gingivitis, oral ulcers, and persistent fever (Friedman-Kien & Farthing, 1990). In addition, a person might experience persistent dizziness, confusion, and blurring of vision or hearing.

In an untreated person, the deterioration of the immune system makes it easier for opportunistic diseases to develop. In general, the incidence of opportunistic illnesses (i.e., those that can make people sick when their immune systems are compromised) are similar in men and women with a few exceptions. In women, cervical cancer may develop as an AIDS-defining condition (Hader et al., 2001). *Pneumocystis carinii* **pneumonia (PCP)** is one type of

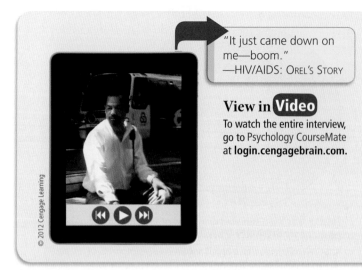

"It just came down on me—boom."
—HIV/AIDS: OREL'S STORY

View in Video

To watch the entire interview, go to Psychology CourseMate at **login.cengagebrain.com.**

© 2012 Cengage Learning

REAL RESEARCH 15.6 A genetic variation found in people of African descent increases the odds of becoming infected with HIV by 40% (WEIJING ET AL., 2008). However, once infected, this genetic variation can slow the progression of the disease and increase life expectancy. This may help explain some of the racial and ethnic differences in the incidence and fatality rates of HIV.

---

opportunistic illness that may develop in untreated men and women who are infected with HIV. PCP is a type of pneumonia that was uncommon before 1980. Other opportunistic diseases include **toxoplasmosis, cryptococcosis, cytomegalovirus,** and **Kaposi's sarcoma (KS).** KS is a rare type of blood vessel cancer that occurs in gay men but is rarely seen in other populations. Lesions from KS frequently occur around the ankle or foot, or they may be on the tip of nose, face, mouth, penis, eyelids, ears, chest, or back. Without treatment, two thirds of male patients with AIDS experience development of KS lesions on the head and neck (Alkhuja et al., 2001). Other STIs may appear or progress quickly, such as genital warts or syphilis, which may be resistant to treatment.

▶▶ DIAGNOSIS

Tests for HIV can either identify the virus in the blood or, more commonly, detect whether the person's body has developed antibodies to fight HIV. The most widely used test for antibodies is the **ELISA (enzyme-linked immunoabsorbent assay).** If an ELISA test result is positive, a second test, known as the **Western blot,** is used to check for accuracy. These tests can determine the presence or absence of HIV antibodies. If there is none, the test results are negative, indicating that the person is probably not infected with HIV. It takes some time for the body to develop antibodies; thus, there is a period in which a person is infected with HIV but the test will not reveal it. If the test is positive, antibodies are present in the body, and the person has HIV. It should be noted that false-negative and false-positive test results are also possible, although tests done within 6 months of infection have a higher accuracy than those performed later.

Since the mid-2000s, the biggest development in diagnosis has been the development of rapid HIV testing (Greenwald et al., 2006). Both the ELISA and Western blot HIV tests require as much as 2 weeks before a result is possible. The OraQuick Rapid HIV Antibody test was the first FDA-approved, noninvasive HIV antibody test. This test detects the presence of antibodies to HIV and requires only a drop of blood. Test results are available within 20 minutes. An oral version of this test, called the OraQuick Advance Rapid HIV Antibody Test, was approved by the FDA in

---

oral candidiasis
An infection in the mouth caused by the excess growth of a fungus that naturally occurs in the body.

Pneumocystis carinii **pneumonia (PCP)**
A rare type of pneumonia; an opportunistic disease that often occurs in people with AIDS.

toxoplasmosis
A parasite that can cause headache, sore throat, seizures, altered mental status, or coma.

cryptococcosis
An acute or chronic infection that can lead to pulmonary or central nervous system infection.

cytomegalovirus
A virus that can lead to diarrhea, weight loss, headache, fever, confusion, or blurred vision.

Kaposi's sarcoma (KS)
A rare form of cancer that often occurs in untreated men with AIDS.

ELISA (enzyme-linked immunoabsorbent assay)
The screening test used to detect HIV antibodies in blood samples.

Western blot
A test used to confirm a positive ELISA test; more accurate than the ELISA test, but too expensive to be used as the primary screening device for infection.

2004. The oral test collects antibodies from the blood vessels in mucous membranes in the mouth (it does not collect saliva). All of these tests must be used by trained professionals and cannot be used at home. Those who test positive are encouraged to follow up with an AIDS blood test.

▶▶ TREATMENT

Since 1995, there has been a tremendous decrease in HIV- and AIDS-related deaths, primarily because of the development of **highly active antiretroviral therapy** (**HAART;** Crum et al., 2006; M. H. Katz et al., 2002; Venkatesh et al., 2008). HAART is the combination of three or more HIV drugs, often referred to as "drug cocktails." This development, in conjunction with the development of **HIV RNA testing** (which allows health care providers to monitor the amount of virus in the bloodstream), has allowed for better control of HIV and has slowed the disease progression.

HAART has also significantly increased the life expectancy of children infected with HIV at birth ("Trends in HIV/AIDS Diagnoses," 2005). Without treatment, one in three HIV-positive African newborns die before the age of 1, half die before their second birthday, and the majority die by the age of 5 (Newell et al., 2004). Today children infected with HIV are surviving longer than earlier in the epidemic, mainly because of HAART (Davies et al., 2008).

Before starting treatment for HIV infection, a person should be given both a viral load test and **CD41 T cell count.** These tests can determine how much HIV is in a person's system and also estimate the T helper white blood cell count (which can show how well a person's immune system is controlling the virus). A baseline CD41 cell count will also give a health care provider a starting measure to compare with later viral load estimates after a person has started drug therapy. This will enable the health care provider to see whether the drug combinations are effective.

In the mid-1990s, HAART involved taking 20 to 30 or more pills with food restrictions (some drugs must be taken on an empty stomach, and others must be taken just after eating). This therapy often includes adverse effects such as fatigue, nausea, fever, nightmares, headaches, diarrhea, changes in a person's fat distribution, elevated cholesterol levels, the development of diabetes, decreased bone density, liver problems, and skin rashes. Newer drug regimens have used fewer pills; and in 2006, the FDA approved the first HIV triple-drug treatment composed of only one pill (Laurence, 2006; Sternberg, 2006). Atripla is a one-pill, once-a-day medicine that combines three antiretroviral drugs.

However, these newer drug regimens are not yet available in many places, and it is estimated that close to 60% of those infected with HIV are on a three-pill-a-day treatment (Sternberg, 2006). Once a person starts this type of drug therapy, it is very important that the dosages are taken every day at the same time (unlike other medications that require an 80% adherence, HIV drugs require a near-perfect adherence to dosing schedules; Mannheimer et al., 2002). Missed dosages can cause a drug resistance, which will destroy the drug's effectiveness. A missed dose could also cause the virus to survive and mutate into a resistant strain that will not respond to drug therapy. Individuals who begin drug therapy will most probably continue it for their entire life.

There are negative side effects to HAART. Two to eight weeks after starting HAART, individuals should have their viral load test redone. This will enable a health care provider to see how effective the drugs are. After this initial test, a person should have a viral load test every 3 to 4 months and a CD41 T cell count every 3 to 6 months to make sure the drugs are still effective. If the viral load is still detectable 4 to 6 months after starting treatment, the drug therapy should be changed. How fast the viral load decreases depends on several factors, including baseline CD41 T cell count, whether the person has any AIDS-related illnesses, and how closely the person has followed the drug therapy protocol.

Many health care providers believe that men and women who have been diagnosed with HIV should be given psychological counseling to explore coping strategies, gain information on the virus, promote a healthier lifestyle, and reduce the risk for transmission to others. Without this intervention, it is possible that people who are diagnosed with HIV will be more likely to become depressed and suicidal (Benton, 2008; Pyne et al., 2008; Rabkin, 2008).

Finally, it is also important to point out that the advent of HAART in the late 1990s brought with it a substantial increase in high-risk behavior among HIV-positive gay men (Elford et al., 2000; M. H. Katz et al., 2002; Stephenson et al., 2003; Wolitski et al., 2001). These behavioral changes were thought to be due to increased feelings of optimism and reduced levels of HIV. Since mid-2005, risky sexual behaviors in HIV-positive gay men have been increasing again (Bezemer et al., 2008; Elford, 2006; Hart & Elford, 2010; Sullivan et al., 2007).

▶▶ PREVENTION

To prevent the further spread of HIV, people's behavior must change. Many programs have been started to achieve this goal, including educational programs, advertising, and mailings. Public service announcements about AIDS have increased on radio stations, and many television programs have agreed to address HIV/AIDS in upcoming episodes. A variety of television shows have also included the topic of HIV/AIDS in their programming. Schools are also working to help prevent HIV and AIDS through education. Many schools today include HIV education in their classes. These programs provide students with information about HIV, risky sexual behaviors, and prevention strategies. Different educational programs emphasize different messages.

*To prevent the further spread of HIV, **people's behavior must change.***

highly active antiretroviral therapy (HAART)
A combination of antiretroviral drugs for the treatment of infections by retroviruses, primarily HIV.

HIV RNA testing
Test that allows health care providers to monitor the amount of virus in the bloodstream.

CD41 T cell count
Test that can determine the T helper white blood cell count, which will show how well a person's immune system is controlling HIV.

Microbicides—compounds that are applied to the vagina or rectum to protect against sexually transmitted infections (STIs)—are one of the most promising new developments in the fight against STIs (Neff et al., 2011). Microbicides will be especially important to women, many of whom do not have the social or economic power necessary to insist their partners remain monogamous or use condoms. They come in many forms, such as creams, gels, suppositories, lubricants, and dissolving film, and work in a variety of ways. Microbicides work by providing a physical barrier that keeps STIs from reaching certain cells, creating an acidic pH level in the vagina to decrease infection, or by preventing replication of the virus. As of mid-2011, there were more than 50 microbicide products in various stages of clinical development around the world. Phase III trials of Carraguard are ongoing in South Africa and Botswana, whereas Phase II and II trials of PRO 2000 and BufferGel were ongoing in India and South Africa (we discussed how FDA approval works in Chapter 13). Some microbicides offer contraceptive protection together with STI prevention, whereas others offer only protection from diseases. Those that do not offer contraceptive protection can be used by women who have an STI (or have a partner with an STI) but desire pregnancy. Microbicides have been found to reduce HIV infection by 39% and HSV-2 infection by 51% (UNAIDS, 2010).

Some traditional spermicides, including nonoxynol-9 (N-9), have antimicrobial properties but do not offer protection from various STIs, including gonorrhea or chlamydia. Research on the safety and effectiveness of nonoxynol-9 for HIV found that frequent use may increase HIV risk by creating vaginal and rectal ulceration (Gayle, 2000; Van Damme et al., 2002; Wilkinson et al., 2002). Condoms have always been the number one defense against STIs; however, their use must be negotiated with a partner, which reduces condom use (Rickert et al., 2002). Microbicides can be used by one partner without negotiation, and studies have shown that microbicides are more accepted than condoms. In fact, 90% of men in one study said they would not object to their partners using these products (Callahan, 2002). Microbicides could help to reduce the number of HIV infections by 2.5 million over 3 years (DePineres, 2002). Experts are hopeful that a microbicide will be available for public use by 2013.

After a diagnosis of HIV has been made, it is important to inform all past sexual contacts to prevent the spread of the disease. Because the virus can remain in the body for several years before the onset of symptoms, some people may not know that they have the virus and are capable of infecting others.

It seems reasonable that before we can determine what will reduce high-risk behaviors that contribute to increases in HIV and AIDS, we need to know the behaviors that people are engaging in. Yet data on sexual practices are lacking in the United States. As discussed in Chapter 2, many of our assumptions about current sexual behaviors are based on the Kinsey studies from the 1940s and 1950s. Little is known about current rates of high-risk behaviors, such as anal intercourse, extramarital or teenage sexuality, and homosexuality. The recent National Survey of Sexual Health and Behavior helped shed some light on these behaviors, and two ongoing surveys, the Behavioral Risk Factor Surveillance Survey (BRFSS) and the Youth Risk Behavior Surveillance Survey (YRBS), continue to collect and monitor information about risk behaviors at the state level (see Chapters 2 and 8 for more information about these studies).

Researchers continue to explore the development of AIDS vaccines. However, HIV is one of the most difficult viruses to eradicate, because it has developed ways of dodging the immune system and becoming immune to specific treatments. In 2009, a clinical trial in Thailand presented the first vaccine to prevent HIV infection. Although the vaccine could effectively reduce HIV infection by 30%, rates were not high enough to approve the vaccine for widespread use. AIDS vaccine trials continued throughout 2011 (see Chapter 13 for more information about the FDA approval process). In the United States, the majority of AIDS vaccine research is funded through the National Institutes of Health. In 2009, the National Institutes of Health and the Bill and Melinda Gates Foundation spent close to $900 million for AIDS vaccine research and development. The Global HIV Vaccine Enterprise, an alliance of independent organizations around the world, has organized to accelerate HIV vaccine research and development. The development of a vaccine is a long process. In fact, the polio vaccine took 47 years to produce, and it is anticipated that the HIV vaccine may take just as long (Markel, 2005).

▶▶ FAMILIES and HIV

Families and friends of people with HIV often do not receive the same social support as do families and friends of people with other devastating illnesses, such as cancer or Alzheimer's disease. There is a great social stigma attached to HIV, and many caregivers find that they have to deal with this pain on their own. Children whose parents become infected with the HIV/AIDS often have difficulties sorting through their own personal feelings about this.

As discussed earlier, with the help of HAART therapies, many parents with HIV are living longer today. This has brought up many new issues, such as disclosure (when and how to tell family members) and adjusting to having a parent with HIV. The majority of parents living with AIDS have discussed their illness with their family members. Mothers are more likely to disclose their HIV status earlier than fathers, and they disclose more often to their daughters than their sons (Lee & Rotheram-Borus, 2002). Many people with HIV-positive family members find it helpful to become involved in support groups. The names of several organizations are provided at the end of this chapter.

1 Explain how HIV is transmitted and how the virus affects the body.

2 Identify the various routes of transmission for HIV, and identify the groups with the highest rates of infection today.

3 Explain what we know about the public's knowledge levels and attitudes about HIV and AIDS.

4 Identify the various symptoms and opportunistic diseases that develop as a result of HIV and AIDS.

5 Explain how HAART works. What other factors are important in the treatment of HIV and AIDS?

6 What work is being done in HIV prevention and research?

7 Identify and explain some of the important issues that face the family of a person with HIV.

▶ GLOBAL ASPECTS of AIDS

Since the 1990s, the annual number of new HIV infections worldwide has steadily declined (UNAIDS, 2010). In 2009, there were approximately 2.6 million people newly infected with HIV, which was significantly less than previous years. Between 2001 and 2009, the HIV incidence around the world declined by more than 25% (UNAIDS, 2010). In sub-Saharan Africa, where the majority of new HIV infections continue to occur (see Figures 15.12 and 15.13), approximately 1.8 million people were infected with HIV in 2009, which was considerably less than the 2.2 million who were infected in 2001. However, there are areas in the world where rates of HIV infection are increasing, such as Eastern Europe and Central Asia (UNAIDS, 2010). Most of these increases are driven by an increase in men having sex with men.

Children are grossly affected by the AIDS epidemic worldwide. In fact, it is estimated that every minute a child becomes infected with HIV and another child dies of an AIDS-related illness (UNAIDS, 2008). By 2005, an estimated 15 million children had lost at least one parent to AIDS worldwide (see accompanying Sexual Diversity in Our World feature; UNAIDS, 2005). The number of children who have been orphaned throughout the world because of AIDS is equivalent to the total number of children younger than 5 living in the United States. In this section, we explore HIV/AIDS in Asia, Eastern Europe and Central Asia, North America, Western and Central Europe, sub-Saharan Africa, the Caribbean, and the Middle East.

▶▶ ASIA

An estimated 5 million people in Asia were living with HIV in 2009, and 360,000 people were newly infected with HIV (which was 20% lower than in 2001; UNAIDS, 2010). HIV rates declined by more than 25% in India, Nepal, and Thailand, and leveled off in Malaysia and Sri Lanka from 2001 to 2009. Increased rates were found in Bangladesh and the Philippines.

The main mode of HIV transmission in Asian countries is unprotected sex, both with intimate partners and paid sex workers (UNAIDS, 2010). High rates of HIV have also been found in injecting drug users and MSM. A large proportion of HIV infections occur in married women whose husbands frequent sex workers or inject drugs. Recently, there has been a push to increase condom use in sex workers, and this has been fairly successful in Cambodia and Thailand (UNAIDS, 2010).

▶▶ EASTERN EUROPE and Central Asia

The number of people living in Eastern Europe and Central Asia has nearly tripled since 2000, and in 2009, there was an estimated total of 1.4 million people living with HIV in this area (UNAIDS, 2010). HIV rates are highest in the Russian Federation and Ukraine, which account for 90% of new HIV diagnoses. The HIV epidemic in Eastern Europe and Central Asia is mainly among people who inject drugs, sex workers and their sexual partners, and MSM.

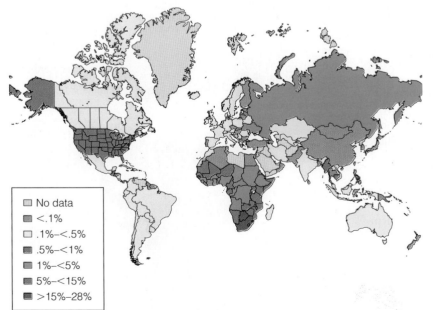

- ☐ No data
- ■ <.1%
- ☐ .1%–<.5%
- ■ .5%–<1%
- ■ 1%–<5%
- ■ 5%–<15%
- ■ >15%–28%

FIGURE **15.12** Global prevalence of HIV in 2009. SOURCE: UNAIDS, 2010.

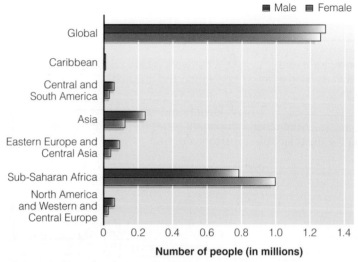

■ Male ■ Female

Number of people (in millions)

FIGURE **15.13** Number of people newly infected with HIV annually by sex and geographical region, 2009. SOURCE: UNAIDS, 2010.

▶▶ NORTH AMERICA AND
Western and Central Europe

The total number of people living with HIV in North America and Western and Central Europe was 2.3 million in 2009, which was 30% more than in 2001 (UNAIDS, 2010). Overall, the main mode of HIV transmission is men having sex with men, heterosexual intercourse, injecting drug use, and paid sex. In the United States, new HIV infections in MSM increased by more than 50% from 1991 to 1993 through 2003 to 2006 (UNAIDS, 2010). High-risk sexual behaviors are the main reason for these increases. Fewer people are dying of HIV infection in these countries because of antiretroviral therapy.

▶▶ SUB-SAHARAN Africa

The majority of the world's HIV-positive people live in sub-Saharan Africa, where close to 68% of the global number of people with HIV are living (UNAIDS, 2010). In 2009, an estimated 11.3 million people were living with HIV in southern Africa. Sub-Saharan Africa has more women than men living with HIV (UNAIDS, 2010). The main mode of HIV transmission is heterosexual intercourse, but injecting drug use, sex work, and men having sex with men also contribute to transmission.

Children are also hard hit in sub-Saharan Africa, where it is estimated 90% of children younger than 15 years who are HIV-positive live (UNAIDS, 2010). One study found that a 15-year-old in Botswana has an 80% chance of dying of AIDS (Piot, 2000). Because sub-Saharan Africa has the world's largest population of HIV-positive children, South Africa's *Sesame Street* unveiled an HIV-positive Muppets character, Kami. Kami is a 5-year-old orphan whose parents died of AIDS. Kami's character was designed to help children in South Africa understand AIDS and teach them that it's all right to play with HIV-positive children.

However, the number of people newly infected with HIV peaked in the 1990s and has been declining over the last few years in several countries in sub-Saharan Africa (UNAIDS, 2010). Most of these reductions in HIV are due to behavioral changes, including increased condom use and a reduction in casual sex. In addi-

tion, antiretroviral therapy and other forms of treatment have also reduced AIDS-related deaths. One of the biggest problems in many parts of Africa is that because of cost, only a small percentage of the many people with HIV are receiving HAART, and many are receiving it late, which limits the impact of treatment.

▶▶ THE Caribbean

There were 240,000 people living with HIV in the Caribbean in 2009, and this number has stayed relatively stable since the late 1990s (UNAIDS, 2010). There are geographical differences in HIV rates, with Cuba having low HIV prevalence with higher HIV rates in the Bahamas. Transmission modes are mainly through unprotected heterosexual sexual behavior, especially paid sex. Like sub-Saharan Africa, there are more women and girls living with HIV than men and boys (UNAIDS, 2010). Other routes of transmission include injecting drug use and men having sex with men. However, many countries in this area are focusing HIV prevention on paid sex workers.

▶▶ THE MIDDLE EAST and Northern Africa

Although reliable data on HIV epidemics in this area are difficult to come by, available evidence has found that an estimated 460,000 people were living with HIV in the Middle East and Northern Africa by the end of 2009, which was an increase from the 180,000 living there in 2001 (UNAIDS, 2010). The main mode of HIV transmission was unprotected paid sex, MSM, and injecting drug use. In Iran, drug-related epidemics have contributed to increasing HIV rates. Although Sudan has increased efforts at educating the public about HIV and AIDS, one study found that only 5% of women knew that condom use could protect them from HIV infection, and more than two thirds of the women had never heard of a condom (UNAIDS, 2005).

In summary, recent research suggests that counseling and educational interventions are being increasingly recognized as important aspects of care for people with HIV and their families in developing countries. In addition, home-based health care is being established to remove some of the burden from the hospitals, increase quality health care, and reduce costs.

In South Africa, an HIV-positive Muppet was added to the cast of *Sesame Street*. Her name is Kami, which is derived from the Tswana word for "acceptance."

AP/Wide World Photos

Despite all the declines in HIV infection and increased access to treatments worldwide, the number of children who have lost their parents to AIDS has not declined (UNAIDS, 2010). In 2009, there were 16.6 million AIDS orphans, and 90% of them lived in sub-Saharan Africa (even though only 10% of the world's population lives there; UNAIDS, 2010). Although we typically think of an orphan as a child without parents, the word is used a bit differently by those involved in the AIDS epidemic. A maternal orphan is a child who has lost a mother to AIDS, a paternal orphan has lost a father to AIDS, and a double orphan has lost both parents to AIDS (Fredriksson et al., 2008). AIDS orphans are often young—15% are newborn to 4 years old, 35% are 5 to 9 years old, and 50% are 10 to 14 years old (Monasch & Boerma, 2004).

At the beginning of the AIDS epidemic in the 1980s, orphanages were set up in many African communities to help care for the many children whose parents had died. However, the number of orphans quickly surpassed the amount of space available in the orphanages. Today, 90% of orphans in sub-Saharan Africa are cared for by extended family members (Heymann et al., 2007). In fact, more than one third of working adults in sub-Saharan Africa care for orphans in their households, but the majority of these families live in poverty and are unable to meet the essential caregiving needs of the orphans in their care (Heymann et al., 2007; Kidman et al., 2007; Roby & Shaw, 2006). Ongoing poverty in sub-Saharan Africa has forced some orphans either into the labor market or to the streets where they may beg, steal, or prostitute themselves for money (Amanpour, 2006).

African orphans are at increased risk for many physical, socioeconomic, and psychological problems (Sherr et al., 2008). Many experience anxiety, depression, fear, anger, and guilt, which can contribute to long-term mental health issues (Foster,

Friedrich Stark/Alamy

2006). Orphans are also at increased risk for social isolation, abuse, neglect, malnutrition, and homelessness, and many lose their opportunities for health care, future employment, and adequate education (Andrews et al., 2006; Cluver & Gardner, 2007; Foster, 2006; Li et al., 2008; Rivers et al., 2008). In fact, because many extended families are unable to afford school and uniform fees, orphans are less likely to attend school than nonorphans (Kürzinger et al., 2008).

Orphans are also at greater risk for negative sexual health outcomes compared with nonorphans. They are more likely to initiate sex early and have multiple sex partners, are less likely to use condoms, and more likely to experience teenage pregnancy (Birdthistle et al., 2008; Gregson et al., 2005). They are also at greater risk for forced sex and have a higher prevalence of HIV and herpes infections (Birdthistle et al., 2008).

As the HIV/AIDS rates continue to climb in many countries around the globe, it is imperative to find ways to both reduce HIV/AIDS infections and increase access to antiretroviral treatment. In addition to this, however, finding care and assistance for orphans also remains a priority. Local and global communities continue to reach out to help AIDS orphans around the globe, ensuring adequate access to services and providing support services for caregivers and families (Roby & Shaw, 2006; UNAIDS, 2008). Some groups provide psychological support, food, and/or clothing and offer resources to keep orphans in school (Foster, 2002). Many believe that finding ways to keep orphans in school may be the key to this crisis, because an adequate education can increase self-esteem and help ensure financial independence in the future (Fredriksson et al., 2008).

◀ review QUESTIONS

1 Explain the global impact of the AIDS epidemic on children.

2 Identify the main mode of HIV transmission in Asian countries. What do you think could be done to decrease HIV infections in this particular area?

3 Identify the main mode of HIV transmission in Eastern Europe and Central Asian countries. What do you think could be done to decrease HIV infections in this particular area?

4 Identify the main mode of HIV transmission in sub-Saharan Africa. What do you think could be done to decrease HIV infections in this particular area?

5 Identify the main mode of HIV transmission in the Caribbean. What do you think could be done to decrease HIV infections in this particular area?

6 Identify the main mode of HIV transmission in the Middle East. What do you think could be done to decrease HIV infections in this particular area?

▶ PREVENTING Sexually Transmitted Infections and AIDS

You might be feeling pretty overwhelmed with all this new information about STIs. It is important not to lose sight of the fact that there is much that you can do to help prevent STIs. If you are sexually active, one of the most important things you can do is to get yourself tested. When you get into a sexual relationship, make sure your partner is also tested. Today's experts recommend full testing for STIs for sexually active men and women, including HIV testing (L. A. Johnson, 2005).

You can also make sure that you carefully choose your sexual partners and use barrier methods such as condoms to reduce your chances of acquiring an STI. Unless you are in a monogamous relationship, it is important to avoid high-risk sexual behaviors (see Sex in Real Life feature, "High-Risk Sexual Behaviors," earlier in the chapter). In addition, it is also important to be sure you are knowledgeable about STIs. Knowledge and education are powerful tools in decreasing the frequency of STIs.

▶▶ EARLY Detection

If you already have an STI, early detection and management of the infection are important and can help lessen the possibility of infecting others. Be sure to notify your sexual partners as soon as a positive diagnosis is made to help reduce the chances that someone else will become infected. As discussed earlier in this chapter,

many college students are apprehensive about getting tested for STIs, especially when they think they might be positive. It is important to be proactive in these matters and seek testing and treatment if you think you may have become infected. Many of the bacterial STIs can be treated with antibiotics. However, delaying treatment may result in more long-term consequences to your health, such as PID or infertility (for you or your partner).

▶▶ TALKING ABOUT Sexually Transmitted Infections

Talking about STIs is not always easy to do, and although people might not always respond positively to such a discussion, it is important. Honesty, trust, and communication are key elements to any successful relationship. To begin a conversation about STIs, choose a time when you can be alone and uninterrupted. Sometimes it's a little easier to start by bringing up the importance of honesty in relationships. You could talk about what you've learned in this class and how it's made you think about your current and future health. Talk about any infections, diseases, and past behaviors that may have put you or your partner at risk. Suggest STI testing and the importance of monogamy in your relationship.

Overall, as we discussed at the beginning of this chapter, it is important that we continue to try to break the silence about STIs and work to reduce the negative beliefs and stigma associated with them. Only then can we help encourage responsibility and safe behaviors.

◀ review QUESTIONS

1 Identify some strategies that a person can use to decrease the possibility of acquiring an STI.

2 If you have already been infected with an STI, what can you do to help manage the infection?

3 Explain how communication can be an important tool in decreasing STIs.

◀◀ chapter REVIEW

SUMMARY POINTS

1 Sexually transmitted infections (STIs) have historically been viewed as symbols of corrupt sexuality, which is why there has been a "punishment concept" of disease. College students are at an increased risk for acquiring STIs because they engage in many behaviors that put them at greater risk, such as having multiple partners and engaging in unprotected sexual behaviors.

2 Large discrepancies have been found in STI prevalence, with higher rates in young people, certain racial/ethnic groups and minority populations, and men who have sex with men (MSM). Young adults are disproportionately affected by STIs, and the incidence of these infections continues to grow in this population, primarily because many engage in high-risk sexual behaviors, such as multiple partners, inconsistent condom use, or both.

3 Birth control methods offer varying levels of protection from STIs. In 1993, the FDA approved labeling contraceptives for STI protection. Barrier methods, such as condoms, diaphragms, or contraceptive sponges, can decrease the risk of acquiring an STI.

4 When a woman does become pregnant, untreated STIs can adversely affect her pregnancy. Syphilis, gonorrhea, chlamydia, herpes, hepatitis B virus (HBV), and HIV can cause miscarriage, stillbirth, early onset of labor, premature rupture of the amniotic sac, mental retardation, and fetal or uterine infection.

5 Ectoparasitic infections are those that are caused by parasites that live on the skin's surface and include pubic lice and scabies. First symptoms include a rash and intense itching. Treatment is with topical creams to kill the parasites and their larvae.

6 Gonorrhea rates declined significantly from 1975 to 1996, leveled off for 10 years, and then began decreasing again. The majority of women who are infected with gonorrhea are asymptomatic, whereas men are symptomatic. Testing for gonorrhea involves collecting a sample of the discharge from the cervix, urethra, or another infected area with a cotton swab. Gonorrhea can be treated effectively with antibiotics. Antibiotics are usually administered orally, but in severe cases, intramuscular injections may be necessary.

7 Syphilis rates decreased in the 1990s, and in 2000, the syphilis rate in the United States was the lowest it had ever been since reporting began in 1941. Syphilis usually infects the cervix, penis, anus, or lips first. It can also infect a baby during birth. Infection with syphilis is divided into three stages: primary or early syphilis, secondary syphilis, and tertiary or late syphilis. Antibiotics are the treatment of choice today.

8 Chlamydia infections are the most common bacterial STI in the United States today. The majority of men and women with a chlamydia infection are asymptomatic. Antibiotics are the treatment of choice today for chlamydia.

9 Chancroid is relatively rare in the United States but is one of the most prevalent STIs in many developing countries. Once infected, women and men often experience development of small lesions where the infection entered the body. The infection may spread to the lymph nodes of the groin, which can cause swelling and pain. Chancroids are treated with antibiotics.

10 Vaginal infections, characterized by a discharge, itching, and/or odor, are most frequently associated with bacterial vaginosis (BV), trichomoniasis, and candidiasis. The majority of women have symptoms, whereas the majority of men are asymptomatic. Treatment includes oral antibiotics or vaginal suppositories.

11 BV is caused by an overgrowth of various types of bacteria in the vagina that replace normal healthy bacteria. BV is the most common cause of vaginal discharge, although many women might be asymptomatic, but it multiplies when the pH balance of the vagina is disturbed. Treatment includes either an antifungal prescription or over-the-counter drugs.

12 Pelvic inflammatory disease (PID) is an infection of the female genital tract, including the endometrium, Fallopian tubes, and lining of the pelvic area. Although the exact rates of PID are unknown, the CDC estimates that 750,000 women experience acute cases of PID each year. Long-term complications of PID include ectopic and tubal pregnancies, chronic pelvic pain, and infertility.

13 Viral infections include herpes simplex virus (HSV), human papillomavirus (HPV), viral hepatitis, and HIV. Herpes is caused by either HSV-1 or HSV-2; however, once a person is infected, the symptoms can overlap. HSV-2 is one of the most common STIs in the United States. The virus can be transmitted even when a person does not have symptoms. Once infected, individuals will always carry the virus in their body. The standard therapy for HSV infection currently is antiviral drugs.

14 More than 40 types of HPV can infect the genitals, anus, mouth, and throat during sexual behaviors. HPV is the most common viral STI in the United States today. The majority of people who are infected do not know they have it. Almost all cervical disease can be attributed to HPV infection. HPV is also a risk factor for several other types of cancer, including oral, penile, and anal cancer. The majority of sexual partners of people with cervical warts experience development of warts within 3 to 4 months of contact. Genital warts can be treated in several ways. An HPV vaccine is now available and recommended for young girls and women.

15 Viral hepatitis is an infection that causes impaired liver function. There are three types of viral hepatitis: hepatitis A (HAV), hepatitis B (HBV), and hepatitis C (HCV). HAV infection is usually symptomatic, whereas infection with HBV and HCV is asymptomatic. Blood tests are used to identify viral hepatitis infections. Vaccines are available for the prevention of both HAV and HBV, and research on a vaccine for HCV is in progress.

16 AIDS is caused by an infection with HIV and is primarily transmitted through body fluids, including semen, vaginal fluid, and blood. HIV attacks the T helper cells in the blood, and antibodies can be detected in the bloodstream anywhere from 2 weeks to 6 months after infection. The attack on the T helper cells causes the immune system to be less effective in its ability to fight disease, and so many infected people develop opportunistic diseases.

17 The CDC estimates that there are approximately 1.1 million adults and teens living with HIV in the United States, with an additional 50,000 to 60,000 more Americans becoming infected each year. Like other STIs, there are age, gender, race/ethnicity, and geographical differences in the prevalence of HIV. From 2006 to 2009, the highest rate of HIV, 15% of diagnoses, were in persons 20 to 24 years old. Overall, the majority of people infected with HIV in 2009 were MSM (57%), followed by heterosexuals (31%).

18 Although perinatal HIV infections have declined in the United States, it is estimated that 8,700 HIV-infected women gave birth in 2006 (Whitmore et al., in press). Worldwide, it is estimated that there are 2.1 million children younger than 15 living with HIV, and every year 430,000 new HIV infections occur in newborns, mostly in Africa.

19 Tests for HIV can look for either the virus itself or for antibodies that the body has developed to fight HIV. One of the biggest developments in diagnosis has been the development of rapid HIV testing. These tests detect the presence of antibodies to HIV and require either a drop of blood or oral fluids. Research continues to work toward developing a home AIDS tests.

20 Since 1995, there has been a tremendous decrease in HIV- and AIDS-related deaths, primarily because of the development of highly active antiretroviral therapy (HAART). However, HAART is much more common in North America and Europe. Newer treatments involve a one-a-day pill. An HIV-infected person must undergo drug therapy for life.

21 Prevention and educational programs have begun to help reduce the spread of AIDS. Educational programs, advertising, mailings, public service announcements, and television shows all have helped to increase knowledge levels about HIV/AIDS. Many schools are beginning to include AIDS education in their classes.

22 Researchers continue to explore the development of AIDS vaccines. However, HIV is one of the most difficult viruses to eradicate because it has developed ways of dodging the immune system and becoming immune to specific treatments. In 2009, a clinical trial in Thailand presented the first vaccine to prevent HIV infection.

23 Families and friends of people with AIDS often do not receive the same social support as do families and friends of people with other devastating diseases. Today, with the help of HAARTs, many parents with HIV are living longer, and this has brought up issues of disclosure and adjusting to having a parent with HIV.

24 Since the 1990s, the annual number of new HIV infections worldwide has steadily declined. In 2009, there were approximately 2.6 million people newly infected with HIV, which was significantly less than previous years. Between 2001 and 2009, the HIV incidence around the world declined by more than 25%.

25 There are ways to protect yourself from becoming infected with an STI. If you do become infected, early treatment can reduce long-term consequences. Although it's not always easy to talk to a sexual partner about STIs, it's important to do so. We need to continue to break the silence about STIs and work to reduce the negative beliefs and stigma associated with these infections.

CRITICAL THINKING QUESTIONS

1 How will reading this chapter affect your own sexual practices? What material has had the biggest impact on you? Why?

2 Suppose that your best friend has never heard of chlamydia. What can you tell him or her about the symptoms, long-term risks, diagnosis, and treatment of chlamydia? Should your friend be worried?

3 Suppose that one late night when you are talking to a group of friends, the topic of STIs comes up. In your argument to encourage your friends to use condoms, what can you say about the asymptomatic nature of STIs? The properties of latency? How women are more at risk? How do you think your friends will respond?

4 Do you think the United States should provide medication to AIDS-infected men and women in sub-Saharan Africa who cannot afford it? Or should the United States provide sexuality education on AIDS prevention to those who do not have the virus? How would the money be best spent? Why?

5 Have you ever dated someone with an STI? If so, when did you find out about it? How did you feel? Did it affect your sex life? How so?

6 The vaccine Gardasil, which protects women from strains of HPV that can cause cervical cancer, has been available for a few years now. If you had daughters, would you get them vaccinated? Health care providers are recommending vaccinating girls as young as 9 years. If you would give your daughter the vaccine, at what age do you think you'd want her to have it and why? If it were available for boys and men, would you want your son to have it? At what age?

MEDIA RESOURCES

CourseMate brings course concepts to life with interactive learning, study, and exam preparation tools that support the printed textbook. A textbook-specific website, Psychology CourseMate includes an integrated interactive eBook and other interactive learning tools including quizzes, flashcards, videos, and more. If your textbook does not include an access code card, go to CengageBrain.com to gain access.

CENGAGENOW   CengageNOW is an easy-to-use online resource that helps you study in less time to get the grade you want—NOW. Take a pre-test for this chapter and receive a personalized study plan based on your results that will identify the topics you need to review and direct you to online resources to help you master those topics. Then take a post-test to help you determine the concepts you have mastered and what you will need to work on. If your textbook does not include an access code card, go to CengageBrain.com to gain access.

View in Video available in CourseMate and CengageNOW:

Testing Positive for HSV: Why Me?: Female college student discusses becoming infected with the herpes virus.

My Side of the Story: Male who infected the student in the chapter opening story tells his side of the story.

Irregular Pap Smears, LEEPs, and the HPV Vaccine: A 26-year-old woman discusses her reaction to an irregular Pap smear.

HIV/AIDS: Orel's Story: Orel describes his initial diagnosis and his struggle coming to terms with being HIV positive.

Websites:

American Social Health Association ▪ The American Social Health Association provides information on sexually transmitted infections (STIs). The website contains support, referrals, resources, and in-depth information about STIs.

Centers for Disease Control and Prevention (CDC) ▪ The CDC's division of STI prevention provides information about STIs, including surveillance reports and disease facts. The CDC's division of HIV/AIDS prevention provides information about HIV and AIDS, including surveillance reports and facts about the infection.

Herpes.org ▪ Herpes.org is an online resource for people with herpes and the human papillomavirus. The website provides information about the infections, what nonprescription and prescription treatments work, and where to find medical help and medication.

Joint United Nations Program on HIV and AIDS (UNAIDS) ▪ UNAIDS provides monitoring and evaluation of AIDS research, and also provides access to various links and information about AIDS. Information on AIDS scenarios for the future, antiretroviral therapy, and HIV/AIDS in children and orphans is available.

LesbianSTDs ▪ This website provides information and resources regarding sexual health and STIs in women who have sex with women.

16 Varieties of Sexual Expression

View in **Video**

View in **Video**

View in **Video**

View in **Video**

View in **Video**

▶ **ABOUT THE CHAPTER OPENING VIDEO** – Kiki is 25-year-old queer, femme-identified woman who works as a professional dominatrix and submissive. For the last 8 years, she has actively been involved in sexual "kink," which can range from playful to intense, and may include spanking, power play, bondage, dominance and submission, and/or sadomasochism. Today she lives with her primary partner in a nonmonogamous relationship.

I really enjoy the experience of various sensations during sexual experiences—either with ice, hot wax, or even needles. A clothespin on your nipple will create an unbearable amount of physical pain, but then hot wax dripping on your thigh requires your attention to another powerful sensation. Being tied up or blindfolded while experiencing these sensations makes your nerves raw, producing a heightened sense of arousal. The range of things you can feel during a "scene," or a single encounter, can take your mind to so many places.

I was recently involved in a "gang-rape" scene with four men and another woman, all of whom were good friends of mine. I felt very comfortable with all of them and I knew they all cared very much about me. The scene took about 2 hours and was done in a hotel room. Throughout the scene I was degraded and humiliated, and at one point I was thrown out in the hall naked. I was also held underwater in the bathtub repeatedly. It was really intense and difficult, but at the same time, exhilarating. The guys knew what my boundaries were and how far they could take it. We all have "safe words," which we can use if I want to stop. If I yell "red," this means to stop everything, "yellow" means that they are getting close to my boundaries, and "green" means it's all a go.

© Roger Cracknell 19/Shambhala/Alamy

I can accept that my sexual interests might be "quirky" and that not all people might understand why I do what I do. But exploring these interests in a healthy, thoughtful way doesn't make me crazy. I've always sought out new and different experiences—this is just another part of that exploration!

Kiki's captivating story had my mind spinning in many directions. How do people decide what sexual behaviors are acceptable for themselves and for others? Listening to Kiki articulate her motivations will help you contemplate the diversity of sexual expression. ▌▌

Janell Cauch

"Fear is an intense part of this, but at the same time there is incredible elation."
—CHAPTER OPENING VIDEO

View in Video

To watch the entire interview, go to Psychology CourseMate at **login.cengagebrain.com.**

© Nicholas Tsacoyeanes

Human sexuality can be expressed in many ways. We tend to celebrate individual and cultural differences in most aspects of human life—in what people eat, how they dress, or how they dance, for example. Yet, we have been less tolerant of sexual diversity, and we have historically considered such behavior "deviant" or "perverted" (Laws & O'Donohue, 2008). More modern views of sexuality, however, do not categorize people as "deviant" versus "normal." For example, the sexual world is not really split into those who become sexually excited from looking at others naked or having sex and those who do not; most people get aroused to some degree from visual sexual stimuli. Some people get more aroused than others, and at the upper limits are those who can get aroused only when watching sexual scenes; such people have taken a normal behavior to an extreme. In this chapter, we explore variations of sexual behavior, including differences in sexual desire and the **paraphilias.**

ON YOUR MIND 16.1

If I fantasize about watching other people having sex or if I get turned on by being spanked, does that mean I have a paraphilia?

A strong and varied fantasy life is the sign of healthy sexuality, and acting out fantasies in a safe sexual situation can add excitement to one's sex life. Problems may arise when the fantasy or desire becomes so prominent or preoccupying that you are unable to function sexually in its absence; sexual play is taken to the point of physical or psychological injury; you feel extreme levels of guilt about the desire; or your compulsion to perform a certain type of sexual behavior interferes with everyday life, disrupts your personal relationships, or risks getting you in trouble with the law. Under any of these circumstances, it is advisable to see a qualified sex therapist or counselor.

▶ WHAT IS "TYPICAL"
Sexual Expression?

Some medical and sexuality texts still categorize certain kinds of behavior as sexual deviance. Many undergraduate texts discuss these behaviors in chapters that include words such as "abnormal," "unusual," or "atypical" sexual behavior in their titles. Yet how exactly do we decide whether a behavior is "normal"? What is "typical" sexual activity? Where do we draw the line? Do we call it "atypical" if 5% of sexually active people do it? Ten percent? Twenty-five percent?

Sexual behaviors increase and decrease in popularity; oral sex, for example, was once considered a perversion, but now it is a commonly reported sexual behavior in adolescent populations

---

REAL RESEARCH 16.1 Although the earliest treatments for paraphilias involved surgical castration, in the 1940s, a shift in treatment led to the popularity of hormonal treatments and soon thereafter to psychotherapy (GORDON, 2008).

(Dake et al., 2011; Song & Halpern-Felsher et al., 2011). Perhaps, then, we should consider as "deviant" only behaviors that may be harmful in some way. Masturbation was once believed to lead to mental illness, acne, and stunted growth; now it is considered a normal, healthy part of sexual expression. If many of these desires exist to some degree in all of us, then any such desire itself is not atypical, just the degree of the desire.

Social value judgments, not science, primarily determine which sexual behaviors are considered "normal" by a society. For example, in 1906, Krafft-Ebing defined sexual deviance as "every

expression of (the sexual instinct) that does not correspond with the purpose of nature—i.e., propagation" (J. C. Brown, 1983, p. 227). Certainly, most people would not go so far today. Freud himself stated that the criterion of normalcy was love and that defenses against "perversion" were the bedrock of civilization because perversion trivializes or degrades love (A. M. Cooper, 1991). Note that Freud's objections to perversion were not medical, as they were to most other mental disturbances, but moral.

Even "modern" definitions can contain hidden value judgments: "The sexually variant individual typically exhibits sexual arousal or responses to inappropriate people (e.g., minors), objects (e.g., leather, rubber, garments), or activities (e.g., exposure in public, coercion, violence)" (Gudjonsson, 1986, p. 192). "Appropriate" or "inappropriate" people, objects, or activities of sexual attention differ in different times, in different cultures, and for different people. Despite these objections, certain groups of behaviors are considered the most common deviations from conventional heterosexual or homosexual behavior.

Society may view these behaviors as either solely the business of the individual in the privacy of his or her bedroom (e.g., sexual excitement from pain or certain clothing), as a sign that the person is mentally ill (e.g., having sex with animals), or as dangerous and illegal (e.g., sex with underage children). The United States Department of Justice coordinates the National Sex Offender Registry, which enables individuals to search for the identity and location of known sex offenders (see the accompanying Sex in Real Life feature). In this chapter, we explore variations in sexual behaviors, theories of why people are attracted to unusual sexual objects, and how therapists have tried to help those who are troubled by their sexual desires.

◀ review QUESTIONS

1 Explain how medical and sexuality texts categorize sexual behaviors and how this might affect popular opinions.

2 Explain how sexual behaviors increase and decrease in frequency, and how this affects society's definition of normal.

3 How do social value judgments determine which sexual behaviors are viewed as normal?

In 1994, 7-year-old Megan Kanka was lured into her neighbor's home in Hamilton Township, New Jersey, by the promise of a puppy. There she was raped, strangled, and suffocated by a two-time convicted sexual offender. Shortly thereafter, the governor of New Jersey, Christine Todd Whitman, signed the toughest sex offender registration act in the country, known as "Megan's Law." In 1996, Megan's Law became federal law and mandated that every community have access to information about the presence of convicted sex offenders in their neighborhoods. Two years earlier, in 1994, a federal statute known as the Jacob Wetterling Crimes against Children and Sexually Violent Offender Registration Program was passed, which also requires all states to create registration programs for convicted sex offenders (Trivits & Reppucci, 2002).

Today, all 50 states require that convicted sex offenders register on their release from prison into the community and require the listing (with the offenders' names, addresses, photographs, crimes, and sometimes physical descriptions) to be made available to the public. Although all require sex offenders to register, the statutes vary in what information is made available and for how long (Trivits & Reppucci, 2002). Many convicted sex offenders have protested the law, claiming that it violates their constitutional rights; however, the government has decided that the safety of children is a higher priority than the privacy of convicted sex offenders. Critics also argue that these listings encourage violent behavior directed at the offenders, although studies have found that the actual incidence of such events is low (Klaas, 2003; J. Miller, 1998). In addition, some argue that having such lists creates instant mailing lists for those who wish to connect with other offenders (Sommerfeld, 1999).

Some states continue to add regulations to their sex offender registry laws. For example, in 2005, certain towns in New York, Florida, and New Jersey banned convicted child molesters from being within 2,500 feet of any school, day-care center, playground, or park (Koch, 2005). Other states use electronic monitoring in addition to their online registries. For example, Florida, Alabama, New Jersey, Missouri, Ohio, and Oklahoma all passed laws requiring electronic monitoring (ankle bands that monitor the offender's whereabouts). In 2006, a federal statute was signed into law called the *Adam Walsh Act*. This law classified sexual offender registries into three tiers, depending on the severity of the offense. Offenders on the top tier must update their whereabouts every 3 months for life, whereas those on middle tier must update their whereabouts every 6 months for 25 years. Those on the bottom tier include minors and those younger than 14, who must update their whereabouts every year for 15 years.

Unfortunately, the registries may have given many parents and caregivers a false sense of security. Sex offender registries contain only those offenders who have been convicted of sexual offenses and not all who commit such crimes. Nonetheless, many of these new laws and tracking devices may help to discourage sexual offenders from engaging in these behaviors.

A sexual offender registry.

Newsmakers/Getty Images

▶ PARAPHILIAS

The word *paraphilia* (pear-uh-FILL-ee-uh) is derived from the Greek "para" (besides) and "philia" (love or attraction). In other words, paraphilias are sexual behaviors that involve a craving for an erotic object that is unusual or different. According to the *Diagnostic and Statistical Manual of Mental Disorders (DSM)*, the essential features involved in a paraphilia are recurrence and intensity of the sexual behavior that involves a nonhuman object, or the suffering or humiliation of oneself or one's partner, a child, or a nonconsenting person. This behavior causes significant distress and interferes with a person's ability to work, interact with friends, and other important areas of one's life. For some people with paraphilias, the fantasy or presence of the object of their desire is necessary for arousal and orgasm; in others, the desire occurs periodically or exists separately from their other sexual relationships.

Although many people, including Kiki from the chapter opening story, view their behaviors as exciting aspects of their sexuality, others may be uncomfortable with their sexual interests or behaviors. However, discomfort or distress about certain sexual interests or behaviors may arise from the fact that their sexual desires are in conflict with current social standards (Wright, 2010). If a person enjoys sexual behaviors that society views as pathological, distress

paraphilia
Clinical term used to describe types of sexual expressions that are seen as unusual and potentially problematic. A person who engages in paraphilias is often referred to as a *paraphiliac*.

Although there has not been much research documenting the incidence, expression, and treatment of paraphilias outside the United States, there have been limited studies. The majority of information available concerns pedophilia and transvestic disorder. A limited amount of research exists on other paraphilias, such as sadomasochism. Here we explore what we do know about paraphilias in a variety of countries.

Brazil

Brazil is a conservative and religious country and, as such, there is not a great deal of acceptance for paraphiliac behaviors. Although there are no legal restrictions against transvestic disorders, researchers estimate that there are few who engage in this practice (de Freitas, 2004). We do know that throughout history, zoophilia has been found to occur in Brazil, and it has been found to be more common in both men and those living in rural areas (de Freitas, 2004).

China

China has very strict policies against behaviors it deems inappropriate, and paraphilias certainly fall into this category. Sex offenders in China are often charged with "hooliganism," which is a term that includes a wide range of uncivil and sexually unrestrained behavior (Ruan & Lau, 2004). China has very severe penalties for those who engage in such behaviors, and harsh punishments are common. For example, one review reported that the Chinese government enforced the death penalty for certain sexual crimes, including forced sex and pedophilia (Ruan & Lau, 2004).

Denmark

Denmark and many of the Scandinavian countries have much more liberal attitudes about sexuality, so they are less likely to sweep behaviors under the carpet if they don't agree with them. Paraphilias are viewed as criminal behaviors, and those found engaging in such behaviors are appropriately charged. Denmark also has high reporting and treatment rates for paraphilias (Graugaard et al., 2004). In reaction to increased rates of child sexual abuse, Denmark opened a center for the treatment of sexually abused children at the University Hospital in Copenhagen in 2000, and today many groups actively educate professionals and the lay public about incest and child sexual abuse (Graugaard et al., 2004).

Czech Republic

Paraphiliacs in the Czech Republic have many more opportunities for communication and contact with other paraphiliacs than they did when they were under communist control (Zverina, 2004). This would include clubs, magazines, newspapers, and the Internet. Sadomasochism and fetishes are the most common paraphilias in the Czech Republic (Zverina, 2004). Sexual offenders who are charged with crimes are referred for counseling and treatments, which are covered under national health insurance plans.

Japan

Sadism and masochism are well-known in Japanese art and literature (Hatano & Shimazaki, 2004). Thousands of sadomasochism magazines are sold each month, and many nightclubs cater to the sadomasochism subculture. Like China, Japan has strict laws and punishments for people who engage in child sexual abuse. In 1999, Japan enacted a Child Prostitution and Child Pornography Prohibition law that prohibits sexual activity with minors and enforces strict punishments for those charged with these behaviors (Hatano & Shimazaki, 2004).

SOURCE: Francoeur & Noonan (2004).

---

can occur. Because of this, there has been a movement to depathologize unusual sexual behaviors (Wright, 2010). Experts have recommended differentiating between paraphilias (which would be consensual) and paraphiliac disorders (which may be coercive) in the revised DSM-5, and have suggested **paraphilic coercive disorder,** in which a person seeks stimulation by forcing sex on various persons.

Individuals who engage in paraphiliac behaviors are a heterogeneous group with no true factors that set them apart from nonparaphiliacs, with the exception of gender—the majority of those with paraphilias are men. Other than this, people with paraphilias come from every socioeconomic bracket, every ethnic and racial group, and from every sexual orientation (Seligman & Hardenburg, 2000).

Although there are no classic profiles that fit all paraphilias, certain factors appear to be related to the development of a paraphilia. Research has found that those with some of the more serious paraphilias have experienced significant family problems during childhood that contribute to poor social skills and distorted views of sexual intimacy (Seligman & Hardenburg, 2000). The intensity of these behaviors varies; someone with a mild case might use certain sexual fantasies during masturbation, whereas someone with a severe case may engage in unwanted sexual behavior with a child.

Some of the extreme cases of paraphilias are similar to many impulse-control disorders, such as substance abuse, gambling, and eating disorders (A. Goodman, 1993). Some people may feel conflicted about their behavior, and develop tension and a preoccupation with certain behaviors. They may repeatedly try to suppress their sexual desires but have not been able to do so (Seligman & Hardenburg, 2000).

Many people find lingerie exciting, enjoy watching sexual scenes, or enjoy being lightly bitten or scratched during sex. However, in an extreme case, the lingerie itself becomes the object of sexual attention, not a means of enhancing the sexuality of the partner. For this reason, some have suggested that the de-

paraphilic coercive disorder
A paraphilia that involves recurrent and intense sexual arousal from fantasies or behaviors involving sexual coercion.

fetishist
A person who engages in a fetishistic behavior.

fining characteristic of paraphilia is that it replaces a whole with a part, that it allows people to distance themselves from complex human sexual contact and replace it with the undemanding sexuality of an inanimate object, a scene, or a single action (L. J. Kaplan, 1991).

Motivations for paraphiliac behaviors vary. Some people with paraphilias claim that their behaviors provide meaning to their lives and give them a sense of self, whereas others say the behaviors relieve their depression and loneliness or help them express rage (A. Goodman, 1993; S. B. Levine et al., 1990). Some violent or criminal paraphiliacs have little ability to feel empathy for their victims and may convince themselves that their victims enjoy the experiences, even though the victims do not consent to them (Seligman & Hardenburg, 2000).

Research on paraphilias has been drawn mostly from clinical and incarcerated samples, which are almost certainly not representative of the population as a whole. The number of people who live comfortably with sexual practices that are outside the realm of what is considered "normal" is hard to determine because many might not be comfortable disclosing their sexual practices, even on confidential questionnaires.

Throughout history, people with paraphilias have been portrayed as sick and/or perverted. There is thus an attempt to draw a clear line between those who engage in such behaviors and "normal" people; yet the line is rarely that clear. Certainly there are paraphiliac behaviors that can be dangerous or can threaten others. Men who expose themselves to young girls, people who violate corpses, strangers who rub against women on buses, or adults who seduce underage children must not be allowed to continue their behavior. There can even be legal problems with the paraphilias that are not in themselves dangerous; some **fetishists** resort to stealing the object of interest to them, and occasionally a voyeur will break into people's homes. A number of therapies have been developed to help these people; but as you will see, it is difficult to change a person's arousal patterns.

Many others live comfortably with their paraphilias. A man who has a fetish for lingerie, for example, may find a partner who very much enjoys wearing it for him. As discussed in the chapter opener, Kiki is engaging in consensual sexual behavior and has no desire to change her behavior. Why should she want to put it to an end just because some other people might find it distasteful, or weird? In what sense is such a person sick?

For this reason, paraphilias have become controversial. Some theorists suggest that the term describes a society's value judgments about sexuality and not a psychiatric or clinical category (Silverstein, 1984). Some theorists deny that terms such as *paraphilia* really describe anything at all. Robert J. Stoller, a well-known psychoanalytic theorist, objected to the idea of trying to create psychological explanations that group people by their sexual habits (Stoller, 1996).

▶▶ THEORIES ABOUT **Paraphilias**

Many researchers have theorized as to why and how paraphilias develop, but very little consensus has been reached. Paraphilias are undoubtedly complex behavior patterns, which may have biological, psychological, or social origins—or aspects of all three.

ON YOUR MIND 16.2

Why are paraphilia disorders more common in men?

No one really knows, although theories abound. Some researchers suggest that perhaps paraphilias are developed visually, and the male tends, for some biological reason, to be more sexually aroused by visual stimuli than the female. Maybe cultural variables give men more sexual latitude in expressing what excites them. It could also have something to do with the way we look at it; women may express their paraphilias in different, less obvious ways than men. There could also be power differentials that contribute to higher rates in men.

Biological Theories

Biological researchers have found that a number of conditions can initiate paraphiliac behavior, such as illnesses, disturbances of brain structure and brain chemistry, and higher levels of certain hormones, such as testosterone (Giotakos et al., 2005; Rahman & Symeonides, 2008; Sartorius et al., 2008). However, this does not mean that everyone with a paraphilia has one of these conditions. At most, these conditions are factors that may lead some people to be more likely to develop a paraphilia, but they do not explain the majority of such behaviors.

Psychoanalytic Theory

Psychoanalytic thought suggests that paraphilias can be traced back to the difficult time the infant has in negotiating his way through the Oedipal crisis and castration anxiety. This can explain why paraphilias are more common among men because both boys and girls identify strongly with their mothers, but girls can continue that identification, whereas boys must, painfully, separate from their mothers to establish a male identity.

Louise Kaplan, a psychoanalyst, suggests that every paraphilia involves issues of masculinity or femininity; as she writes, "Every male perversion entails a masquerade or impersonation of masculinity and every female perversion entails a masquerade or impersonation of femininity" (1991, p. 249). For example, a man who exposes himself in public may be coping with castration anxiety by evoking a reaction to his penis from women. The exhibitionist in this view is "masquerading" as a man to cover up feelings of nonmasculinity; he is saying, in effect, "Let me prove that I am a man by showing that I possess the instrument of masculinity." He even needs to demonstrate that his penis can inspire fear, which may be why exhibitionists disproportionately choose young girls, who are more likely to display a fear reaction (Kline, 1987). This confirms to the exhibitionist the power of his masculinity.

In contrast, voyeurs, who are excited by looking at others nude or having sex, may be fixated on the experience that aroused their castration anxieties as children—the sight of genitals and sexuality (Kline, 1987). Looking allows the person to gain power over the fearful and hidden world of sexuality while safe from the possibility of contact. The visual component of castration anxiety occurs when the boy sees the power and size of the father's genitals and the lack of a penis on his mother or sisters. The act of looking initiates

*Throughout history, people with paraphilias have been **portrayed as sick and/or perverted.***

It is common for young children to play around with clothing and sometimes dress as the other sex. The majority of them do not develop an erotic attraction to the clothing.

castration anxiety, and in the voyeur, the looking has never ceased. Yet looking itself cannot really relieve the anxiety permanently, and so the voyeur is compelled to peep again and again.

Developmental Theories

Freud suggested that children are polymorphously perverse; that is, at birth we have a general erotic potential that can be attached to almost anything. We learn from an early age which sexual objects society deems appropriate for us to desire, but society's messages can get off track. For example, advertising tries to "sexualize" its products—we have all seen shoe commercials, for example, that emphasize the long, sexy legs of the model while focusing on the shoes she wears. Some boys may end up focusing on those shoes as objects of sexual fantasy, which can develop into a fetish.

A theory that builds on similar ideas is John Money's (1984, 1986, 1990) **lovemaps.** Money suggests that the auditory, tactile, and (especially) visual stimuli we experience during childhood sex play form a template in our brain that defines our ideal lover and ideal sexual situation. If our childhood sex play remains undisturbed, development goes on toward heterosexual desires. If, however, the child is punished for normal sexual curiosity or if there are traumas during this stage, such as sexual abuse, the development of the lovemap can be disrupted in one of three ways.

In **hypophilia** (high-po-FILL-ee-uh), negative stimuli prevent the development of certain aspects of sexuality, and the genitals may be impaired from full functioning. Overall, females are more likely to experience hypophilia than men, resulting in an inability to orgasm, vaginal pain, or lubrication problems later in life. A lovemap can also be disrupted to cause a condition called **hyperphilia** (high-per-FILL-ee-uh), in which a person defies the negative sexual stimulus and becomes overly sexually active, even becoming compulsively sexual. Finally, a lovemap can be disrupted when there is a substitution of new elements into the lovemap, and a paraphilia can develop. Because normal sexual curiosity has been discouraged or made painful, the child

lovemap
Term coined by John Money to refer to the template of an ideal lover and sexual situation we develop as we grow up.

hypophilia
Lack of full functioning of the sexual organs because of missing stages of childhood development.

hyperphilia
Compulsive sexuality caused by overcompensating for negative reactions to childhood sexuality.

courtship disorder
Theory that asserts that paraphilias develop from abnormalities in the normal courtship process, which involves looking for sexual partners, interacting with partners, touching or embracing them, and sexual intercourse.

conditioning
In behaviorism, a type of associative learning in which a person associates a particular behavior with a positive response.

redirects erotic energy toward other objects that are not forbidden, such as shoes, rubber, or just looking; in other cases, the child turns his or her erotic energy inward and becomes excited by pain or humiliation.

Once this lovemap is set, it becomes very stable, which explains why changing it is so difficult. For example, Money (1984) suggests that sexual arousal to objects may arise when a parent makes a child feel shame about interest in an object. For example, a boy may be caught with his mother's panties in the normal course of curiosity about the woman's body, but when he is severely chastised, the panties become forbidden, dirty, and promising of sexual secrets, and he may begin to seek them out.

Another theory about how these fixations occur is the idea of **courtship disorders** (K. Freund & Blanchard, 1986; K. Freund et al., 1983, 1984). Organizing paraphilias into "courtship" stages suggests that the paraphiliac's behavior becomes fixed at a preliminary stage of mating that would normally lead to vaginal intercourse. Thus, a person becomes fixated on a particular person, object, or activity and does not progress to typical mating behaviors.

Behavioral Theories

Behaviorists suggest that paraphilias develop because some behavior becomes associated with sexual pleasure through **conditioning** (G. D. Wilson, 1987). For example, imagine that a boy gets a spanking. While receiving it, the boy has an erection, either by coincidence or because he finds the stimulus of the spanking pleasurable (it becomes a reinforcement). Later, remembering the spanking, he becomes excited and masturbates. As he repeats his masturbatory fantasy, a process called *conditioning* occurs, whereby sexual excitement becomes so associated with the idea of the spanking that he has trouble becoming excited in its absence.

You can imagine how similar situations could lead to other types of fetishes: A boy lies naked on a fur coat, or takes a "pony" ride on his aunt's leg while she's wearing her black leather boots, or puts on his sister's panties, or spies on a female houseguest through the bathroom keyhole. All of these behaviors become positively reinforced, and thus are more likely to be repeated.

Sociological Theories

Another way of looking at the causes of paraphilias is to examine the ways society encourages certain behaviors. Feminists, for example, argue that in societies that treat women as sexual objects, it can be a natural development to replace the woman with another, inanimate sexual object. When men and their sexual organs are glorified, some men may need to reinforce their masculinity by exposing themselves and evoking fear.

American society is ruled by images, saturated with television, movies, commercials, advertisements, and magazines; most of these images have highly charged sexual imagery (R. Collins, 2005). The result, some argue, is a world where the image takes the place of the reality, where it becomes common to substitute fantasies for reality. Surrounded by media, the society experiences things vicariously, through reading about it or seeing it rather than actually doing it. In such a climate, representations of eroticism may be easily substituted for sex itself, and so paraphilias become common.

◀ review QUESTIONS

1 Define a paraphilia and explain the essential features of a paraphilia as determined by the *DSM*.

2 Identify and explain some of the motivations for paraphiliac behaviors.

3 Differentiate between consensual and nonconsensual paraphilias.

4 Compare and contrast how the biological and psychoanalytic theories explain paraphilias and provide an example.

5 Compare and contrast how the developmental and sociological theories explain paraphilias and provide an example.

▶ TYPES of Paraphilias

Paraphilias have been grouped into a number of major categories by researchers and clinicians. We review in this section some of the more common types of paraphilias, including fetishism, transvestic fetishism, sadism and masochism, exhibitionism and voyeurism, and pedophilia.

▶▶ FETISHISTIC Disorder

A **fetishistic** (FEH-tish-is-tic) **disorder** involves a recurrent and intense sexual arousal manifested in fantasies, urges, or behaviors that involve the use of nonliving objects (such as shoes, boots, panties, or bras; to a fabric, such as leather, silk, fur, or rubber), or focus on nongenital body parts (such as feet or hair). As with most paraphilias, the majority of fetishists are male (Darcangelo, 2008). The strength of the preference for the object varies from thinking about or holding the object to a need to use it during all sexual acts.

fetishistic disorder
A recurrent and intense sexual arousal manifested in fantasies, urges, or behaviors involving the use of nonliving objects or nongenital body parts.

A person with a foot fetish often has an inability to experience sexual arousal or orgasm without contact or a sexual fantasy about feet.

Many people enjoy using lingerie or other fabrics as part of their lovemaking without becoming dependent on them for arousal. The fetishist, in contrast, needs the presence or the fantasy

---

REAL RESEARCH 16.2 Men and women who are knowledgeable about sadomasochistic behavior or who know someone who has engaged in it have more positive attitudes about sadomasochism than those with less knowledge or acquaintances (YOST, 2010).

---

of the object to achieve arousal and sometimes cannot achieve orgasm in its absence. Some fetishists integrate the object of their desire into their sexual life with a partner; for others it remains a secret fetish, with hidden collections of shoes, or panties, or photographs of a body part, over which they masturbate in secret, ever fearful of discovery.

Many fetishists see their sexual habits as a major part of their life, a source of their sense of identity; yet because fetishism is often regarded by society as shameful, they may be embarrassed to admit to their sexual desires. It is therefore rare to find individuals who are open about their fetishes.

Different cultures hold up different body parts, objects, colors, or smells as symbols of attraction and sexuality for mating (see Chapter 7 for more information about attraction in different cultures). Fetishism involves a person becoming sexually attracted to a symbol itself instead of what it represents. Put another way, for the fetishist, the object—unlike the living, breathing person—is itself erotic, rather than the person, which also eliminates having to deal with another person's feelings, wants, and needs. It can be a refuge

from the complexity of interpersonal sexual relations. In that sense, all the paraphilias we discuss can be seen as a type of fetishism; pain and humiliation, or women's clothes, or looking at people having sex can each be a substitute for interpersonal sexuality.

▶▶ TRANSVESTIC Disorder

In Chapter 4, we discussed the transgender community that includes a variety of gender diverse individuals. This is different from a **transvestic** (trans-VESS-tick) **disorder,** which involves wearing clothes of the other gender and recurrent and intense sexual arousal from the cross-dressing, which typically causes significant distress or impairment in functioning (American Psychiatric Association, 2010).

Transvestic disorder is usually harmless, and most transvestites are not anxious to seek out therapy to stop their behavior (Newring et al., 2008). Many times treatment is sought only when a transvestite's partner is upset or the cross-dressing causes stress in the relationship. Many female partners of male transvestites do not understand his need to dress in women's clothing, even though they are accepting of the behavior (Dzelme & Jones, 2001; Newring et al., 2008). In any case, transvestic disorder is usually so firmly fixed in a man's personality that eradication is neither possible nor desirable. The goal of therapy is to cope with the anxieties and guilt of the transvestite and the way he relates interpersonally and sexually with his partner and family (Newring et al., 2008). Transvestite support groups have been organized in cities all over the country and may offer a good support system for these men (Newring et al., 2008).

▶▶ SADISM and Masochism

Sexual sadism disorder refers to a recurrent and intense sexual arousal from the physical or psychological suffering of another person, which can be manifested by fantasies or behaviors (American Psychiatric Association, 2010). Sadistic behaviors may include restraint, blindfolding, strangulation, spanking, whipping, pinching, beating, burning, and electrical shocks (Kleinplatz & Moser, 2006).

The term **sadism** is derived from a man named Donatien Alphonse François de Sade (1740–1814), known as the Marquis de Sade. De Sade was sent to prison for kidnapping and terrorizing a beggar girl and then later for tricking some prostitutes into eating "Spanish fly," supposedly an aphrodisiac, but which caused such burning and blistering that one threw herself out a window. While in prison, de Sade wrote novels describing such tortures as being bound hand and foot, suspended between trees, set upon by dogs, almost being eviscerated (cut open), and so on. De Sade believed that the highest form of sexual ac-

---

transvestic disorder
A paraphilia that involves recurrent and intense sexual arousal from fantasies or behaviors involving cross-dressing, which often causes significant distress.

sexual sadism disorder
A paraphilia that involves a recurrent and intense sexual arousal from fantasies or behaviors involving the physical or psychological suffering of another person.

sadism
Deriving sexual pleasure from administering or watching pain and humiliation.

sexual masochism disorder
A paraphilia that involves recurrent and intense sexual arousal from fantasies or behaviors involving the act of being humiliated, beaten, bound, or suffering in other ways.

masochism
Deriving sexual pleasure from receiving pain or being humiliated.

Sadomasochists often use props, like leather clothes, studs, chains, and nipple clamps.

tivity for women was pain, not pleasure, because pleasure could be too easily faked. De Sade spent much of his life in prison (Bullough, 1976).

Sexual masochism disorder (MASS-oh-kiz-um) refers to a recurrent and intense sexual arousal from the act of being humiliated, beaten, bound, or suffering in other ways (American Psychiatric Association, 2010). **Masochism** was named after another novelist, Leopold Baron Von Sacher-Masoch (1836–1895), who believed that women were created to subdue men's "animal passions" (Bullough, 1976). The *DSM* criteria specifies that these behaviors typically cause significant distress or impairment in life functioning for a period of at least six months (American Psychiatric Association, 2010).

Sadism and masochism both associate sexuality and pain, and most people who practice one are also involved with the other. Therefore, the phenomenon as a whole is often referred to as **sadomasochism** (say-doe-MASS-oh-kiz-um), or S&M. The acronym BDSM—bondage, discipline, sadism, and masochism—is commonly used today because it illustrates the diverse range of possible experiences (Kleinplatz & Moser, 2006; Wiseman, 2000). Some individuals may participate in only one aspect of BDSM, whereas others may engage in a variety of BDSM practices (Kleinplatz & Moser, 2006; Wiseman, 2000).

Because BDSM encompasses a wide variety of behaviors, the number of people who engage in it depends on how one defines it. Kinsey and his colleagues (1953) found that 3% to 12% of women and 10% to 20% of men reported getting sexually aroused to S&M narratives. However, researchers today believe that BDSM is much more prevalent than studies indicate (Chancer, 2006; Kleinplatz & Moser, 2006; Yates et al., 2008).

Freud and his followers made sadomasochism central to their theories about adult sexuality. Freud believed that to some degree

*Sexual responses to pain exist, to some degree, **in many sexual relationships.***

we all feel ambivalent about the ones we love and even, at times, feel the desire to hurt them. However, we also feel guilty about it, especially in early childhood, and the guilt we feel is satisfied by turning that hurt on ourselves. Later psychoanalytic theorists believed that the goal of masochism was not pain or punishment itself, but rather relinquishing the self to someone else to avoid responsibility or anxiety for sexual desires.

Sexual responses to pain exist, to some degree, in many sexual relationships. Kinsey and his colleagues (1953), for example, found that about half the men and women in his sample experienced erotic response to sexual biting, and 24% of men and 12% of women had some erotic response to sadomasochistic stories. Another study found that 25% of men and women reported occasionally engaging in sadomasochistic behavior (L. Rubin, 1990). For example, some couples use bondage as a variation on their lovemaking without any other sadomasochistic elements (Comfort, 1987).

In most S&M encounters, one partner plays the **dominant** role ("master" or "top") and the other the **submissive** ("slave" or "bottom"). Female dominants are often referred to as Mistress, and male dominants are referred to as Master or Lord. Bondage and restraint are the most common expressions of BDSM, although it is power, rather than pain, that is the most important aspect of BDSM behaviors (Cross & Matheson, 2006; Seligman & Hardenburg, 2000).

A variety of techniques are commonly used to physically dominate the submissive partner. Tying the submissive partner up or using restraints to render him or her helpless is often referred to as B&D (for bondage and discipline). B&D may be accompanied by **flagellation, caning, birching,** or other painful or shocking stimuli on the skin such as the use of hot wax, ice, or biting (Wise-

sadomasochism	**dominant**	**flagellation**	**caning**	**birching**
Broad term that refers to the receiving of sexual pleasure from acts involving the infliction or receiving of pain and humiliation.	Describes the active role in sadomasochistic sexuality.	Striking a partner, usually by whipping.	Beating someone with a rigid cane.	Whipping someone using the stripped branch of a tree.
	submissive			
	Describes the passive role in sadomasochistic activity.			

A dominatrix is paid by submissive clients to engage in bondage and discipline fantasy play.

"At the core of every BDSM relationship, there's a power exchange."
—BDSM

View in Video

To watch the entire interview, go to Psychology CourseMate at **login.cengagebrain.com.**

man, 2000). Psychological techniques can include sensory deprivation (through the use of face masks, blindfolds, earplugs), humiliation (being subject to verbal abuse or being made to engage in embarrassing behaviors such as boot-licking, **scatophagia** [scat-oh-FAJ-ee-uh], **urolagnia** [yur-oh-LOG-nee-uh], or acting like a dog), forced cross-dressing, or **infantilism** (American Psychiatric Association, 2000; Moser, 1988). This is accompanied by verbal descriptions of what is to come and why the person deserves it, increasing in intensity over time to eventual sexual climax. Note that the pain is used as part of a technique to enhance sexuality—the pain itself is not exciting.

People can participate in BDSM to different degrees. For some couples, BDSM is an occasional diversion in their lovemaking. Others pursue it outside of a committed relationship; for example, most big cities have active kink subcultures that offer a variety of sadomasochistic services, including **dominatrix** and submissives.

A sadomasochistic (or "kink") subculture exists for those who have adopted BDSM as a lifestyle. A variety of organizations cater to consensual BDSM (such as the Eulenspiegel Society or the Society of Janus), and partners can meet at conferences and learn more in various BDSM newsletters and magazines. Specialty shops cater to BDSM advocates, selling restraints, whips, leather clothing, and other items. Like Kiki described in the chapter opening story, the sadomasochistic encounter, or "scene," is really a kind of drama or performance, and is enhanced by both sides knowing their roles and dressing the part.

scatophagia
A paraphiliac behavior that involves recurrent and intense sexual arousal from fantasies or behaviors involving feces.

urolagnia
A paraphiliac behavior that involves recurrent and intense sexual arousal from fantasies or behaviors involving urine.

infantilism
A paraphiliac behavior that involves recurrent and intense sexual arousal from fantasies or behaviors involving being treated like a baby (such as dressing in diapers).

dominatrix
A woman who takes the dominant role in bondage and discipline behaviors with male or female submissives.

Much of BDSM is about playing roles, usually with appropriate attitude, costuming, and scripted talk (Hoff, 2003). The encounter is carefully planned, and the dominant partner is usually very careful not to actually hurt the submissive partner while "torturing" him or her. As Kiki explained, a "safe word" is usually agreed on so that the submissive partner can signal if he or she is in real distress. The *Master's and Mistress' Handbook,* a guide to S&M encounters, offers a set of rules on how to torture one's partner without really causing harm:

Remember that a slave may suddenly start to cough or feel faint. If masked and gagged, choking or lack of oxygen may result in serious consequences within seconds....Never leave a bound and gagged slave alone in a room....It is essential that gags, nostril tubes, enema pipes, rods and other insertions should be scrupulously clean and dipped into mild antiseptic before use....Never use cheap or coarse rope. This has no "give" and can quickly cause skin-sores. (Quoted in Gosselin, 1987, pp. 238–239)

Sadomasochistic subcultures exist among gays, lesbians, and heterosexuals (Nordling et al., 2006; Sandnabba et al., 2002). In heterosexual BDSM, power relations between the sexes may be overturned, with the female being the dominant partner and the male submissive. The sadomasochistic "scene" is used to explore the nature of social relations by using sex as a means to explore power. Gay men who engage in BDSM have been found to prefer the use of leather, dildos, and wrestling, whereas heterosexual men tend to prefer humiliation, masks, gags, and straight jackets (Nordling et al., 2006). Both straight and gay BDSM participants derive sexual excitement from playing with power relations, from either being able to dominate another completely or to give in completely to another's will.

The BDSM subculture takes symbols of authority and dominance from the general culture, such as whips, uniforms, and handcuffs, and uses them in a safe erotic drama in which scripted roles take the place of "real self." It even mocks these symbols of authority by using them for erotic pleasure. Well-known social psychologist R. F. Baumeister (1988) suggests that sadomasochism is a reaction to modern society itself. Noting that sexual masochism proliferated when Western culture became highly individualistic, Baumeister suggests that it relieves the submissive partner of a sense of responsibility for the self by placing one's behavior completely under someone else's control. The majority of men and women who engage in BDSM behaviors are well adjusted and well educated (Allison et al., 2001; Kleinplatz & Moser, 2006; Santilla et al., 2000).

▶▶ EXHIBITIONISM and Voyeurism

Visual stimuli are basic aspects of sexuality; most sexually active people enjoy looking at the nude bodies of their partners, and such things as lingerie and the act of undressing one's partner can enhance the sexual nature of the human form. The enormous industry of adult magazines and books, the almost obligatory nude scene in modern movies, the embarrassment most people feel when seen naked inappropriately, and even the common nighttime dream of being caught naked in public all show the fundamental psychological power of visual sexual stimuli.

For some people, looking at nudity or sexual acts, or being seen naked or engaging in sex, become the paramount activities of sexuality. The person who becomes sexually aroused primarily from displaying his (or, more rarely, her) genitals, nudity, or sexuality to strangers is an **exhibitionist**; the person whose primary mode of sexual stimulation is to watch others naked or engaging in sex is called a **voyeur**. Langevin and Lang (1987) reviewed a number of studies that show that there is a close connection between exhibitionism and voyeurism; most exhibitionists engaged in voyeuristic habits before beginning to expose themselves.

Exhibitionism

Exhibitionism (or exhibitionistic disorder) involves recurrent and intense arousal from exposing one's genitals to an unsuspecting stranger (American Psychiatric Association, 2010). As such, this behavior is nonconsensual. The exhibitionist (or "flasher"), who is usually male, achieves sexual gratification from exposing his genitals in public or to unsuspecting people, who are usually female (Murphy & Page, 2008). What excites the exhibitionist is not usually the nudity itself but the lack of consent of the victim as expressed in her shocked or fearful reaction. True exhibitionists would not get the same sexual charge being naked on a nude beach, for example, where everyone is naked.

Exhibitionists usually have erections while exposing themselves, and they masturbate either then and there or later, while thinking about the reactions of their victims. Usually exhibitionism begins in the teen years and decreases as a man ages; however, it may worsen in times of stress or disappointment (Murphy & Page, 2008; Seligman & Hardenburg, 2000).

Exhibitionism is legally classified as "indecent exposure" and accounts for up to one third of all sex convictions in the United States, Canada, and Europe (Bogaerts et al., 2006; Langevin & Lang, 1987; Murphy & Page, 2008). However, it is important to keep in mind that exhibitionists have a witness to their crimes, unlike some of the other paraphilias (such as voyeurism). As such, there is a higher likelihood of being caught. Research has

AP/Wide World Photos

Although female exhibitionism is rare, it is interesting how much more acceptable it is for a woman to expose her body in U.S. society. Few people would complain about this woman exposing her breasts in public.

REAL RESEARCH 16.3 One study found that sadists and masochists have been found to have unique personality styles that contribute to their behaviors. Sadists are more likely to have aggressive personality styles, whereas masochists are more likely to experience self-image problems (RASMUSSEN, 2005).

---

failed to confirm any personality characteristics that might be common to exhibitionists except that the behavior is compulsive and difficult to stop (Rabinowitz et al., 2002). Many exhibitionists have normal dating and sexual histories, are married or in committed partnerships, and have normal sexual relations with their spouses or partners (Langevin & Lang, 1987). The majority of exhibitionists are shy and withdrawn, and many have been found to have borderline or avoidant personality disorders (or both; Bogaerts et al., 2006; Murphy & Page, 2008). Although we don't know exactly how many exhibitionists there are, we do know that many women are "flashed"—in fact, 40% to 60% of female college students report having been flashed at some point (Murphy & Page, 2008).

Exhibitionism in women is rare, although cases of it are reported in the literature (Grob, 1985; Rhoads & Boekelheide, 1985). Female exhibitionists may seek approval to feel feminine and appreciated, and seeing men admire her naked body reinforces her sense of sexual value and femininity. Perhaps, then, exhibitionism in women just takes a different form than in men. Women have more legitimate ways to expose their bodies than men do. After all, women exposing breast (and even buttock) cleavage is often acceptable by today's fashion standards. This type of exposure may be enough for female exhibitionists.

---

exhibitionist
A person who experiences recurrent and intense arousal from exposing his or her genitals to an unsuspecting stranger.

voyeur
A person who experiences a recurrent and intense arousal from observing unsuspecting persons undressing or engaging in sex acts.

In 2006, a new Dutch political party, known as the *Party for Neighbourly Love, Freedom, and Diversity* (*PNVD or Partij voor Naastenliefde*),[1] was founded in the Netherlands by three known pedophiles, Ad van den Berg, Martin Uittenbogaard, and Nobert de Jonge. The party became known as the "pedophilia" party in the media, since the two major issues on their platform involved lowering the age of consent and legalizing child pornography in the Netherlands. The main rationale for the development of the party was to give a voice to pedophiles, many of whom felt they had been ignored and silenced over the years. Creating a political party gave them an opportunity to have their voices heard. Although many Dutch men and women believed that the PNVD was a one-issue party, the group's founders argued that they had several additional proposed provisions including:

- Allowing the private possession of child pornography.

- Everybody will have the freedom to appear naked in public.

- People, aged 16 and older, can appear in pornographic productions.

- Pornography can be broadcast during the daytime hours.

- Allowing sexual contact for young people from the age of 12 on.

- Legalizing soft drugs (for those aged 12 and older) and hard drugs (for those 16 and over).

- Legalizing smoking, gambling, and alcohol consumption from the age of 12 on.

- Allowing sexual contact in public nature reserves (intervention only when the nuisance becomes too great).

- Punishing the circumcision of boys and girls under the age of 16.

- Legalizing prostitution for those over the age of 16.

- Providing sexual education beginning in nursery school.

As you can imagine, the PNVD created a significant amount of controversy in Holland. To become a legally recognized party they needed at least 60,000 signatures. However, very few people were willing to support the PNVD. In 2010, the party disbanded due to a lack of public support. During a recent visit to the Netherlands, I had the opportunity to meet with two of the party's founders, Ad van den Berg and Martin Uittenbogaard. I really wanted to understand more about them and their ideas for creating such a group.

Martin Uittenbogaard told me that it has been very difficult being so open and public about his interests in pedophilia. He has experienced multiple death threats and several of his windows have been broken with rocks. But the main reason he believes that society is against pedophilia is because it is "taboo." Martin explained that young children experience sexual interest and several do engage in sexual relationships with other young children. The problem, he believes, is that the government wants to control *who* people have sex with. That is why he thinks certain sexual behaviors, such as homosexuality or pornography, were illegal—so the government could control it.

Ad van den Berg agreed with Martin and said that it was difficult to explain why he was attracted to young boys. He remembers the attractions started when he was young but he didn't act on them until he was about 32-years-old. He has never been attracted to girls, women, or adult men—only young boys. He was 65-years-old when I spoke with him and he told me about several platonic and sexual relationships he had with young boys. The youngest was 10-years-old, but most are 11- to 13-years-old. When I asked him what they talked about he told me they mostly talk about the boy's day and he helps them with homework. Most of the boys are not interested in his life or work, but they do like the attention he gives them. He doesn't see himself as a predator or a "hunter." When a boy tells him he doesn't want to be touched, he respects this. Some boys just like to be with him, while others are looking simply for sex without a relationship.

One 11-year-old boy came to his house one day after a soccer game and asked him why he didn't have a wife. Ad explained that he didn't like women and that he liked boys instead. He explained that being honest about his feelings didn't scare the boy off. They trusted each other. One day the boy came over and told him that he was going to show himself to Ad. He undressed himself and walked around naked in the house. Ad stresses that he didn't ask the boy to do this—he did it on his own free will.

Both men told me if there is a power issue involved, it is the minor child who has all the power. If a boy goes to the police and tells them they were touched by an adult, the adult can be arrested. But the main point that both Martin and Ad wanted others to understand is that their love for boys is real and they feel they should be allowed to have loving relationships with them.

You might be wondering how a party with such a controversial platform could even exist. Their beliefs are disturbing to most of us, and many would argue that known pedophiles who are openly advocating child pornography and sexual contact with children belong in prison. What do you think? Does everyone have the right to express themselves, or does the safety of children preclude this right?

[1]Although the PNVD has disbanded, you can learn more about this group by visiting their website at www.pnvd.nl.

Voyeurism

Voyeurism, or voyeuristic disorder, involves individuals whose main means of sexual gratification is watching unsuspecting persons undressing, naked, or engaging in sexual activity. Some would argue that we are a voyeuristic society; our major media—newspapers, television, movies, advertisements—are full of sexual images that are intended to interest and arouse us. Magazines and movies featuring nude women or couples are popular. Even television shows display far more nudity and sexuality than would have been allowed just a few years ago. In modern society, it seems, we have all become casual voyeurs to some degree.

Clinical voyeurs, however, are those for whom watching others naked or viewing erotica is a compulsion. Voyeurs are often called "Peeping Toms," a revealing term because implicit in it are two important aspects of voyeurism. First, a "peeper" is one who looks without the knowledge or consent of the person being viewed, and true voyeurs are excited by the illicit aspect of their peeping. Second, voyeurs are usually male. Although it is becoming more acceptable for women in society to watch porn or to go to see male strippers, clinically speaking, there are few "Peeping Janes" (Lavin, 2008).

The typical voyeur is a heterosexual male who begins his voyeuristic behaviors before age 15 (Lavin, 2008; Seligman & Hardenburg, 2000). **Primary voyeurism** is rare. More often, voyeurism is mixed in with a host of other paraphiliac behaviors (Langevin & Lang, 1987; Lavin, 2008). Still, voyeurs are generally harmless and are satisfied just with peeping, although they certainly can scare an un-

---

REAL RESEARCH 16.4 Approximately 10% of high school students have experienced some form of "educator sexual misconduct," which are behaviors directed at students for purposes of sexually arousing the educator or student (WEST ET AL., 2010). These behaviors may be perpetuated by teachers, coaches, administrators, tutors, or counselors.

---

suspecting person who sees a strange man peering in the window. In a few cases, however, voyeurism can lead to more and more intrusive sexual activity, including rape (Holmes, 1991). Voyeurs, when caught, are usually not charged with a sex crime but with trespassing or sometimes breaking and entering (Lavin, 2008). Therefore, how many actually get in trouble with the law is difficult to determine.

Many voyeurs satisfy some of their urges by watching pornography. For most voyeurs, however, this is ultimately unsatisfying, for part of the excitement is the knowledge that the victim does not know or approve of the fact that the voyeur sees them. Like exhibitionists, voyeurs tend to be immature, sexually frustrated, poor at developing relationships, and chronic masturbators (Lavin, 2008). Some voyeurs have turned to voyeuristic webcam sites that capture unsuspecting sexual activity and broadcast it live over the Internet (M. D. Griffiths, 2000).

primary voyeurism
Voyeurism as the main and exclusive paraphilia.

troilism
Any sex sessions involving multiple partners, typically witnessed by others.

pedophilia
A paraphilia that involves recurrent and intense sexual arousal from prepubescent or pubescent children, which usually causes distress or impairment in important areas of functioning. People who engage in this behavior are called *pedophiles*, or *sexual offenders*.

Although it technically refers to a single couple copulating in front of others, **troilism** (TROY-ill-iz-um) has come to mean any sex sessions involving multiple partners. Troilism is not new; in 1631, Mervyn Touchet, the Second Earl of Castlehaven, was executed in England for ordering his servants to have sex with his wife while he watched. The fact that they were servants and thus beneath his station was as damaging to him as the actual act (Bullough, 1976).

Troilism may involve aspects of voyeurism, exhibitionism, and, sometimes, latent homosexual desires; an observer who gets excited, for example, by watching his wife fellate another man may be subconsciously putting himself in his wife's place. Some troilists install ceiling mirrors, video cameras, and other means to capture the sexual act for viewing later on. Others engage in sharing a sexual partner with a third party while they look on, or they engage in swinging (see Chapter 9). Many couples experiment with group sex, but to the troilist, engaging in or fantasizing about such sexual activity is the primary means of sexual arousal.

▶▶ PEDOPHILIA

Throughout history, **pedophilia** (pee-doh-FILL-ee-uh) has been called many things, including child-love, cross-generational sex, man–child (or adult–child) interaction, boy-love, pederasty, and Greek love (Bullough, 1990). The variety of terms shows how differently adult–child sexual interactions have been viewed in different periods of history. In Chapter 17, we discuss child sexual abuse and incest, whereas in this chapter we concentrate our attention on pedophilia.

Pedophilia involves recurrent and intense sexual arousal from prepubescent or pubescent children, which usually causes distress or impairment in important areas of functioning (American Psychological Association, 2010). Pedophilia is one of the most common paraphilias and is most likely to be seen in treatment because of its harmful and illegal nature (O'Grady, 2001).

Pedophiles are often 18 years or older and at least 5 years older than their victims (American Psychiatric Association, 2010). However, even though many people consider sexual contact between adults and children to be one of the most objectionable of crimes today, in many periods of history and in different cultures today, various types of child–adult sexual contact have been seen as acceptable (see Chapter 1 for more information about Greek pederasty, or Chapter 11 for more information on the Sambian culture). Even so, pedophilia is illegal in every country in the world (O'Grady, 2001).

What exactly constitutes such contact in a society may be unclear. For example, as recently as the 1980s, a girl in the state of New Mexico could get married at age 13. If a 30-year-old man marries a 13-year-old girl and has legal, consensual marital intercourse with her, is it pedophilia? What if they have consensual sex but are not married? Why should a piece of paper—a marriage certificate—make a difference in our definition?

Throughout most of history, a girl was considered ready for marriage and an adult sexual relationship as soon as she "came of age," that is, at menarche. It was common for much older men to be betrothed to very young women, and such marriages were seen as proper. For example, Saint Augustine decided to get married to try to curb his sexual promiscuity, and so he was betrothed to a prepubertal girl. Although intercourse was not permitted until she reached puberty, such early marriages were apparently common (Bullough, 1990). In England in the 18th to 19th centuries, 12 years was considered the age of consent. In the 18th century as well, adult–child sex (especially same-sex pairings) were accepted in China, Japan, parts of Africa, Turkey, Arabia, Egypt, and the Islamic areas of India (Ames & Houston, 1990).

To some degree or another, then, what legally constitutes pedophilia is a matter of the laws in different societies. Yet, clinically speaking, pedophilia refers to sexual activity with a prepubescent child (under age 14). Many times these behaviors are also referred to as child sexual abuse. In fact, it has been shown that heterosexual males in almost all cultures are attracted to younger females, and homosexual males are attracted to younger (or younger appearing) males (O'Grady, 2001) (see the nearby Sexual Diversity in Our World feature).

Pedophiles often report an attraction to children of a particular age range, most often 8- to 10-year-olds in those attracted to girls, and slightly older in those attracted to boys (attraction to prepubescent girls is more common; Murray, 2000). Some pedophiles are unable to function sexually with an adult, whereas others also maintain adult sexual relationships (Seligman & Hardenburg, 2000). Many pedophiles believe that pedophilia will become more socially acceptable over time, much like homosexuality did (O'Grady, 2001).

Pedophiliac behavior is often obsessive. Pedophiles are usually obsessed with their fantasies, and they tend to dominate their lives. They are also predators—they know which child they like, and they work hard to get the trust and support from the parents or caretakers first. Pedophiles are good at winning the trust of parents. In fact, parents often trust the pedophile so much that they often take the pedophile's word over their own child's (O'Grady, 2001).

Many pedophiles threaten their victims and tell them they must keep their sexual activity secret. One therapist tells of a patient who had been repeatedly threatened by her assailant:

As a young teen, she and a friend were raped repeatedly by a friend of their parents. It went on for years. He would rape the

"He gave everyone on the bus his screen name, which was a really perverted name."
—The Sexual Offender Registry

View in Video
To watch the entire interview, go to Psychology CourseMate at **login.cengagebrain.com**.

© Janell Carroll

girls in front of each other and threatened the lives of both of them if they told. They didn't. They were both afraid of him and convinced they wouldn't be believed anyway, given his high standing in the community and his friendship with their parents. There is a song she still hates, she tells me, because he used to sing it as he undressed them. (Salter, 2003, p. 13)

In the United States, an adult who has sexual contact with a boy or girl younger than the age of consent (see Table 17.1 for more information about the age of consent) to whom he or she is not married is guilty of child sexual abuse. A child sexual abuser may or may not be a pedophile; a person may sexually abuse a child because an adult is not available, because children are easier to seduce than adults, out of anger, or because of other sexual, psychological, or familial problems.

Girls are twice as likely as boys to be victims of pedophiliac behavior (Murray, 2000). In one study, 44% of pedophiles chose only girls, 33% chose only boys, and 23% abused both boys and girls (Murray, 2000). Boys are less likely to reject sexual advances and to report their sexual advances to authorities than girls (Brongersma, 1990). This may be the reason that violence is less common in sexual contact between men and boys than between men and girls.

Some pedophiles only look at children and never touch, whereas others engage in a variety of sexual acts with their victims, with the most common behavior being fondling and exhibitionism, rather than penetration (Murray, 2000). As we discussed earlier, pedophiles often have a lack of empathy and believe that their behavior does not cause any negative psychological or physical consequences for their victims (Miranda & Fiorello, 2002).

Unfortunately, some pedophiles, realizing the chance of the child reporting the act, kill their victims. After one such murder of a young New Jersey girl named Megan Kanka in July 1994, her parents spearheaded "Megan's Law," which was signed into state law in October 1994. This law made it mandatory for authorities in New Jersey to tell parents when a convicted child molester moved into the neighborhood and increased penalties for child molesters. In 1996, Megan's Law became federal law (see the accompanying Sex in Real Life feature, "Megan's Law," for more information).

Female pedophiles also exist, although they often abuse children in concert with another person, usually their male partner. They may act to please their adult sexual partners rather than to

Toys that sexualize girls, such as Bratz dolls, can encourage girls to think and treat their bodies as sexual objects.

AP Photo/MGM Entertainment

satisfy their own pedophilic desires. Although less common, female pedophiles have been found to have a higher incidence of psychiatric disorders than male pedophiles (Chow & Choy, 2002).

A number of small organizations in Western countries, usually made up of pedophiles, argue that man–boy love should be legalized, usually under the pretense of guarding "the sexual rights of children and adolescents" (Okami, 1990). In America, the North American Man–Boy Love Association (NAMBLA) supports the abolition of age-of-consent laws. NAMBLA believes that there is a difference between those who simply want to use children for sexual release and those who develop long-lasting, often exclusive, and even loving relationships with a single boy. Suppe (1984) agrees that pederasty among postpubescent boys need not necessarily be harmful (which is not to deny that it often may be). In contrast, those who work with sexually abused children vehemently deny the claim, pointing to children whose lives were ruined by sex with adults.

Several factors may go into pedophilic behavior. Pedophiles have been described as having had arrested psychological development, which makes them childlike with childish emotional needs. They may also have low self-esteem and poor social relations with adults, may be trying to overcome their own humiliations and pains from their childhood, or may exaggerate the social male role of dominance and power over a weaker sexual partner. Conditions such as alcoholism may lessen the barriers to having sex with children. Other studies have found that pedophiles have brain abnormalities that contribute to their sexual behaviors (Eastvold et al., 2011). Another study asked pedophiles why they engaged in sex with children and found the most common response was that the children didn't fight it, followed by a lack of sexual outlets with adults, intoxication, and victim initiation of sexual behavior (Pollack & Hashmall, 1991).

Over the years, research has found that being a victim of sexual abuse in childhood is one of the most frequently reported risk factors for becoming a pedophile (Glasser et al., 2001; Langstrom et al., 2000; Seto, 2004). It is estimated that 35% of pedophiles were sexually abused as children (Keegan, 2001). Studies have also found that the choice of gender and age of victims often reflects the pattern of past sexual abuse in the pedophile's life (Pollock & Hashmall, 1991). Although past sexual abuse is a risk factor, it is important to point out that the majority of male victims of child sexual abuse do not become pedophiles (Salter et al., 2003). Pedophiles have high **recidivism** (re-SID-iv-iz-um) rates, and for some unknown reason, these rates are higher in homosexual men (Murray, 2000). The recidivism rate is the main impetus for legislation such as Megan's Law (M. A. Alexander, 1999).

The Internet has been a two-edged sword when it comes to pedophilia. On one hand, it has helped pedophiles find each other and talk about their behaviors. This can validate their behaviors because they are no longer feeling isolated, as though they are the only person who engages in child sex behaviors. Pedophiles are also able to gather information and can actually share images with each other (O'Grady, 2001). On the other hand, the Internet has also become a powerful tool to combat pedophilia, both in the online reporting of sex offenders and the ability of law officials to go undercover and seek out pedophiles online (Trivits & Reppucci, 2002; see Real Research 16.5).

ON YOUR MIND 16.3

What should I do if I receive an obscene telephone call?

You should react calmly and not exhibit the reactions of shock, fright, or disgust that the caller finds exciting. Do not slam the phone down; simply replace it gently in the cradle. An immediate ring again is probably a callback; ignore it, or pick up the phone and hang up quickly without listening. Sometimes a gentle suggestion that the person needs psychological help disrupts the caller's fantasy. Persistent callers can be discouraged by suggesting that you have contacted the police. If you do get more than one call, notify the telephone company. The popularity of caller ID today has been helpful in reducing the rates of obscene phone calls.

OTHER PARAPHILIAS and Sexual Variations

People can be sexually attracted to almost anything. An article in the *Journal of Forensic Sciences* tells of a man who was erotically attracted to his tractor; he wrote poetry to it, he had a pet name for it,

REAL RESEARCH 16.5   Federal investigators have found that many pedophiles are using powerful encryption tools in social media and other programs to illegally share child pornography online (VEDANTAM, 2011). Because law enforcement officers are prohibited from providing images of child porn, would-be members to these sites are required to share photos and videos of children being sexually abused to gain access to the sites.

and his body was found after he was asphyxiated by suspending himself by the ankles from the tractor's shovel to masturbate (O'Halloran & Dietz, 1993). However, a number of other paraphilias are relatively more common, and we now review a sample of them.

Obscene Telephone Callers

Scatolophilia (scat-oh-low-FILL-ee-uh), or obscene telephone calling, is when a person, almost always male, calls women and becomes excited as the victims react to his obscene suggestions. Most scatolophiliacs masturbate either during the call or afterward. Like exhibitionism, scatolophilia is nonconsensual, and the scatolophiliac becomes excited by the victim's reactions of fear, disgust, or outrage.

Most scatolophiliacs have problems in their relationships and suffer from feelings of isolation and inadequacy. For many, scatolophilia is the only way they can express themselves sexually (Holmes, 1991). Scatolophiliacs often have coexisting paraphilias, such as exhibitionism or voyeurism (M. Price et al., 2002).

recidivism
A tendency to repeat crimes, such as sexual offenses.

scatolophilia
Sexual arousal from making obscene telephone calls.

Women-only passenger cars are subway and railway cars that do not allow male passengers. Problems with groping and frotteurism on public transportation has led to the establishment of women-only passenger cars in places such as Tokyo, Japan and Seoul, South Korea.

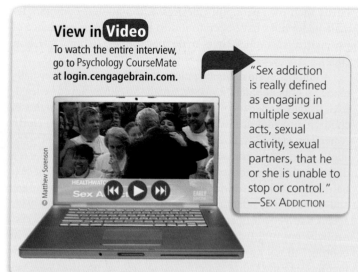

View in Video

To watch the entire interview, go to Psychology CourseMate at **login.cengagebrain.com.**

"Sex addiction is really defined as engaging in multiple sexual acts, sexual activity, sexual partners, that he or she is unable to stop or control."
—SEX ADDICTION

The obscene telephone caller may boast of sexual acts he will perform on the victim, may describe his masturbation in detail, may threaten the victim, or may try to entice the victim to reveal aspects of her sexual life or even perform sexual acts such as masturbating while he listens on the phone. Some callers are very persuasive; many have great success in talking women into performing sexual acts while posing as product representatives recalling certain products, as the police, or even as people conducting a sexual survey. (Note: No reputable sexuality researchers conduct surveys over the phone. If you receive such a call, do not answer any sexually explicit questions.). Others threaten harm to the victim or her family if she does not do what he asks (obscene callers often know the victim's address, if only from the phone book). Some will get a woman's phone number while observing her writing a check at a place like the supermarket and then will frighten her more because he knows her address, appearance, and even some of her food preferences (Matek, 1988).

Frotteurism

Frotteurism (frah-TOUR-iz-um) involves a man rubbing his genitals against a woman's thighs or buttocks in a crowded place (such as a subway) where he can claim it was an accident and get away quickly. In some cases, he may fondle a woman's breasts with his hand while he is rubbing up against her. This is similar to **toucheurism,** which is the compulsive desire to touch strangers with one's hands for sexual arousal. This desire, usually in men, finds expression on buses, trains, in shopping malls, while waiting in line, at crowded concerts, anyplace where bodies are pressed together. There have also been cases of frotteurism or toucheurism among doctors or dentists who rub against or touch their patients. Frotteurism, however, does not usually appear in isolation but as

one of a number of paraphilias in an individual (Langevin & Lang, 1987).

Zoophilia

Zoophilia (zoo-uh-FILL-ee-uh; also referred to as bestiality), or sexual contact with animals, is rare, although Kinsey and his colleagues (1948, 1953) found that 1 man in every 13 engages in this behavior. Contact between people and animals has been both practiced and condemned since earliest times.

Studies of people who engage in sex with animals have found that a male dog is the most popular animal sex partner for both men and women (Miletski, 2002). Sexual behaviors included masturbating the animal, submitting to anal sex performed by the animal, or active or passive oral sex with the animal (Miletski, 2002).

Necrophilia

Tales of **necrophilia** (neck-row-FILL-ee-uh), or having sex with corpses, have been found even in ancient civilizations. The Egyptians prohibited embalmers from taking immediate delivery of corpses of the wives of important men for fear that the embalmers would violate them (Rosman & Resnick, 1989). More recently, the legends of the vampires imply necrophilia in the highly sexual approaches of the "undead." The stories of Sleeping Beauty, Snow White, and Romeo and Juliet all convey a sense of the restorative powers of loving the dead and thereby bringing the corpse back to life.

Rosman and Resnick (1989) suggest that necrophiliacs desire a partner who is unresisting and unrejecting; to find one, many seek out professions that put them in contact with corpses. They identify three types of genuine necrophilia: necrophiliac fantasy, in which a person has persistent fantasies about sex with dead bodies without

---

frotteurism
A paraphiliac behavior that involves recurrent and intense sexual arousal from fantasies or behaviors that involve touching and/or rubbing the genitals against a nonconsenting person in a crowded place.

toucheurism
A paraphiliac behavior that involves recurrent and intense sexual arousal from fantasies or behaviors involving compulsively touching strangers.

zoophilia
A paraphiliac behavior that involves recurrent and intense sexual arousal from fantasies or behaviors involving sexual contact with animals (also referred to as *bestiality*).

necrophilia
A paraphiliac behavior that involves recurrent and intense sexual arousal from fantasies or behaviors involving sexual contact with dead bodies.

For some people, obsessions develop for online sexual behavior, such as cybersex, pornography, or telephone sex. It's not hard to understand how an addiction might develop when we learn that hundreds of new sex-related sites are added to the Internet every day.

A person who has an Internet sexual addiction routinely spends significant amounts of time in chat rooms and instant messaging with the intent of getting sex; feels preoccupied with using the Internet to find online sexual partners; discusses personal sexual fantasies not typically expressed offline; masturbates while engaging in online chats; obsesses about the next opportunity to engage in online sex; moves from cybersex to phone sex or face-to-face meetings; hides online chat sessions from others; obsessively seeks out Internet pornography sites; feels guilty; and has decreasing interest in real-life sexual partners (Griffiths, 2001; Grove et al., 2011). Men and women with low self-

esteem, a distorted body image, an untreated sexual dysfunction, or a prior diagnosed sexual addiction are at greater risk for development of an Internet sexual addiction, and those who seek out Internet pornography have been found to have higher levels of loneliness compared with those who do not (Paul, 2009; Paul & Shim, 2008; Yoder et al., 2005; Young et al., 2000).

Many people with paraphilias turn to the Internet as a "safe" outlet for their sexual fantasies and urges. Psychotherapy and support groups often offer the

most help for those with Internet sexual addictions. More research is needed into this new and growing problem. Research has shown that there is a small minority of men and women who experience significant disturbances caused by their online sexual activity (Griffiths, 2001).

© vario images GmbH & Co.KG/Alamy

---

actually engaging in such behavior; "regular" necrophilia, which involves the use of already-dead bodies for sexual pleasure; and necrophiliac homicide, in which the person commits murder to obtain a corpse for sexual pleasure. However, necrophilia is extremely rare and accounts for only a tiny fraction of murders (Milner et al., 2008).

An infamous case of necrophiliac homicide was that of serial killer Jeffrey Dahmer. Dahmer admitted to killing 17 men and having sex with their corpses; he also mutilated their bodies, tried to create a "shrine" out of their organs that he thought would give him "special powers," and ate their flesh. In keeping with Rosman and Resnick's claim that necrophiliacs desire a partner who is unresisting and unrejecting, Dahmer bored holes into his victims' skulls while they were alive and poured in acid or boiling water, trying to create "zombies" who would fulfill his every desire.

On the other hand, Dahmer also had sex with his victims while they were alive; perhaps he was an **erotophonophiliac**, which is someone who gets sexual excitement from the act of murder itself. Dahmer admitted his deeds but claimed he was insane. A jury found him sane and guilty, and he was sentenced to life in prison with no chance of parole; he was killed by another inmate in 1994.

Sexual Addictions

Although there is a great range in frequency of sexual contact in the general population (see Chapter 10), some argue that certain people cross over the line from a vigorous sex life to an obsessed sex life. Sexuality, like drugs, alcohol, gambling, and all other be-

haviors that bring a sense of excitement and pleasure, should involve some degree of moderation. Yet for some people, the need for repeated sexual encounters, which often end up being fleeting and unfulfilling, becomes almost a compulsion (Bancroft & Vukadinovic, 2004; G. H. Golden, 2001). An addiction involves an uncontrollable craving and compulsive need for a specific object. A typical sexual addict is a married man whose obsession with masturbation increases to an obsession with pornography, cybersex, prostitute visits, or multiple sexual affairs (Keane, 2004).

In the past, derogatory terms, mostly for women, were used to describe these people; an example is **nymphomaniac.** Terms for men were more flattering and included **Don Juanism, satyriasis,** or in other cases, "studs." Perhaps nowhere else is the double standard between the sexes so blatant—women who enjoy frequent sexual encounters are considered "whores" or "sluts," whereas men who enjoy similar levels of sexual activity have been admired. However, on some college campuses across the United States, men who engage in sex with many partners are often referred to as "man-whores" or male "sluts" (Author's files).

erotophonophiliac
A paraphilia that involves recurrent and intense sexual arousal from real or imagined acts of committing murder.

nymphomaniac
A pejorative term used to describe women who engage in frequent or promiscuous sex.

Don Juanism, or satyriasis
Terms used to describe men who engage in frequent or promiscuous sex.

Recent cases of sexual addiction in the media involving celebrities such as Charlie Sheen, Tiger Woods, and Arnold Schwarzenegger have prompted experts to include "hypersexual disorder" in the DSM-5 due out in 2013.

WireImage/Getty Images

Sexual addiction, or hypersexual disorder, involves recurrent and intense sexual fantasies, sexual urges, and sexual behavior, and excessive time spent on these behaviors and an inability to control these fantasies (American Psychiatric Association, 2010). Sexual addiction was first written about by Patrick Carnes (2001) in his book, *Out of the Shadows: Understanding Sexual Addiction.* Carnes wrote about the parallels between sexual addiction and compulsive gambling, both of which involve an obsessive and compulsive addiction.

According to Carnes, sexual addicts go through four cycles repeatedly: a preoccupation with thoughts of sex, ritualization of preparation for sex (such as primping oneself and going to bars), compulsive sexual behavior over which addicts feel they have no control, and despair afterward as the realization hits that they have again repeated the destructive sequence of events.

Although hypersexual disorder is not a paraphilia, it is seen as a compulsive sexual behavior. It typically interferes with a person's daily functioning and may include compulsive masturbation or an obsession with pornography, whereas for others it may progress to multiple sex partners or exhibitionistic behaviors. Hypersexual disorder can lead to emotional suffering and problems in one's occupational functioning and marital and family relationships (Bird, 2006; Miner et al., 2007).

Although there are no definite numbers, the Society for the Advancement of Sexual Health estimates that 3% to 5% of Americans have a sexual addiction, with men outnumbering women five to one (Beck, 2008; Society for the Advancement of Sexual Health, 2008). However, these numbers are based only on those who seek treatment, so actual numbers are probably much higher. The availability of sex on the Internet has increased the number of cases of sexual addiction (Landau, 2008).

Typically, treatment for sexual addiction involves individual or group therapy as part of a 12-step recovery process (similar to the Alcoholics Anonymous program), originated by Carnes (2001). Medications may also be used, especially if a person also has bipolar disorder or depression, each of which is commonly associated with compulsive sexual behavior.

Many have criticized the idea of hypersexuality, however. They argue that terms such as "sexual addiction" are really disguised social judgments. Before the sexual freedom of the 1960s, those who engaged in promiscuous sex were often considered physically, mentally, or morally sick. Some scholars suggest that there has been an attempt to return to a pathological model of sexuality using the concept of addiction (Irvine, 1995). Although this is a growing area of research, limited research is available on hypersexuality. A number of self-help groups have been organized, including Sexaholics Anonymous, Sex Addicts Anonymous, Sex and Love Addicts Anonymous, and Co-Dependents of Sexual Addicts.

◀ review QUESTIONS

1 Define a fetish and identify the key features of this paraphilia. What are the most common fetish items? Define transvestic fetishism.

2 Define sadism and masochism, and identify the key features of these paraphilias.

3 Define exhibitionism and voyeurism, and identify the key features of these paraphilia.

4 Define pedophilia and identify the key features of this paraphilia.

5 Identify some of the other less common paraphilias and identify the key features of these disorders.

6 Explain how sexuality can be viewed as a behavior that brings excitement and pleasure, similar to gambling, drugs, and alcohol.

7 What is hypersexuality, and how is it manifested in a man or woman? Explain any gender differences in the perceptions of hypersexuality.

8 Explain Carne's treatment methods and the four cycles of repair.

9 Explain the issues contributing to the debate about whether sexual addiction exists.

ASSESSING AND TREATING
Paraphilias and Sexual Variations

Although the majority of those with paraphilias and sexual variations do not seek treatment and are content with balancing the pleasure and guilt of their behaviors, others find their behaviors to be an unwanted disruption to their lives. Their sexual desires may get in the way of forming relationships, may get them into legal trouble, or may become such a preoccupation that they dominate their lives. For these people, a number of therapeutic solutions have been tried, with varying success.

ASSESSMENT

It is very difficult to assess and measure sexual variations (Laws & O'Donahue, 2008). Part of the problem is that many people tend to feel uncomfortable talking about their sexual practices, especially if they are socially stigmatized. In addition, sexual behaviors often occur in private and may involve the use of sexual fantasy, which is nearly impossible to measure (Laws & O'Donahue, 2008). There are also ethical issues that make assessment difficult.

Although some people with paraphilias are referred to clinicians by law enforcement, for others, assessment is often done through self-report, through behavioral observation, or by physiological tests or personality inventories (Laws & O'Donahue, 2008; Seligman & Hardenburg, 2000). Self-reports may not be reliable, however; individuals under court order to receive treatment for pedophilia may be highly motivated to report that the behavior has ceased. Also, people are not necessarily the best judge of their own desires and behavior; some may truly believe they have overcome their sexual desires when, in fact, they have not. The second technique, behavioral observation, is limited by the fact that it cannot assess fantasies and desires; also, most people can suppress these behaviors for periods of time.

Physiological tests may be a bit more reliable. The most reliable technique for men is probably **penile plethysmography,** which is often used with male sex offenders. For example, a pedophile can be shown films of nude children and the plethysmograph can record his penile blood volume. If he becomes excited at the pictures, then he is probably still having pedophilic desires and fantasies. A similar test is also available to test the sexual response of female offenders. However, both of these physiological tests have been found to be of limited use in this population because there are no outward signs of arousal (Laws & O'Donahue, 2008; Seligman & Hardenburg, 2000).

Personality inventories, such as the **Minnesota Multiphasic Personality Inventory (MMPI),** can help establish personality patterns and determine whether there are additional psychological disorders (Seligman & Hardenburg, 2000). Other psychological inventories for depression and anxiety are often also used. In the future, the development of methodologies to assess these behaviors will be a priority in this field (Laws & O'Donahue, 2008).

TREATMENT Options

For the most part, treatment for paraphilias today is multifaceted and may include group, individual, and family therapy; medication; education; and self-help groups (Laws & O'Donahue, 2008; Seligman & Hardenburg, 2000; see Table 16.1). Overall, treatment is aimed at the reduction or elimination of the paraphiliac symptoms, relapse prevention, and increasing victim empathy (d'Amora & Hobson, 2003).

Whatever the technique, the most important goal of therapy must be to change a person's behavior. If behavior can be changed, even if fantasies and inner emotional life are not altered, then at least the individuals will not be harming others or themselves. That is why behavioral techniques have been the most commonly used and most successful of the paraphilia treatments.

Therapy to resolve earlier childhood trauma or experiences that help maintain the paraphiliac behaviors is also helpful (H. Kaplan et al., 1994). This therapy can help increase self-esteem and social skills, which are often lacking in people with paraphilias. Positive behaviors can be encouraged by teaching them how to improve their social skills, allowing them to meet more men or women as potential sexual partners. Counseling, modeling (taking after a positive role model), or feedback to change emotions and thoughts can be used to change a person's attitudes toward the sexual object. In empathy training, which is useful when there is a victim, individuals are taught to increase their compassion by putting themselves in the same situation as the victim. Incarcerated sex offenders may be exposed to relapse prevention therapies, which focus on controlling the cycle of troubling emotions, distorted thinking, and fantasies that accompany their activities (Goleman, 1992). These techniques can be used in either group psychotherapy or individual counseling sessions. Group therapy has been found to be an important tool in reducing isolation, improving social skills, and reducing shame and secrecy (Seligman & Hardenburg, 2000).

Yet most find their desires difficult to suppress, and for them aversion therapy is one of the most common treatment strategies (Laws & O'Donahue, 2008; Seligman & Hardenburg, 2000). In aversion therapy, the undesirable behavior is linked with an unpleasant stimulus. For example, the person might be shown pictures of nude boys or asked to fantasize about exposing himself to a girl while an unpleasant odor, a drug that causes nausea, or an

> *Behavioral techniques have been the most commonly used and most successful of the paraphilia treatments.*

penile plethysmography
A test performed by measuring the amount of blood that enters the penis in response to a stimulus, which can indicate how arousing the stimulus is for the male.

Minnesota Multiphasic Personality Inventory (MMPI)
Psychological test used to assess general personality characteristics.

table 16.1 ■ Paraphilia Treatment Options

Treatment for paraphilias may often involve several approaches. Overall, the goal of treatment is to reduce or eliminate the paraphiliac behaviors, reduce or eliminate the chances of relapse, and increase personal feelings of self-esteem, as well as victim empathy. Although many sexual offenders are mandated by courts to go to therapy, those who seek out therapy on their own have been found to be more motivated and successful in their treatment. Although many convicted sex offenders will reduce their paraphiliac behavior after treatment, some may not. Those who are engaging in high levels of paraphiliac behavior and/or those with multiple psychological disorders are often less successful in therapy. Following are the various treatment options for paraphilias.

Type of Therapy	Therapeutic Methods
Individual	One-on-one therapy with a psychologist or counselor; work on improving self-esteem and social skills. Often uses modeling, empathy, and social-skills training, controlling the cycle of troubling emotions, distorted thinking, and fantasies that accompany their activities.
Group	A form of psychotherapy in which a therapist works with multiple paraphiliacs with similar conditions. The interactions between the members of the group are analyzed and considered to be therapeutic.
Family	Treatment of more than one member of a family in the same session. Family relationships and processes are explored and evaluated for their potential role in the paraphiliac's behavior.
Cognitive behavioral	Combination of cognitive and behavior therapy. Works to help weaken the connections between certain situations and emotional/physical reactions to them (including depression, self-defeating, or self-damaging behaviors), whereas also examining how certain thinking patterns help contribute to behavior. Emphasizes relaxation and improving emotional health.
Systematic desensitization	A technique used in behavior therapy to treat behavioral problems involving anxiety. Clients are exposed to threatening situations under relaxed conditions until the anxiety reaction is extinguished.
Aversion	A behavior-modification technique that uses unpleasant stimuli in a controlled fashion to change behavior in a therapeutic way. An example would be a pedophile who is given an electric shock or a nausea drug while looking at naked pictures of children.
Shame aversion	A behavior-modification technique that uses shame as the unpleasant stimuli to change behavior in a therapeutic way. An example would be an exhibitionist who is asked to expose himself in front of an audience.
Orgasmic reconditioning	A behavioral technique that involves reprogramming a person's fantasies. An example would be to have a paraphiliac masturbate, and when orgasm is inevitable, he would switch his fantasy to a more socially desirable one, hoping thereby to increasingly associate orgasm and, later, erection with the desirable stimulus.
Satiation	A behavioral technique in which a person masturbates to a conventional fantasy and then immediately masturbates again to an undesirable fantasy. The decreased sex drive and low responsiveness of the second attempt makes the experience less exciting than usual, and eventually the behavior may lose its desirability.
Pharmacotherapy	Medications may be used to improve symptoms, delay the progression, or reduce the urge to act on paraphiliac behaviors. A variety of medications have been used, including antidepressants and testosterone-suppressing drugs.
Surgical	Procedures such as castration are used to stop the paraphiliac behavior.
Chemotherapy	Using medication to either decrease sexual drive or to treat psychological pathologies that are believed to underlie the paraphiliac behavior.

electric shock is administered. This technique has had some success, although its effectiveness decreases over time (Laws & O'Donahue, 2008). In **shame aversion,** the unpleasant stimulus is shame; for example, an exhibitionist may be asked to expose himself in front of an audience.

Although removing the behavior itself may protect any victims, the person who still fantasizes about the behavior or has the same underlying attitude that led to it (such as fear of women) may not really be that much better off. The psychological underpinnings of the paraphilia also must be changed. In systematic desensitization (Wolpe, 1958), the person is taught to relax and is then taken through more and more anxiety-provoking or arousing situations until eventually the person learns to relax during even the most extreme situations (Hawton, 1983).

A number of therapies incorporate masturbation to try to reprogram a person's fantasies. In **orgasmic reconditioning,** the paraphiliac masturbates; just as he feels orgasm is inevitable, he switches his fantasy to a more socially desirable one, hoping thereby to increasingly associate orgasm and, later, erection with the desirable stimulus. Similarly, in **satiation therapy,** the person masturbates to a conventional fantasy and then right away masturbates again to the undesirable fantasy (Marshall, 1979). The decreased sex drive and low responsiveness of the second attempt makes the experience less exciting than usual, and eventually the behavior may lose its desirability.

In addition to these behavioral therapies, pharmacotherapy (drug therapy) has become more popular (Chopin-Marcé, 2001). The research shows that certain drugs can lead to a significant decrease in deviant sexual fantasies, urges, and behaviors (Keegan, 2001). Testosterone-suppressing drugs (antiandrogen) can produce castration levels of testosterone for up to 5 years (Reilly et al., 2000).

Antidepressants have also been found to be helpful. In fact, many therapists believe that the compulsive nature of many paraphilias is related to a psychological condition known as **obsessive–compulsive disorder (OCD).** Because of these similarities, treatment options for sexual paraphilias have begun to evaluate the use of selective serotonin reuptake inhibitors (SSRIs; these antidepressant drugs have been successful in the treatment of OCD; Abouesh & Clayton, 1999). Selective serotonin reuptake inhibitors have been found to reduce deviant sexual fantasies, urges, and behaviors (Keegan, 2001).

> *Ultimately, **there is no certain way** to change a person's sexual desires.*

Surgery has also been used in the treatment of paraphilias. Castration may not be the answer to the violent or pedophilic offender; some use foreign objects on their victims, and so the inability to achieve erection is not necessarily an impediment to their activity. Others cite the fact that although castration may cause a decrease in testosterone, it does not always result in a decrease in sex drive (Santen, 1995). To the degree that such crimes are crimes of aggression, rather than of sex, castration may not address the underlying cause.

Ultimately, there is no certain way to change a person's sexual desires. For many people with paraphilias whose desires are socially or legally unacceptable, life is a struggle to keep their sexuality tightly controlled. As we mentioned earlier, recidivism rates for those with paraphilias are generally high, so long-term treatment is often necessary (McGrath, 1991; Rabinowitz et al., 2002). Those who do best are motivated and committed to treatment (as opposed to being mandated by the court to appear in therapy), seek treatment early, and have normal adult sexual outlets (Seligman & Hardenburg, 2000). Those with less treatment success often have multiple psychological disorders, low empathy levels, and a high frequency of paraphiliac behavior (H. Kaplan et al., 1994).

Overall, this is an area of research that is also in need of further study. Unfortunately, few studies have shown promising treatment results for paraphilias. In fact, current research does not support the fact that treatments lead to long-term behavioral changes (Laws & O'Donahue, 2008). Treatment modalities for paraphilias will be another priority research area in the future.

---

shame aversion
A type of aversion therapy in which the behavior that one wishes to extinguish is linked with strong feelings of shame.

orgasmic reconditioning
A sex therapy technique in which a person switches fantasies just at the moment of masturbatory orgasm to try to condition himself or herself to become excited by more conventional fantasies.

satiation therapy
A therapy to lessen excitement to an undesired stimulus by masturbating to a desired stimulus and then immediately masturbating again, when desire is lessened, to an undesired stimulus.

obsessive–compulsive disorder (OCD)
A psychological disorder in which a person experiences recurrent and persistent thoughts, impulses, or images that are intrusive and inappropriate, and that cause marked anxiety and repetitive behaviors.

◀ review QUESTIONS

1 Explain some of the reasons a paraphiliac may, or may not, seek out therapy.

2 How are paraphilias assessed? Are self-reports reliable? Why or why not?

3 Identify the various treatment options for the paraphilias.

4 Explain how aversion therapy has been used for the treatment of the paraphilias.

5 What is often the main goal of therapy for a paraphiliac?

VARIATIONS or Deviations

What criteria should we use to decide whether a sexual behavior is "normal"? The number of people who engage in it? What a particular religion says about it? Popular opinion? Should we leave it up to the courts or psychiatrists? Stoller (1991) suggests that we are all perverse to some degree. Why should some people be singled out as being too perverse, especially if they do no harm to anyone else?

Perhaps the need we feel to brand some sexual behaviors as perverse is summed up by S. B. Levine and colleagues (1990, p. 92): "Paraphiliac images often involve arousal without the pretense of caring or human attachment." We tend to be uncomfortable with sex for its own sake, separate from ideas of love, intimacy, or human attachment (Laws & O'Donohue, 2008), which is one reason that masturbation was seen as evil or sick for so many years.

Paraphilias are still labeled "perversions" by law and often carry legal penalties. Because even consensual adult sexual behavior, such as anal intercourse, is illegal in some states, it is not surprising that paraphilias are as well. Yet these laws also contain contradictions; for example, why is it illegal for men to expose

ON YOUR MIND 16.4

I think about sex a lot—it seems like it is almost all the time. I also like to have sex as often as I can. Do I have a sexual addiction?

Probably not. Thinking about sex is a universal human pastime, especially when a person is younger and just beginning to mature as a sexual being. Sexual addiction becomes a problem when people find their sexual behavior becoming dangerous or uncomfortable. People who find that they cannot stop themselves from engaging in behaviors that put them at physical risk, that they find immoral, that make them feel extremely guilty, or that intrude on their ability to do other things in their life should probably seek counseling—but that is true whether or not the behavior is sexual.

themselves, yet women are not arrested for wearing a see-through blouse? We must be careful in deciding that some sexual behaviors are natural and others are unnatural, or some normal and others abnormal. Those that we call paraphilias may simply be part of human sexual diversity, unproblematic unless they cause distress, injury, or involve an unconsenting or underage partner.

◀ review QUESTIONS

1 Identify some of the ways that people may determine whether a sexual behavior is "normal."

2 Explain how there are contradictions in laws regulating sexual behaviors.

3 How might paraphilias be viewed as a normal variation of human sexual behavior?

◄◄ chapter REVIEW

SUMMARY POINTS

1 People celebrate individual differences for most aspects of human life, with the exception of sexual diversity. Sexual behavior can be viewed as a continuum, but social value judgments, rather than science, determine which sexual behaviors are considered acceptable in society. Attitudes about which behaviors are acceptable vary over time, and there are cultural variations.

2 Paraphilias are recurrent, intense sexually arousing fantasies, sexual urges, or behaviors that involve a craving for an erotic object for 6 months or more that involves a nonhuman object, the suffering or humiliation of oneself or one's partner, or children or other

nonconsenting persons. This behavior causes significant distress and interferes with a person's ability to work, interact with friends, and other important areas.

3 Discomfort or distress about certain sexual interests or behaviors may arise from the fact that the sexual desires are in conflict with current social standards. If a person enjoys sexual behaviors that society views as pathological, distress can occur. There has been a movement to depathologize unusual sexual behaviors.

4 People with paraphilias come from every socioeconomic bracket, every ethnic and racial group, and every sexual orientation. The factors

that have been found to be related to the development of a paraphilia include a person's sex, growing up in a dysfunctional family or experiencing family problems during childhood, and past sexual abuse.

5 Several theories attempt to explain the development of paraphilias. The biological theories claim physical factors are responsible for the development of paraphiliac behavior. Psychoanalytic theorists suggest that the causes can be traced back to problems during the Oedipal crisis and with castration anxiety. Developmental theories claim that individuals form a template in their brain that defines their ideal lover and sexual situation, and this can be disrupted in several ways. Paraphilias may also be caused by courtship disorders in which the behavior becomes fixed at a preliminary stage of mating that would normally lead to sexual intercourse. Behaviorists suggest that paraphilias develop because a behavior becomes associated with sexual pleasure through conditioning. Sociologists look at the ways in which society shapes and encourages certain behaviors.

6 Some of the most common paraphilias include fetishistic disorder, transvestic disorder, sexual sadism disorder, sexual masochism disorder, exhibitionistic disorder, voyeuristic disorder, and pedophilia. A fetish is an inanimate object or a body part (not usually associated with the sex act) that becomes the primary or exclusive focus of sexual arousal and orgasm in an individual. A transvestic disorder involves recurrent and intense sexual arousal from cross-dressing.

7 Sadism refers to the intentional infliction of physical or psychological pain on another person to achieve sexual excitement. Masochists derive sexual pleasure through their own physical pain or psychological humiliation. Exhibitionism is the most common of all reported sexual offenses, and it involves a person becoming sexually aroused primarily from displaying his (or, more rarely, her) genitals. Voyeurs' main means of sexual gratification are in watching unsuspecting persons undressing, naked, or engaging in sexual activity.

8 Pedophilia involves recurrent and intense sexual arousal from prepubescent or pubescent children, which usually causes distress or impairment in important areas of functioning. Pedophiles most often report an attraction to children of a particular age range. Many choose children because they are available and vulnerable; some pedophiles are unable to function sexually with an adult. The Internet has been both helpful and detrimental in the elimination of pedophilia: Pedophiles use it to find each other and talk about their behaviors, but it has also helped to identify pedophiles.

9 People can be sexually attracted to almost anything. Other paraphilias include scatolophilia (obscene telephone calling), frotteurism (rubbing of the genitals on unsuspecting persons), zoophilia (sexual contact with animals), and necrophilia (sexual contact with dead bodies).

10 Although there is a great range in frequency of sexual contact in the general population, some argue that certain people cross over the line from a vigorous sex life to an obsessed sex life. Sexuality, like drugs, alcohol, gambling, and all other behaviors that bring a sense of excitement and pleasure, should involve some degree of moderation. Yet for some people, the need for repeated sexual encounters, which often end up being fleeting and unfulfilling, becomes almost a compulsion; this is often referred to as a sexual addiction or hypersexuality. Many have criticized this concept and argue that terms such as these are really disguised social judgments.

11 Treatment for paraphilias first involves an assessment. This can be done through self-report, behavioral observation, physiological tests, or personality inventories. Overall, the most important goal of therapy must be to change a person's behavior. Treatments for paraphilias may include group, individual, and family therapy; medication; education; and self-help groups. Behavioral methods are most common; techniques include aversion therapy, shame aversion, systematic desensitization, orgasmic reconditioning, and satiation therapy. Pharmacological and surgical interventions, such as testosterone-suppressing drugs, antidepressants, and chemotherapy are also used.

12 It is difficult to determine how to decide whether a sexual behavior is normal or abnormal. Much of society feels uncomfortable with the idea of sex for its own sake, separate from love, intimacy, and human attachment.

CRITICAL THINKING QUESTIONS

1 How do you decide whether a sexual behavior is "normal"? What is your definition of "typical" sexual activity, and where do you draw the line for yourself?

2 Do you think people should be allowed to engage in any sexual behaviors they choose, as long as they don't hurt anyone? Explain.

3 If the majority of people feel that Kiki's behavior (described in the chapter opening story) is distasteful, perverted, or abnormal, should we as a society make her stop doing it? Do you think she is sick? Should she stop engaging in such behaviors? Why or why not?

4 Which theory do you think best explains why a paraphilia might develop? What aspects of this theory make the most sense to you? Why?

5 Suppose that tonight when you are walking by yourself, you are approached by a middle-aged man who flashes you and begins stroking his erect penis. What do you think you would be thinking as he stands in front of you stroking his penis? What do you do? Whom do you tell?

6 Do you think a pedophile's address and photograph should be made public so that neighbors can be aware of his or her crimes against young children? How long should this information be listed? For 1 year? 5 years? 10 years? The rest of the person's life? Explain.

MEDIA RESOURCES

CourseMate brings course concepts to life with interactive learning, study, and exam preparation tools that support the printed textbook. A textbook-specific website, Psychology CourseMate includes an integrated interactive eBook and other interactive learning tools including quizzes, flashcards, videos, and more. If your textbook does not include an access code card, go to CengageBrain.com to gain access.

CENGAGENOW
CengageNOW is an easy-to-use online resource that helps you study in less time to get the grade you want—NOW. Take a pre-test for this chapter and receive a personalized study plan based on your results that will identify the topics you need to review and direct you to online resources to help you master those topics. Then take a post-test to help you determine the concepts you have mastered and what you will need to work on. If your textbook does not include an access code card, go to CengageBrain.com to gain access.

View in Video available in CourseMate and CengageNOW:

Kiki and Kink: A young woman explains her interest in sexual kink and describes various "scenes" she has been involved in.

Professional Dominatrix: Hear from a professional dominatrix about her job.

BDSM: A couple discusses their master/slave relationship.

The Sexual Offender Registry: Student discusses learning her bus driver in H.S. was a registered sex offender.

Sex Addiction: Defining sex addiction, the symptoms, who is susceptible, and whether or not Bill Clinton is considered a sex addict.

Websites:

Community-Academic Consortium for Research on Alternative Sexualities (CARAS) ■ CARAS is dedicated to the support and promotion of excellence in the study of alternative sexualities and the dissemination of research results to the alternative sexuality communities, the public, and the research community.

Sexaholics Anonymous (SA) ■ SA is a fellowship of men and women who share their experience, strength, and hope with each other so they may overcome their sexual addiction and help others recover from sexual addiction or dependency.

Silent Lambs ■ Silent Lambs is a website dedicated to reducing the ability of churches to adopt a "code of silence" when it comes to child sexual abuse that occurs within the church. This website has a variety of links and helpful information; a variety of videos and transcripts are available from recent clergy sexual abuse cases.

Vegan Erotica ■ VeganErotica.com manufactures handcrafted vegan bondage gear, whips, belts, harnesses, and other vegan leather (also known as "pleather") items. Vegan condoms and other sex products are also available. All products are 100% vegetarian and do not contain animal products, nor were they tested on animals.

National Sex Offender Public Registry ■ The National Sex Offender Public Registry, coordinated by the Department of Justice, is a cooperative effort between the state agencies hosting public sexual offender registries and the federal government. This website's search tool has a number of search options that allow a user to submit a single national query to obtain information about sex offenders.

17 Power and Sexual Coercion

View in **Video**

View in **Video**

View in **Video**

View in **Video**

View in **Video**

ABOUT THE CHAPTER OPENING VIDEO – I worked as a rape crisis counselor for many years, and while I found it enormously rewarding, it was also one of the hardest jobs I've ever had. The self-blame that many women experienced after a rape was one of the most difficult aspects of this work. We live in a blame-the-victim society that seems to take rape seriously only when a person is overcome by a stranger in a dark alley. But we all know that rapists can also be our friend, date, or classmate. Each of us makes hundreds of decisions every day, and while many of these are good decisions (such as driving the speed limit or wearing a seat belt), some may be neutral. Going to a particular party, having one too many drinks, walking home alone may not be good decisions, but a person doesn't deserve to be punished for such decisions. When something bad happens to us as a result of that decision, we often second-guess ourselves, wondering, *Why did I go to that party?* or *Why did I get drunk?* Although second-guessing is normal, many people fail to realize that rape often involves one person disrespecting another person. All of these thoughts were running through my head when I met Meg last fall. Although she had agreed to talk to me about her recent experience being raped by an acquaintance, I knew it was going to be difficult for her to share her story with me. As she started to talk to me I could see the pain in her eyes, but I also heard hope in her voice.

Last summer, a group of friends and I decided we were going to cut loose and have fun. All the kids we invited were friends, and many of us had little time to hang out together. We organized a party at a campsite out in the woods so that our loud music and noise wouldn't bother anyone. On the drive there we drank Jäger and Red Bull. Usually I'm the one who is the designated driver because everyone thinks I'm the most responsible of our friends. But this night I decided I was going to have a good time. I

© Masterfile

wasn't worried at all because I was with friends. When we got to the campsite we brought out our coolers of beer and some food and made a fire. Everyone was talking, drinking, laughing, and dancing. But at one point I just knew I had too much to drink. I felt really sick and I wanted to lie down. One couple had brought a tent and my friends took me there to lay down for a bit. I don't remember getting into the tent. What I do remember is waking up with a man on top of me and feeling absolutely terrified._

Although Meg's story is difficult to hear, it also helps motivate us to continue to work toward overcoming our blame-the-victim mentality. ▌

Janell Caroll

"What I do remember is waking up with a man on top of me and feeling absolutely terrified."
—CHAPTER OPENING VIDEO

View in **Video**
To watch the entire interview, go to Psychology CourseMate at **login.cengagebrain.com.**

© Matthew Sorenson

Power is an aspect of all sexual relationships. Sexual relationships are healthy when power is shared and when the relationship empowers the partners. In sexuality, however, as everywhere in human life, power can also be used to degrade and oppress. For example, the act of seduction is usually an interaction between each partner's power, which is partly what makes dating and sexual anticipation so exciting. However, coercive sexuality involves the clash of personal power, with one partner overpowering the other.

Physically or psychologically forcing sexual relations on another person is usually referred to as *rape*. Sexual contact with a minor by an adult is called *child sexual abuse* and, in some societies, is also considered rape. There are also instances in which a person with more power entices, pressures, or encourages another person with less power into sexual activities, ranging from an unwanted glance or word to actual sexual contact. This is sexual harassment. This chapter begins with discussions of rape and sexual assault, and then goes on to explore other ways that power can be misused in relationships.

RAPE AND SEXUAL ASSAULT: Incidence and Theories

For most mammals, penile penetration of a female by a male is done only when the female is in estrus, or "heat," as it is commonly called. However, forced penetration is common in a wide variety of animal species (Lalumière et al., 2005b); for instance, male orangutans often engage in forced mating and vicious biting of the female. Humans can have sexual intercourse at any point in the menstrual cycle, which means other motivations determine when intercourse might take place. However, in humans, male and female desire for sexual contact may not coincide.

DEFINING RAPE and Sexual Assault

The line that separates **rape** from other categories of sexual activity can be blurry because of the fine distinctions between forced and consensual sex, as well as societal patterns of female passivity and male aggression (LaFree, 1982). For instance, societal and cultural rules often dictate that men, not women, should initiate sexual activity. These beliefs about how sex is supposed to be can make defining rape a difficult task. Defining rape is also complicated by the fact that sometimes unwanted sex is consensual. Studies have found that a significant percentage of college students engage in unwanted sexual activity in dating relationships (Brousseau et al., 2011; O'Sullivan & Allgeier, 1998).

The U.S. Department of Justice defines rape as forced sexual intercourse that can include psychological and physiological coercion. This would include forced vaginal, anal, or oral penetration. Psychological coercion would include pressuring someone who has not consented to sexual activity or taking advantage of someone because of his or her intellectual abilities, intoxication, or age (see Table 17.1). **Sexual assault** is defined as any type of sexual contact or behavior that occurs without the consent of the recipient of the unwanted sexual activity. Behaviors that are included in the definition of sexual assault are unwanted penetration, forced oral sex, masturbation, touching, fondling, or kissing. It would also include forcing

someone to view sexually explicit materials, such as pornography. These definitions apply to both male and female victims, and include heterosexual and homosexual rape and sexual assault.

However, these definitions are proposed as guidelines by the U.S. Department of Justice, and exact definitions of rape and sexual assault are determined by individual states. Typically, state definitions include lack of consent, force or threat of force, and vaginal penetration in the definition of rape and sexual assault. Regardless of state definitions, some women do not consider an assault to be rape if a penis was not involved (Bart & O'Brien, 1985). This is because many women view rape as something that is done by a penis (intercourse, fellatio, anal sex) rather than something done to a vagina (digital penetration, cunnilingus, touching).

Debate is ongoing about the appropriate term for a person who has experienced a rape or sexual assault. Although the word *victim* emphasizes the person's lack of responsibility for the incident, it may also imply that the person was a passive recipient of the attack. The term *victim* can also become a permanent label. Some prefer the term *survivor*, which implies that the person had within herself or himself the strength to overcome and to survive the rape. However, for clarity, in this chapter we use the term *victim* to refer to a person who has survived a rape.

RAPE AND Sexual Assault Statistics

In 2008, there were 203,830 victims of rape or sexual assault in the United States, which is 53% less than the number 10 years earlier (Rand, 2009). Although both women and men can be raped, by far the majority of victims are female (Figure 17.1). In the majority of cases, the victims know their assailants (Lawyer et al., 2010). In

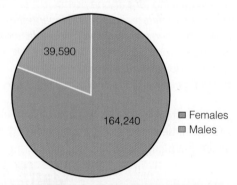

FIGURE **17.1** Reported rapes by sex of victim in the United States, 2008. SOURCE: U.S. Department of Justice, Bureau of Justice Statistics. Criminal Victimization, 2008.

table 17.1 ■ Age of Consent

Many countries, and states within the United States, have legal ages of consent. The age of consent is how old a person must be to be considered capable of legally giving informed consent to engage in sexual acts with another person. It is considered a crime for a person to engage in sexual behavior with someone younger than the age of consent. Many countries and states provide ages of consent for male–male and female–female sex. In some countries, there is no information on specific ages for certain behaviors.

Country	Male–Female Sex	Male–Male Sex	Female–Female Sex
Queensland, Australia	16	18	16
Austria	14	14	14
Bahamas	16	18	18
Botswana	16 for females 14 for males	Illegal for all ages	No information
Denmark	15	15	15
Hong Kong	18 for males 16 for females	21	No information
Croatia	14	14	14
India	16	Illegal for all ages	Illegal for all ages
Italy	14	14	14
Kenya	16	Illegal for all ages	Illegal for all ages
Madagascar	21	21	21
Puerto Rico	14	Illegal for all ages	Illegal for all ages
Saudi Arabia	No age minimum but must be married	Illegal for all ages	Illegal for all ages
South Africa	16	19	19
Swaziland	18	Illegal for all ages	Illegal for all ages
U.S.A.—California	18	18	18
U.S.A.—Connecticut	16	16	16
U.S.A.—Illinois	17	17	17
U.S.A.—New Hampshire	16	18	18
U.S.A.—Pennsylvania	16	16	16

SOURCE: "Legal age of consent." (1998–2000). Retrieved August 3, 2011, from http://www.ageofconsent.com/ageofconsent.htm.

one study, 63% of rapes against women and 100% of rapes against men were committed by someone they knew (Figure 17.2; Rand, 2009). We will primarily discuss the rape of women by men here and later in the chapter will explore the rape of men.

Keep in mind, however, that rape and sexual assault are some of the most underreported crimes in the United States, so it is difficult to assess the actual number of victims (Gonzales et al., 2005). Why are close to half of victims unlikely to report rape? Like Meg, some do not report it because they feel shameful, guilty, embarrassed, or humiliated and don't want people to know (Sable et al., 2006; Shechory & Idisis, 2006). Because victims often know their

assailants and may blame themselves for being with them, these factors can make them less comfortable reporting their attacks (see Figure 17.2). Victims who were using drugs or alcohol before the rape are much less likely to report the rape (Wolitzky-Taylor et al., 2011). Many also worry that their reports will not be taken seriously, their confidentiality will not be maintained, or the attacker will retaliate (Sable et al., 2006).

rape
Forced sexual behavior without a person's consent.

sexual assault
Coercion of a nonconsenting victim to have sexual contact.

table 17.2 ■ Rape Myths

Martha Burt (1980) defined rape myths as prejudicial and stereotyped beliefs about rape, rape victims, and rapists. They often lead people to justify rape by rationalizing what happened and who might be at fault. Frequently they shift the blame for rape to the victims.

Although there are many rape myths, below are some common most common myths.

- Only "bad" women get raped.
- Women make false reports of rape.
- Women fantasize about rape.
- Men can't be raped.
- You can tell a rapist by the way he looks.
- No woman or man can be raped against his or her will.
- A man can't rape his wife.
- Rape only happens to young, attractive women.
- Most rapists rape only once.
- False reporting of rape is common.

Copyright © Cengage Learning 2013

▶▶ CHARACTERISTICS of Rapists

What is your image of a "rapist"? Who is it that rapes? A stranger who jumps out of a bush? A drunk at a fraternity party? What drives someone to commit rape? Anger? Frustration? Even today, the question of why someone would rape remains largely unanswered.

Rapists are primarily male, single, and between the ages of 15 and 30 (Amir, 1971; D. E. H. Russell, 1984). They have been found to have high levels of impulsivity and aggression, sexist views about women, and high levels of rape myth acceptance (see Table 17.2; Beech et al., 2006; Giotakos et al., 2005; Lalumière et al., 2005d; Langevin et al., 2007; Masser et al., 2006). Men who commit sexual assault and rape often have histories of personal violence, such as child physical abuse, child sexual abuse, dating violence, or intimate partner violence (IPV; we will discuss IPV further later in this chapter; Cavanaugh et al., 2011; Lisak & Miller, 2002). Even so, despite the assumption that rapists are psychologically disturbed individuals, research does not support the assumption that they are very different from nonoffenders (Oliver et al., 2007; Voller & Long, 2010).

Rapists often have multiple victims. In fact, research has found that the majority of rapes are perpetrated by serial offenders who have an average of six victims (Lisak & Miller, 2002). Thus, a relatively small number of men are responsible for a large number of rapes, which explains the disparities between the number of men who say they rape and the number of women who say they are raped (Lisak & Miller, 2002). Within this group of men, there are a variety of rapist "types," including the power, anger, and sadistic rapists, which differentiate motivations for rape (J. Douglas & Olshaker, 1998; Hazelwood & Burgess, 1987; McCabe & Wauchope, 2005; Pardue & Arrigo, 2008). Power rapists are motivated by domination and control; anger rapists are motivated by anger and use it in overt ways (i.e., force or weapons); and sadistic rapists are motivated by sexual and aggressive fantasies.

The idea of forcing or coercing a woman to engage in sex is not unusual. In a classic study about the potential to rape, 356 college-age heterosexual men were asked, "If you could be assured that no one would know and that you could in no way be punished for forcing a woman to do something she really didn't want to do (rape), how likely, if at all, would you be to commit such acts?" Sixty percent indicated that under the right circumstances, there was some likelihood that they would use force, rape, or both (Briere & Malamuth, 1983:318). However, this study is dated, so it is difficult to know whether the results would be significantly different today. One study on forcing sex found that 30% of men admitted they might force sex under certain circumstances (Lev-Wiesel, 2004), whereas another study found that 58% of men reported having forced sex on a woman who was unable to consent or who had made her lack of consent clear (Parkhill & Abbey, 2008).

REAL RESEARCH 17.1 One study found that 45% of females and 30% of males who were in a relationship reported being forced into sexual activity by their partner when they didn't want it (BROUSSEAU ET AL., 2011). Such sexual coercion can lead to depression, anxiety, low self-esteem, and a negative view of one's sexual self.

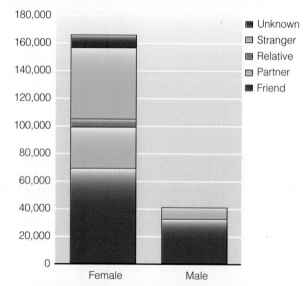

Relationship between Victim and Offender

■ Unknown
□ Stranger
■ Relative
□ Partner
■ Friend

FIGURE **17.2** Number of rapes/sexual assaults by relationship to offender. SOURCE: U.S. Department of Justice, Bureau of Justice Statistics. Criminal Victimization, 2008.

The term *date-rape drug* is slang for any drug that may be used during a sexual assault. This would include Rohypnol (also called *roofies, Forget Pill,* or *Mind Eraser*), gamma-hydroxybutyric acid (GHB; also called *Liquid Ecstasy, Georgia Home Boy,* or *Easy Lay*), and ketamine (also called *Special K, Kit Kat,* or *Cat Valium*). Today, experts refer to rapes using these drugs as "drug-facilitated sexual assault." The effects of these drugs are similar to those of Valium, but they are much more powerful. The drugs go to work quickly, and the time they last varies. If a person has been drinking alcohol when the drugs were ingested, the drug effects will last longer. Adverse effects of these drugs may include drowsiness, memory problems, lower blood pressure, sleepiness, problems talking, dizziness, and impaired motor functions. With higher doses, convulsions, vomiting, loss of consciousness, and coma or death can occur.

Rohypnol is illegal in the United States but is legal in several countries and has been smuggled into the United States. Rohypnol comes in tablet form and is typically placed in a drink, where it quickly dissolves. Once dissolved, the tablets are undetectable—there is no taste or color change to the liquid. Ketamine is a white powder that easily dissolves in a drink, whereas GHB can come in tablet, liquid, or powder form. Ketamine and GHB are both legal and used for different medical purposes. The effects of these drugs usually begin within

Coasters like these include test patches that can show the presence of date-rape drugs in a drink.

30 minutes, peak within 2 hours, and can last a total of 8 hours. An individual may feel nauseous, hot or cold, and dizzy within 10 minutes after ingesting these drugs.

You can protect yourself from drug-facilitated sexual assault by never accepting drinks from other people, opening your drinks yourself, and never leaving your drink unattended. If you think you have been drugged, it is important to go to a police station or hospital as soon as possible because a urine test can check for the presence of the drugs. These drugs can leave your body within 12 to 72 hours, so it is important to get a urine test as soon as possible. For more information about date-rape drugs, check the website listings at the end of this chapter.

Although it is important to be aware of these drugs, many experts argue that focusing on these drugs in sexual crimes often turns our attention away from other drugs, such as alcohol and/or street drugs, that are often associated with sexual assault (Németh et al., 2010). In fact, alcohol is the most common "rape drug" (Littleton et al., 2009a).

▶▶ THEORIES **about Rape**

What drives someone to rape another person? We discuss the most prominent theories of why rape occurs, including rapist psychopathology, victim precipitation, and feminist, sociological, and evolutionary theories.

Rapist Psychopathology: A Disease Model

Modern ideas about why rape occurs evolved first from psychiatric theories, which suggested that men rape because of mental illness, uncontrollable sexual urges, or alcohol intoxication. This theory of **rapist psychopathology** suggests that it is either disease or intoxication that forces men to rape, and that if they did not have these problems, they would not rape.

According to this theory, the rape rate can be reduced by finding these sick individuals and rehabilitating them. The theory makes people feel safer because it suggests that only sick individuals rape, not "normal" people. However, research consistently fails to identify any significant distinguishing characteristics of rapists (Fernandez & Marshall, 2003). Having psychological or alcohol problems does not predispose a person to be a rapist. In fact, men who rape are often found to be

ON YOUR MIND **17.2**

My ex-boyfriend forced me to have sex with him. Since I dated him in the past, does that mean this is not rape?

It does not matter if you have had a sexual relationship with someone in the past—if it is nonconsensual, it is rape. Rape can, and does, occur between an offender and victim who have a preexisting relationship (often referred to as "date rape" or "acquaintance rape"), and even between spouses and partners, which we will talk about later in this chapter.

nearly "normal" in every other way. Perhaps it is easier to see rapists as somehow sick than realize that the potential to rape exists in many of us.

Theories of rapist psychopathology were very common until the 1950s, when feminist researchers began to refocus attention on rape's effect on the victim rather than on the offender. However,

rapist psychopathology
A theory of rape that identifies psychological issues in a rapist that contribute to rape behavior.

there are still those who accept psychopathological theories today. In fact, college students often report that this theory helps to explain stranger rape but does not help us to understand date or acquaintance rape (Cowan, 2000).

Victim Precipitation Theory: Blaming the Victim

In the chapter opening story, I discussed how many people might believe that a woman does something to put herself at risk for rape. The **victim precipitation theory** explores the ways victims make themselves vulnerable to rape, such as how they dress or act or where they walk (Wakelin, 2003). By focusing on the victim and ignoring the motivations of the attacker, many have labeled this a blame-the-victim theory.

The victim precipitation theory of rape shifts the responsibility from the person who knowingly attacked to the innocent victim (Sawyer et al., 2002): *"She was walking home too late at night," "She was drunk," "She was wearing a really short skirt,"* or *"She was flirting."* Women who wear suggestive clothing and drink alcohol are perceived as having greater sexual intent than women who wear neutral attire and do not drink alcohol (Maurer & Robinson, 2008). The women who wear suggestive clothing and drink alcohol are also viewed as being more responsible for a sexual assault (Maurer & Robinson, 2008).

The victim precipitation theory of rape shifts the responsibility from the person who knowingly attacked to the innocent victim.

The victim precipitation theory also serves to distance people from the reality of rape and lulls them into the false assumption that it could not happen to them or someone close to them because they would not act like "those other women." If we believe bad things happen to people who take risks, then we are safe if we do not take those risks.

In Susan Brownmiller's (1975) classic work on gender and rape, she argues that rape forces a woman to stay in at night, to monitor her behavior, and to look to men for protection. This attitude also contributes to a rape victim's guilt because she then wonders, *If I hadn't worn what I did, walked where I walked, or acted as I did, maybe I wouldn't have been raped.* Overall, men are more likely than women to believe in the victim precipitation theory and to view sexual coercion as acceptable (Auster & Leone, 2001; Proto-Campise et al., 1998).

Feminist Theory: Keeping Women in Their Place

Feminist theorists contend that rape and the threat of rape are tools used in our society to keep women in their place. This fear keeps women in traditional sex roles, which are subordinate to men's. Feminist theorists believe that the social, economic, and political separation of the genders has encouraged rape, which is viewed as an act of domination of men over women (Hines, 2007; Murnen et al., 2002). Sex-role stereotyping—which reinforces the idea that men are supposed to be strong, aggressive, and assertive, whereas women are expected to be slim, weak, and passive—encourages rape in our culture (Murnen et al., 2002).

Sociological Theory: Balance of Power

Sociological theory and feminist theory have much in common; in fact, many feminist theorists are sociologists. Sociologists believe that rape is an expression of power differentials in society (T. A. Martin, 2003). When men feel disempowered by society, by changing sex roles, or by their jobs, overpowering women with the symbol of their masculinity (a penis) reinforces, for a moment, men's control over the world.

Sociologists explore the ways people guard their interests in society. For example, the wealthy class in a society may fear the poorer classes, who are larger in number and envy the possessions of the upper class. Because women have been viewed as "possessions" of men throughout most of Western history, fear of the lower classes often manifested itself in a belief that lower-class males were "after our wives and daughters." During the slavery period in the United States, for example, it was widely believed that, if given the chance, Black males would rape White women, whereas White males did not find Black women attractive. Yet the truth was just the opposite: Rape of White women by Black males was relatively rare, whereas many White slave masters routinely raped their Black slaves. Once again, this supports the idea that rape is a reflection of power issues rather than just sexual issues.

Evolutionary Theory: Product of Evolution

Finally, a controversial theory on the origins of rape came out of evolutionary theory. Randy Thornhill and Craig Palmer, authors of *Natural History of Rape: Biological Bases of Sexual Coercion*, propose that rape is rooted in human evolution (Thornhill & Palmer, 2000). According to evolutionary theory, men and women have developed differing reproductive strategies, wherein men desire frequent mating to spread their seed, and women are designed to protect their eggs and be more selective in choosing mates (see Chapter 2 for more information about evolutionary theory). Rape has developed as a consequence of these differences in reproductive strategies. The majority of rapists are male, Thornhill and Palmer assert, because men are designed to impregnate and spread their seed.

As we pointed out, this theory is controversial, and many feminists and sociologists alike are upset about ideas proposed in this theory (Brownmiller, 2000; Roughgarden, 2004). However, controversial or not, it is an interesting argument for us to consider when discussing theories on the development of rape.

victim precipitation theory
A theory of rape that identifies victim characteristics or behaviors that contribute to rape.

feminist theory
A theory of rape that contends that rape is a tool used in society to keep a woman in her place.

sociological theory
A theory of rape that identifies power differentials in society as causing rape.

1 Explain why there is no single definition of rape.

2 Describe the problems that have been encountered in attempting to identify the actual number of rapes.

3 Identify what researchers have found about the characteristics of rapists.

4 Explain the disparities between the number of women who say they were raped and the number of men who say they have raped.

5 Identify and differentiate between the five theories of rape.

▶ RAPE ATTITUDES
and Cultural Variations

Studies have found gender and ethnic variations in attitudes about rape. In addition, cultural issues can affect how a society defines rape and the attitudes toward it. We discuss these issues in the following sections.

▶▶ GENDER DIFFERENCES
in Attitudes about Rape

Researchers have used many techniques to measure attitudes about rape and rape victims, such as questionnaires, written vignettes, mock trials, videotaped scenarios, still photography, and newspaper reports. Overall, men are less empathetic and sensitive than women toward rape (Black & Gold, 2008; Davies et al., 2009; Earnshaw et al., 2011; Schneider et al., 2009). Men believe more rape myths and tend to blame victims more than women (see Table 17.2; Earnshaw et al., 2011; Franiuk et al., 2008). Studies have found that heterosexual men are more likely than heterosexual women to believe that a man should expect sexual intercourse if the man pays for an expensive date (Basow & Minieri, 2011; Emmers-Sommer et al., 2010); however, there were no expectations for sex when the expenses were split.

However, some hope exists about changing these attitudes about rape. Men who take rape education workshops or college courses on violence against women have less rape myth acceptance than men who do not take such workshops or courses (Currier & Carlson, 2009; Foubert & Cremedy, 2007). Rape prevention programs for male college students have also been related to both attitudinal and behavioral changes (Foubert et al., 2010a, 2010b). Men who took these classes also reported less likelihood to commit sexual assault when they or a potential partner was under the influence of alcohol.

▶▶ ETHNIC DIFFERENCES
in Attitudes about Rape

Although the majority of the research has examined gender differences in attitudes about rape, there is also research on ethnicity differences in rape attitudes. Overall, ethnic minorities have been found to have more traditional attitudes toward women, which have been found to affect rape attitudes. For example, among college students, non-Hispanic Whites are more sympathetic than Blacks to women who have been raped (Nagel et al., 2005). However, Blacks are more sympathetic than either Hispanic or Japanese American college students (Fischer, 1987; Littleton et al., 2007; Yamawaki & Tschanz, 2005). Asian American students have the least sympathy for women who have been raped and are more likely to hold a rape victim responsible for the rape and excuse the rapist (Devdas & Rubin, 2007; J. Lee et al., 2005; Yamawaki & Tschanz, 2005).

Researchers suggest that these differences are due to variations in cultural gender roles and conservative attitudes about sexuality. It is important to keep in mind that within these ethnic groups, there are also gender differences in attitudes about rape, with women more supportive of rape victims than men.

▶▶ RAPE IN
Different Cultures

Rape is defined differently around the world, so the incidence of rape varies depending on a culture's definition (see Figure 17.3 for more information). One culture might accept sexual behavior that is considered rape in another culture. For example, rape has been accepted as a punishment in some cultures throughout history. Among the Cheyenne Indians, a husband who suspected his wife of infidelity could put her "out to field," where other men were encouraged to rape her (Hoebel, 1954). In the Marshall Islands of the Pacific Ocean, women were seen as the property of the males, and any male could force sexual intercourse on them (Sanday, 1981). In Kenya, the Gusii people view intercourse as an act in which males overpower their female partners and cause them considerable pain. In fact, if the female has difficulty walking the next morning, the man is seen as a "real man" and will boast of his ability to make his partner cry (Bart & O'Brien, 1985). In 2002, an 11-year-old Pakistani boy was found guilty of walking unchaperoned with a girl from a different tribe. His punishment involved the gang-raping of his 18-year-old sister, which was done to shame his family. The gang rape took place in a mud hut while hundreds of people stood by and laughed and cheered (Tanveer, 2002).

South Africa has one of the highest reported rape rates in the world. In fact, a female born in South Africa has a greater chance of being raped in her lifetime than of learning to read (Dempster, 2002). High rape rates are primarily due to a wide variety of social and cultural issues, including economic issues, gender inequality, the sexual entitlement of men, and an acceptance of violence against women (Jewkes et al., 2009a, 2009b). Poverty and economic issues often force large families to sleep in the same bedroom, which exposes young children to sex at an early age (Phillips, 2001). South African men are raised with a strong sense of male sexual entitlement. This shouldn't be surprising, especially when you consider that South Africa's president, Jacob Zuma, was tried for rape in 2006, but later acknowledged engaging in unprotected sex with the HIV-positive daughter of a family friend (McDougall, 2010). Throughout the trial, Zuma's supporters burned photographs of the woman who accused him (McDougall, 2010).

Overall, a female born in South Africa has a 50% chance of being raped in her lifetime (Shields, 2010). Many of these rapes involve gang rapes or involve multiple acts of penetration (Vetten et al., 2008). Gang rapes are often viewed as a part of the culture and may be considered a form of male bonding (Jewkes et al., 2009b). In addition to high rape rates, South Africa also has the largest number of people living with HIV. In fact, a woman who is raped by a man older than 25 years has a 25% chance of her rapist being HIV-positive (Jewkes et al., 2009b). Women who are raped in South Africa often do not report the rape and instead live in social isolation and fear. Those who do report the rape often face retribution and threats of murder.

A study by the Medical Research Council of South Africa found that 1 in 4 men had raped a woman or a girl in their lifetime, and nearly half of these men said they raped more than once (Jewkes et al., 2009a). Several factors were associated with the likelihood of having committed rape, including age, levels of education, and early childhood experiences. Men who raped were more likely to be between the ages of 20 and 40 years and have higher levels of education than those who did not rape (Jewkes et al., 2009a). They were also more likely to have experienced teasing, harassment, or bullying in childhood, and engage in various risky sexual behaviors, including multiple sex partners, sex with a prostitute, and a lack of condom use.

South Africa also has the highest rates of child rape in the world. It is estimated that a child is raped every 26 seconds (Jewkes et al., 2009a; McDougall, 2010). Studies have found that approximately 40% of girls and boys report being sexually abused at some point in their childhood (for comparison, sexual abuse rates in U.S. children are 28% and 17% in girls and boys, respectively; Lichtenberg, 2011). Children are often raped first by relatives in South Africa. One father, who had been raping his 11-year-old daughter for a year, said, *"My child cannot sleep with other men until I have slept with her first"* (Shields, 2010). Even Oprah Winfrey was forced to take notice of these events when several girls at her exclusive school for underprivileged

© Mike Hutchings/Reuters/Corbis

Rapex, an antirape condom worn by women, was unveiled in South Africa in 2005. The South African inventor, shown here, advises women to insert the device as part of their daily security routine. During rape, metal barbs in the condom will hook into the skin of the penis and immediately disable the man, allowing the woman to get away. The barbs must be surgically removed, so a rapist will need to seek medical attention, enabling the police to identify him.

Rape has also been used for initiation purposes. In East Africa, the Kikuyu previously had an initiation ritual in which a young boy was expected to rape to prove his manhood (Broude & Greene, 1976). Until he did this, he could not engage in sexual intercourse or marry a woman. In Australia, among the Arunta, rape serves as an initiation rite for girls. After the ceremonial rape, she is given to her husband, and no one else has access to her (Broude & Greene, 1976).

Many cultural beliefs and societal issues are responsible for the high rape rates in South Africa, including the fact that South African women have a difficult time saying no to sex; many men

girls outside of Johannesburg were victims of sexual violence (Lichtenberg, 2011). For many years, a persistent myth existed that having sex with a virgin can cure AIDS (Phillips, 2001). As a result, babies, some as young as 8 months old, were being gang-raped by HIV-positive men. The rape of infants poses many challenges, including the inability of the child to identify the rapist and a lack of DNA evidence because highly absorbent, disposable diapers often make it impossible to retrieve evidence (McDougall, 2010). Overall, conviction rate of child and baby rapists in South Africa is extremely low—only about 7% of rapists are ever found guilty (Ghanotakis, 2008).

Finally, another troubling practice in South Africa is that of *corrective rape,* in which a lesbian woman is raped to "cure" her of her sexual orientation

(Kelly, 2009). Homophobia is rampant in South Africa, and this became painfully clear when Eudy Simelane, a star of South Africa's national female soccer team who was living openly as a lesbian, was gang-raped and brutally beaten and stabbed in 2008 (Bearak, 2009). A South African gay rights organization found that 86% of Black lesbians say they live in fear of sexual assaults (Kelly, 2009).

Efforts to reduce the rape rates include educational campaigns, improved legislation, and increasing the prosecution of rapists and the penalties for rape. Educational interventions are now available to empower children and other adults and help them to understand sexual violence. It is hoped that all of these efforts will eventually decrease the skyrocketing rape rates in South Africa.

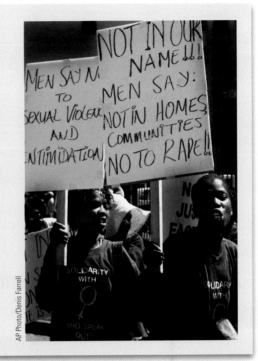

believe they are entitled to sex and believe that women enjoy being raped (Meier, 2002). In 2005, an anti-rape female condom was unveiled in South Africa (Dixon, 2005). This device was controversial, with some believing that it put the responsibility for the problem on the shoulders of South African women, and others believing that the device was a valuable tool in decreasing the climbing rape rates in South Africa. (See the accompanying Sexual Diversity in Our World feature for more information about rape in South Africa.)

Asian cultures often have more conservative attitudes about sex; because of this, there is often more tolerance for rape myths (M. A. Kennedy & Gorzalka, 2002; Uji et al., 2007; Yamawaki, 2007). Research by Sanday (1981) indicates that the primary cultural factors that affect the incidence of rape in a society include relations between the sexes, the status of women, and male attitudes in the society. Societies that promote male violence have higher incidences of rape because men are socialized to be aggressive, dominating, and to use force to get what they want.

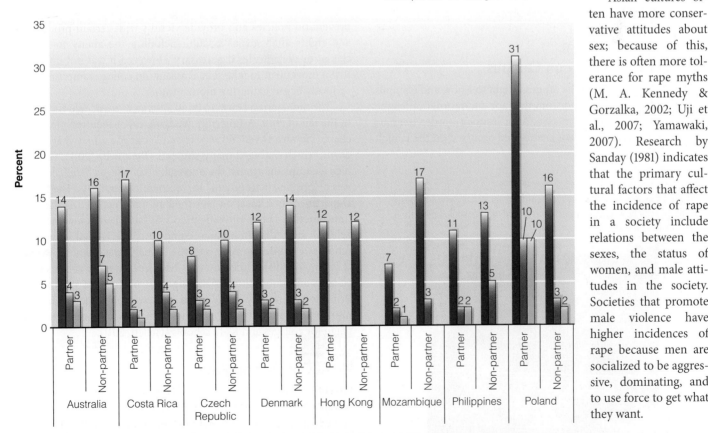

FIGURE **17.3** Reported rapes and convictions in select countries. SOURCE: Johnson, H., Ollus, N., & Nevala, S. (2008). *Violence against women: An international perspective.* New York: Springer Science and Business.

1 Discuss the research on gender differences in attitudes about rape.

2 Explain the impact of educational programs on attitudes and behaviors about rape.

3 Discuss the research on ethnicity differences in attitudes about rape.

4 Explain how rape is defined differently around the world and how rape rates vary depending on a culture's definition.

▶ RAPE AND SEXUAL ASSAULT on Campus

Female college students are at greater risk for rape than their non-college peers (Gonzales et al., 2005). It is estimated that 1 of every 5 college women will experience a rape during college. The majority of these rapes will be perpetrated by someone the women know, which is why most cases are never reported (B.S. Fisher et al., 2000).

In Chapter 7, we discussed stalking in intimate relationships. Some women report being stalked on campus, either physically or through notes and e-mails. Overall, a total of 8% to 16% of women and 2% to 7% of men report being stalked at some point in their lives (Dennison & Thomson, 2005). Stalking is a serious problem, especially given that 81% of women who have been stalked by a heterosexual partner were also physically assaulted by that partner and 31% were sexually assaulted by him (Tjaden & Thoennes, 1998).

▶▶ RAPE AND SEXUAL ASSAULT Legislation on Campus

In 1990, Congress passed the Student Right to Know and Campus Security Act, which resulted from the rape and murder of Jeanne Clery at Lehigh University in 1986. After Jeanne's murder, her parents found out that 38 violent crimes had occurred on the Lehigh

Alcohol can sexualize the environment for men. A man who has been drinking may believe that a woman is signaling she is available when she is acting friendly.

© Peter M. Fisher/Corbis

ON YOUR MIND 17.3

What if you are drunk and she is, too, and when you wake up in the morning, she says you raped her?

Claims of rape must be taken seriously. This is why men and women should be very careful in using alcohol and engaging in sexual activity. The best approach would be to delay engaging in sexual activity if you have been drinking. This way, you will not find yourself in this situation.

campus in the 3 years before her murder. Working with other parents and groups, they fought for Congress to pass a law requiring colleges and universities to make information about sexual crimes public. In 1992, the Campus Sexual Assault Victims' Bill of Rights was added, which required colleges and universities to develop prevention policies and provide victims with certain protections and rights after sexual assault, including the ability to change classes or dormitories if necessary. However, it was not until 2011 that a movement to take sexual assault on college campuses more seriously began gathering momentum.

The momentum began to build after an event at Yale University in the fall of 2010. A fraternity pledging event required pledges to chant *"No means yes! Yes means anal!"* outside a first-year female dorm, which outraged many students (Berkowitz, 2011). Students filed a complaint against the university that alleged Yale University was a "hostile environment" for women (Slater, 2011). The federal Department of Education launched an investigation. At the same time, another federal investigation was launched at Harvard Law School, after discrimination complaints were filed about the school's responses to rape and the sexual harassment of women (Lauerman, 2011). Other lawsuits have been filed at various other colleges and universities, including the University of Virginia and Princeton University. In response to these events, the Obama Administration announced a national sexual assault awareness campaign for colleges and K–12 schools (Hallett, 2011).

▶▶ ALCOHOL and Rape

On college campuses, alcohol use is one of the strongest predictors of rape—up to two thirds of rape victims have voluntarily consumed alcohol before an assault (Lawyer et al., 2010; Littleton et al., 2009a). Women who are drunk are more likely to be viewed as "loose" or sexually "easy" (Parks & Scheidt, 2000). For men, alco-

Yale University student, Hannah Zeavin, was one of a handful of students who signed the complaint accusing the university of violating Title IX in 2011. She knew of several women who had been sexually assaulted on campus.

hol seems to "sexualize" the environment around them. Cues that might be taken as neutral if the men were not drunk (such as a certain woman talking to them or dancing with them) may be seen as an indication of sexual interest (Abbey et al., 2005; Montemurro & McClure, 2005; Peralta, 2008). Alcohol also reduces inhibitions, which increases the chances of engaging in risky sexual behaviors for both men and women (Klein et al., 2007; Maisto et al., 2004; O'Hare, 2005; see Chapter 15 for a discussion of high-risk sexual behaviors).

Alcohol use on college campuses, as it relates to rape, is viewed very differently for men and women. A man who is drunk and is accused of rape is seen as less responsible because he was drinking ("*Lighten up; he didn't even know what he was doing.*"), whereas a woman who has been drinking is seen as more responsible for her behavior ("*Can you believe her? She's had so much to drink that she's flirting with everyone—what a slut!*"; Peralta, 2008; D. Richardson & Campbell, 1982; Scully & Marolla, 1983).

> *Alcohol reduces inhibitions,* which increases the chances of engaging in risky sexual behaviors for both men and women.

Being impaired or incapacitated during a rape has been associated with self-blame, stigma, and problematic alcohol use in victims post-assault (Littleton et al., 2009a). In addition, many women might not even label the event as a rape even when it clearly was (L. G. Hensley, 2002).

▶▶ FRATERNITIES and Rape

Initially, Greek organizations were established to help students join together to participate in social issues that they felt were largely ignored by their respective universities (Bryan, 1987). Today, however, many fraternities and sororities operate primarily for socializing. Although rape does occur in residence halls and off-campus apartments, there are several ways in which fraternities create a riper environment for rape. Many fraternities revolve around an ethic of masculinity. Values that the members see as important include competition, dominance, willingness to drink alcohol, and sexual prowess. There is considerable pressure to be sexually successful, and the members gain respect from other

members through sex (Flanagan, 2011; Murnen & Kohlman, 2007). The emphasis on masculinity, secrecy, and the protection of the group often provides a fertile environment for coercive sexuality (Adams-Curtis & Forbes, 2004). In addition, fraternity men have been found to be more accepting of rape myths (Bleecker & Murnen, 2005).

Many fraternities today sponsor rape and sexual assault prevention programs, and invite guest speakers from **rape crisis centers** to discuss the problem of date rape. As we discussed earlier, studies have found that these programs contribute to positive attitudinal and behavioral changes (Foubert et al., 2010a, 2010b). Men who attend such programs are less likely to commit sexual assaults (Currier & Carlson, 2009; Foubert & Cremedy, 2007).

▶▶ ATHLETES and Rape

Over the last few years it has become increasingly more common to hear stories in the news about college and professional athletes who are accused of rape or sexual assault (Farr & Kern, 2010; Lundstrom & Walsh, 2010; Namuo, 2010; Tramel, 2011). Participation in athletics has been found to be associated with rape-supportive attitudes and, to a lesser degree, sexually aggressive behavior (Murnen & Kohlman, 2007). In addition, athletes who participate on teams that produce revenue have higher rates of sexually abusive behavior than athletes on teams that do not produce revenue (McMahon, 2004). Researchers suggest that perhaps it is the sense of privilege that contributes to a view of the world in which rape is legitimized. Playing sports may also help connect aggression and sexuality.

Some researchers suggest that all male groups may foster "hypermasculinity," which promotes the idea that violence and aggression are "manly" (Muehlenhard & Cook, 1988). The need to be aggressive and tough while playing sports may also help create problems off the field (Boeringer, 1999; T. J. Brown et al., 2002). Many male athletes may also have a distorted view of women, which often revolves around views expressed in the locker room. Locker room talk often includes derogatory language about women (including the use of words such as "sluts" or "bitches" to describe them), whereas those athletes who are not playing well are referred to as "girls" (McMahon, 2004; Murnen & Kohlman, 2007).

Research on female athletes has found that these athletes often believe they are less at risk than female nonathletes (McMahon, 2004). When asked about the potential for a female athlete to be raped, one woman said:

> *I think it would be a shock to a female athlete—because, we feel that we're so tough.…I always am kidding around that like, I could sit on a guy and knock the wind out of him and the idea of a guy taking advantage of me seems…well, that could never happen.…I work out all the time, I'm so strong.…I'm not some little girl. I'm tough.* (McMahon, 2004, p. 16)

rape crisis centers
Organizations that offer support services to victims of sexual assault, their families, and friends. Many offer information, referrals, support groups, counseling, educational programs, and workshops.

Female athletes are also more likely to blame-the-victim for a rape than female nonathletes, and believe that some women who are raped have put themselves in a bad situation (McMahon, 2004).

REAL RESEARCH 17.2   When college students were asked described a bad hookup scenario, the majority focused on negative psychological consequences, such as shame, and did not identify the possibility of rape (LITTLETON, ET AL., 2009B).

◀ review QUESTIONS

1 Explain what we know about rape on campus.

2 Explain the role that alcohol plays in rape on college campuses.

3 Explain the research on fraternity membership and rape on college campuses.

4 Explain the research on athletes, athletics, and rape on college campuses.

▶ EFFECTS of Rape

Rape is an emotionally, physically, and psychologically shattering experience for the victim. Some deny that the rape occurred at all, to avoid the pain of dealing with it. Others express self-blame, disbelief, anger, vulnerability, and increased feelings of dependency. As time goes by, the healing process begins, and feelings may shift to self-pity, sadness, and guilt. Anxiety attacks, nightmares, and fear slowly begin to decrease, although the incident is never forgotten. Some women never return to prior functioning levels and must create an entirely new view of themselves.

▶▶ RAPE TRAUMA Syndrome

Researchers Burgess and Holmstrom (1979) coined the term **rape trauma syndrome (RTS),** which describes the effects of rape. RTS is a two-stage stress response pattern characterized by physical, psychological, behavioral, sexual problems, or a combination of these, and it occurs after forced, nonconsenting sexual activity. Although the *Diagnostic and Statistical Manual of Mental Disorders* does not recognize RTS, symptoms are similar to posttraumatic stress disorder (PTSD), which occurs after a traumatic event. Research has found that a significant number of rape survivors develop PTSD within 2 weeks after the rape (Littleton & Henderson, 2009; Taft et al., 2009).

Although not all victims respond to rape in the same manner, what follows is a description of what typically occurs. During the

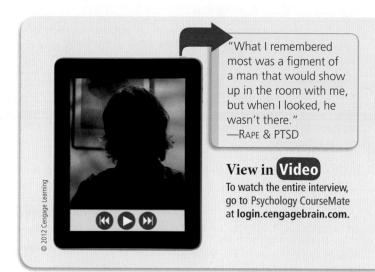

"What I remembered most was a figment of a man that would show up in the room with me, but when I looked, he wasn't there."
—RAPE & PTSD

View in Video
To watch the entire interview, go to Psychology CourseMate at **login.cengagebrain.com.**

© 2012 Cengage Learning

rape trauma syndrome (RTS)
A two-stage stress response pattern that occurs after a rape.

acute phase
First stage of the rape trauma syndrome, in which a victim often feels shock, fear, anger, or other related feelings.

long-term reorganization
The second stage of the rape trauma syndrome, which involves a restoration of order in the victim's lifestyle and reestablishment of control.

first stage of RTS, the **acute phase,** most victims fear being alone, strangers, or even their bedroom or their car if that is where the rape took place. Other emotional reactions to rape include anger (at the assailant, the rape, health care workers, family, oneself, court), anxiety, depression, confusion, shock, disbelief, incoherence, guilt, humiliation, shame, and self-blame (Frazier, 2000). A victim may also experience wide mood fluctuations. Difficulties with sleeping, including recurrent nightmares, are common. This phase begins immediately after the assault, may last from days to weeks, and involves several stress-related symptoms.

The majority of victims eventually talk to someone about the rape (B. S. Fisher et al., 2003). Most of the time a victim will talk to friends or family members rather than to the police. Younger victims are more likely to tell someone than are older victims, perhaps because older victims blame themselves more for the rape and may fear that others also will blame them. One study found that half of the

During the first stage of rape trauma syndrome, victims may feel depressed, confused, angry, guilty, or humiliated. Taking to a counselor can be very helpful in working through these feelings.

ON YOUR MIND **17.4**

Do women who are raped eventually have a normal sex life?

Although it may take anywhere from a few days to months, most rape victims report that their sex lives get back to what is normal for them (van Berlo & Ensink, 2000). However, research indicates that lesbian women may have more difficulties with sexual problems post-rape (Long et al., 2007). Counseling, a supportive partner, and emotional support are extremely helpful.

(if there was oral sex), genital itching or burning, and rectal bleeding or pain (if there was anal sex). In women, the emotional stress of the rape may also cause menstrual irregularities. However, some of these symptoms (nausea and menstrual irregularities) are also signs of pregnancy, which is why a pregnancy test is of utmost importance after a victim has been raped. Research has found there is a greater incidence of pregnancy in women who have been raped than in women who engage in consensual unprotected vaginal intercourse (Gottschall & Gottschall, 2003). However, it is also true that women in prime fertile ages are overrepresented in rape victim statistics.

Long-term reorganization, stage two of RTS, involves restoring order in the victim's lifestyle and reestablishing control. Many victims report that changing some aspect of their lives, such as changing addresses, roommates, universities, or even phone numbers, helped them to gain control. Symptoms from both stages can persist for 1 to 2 years after the rape (Nadelson et al., 1982), although Burgess and Holmstrom (1979) found that 74% of rape victims recovered within 5 years. Recovery is affected by the amount and quality of care that the victim received after the rape. Positive crisis intervention and the support of others decrease the symptoms of the trauma.

In the past, many researchers have argued that rape is a violent crime, not a sexual one. "Desexualizing" rape, or taking the sexual aspect out of it, has de-emphasized post-rape sexual concerns (Wakelin, 2003). Rape is indeed both a violent and a sexual crime, and the majority of victims report experiencing sexual problems post-rape, even though these problems may not be lifelong (J. V. Becker et al., 1986; Burgess & Holmstrom, 1979; Van Berlo & Ensink, 2000).

Changes in sexual behaviors and sexual difficulties can persist for a considerable period after the rape (Campbell et al., 2004). It can take weeks, months, or even years to work through sexual difficulties such as fear of sex, desire and arousal disorders, and specific problems with sexual behaviors such as sexual intercourse, genital fondling, and oral sex. Counseling can be helpful for women suffering from post-rape sexual difficulties. It is not uncommon for a woman to seek help for a sexual problem, such as anorgasmia (lack of orgasm), and during the course of therapy reveal an experience with rape that she had never discussed. Some women may become more sexual after a rape. In fact, one study found an increase in alcohol consumption post-rape, which increased the likelihood of engaging in risky sexual behaviors with multiple partners (Deliramich & Gray, 2008).

women who were raped waited years before telling anyone (Monroe et al., 2005). Overall, women who speak out about their rape experiences and experience negative reactions often stop talking about it (Ahrens, 2006). Negative reactions lead to increased self-blame and uncertainty about whether the experience qualified as rape, and they increase the likelihood of PTSD (Ullman et al., 2007).

Depression often follows a rape, and some victims report still feeling depressed 8 to 12 months after the rape. Women who have a history of prior psychological problems, prior victimization, and/or a tendency to self-blame have a greater risk for depression (Cheasty et al., 2002; Frazier, 2000). Sometimes depression is so severe that victims' thoughts turn to suicide (Bridgeland et al., 2001).

Emotional reactions also vary depending on whether the victims knew their assailants. Women who report being raped by strangers experience more anxiety, fear, and startle responses, whereas those raped by acquaintances usually report more depression and guilt and decreased self-confidence (Sorenson & Brown, 1990). The majority of women who are raped know their assailant and may have initially trusted him and agreed to be with him. After the rape, they may second-guess themselves, wondering how they could have had such bad judgment or why they didn't see it coming. Many also feel a sense of betrayal. Women who feel guilty or responsible for a rape have lower levels of psychological well-being than women who do not feel responsible or guilty (Glenn & Byers, 2009).

Physical symptoms after a rape include general body soreness, bruises, nausea, throat soreness and difficulties swallowing

Depression often follows a rape with *some victims feeling depresssed 8 to 12 months after the rape.*

▶▶ SILENT Rape Reaction

Some victims never discuss their rape with anyone and carry the burden of the assault alone. Burgess and Holmstrom (1974) call this the **silent rape reaction,** and in many ways, it is similar to RTS. Feelings of fear, anger, and depression and physiological symptoms still exist; however, they remain locked inside. In fact, those who take longer to confide in someone usually suffer a longer recovery period (L. Cohen & Roth, 1987).

The silent rape reaction occurs because some victims deny and repress the incident until a time when they feel stronger emotionally. This may be months or even years later. A student of mine, who had been raped 3 years earlier, was taking a course in psychology and noticed with frustration that as she read each chapter of the textbook, she would become extremely anxious when she saw the word *therapist.* When she explored why this produced anxiety, she realized that she could read the word only as *the rapist,* and it frightened her. Perhaps her subconscious was letting her know that she was finally ready to work through the repressed experience. Slowly the memories of the rape came back, as did all of the pain and sorrow from the attack. After 2 months in counseling, she had worked through the memories sufficiently to feel that she was on her way to resolving her feelings about the rape.

▶▶ RAPE OF PARTNERS
and Other Special Populations

Although we have learned from the research that certain groups are at greater risk for rape and sexual assault, we also know that some special populations are also at risk, including spouses, lesbians, older women, women with disabilities, and prostitutes.

Marital Rape

Marital rape has been a crime in all 50 states since 1993. However, 30 states have exemptions for husbands who force sex under certain conditions (e.g., his wife is unconscious, asleep, or mentally impaired; Bergen, 2006). A woman's consent is often assumed when there is a marital contract (Bergen, 2006). It has been estimated that 10% to 14% of all married women are raped by their husbands, although this number is much higher in battered women (D. E. H. Russell & Howell, 1983; Yllo & Finkelhor, 1985).

Although their symptoms are similar to those who are victims of nonmarital rape, many of these women report feeling extremely betrayed and may lose the ability to trust others, especially men. In addition, there is often little social support for wives who are raped, and those who stay with their husbands often endure repeated attacks (Bergen & Bukovec, 2006). Unfortunately, marital rape may be one of the least discussed types of rape.

Lesbians and Bisexuals

Rape is a common experience in both lesbian and bisexual women. In fact, adult sexual assault by men is slightly higher in lesbian and bisexual women compared with heterosexual women (Balsam et al., 2005). Like heterosexual women, lesbian and bisexual women experience RTS after a rape. However, there may be more intense emotional repercussions compared with heterosexual women (Campbell, 2008; Long et al., 2007). Lesbians may also experience difficulties in assimilating the experience of rape into their own

Mel Curtis/Getty Images

Older women are also victims of rape and may experience increased trauma because of declining physical health and more conservative attitudes about sexuality.

self-image (Long et al., 2007). They may be "feminist-identified" in most areas of their lives, and the rape may force them to reexamine the patriarchal society and their feelings about men. Some lesbians may have never experienced vaginal intercourse with a man and may be unaccustomed to dealing with the fear of pregnancy, let alone the extreme feelings of being violated and abused. Although very little research on this topic is available, lesbians can also be raped by women (Campbell, 2008).

Older Women

Many people believe that rape happens only to younger women. It is difficult to think about our mothers or grandmothers being raped. The stereotype that only young, attractive women are raped prevents our thinking about the risk for rape for older women. Although it is true that younger women are more at risk for rape, older women are also raped (Ball, 2005; Burgess & Morgenbesser, 2005; Jeary, 2005). Older women are likely to be even more traumatized by rape than younger women because many have very conservative attitudes about sexuality, have undergone physical changes in the genitals (lack of lubrication and/or thinning of the walls of the vagina) that can increase the severity of physical injury, and have less social support after a rape, which reinforces and intensifies their sense of vulnerability (Burgess & Morgenbesser, 2005).

Women with Disabilities

Women with disabilities, regardless of their age, race, ethnicity, sexual orientation, or socioeconomic class, are assaulted, raped, and abused at a rate two times greater than women without disabilities (Cusitar, 1994; Sobsey, 1994; Wacker et al., 2008). They may be more vulnerable because of their diminished ability to fight back. In addition, mentally handicapped persons may have a more difficult time reading the preliminary cues that would alert them to danger. The impact of a rape may be intense for these people because of a lack of knowledge about sexuality, loss of a sense of trust in others, and the lack of knowledgeable staff who can effectively

silent rape reaction
A type of rape trauma syndrome in which a victim does not talk to anyone after the rape.

work with them. In many cases, women with severe mental disabilities who have been sexually assaulted may not realize that their rights have been violated and, therefore, may not report the crime. Because of these factors, the intensity and length of time of RTS is usually prolonged. Educational interventions, together with solid support networks, have been found to help women with disabilities cope with sexual assaults (Foster & Sandel, 2010).

Prostitutes

Studies have found that between 68% and 70% of female prostitutes have been victims of rape (Farley & Barkan, 1998; Silbert, 1998). Because a prostitute's job is to provide sex in exchange for payment, the question of consent is often difficult to judge. Sexual assaults are also common from a prostitute's pimp. In fact, one study found that prostitutes reported being raped an average of 16 times and beaten 58 times each year by their pimps (Chesler, 1993). Also, because of the general disapproval of prostitution, a prostitute who reports rape is often treated with disdain. People tend not to believe that she was raped or may think that she is angry because she was not paid. Many prostitutes who are raped begin to question their involvement in prostitution. Believing and trusting all women's reports of rape and performing a comprehensive medical checkup are imperative.

▶▶ HOW PARTNERS React to Rape

When a man or woman's sexual partner is raped, the partner often feels anger, frustration, and intense feelings of revenge (M. E. Smith, 2005). Many partners express a strong desire to make the rapist "pay" for his or her crime. In addition, some partners experience a sense of loss, guilt, self-blame, and jealousy. Emotional reactions to the rape may affect their feelings about their partner (M. E. Smith, 2005). In cases of acquaintance rape, people may lose trust in their partners and worry that they might have expressed sexual interest in the rapist. Overall, after a date rape experience, negative judgments and reactions by a rape victim's partner are common (A. Brown & Testa, 2008). These reactions further isolate the victim and reinforce feelings of guilt.

All in all, rape places a great deal of stress on a relationship. Couples often avoid dealing with rape entirely, believing that talking about it would be too stressful. Many men feel uncomfortable sharing their feelings about a rape because they worry about burdening their partners. However, open communication is extremely beneficial and should be encouraged. Even though dealing with a rape in a relationship can be traumatic, it has been found that women who have a stable and supportive partner recover from a rape more quickly than those who do not.

◀ review QUESTIONS

1 Define and describe the rape trauma syndrome (RTS).

2 Identify the stages of the RTS and explain what typically happens during these stages.

3 Define and describe the silent rape reaction and discuss the long-term effects of the silent rape reaction.

4 Describe the effects of rape in special populations, including married partners, lesbians, older women, women with disabilities, and prostitutes.

5 Describe the typical reactions of men and women whose partners have been raped.

▶ WHEN MEN Are Rape Victims

Can a man be raped? Although male rape is more underreported than female rape in the United States, it is estimated that 1 of every 33 men has been a victim of a completed or attempted rape (Tewksbury, 2007; U.S. Department of Justice, 2006). One study found a lifetime prevalence rate of sexual assault in men of 13% (Masho & Anderson, 2009). Male rapes account for approximately 8% of all noninstitutional rapes in the United States (Masho & Anderson, 2009).

The majority of men who are sexually assaulted are assaulted for the first time before the age of 18 (Masho & Anderson, 2009). Male victims of rape are more likely to be Black (Scarce, 1997). However, the higher frequency of rape in Black men may be because much of the research on male rape has been done in African American communities.

Although the long-term effects of rape are common in men and can include depression, anger, anxiety, self-blame, and increased vulnerability, few men ever seek out medical care or counseling (Masho & Anderson, 2009; J. Walker et al., 2005). Like for women, sexual dysfunction is common in male rape victims and can continue for years after the rape (Walker et al., 2005). Also, unlike for women, some male rape victims may increase their subsequent sexual activity to reaffirm their manhood.

▶▶ RAPE OF MEN by Women

Students often dismiss the idea that a man could be raped by a woman because they believe that because men are always willing to have sex, a woman would never need to rape a man. However, this belief actually serves to make male rape more humiliating and painful for many men.

Female rapists have been found to engage in a wide range of sexually aggressive behaviors, including forced sex and the use of verbal coercion (P. B. Anderson & Savage, 2005). In a study of male college students, 34% reported coercive sexual contact: 24% from women, 4% from men, and 6% from both sexes (Struckman-Johnson & Struckman-Johnson, 1994). The majority of male rapes by women use psychological or pressured contact, such as verbal persuasion or emotional manipulation, rather than physical force. Although the majority of college men had no reaction, or a very mild negative reaction, to the unwanted female contact, 20% of the men experienced strong negative reactions. Because men who are raped by women are often unwilling to define themselves as victims, many do not report these rapes even though physical and psychological symptoms are common (P. B. Anderson & Savage, 2005).

▶▶ RAPE OF MEN by Men

Gay men have been found to be raped at a higher rate than heterosexual men (Scarce, 1997). Hickson and colleagues (1994) found that in a sample of 930 gay men, close to 30% claimed they had been sexually assaulted at some point in their lives. Close to one third of the victims had been sexual with the perpetrator before the sexual assault. The victims reported forced anal and oral sex and masturbation to ejaculation. The most common type of activity in the sexual assault of men by men is anal penetration followed by oral penetration (N. Groth & Burgess, 1980; Scarce, 1997).

As in the case of female rape, male rape is an expression of power, a show of strength and masculinity that uses sex as a weapon. The most common emotional reactions to the rape of men by men include shame, embarrassment, self-blame, hostility, and depression (Scarce, 1997; Tewksbury, 2007). Like women, men who have been raped may go through RTS (Tewksbury, 2007). Many victims question their sexual orientation and feel that the rape makes them less of a "real man." Fearing others will think they are gay is a barrier to reporting for some men (Sable et al., 2006).

Male rape is an expression of power that uses sex as a weapon.

▶▶ PRISON Rape

The Prison Rape Elimination Act, a federal law that reduces tolerance for prison sexual assault, became effective in 2003. It mandated the collection of national data on the incidence of prison rape, and provides funding for research and program development. This law has helped reduce prison rape and support those who have been raped in prison. Studies have found that approximately 18% of prison inmates report sexual threats from other prisoners, whereas 8.5% report sexual assaults in prison (C. Hensley et al., 2005).

ON YOUR MIND 17.5

Technically, can a man really be raped?

Some people think that it is impossible for a woman to rape a man because he just would not get an erection. Even though men are anxious, embarrassed, or terrorized during a rape, they are able to have erections. Having an erection while being raped may be confusing and humiliating, just as an orgasm is for females. In fact, for some, it may be the most distressing aspect of the assault (Sarrel & Masters, 1982). Women who rape men can also use dildos, hands, or other objects to penetrate the anus. In addition, men can be orally or anally raped by men and forced to perform various sexual behaviors.

Although prison rape occurs most frequently in the male population, it also occurs between female inmates using a variety of different objects to penetrate the vagina or anus. Women who are in U.S. prisons are often victims of sexual harassment, molestation, coercive sexual behaviors, and forced intercourse, with the majority of this abuse being perpetuated by prison staff (Struckman-Johnson & Struckman-Johnson, 2002). Female inmates also experience sexual pressure in their interactions with other female inmates (Alarid, 2000). The majority of women who are raped in prison never report the crime for fear of retaliation.

Men in prison learn avoidance techniques that women use in society—physical modesty, no eye contact, no accepting of gifts, and tempering of friendliness (Bart & O'Brien, 1985). Prison rape has been found to be an act of asserting one's own masculinity in an environment that rewards dominance and power (Peeples & Scacco, 1982). Sex, violence, and conquest are the only avenues open to men in the restrictive confines of prison. To rape another man is seen as the "ultimate humiliation" because it forces the victim to assume the role of a woman. The victim becomes the "property" of his assailant, who will, in turn, provide protection in return for anal or oral sex. However, the rapist often will "sell" sexual favors from his man to other inmates in exchange for cigarettes or money.

Like rape in other populations, inmates who have been raped also experience RTS. Because these men and women must continue to interact with their assailants, long-term reorganization may take longer to work through. In addition, oftentimes there are no rape crisis services for those who have been raped in prison and little sympathy from prison employees.

Prison rape has also contributed to the increased prevalence of HIV and other sexually transmitted infections in U.S. prisons (Pinkerton et al., 2007). Rectal and vaginal trauma is common during prison rape, which increases the risk for sexually transmitted infections and HIV (Dumond & Dumond, 2002).

1 How has the myth that a man could never be raped by a woman made male rape more humiliating for the victims?

2 Explain how female rapists use verbal persuasion or emotional manipulation more often than physical force.

3 Explain how the male rape of men has been viewed as an expression of power.

4 What does the research tell us about rape in prison?

5 Explain how prison rape has been associated with posttraumatic stress disorder (PTSD).

▶ COPING WITH RAPE,
Reporting Rape, and Treating Rapists

As discussed earlier in the chapter, the majority of rape victims do not report the rape to the police. We now explore coping with rape, reporting statistics and reasons for nonreporting, and the process of telling the police, pressing charges, and going to court. We also examine the treatment of rapists.

▶▶ COPING with Rape

Rape is the only violent crime in which the victim is expected to fight back. If a woman does not struggle, people question whether she wanted to have sex. Only with visible proof of a struggle (bruises and cuts) does society seem to have sympathy. Some victims of rape have said that at the time of the rape, they felt frozen with fear, that it was impossible to move because they just could not believe what was happening to them. One victim explains:

> *Did you ever see a rabbit stuck in the glare of your headlights when you were going down a road at night? Transfixed—like it knew it was going to get it—that's what happened.* (Brownmiller, 1975, p. 358)

How do people know when to fight back? What should their strategies be? If you are confronted with a potential or attempted rape, the first and best strategy is to try to escape. However, this may not be possible if you are in a deserted area, if there are multiple attackers, or if your attacker has a weapon. If you cannot escape, effective strategies include verbal strategies such as screaming, dissuasive techniques ("I have my period," or "I have herpes."), empathy (listening or trying to understand), negotiation ("Let's discuss this."), and stalling for time. However, if the rapist does not believe the victim, these techniques may cause more harm than good.

Prentky and Knight (1986) assert that the safest strategy is to attempt to talk to the attacker and try to make yourself a real person to the attacker ("I'm a stranger; why do you want to hurt me?"). Self-defense classes can help people feel more confident in their ability to fight back.

▶▶ REPORTING a Rape

It is estimated that about 1 in 7 rapes is reported (Resnick et al., 2005); the likelihood of reporting is increased if the assailant was a stranger, if there was violence, or if a weapon was involved (U.S. Department of Justice—Office of Justice Programs, 2002). This probably has to do with the fact that victims are clearer about intent under these conditions.

Gender differences in reporting are also common. Women are less likely to report a rape if they know the attacker, whereas men are less likely to report if it jeopardizes their masculine self-identity (Pino & Meier, 1999). Women who report their rape to the police have been subsequently found to have a better adjustment and fewer emotional symptoms than those who do not report it (see Table 17.3 for more information; Sable et al., 2006).

It is also important for a victim to write out exactly what happened in as much detail as possible. When did the rape occur? Where was the victim? What time was it? Who was with the victim? What did the rapist look like? What was the rapist wearing? Exactly what happened? Was alcohol involved? Was anyone else present? Victims should keep this for their own records, for if they decide to press charges, it will come in handy. Over time memories fade, and victims can lose the important small details.

Telling the Police

On college campuses, campus police are often notified before the local police. Campus police may be able to take disciplinary action, such as fines or dismissal if the assailant is a student, but they are not able to press formal charges. Pressing charges with the local police may be important for two reasons. First, it alerts the police to a crime, and thus may prevent other women from being victimized. Second, if the victim decides to take legal action, he or she will need to have a formal report from the local police (not the campus police).

Although police officers have become more sensitive to the plight of rape victims in the past few years, some victims still report negative experiences (Monroe et al., 2005). Society's victim-precipitated view of rape also affects the attitudes of the police. To make sure that a crime did indeed occur, police must interrogate each case completely, which can be very difficult for a victim who has just been through a traumatic experience. Still, many report that taking such legal action makes them feel back in control, that they are doing something about their situation.

table **17.3** ■ **What to Do If You Are Raped**

1. Know that it was not your fault. When a woman is raped, she often spends a long time trying to figure out exactly what she did to put herself at risk for a rape. This is probably because women have always been told to "be careful," "watch how you dress," or "don't drink too much." In reality, a rape might happen anywhere and at any time. No one asks to be raped.

2. Talk to a rape crisis counselor. Some women like to talk to a rape crisis counselor before going to the hospital or police. This is very helpful because counselors can often give you advice. Besides this, they are knowledgeable about rape and the aftermath of symptoms. Many hospitals have on-site counselors, usually volunteers from Women Organized Against Rape. Talking to a counselor also helps give the victim back her sense of control (see the Media Resources at the end of this chapter).

3. Go to a hospital for a medical examination. An immediate medical evaluation is imperative. If there is a nurse or health care provider on campus, you can see either of them, but it is better to go to a local emergency department to have a thorough physical examination. New federal requirements beginning in 2009 have made states pay for "Jane Doe Rape Kits," which allow for an anonymous collection of evidence during the medical evaluation (U.S. Department of Justice, 2008; Wyatt, 2008). This allows women to have a medical examination, but the evidence will be released only if she decides to press charges. Medical evaluations are important for two reasons: to check for sexually transmitted infections that may have been transmitted during the rape and to check for the presence of date-rape drugs. Because some of the sexually transmitted infections take time to show up positive on a culture, it is important to be retested in the following weeks. Recently, some women have requested AIDS tests post-rape, although infection with HIV also takes time to show up. If a woman was not using birth control or has reason to suspect that she may have become pregnant, the hospital can administer the morning-after pill (see Chapter 12 for more information about the morning-after pill). Also, if you think you might have been drugged, you can also have a urine test to check for the drug's presence. Try not to urinate before having this test.

4. Do not throw away any evidence of the rape. Do not shower before you go to the hospital. If you decide to change your clothes, do not wash or destroy what you were wearing. If anything was damaged in the assault, such as glasses, jewelry, or book bags, keep these, too. Put everything in a plastic bag and store it in a safe place. It is necessary to preserve the evidence of the rape, which will be very important if you decide to press charges against the rapist.

5. Decide whether you want to file a police report. You have a choice of filing either a formal or informal report. This is something that you will need to sort through and decide. A rape crisis counselor can be very helpful in this decision process.

6. Decide whether you want to press charges. Although you do not need to decide this right away, you will need to think about it as soon as possible. It is important to review this decision with a lawyer experienced in rape cases.

Pressing Charges

The decision to press official charges is a difficult one that takes much consideration. It has often been said that rape victims go through a second rape because they can be put on trial more than the accused rapist. Court proceedings take up a great deal of time and energy, and they create considerable anxiety.

Re-living a rape during a legal trial is emotionally draining. Many victims feel isolated and alone with increased feelings of guilt and self-blame.

Victims of rape report that they pressed charges because they were angry, to protect others, or they wanted justice to be served. Reasons for refusing to press charges include being afraid of revenge, wanting to just forget, feeling sorry for the rapist, or feeling as though it would not matter anyway because nothing would be done. Victims of rape can also file a civil lawsuit and sue the assailant for monetary damages. Civil lawsuits are generally easier to prove than criminal lawsuits (Wagner, 1991).

Going to Court

If a victim is undecided about whether to press charges, it may be helpful to sit in on a rape trial. Rape trials can be extremely difficult for all involved. However, the purpose of sitting in is not to scare a person but to prepare oneself. It is not easy to proceed with legal action, so it can be really helpful to gather support from friends and family.

▶▶ TREATING Rapists

Can people who rape be treated so they lose their desire to rape? Because the majority of rapists are male, this section concentrates on treating male rapists. Many therapies have been tried, including psychotherapy, behavioral treatment, support groups, shock treatment, and the use of Depo-Provera, a drug that can diminish a man's sex drive. The idea behind Depo-Provera is that if the sex drive is reduced, so, too, is the likelihood of rape. So far these treatments have yielded inconclusive results. Many feminists argue that because violence, not sexual desire, causes rape, taking away sexual desire will not decrease the incidence of rape. For many men in treatment, the most important first step is to accept responsibility for their actions.

Many programs have been developed to decrease myths about rape and increase knowledge levels. All-male programs have been found to reduce significantly the belief in rape myths (Foubert & Cremedy, 2007). In another study evaluating post-education out-comes, among the 20% of men who indicated a possible likelihood of committing a rape before participating in an educational program, 75% reported less likelihood of committing a rape after the program (Foubert & McEwen, 1998). However, although attitudes about rape myths appear to change after these programs, research has yet to show that these attitude changes result in changes in sexually coercive behavior (Foubert, 2000; Foubert & Cremedy, 2007). Treatments for high-risk rapists (that is, those who are repeat offenders) have not been found to be overwhelmingly successful (Lalumière et al., 2005a).

◀ **review** QUESTIONS

1 What gender differences have been found in the reporting of rape?

2 Explain how a victim-precipitated view of rape might affect police attitudes.

3 Identify some of the reasons a victim might press (and not press) charges after a rape.

4 Explain the process of telling the police, pressing charges, and going to court. What are some of the problems a rape victim might experience along the way?

5 Explain some of the strategies given for avoiding a rape. When might these strategies cause more harm than good?

6 Identify some of the therapies that have been used in the treatment of rapists.

▶ SEXUAL ABUSE of Children

So far we have been talking about forced sexual relations between adults. But what happens when the coercive behavior involves children? **Child sexual abuse** is defined as sexual behavior that occurs between an adult and a minor. One important characteristic of child sexual abuse is the dominant, powerful position of the adult or older teen that allows him or her to force a child into sexual activity. The sexual activity can include inappropriate touching, removing a child's clothing, genital fondling, masturbation, digital penetration with fingers or sex toys, oral sex, vaginal intercourse, or anal intercourse (Valente, 2005).

As straightforward as this seems, the definition of child sexual abuse can become fuzzy. For instance, do you consider sexual play between a 13-year-old brother and his 7-year-old sister sexual abuse? How about an adult male who persuades a 14-year-old girl to touch his genitals? Or a mother who caresses her 2-year-old son's genitals? How about a 14-year-old-boy who willingly has sex with a 25-year-old woman? How would you define the sexual abuse of children? Personal definitions of sexual abuse affect how we perceive those who participate in this behavior (Finkelhor, 1984).

Many researchers differentiate between child sexual abuse or molestation, which usually involves nonrelatives; pedophilia, which involves a compulsive desire to engage in sex with a particular age of child; and **incest,** which is sexual contact between a child or adolescent who is related to the abuser. There are several types of incest, including father–daughter, father–son, brother–sister, grandfather–grandchild, mother–daughter, and mother–son. Incest can also occur between stepparents and stepchildren or aunts and uncles and their nieces and nephews. Sexual activity between a child and someone who is responsible for the child's care (such as a babysitter) may also be considered incest, although definitions for incest vary from state to state.

Because most children look to their parents for nurturing and protection, incest involving a parent, guardian, or someone else the child trusts can be extremely traumatic. The incestuous parent exploits this trust to fulfill sexual or power needs of his or her own. The particularly vulnerable position of children in relation to their parents has been recognized in every culture. The **incest taboo**—the absolute prohibition of sex between family members—is universal (J. L. Herman, 1981).

Sociologists suggest that social restrictions against incest may have originally formed to reduce role conflicts (Henslin, 2005). Parents who have sexual relationships with their child will have one role (i.e., parent) that conflicts with another (i.e., lover), which can interfere with responsibilities. We must also understand, however, that definitions of incest vary cross-culturally. The Burundi, a tribal group in tropical Africa, believe that a mother causes her son's erectile dysfunction by allowing the

child sexual abuse
Sexual contact with a minor by an adult.

incest
Sexual contact between persons who are related or have a caregiving relationship.

incest taboo
The absolute prohibition of sex between family members.

umbilical cord to touch his penis during birth (Henslin, 2005). To rectify this situation, the mother must engage in sexual intercourse with her son. Although this practice may sound bizarre to us, the culture of the Burundi supports this practice and does not view it as incestuous.

Although there are various types of incest, father–daughter and sibling incest are two of the most common types of incest in the United States (Caffaro & Conn-Caffaro, 2005; Thompson, 2009). Many siblings play sex games with each other while growing up, and the line between harmless sex play and incest can be difficult to ascertain. Sex play often involves siblings who are no more than 5 years apart, is nonabusive, is mutually desired, and often involves experimentation (Kluft, 2010). Sibling incest, in contrast, often involves siblings with a large age difference, repeated sexual contact, and motivations other than curiosity (Kluft, 2010; Rudd & Herzberger, 1999; Thompson, 2009).

Although the majority of incest offenders are male, some women do engage in such behaviors. Mother–son incest is more likely to be subtle, including behaviors that may be difficult to distinguish from normal mothering behaviors (including genital touching; R. J. Kelly et al., 2002). Men who have been sexually abused by their mothers often experience more trauma symptoms than do other sexually abused men.

▶▶ INCIDENCE OF **Child Sexual Abuse**

Accurate statistics on the prevalence of child sexual abuse are difficult to come by for many reasons: Some victims are uncertain about the precise definition of sexual abuse, might be unwilling to report, or are uncomfortable about sex and sexuality in general (Ephross, 2005; Finkelhor, 1984). The overall reported incidence has been increasing. In Kinsey and colleagues' (1953) study of 441 females, 9% reported sexual contact with an adult before the age of 14. By the late 1970s and early 1980s, reports of child sexual abuse were increasing dramatically; 1,975 cases were reported in 1976, 22,918 in 1982 (Finkelhor, 1984), and 130,000 by 1986 (Jetter, 1991). It is estimated that 1 of every 4 girls and 1 of every 10 boys experiences sexual abuse as a child (Fieldman & Crespi, 2002; Valente, 2005).

Perhaps the increase in the incidence of child sexual abuse is a reflection of the changing sexual climate (in which there is less tolerance for such behavior), rather than an actual increase in the number of sexual assaults on children. The women's movement and the child protection movement both have focused attention on child sexual abuse issues (Finkelhor, 1984). Women's groups often teach that child sexual abuse is due to the patriarchal social structure and must be treated through victim protection. The child protection movement views the problem as one that develops out of a dysfunctional family and is treated through family therapy.

Recently, there has been some doubt about the credibility of child sex abuse reporting. Would a child ever "make up" a story of sexual abuse? Research has shown that false reports occur in less than 10% of reported cases (Besharov, 1988). This is important because a child's report of sexual abuse remains the single most important factor in diagnosing abuse (Heger et al., 2002).

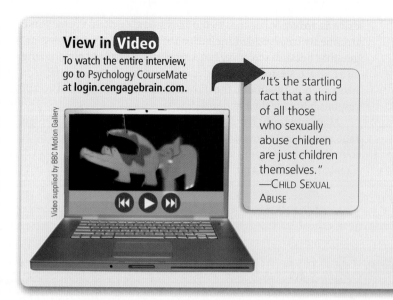

View in Video
To watch the entire interview, go to Psychology CourseMate at **login.cengagebrain.com.**

Video supplied by BBC Motion Gallery

"It's the startling fact that a third of all those who sexually abuse children are just children themselves."
—CHILD SEXUAL ABUSE

▶▶ VICTIMS OF **Child Sexual Abuse**

Although research is limited because of sampling and responding rates, we do know that the median age for sexual abuse of both girls and boys is around 8 or 9 years old (Feinauer, 1988; Finkelhor et al., 1990). Boys are more likely to be sexually abused by strangers (40% of boys, 21% of girls), whereas girls are more likely to be sexually abused by family members (29% of girls, 11% of boys; Finkelhor et al., 1990).

Finkelhor (1984) proposes three reasons why the reported rates of male sexual abuse may be lower than those for females: Boys often feel they should be more self-reliant and should be able to handle the abuse; the stigma of homosexuality; and the fear of a loss of freedoms.

Reactions to abuse vary. Many victims are scared to reveal the abuse, because of shame, fear of retaliation, belief that they themselves are to blame, or fear that they will not be believed. Some incest victims try to get help only if they fear that a younger sibling is threatened. When they do get help, younger victims are more likely to go to a relative for help, whereas older victims may run away or enter into early marriages to escape the abuse (J. L. Herman, 1981). Victims of incest with a biological father delay reporting the longest, whereas those who have been victims of stepfathers or live-in partners have been found to be more likely to tell someone more readily (Faller, 1989).

▶▶ HOW CHILDREN **Are Affected**

There have been conflicting findings regarding the traumatic effects of sexual abuse. Some studies indicate that children are not severely traumatized by sexual abuse (Fritz et al., 1981), whereas more recent studies indicate that it may have long-lasting effects that may lead to other psychological problems. Keep in mind that what follows is a discussion of what is typically experienced by a victim of childhood sexual abuse or incest. As we have discussed before, it is impossible to predict what a child's experience will be; the reaction of each child is different. A few factors make the abuse more traumatic, including the intensity of the sexual contact and how the sexual abuse is handled in the family. If a family handles the sexual abuse in a caring and sensitive manner, the effects on the child are often reduced.

Psychological and Emotional Reactions

Sexual abuse can be devastating for a child and often causes feelings of betrayal, powerlessness, fear, anger, self-blame, low self-esteem, and problems with intimacy and relationships later in life (Martens, 2007; Thompson, 2009; Valente, 2005). Many children who were sexually abused experience antisocial behavior, drug abuse, and prostitution later in life (Hardt et al., 2008; Jonas et al., 2011; Lu et al., 2008; Thompson, 2009). Overall, incest behaviors are the most traumatic when they occur over a long period, the offender is a person who is trusted, penetration occurs, and there is aggression (A. N. Groth, 1978). Children who hide their sexual abuse often experience shame and guilt, and fear the loss of affection from family and friends (Seymour et al., 2000). They also feel frustrated about not being able to stop the abuse.

Regardless of whether they tell someone about their sexual abuse, many victims experience psychological symptoms such as depression, increased anxiety, nervousness, emotional problems, and personality and intimacy disorders. Similar to reactions of rape victims, PTSD and depression are common symptoms, and may occur more often in victims who are abused repeatedly (Jonas et al., 2011; Thompson, 2009). Guilt is usually severe, and many children blame themselves for the sexual abuse (Thompson, 2009; Valente, 2005). Victims of sexual abuse are also more likely than nonabused children to abuse alcohol and drugs, experience eating disorders, and contemplate suicide (Jonas et al., 2011).

Victims may also try to cut themselves off from a painful or unbearable memory, which can lead to what psychiatrists refer to as a **dissociative disorder.** In its extreme form, dissociative disorder may result in a **dissociative identity disorder,** in which a person maintains two or more distinct personalities. Although it has long been a controversial issue in psychology, there is research to support the claim that some abuse victims are unable to remember past abuse (Malmo & Laidlaw, 2010). In one study of incest victims, 64% were found to partially repress their abuse, whereas 28% severely repressed it (J. Herman & Schatzow, 1987). Some experts claim that although the memories are classified as bad, disgusting, and confusing, many times they are not "traumatic." Because of this, the memories are simply forgotten and not repressed (McNally et al., 2004, 2005). This issue continues to be controversial, even though many victims of sexual abuse often report an inability to remember details or the entirety of the abuse.

Children who are sexually abused have been found to experience sexual problems in adulthood.

dissociative disorder
Psychological disorder involving a disturbance of memory, identity, and consciousness, usually resulting from a traumatic experience.

dissociative identity disorder
A disruption of identity characterized by two or more distinct personality states.

traumatic sexualization
A common result of sexual abuse in which a child displays compulsive sex play or masturbation and shows an inappropriate amount of sexual knowledge.

Women who were sexually abused as children have higher rates of personality disorders and PTSD than those who experienced sexual abuse later in life (Jonas et al., 2011; McLean & Gallop, 2003). Earlier in this chapter, we discussed the increased risk for engaging in risky sexual behaviors post-rape. Both antisocial and promiscuous sexual behaviors are also related to a history of childhood sexual behavior (Deliramich & Gray, 2008; Valente, 2005). The most devastating emotional effects occur when the sexual abuse is done by someone the victim trusts. In a study of the effects of sexual abuse by relatives, friends, or strangers, it was found that the stronger the emotional bond and trust between the victim and the assailant, the more distress the victim experienced (Feinauer, 1989).

Long-Term Effects

It is not uncommon for children who are sexually abused to display what Finkelhor and Browne (1985) refer to as **traumatic sexualization.** Children may begin to exhibit compulsive sex play or masturbation and show an inappropriate amount of sexual knowledge. When they enter adolescence, they may begin to show promiscuous and compulsive sexual behavior, which may lead to sexually abusing others in adulthood (Rudd & Herzberger, 1999; Valente, 2005). These children have learned that it is through their sexuality that they get attention from adults.

Children who are sexually abused have been found to experience sexual problems in adulthood. The developmentally inappropriate sexual behaviors that they learned as children can contribute to a variety of sexual dysfunctions later in life (Najman et al., 2005). Research has found that a large proportion of patients who seek sex therapy have histories of incest, rape, and other forms of sexual abuse (Maltz, 2002).

Research demonstrates a connection between eating disorders and past sexual abuse (Kong & Berstein, 2009; Ross, 2009; Steiger et al., 2010; Vrabel et al., 2010). Gay and bisexual men who experience childhood sexual abuse are significantly more likely to have an eating disorder than men without a history of sexual abuse (Feldman & Meyer, 2007). Women and men who can discuss the sexual abuse are often able to make significant changes in their eating patterns.

Problems with drug and alcohol addiction are also more common in adults with a history of child sexual abuse. In fact, high rates of alcohol and drug use have been found even as early as age 10 (Valente, 2005). Finkelhor and Browne (1985) hypothesize that because of the stigma that surrounds the early sexual abuse, the children believe they are "bad," and the thought of "badness" is incorporated into their self-concept (Kluft, 2010). As a result, they often gravitate toward behaviors that society sees as deviant.

It is not unusual for adults who had been abused as children to confront their offenders later in life, especially among those who have undergone some form of counseling or psychotherapy to work through their own feelings about the experience. They may feel a strong need to deal with the experience and often get help to work through it. The accompanying *Sex in Real Life* feature is a letter written by an 18-year-old woman who had been sexually abused by her father throughout her childhood. This letter was the first time that she had confronted him.

The following letter was written by an 18-year-old college student to her father. She had just begun to recall past sexual abuse by her father and was in counseling working on her memories. She decided to confront her father with this letter.

Dad: I can't hide it any longer! I remember everything about when I was a little girl. For years I acted as if nothing ever happened; it was always there deep inside but I was somehow able to lock it away for many years. But Daddy, something has pried that lock open, and it will never be able to be locked away again. I remember being scared or sick and crawling into bed with my parents only to have my father's hands touch my chest and rear. I remember going on a Sunday afternoon to my father's office, innocently wanting to spend time with him, only to play with some machine that vibrated.

I remember sitting on my father's lap while he was on the phone. I had a halter top on at the time. I remember wondering what he was doing when he untied it then turned me around to face him so he could touch my

stomach and chest. I remember many hugs, even as a teenager, in which my father's hand was on my rear. I remember those words, "I like what is underneath better," when I asked my father if he liked my new outfit. But Daddy, more than anything, I remember one night when mom wasn't home. I was scared so I crawled into bed with my father who I thought was there to protect me. I remember his hands caressing my still undeveloped breast. I remember his hand first rubbing the top of my underwear then the same hand working its way down my underwear. I remember thinking that it tickled, but yet it scared me.

Others had never tickled me like this. I felt frozen until I felt something inside me. It hurt, and I was scared. I said stop and started shaking. I remember jumping out of bed and running to my room where I cried myself to sleep. I also remember those words I heard a few days later, "I was just trying to love you. I didn't mean to hurt you. No one needs to know about this. People would misunderstand what happened."

You don't have to deal with the memories of what this has done to my life, my relationships with men, my many sleepless nights, my days of depression, my feelings of filth being relieved through making myself throw up and the times of using—abusing— alcohol in order to escape. You haven't even had to see the pain and confusion in my life because of this. I have two feelings, pain and numbness. You took my childhood away from me by making me lock my childhood away in the dark corners of my mind. Now that child is trying to escape, and I don't know how to deal with her.

I felt it was only fair that you know that it is no longer a secret. I have protected you long enough. Now it is time to protect myself from all of the memories. Daddy, I must tell you, even after all that has happened, for some reason I'm not sure of, I still feel love for you—that is, if I even know what love is.

SOURCE: Author's files.

►► CHARACTERISTICS of Child Sexual Abusers

Research on child sexual abusers has found several factors that distinguish abusers from those who do not abuse children. Sexual abusers are more likely to have poor social skills, low IQs, unhappy family histories, low self-esteem, and less happiness in their lives than nonabusers (Finkelhor et al., 1990; Hunter et al., 2003; Langevin et al., 1988; Milner & Robertson, 1990). The majority of abusers are heterosexual males (Valente, 2005).

Several motivations have been identified for engaging in incestuous child sexual abuse (Kluft, 2010). An abuser with an affection motivation views the behaviors as a part of family closeness with an emphasis on the "special" relationship between the victim and abuser. An erotic-based motivation usually involves sexual contact between several family members and is motivated by an eroticization of family roles. Aggression-based and rage-based motivations revolve around the abuser's sexualized anger and frustration, which is often taken out on a victim. Rage-based motivations also involve an overly hostile and sadistic abuser.

Denying responsibility for the offense and claiming they were in a trancelike state is also common. The majority of offenders are

also good at manipulation, which they develop to prevent discovery by others. One man told his 13-year-old victim, "I'm sorry this had to happen to you, but you're just too beautiful," demonstrating the typical abuser's trait of blaming the victim for the abuse (Vanderbilt, 1992, p. 66).

The Development of a Sexual Abuser

Three prominent theories—learning, gender, and biological—propose factors that make abuse more likely. Proponents of learning theories believe that what children learn from their environment or those around them contributes to their behavior later in life. Many child sex abusers were themselves sexually abused as children (Seto, 2008). Many reported an early initiation into sexual behavior that taught them about sex at a young age. Many learned that such behavior was how adults show love and affection to children.

Proponents of gender theories identify gender as an important aspect in the development of an abuser—sexual abusers are overwhelmingly male (Finkelhor et al., 1990; Seto, 2008). Males often are not taught how to express affection without sexuality, which leads to needing sex to confirm their masculinity, being more focused on the sexual aspect of relationships, and being socialized to be attracted to mates who are smaller (Finkelhor, 1984; Seto, 2008). Keep in mind that the incidence of female offenders may be lower because of lower reporting rates for boys or because society accepts intimate female interaction with children as normal (A. N. Groth, 1978). Although it was previously thought that about 4% of offenders were female (D. E. H. Russell, 1984), newer studies have found that these numbers may be significantly higher. In one

---

REAL RESEARCH 17.3   Victims of childhood sexual, physical, and emotional abuse lose at least 2 years of quality of life (CORSO ET AL., 2008). This typically occurs because of the increased risk for obesity, depression, and heart disease, in addition to the development of unhealthy behaviors such as substance abuse or sexual promiscuity.

---

study, a review of 120,000 cases of child sexual abuse, 25% of cases were found to involve a female offender (Boroughs, 2004).

Proponents of biological theories suggest that physiology contributes to the development of sexual abusers. One study found that male offenders had normal levels of the male sex hormone testosterone but increased levels of other hormones (Lang et al., 1990). There have also been reports of neurological differences between incest offenders and non–sex criminal offenders that are thought to contribute to violence (Langevin et al., 1988).

▶▶ TREATING Child Sexual Abuse

We know that sexual abuse can have many short- and long-term consequences—for victims and abusers. As a result, it is important to help victims of child sexual abuse to heal and help abusers learn ways to eliminate their abusive behaviors.

Helping the Victims Heal

Currently, the most effective treatments for victims of child sexual abuse include a combination of cognitive and behavioral psychotherapies, which teach victims how to understand and handle the trauma of their assaults more effectively. Many victims of sexual abuse also have difficulties developing and maintaining intimate relationships. Being involved in a relationship that is high in emotional intimacy and low in expectations for sex is beneficial (W. Maltz, 1990). Learning that they have the ability to say no to sex is very important and usually develops when they establish relationships based first on friendship, rather than sex. Many times the partners of victims of sexual abuse are confused; they do not fully

understand the effects of abuse in the lives of their mates, and so they may also benefit from counseling (L. Cohen, 1988).

Treating the Abusers

In Chapter 16, we discussed treatment for pedophilia. The treatment of child sexual abusers is similar in that the primary goal is to decrease the level of sexual arousal to inappropriate sexual objects—in this case, children. This is done through behavioral treatment, psychotherapy, or drugs. Other goals of therapy include teaching sexual abusers to interact and relate better with adults, assertiveness skills training, empathy and respect for others, increasing sexual education, and evaluating and reducing any sexual difficulties that they might be experiencing with their sexual partners (Abel et al., 1980). Because recidivism is high in these abusers, it is also important to find ways to reduce the incidence of engaging in these behaviors (Firestone et al., 2005).

▶▶ PREVENTING Child Sexual Abuse

How can we prevent child sexual abuse? One program that has been explored is the "just say no" campaign, which teaches young children how to say no to inappropriate sexual advances by adults. This program has received much attention. How effective is such a strategy? Even if we can teach children to say no to strangers, can we also teach them to say no to their fathers or sexually abusive relatives? Could there be any negative effects of educating children about sexual abuse? These are a few questions that future research will need to address.

Increasing the availability of sex education has also been cited as a way to decrease the incidence of child sexual abuse. Children from traditional, authoritarian families who have no sex education are at greater risk for sexual abuse. Education about sexual abuse—teaching that it does not happen to all children—may help children to understand that it is wrong. Telling children where to go and whom to talk to is also important.

Another important factor in prevention is adequate funding and staffing of child welfare agencies. Social workers may be among the first to become aware of potentially dangerous situations. Physicians and educators must also be adequately trained to identify the signs of abuse.

◀ review QUESTIONS

1 Define child sexual abuse and discuss its incidence.

2 Discuss victims' psychological and emotional reactions to child sexual abuse.

3 Explain what the research tells us about sexual abusers and the development of such behavior.

4 Describe the most effective treatments for victims and perpetrators of childhood sexual abuse.

5 Identify some ways in which society can help prevent childhood sexual abuse.

▶ INTIMATE Partner Violence

Intimate partner violence (**IPV,** which may also be referred to as domestic violence) is found among all racial, ethnic, and socioeconomic classes. It is estimated that close to 5 million women and men are victims of IPV each year (Armour et al., 2008; Centers for Disease Control and Prevention, 2011a). However, the numbers of unreported IPV incidents are much higher. In fact, national studies have found that 29% of both women and men have experienced IPV in their lifetime (Reid et al., 2008).

Although IPV is common in adolescent and college-age populations, it can happen to men and women at any age (Bonomi et al., 2007; Forke et al., 2008). It is often related to stress (Harville et al., 2011). Studies have found that women with disabilities are significantly more likely to report experiencing IPV in their lifetime, compared with women without disabilities (Armour et al., 2008; Friedman et al., 2011).

Many women and men are killed by their violent partners (known as intimate partner homicide [IPH])—76% of IPH victims were women, whereas 24% were men (Fox & Zawitz, 2004). Studies on men who commit IPH have found that 42% have past criminal charges, 15% have a psychiatric history, and 18% have both (Eke et al., 2011).

REAL RESEARCH 17.4   Two thirds of women with serious mental illness have histories of sexual violence (FRIEDMAN ET AL., 2011).

▶▶ DEFINING INTIMATE Partner Violence

IPV is coercive behavior that uses threats, harassment, or intimidation. It can involve physical (shoving, hitting, hair pulling), emotional (extreme jealousy, intimidation, humiliation), or sexual (forced sex, physically painful sexual behaviors) abuse. Some of-

Although less is known about the prevalence and experience of intimate partner violence in lesbian relationships, it is known that IPV in lesbian relationships looks similar to IPV in heterosexual relationships.

© Joel Gordon

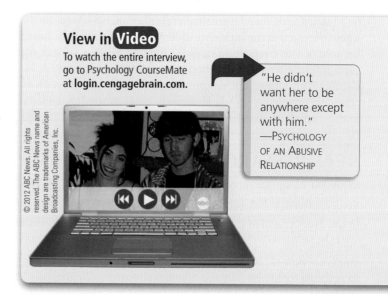

View in Video
To watch the entire interview, go to Psychology CourseMate at login.cengagebrain.com.

"He didn't want her to be anywhere except with him." —PSYCHOLOGY OF AN ABUSIVE RELATIONSHIP

fenders even are violent toward pets, especially pets that are close to the victim. Generally there is a pattern of abuse rather than a single isolated incident.

Many women in abusive relationships claim their relationship started off well and that they believed the first incidence of violence was a one-time occurrence that would not happen again. They often excuse their partner's behavior and accept their partner's apologies. In time, the abuser convinces his partner that it is really her fault that he became violent and that if she changes, it won't happen again. Most women in this situation begin to believe that the problems are indeed their fault, so they stay in the abusive relationship. Many actually believe that it is safer in the relationship than outside of it. Things that may make it more difficult for some heterosexual women to leave include issues such as finances, low self-esteem, fear, or isolation.

This type of violence and abuse also occurs among college students. One 21-year-old college student told me:

> No one could understand why I wanted my relationship with Billy to work. After all, no relationship is perfect. He didn't mean to slam me that hard. Why would he want to leave bruises on me? Look at him. He's a big guy. Anyone can tell he might have trouble seeing his own strength. He means well. He gives the best hugs, like a big sweet bear. He always says he's sorry. He loves me and tells me this in letters all the time. He thinks I'm sweet, pretty, and kind. Maybe my friends are just jealous. After all, he is a really good-looking guy. I know a lot of girls who want him. He tells me girls throw themselves at him every day. Why would he lie? (Author's files)

IPV in same-sex relationships looks similar to IPV in heterosexual relationships (Eaton et al., 2008; St Pierre & Senn, 2010).

---

intimate partner violence (IPV)
A pattern of coercive behavior designed to exert power and control over a person in an intimate relationship through the use of intimidation, threats, or harmful or harassing behavior.

Although we don't often hear much about it, domestic violence occurs at about the same rate in lesbian relationships as it does in heterosexual relationships (Eaton et al., 2008; Hewlett, 2008). Many women in same-sex relationships do not feel comfortable discussing the violence with others and worry about being outed by their partner (C. Brown, 2008). Following is one woman's story about the violence in her relationship.

I met my girlfriend at a party that a friend hosted. She was intelligent, beautiful, and had a wonderful sense of humor. Our relationship developed rapidly and the closeness we shared was something I had never experienced before. It is difficult to remember exactly when the abuse began because it was subtle. She criticized me because she didn't like my cooking, and she occasionally called me names when we argued. I didn't think much about it because she had recently lost custody of her daughter to her ex-husband because of her sexual orientation and was angry, irritable,

and depressed. She often threatened suicide and attempted it during an argument that we had and then blamed me for calling 911 for help. Despite the stress she was experiencing, she was very supportive of me when my family "disowned" me after I came out to them. When I bought my first car, she insisted I put it in her name. Although we had periods of profound happiness, our arguments increased in frequency as did her drinking and drug use. I kept telling myself that things would get better but they never did. She continually accused me of being unfaithful (I wasn't) and even once raped me after claiming I had flirted with a supermarket cashier. The first time she hit me I grabbed her wrist and twisted her arm to keep from being hit again. My response frightened me so much I suggested we see a couple's counselor, and she agreed.

Couple counseling was not helpful, and although things felt worse, our therapist said that was normal so we persevered. I began scrutinizing my

own behavior believing that if I could only do things better or differently, our life together would improve. It wasn't until she pulled a knife on me that I realized that it wasn't going to change for the better…it was only going to get worse. I called a crisis line and the counselor suggested that what I was experiencing was domestic violence. That had actually never occurred to me because we were both women. Leaving her was the hardest thing I have ever done.

It's still difficult to think of my situation as domestic violence but with the help of my counselor and support group, I am learning that women can be violent to other women, that anger, stress, depression, alcohol and drugs do not cause violence, that violence is a choice the abuser makes, and finally, that I am not to blame.

SOURCE: National Coalition of Anti-Violence Programs (1998).

However, in same-sex relationships, additional issues may arise, including fewer social supports, less availability of medical and psychological services, and the fear of being "outed" when seeking help (C. Brown, 2008; St Pierre & Senn, 2010). Although we know less about IPV in gay relationships, studies have found that 1 in 3 men in same-sex relationships have been abused (Houston & McKirnan, 2008). Unfortunately, many gay and bisexual men are reluctant to seek help for violence in intimate relationships because there is often little social support to do so (Cruz, 2003).

▶▶ REACTIONS TO INTIMATE Partner Violence

Victims of IPV experience both physical and psychological symptoms, and the symptoms depend on both the frequency and severity of the violence (Beeble et al., 2011; J. C. Campbell et al., 2002). Common psychological symptoms, similar to those experienced by victims of other coercive sexual behaviors, include depression, antisocial behavior, increased anxiety, low self-esteem, and a fear of intimacy (Cavanaugh et al., 2011; Tjaden & Thoennes, 2000). PTSD is also common (Cavanaugh et al., 2011). Physical symptoms may include headaches, back pain, broken bones, gynecological disorders, and stomach problems.

▶▶ PREVENTING INTIMATE Partner Violence

Earlier in this chapter, we discussed the fact that violence tends to repeat itself in people's lives—victims of violence often experience it more than once, known as *poly-victimization* (Cavanaugh et al., 2011). IPV victims often have a history of violence in their families, child sexual abuse, and/or teen dating violence (Gómez, 2011; Leonard, 2005; Lipsky et al., 2005). In fact, men and women who are victims of child sexual abuse or teen dating violence are significantly more likely to perpetrate or become victims of IPV as adults than those who were not victims of child sexual abuse (Gómez, 2011).

Educational programs can help educate the public about IPV, and prevention programs can be designed to reach out to those who have been victimized to help them learn ways to reduce violent tendencies. Safe housing for victims of IPV can also reduce the likelihood of future abuse. Today, there are thousands of battered women's shelters across the United States. These shelters provide women with several important things, including information and a safe haven. Often these centers have 24-hour hotlines that can help women who are struggling with issues related to domestic violence (see the Media Resources at the end of this chapter for other hotline options). Increasing the availability of safe houses and counseling and education is imperative. In addition, increasing the availability of services for gay, lesbian, bisexual, transgendered, elderly, and disabled women and men will help ensure that help is available for all who may need it.

Finally, because we know that IPV increases during times of stress, it is important to have educational and prevention programs available during times of heightened stress. In addition, it is important to become aware of how various events, such as natural disasters, can increase stress. For example, the incidence of IPV increased significantly during Hurricane Katrina and its aftermath (Harville et al., 2011).

REAL RESEARCH 17. 5   A longitudinal study found that aggression and suicide attempts during male adolescence were related to poor intimate partner relationships and an increased likelihood of partner violence in young adulthood (KERR & CAPALDI, 2011).

◀ review QUESTIONS

1 Define intimate partner violence (IPV) and give one example.

2 Identify some common psychological and physiological symptoms of IPV.

3 How is IPV in same-sex relationships similar to and different from heterosexual relationships?

4 Explain how IPV relates to sexual and physical abuse.

▶ SEXUAL Harassment

Sexual harassment is a broad term that includes anything from jokes, unwanted sexual advances, a "friendly" pat, an "accidental" brush on a person's body, or an arm around a person (Cammaert, 1985). It can also include unwanted sexual attention online (Barak, 2005). Because of the wide variety of actions that fall under this definition, many people are confused about what exactly constitutes sexual harassment.

In the United States, the courts recognize two types of sexual harassment, including **quid pro quo harassment** and **hostile environment harassment.** Quid pro quo (meaning "this for that") harassment occurs when a person is required to engage in some type of sexual conduct in exchange for a certain grade, employment, or other benefit. For example, a teacher or employer might offer you a better grade for engaging in sexual behavior. Another type of sexual harassment involves being subjected to unwelcome repeated sexual comments or visually offensive material that creates a hostile work environment and interferes with work or school. For example, a student or employee might repeatedly tell sexual jokes or send them electronically.

It may seem that sexual harassment is not as troubling as other forms of sexual coercion, but the effects of harassment on the victim can be traumatic and often cause long-term difficulties. Fitzgerald and Ormerod (1991) claim, *"There are many similarities between sexual harassment and other forms of sexual victimization, not only in the secrecy that surrounds them but also in the [myth] that supports them"* (p. 2). Severe or chronic sexual harassment can cause psychological side effects similar to rape and sexual assault, and in extreme cases, it has been known to contribute to suicide.

REAL RESEARCH 17.6   Cross-cultural studies on attitudes about sexual harassment have found that students from individualist countries (such as the United States, Canada, Germany, and the Netherlands) are less accepting of sexual harassment, whereas students from collectivist countries (such as Ecuador, Pakistan, the Philippines, Taiwan, and Turkey) are more accepting (SIGAL ET AL., 2005).

---

sexual harassment
Unwanted sexual attention from someone in school or the workplace; also includes unwelcome sexual jokes, glances, or comments, or the use of status or power to coerce or attempt to coerce a person into having sex.

quid pro quo harassment
A type of sexual harassment that involves submission to a particular type of conduct, either explicitly or implicitly, to get education or employment.

hostile environment harassment
A type of sexual harassment that occurs when an individual is subjected to unwelcome repeated sexual comments, innuendoes, or visually offensive material or touching that interferes with school or work.

▶▶ INCIDENCE AND
Reporting of Sexual Harassment

It is estimated that 25% to 30% of college students report experiences of sexual harassment (Mènard et al., 2003). Sexual harassment on campus usually involves sexist comments, jokes, or touching, and the majority of students do not report it (Mènard et al., 2003). Federal law prohibits the sexual harassment of college students, and victims of sexual harassment can sue their schools for damages for sexual harassment (Hogan, 2005).

In the United States, sexual harassment has increased in recent years, probably in relation to the increase in women in the workforce. Because of sexual harassment, women are nine times more likely than men to quit a job, five times more likely to transfer, and three times more likely to lose their jobs (Parker & Griffin, 2002). Although the majority of people who are sexually harassed are female, it can also happen to men. Same-sex harassment also occurs (Foote & Goodman-Delahunty, 2005).

As we have discussed, many victims of sexual harassment never say anything to authorities, although they may tell a friend; this may be partly because women are socialized to keep harmony in relationships. Others verbally confront the offender or leave their jobs to get away from it. Assertiveness is the most effective strategy, either by telling someone about it or confronting the offender. Many fear, however, that confronting a boss or teacher who is harassing them could jeopardize their jobs or their grades. Also, although these strategies increase the chances that the behavior will stop, they do not guarantee it. If you are being sexually harassed by someone in a university setting, the best advice is to talk to a counselor or your advisor about it. Remember that you are protected by federal law. Colleges and universities today will not tolerate the sexual harassment of any student, regardless of sex, ethnicity, religion, or sexual orientation.

Women and men think differently about sexual harassment. In one study, females were more likely than males to experience sexual harassment and to perceive it as harmful (Hand & Sanchez, 2000). Researchers have found that a behavior might be interpreted as sexual harassment by a woman, whereas it is interpreted as flattering to a man (Lastella, 2005).

▶▶ PREVENTING Sexual Harassment

The first step in reducing the incidence of sexual harassment is to acknowledge the problem. Too many people deny its existence. Because sexual harassers usually have more power, it is difficult for victims to come forward to disclose their victimization. University officials and administrators need to work together to provide educational opportunities and assistance for all students, staff, and employees. Establishing policies for dealing with these problems is necessary. Workplaces also need to design and implement strong policies against sexual harassment.

Education, especially about the role of women, is imperative. Studies have shown that sexual harassment education and training can reduce these behaviors (Lonsway et al., 2008). As our society continues to change and as more and more women enter the workforce, we need to prepare men for this adjustment. Throughout history, when women have broken out of their traditional roles, there have always been difficulties. Today, we need research to explore the impact of women on the workforce.

Throughout this chapter we have explored how power can be used in sexual relationships to degrade and oppress. Rape, the sexual abuse of children, incest, IPV, and sexual harassment are problems in our society today. The first step in reducing these crimes is to acknowledge the problems and not hide them. Education, especially about the role of women, is necessary; without it, these crimes will undoubtedly continue to escalate.

DANGER ONLINE
IS HE DATING YOU TO GET YOUR CHILD?

"People are caught off-guard, even the smartest, savviest online dater can be a victim of sexual assault."
—ONLINE DATING: SEXUAL PREDATORS

View in Video
To watch the entire interview, go to Psychology CourseMate at **login.cengagebrain.com.**

◀ review QUESTIONS

1 Define sexual harassment and differentiate between the various types of sexual harassment.

2 Explain how sexual harassment can affect a woman's employment.

3 Identify gender differences in thoughts about sexual harassment.

4 Identify some strategies for dealing with, and preventing, sexual harassment.

SUMMARY POINTS

1 Physically or psychologically forcing sexual relations on another person is usually referred to as rape. Sexual assault refers to sexual penetration (vaginal, oral, or anal), as well as unwanted sexual touching. However, exact definitions of rape and sexual assault are determined by individual states.

2 In the United States, the rape rate in 2008 was 53% lower than it was 10 years earlier. In the majority of cases, the victims know their assailants. Actual incidence rates for rape are difficult to determine because forcible rape is one of the most underreported crimes in the United States.

3 Women do not report rape for several reasons, including that they do not think that they were really raped, they blame themselves, they fear no one will believe them, they worry that no legal action will be taken, or they feel shame or humiliation. Women who were using drugs or alcohol before the rape are much less likely to report the rape.

4 Four theories that explain why rape occurs are the rapist psychopathology, victim precipitation, feminist, and sociological theories. The rapist psychopathology theory suggests that either disease or intoxication forces men to rape. Victim precipitation theory shifts the responsibility from the person who knowingly attacked to the innocent victim. Feminists believe that rape and the threat of rape are tools used in our society to keep women in their place. The social, economic, and political separation of the sexes has also encouraged rape, which is viewed as an act of domination of men over women. Finally, sociologists believe that rape is an expression of power differentials in society. When men feel disempowered by society, by changing sex roles, or by their jobs, overpowering women with the symbol of their masculinity (a penis) reinforces, for a moment, men's control over the world.

5 There are also strong gender differences in attitudes toward rape. Men have been found to be less empathetic and sensitive toward rape than women and to attribute more responsibility to the victim than women do. Men are more likely than women to believe that a man should expect sexual intercourse if he pays for an expensive date. Rape prevention programs for male college students have also been related to both attitudinal and behavioral changes.

6 Ethnic minorities have been found to have more traditional attitudes toward women, which has been found to affect rape attitudes. Non-Hispanic Whites are more sympathetic than Blacks to women who have been raped, whereas Blacks are more sympathetic than either Hispanic or Japanese American college students. Asian American students have the least sympathy for women who have been raped and are more likely to hold a rape victim responsible for the rape and excuse the rapist.

7 Rape is defined differently around the world, so the incidence of rape varies depending on a culture's definition. In some cultures, rape is accepted as a punishment for women or is used for initiation purposes. Rape has also been used during times of war as a weapon. This is referred to as persecutory rape. The rape of children is also common in some places around the globe.

8 Female college students are at greater risk for rape than their noncollege peers. The majority of women know the person who sexually victimized them. Because many of these women know their attackers, few feel comfortable reporting or pressing charges.

9 Recent events on various college campuses have resulted in a variety of lawsuits. In response to these events, the Obama Administration announced a national sexual assault awareness campaign for colleges and K–12 schools.

10 Alcohol use is one of the strongest predictors of acquaintance rape on college campuses. Up to two thirds of rape victims have voluntarily consumed alcohol before an assault. Alcohol use on college campuses, as it relates to rape, is viewed very differently for men and women. Being impaired or incapacitated during a rape has been associated with self-blame, stigma, and problematic alcohol use in victims post-assault.

11 Fraternities tend to tolerate and may actually encourage the sexual coercion of women, because they tend to host large parties with lots of alcohol and little university supervision. The ethic of masculinity also helps foster an environment that may increase the risk for rape.

12 Male athletes have been found to be disproportionately overrepresented as assailants of rape by women surveyed. Many athletes have been found to view the world in a way that helps to legitimize rape, and many feel a sense of privilege. Female athletes have been found to be more likely than nonathletes to believe in the blame-the-victim theory of rape and believe that some women put themselves in a bad situation.

13 Rape trauma syndrome (RTS) is a two-stage stress response pattern characterized by physical, psychological, behavioral, or sexual problems (or a combination of these). Two stages, the acute and long-term reorganization, detail the symptoms that many women feel after a rape. Rape may cause sexual difficulties that can persist for a considerable period after the rape. Some victims have a silent rape reaction because they never report or talk about their rape.

14 The effects of rape are similar in special populations, including rape between marital partners and rape of lesbians, older women, women with disabilities, and prostitutes. Partners of women who have been raped also experience emotional symptoms. Overall, rape places a great deal of stress on a relationship.

15 Men can be raped by women and also by other men. The majority of male rapes by women use psychological or pressured contact, such as verbal persuasion or emotional manipulation, rather than physical force. The true incidence is unknown because the rape of men by men is infrequently reported to the police. Male rape is an expression of power; a show of strength and masculinity that uses sex as a weapon. Rape also occurs in prison.

16 Rapists are primarily from younger age groups and tend to reduce their rape behavior as they get older. They have also been found to have experienced overwhelmingly negative early interpersonal experiences, most of which were with their fathers; have sexist views about women; accept myths about rape; have low self-esteem; and be politically conservative.

17 Different therapies for rapists include shock treatment, psychotherapy, behavioral treatment, support groups, and the use of medications. Many programs have been developed to decrease myths about rape and increase knowledge levels. All-male programs have been found to reduce significantly the belief in rape myths.

18 The likelihood that a rape will be reported increases if the assailant was a stranger, if there was violence, or if a weapon was involved. Women who report their rapes to the police have been found to have a better adjustment and fewer emotional symptoms than those who do not report. Some victims refuse to press charges because they are afraid of revenge, want to forget the event, feel sorry for the rapist, or feel as though it would not matter anyway because nothing will be done.

19 Incest refers to sexual contact between a child or adolescent who is related to the abuser. There are several types of incest, including father–daughter, father–son, father–sister, grandfather–grandchild, mother–daughter, and mother–son. Sexual abuse can include undressing, inappropriate touch, oral and genital stimulation, and vaginal or anal penetration.

20 Accurate statistics on the prevalence of child sexual abuse are difficult to come by because some victims are uncertain about the definition of sexual abuse, unwilling to report, or uncomfortable about sex and sexuality in general.

21 The median age for sexual abuse of both girls and boys is around 8 or 9 years old, and many victims are scared to reveal the abuse. Victims of incest with a biological father delay reporting the longest, whereas those who have been victims of stepfathers or live-in partners tell more readily.

22 Children who hide their sexual abuse often experience shame and guilt and fear the loss of affection from family and friends. They also have low self-esteem and feel frustrated about not being able to stop the abuse.

23 Regardless of whether they tell someone about their sexual abuse, many victims experience psychological symptoms such as depression, increased anxiety, nervousness, emotional problems, low self-esteem, and personality and intimacy disorders. Guilt is usually severe, and many females develop a tendency to blame themselves for the sexual abuse. Men and women who have been sexually abused may not be able to recall the abuse. The most devastating emotional effects occur when the sexual abuser is someone the victim trusts.

24 Research comparing child sexual abusers with nonabusers has shown that molesters tend to have poorer social skills, lower IQs, unhappy family histories, lower self-esteem, and less happiness in their lives. As surprising as it may seem, many abusers have strict religious codes, yet still violate sexual norms. Three prominent theories that propose factors that make abuse more likely are learning, gender, and biological theories.

25 Currently, the most effective treatments for victims of sexual abuse include a combination of cognitive and behavioral psychotherapies. Many victims of sexual abuse also have difficulties developing and maintaining intimate relationships. Goals for therapy of child sex abusers include decreasing sexual arousal to inappropriate sexual objects, teaching them to interact and relate better with adults, assertiveness skills training, empathy and respect for others, increasing sexual education, and evaluating and reducing any sexual difficulties that they might be experiencing with their sexual partners.

26 Increasing the availability of sex education can also help decrease child sexual abuse. Adequate funding and staffing of child welfare agencies may also be helpful.

27 Although IPV is common in adolescent and college-age populations, it can happen to men and women at any age. It is often related to stress. Studies have found that women with disabilities are significantly more likely to report experiencing IPV in their lifetime, compared with women without disabilities.

28 Many women and men are killed by their violent partners (known as *intimate partner homicide* [IPH]). Studies on men who commit IPH often have past criminal charges, a psychiatric history, or both.

29 Sexual harassment includes anything from jokes, unwanted sexual advances, a friendly pat, an "accidental" brush on a person's body, or an arm around a person. Severe or chronic sexual harassment can cause psychological side effects similar to those experienced by rape and sexual assault victims, and in extreme cases, it has been known to contribute to suicide. It is estimated that 25% to 30% of college students report experiences with sexual harassment.

30 The first step in reducing the incidence of sexual harassment is to acknowledge the problem. Too many people deny its existence. Because sexual harassers usually have more power, it is difficult for victims to come forward to disclose their victimization.

CRITICAL THINKING QUESTIONS

1 If a woman who was alone and drunk at a bar dancing very seductively with several men is raped, do you think she is more to blame than a woman who was raped in the street by an unknown assailant? Explain.

2 In 2003, a woman accused Kobe Bryant of the Los Angeles Lakers of rape. Do you think professional athletes make poor decisions with women who flock to them? Do you think a woman would cry rape without just cause? Why or why not?

3 Do you consider a 17-year-old male who has sexual intercourse with his 14-year-old girlfriend sexual abuse? How would you define the sexual abuse of children?

4 In a handful of divorce cases, one spouse accuses the other of child sexual abuse. Do you think that these accusations originate from a vengeful ex-spouse wanting custody, or do you think it might be easier to discuss the sexual abuse once the "bonds of secrecy" have been broken, as they typically are during divorce?

MEDIA RESOURCES

CourseMate brings course concepts to life with interactive learning, study, and exam preparation tools that support the printed textbook. A textbook-specific website, Psychology CourseMate includes an integrated interactive eBook and other interactive learning tools including quizzes, flashcards, videos, and more. If your textbook does not include an access code card, go to CengageBrain.com to gain access.

CENGAGENOW   CengageNOW is an easy-to-use online resource that helps you study in less time to get the grade you want—NOW. Take a pre-test for this chapter and receive a personalized study plan based on your results that will identify the topics you need to review and direct you to online resources to help you master those topics. Then take a post-test to help you determine the concepts you have mastered and what you will need to work on. If your textbook does not include an access code card, go to CengageBrain.com to gain access.

View in Video available in CourseMate and CengageNOW:

Date Rape: Meg's Story: College student describes a date rape experience.

Rape & PTSD: Listen to a young woman describe her symptoms of posttraumatic stress disorder after being raped.

Child Sexual Abuse: A short clip featuring surprising statistics about sexual abusers.

Psychology of an Abusive Relationship: A teenager deals with the repercussions of an abusive relationship.

Online Dating: Sexual Predators: The psychology of an online predator is explored through an interview with him and the woman he married in order to have access to her daughter.

Websites:

Adult Survivors of Child Abuse (ASCA) ■ Designed specifically for adult survivors of physical, sexual, and emotional child abuse or neglect, ASCA offers an effective support program. This website's mission is to reach out to as many survivors of child abuse as possible, and it offers information on individual and group support groups.

American Women's Self-Defense Association (AWSDA) ■ The AWSDA began with the realization that women's self-defense needs were not being met. Founded in 1990, AWSDA is an educational organization dedicated to furthering women's awareness of self-defense and rape prevention.

National Violence Against Women Prevention Research Center ■ National Violence Against Women Prevention Research Center provides information on current topics related to violence against women and its prevention. The website contains statistics and information on many topics, including evaluations of college sexual assault programs across the nation.

Rape, Abuse & Incest National Network (RAINN) ■ RAINN is the nation's largest anti–sexual assault organization. It operates the National Sexual Assault Hotline at 1-800-656-HOPE, and carries out programs to prevent sexual assault, help victims, and ensure that rapists are brought to justice. The website includes statistics, counseling resources, prevention tips, news, and more.

Men Can Stop Rape (MCSR) ■ MCSR is a nonprofit organization that works to increase men's involvement and efforts to reduce male violence. MCSR empowers male youths and the institutions that serve them to work as allies with women in preventing rape and other forms of men's violence. MCSR uses education and community groups to build men's capacity to be strong without being violent.

Security on Campus ■ Security on Campus is a nonprofit organization that works to make campuses safe for college and university students. It was cofounded in 1987 by Connie and Howard Clery, following the murder of their daughter at Lehigh University. Jeanne Clery was a freshman when she was beaten, raped, and murdered by another student in her dormitory room. Security on Campus educates students and parents about crime on campus and assists victims in understanding laws pertaining to these crimes.

Male Survivor ■ Male Survivor works to help people better understand and treat adult male survivors of childhood sexual abuse. Information about male sexual abuse and a variety of helpful links are available.

Northwest Network of Bi, Trans, Lesbian and Gay Survivors of Abuse ■ The Northwest Network provides support and advocacy for bisexual, transsexual, lesbian, and gay survivors of abuse. Information about sexual abuse and a variety of helpful links are available.

18 Sexual Images and Selling Sex

View in **Video**

View in **Video**

View in **Video**

ABOUT THE CHAPTER OPENING VIDEO – I have a secret to share—I'm fascinated by reality television shows. I'm curious about the people who are in them and the reasons why the shows are so popular. A few years ago, I was invited to participate in *Wife Swap,* a show that swaps wives/mothers for 2 weeks with a family with a different lifestyle. Although my kids thought this would be a great idea, they were disappointed when I flatly refused. Why would I ever want to go live in someone else's house and have another person come live in mine? But many people would jump at the chance to be on a reality show. It's interesting to me because such shows are completely unrealistic, using sensationalism to attract viewers and advertisers. One very popular show, *Jersey Shore,* follows a group of housemates. The show has been called a "cultural phenomenon," generating record ratings for MTV and earning the title as the "most watched television series EVER" (Gorman, 2011). Not surprisingly, many college students spend hours watching the show and analyzing its content. Two students of mine, Alex and Raelynn, agreed to talk to me about how reality shows affect men's and women's attitudes about gender, sexuality, and relationships.

The way women are portrayed on reality shows is ridiculous. All the women have fake boobs, big hair, and fake tans. But the funny thing is that women love to watch it. One girl I know set her Facebook status to "I want to be like JWOWW"! Even younger high school girls look up to JWOWW and Deena. But these girls are such bad influences for them. Who would choose that for their life?

Shows like Jersey Shore *also have a horrible effect on guys. Many of them look up to the male characters and end up treating girls just like they do on the show! They think it's okay to treat girls like that. It's completely disrespectful. They call*

girls "grenades" and blow a whistle to announce the presence of a grenade [a *Jersey Shore* term referring to an unattractive female]. *I know some guys that bring girls home, kick them out, and then go out and get more girls to bring home. The show makes it seem like it's totally okay to treat a girl like that. A friend of mine even made a poster for his dorm door that said "No Grenades!" I felt bad when I saw it because I started to wonder if it was okay for me to be in his room!*

Alex and Raelynn offer an interesting perspective on reality television, one that I'm sure you might agree with. The popularity of reality shows definitely makes us wonder about the future of American television. ‖

Janell Cauth

"The way women are portrayed on reality shows is ridiculous."
—CHAPTER OPENING VIDEO

View in Video

To watch the entire interview, go to Psychology CourseMate at **login.cengagebrain.com.**

Our lives today are full of visual media: magazines, newspapers, book covers, CD and DVD packaging, cereal boxes, and food products. Even medicines are adorned with pictures of people, scenes, or products. Advertisements peer at us from magazines, billboards, buses, matchbook covers, and anywhere else that advertisers can buy space. Television, movies, computers, and other moving visual images surround us almost everywhere we go, and we will only depend on them more as information technology continues to develop. We live in a visual culture with images we simply cannot escape.

We begin this chapter with a brief history of erotic representations. Next, we examine how erotic representations are presented to us every day in books, television, advertising, and other media. Only then do we turn to the graphic sexual images of pornography. We also explore how sex itself is sold today, from lap dances in strip clubs to prostitution. Along the way, ask yourself the following questions: What influence do sexual representations and selling sex have on us? What are they trying to show us about ourselves? How do they subtly affect the way we think about men, women, and sexuality?

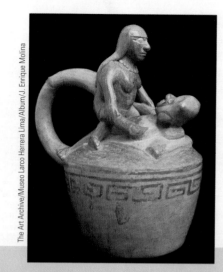

Early erotic art was often public art. The city of Pompeii included large, erect phalluses on street corners, and erotic frescoes adorned many people's homes.

EROTIC REPRESENTATIONS in History

Human beings have been making representations of themselves and the world around them since ancient times. Many of the earliest cave drawings and animal bone sculptures have been representations of the human form, usually scantily dressed or naked. Often, the poses or implications of the art seem explicitly erotic. Yet it is hard to know to what degree these images were considered erotic by preliterate people, for early erotic art was also sacred art in which the purpose was to represent those things most important to early people—the search for food and the need to reproduce (Lucie-Smith, 1991). However, by the dawn of the great ancient civilizations such as Egypt, people were drawing erotic images on walls or pieces of papyrus just for the sake of eroticism (Manniche, 1987). Since that time, human beings have been fascinated with representations of the human form naked or engaged in sexually explicit behavior; in turn, many governments have been equally intent on limiting or eradicating those images.

Erotic representations have appeared in most societies throughout history, and they have been greeted with different degrees of tolerance. Ancient cultures often created public erotic tributes to the gods, including temples dedicated to phallic worship. India's sacred writings are full of sexual accounts, and some of the most explicit public sculptures in the world adorn its temples. Greece is famous for the erotic art that adorned objects like bowls and urns. When archaeologists in the 18th and 19th centu-

ries uncovered the Roman city of Pompeii, buried in a volcanic blast in 79 A.D., they were startled and troubled to find that this jewel of the Roman Empire, which they had so admired, was full of brothels, had carved phalluses protruding at every street corner, and had private homes full of erotic **frescoes** (FRESS-cohs; Kendrick, 1987). Authorities hid these findings for years by keeping the erotic objects in locked museum rooms and publishing pictures of the city in which the phalluses were made to taper off like candles.

Not all sexual representations are explicit, and many of our greatest artists and writers included sexual components in their creations. The plays of Shakespeare, although hardly shocking by today's standards, do contain references to sexuality and sexual intercourse. The art of Michelangelo and Leonardo da Vinci also included graphic nudity without being titillating. Still, in their day, these pictures caused controversy; in the 16th century, for example, priests painted loincloths over nude pictures of Jesus and the angels. What people in one society or one period in history see as obscene, another group—or the same group later—can view as great art.

DEVELOPMENT of Pornography

Most sexual representations created throughout history had a specific purpose, whether it was to worship the gods, to adorn pottery, or, later, to criticize the government or religion. Very little erotic art seems to have been created simply for the purpose of arousing the viewer, as much of modern erotic art is. So most of history's erotic art cannot be considered "pornographic" in the modern sense (L. Hunt, 1993).

---

fresco
A type of painting done on wet plaster so that the plaster dries with the colors incorporated into it.

pornography
Any sexually oriented material that is created simply for the purpose of arousing the viewer.

decency
Conformity to recognized standards of propriety, good taste, and modesty—as defined by a particular group (standards of decency differ among groups).

obscenity
A legal term for materials that are considered offensive to standards of sexual decency in a society.

hard core
Describes explicit, genitally oriented sexual depictions, more explicit than soft core, which displays sexual activity often without portrayals of genital penetration.

Pornography, which tends to portray sexuality for its own sake, did not emerge as a distinct, separate category until the middle of the 18th century in the United States. For most of history, sexuality itself was so imbedded in religious, moral, and legal contexts that it was not thought of as a separate sphere of life (Kendrick, 1987). Explicit words and pictures (together with other forms of writing, such as political writings) were controlled in the name of religion or in the name of politics, not in the name of public **decency** (L. Hunt, 1993). For example, **obscenity** was illegal among the Puritans (punishable originally by death and later by boring through the tongue with a hot iron) because it was an offense against God. That is why before the 19th century, **hard-core** sexual representations were rare.

Another strong influence on the development of pornography in the United States was the development of the printing press and the mass availability of the printed word (sexually explicit books were printed within 50 years of the invention of movable type in the Western world). For most of history, written or printed work was available only to a small elite because only they could afford it and, more important, only they could read.

The most famous pornographic work of the 18th century was John Cleland's *Memoirs of a Woman of Pleasure* (better known as Fanny Hill), first published in 1748. Cleland's work was solely aimed at sexually arousing the reader. Before Cleland, most sexually explicit books were about prostitutes because these women did "unspeakable" things (that could be described in graphic detail) and because they could end up arrested, diseased, and alone, thereby reinforcing society's condemnation of their actions. In fact, the word *pornography* literally means "writing about harlots."

*The U.S. entertainment media seems to be **almost obsessed by sexual imagery.***

Cases such as Fanny Hill teach us that to really understand the meaning of "pornography," we must understand the desire of the U.S. government and other groups to control it and suppress it. In other words, the story of pornography is not just about publishing erotic material but also about the struggle between those who try to create it and those who try to stop them. Both sides must be included in any discussion of pornography; without those who try to suppress it, pornography just becomes erotic art. In fact, the term **erotica,** often used to refer to sexual representations that are not pornographic, really just means pornography that a particular person finds acceptable. One person's pornography can be another person's erotica. As we shall see in this chapter, the modern arguments about pornography are some of the most divisive in the country, pitting feminists against feminists, allying some of the most radical feminist scholars with fundamentalist preachers of the religious right, and pitting liberals against liberals and conservatives against conservatives in arguments over the limits of free speech.

But sexually explicit representations are not the only sexual images in U.S. society. Sexuality is present in almost all of our **media,** from the model sensuously sipping a bottle of beer to the offhand sexual innuendos that are a constant part of television sitcoms. In fact, the U.S. entertainment media seems to be almost obsessed by sexual imagery; Michel Foucault (1998), French philosopher and historian of sexuality, has called it a modern compulsion to speak incessantly about sex. Before we discuss the sexually explicit representations of "pornography" with the heated arguments they often inspire, let us turn to the erotic images that present themselves to us in the popular media every day.

◀ review QUESTIONS

1 Explain how erotic representations have appeared throughout history.

2 Differentiate among pornography, obscenity, and erotica.

3 Describe the development of pornography.

▶ SEXUALITY IN THE MEDIA and the Arts

Since the early 1990s, representations in the U.S. **mass media** have become more explicitly erotic. Many of the images we see today are explicitly or subtly sexual. Barely clothed females and shirtless, athletic males are so common in our ads that we scarcely notice them anymore. Some even feature full nudity (in fact, some clothing companies, such as Abercrombie, are notorious for using naked models or models with very little clothing—which appears rather odd when you remember they want to sell clothes!). The majority of movies, even those directed at children, have sexual scenes that would not have been permitted in movie theaters even 20 years ago. The humor in television sitcoms has become more and more sexual, and nudity has begun to appear on primetime

network television shows. In addition, graphic depictions of sexuality, which until recently could be found only in adult bookstores and theaters, are now available at neighborhood video stores.

We like to believe that we are so used to the media that we are immune to its influences. Does sex (or violence) on television, for example, really influence how promiscuous (or violent) our society becomes? Do the constant sexual stereotypes paraded before us in commercials and advertisements really help shape our attitudes toward gender relations? Does constant exposure to sexual

erotica
Sexually oriented media that are considered by a viewer or society as within the acceptable bounds of decency.

media
All forms of public communication.

mass media
Media intended for a large, public audience.

images erode family life, encourage promiscuity, and lead to violence against women, as some conservative and feminist groups claim? Also, if we find out that sex and violence in the media do have an effect on how we behave, what should we do about it?

▶▶ EROTIC Literature

Although the portrayal of sexuality is as old as art itself, pornography and censorship are more modern concepts, products of the mass production of erotic art in society. Throughout Western history, reactionary forces (usually the clergy) often censored nudity in public art, especially when it featured religious figures. For example, on the walls of Michelangelo's Sistine Chapel, clerics painted over the genitals of nudes with loincloths and wisps of fabric. Still, because there was no way to mass-produce these kinds of art, the Church's reactions varied on a case-by-case basis.

Pornography in the modern sense began to appear when printing became sophisticated enough to allow fairly large runs of popular books, beginning in the 16th century. Intellectuals and clergy were often against this mass production of books. They worried that if everybody had books and could learn about things for themselves, why would anyone need teachers, scholars, or theologians? Religious and secular intellectuals quickly issued dire warnings about the corrupting effects of allowing people direct access to knowledge and established censorship mechanisms. By the 17th century, the Church was pressuring civic governments to allow them to inspect bookstores, and soon forbidden books, including erotica, were being removed; such books then became rarer and more valuable, and a clandestine business arose in selling them. It was this struggle between the illicit market in sexual art and literature and the forces of censorship that started what might be called a pornographic subculture—one that still thrives today. TV and movie producers in the United States believe that "sex sells."

Today, erotic literature of almost any kind is readily available in the United States. The sexual scenes described in the average romance novel today would have branded it as pornographic only a few decades ago. One would think that such books would be the main targets of people trying to censor sexually explicit materials. Yet, most censorship battles over sexually explicit material involve images rather than written word.

The popular television show, *Glee,* boldly explores many sex-related themes. One episode starring Britney Spears and John Stamos was watched by a record 13.3 million viewers—which was the highest ever ratings for the show.

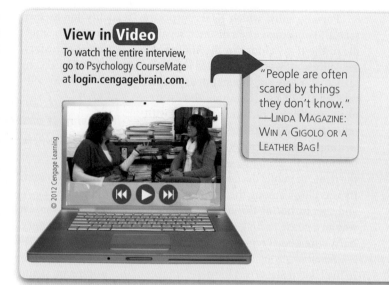

View in Video
To watch the entire interview, go to Psychology CourseMate at **login.cengagebrain.com.**

"People are often scared by things they don't know." —LINDA MAGAZINE: WIN A GIGOLO OR A LEATHER BAG!

Although the early court cases that established the U.S. legal attitudes toward pornography in the United States were often about books (especially about sending them through the mail), modern debates about pornography tend to focus more on explicit pictures and movies. Still, it was the erotic novel that first established pornographic production as a business in the Western world and provoked a response from religious and governmental authorities.

▶▶ TELEVISION and Film

Television is the single strongest influence on the modern American outlook toward life. Yet, the world we see on TV is only a small slice of the real world; television, like the movies, edits the world it displays. For example, although literally hundreds of acts of sexual intercourse are portrayed or suggested on television shows and in movies every day, we rarely see a couple discuss or use contraception, discuss the morality of their actions, contract a sexually transmitted infection (STI), worry about AIDS, experience erectile dysfunction, or regret the act afterward. Most couples fall into bed shortly after initial physical attraction and take no time to build an emotional relationship before becoming sexually active. Values and morals about sexuality seem nonexistent. The majority of sex on television, and in the movies, is provided in an artificial and unrealistic light (Kunkel et al., 2005).

Relatively new shows, such as *Jersey Shore* (MTV), *Hung* (HBO), *The Hard Times of RJ Berger* (MTV), *Blue Mountain State* (Spike), *Gossip Girl* (CW), and *Secret Diary of a Call Girl* (Showtime), are graphically explicit in their treatment of sex. Full frontal nudity is not uncommon in many of these shows and various sexual issues, such as masturbation and oral sex, are commonly explored in storylines (Strauss, 2010). Even *Glee* (Fox), a popular and highly sexualized teen show, boldly explores sex-related themes. One episode, entitled "Sexy," explored sex education with Gwyneth Paltrow doing a guest appearance as the health and wellness teacher (who tells students that celibacy is a valid but unrealistic choice for the students; the character claims, "It's like saying vegetarianism is an option for lions."). When talking about the amount of sex allowed on television today, Doug Herzog, president of MTV Networks Entertainment Group, said, "The line moves every day, so you go to move with it" (quoted in Strauss, 2010).

Chapter 1 opened with a cross-cultural exploration of sexuality in three countries: Japan, the Netherlands, and the United States. Each of these countries has rules about how much sex is tolerated on television. In a conservative country, such as Japan, there is less tolerance, whereas in more liberal countries, such as the Netherlands, there is more tolerance. On a recent trip to the Netherlands, I had the opportunity to attend the taping of a popular Dutch television show *Spuiten en Slikken*. The title of the show is a play on words that can mean either "Shoot Up and Swallow" or "Ejaculate and Swallow," referencing sex and drugs. *Spuiten en Slikken* explores sex and drugs in a very open and matter-of-fact fashion, and is aimed at 13- to 19-year-olds. The weekly show has between 500,000 and 750,000 viewers each week, representing about 4% of the Netherlands population (for comparison, MTV's hit show *Jersey Shore* averages about 3 million viewers, which is roughly 1% of the U.S. population; Henke, 2011).

Hosts of the show experiment with sex and drugs in every show, while young audience members watch and learn what can happen. Typical sex storylines for the show involve oral and anal sex, partner swapping, pornography, and semen tasting, whereas typical drug storylines include exploring the effects of psychedelic mushrooms, hash, or marijuana. On one show, the host smoked pot to show audience members the effect of marijuana use on memory (she forgot most of her lines).

To come up with show topics, a group of researchers keeps tabs on sexual and drug trends in the young adult population. Noticing that many teens had been experimenting with videotaping their sexual interactions, producers decided to explore these practices in more depth. The show explored the reasons why a teen might decide to videotape themselves having sex and the consequences of doing so. Hosts discussed the negative possibilities of doing so (i.e., it could get into the wrong hands), as well as the suggestions for doing it right (i.e., getting the lighting right).

© Janell Carroll

I had the opportunity to talk with Pim Castelijn, the Director of Programming for the station that broadcasts the show in the Netherlands. I told him that critics might think the show "glorified" sex and drugs. Did he think it made kids want to experiment with things they showcased? He told me that teens already know that sex and drugs *are* glorious, and that's what draws them toward experimentation. He wondered why so many people are afraid to talk to teens about the positives. Ignoring them only makes teens distrustful; Americans ignore the positives, Pim said, because they're afraid talking about them will make kids run out and experiment. *Spuiten en Slikken* attempts to highlight both the good and the bad associated with various sexual behaviors (and drug use) and doesn't automatically claim that all sex and drugs are bad. It presents a balanced approach in hope that kids who watch will be able to make up their own minds.

Probably the most interesting thing I learned about the show that day was that the station it airs on, BNN, is a public television station, funded with taxpayer money. Do you think a show like this would air in the United States? Why or why not?

SOURCE: P. Castelijn, personal communication, September 26, 2008; A. Gnocchi, personal communication, September 26, 2008.

Television magazine shows that imitate news reports but concentrate on two or three stories (for example, *Dateline* or *20/20*) often search for stories with lurid content, and if there is a sexual scandal or a rape accusation in the news, they are sure to feature it. Even the "hard" news shows, such as the networks' evening news reports, have turned a corner in their willingness to use graphic descriptions of sexual events. News shows, after all, also need ratings to survive, and one way to interest audiences is to report legitimate news stories that have a sexual content in a graphic and provocative way. These news reports deliver the sexually explicit information with the implicit message that they disapprove of it; but they still deliver it.

In 2005, Sex on TV 4, a biennial study of sexual content on American television, analyzed more than 1,000 hours of programming including all genres of television shows. Overall, 70% of the shows studied included some sexual content, and shows averaged five sexual scenes per hour (Kunkel et al., 2005). These numbers were up from 1998, when 56% of shows included sexual content, and 3.2 sexual scenes occurred every hour. During primetime programming, 77% of shows included sexual content and averaged close to six sexual scenes per hour (Kunkel et al., 2005). This study also found that only 11% of primetime network shows made references to sexual risks or responsibilities, and this percentage has remained virtually the same since 1998 (Kunkel et al., 2005). Interestingly, approximately 53% of sexual scenes that included intercourse were between couples with an established relationship; 20% were between couples who have met but who have no relationship; 15% were between couples who have just met; and in 12% of cases, it was unclear what the couple's relationship is (Kunkel et al., 2005).

The AIDS epidemic was a key factor in opening up the way in which news organizations speak about sexuality (for example, the word *condom* would never have appeared on a major news network before the outbreak of AIDS). Another landmark came in 1998 when news broke of a sex scandal between then-President Bill Clinton and Monica Lewinsky. The Clinton–Lewinsky story was one of the biggest of the decade and was covered by most evening news shows in explicit detail. This story broke precedent and allowed the networks to use language and sexual references that would have been unthinkable just a few years earlier.

Television, Film, and Minority Sexuality

As sexually explicit as the U.S. visual media has become, it has generally had a very poor track record in its portrayals of certain sexual behaviors, such as same-sex behavior and sexuality among certain minorities, such as the elderly, the disabled, and racial and ethnic minorities. Today, popular shows such as *House, Desperate Housewives,* and *The L Word* help bisexual, lesbian, and gay men become more mainstream on television.

One place where minorities, especially female minorities, have had a high representation has been in reality television. Reality shows, such as *Bad Girl's Club* (Oxygen), often portray Black

---

REAL RESEARCH 18.1 Even with Internet blocks and filters, 70% of teenagers (10–17 years old) claim to have viewed pornography on the Internet (DELMONICO & GRIFFIN, 2008).

---

women as bossy, manipulative, and stubborn (Samuels, 2011). Although many White women are portrayed in equally negative ways in reality shows (take *Jersey Shore,* for example), the difference lies in the fact that White women have a less stereotyped presence on many major television networks. Black women often do not have as much access to major networks, so the image of Black women in reality shows can influence our attitudes about Black women (Samuels, 2011).

Television, Film, and Gender

American television offers its viewers sexual information both explicitly (through such things as news, documentaries, and public service announcements) and implicitly (through the ways it portrays sexuality or gender relations in its programming; Gunter & McAleer, 1990; Peter & Valkenburg, 2007). One implicit message of American television programming, almost since its inception, has been that men are in positions of leadership (whether they are chief legal counsel or the head of the family), whereas women, even if they are high ranking, are sexual temptations for men. Even today, the stereotyping of women is often extreme in television commercials, which is considered in the "Advertising" section later in this chapter. Although the types of portrayals of women's roles are changing and improving on television today, men

still outnumber women in major roles, and the traditional role of woman as sex object still predominates on television.

Many gender stereotypes persist on American television. This is especially true in reality television shows such as *Jersey Shore* (MTV) or *You're Cut Off* (VH1), where women are often portrayed as brainless and backstabbing. The only place gender stereotypes are less prevalent is on soap operas. Because soap operas have been aimed at women, they often portray women as more competent than other programming (Stern et al., 2007).

Fortunately, some gender stereotypes on other television shows are changing. Men are now being shown as single or stay-at-home dads, and there is a tendency to mock the old "macho man" stereotypes on shows such as *The Family Guy.* Shows like *Bones, CSI,* and *Law & Order* regularly feature women in leading roles and have helped establish the new television woman: forceful, working outside the home, and dealing with the real-life problems of balancing social life, personal issues, and work. These women are smart, motivated, and self-confident. Gender stereotypes have also been changing with the increasing popularity of reality television shows, such as *Survivor* and *The Amazing Race.* Shows like these portray the majority of women as strong, independent, and self-confident people who are willing to take risks.

Television and Children

American teenagers watch an average of 4.5 hours of television each day (Rideout et al., 2010). The proliferation of new technologies on which to watch television shows, such as iPods, iPads, and cell phones, has significantly increased the overall amount of time that teens spend watching television shows since 2003 (Rideout et al., 2010). Almost half of teens record and watch their shows later, or watch them on devices other than television sets.

Television viewing also begins early in the United States: 2- to 5-year-olds spend almost 28 hours a week watching television and teenagers about 22 hours. In 1961, the average age to begin watching television was 3 years old, but by 2007, it was 9 months old (Zimmerman et al., 2007). The biggest leap in hours spent watching television occurs from 11 to 14 years old when children watch an average of 5 hours of television and movie content—either live or recorded—each day (Rideout et al., 2010). When these numbers are evaluated by ethnicity and race, Black and Hispanic youths have been found to watch nearly 6 hours of television per day, compared with 3.5 for Whites (Rideout et al., 2010).

Researchers have begun to ask serious questions about the impact of all this television watching, especially because television is so inundated with sexuality and sexual stereotypes. For example, children are concerned with gender roles, and they often see the world in terms of "boy's" behavior and "girl's" behavior. As discussed in Chapter 4, children are taught early to behave in gender-appropriate ways, and they quickly begin to tease other children who do not follow these stereotypes (such as effeminate boys). Still, research shows that when children are exposed to books or films that portray nonstereotyped gender behaviors, their gender stereotypes are reduced (Comstock & Paik, 1991).

Historically, many children's shows lacked positive female role models and offered stereotyped portrayals of men and women. For example, although *Sesame Street* has had a human cast of

The face of media is quickly changing all around us. Today we can hear music from devices smaller than our finger and access the Internet through our cell phones. Many cars and vans have optional built-in television monitors on seat backs, and cell phones download e-mails and can record both digital images and video. Today's adolescents spend an average of 7.5 hours per day using media, including television, movies, Internet, video, cell phones, iPods, MP3 players, GameCubes, and PlayStations (not including the time they spend using computers for school work or the time spent texting and talking on a cell phone; Rideout et al., 2010). When you add in the fact that they are often multitasking and using more than one medium at a time, the overall time spent with media is 10 hours and 45 minutes each day.

In 2010, the Henry J. Kaiser Family Foundation released "Generation M: Media in the Lives of 8–18-Year-Olds," the results of a study that included responses to anonymous questionnaires

© Janell Carroll

from more than 2,000 8- to 18-year-olds. Whereas 39% of teens had their own cell phone in 2005, by 2010, 66% had cell phones (Rideout et al., 2010). Following are other interesting findings from this important study. On average, adolescents between the ages of 8 and 18 were found to:

- Watch 4 hours 29 minutes of television each day
- Listen to 2 hours 31 minutes of music each day
- Spend 1 hour 29 minutes using the computer for recreational use per day
- Play video games for 1 hour 13 minutes per day
- Read recreational material for 38 minutes a day

In the average home in America, 84% have Internet access (59% have high-speed Internet), 84% have cable or satellite (47% of these also get premium cable channels, such as HBO), and 52% have TiVo or other DVRs. What is interesting, however, is the number of adolescents who have access to this material in their bedrooms. Forty-five percent of 8- to 18-year-olds report there

are no rules about television watching (Rideout et al., 2010). The study also found that in the average adolescent bedroom:

- 71% have a television
- 49% have cable television
- 50% have a video game console
- 36% have a computer

Gender differences were found: Boys were twice as likely as girls to play video games, but girls spent more time listening to music than boys. As for the overall types of music listened to by both girls and boys, rap and hip-hop were the clear favorites (60% of Caucasians, 70% of Hispanics, and 81% of African Americans reported this genre of music as their favorite; Rideout et al., 2005). Ethnic differences revealed that African American youths spent more time watching television than Hispanic or White Americans.

Adolescents' increased access to computers and the Internet gives them much greater access to information. Many adolescents report that their parents are unaware of what they see online (Cameron et al., 2005). Because research has shown that the exposure to sexuality in the media has been found to be related to adolescent sexual behavior (Pardun et al., 2005), the content of these media is worth exploring. This generation of adolescents is certainly a media generation, but now the question for researchers is this: What long-term impact will this have on adolescents?

SOURCE: Rideout et al. (2005, 2010).

mixed ethnicities and genders, and even a number of female Muppets, its most notable Muppet figures (from Kermit to Bert and Ernie to Big Bird to the Count) have all been male. It was only with the introduction of Zoe in 1993 that a female Muppet managed to gain a high profile.

Television executives argue that boys will not watch cartoons with a female lead, but girls will watch cartoons with a male lead, and so it makes economic sense to produce cartoons featuring males. The result is that it is hard for young girls to find good gender role models in cartoons. It is understandable that researchers have found that more television viewing is correlated with greater sexual stereotyping in certain groups of children (Gunter & McAleer, 1990). However, the situation is slowly improving, with *Blue's Clues*

(Blue is a girl), *Bob the Builder* (Wendy, Bob's sidekick, is more handy than Bob), and *Dora the Explorer*. However, *Go Diego Go*, a spin-off of *Dora the Explorer*, was developed primarily so that boys would have a character to identify with (Fernández, 2005).

One might also wonder what effect television has on the developing sexuality of children and adolescents. Sex is a common theme on many television programs today. How does this affect the sexual behavior of teens? Research has shown that increasing sexual content on television is related to early sexual initiation in adolescents (Collins et al., 2004). Teens who watch a lot of television are likely to believe their peers are sexually active. One study found that the more hours of television teens watched, the more likely they were to perceive their peers as being sexually active (Eggermont, 2005).

Movement against the Sexualization of the Visual Media

The irony is that American networks have turned to sex to increase their ratings, yet the constant presence of sexual themes on television is beginning to turn viewers away. The majority of Americans want stronger regulation of sexual content and profanity (Kunkel et al., 2005).

Portrayal of sexuality in movies has also long been a source of controversy. There was no control over motion picture content until the 1930s, when the industry began policing itself with the Motion Picture Code. However, the rating system has not stopped the filmmakers from trying to be as sexually explicit as they can within the rating categories. Hollywood seems to try to push the limits of the R rating as far as possible, and a number of directors have had to cut sexually explicit scenes out of their movies. In fact, some movies are made in two or three versions; the least sexually explicit version is for release in the United States, a more explicit copy is released in Europe (where standards are looser), and a third, even more explicit version, is released on DVD.

A backlash does seem to be developing, and Hollywood has been reducing the sexual explicitness of its general release movies. Michael Medved (1992), a noted movie critic, argued in his book *Hollywood vs. America* that the movie and television industries are out of touch; too dedicated to violence, profanity, and sex; and do not really understand what consumers want to see on television and in the movies. He claimed that G- and PG-rated movies actually make more money than R-rated movies.

However, some of the shows boycotted by groups such as the American Family Association get high ratings for the very reasons that they are boycotted—they are willing to deal with complex issues such as abortion and homosexuality in a frank and honest (if sometimes sensationalistic) manner. It will be interesting to see whether advertisers are scared away by these groups or continue to sponsor provocative and controversial programs.

After a controversial season full of negative reviews for the scandalous nature of the show, *Gossip Girl* launched a highly successful ad campaign that used negative quotes from several watchdog organizations to promote the show. Scandalous ad campaigns involved the acronyms "OMFG" and "WTF." Producers claimed that "WTF" simply referred to "Watch This Fall."

© Janell Carroll

▶▶ ADVERTISING

Advertising is a modern medium, and its influence pervades modern life. There is practically no area free from its effects, from mass media to consumer products and even to nature itself—billboards obscure our views from highways, and planes drag advertising banners at our beaches. People proudly wear advertisements for soft drinks or fashion designers on their shirts, sneakers, or hats, not realizing that they often spend more for such clothing, paying money to help the company advertise.

According to estimates, children watch more than 40,000 commercials on television every year (Bakir & Palan, 2010). Studies have shown that advertising has a profound effect on the way children think about the world (forming a mind-set of "products I want to have," for example), and it influences the way they begin to form their ideas of sexuality and gender roles (Bakir & Palan, 2010; Gunter & McAleer, 1990).

Advertising and Gender Role Portrayals

In his groundbreaking book *Gender Advertisements*, Erving Goffman (1976) used hundreds of pictures from print advertising to show how men and women are positioned or displayed to evoke sexual tension, power relations, or seduction. Advertisements, Goffman suggested, do not show actual portrayals of men and women, but present clear-cut snapshots of the way we think they behave. Advertisements try to capture ideals of each sex: Men are shown as more confident and authoritative, whereas women are more childlike and deferential (Belknap & Leonard, 1991). Since Goffman's book was published, advertisements have become more blatantly sexual, and analyzing the gender role and sexual content of advertisements has become a favorite pastime of those who study the media.

Although studies indicate that advertising is becoming less sexist today, gender differences still exist (Eisend, 2010). An examination of gender-role portrayals in television advertising from seven countries, including Brazil, Canada, China, Germany, South Korea, Thailand, and the United States, found that females were still portrayed in stereotypical ways (Paek et al., 2011).

As you flip through popular magazines today, it's obvious that advertising companies are trying to put more women into ads in

A recent advertising campaign for the Pirelli fashion collection featured Naomi Campbell and Tyson Beckford naked, wearing only sneakers.

positions of authority and dominance. Men are also being shown in less stereotypic roles, such as cuddling babies or cooking. However, the naked body is still a primary means of selling products, and even if gender roles are becoming more egalitarian, portrayals of sexuality are still blatant.

Advertising and Portrayals of Sexuality

The purpose of advertising is threefold—to get your attention, to get you physiologically excited, and to associate that excitement with the product being advertised. The excitement can be intellectual, emotional, physical (sports, for example), or visual (fast-moving action, wild colors). But when you think of "getting excited," what immediately comes to mind? Well, that is what comes to the mind of advertising executives also, and so ads often use sexual images or suggestions to provoke, to entice—in short, to seduce.

Sexuality (especially female sexuality) has been used to sell products for decades. In an analysis comparing magazine advertisements in 1964 with advertisements in 1984, Soley and Kurzbard (1986) found that although the percentage of advertisements portraying sexuality did not change, sexual illustrations had become more overt and visually explicit by 1984. By the late 1990s, a variety of advertisers, including Calvin Klein and Abercrombie & Fitch, were challenging the limits with advertising campaigns that featured graphic nudity or strong sexual implications. Although Abercrombie & Fitch was forced to withdraw many of its catalogs because of public outcry, today clothing manufacturers and perfume companies constantly try to out-eroticize each other.

Not all portrayals of sexuality are this blatant, however. Some are suggestive, such as sprays of soda foam near the face of an ecstatic looking woman, models posing with food or appliances placed in obviously phallic positions, models posed in sexual

subliminal
Existing or functioning below the threshold of consciousness, such as images or words, often sexual, that are not immediately apparent to the viewer of an advertisement, intended to excite the subconscious mind and improve the viewer's reaction to the ad.

positions even if clothed, or ads that show women and, less often, men whose faces are contorted in sexual excitement. Some authors even claim that advertisements have tried to use **subliminal** sexuality—pictures of phalluses or breasts or the word *sex* worked into advertisements so they cannot be seen without extreme scrutiny (J. Levine, 1991). Whether these strategies work is a matter of much debate, but Calvin Klein's ads were so provocative that news reports about them appeared in newspapers and on television news shows—and that is just what advertisers want most for their ads and the products they represent, for people to talk and think about them.

In early 2011, a J. Crew ad led to such a controversy. The ad featured J. Crew's president painting her son's toenails pink (see accompanying photo). Critics argued that painting a boy's toenails would increase the chances of the boy being gay or transgender (James, 2011). Although critics were vocal and debate was strong, in the end, the ad did exactly what it was supposed to do—it created a buzz, drawing more attention to the brand.

▶▶ OTHER MEDIA:
Music Videos, Virtual Reality, and More

Other forms of media exist that have not been discussed so far in this chapter. Because sexuality pervades our lives, it also pervades our art and our media. Today, sex-advice columns run in many newspapers and magazines across the country. There are also thousands of "900 number" telephone lines offering sexual services of various kinds across the country. People call the number and pay a certain amount per minute (or use their credit cards for

In early 2011, a J. Crew ad created controversy by showing a woman painting her son's toenails pink. Critics argued this could increase the chances of the boy being gay or transgender.

SATURDAY
with jenna

See how she and son Beckett go off duty in style.

quality time

"Lucky for me, I ended up with a boy whose favorite color is pink. Toenail painting is way more fun in neon."

a flat fee) and can talk either to other people who have called in on a party line or to professionals who will discuss sex or play the part of the caller's sexual fantasy. These phone lines cater mostly to both heterosexual and homosexual men. Even cell phones are now capable of receiving pornographic images and video clips.

The power of the Internet has been discussed throughout this text, but it is mentioned here once again because the Internet allows for completely unregulated interaction between millions of people. The Internet has generated whole new forms of communications, and as new forms of media are developed, sexual and gender issues are arising there, too. Literally thousands of sexually explicit conversations, artworks, and computer games go zipping through the Internet between the users of computer networks every day.

Computer technology has been taken even one step further: virtual reality (VR). In VR, pictures generated by computer are projected into goggles put over the eyes, and as the head and eyes move, the picture moves accordingly. Users are given the illusion of actually being in the scene before them. Recently, enterprising VR producers have been making sexually explicit VR movies that are coordinated with "stimulators" (vibrators) attached to sensors at the groin; one can actually feel as though one is acting in the pornographic scene while the computer responds to the user's own physical states of excitement and stimulates the user to

ON YOUR MIND 18.2

I've heard that men and women who are looking for child pornography often use the Internet. What kind of images do they look for? How often do they get caught?

Although the distribution of child pornography is illegal and banned by federal law in all 50 states, the crimes still occur. Research has found that from 2000 to 2001, an estimated 1,713 nationwide arrests were made for Internet-related crimes involving the possession of child pornography (Wolak et al., 2005). Those who were arrested all had access to minor children, either by living with them, through a job, or in organized youth activities. The majority were White (91%), older than 25 (86%), and unmarried (Wolak et al., 2005). When law officials reviewed the child pornography that offenders had in their possession, they found 83% had images of 6- to 12-year-olds, 39% had images of 3- to 5-year-olds, and 19% had images of children younger than 3. These images contained children involved in a range of sexual behaviors including oral sex, genital touching, and penetration (Wolak et al., 2005).

orgasm. Certainly, new forms of media will present challenges to those who want to regulate or control the public's access to sexually explicit materials.

◀ review QUESTIONS

1 Identify the early reactionary forces that began a censorship of erotic literature.

2 Explain how television uses sex to attract viewers and increase their ratings.

3 In what ways do television and movies influence our perceptions of gender?

4 Identify and explain how television has been found to socialize children from a young age.

5 Explain how gender roles have been portrayed in various types of advertising.

6 Explain how advances in technology have provided people with greater access to sexual content.

▶ PORNOGRAPHY:
Graphic Images and Obscenity

Pornography has always aroused passions, but the debate over pornography is particularly active today because pornography is so widely available. Pornography can be purchased in stores, and viewed and downloaded online. Worldwide, more than $3,000 is spent on pornography each second, and in the United States, a new pornographic video is created every 39 minutes (Ropelato, 2008). In addition, throw in arguments from free-speech advocates, antiporn (and anti-antiporn) feminists, religious groups, presidential commissions, the American Civil Liberties Union, and a powerful pornography industry, and you can begin to see the extent of the conflicts that have developed over this issue.

▶▶ DEFINING Obscenity

This section begins by reviewing the disputes over the legal and governmental definitions of pornography as they have been argued in presidential commissions and in the highest courts in the country. Then we look at how those same debates are discussed among the scholars and activists who try to influence the country's policies toward pornography. We also examine the basic claim of modern opponents of pornography: that pornography is harmful in its effects on individuals and society as a whole. Finally, we examine the public's attitudes toward pornography.

Court Decisions

The First Amendment to the Constitution of the United States, enacted in 1791, includes the words: "Congress shall make no

Sex in Real Life ▶▶ My Short-Lived Porn Career

A few years ago, one of my students came to me to discuss an issue that came up in her relationship with her boyfriend. He had gone to Los Angeles to star in some adult films and she was distressed. How would this affect their relationship? The two of them came to talk with me and he shared the story of his short-lived porn career. Unfortunately, in the end he lost his girlfriend, who was really unhappy about his decision to participate in the films. What would you have done in this situation? Would you have supported him or told him not to go? If you're a man, would you have wanted to go? Why or why not?

It's not like I've always wanted to be a porn star. Of course I've wondered what the lifestyle would be like, and how I would perform if I were one. One night I found out that a famous porn star, Ginger Lynn, was dancing at a local strip club. We go to see her, and after her dance she offers to sign autographs. She also mentions that she is sponsoring a competition to earn a chance to star in an adult porno film with her. I was intrigued and decided to approach her to ask her about it. After speaking with her for a while about the opportunity she took some information from me and told me that she would call me.

After a battery of tests to check for STIs, I flew out west to make my porn debut a few months later. I was given $700 to pay for travel expenses and my "services." My head was spinning on the plane because I was consumed by anticipation, excitement, nervousness, and fear. I was mostly worried about my relationship with my girlfriend. I knew that she was having a hard time understanding why I wanted to do this. To be honest, I wasn't even

sure why I wanted to do it. I guess I looked at it as the opportunity of a lifetime. But I still questioned it. Was I trying to prove something?

It is hard to explain the feelings I had when I first arrived to the set where the filming would take place. There were many people walking around freely observing the sex scenes. The people there were all very courteous and professional. Each of us was taken aside and asked about what types of scenes and sex acts we were willing to participate in. The producers stressed that we should not participate in anything we were uncomfortable with.

© Frédéric Neema/Sygma/Corbis

The days on the set were long. There were about two dozen males and females participating, and each of us had to do a minimum of three scenes. Each scene lasted about an hour. The male performers were encouraged to take a Viagra pill for insurance after consulting the onsite doctor. On this first day I participated in two scenes. The first involved an oral sex competition with seven girls and seven guys. The guys serviced the girls first while the girls were blindfolded. We had to kneel and perform cunnilingus on each girl for three minutes. By a show of

fingers in the air the girls were asked to "score" the guys on a scale of 1 to 10. There was a cash prize for the guy with the highest score.

The second scene was much like the first only it involved the guys seated on the couches and the girls on their knees. I was blindfolded and each of the seven girls came around and gave me oral sex for three minutes each. When each of the girls had given action to each of us, we removed our blindfolds to watch the grand finale— our ejaculations. During all the scenes the cameramen moved around freely filming video and taking still photos.

My third scene was filmed on the final day of shooting. I was to be dominated by two women. We participated in a kinky threesome the likes of which I have never known. The women performed oral sex on each other and on me. We switched positions repeatedly, and there was much groping and licking. The scene lasted for about an hour, but the time seemed to go by very quickly. At one point I was lying down and one girl was sitting on my face while the other was sucking my cock.

The experience was very interesting. Although I was glad to have the experience I did not find that it was an appealing career for me to pursue, and I have been troubled by the potential aftermath of my participation. I realize that I might lose my relationship with my girlfriend. I wonder if she'll decide to let me go because she is so unhappy that I even wanted to do it in the first place.

SOURCE: Author's files.

---

law…abridging the freedom of speech, or of the press." Ever since, the court system has struggled with the meaning of those words, for it is obvious that they cannot be taken literally; we do not have the right to make false claims about other people, lie in court under oath, or in the most famous example, yell "fire" (falsely) in a crowded theater, even though that limits our freedom of speech.

Court cases in the United States have established the following three-part definition of obscenity that has determined how courts

define pornography. For something to be obscene, it must: (a) appeal to the **prurient** (PRURE-ee-ent) interest; (b) offend contemporary community standards; and (c) lack serious literary, artistic, political, or scientific value.

prurient
Characterized by lascivious thoughts; used as criterion for deciding what is pornographic.

However, these criteria are not without critics. Important questions remain about topics such as the definitions of community standards and prurient interest, and who gets to decide. Some argue that the criteria of prurience, offensiveness, and community standards turn moral fears into legal "harms," which are more imaginary than real, and so we end up with arbitrary discussions of what is "prurient" and which speech has "value" (I. Hunter et al., 1993). In contrast, antiporn feminists argue that pornography laws were made to reflect a male preoccupation with "purity" of thought and insult to moral sensibilities, and to ignore the true harms of pornography: the exploitation of women (see later in this chapter for a more detailed discussion of female exploitation; R. J. Berger et al., 1991).

REAL RESEARCH 18.2 One study found that 87% of male students and 31% of female students reported using pornography in their lifetimes (CARROLL ET AL., 2008). However, whereas 20% of male students reported using pornography daily or almost daily, only 3% of women did so.

Presidential Commissions

Although presidential commissions date back to George Washington, they became more popular in the 20th century (Rosenbaum, 2005). As of 2005, a total of 46 presidential commissions had been established, examining issues such as bioethics, chemical warfare, and terrorist attacks. These commissions issued detailed reports and recommended changes in public policy. Even though presidential commissions often do not lead to an adoption of new policies, they do help educate Americans about important issues. Now we'll explore two of the commissions on pornography.

1970 COMMISSION ON OBSCENITY AND PORNOGRAPHY In 1967, President Lyndon Johnson set up a commission to study the impact of pornography on American society. The commission was headed by a behavioral scientist who brought on other social scientists, and although the commission also included experts in law, religion, broadcasting, and publishing, its findings were based on empirical research, and much of its $2 million budget was used to fund more scientific studies (Einsiedel, 1989). The commission (which used the terms "erotica" or "explicit sexual material" rather than "pornography"), studied four areas: pornography's effects, traffic and distribution of pornography, legal issues, and positive approaches to cope with pornography (R. J. Berger et al., 1991).

The 1970 Commission operated without the benefit of the enormous research on pornography that has appeared since that time, and so it has been criticized for such things as not distinguishing between different kinds of erotica (for example, violent versus nonviolent); for including homosexuals, exhibitionists, and rapists all under the same category of "sex offenders"; and for relying on poor empirical studies. Still, although calling for more research and better designed and funded studies in the future, the commission did perform the most comprehensive study of the evidence up until that time, and concluded that no reliable evidence was found to support the idea that exposure to explicit sexual materials is related to the development of delinquent or criminal sexual behavior among youths or adults, so adults should be able to decide for themselves what they will or will not read (Einsiedel, 1989).

In other words, the commission recommended that the state stop worrying so much about pornography, which the commission saw as a relatively insignificant threat to society. The U.S. Senate was not happy with the commission's conclusions and condemned its members.

1986 ATTORNEY GENERAL'S COMMISSION ON PORNOGRAPHY (THE "MEESE COMMISSION") In 1985, President Ronald Reagan appointed Attorney General Edwin Meese to head a new commission that he expected to overturn the 1970 Commission's findings. In fact, the official charter of the Meese Commission was to find "more effective ways in which the spread of pornography could be contained" (R. J. Berger et al., 1991, p. 25); thus, it already assumed that pornography was dangerous or undesirable and needed containment. Whereas the 1970 Commission focused on social science, the Meese Commission listened to experts and laypeople through public hearings around the country, most of whom supported restricting or eliminating sexually graphic materials. Virtually every claim made by antipornography activists was cited in the report as fact with little or no supporting evidence, and those who did not support the commission's positions were treated rudely or with hostility (R. J. Berger et al., 1991).

The Meese Commission divided pornography into four categories: violent pornography, "degrading" pornography (e.g., anal sex, group sex, homosexual depictions), nonviolent/nondegrading pornography, and nudity. The commission used a selection of scientific studies to claim that the first two categories are damaging and may be considered a type of social violence, and that they hurt women most of all. Overall, the Meese Commission came to the opposite conclusions of the 1970 Commission and made a number of recommendations:

- Antipornography laws were sufficient as they were written, but law enforcement efforts should be increased at all levels.

- Convicted pornographers should forfeit their profits and be liable to have property used in production or distribution of pornography confiscated, and repeat offenses against the obscenity laws should be considered felonies.

- Religious and civic groups should picket and protest institutions that peddle offensive materials.

- Congress should ban obscene cable television, telephone sex lines, and child pornography in any form.

Reaction to the Meese Commission was immediate and strong. Many of the leading sexuality researchers cited by the commission in support of its conclusions condemned the report and accused the commission of intentional misinterpretation of their scientific evidence. The Moral Majority, the religious right, and conservative supporters hailed the findings as long overdue. Women's groups were split on how to react to the report. On the one hand, the report used feminist language and adopted the position that pornography damages women. Antiporn feminists saw in Meese a possible ally to get pornography banned or at

Jenna Jameson, the world's most famous adult-entertainment performer, has been called the "Queen of Porn."

least restricted, and thus supported the Meese Commission's conclusions, if not its spirit. Other women's groups, however, were very wary of the commission's antigay postures and conservative bent, and they worried that the report would be used to justify wholesale censorship.

▶▶ THE PORNOGRAPHY Debates

The religious conservative opposition to pornography is based on a belief that people have an inherent human desire to sin, and that pornography reinforces that tendency and so undermines the family, traditional authority, and the moral fabric of society (R. J. Berger et al., 1991). Unless strong social standards are kept, people will indulge themselves in individual fulfillment and pleasure, promoting material rather than spiritual or moral values (Downs, 1989). Users of pornography become desensitized to shocking sexual behaviors, and pornography teaches them to see sex as simple physical pleasure rather than a part of a loving, committed relationship. This leads to increased teen pregnancy rates, degradation of females, and rape; in this, at least, the religious conservative antipornography school agrees with the antiporn feminists.

*Pornography teaches users to **see sex as simple physical pleasure** rather than a **part of a loving, committed relationship.***

Nowhere has the issue of pornography been as divisive as among feminist scholars, splitting them into two general schools. The antipornography feminists see pornography as an assault on women that silences them, renders them powerless, reinforces male dominance, and indirectly encourages sexual and physical abuse against women. The other side, which includes groups such as the Feminist Anticensorship Taskforce (FACT), argues that censorship of sexual materials will eventually (if not immediately) be used to censor such things as feminist writing and gay erotica, and would therefore endanger women's rights and freedoms of expression (Cowan, 1992). Some who argue against the antipornography feminists call themselves the "anti-antiporn" contingent, but for simplicity's sake, we refer to them simply as the "anticensorship" group.

ON YOUR MIND 18.3

I've watched pornography, and I'm just curious about condom use. Are there any rules about using condoms on the sets of pornographic movies?

Male and female adult film actors are not legally required to wear condoms during filming. Some production companies may require condoms, but producers argue that viewers don't want to watch safe sex in porn and scenes with condoms take too long to shoot (Liu, 2004; Madigan, 2004). Actors are required to undergo monthly testing for STIs, but as you learned from Chapter 15, many infections may not show up in testing until many weeks after a person becomes infected. Some states have begun exploring legislation to require condom use during filming. In fact, in 2004, the California Assembly warned the pornographic film industry that condoms must be worn or they will write a law to require it (Liu, 2004; Madigan, 2004).

Antipornography Arguments

One of the scholars who has written most forcefully and articulately against pornography is Catherine MacKinnon (1985, 1987, 1993). MacKinnon argues that pornography cannot be understood separately from the long history of male domination of women, and that it is, in fact, an integral part and a reinforcing element of women's second-class status. According to MacKinnon, pornography is less about sex than power. She argues that pornography is a discriminatory social practice that institutionalizes the inferiority and subordination of one group by another, the way segregation institutionalized the subordination of Blacks by Whites.

MacKinnon suggests that defending pornography on First Amendment terms as protected free speech is to misunderstand the influence of pornography on the everyday lives of women in society. She suggests thinking of pornography itself as a violation of a woman's right not to be discriminated against, guaranteed by the Fourteenth Amendment. Imagine, she suggests, if the thousands of movies and books produced each year by the pornographic industry were not showing women, but rather Jews, African Americans, the handicapped, or some other minority splayed naked, often chained or tied up, urinated and defecated on, with foreign objects inserted into their orifices, while at the same time physical and sexual assaults against that group were epidemic in society (as they are against women). Would people still appeal to the First Amendment to prevent some kind of action?

Other feminists take this argument a step further and claim that male sexuality is by its nature subordinating; Andrea Dworkin (1981, 1987), for example, is uncompromising about men and their sexuality. Dworkin, like MacKinnon, sees pornography as a central aspect of male power, which she sees as a long-term strategy to elevate men to a superior position in society by forcing even strong women to feign weakness and dependency. Even sexuality reflects male power: Dworkin sees every act of intercourse as an assault, because men are the penetrators and women are penetrated.

Because pornography is harmful in and of itself, such authors claim it should be controlled or banned. Although they have not had much success passing such laws in the United States, their strong arguments have set the agenda for the public debate over pornography.

Anticensorship Arguments

A number of critics have responded to the arguments put forth by people like MacKinnon and Dworkin (Kaminer, 1992; Posner, 1993; Wolf, 1991). First, many argue that a restriction against pornography cannot be separated from a restriction against writing or pictures that show other oppressed minorities in subordinate positions. Once we start restricting all portrayals of minorities being subordinated, we are becoming a society ruled by censorship. Many Hollywood movies, television shows, and even women's romance novels portray women as subordinate or secondary to men.

REAL RESEARCH 18.3   The average age for a child's first exposure to online pornography is 11 years old (MITCHELL ET AL., 2003).

Are all of those to be censored, too? MacKinnon seems to make little distinction between *Playboy* and movies showing violent rape. Are all sexual portrayals of the female body or of intercourse harmful to women?

Also, what about lesbian pornography, in which the models and the intended audience are female, and men almost wholly excluded? Many of these portrayals are explicitly geared toward resisting society's established sexual hierarchies (Henderson, 1991). Should they also be censored? Once sexually explicit portrayals are suppressed, anticensorship advocates argue, so are the portrayals that try to challenge sexual stereotypes.

A more complicated issue is the antiporn group's claim that pornography harms women. One response is to suggest that such an argument once again casts men in a more powerful position than women and, by denying women's power, supports the very hierarchy it seeks to dismantle. But the question of whether it can be demonstrated that pornography actually harms women is a difficult one.

▶▶ STUDIES ON THE HARMFUL Effects of Pornography

Both sides of the pornography debate have produced reams of studies that support their side; the Meese Commission and antiporn feminists such as MacKinnon and Dworkin have produced papers showing that pornography is tied to rape, assault, and negative attitudes toward women, and others have produced studies showing that pornography has no effects or is secondary to more powerful forces (W. A. Fisher & Barak, 1991). More recent experts argue that pornography is linked to failed relationships and negative attitudes about women (P. Paul, 2005). Who is right?

Society-Wide Studies

In 1969, J. Edgar Hoover, director of the FBI, submitted evidence to the Presidential Commission on Obscenity and Pornography claiming that police observation had led him to believe the following:

A disproportionate number of sex offenders were found to have large quantities of pornographic materials in their residences… more, in the opinion of witnesses, than one would expect to find in the residences of a random sample of non-offenders of the same sex, age, and socioeconomic status, or in the residences of a random sample of offenders whose offenses were not sex offenses. (Quoted in I. Hunter et al., 1993, p. 226)

Correlations like these have been used since the early 19th century to justify attitudes toward pornography (I. Hunter et al., 1993). Such claims are easily criticized on scientific grounds because a "witness's opinion" cannot be relied on (and there has never been a study that has reliably determined the amount of pornography in the "average" nonoffender or non–sex offender's home). Better evidence is suggested in the state-by-state studies (L. Baron & Straus, 1987; J. E. Scott & Schwalm, 1988). Both groups of researchers found a direct nationwide correlation between rape and sexually explicit magazines: Rape rates are highest in those places with the highest circulation of sex magazines.

However, Denmark, which decriminalized pornography in the 1960s, and Japan, where pornography is sold freely and tends to be dominated by rape and bondage scenes, have low rates of reported rape, relative to the United States (Davies, 1997; Posner, 1993). In a study of four countries over 20 years, Kutchinsky (1991) could find no increase in rape relative to other crimes in any of the countries, even as the availability of pornography increased dramatically. L. Baron (1990), the same researcher who found that rape rates correlated with explicit magazines, did a further study, which showed that gender equality was higher in states with higher circulation rates of sexually explicit magazines. This may be because those states are generally more liberal. Women in societies that forbid or repress pornography (such as Islamic societies) tend to be more oppressed than those in societies in which it is freely available. All in all, the effects of pornography on a society's violence toward women are far from clear.

Individual Studies

Several laboratory studies have sought to determine the reactions of men exposed to different types of pornography. In most cases, men are shown pornography and then a test is done to determine whether their attitudes toward women, sex crimes, and the like are altered. Although little evidence indicates that nonviolent, sexually explicit films provoke antifemale reactions in men, many studies have shown that violent or degrading pornography does influence attitudes (Davies, 1997; Padgett et al., 1989). Viewing sexual violence and degradation increases fantasies of rape, the belief that some women secretly desire to be raped, acceptance of violence against women, insensitivity to rape victims, desire for sex without emotional involvement, the treatment of women as sex objects, and desire to see more violent pornography (R. J. Berger et al., 1991; W. A. Fisher & Barak, 1991; Linz, 1989).

However, these studies take place under artificial conditions (Would these men have chosen to see such movies if not in a study?), and feelings of sexual aggression in a laboratory may not mirror a person's activities in the real world. It is also unclear how long such feelings last and whether they really influence behavior (Kutchinsky, 1991). Other studies show that men's aggression tends to increase after seeing any violent movie, even if it is not sexual, and so the explicit sexuality of the movies may not be the important factor (Linz & Donnerstein, 1992). A recent study on the self-perceived effects of pornography use in Danish men and women 18 to 30 years old found few negative effects (Hald & Malamuth, 2008). In fact, participants reported that the use of pornography had an overall positive effect on various aspects of their lives.

Are We Missing the Point?

Lahey (1991) argues that the attempt to determine the effects of viewing pornography misses the point because, once again, the focus is on men and their reactions. Is it not enough that women feel belittled, humiliated, and degraded? The voice of women is silent in pornography studies. The questions focus on whether pornography induces sexual violence in men. Pornography, Lahey (after MacKinnon and Dworkin) argues, harms women by teaching falsehoods about them (that they enjoy painful sex, are not as worthy as men, secretly desire sex even when they refuse it, and do not know what they really like); it harms women's self-esteem; and it harms women by reproducing itself in men's behavior toward women.

Certainly, there is an argument to be made that certain kinds of sexually explicit materials contribute little to society and cause much pain directly and indirectly to women. Many who defend sexually explicit materials that show consensual sex abhor the violent and degrading pornography that is the particular target of feminist ire. Whether the way to respond to such materials is through new laws (which may do little to stop its production; for example, child pornography, which is illegal, flourishes in the United States; Wolak et al., 2005) or through listening to the voices of women, who are its victims, is an open question.

▶▶ ONLINE Pornography

The adult entertainment industry includes pornographic videos, magazines, online content, novelties, and merchandise. Probably the fastest growing area of the adult entertainment industry involves online pornography, which was worth approximately $3 billion in 2006 (a 13% increase from 2005; Edelman, 2009). Many of the online buying features available through websites today (such as real-time credit card processing) were developed by the pornography industry (Griffiths, 2003). The accessibility, anonymity, and ease of use have all contributed to the growing popularity of the Internet. It is estimated that 36% of Internet users visit one or more pornographic websites each month (Edelman, 2009). The average website visit lasts approximately 12 minutes.

Of those adults who visit at least one pornographic website per month, the average user views pornographic websites approxi-

---

REAL RESEARCH 18.4 Heterosexual men who watch pornographic videos containing images of naked men with a woman have been found to have higher quality sperm than heterosexual men who watch similar videos containing only women (KILGALLON & SIMMONS, 2005). Researchers suggest this is due to a perceived sperm competition, wherein a heterosexual male produces higher quality sperm when there is a threat of a female choosing another male.

---

mately 8 times per month (Edelman, 2009). Individuals who have high levels of online pornography use often experience difficulties in their intimate relationships. In fact, one study found 68% of users lost interest in sex with their partner (J. P. Schneider, 2000b). Partners and children of users also experience adverse psychological effects as well, including depression and loneliness (P. Paul, 2005; see Chapter 16 for more information about Internet sexual addictions). Users of online pornography also report desensitization to pornography over time (J. P. Schneider, 2000b).

Over the next few years it will be interesting to see what happens to online pornography. The Internet has helped to solve the problems of distribution and privacy (Chmielewski & Hoffman, 2006). Online pornography reduces embarrassment and allows individuals to watch and buy pornography in the privacy of their own home.

▶▶ PUBLIC ATTITUDES about Pornography

It is not only scholars and activists who disagree about pornography; the general public seems profoundly ambivalent about it as well. The majority want to ban violent pornography and feel that such pornography can lead to a loss of respect for women, acts of violence, and rape. Female erotica and soft-core pornography are generally not viewed as negatively. One of the biggest producers of female erotica is Candida Royalle, who had previously been an adult film actress. Royalle is the founder of Femme Productions, which has produced a number of soft-core pornography videos for women and couples.

Unlike many other businesses today, America's pornography industry continues to do well. One study found that the porn industry generated $97 billion in 2006 alone (Ropelato, 2008). Video and computer technology continues to open doors to millions and millions of customers throughout the world. Even so, pornography is a difficult, controversial problem in American society. By arguing that sex is the only part of human life that should not be portrayed in our art and media, the core conflict over sexuality is revealed: People seem to believe that although sexuality is a central part of human life, it should still be treated differently than other human actions, as a category unto itself.

1 Explain how courts define *pornography* and *obscenity.*

2 Discuss and differentiate between the two commissions on pornography, and explain the findings of each.

3 Identify the two schools of thought regarding the pornography debate.

4 Differentiate between the antipornography and anticensorship arguments.

5 Describe the studies that have been done on the harmful effects of pornography.

6 Discuss public attitudes about pornography.

▶ SEX WORK: Trading Sex for Money

Thus far we have explored how sexual images have been used to sell everything from blue jeans to perfume and how sex has been used in television and films to increase viewership and ratings. We also looked at pornography's history, its growing presence on the Internet, and the public's response to it. Now we turn our attention to those who work in the sex industry, such as prostitutes, escorts, phone sex operators, strippers, and porn stars (in the accompanying Sex in Real Life feature, one college student talks about working in the porn industry). One of the oldest forms of sex work is prostitution (also referred to as "hooking," with prostitutes being referred to as "hookers"), which we focus on in this section.

Defining sex work or prostitution is not easy. The U.S. legal code is ambiguous about what constitutes sex work and prostitution; for instance, some state penal codes define it as the act of hiring out one's body for sexual intercourse, whereas other states define it as sexual intercourse in exchange for money or as any sexual behavior that is sold for profit. This text defines sex work as the exchange of money or goods for sexual services. This can include a wide range of sexual behaviors from erotic interactions without physical contact to high-risk sexual behaviors (Harcourt & Donovan, 2005). Sex workers may be female, male, or transgendered.

Researchers have found the study of sex work a challenge, because the exact size of the population is unknown, making a representative sample difficult to come by (Shaver, 2005). Also, because sex work is illegal in the United States, except for certain counties in Nevada, many sex workers are hidden, so their behaviors cannot be measured. It is estimated that there are as many as 2 million sex workers in the United States today, some full time and some part time. Overall, there are more female sex workers (FSWs) working with male clients than all other forms combined (Goode, 1994; Perkins & Bennett, 1985). Although the use of sex workers is significantly underreported, studies have found that 2% to 3% of adult male residents of large metropolitan areas in the United States have patronized local sex workers (Brewer et al., 2008).

▶▶ SOCIOLOGICAL ASPECTS of Sex Work

Society has created social institutions such as marriage and the family in part to regulate sexual behavior. However, it is also true that, throughout history, people have had sexual relations outside these institutions. Sex work has existed, in one form or another, as long as marriage has, which has led some to argue that it provides a needed sexual release. Whether a society should recognize this by allowing legal, regulated sex work, however, raises a number of controversial social, political, economic, and religious questions.

Some sociologists suggest that sex work developed out of the patriarchal nature of most societies. In a society in which men are valued over women and men hold the reins of economic and political power, some women exploit the only asset that cannot be taken away from them—their sexuality. Other sociologists used to claim that women actually benefited from sex work because, from a purely economic point of view, they get paid for giving something away that is free to them. Kingsley Davis, one of the most famous sociologists of the 20th century, wrote:

> *The woman may suffer no loss at all, yet receive a generous reward, resembling the artist who, paid for his work, loves it so well that he would paint anyway. Purely from the angle of economic return, the hard question is not why so many women become prostitutes, but why so few of them do.* (Quoted in Benjamin, 1961, p. 876)

Xaveria Hollander, one of New York's leading madams for many years, opened the *Vertical Whorehouse* in 1969 but was arrested for prostitution and thrown out of the country a few years later. Today, she operates *Xaveria's Happy House,* a bed and breakfast out of her home in Amsterdam, where I met with her and talked about her life in prostitution.

© Petra Lambert

Lee is a 37-year-old prostitute. She also raises a family at home. Here she talks about her life of prostitution.

I began prostituting when I was nineteen and met some working ladies. I was intrigued by what they were doing and saw the money they had and what they could do with it....

I've made $2,000 in one week, which is very good money. I charge $20 minimum, short time, just for straight sex. That's ten minutes, which will not sound very long to most people, but when you consider that the average male only needs two or three minutes in sex—I had some guys finishing even before they get on the bed. I make all my clients wear a condom and I've put the condom on them and by the time I've turned around to get on the bed they've already blown it. In most of these cases it's the guys who are most apologetic and feel they have fallen down on the job.

I always check my clients both for any disease or body lice. If I am at all wary of a client I always get another girl to double-check. I go to the doctor once a week and get a report within ten minutes. There are some girls who will take anybody and don't use any protection, and they don't know how to check a client properly anyway. Girls on drugs are less careful than they should be, and in the parlors condoms are generally not insisted on.

Clients ask for a range of different sexual activities. It can range from good old-fashioned straight-out sex to swinging from the chandeliers. Apart from bondage and discipline there are some weird requests such as golden showers, spankings and whippings, and the guy who wants a girl to shit on a glass-top table with him underneath the table. There's money to be made in these things, but I won't do them because it's my own individual choice.

As for a typical day for me, I get up between seven and seven-thirty and have the usual argument with getting kids off to school. I do my housework like any other housewife. I have pets, and I have a normal home. I eat, sleep, and breathe like any normal human being. I enjoy cooking a lot. I keep my business quite separate from my home life, and the kids don't know what I do, my husband doesn't want to know about it, and I don't want to discuss it with him. Work is work. I go to work to work and when I go home and close the doors on the house that's it. My occupation is not all that different from any nine-to-five worker except the hours are better, I'm my own boss, and the pay's better.

SOURCE: Perkins and Bennett (1985, pp. 71–85).

▶▶ TYPES of Sex Workers

Sex work is mostly a gendered phenomenon, with women selling and men buying (Oselin, 2010). By far, the main motivation for becoming a sex worker is economic (Harcourt & Donovan, 2005; Oselin, 2010). In this section, we discuss female, male, and adolescent sex workers.

Female Sex Workers

In the United States, most FSWs are young. The average age of entry into sex work is 14 years old (Dittmann, 2005). One study found that 75% of FSWs were younger than 25 and single (Medrano et al., 2003; Potterat et al., 1990).

Typically, FSWs live in an apartment or home with several other sex workers and one pimp. This is known as a **pseudofamily** (Romenesko & Miller, 1989). The pseudofamily operates much like a family does; there are rules and responsibilities for all family members. The pimp is responsible for protecting the FSWs, whereas the women are responsible for bringing home the money. Other household responsibilities are also agreed on. When the female ages or the pimp tires of her, she may be traded like a slave or simply disowned.

pseudofamily
A type of family that develops when prostitutes and pimps live together; rules, household responsibilities, and work activities are agreed on by all members of the family.

Psychological problems are more common to FSWs compared with those not in the industry and more common in older FSWs (de-Schampheleire, 1990). There are dangers associated with a life of sex work, including stressful family situations and mistreatment by clients or pimps. To deal with these pressures, many sex workers turn to drugs or alcohol, although many enter sex work to enable them to make enough money to support their preexisting addictions. Many women who become sex workers have drug addictions and use the sex work as a way to help pay for their drugs (Potterat et al., 1998).

Entry into sex work is often a gradual process (Goode, 1994). At first, the activity may bother FSWs, but as time goes by, they

ON YOUR MIND 18.4

Do sex workers enjoy having sex?

Having sex with whom? Eighty percent of sex workers have sexual lives outside of their professional lives (Savitz & Rosen, 1988). As for sex with clients, although some sex workers report that they enjoy both sexual intercourse and oral sex, the majority do not. Some do experience orgasms in their interactions with clients, but again, the majority do not. In fact, in Masters and Johnson's early research on sexual functioning, they included sex workers (see Chapter 2) but found that the pelvic congestion in sex workers, which resulted from having sex without orgasms, made them poor subjects for their studies.

become accustomed to the life and begin to see themselves and the profession differently. Most work full time, with 49% of their clients repeat customers, including some long-term customers (M. Freund et al., 1989). A regular customer visits the FSW at least once a week, and some have sexual encounters two or three times each week or spend several hours at a hotel (or one of their homes) together. Many FSWs want to escape from sex work (Farley et al., 2003). In the accompanying Sex in Real Life feature, "Female Prostitution: Lee's Story," one woman shares her feelings about her work.

PREDISPOSING FACTORS FOR ENGAGING IN FEMALE SEX WORK Some common threads run through the lives of many FSWs. The most common factor, according to researchers, is an economically deprived upbringing (Goode, 1994). However, because high-class sex workers, who often come from wealthy backgrounds, are less likely to be caught and arrested, research studies may concentrate too much on poorer women.

Early sexual contact with multiple partners has also been found to be related to female sex work. FSWs are also more often victims of sexual abuse, initiate sexual activity at a younger age, and experience a higher frequency of rape. Intrafamilial violence and past physical and sexual abuse are also common (Mitchell et al., 2010; Murphy, 2010; R. L. Simons & Whitbeck, 1991). Overall, Black women who have a history of emotional or physical abuse have been found to be more likely to engage in sex work than White or Hispanic women with similar abuse (Medrano et al., 2003).

Keep in mind that although these factors contribute to a predisposition to sex work, they do not cause a woman to become a sex worker. For example, it is known that many FSWs have had no early sex education either in school or from their family; however, this does not mean that the lack of sex education caused them to become FSWs. Many different roads lead to a life of sex work.

*Early sexual contact with multiple partners has also been found to **be related to female sex work.***

TYPES OF FEMALE SEX WORKERS There are a variety of different types of FSWs. FSWs can solicit their services in the street, clubs, brothels, on CB radios, as **call girls** or **courtesans,** or out of an **escort agency** (Harcourt & Donovan, 2005; Perkins & Bennett, 1985). These types of FSWs differ with respect to the work setting, prices charged, and safety from violence and arrest.

The most widespread type of FSWs is streetwalkers (Harcourt & Donovan, 2005). To attract customers, they dress in tight clothes and high heels and may work on street corners or transportation stops (Riccio, 1992). This type of sex work is considered the most dangerous type because streetwalkers are often victims of violence, rape, and robbery (Dalla, 2002; Romero-Daza et al., 2003).

Streetwalkers generally approach customers and ask them questions, such as "Looking for some action?" or "Do you need a date?" If the client is interested, the prostitute will suggest a price,

"Life in the street is hard when you're hardcore."
—STREETWALKERS: LORETTA'S STORY

View in Video
To watch the entire interview, go to Psychology CourseMate at **login.cengagebrain.com.**

and they will go to a place where the service can be provided (an alley, car, or cheap hotel room). In places where there is a lack of privacy, streetwalkers often provide oral sex or "hand relief" (Harcourt & Donovan, 2005). Other sex workers actively seek out clients via CB radio while driving on the highway, stopping at truck or rest stops to service the clients (Harcourt & Donovan, 2005; Luxenburg & Klein, 1984).

Indoor sex work offers more protection from violence and less police arrests. It includes club or bar sex workers, who solicit clients and perform services on site or at an agreed-on location (Harcourt & Donovan, 2005). **Brothel** sex work is another type of indoor sex work. Brothels vary with respect to their size and design, but it is typically found in places where there is an active sex industry and is regulated by the state (Harcourt & Donovan, 2005). In the United States, Nevada is the only state with counties in which brothels are legal, and sex workers carry identification cards and are routinely examined for STIs. When a customer walks into a brothel in Nevada, he may be given a "menu" of choices. From this menu he picks an appetizer (such as a hot bath or a pornographic video) and a main course (such as the specific sexual position). Then he can choose a woman from a **lineup,** and the couple goes into a private room. The typical rate is $2 per minute, with more exotic services being more expensive. Usually conventional sexual intercourse costs $30 to $40, and oral sex may cost $50 or more.

Probably the most covert form of sex work is done through escort agencies (Harcourt & Donovan, 2005). High-class call girls and courtesans can be reached by phone and services are performed in a client's home or hotel room. In 2008, New York governor Eliot Spitzer was found to have had multiple liaisons with a variety of prostitutes working with the Emperor's Club V.I.P. The

call girl	courtesan	escort agency	brothel	lineup
A higher class female prostitute who is often contacted by telephone and may either work by the hour or the evening or for longer periods.	A prostitute who often interacts with men of rank or wealth.	An agency set up to arrange escorts for unaccompanied males; sexual services are often involved.	A house of prostitution.	The lining up of prostitutes in a brothel so that when clients enter a brothel, they can choose the prostitute they want.

Investigators believe that Eliot Spitzer spent up to $80,000 for prostitutes over a period of several years. One woman he hired was Ashley Dupré, a $1,000-an-hour call girl working with the Emperor's Club V.I.P.

Emperor's Club operated out of New York, Washington, Miami, Paris, and London, and offered prostitutes for anywhere from $1,000 to $5,500 per hour.

Finally, less common types of FSW include **bondage and discipline (B&D) sex workers** who provide B&D services, using such things as leather, whips, and chains. Women who specialize in B&D will advertise with pseudonyms such as Madam Pain or Mistress Domination (Perkins & Bennett, 1985). B&D sex workers may have dungeons, complete with whips, racks, and leg irons, and wear black leather, studded belts, and masks. Lesbian and transgendered sex workers also exist, but little is known about them. Lesbian sex workers tend to be older, and many take younger women on as clients (Perkins & Bennett, 1985).

Male Sex Workers

Male sex workers (MSWs) may service both men and women. MSWs who service men are referred to as **hustlers** or "boys." Many MSWs who have sex with men may identify as heterosexual. Approximately 50% of MSWs are homosexual, 25% are bisexual, and 25% are heterosexual (Pleak & Meyer-Bahlburg, 1990). In many beach resorts around the globe, male "beachboys" or **gigolos** (JIG-uh-lows) are available to wealthier women for both social and sexual needs (Harcourt & Donovan, 2005). Like women, men tend to enter into the life of sex work early, usually by the age of 16 (with a range from 12 to 19; J. A. Cates & Markley, 1992). The majority of MSWs are between the ages of 16 and 29 and are White (D. J. West, 1993). Like the pimp for FSWs, many MSWs also have mentors, or "sugar daddies."

When MSWs are asked what types of sexual behavior they engage in with their clients, 99% say that they perform fellatio, either alone or in combination with other activities; 80% say that they engage in anal sex, and 63% participate in anal rimming (anal oral sex; Morse et al., 1992).

PREDISPOSING FACTORS FOR ENGAGING IN MALE SEX WORK Like females, males engage in sex work mainly for economic reasons (Kaye, 2007). They typically view their work as a valid source of income (Bimbi, 2007). Several factors predispose a man to become a sex worker, including early childhood sexual experience (such as coerced sexual behavior) combined with a homosexual orientation (Earls & David, 1989). MSWs often experience their first sexual experience at a young age (approximately 12 years old) and have older partners. They often have fewer career aspirations than those not in the sex worker industry and are more likely to view themselves as addicted to either drugs or alcohol (Cates & Markley, 1992).

Like female streetwalkers, male streetwalkers have more psychopathologies than non–sex workers, which may have to do with their dangerous and chaotic environments (P. M. Simon et al., 1992). They are more suspicious, mistrustful, hopeless, lonely, and often lack meaningful interpersonal relationships (Leichtentritt & Arad, 2005). These feelings may develop out of the distrust that many have for their clients; clients may refuse to pay for services, hurt them, or force them to do things that they do not want to do. In fact, more than half of MSWs report a fear of violence while they are hustling (J. R. Scott, 2005). Although many would like to stop prostituting, they feel that they would not be able to find other employment (P. M. Simon et al., 1992).

TYPES OF MALE SEX WORKERS MSWs, like FSWs, may engage in street hustling, bar hustling, and escort prostitution. The differences between these types of prostitution are in income potential and personal safety.

Male street and bar hustlers solicit clients on the street or in parks that are known for the availability of the sexual trade. The majority of male prostitutes begin with street hustling, especially if they are too young to get into bars. MSWs, like FSWs, ask their clients if they are "looking for some action."

Because of increasing fear and danger on the streets, many street hustlers eventually move into bars. One MSW explains:

You got a lot of different kinds of assholes out there. When someone pulls up and says "get in," you get in. And you can look at their eyes, and they can be throwing fire out of their eyes, and have a knife under the seat. You're just in a bad situation. I avoid it by not hustling in the street. I hustle in the bars now. (Luckenbill, 1984, p. 288)

bondage and discipline (B&D) sex worker
A prostitute who is paid to engage in bondage and discipline fantasy play with clients.

hustler
A male sex worker who provides sexual services to men.

gigolo
A man who is hired to have a sexual relationship with a woman and receives financial support from her.

MSWs also report that bar hustling enables them to make more money than street hustling because they get to set their own prices. The average price for a bar trick ranges from $50 to $75. A natural progression after bar hustling is working as an escort, which involves finding someone who arranges clients but also takes a share of the profits. Each date that is arranged for an escort can bring from $150 to $200, and the sex worker usually keeps 60% for himself. However, escort services are not always well-run or honest operations, and problems with escort operators may force a MSW to return to bar hustling. Compared with other types of MSWs, however, escorts are least likely to be arrested.

Adolescent Sex Workers

What is known about adolescent sex workers is disheartening. For adolescents who run away from home, sex work offers a way to earn money and to establish their autonomy. Many of these adolescents have been sexually abused and have psychological problems (S. J. Thompson, 2005; Walker, 2002). Adolescent sex work can have long-term psychological and sociological effects on the adolescents and their families (Landau, 1987).

It is estimated that between 1.6 and 2.8 million teens run away from home each year in the United States, and that more than 85% eventually become involved in sex work (Hammer et al., 2002; Landau, 1987). Others engage in sex work while living at home. Stories about adolescent prostitution are often tragic, like the following one from Lynn, a 13-year-old prostitute:

> It was freezing cold that Friday afternoon as I stood on the street corner looking for buyers. The harsh wind made the temperature feel as though it was below zero, and I had been outdoors for almost two and a half hours already. I was wearing a short fake fur jacket, a brown suede miniskirt and spike heels. Only a pair of very sheer hose covered my legs, and I shook as I smiled and tried to flag down passing cars with male drivers.
>
> Finally, a middle-aged man in an expensive red sports car pulled up to the curb. He lowered the car window and beckoned me over to him with his finger. I braced myself to start my act. Trying as hard as I could to grin and liven up my walk, I went over to his car, rested my chest on the open window ledge and said, "Hi ya, Handsome." He answered, "Hello, Little Miss Moffet. How'd you like Handsome to warm you up on a cold day like this?" I wished that I could have told him that I wouldn't like it at all. That even the thought of it made me sick to my stomach. I hid my feelings and tried to look enthusiastic. So with the broadest smile I could manage, I answered, "There's nothing I'd like better than to be with you, Sir." I started to get into his car, but he stopped me, saying, "Not so fast, Honey, how much is this going to cost me?" I hesitated for a moment. I really wanted twenty dollars, but it had been a slow day and I had a strong feeling that this guy wasn't going to spring for it, so I replied, "Fifteen dollars, and the price of the hotel room."
>
> We had sex in the same run-down dirty hotel that I always take my tricks to. It doesn't cost much, and usually that's all

> that really matters to them. Being with that guy was horrible, just like it always turns out to be. That old overweight man sweated all over me and made me call him Daddy the whole time. He kept calling me Marcy, and later he explained that Marcy was his youngest daughter. Once he finished with me, the guy seemed in a big hurry to leave. He dressed quickly, and just as he was about to rush out the door, I yelled out, "But what about my money?" He pulled a ten-dollar bill out of his back pocket and laid it on the dresser, saying only, "Sorry, kid, this is all I've got on me right now."
>
> At that moment I wished that I could have killed him, but I knew that there was nothing I could do. The middle-class man in the expensive red sports car had cheated his 13-year-old hooker. That meant that I had to go back out on the street and brave the cold again in order to find another taker. (Landau, 1987, pp. 25–26)

Pimps look for scared adolescent runaways on the street or at train and bus stations, luring them with promises of friendship and potential love relationships. A pimp will approach a runaway in a very caring and friendly way, offering to buy her a meal or give her a place to stay. At first, he makes no sexual demands whatsoever. He buys her clothes and meals and does whatever it takes to make her feel indebted to him. To him, all of his purchases are a debt she will one day repay. As soon as the relationship becomes sexual and the girl has professed her love for the pimp, he begins asking her to "prove" her love by selling her body. The girl may agree to do so only once, not realizing the destructive cycle she is beginning. This cycle is based on breaking down her self-esteem and increasing her feelings of helplessness. Male adolescents may enter into the life of prostitution in similar ways. Some may choose a life of sex work to meet their survival needs or to support a drug habit.

Outside the United States, adolescent sex work is prevalent in many countries, such as Brazil and Thailand. Female adolescents in Brazil are drawn to sex work primarily for economic reasons (Penna-Firme et al., 1991; sex trafficking is discussed later in this chapter). In Thailand, some parents sell their daughter's virginity for money or act as their managers and arrange jobs for them.

▶▶ OTHER PLAYERS in the Business

Sex workers are not the only people involved in the business. Other players include pimps and clients.

Pimps

Pimps play an important role in sex work, although not all sex workers have pimps. In exchange for money, a pimp offers a sex worker protection from both clients and the police. Many pimps take all of an FSWs earnings and manage the money, providing

pimp
A slang term that refers to the male in charge of organizing clients for a female prostitute.

her with clothes, jewels, food, and sometimes a place to live. Many pimps feel powerful within their peer group and enjoy the fact that their job is not particularly stressful for them. Pimps often require that their FSWs make a certain amount of money (Dalla, 2002). A pimp recruits FSWs and will often manage a group of sex workers, known as his "stable" (Ward et al., 1994). He is typically sexually involved with many of them.

Clients

Clients of sex workers are often referred to as **johns** or **tricks** (Brooks-Gordon & Geisthorpe, 2003). The term *trick* has also been used to describe the behavior requested by the client. This term originated from the idea that the client was being "tricked" out of something, mainly his money (Goode, 1994).

What motivates people to use sex workers? Sigmund Freud believed that some men preferred sex with prostitutes because they were incapable of sexual arousal without feeling that their partner was inferior or a "bad" woman. Carl Jung went a step further and claimed that prostitution was tied to various unconscious **archetypes,** such as the "Great Mother." This archetype includes feelings of hatred and sexuality, which are connected to mother figures. This, in turn, leads men to have impersonal sex with partners whom they do not love or to whom they have no attraction.

There is much confusion about clients and the reasons they visit sex workers (Brooks-Gordon & Geisthorpe, 2003). What is known is that the majority of clients of sex workers are male, and they visit sex workers for a variety of reasons: for guaranteed sex, to eliminate the risk for rejection, for greater control in sexual encounters, for companionship, to have undivided attention, a lack of sexual outlets, physical or mental handicaps, for adventure or curiosity, or to relieve loneliness (Jordan, 1997; McKeganey & Bernard, 1996; Monto, 2000, 2001). Married men may seek out sex workers when their wives will not perform certain sexual behaviors, when they feel guilty about asking their wives to engage in an activity, or when they feel the behaviors are too deviant to discuss with their wives (Jordan, 1997). A nonscientific study done in 2008 interviewed men who had paid for sex and found that the majority of men felt highly conflicted about their behavior (Heinzmann, 2008). Eighty-three percent of men said they kept returning to sex workers because it was an "addiction," and 40% said they were drunk when they went. One client felt it was all about business: "Prostitutes are a product, like cereal. You go to the grocery, pick the brand you want and pay for it. It's business" (Heinzmann, 2008).

When men who were arrested for soliciting sex workers were asked which sexual behaviors they engaged in, 81% had received fellatio, 55% had engaged in sexual intercourse, whereas others engaged in a little of both, or manual masturbation (i.e., hand jobs; Monto, 2001). Sadomasochistic behavior, with the woman as dominant and the man submissive, is the most common form of "kinky" sexual behavior requested from sex workers (Goode, 1994). Other commonly requested behaviors include clients dressing as women, masturbating in front of nude clients, and rubber fetishes. One FSW recalled a job in which she was paid $300 to dress up in a long gown and urinate in a cup while her client masturbated, and another was asked to have sex with a client in his daughter's bed (Dalla, 2002).

Clients may also seek out sex workers because they are afraid of emotional commitments and want to keep things uninvolved (which is what Eliot Spitzer, the governor of New York, said about his liaisons with call girls); to build up their egos (many FSWs fake orgasm and act very sexually satisfied); because they are starved for affection and intimacy; or because they travel a great deal or work in heavily male-populated areas (such as in the armed services) and desire sexual activity.

Kinsey found that clients of sex workers are predominantly White, middle-class, unmarried men who are between the ages of 30 and 60 (Kinsey et al., 1948). More recent research supports Kinsey's findings—the majority of men who visit sex workers are middle-aged and unmarried (or unhappily married; Monto & McRee, 2005). They also tend to be regular or repeat clients:

REAL RESEARCH 18.5 The National Health and Social Life Survey found a substantial discrepancy between men's and women's interest in fellatio. Although 45% of men reported receiving fellatio as very appealing, only 17% of women found giving it appealing (Monto, 2001). Not surprisingly, fellatio is the most requested sexual behavior from prostitutes (MONTO, 2001).

Almost 100% go monthly or more frequently, and half of these go weekly or more frequently (M. Freund et al., 1991). "Regulars" often pay more than new customers and are a consistent source of income (Dalla, 2002).

The majority of clients are not concerned with the police because law enforcement is usually directed at the sex workers rather than clients. However, some authorities have gone so far as videotaping license plates and enrolling clients in "john school" to stop their behaviors (B. Fisher et al., 2002).

▶▶ THE GOVERNMENT'S ROLE in Sex Work

Sex work is illegal in every state in the United States, except, as noted earlier, for certain counties in Nevada. However, even though it is illegal, it still exists in almost every large U.S. city. In general, the government could address the issue of sex work in two ways. It could remain a criminal offense, or it could be legalized and regulated. If sex work were legalized, it would be subject to government regulation over such things as licensing, location, health standards, and advertising.

john
A slang term that refers to a prostitute's client.

trick
A slang term that refers to the sexual services of a prostitute; also may refer to a john.

archetypes
Ancient images that Carl Jung believed we are born with and influenced by.

The biggest roadblock to legalized sex work in the United States is that it is viewed as an immoral behavior by the majority of people (Rio, 1991). Laws that favor legal sex work would, in effect, be condoning this immoral behavior. Overall, however, the strongest objections to legalized sex work are reactions to streetwalking. Today the majority of Americans believe that the potential benefits of legalized sex work should be evaluated.

Those who feel that sex work should be legalized believe that this would result in lower levels of STIs (because sex workers could be routinely checked for STIs) and less disorderly conduct. Another argument in favor of legalization is that if sex work were legal, the government would be able to collect taxes on the money earned by both sex workers and their pimps. Assuming a 25% tax rate, this gross income would produce more than $20 billion each year in previously uncollected taxes.

In parts of Nevada where sex work is legal, the overwhelming majority of people report that they favor legalized sex work. Ordinances in Nevada vary by county, with each county responsible for deciding whether sex work is legal throughout the county, only in certain districts, or not at all. For instance, there are no legal broth-

---

REAL RESEARCH 18.6 More than 1 in 12 U.S. men report exchanging drugs, money, or a place to stay for sex with a female in the last year (DECKER ET AL., 2008).

---

els in Reno or Las Vegas, perhaps because these cities enjoy large conventions and because many men attend these conventions without their partners. City officials felt that if a convention was held in a town with legalized sex work, many partners might not want the men to attend; thus, there would be a decrease in the number of convention participants. Even so, there are several brothels near Reno and Las Vegas, and also several that are close to state borders. Usually, these are the largest of all the Nevada brothels. Brothels are locally owned small businesses that cater to both local and tourist customers. Although sex work in Nevada is not a criminal offense, there are laws against enticing people into sex work, such as pimping or advertising for sex workers (H. Reynolds, 1986).

Crackdowns on sex work in other areas of the United States (where it is not legal) often result in driving it further underground. This is exactly what happened in New York City in the 1980s. After law officials closed down several brothels in Manhattan, many of them moved to Queens. Some of the sex workers began operating out of "massage parlors" or private homes, which were supported through drug money.

Many groups in the United States and abroad are working for the legalization of prostitution. In San Francisco in 1973, an organization called COYOTE ("Call Off Your Old Tired Ethics") was formed by an ex-prostitute named Margo St. James to change the public's views of prostitution. Today, COYOTE is regarded as the best-known sex workers' rights group in the United States. COYOTE's mission is to repeal all laws against sex work, to reshape sex work into a credible occupation, and to protect the rights of sex workers. Members argue that contrary to popular belief, not all sex work is forced—some women voluntarily choose to become sex workers, and it should be respected as a career choice.

Delores French, a prostitute, author, president of the Florida COYOTE group, and president of HIRE ("Hooking Is Real Employment") argues:

> *A woman has the right to sell sexual services just as much as she has the right to sell her brains to a law firm when she works as a lawyer, or to sell her creative work to a museum when she works as an artist, or to sell her image to a photographer when she works as a model, or to sell her body when she works as a ballerina. Since most people can have sex without going to jail, there is no reason except old fashioned prudery to make sex for money illegal.* (Quoted in Jenness, 1990, p. 405)

▶▶ SEX WORK and Sexually Transmitted Infections

Most U.S. sex workers are knowledgeable about STIs and AIDS. They try to minimize their risks by using condoms, rejecting clients with obvious STIs, and routinely taking antibiotics. However, although FSWs often do feel they are at risk for infection with STIs or AIDS with clients, they usually do not feel this way with their husbands or boyfriends (Dorfman et al., 1992). Condoms are used less frequently with their own sexual partners than with clients. Among MSWs who have sex with men, receptive anal intercourse without a condom is the most common mode of HIV transmission (Elifson et al., 1993), whereas among FSWs, intravenous drug use is the most common mode of HIV transmission.

Many opponents of legalized sex work claim that legalization would lead to increases in the transmission of various STIs. However, STI transmission and sex work have been found to have less of a relationship than you might think. Rates of STIs in Europe were found to decrease when sex work was legalized and to increase when it was illegal (Rio, 1991). This is probably because legalization can impose restrictions on the actual practice and require medical evaluations. Many sex workers take antibiotics sporadically to reduce the risk for STIs; however, this practice has led some strains of STIs to become resistant to various antibiotics. Also, viral STIs, such as AIDS and herpes, are not cured by antibiotics.

▶▶ QUITTING Sex Work

Sex work is considered by many to be a deviant, and often low-status, line of work. Women and men in this industry are often labeled and stigmatized for working in an area that violates societal norms (Ebaugh, 1988; Oselin, 2010). Their job creates a role for them in society, which influences their view of the world and the behaviors they engage in. Because many sex workers see themselves as deviant, this makes it especially difficult to leave. In addition, few have support systems that could help them get out.

Women who do leave often have many reasons for doing so. One common reason involves religion and wanting to reestablish a religious lifestyle. One FSW who left the industry said:

When I was working on the streets, I kept praying to God: This is not me. Why do I keep doing this? Why can't I stop? God help me stop…He was always there knocking I just had to open up the door to allow him to come in and help me stop. (Oselin, 2010, p. 532)

Other women leave because of fear and the experience of seeing all the violence on the streets. One FSW who left for this reason said:

I thought I was going to die in the life because I didn't see anyway out no matter how much I wanted it to end. Things were getting worse on the streets day by day. I've seen about five prostitutes I knew end up dead in garbage cans. (Oselin, 2010, p. 533)

Other women cite personal and family relationships, exhaustion, sobriety, and feeling too old to continue as reasons for quitting (Oselin, 2010). Research has found that between 60% and 75% of FSWs were raped, whereas 70% to 95% were physically assaulted (U.S. Department of State, 2005). These experiences, along with jail time, multiple pregnancies, and STIs can also be turning points for quitting the industry.

Another key factor in leaving sex work is finding an agency that offers assistance, such as a prostitution-helping organization (PHO; Oselin, 2010). These organizations provide information, assistance, and shelter for women who want to leave sex work. Sometimes their first interaction with a PHO is through a mobile outreach unit that appears in their neighborhood (Oselin, 2010). Other women find out about PHOs from counselors, jail personnel, friends, or advertising. One woman who found a PHO said:

I couldn't do it alone. I tried before but it didn't work. I started to get back on drugs. And the only thing I knew was to go and get money from men [through sex] and once I started doing that I started using drugs too. The program offered me a different way out. I knew they helped you get an education, a job, and maintain sobriety. (Oselin, 2010, p. 544)

▶▶ SEX WORK AROUND the World

During World War II, it is estimated that 200,000 women from Japan, Korea, China, the Philippines, Indonesia, Taiwan, and the Netherlands were taken by the Imperial Japanese Army from their hometowns and put in brothels for Japanese soldiers (Kakuchi, 2005). In 1993, Japan finally admitted to having forced women to prostitute themselves as **comfort girls,** and in the early 2000s, these women demanded compensation for the suffering they were forced to endure. In 2005, the Women's Active Museum on War and Peace in Tokyo was opened to honor the women who worked as sex slaves during World War II.

A group named GABRIELA (General Assembly Binding Women for Reforms, Integrity, Equality, Leadership, and Action) has formed in the Philippines in an attempt to fight sex work, sexual harassment, rape, and battering of women. More than 100 women's organizations belong to GABRIELA, which supports the economic, health, and working conditions of women. GABRIELA operates free clinics for sex workers and also provides seminars and activities to educate the community about sex work (L. West, 1989).

© AFP/Getty Images

At a beach resort in Thailand, young prostitutes wait for a buyer.

Sex work has long been a part of the cultural practices in Thailand. Many countries, including the United States, Japan, Taiwan, South Korea, Australia, and Europe, organize "sex tours" to Thailand. Sex workers are so prevalent in Thailand that Thai men view a trip to a sex worker almost in the same regard as going to the store for milk (Sexwork.com, 1999). It has also been suggested that because many Thais are Buddhists, they believe in reincarnation and hope that they will not be a sex worker in their next life. This belief in reincarnation often reduces the fear of death (Kirsch, 1985; Limanonda et al., 1993). Sex work is endorsed by both men and women in Thailand, mainly because of the prevailing belief that men have greater sex drives than women (Taywaditep et al., 2004). In fact, college students in Thailand often report that sex work protects "good women" from being raped (Taywaditep et al., 2004).

It is estimated that there are between 500,000 and 700,000 FSWs and between 5,000 and 8,000 MSWs in Thailand—working "direct" (in brothels or massage parlors) or "indirect" (available for dates and also offering sex for their customers). Direct sex workers make between $2 and $20 for a service, whereas indirect sex workers make between $20 and several hundred dollars (Taywaditep, 2004). Sex workers in Thailand are required to participate in the governmental STI monitoring system, which has helped decrease STI prevalence. Thailand has instituted a "100% condom use" program targeted at the sex work industry (Sharma, 2001). As a result, condom use by sex workers and clients is high. One study found that 79% of men used condoms with sex workers (compared with 4% of men using them with regular partners; Ford & Chamrathrithirong, 2007).

In Amsterdam, Holland, De Wallen is the largest and best known red-light district. This area is crowded with sex shops, adult movie and live theater shows, and street and window prostitutes. These prostitutes are called "window" prostitutes because

comfort girl
A woman in Japan or the Philippines during World War II who was forced into prostitution by the government to provide sex for soldiers; also called a *hospitality girl.*

De Wallen, also known as *Rosse Buurt* or the Red Light District, is a designated area for legalized prostitution in Amsterdam, Holland.

they sit behind a window and sell their bodies. There are approximately 200 such windows in the red-light district, which is one of the biggest tourist attractions in Amsterdam. Travel services run tours through the red-light district, although these tourists do not generally hire the sex workers. Sex work in Amsterdam is loosely regulated by authorities. Sex workers pay taxes, get regular checkups, and participate in government-sponsored health and insurance plans (McDowell, 1986).

In Cuba, MSWs and FSWs who solicit tourists are known as *jineteros* (Espín et al., 2004). *Jineteros* exchange sex for clothing or other luxuries brought over from other countries. In Havana, teenagers offer sex to older tourists in exchange for a six-pack of cola or a dance club's cover charges. FSWs in Cuba also ply the tourist trade.

Although sex work exists all over the world, it is dealt with differently in each culture. We have much to learn from the way that other cultures deal with sex work. There are many places throughout the world where young girls are forced into sexual slavery against their will, which is discussed next.

◄ review QUESTIONS

1 Define sex work and explain some of the problems with legal definitions.

2 Identify the factors that sociologists believe helped foster the development of sex work.

3 Describe what the research has found about FSWs, MSWs, and adolescent prostitutes, and differentiate among the various types of sex workers.

4 Describe the responsibilities of a pimp.

5 Identify the factors that research has found motivate people to hire sex workers.

6 Identify the pros and cons of legalized sex work.

7 Explain what has been found about STI knowledge and condom usage in prostitutes.

8 Identify and explain the issues that arise after a prostitute stops prostituting.

9 Describe what is known about prostitution outside the United States.

▶ SEX TRAFFICKING:
Modern-Day Slavery

Sex trafficking is the most common form of modern-day slavery and is one of the fastest growing organized crimes (Schauer & Wheaton, 2006; Walker-Rodriguez & Hill, 2011). Victims tend to come from countries such as Asia, the former Soviet Union, Africa, Eastern Europe, and the United States, and are most commonly trafficked to Italy, the United States, Germany, and the Netherlands (Hodge, 2008). The United States is the second largest destination and market country in the world for women and children trafficked by the sex industry (Germany is number one; Schauer & Wheaton, 2006).

Some victims are recruited via false-front agencies (such as modeling or employment agencies that pose as legitimate organizations), or they are approached because they are already working in prostitution in their native country and are promised more money in wealthier nations (Hodge, 2008). Because many cannot afford the trip, they agree to work off their debts once they arrive in their new location (referred to as "debt bondage"; Hodge, 2008). For many others, there is no choice involved in the process—they are sold by poor family members or kidnapped.

▶▶ STATISTICS

It is estimated that between 600,000 and 800,000 people are trafficked across international borders every year—80% of whom are female and 50% children (Hodge, 2008). Although we tend to think of sex trafficking as only an international problem, it is estimated that between 100,000 to 300,000 children are trafficked in the United States each year (Carr, 2009).

▶▶ VICTIMS

Traffickers often use force, drugs, and financial methods to control their victims (Walker-Rodriguez & Hill, 2011). Gang rapes and other forms of violence are common to force the victims to stay. Continuous abuse makes victims more likely to comply with the demands of the traffickers. One victim, a teen runaway from Baltimore, Maryland, was gang-raped by an acquaintance of the trafficker, who "rescued" her and demanded she repay him by working as his prostitute (Walker-Rodriguez & Hill, 2011). Many of the women and girls are frightened and afraid to speak out against the traffickers.

The physical and psychological costs to victims of sexual trafficking are high. Many are locked in homes or brothels for weeks or months and are beaten and raped. Physical symptoms often include broken bones, bruises, cuts, and vaginal bleeding (Raymond & Hughes, 2001), whereas emotional symptoms include depression, anxiety, and posttraumatic stress disorder (Hodge, 2008).

Following is one young woman's testimony before the U.S. Senate Foreign Relations Committee in 2000:

When I was 14, a man came to my parents' house in Veracruz, Mexico, and asked me if I was interested in making money in the United States. He said I could make many times as much money doing the same things that I was doing in Mexico. At the time, I was working in a hotel cleaning rooms and I also helped around my house by watching my brothers and sisters. He said I would be in good hands, and would meet many other Mexican girls who had taken advantage of this great opportunity. My parents didn't want me to go, but I persuaded them.

A week later, I was smuggled into the United States through Texas to Orlando, Florida. It was then the men told me that my employment would consist of having sex with men for money. I had never had sex before, and I had never imagined selling my body. And so my nightmare began. Because I was a virgin, the men decided to initiate me by raping me again and again, to teach me how to have sex. Over the next three months, I was taken to a different trailer every 15 days. Every night I had to sleep in the same bed in which I had been forced to service customers all day. I couldn't do anything to stop it. I wasn't allowed to go outside without a guard. Many of the bosses had guns. I was constantly afraid. One of the bosses carried me off to a hotel one night, where he raped me. I could do nothing to stop him.

Because I was so young, I was always in demand with the customers. It was awful. Although the men were supposed to wear condoms, some didn't, so eventually I became pregnant and was forced to have an abortion. They sent me back to the brothel almost immediately. I cannot forget what has happened. I can't put it behind me. I find it nearly impossible to trust people. I still feel shame. I was a decent girl in Mexico. I used to go to church with my family. I only wish none of this had ever happened. (Polaris Project, 2005)

▶▶ LOOKING Forward

In 2000, the U.S. Congress passed the Trafficking Victims Protection Act, which was the first federal law that specifically addressed trafficking (Walker-Rodriguez & Hill, 2011). This law has helped protect victims of sexual trafficking by increasing awareness and enforcing laws against sexual trafficking (Hodge, 2008). It has also helped to create a "T-visa," which allows international victims to stay in the United States to assist federal authorities in the prosecution of traffickers. Victims may be moved into the witness protection program and granted permanent residency after 3 years (Hodge, 2008). The law helped to increase awareness, monitor the situation, and improve prosecution.

The Federal Bureau of Investigation with the U.S. Immigration and Customs Enforcement agencies and other local, state, and federal law enforcement agencies work together to help combat sex trafficking of both U.S. and international victims.

Throughout this chapter, we have explored erotic representations in books, television, advertising, other media, and how sex is used to sell products. We have also examined the sale of sex itself through sex work. There are many effects to living in a society so saturated with sexual representations, and these effects certainly help shape our opinions and thoughts about men, women, and sexuality today.

The physical and psychological costs to victims of sexual trafficking **are high.**

◀ review QUESTIONS

1 Define sex trafficking and identify countries that are often involved in such practices.

2 Provide one way in which women become victims of sex trafficking.

3 Explain the methods that traffickers use to control their victims.

4 What is the U.S. government doing to help protect victims of trafficking?

SUMMARY POINTS

1 Erotic representations have existed in almost all societies at almost all times; they have also been the subject of censorship by religious or governmental powers.

2 Pornography emerged as a separate category of erotic art during the 18th century. The printing press made it more readily available. The erotic novel first established pornography production as a business in the Western world, and it provoked a response of censorship from church and governmental authorities.

3 Television and, to a lesser extent, movies have become the primary media in the United States, and they contain enormous amounts of sexually suggestive material. Certain groups have begun to organize to change the content of television programming.

4 Advertising has commercialized sexuality and uses an enormous amount of sexual imagery to sell products. Advertisements are becoming more sexually explicit in the general media in the United States.

5 Pornography is one of the most difficult issues in public life in America. Feminists, conservatives, and the religious right argue that pornography is destructive, violates the rights of women, corrupts children, and should be banned or severely restricted. Liberals and critics of banning pornography argue that creating a definition of pornography that protects art and literature is impossible, that people have the right to read whatever materials they want in their own homes, and that censorship is a slippery slope that leads to further censorship. The public is split between these positions.

6 The online pornography industry continues to grow. The accessibility, anonymity, and ease of use have all contributed to the growing popularity of the Internet. Some view online pornography, visit sexually oriented chat rooms, or may engage in sexual activities with an anonymous person online. Users of online pornography also report desensitization to pornography over time.

7 Defining sex work or prostitution is not easy. The U.S. legal code is ambiguous about what constitutes sex work and prostitution; for instance, some state penal codes define it as the act of hiring out one's body for sexual intercourse, whereas other states define it as sexual intercourse in exchange for money or as any sexual behavior that is sold for profit.

8 Sex work involves the exchange of money or goods for sexual services. This can include a wide range of sexual behaviors from erotic interactions without physical contact to high-risk sexual behaviors. Sex workers may be female, male, or transgendered.

9 The sex industry includes prostitutes, escorts, phone sex operators, strippers, and porn stars. One of the oldest forms of sex work is prostitution. Sex work is mostly a gendered phenomenon, with women selling and men buying. By far, the main motivation for becoming a sex worker is economic.

10 Female sex workers (FSWs) often experience an economically deprived upbringing. Although high-class sex workers, who often come from wealthy backgrounds, are less likely to be caught and arrested, research studies may concentrate too much on poorer women.

11 FSWs are also more often victims of sexual abuse, initiate sexual activity at a younger age, and experience a higher frequency of rape. Intrafamilial violence and past physical and sexual abuse are also common.

12 FSWs can solicit their services in the street, clubs, brothels, on CB radios, as call girls or courtesans, or out of an escort agency. These types of FSWs differ with respect to the work setting, prices charged, and safety from violence and arrest. The most widespread type of FSWs is streetwalkers.

13 MSWs engage in sex work mainly for economic reasons and view their work as a valid source of income. Many experienced early childhood sexual experience (such as coerced sexual behavior) combined with a homosexual orientation, first sexual experience at a young age (approximately 12 years old), and have older partners. They often have fewer career aspirations than those not in the sex worker industry, and are more likely to view themselves as addicted to either drugs or alcohol. MSWs, like FSWs, may engage in street hustling, bar hustling, and escort prostitution. The differences between these types of prostitution are in income potential and personal safety.

14 It is estimated that between 1.6 and 2.8 million teens run away from home each year in the United States, and that more than 85% eventually become involved in sex work. Outside the United States, adolescent sex work is prevalent in many countries, such as Brazil and Thailand. Female adolescents in Brazil are drawn to sex work primarily for economic reasons.

15 Pimps play an important role in sex work. They offer protection, recruit other prostitutes, may manage a group of sex workers, and try to keep them hustling to make money. Successful pimps can make a great deal of money and often feel powerful in their role as a pimp.

16 Clients go to sex workers for a variety of reasons, including guaranteed sex, to eliminate the risk for rejection, for companionship, to have the undivided attention of the prostitute, because they have no other sexual outlets, for adventure or curiosity, or to relieve loneliness.

17 Many people believe that sex work should be legalized so that it can be subjected to government regulation and taxation. However, others think that it would be immoral to legalize it.

18 Different groups, such as COYOTE, have organized to change the public's views of prostitution and to change the laws against it. These groups are also common outside the United States.

19 Sex workers are at high risk for acquiring STIs and AIDS. Overall, they are knowledgeable about these risks and use condoms some of the time. STIs have been found to decrease when sex work is legalized and increase when it is illegal.

20 FSWs cite personal and family relationships, exhaustion, sobriety, and feeling too old to continue as reasons for quitting sex work. Research has found that between 60% and 75% of FSWs were raped, whereas 70% to 95% were physically assaulted (U.S. Department of State, 2005). These experiences, along with jail time, multiple pregnancies, and/or sexually transmitted infections (STIs), can also be turning points for quitting the industry.

21 An important factor in quitting sex work is finding an agency that offers assistance, such as a prostitution-helping organization.

22 Sex workers exist all over the world. "Comfort girls" were forced into sex work in Japan during World War II. "Hospitality girls" were used for the same purposes in the Philippines.

23 Sex work has long been a part of the cultural practices in Thailand. Sex work is legal and supported by both men and women in Thailand mainly because of the prevailing belief that men have greater sex drives than women. College students in Thailand often report that sex work protects "good women" from being raped. Sex workers in Thailand are required to be under a governmental STI monitoring system, which has helped decrease STI prevalence.

24 Sex trafficking is the most common form of modern-day slavery and is one of the fastest growing organized crimes. Victims tend to come from countries such as Asia, the former Soviet Union, Africa, Eastern Europe, and the United States, and are most commonly trafficked to Italy, the United States, Germany, and the Netherlands.

25 The United States is the second largest destination and market country in the world for women and children trafficked by the sex industry. It is estimated that between 600,000 and 800,000 people are trafficked across international borders every year—80% of whom are female and 50% children.

26 Traffickers often use force, drugs, and financial methods to control their victims. Many of the victims are drugged and/or beaten and raped. Gang rapes and other forms of violence are common to force the victims to stay.

27 The Federal Bureau of Investigation with the U.S. Immigration and Customs Enforcement agencies and other local, state, and federal law enforcement agencies work together to help combat sex trafficking of both U.S. and international victims.

CRITICAL THINKING QUESTIONS

1 When you read through one of your favorite magazines and see the various advertisements that use sex to sell their products, what effect do these ads have on you? Do you think there are any effects of living in a society so saturated with sexual images? Why or why not?

2 Do you think that sex or violence on television influences how promiscuous or violent our society becomes? Do the sexual stereotypes paraded before us in commercials and advertisements shape our attitudes toward gender relations? What do you think can be done about this?

3 What television shows did you watch as a child? What messages about gender, sexuality, and relationships did you learn from these shows? Would you let your own child watch these shows today? Why or why not?

4 Would you ever want to go to a strip club? If so, what would be your reasons for going? For not going? If you have been, what types of reactions did you have?

5 The U.S. is the second largest destination and market country in the world for women and children trafficked by the sex industry. If you were to design a strategy to reduce trafficking in the United States, what would you do?

MEDIA RESOURCES

CourseMate brings course concepts to life with interactive learning, study, and exam preparation tools that support the printed textbook. A textbook-specific website, Psychology CourseMate includes an integrated interactive eBook and other interactive learning tools including quizzes, flashcards, videos, and more. If your textbook does not include an access code card, go to CengageBrain.com to gain access.

CENGAGENOW   CengageNOW is an easy-to-use online resource that helps you study in less time to get the grade you want—NOW. Take a pre-test for this chapter and receive a personalized study plan based on your results that will identify the topics you need to review and direct you to online resources to help you master those topics. Then take a post-test to help you determine the concepts you have mastered and what you will need to work on. If your textbook does not include an access code card, go to CengageBrain.com to gain access.

View in Video available in CourseMate and CengageNOW:

Are Reality Shows Realistic?: Two college students discuss the impact of reality shows on college student attitudes about gender and sexuality.

Linda Magazine: Win a Gigolo or a Leather Bag!: An interview with Margot Jamnisek, who works at *Linda*, a successful Dutch magazine. She discusses the sexual content of the magazine and strategies to increase readership.

Streetwalkers: Loretta's Story: A streetwalker describes her life and how she got into prostitution.

Websites:

STORM: Sex Trade Opportunities for Risk Minimization ▪ STORM is a harm-reduction advocacy, education, direct services, and activist organization for individuals and issues involving the sex trade. Its website contains harm-reduction information and strategies offered by current or former sex workers.

Coalition Against Trafficking in Women (CATW) ▪ Founded in 1988, CATW was the first international, nongovernmental organization to focus on human sex trafficking, especially in women and children. CATW promotes women's human rights by working internationally to combat sexual exploitation in all its forms.

GABRIELA Network, USA (GABNet) ▪ The GABRIELA (General Assembly Binding Women for Reforms, Integrity, Equality, Leadership, and Action) Network is a United States–based multiracial, multiethnic women's solidarity organization that works on issues that affect women and children of the Philippines but have their roots in decisions made in the United States. The Purple Rose Campaign, spearheaded by GABRIELA, addresses the issue of sex trafficking of Filipino women and children.

Henry J. Kaiser Family Foundation ▪ The Kaiser Foundation conducts original survey research on a wide range of topics related to health policy and public health, as well as major social issues, including sexuality. In 2005, the Kaiser Foundation published Sex on TV 4, the fourth study on sex on television. The goal of Kaiser's surveys is to better understand the public's knowledge, attitudes, and behaviors.

Prostitution Research and Education ▪ Prostitution Research and Education, sponsored by the San Francisco Women's Centers, develops research and educational programs to document the experiences of people in prostitution through research, public education, and arts projects. Links are provided to fact sheets about prostitution, arguments for and against legalization, outreach programs for those who want to leave the business, information on female slavery outside the United States, and many other important topics.

Victims of Pornography ▪ Victims of Pornography is a website aimed to educate and create awareness that there are real victims of pornography. The site includes news; letters from men, women, and children who have been involved with pornography; and links to advocacy and outreach groups.

Aaronson, I., & Aaronson, A. (2010). How should we classify intersex disorders? *Journal of Pediatric Urology, 6*(5), 443–446.

Abbey, A., Zawacki, T., & Buck, P. O. (2005). The effects of past sexual assault perpetration and alcohol consumption on men's reactions to women's mixed signals. *Journal of Social & Clinical Psychology, 24*(2), 129–155.

Abboud, L. N., & Liamputtong, P. (2003). Pregnancy loss: What it means to women who miscarry and their partners. *Social Work in Health Care, 36*(3), 37–62.

Abdel-Hamid, I. A., & Saleh, E. S. (2011). Primary lifelong delayed ejaculation: Characteristics and response to bupropion. *Journal of Sexual Medicine, 8*(6), 1772–1779.

Abel, G., Becker, J., & Skinner, L. (1980). Aggressive behavior and sex. *Psychiatric Clinics of North America, 3,* 133–135.

Abma, J. C., Martinez, G. M., & Copen, C. E. (2010). Teenagers in the United States: Sexual activity, contraceptive use, and childbearing, National Survey of Family Growth 2006–2008. National Center for Health Statistics. *Vital Health Statistics, 23*(30), 1–47.

"Abortion Policy in the Absence of *Roe*." (2011, March 1). State policies in brief. Alan Guttmacher Institute. Retrieved March 18, 2011, from http://www.guttmacher.org/statecenter/spibs/spib_APAR.pdf.

Abouesh, A., & Clayton, A. (1999). Compulsive voyeurism and exhibitionism: A clinical response to paroxetine. *Archives of Sexual Behavior, 28*(1), 23–30.

AbouZeid, A. A., Mousa, M. H., Soliman, H. A., Hamza, A. F., & Hay, S. A. (2011). Intra-abdominal testis: Histological alterations and significance of biopsy. *Journal of Urology, 185*(1), 269–274.

Abramson, A. (2003). *The history of television: 1942–2000.* Jefferson, NC: McFarland Publishers.

Adair, L. S., & Gordon-Larsen, P. (2001). Maturational timing and overweight prevalence in U.S. adolescent girls. *American Journal of Public Health, 91*(4), 642–645.

Adam, B. D. (1987). *The rise of a gay and lesbian movement.* Boston: Twayne.

Adams, H. E., Wright, L. W., Jr., & Lohr, B. A. (1996). Is homophobia associated with homosexual arousal? *Journal of Abnormal Psychology, 105,* 440–445.

Adams-Curtis, L. E., & Forbes, G. B. (2004). College women's experiences of sexual coercion: A review of cultural, perpetrator, victim, and situational variables. *Trauma, Violence & Abuse, 5*(2), 91–122.

ADD Health. (2002). Add Health and Add Health 2000: A national longitudinal study of adolescent health. Retrieved June 14, 2002, from http://www.cpc.unc.edu/addhealth.

Addo, W. (2010). Body mass index, weight gain during pregnancy and obstetric outcomes. *Ghana Medicine Journal, 44*(2), 64–69.

Adler, R. B., Rosenfeld, L. B., & Proctor, R. F. (2007). *Interplay: The process of interpersonal communication* (10th ed.). New York: Oxford University Press.

Afifi, T., McManus, T., Steuber, K., & Coho, A. (2009). Verbal avoidance and dissatisfaction in intimate conflict situations. *Human Communication Research, 35*(3), 357.

Agarwal, A., Deepinder, F., Sharma, R. K., Ranga, G., & Li, J. (2008). Effect of cell phone usage on semen analysis in men attending infertility clinic: An observational study. *Fertility and Sterility, 89,* 124–128.

Ahmed, J. (1986). Polygyny and fertility differentials among the Yoruba of western Nigeria. *Journal of Biosocial Sciences, 18,* 63–73.

Ahmetoglu, G., Swami, V., & Chamorro-Premuzic, T. (2010). The relationship between dimensions of love, personality, and relationship length. *Archives of Sexual Behavior, 39*(5), 1181–1190.

Ahrens, C. E. (2006). Being silenced: The impact of negative social reactions on the disclosure of rape. *American Journal of Community Psychology, 38,* 263–274.

Aicken, C., Nardone, A., & Mercer, C. (2011). Alcohol misuse, sexual risk behavior, and adverse sexual health outcomes, *Journal of Public Health, 33*(2), 262–271.

Ainsworth, M. D. S., Blehar, M. C., Waters, E., & Wall, S. (1978). *Patterns of attachment: A psychological study of the strange situation.* Hillsdale, NJ: Erlbaum.

Akbag, M., & Imamoglu, S. (2010). The prediction of gender and attachment styles on shame, guilt, and loneliness. *Educational Sciences: Theory and Practice, 10*(2), 669–682.

Akers, A. Y., Gold, M. A., Bost, J. E., Adimora, A. A., Orr, D. P., & Fortenberry, J. D. (2011). Variation in sexual behaviors in a cohort of adolescent females: The role of personal, perceived peer, and perceived family attitudes. *Journal of Adolescent Health, 48*(1), 87–93.

Ako, T., Takao, H., Yoshiharo, M., Osamu, I., & Yutaka, U. (2001). Beginnings of sexual reassignment surgery in Japan. *International Journal of Transgenderism.* Retrieved June 1, 2003, from http://www.symposion.com/ijt/ijtvo05no01_02.htm.

Alan Guttmacher Institute. (2002). Facts in brief: Contraceptive use. Retrieved January 14, 2003, from http://www.agi-usa.org/pubs/fb_contr_use.html.

Alan Guttmacher Institute. (2006). U.S. Teenage pregnancy statistics: National and state trends and trends by race and ethnicity. Retrieved May 29, 2008, from http://www.guttmacher.org/pubs/2006/09/12/USTPstats.pdf.

Alan Guttmacher Institute. (2008a, January). Facts in brief: Facts on contraceptive use. Retrieved July 20, 2008, from http://www.guttmacher.org/pubs/fb_contr_use.html.

Alan Guttmacher Institute. (2008b, July 1). State Policies in Brief: Abortion policy in the absence of Roe. Retrieved July 28, 2008, from http://www.guttmacher.org/statecenter/spibs/spib_APAR.pdf.

Alan Guttmacher Institute. (2008c). State Policies in Brief: An overview of abortion laws. Retrieved October 28, 2008, from http://www.guttmacher.org/statecenter/spibs/spib_OAL.pdf.

Alan Guttmacher Institute. (2008d). State Policies in Brief: Counseling and waiting periods for abortion. Retrieved October 28, 2008 from http://www.guttmacher.org/statecenter/spibs/spib_MWPA.pdf.

Alan Guttmacher Institute. (2008e, May 1). State Policies in Brief: Sex and STI/HIV education. Retrieved May 29, 2008, from http://www.guttmacher.org/statecenter/spibs/spib_SE.pdf.

Alan Guttmacher Institute. (2008f). Trends in abortion in the United States, 1975–2005. Retrieved August 3, 2008, from http://www.guttmacher.org/presentations/trends.html.

Alan Guttmacher Institute. (2010, October 1). A key step forward in overhauling US teen pregnancy prevention efforts. *Media Center: News in Context.* Retrieved January 24, 2011, from http://www.guttmacher.org/media/inthenews/2010/10/01/index.html.

Alan Guttmacher Institute. (2011). Abortion policy in the absence of Roe. *State Policies in Brief.* Retrieved August 1, 2011, from http://www.guttmacher.org/statecenter/spibs/spib_APAR.pdf.

Alan Guttmacher Institute. (2011, January 1). Sex and HIV education. *State Policies in Brief.* Retrieved January 24, 2011, from http://www.guttmacher.org/statecenter/spibs/spib_SE.pdf.

Alanis, M. C., & Lucidi, R. S. (2004, May). Neonatal circumcision: A review of the world's oldest and most controversial operation. *Obstetrical & Gynecological Survey, 59*(5), 379–395.

Alanko, K., Santtila, P., Harlaar, N., Witting, K., Varjonen, M., Jern, P., Johansson, A., von der Pahlen, B., & Sandnabba, N. K. (2010). Common genetic effects of gender atypical behavior in childhood and sexual orientation in adulthood: A study of Finnish twins. *Archives of Sexual Behavior, 39*(1), 81–92.

Alarid, L. F. (2000). Sexual assault and coercion among incarcerated women prisoners: Excerpts from prison letters. *The Prison Journal, 80*(4), 391–406.

Albada, K. F., Knapp, M. L., & Theune, K. E. (2002). Interaction appearance theory: Changing perceptions of physical attractiveness through social interaction. *Communication Theory, 12*, 8–40.

Albers, K. (2007). Comprehensive care in the prevention of ectopic pregnancy and associated negative outcomes. *Midwifery Today with International Midwife.* (84), 26–27, 67.

Albert, A., & Porter, J. R. (1988). Children's gender-role stereotypes: A sociological investigation of psychological models. *Sociological Forum, 3,* 184–210.

Albert, B. (2009). With one voice: A 2009 survey of adults and teens on parental influence, abstinence, contraception, and the increase in the teen birth rate. National Campaign to Prevent Teen Pregnancy. Retrieved January 24, 2011, from http://www.thenationalcampaign.org/resources/pdf/pubs/WOV_Lite_2009.pdf.

Albert, R. T., Elwell, S. L., & Idelson, S. (2001). *Lesbian rabbis: The first generation.* Piscataway, NJ: Rutgers University Press.

Alexander, C. J., Sipski, M. L., & Findley, T. W. (1993). Sexual activities, desire, and satisfaction in males pre- and post-SCI. *Archives of Sexual Behavior, 22,* 217–228.

Alexander, M., & Rosen, R. (2008). Spinal cord injuries and orgasm: A review. *Journal of Sex and Marital Therapy, 24,* 308–324.

Alexander, M. A. (1999). Sexual offender treatment efficacy revisited. *Sexual Abuse: A Journal of Research and Treatment, 11,* 101–116.

Alexander, M. S., Brackett, N. L., Bodner, D., Elliott, S., Jackson, A., Sonksen, J.; National Institute on Disability and Rehabilitation Research. (2009). Measurement of sexual functioning after spinal cord injury: Preferred instruments. *Journal of Spinal Cord Medicine, 32*(3), 226–236.

Alexander, M. S., Rosen, R. C., Steinberg, S., Symonds, T., Haughie, S., & Hultling, C. (2011). Sildenafil in women with sexual arousal disorder following spinal cord injury. *Spinal Cord, 49*(2), 273–279.

Alexandre, B., Lemaire, A., Desvaux, P., & Amar, E. (2007). Intracavernous injections of prostaglandin E1 for erectile dysfunction: Patient satisfaction and quality of sex life on long-term treatment. *Journal of Sexual Medicine, 4,* 426–431.

Alkhuja, S., Mnekel, R., Patel, B., & Ibrahimbacha, A. (2001). Stidor and difficult airway in an AIDS patient. *AIDS Patient Care and Sexually Transmitted Diseases, 15*(6), 293–295.

Allan, C., Forbes, E., Strauss, B., & McLachlan, R. (2008). Testosterone therapy increases sexual desire in ageing men with low-normal testosterone levels and symptoms of androgen deficiency. *International Journal of Impotence Research, 20,* 396–401.

Allen, C., Bowdin, S., Harrison, R., Sutcliffe, A., Brueton, L., Kirby, G., et al. (2008, June 3). Pregnancy and perinatal outcomes after assisted reproduction: A comparative study. *Irish Journal of Medical Science, 177*(3), 233–241.

Allen, D. J., & Oleson, T. (1999). Shame and internalized homophobia in gay men. *Journal of Homosexuality, 37*(3), 33–34.

Allen, M., Emmers-Sommer, T. M., & Crowill, T. L. (2002). Couples negotiating safer sex behaviors: A meta-analysis of the impact of conversation and gender. In M. Allen & R. Preiss (Eds.), *Interpersonal communication research.* Mahwah, NJ: Erlbaum.

Allen, P. L. (2000). *The wages of sin: Sex and disease, past and present.* Chicago: University of Chicago Press.

Allison, L., Santilla, P., Sandnabba, N., & Nordling, N. (2001). Sadomasochistically oriented behavior: Diversity in practice and meaning. *Archives of Sexual Behavior, 30,* 1–12.

Allyn, D. (1996). Private acts—public policy: Alfred Kinsey, the American Law Institute and the privatization of American sexual morality. *Journal of American Studies, 30,* 405–428.

Allyn, D. (2000). *Make love not war: The sexual revolution: An unfettered history.* Boston: Little, Brown.

Almeida, O. P., Alfonso, H., Flicker, L., Hankey, G. J., & Norman, P. E. (In press). Cardiovascular disease, depression and mortality: The Health in Men Study. *American Journal of Geriatric Psychiatry.*

Aloni, M., & Bernieri, F. J. (2004). Is love blind? The effects of experience and infatuation on the perception of love. *Journal of Nonverbal Behavior, 28*(4), 287–295.

Alonso-Zaldivar, R., & Neuman, J. (2005, November 11). FDA suggests warning for condoms. *Los Angeles Times,* p. A-15.

Al-Saleh, N. (2011). Bilateral ductal carcinoma in situ in a male breast: A case report. *Gulf Journal of Oncology, 1*(9), 68–72.

Al-Shawaf, T., Zosmer, A., Dirnfeld, M., & Grudzinskas, G. (2005). Safety of drugs used in assisted reproduction techniques. *Drug Safety, 28*(6), 513–528.

Althaus, F. (1997). Most Japanese students do not have intercourse until after adolescence. *Family Planning Perspectives, 29*(3), 145–147.

Althof, S., Abdo, C., Dean, J., Hackett, G., McCabe, M., McMahon, C., Rosen, R., Sadovsky, R., Waldinger, M., Becher, E., Broderick, G., Buvat, J., et al. (2010). International society for sexual medicine's guidelines for the diagnosis and treatment of premature ejaculation. *Journal of Sexual Medicine, 7*(9), 2947–2969.

Althuis, M. D., Brogan, D. D., Coates, R. J., Daling J. R., Gammon M. D., Malone K. E., et al. (2003). Breast cancers among very young premenopausal women (United States). *Cancer Causes and Control, 14,* 151–160.

Altman, C. (2000). Gay and lesbian seniors: Unique challenges of coming out in later life. *SIECUS Report, 4,* 14.

Altman, D. (1986). *AIDS in the mind of America.* New York: Anchor Press, Doubleday.

Amador, J., Charles, T., Tait, J., & Helm, H. (2005). Sex and generational differences in desired characteristics in mate selection. *Psychological Reports, 96*(1), 19–25.

Amanpour, C. (2006). World fails to save Africa's AIDS orphans: Africa's HIV-infected children also ignored. *CNN Online.* Retrieved November 3, 2008 from http://www.cnn.com/2006/WORLD/africa/07/17/amanpour.africa.btsc/index.html.

Amato, P., & DeBoer, D. (2001). The transmission of marital instability across generations: Relationship skills or commitment to marriage? *Journal of Marriage and the Family, 63,* 1038–1051.

Amato, P., Johnson, D., Booth, A., & Rogers, S. (2003). Stability and change in marital quality between 1980 and 2000. *Journal of Marriage and Family, 65,* 1–22.

Amato, P. R., & Hohmann-Marriott, B. (2007). A comparison of high- and low-distress marriages that end in divorce. *Journal of Marriage and Family, 69,* 621–639.

Ambady, N., Koo, J., Lee, F., & Rosenthal, R. (1996). More than words: Linguistic and nonlinguistic politeness in two cultures. *Journal of Personality and Social Psychology, 70,* 996–1011.

American Academy of Pediatrics. (1999). Task Force on Circumcision. Circumcision Policy Statement (RE 9850), *Pediatrics, 103,* 686–693.

American Cancer Society. (2005). Testicular cancer has high cure rate—in America. Retrieved April 6, 2008, from http://www.cancer.org/docroot/NWS/content/update/NWS_1_1xU_Testicular_Cancer_Has_High_Cure_Rate_%E2%80%94_In_America.asp.

American Cancer Society. (2007a). *How to perform a breast self exam.* Retrieved March 22, 2008, from http://www.cancer.org/docroot/CRI/content/CRI_2_6x_How_to_perform_a_breast_self_exam_5.asp.

American Cancer Society. (2007b). Overview: Prostate Cancer. Retrieved October 15, 2008, from http://www.cancer.org/docroot/CRI/CRI_2_1x.asp?dt=36.

American Cancer Society. (2007c). Overview: Testicular cancer. Retrieved April 6, 2008, from http://www.cancer.org/docroot/CRI/content/CRI_2_2_1x_How_Many_People_Get_Testicular_Cancer_41.asp?sitearea=.

American Cancer Society. (2007d). What are the Key Statistics about Breast Cancer in Men? Retrieved August 11, 2008, from http://www.cancer.org/docroot/CRI/content/CRI_2_4_IX_What_are_the_key_statistics_for_male_breast_cancer_28.asp.

American Cancer Society. (2010). *Cancer: Facts and figures, 2010.* Atlanta, GA: American Cancer Society. Retrieved January 5, 2011, from http://www.cancer.org/acs/groups/content/@epidemiologysurveilance/documents/document/acspc-026238.pdf.

American Cancer Society. (2011). *Breast cancer in men.* Retrieved April 19, 2011, from http://www.cancer.org/acs/groups/cid/documents/webcontent/003091-pdf.pdf.

American College Health Association. (2009). American College Health Association National College Health Assessment Spring 2008 reference group data report. *Journal of American College Health, 57*(5), 477–488.

American College of Obstetricians and Gynecologists. (2006). ACOG practice bulletin. Episiotomy. Clinical managment guidelines for obstetrician-gynecologists. *Obstetrics and Gynecology, 107*(4), 957–962.

American College of Obstetricians and Gynecologists. (2007). Screening for fetal chromosomal abnormalities. Washington, DC: American College of Obstetricians and Gynecologists (ACOG); 2007 Jan. 11. (*ACOG Practice Bulletin; No. 77*).

American Psychiatric Association. (1994). *Diagnostic and statistical manual of mental disorders* (4th ed.). Washington, DC: Author.

American Psychiatric Association. (1998). *Media information: Position statement on hate crimes.* Retrieved October 4, 2008, from http://www.apa.org/releases/hate.html.

American Psychiatric Association. (2000). *Diagnostic and statistical manual of mental disorders* (4th ed., Text. Rev.). Washington, DC: Author.

American Psychiatric Association. (2008). DSM-V: The future manual. Retrieved August 25, 2008, from http://www.psych.org/dsmv.asp.

American Psychiatric Association. (2010). About the DSM. Retrieved June 18, 2011, from http://www.dsm5.org/about/Pages/Default.aspx.

American Psychological Association. (2005). Lesbian and gay parenting. Committee on Lesbian, Gay, and Bisexual Concerns. Retrieved September 1, 2008, from http://www.apa.org/pi/lgbc/publications/lgparenting.pdf.

American Society for Aesthetic Plastic Surgery. (2009, March 16). Liposuction no longer the most popular surgical procedure according to new statistics. American Society for Aesthetic Plastic Surgery reports 10.2 Million Cosmetic Procedures in 2008. Retrieved December 26, 2010, from http://www.cosmeticplasticsurgerystatistics.com/statistics.html#2008-GRAPHS.

Ames, M. A., & Houston, D. A. (1990). Legal, social, and biological definitions of pedophilia. *Archives of Sexual Behavior, 19,* 333–342.

Amir, M. (1971). *Patterns in forcible rape.* Chicago: University of Chicago Press.

Amis, D. (2007). Care practice #1: Labor begins on its own. *Journal of Perinatal Education, 16,* 16–20.

An, G., Huang, T. H., Wang, D. G., Xie, Q. D., Ma, L., & Chen, D. Y. (2009). In vitro and in vivo studies evaluating recombinant plasmid pCXN2-mIzumo as a potential immunocontraceptive antigen. *American Journal of Reproductive Immunology, 61*(3), 227–235.

"An Overview of Abortion Laws." (2011, March 1). State policies in brief. Alan Guttmacher Institute. Retrieved March 18, 2011, from http://www.guttmacher.org/statecenter/spibs/spib_OAL.pdf.

Anderson, F. D., Gibbons, W., & Portman, D. (2006). Long-term safety of an extended-cycle oral contraceptive (Seasonale): A 2-year multimember open-label extension trial. *American Journal of Obstetrics and Gynecology, 195,* 92–96.

Anderson, P. B., & Savage, J. S. (2005). Social, legal, and institutional context of heterosexual aggression by college women. *Trauma, Violence, & Abuse, 6*(2), 130–140.

Anderton, D., & Emigh, R. (1989). Polygynous fertility: Sexual competition vs. progeny. *American Journal of Sociology, 94*(4), 832–855.

Andre, A. (2006). The study of sex. Retrieved January 2, 2008, from http://www.alternet.org/story/33347/.

Andrews, G., Skinner, D., & Zuma, K. (2006). Epidemiology of health and vulnerability among children orphaned and made vulnerable by HIV/AIDS in sub-Saharan Africa. *AIDS Care, 18*(3), 269–276.

Angier, N. (1999). *Woman: An intimate geography.* New York: Anchor Books.

Ankum, W. M., Hajenius, P. J., Schrevel, L. S., & Van der Veen, F. (1996). Management of suspected ectopic pregnancy. Impact of new diagnostic tools in 686 consecutive cases. *Journal of Reproductive Medicine, 41*(10), 724–728.

Antheunis, M., Valkenburg, P. M., & Peter, J. (2007). Computer-mediated communication and interpersonal attraction: An experimental test of two explanatory hypotheses. *CyberPsychology & Behavior, 10,* 831–836.

Apfel, R. J., & Handel, M. H. (1993). *Madness and loss of motherhood.* Washington, DC: American Psychiatric Press.

Arena, J. M., & Wallace, M. (2008). Issues regarding sexuality. In E. Capezuti, D. Zwicker, M. Mezey, T. Fuller, D. Gray-Miceli, & M. Kluger (Eds.). *Evidence-based geriatric nursing protocols for best practice* (3rd ed., pp. 629–647). New York: Springer Publishing Company.

Aries, E. (1996). *Men and women in interaction: Reconsidering the differences.* New York: Oxford University Press.

Aries, P. (1962). *Centuries of childhood: A social history of family life.* New York: Vintage Books.

Armour, B.S., Wolf, L., Mitra, M., Brieding, M. (2008). Differences in intimate partner violence among women with and without a disability. American Public Health Association's 136th Annual Meeting, San Diego, CA. October 27. Retrieved November 14, 2008, from http://apha.confex.com/ apha/136am/webprogram/Paper182004. html.

Aron, A., Fisher, H., Mashek, D, Strong, G., Li, H., & Brown, L. (2005). Reward, motivation and emotion systems associated with early-stage intense romantic love. *Journal of Neurophysiology, 94(1),* 327–337.

Arpino, C., Compagnone, E., Montanaro, M., Cacciatore, D., DeLuca, A., Cerulli, A., Di-Girolamo, S., & Curatoio, P. (2010). Preterm birth and neurodevelopmental outcome: A review. *Child's Nervous System, 26*(9), 1139–1149.

Arrington-Sanders, R., Dyson, J., & Ellen, J. (2007). STDs in adolescents. In J. Klausner & E. Hook (Eds.), *Current diagnosis and treatment of STDs (pp. 160–166).* New York: McGraw-Hill.

Arroba, A. (2004). Costa Rica. In R. T. Francoeur & R. J. Noonan (Eds.), *The Contin-uum international encyclopedia of sexuality* (pp. 227–240). New York/London: Continuum International.

Atanackovic, G., Wolpin, J., & Koren, G. (2001). Determinants of the need for hospital care among women with nausea and vomiting of pregnancy. *Clinical and Investigative Medicine, 24*(2), 90–94.

Athenstaedt, U., Haas, E., & Schwab, S. (2004). Gender role self-concept and gender-typed communication behavior in mixed-sex and same-sex dyads. *Sex Roles, 50*(1–2), 37–52.

Aust, T. R., & Lewis-Jones, D. I. (2004). Retrograde ejaculation and male infertility. *Hospital Medicine, 65*(6), 361–364.

Auster, C. J., & Leone, J. M. (2001). Late adolescents' perspectives on marital rape. *Adolescence, 36,* 141–152.

Auster, C. J., & Ohm, S. C. (2000). Masculinity and femininity in contemporary American Society. *Sex Roles, 43*(7–8), 499–528.

Austoni, E., Colombo, F., Romano, A. L., Guarneri, A., Goumas, I. K., & Cazzaniga, A. (2005). Soft prosthesis implant and relaxing albugineal incision with saphenous grafting for surgical therapy of Peyronie's disease. *European Urology, 47*(2), 223–230.

Aviram, I. (2005). Online infidelity: Aspects of dyadic satisfaction, self-disclosure, and narcissism. Retrieved May 9, 2005, from http://jcmc.indiana.edu/vol10/issue3/ aviram.html.

Ayala, M. (2009). Brain serotonin, psychoactive drugs, and effects on reproduction. *Central Nervous System Agents in Medical Chemistry, 9*(4), 258–276.

Azam, S. (2000). What's behind retro virginity? The Toronto Star Life Story. Retrieved December 29, 2002, from http://www.psurg. com/star2000.html.

Back, M., Stopfer, J., Vazire, S., Gaddis, S., Schmukle, B., & Gosling, S. (2010). Facebook profiles reflect actual personality, not self-idealization. *Psychological Science, 21*(3), 372–374.

Bacon, C. G., Mittleman, M. A., Kawachi, I., et al. (2003). Sexual function in men older than 50 years of age: Results from the health professionals follow-up study. *Annals of Internal Medicine, 139,* 161–168.

Badawy Z. S., Chohan K. R., Whyte D. A., Penefsky H. S., Brown O. M., & Souid A. K. (2008). Cannabinoids inhibit the respiration of human sperm. Fertility and Sterility. Retrieved October 13, 2008, from http://www.fertstert.org/article/S0015–0282(08)00750–4/abstract.

Bagemihl, B. (1999). *Biological exuberance: Animal homosexuality and natural diversity.* New York: St. Martin's Press.

Bagley, D. (2005). Personal communication.

Bailey, A., & Hurd, P. (2005). Finger length ratio correlates with physical aggression in men but not in women. *Biological Psychology, 68*(3), 215–222.

Bailey, B. P., Gurak, L. J., & Konstan, J. A. (2003). Trust in cyberspace. In J. Ratner (Ed.), *Human factors and Web development* (2nd ed., pp. 311–321). Mahwah, NJ: Erlbaum.

Bailey, J. M., & Pillard, R. C. (1993). A genetic study of male sexual orientation. *Archives of General Psychiatry 50*(3), 240–241.

Bailey, J. M., & Pillard, R. C. (1995). Genetics of human sexual orientation. *Annual Review of Sex Research, 6,* 126–150.

Bailey, R., Egesah, O., & Rosenberg, S. (2008). Male circumcision for HIV prevention: A prospective study of complications in clinical and traditional settings in Bungoma, Kenya. *Bulletin of the World Health Organization, 86,* 669–677.

Bain, J. (2001). Testosterone replacement therapy for aging men. *Canadian Family Physician, 47,* 91–97.

Baker, E., Sanchez, L., Nock, S., & Wright, J. (2009). Covenant marriage and the sanctification of gendered marital roles. *Journal of Family Issues, 30*(2), 147–178.

Bakir, A., & Palan, K. (2010). How are children's attitudes toward ads and brands affected by gender-related content in advertising? *Journal of Advertising, 39*(1), 35–48.

Balaban, B., Yakin, K., Alatas, C., Oktem, O., Isiklar, A., & Urman, B. (In press). Clinical outcome of intracytoplasmic injection of spermatozoa morphologically selected under high magnification: A prospective randomized study. *Reproductive Biomedicine Online.* Retrieved February 25, 2011, from http://www.ncbi.nlm.nih.gov/ pubmed/21324747.

Baladerian, N. J. (1991). Sexual abuse of people with developmental disabilities. *Sexuality and Disability, 9,* 323–335.

Ball, H. (2005). Sexual offending on elderly women: A review. *Journal of Forensic Psychiatry & Psychology, 16*(1), 127–138.

Balsam, K. F., Beauchaine, T., Rothblum, E., & Solomon, S. (2008). Three-year follow-up of same-sex couples who had civil unions in Vermont, same-sex couples not in civil unions, and heterosexual married couples. *Developmental Psychology, 44,* 101–116.

Balsam, K., Rothblum, E., & Beauchaine, T. (2005). Victimization over the life span: A comparison of lesbian, gay, bisexual and heterosexual siblings. *Journal of Counseling and Clinical Psychology, 73,* 477–487.

Bancroft, J. (2004). Alfred C. Kinsey and the politics of sex research. *Annual Review of Sex Research, 15,* 1–39.

Bancroft, J. (2007). Sex and aging. *New England Journal of Medicine, 357,* 820–822.

Bancroft, J., & Vukadinovic, Z. (2004). Sexual addiction, sexual compulsivity, or what? Toward a theoretical model. *Journal of Sex Research, 41*(3), 225–234.

Bancroft, J., Herbenick, D., Barnes, T., Hallam-Jones, R., Wylie, K., & Janssen, E. (2005). The relevance of the dual control model to male sexual dysfunction: The Kinsey Institute/BASRT collaborative project. *Sexual & Relationship Therapy, 20*(1), 13–30.

Bandura, A. (1969). *Principles of behavior modification.* Austin, TX: Holt, Rinehart & Winston.

Banerjee, N. (2007, March 13). A place to turn when a newborn is fated to die. *New York Times.* Retrieved from http://www.nytimes.com/2007/03/13/health/13hospice.html.

Baptista, M., & Ramalho-Santos, J. (2009). Spermicides, microbicides and antiviral agents: Recent advances in the development of novel multi-functional compounds. *Mini Reviews in Medicinal Chemistry, 9*(13), 1556–1567.

Barak, A. (2005). Sexual harassment on the Internet. *Social Science Computer Review, 23*(1), 77–92.

Barbach, L. (1982). *For each other: Sharing sexual intimacy.* New York: Penguin Group.

Barber, N. (2008). Explaining cross-national differences in polygyny intensity. *Cross-Cultural Research, 42,* 103.

Bardeguez, A., Lindsey, J., Shannon, M., Tuomala, R., Cohn, S., Smith, E., et al. (2008). Adherence to antiretrovirals among US women during and after pregnancy. *Journal of Acquired Immune Deficiency Syndrome, 48,* 408–417.

Barford, V. (2008, February, 25). Iran's 'diagnosed transsexuals.' BBC News. Retrieved December 20, 2010, from http://news.bbc.co.uk/2/hi/7259057.stm.

Barker, D. J. (1997). Maternal nutrition, fetal nutrition, and disease in later life. *Nutrition, 13*(9), 807–813.

Barner, J. M. (2003). Sexual fantasies, attitudes, and beliefs: The role of self-report sexual aggression for males and females. *Dissertation Abstracts International, 64*(4-B), 1887 (#0419–4217).

Baron, L. (1990). Pornography and gender equality: An empirical analysis. *The Journal of Sex Research, 27,* 363–380.

Baron, L., & Straus, M. A. (1987). Four theories of rape: A macrosociological analysis. *Social Problems, 34,* 467–489.

Baron, N. S. (2004). See you online: Gender issues in college student use of instant messaging. *Journal of Language & Social Psychology, 23*(4), 397–423.

Barratt, C., Mansell, S., Beaton, C., Tardif, S., & Oxenham, S. (2011). Diagnostic tools in male infertily—the question of sperm dysfunction. *Asian Journal of Andrology, 13*(1), 53–58.

Barrow, R., Newman, L., & Douglas, J. (2008). Taking positive steps to address STD disparities for African-American communities. *Sexually Transmitted Diseases, 35*(12), S1-S3.

Bart, P. B., & O'Brien, P. H. (1985). *Stopping rape: Successful survival strategies.* New York: Pergamon Press.

Barth, K. R., Cook, R. L., Downs, J. S., Switzer, G. E., & Fischoff, B. (2002). Social stigma and negative consequences: Factors that influence college students' decision to seek testing for STIs. *Journal of American College Health, 50*(4), 153–160.

Bartholomew, K., & Horowitz, L. (1991). Attachment styles among young adults: A test of a four-category model. *Journal of Personality and Social Psychology, 61,* 226–244.

Bar-Yosef, Y., Greenstein, A., Beri, A., Lidawi, G., Matzkin, H., & Chen, J. (2007). Doral vein injuries observed during penile exploration for suspected penile fracture. *Journal of Sexual Medicine, 4,* 1142–1146.

Basaria, S, Coviello, A., Travison, T., Storer, T., Farwell, W., Jette, A. M., et al. (2010). Adverse events associated with testosterone administration. *New England Journal of Medicine, 363,* 109–122.

Basow, S., & Minieri, A. (2011). "You owe me": Effects of date cost, who pays, participant gender, and rape myth beliefs on perceptions of rape. *Journal of Interpersonal Violence, 26*(3), 479–497.

Bassil, N., & Morley, J. E. (2010). Late-life onset hypogonadism: A review. *Clinical Geriatric Medicine, 26*(2), 197–222.

Basson, R. (2000a). The female sexual response: A different model. *Journal of Sex and Marital Therapy, 26,* 51–65.

Basson, R. (2000b). The female sexual response revisited. *Journal of Obstetrics and Gynaecology of Canada, 22,* 383–387.

Basson, R. (2001). Using a different model for female sexual response to address women's problematic low sexual desire. *Journal of Sex and Marital Therapy, 27,* 395–403.

Basson, R. (2005). Women's sexual dysfunction: Revised and expanded definitions. *Canadian Medical Association Journal, 172*(10), 1327–1333.

Basson, R., McInnes, R., Smith, M., Hodgson, G., & Koppiker, N. (2002). Efficacy and safety of sildenafil citrate in women with sexual dysfunction associated with female sexual arousal disorder. *Journal of Women's Health and Gender-Based Medicine, 11*(4), 367–377.

Basson, R., Rees, P., Wang, R., Montejo, A. L., & Incrocci, L. (2010). Sexual function in chronic illness. *Journal of Sexual Medicine, 7*(1 Pt 2), 374–388.

Batabyal, A. A. (2001). On the likelihood of finding the right partner in an arranged marriage. *Journal of Socio-Economics, 30*(3), 273–281.

Bates, K. G. (2010). MTV's 'teen mom' makes for teaching moments. National Public Radio. Retrieved August 10, 2010, from http://www.npr.org/templates/story/story.php?storyId5128626258.

Bauer, G. R., & Welles, S. L. (2001). Beyond assumptions of negligible risk: STDs and women who have sex with women. *American Journal of Public Health, 91*(8), 1282–1287.

Bauer, G. R., Jairam, J. A., & Baidoobonso, S. M. (2010). Sexual health, risk behaviors, and substance use in heterosexual-identified women with female sex partners: 2002 US National Survey of Family Growth. *Sexually Transmitted Diseases, 37*(9), 531–537.

Bauermeister, J. A., Johns, M. M., Sandfort, T. G., Eisenberg, A., Grossman, A. H., & D'Augelli, A. R. (2010). Relationship trajectories and psychological well-being among sexual minority youth. *Journal of Youth and Adolescence, 39*(10), 1148–1163.

Baumeister, L. M., Flores, E., & Marin, B. V. (1995). Sex information given to Latina adolescents by parents. *Health Education Research, 10*(2), 233–239.

Baumeister, R. F. (1988). Masochism as escape from self. *Journal of Sex Research, 25,* 28–59.

Baxter, J., & Hewitt, B. (2010). Pathways into marriage: Cohabitation and the domestic division of labor. *Journal of Family Issues, 31*(11), 1507–1529.

Bayer, R. (1981). *Homosexuality and American psychiatry: The politics of diagnosis.* New York: Basic Books.

Baylin, A., Hernandez-Diaz, S., Siles, X., Kabagambe, E., & Campos, H. (2007). Triggers of nonfatal myocardial infarction in Costa Rica: Heavy physical exertion, sexual activity, and infection. *Annals of Epidemiology, 17,* 112–118.

Beals, K. P., & Peplau, L. A. (2005). Identity support, identity devaluation, and well-being among lesbians. *Psychology of Women Quarterly, 29*(2), 140–148.

Bearak, B. (2009, September 22). Mixed verdict in S. African lesbian's murder trial. *New York Times.* Retrieved April 20, 2011, from http://www.nytimes.com/2009/09/23/world/africa/23safrica.html.

Bearman, P., & Bruckner, H. (2001). Promising the future: Virginity pledges and first intercourse. *American Journal of Sociology, 106*(4), 859–912.

Beaton, A. A., & Mellor, G. (2007). Direction of hair whorl and handedness. *Laterality, 12,* 295–301.

Beaudreau, S. A., Rideaux, T., & Zeiss, R. A. (2011). Clinical characteristics of older male military veterans seeking treatment for erectile dysfunction. *International Psychogeriatrics, 23*(1), 155–160.

Beck, M. (2008, September 30). Is sex addiction a sickness, or excuse to behave badly? *Wall Street Journal,* (Eastern edition). New York, p. B.9.

Becker, G., Landes, E., & Michael, R. (1977). An economic analysis of marital stability. *Journal of Political Economy, 85,* 1141–1187.

Becker, J. V., et al. (1986). Level of postassault sexual functioning in rape and incest victims. *Archives of Sexual Behavior, 15,* 37–50.

Beckett, M. K., Elliott, M. N., Martino, S., Kanouse, D. E., Corona, R., Klein, D. J., & Schuster, M. A. (2010). Timing of parent and child communication about sexuality relative to children's sexual behaviors. *Pediatrics, 125*(1), 34–42.

Beeble, M., Sullivan, C., & Bybee, D. (2011). The impact of neighborhood factors on the well-being of survivors of intimate partner violence over time. *American Journal of Community Psychology, 47*(3–4), 287–306.

Beech, A., Ward, T., & Fisher, D. (2006). The identification of sexual and violent motivations in men who assault women: Impli-

cation for treatment. *Journal of Interpersonal Violence, 21,* 1635.

Begley, S. (2007, May 7). Just say no—to bad science. *Newsweek,* p. 57.

Begley, S. (2010, July 2). The anti-lesbian drug. *Newsweek.* Retrieved November 16, 2010, from http://www.newsweek.com/2010/07/02/the-anti-lesbian-drug.html.

Belkin, L. (2011, February 11). The IRS, breast pumps and other updates. *New York Times.* Retrieved May 30, 2011, from http://parenting.blogs.nytimes.com/2011/02/11/the-irs-breast-pumps-and-other-updates/.

Belknap, P., & Leonard II, W. M. (1991). A conceptual replication and extension of Erving Goffman's study of gender advertisements. *Sex Roles, 25,* 103–118.

Bell, A. P., Weinberg, M. S., & Hammersmith, S. K. (1981). *Sexual preference: Its development in men and women.* Bloomington: Indiana University Press.

Bellino, S., Renocchio, M., Zizzo, M., Rocca, G., Bogetti, P., & Bogetto, F. (2010). Quality of life of patients who undergo breast reconstruction after mastectomy: Effects of personality characteristics. *Plastic Reconstructive Surgery, 127*(1), 10–17.

Belsky, J., Houts, R., & Fearon, R. (2010). Infant attachment security and the timing of puberty: Testing an avolutional hypothesis. *Psychological Science, 21*(9), 1195–1201.

Bem, D. J. (2000). Exotic becomes erotic: Interpreting the biological correlates of sexual orientation. *Archives of Sexual Behavior, 29*(6), 531–548.

Bem, S. L. (1974). The measurement of psychological androgyny. *Journal of Consulting and Clinical Psychology, 42,* 155–162.

Bem, S. L. (1977). On the utility of alternative procedures for assessing psychological androgyny. *Journal of Consulting and Clinical Psychology, 45,* 196–205.

Bem, S. L. (1981). Gender schema theory: A cognitive account of sex-typing. *Psychological Review, 88,* 354–364.

Benevento, B. T., & Sipski, M. L. (2002). Neurogenic bladder, neurogenic bowel, and sexual dysfunction in people with spinal cord injury. *Physical Therapy, 82*(6), 601–612.

Benjamin, H. (1961). *Encyclopedia of sexual behavior.* New York: Hawthorn Books.

Bennett, J. (2009). Only you. And you. And you. *Newsweek.* Retrieved July 3, 2011, from http://www.newsweek.com/2009/07/28/only-you-and-you-and-you.html.

Benokraitis, N. V. (1993). *Marriages and families.* Englewood Cliffs, NJ: Prentice Hall.

Benson, A., Ost, L., Noble, M., & Laakin, M. (2009). Premature ejaculation. *Emedicine.* Retrieved March 25, 2010, from http://emedicine.medscape.com/article/435884-overview.

Benton, T. (2008). Depression and HIV/AIDS. *Current Psychiatry Reports, 10,* 280–285.

Ben-Zion, I., & Shiber, A. (2006). Heart to heart: Rehabilitation of sexuality in cardiac patients. *Harefuah, 145,* 350–351.

Ben-Zion, I., Rothchild, S., Chudakov, B., & Aloni, R. (2007). Surrogate versus couple therapy in vaginismus. *Journal of Sexual Medicine, 4,* 728–733.

Berenbaum, S. A., & Snyder, E. (1995). Early hormonal influences on childhood sex-typed activity and playmate preferences. *Developmental Psychology, 31*(1), 31–43.

Bergen, R. (2006). Marital rape: New research and directions. National Sexual Violence Resource Center. Retrieved June 26, 2011, from http://new.vawnet.org/Assoc_Files_VAWnet/AR_MaritalRapeRevised.pdf.

Bergen, R., & Bukovec, P. (2006). Men and intimate partner rape: Characteristics of men who sexually abuse their partner. *Journal of Interpersonal Violence, 21,* 1375.

Berger, R. J., Searles, P., & Cottle, C. E. (1991). *Feminism and pornography.* New York: Praeger.

Bergmann, M. S. (1987). *The anatomy of living.* New York: Fawcett Columbine.

Bergmark, K., Avall-Lundqvist, E., Dickman, P., Henningsohn, L., & Steineck, G. (1999). Vaginal changes and sexuality in women with a history of cervical cancer. *New England Journal of Medicine, 340,* 1383–1389.

Bergstrand, C., & Williams, B. (2000, October 10). Today's alternative marriage styles: The case of swingers. *Electronic Journal of Human Sexuality, 3.* Retrieved September 14, 2008, from http://www.ejhs.org/volume3/swing/body.htm.

Berkey, B. R., Perelman-Hall, T., & Kurdek, L. A. (1990). The multidimensional scale of sexuality. *Journal of Homosexuality, 19,* 67–87.

Berkow, R., Beers, M. H., Fletcher, A. J., & Bogin, R. M. (Eds). (2000). *Merck manual of medical information* (Home ed.). Whitehouse Station, NJ: Merck & Co.

Berkowitz, D., & Marsiglio, W. (2007). Gay men: Negotiating procreative, father, and family identities. *Journal of Marriage and Family, 69,* 366–382.

Berkowitz, P. (2011, April 16). Is Yale University sexist? *Wall Street Journal.* Retrieved

April 24, 2011, from http://online.wsj.com/article/SB10001424052748704529204576257121944716258.html.

Berman, J., Berman, L., Toler, S., Gill, J., Haughie, S., & the Sildenafil Study Group. (2003). Safety and efficacy of sildenafil citrate for the treatment of female sexual arousal disorder: A double-blind, placebo controlled study. *Journal of Urology, 170(6 Pt 1),* 2333–2338.

Bernstein, D. I., Earwood, J. D., Bravo, F. J., Cohen, G. H., Eisenberg, R. J., Clark, J. R., Fairman, J., & Cardin, R. D. (2011). Effects of herpes simplex virus type 2 glycoprotein vaccines and CLDC adjuvant on genital herpes infection in the guinea pig. *Vaccine, 29(11),* 2071–2078.

Bernstein, E. (2010, October 19). I'm very, very, very sorry—really? *Wall Street Journal,* D1.

Bersamin, M. M., Paschall, M. J., Saltz, R. F., & Zamboanga, B. L. (2011). Young adults and casual sex: The relevance of college drinking settings. *Journal of Sex Research, 20,* 1–8.

Besharov, D. (1988). *Protecting children from abuse and neglect: Policy and practices.* Springfield, IL: Charles C. Thomas.

Bessede, T., Massard, C., Albouy, B., Leborgne, S., Gross-Goupil, M., Droupy, S., Patard, J. J., Fizazi, K., & Escudier, B. (In press). Sexual life of male patients with advanced renal cancer treated with angiogenesis inhibitors. *Annals of Oncology.*

Bestic, L. (2005). When a patch works. Retrieved August 30, 2005, from http://www.timesonline.co.uk/article/0,,8124–1716899,00.html

Bettocchi, C., Palumbo, F., Spilotros, M., Lucarelli, G., Palazzo, S., Battaglia, M., Selvaggi, F., & Ditonno, P. (2010). Patient and partner satisfaction after AMS inflatable penile prosthesis implant. *Journal of Sexual Medicine, 7(1 Pt 1),* 304–309.

Bettocchi, C., Verze, P., Palumbo, F., Arcaniolo, D., & Mirone, V. (2008). Ejaculatory disorders: Pathophysiology and management. *Nature Clinical Practice Urology, 5(2),* 93–103.

Bezemer, D., de Wolf, F., Boerlijst, M. C., van Sighem, A., Hollingsworth, T. D., Prins, M., Geskus, R. B., Gras, L., Coutinho, R. A., & Fraser, C. (2008). A resurgent HIV-1 epidemic among men who have sex with men in the era of potent antiretroviral therapy. *AIDS, 22(9),* 1071–1077.

Bhide, A., Nama, V., Patel, S., & Kalu, E. (2010). Microbiology of cysts/abscesses of Bartholin's gland: Review of empirical antibiotic therapy against microbial culture. *Journal of Obstetrics and Gynecology, 30(7),* 701–703.

Bialik, C. (2007). Sorry you have gone over your limit of network friends. *Wall Street Journal.* Retrieved February 10, 2008, from http://online.wsj.com/article/SB119518271549595364.html?mod=googlenews_wsj.

Bialik, C. (2010a, October 8). Sex, and studying it, are complicated. *Wall Street Journal.* Retrieved October 10, 2010, from http://blogs.wsj.com/numbersguy/sex-and-studying-it-is-complicated-998/.

Bialik, C. (2010b, October 9). Research into human sexuality leaves a lot to be desired. *Wall Street Journal,* p. A2.

Bick, R. L., Maden, J., Heller, K. B., & Toofanian, A. (1998). Recurrent miscarriage: Causes, evaluation, and treatment. *Medscape Women's Health, 3(3),* 2.

Bieber, I., et al. (1962). *Homosexuality: A psychoanalytic study.* New York: Basic Books.

Biello, D. (2007, December 5). What is the best age difference for husband and wife? *Scientific American.* Retrieved May 11, 2011, from http://www.scientificamerican.com/article.cfm?id5what-is-the-best-age-difference-for-husband-and-wife.

Bigelow, B. J. (1977). Children's friendship expectations: A cognitive developmental study. *Child Development, 48,* 246–253.

Biglia, N., Moggio, G., Peano, E., Sgandurra, P., Ponzone, R., Nappi, R. E., & Sismondi, P. (2010). Effects of surgical and adjuvant therapies for breast cancer on sexuality, cognitive functions, and body weight. *Journal of Sexual Medicine, 7(5),* 1891–1900.

Bimbi, D. S. (2007). Male prostitution: Pathology, paradigms and progress in research. *Journal of Homosexuality, 53(1–2),* 7–35.

Binik, Y. M. (2010a). The DSM diagnostic criteria for vaginismus. *Archives of Sexual Behavior, 39(2),* 278–291.

Binik, Y. M. (2010b). The DSM diagnostic criteria for dyspareunia. *Archives of Sexual Behavior, 39(2),* 292–303.

Bird, M. H. (2006). Sexual addiction and marriage and family therapy: Facilitating individual and relationship healing through couple therapy. *Journal of Marital and Family Therapy, 32(3),* 297–310.

Birdthistle, I., Floyd, S., Machingura, A., Mudziwapasi, N., Gregson, S., Glynn, J. R. (2008). From affected to infected? Orphanhood and HIV risk among female adolescents in urban Zimbabwe. *Epidemiology and Social AIDS, 22(6),* 759–766.

Birnbaum, G., Glaubman, H., & Mikulincer, M. (2001). Women's experience of heterosexual intercourse. *Journal of Sex Research, 38(3),* 191–194.

Biro, F., Galvez, M., Greenspan, L., Succop, P., Vangeepuram, N., Pinney, S., Teitelbaum, S., Windham, G., Kushi, L., & Wolff, M. (2010). Pubertal assessment method and baseline characteristics in a mixed longitudinal study of girls. *Pediatrics, 6(11),* 595.

Bish, C. L., Chu, S. Y., Shapiro-Mendoza, C., Sharma, A., & Blanck, H. (May 1, 2008). Trying to lose or maintain weight during pregnancy—United States, 2003. *Maternal and Child Health Journal.* Retrieved October 14, 2008, from http://www.springerlink.com/content/n76tk678r07j87v1/?p=13a04154744143e6be60537c74733c0d&pi=1.

Biswas, S. (2005, May 17). Fear and loathing in gay India. *BBC News.* Retrieved September 15, 2008, from http://news.bbc.co.uk/2/hi/south_asia/4304081.stm.

Bittles, A. H., Mason, W. M., & Greene, J. (1991). Reproductive behavior and health in consanguineous marriages. *Science, 252(5007),* 789–794.

Black, K., & Gold, D. (2008). Gender differences and socioeconomic status biases in judgments about blame in date rape scenarios. *Violence and Victims, 23(1),* 115–128.

Black, M., Shetty, A., & Bhattacharya, S. (2008). Obstetric outcomes subsequent to intrauterine death in the first pregnancy. *British Journal of Gynecology, 115,* 269–274.

Blackwood, E. (1994). Sexuality and gender in Native American tribes: The case of cross-gender females. In A. C. Herrmann & A. J. Stewart (Eds.), *Theorizing feminism: Parallel trends in the humanities and social sciences.* (pp. 301–315). Boulder, CO: Westview Press.

Blair, A. (2000) Individuation, love styles and health-related quality of life among college students. *Dissertation Abstracts International,* University of Florida, #0–599–91381–9.

Blake, S. M., Ledsky, R., Lehman, T., Goodenow, C., Sawyer, R., & Hack, T. (2001). Preventing sexual risk behaviors among gay, lesbian, and bisexual adolescents: The benefits of gay-sensitive HIV instruction in schools. *American Journal of Public Health, 91,* 940–946.

Blakemore, J. E. (2003). Children's beliefs about violating gender norms: Boys shouldn't look like girls, and girls shouldn't act like boys. *Sex Roles, 48*(9–10), 411–419.

Blanchard, M. A., & Semoncho, J. E. (2006). Anthony Comstock and his adversaries: The mixed legacy of the battle for free speech. *Communication and Public Policy, 11*, 317–366.

Blanchard, R. (1997). Birth order and sibling sex ratio in homosexual versus heterosexual males and females. *Annual Review of Sex Research, 8*, 27–67.

Blanchard, R. (2004). Quantitative and theoretical analyses of the relation between older brothers and homosexuality in men. *Journal of Theoretical Biology, 230*(2), 173–187.

Blanchard, R. (2008). Review and theory off-handedness, birth order, and homosexuality in men. *Laterality, 13*, 51–70.

Blanchard, R., Cantor, J. M., Bogaert, A., Breedlove, S., & Ellis, L. (2006). Interaction of fraternal birth order and handedness in the development of male homosexuality. *Hormones & Behavior, 49*, 405–414.

Bleakley, A., Hennessey, M., & Fishbein, M. (2006). Public opinion on sex education in U.S. schools. *Archives of Pediatrics and Adolescent Medicine, 160*, 1151–1156.

Blecher, S. R., & Erickson, R. P. (2007). Genetics of sexual development: A new paradigm. *American Journal of Medical Genetics, 143*, 3054–3068.

Bleecker, E., & Murnen, S. (2005). Fraternity membership, the display of degrading sexual images of women, and rape myth acceptance. *Sex Roles, 53*, 487–493.

Blell, M., Pollard, T., & Pearce, M. (2008). Predictors of age at menarche in the Newcastle Thousand Families Study. *Journal of Biosocial Science, 40*, 563–575.

Block, J. D. (1999). *Sex over 50.* Paramus, NJ: Reward Books.

Blow, A. J., & Hartnett, K. (2005). Infidelity in committed relationships: A methodological review. *Journal of Marital and Family Therapy, 31*(2), 183–216.

Blumstein, H. (2001). Bartholin gland disease. Retrieved September 9, 2002, from http://www.emedicine.com/emeg/topic54.htm.

Blumstein, P., & Schwartz, P. (1983). *American couples.* New York: William Morrow.

Boardman, L. A., & Stockdale, C. K. (2009). Sexual pain. *Clinical Obstetrics and Gynecology, 52*(4), 682–690.

Bocklandt, S., & Vilain, E. (2007). Sex differences in brain and behavior: Hormones versus genes. *Advances in Genetics, 59*, 245–266.

Bodenmann, G., Meuwly, N., Bradbury, T., Gmelch, S., & Ledermann, T. (2010). Stress, anger, and verbal aggression in intimate relationships: Moderating effects of individual and dyadic coping. *Journal of Social and Personal Relationships, 27*(3), 408–424.

Bodner, E., & Lazar, A. (2008). Ageism among Israeli students: Structure and demographic influences. *International Psychogeriatrics, 20*(5), 1046–1058.

Boehmer, U. (2002). Twenty years of public health research: Inclusion of lesbian, gay, bisexual and transgender populations. *American Journal of Public Health, 92*(7), 1125–1131.

Boeke, A. J., van Bergen, J. E., Morre, S. A., & van Everdingen, J. J. (2005). The risk of pelvic inflammatory disease associated with urogenital infection with chlamydia trachomatis: Literature review. *Ned Tijdschr Geneeskd, 149*(16), 878–884.

Boeringer, S. (1999). Associations of rape-supportive attitudes with fraternal and athletic participation. *Violence Against Women, 5*(1), 81–90.

Bogaert, A. (1996). Volunteer bias in human sexuality research: Evidence for both sexuality and personality differences in males. *Archives of Sexual Behavior, 25*(2), 125–140.

Bogaert, A. (2010). Physical development and sexual orientation in men and women: An analysis of NATSAL-2000. *Archives of Sexual Behavior, 39*(1), 110–116.

Bogaert, A. F. (2005). Gender role/identity and sibling sex ratio in homosexual men. *Journal of Sex and Marital Therapy, 31*, 217–227.

Bogaert, A. F., & Skorska, M. (2011). Sexual orientation, fraternal birth order, and the maternal immune hypothesis: A review. *Frontiers in Neuroendocrinology, 32*(2), 247–254.

Bogaert, A. F., Blanchard, R., & Crosthwait, L. (2007). Interaction of birth order, handedness, and sexual orientation in the Kinsey interview data. *Behavioral Neuroscience, 121*, 845–853.

Bogaerts, S., Vanheule, S., Leeuw, F., & Desmet, M. (2006). Recalled parental bonding and personality disorders in a sample of exhibitionists: A comparative study. *Journal of Forensic Psychiatry & Psychology, 17*(4), 636–646.

Bohm-Starke, N. (2010). Medical and physical predictors of localized provoked vulvodynia. *Acta Obstetrics and Gynecology Scandinavia, 89*(12), 1504–1510.

Bolso, A. (2005). Orgasm and lesbian sexuality. *Sex Education, 5*(1), 29–48.

Bolton, M., van der Straten, A., & Cohen, C. (2008). Probiotics: Potential to prevent HIV and sexually transmitted infections in women. *Sexually Transmitted Diseases, 35*(3), 214–225.

Bonetti, A., Tirelli, F., Catapano, A., Dazzi, D., Dei Cas, A., Solito, F., et al. (2007). Side effects of anabolic androgenic steroids abuse. *International Journal of Sports Medicine, 29*(8), 679–687.

Bonomi, A., Anderson, M., Reid, R., Carrell, D., Fishman, P., Rivara, F., & Thompson, R. (2007). Intimate partner violence in older women. *The Gerontologist, 47*, 34–41.

Boomer, D. S. (1963). Speech disturbances and body movement in interviews. *Journal of Nervous and Mental Disease, 136*, 263–266.

Boon, S., & Alderson, K. (2009). A phenomenological study of women in same-sex relationships who were previously married to men. *Canadian Journal of Human Sexuality, 18*(4), 149–169.

Boon, S., Deveau, V., & Alibhai, A. (2009). Payback: The parameters of revenge in romantic relationships. *Journal of Social and Personal Relationships, 26*(6–7), 747–768.

Boonstra, H. (2005, May). Condoms, contraceptives and nonoxynol-9: Complex issues obscured by ideology. *The Guttmacher Report on Public Policy, 8*(2), pp. 4–7.

Boonstra, H., Gold, R., Richard, C., & Finer, L. (2006). *Abortion in women's lives.* New York: Guttmacher Institute. Retrieved June 4, 2011, from http://www.guttmacher.org/pubs/2006/05/04/AiWL.pdf.

Borg, C., de Jong, P. J., & Schultz, W. W. (2010). Vaginismus and dyspareunia: Automatic vs. deliberate disgust responsivity. *Journal of Sexual Medicine, 7*(6), 2149–2157.

Borg, C., de Jong, P. J., & Weijmar Schultz, W. (2011). Vaginismus and dyspareunia: Relationship with general and sex-related moral standards. *Journal of Sexual Medicine, 8*(1), 223–231.

Borini, A., Cattoli, M., Bulletti, C., & Coticchio, G. (2008). Clinical efficiency of oocyte and embryo cryopreservation. *Annals of the New York Academy of Sciences, 1127*, 49–58.

Borisoff, J., Elliott, S., Hocaloski, S., & Birch, G. (2010). The development of a sensory substitution system for the sexual rehabilitation of men with chronic spinal cord injury. *Journal of Sexual Medicine, 7*(11), 3647–3658.

Bornstein, D. (Ed.). (1979). *The feminist controversy of the Renaissance.* Delmar, NY: Scholars' Facsimiles & Reprints.

Boroughs, D. S. (2004). Female sexual abusers of children. *Children & Youth Services Review, 26*(5), 481–487.

Bos, H., & Gartrell, N. (2010). Adolescents of the USA National Longitudinal Lesbian Family Study: Can family characteristics counteract the negative effects of stigmatization? *Family Process, 49*(4), 559–572.

Bosello, R., Favaro, A., Zanetti, T., Soave, M., Vidotto, G., Huon, G., & Santanastaso, P. (2010). Tattoos and piercings in adolescents: Family conflicts and temperament. *Rivesta di Psichiatria, 45*(2), 102–106.

Boswell, J. (1980). *Christianity, social tolerance, and homosexuality: Gay people in western Europe from the beginning of the Christian era to the fourteenth century.* Chicago: The University of Chicago Press.

Bouchlariotou, S., Tsikouras, P., Dimitraki, M., Athanasiadis, A., Papoulidis, I., Maroulis, G., Liberis, A., & Liberis, V. (2011). Turner's syndrome and pregnancy: Has the 45,X/47,XXX mosaicism a different prognosis. *Journal of Maternal and Fetal Neonatal Medicine, 24*(5), 668–672.

Bounhoure, J., Galinier, M., Roncalli, J., Assoun, B., & Puel, J. (2008). Myocardial infarction and oral contraceptives. *Bulletin of the Academy of National Medicine, 192,* 569–579.

Boushey, H., & O'Leary, A. (2010, March 8). How working women are reshaping America's families and economy and what it means for policymakers. Center for American Progress. Retrieved December 20, 2010, from http://www.american-progress.org/issues/2010/03/our_working_nation.html/print.html.

Bower, B. (1992). Depression, early death noted in HIV cases. *Science News, 142,* 53.

Bowlby, J. (1969). *Attachment and loss: Attachment.* New York: Basic Books.

Boxer, D. (1996). Ethnographic interviewing as a research tool in speech act analysis: The case of complaints. In S. M. Gass and J. Neu (Eds.), *Speech Acts Across Cultures* (pp. 217–239). New York: de Gruyter.

Boyd, L. (2000). Morning sickness shields fetus from bugs and chemicals. *RN, 63*(8), 18–20.

Boyle, C., Berkowitz, G., & Kelsey, J. (1987). Epidemiology of premenstrual symptoms. *American Journal of Public Health, 77*(3), 349–350.

Bradshaw, C., Kahn, A., & Saville, B. (2010). To hook up or date: Which gender benefits? *Sex Roles, 62*(9–10), 661–669.

Brandberg, Y., Sandelin, K., Erikson, S., Jurell, G., Liljegren, A., Lindblom, A., et al. (2008). Psychological reactions, quality of life, and body image after bilateral prophylactic mastectomy in women at high risk for breast cancer: A prospective 1-year follow-up study. *Journal of Clinical Oncology, 26,* 3943–3949.

Brandes, M., Hamilton, C. J., Bergevoet, K. A., de Bruin, J. P., Nelen, W. L., & Kremer, J. A. (2010). Origin of multiple pregnancies in a subfertile population. *Acta Obstetricia et Gynecologica Scandinavica, 89*(9), 1149–1154.

Brandt, A. M. (1985). *No magic bullet: A social history of venereal disease in the United States.* New York: Oxford University Press.

Brans, R., & Yao, F. (2010). Immunization with a dominant-negative recombinant Herpes Simplex Virus (HSV) type 1 protects against HSV-2 genital disease in guinea pigs. *BMC Microbiology, 10,* 163.

Branson, K. (2011, March 4). Gender-neutral housing. *Rutgers Today.* Retrieved April 17, 2011, from http://news.rutgers.edu/medrel/special-content/hot-topic-gender-neu-20110304.

Bratter, J. L., & King, R. B. (2008). "But will it last?": Marital instability among interracial and same-race couples. *Family Relations, 57,* 160–172.

Brecher, E. M., & Brecher, J. (1986). Extracting valuable sexological findings from severely flawed and biased population samples. *Journal of Sex Research, 22,* 6–20.

Brecklin, L. R., & Ullman, S. E. (2005). Self-defense or assertiveness training and women's responses to sexual attacks. *Journal of Interpersonal Violence, 20*(6), 738–762.

Breech, L., & Braverman, P. (2010). Safety, efficacy, actions, and patient acceptability of drospirenone/ethinyl estradiol contraceptive pills in the treatment of premenstrual dysphoric disorder. *International Journal of Women's Health, 1,* 85–95.

Brener, N., Grunbaum, J., Kann, L., McManus, T., & Ross, J. (2004). Assessing health risk behaviors among adolescents: The effect of question wording and appeals for honesty. *Journal of Adolescent Health, 35*(2), 91–100.

Brennan, A., Ayers, S., Ahmed, H., & Marshall-Lucette, S. (2007). A critical review of the Couvade syndrome: The pregnant male. *Journal of Reproductive and Infant Psychology, 25*(3), 173–189.

Brennan, B. P., Kanayama, G., Hudson, J. I., & Pope, H. G., Jr. (2011). Human growth hormone abuse in male weightlifters. *American Journal of Addiction, 20*(1), 9–13.

Breuss, C. E., & Greenberg, S. (1981). *Sex education: Theory and practice.* Belmont, CA: Wadsworth.

Brewer, D., Roberts, J., Muth, S., & Potterat, J. (2008). Prevalence of male clients of street prostitute women in the United States. *Human Organization, 67,* 346–357.

Brewis, A., & Meyer, M. (2005). Marital coitus across the life course. *Journal of Biosocial Sciences, 37,* 499–518.

Brewster, K. L., & Tillman, K. H. (2008). Who's doing it? Patterns and predictors of youths' oral sexual experiences. *Journal of Adolescent Health, 42,* 73–80.

Brewster, P., Mullin, C., Dobrin, R., & Steeves, J. (2010). Sex differences in face processing are mediated by handedness and sexual orientation. *Laterality, 9,* 1–13.

Bridgeland, W. M., Duane, E. A., & Stewart, C. S. (2001). Victimization and attempted suicide among college students. *College Student Journal, 35*(1), 63–76.

Briere, J., & Malamuth, N. (1983). Self-reported likelihood of sexually aggressive behavior: Attitudinal versus sexual explanations. *Journal of Research in Personality, 17,* 315–323.

Brinig, M. F., & Allen, D. A. (2000). "These boots are made for walking": Why most divorce filers are women. *American Law and Economics Review, 2,* 126–169.

Brinton, L. (2007). Long-term effects of ovulation-stimulating drugs on cancer risk. *Reproductive Biomedicine Online, 15,* 38–44.

Brinton, L. A., & Schairer, C. (1997). Postmenopausal hormone-replacement therapy: Time for a reappraisal? *New England Journal of Medicine, 336*(25), 1821–1822.

Brinton, L., Richesson, D., Gierach, G., & Lacey, J. (2008). Prospective evaluation of risk factors for male breast cancer. *Journal of the National Cancer Institute, 100*(20), 1477–1482.

Brizendine, L. (2006). *The female brain.* New York, NY: Broadway Publishing.

Brizendine, L., & Allen, B. J. (2010). Are gender differences in communication biologically determined? In B. Slife (Ed.), *Taking sides: Clashing views on psychological issues* (16th ed., pp. 71–88). New York: McGraw-Hill.

Brockman, N. (2004). Kenya. In R. T. Francoeur & R. J. Noonan (Eds.), *The Continuum international encyclopedia of sexuality* (pp. 679–691). New York/London: Continuum International.

Brongersma, E. (1990). Boy-lovers and their influence on boys: Distorted research and anecdotal observations. *Journal of Homosexuality, 20,* 145–173.

Brooks, R., Lee, S., Newman, P., & Leibowitz, A. (2008). Sexual risk behavior has decreased among men who have sex with men in Los Angeles but remains greater than that among heterosexual men and women. *AIDS Education and Prevention, 20,* 312–324.

Brooks-Gordon, B., & Geisthorpe, L. (2003). What men say when apprehended for kerb crawling: A model of prostitutes' clients' talk. *Psychology, Crime and Law, 9*(2), 145–171.

Brooks-Gunn, J., & Furstenberg, F. F. (1989). Adolescent sexual behavior. *American Psychologist, 44,* 249–257.

Brooks-Gunn, J., & Furstenberg, F. F. (1990). Coming of age in the era of AIDS: Puberty, sexuality, and contraception. *Milbank Quarterly, 68,* 59–84.

Broude, G. J., & Greene, S. J. (1976). Cross-cultural codes on twenty sexual attitudes and practices. *Ethnology, 15,* 409–428.

Brousseau, M., Bergeron, S., & Hebert, M. (2011). Sexual coercion victimization and perpetration in heterosexual couples: A dyadic investigation. *Archives of Sexual Behavior, 40*(2), 363–372.

Brown, A., & Testa, M. (2008). Social influences on judgments of rape victims: The role of the negative and positive social reactions of others. *Sex Roles, 58,* 490–501.

Brown, B. B., Dolcini, M. M., & Leventhal, A. (1997). Transformations in peer relationships at adolescence: Implications for healthrelated behavior. In J. Schulenberg, J. L. Maggs, & K. Hurrelmann (Eds.), *Health risks and developmental transitions during adolescence* (pp. 161–189). Cambridge, U.K.: Cambridge University Press.

Brown, C. (2008). Gender-role implications on same-sex intimate partner abuse. *Journal of Family Violence, 23,* 457–463.

Brown, D. J., Hill, S. T., & Baker, H. W. (2005). Male fertility and sexual function after spinal cord injury. *Progress in Brain Research, 152,* 427–439.

Brown, D. L., & Frank, J. E. (2003). Diagnosis and management of syphilis. *American Family Physician, 68*(2), 283–290.

Brown, H. G. (1962). *Sex and the single girl.* New York: Giant Cardinal.

Brown, J., & Trevethan, R. (2010). Shame, internalized homophobia, identity forma-

tion, attachment style, and the connection to relationship status in gay men. *American Journal of Men's Health, 4*(3), 267–276.

Brown, J., Pan, A., & Hart, R. J. (2010). Gonadotrophin-releasing hormone analogues for pain associated with endometriosis. *Cochrane Database of Systematic Reviews, 12,* CD008475.

Brown, J. C. (1983). Paraphilias: Sadomasochism, fetishism, transvestism and transsexuality. *British Journal of Psychiatry, 143,* 227–231.

Brown, M. S., & Brown, C. A. (1987). Circumcision decision: Prominence of social concerns. *Pediatrics, 80,* 215–219.

Brown, S. L., Lee, G. R., & Bulanda, J. R. (2006). Cohabitation among older adults: A national portrait. *Journals of Gerontology Series B: Psychological Sciences and Social Science, 61,* S71-S79.

Brown, T. J., Sumner, K. E., & Nocera, R. (2002). Understanding sexual aggression against women: An examination of the role of men's athletic participation and related variables. *Journal of Interpersonal Violence, 17*(9), 937–952.

Brownmiller, S. (1975). *Against our will: Men, women, and rape.* New York: Simon & Schuster.

Brownmiller, S. (2000). Rape on the brain: A review of Randy Thornhill and Craig Palmer. Retrieved December 5, 2005, from http://www.susanbrownmiller.com/html/review-thornhill.html.

Brubaker, L., Handa, V., Bradley, C., Connolly, A., Moalli, P., Brown, M., & Weber, A. (2008). Sexual function 6 months after first delivery. *Obstetrics and Gynecology, 111,* 1040–1044.

Bruce, K., & Walker, L. (2001). College students' attitudes about AIDS: 1986 to 2000. *AIDS Education and Prevention, 13*(5), 428–437.

Brucker, C., Karck, U., & Merkle, E. (2008). Cycle control, tolerability, efficacy and acceptability of the vaginal contraceptive ring, NuvaRing: Results of clinical experience in Germany. *European Journal of Contraceptive Reproductive Health Care, 13,* 31–38.

Brückner, H., & Bearman, P. (2005). After the promise: The STD consequences of adolescent virginity pledges. *Journal of Adolescent Health, 36*(4), 271–278.

Brugman, M., Caron, S., & Rademakers, J. (2010). Emerging adolescent sexuality: A comparison of American and Dutch college women's experiences. *International Journal of Sexual Health, 22*(1), 32–46.

Brumbaugh, C., & Fraley, C. (2010). Adult attachment and dating strategies: How do insecure people attract dates? *Personal Relationships, 17*(4), 599–614.

Brumberg, J. J. (1997). *The body project: An intimate history of American girls.* New York: Vintage Books.

Bruni, V., Pontello, V., Luisi, S., & Petraglia, F. (2008). An open-label multicentre trial to evaluate the vaginal bleeding pattern of the combined contraceptive vaginal ring NuvaRing. *European Journal of Obstetrics and Gynecological Reproductive Biology, 139,* 65–71.

Brunner Huber, L. R., & Ersek, J. L. (2011). Perceptions of contraceptive responsibility among female college students: An exploratory study. *Annals of Epidemiology, 21*(3), 197–203.

Brunner-Huber, L., & Toth, J. (2007). Obesity and oral contraceptive failure: Findings from the 2002 National Survey of Family Growth. *American Journal of Epidemiology, 166,* 1306–1311.

Bryan, W. A. (1987). Contemporary fraternity and sorority issues. *New Directions for Student Services, 40,* 37–56.

Bryant, C. (2010). Understanding the intersection of race and marriage: Does one model fit all? *Psychological Science Agenda.* Retrieved May 11, 2011, from http://www.apa.org/science/about/psa/2010/10/race-marriage.aspx.

Buckett, W., Chian, R., Holzer, H., Dean, N., Usher, R., & Tan, S. (2007). Obstetric outcomes and congenital abnormalities after in vitro maturation, IVF, and ICSI. *Obstetrics and Gynecology, 110,* 885–891.

Buffardi, A. L., Thomas, K. K., Holmes, K. K., & Manhart, L. E. (2008). Moving upstream: Ecosocial and psychosocial correlates of sexually transmitted infections among young adults in the United States. *American Journal of Public Health, 98,* 1128–1137.

Buisson, O., Foldes, P., Jannini, E., & Mimoun, S. (2010). Coitus as revealed by ultrasound in one volunteer couple. *Journal of Sexual Medicine, 7*(8), 2750–2754.

Bull, S. S., & Melian, L. M. (1998). Contraception and culture: The use of Yuyos in Paraguay. *Health Care for Women International, 19*(1), 49–66.

Bullivant, S., Sellergren, S., Stern, K., Spencer, N., Jacob, S., Mennella, J., & McClintock, M. (2004). Women's sexual experience during the menstrual cycle: Identification of the sexual phase by noninvasive measurement of luteinizing hormone. *Journal of Sex Research, 41*(1), 82–93.

Bullough, V. (1994). *Science in the bedroom: The history of sex research.* New York: Basic Books.

Bullough, V. L. (1973). *The subordinate sex: A history of attitudes toward women.* Urbana: University of Illinois Press.

Bullough, V. L. (1976). *Sexual variance in society and history.* New York: Wiley.

Bullough, V. L. (1979). *Homosexuality: A history.* New York: New American Library.

Bullough, V. L. (1990). History in adult human sexual behavior with children and adolescents in Western societies. In J. Feierman (Ed.), *Pedophilia biosocial dimensions* (pp. 69–90). New York: Springer-Verlag.

Bullough, V. L. (1998). Alfred Kinsey and the Kinsey Report: Historical overview and lasting contributions. *Journal of Sex Research, 35*(2), 127–131.

Bumpass, L., & Lu, H.-H. (2000). Trends in cohabitation and implications for children's family contexts in the U.S. *Population Studies, 54,* 29–41.

Bumpass, L., & Lu, H-H. (2000). Trends in cohabitation and implications for children's family contexts in the United States. *Population Studies, 54*(1), 29–41.

Burbidge, M., & Walters, J. (1981). *Breaking the silence: Gay teenagers speak for themselves.* London, U.K.: Joint Council for Gay Teenagers.

Burch, B. (1998). Lesbian sexuality. *Psychoanalytic Review, 85*(3), 349–372.

Burdette, A. M., Ellison, C. G., Sherkat, D. E., & Gore, K. A. (2007). Are there religious variations in marital infidelity? *Journal of Family Issues, 28,* 1553.

Burgess, A. W., & Holmstrom, L. L. (1979). *Rape: Crisis and recovery.* Bowie, MD: Robert J. Brady.

Burgess, A. W., & Morgenbesser, L. I. (2005). Sexual violence and seniors. *Brief Treatment & Crisis Intervention, 5*(2), 193–202.

Burgess, A., & Holmstrom, L. (1979). Rape: Sexual disruption and recovery. *American Journal of Orthopsychiatry, 131,* 981–986.

Burke, A. E., Barnhart, K., Jensen, J. T., Creinin, M. D., Walsh, T. L., Wan, L. S., Westhoff, C., Thomas, M., Archer, D., Wu, H., Liu, J., Schlaff, W., Carr, B. R., & Blithe, D. (2010). Contraceptive efficacy, acceptability, and safety of C31G and non-oxynol-9 spermicidal gels: A randomized controlled trial. *Obstetrics and Gynecology, 116*(6), 1265–1273.

Burke, D. (2008, July 26). Birth control ban marks 40 years. *The Ledger.* Retrieved Oc-

tober 28, 2008, from http://www.theledger.com/article/20080726/NEWS/807260367/1326&title=Birth_Control_Ban_Marks_40_Years.

Burkeman, O., & Younge, G. (2005). Being Brenda. Retrieved February 24, 2005, from http://www.godspy.com/life/Being-Brenda.cfm.

Burkman, R. T. (2002). The transdermal contraceptive patch: A new approach to hormonal contraception. *International Journal of Fertility and Women's Medicine, 47*(2), 69–76.

Burkman, R., Schlesselman, J. J., & Zieman, M. (2004). Safety concerns and health benefits associated with oral contraception. *American Journal of Obstetrics and Gynecology, 190*(Suppl. 4), S5–22.

Burleson, B. R. (2003). The experience and effects of emotional support: What the study of cultural and gender differences can tell us about close relationships, emotion and interpersonal communication. *Personal Relationships, 10*(1), 1–23.

Burleson, B. R., Kunkel, A. W., Samter, W., & Werking, K. (1996). Men's and women's evaluations of communication skills in personal relationships: When sex differences make a difference—and when they don't. *Journal of Social and Personal Relationships, 13,* 201–224.

Burns, M., Costello, J., Ryan-Woolley, B., & Davidson, S. (2007). Assessing the impact of late treatment effects in cervical cancer: An exploratory study of women's sexuality. *European Journal of Cancer Care, 16,* 364–372.

Burris, H., Collins, J., & Wright, R. (2011). Racial/ethnic disparities in preterm birth: Clues from environmental exposures. *Current Opinions in Pediatrics, 23,* 227–232.

Burt, M. (1980). Cultural myths and support for rape. *Journal of Personality and Social Psychology, 38,* 217–230.

Burton, K. (2005). Attachment style and perceived quality of romantic partner's opposite-sex best friendship: The impact on romantic relationship satisfaction. *Dissertation Abstracts International, 65*(8-B), 4329, # 0419–4217.

Busby, D., Carroll, J., & Willoughby, B. (2010). Compatibility or restraint? The effects of sexual timing on marriage relationships. *Journal of Family Psychology, 24*(6), 766–774.

Buss, D. (1989). Sex differences in human mate preferences: Evolutionary hypotheses

tested in 37 cultures. *Behavioral and Brain Sciences, 12,* 1–49.

Buss, D. M. (1994). *The evolution of desire: Strategies of human mating.* New York: Basic Books.

Buss, D. M. (2003). The dangerous passion: Why jealousy is as necessary as love and sex. *Archives of Sexual Behavior, 32*(1), 79–80.

Buss, D. M., Shackelford, T. K., Kirkpatrick, L., & Larsen, R. J. (2001). A half century of mate preferences: The cultural evolution of values. *Journal of Marriage & the Family, 63*(2), 491–503.

Busse, P., Fishbein, M., Bleakley, A., & Hennessy, M. (2010). The role of communication with friends in sexual initiation. *Communication Research, 37*(2), 239–255.

Butrick, C. W. (2009). Pelvic floor hypertonic disorders: Identification and management. *Obstetrics and Gynecology Clinics of North America, 36*(3), 707–722.

Byers, E., Henderson, J., & Hobson, K. (2009). University students' definitions of sexual abstinence and having sex. *Archives of Sexual Behavior, 38*(5), 665–674.

Byrne, D., & Murnen, S. K. (1988). Maintaining loving relationships. In R. Sternberg & M. L. Barnes (Eds.), *Psychology of love* (pp. 293–310). New Haven, CT: Yale University Press.

Cabaret, A. S., Leveque, J., Dugast, C., Blanchot, J., & Grall, J. Y. (2003). Problems raised by the gynaecologic management of women with BRCA 1 and 2 mutations. *Gynecology, Obstetrics and Fertility, 31*(4), 370–377.

Cado, S., & Leitenberg, H. (1990). Guilt reactions to sexual fantasies during intercourse. *Archives of Sexual Behavior 19*(1), 49–63.

Caffaro, J., & Conn-Caffaro, A. (2005). Treating sibling abuse families. *Aggression and Violent Behavior, 10*(5), 604–623.

Cahill, S., South, K., & Spade, J. (2000). *Outing age: Public policy issues affecting gay, lesbian, bisexual and transgender elders.* Washington, DC: National Gay and Lesbian Task Force.

Cai, D., Wilson, S. R., & Drake, L. E. (2000). Culture in the context of intercultural negotiation: Individualism-collectivism and paths to integrative agreements. *Human Communication Research, 26*(4), 591–617.

Cakin-Memik, N., Yildiz, O., Sişmanlar, S. G., Karakaya, I., & Ağaoğlu, B. (2010). Priapism associated with methylphenidate: A case report. *Turkish Journal of Pediatrics, 52*(4), 430–434.

Calderone, M. (1983). On the possible prevention of sexual problems in adolescence. *Hospital and Community Psychiatry, 34,* 528–530.

Callahan, M. M. (2002). Safety and tolerance studies of potential microbicides following multiple penile applications. Annual Conference on Microbicides, May 12–15, 2002, Antwerp, Belgium.

Calzavara, L. M., Burchell, A. N., Lebovic, G., Myers, T., Remis, R. S., Raboud, J., Corey, P., Swantee, C., & Hart, T. A. (2011). The impact of stressful life events on unprotected anal intercourse among gay and bisexual men. *AIDS Behavior.* Retrieved February 20, 2011, from http://www.ncbi.nlm.nih.gov/pubmed/21274612.

Camacho, M., & Reyes-Ortiz, C. (2005). Sexual dysfunction in the elderly: Age or disease? *International Journal of Impotence Research, 17,* S52–S56.

Cameron, K. A., Salazar, L. F., Bernhardt, J. M., Burgess-Whitman, N., Wingood, G. M., & DiClemente, R. J. (2005). Adolescents' experience with sex on the web: Results from online focus groups. *Journal of Adolescence, 28*(4), 535–540.

Cameron, P. (2006). Children of homosexuals and transsexuals more apt to be homosexual. *Journal of Biosocial Science, 38*(3), 413–418.

Cameron, S., Glasier, A., Dewart, H., & Johnstone, A. (2010). Women's experiences of the final stage of early medical abortion at home: Results of a pilot survey. *Journal of Family Planning and Reproductive Health Care, 36*(4), 213–216.

Cammaert, L. (1985). How widespread is sexual harassment on campus? Special issue: Women in groups and aggression against women. *International Journal of Women's Studies, 8,* 388–397.

Campbell, J. C., Webster, D., Koziol-McLain, J., Block, C., Campbell, D., Curry, M. A., et al. (2002). Intimate partner violence and physical health consequences. *Archives of Internal Medicine, 162*(10), 1157–1163.

Campbell, L., Simpson, J., Boldry, J., & Rubin, H., (2010). Trust, variability in relationship evaluations, and relationship processes. *Journal of Personality and Social Psychology, 99*(1), 14–21.

Campbell, P. P. (2008). Sexual violence in the lives of lesbian rape survivors. St. Louis: Saint Louis University, AAT #3324148.

Campbell, R., Lichty, L., Sturza, M., & Raja, S. (2006). Gynecological health impact of sexual assault. *Research in Nursing and Health, 29,* 399–413.

Campbell, R., Sefl, T., & Ahrens, C. E. (2004). The impact of rape on women's sexual health risk behaviors. *Health Psychology, 23*(1), 67–74.

Camperio-Ciani, A., Corna, F., & Capiluppi, C. (2004). Evidence for maternally inherited factors favouring male homosexuality and promoting female fecundity. *Proceedings: Biological Sciences, 271*(1554), 2217–2221.

Campos, B., Graesch, A., Repetti, R., Bradbury, T., & Ochs, E. (2009). Opportunity for interaction? A naturalistic observation study of dual-earner families after work and school. *Journal of Family Psychology, 23*(6), 798–807.

Caplan, A., & Patrizio, P. (2010). Are you ever too old to have a baby? The ethical challenges of older women using infertility services. *Seminars in Reproductive Medicine, 28*(4), 281–286.

Carcopino, X., Shojai, R., & Boubli, L. (2004). Female genital mutilation: Generalities, complications and management during obstetrical period. *Journal of Gynecology, Obstetrics, & Biological Reproduction, 33*(5), 378–383.

Cardoso, F. L., Savall, A. C., & Mendes, A. K. (2009). Self-awareness of the male sexual response after spinal cord injury. *International Journal of Rehabilitation Research, 32*(4), 294–300.

Carey, B. (2005). Straight, gay or lying? Bisexuality revisited. Retrieved July 5, 2005, from http://www.thetaskforce.org/downloads/07052005NYTBisexuality.pdf.

Carlson, H. (2011). Approach to the patient with gynecomastia. *Journal of Clinical Endocrinological Metabolism, 96*(1), 15–21.

Carlton, C. L., Nelson, E. S., & Coleman, P. K. (2000). College students' attitudes toward abortion and commitment to the issue. *Social Science Journal, 37*(4), 619–625.

Carnes, P. (2001). *Out of the shadows: Understanding sexual addiction.* Center City, MN: Hazelden Information Education.

Carpentier, M. Y., & Fortenberry, J. D. (2010). Romantic and sexual relationships, body image, and fertility in adolescent and young adult testicular cancer survivors: A review of the literature. *Journal of Adolescent Health, 47*(2), 115–125.

Carr, B. (2009, November 25). Sex trafficking: An American problem too. CNN Online. Retrieved May 7, 2011, from http://articles.cnn.com/2009–11–25/opinion/carr.human.trafficking_1_trafficking-victims-protection-act-tvpa-lena?_s5PM:OPINION.

Carr, R. R., & Ensom, M. H. (2002). Fluoxetine in the treatment of premenstrual dysphoric disorder. *Annuals of Pharmacotherapy, 36*(4), 713–717.

Carrell, D. T., Wilcox, A. L., Lowry, L., Peterson, C. M., Jones, K. P., Erickson, L., et al. (2003). Elevated sperm chromosome aneuploidy and apoptosis in patients with unexplained recurrent pregnancy loss. *Obstetrics and Gynecology, 101*(6), 1229–1235.

Carrier, J. M. (1989). Gay liberation and coming out in Mexico. *Journal of Homosexuality, 17,* 225–252.

Carroll, J. (2009). *The day Aunt Flo comes to visit.* Avon, CT: Best Day Media.

Carroll, J., Padilla-Walker, L., Nelson, L., Olsen, C., Barry, C., & Madsen, S. (2008). Generation XXX. *Journal of Adolescent Research, 23*(1), 6–30.

Carter, F., Carter, J., Luty, S., Jordan, J., McIntosh, V., Bartram, A., et al. (2007). What is worse for your sex life: Starving, being depressed, or a new baby? *International Journal of Eating Disorders, 40,* 664–667.

Carter, J. S., Corra, M., & Carter, S. K. (2009). The interaction of race and gender: Changing gender-role attitudes, 1974–2006. *Social Science Quarterly, 90*(1), 196–212.

Carter, J., Goldfrank, D., & Schover, L. (2011). Simple strategies for vaginal health promotion in cancer survivors. *Journal of Sexual Medicine, 8*(2), 549–559.

Caruso, S., Iraci Sareri, M., Agnello, C., Romano, M., Lo Presti, L., Malandrino, C., & Cianci, A. (2011). Conventional vs. extended-cycle oral contraceptives on the quality of sexual life: Comparison between two regimens containing 3 mg drospirenone and 20 mg ethinyl estradiol. *Journal of Sexual Medicine, 8*(5), 1478–1485.

Caruso, S., Rugolo, S., Agnello, C., Intelisano, G., DiMari, L., & Cianci, A. (2006). Sildenafil improves sexual functioning in premenopausal women with type 1 diabetes who are affected by sexual arousal disorder: A double-blind, crossover, placebo-controlled pilot study. *Fertility and Sterility, 85,* 1496–1501.

Case, P., Austin, S. B., Hunter, D., Manson, J., Malpeis, S., Willett, W., & Spiegelman, D. (2004). Sexual orientation, health risk factors, and physical functioning in the nurses' health study II. *Journal of Women's Health, 13*(9), 1033–1047.

Casey, B., Getz, S., & Galvan, A. (2008). The adolescent brain. *Developmental Review, 28,* 62–77.

Caspi, A., Williams, B., Kim-Cohen, J., Craig, I., Milne, B., Poulton, R., et al. (2007). Moderation of breastfeeding effects on the IQ by genetic variation in fatty acid metabolism. *Proceedings of the National Academy of Sciences of the United States of America, 104,* 18860–18865.

Cass, V. C. (1979). Homosexual identity formation: A theoretical model. *Journal of Homosexuality, 4,* 219–235.

Cass, V. C. (1984). Homosexual identity formation: Testing a theoretical model. *The Journal of Sex Research, 20,* 143–167.

Casteels, K., Wouters, C., VanGeet, C., & Devlieger, H. (2004). Video reveals self-stimulation in infancy. *Acta Paediatrics, 93*(6), 844–846.

Catania, J. A., Binson, D., Van Der Straten, A., & Stone, V. (1995). Methodological research on sexual behavior in the AIDS era. *Annual Review of Sex Research, 6,* 77–125.

Catania, J. A., Coates, T. J., Kegeles, S. M., et al. (1989). Implications of the AIDS risk-reduction model for the gay community: The importance of perceived sexual enjoyment and help-seeking behaviors. In V. M. Mays, G. W. Albee, & S. F. Schneider (Eds.), *Primary prevention of AIDS: Psychological approaches* (pp. 242–261). Newbury Park, CA: Sage.

Catania, J. A., McDermott, L. J., & Pollack, L. M. (1986). Questionnaire response bias and face-to-face interview sample bias in sexuality research. *Journal of Sex Research, 22,* 52–72.

Cates, J. A., & Markley, J. (1992). Demographic, clinical, and personality variables associated with male prostitution by choice. *Adolescence, 27,* 695–706.

Cathcart, R. (2008, February 23). Boy's killing, labeled a hate crime, stuns a town. *New York Times.* Retrieved February 23, 2008, from http://www.nytimes.com/2008/02/23/us/23oxnard.html?ref=us.

Caughey, A., Hopkins, L., & Norton, M. (2006). Chorionic villus sampling compared with amniocentesis and the difference in the rate of pregnancy loss. *Obstetrics and Gynecology, 108,* 612–616.

Cauley, L. (2009, June 4). Internet use triples in decade; broadband surges. *USA Today.* Retrieved October 12, 2010, from http://www.usatoday.com/tech/news/2009–06–03-internet-use-broadband_N.htm.

Cavanaugh, C., Messing, J., Petras, H., Fowler, B., LaFlair, L., Kub, J., Agnew, J., Fitzgerald, S., Bolyard, R., & Campbell, J. (2011). Patterns of violence against women: A la-

tent class analysis. *Psychological Trauma: Theory, Research, Practice, and Policy.* Retrieved August 26, 2011, from http://psycnet.apa.org/index.cfm?fa=buy.optionToBuy&id=2011-07605-001.

CBS. (2010, August). CBS News Poll. Should gays be allowed to married? Retrieved January 31, 2011, from http://www.cbsnews.com/stories/2007/10/12/politics/main3362530.shtml?tag5featuredPostArea.

Cecchetti, J. A. (2007). Women's attachment representations of their fathers and the experience of passionate love in adulthood. *Dissertation Abstracts International: Section B: The Sciences and Engineering, 68,* 3389.

Cederroth, C. R., Auger, J., Zimmermann, C., Eustache, F., & Nef, S. (2010). Soy, phyto-oestrogens and male reproductive function: A review. *International Journal of Andrology, 33*(2), 304–316.

Ceniti, J., & Malamuth, N. (1984). Effects of repeated exposure to sexually violent or nonviolent stimuli on sexual arousal to rape or nonrape depictions. *Behavior Research and Therapy, 22,* 535–548.

Centers for Disease Control and Prevention, Division of STD Prevention. (2007). *Sexually transmitted disease surveillance, 2006.* Retrieved September 17, 2008, from http://www.cdc.gov/STD/stats/toc2006.htm.

Centers for Disease Control and Prevention. (2007a). *2005 assisted reproductive technology success rates: National summary and fertility clinic reports.* Atlanta, GA: Author.

Centers for Disease Control and Prevention. (2007b). *Chlamydia—CDC fact sheet.* Retrieved September 18, 2008, from http://www.cdc.gov/std/Chlamydia/STDFact-Chlamydia.htm.

Centers for Disease Control and Prevention. (2007c). *Trends in reportable sexually transmitted diseases in the U.S., 2006.* Retrieved September 18, 2008, from http://www.cdc.gov/STD/STATS/pdf/trends2006.pdf.

Centers for Disease Control and Prevention. (2007d). Trichomoniasis—CDC fact sheet. Retrieved September 18, 2008, from http://www.cdc.gov/std/trichomonas/STDFact-Trichomoniasis.htm.

Centers for Disease Control and Prevention. (2008a). *Genital HPV infection—CDC fact sheet.* Retrieved September 18, 2008, from http://www.cdc.gov/std/HPV/STDFact-HPV.htm.

Centers for Disease Control and Prevention. (2008b). *Hepatitis A.* National Center for

HIV/AIDS, Viral Hepatitis, STD, and TB Prevention, Division of Viral Hepatitis. Retrieved September 16, 2008, from http://www.cdc.gov/hepatitis/HAV/HAV-faq.htm#general.

Centers for Disease Control and Prevention. (2008c). *Hepatitis B.* National Center for HIV/AIDS, Viral Hepatitis, STD, and TB Prevention, Division of Viral Hepatitis. Retrieved September 16, 2008, from http://www.cdc.gov/hepatitis/HBV/HBV-faq.htm#overview.

Centers for Disease Control and Prevention. (2008d). *Hepatitis C.* National Center for HIV/AIDS, Viral Hepatitis, STD, and TB Prevention, Division of Viral Hepatitis. Retrieved September 16, 2008, from http://www.cdc.gov/hepatitis/HCV.htm.

Centers for Disease Control and Prevention. (2008e). HIV/AIDS among women. *CDC HIV/AIDS Fact Sheet.* Retrieved September 16, 2008, from http://www.cdc.gov/hiv/topics/women/resources/factsheets/pdf/women.pdf.

Centers for Disease Control and Prevention. (2008f). *HIV and AIDS in the U.S.: A picture of today's epidemic.* Retrieved on September 18, 2008, from http://www.cdc.gov/hiv/topics/surveillance/united_states.htm.

Centers for Disease Control and Prevention. (2008g). *HPV vaccine—questions and answers.* Retrieved September 18, 2008, from http://www.cdc.gov/vaccines/vpd-vac/hpv/vac-faqs.htm.

Centers for Disease Control and Prevention. (2008h, February). Male circumcision and risk for HIV transmission and other health conditions: Implications for the United States. Department of Health and Human Services. Retrieved December 18, 2008, from http://www.cdc.gov/hiv/resources/factsheets/circumcision.htm.

Centers for Disease Control and Prevention. (2008i). MMWR analysis provides new details on HIV incidence in U.S. populations. *CDC HIV/AIDS Facts.* Retrieved September 16, 2008, from http://www.cdc.gov/hiv/topics/surveillance/resources/factsheets/pdf/mmwr-incidence.pdf.

Centers for Disease Control and Prevention. (2008j). *Pelvic inflammatory disease—CDC fact sheet.* Retrieved September 18, 2008, from http://www.cdc.gov/std/PID/STDFact-PID.htm.

Centers for Disease Control and Prevention. (2008k). Syncope after vaccination—United States, January 2005–July 2007.

Morbidity and Mortality Weekly Report, 57, 457–460.

Centers for Disease Control and Prevention. (2008l). Update on overall prevalence of major birth defects—Atlanta, Georgia, 1978–2005. *MMWR Morbidity and Mortality Weekly, 57*(1), 1–5.

Centers for Disease Control and Prevention. (2008m). *Viral hepatitis.* National Center for HIV/AIDS, Viral Hepatitis, STD, and TB Prevention, Division of Viral Hepatitis. Retrieved September 16, 2008, from http://www.cdc.gov/hepatitis/index.htm.

Centers for Disease Control and Prevention. (2009a). *Genital HPV infection—fact sheet.* Centers for Disease Control and Prevention. Retrieved April 1, 2011, from http://www.cdc.gov/std/HPV/STDFact-HPV.htm#common.

Centers for Disease Control and Prevention. (2009b). HIV surveillance report, 2009 (Vol. 21). Retrieved March 26, 2011, from http://www.cdc.gov/hiv/topics/surveillance/resources/reports/.

Centers for Disease Control and Prevention. (2009c). *Oral sex and HIV risk. CDC HIV/AIDS facts.* Retrieved April 1, 2011, from http://www.cdc.gov/hiv/resources/factsheets/PDF/oralsex.pdf.

Centers for Disease Control and Prevention. (2009d). Sexually transmitted diseases in the United States, 2008: National surveillance data for chlamydia, gonorrhea, and syphilis. Atlanta, GA: U.S. Department of Health and Human Services. Retrieved April 1, 2011, from http://www.cdc.gov/std/stats08/trends.htm.

Centers for Disease Control and Prevention. (2009e). Sexually transmitted disease surveillance, 2008. Atlanta, GA: U.S. Department of Health and Human Services.

Centers for Disease Control and Prevention. (2010a). 2008 assisted reproductive technology success rates: National summary and fertility clinic reports. Atlanta, GA: U.S. Department of Health and Human Services. Retrieved March 1, 2011, from http://www.cdc.gov/art/ART2008/PDF/ART_2008_Full.pdf.

Centers for Disease Control and Prevention. (2010b). Breastfeeding report card—United States, 2010. Department of Health and Human Services. Retrieved February 24, 2010, from http://www.cdc.gov/breastfeeding/pdf/BreastfeedingReportCard2010.pdf.

Centers for Disease Control and Prevention. (2010c). Hepatitis A information for health professionals. Retrieved April 1, 2011, from http://www.cdc.gov/hepatitis/Statistics/2008Surveillance/Commentary.htm.

Centers for Disease Control and Prevention. (2010d). *HIV in the United States. National Center for HIV/AIDS, hepatitis, STD, and TB prevention.* Retrieved March 30, 2011, from http://www.cdc.gov/hiv/topics/surveillance/resources/factsheets/pdf/us_overview.pdf.

Centers for Disease Control and Prevention. (2010e). Sexually transmitted disease surveillance 2009. Atlanta, GA: U.S. Department of Health and Human Services.

Centers for Disease Control and Prevention. (2010f). Sexually transmitted diseases treatment guidelines, 2010. *Morbidity and Mortality Weekly Report: Recommendations and Reports, 59*(RR12), 1–110.

Centers for Disease Control and Prevention. (2010g). Youth Risk Behavior Surveillance—United States, 2009. *Morbidity and Mortality Weekly Report Surveillance Summaries, 59*(5), 1–142.

Centers for Disease Control and Prevention. (2011a). *Pelvic inflammatory disease—CDC fact sheet.* Centers for Disease Control and Prevention. Retrieved April 1, 2011, from http://www.cdc.gov/std/pid/stdfact-pid.htm.

Centers for Disease Control and Prevention. (2011b). *Understanding intimate partner violence fact sheet.* CDC Violence Prevention. Retrieved April 29, 2011, from http://www.cdc.gov/violenceprevention/pdf/IPV_factsheet-a.pdf.

Centers for Disease Control. (2006). HIV prevalence estimates—*U.S. Morbidity and Mortality Weekly Report, 57*(39), 1073–1076.

Chakraborty, A., McManus, S., Brugha, T. S., Bebbington, P., & King, M. (2011). Mental health of the non-heterosexual population of England. *British Journal of Psychiatry, 198,* 143–148.

Chalett, J. M., & Nerenberg, L. T. (2000). "Blue balls": A diagnostic consideration in testiculoscrotal pain in young adults: A case report and discussion. *Pediatrics, 106,* 843.

Chan, C. S. (1989). Issues of identity development among Asian-American lesbians and gay men. *Journal of Counseling and Development, 68,* 16–20.

Chan, J., Olivier, B., deJong, R., Snoeren, E., Kooijman, E., vanHasselt, F., et al. (2008). Translational research into sexual disorders: Pharmacology and genomics. *European Journal of Pharmacology, 585,* 426–435.

Chancer, L. S. (2006). *Sadomasochism in everyday life: The dynamics of power and powerlessness.* New Brunswick, NJ: Rutgers University Press.

Chandra, A., Mosher, W. D., Copen, C., & Sionean, C. (2011). Sexual behavior, sexual attraction, and sexual identity in the United States: Data from the 2006–2008 National Survey of Family Growth [National health statistics reports; no 36]. Hyattsville, MD: National Center for Health Statistics.

Chang, Q., Qian, X., Xu, Z., & Zhang, C. (2010). Effects of combined administration of low-dose gossypol with steroid hormones on the mitotic phase of spermatogenesis of rat. *Journal of Experimental Zoology, 313*(10), 671–679.

Chang, S., Chen, K., Lin, H., Chao, Y., & Lai, Y. (2011). Comparison of the effects of episiotomy and no episiotomy on pain, urinary incontinence, and sexual function 3 months postpartum: A prospective follow-up study. *International Journal of Nursing Studies, 48*(4), 409–418.

Chaplin, S. (2007). *Japanese love hotels: A cultural history.* London: Routledge.

Chaudhury, R. R. (1985). Plant contraceptives translating folklore into scientific application. In D. B. Jelliffe & E. F. Jelliffe (Eds.), *Advances in international maternal and child health* (pp. 107–114). Oxford, U.K.: Claredon Press.

Chavarro, J., Sadio, S. M., Toth, T. L., & Hauser, R. (2007a, October). Soy food and soy isoflavone intake in relation to semen quality parameters. Presentation at the Annual Meeting of the American Society for Reproductive Medicine, Washington, D.C.

Chavarro, J. E., Toth, T. L., Sadio, S. M., & Hauser, R. (2008). Soy food and isoflavone intake in relation to semen quality parameters among men from an infertility clinic. *Human Reproduction, 23*(11), 2584–2590.

Chavarro, J. E., Willett, W. C., & Skerrett, P. J. (2007b). *The fertility diet.* New York: McGraw Hill.

Cheasty, M., Clare, A. W., & Collins, C. (2002). Child sexual abuse: A predictor of persistent depression in adult rape and sexual assault victims. *Journal of Mental Health, 11*(1), 79–84.

Check, J. H. (2010). The future trends of induction of ovulation. *Minerva Endocrinology, 35*(4), 227–246.

Chemes, H., & Rawe, V. (2010). The making of abnormal spermatozoa: Cellular and molecular mechanisms. *Cell Tissue Research, 341*(3), 349–357.

Chen, J., & Danish, S. (2010). Acculturation, distress disclosure, and emotional self-disclosure within Asian populations. *Asian American Journal of Psychology, 1*(3), 200–211.

Chen, S. (2010, May 3). Serious legal hurdles for gay divorce. CNN. Retrieved January 31, 2011, from http://articles.cnn.com/2010–05–03/living/texas.gay.divorce_1_gay-marriage-gay-divorce-same-sex-divorce?_s5PM:LIVING.

Chen, Z., & Shi, Y. (2010). Polycystic ovary syndrome. *Front Medicine China, 4*(3), 280–284.

Cheng, D., Kettinger, L., Uduhiri, K., & Hurt, L. (2011). Alcohol consumption during pregnancy: Prevalence and provider assessment. *Obstetrics and Gynecology, 117*(2 Pt 1), 212–217.

Cheng, W., & Warren, M. (2001). She knows more about Hong Kong than you do isn't it: Tags in Hong Kong conversational English. *Journal of Pragmatics, 33,* 1419–1439.

Cherlin, A. (2009). The origins of the ambivalent acceptance of divorce. *Journal of Marriage and Family, 71*(2), 226–229.

Chesler, P. (1993, October). Sexual violence against women and a woman's right to self-defense: The case of Aileen Carol Wuornos. *Criminal Practice Law Report, 1*(9). Retrieved May 1, 2011, from http://www.phyllis-chesler.com/114/sexual-violence-against-women-self-defense-wuornos.

Chia, M., & Abrams, D. (1997). *The multiorgasmic man: Sexual secrets every man should know.* San Francisco: HarperCollins.

Chin-Hong, P., Berry, J., Cheng, S., Catania, J., DaCosta, M., Darragh, T., et al. (2008). Comparison of patient- and clinician-collected anal cytology samples to screen for human papillomavirus-associated anal intraepithelial neoplasia in men who have sex with men. *Annals of Internal Medicine, 149,* 300–306.

Chmielewski, D. C., & Hoffman, C. (2006). Porn industry again at the tech forefront. *Los Angeles Times,* p. A1. Retrieved November 15, 2008, from http://articles.latimes.com/2006/apr/19/business/fi-porn19.

Choi, N. (2004). Sex role group differences in specific, academic, and general self-efficacy. *Journal of Psychology: Interdisciplinary & Applied, 138*(2), 149–159.

Chopin-Marcé, M. J. (2001). Exhibitionism and psychotherapy: A case study. *International Journal of Offender Therapy & Comparative Criminology, 45*(5), 626–633.

Chow, E. W., & Choy, A. L. (2002). Clinical characteristics and treatment response to SSRI in a female pedophile. *Archives of Sexual Behavior, 31*(2), 211–215.

Christiansen, O. B. (1996). A fresh look at the causes and treatments of recurrent miscarriage, especially its immunological aspects. *Human Reproduction Update, 2*(4), 271–293.

Christofides, E., Muise, A., & Desmarais, S. (2009). Information disclosure and control on Facebook: Are they two sides of the same coin or two different processes? *CyberPsychology & Behavior, 12*(3), 341–345.

Chudakov, B., Cohen, H., Matar, M., & Kaplan, Z. (2008). A naturalistic prospective open study of the effects of adjunctive therapy of sexual dysfunction in chronic PTSD patients. *Israel Journal of Psychiatry Related Sciences, 45,* 26–32.

Chumlea, W. C., Schubert, C. M., Roche, A. F., Kulin, H. E., Lee, P. A., Himes, J. H., & Sun, S. S. (2003). Age at menarche and racial comparisons in U.S. girls. *Pediatrics, 111,* 110–113.

Cianciotto, J., & Cahill, S. (2006). *Youth in the crosshairs: The third wave of the ex-gay movement.* National Gay and Lesbian Task Force Policy Institute. Retrieved October 2, 2008, from http://www.thetaskforce.org/downloads/reports/reports/YouthInTheCrosshairs.pdf.

Cibula, D., Gompel, A., Mueck, A. O., La Vecchia, C., Hannaford, P. C., Skouby, S. O., Zikan, M., & Dusek, L. (2010). Hormonal contraception and risk of cancer. *Human Reproduction Update, 16*(6), 631–650.

Cigna, E., Tarallo, M., Fino, P., DeSanto, L., & Scuderi, N. (In press). Surgical correction of gynecomastia in thin patients. *Aesthetic Plastic Surgery.*

Clapp, I., & Lopez, B. (2007). Size at birth, obesity and blood pressure at age five. *Metabolic Syndrome and Related Disorders, 5,* 116–126.

Clapp, J. F. (1996). Morphometric and neurodevelopmental outcome at age five years of the offspring of women who continued to exercise regularly throughout pregnancy. *Journal of Pediatrics, 129*(6), 856–863.

Clark, A. M., Ledger, W., Galletly, C., Tomlinson, L., Blaney, F., Wang, X., & Norman R.J. (1995). Weight loss results in significant improvement in pregnancy and ovulation rates in anovulatory obese women. *Human Reproduction, 10,* 2705–2712.

Clark, M. S., & Reis, H. T. (1988). Interpersonal processes in close relationships. *Annual Review of Psychology, 39,* 609–672.

Clark, P. M., Atton, C., Law, C. M., Shiell, A., Godfrey, K., & Barker, D. J. (1998). Weight gain in pregnancy, triceps skinfold thickness, and blood pressure in offspring. *Obstetrics and Gynecology, 91*(1), 103–107.

Clarke, A. K., & Miller, S. J. (2001). The debate regarding continuous use of oral contraceptives. *Annals of Pharmacotherapy, 35,* 1480–1484.

Clarke, L., & Korotchenko, A. (2010). Shades of grey: To dye or not to dye one's hair in later life. *Ageing and Society, 30*(6), 1011–1026.

Claxton, A., & Perry-Jenkins, M. (2008). No fun anymore: Leisure and marital quality across the transition to parenthood. *Journal of Marriage and Family, 70,* 28–44.

Clayton, A. H. (2008). Symptoms related to the menstrual cycle: Diagnosis, prevalence, and treatment. *Journal of Psychiatric Practices, 14,* 13–21.

Clinton, C., & Gillespie, M. (1997). *Sex and race in the early South.* Oxford, England: Oxford University Press.

Cluver, L., & Gardner, F. (2007). Risk and protective factors for psychological well-being of children orphaned by AIDS in Cape Town: A qualitative study of children and caregivers' perspectives. 19(3), 318–325.

Coast, E. (2007). Wasting semen: Context and condom use among the Maasai. *Culture, Health and Sexuality, 9,* 387–401.

Coccia, M., & Rizzello, F. (2008). Ovarian reserve. Assessment of human reproductive function. *Annals of the New York Academy of Science, 1127,* 27–30.

Coccia, M., Rizzello, F., Cammilli, F., Bracco, G., & Scarselli, G. (2008). Endometriosis and infertility surgery and ART: An integrated approach for successful management. *European Journal of Obstetrics, Gynecology, and Reproductive Biology, 138,* 54–59.

Cochran, B. M., Ginzler, J., & Cauce, A. (2002). Challenges faced by homeless sexual minorities: Comparison of gay, lesbian, bisexual, and transgendered homeless sexual minorities with their heterosexual counterparts. *Journal of Public Health, 92,* 773–777.

Cochran, S. D., Mays, V. M., Alegria, M., Ortega, A. N., & Takeuchi, D. (2007). Mental health and substance use disorders among Latino and Asian American lesbian, gay, and bisexual adults. *Journal of Consulting and Clinical Psychology, 75*(5), 785–794.

Cohan, C., & Kleinbaum, S. (2002). Toward a greater understanding of the cohabitation effect. *Journal of Marriage and Family, 64*(1), 180–193.

Cohen, C., Brandhorst, B., Nagy, A., Leader, A., Dickens, B., Isasi, R., Evans, D., & Knoppers, B. (2008a). The use of fresh embryos in stem cell research: Ethical and policy issues. *Cell Stem Cell, 2,* 416–421.

Cohen, F., Kemeny, M., Kearney, K., Zegans, L., Neuhaus, J., & Conant, M. (1999). Persistent stress as a predictor of genital herpes recurrence. *Archives of Internal Medicine, 159,* 2430–2436.

Cohen, J., Byers, E., & Walsh, L. (2008). Factors influencing the sexual relationships of lesbians and gay men. *International Journal of Sexual Health, 20*(3), 162–176.

Cohen, J. K., Miller, R. J., Ahmed, S., Lotz, M. J., & Baust, J. (2008c). Ten-year biochemical disease control for patients with prostate cancer treated with cryosurgery as primary therapy. *Urology, 71,* 515–518.

Cohen, K. M., & Savin-Williams, R. C. (1996). Developmental perspectives on coming out to self and others. In R. C. Savin-Williams & K. M. Cohen (Eds.), *The lives of lesbians, gays, and bisexuals: Children to adults* (pp. 113–151). Fort Worth, TX: Harcourt Brace.

Cohen, L. (1988). Providing treatment and support for partners of sexual-assault survivors. *Psychotherapy, 25,* 94–98.

Cohen, L., & Roth, S. (1987). The psychological aftermath of rape: Long-term effects and individual differences in recovery. *Journal of Social and Clinical Psychology, 5,* 525–534.

Cohen, L. S., Soares, C., Otto, M., Sweeney, B., Liberman, R., & Harlow, B. (2002). Prevalence and predictors of premenstrual dysphoric disorder (PMDD) in older premenopausal women. The Harvard Study of Moods and Cycles. *Journal of Affective Disorders, 70*(2), 125–132.

Cohen, M. S., Hellmann, N., Levy, J. A., Decock, K., & Lange, J. (2008d). The spread, treatment, and prevention of HIV-1: Evolution of a global pandemic. *Journal of Clinical Investigation, 118,* 1244–1254.

Cohen, S. A. (2008, Summer). Abortion and women of color: The bigger picture. *Guttmacher Policy Review, 11*(3). Retrieved March 14, 2011, from http://www.guttmacher.org/pubs/gpr/11/3/gpr110302.html.

Cohen, S. A. (2009). Facts and consequences: Legality, incidence and safety of abortion worldwide. *Guttmacher Policy Review, 12*(4). Retrived June 4, 2010, from http:// www.guttmacher.org/pubs/gpr/12/4/gpr120402.html.

Cohen-Bendahan, C., van de Beek, C., & Berenbaum, S. (2005). Prenatal sex hormone effects on child and adult sex-typed behavior: Methods and findings. *Neuroscience & Biobehavioral Reviews, 29*(2), 353–384.

Cohn, D. (2009). The states of marriage and divorce. Pew Research Council, October 15, Retrieved July 4, 2011, from http://pewresearch.org/pubs/1380/marriage-and-divorce-by-state.

Coker, A. L. (2007). Does physical intimate partner violence affect sexual health? A systematic review. *Trauma Violence Abuse, 8,* 149–177.

Cokkinos, D. D., Antypa, E., Tserotas, P., Kratimenou, E., Kyratzi, E., Deligiannis, I., Kachrimanis, G., & Piperopoulos, P. N. (2011). Emergency ultrasound of the scrotum: A review of the commonest pathologic conditions. *Current Problems in Diagnostic Radiology, 40*(1), 1–14.

Colapinto, J. (2001). *As nature made him: The boy who was raised as a girl.* New York: HarperCollins.

Coleman, E. (1982). Developmental stages of the coming-out process. *American Behavioral Scientist, 25,* 469–482.

Coleman, M., & Ganong, L. H. (1985). Love and sex role stereotypes: Do macho men and feminine women make better lovers? *Journal of Personality & Social Psychology, 49*(1), 170–176.

Coleman, M., Ganong, L., & Fine, M. (2000). Reinvestigating remarriage: Another decade of progress. *Journal of Marriage and Family, 62*(4), 1288–1308.

Coleman, P. (2002). *How to say it for couples.* New York: Prentice Hall Press.

Coleman, P. K. (2006). Resolution of unwanted pregnancy during adolescence through abortion versus childbirth: Individual and family predictors and psychological consequences. *Journal of Youth and Adolescence, 35,* 903–911.

Coles, M., Makino, K., Stanwood, N., Dozier, A., & Klein, J. (2010). How are restrictive abortion statutes associated with unintended teen birth? *Journal of Adolescent Health, 47*(2), 160–167.

Coles, R., & Stokes, G. (1985). *Sex and the American teenager.* New York: Harper & Row.

Collaborative Group on Hormonal Factors in Breast Cancer. (2001). Familial breast cancer. *The Lancet, 358*(9291), 1389–1399.

Colley, A., Todd, Z., White, A., & Turner-Moore, T. (2010). Communication using camera phones among young men and women: Who sends what to whom? *Sex Roles, 63*(5/6), 348–360.

Collier, J. F., & Rosaldo, M. Z. (1981). Politics and gender in simple societies. In S. Ortner & H. Whitehead (Eds.), *Sexual meanings* (pp. 275–329). Cambridge, U.K.: Cambridge University Press.

Collins, P. H. (1998). The tie that binds: Race, gender and U.S. violence. *Ethnic and Racial Studies, 21*(5), 917–939.

Collins, P. H. (2000). It's all in the family. *Women and Language, 23*(2), 65–69.

Collins, R. (1988). *Sociology of marriage and the family.* Chicago: Nelson-Hall.

Collins, R. (2005). Sex on television and its impact on American youth: Background and results from the RAND television and adolescent sexuality study. *Child & Adolescent Psychiatric Clinics of North America, 14*(3), 371–385.

Collins, R. L., Ellickson, P. L., & Klein, D. J. (2007). Research report: The role of substance use in young adult divorce. *Addiction, 102,* 786.

Collins, R. L., Elliott, M. N., Berry, S. H., Kanouse, D. E., Kunkel, D., Hunter, S. B., & Miu, A. (2004). Watching sex on television predicts adolescent initiation of sexual behavior. *Pediatrics, 114*(3), 280–289.

Comfort, A. (1987). Deviation and variation. In G. D. Wilson (Ed.), *Variant sexuality: Research and theory* (pp. 1–20). Baltimore: Johns Hopkins University Press.

Comfort, A., & Rubenstein, J. (1992). The new joy of sex: A gourmet guide to lovemaking in the nineties. New York: Simon & Schuster.

Comstock, G., & Paik, H. (1991). *Television and the American child.* San Diego, CA: Academic Press.

Condon, P. (2010, July 8). Presbyterian church's general assembly oks gay clergy. *Huffington Post.* Retrieved February 20, 2011, from http://www.huffingtonpost.com/2010/07/08/presbyterian-gay-clergy_n_640189.html.

Conron, K. J., Mimiaga, M. J., & Landers, S. J. (2010). A population-based study of sexual orientation identity and gender differences in adult health. *American Journal of Public Health, 100*(10), 1953–1960.

Conway, A. M. (2005). Girls, aggression, and emotional regulation. *American Journal of Orthopsychiatry, 75*(2), 334–339.

Conway, G., Band, M., Doyle, J., & Davies, M. (2010). How do you monitor the patient with Turner's syndrome in adulthood? *Clinical Endocrinology, 73*(6), 696–699.

Cook, R., & Dickens, B. (2009). Hymen reconstruction: Ethical and legal issues. *International Journal of Gynecology and Obstetrics, 107*(3), 266–269.

Cooksey, C., Berggren E., & Lee, J. (2010). Chlamydia trachomatis infection in minority adolescent women: A public health challenge. *Obstetrics and Gynecology Survey, 65*(11), 729–735.

Cooper, A. M. (1991). The unconscious core of perversion. In G. I. Fogel & W. A. Myers (Eds.), *Perversions and near-perversions in clinical practice: New psychoanalytic perspectives* (pp. 17–35). New Haven: Yale University Press.

Cooper, A., Putnam, D. E., Planchon, L., & Boies, S. C. (1999). Online sexual compulsivity: Getting tangled in the net. *Sexual Addiction & Compulsivity, 6*(2), 79–104.

Coordt, A. K. (2005). Young adults of childhood divorce: Intimate relationships prior to marriage. *Dissertation Abstracts International, Section A: Humanities and Social Sciences, 66,* 500.

Coppola, M. A., Klotz, K. L., Kim, K. A., Cho, H. Y., Kang, J., Shetty, J., Howards, S. S., Flickinger, C. J., & Herr, J. C. (2010). SpermCheck Fertility, an immunodiagnostic home test that detects normozoospermia and severe oligozoospermia. *Human Reproduction, 25*(4), 853–861.

Corey, L., & Handsfield, H. (2000). Genital herpes and public health. *Journal of the American Medical Association, 283,* 791–794.

Corneanu, L. M., Stănculescu, D., & Corneanu, C. (2011). HPV and cervical squamous intraepithelial lesions: Clinicopathological study. *Romanian Journal of Morphology and Embryology, 52*(1), 89–94.

Cornelius, T., Shorey, R., & Beebe, S. (2010). Self-reported communication variables and dating violence: Using Gottman's marital communication conceptualization. *Journal of Family Violence, 25*(4), 439.

Corona, G., Jannini, E. A., Lotti, F., Boddi, V., De Vita, G., Forti, G., Lenzi, A., Mannucci, E., & Maggi, M. (2011). Premature and delayed ejaculation: Two ends of a single continuum influenced by hormonal milieu. *International Journal of Andrology, 34*(1), 41–48.

Corra, M., Carter, S., Carter, J., & Knox, D. (2009). Trends in marital happiness by gender and race, 1973 to 2006. *Journal of Family Issues, 30*(10), 1379–1404.

Corso, P., Edwards, V., Fang, X., & Mercy, J. (2008). Health-related quality of life among adults who experience maltreatment during childhood. *American Journal of Public Health, 98,* 1094–1100.

Corty, E. W., & Guardiani, J. M. (2008). Canadian and American sex therapists' perceptions of normal and abnormal ejaculatory latencies: How long should intercourse last? *Journal of Sexual Medicine, 5,* 1251–1256.

Costabile, R., Mammen, T., & Hwang, K. (2008). An overview and expert opinion on the use of alprostadil in the treatment of sexual dysfunction. *Expert Opinions in Pharmacotherapy, 9,* 1421–1429.

Costello, C., Hillis, S. D., Marchbanks, P. A., Jamieson, D. J., & Peterson, H. B. (2002). The effect of interval tubal sterilization on sexual interest and pleasure. *Obstetrics and Gynecology, 100*(3), 511–518.

Coulson, N. J. (1979). Regulation of sexual behavior under traditional Islamic law. In Al- Sayyid-Marsot & A. Lutfi (Eds.), *Society and the sexes in medieval Islam* (pp. 63–68). Malibu, CA: Undena Publications.

Courtenay, W. H. (2000). Behavioral factors associated with disease, injury, and death among men: Evidence and implications for prevention. *The Journal of Men's Studies, 9*(1), 81–142.

Cowan, G. (1992). Feminist attitudes toward pornography control. *Psychology of Women Quarterly,* 165–177.

Cowan, G. (2000). Beliefs about the causes of four types of rape. *Sex Roles, 42*(9–10), 807–823.

Cox, N., Vanden Berghe, W., Dewaele, A., & Vincke, J. (2010). Acculturation strategies and mental health in gay, lesbian, and bisexual youth. *Journal of Youth and Adolescence, 39*(10), 1199–1210.

Cramer, R., Golom, F., LoPresto, C., & Kirkley, S. (2008). Weighing the evidence: Empirical assessment and ethical implications of conversion therapy. *Ethics & Behavior, 18,* 93–114.

Crary, D. (2010, October 4). Indiana University survey on sex in U.S., biggest since 1994. *Courier-Journal.com.* Retrieved October 9, 2010, from http://www.courier-journal.com/article/20101004/FEATURES03/310040046/1010/Indiana1University1survey1on1sex1in1US11biggest1since11994.

Crawford, A. (2008, July 13). Male fertility options growing. *Chicago Tribune.* Retrieved July 29, 2008, from http://www.chicagotribune.com/features/lifestyle/chi-0713-guy-birth-control-for-mjul13,0,1337399.story.

Crawford, J., Boulet, M., & Drea, C. (2011). Smelling wrong: Hormonal contraception in lemurs alters critical female odour cues. *Proceedings of the Royal Society B, 278,* 122–130.

Crawford, J. T., Leynes, P. A., Mayhorn, C. B., & Bink, M .L. (2004). Champagne, beer, or coffee? A corpus of gender-related and neutral words. *Behavior Research Methods, Instruments & Computers, 36*(3), 444–459.

Crawford, M. (2006). *Transformations: Women, gender & psychology.* New York: McGraw-Hill.

Cremer, M., Phan-Weston, S., & Jacobs, A. (2010). Recent innovations in oral contraception. *Seminars in Reproductive Medicine, 28*(2), 140–146.

Crepaz, N., Hart, T. A., & Marks, G. (2004). Highly active antiretroviral therapy and sexual risk behavior: A meta-analytic review. *Journal of the American Medical Association, 292*(2), 224–236.

Critelli, J. W., Myers, E. J., & Loos, V. E. (1986). The components of love: Romantic attraction and sex role orientation. *Journal of Personality, 54*(2), 354–370.

Crittenden, A. (2001). *The price of motherhood.* New York: Metropolitan Books.

Croft, M. L., Morgan, V., Read, A. W., & Jablensky, A. S. (2010). Recorded pregnancy histories of the mothers of singletons and the mothers of twins. *Twin Research and Human Genetics, 13*(6), 595–603.

Crosby, R., & Danner, F. (2008). Adolescents' STD protective attitudes predict sexually transmitted disease acquisition in early adulthood. *Journal of School Health, 78,* 310–313.

Crosby, R., & Diclemente, R. (2004). Use of recreational Viagra among men having sex with men. *Sexually Transmitted Infections, 80,* 466–468.

Crosby, R., Diclemente, R., Wingood, G., Salazar, L., Lang, D., Rose, E., et al. (2008a). Co-occurrence of intoxication during sex and sexually transmitted infections among young African American women: Does partner intoxication matter? *Sexual Health, 5,* 285–289.

Crosby, R., Milhausen, R., Yarber, W., Sanders, S., & Graham, C. (2008b). Condom "turn offs" among adults: An exploratory study. *International Journal of STDs and AIDS, 19,* 590–594.

Cross, P., & Matheson, K. (2006). Understanding sadomasochism: An empirical examination of four perspectives. *Journal of Homosexuality, 50,* 133–166.

Crow, S., Agras, W., Crosby, R., Halmi, K., & Mitchell, J. (2008). Eating disorder symptoms in pregnancy: A prospective study.

International Journal of Eating Disorders, 41, 277–279.

Crowley, I. P., & Kesner, K. M. (1990). Ritual circumcision (umkhwetha) amongst the Xhosa of the Ciskei. *British Journal of Urology, 66*(3), 318–321.

Crum, N., Riffenburgh, R., Wegner, S., Agan, B., Tasker, S., Spooner, K., et al.; Triservice AIDS Clinical Consortium. (2006). Comparisons of causes of death and mortality rates among HIV-infected patients. Analysis of the pre-, early, and late HAART (highly active antiretroviral therapy) eras. *Journal of Acquired Immune Deficiency Syndromes, 41*, 194–200.

Cruz, J. M. (2003). "Why doesn't he just leave?": Gay male domestic violence and the reasons victims stay. *Journal of Men's Studies, 11*, 309.

Cuddy, A. J. C., Norton, M. I., & Fiske, S. T. (2005) This old stereotype: The pervasiveness and persistence of the elderly stereotype. *Journal of Social Issues, 61*(2), 267–285.

Cunningham, G. R., & Toma, S. M. (2011). Why is androgen replacement in males controversial? *Journal of Clinical Endocrinological Metabolism, 96*(1), 38–52.

Cunningham, S. D., Kerrigan, D. L., Jennings, J. M., & Ellen, J. M. (2009). Relationships between perceived STD-related stigma, STD-related shame and STD screening among a household sample of adolescents. *Perspectives on Sexual and Reproductive Health, 41*(4), 225–230.

Currier, D., & Carlson, J. (2009). Creating attitudinal change through teaching: How a course on "women and violence" changes students' attitudes about violence against women. *Journal of Interpersonal Violence, 24*(10), 1735–1754.

Cusitar, L. (1994). *Strengthening the link: Stopping the violence.* Toronto: Disabled Women's Network.

D'Aloisio, A., Baird, D., DeRoo, L., & Sandler, D. (2010). Association of intrauterine and early-life exposures with diagnosis of uterine leiomyomata by 35 years of age in the sister study. *Environmental Health Perspectives, 118*(3), 375–381.

d'Amora, D., & Hobson, B. (2003). Sexual offender treatment. Retrieved March 31, 2003, from http://www.smith-lawfirm.com/Connsacs_offender_treatment.htm.

D'Augelli, A. R. (2005). Stress and adaptation among families of lesbian, gay, and bisexual youth: Research challenges. *Journal of GLBT Family Studies, 1,* 115–135.

D'Augelli, A. R., Grossman, A. H., & Starks, M. (2006). Childhood gender atypicality, victimization, and PTSD among lesbian, gay, and bisexual youth. *Journal of Interpersonal Violence, 21*, 1462–1482.

D'Augelli, A. R., Grossman, A. H., Hershberger, S., & O'Connell, T. (2001). Aspects of mental health among older lesbian, gay, and bisexual adults. *Aging and Mental Health, 5*, 149–158.

D'Augelli, A. R., Grossman, A., Salter, N., Vasey, J., Starks, M., & Sinclair, K. (2005b). Predicting the suicide attempts of lesbian, gay, and bisexual youth. *Suicide and Life-Threatening Behavior, 35*, 646–660.

D'Augelli, A. R., Rendian, J., Sinclair, K., & Grossman, A. (2007). Lesbian and gay youth's aspirations for marriage and raising children. *Journal of LGBT Issues in Counseling, 1(4)*, 77–98.

D'Augelli, A., Grossman, A., & Starks, M. (2005a). Parents' awareness of lesbian, gay, and bisexual youths' sexual orientation. *Journal of Marriage & Family, 67*(2), 474–482.

Dade, L. R., & Sloan, L. R. (2000). An investigation of sex-role stereotypes in African Americans. *Journal of Black Studies, 30*(5), 676.

Dahl, A., Bremnes, R., Dahl, O., Klepp, O., Wist, E., & Fossa, S. (2007). Is the sexual function compromised in long-term testicular cancer survivors? *European Urology, 52*, 1438–1447.

Dahlen, H., Homer, C., Leap, N., & Tracy, S. (In press). From social to survival: Historical perspectives on perineal care during labour and birth. *Women and Birth.*

Dake, J. A., Price, J. H., Ward, B. L., & Welch, P. J. (2011). Midwestern rural adolescents' oral sex experience. *Journal of School Health, 81*(3), 159–165.

Dalla, R. L. (2002). Night moves: A qualitative investigation of street-level sex work. *Psychology of Women Quarterly, 26*(1), 63–74.

Daltveit, A., Tollances, M., Pihlstrom, H., & Irgens, L. (2008). Cesarean delivery and subsequent pregnancies. *Obstetrics and Gynecology, 111*, 1327–1334.

Danby, C., & Margesson, L. (2010). Approach to the diagnosis and treatment of vulvar pain. *Dermatology Therapy, 23*(5), 485–504.

Dancey, C. P. (1990). Sexual orientation in women: An investigation of hormonal and personality variables. *Biological Psychology, 30*, 251–264.

Daniels M. C., & Adair, L. S. (2005). Breast-feeding influences cognitive development in Filipino children. *Journal of Nutrition, 135*(11), 2589–2595.

Daniluk, J., & Browne, N. (2008). Traditional religious doctrine and women's sexuality reconciling the contradictions. *Women and Therapy, 31*(1), 129–142.

Dante, G., & Facchinetti, F. (2011). Herbal treatments for alleviating premenstrual symptoms: A systematic review. *Journal of Psychosomatic Obstetrics and Gynecology, 32*(1), 42–51.

Daragahi, B., & Dubin, A. (2001). Can prenups be romantic? *Money, 30*(2), 30–38.

Darcangelo, S. (2008). Fetishism: Psychopathology and theory. In D. Laws & W. O'Donohue (Eds.), *Sexual deviance: Theory, assessment and treatment* (2nd ed., pp. 108–118). New York: Guilford Press.

Dare, R. O., Oboro, V. O., Fadiora, S. O., Orji, E. O., Sule-Edu, A. O., & Olabode, T. O. (2004). Female genital mutilation: An analysis of 522 cases in South-Western Nigeria. *Journal of Obstetrics & Gynaecology, 24*(3), 281–283.

Das, A. (2007). Masturbation in the U.S. *Journal of Sex and Marital Therapy, 33*(4), 301–317.

Das, A., Parish, W., & Laumann, E. (2009). Masturbation in urban China. *Archives of Sexual Behavior, 38*(1), 108–120.

Das, M. (2010) Gender role portrayals in Indian television ads. *Sex Roles, 64,* 208–222.

Dattijo, L. M., Nyango, D. D., & Osagie, O. E. (2010). Awareness, perception and practice of female genital mutilation among expectant mothers in Jos University Teaching Hospital Jos, north-central Nigeria. *Nigerian Journal of Medicine, 19*(3), 311–315.

Davé, S., Petersen, I., Sherr, L., & Nazareth, I. (2010). Incidence of maternal and paternal depression in primary care. *Archives of Pediatriac Adolescent Medicine, 164*(11), 1038–1044.

Davidsen, L., Vistulien, B., & Kastrup, A. (2007). Impact of the menstrual cycle on determinants of energy balance: A putative role in weight loss attempts. *International Journal of Obesity, 31*, 1777–1785.

Davidson, J. (2002). Working with polyamorous clients in the clinical setting. *Electronic Journal of Human Sexuality, 5.* Retrieved September 13, 2008, from http://www.ejhs.org/volume5/polyoutline.html.

Davidson, J., Moore, N., Earle, J., & Davis, R. (2008). Sexual attitudes and behavior at four universities: Do region, race, and/or religion matter? *Adolescence, 433*(170), 189–220.

Davies, J., Knight, E., Savage, A., Brown, J., & Malone, P. (2011). Evaluation of terminology used to describe disorders of sex development. *Journal of Pediatric Urology, 7*(4), 412–415.

Davies, K. A. (1997). Voluntary exposure to pornography and men's attitudes toward feminism and rape. *Journal of Sex Research, 34*(2), 131–138.

Davies, M., Boulle, A., Fakir, T., Nuttall, J., & Eley B. (2008). Adherence to antiretroviral therapy in young children in Cape Town, South Africa, measured by medication return and caregiver self-report: A prospective cohort study. *BMC Pediatrics, 4*(8), 34.

Davies, M., Rogers, P., & Whitelegg, L. (2009). Effects of victim gender, victim sexual orientation, victim response and respondent gender on judgments of blame in a hypothetical adolescent rape. *Legal and Criminological Psychology, 14*(2), 331–338.

Davis, K. E., & Latty-Mann, H. (1987). Love styles and relationship quality: A contribution to validation. *Journal of Social & Personal Relationships, 4*(4), 409–428.

Davis, K. E., & Todd, M. J. (1982). Friendship and love relationships. *Advances in Descriptive Psychology, 2*, 79–122.

Davis, M. G., Reape, K. Z., & Hait, H. (2010a). A look at the long-term safety of an extended-regimen OC. *Journal of Family Practitioner, 59*(5), E3.

Davis, S. C., Meneses, K., & Hilfinger Messias, D. K. (2010b). Exploring sexuality & quality of life in women after breast cancer surgery. *Nurse Practitioner, 35*(9), 25–31.

Daw, J. (2002). Hormone therapy for men? *Monitor on Psychology, 33*(9), 53.

Dawar, A. (2006, November 28). British scientists invent male pill. *Telegraph.* Retrieved October 28, 2008, from http://www.telegraph.co.uk/news/migrationtemp/1535304/British-scientists-invent-male-pill.html.

Day, R. D., & Padilla-Walker, L. M. (2009). Mother and father connectedness and involvement during early adolescence. *Journal of Family Psychology, 23*(6), 900–904.

D'Cruz, H., & Stagnitti, K. (2010). When parents love and don't love their children: Some children's stories. *Child & Family Social Work, 15*(2), 216.

de Freitas, S. (2004). Brazil. In R. T. Francoeur & R. J. Noonan (Eds.), *The Continuum complete international encyclopedia of sexuality* (pp. 98–113). New York/London: Continuum International.

de Vries, B. (2009). Brain sexuality and aging: A late blooming relationship. *Sexuality Research & Social Policy, 6*(4), 1–4.

DeBellis, M. D., Keshavan, M. S., Beers, S. R., Hall, J., Frustaci, K., Masalehdan, A., et al. (2001) Sex differences in brain maturation during childhood and adolescence. *Cerebral Cortex, 11*(6), 552–557.

Decker, M., Raj, A., Gupta, J., & Silverman, J. (2008). Sex purchasing and associations with HIV/STI among a clinic-based sample of U.S. men. *Journal of Acquired Immune Deficiency Syndrome, 48*(3), 355–359.

DeCuypere, G., T'Sjoen, G., Beerten, R., Selvaggi, G., Sutter, P., Hoebeke, P., et al. (2005). Sexual and physical health after sex reassignment surgery. *Archives of Sexual Behavior, 34*, 679–690.

Deepinder, R., Makker, K., & Agarwal, A. (2007). Cell phones and male infertility: Dissecting the relationship. *Reproductive BioMedicine Online, 15*(3), 266–270.

Degges-White, S., & Marszalek, J. (2008). An exploration of long-term, same-sex relationships: Benchmarks, perceptions, and challenges. *Journal of Lesbian, Gay, Bisexual, and Transgendered Issues in Counseling, 1*, 99–119.

DeJonge, A., Teunissen, D., van Diem, M., Scheepers, P., & Lagro-Janssen, A. (2008). Woman's positions during the second stage of labour: Views of primary care midwives. *Journal of Advanced Nursing, 63*, 347–356.

DeLamater, J. (1987). A sociological approach. In J. H. Geer & W. T. O'Donohue (Eds.), *Theories of human sexuality* (pp. 237–253). New York: Plenum Press.

DeLange, J. (1995). Gender and communication in social work education: A cross-cultural perspective. *Journal of Social Work Education, 31*(1), 75–82.

Deligeoroglou, E., Michailidis, E., & Creatsas, G. (2003). Oral contraceptives and reproductive system cancer. *Annals of New York Academy of Science, 997*, 199–208.

Deliramich, A., & Gray, M. (2008). Changes in women's sexual behavior following sexual assault. *Behavior Modification, 32*(5), 611–621.

Delmonico, D. L., & Griffin, E. J. (2008). Cybersex and the e-teen: What marriage and family therapists should know. *Journal of Marital and Family Therapy, 34*(4), 431–444.

D'Emilio, J. (1998). *Sexual politics, sexual communities.* Chicago: University of Chicago Press.

D'Emilio, J., & Freedman, E. (1988). *Intimate matters: A history of sexuality in America.* New York: Harper & Row.

D'Emilio, J., & Freedman, S. (1988). *A history of sexuality in America.* Chicago: The University of Chicago Press.

Dempster, C. (2002). Silent war on South African women. Retrieved April 10, 2003, from www.new.bbc.co.uk/hi/english/world/africa/newsid_190900011909220.stm.

Denizet-Lewis, B. (2009, September 23). Coming out in middle school. *New York Times.* Retrieved February 20, 2011, from http://www.nytimes.com/2009/09/27/magazine/27out-t.html?pagewanted54&_r51.

Dennerstein, L., Dudley, E., Guthrie, J., & Barrett-Connor, E. (2000). Life satisfaction, symptoms, and the menopausal transition. *Medscape Women's Health, 5*(4), E4.

Dennison, S. M., & Tomson, D. M. (2005). Criticisms of plaudits for stalking laws? What psycholegal research tells us about proscribing stalking. *Psychology, Public Policy, & Law, 11*(3), 384–406.

DePineres, T. (2002). Reproductive health 2002: Update on contraception and medical abortion from the ARHD Annual Meeting. *Medscape Ob/Gyn and Women's Health, 7*(2). Retrieved May 20, 2003, from http://www. medscape.com/viewarticle/442100.

de-Schampheleire, D. (1990). MMPI characteristics of professional prostitutes: A cross-cultural replication. *Journal of Personality Assessment, 54*, 343–350.

DeSteno, D., Barlett, M. T., Braverman, J., & Salovey, P. (2002). Sex differences in jealousy: Evolutionary mechanism or artifact of measurement? *Journal of Personality and Social Psychology, 83*(5), 1103–116.

Devdas, N., & Rubin, L. (2007). Rape myth acceptance among first-and second-generation south Asian American women. *Sex Roles, 56*, 701–705.

deVisser, R., & McDonald, D. (2007). Swings and roundabouts: Management of jealousy in heterosexual "swinging" couples. *British Journal of Social Psychology, 46*, 459–476.

Dhir, R. R., Lin, H. C., Canfield, S. E., & Wang, R. (2011). Combination therapy for erectile dysfunction: An update review. *Asian Journal of Andrology, 13*(3), 382–390.

Diamanduros, T., Jenkins, S. J., & Downs, E. (2007). Analysis of technology ownership and selective use among undergraduates. *College Student Journal, 41*, 970–976.

Diamanti-Kandarakis, E. (2007). Role of obesity and adiposity in polycystic ovary syndrome. *International Journal of Obesity, 31,* s8–s13.

Diamond, L., & Fagundes, C. (2010). Psychobiological research on attachment. *Personal Relationships, 27*(2), 218.

Diamond, L., Earle, D., Heiman, J., Rosen, R., Perelman, M., & Harning, R. (2006). An effect on the subjective sexual response in premenopausal women with sexual arousal disorder by bremelanotide (PT-141), a melanocortin receptor agonist. *Journal of Sexual Medicine, 3,* 628–638.

Diamond, L. M. (2000). Sexual identity, attractions, and behavior among young sexual minority women over a 2-year period. *Developmental Psychology, 36*(2), 241–250.

Diamond, L. M. (2005). A new view of lesbian subtypes: Stable versus fluid identity trajectories over an 8-year period. *Psychology of Women Quarterly, 29*(2), 119–128.

Diamond, M. (1993). Homosexuality and bisexuality in different populations. *Archives of Sexual Behavior, 22,* 291–310.

Diamond, M., & Diamond, G. H. (1986). Adolescent sexuality: Biosocial aspects and intervention. In P. Allen-Meares & D. A. Shore (Eds.), *Adolescent sexualities: Overviews and principles of intervention* (pp. 3–13). New York: Haworth Press.

Diamond, M., & Sigmundson, H. K. (1997). Sex reassignment at birth: Long-term review and clinical implications. *Archives of Pediatric Medicine, 151,* 290–297.

Diaz, R. M., Ayala, G., Bein, E., Henne, J., & Marin, B. V. (2001). The impact on homophobia, poverty, and racism on the mental health of gay and bisexual Latino men. *American Journal of Public Health, 41*(6), 927–933.

Dibble, S. L., & Swanson, J. M. (2000). Gender differences for the predictors of depression in young adults with genital herpes. *Public Health Nursing, 17*(3), 187–194.

Dietz, A., & Nyberg, C. (2011). Genital, oral, and anal human papillomavirus infection in men who have sex with men. *Journal of the American Osteopathic Association, 111*(3 Suppl. 2), S19–S25.

Dietz, H. P. (2006). Pelvic floor trauma following vaginal delivery. *Current Opinions in Obstetrics and Gynecology, 18,* 528–537.

Dillow, M., Dunleavy, K., & Weber, K. (2009). The impact of relational characteristics and reasons for topic avoidance on relational closeness. *Communication Quarterly, 57*(2), 205.

Dimah, K., & Dimah, A. (2004). Intimate relationships and sexual attitudes of older African American men and women. *The Geronotologist, 44,* 612–613.

diMauro, D. (1995). *Sexuality research in the United States: An assessment of the social and behavioral sciences.* New York: Social Science Research Council.

DiNapoli, L., & Capel, B. (2008). SRY and the standoff in sex determination. *Molecular Endocrinology, 22,* 1–9.

Dindia, K. & Canary, D.J. (2006). (Eds.), *Sex differences and similarities in communication* (2nd. ed.). Mahwah, NJ: Erlbaum.

Dindyal, S. (2004). The sperm count has been decreasing steadily for many years in Western industrialised countries: Is there an endocrine basis for this decrease? *The Internet Journal of Urology 2*(1). Retrieved December 18, 2008, from http://www.ispub.com/ostia/index.php?xmlFilePath=journals/iju/vol2n1/sperm.xml.

Dinger, J., Minh, T. D., Buttmann, N., & Bardenheuer, K. (2011). Effectiveness of oral contraceptive pills in a large U.S. cohort comparing progestogen and regimen. *Obstetrics and Gynecology, 117*(1), 33–40.

Dinh, M., Fahrbach, K., & Hope, T. (2011). The role of the foreskin in male circumcision: An evidence-based review. *American Journal of Reproductive Immunlogy, 65*(3), 279–283.

Dion, K., & Dion, K. (2010). Individualistic and collectivistic perspectives on gender and the cultural context of love and intimacy. *Journal of Social Issues, 49*(3), 53–69.

Dion, K. L., & Dion, K. K. (1988). Romantic love: Individual and cultural perspectives. In R. J. Sternberg & R. J. Barnes (Eds.), *Psychology of love* (pp. 264–289). New Haven, CT: Yale University Press.

Dittmann, M. (2005). Getting prostitutes off the streets. *Monitor on Psychology, 35*(9), 71.

Dittmar, M. (2000). Age at menarche in a rural Aymara-speaking community located at high altitude in northern Chile. *Mankind Quarterly, 40*(4), 38–52.

Dixit, A. K., & Pindyck, R. S. (1994). *Investment under uncertainty.* Princeton, NJ: Princeton University Press.

Dixon, R. (2005). Controversy in South Africa over device to snare rapists. Retrieved October 19, 2005, from http://www.smh.com.au/news/world/controversy-in-south-africa-over-device-to-snare-rapists/2005/09/01/1125302683893.html.

Dodd, S. M. (2010). Ambivalent social support and psychneuroimmunologic relationships among women undergoing surgery for suspected endometrial cancer. University of Florida, AAT #34366330.

Dodge, B., Reece, M., Herbenick, D., Schick, V., Sanders, S. A., & Fortenberry, J. D. (2010). Sexual health among U.S. black and Hispanic men and women: A nationally representative study. *Journal of Sexual Medicine, 7*(Suppl. 5): 330–345.

Dodson, B. (1993). *Sex for one: The joy of self-loving.* New York: Crown.

Dolnick, S. (2007, December 31). India leads way in making commercial surrogacy a viable industry. *Hartford Courant,* p. A3.

Dong, Q., Deng, S., Wang, R., & Yuan, J. (2011). In vitro and in vivo animal models in priapism research. *Journal of Sexual Medicine, 8*(2), 347–359.

Donnan, H. (1988). *Marriage among Muslims: Preference and choice in Northern Pakistan.* New York: E. J. Brill.

Donnelly, D. A., & Burgess, E. O. (2008). The decision to remain in an involuntarily celibate relationship. *Journal of Marriage and Family, 70,* 519–536.

Donovan, K., Taliaferro, L., Alvarez, E., Jacobsen, P., Roetzheim, R., & Wenham, R. (2007). Sexual health in women treated for cervical cancer: Characteristics and correlates. *Gynecological Oncology, 104,* 428–434.

Dording, C. M., Mischoulon, D., Shyu, I., Alpert, J. E., & Papakostas, G. I. (In press). SAMe and sexual functioning. *European Psychiatry.*

Dorfman, L. E., Derish, P. A., & Cohen, J. B. (1992). Hey girlfriend: An evaluation of AIDS prevention among women in the sex industry. *Health Education Quarterly, 19,* 25–40.

Dorgan, M. (2001, June 13). New divorce laws in China give rise to spying. *Hartford Courant,* A13.

Dorner, G., Schenk, B., Schmiedel, B., & Ahrens, L. (1983). Stressful events in perinatal life of bi- and homosexual men. *Experimental and Clinical Endocrinology, 81*(1), 83–87.

Dorr, C. (2001). Listening to men's stories: Overcoming obstacles to intimacy from childhood. *Families in Society, 82,* 509–515.

Doty, N. D., Willoughby, B. L., Lindahl, K. M., & Malik, N. M. (2010). Sexuality related social support among lesbian, gay, and bisexual youth. *Journal of Youth and Adolescence, 39*(10), 1134–1147.

Dougherty, C. (2010, September 29). New vow: I don't take thee. *Wall Street Journal.* Retrieved October 5, 2010, from http://online.wsj.com/article/SB10001424052748703882404575519871444705214.html.

Douglas, J., & Olshaker, M. (1998). *Obsession.* Sydney: Pocket Books.

Douglas, M., & Swenerton, J. (2002). Epidural anesthesia in three parturients with lumbar tattoos: A review of possible implications. *Canadian Journal of Anesthesia, 49,* 1057–1060.

Downs, D. A. (1989). *The new politics of pornography.* Chicago: The University of Chicago Press.

Doyle, D. (2005). Ritual male circumcision: A brief history. *Journal of the Royal College of Physicians, 35,* 279–285. Retrieved April 8, 2008, from http://www.rcpe.ac.uk/publications/articles/journal_35_3/doyle_circumcision.pdf.

Draganowski, L. (2004). Unlocking the closet door: The coming out process of gay male adolescents. *Dissertation Abstracts International, 64*(11-B). (#0419–4217)

Drain, P. K., Halperin, D. T., Hughes, J. P., Klausner, J. D., & Bailey, R. C. (2006). Male circumcision, religion, and infections diseases: An ecologic analysis of 118 developing countries. *BMC Infectious Diseases, 6,* 172.

Dreger, A., Feder, E., & Tamar-Mattis, A. (2010, June 29). Preventing homosexuality (and uppity women) in the womb? The Hastings Center. Retrieved November 13, 2010, from http://www.thehastingscenter.org/Bioethicsforum/Post.aspx?id54754.

Dresner, E., & Herring, S. (2010). Functions of the nonverbal in CMC: Emoticons and illocutionary force. *Communication Theory, 20*(3), 249.

Drew, P. E. (2004). Iran. In The International Encyclopedia of Sexuality. In R. T. Francoeur & R. J. Noonan (Eds.), *The Continuum international encyclopedia of sexuality* (pp. 554–568). New York/London: Continuum International.

Droupy, S. (2010). [Sexual dysfunctions after prostate cancer radiation therapy]. *Cancer Radiotherapy, 14*(6–7), 504–509.

Duarte Freitas, P., Haida, A., Bousquet, M., Richard, L., Mauriège, P., & Guiraud T. (2011). Short-term impact of a 4-week intensive cardiac rehabilitation program on quality of life and anxiety-depression. *Annals of Physical and Rehabilitation Medicine, 54*(3), 132–143.

Dubuc, S., & Coleman, D. (2007). An increase in the sex ratio of births to India-born mothers in England and Wales: Evidence for sex-selective abortion. *Population and Development Review, 33,* 383–400.

Duffy, J., Warren, K., & Walsh, M. (2001). Classroom interactions: Gender of teacher, gender of student and classroom subject. *Sex Roles, 45*(9–10), 579–593.

Duijts, L., Jaddoe, V., Hofman, A., & Moll, H. (2010). Prolonged and exclusive breastfeeding reduces the risk of infectious diseases in infancy. *Pediatrics, 126,* e18-e25.

Dumond, R., & Dumond, D. (2002). The treatment of sexual assault victims. In C. Hensley (Ed.), *Prison sex: Practice and policy* (pp. 67–87). Boulder, CO: Lynne Reinner.

Dunbar, R. (1998). *Grooming, gossip, and the evolution of language.* Boston: Harvard University Press.

Dunham, C., Myers, F., McDougall, A., & Barnden, N. (1992). *Mamatoto: A celebration of birth.* New York: Penguin Group.

Dunn, M. E., & Trost, J. E. (1989). Male multiple orgasms: A descriptive study. *Archives of Sexual Behavior, 18,* 377–387.

Dunne, E. (2007). *Genital warts.* U.S. Centers for Disease Control, Division of STD Prevention. Retrieved September 17, 2008, from http://www.cdc.gov/vaccines/recs/acip/downloads/mtg-slides-oct07/23HPV.pdf.

Dunne, E., Nielson, C., Stone, K., Markowitz, L., & Giuliano, A. (2006). Prevalence of HPV infection among men: A systematic review of the literature. *Journal of Infectious Diseases, 194,* 1044–1054.

Dupre, M. E., & Meadows, S. O. (2007). Disaggregating the effects of marital trajectories on health. *Journal of Family Issues, 28,* 623–652.

Durex Network. (2008). The face of global sex 2008: The path to sexual confidence. Retrieved October 13, 2010, from http://www.durexnetwork.org/SiteCollectionDocuments/Research%20-%20Face%20of%20Global%20Sex%202008.pdf.

Durex.com. (2007). *Sexual wellbeing global study 2007–2008.* Retrieved on January 20, 2008, from http://durex.com/cm/sexual_wellbeing_globeflash.asp.

Durham, L., Veltman, L., Davis, P., Ferguson, L., Hacker, M., Hooker, D., et al. (2008). Standardizing criteria for scheduling elective labor inductions. *American Journal of Maternal Child Nursing, 33,* 159–165.

Durmaz, E., Oxzmert, E., Erkekoglu, P., Giray, B., Derman, O., Hincal, F., & Yurdaök, K. (2010). Plasma phthalate levels in pubertal gynecomastia. *Pediatrics, 125*(1), 122.

Dush, C., & Amato, P. R. (2005). Consequences of relationship status and quality for subjective well-being. *Journal of Social and Personal Relationships, 22,* 607.

Dworkin, A. (1981). *Pornography: Men possessing women.* New York: Putnam.

Dworkin, A. (1987). *Intercourse.* New York: The Free Press.

Dzelme, K., & Jones, R. A. (2001). Male crossdressers in therapy: A solution-focused perspective for marriage and family therapists. *American Journal of Family Therapy, 29,* 293–305.

Eaker, E. D., Sullivan, L. M., Kelly-Hayes, M., D'Agostino, R. B., Sr., & Benjamin, E. J. (2007). Marital status, marital strain and the risk of coronary heart disease or total mortality: The Framingham Offspring Study. *Psychosomatic Medicine, 69,* 509–513.

Eardley, I. (2010). Oral therapy for erectile dysfunction. *Archives of Españoles Urology, 63*(8), 703–714.

Earls, C. M., & David, H. (1989). A psychosocial study of male prostitution. *Archives of Sexual Behavior, 18,* 401–419.

Earnshaw, V., Pitipitan, E., & Chaudoir, S. (2011). Intended responses to rape as functions of attitudes, attributions of fault, and emotions. *Sex Roles, 64*(5–6), 382–393.

Easton, J. A., Confer, J. C., Goetz, C. D., & Buss, D. M. (2010). Reproduction expediting: Sexual motivations, fantasies, and the ticking biological clock. *Personality and Individual Differences, 49,* 516–520.

Eastvold, A., Suchy, Y., & Strassberg, D. (2011). Executive function profiles of pedophilic and nonpedophilic child molesters. *Journal of the International Neuropyshochological Society, 17*(2), 295–308.

Eaton, D. K., Kann, L., Kinchen, S., Ross, J., Hawkins, J., Harris, W., et al. (2006, June 9). Youth risk behavior surveillance—United States, 2005. Surveillance Summaries. *Morbidity and Mortality Weekly Report, 55*(no. SS-5). Hyattsville, MD: U.S. Department of Health and Human Services, Centers for Disease Control. Retrieved September 2, 2008, from http://www.cdc.gov/mmwr/PDF/SS/SS5505.pdf.

Eaton, D. K., Kann, L., Kinshen, S., Shanklin, S., Ross, J., Hawkins, J., Harris, W., Lowry, R., McManus, T., Chyen, D., et al. (2009). Youth risk behavior surveillance—United States, 2009. *Morbidity and Mortality Weekly Report Surveillance Summaries, 59*(SS-5), 1–142.

Eaton, L., Kaufman, M., Fuhrel, A., Cain, D., Cherry, C., Pope, H., & Kalichman, S. (2008). Examining factors co-existing with interpersonal violence in lesbian relationships. *Journal of Family Violence, 23,* 697–706.

Ebaugh, H. (1988). *Becoming an ex: The process of role exit.* Chicago: University of Chicago Press.

Eckholm, E. (2011, January 1). In isolated Utah city, new clubs for gay students. *New York Times.* Retrieved February 16, 2011, from http://www.nytimes.com/2011/01/02/us/02utah.html.

Eckstein, D., & Goldman, A. (2001). The couples' gender-based communication questionnaire. *Family Journal of Counseling and Therapy for Couples and Families, 9*(1), 62–74.

Edelman, B. (2009). Red light states: Who buys online adult entertainment? *Journal of Economic Perspectives, 23*(1), 209–220.

Edwards, J. (2010, March 12). Sequenom's disappearing Down syndrome test mystery—solved! CBS Business Network. Retrieved March 1, 2011, from http://www.bnet.com/blog/drug-business/sequenom-8217s-disappearing-down-syndrome-test-mystery-8212-solved/4388.

Edwards, R. (1998). The effects of gender, gender role, and values. *Journal of Language and Social Psychology, 17*(1), 52–72.

Edwards, R., & Hamilton, M. A. (2004). You need to understand my gender role: An empirical test of Tannen's model of gender and communication. *Sex Roles, 50*(7–8), 491–504.

Eggermont, S. (2005). Young adolescents' perceptions of peer sexual behaviours: The role of television viewing. *Child: Care, Health and Development, 31*(4), 459–468.

Ehrich, K., Williams, C., Farsides, B., Sandall, J., & Scott, R. (2007). Choosing embryos: Ethical complexity and relational autonomy in staff accounts of PGD. *Sociology of Health and Illness, 29,* 1091–1106.

Einsiedel, E. (1989). Social science and public policy: Looking at the 1986 commission on pornography. In S. Gubar & J. Hoff (Eds.), *For adult users only* (pp. 87–107). Bloomington: Indiana University Press.

Eisenberg, M. (2001). Differences in sexual risk behaviors between college students with same-sex and opposite-sex experience. *Archives of Sexual Behavior, 30*(6), 575–589.

Eisend, M. (2010). A meta-analysis of gender roles in advertising. *Journal of the Academy of Marketing Science, 38*(4), 418–440.

Eisenman, R., & Dantzker, M. (2006). Gender and ethnic differences in sexual attitudes at a Hispanic-Serving University. *Journal of General Psychology, 133*(2), 153–163.

Eisinger, F., & Burke, W. (2002). Breast cancer and breastfeeding. *Lancet, 360*(9328), 187–195.

Eke, A., Hilton, N., Harris, G., Rice, M., & Houghton, R. (2011). Intimate partner homicide: Risk assessment and prospects for prediction. *Journal of Family Violence, 26*(3), 211–216.

Ekman, P., & Friesen, W. (1969). The repertoire of nonverbal behavior: Categories, origins, usage and coding. *Semiotica, 1,* 49–98.

Eldar-Avidan, D., Haj-Yahia, M., & Greenbaum, C. (2009). Divorce is a part of my life. Resilience, survival, and vulnerability. Young adults' perception of the implications of parental divorce. *Journal of Marital and Family Therapy, 35*(1), 30–47.

Eley, A., & Pacey, A. A. (In press). The value of testing semen for Chlamydia trachomatis in men of infertile couples. *International Journal of Andrology,* Retrieved May 29, 2011, from http://onlinelibrary.wiley.com/doi/10.1111/j.1365-2605.2010.01099.x/abstract.

Elford, J. (2006). Changing patterns of sexual behaviour in the era of highly active antiretroviral therapy. *Current Opinions in Infectious Disease, 19*(1), 26–32.

Elford, J., Bolding, G., Maguire, M., & Sherr, L. (2000). Combination therapies for HIV and sexual risk behavior among gay men. *Journal of Acquired Immune Deficiency Syndrome, 23,* 266–271.

Elhanbly, S., Elkholy, A., Elbayomy, Y., Elsaid, M., & Abdel-gaber, S. (2009). Nocturnal penile erections: The diagnostic value of tumescence and rigidity activity units. *International Journal of Impotence Research, 21*(6), 376–381.

El-Helaly, M., Awadalla, N., Mansour, M., & El-Biomy, Y. (2010). Workplace exposures and male infertility: A case-control study. *International Journal of Occupational Medicine and Environmental Medicine, 23*(4), 331–338.

Elias, M. (2007, February 11). Gay teens coming out earlier to peers and family. *USA Today.* Retrieved October 2, 2008, from http://www.usatoday.com/news/nation/2007-02-07-gay-teens-cover_x.htm.

Eliason, M. J. (1997). The prevalence and nature of biphobia in heterosexual undergraduate students. *Archives of Sexual Behavior, 26,*(3), 317–326.

Elifson, K. W., Boles, J., Posey, E., Sweat, M., et al. (1993). Male transvestite prostitutes and HIV risk. *American Journal of Public Health, 83,* 260–261.

Eliot, L. (2009). *Pink brains, blue brains: How small differences grow into troublesome gaps—and what we can do about it.* Orlando, FL: Houghton Mifflin Harcourt.

Elliott, S. (2010). Parents' constructions of teen sexuality: Sex panics, contradictory discourses, and social inequality. *Symbolic Interaction, 33*(2), 191–212.

Elliott, S., & Umberson, D. (2008). The performance of desire: Gender and sexual negotiation in long-term marriages. *Journal of Marriage and Family, 70,* 392–407.

Elliott, S., Latini, D., Walker, L., Wassersug, R., & Robinson, J. (2010). Androgen deprivation therapy for prostate cancer: Recommendations to improve patient and partner quality of life. *Journal of Sexual Medicine, 7*(9), 2996–3010.

Ellis, B. J., & Essex, M. J. (2007). Family environments, adrenarche, and sexual maturation: A longitudinal test of a life history model. *Child Development, 78,* 1799–1817.

Ellis, D. G., & McCallister, L. (1980). Relational control sequences in sex-typed and androgynous groups. *Western Journal of Speech Communication, 44,* 35–49.

Ellis, H. (1910). *Studies in the psychology of sex* (Vols. I-VI). Philadelphia: F. A. Davis.

Ellis, L. (1988). Sexual orientation of human offspring may be altered by severe maternal stress during pregnancy. *Journal of Sex Research, 25*(1), 152–157.

Ellis, L., Burke, D., & Ames, M. (1987). Sexual orientation as a continuous variable: A comparison between the sexes. *Archives of Sexual Behavior, 16,* 523–529.

Ellison, C. R. (2000). *Women's sexualities.* Oakland, CA: New Harbinger.

Ellison, C. R. (2006). *Women's sexualities: Generations of women share intimate secrets of sexual self-acceptance.* Oakland, CA: New Harbinger Publications.

Elmslie, B., & Tebaldi, E. (2007). Sexual orientation and labor market discrimination. *Journal of Labor Research, 28*(3), 436–453.

Eloi-Stiven, M., Channaveeraiah, N., Christos, P., Finkel, M., & Reddy, R. (2007). Does marijuana use play a role in the recreational use of sildenafil? *Journal of Family Practitioner, 56,* E1–E4.

Ely, G., Flaherty, C., & Cuddeback, G. (2010). The relationship between depression and other psychosocial problems in a sample of adolescent pregnancy termination patients. *Child and Adolescent Social Work Journal, 27*(4), 269–282.

Emilee, G., Ussher, J. M., & Perz, J. (2010). Sexuality after breast cancer: A review. *Maturitas, 66*(4), 397–407.

Emmers-Sommer, T., Farrell, J., Gentry, A., Stevens, S., Eckstein, J., Battocletti, J., & Gardener, C. (2010). First date sexual expectations: The effects of who asked, who paid, date location, and gender. *Communication Studies, 61*(3), 339–355.

Emons, G., Fleckenstein, G., Hinney, B., Huschmand, A., & Heyl, W. (2000). Hormonal interactions in endometrial cancer. *Endocrine-Related Cancer, 7,* 227–242.

Engel, J. W., & Saracino, M. (1986). Love preferences and ideals: A comparison of homosexual, bisexual, and heterosexual groups. *Contemporary Family Therapy: An International Journal, 8*(3), 241–250.

Engman, M., Wijma, K., & Wijma, B. (2010). Long-term coital behaviour in women treated with cognitive behaviour therapy for superficial coital pain and vaginismus. *Cognitive and Behavioral Therapy, 39*(3), 193–202.

Ensign, J., Scherman, A., & Clark, J. (1998). The relationship of family structure and conflict to levels of intimacy and parental attachment in college students. *Adolescence, 33*(131), 575–582.

Ephross, P. H. (2005). Group work with sexual offenders. In G. L. Greif (Ed.), *Group work with populations at risk* (pp. 253–266). New York: Oxford University Press.

Epp, A., Larochelle, A., Lovatsis, D., Walter, J., Easton, W., Farrell, S., Girouard, L., Gupta, C., Harvey, M., Robert, M., et al. (2010). Recent urinary tract infections. *Journal of Obstetrics and Gynecology, 32*(11), 1082–1090.

Epps, J., & Kendall, P. C. (1995). Hostile attributional bias in adults. *Cognitive Therapy and Research, 19,* 159–178.

Epstein, C. F. (1986). Symbolic segregation: Similarities and differences in the language and non-verbal communication of women and men. *Sociological Forum, 1,* 27–49.

Epstein, C. F. (1988). *Deceptive distinctions: Sex, gender, and the social order.* New Haven, CT: Yale University Press.

Epstein, H., & Morris, M. (2011). Concurrent partnerships and HIV: An inconvenient truth. *Journal of the International AIDS Society, 14,* 13.

Epstein, M., & Ward, L. M. (2008). "Always use protection": Communication boys receive about sex from parents, peers, and the media. *Journal of Youth and Adolescence, 37,* 113–127.

Ericksen, J. A. (1999). *Kiss and tell: Surveying sex in the twentieth century.* Cambridge, MA: Harvard University Press.

Erogul, O., Oztas, E., Yildirim, I., Kir, T., Aydur, E., Komesli, G., et al. (2006). Effects of electromagnetic radiation from a cellular phone on human sperm motility: An in vitro study. *Archives of Medical Research, 37,* 840–843.

Ersoy, B., Balkan, C., Gunay, T., & Egemen, A. (2005). The factors affecting the relation between the menarcheal age of mother and daughter. *Child: Care, Health & Development, 31*(3), 303–308.

Escoffier, J. (2003). *Sexual revolution.* New York: Thunder's Mouth Press.

Eshbaugh, E. M., & Gute, G. (2008). Hookups and sexual regret among college women. *Journal of Social Psychology, 148,* 77–89.

Eskenazi, B., Wyrobek, A. J., Sloter, E., Kidd, S. A., Moore, L., Young, S., & Moore, D. (2003). The association of age and semen quality in healthy men. *Human Reproduction, 18,* 447–454.

Espelage, D. L., Aragon, S. R., Birkett, M., & Koenig, B. W. (2008). Homophobic teasing, psychological outcomes, and sexual orientation among high school students: What influence do parents and schools have? *School Psychology Review, 37,* 202–216.

Espín, M. C., Llorca, M. D. C., Simons, B. C., Borrego, N. G., Cueto, G. M., Guerra, E. A., Rodríguez, B. T., et al. (2004). Cuba. In R. T. Francoeur & R. J. Noonan (Eds.), *The Continuum complete international encyclopedia of sexuality* (pp. 259–279). New York/London: Continuum International.

Esposito, K., Maiorino, M. I., Bellastella, G., Giugliano, F., Romano, M., & Giugliano, D. (2010). Determinants of female sexual dysfunction in type 2 diabetes. *International Journal of Impotence Research, 22*(3), 179–184.

Essén, B., Blomkvist, A., Helström, L., & Johnsdotter, S. (2010). The experience and responses of Swedish health professionals to patients requesting virginity restoration. *Reproductive Health Matters, 18*(35), 38–46.

Estacion, A., & Cherlin, A. (2010). Gender distrust and intimate unions among low-income Hispanic and African American women. *Journal of Family Issues, 31*(4), 475.

Estephan, A., & Sinert, R. (2010, February 1). *Dysfunctional uterine bleeding.* Retrieved December 26, 2010, from http://emedicine.medscape.com/article/795587-overview.

Ethics Committee Report. (2006). *Access to fertility treatment by gays, lesbians, and unmarried persons.* Ethics Committee of the American Society for Reproductive Medicine. Retrieved from http://www.asrm.org/Media/Ethics/fertility_gaylesunmarried.pdf.

Evans, A., Scally, A., Wellard, S., & Wilson, J. (2007). Prevalence of bacterial vaginosis in lesbians and heterosexual women in a community setting. *Sexually Transmitted Infections, 83,* 424–425.

Eyada, M., & Atwa, M. (2007). Sexual function in female patients with unstable angina or non-ST-elevation myocardial infarction. *Journal of Sexual Medicine, 4*(5), 1373–1380.

Fabes, R., Martin, C., & Hanish, L. (2003). Young children's play qualities in same-, other-, and mixed-sex peer groups. *Child Development, 74*(3), 921–932.

Fabre, L. F., Brown, C. S., Smith, L. C., & Derogatis, L. R. (2011). Gepirone-ER treatment of hypoactive sexual desire disorder (HSDD) associated with depression in women. *Journal of Sexual Medicine, 8*(5), 1411–1419.

Faderman, L. (1981). *Surpassing the love of men: Romantic friendship and love between women from the Renaissance to the present.* New York: William Morrow.

Falagas, M., Betsi, G., & Athanasiou, S. (2006). Probiotics for prevention of recurrent vulvovaginal candidiasis: A review. *Journal of Antimicrobial Chemotherapy, 58*(2), 266–272.

Faller, K. C. (1989). The role relationship between victim and perpetrator as a predictor of characteristics of intrafamilial sexual abuse. *Child and Adolescent Social Work Journal, 6,* 217–229.

Faludi, S. (1991). *Backlash: The undeclared war against American women.* New York: Crown.

Farah, M. (1984). *Marriage and sexuality in Islam.* Salt Lake City: University of Utah Press.

Farley, M., & Barkan, H. (1998). Prostitution, violence, and post-traumatic stress disorder. *Women and Health, 27*(3), 37–49.

Farley, M., Cotton, A., Lynne, J., et al. (2003). Prostitution and trafficking in nine countries: An update on violence and posttraumatic stress disorder. In M. Farley (Ed.), *Prostitution, trafficking and traumatic stress* (pp. 33–74). Binghamton, NY: Haworth Press.

Farr, C., Brown, J., & Beckett, R. (2004). Ability to empathise and masculinity levels: Comparing male adolescent sex offenders with a normative sample of non-offending adolescents. *Psychology, Crime & Law, 10*(2), 155–168.

Farr, R., Forssell, S., & Patterson, C. (2010). Parenting and child development in adoptive families: Does parental sexual orientation matter? *Applied Developmental Science, 14*(3), 164–178.

Farr, S., & Kern, M. (2010, November 24). Temple football players eyed in rape of student. *McClatchy-Tribune Business News.* Retrieved April 13, 2011, from http://articles.philly.com/2010-11-24/news/24955668_1_temple-students-temple-officials-al-golden.

Faulkner, A. H., & Cranston, K. (1998). Correlates of same-sex sexual behavior in a random sample of Massachusetts high school students. *American Journal of Public Health, 88*(2), 262–266.

Faulkner, S., & Lannutti, P. (2010). Examining the content and outcomes of young adults' satisfying and unsatisfying conversations about sex. *Qualitative Health Research, 20*(3), 375.

Fava, M., Dording, C., Baker, R., Mankoski, R., Tran, Q., Forbes, R., et al. (2011). Effects of adjunctive aripiprazole on sexual functioning in patients with major depressive disorder and an inadequate response to standard antidepressant monotherapy. *Primary Care Companion for CHS Disorders, 13*(1). Retrieved August 2, 2011, from http://www.ncbi.nlm.nih.gov/pmc/articles/PMC3121211/?tool5gateway.

Fay, R. E., Turner, C. F., Klassen, A. D., & Gagnon, J. H. (1989). Prevalence and patterns of same-gender sexual contact among men. *Science, 243,* 338–348.

Fechner, A. J., & McGovern, P. G. (2011). The state of the art of in vitro fertilization. *Frontiers in Bioscience, 3,* 264–278.

Federation of Feminist Women's Health Centers. (1991). *A new view of a woman's body: An illustrated guide.* Los Angeles: The Feminist Press.

Feeney, J. A., & Noller, P. (1990). Attachment style as a predictor of adult romantic relationships. *Journal of Personality & Social Psychology, 58*(2), 281–291.

Feige, A. M., Pinsky, M. R., & Hellstrom, W. J. (2011). Dapoxetine for premature ejaculation. *Clinical Pharmacology and Therapeutics, 89*(1), 125–128.

Feijoo, A. (2008). Adolescent sexual health in Europe and the U.S.—Why the difference? *Advocates for Youth.* Retrieved May 10, 2011, from http://www.circumcision-andhiv.com/files/fsest.pdf.

Feiler, B. (2010, August 27). The joys of vicarious divorce. *New York Times.* Retrieved September 16, 2010, from http://community.nytimes.com/comments/www.nytimes.com/2010/08/29/fashion/29FamilyMatters.html.

Feinauer, L. (1988). Relationship of long term effects of childhood sexual abuse to identity of the offender: Family, friend, or stranger. *Women and Therapy, 7,* 89–107.

Feinauer, L. (1989). Comparison of long-term effects of child abuse by type of abuse and by relationship of the offender to the victim. *American Journal of Family Therapy, 17,* 46–48.

Feldhaus-Dahir, M. (2010). Treatment options for female sexual arousal disorder: Part II. *Urologic Nursing, 30*(4), 247–251.

Feldman, M., & Meyer. I. (2007). Childhood abuse and eating disorders in gay and bisexual men. *International Journal of Eating Disorders, 40*(5), 418–423.

Ferdenzi, C., Schaal, B., & Roberts, S. C. (2009). Human axillary odor: Are there side-related perceptual differences? *Chemical Senses, 34*(7), 565–571.

Ferguson, D. M., Hosmane, B., & Heiman, J. R. (2010). Randomized, placebo-controlled, double-blind, parallel design trial of the efficacy and safety of Zestra in women with mixed desire/interest/arousal/orgasm disorders. *Journal of Sex and Marital Therapy, 36*(1), 66–86.

Ferguson, D. M., Steidle, C. P., Singh, G. S., Alexander, J. S., Weihmiller, M. K., & Crosby, M. G. (2003). Randomized placebo-controlled, double blind, crossover design trial of the efficacy and safety of Zestra for women with and without female sexual arousal disorder. *Journal of Sex and Marital Therapy, 29*(Suppl. 1), 33–44.

Ferguson, R. B. (2004). The associations among members' perceptions of intragroup relationship conflict, leader-member exchange quality, and leader gossiping behavior. *Dissertation Abstracts International, 64*(10-A), (#0419–4209).

Fergusson, D. M., Horwood, L. J., & Boden, J. M. (2009). Reactions to abortion and subsequent mental health. *British Journal of Psychiatry, 195*(5), 420–426.

Fernández, I. (2005). Go, Diego go. *Hispanic, 18, 20,* 68.

Fernandez, Y. M., & Marshall, W. L. (2003). Victim empathy, social self-esteem, and psychopathology in rapists. *Sexual Abuse: Journal of Research and Treatment, 15*(1), 11–26.

Ferree, M. M., & Hess, B. B. (1985). *Controversy and coalition: The new feminist movement.* Boston: Twayne.

Ferreira-Poblete, A. (1997). The probability of conception on different days of the cycle with respect to ovulation: An overview. *Advances in Contraception, 13*(2–3), 83–95.

Ferreiro-Velasco, M. E., Barca-Buyo, A., de la Barrera, S. S., Montoto-Marques, A., Vazquez, X. M., & Rodriguez-Sotillo, A. (2005). Sexual issues in a sample of women with spinal cord injury. *Spinal Cord, 43*(1), 51–55.

Ferro, C., Cermele, J., & Saltzman, A. (2008). Current perceptions of marital rape. *Journal of Interpersonal Violence, 23,* 764.

Fieldman, J. P., & Crespi, T. D. (2002). Child sexual abuse: Offenders, disclosure and school-based initiatives. *Adolescence, 37*(145), 151–160.

Fincham, F., & Beach, S. (2010). Marriage in the new millennium: A decade of review. *Journal of Marriage and Family, 72*(3), 630–650.

Finer, L., Frohwirth, L., Dauphinee, L., Singh, S., & Moore, A. (2006). Timing of steps and reasons for delays in obtaining abortions in the United States. *Contraception, 74*(4), 334–344.

Finer, L. B., & Henshaw, S. K. (2006). Disparities in rates of unintended pregnancy in the United States, 1994 and 2001. *Perspectives on Sexual and Reproductive Health, 38,* 90–96.

Fink, H. A., MacDonald, R., Rutks, I. R., & Nelson, D. B. (2002). Sildenafil for male erectile dysfunction: A systematic review and meta-analysis. *Archives of Internal Medicine, 162*(12), 1349–1360.

Finkelhor, D. (1980). Sex among siblings: A survey on prevalence, variety, and effects. *Archives of Sexual Behavior, 9,* 171–194.

Finkelhor, D. (1984). *Child sexual abuse: New theory and research.* New York: The Free Press.

Finkelhor, D., & Browne, A. (1985). The traumatic impact of child sexual abuse. *American Journal of Ortho-Psychiatry, 55,* 530–541.

Finkelhor, D., Hotaling, G., Lewis, I. A., & Smith, C. (1990). Sexual abuse in a national survey of adult men and women:

Prevalence, characteristics, and risk factors. *Child Abuse and Neglect, 14,* 19–28.

Finster, M., & Wood, M. (2005). The Apgar score has survived the test of time. *Anesthesiology, 102*(4), 855–857.

Firestone, P., Nunes, K. L., Moulden, H., Broom, I., & Bradford, J. M. (2005). Hostility and recidivism in sexual offenders. *Archives of Sexual Behavior, 34*(3), 277–283.

Fischer, G. J. (1987). Hispanic and majority student attitudes toward forcible date rape as a function of differences in attitudes toward women. *Sex Roles, 17*(1–2), 93–101.

Fisher, B., Wortley, S., Webster, C., & Kirst, M. (2002). The socio-legal dynamics and implications of "diversion": The case study of the Toronto "John School" diversion programme for prostitution offenders. *Criminal Justice: International Journal of Policy and Practice, 2*(34), 385–410.

Fisher, B. S., Cullen, F. T., & Turner, M. G. (2000). *Sexual victimization of college women.* Washington, DC: U.S. Department of Justice, National Institute of Justice.

Fisher, B. S., Daigle, L. E., Cullen, F. T., & Turner, M. G. (2003). Reporting sexual victimization to the police and others: Results from a national-level study of college women. *Criminal Justice & Behavior, 30*(1), 6–38.

Fisher, D., Malow, R., Rosenberg, R., Reynolds, G., Farrell, N., & Jaffe, A. (2006). Recreational Viagra use and sexual risk among drug abusing men. *American Journal of Infectious Disease, 2,* 107–114.

Fisher, H. (2004). *Why we love: The nature and chemistry of romantic love.* New York: Henry Holt.

Fisher, H., Brown, L., Aron, A., Strong, G., & Mashek, D. (2010). Reward, addiction, and emotion regulation systems associated with rejection in love. *Journal of Neurophysiology, 104*(1), 51–60.

Fisher, W. A., & Barak, A. (1991). Pornography, erotica, and behavior: More questions than answers. *International Journal of Law and Psychiatry, 14,* 65–83.

Fitzgerald, L. F., & Ormerod, A. J. (1991). Perceptions of sexual harassment: The influence of gender and academic context. *Psychology of Women Quarterly, 15,* 281–294.

Flanagan, C. (2011, April 23). Shutter fraternities for young women's good. *Wall Street Journal.* Retrieved April 24, 2011, from http://online.wsj.com/article/SB10001424052748704658704576275152354071470.

html?mod5WSJ_WSJ_News_BlogsModule.

Flanigan, C., Suellentrop, K., Albert, B., Smith, J., & Whitehead, M. (2005, September 15). Science says #17: Teens and oral sex. Retrieved September 17, 2005, from http://www.teenpregnancy.org/works/pdf/ScienceSays_17_OralSex.pdf.

Fleischmann, A. A., Spitzberg, B. H., Andersen, P. A., Roesch, S. C., & Metts, S. (2005). Tickling the monster: Jealousy induction in relationships. *Journal of Social and Personal Relationships, 22*(1), 49–73.

Foldes, P., & Buisson, O. (2009). The clitoral complex: A dynamic sonographic study. *Journal of Sexual Medicine, 6*(5), 1223–1231.

Food and Drug Administration. (2006, August 24). *FDA approves over-the-counter access for Plan B for women 18 and older: Prescription remains required for those 17 and under.* Retrieved October 28, 2008, from http://www.fda.gov/bbs/topics/news/2006/new01436.html.

Food and Drug Administration. (2007a, December 18). *FDA mandates new warning for nonoxynol 9 OTC contraceptive products.* Retrieved October 28, 2008, from http://www.fda.gov/bbs/topics/NEWS/2007/NEW01758.html.

Food and Drug Administration. (2007b). Over-the-counter vaginal contraceptive and spermicide drug products containing nonoxynol 9; required labeling. Final rule. *Federal Register, 72,* 71769–71785.

Food and Drug Administration. (2008, January 18). *FDA approves update to label on birth control patch.* Retrieved October 28, 2008, from http://www.fda.gov/bbs/topics/NEWS/2008/NEW01781.html.

Food and Drug Administration, Office of Women's Health. (2006, June). *Human papillomavirus.* Retrieved September 16, 2008, from http://www.fda.gov/WOMENS/getthefacts/hpv.html.

Foote, W. E., & Goodman-Delahunty, J. (2005). Harassers, harassment contexts, same-sex harassment, workplace romance, and harassment theories. In W. E. Foote & J. Goodman-Delahunty (Eds.), *Evaluating sexual harassment: Psychological, social, and legal considerations in forensic examinations* (pp. 27–45). Washington, DC: American Psychological Association.

Ford, C. L., Whetten, K. D., Kaufman, J. S., & Thrasher, A. D. (2007). Black sexuality, social construction, and research targeting 'The down low' ('The DL'). *Annals of Epidemiology, 17*(3), 209–216.

Ford, K., & Chamrathrithirong, A. (2007). Sexual partners and condom use of migrant workers in Thailand. *AIDS Behavior, 11,* 905–914.

Forhan, S. (2008, March). *Prevalence of STIs and bacterial vaginosis among female adolescents in the U.S.: Data from the National Health and Nutritional Examination Survey 2003–2004.* Presented at the 2008 National STD Prevention Conference, Chicago, IL. Retrieved May 29, 2008, from http://www.cdc.gov/STDConference/2008/media/summaries-11march2008.htm#tues1.

Forke, C., Myers, R., Catallozzi, M., & Schwarz, D. (2008). Relationship violence among female and male college undergraduate students. *Archives of Pediatric Adolescent Medicine, 162,* 634–641.

Forry, N. D., Leslie, L. A., & Letiecq, B. L. (2007). Marital quality in interracial relationships. *Journal of Family Issues, 28,* 1538.

Forstein, M. (1988). Homophobia: An overview. *Psychiatric Annals, 18,* 33–36.

Fortenberry, J., Schick, V., Herbenick, D., Sanders, S., Dodge, B., & Reece, M. (2010). Sexual behaviors and condom use at least vaginal intercourse: A national sample of adolescents age 14 to 17 years. *Journal of Sexual Medicine, 7*(Suppl. 5), 305–314.

Fortenberry, J. D. (2002). Unveiling the hidden epidemic of STDs. *Journal of the American Medical Association, 287*(6), 768–769.

Forti, G., & Krausz, C. (1998). Clinical review 100: Evaluation and treatment of the infertile couple. *Journal of Clinical Endocrinology Medicine, 83*(12), 4177–4188.

Forti, G., Corona, G., Vignozzi, L., Krausz, C., & Maggi, M. (2010). Klinefelter's syndrome: A clinical and therapeutical update. *Sex Development, 4*(4–5), 249–258.

Foster, G. (2002). Supporting community efforts to assist orphans in Africa. *New England Journal of Medicine, 346,* 1907–1911.

Foster, G. (2006). Children who live in communities affected by AIDS. *The Lancet, 367*(9511), 700–701.

Foster, K., & Sandel, M. (2010). Abuse of women with disabilities: Toward an empowerment perspective. *Sexuality and Disability, 28*(3), 177–187.

Foster, R. T. (2008). Noncomplicated urinary tract infections in women. *Obstetrics and Gynecology Clinics of North America, 35,* 235–248.

Foubert, J., & Cremedy, B. (2007). Reactions of men of color to a commonly used rape prevention program. *Sex Roles, 57,* 137–144.

Foubert, J., Godin, E., & Tatum, J. (2010a). In their own words: Sophomore college men describe attitude and behavior changes resulting from a rape prevention program 2 years after their participation. *Journal of Interpersonal Violence, 25*(12), 2237–2257.

Foubert, J., Tatum, J., & Godin, E. (2010b). First-year male students' perceptions of a rape prevention program 7 months after their participation: Attitude and behavior changes. *Journal of College Student Development, 51*(6), 707–715.

Foubert, J. D. (2000). The longitudinal effects of a rape: Prevention program on fraternity men's attitudes. *Journal of American College Health, 48*(4), 158–163.

Foubert, J. D., & McEwen, M. K. (1998). An all-male rape prevention peer education program: Decreasing fraternity men's behavioral intent to rape. *Journal of College Student Development, 39,* 548–556.

Foucault, M. (1998). *The history of sexuality, Vol. 1: An introduction.* London: Penguin Books.

Fowers, B. J. (1998). Psychology and the good marriage. *American Behavioral Scientist, 41*(4), 516.

Fowler, M. G., Gable, A. R., Lampe, M. A., Etima, M., & Owor, M. (2010). Perinatal HIV and its prevention: Progress toward an HIV-free generation. *Clinical Perinatology, 37*(4), 699–719.

Fox, J. A., & Zawitz, M. W. (2004). Homicide trends in the United States. Retrieved October 23, 2005, from www.ojp.usdoj.gov/bjs/homicide/homtrnd.htm.

Fox, M., & Thomson, M. (2010). HIV/AIDS and circumcision: Lost in translation. *Journal of Medical Ethics, 36*(12), 798–801.

Frackiewicz, E. J. (2000). Endometriosis: An overview of the disease and its treatment. *Journal of the American Pharmaceutical Association, 40*(5), 645–657.

France-Presse, A. (2010, September 28). Bishops to support protests against birth control. ABS/CBN News. Retrieved March 2, 2011, from http://www.abs-cbnnews.com/nation/09/28/10/bishops-support-protests-against-birth-control.

Franceschi, S. (2005). The IARC commitment to cancer prevention: The example of papillomavirus and cervical cancer. *Recent Results in Cancer Research, 166,* 277–297.

Francis, A. (2008). Family and sexual orientation: The family-demographic correlates of homosexuality in men and women. *Journal of Sex Research, 45*(4), 371–377.

Francoeur, R. T., & Noonan, R. J. (Eds.). (2004). *The Continuum International encyclopedia of sexuality.* New York/London: Continuum International.

Francucci, C. M., Ceccoli, L., Caudarella, R., Rilli, S., & Boscaro, M. (2010). Skeletal effect of natural early menopause. *Journal of Endocrinological Investigations, 33*(7 Suppl.), 39–44.

Franiuk, R., Seefelt, J., & Vandello, J. (2008). Prevalence of rape myths in headlines and their effects on attitudes toward rape. *Sex Roles, 58,* 790–802.

Frank, E., Anderson, C., & Rubinstein, D. N. (1978). Frequency of sexual dysfunction in normal couples. *New England Journal of Medicine, 299,* 111–115.

Frankel, L. (2002). "I've never thought about it": Contradictions and taboos surrounding American males' experiences of first ejaculation (semenarche). *Journal of Men's Studies, 11*(1), 37–54.

Frazier, P. A. (2000). The role of attributions and perceived control in recovery from rape. *Journal of Personal and Interpersonal Loss, 5*(2/3), 203–225.

Fredriksson, J., Kanabus, A., Pennington, J., & Pembrey, G. (2008). AIDS orphans. Avert International AIDS Charity. Retrieved November 3, 2008, from http://www.avert.org/aidsorphans.htm.

Freedman, D., Khan, L., Serdula, M., Dietz, W., Srinivasan, S. R., & Berenson, G. S. (2002). Relation of age at menarche to race, time period, and anthropometric dimensions: The Bogalusa Heart Study. *Pediatrics, 110*(4), E43.

Freedman, D. H. (2010, November). Lies, damned lies, and medical science. *The Atlantic.* Retrieved January 2, 2011, from http://www.theatlantic.com/magazine/archive/2010/11/lies-damned-lies-and-medical-science/8269/.

Freeman, N. (2007). Preschoolers' perceptions of gender appropriate toys and their parents' beliefs about genderized behaviors: Miscommunication, mixed messages, or hidden truths? *Early Childhood Education Journal, 34*(5), 357–366.

Freeman, S. B. (2008). Continuous oral contraception. Strategies for managing breakthrough bleeding. *Advance for Nurse Practitioners 16*(8), 36–38.

Fretts, R. C., Boyd, M. E., Usher, R. H., & Usher, H. A. (1992). The changing pattern of fetal death, 1961–1988. *Obstetrics and Gynecology, 79*(1), 35–39.

Freud, S. (1953). Three essays on the theory of sexuality. In J. Strachey (Ed. & Trans.), *The standard edition of the complete psychological works of Sigmund Freud* (Vol. 7, pp. 130–243). London: Hogarth Press. (Original work published 1905.)

Freund, K., & Blanchard, R. (1986). The concept of courtship disorder. *Journal of Sex and Marital Therapy, 12,* 79–92.

Freund, K., Scher, H., & Hucker, S. (1983). The courtship disorders. *Archives of Sexual Behavior, 12,* 369–379.

Freund, K., Scher, H., & Hucker, S. (1984). The courtship disorders: A further investigation. *Archives of Sexual Behavior, 13,* 133–139.

Freund, M., Lee, N., & Leonard, T. (1991). Sexual behavior of clients with street prostitutes in Camden, New Jersey. *Journal of Sex Research, 28,* 579–591.

Freund, M., Leonard, T. L., & Lee, N. (1989). Sexual behavior of resident street prostitutes with their clients in Camden, New Jersey. *Journal of Sex Research, 26,* 460–478.

Freymiller, L. (2005, May). Separate or equal?: Gay viewers respond to same-sex and gay/straight relationships on TV. Presented at the 2005 Annual Meeting of the International Communication Association, New York, NY.

Frick, K. D., Clark, M. A., Steinwachs, D. M., Langenberg, P., Stovall, D., Munro, M. G., & Dickersin, K.; STOP-DUB Research Group. (2009). Financial and quality-of-life burden of dysfunctional uterine bleeding among women agreeing to obtain surgical treatment. *Womens Health Issues, 19*(1), 70–78.

Friebe, A., & Arck, P. (2008). Causes for spontaneous abortion: What the bugs 'gut' to do with it? *International Journal of Biochemistry and Cell Biology, 40*(11), 2348–2352.

Frieden, T. R. (2011). CDC health disparities and inequalities report—United States, 2011. *Morbidity and Mortality Weekly Report, 60*(Suppl.), 1–2.

Friedler, S., Glasser, S., Azani, L., Freedman, L., Raziel, A., Strassburger, D., Ron-El, R., & Lerner-Geva, L. (2011). The effect of medical clowning on pregnancy rates after in vitro fertilization and embryo transfer. *Fertility and Sterility, 95*(6), 2127–2130.

Friedman, C. (2007). First comes love, then comes marriage, then comes baby carriage: Perspectives on gay parenting and reproductive technology. *Journal of Infant, Child, and Adolescent Psychotherapy, 6,* 111–123.

Friedman, S., Loue, S., Heaphy, E., & Mendez, N. (2011). Intimate partner violence victimization and perpetration by Puerto Rican women with severe mental illnesses. *Community Mental Health Journal, 47*(2), 156–163.

Friedman-Kien, A. E., & Farthing, C. (1990). Human immunodeficiency virus infection: A survey with special emphasis on mucocutaneous manifestations. *Seminars in Dermatology, 9,* 167–177.

Friedrich, W. N. (1998). Behavioral manifestations of child sexual abuse. *Child Abuse and Neglect, 22*(6), 523–531.

Friedrich, W. N., Grambsch, P., Broughton, D., Kuiper, J., & Beilke, R. L. (1991). Normative sexual behavior in children. *Pediatrics, 88,* 456–464.

Fritz, G. S., Stoll, K., & Wagner, N. N. (1981). A comparison of males and females who were sexually molested as children. *Journal of Sex & Marital Therapy, 7*(1), 54–59.

Frohlich, P. F., & Meston, C. M. (2000). Evidence that serotonin affects female sexual functioning via peripheral mechanisms. *Physiology and Behavior, 71*(3–4), 383–393.

Frost, J. J., & Driscoll, A. K. (2006). *Sexual and reproductive health of U.S. Latinas: A literature review.* New York: Alan Guttmacher Institute. Retrieved May 27, 2008, from http://www.guttmacher.org/pubs/2006/02/07/or19.pdf.

Frost, J. J., Darroch, J. E., & Remez, L. (2008). Improving contraception use in the United States. *In Brief, 1.* New York: Alan Guttmacher Institute.

Frostino, A. (2007). Guilt and jealousy associated with sexual fantasies among heterosexual married individuals. Widener University. *Dissertation Abstracts International: Section B: The Sciences and Engineering, 68*(3-B), 1924.

Fruth, A. (2007). Dating and adolescents' psychological well-being. *Dissertation Abstracts International Section A: Humanities and Social Sciences, 68*(1-A), 360.

Fryar, C. D., Hirsch, R., Porter, K. S., Kottiri, B., Brody, D., & Louis, T. (2007, June 28). Drug use and sexual behaviors reported by adults: United States, 1999–2002. Advance Data from Vital and Health Statistics, Centers for Disease Control, 384. Retrieved October 3, 2008, from http://www.cdc.gov/nchs/data/ad/ad384.pdf.

Fu, Y. (2010). Interracial marriage formation: Entry into first union and transition from cohabitation to marriage. University of North Carolina at Chapel Hill, AAT #1483777.

Fuller-Fricke. R. L. (2007). Interaction of relationship satisfaction, depressive symptoms, and self-esteem in college-aged women. *Fuller Theological Seminary, Dissertation Abstracts,* UMI #3267404.

Gaetz, S. (2004). Safe streets for whom? Homeless youth, social exclusion, and criminal victimization. *Canadian Journal of Criminology and Criminal Justice, 46,* 423–456.

Gaffield, M. E., Culwell, K. R., & Ravi, A. (2009). Oral contraceptives and family history of breast cancer. *Contraception, 80*(4), 372–380.

Gähler, M., Hong, Y., & Bernhardt, E. (2009). Parental divorce and union disruption among young adults in Sweden. *Journal of Family Issues, 30*(5), 688–713.

Gaither, G. A. (2000). The reliability and validity of three new measures of male sexual preferences (Doctoral dissertation, University of North Dakota). *Dissertation Abstracts International, 61,* 4981.

Gaither, G. A., Sellbom, M., & Meier, B. P. (2003). The effect of stimulus content on volunteering for sexual interest research among college students. *Journal of Sex Research, 40*(3), 240–249.

Galis, F., Broek, C., Van Dongen, S., & Wijnaendts, L. (2010). Sexual dimorphism in the prenatal digit ratio (2D:4D). *Archives of Sexual Behavior, 39,* 57–62.

Gallagher, J. (2001). Normal, China—The Chinese Psychiatric Association decides that being gay is no longer a disease. *The Advocate.* p. 22.

Gallagher, M., & Baker, J. K. (2004, May 4). Same-sex unions and divorce risk: Data from Sweden. *iMAPP Policy Brief.* Retrieved September 14, 2008, from http://www.marriagedebate.com/pdf/SSdivorcerisk.pdf.

Gallo, R. V. (2000). Is there a homosexual brain? *Gay and Lesbian Review, 7*(1), 12–16.

Galloway, T., Cipelli, R., Guralnick, J., Ferrucci, L., Bandinelli, S., Corsi, A. M., Money, C., McCormack, P., & Melzer, D. (2010). Daily bisphenol A excretion and associations with sex hormone concentrations: Results from the InCHIANTI Adult Population Study. *Environmental Health Perspectives, 118*(11), 1603–1608.

Galupo, M. P. (2006). Sexism, heterosexism, and biphobia: The framing of bisexual women's friendships. *Journal of Bisexuality, 6,* 35–45.

Gamel, C., Hengeveld, M., Davis, B. (2000). Informational needs about the effects of gynaecological cancer on sexuality: A review of the literature. *Journal of Clinical Nursing, 9*(5), 678–688.

Gan, C., Zou, Y., Wu, S., Li, Y., & Liu, Q. (2008). The influence of medical abortion compared with surgical abortion on subsequent pregnancy outcome. *International Journal of Gynecology and Obstetrics, 101,* 231–238.

Garbin, C., Deacon, J., Rowan, M., Hartmann, P., & Geddes, D. (2009). Association of nipple piercing with abnormal milk production and breastfeeding. *Journal of the American Medical Association, 301*(24), 2550–2551.

Garcia-Falgueras, A., & Swaab, D.F. (2010). Sexual hormones and the brain: An essential alliance for sexual identity and sexual orientation. *Endocrine Development, 17,* 22–35.

Gard, C. (2000). What is he/she saying? *Current Health, 26*(8), 18–20.

Gardiner, P., Stargrove, M., & Low, D. (2011). Concomitant use of prescription medications and dietary supplements in menopausal women: An approach to provider preparedness. *Maturitas, 68*(3), 251–255.

Gardner, A. (2004). *Excess weight can compromise birth control pills.* Sexual Health Network. Retrieved October 1, 2008, from http://sexualhealth.e-healthsource.com/?p=news1&id=523135.

Garner, M., Turner, M. C., Ghadirian, P., Krewski, D., & Wade, M. (2008). Testicular cancer and hormonally active agents. *Journal of Toxicology and Environmental Health, 11,* 260–275.

Garnock-Jones, K. P., & Giuliano, A. R. (2011) Quadrivalent human papillomavirus (HPV) types 6, 11, 16, 18 vaccine: For the prevention of genital warts in males. *Drugs, 71*(5), 591–602.

Gartrell, N., & Bos, H. (2010). The US national longitudinal lesbian family study: Psychological adjustment of the 17-year-old adolescents. Retrieved June 7, 2010, from http://pediatrics.aappublications.org/cgi/content/abstract/peds.2009-3153v1.

Garver-Apgar, C. E., Gangestad, S. W., Thornhill, R., Miller, R. D., & Olp, J. J. (2006). Major histocompatibility complex alleles, sexual responsivity, and unfaithfulness in romantic couples. *Psychological Science, 17,* 830–835.

Gates, G., & Renna, C. (2010). 2010 census analysis of same-sex couples: 1 in 7 not identified. Williams Institute. Retrieved

May 11, 2011, from http://www3.law.ucla.edu/williamsinstitute/pdf/2010CensusAnalysis_PR_Sept7.pdf.

Gates, G., Badgett, L., Macomber, J. E., & Chambers, K. (2007, March 27). Adoption and foster care by lesbian and gay parents in the United States. Urban Institute. Retrieved October 2, 2008, from http://www.urban.org/url.cfm?ID=411437.

Gates, G. J. (2008). Same-sex couples: U.S. census and the American Community Survey. Retrieved January 31, 2011, from http://www2.law.ucla.edu/williamsinstitute/pdf/CensusPresentation_LGBT.pdf.

Gates, G. J., & Sonenstein, F. L. (2000). Heterosexual genital sexual activity among adolescent males: 1998–1995. *Family Planning Perspectives, 32*(6), 295–304.

Gavard, J., & Artal, R. (2008). Effect of exercise on pregnancy outcome. *Clinical Obstetrics and Gynecology, 51,* 467–480.

Gayle, H. (2000). Letter to colleagues from Helene Gayle, M.D. Retrieved March 4, 2000, from http://www.cdc.gov/washington/testimony/ha030200.htm.

Gebhard, P., & Johnson, A. (1979). *The Kinsey data: Marginal tabulations of the 1938–1963 interviews conducted by the Institute for Sex Research.* Philadelphia: W. B. Saunders.

Geer, J. H., & O'Donohue, W. T. (1987). A sociological approach. In J. H. Geer & W. T. O'Donohue (Eds.), *Theories of human sexuality* (pp. 237–253). New York: Plenum Press.

Gelbard, M. (1988). Dystrophic penile classification in Peyronie's disease. *Journal of Urology, 139,* 738–740.

Gemelli, R. J. (1996). *Normal child and adolescent development.* Arlington, VA: American Psychiatric Press.

Gentzler, A., Kerns, K., & Keener, E. (2010). Emotional reactions and regulatory responses to negative and positive events: Associations with attachment and gender. *Motivation and Emotion, 34*(1), 78.

Geraghty, P. (2010). Beyond birth control. The health benefits of hormonal contraception. *Advanced Nurse Practitioner, 17*(2), 47–48, 50, 52.

Getahun, D. Ananth, C. V., Selvam, N., & Demissie, K. (2005). Adverse perinatal outcomes among interracial couples in the United States. *Obstetrics and Gynecology, 106*(1), 81–88.

Ghanotakis, E. (2008, January 10). South Africa: An everyday crime. *Frontline Rough Cut.* Retrieved April 30, 2011, from http://www.pbs.org/frontlineworld/rough/2008/01/south_africa_ev.html.

Ghaziani, A. (2005). Breakthrough: The 1979 national march. *Gay & Lesbian Review Worldwide, 12*(2), 31–33.

Ghidini, A., & Bocchi, C. (2007). Direct fetal blood sampling: Cordocentesis. In J. T. Queenan, C. Y. Spong, & C. J. Lockwood (Eds.), *Management of high-risk pregnancy: An evidence-based approach.* Hoboken, NJ: Wiley Blackwell.

Ghosh, M. K. (2005). Breech presentation: Evolution of management. *Journal of Reproductive Medicine, 50*(2), 108–116.

Gibbs, J. L., Ellison, N. B., & Heino, R. D. (2006). Self-presentation in online personals: The role of anticipated future interaction, self-disclosure, and perceived success in Internet dating. *Communication Research, 33,* 152–177.

Gibbs, N. (2010, April 22). The pill at 50: Sex, freedom and paradox. *Time Magazine.* Retrieved September 6, 2010, from http://www.time.com/time/health/article/0,8599,1983712,00.html.

Gibson, B. (2010). Care of the child with the desire to change genders—female to male transition. *Pediatric Nursing, 36*(2), 112–119.

Gill, S. (2009). Honour killings and the quest for justice in black and minority ethnic communities and in the UK. United Nations Division for the Advancement of Women, Expert Group Meeting on good practices in legislation to address harmful practices against women. Retrieved March 30, 2011, from http://www.un.org/womenwatch/daw/egm/vaw_legislation_2009/Expert%20Paper%20EGMGPLHP%20_Aisha%20Gill%20revised_.pdf.

Gilleard, C., & Higgs, P. (2000). *Cultures of ageing: Self, citizen and the body.* Upper Saddle River, NJ: Prentice Hall Publishers.

Gilmore, A. K., Schacht, R. L., George, W. H., Otto, J. M., Davis, K. C., Heiman, J. R., Norris, J., & Kajumulo, K. F. (2010). Assessing women's sexual arousal in the context of sexual assault history and acute alcohol intoxication. *Journal of Sexual Medicine, 7*(6), 2112–2119.

Gilmore, D. D. (1990). *Manhood in the making: Cultural concepts of masculinity.* New Haven, CT: Yale University Press.

Gilson, R. J., & Mindel, A. (2001). Sexually transmitted infections. *British Medical Journal, 322*(729S), 1135–1137.

Giltay, J. C., & Maiburg, M. C. (2010). Klinefelter syndrome: Clinical and molecular aspects. *Expert Review of Molecular Diagnostics, 10*(6), 765–776.

Ginsberg, T. B., Pomerantz, S. C., & Kramer-Feeley, V. (2005). Sexuality in older adults: Behaviours and preferences. *Age and Ageing, 34,* 475–480.

Ginty, M. M. (2005). New pills launch debate over menstruation. Retrieved March 19, 2005, from http://www.womensenews.org/article.cfm/dyn/aid/1879/context/archive.

Giotakos, O., Markianos, M., & Vaidakis, N. (2005). Aggression, impulsivity, and plasma sex hormone levels in a group of rapists, in relation to their history of childhood attention-deficit/hyperactivity disorder symptoms. *Journal of Forensic Psychiatry & Psychology, 16*(2), 423–433.

Giraldi, A., & Kristensen, E. (2010). Sexual dysfunction in women with diabetes mellitus. *Journal of Sex Research, 47*(2), 199–211.

Girsh, E., Katz, N., Genkin, L., Girtler, O., Bocker, J., Bezdin, S., & Barr, I. (2008). Male age influences oocyte-donor program results. *Journal of Assisted Reproductive Genetics, 25*(4), 137–143.

Girshick, L. B. (1999). *No safe haven: Stories of women in prison.* Lebanon, NH: University Press of New England.

Giuliano, A., Lazcano-Ponce, E., Villa, L., Flores, R., Salmeron, J., Lee, J., et al. (2008a). The human papillomavirus infection in men study: Human papillomavirus prevalence and type distribution among men residing in Brazil, Mexico, and the United States. *Cancer Epidemiology Biomarkers Prevention, 17,* 2036–2043.

Giuliano, A., Lu, B., Nielson, C., Flores, R., Papenfuss, M., Lee, J., et al. (2008b). Age-specific prevalence, incidence, and duration of human papillomavirus infections in a cohort of 290 U.S. men. *Journal of Infectious Disease, 198,* 827–835.

Giuliano, A. R., Palefsky, J. M., Goldstone, S., Moreira, E. D., Jr., Penny, M. E., Aranda, C., Vardas, E., Moi, H., Jessen, H., Hillman, R., Chang, Y. H., Ferris, D., Rouleau, D., Bryan, J., Marshall, J. B., Vuocolo, S., Barr, E., Radley, D., Haupt, R. M., & Guris, D. (2011). Efficacy of quadrivalent HPV vaccine against HPV infection and disease in males. *New England Journal of Medicine, 364*(5), 401–411.

Glasser, M., Kolvin, I., Campbell, D., Glasser, A., Leitch, I., & Farrelly, S. (2001). Cycle of child sexual abuse: Links between being a victim and becoming a perpetrator. *British Journal of Psychiatry, 179,* 482–494.

Gleicher, N., Weghofer, A., & Barad, D. (2008). Preimplantation genetic screening: "Established" and ready for prime time? *Fertility and Sterility, 89,* 780–788.

Glenn, N., & Marquardt, E. (2001). Hooking up, hanging out and hoping for Mr. Right: College women on mating and dating today. Retrieved October 19, 2005, from http://www. americanvalues.org/Hooking_Up.pdf.

Glenn, S., & Byers, E. (2009). The roles of situational factors, attributions, and guilt in the well-being of women who have experienced sexual coercion. *Canadian Journal of Human Sexuality, 18*(4), 201–220.

Glenwright, M., & Pexman, P. M. (2010). Development of children's ability to distinguish sarcasm and verbal irony. *Journal of Child Language, 37*(2), 429–451.

Godeau, E., Gabhainn, S., Vignes, C., Ross, J., Boyce, W., & Todd, J. (2008). Contraceptive use by 15-year old students at their last sexual intercourse. *Archives of Pediatric and Adolescent Medicine, 162*(1), 66–73.

Godfrey, K., Robinson, S., Barker, D. J., Osmond, C., & Cox, V. (1996). Maternal nutrition in early and late pregnancy in relation to placental and fetal growth. *British Medical Journal, 312*(7028), 410–414.

Goffman, E. (1976). *Gender advertisements.* New York: Harper Colophon Books.

Gokyildiz, S., & Beji, N. K. (2005). The effects of pregnancy on sexual life. *Journal of Sex and Marital Therapy, 31*(3), 201–215.

Gold, J. C. (2004). Kiss of the yogini: "Tantric sex" in its South Asian contexts. *Journal of Religion, 84*(2), 334–336.

Gold, M., Wolford, J., Smith, K., Parker, A. (2004). The effects of advance provision of emergency contraception on adolescent women's sexual and contraceptive behaviors. *Journal of Pediatric and Adolescent Gynecology, 17,* 87–96.

Gold, R. (2009). All that's old is new again: The long campaign to persuade women to forego abortion. *Guttmacher Policy Review, 12*(2). Retrieved March 17, 2011, from http://www.guttmacher.org/pubs/gpr/12/2/gpr120219.html.

Gold, R. B. (2003, March). Lessons from before Roe: Will past be prologue? Retrieved September 3, 2005, from http://www.agi-usa.org/pubs/ib_5–03.html.

Goldberg, A., Smith, J., & Kashy, D. (2010). Preadoptive factors predicting lesbian, gay, and heterosexual couples' relationship quality across the transition to adoptive parenthood. *Journal of Family Psychology, 24*(3), 221–232.

Golden, G. H. (2001). Dyadic-dystonic compelling eroticism: Can these relationships be saved? *Journal of Sex Education & Therapy, 26*(1), 50.

Goldman, R. (1999). The psychological impact of circumcision. *British Journal of Urology International, 83,* 93–102.

Goldman-Mellor, S., Brydon, L., & Steptoe, A. (2010). Psychological distress and circulating inflammatory markers in healthy young adults. *Psychological Medicine, 40,* 2079–2087.

Goldstein, A. T., & Burrows, L. (2008). Vulvodynia. *Journal of Sexual Medicine, 5,* 5–15.

Goleman, D. (1992, April 14). Therapies offer hope for sexual offenders. *The New York Times,* pp. C1, C11.

Golen, S. (1990). A factor analysis of barriers to effective listening. *Journal of Business Communication, 27,* 25–36.

Gollapalli, V., Liao, J., Dudakovic, A., Sugg, S., Scott-Conner, C., & Weigel, R. (2010). Risk factors for development and recurrence of primary breast abscesses. *Journal of the American College of Surgeons, 211*(1), 41–48.

Gómez, A. (2011). Testing the cycle of violence hypothesis: Child abuse and adolescent dating violence as predictors of intimate partner violence in young adulthood. *Youth and Society, 43*(1), 171–192.

Gonzaga, G., Haselton, M., Smurda, J., Davies, M., & Poore, J. (2008). Love, desire, and the suppression of thoughts of romantic alternatives. *Evolution and Human Behavior, 29,* 119–126.

Gonzales, A., Schofield, R., & Schmitt, G. (2005). Sexual assault on campus: What colleges and universities are doing about it. U.S. Department of Justice. Retrieved April 25, 2011, from http://www.publicintegrity.org/investigations/campus_assault/assets/pdf/Fisher_report_3.pdf.

González, M., Viáfara, G., Caba, F., Molina, T., & Ortiz, C. (2006). Libido and orgasm in middle-aged women. *Maturitas, 53,* 1–10.

Goode, E. (1994). *Deviant behavior.* Englewood Cliffs, NJ: Prentice Hall.

Goodman, A. (1993). Diagnosis and treatment of sexual addiction. *Journal of Sex and Marital Therapy, 19*(3), 225–251.

Goodman, M., Shvetsov, Y., McDuffie, K., Wilkens, L., Zhu, X., Ning, L., et al. (2008). Acquisition of anal human papillomavirus infection in women: The Hawaii HPV cohort study. *Journal of Infectious Diseases, 197,* 957–966.

Goodman, M. P. (2009). Female cosmetic genital surgery. *Obstetrics and Gynecology, 113*(1), 154–159.

Goodman, M. P., Placik, O., Benson, R., Miklos, J., Moore, R., Jason, R., Matlock, D., Simopoulos, A., Stern, B., Stanton, R., et al. (2010). A large multicenter outcome study of female genital plastic surgery. *Journal of Sexual Medicine, 7*(4 Pt 1), 1565–1577.

Goodwin, J. (2007, June). Kill yourself or your family will kill you. *Marie Claire,* 155–157.

Goodwin, P. Y., Mosher, W. D., & Chandra, A. (2010). Marriage and cohabitation in the United States: A statistical portrait based on Cycle 6 (2002) of the National Survey of Family Growth. National Center for Health Statistics. DHHS Publication No. 2010–1980. *Vital Health Statistics 23*(28), 1–45.

Gooren, L. (2006). The biology of human psychosexual differentiation. *Hormones & Behavior, 50,* 589–601.

Gordon, B. N., & Schroeder, C. S. (1995). *Sexuality: A developmental approach to problems.* Chapel Hill, NC: Clinical Child Psychology Library.

Gordon, H. (2008). The treatment of paraphilias: A historical perspective. *Criminal Behaviour and Mental Health, 18,* 79–87.

Gordon, L. (2010, March 15). Mixed-gender dorm rooms are gaining acceptance. *Los Angeles Times.* Retrieved November 6, 2010, from http://articles.latimes.com/2010/mar/15/local/la-me-dorm-gender15–2010mar15.

Gordon, S. (1986). What kids need to know. *Psychology Today, 20,* 22–26.

Gorman, B. (January 7, 2011). "'Jersey Shore' Season Premiere Draws 8.45 Million Viewers; 4.2 Adults 18–49 Rating." TVbytheNumbers.com. Retrieved January 7, 2011, from http://tvbythenumbers.zap2it.com/2011/01/07/jersey-shore-season-premiere-draws-8–4-million-sets-mtv-all-time-series-high/77688.

Gosselin, C. C. (1987). The sadomasochistic contract. In G. D. Wilson (Ed.), *Variant sexuality: Research and theory* (pp. 229–257). Baltimore: Johns Hopkins University Press.

Gottman, J. M. (1994). *Why marriages succeed or fail.* New York: Simon & Schuster.

Gottman, J. M. (1999). *The seven principles for making marriage work.* New York: Random House.

Gottman, J., & Silver, N. (2000). *The seven principles for making marriage work.* New York: Crown.

Gottman, J., Levenson, R., Swanson, C., Swanson, K., Tyson, R., & Yoshimoto, D. (2003). Observing gay, lesbian and heterosexual couples' relationships: Mathematical modeling of conflict interaction. *Journal of Homosexuality, 45*, 65–91.

Gottschall, J. A., & Gottschall, T. A. (2003). Are per-incident rape-pregnancy rates higher than per-incident consensual pregnancy rates? *Human Nature, 14*(1), 1–20.

Gould, S. J. (1981). *The mismeasure of man.* New York: Norton.

Gourley, C. (2007). *Flappers and the new American woman: Perceptions of women from 1918 through the 1920s.* Breckenridge, CO: Twenty-First Century Books.

Graham, C., Bancroft, J., Doll, H., Greco, T., & Tanner, A. (2007). Does oral contraceptive-induced reduction in free testosterone adversely affect the sexuality or mood of women? *Psychneuroendocrinology, 32*, 246–255.

Graugaard, C., Eplov, L. F., Giraldi, A., Mohl, B., Owens, A., Risor, H., & Winter, G. (2004). Denmark. In R. T. Francoeur & R. J. Noonan (Eds.), *The Continuum complete international encyclopedia of sexuality* (pp. 329–344). New York/London: Continuum International.

Graziottin, A. (2007). Prevalence and evaluation of sexual health problems—HSDD in Europe. *Journal of Sexual Medicine, 4*(Suppl 3), 211–219.

Grce, M., & Davies, P. (2008). Human papillomavirus testing for primary cervical cancer screening. *Expert Review of Molecular Diagnostics, 8*, 599–605.

Green, R. (1987). *The "sissy boy syndrome" and the development of homosexuality.* New Haven, CT: Yale University Press.

Green, R. (1988). The immutability of (homo)-sexual orientation: Behavioral science implications for a constitutional (legal) analysis. *The Journal of Psychiatry and the Law, 16*, 537–575.

Green, R. J. (2008a). Gay and lesbian couples: Developing resilience in response to social injustice. In M. McGoldrick & K. Hardy (Eds.), *Revisioning family therapy: Race, culture, and gender in clinical practice* (2nd ed.). New York: Guilford Press.

Green, R. J. (2008b, January 11). *What straights can learn from gays about relationships and parenting.* San Francisco: Rockway Institute. Retrieved December 19, 2008, from http://www.newswise.com/articles/view/536799/.

Green, R. J., & Mitchell, V. (2002). Gay and lesbian couples in therapy: Homophobia, re-lational ambiguity, and social support. In A. S. Gurman & N. S. Jacobson (Eds.), *Clinical handbook of couple therapy* (3rd ed., pp. 546–568). New York: Guilford Press.

Green, R. J., Bettinger, M., & Zacks, E. (1996). Are lesbian couples fused and gay male couples disengaged? Questioning gender straightjackets. In J. Laird & R. J. Green (Eds.), *Lesbians and gays in couples and families: A handbook for therapists* (pp. 185–230). New York: Jossey-Bass.

Greenberg, M., Cheng, Y., Hopkins, L., Stotland, N., Bryant, A., & Caughey, A. (2006). Are there ethnic differences in the length of labor? *American Journal of Obstetrics and Gynecology, 195*, 743–748.

Greenberg, M., Cheng, Y., Sullivan, M., Norton, L., & Caughey, A. (2007). Does length of labor vary by maternal age? *American Journal of Obstetrics and Gynecology, 197*, 428.

Greenfeld, D. A. (2005). Reproduction in same sex couples: Quality of parenting and child development. *Current Opinions in Obstetrics and Gynecology, 17*, 309–312.

Greenwald, E., & Leitenberg, H. (1989). Long-term effects of sexual experiences with siblings and nonsiblings during childhood. *Archives of Sexual Behavior, 18*, 289–400.

Greenwald, H., & McCorkle, R. (2008). Sexuality and sexual function in long-term survivors of cervical cancer. *Journal of Women's Health, 17*, 955–963.

Greenwald, J. L., Burstein, G., Pincus, J., & Branson, G. (2006). A rapid review of rapid HIV antibody tests. *Current Infectious Disease Reports, 8*, 125–131.

Greer, J. B., Modugno, F., Allen, G. O., & Ness, R. B. (2005). Androgenic progestins in oral contraceptives and the risk of epithelial ovarian cancer. *Obstetrics and Gynecology, 105*, 731–740.

Gregson, S., Nyamukapa, C., Garnett, G., Wambe, M., Lewis, J., Mason, P., Chandiwana, S., & Anderson, R. (2005). HIV infection and reproductive health in teenage women orphaned and made vulnerable by AIDS in Zimbabwe. *AIDS Care, 17*(7), 785–794.

Grenier, G., & Byers, E. (2001). Operationalizing premature or rapid ejaculation. *Journal of Sex Research, 38*(4), 369–378.

Griffin, J., Umstattd, M., & Usdan, S. (2010). Alcohol use and high-risk sexual behavior among collegiate women: A review of research on alcohol myopia theory. *Journal of American College Health, 58*(6), 523–533.

Griffin, S. A. (2006). A qualitative inquiry into how romantic love has been portrayed by contemporary media and researchers. *Dissertation Abstracts International Section A: Humanities and Social Sciences, 67*, 2272.

Griffith, R. S., Walsh, D. E., Myrmel, K. H., Thompson, R. W., & Behforooz, A. (1987). Success of L-lysine therapy in frequently recurrent herpes simplex infection. Treatment and prophylaxis. *Dermatologica, 175*(4), 183–190.

Griffiths, M. (2001). Sex on the Internet: Observations and implications for Internet sex addiction. *Journal of Sex Research, 38*(4), 333–343.

Griffiths, M. (2003). Internet abuse in the workplace and concern for employers and employment counselors. *Journal of Employment Counseling, 40*(2), 87–97.

Griffiths, M. D. (2000). Excessive Internet use: Implications for sexual behavior. *Cyberpsychology and Behavior, 3*, 537–552.

Griffitt, W., & Veitch, R. (1971). Hot and crowded: Influences of population density and temperature on interpersonal affective behavior. *Journal of Personality and Social Psychology, 17*, 92–98.

Grimbizis, G. F., & Tarlatzis, B. C. (2010). The use of hormonal contraception and its protective role against endometrial and ovarian cancer. *Best Practice & Research: Clinical Obstetrics & Gynaecology, 24*(1), 29–38.

Grimbos T., Dawood K., Burriss R. P., Zucker K. J., & Puts D. A. (2010). Sexual orientation and the second to fourth finger length ratio: A meta-analysis in men and women. *Behavioral Neuroscience, 124*(2), 278–287.

Grob, C. S. (1985). Single case study: Female exhibitionism. *Journal of Nervous and Mental Disease, 173*, 253–256.

Groer, M. W. (2005). Differences between exclusive breastfeeders, formula-feeders, and controls: A study of stress, mood, and endocrine variables. *Biological Research for Nursing, 7*(2), 106–117.

Gross, J. (2007, October 9). Aging and gay, and facing prejudice in twilight. *New York Times.* Retrieved September 3, 2008, from http://www.nytimes.com/2007/10/09/us/09aged.html.

Grosskurth, P. (1980). *Havelock Ellis: A biography.* New York: Alfred A. Knopf.

Groth, A. N. (1978). Patterns of sexual assault against children and adolescents. In A. W. Burgess, A. N. Groth, L. L. Holmstrom, &

S. M. Sgroi (Eds.), *Sexual assault of children and adolescents*. Toronto: Lexington Books.

Groth, N., & Burgess, A. (1980). Male rape: Offenders and victims. *American Journal of Psychiatry, 137*, 806–810.

Grove, C., Gillespie, B., Royce, T., & Lever, J. (2011). Perceived consequences of casual online sexual activities on heterosexual relationships: A US online survey. *Archives of Sexual Behavior, 40*(2), 429–439.

Groysman, V. (2010). Vulvodynia: New concepts and review of the literature. *Dermatology Clinics, 28*(4), 681–696.

Gruber, A. J., & Pope, H. G. (2000). Psychiatric and medical effects of anabolic-androgenic steroid use in women. *Psychotherapy and Psychosomatics, 69*(1), 19–26.

Gruenbaum, E. (2006). Sexuality issues in the movement to abolish female genital cutting in Sudan. *Medical Anthropology Quarterly, 20*, 121.

Grunbaum, J. A., Kann, L., Kinchen, S. A., Williams, B., Ross, J. G., Lowry, R., & Kolbe, L. (2002). Youth risk behavior surveillance: United States, 2001. *Morbidity and Mortality Weekly Report, 51*(no. SS-4).

Guadagno, R., & Sagarin, B. (2010). Sex differences in jealousy: An evolutionary perspective on online infidelity. *Journal of Applied Social Psychology, 40*(10), 2636–2655.

Gudjonsson, G. H. (1986). Sexual variations: Assessment and treatment in clinical practice. *Sexual and Marital Therapy, 1*, 191–214.

Gudykunst, W., Ting-Toomey, S., & Nishida, T. (1996). *Communication in personal relationships across cultures*. Thousand Oaks, CA: Sage Publications.

Guerrero, L., & Bachman, G. (2010). Forgiveness and forgiving communication in dating relationships: An expectancy-investment explanation. *Journal of Social and Personal Relationships, 27*(6), 801.

Guerrero, L. K., & Afifi, W. (1999). Toward a goal-oriented approach for understanding communicative responses to jealousy. *Western Journal of Communication, 63*(2), 216–248.

Guerrero, L. K., Spitzberg, B. H., & Yoshimura, S. M. (2004). Sexual and emotional jealousy. In J. H. Harvey, A. Wenzel, & S. Sprecher (Eds.), *The handbook of sexuality in close relationships* (pp. 311–345). Mahwah, NJ: Erlbaum.

Guffey, M. E. (1999). *Business communication: Process & product* (3rd ed.). Belmont, CA: Wadsworth.

Guha, C., Shah, S. J., Ghosh, S. S., Lee, S. W., Roy-Chowdhury, N., & Roy-Chowdhury, J. (2003). Molecular therapies for viral hepatitis. *BioDrugs, 17*(2), 81–91.

Gundersen, B. H., Melas, P. S., & Skar, J. E. (1981). Sexual behavior of preschool children: Teachers' observations. In L. L. Constantine & F. M. Martinson (Eds.), *Children and sex: New findings, new perspectives* (pp. 45–61). Boston: Little, Brown.

Gunter, B., & McAleer, J. L. (1990). *Children and television: The one-eyed monster?* London: Routledge, Chapman, Hall.

Gunter, J. (2007). Vulvodynia: New thoughts on a devastating condition. *Obstetrics and Gynecological Survey, 62*, 812–819.

Gupta, J. K., & Nikodem, V. C. (2000). Woman's position during second stage of labour. *Cochrane Database of Systematic Reviews, 2*, CD002006.

Gutkin, M. (2010). Internet versus face-to-face dating: A study of relationship satisfaction, commitment, and sustainability. *Dissertation Abstracts International, 71*(08). University of Delaware, AAT #3417180.

Guzzo, K. (2009). Marital intentions and the stability of first cohabitations. *Journal of Family Issues, 30*(2), 179–205.

Hack, W. W., Meijer, R. W., Bos, S. D., & Haasnoot, K. (2003). A new clinical classification for undescended testis. *Scandinavian Journal of Nephrology, 37*(1), 43–47.

Hader, S. L., Smith, D. K., Moore, J. S., & Holmberg, S. D. (2001). HIV infection in women in the U.S.: Status at the millennium. *Journal of the American Medical Association, 285*(9), 1186–1192.

Haeberle, E. J. (1982). The Jewish contribution to the development of sexology. *Journal of Sex Research, 18*, 305–323.

Haggerty, C. L., Gottlieb, S. L., Taylor, B. D., Low, N., Xu, F., & Ness, R. B. (2010). Risk of sequelae after Chlamydia trachomatis genital infection in women. *Journal of Infectious Disease, 201*(Suppl. 2), S134-S155.

Hahlweg, K., Kaiser, A., Christensen, A., Fehm-Wolfsdorf, G., & Grother, T. (2000). Self-report and observational assessment of couples' conflict. *Journal of Marriage and Family, 62*(1), 61.

Hahm, H., Lee, J., Zerden, L., & Ozonoff, A. (2008). Longitudinal effects of perceived maternal approval on sexual behaviors of Asian and Pacific Islander (API) young adults. *Journal of Youth and Adolescence, 37*, 74–85.

Hald, G. M., & Malamuth, N. M. (2008). Self-perceived effects of pornography consumption. *Archives of Sexual Behavior, 37*(4), 614–626.

Hall, E. T. (1976). *Beyond culture*. New York: Doubleday.

Hall, E. T. (1990). *Understanding cultural differences, Germans, French and Americans*. Yarmouth, ME: Intercultural Press.

Hall, H., Hughes, D., Dean, H., Mermin, J., & Fenton, K. (2011). HIV infection—United States, 2005 and 2008. *Morbidity and Mortality Weekly Report, 60*(01), 87–89.

Hall, H., Song, R., Rhodes, P., Prejean, J., An, Q., Lee, L., Karon, J., et al. (2008). Estimation of HIV incidence in the U.S. *Journal of the American Medical Association, 300*, 520–529.

Hall, J. (2005). Neuroscience and education (SCRE Research Report No. 121). Glasgow, Scotland: University of Glasgow, the Scottish Council for Research in Education Centre.

Hall, P., & Schaeff, C. (2008). Sexual orientation and fluctuating symmetry in men and women. *Archives of Sexual Behavior, 37*(1), 158–165.

Halldorsson, T. I., Strøm, M., Petersen, S. B., & Olsen, S. F. (2010). Intake of artificially sweetened soft drinks and risk of preterm delivery: A prospective cohort study in 59,334 Danish pregnant women. *American Journal of Clinical Nutrition, 92*(3), 626–633.

Hallett, S. (2011, April 4). Joe Biden urges schools to address sexual assault epidemic. *Ms. Magazine*. Retrieved April 29, 2011, from http://msmagazine.com/blog/blog/2011/04/04/joe-biden-urges-schools-to-address-sexual-assault-epidemic/.

Halpern-Felsher, B., Kropp, R., Boyer, C., Tschann, J., & Ellen, J. (2004). Adolescents' self-efficacy to communicate about sex: Its role in condom attitudes, commitment, and use. *Adolescence, 39*(155), 443–457.

Halsall, P. (1996). *Thomas Aquinas: Summa theologiae*. Retrieved April 10, 2008, from http://www.fordham.edu/halsall/source/aquinas1.html.

Hamachek, D. E. (1982). *Encounters with others: Interpersonal relationships and you*. New York: Holt, Rinehart & Winston.

Hamberg, K. (2000). Gender in the brain: A critical scrutiny of the biological gender differences. *Lakartidningen, 97*, 5130–5132.

Hamburg, B. A. (1986). Subsets of adolescent mothers: Developmental, biomedical, and psychosocial issues. In J. B. Lancaster & B. A. Hamburg (Eds.), *School-age preg-*

nancy and parenthood: Biosocial dimensions (pp. 115–145). New York: Aldine DeGruyter.

Hamer, D. H., et al. (1993). A linkage between DNA markers on the X chromosome and male sexual orientation. *Science, 261,* 321–327.

Hamilton B., Martin J., & Ventura S. (2010a). Births: Preliminary data for 2008. *National Vital Statistics Reports, 58*(16). Retrieved May 10, 2011, from http://www.cdc.gov/ nchs/data/nvsr/nvsr58/nvsr58_16.pdf.

Hamilton, B., Martin, J., & Ventura, S. (2010b). Births: Preliminary data for 2009. *National Vital Statistics Report, 59*(3). Retrieved March 1, 2011, from http://www.cdc.gov/ nchs/data/nvsr/nvsr59/nvsr59_03.pdf.

Hamilton, L., & Armstrong, E. (2009). Gendered sexuality in young adulthood: Double binds and flawed options. *Gender and Society, 23*(5), 589–616.

Hamilton, T. (2002). *Skin flutes and velvet gloves.* New York: St. Martin's Press.

Hammer, H., Finkelhor, D., & Sedlak, A. (2002). Runaway/thrownaway children: National estimates and characteristics. National incidence studies of missing, abducted, runaway, and thrownaway children. Retrieved June 28, 2011, from http:// www.ncjrs.gov/html/ojjdp/nismart/04/.

Hand, J. Z., & Sanchez, L. (2005). Badgering or bantering? Gender differences in experience of, and reactions to, sexual harassment among U.S. high school students. *Gender & Society, 14*(6), 718–746.

Handler, A., Davis, F., Ferre, C., & Yeko, T. (1989). The relationship of smoking and ectopic pregnancy. *American Journal of Public Health, 79,* 1239–1242.

Handwerk, B. (2005, February 25). 4-D ultrasound gives video view of fetuses in the womb. *National Geographic News.* Retrieved October 14, 2008, from http:// news.nationalgeographic.com/news/ pf/80752382.html.

Hankins, G. (1995). *Operative obstetrics.* Appleton and Lange, Stamford, CT.

Hannaford, P. C., Iversen, L., Macfarlane, T. V., Elliott, A. M., Angus, V., & Lee, A. J. (2010). Mortality among contraceptive pill users: Cohort evidence from Royal College of General Practitioners' Oral Contraception Study. *British Medical Journal, 340,* c927.

Hans, J., Gillen, M., & Akande, K. (2010). Sex redefined: The reclassification of oral-genital contact. *Perspectives on Sexual and Reproductive Health, 42*(2). Retrieved February 6, 2011, from http://www .guttmacher.org/pubs/psrh/full/ 4207410.pdf.

Hansen, B. (1989). American physicians' earliest writings about homosexuals, 1880–1900. *Milbank Quarterly, 67*(Suppl 1), 92–108.

Harcourt, C., & Donovan, B. (2005). The many faces of sex work. *Sexually Transmitted Diseases, 81,* 201–206.

Hardt, J., Sidor, A., Nickel, R., Kappis, B., Petrak, P., & Egle, U. T. (2008). Childhood adversities and suicide attempts: A retrospective study. *Journal of Family Violence, 23,* 713–719.

Hardy, S., & Raffaelli, M. (2003). Adolescent religiosity and sexuality: An investigation of reciprocal influences. *Journal of Adolescence, 26*(6), 731–739.

Harlan, L. C., Potosky, A., Cilliland, F. D., Hoffman, R., Albertsen, P. C., Hamilton, A. S., Eley, J. W., Stanford, J. L., & Stephenson, R. A. (2001). Factors associated with initial therapy for clinically localized prostate cancer: Prostate cancer outcomes study. *Journal of the National Cancer Institute, 93*(24), 1864–1871.

Harlow, H. F. (1959). Love in infant monkeys. *Scientific American, 200,* 68–70.

Harmon, A. (2007, September 16). Cancer free at 33, but weighing a mastectomy. *New York Times.* Retrieved March 20, 2008, from http://www.nytimes.com/2007/ 09/16/health/16gene.html.

Harris, C. R. (2003). A review of sex differences in sexual jealousy, including self-report data, psychophysiological responses, interpersonal violence, and morbid jealousy. *Personality and Social Psychology Review, 7*(2), 102–128.

Harrison, F. (2005). Iran's sex-change operations. *BBC News.* Retrieved May 25, 2008, from http://news.bbc.co.uk/2/hi/ programmes/newsnight/4115535.stm.

Hart, C. W. M., & Pilling, A. R. (1960). *The Tiwi of North Australia.* New York: Holt, Rinehart & Winston.

Hart, G. J., & Elford, J. (2010). Sexual risk behaviour of men who have sex with men: Emerging patterns and new challenges. *Current Opinions in Infectious Disease, 23*(1), 39–44.

Hartmann, K., Viswanathan, M., Palmieri, R., Gartlehner, G., Thorp, J., & Lohr, K. (2005). Outcomes of routine episiotomy: A systematic review. *Journal of the American Medical Association, 293*(17), 2141–2148.

Harville, E., Taylor, C., Tesfai, H., Xiong, X., & Buekens, P. (2011). Experience of hurricane Katrina and reported intimate partner violence. *Journal of Interpersonal Violence, 26*(4), 833–845.

Haselton, M. G., Mortezaie, M., Pillsworth, E. G., Bleske-Recheck, A. E., & Frederick, D. A. (2007). Ovulation and human female ornamentation: Near ovulation, women dress to impress. *Hormones and Behavior, 51,* 40–45.

Hatano, Y., & Shimazaki, T. (2004). Japan. In R. T. Francoeur & R. J. Noonan (Eds.), *The Continuum International encyclopedia of sexuality* (pp. 636–678). New York/London: Continuum International.

Hatcher, R. (2004). Depo-Provera injections, implants, and progestin-only pills (minipills). In R. A. Hatcher et al. (Eds.), *Contraceptive technology* (18th Rev. ed., pp. 461–494). New York: Ardent Media.

Hatcher, R. A., Trussell, J., Nelson, A., Cates, W., Steward, F., & Kowal, D. (2007). *Contraceptive technology* (19th ed.). New York: Ardent Media.

Hatcher, R. A., Trussell, J., Nelson, A., Cates, W., Kowal, D., & Policar M. (2011). *Contraceptive technology* (20th ed.). New York: Ardent Media.

Hatcher, R. A., Trussell, J., Stewart, F. H., Nelson, A. L., Cates, W., Guest, F., & Kowal, D. (2004). *Contraceptive technology* (18th Rev. ed.). New York: Ardent Media.

Hatfield, E. (1988). Passionate and companionate love. In R. J. Sternberg & R. J. Barnes (Eds.), *Psychology of love* (pp. 191–217). New Haven, CT: Yale University Press.

Hatfield, E., & Sprecher, S. (1986). Measuring passionate love in intimate relationships. *Journal of Adolescence, 9*(4), 383–410.

Hathaway, J. E., Willis, G., Zimmer, B., & Silverman, J. G. (2005). Impact of partner abuse on women's reproductive lives. *Journal of the American Medical Women's Association, 60*(1), 42–45.

Hawkins, A. J., Nock, S. L., Wilson, J. C., Sanchez, L., & Wright, J. D. (2002). Attitudes about covenant marriage and divorce: Policy implications from a three-state comparison. *Family Relations, 51*(2), 166–176.

Hawkins, N. A., Cooper, C. P., Saraiya, M., Gelb, C. A., & Polonec, L. (2011). Why the Pap test? Awareness and use of the Pap test among women in the United States. *Journal of Womens Health, 20,* 511–515.

Hawton, K. (1983). Behavioural approaches to the management of sexual deviations. *British Journal of Psychiatry, 143,* 248–255.

Hayashi, A. (2004, August 20). Japanese women shun the use of the pill. *CBS News.* Retrieved October 28, 2008, from http://

www.cbsnews.com/stories/2004/08/20/health/main637523.shtml.

Hazelwood, R., & Burgess, A. (1987). *Practical aspects of rape investigation: A multidisciplinary approach.* New York: Elsevier.

Hebert, K., Lopez, B., Castellanos, J., Palacio, A., Tamariz, L., & Arcement, L. (2008). The prevalence of erectile dysfunction in heart failure patients by race and ethnicity. *International Journal of Impotence Research, 20*(5), 507–511.

Heger, A., Ticson, L., Velasquez, O., & Bernier, R. (2002). Children referred for possible sexual abuse: Medical findings in 2384 children. *Child Abuse & Neglect, 26*(6–7), 645–659.

Hegna, K., & Rossow, I. (2007). What's love got to do with it? Substance use and social integration for young people categorized by same-sex experience and attractions. *Journal of Drug Issues, 37,* 229–256.

Heidari, M., Nejadi, J., Ghate, A., Delfan, B., & Iran-Pour, E. (2010). Evaluation of intralesional inject of verapamil in treatment of Peyronie's disease. *Journal of the Pakistan Urological Association, 60*(4), 291–293.

Heiman, J. (2002). Sexual dysfunction: Overview of prevalence, etiological factors, and treatments. *Journal of Sex Research, 39*(1), 73–79.

Heiman, J., & LoPiccolo, J. (1992). *Becoming orgasmic: A sexual and personal growth program for women.* New York: Simon & Schuster.

Heiman, J., & Meston, M. (1997). Empirically validated treatment for sexual dysfunction. *Annual Review of Sex Research, 8,* 148–194.

Heinzmann, D. (2008, May 6). Some men say using prostitutes is an addiction: 200 take part in a study about motivation. *Chicago Tribune.* Retrieved October 7, 2008, from http://libill.hartford.edu:2083/pqdweb?index=7&did=1473639221&SrchMode=1&sid=4&Fmt=3&VInst=PROD&VType=PQD&RQT=309&VName=PQD&TS=1223437846&clientId=3309.

Hellerstein, E., Olafson, L., Parker, H., & Offen, K. M. (1981). *Victorian women: A documentary account of women's lives in nineteenth-century England, France, and the United States.* Stanford, CA: Stanford University Press.

Hellstrom, W. J. (2006). Current and future pharmacotherapies of premature ejaculation. *Journal of Sexual Medicine, 3*(Suppl 4), 332–341.

Helmore, K. (2010, July 1). Empowering women to protect themselves: Promoting the female condom in Zimbabwe. United Nations Population Fund. Retrieved March 15, 2011, from http://www.unfpa.org/public/News/pid/3913.

Hemphill, E. (1991). *Brother to brother: New writings by black gay men.* Boston: Alyson.

Hemstrom, O. (1996). Is marriage dissolution linked to differences in mortality risks for men and women? *Journal of Marriage and the Family, 58,* 366–378.

Henderson, A., Lehavot, K., & Simoni, J. (2009). Ecological models of sexual satisfaction among lesbian/bisexual and heterosexual women. *Archives of Sexual Behavior, 38*(1), 50–66.

Henderson, L. (1991). Lesbian pornography: Cultural transgression and sexual demystification. *Women and Language, 14,* 3–12.

Hendrick, C., & Hendrick, S. S. (1989). Research on love: Does it measure up? *Journal of Personality & Social Psychology, 56*(5), 784–794.

Hendrick, C., & Hendrick, S.S. (2000). *Close relationships: A sourcebook.* Thousand Oaks, CA: Sage.

Henke, G. (2010, November 7). Personal communication.

Henke, G. (2011, May 11). Personal communication.

Henline, B., Lamke, L., & Howard, M. (2007). Exploring perceptions of online infidelity. *Personal Relationships, 14,* 113–238.

Hennessy, M., Bleakley, A., Fishbein, M., & Jordan, A. (2009). Estimating the longitudinal association between adolescent sexual behavior and exposure to sexual media content. *Journal of Sex Research, 46,* 586–596.

Hensel, D. J., Fortenberry, J. D., Harezlak, J., Anderson, J. G., & Orr, D. P. (2004). A daily diary analysis of vaginal bleeding and coitus among adolescent women. *Journal of Adolescent Health, 34*(5), 392–394.

Hensley, C., Koscheski, M., & Tewksbury, R. (2005). Examining the characteristics of male sexual assault targets in a Southern maximum-security prison. *Journal of Interpersonal Violence, 20*(6), 667–679.

Hensley, L. G. (2002). Treatment of survivors of rape: Issues and interventions. *Journal of Mental Health Counseling, 24*(4), 331–348.

Henslin, J. M. (2005). The sociology of human sexuality. In J. M. Henslin, *Sociology: A down-to-earth approach.* Online chapter retrieved November 30, 2005, from http://www.ablongman.com/html/henslintour/henslinchapter/ahead3.html.

Herbenick, C., Reece, M., Sanders, S., Dodge, B., Ghassemi, A., & Fortenberry, J. (2009). Prevalence and characteristics of vibrator use by women in the US.: Results from a nationally representative study. *Journal of Sexual Medicine, 6,* 1857–1866.

Herbenick, D., Reece, M., Schick, V., Sanders, S., Dodge, B., & Fortenberry, D. (2010a). Sexual behavior in the United States: Results from a National Probability Sample of men and women ages 14–94. *Journal of Sexual Medicine, 7*(Suppl. 5), 255–265.

Herbenick, D., Reece, M., Schick, V., Sanders, S., Dodge, B., & Fortenberry, J. D. (2010b). Sexual behaviors, relationships, and perceived health status among adult women in the U.S.: Results from a national probability sample. *Journal of Sexual Medicine, 7*(Suppl. 5), 277–290.

Herbruck, L. F. (2008). The impact of childbirth on the pelvic floor. *Urlogical Nursing, 28,* 173–184.

Herdt, G. (1981). *Guardians of the flutes: Idioms of masculinity.* New York: McGraw-Hill.

Herdt, G. (1988). Cross-cultural forms of homosexuality and the concept "gay." *Psychiatric Annals, 18,* 37–39.

Herdt, G. (1989). Introduction: Gay and lesbian youth, emergent identities, and cultural scenes at home and abroad. In G. Herdt (Ed.), *Gay and lesbian youth* (pp. 1–42). New York: Harrington Park Press.

Herdt, G., & Stoller, R. (1990). *Intimate communications: Erotics and the study of culture.* New York: Columbia University Press.

Herek, G. (2002). Heterosexuals' attitudes toward bisexual men and women in the United States. *Journal of Sex Research, 39*(4), 264–274.

Herek, G. (2006). Legal recognition of same-sex relationship in the United States: A social science perspective. *American Psychologist, 61,* 606–621.

Herek, G. M. (1984). Beyond "homophobia": A social psychological perspective on attitudes toward lesbians and gay men. In J. P. DeCecco (Ed.), *Homophobia: An overview* (pp. 1–21). New York: The Haworth Press.

Herek, G., Cogan, J. C., & Gillis, J. (2002). Victim experiences in hate crimes based on sexual orientation. *Journal of Social Issues, 58*(2), 319–339.

Herman, J. L. (1981). *Father-daughter incest.* Cambridge, MA: Harvard University Press.

Herman, J., & Schatzow, E. (1987). Recovery and verification of memories of childhood sexual trauma. *Psychoanalytic Psychology, 4,* 1–14.

Heron, J., McGuinness, M., Blackmore, E., Craddock, N., & Jones, I. (2008). Early postpartum symptoms in puerperal psychosis. *British Journal of Obstetrics and Gynecology, 115,* 348–353.

Herrick, A. L., Matthews, A. K., & Garofalo, R. (2010). Health risk behaviors in an urban sample of young women who have sex with women. *Journal of Lesbian Studies, 14*(1), 80–92.

Herz, R. (2007). *The scent of desire: Discovering our enigmatic sense of smell.* New York: William Morrow Publishers.

Hetherington, E. (2003). Intimate pathways: Changing patterns in close personal relationships across time. *Family Relations, 52,* 318–331.

Hewlett, M. (2008, September 17). Getting help is hard for gay domestic violence victims. *McClatchy—Tribune Business News.* Retrieved October 5, 2008, from http://libill. hartford.edu:2083/pqdweb?index=2&did= 1556431461&SrchMode=1&sid=1&Fmt=3 &VInst=PROD&VType=PQD&RQT=309 &VName=PQD&TS=1223252228&clientI d=3309.

Heymann, J., Earle, A., Rajaraman, D., Miller, C., & Bogen, K. (2007). Extended family caring for children orphaned by AIDS: Balancing essential work and caregiving in a high HIV prevalence nation. *AIDS Care, 19*(3), 337–345.

Hickman, S. E., & Muehlenhard, C. L. (1999). By the semi-mystical appearance of a condom: How young women and men communicate sexual consent in heterosexual situations. *Journal of Sex Research, 36*(3), 258–272.

Hicks, C. W., & Rome, E. S. (2010). Menstrual manipulation: Options for suppressing the cycle. *Cleveland Clinic Journal of Medicine, 77*(7), 445–453.

Hicks, S. (2005). Is gay parenting bad for kids? Responding to the "very idea of difference" in research on lesbian and gay parents. *Sexualities, 8*(2), 153–168.

Hicks, T., & Leitenberg, H. (2001). Sexual fantasies about one's partner versus someone else: Gender differences in incidence and frequency. *Journal of Sex Research, 38,* 43–50.

Hickson, F. C. I., Davies, P. M., & Hunt, A. J. (1994). Gay men as victims of nonconsensual sex. *Archives of Sexual Behavior, 23*(3), 281–294.

Hill, B. F., & Jones, J. S. (1993). Venous air embolism following orogenital sex during pregnancy. *American Journal of Emergency Medicine, 11,* 155–157.

Hill, S. (2007). Overestimation bias in mate competition. *Evolution and Human Behavior, 28*(2), 118–123.

Hill, S. A. (2002). Teaching and doing gender in African American families. *Sex Roles, 47,* 493–506.

Hillebrand, R. (2008). The Oneida community. Retrieved April 10, 2008, from http:// www.nyhistory.com/central/oneida.htm.

Hinchley, G. (2007). Is infant male circumcision an abuse of the rights of the child? Yes. *British Medical Journal, 8,* 335(7631), 1180.

Hines, D. A. (2007). Predictors of sexual coercion against women and men: A multilevel, multinational study of university students. *Archives of Sexual Behavior, 36,* 403–422.

Hinshelwood, M. (2002). Early and forced marriage: The most widespread form of sexual exploitation of girls? Retrieved August 27, 2003, from http://www.kit.nl/ils/ exchange_content/html/forced_marriage_ -_sexual_healt.asp.

Hirayama, H., & Hirayama, K. (1986). The sexuality of Japanese Americans. Special issue: Human sexuality, ethnoculture, and social work. *Journal of Social Work and Human Sexuality, 4*(3), 81–98.

Hirshkowitz, M., & Schmidt, M. H. (2005). Sleep-related erections: Clinical perspectives and neural mechanisms. *Sleep Medicine Reviews, 9*(4), 311–329.

Hisasue, S., Furuya, R., Itoh, N., Kobayashi, K., Furuya, S., & Tsukamoto, T. (2006). Ejaculatory disorder caused by alpha-1 adrenoceptor antagonists is not retrograde ejaculation but a loss of seminal emission. *International Journal of Urology, 13*(10), 1311–1316.

Hitsch, G., Hortacsu, A., & Ariely, D. (2010). What makes you click? Mate preferences in online dating. *Quantitative Marketing and Economics, 8*(4), 393.

Hitti, M. (2008, January 18). *FDA strengthens warning on blood clot risk for users of Ortho Evra birth control skin patch.* WebMD. Retrieved October 28, 2008, from http:// www.webmd.com/sex/birth-control/ news/20080118/birth-control-patch- stronger-warning.

Hjelmstedt, A., Andersson, L., Skoog-Syanberg, A., Bergh, T., Boivin, J., & Collins, A. (1999). Gender differences in psychological reactions to infertility among couples seeking IVF and ICSI treatment. *Acta Ob-*

stetricia et Gynecologica Scandinavica, 78(1), 42–48.

Ho, V. P., Lee, Y., Stein, S. L., & Temple, L. K. (2011). Sexual function after treatment for rectal cancer: A review. *Diseases of the Colon and Rectum, 54*(1), 113–125.

Hobbs, K., Symonds, T., Abraham, L., May, K., & Morris, M. (2008). Sexual dysfunction in partners of men with premature ejaculation. *International Journal of Impotence Research, 20*(5):512–517.

Hoburg, R., Konik, J., Williams, M., & Crawford, M. (2004). Bisexuality among self-identified heterosexual college students. *Journal of Bisexuality, 4,* 25–36.

Hodge, D. R. (2008). Sexual trafficking in the U.S.: A domestic problem with transnational dimensions. *Social Work, 53*(2), 143–152.

Hoebel, E. A. (1954). *The law of primitive man.* Cambridge, MA: Harvard University Press.

Hoff, C., Beougher, S., Chakravarty, D., Darbes, L., & Neilands, T. (2010). Relationship characteristics and motivations behind agreements among gay male couples: Differences by agreement type and couple serostatus. *AIDS Care, 22*(7), 827–835.

Hoff, G. (2003). Power and love: Sadomasochistic practices in long-term committed relationships. *Dissertation Abstracts: Section B, 64*(1-B), #0419–4217.

Hoffman, M. C. (2008, July 23). Philippines in struggle against abortionist population control initiative. *LifeSite News.com.* Retrieved October 28, 2008, from http:// www.lifesitenews.com/ldn/2008/ jul/08072201.html.

Hoffstetter, S., Barr, S., LeFevre, C., Leong, F., & Leet, T. (2008). Self-reported yeast symptoms compared with clinical wet mount analysis and vaginal yeast culture in a specialty clinic setting. *Journal of Reproductive Medicine, 53,* 402–406.

Hofman, B. (2005). "What is next?": Gay male students' significant experiences after coming-out while in college. *Dissertation Abstracts International Section A: Humanities & Social Sciences, 65*(8-A), #0419– 4209.

Hogan, H. (2005). Title IX requires colleges & universities to eliminate the hostile environment caused by campus sexual assault. Retrieved October 25, 2005, from http:// www.securityoncampus.org/victims/title- ixsummary.html.

Hollander, D. (2000, March/April). Fertility drugs do not raise breast, ovarian or uterine cancer risk. *Family Planning Perspectives, 32*(2), 100–103.

Hollander, D. (2001). Users give new synthetic and latex condoms similar ratings on most features. *Family Planning Perspectives, 33*(1), 45–48.

Holmberg, D., & Blair, K. (2009). Sexual desire, communication, satisfaction, and preferences of men and women in same-sex versus mixed-sex relationships. *Journal of Sex Research, 46*(1), 57–66.

Holmes, J. G., & Rempel, J. K. (1989). Trust in close relationships. In C. Hendrick (Ed.), *Close relationships* (Vol. 10, pp. 187–219). Newbury Park, CA: Sage.

Holmes, M. C. (2004). Reconsidering a "woman's issue:" Psychotherapy and one man's postabortion experiences. *American Journal of Psychotherapy, 58*(1), 103–115.

Holmes, R. (1991). *Sex crimes.* Newbury Park, CA: Sage.

Holmstrom, A. (2009). Sex and gender similarities and differences in communication values in same-sex and cross-sex friendships. *Communication Quarterly, 57*(2), 224–238.

Hooker, E. (1957). The adjustment of the male overt homosexual. *Journal of Projective Techniques, 21,* 18–31.

Hooton, T. M. (2003). The current management strategies for community-acquired urinary tract infection. *Infectious Disease Clinics of North America, 17*(2), 303–332.

Hope, M. E., Farmer, L., McAllister, K. F., & Cumming, G. P. (2010). Vaginismus in peri- and postmenopausal women: A pragmatic approach for general practitioners and gynaecologists. *Menopause International, 16*(2), 68–73.

Horan, S., & Booth-Butterfield, M. (2010). Investing in affection: An investigation of affection exchange theory and relationship qualities. *Communication Quarterly, 58*(4), 394.

Horowitz, S. M., Weis, D. L., & Laflin, M. T. (2001). Differences between sexual orientation behavior groups and social background, quality of life, and health behaviors. *Journal of Sex Research, 38*(3), 205–219.

Horrigan, J. B., Rainie, L., & Fox, S. (2001). Online communities: Networks that nurture long-distance relationships and local ties. Pew Internet and American Life Project. Retrieved April 26, 2008, from http://www.pewinternet.org/pdfs/pip_communities_report.pdf.

Houston, E., & McKirnan, D. (2008). Intimate partner abuse among gay and bisexual men: Risk correlates and health outcomes. *Journal of Urban Health, 84,* 681–690.

Howard, L. M., Hoffbrand, S., Henshaw, C., Boath, L., & Bradley, E. (2005). Antidepressant prevention of postnatal depression. *The Cochrane Database of Systematic Reviews, 2,* art. no. CD004363.

Howe, N., Rinaldi, C., & Recchia, H. (2010). Patterns in mother-child internal state discourse across four contexts. *Merrill-Palmer Quarterly, 56*(1), 1–20.

Howell, E. A., Mora, P. A., Horowitz, C. R., & Leventhal, H. (2005). Racial and ethnic differences in factors associated with early postpartum depressive symptoms. *Obstetrics & Gynecology, 105*(6), 1442–1450.

Howlett, K., Koetters, T., Edrington, J., West, C., Paul, S., Lee, K., Aouizerat, B. E., Wara, W., Swift, P., & Miaskowski, C. (2010). Changes in sexual function on mood and quality of life in patients undergoing radiation therapy for prostate cancer. *Oncology Nursing Forum 37*(1):E58–E66.

Htay, T., Aung, K., Carrick, J., & Papica, R. (2009, September 29). *Premenstrual dysphoric disorder.* Retrieved January 4, 2011, from http://emedicine.medscape.com/article/293257-overview.

Hu, K., He, X., Yu, F., Yuan, X., Hu, W., Liu, C., Zhao, F., & Dou, J. (2011). Immunization with DNA vaccine expressing herpes simplex virus type 1 gD and IL-21 protects against mouse herpes keratitis. *Immunology Invest, 40*(3), 265–278.

Hu, S., Wei, N., Wang, Q., Yan, L., Wei, E., Zhang, M., Hu, J., Huang, M., Zhou, W., & Xu, Y. (2008). Patterns of brain activation during visually evoked sexual arousal differ between homosexual and heterosexual men. *American Journal of Neuroradiology, 29,* 1890–1896.

Hu, X., Cheng, L., Hua, X., & Glasier, A. (2005). Advanced provision of emergency contraception to postnatal women in China makes no difference in abortion rates: A randomized controlled trial. *Contraception, 72,* 111–116.

Huang, C. Y., Yao, C. J., Wang, C., Jiang, J. K., & Chen, G. (2010). Changes of semen quality in Chinese fertile men from 1985 to 2008. *National Journal of Andrology, 16*(8), 684–688.

Huang, J. (2007). Hormones and female sexuality. In M. Tepper & A. F. Owens (Eds.), *Sexual Health, Vol 2: Physical Foundations* (pp. 43–78). Westport, CT: Praeger.

Huang, L. W., Lin, Y. H., Pan, H. S., Seow, K. M., & Lin, C. Y. (In press). Human papillomavirus genotyping as a predictor of high-grade cervical dysplasia in women with mildly cytologic abnormalities: A two-year follow-up report. *Diagnostic Cytopathology.*

Hubacher, D., Finerb, L., & Espeyc, E. (2010). Renewed interest in intrauterine contraception in the United States: Evidence and explanation. *Contraception, 83*(4), 291–294.

Hubayter, Z., & Simon, J. (2008). Testosterone therapy for sexual dysfunction in postmenopausal women. *Climacteric, 11,* 181–191.

Hudson, D. J. (2010). Standing OUT/fitting IN: Identity, appearance, and authenticity in gay and lesbian communities. *Symbolic Interaction, 33*(2), 213–233.

Huff-Hannon, J. (2011). A campaign goes viral to stop 'corrective rape,' used to 'cure' south African women of homosexuality. Retrieved February 20, 2011, from http://www.alternet.org/rights/149491/a_campaign_goes_viral_to_stop_%2527corrective_rape%252C%2527_used_to_%2527cure%2527_south_african_women_of_homosexuality/.

Huffstutter, P. J. (2004). Smallest surviving preemie will go home soon. Retrieved December 23, 2004, from http://www.latimes.come/news/nationworld/nation/la-na-baby22dec,0,3320847,print.story.

Hughes, J. R. (2006). A general review of recent reports on homosexuality and lesbianism. *Sexuality and Disability, 24,* 195–205.

Hughes, L. M., Griffith, R., Aitken, R. (2007). The search for a topical dual action spermicide/microbicide. *Current Medicinal Chemistry, 14,* 775–786.

Hulbert, F. (1989). Barriers to effective listening. *Bulletin for the Association for Business Communication, 52,* 3–5.

Hull, S., Hennessy, M., Bleakley, A., Fishbein, M., & Jordan, A. (2010). Identifying the causal pathways from religiosity to delayed adolescent sexual behavior. *Journal of Sex Research, 19,* 1–11.

Human Genome Project. (2003). How many genes are in the human genome? Retrieved October 1, 2005, from http://www.ornl.gov/sci/techresources/Human_Genome/faq/genenumber.shtml.

Human Rights Campaign. (2009). FBI reports 11 percent increase in victims of hate crimes based on sexual orientation in 2008. Retrieved February 19, 2011, from http://www.hrc.org/issues/hate_crimes/13826.htm.

Human Rights Campaign. (2010). Surrogacy laws and legal considerations. Retrieved

February 24, 2011, from http://www.hrc .org/issues/parenting/surrogacy/2485.htm.

Human Rights Campaign. (2011). Employment non-discrimination act. Retrieved February 16, 2011, from http://www.hrc.org/ laws_and_elections/enda.asp.

Hunt, L. (1993). Introduction: Obscenity and the origins of modernity, 1500–1800. In L. Hunt (Ed.), *The invention of pornography* (pp. 9–45). New York: Zone Books.

Hunt, M. (1974). *Sexual behavior in the 1970's.* New York: Dell.

Hunter, I., Saunders, D., & Williamson, D. (1993). *On pornography: Literature, sexuality and obscenity law.* New York: St. Martin's Press.

Hunter, J. A., Figueredo, A. J., Malamuth, N. M., & Becker, J. V. (2003). Juvenile sex offenders: Toward the development of a typology. *Sexual Abuse: Journal of Research & Treatment, 15*(1), 27–48.

Huober-Zeeb, C., Lawrenz, B., Popovici, R. M., Strowitzki, T., Germeyer, A., Stute, P., & von Wolff, M. (2011). Improving fertility preservation in cancer: Ovarian tissue cryobanking followed by ovarian stimulation can be efficiently combined. *Fertility and Sterility, 95*(1), 342–344.

Huppertz, B. (2011). Placental pathology in pregnancy complications. *Thombosis Research, 127*(Suppl. 3), S96-S99.

Hussain, A., Nicholls, J., & El-Hasani, S. (2010). Technical tips following more than 2000 transabdominal preperitoneal (TAPP) repair of the groin hernia. *Surgical Laparoscopy, Endoscopy, and Percutaneous Techniques, 20*(6), 384–388.

Hutcheon, J. A., Lisonkova, S., & Joseph, K. S. (2011). Epidemiology of pre-eclampsia and the other hypertensive disorders of pregnancy. *Best Practice and Research in Clinical Obstetrics and Gynecology, 25*(4), 391–403.

Hutson J. M., & Hasthorpe S. J. (2005). Testicular descent and cryptorchidism: The state of the art in 2004. *Pediatric Surgery, 40*(2), 297–302.

Hutson, J. M., Baker, M., Terada, M., Zhou, B., & Paxton, G. (1994). Hormonal control of testicular descent and the cause of cryptorchidism. *Reproduction, Fertility and Development, 6*(2), 151–156.

Hutter, M. (1981). *The changing family: Comparative perspective.* New York: Wiley.

Huyghe, E., Delannes, M., Wagner, F., Delaunay, B., Nohra, J., Thoulouzan, M., Shut-Yee, J. Y., Plante, P., Soulie, M., Thonneau, P., & Bachaud, J. M. (2009). Ejaculatory function after permanent 125I prostate brachytherapy for localized prostate cancer. *International Journal of Radiation Oncology, 74*(1), 126–132.

Hwu, J. R., Lin, S. Y., Tsay, S. C., De Clercq, E., Leyssen, P., & Neyts, J. (2011). Coumarin-purine riboficanoside conjugates as new agents against hepatitis C virus. *Journal of Medical Chemistry, 54*, 2114–2126.

Hyde, J., & Mertz, J. (2008). Gender, culture, and mathematics. *Proceedings of the National Academy of Science, 106*(22), 8801–8807.

Ignatius, E., & Kokkonen, M. (2007). Factors contributing to verbal self-disclosure. *Nordic Psychology, 59*(4), 362–391.

Impett, E. A., Beals, K. P., & Peplau, L. A. (2001). Testing the investment model of relationship commitment and stability in a longitudinal study of married couples. *Current Psychology, 20*(4), 312–327.

Incerpi, M. H., Miller, D. A., Samadi, R., Settlage, R. H., & Goodwin, T. M. (1999). Stillbirth evaluation: What tests are needed? *American Journal of Obstetrics and Gynecology, 180*(6 Pt 1), 1595–1596.

International Gay and Lesbian Human Rights Commission. (2010). Middle East and North America. Retrieved August 26, 2011, from http://www.iglhrc.org/cgi-bin/ iowa/region/10.html.

Ireland, M., Slatcher, R., Eastwick, P., Scissors, L., Finkel, E., & Pennebaker, J. (2010). Language style matching predicts relationship initiation and stability. *Communication Reports, 22*(1), 39–44.

Irvine, J. (1990). *Disorders of desire, sex, and gender in modern American sexology.* Philadelphia: Temple University Press.

Irving, C., Basu, A., Richmond, S., Burn, J., & Wren, C. (2008, July 2). Twenty-year trends in prevalence of survival of Down syndrome. *European Journal of Human Genetics.* Retrieved October 14, 2008, from http://www.nature.com/ejhg/journal/ vaop/ncurrent/abs/ejhg2008122a.html.

Irwig, M. S., & Kolukula, S. (2011). Persistent sexual side effects of finasteride for male pattern hair loss. *Journal of Sexual Medicine, 8*(6), 1747–1753.

Isaiah Green, A. (2007). Queer theory and sociology: Locating the subject and the self in sexuality studies. *Sociological Theory, 25*, 26–45.

Isay, R. A. (1989). *Being homosexual.* New York: Farrar, Straus, & Giroux.

Ishak, W., Bokarius, A., Jeffrey, J., Davis, M., & Bakhta, Y. (2010). Disorders of orgasm in women: A literature review of etiology and current treatments. *Journal of Sexual Medicine, 7*(10), 3254–3268.

Ishak, W. W., Berman, D. S., & Peters, A. (2008). Male anorgasmia treated with oxytocin. *Journal of Sexual Medicine, 5*, 1022–1024.

Ishibashi, K. L., Koopmans, J., Curlin, F. A., Alexander, K., & Ross, L. (2008). Paediatricians' attitudes and practices towards HPV vaccination. *Acta Paediatrician, 97*(11), 1550–1556.

Isidori, A., Giannetta, E., Gianfrilli, D., Greco, E., Bonifacio, V., Aversa, A., et al. (2005). Effects of testosterone on sexual function in men: Results of a meta-analysis. *Clinical Endocrinology, 63*, 381–394.

Islam, A., Mitchel, J., Rosen, R., Phillips, N., Ayers, C., Ferguson, D., et al. (2001). Topical alprostadil in the treatment of female sexual arousal disorder. *Journal of Sex and Marital Therapy, 27*(5), 531–540.

Israilov, S., Niv, E., Livne, P. M., Shmeuli, J., Engelstein, D., Segenreich, E., & Baniel, J. (2002). Intracavernous injections for erectile dysfunction in patients with cardiovascular diseases and failure or contraindications for sildenafil citrate. *International Journal of Impotence Research, 14*(1), 38–43.

Ivarsson, B., Fridlund, B., & Sjöberg, T. (2010). Health professionals' views on sexual information following MI. *British Journal of Nursing, 19*(16), 1052–1054.

Iverson, J. S. (1991). A debate on the American home: The antipolygamy controversy, 1880–1890. *Journal of the History of Sexuality, 1*, 585–602.

Jackman, L. P., Williamson, D. A., Netemeyer, R. G., & Anderson, D. A. (1995). Do weight-preoccupied women misinterpret ambiguous stimuli related to body size? *Cognitive Therapy and Research, 19*, 341–355.

Jackson, B. (1998). *Splendid slippers: A thousand years of an erotic tradition.* Berkeley, CA: Ten Speed Press.

Jackson, M. (1984). Sex research and the construction of sexuality: A tool of male supremacy? *Women's Studies International Forum, 7*, 43–51.

Jacobs, S. E., Thomas, W., & Lang, S. (1997). *Two-spirit people: Native American gender identity, sexuality, and spirituality.* Chicago: University of Illinois Press.

Jacquet, S. E., & Surra, C. A. (2001). Parental divorce and premarital couples: Commitment and other relationship characteristics. *Journal of Marriage and Family, 63*(3), 627–639.

Jain, J. K., Minoo, P., Nucatola, D. L., & Felix, J. C. (2005). The effect of nonoxynol-9 on human endometrium. *Contraception, 71*(2), 137–142.

Jakimiuk, A., Fritz, A., Grzybowski, W., Walecka, I., & Lewandowski, P. (2007). Diagnosing and management of iatrogenic moderate and severe ovarian hyperstymulation syndrome in clinical material. *Polish Academy of Sciences, 45*(Suppl. 1), S105–108.

Jamanadas, K. (2008). Sati was started for preserving caste. Retrieved April 8, 2008, from http://www.ambedkar.org/research/Sati_Was_Started_For_Preserving_Caste.htm.

James, S. D. (2011, April 13). J Crew ad with boy's pink toenails creates stir. *ABC News.* Retrieved May 5, 2011, from http://abcnews.go.com/Health/crew-ad-boy-painting-toenails-pink-stirs-transgender/story?id513358903.

Jamieson, D., Kaufman, S., Costello, C., Hillis, S., Marchbanks, P., & Peterson, H. (2002). A comparison of women's regret after vasectomy versus tubal sterilization. *Obstetrics and Gynecology, 99,* 1073–1079.

Jannini, E., Whipple, B., Kingsberg, S., Buisson O., Foldès, & Vardi, Y. (2010).Who's afraid of the g-spot? *Journal of Sexual Medicine, 7*(1 Pt 1), 25–34.

Janus, S. S., & Janus, C. L. (1993). *The Janus report on sexual behavior.* New York: Wiley.

Japsen, B. (2003). Viagra faces 1st rivals by year's end. Retrieved July 18, 2003, from http://www.webprowire.com/summaries/5357111.html.

Jaworowicz, D. (2007). Novel risk factors for breast cancer. Presented at the 40th Annual Meeting of the Society for Epidemiologic Research, Boston, MA.

Jaworski, A., & Coupland, J. (2005). Othering in gossip: "You go out you have a laugh and you can pull yeah okay but like...." *Language and Society, 34,* 667–695.

Jayne, C. (1981). A two-dimensional model of female sexual response. *Journal of Sex and Marital Therapy, 7,* 3–30.

Jeary, K. (2005). Sexual abuse and sexual offending against elderly people: A focus on perpetrators and victims. *Journal of Forensic Psychiatry & Psychology, 16*(2), 328–343.

Jelovsek, J. E., Walters, M. D., & Barber, M. D. (2008). Psychosocial impact of chronic vulvovaginal conditions. *Journal of Reproductive Medicine, 53,* 75–82.

Jemal, A., Murray, T. Ward, E., Samuels, A., Tiwari, R. C., Ghafoor, A., Feuer, E. J., &

Thun, M. J. (2005). Cancer statistics, 2005. *CA: A Cancer Journal for Clinicians, 55,* 10–30.

Jenkins, D., & Johnston, L. (2004). Unethical treatment of gay and lesbian people with conversion therapy. *Families in Society, 85*(4), 557–561.

Jenkins, S. (2009). Marital splits and income changes over the longer term. In M. Brynin & J. Ermisch (Eds.), *Changing relationships.* London: Routledge.

Jenkins, W. (2010). Can anyone tell me why I'm gay? What research suggests regarding the origins of sexual orientation. *North American Journal of Psychology, 12*(2), 279–296.

Jenness, V. (1990). From sex as sin to sex as work: COYOTE and the reorganization of prostitution as a social problem. *Social Problems, 37,* 403–420.

Jensen, J. T. (2008). A continuous regimen of levonorgestrel/ethinyl estradiol for contraception and elimination of menstruation. *Drugs Today, 44,* 183–195.

Jern, P., Santtila, P., Johansson, A., Varjonen, M., Witting, K., von der Pahlen, B., & Sandnabba, N. K. (2009). Evidence for a genetic etiology to ejaculatory dysfunction. *International Journal of Impotence Research, 21*(1), 62–67.

Jetter, A. (1991). Faye's crusade. *Vogue,* 147–151, 202–204.

Jewkes, R., Abrahams, N., Mathews, S., Seedat, M., Niekerk, A., Suffla, S., & Ratele, K. (2009a). Preventing rape and violence in South Africa: Call for leadership in a new agenda for action. MRC Policy Brief. Retrieved April 30, 2011, from http://www.mrc.ac.za/gender/prev_rapedd041209.pdf.

Jewkes, R., Sikweyiya, Y., Morrell, R., & Dunkle, K. (2009b). Understanding men's health and use of violence: Interface of rape and HIV in South Africa. Medical Research Council of South Africa. Retrieved April 30, 2011, from http://gender.care2share.wikispaces.net/file/view/MRC-1SA1men1and1rape1ex1summary-1june2009.pdf.

Jha, A. (2010, October 4). British IVF pioneer Robert Edwards wins Nobel prize for medicine. Retrieved March 1, 2011, from http://www.guardian.co.uk/science/2010/oct/04/ivf-pioneer-robert-edwards-nobel-prize-medicine.

Jha, P., Kumar, R., Vasa, P., Dhingra, N., Thiruchelvam, D., & Moineddin, R. (2006). Low male-to-female sex ratio of children born in India: National survey of 1.1 million households. *The Lancet, 367,* 211–218.

Jha, R. K., Jha, P. K., & Guha, S. K. (2009). Smart RISUG: A potential new contraceptive and its magnetic field-mediated sperm interaction. *International Journal of Nanomedicine, 4,* 55–64.

Jick, S., & Hernandez, R. (2011). Risk of nonfatal venous thromboembolism in women using oral contraceptives containing drospirenone compared with contraceptives containing levonorgestrel. *British Medical Journal.* Retrieved June 5, 2011, from http://www.bmj.com/content/342/bmj.d2151.full.

Johannsen, T., Ripa, C., Carlsen, E., Starup, J., Nielsen, O., Schwartz, M., Drzewiecki, K., Mortensen, E., & Main, K. (2010). Long-term gynecological outcomes in women with congenital adrenal hyperplasia due to 21-hydroxylase deficiency. *International Journal of Pediatric Endocrinology.* Retrieved November 13, 2010, from http://www.ncbi.nlm.nih.gov/pmc/articles/PMC2963122/.

Johansen, R. E. B. (2007). Experiencing sex in exile—Can genitals change their gender? In Y. Hernlund & B. Shell-Duncan (Eds.), *Transcultural bodies: Female cutting in global context* (pp. 248–277). New Brunswick, NJ: Rutgers University Press.

Johansson, A., Sundbom, E., Hojerback, T., & Bodlund, O. (2010). A five-year follow-up study of Swedish adults with gender identity disorder. *Archives of Sexual Behavior, 39*(6), 1429–1437.

John, E. M., Miron, A., Gong, G., Phipps, A. I., Felberg, A., Li, R. P., et al. (2007). Prevalence of pathogenic BRCA1 mutation carriers in 5 U.S. racial/ethnic groups. *Journal of the American Medical Association, 298,* 2910–2911.

Johnson, A. J. (2009). A functional approach to interpersonal argument: Differences between public-issue and personal-issue arguments. *Communication Reports, 22*(1), 13.

Johnson, A. M. (2001a). Popular belief in gender-based communication differences and relationship success. *Dissertation Abstracts,* University of Massachusetts, Amherst, #0–599–95739–5.

Johnson, A. M., Mercer, C. H., Erens, B., Copas, A. J., McManus, S., Wellings, K., Fenton, K. A., Korovessis, C., Macdowall, W., Nanchahal, K., Purdon, S., & Field, J. (2001). Sexual behaviour in Britain: Partnerships, practices, and HIV-risk behaviours. *Lancet, 358,* 1835–1842.

Johnson, H., Ollus, N., & Nevala, S. (2008). *Violence against women: An international perspective.* New York: Springer Science and Business.

Johnson, J. (2001b). *Male multiple orgasm: Step by step* (4th ed). Jack Johnson Seminars.

Johnson, J., & Alford, R. (1987). The adolescent quest for intimacy: Implications for the therapeutic alliance. *Journal of Social Work and Human Sexuality* (Special issue: Intimate Relationships), *5,* 55–66.

Johnson, K., Gill, S., Reichman, V., Tassinary, L. (2007). Swagger, sway, and sexuality: Judging sexual orientation from body motion and morphology. *Journal of Personality and Social Psychology, 93*(3), 321–334.

Johnson, K. C., & Daviss, B. A. (2005). Outcomes of planned home births with certified professional midwives: Large prospective study in North America. *British Medical Journal, 330*(7505), 1416–1420.

Johnson, L. A. (2005). Experts urge routine HIV tests for all. Retrieved February 11, 2005, from http://abcnews.go.com/Health/wireStory?id=485527.

Johnson, N. (2010, September 11). For-profit hospitals leading in cesareans. *Daily News Los Angeles.* Retrieved September 13, 2010, from http://www.dailynews.com/news/ci_16051899.

Johnson, R., & Murad, H. (2009). Gynecomastia: Pathophysiology, evaluation, and management. *Mayo Clinic Proceedings, 84*(11), 1010–1015.

Johnson, S. E. (1996). *Lesbian sex: An oral history.* Tallahassee, FL: Naiad Press.

Jonas, S., Bebbington, P., McManus, S., Meltzer, H., Jenkins, R., Kuipers, E., Cooper, C., King, M., & Brugha, T. (2011). Sexual abuse and psychiatric disorder in England: Results from the 2007 adult psychiatric morbidity survey. *Psychological Medicine, 41*(4), 709–720.

Jones, J. H. (1997). *Alfred C. Kinsey: A public/private life.* New York: W. W. Norton.

Jones, R. (1984). *Human reproduction and sexual behavior.* Englewood Cliffs, NJ: Prentice Hall.

Jones, R., & Kooistra, K. (2011). Abortion incidence and access to services in the U.S., 2008. *Perspectives in Sex and Reproductive Health, 43*(1), 41–50.

Jones, R., Darroch, J., & Singh, S. (2005). Religious differentials in the sexual and reproductive behaviors of young women in the United States. *Journal of Adolescent Health, 36*(4), 279–288.

Jones, R., Finer, L., & Singh, S. (2010, May). Characteristics of U.S. abortion patients, 2008. New York: Alan Guttmacher Institute. Retrieved June 5, 2011, from http://www.guttmacher.org/pubs/US-Abortion-Patients.pdf.

Jones, R. K., Moore, A. M., & Frohwirth, L. F. (2011). Perceptions of male knowledge and support among U.S. women obtaining abortions. *Women's Health Issues, 21*(2), 117–123.

Jongpipan, J., & Charoenkwan, K. (2007). Sexual function after radical hysterectomy for early-stage cervical cancer. *Journal of Sexual Medicine, 4,* 1659–1665.

Jordan, J. (1997). User buys: Why men buy sex. *Australian and New Zealand Journal of Criminology, 30,* 55–71.

Jorgensen, C. (1967). *Christine Jorgenson: Personal biography.* New York: Erickson.

Joung, I. M., Stronks, K., & van de Mheen, H. (1995). Health behaviours explain part of the differences in self-reported health associated with partner/marital status in the Netherlands. *Journal of Epidemiology and Community Health, 49*(5), 482–488.

Juntti, S. A., Tollkuhn, J., Wu, M. V., Fraser, E., Soderborg, T., Tan, S., Honda, S., Harada, N., & Shah, N. M. (2010). The androgen receptor governs the execution, but not the programming, of male sexual and territorial behavior. *Neuron, 66*(2), 167–169.

Kaats, G. R., & Davis, K. E. (1971). Effects of volunteer biases in studies of sexual behavior and attitudes. *Journal of Sex Research, 7,* 26–34.

Kaestle, C., & Allen, K. (In press). The role of masturbation in healthy sexual development: Perceptions of young adults. *Archives of Sexual Behavior,* Retrieved February 4, 2011, from http://www.springerlink.com/content/a61r62w728335l00/.

Kahn, Y. (1989–90). Judaism and homosexuality: The traditionalist/progressive debate. *Journal of Homosexuality, 18,* 47–82.

Kahr, B. (2008). *Who's been sleeping in your head: The secret world of sexual fantasies.* New York: Basic Books.

Kain, E. L. (1987). A note on the integration of AIDS into the Sociology of Human Sexuality. *Teaching Sociology, 15,* 320–323.

Kakuchi, S. (2005). New museum documents lives of Japan's "comfort women." Retrieved November 6, 2005, from http://www.womensenews.org/article.cfm?aid=2509.

Kalsi, J., Thum, M. Y., Muneer, A., Pryor, J., Abdullah, H., & Minhas, S. (2011). Analysis of the outcome of intracytoplasmic sperm injection. *British Journal of Urology, 107*(7), 1124–1128.

Kalu, E., Thum, M., & Abdalla, H. (2011). Prognostic value of first IVF cycle on success of a subsequent cycle. *Journal of Assisted Reproductive Genetics, 28*(4), 379–382.

Kalyani, R., Basavaraj, P. B., & Kumar, M. L. (2007). Factors influencing quality of semen: A two year prospective study. *Indian Journal of Pathology and Microbiology, 50,* 890–895.

Kamali, H. (2010, December 20). Personal communication.

Kaminer, W. (1992, November). Feminists against the first amendment. *Atlantic Monthly,* pp. 111–117.

Kanayama, G., Hudson, J. I., & Pope, H. G., Jr. (2010). Illicit anabolic-androgenic steroid use. *Hormones and Behavior, 58*(1), 111–121.

Kandaraki, E., Chatzigeorgiou, A., Livadas, S., Palioura, E., Economou, F., Koutsilieris, M., Palimeri, S., Panidis, D., & Diamanti-Kandarakis, E. (2011). Endocrine disruptors and polycystic ovary syndrome: Elevated serum levels of bisphenol A in women with PCOS. *Journal of Clinical Endocrinology and Metabolism, 96*(3), E480–E484.

Kantor, L. (1992). Scared chaste? Fear based educational curricula. *SIECUS Reports, 21,* 1–15.

Kaplan, G. (1977). Circumcision: An overview. *Current Problems in Pediatrics, 1,* 1–33.

Kaplan, H., Kohl, R., Pomeroy, W., Offit, A., & Hogan, B. (1974). Group treatment of premature ejaculation. *Archives of Sexual Behavior, 3*(5), 443–452.

Kaplan, H., Sadock, B., & Grebb, J. (1994). *Synopsis of psychiatry* (7th ed.). Baltimore, MD: Williams and Wilkins.

Kaplan, H. S. (1974). *The new sex therapy.* New York: Bruner/Mazel.

Kaplan, L. J. (1991). Women masquerading as women. In G. I. Fogel & W. A. Meyers (Eds.), *Perversions and near-perversions in clinical practice: New psychoanalytic perspectives* (pp. 127–152). New Haven, CT: Yale University Press.

Kaplan, S. A. (2009). Side effects of alpha-blocker use: Retrograde ejaculation. *Reviews in Urology, 11*(Suppl. 1), S14-S18.

Kaplowitz, P. B. (2008). Link between body fat and the timing of puberty. *Pediatrics, 121*(Suppl 3), S208–217.

Kaplowitz, P. B., Slora, E. J., Wasserman, R. C., Pedlow, S. E., & Herman-Giddens, M. E. (2001). Earlier onset of puberty in girls: Relation to increased body mass index and race. *Pediatrics, 2108*(2), 347–354.

Kapoor, S. (2008). Testicular torsion: A race against time. *International Journal of Clinical Practices, 62,* 821–827.

Kapsimalakou, S., Grande-Nagel, I., Simon, M., Fischer, D., Thill, M., & Stökelhuber, B. (2010). Breast abscess following nipple piercing: A case report and review of the literature. *Archives of Gynecology and Obstetrics, 282*(6), 623–626.

Karatas, O., Baltaci, G., Ilerisoy, Z., Bayrak, O., Cimentepe, E., Irmak, R., & Unal, D. (2010). The evaluation of clitoral blood flow and sexual function in elite female athletes. *Journal of Sexual Medicine, 7*(3), 1185–1189.

Karlsson, A., Sterlund, A., & Forss, N. (2011). Pharyngeal chlamydia trachomatis is not uncommon any more. *Scandinavian Journal of Infectious Disease, 43,* 344–348.

Karniol, R. (2001). Adolescent females' idolization of male media stars as a transition into sexuality. *Sex Roles, 44*(1–2), 61–77.

Kaschak, E., & Tiefer, L. (2001). *A new view of women's sexual problems.* Binghamton, NY: Haworth Press.

Kask, A. S., Chen, X., Marshak, J. O., Dong, L., Saracino, M., Chen, D., Jarrahian, C., Kendall, M. A., & Koelle, D. M. (2010). DNA vaccine delivery by densely-packed and short microprojection arrays to skin protects against vaginal HSV-2 challenge. *Vaccine, 28*(47), 7483–7491.

Kaslow, F. (2000). *Handbook of couple and family forensics: A sourcebook for mental health and legal professionals.* Hoboken, NJ: John Wiley & Sons Inc.

Kassler, W. J., & Cates, W. (1992). The epidemiology and prevention of sexually transmitted diseases. *Urologic Clinics of North America, 19,* 1–12.

Katz, M. H., Schwarcz, S. K., Kellogg, T. A., Klausner, J. D., Dilley, J. W., Gibson, S., et al. (2002). Impact of highly active antiretroviral treatment on HIV seroincidence among men who have sex with men. *American Journal of Public Health, 92*(3), 388–395.

Kaufman, B. S., Kaminsky, S. J., Rackow, E. C., & Weil, M. H. (1987). Adult respiratory distress syndrome following orogenital sex during pregnancy. *Critical Care Medicine, 15,* 703–704.

Kaufman, M. (2005). FDA investigates blindness in Viagra users. Retrieved November 15, 2005, from http://www.washingtonpost.com/wp-dyn/content/article/2005/05/27/AR2005052701246_pf.html.

Kaunitz, A. (2002). Current concepts regarding use of DMPA. *Journal of Reproductive Medicine, 47*(9 Suppl.), 785–789.

Kaunitz, A. M., Arias, R., & McClung, M. (2008). Bone density recovery after depot medroxyprogesterone acetate injectable contraception use. *Contraception, 77,* 67–76.

Kaushic, C., Roth, K. L., Anipindi, V., & Xiu, F. (2011). Increased prevalence of sexually transmitted viral infections in women: The role of female sex hormones in regulating susceptibility and immune responses. *Journal of Reproductive Immunology, 88*(2), 204–209.

Kavanaugh, M. L., & Schwarz, E. B. (2008). Counseling about and use of emergency contraception in the United States. *Perspectives on Sexual Reproductive Health, 40,* 81–86.

Kaye, K. (2007). Sex and the unspoken in male street prostitution. *Journal of Homosexuality, 53,* 37–73.

Kayongo-Male, D., & Onyango, P. (1984). *The sociology of the African family.* London: Longman.

Kazemi-Saleh, D., Pishgou, B., Assari, S., & Tavallaii, S. (2007). Fear of sexual intercourse in patients with coronary artery disease: A pilot study of associated morbidity. *Journal of Sexual Medicine, 4,* 1619–1625.

Keane, H. (2004). Disorders of desire: Addiction and problems of intimacy. *Journal of Medical Humanities, 25*(3), 189–197.

Keasler, M. (2006). *Love hotels.* San Francisco: Chronicle Books.

Keegan, J. (2001). The neurobiology, neuropharmacology and pharmacological treatment of the paraphilias and compulsive sexual behavior. *Canadian Journal of Psychiatry, 46*(1), 26–33.

Keller, J. (2011). Facebook adds same-sex relationship statuses. *The Atlantic.* Retrieved February 18, 2011, from http://www.theatlantic.com/technology/archive/2011/02/facebook-adds-same-sex-relationship-statuses/71431/.

Keller, J. C. (2005). Straight talk about the gay gene. *Science & Spirit, 16,* 21.

Kelly, A. (2009, March 12). Raped and killed for being a lesbian: South Africa ignores 'corrective' attacks. *The Guardian.* Retrieved April 30, 2011, from http://www.guardian.co.uk/world/2009/mar/12/eudy-simelane-corrective-rape-south-africa.

Kelly, B., Leader, A., Mittermaier, D., Hornik, R., & Cappella, J. (2009). The HPV vaccine and the media: How has the topic been covered and what are the effects on knowledge about the virus and cervical cancer? *Patient Education and Counseling, 77,* 308–313.

Kelly, J. M. (2005). *Zest for life: Lesbians' experiences of menopause.* North Melbourne, Australia: Spinifex Press.

Kelly, M. P., Strassberg, D. S., & Kircher, J. R. (1990). Attitudinal and experiential correlates of anorgasmia. *Archives of Sexual Behavior, 19,* 165–177.

Kelly, R. J., Wood, J., Gonzalez, L., MacDonald, V., & Waterman, J. (2002). Effects of mother-son incest and positive perceptions of sexual abuse experiences on the psychosocial adjustment of clinic-referred men. *Child Abuse and Neglect, 26*(4), 425–441.

Kelly-Vance, L., Anthis, K. S., & Needelman, H. (2004). Assisted reproduction versus spontaneous conception: A comparison of the developmental outcomes in twins. *Journal of Genetic Psychology, 165*(2), 157–168.

Kempeneers, P., Andrianne, R., & Mormont, C. (2004). Penile prosthesis, sexual satisfaction and representation of male erotic value. *Sexual & Relationship Therapy, 19*(4), 379–392.

Kendrick, W. M. (1987). *The secret museum: Pornography in modern culture.* New York: Viking.

Kennedy, H. (2002). Research and commentaries on Richard von Krafft-Ebing nand Karl Heinrich Ulrichs. *Journal of Homosexuality, 42*(1), 165–178.

Kennedy, M. A., & Gorzalka, B. B. (2002). Asian and non-Asian attitudes toward rape, sexual harassment and sexuality. *Sex Roles, 46*(7–8), 227–238.

Kerckhoff, A. (1964). Patterns of homogamy and the field of eligibles. *Social Forces, 42*(3), 289–297.

Kerr, D., & Capaldi, D. (2011). Young men's intimate partner violence and relationship functioning: Long-term outcomes associated with suicide attempt and aggression in adolescence. *Psychological Medicine, 41*(4), 759–769.

Kerrigan, D., Mobley, S., Rutenberg, N., Fisher, A., & Weiss, E. (2000). The female condom: Dynamics of use in urban Zimbabwe. New York: The Population Council. Retrieved July 24, 2008, from http://www.popcouncil.org/pdfs/horizons/fcz.pdf.

Kershaw, S. (2009, October 15). Rethinking the older woman-young man relationship. *New York Times.* Retrieved October 15,

2009, from http://www.nytimes.com/2009/10/15/fashion/15women.html.

Kertzner, R. M., Meyer, I. H., Frost, D. M., & Stirratt, M. J. (2009). Social and psychological well-being in lesbians, gay men, and bisexuals: The effects of race, gender, age, and sexual identity. *American Journal of Orthopsychiatry, 79*(4), 500–510.

Khadivzadeh, T., & Parsai, S. (2005). Effect of exclusive breastfeeding and complementary feeding on infant growth and morbidity. *Eastern Mediterranean Health Journal, 10*(3), 289–294.

Kidman, R., Petrow, S., & Heymann, S. (2007). Africa's orphan crisis: Two community-based models of care. *AIDS Care, 19*(3), 326–329.

Kilgallon, S., & Simmons, L. (2005). Image content influences men's semen quality. *Biology Letters, 1*(3), 253–255.

Killick, S., Leary, C., Trussell, J., & Guthrie, K. (2010). Sperm content of pre-ejaculatory fluid. *Human Fertility, 14*(1), 48–52.

Kim, J., & Hatfield, E. (2004). Love types and subjective well-being: A cross-cultural study. *Social Behavior and Personality, 32,* 173–182.

Kim, K., & Smith, P. K. (1999). Family relations in early childhood and reproductive development. *Journal of Reproductive and Infant Psychology, 17*(2), 133–149.

Kim, Y., Yang, S., Lee, J., Jung, T., & Shim, H. (2008). Usefulness of a malleable penile prosthesis in patients with a spinal cord injury. *International Journal of Urology, 15*(10), 919–923.

Kimberlin, D. W. (2007). Herpes simplex virus infections of the newborn. *Seminars in Perinatology, 31*(1), 19–25.

Kimmel, M. S., & Plante, R. F. (2007). Sexualities. *Contexts, 6,* 63–65.

King, M., & Bartlett, A. (2005). What same sex civil partnerships may mean for health. *Journal of Epidemiology & Community Health, 60,* 188–191.

King, M., Semlyen, J., Tai, S., Killaspy, H., Osborn, D., Popelyuk, D., & Nazareth, I. (2008). A systematic review of mental disorder, suicide, and deliberate self harm in lesbian, gay and bisexual people. *BMC Psychiatry, 8,* 70. Retrieved January 24, 2011, from http://www.biomedcentral.com/1471-244X/8/70.

King, P., & Boyatzis, C. (2004). Exploring adolescent spiritual and religious development: Current and future theoretical and empirical perspectives. *Applied Developmental Science, 8,* 2–6.

Kingsberg, S. A., & Knudson, G. (2011). Female sexual disorders: Assessment, diagnosis, and treatment. *Urological Clinics of North America, 34*(4), 497–506.

Kinkade, S., & Meadows, S. (2005). Does neonatal circumcision decrease morbidity? *The Journal of Family Practice, 54*(1), 81–82.

Kinnunen, L. H., Moltz, H., Metz, J., & Cooper, M. (2004). Differential brain activation in exclusively homosexual and heterosexual men produced by the selective serotonin reuptake inhibitor, fluoxetine. *Brain Research, 1024*(1–2), 251–254.

Kinsey, A., Pomeroy, W. B., & Martin, C. E. (1948). *Sexual behavior in the human male.* Philadelphia: Saunders.

Kinsey, A. C., Pomeroy, W., Martin, C. E., & Gebhard, P. (1953). *Sexual behavior in the human female.* Philadelphia: Saunders.

Kirby, D. (1992). Sexuality education: It can reduce unprotected intercourse. *SIECUS Report, 21,* 19–25.

Kirby, D. (2001, May). Emerging answers: Research findings on programs to reduce teen pregnancy. National Campaign to Prevent Teen Pregnancy.

Kirby, D. (2007). Emerging answers: 2007. Research findings on programs to reduce teen pregnancy and sexually transmitted diseases. Washington, DC: National Campaign to Prevent Teen and Unplanned Pregnancy. Retrieved May 29, 2008, from http://www.thenationalcampaign.org/EA2007/EA2007_full.pdf.

Kirsch, A. T. (1985). Text and context: Buddhist sex roles/culture of gender revisited. *American Ethnologist, 12*(2), 302–320.

Kitazawa, K. (1994). Sexuality issues in Japan. *SIECUS Report,* 7–11.

Kito, M. (2005). Self-disclosure in romantic relationships and friendships among American and Japanese college students. *Journal of Social Psychology, 145,* 127–140.

Klaas, M. (2003). *Klaas Action Review Newsletter, 9*(1). Retrieved May 23, 2003, from http://www.pollyklaas.org/newsletter.htm.

Klausen, P. (2007). *Trends in birth defect research.* Hauppauge, NY: Nova Science Publishers.

Klein, C., & Gorzalka, B. (2009). Sexual functioning in transsexuals following hormone therapy and genital surgery: A review. *Journal of Sexual Medicine, 6*(11), 2922–2932.

Klein, F. (1978). *The bisexual option: A concept of one-hundred percent intimacy.* New York: Arbor House.

Klein, F. (1990). The need to view sexual orientation as a multivariable dynamic process: A theoretical perspective. In D. P. McWhirter, S. A. Sanders, & J. M. Reinisch (Eds.), *Homosexuality/heterosexuality: Concepts of sexual orientation* (pp. 277–282). New York: Oxford University Press.

Klein, F. (1993). *The bisexual option* (2nd ed.). Philadelphia: Haworth Press.

Klein, W., Geaghan, T., & MacDonald, T. (2007). Unplanned sexual activity as a consequence of alcohol use: A prospective study of risk perceptions and alcohol use among college freshman. *Journal of American College Health, 56,* 317–323.

Kleinfeld, J. (2002). Six degrees: Urban myth? *Psychology Today.* Retrieved February 10, 2008, from http://psychologytoday.com/articles/pto-20020301-000038.html.

Kleinplatz, P., & Moser, C. (2006). *Sadomasochism: Powerful pleasures,* Routledge, NY: Haworth Press.

Klimkiewicz, J. (2008, April 24). Outsourcing labor. *Hartford Courant,* p. D1–D4.

Kline, P. (1987). Sexual deviation: Psychoanalytic research and theory. In G. D. Wilson (Ed.), *Variant sexuality: Research and theory* (pp. 150–175). Baltimore: Johns Hopkins University Press.

Klonoff-Cohen, H., Natarajan, L., & Chen, R. (2006). A prospective study of the effects of female and male marijuana use on in vitro fertilization (IVF) and gamete intrafallopian transfer (GIFT) outcomes. *American Journal of Obstetrics and Gynecology, 194*(2), 369–376.

Kluft, R. (2010). Ramifications of incest. *Psychiatric Times, 27*(12), 48–56.

Kluger, J. (2008, January 17). The science of romance: Why we love. *Time Magazine.* Retrieved August 17, 2008, from http://www.time.com/time/magazine/article/0,9171,1704672-2,00.html.

Kluger, N. (2010). Body art and pregnancy. *European Journal of Obstetrics and Gynecological Reproductive Biology, 153*(1), 3–7.

Knaapen, L., & Weisz, G. (2008). The biomedical standardization of premenstrual syndrome. *Studies in History and the Philosophy of Biology and Biomedical Science, 39,* 120–134.

Knapp, M. L., & Hall, J. A. (2005). *Nonverbal communication in human interaction* (6th ed.). Belmont, CA: Wadsworth.

Knight, S. J., & Latini, D. M. (2009). Sexual side effects and prostate cancer treatment decisions: Patient information needs and preferences. *Cancer Journal, 15*(1), 41–44.

Knoester, M., Helmerhorst, F., Vandenbroucke, J., van der Westerlaken, L., Walther, F., Veen, S., et al. (2008). Perinatal outcome, health growth, and medical care utilization of 5- to 8- year old intracytoplasmic sperm injection singletons. *Fertility and Sterility, 89,* 1133–1146.

Knöfler, T., & Imhof, M. (2007). Does sexual orientation have an impact on nonverbal behavior in interpersonal communication? *Journal of Nonverbal Behavior, 31,* 189–204.

Knox, D., Breed, R., & Zusman, M. (2007). College men and jealousy. *College Student Journal, 41,* 435–444.

Knox, D., Zusman, M. E., Buffington, C., & Hemphill, G. (2000). Interracial dating attitudes among college students. *College Student Journal, 434*(1), 69–72.

Knox, D., Zusman, M. E., & Mabon, L. (1999). Jealousy in college student relationships. *College Student Journal, 33*(3), 328–329.

Knox, D., Zusman, M., & McNeely, A. (2008). University student beliefs about sex: Men vs. women. *College Student Journal, 42,* 181–186.

Ko, D. (2001). *In every step a lotus: Shoes for bound feet.* Berkeley: University of California Press.

Ko, D. (2007). *Cinderella's sisters: A revisionist history of footbinding.* Berkeley: University of California Press.

Koch, W. (2005). Despite high-profile cases, sex-offense crimes decline. Retrieved October 9, 2005, from http://www.usatoday.com/news/nation/2005-08-24-sex-crimes-cover_x. htm?POE=NEWISVA.

Koci, A. F. (2004). Marginality, abuse and adverse health outcomes in women. *Dissertations Abstracts International,* 0419–4217.

Kocieniewski, D. (2010, October 26). Acne cream? Tax-sheltered. Breast pump? No. *New York Times.* Retrieved February 24, 2011, from http://www.nytimes.com/2010/10/27/business/27breast.html.

Koda, T., Ishida, T., Rehm, M., & Andre, E. (2009). Avatar culture: Cross-cultural evaluations of avatar facial expressions. *Artificial Intelligence & Society, 24,* 237–250.

Koerner, A., & Fitzpatrick, M. (1997). Family type and conflict: The impact of conversation orientation and conformity orientation on conflict in the family. *Communication Studies, 48,* 59–75.

Koh, A. S., Gomez, C. A., Shade, S., & Rowley, E. (2005). Sexual risk factors among self-identified lesbians, bisexual women, and heterosexual women accessing primary care settings. *Sexually Transmitted Diseases, 32*(9), 563–569.

Kohl, J. V., & Francoeur, R. (2002). *The scent of eros: Mysteries of odor in human sexuality.* Lincoln, NE: iUniverse, Author's Choice Press.

Kohler, P. K., Manhart, L. E., & Lafferty, W. E. (2008). Abstinence-only and comprehensive sex education and the initiation of sexual activity and teen pregnancy. *Journal of Adolescent Health, 42,* 344–351.

Kohn, C., Hasty, S., & Henderson, C. W. (2002, September 3). Study confirms infection from receptive oral sex occurs rarely. *AIDS Weekly,* 20–22.

Kolata, G. (2007, August 12). The myth, the math, the sex. *New York Times.* Retrieved October 14, 2010, from http://www.nytimes.com/2007/08/12/weekinreview/12kolata.html.

Kon, I. S. (2004). Russia. In R. T. Francoeur & R. J. Noonan (Eds.), *The Continuum International encyclopedia of sexuality* (pp. 888–908). New York/London: Continuum International.

Kong, S., & Bernstein, K. (2009). Childhood trauma as a predictor of eating psychopathology and its mediating variables in patients with eating disorders. *Journal of Clinical Nursing, 18*(13), 1897–1907.

Kontula, O., & Haavio-Mannila, E. (2004). Finland. In R. T. Francoeur & R. J. Noonan (Eds.), *The Continuum International encyclopedia of sexuality* (pp. 381–411). New York/London: Continuum International.

Kopelman, L. (1988). The punishment concept of disease. In C. Pierce & D. Vandeveer (Eds.), *AIDS, ethics, and public policy.* Belmont, CA: Wadsworth.

Koppel, N. (2010). Appeals court rejects Florida's ban on gay adoptions. *Wall Street Journal,* A7.

Koropeckyj-Cox, T., Romano, V., & Moras, A. (2007). Through the lenses of gender, race, and class. Students' perceptions of childless/childfree individuals and couples. *Sex Roles, 56,* 415–428.

Kosfeld, M., Heinrichs, M., Zak, P. J., Fischbacher, U., & Fehr, E. (2005). Oxytocin increases trust in humans. *Nature, 435,* 676–676.

Koskimäki, J., Shiri, R., Tammela, T., Häkkinen, J., Hakama, M., & Auvinen, A. (2008). Regular intercourse protects against erectile dysfunction: Tampere aging male urologic study. *American Journal of Medicine, 121,* 592–596.

Kotchick, B. A., Dorsey, S., & Miller, K. S. (1999). Adolescent sexual risk-taking behavior in single-parent ethnic minority families. *Journal of Family Psychology, 13*(1), 93–102.

Kreider, R. M. (2005). Number, timing and duration of marriages and divorces: 2001. *Current Population Reports* (P70–97). Washington, DC: U.S. Census Bureau.

Kreuter, M., Siosteen, A., & Biering-Sorensen, F. (2008). Sexuality and sexual life in women with spinal cord injury: A controlled study. *Journal of Rehabilitative Medicine, 40,* 61–69.

Kreuter, M., Taft, C., Siösteen, A., & Biering-Sørensen, F. (2011). Women's sexual functioning and sex life after spinal cord injury. *Spinal Cord, 49*(1), 154–160.

Kriebs, J. (2008). Understanding herpes simplex virus: Transmission, diagnosis, and considerations in pregnancy management. *Journal of Midwifery Women's Health, 53,* 202–208.

Krikorian, T. (2004, February 25). Hymenoplasty surgery result of a sexist society. *Spartan Daily.* Retrieved January 13, 2011, from http://www.urogyn.org/documents/Hymenoplasty_surgery_result_of_sexist_society.pdf.

Krilov, L. (1991). What do you know about genital warts? *Medical Aspects of Human Sexuality, 25,* 39–41.

Kristof, N. D. (1996, February 11). Who needs love! In Japan, many couples don't. *New York Times,* p. A1.

Krone, N., Hanley, N. A., & Arlt, W. (2007). Age-specific changes in sex steroid biosynthesis and sex development. *Best Practice & Research: Clinical Endocrinology Metabolism, 21,* 393–401.

Krone, N., Hanley, N., & Arlt, W. (2007). Age-specific changes in sex steroid biosynthesis and sex development. *Clinical Endocrinology and Metabolism, 21*(3), 393–401.

Krstic, Z. D., Smoljanic, Z., Vukanic, D., Varinac, D., & Janiic, G. (2000). True hermaphroditism: 10 years' experience. *Pediatric Surgery International, 16*(8), 580–583.

Krüger, T., Schiffer, B., Eikermann, M., Haake, P., Gizewski, E., & Schedlowsk, M. (2006). Serial neurochemical measurement of cerebrospinal fluid during the human sexual response cycle. *European Journal of Neuroscience, 24,* 3445–3452.

Kuczkowski, K. M. (2006). Labor analgesia for the parturient with lumbar tattoos: What does an obstetrician need to know? *Archives of Gynecology and Obstetrics, 274,* 310–312.

Kuefler, M. (2006). *The Boswell thesis: Essays on Christianity, social tolerance, and homosex-*

uality. Chicago: University of Chicago Press.

Kuliev, A., & Verlinsky, Y. (2008). Impact of preimplantation genetic diagnosis for chromosomal disorders on reproductive outcome. *Reproductive Biomedical Online, 16*, 9–10.

Kumar, S., Roy, S., Chaudhury, K., Sen, P., & Guha, S. K. (2008). Study of the microstructural properties of RISUG—a newly developed male contraceptive. *Journal of Biomedical Materials Research, 86*(1), 154–161.

Kunin, C. M. (1997) *Urinary tract infections: Detection, prevention and management.* (5th ed.) Baltimore: Williams & Wilkins.

Kunkel, A. W., & Burleson, B. R. (1998). Social support and the emotional lives of men and women: An assessment of the different cultures perspective. In D. Canary & K. Dindia (Eds.), *Sex differences and similarities in communication: Critical essays and empirical investigations of sex and gender in interaction* (pp. 101–125). Mahwah, NJ: Lawrence Erlbaum Associates.

Kunkel, D., Eyal, K., Finnerty, K., Biely, E., & Donnerstein, E. (2005). Sex on TV4. Retrieved November 9, 2005, from http://www.kff.org/entmedia/upload/Sex-on-TV-4-Full-Report.pdf.

Kurdek, L. (2004). Are gay and lesbian cohabiting couples really different from heterosexual married couples? *Journal of Marriage and Family, 66*, 880–900.

Kurdek, L. A. (2006). Differences between partners from heterosexual, gay, and lesbian cohabiting couples. *Journal of Marriage and Family, 68*, 509–528.

Kurdek, L. A. (2008). Change in relationship quality for partners from lesbian, gay male, and heterosexual couples. *Journal of Family Psychology, 22*(5), 701–711.

Kürzinger, M., Pagnier, J., Kahn, J., Hampshire, R., Wakabi, T., & Dye, T. (2008). Education status among orphans and non-orphans in communities affected by AIDS in Tanzania and Burkina Faso. *AIDS Care, 20*(6), 726–732.

Kutchinsky, B. (1991). Pornography and rape: Theory and practice? *International Journal of Law and Psychiatry, 14*, 47–64.

Kwan, I., Bhattacharya, S., McNeil, A., & van Rumste, M. (2008). Monitoring of stimulated cycles in assisted reproduction. *Cochrane Database of Systematic Reviews, 16*, CD005289.

Labbate, L. (2008). Psychotropics and sexual dysfunction: The evidence and treatments.

Advances in Psychosomatic Medicine, 29, 107–130.

Lacerda, H. M., Richiardi, L., Pettersson, A., Corbin, M., Merletti, F., & Akre, O. (2010). Cancer risk in mothers of men operated for undescended testis. *PLoS One, 5*(12), e14285.

Lacey, R. S., Reifman, A., Scott, J. P., Harris, S. M., & Fitzpatrick, J. (2004). Sexual-moral attitudes, love styles, and mate selection. *The Journal of Sex Research, 41*(2), 121–129.

Lachance-Brzela, M., & Bouchard, G. (2010). Why do women do the lion's share of housework? A decade of research. *Sex Roles, 63*(11–12), 767.

LaFree, G. (1982). Male power and female victimization. *American Journal of Sociology, 88*, 311–328.

Lahaie, M. A., Boyer, S. C., Amsel, R., Khalifé, S., & Binik, Y. M. (2010). Vaginismus: A review of the literature on the classification/diagnosis, etiology and treatment. *Womens Health, 6*(5), 705–719.

Lahey, K. A. (1991). Pornography and harm—learning to listen to women. *International Journal of Law and Psychiatry, 14*, 117–131.

Lai, C. H. (2011). Major depressive disorder: Gender differences in symptoms, life quality, and sexual function. *Journal of Clinical Psychopharmacology, 31*(1), 39–44.

Lakhey, M., Ghimire, R., Shrestha, R., & Bhatta, A. D. (2010). Correlation of serum free prostate-specific antigen level with histological findings in patients with prostatic disease. *Kathmandu University Medical Journal, 8*(30), 158–163.

Lakoff, R. (1975). *Language and woman's place.* New York: Harper.

Lalumière, M. L., Harris, G. T., Quinsey, V., & Rice, M. E. (2005a). Clinical assessment and treatment of rapists. In M. L. Lalumière & G. Harris (Eds.), *Causes of rape: Understanding individual differences in male propensity for sexual aggression* (pp. 161–181). Washington, DC: American Psychological Association.

Lalumière, M. L., Harris, G. T., Quinsey, V., & Rice, M. E. (2005b). Forced copulation in the animal kingdom. In M. L. Lalumière & G. Harris (Eds.), *Causes of rape: Understanding individual differences in male propensity for sexual aggression* (pp. 31–58). Washington, DC: American Psychological Association.

Lalumière, M. L., Harris, G. T., Quinsey, V., & Rice, M. E. (2005c). Rape across cultures and time. In M. L. Lalumière & G. Harris

(Eds.), *Causes of rape: Understanding individual differences in male propensity for sexual aggression* (pp. 9–30). Washington, DC: American Psychological Association.

Lalumière, M. L., Harris, G. T., Quinsey, V., & Rice, M. E. (2005d). Sexual interest in rape. In M. L. Lalumière & G. Harris (Eds.), *Causes of rape: Understanding individual differences in male propensity for sexual aggression* (pp. 105–128). Washington, DC: American Psychological Association.

Lam, A. G., Russell, S. T., Tan, T. C., & Leong, S. J. (2008). Maternal predictors of noncoital sexual behavior: Examining a nationally representative sample of Asian and White American adolescents who have never had sex. *Journal of Youth and Adolescence, 37*, 62–74.

Lambda. (2001). State-by-state map of sodomy laws. Retrieved October 15, 2003, from http://lambdalegal.org/cgi_bin/pages/states/sodomy-map.

Lampiao, F. (2009). Variation of semen parameters in healthy medical students due to exam stress. *Malawi Medical Journal, 21*(4), 166–170.

Lance, L. M. (2007). College student sexual morality revisited: A consideration of premarital sex, extramarital sex and childlessness between 1940 and 2000–2005. *College Student Journal, 41*, 727–734.

Landau, E. (1987). *On the streets: The lives of adolescent prostitutes.* New York: Julian Messner.

Landau, E. (2008, September 5). When sex becomes an addiction. CNN.com. Retrieved October 2, 2008, from http://www.cnn.com/2008/HEALTH/09/05/sex.addiction/.

Lang, R., Flor-Henry, P., & Frenzel, R. (1990). Sex hormone profiles in pedophilic and incestuous men. *Annals of Sex Research, 3*, 59–74.

Langevin, R., & Lang, R. A. (1987). The courtship disorders. In G. D. Wilson (Ed.), *Variant sexuality: Research and theory* (pp. 202–228). Baltimore: Johns Hopkins University Press.

Langevin, R., Langevin, M., & Curnoe, S. (2007). Family size, birth order, and parental age among male paraphilics and sex offenders. *Archives of Sexual Behavior, 36*, 599–609.

Langevin, R., Wortzman, G., Dickey, R., Wright, P., et al. (1988). Neuropsychological impairment in incest offenders. *Annals of Sex Research, 1*, 401–415.

Langstrom, N., Grann, M., & Lindblad, F. (2000). A preliminary typology of young sex offenders. *Journal of Adolescence, 23,* 319–329.

Lanz, M., & Tagliabue, S. (2007). Do I really need someone in order to become an adult? Romantic relationships during emerging adulthood in Italy. *Journal of Adolescent Research, 22,* 531–549.

Laqueur, T. W. (2003). *Solitary sex: A cultural history of masturbation.* Cambridge, MA: Zone Books.

Larkin, M. (1992). Reacting to patients with sexual problems. *Headlines, 3,* 2, 3, 6, 8.

LaSala, M. C. (2000). Lesbians, gay men and their parents: Family therapy for the coming out crisis. *Family Process, 39*(2), 257–266.

LaSala, M. C. (2001). The importance of partners to lesbians' intergenerational relationships. *Social Work Research, 25*(1), 27–36.

Lastella, D. D. (2005). Sexual harassment as an interpersonal dynamic: The effect of race, attractiveness, position power and gender on perceptions of sexual harassment. *Dissertation Abstracts International: Section B., #0419–4217.*

Lau, J., Kim, J. H., & Tsui, H. Y. (2005). Prevalence of male and female sexual problems, perceptions related to sex and association with quality of life in a Chinese population. *International Journal of Impotence Research, 17*(6), 494–505.

Lauerman, J. (2011, April, 25). Harvard law school target of US probe into discrimination against women. *Bloomberg News.* Retrieved April 27, 2011, from http://www.bloomberg.com/news/2011–04–25/harvard-law-school-faces-u-s-probe-of-response-to-harassment-rape-claims.html.

Laughlin, S., Schroeder, J., & Baird, D. (2010). New directions in the epidemiology of uterine fibroids. *Seminars in Reproductive Medicine, 28*(3), 204–217.

Laumann, E., Nicolosi, A., Glasser, D., Paik, A., Gingell, C., Moreira, E., Wang, T., for the GSSAB Investigators' Group. (2005). Sexual problems among women and men aged 40–80-y: Prevalence and correlates identified in the Global Study of Sexual Attitudes and Behaviors. *International Journal of Impotence Research, 17,* 39–57.

Laumann, E. O., Gagnon, J., Michael, R., & Michaels, S. (1994). *The social organization of sexuality: Sexual practices in the United States.* Chicago: University of Chicago Press.

Laumann, E. O., Paik, A., & Rosen, R. (1999). Sexual dysfunction in the United States. *Journal of the American Medical Association, 281,* 537–544.

Laumann, E. O., Paik, A., Glasser, D. B., Kang, J., Wang, T., Levinson, B., et al. (2006). A cross-national study of subjective sexual well-being among older women and men: Findings from the Global Study of Sexual Attitudes and Behaviors. *Archives of Sexual Behavior, 35,* 145–161.

Laurence, J. (2006). Treating HIV infection with one pill per day. *AIDS Patient Care and STDs, 20,* 601–603.

Lavee, Y. (1991). Western and non-Western human sexuality: Implications for clinical practice. *Journal of Sex and Marital Therapy, 17,* 203–213.

Lavin, M. (2008). Voyeurism: Psychopathology and theory. In D. Laws & W. O'Donohue (Eds.), *Sexual deviance: Theory, assessment and treatment* (2nd ed., pp. 305–319). New York: Guilford Press.

Lawrence, A. A. (2006). Patient-reported complications and functional outcomes of male and female sex reassignment surgery. *Archives of Sexual Behavior, 35,* 717–727.

Laws, D., & O'Donohue, W. (2008). *Sexual deviance: Theory, assessment, and treatment.* New York: Guilford Press.

Lawyer, S., Resnick, H., Bakanic, V., Burkett, T., & Kilpatrick, D. (2010). Forcible, drug-facilitated, and incapacitated rape and sexual assault among undergraduate women. *Journal of American College Health, 58*(5), 453–461.

Layton-Tholl, D. (1998). Extramarital affairs: The link between thought suppression and level of arousal. *Dissertation Abstracts,* Miami Institute of Psychology of the Caribbean Center for Advanced Studies, #AAT9930425.

Lazarou, S,. & Morgentaler, A. (2008). The effect of aging on spermatogenesis and pregnancy outcomes. *Urologic Clinics of North America, 35*(2), 331–339.

Leaper, C. (2000). The social construction and socialization of gender during development. In P. H. Miller & E. K. Scholnick (Eds.), *Toward a feminist developmental psychology* (pp. 127–152). New York: Routledge.

Lechuga, J., Swain, G., & Weinhardt, L. S. (In press). Perceived need of a parental decision aid for the HPV vaccine: Content and format preferences. *Health Promotions Practice.*

Ledbetter, A. (2010). Communication patterns and communication competence as predictors of online communication attitude: Evaluating a dual pathway model. *Journal of Family Communication, 10*(2), 99–115.

Ledermann, T., Bodenmann, G., Rudaz, M., & Bradbury, T. (2010). Stress, communication, and martial quality in couples. *Family Relations, 59*(2), 195–207.

Ledger, W. (2004). Implications of an irreversible procedure. *Fertility and Sterility, 82,* 1473.

Lee, J., Pomeroy, E. C., Yoo, S., & Rheinboldt, K. (2005). Attitudes toward rape: A comparison between Asian and Caucasian college students. *Violence Against Women, 11*(2), 177–196.

Lee, J. A. (1974). The styles of loving. *Psychology Today, 8,* 43–51.

Lee, J. A. (1988). Love-styles. In R. Sternberg & M. Barnes (Eds.), *The psychology of love.* New Haven, CT: Yale University Press.

Lee, J. A. (1998). Ideologies of lovestyle and sexstyle. In V. de Munck (Ed.), *Romantic love and sexual behavior* (pp. 33–76). Westport, CT: Praeger.

Lee, M. B., & Rotheram-Borus, M. J. (2002). Parents' disclosure of HIV to their children. *AIDS, 16*(16), 2201–2207.

Lee, P., Houk, C., Ahmed, S., Hughes, I., & the International Consensus Conference on Intersex Organized by the Lawson Wilkins Pediatric Endocrine Society and the European Society of Paediatric Endocrinology. (2006). Consensus statement on management of intersex disorders. *Pediatrics, 118,* 488–500.

Lee, S., Liong, M., Yuen, K., Leong, W., Cheah, P., Khan, N., & Krieger, J. (2008). Adverse impact of sexual dysfunction in chronic prostatitis/chronic pelvic pain syndrome. *Urology, 71,* 79–84.

Leiblum, S. (2007). Persistent genital arousal disorder: Perplexing, distressing, and underrecognized. In S. Leiblum (Ed.). *Principles and practice of sex therapy* (4th Ed., 54–83.). New York: Guilford Press.

Leiblum, S., Koochaki, P., Rodenberg, X., Barton, I., & Rosen, R. (2006). Hypoactive sexual desire disorder in postmenopausal women: US results from the women's international study of health and sexuality. *Menopause, 13,* 46–56.

Leiblum, S. R., & Goldmeier, D. (2008). Persistent genital arousal disorder in women: Case reports of association with antidepressant usage and withdrawal. *Journal of Sex and Marital Therapy, 34*(2), 150–159.

Leiblum, S. R., & Seehuus, M. (2009). FSFI scores of women with persistent genital arousal disorder compared with published scores of women with female sexual arousal disorder and healthy controls. *Journal of Sexual Medicine, 6,* 469–473.

Leibo, S. P. (2008). Cryopreservation of oocytes and embryos: Optimization by theoretical versus empirical analysis. *Theriogenology, 69*, 37–47.

Leichtentritt, R. D., & Arad, B. D. (2005). Young male street workers: Life histories and current experiences. *British Journal of Social Work, 35*(4), 483–509.

Leite, R., Prestes, J., Pereira, G., Shiguemoto, G., & Perez, S. (2010). Menopause: Highlighting the effects of resistance training. *International Journal of Sports Medicine, 31*(11), 761–767.

Leitenberg, H., & Henning, K. (1995). Sexual fantasy. *Psychological Bulletin, 117*(3), 469–496.

Leo, S., & Sia, A. (2008). Maintaining labour epidural analgesia: What is the best option? *Current Opinions in Anesthesiology, 21*, 263–269.

Leonard, A. S. (2006, September 25). Hong Kong appeals court strikes down differential age of consent law on "buggery." Leonard Link, New York Law School. Retrieved October 2, 2008, from http://newyorklawschool.typepad.com/leonardlink/2006/09/hong_kong_appea.html.

Leonard, K. E. (2005). Editorial: Alcohol and intimate partner violence: When can we say that heavy drinking is a contributing cause of violence? *Addiction, 100*(4), 422–425.

Leonard, T. M. (2006). *Encyclopedia of the developing world* (Vol. 2). Philadelphia: Taylor & Francis.

Leone, T., & Padmadas, S. (2007). The proliferation of a sterilization culture in women's lives: A comparison of Brazil and India. London School of Economics. *Genus, 63*(3/4), 77–97.

Lepkowski, J. M., Mosher, W. D., Davis, K. E., Groves, R. M., & Van Hoewyk, J. (2010). The 2006–2010 National Survey of Family Growth: Sample design and analysis of a continuous survey. National Center for Health Statistics. *Vital Health Statistics, 2*(150), 1–36.

Lerner, H. (1998). *The mother dance: How children change your life.* New York: HarperCollins.

Lerner-Geva, L., Keinan-Boker, L., Blumstein, T., Boyko, V., Olmar, L., Mashiach, S., et al. (2006). Infertility, ovulation induction treatments and the incidence of breast cancer—a historical prospective cohort of Israeli women. *Breast Cancer Research and Treatment, 100*, 201–212.

Leslie, G. R., & Korman, S. K. (1989). *The family in social context.* New York: Oxford University Press.

LeVay, S. (1991). A difference in hypothalamic structure between heterosexual and homosexual men. *Science, 253*, 1034–1037.

Lever, J., Grov, C., Royce, T., & Gillespie, B. (2008). Searching for love in all the "write" and "wrong" places: Exploring Internet personals use by sexual orientation, gender, and age. *International Journal of Sexual Health, 20*(4), 233.

Levin, R., & Wylie, K. (2010). Persistent genital arousal disorder: A review of the literature and recommendations for management. *International Journal of STDs and AIDS, 21*(5), 379–380.

Levin, R. J. (2007). Sexual activity, health and well-being—the beneficial roles of coitus and masturbation. *Sexual and Relationship Therapy, 22*, 135–148.

Levine, D. (2007). Ectopic pregnancy. *Radiology, 245*, 385–397.

Levine, D. A., & Gemignani, M. L. (2003). Prophylactic surgery in hereditary breast/ovarian cancer syndrome. *Oncology, 17*(7), 932–941.

Levine, J. (1991). Search and find. *Forbes, 148*, 134–135.

Levine, R., Sato, S., & Hashimoto, T. (1995). Love and marriage in eleven cultures. *Journal of Cross-Cultural Psychology, 26*(5), 554–571.

Levine, S. B., Risen, C. B., & Althof, S. E. (1990). Essay on the diagnosis and nature of paraphilia. *Journal of Sex and Marital Therapy, 16*(2), 89–102.

Lev-Wiesel, R. (2004). Male university students' attitudes toward rape and rapists. *Child & Adolescent Social Work Journal, 21*, 199.

Lewes, K. (1988). *The psychoanalytic theory of male homosexuality.* New York: Meridian.

Lewin, R. (1988). New views emerge on hunters and gatherers. *Science, 240*(4856), 1146–1148.

Lewis, D. A. (2000). Chancroid: From clinical practice to basic science. *AIDS Patient Care and STDs, 14*(1), 19–36.

Lewis, M. (1987). Early sex role behavior and school age adjustment. In J. M. Reinish, L. A. Rosenblum, & S. A. Sanders (Eds.), *Masculinity/femininity: Basic perspectives* (pp. 202–226). New York: Oxford University Press.

Lewis, R., & Ford-Robertson, J. (2010). Understanding the occurrence of interracial marriage in the United States through differential assimilation. *Journal of Black Studies, 41*(2), 405–420.

Lewis, R. J., & Janda, L. H. (1988). The relationship between adult sexual adjustment and childhood experiences regarding exposure to nudity, sleeping in the parental bed, and parental attitudes toward sexuality. *Archives of Sexual Behavior, 17*, 349–362.

Lewis, S. E., Agbaje, I., & Alvarez, J. (2008). Sperm DNA tests as useful adjuncts to semen analysis. *Systems Biology in Reproductive Medicine, 54*, 111–125.

Leyendecker, G., Kunz, G., Herbertz, M., Beil, D., Huppert, P., Mall, G., Kissler, S., Noe, M., & Wildt, L. (2004, December). Uterine peristaltic activity and the development of endometriosis. *Annals of the New York Academy of Sciences, 1034*, 338–355.

Leyson, J. F. (2004). Philippines. In R. T. Francoeur & R. J. Noonan (Eds.), *The Continuum International encyclopedia of sexuality* (pp. 825–845). New York/London: Continuum International.

Li, C. C., & Rew, L. (2010). A feminist perspective on sexuality and body image in females with colorectal cancer: An integrative review. *Journal of Wound Ostomy and Continence Nursing, 37*(5), 519–525.

Li, C. I., Chlebowski, R. T., Freiberg, M., Johnson, K. C., Kuller, L., Lane, D., Lessin, L., O'Sullivan, M. J., Wactawski-Wende, J., Yasmeen, S., & Prentice, R. (2010a). Alcohol consumption and risk of postmenopausal breast cancer by subtype: The Women's Health Initiative Observational Study. *Journal of the National Cancer Institute, 102*(18), 1422.

Li, C. I., Malone, K. E., Daling, J. R., Potter, J. D., Bernstein, L., Marchbanks, P. A., et al. (2008). Timing of menarche and first full-term birth in relation to breast cancer risk. *Journal of Epidemiology, 167*, 230–239.

Li, D. K., Zhou, Z., Miao, M., He, Y., Wang, J., Ferber, J., Herrinton, L. J., Gao, E., & Yuan, W. (2011). Urine bisphenol-A (BPA) level in relation to semen quality. *Fertility and Sterility, 95*(2), 625–630.e1-e4.

Li, G., Li, G. Y., Ji, H. J., Zhao, W. J., Chu, S. F., & Chen, N. H. (2010b). [Effect of testosterone on the expression of CMTM family of the male spermatogenesis suppression rats]. *Yao Xue Xue Bao, 45*(8), 995–1000.

Liao, C., Wei, J., Li, Q., Li, L., Li, J., & Li, D. (2006). Efficacy and safety of cordocentesis for prenatal diagnosis. *International Journal of Gynecology and Obstetrics, 93*, 13–17.

Liao, L., Michala, L., & Creighton, S. (2010). Labial surgery for well women: A review of the literature. *British Journal of Obstetrics and Gynecology, 117*(1), 20–25.

Liao, L. M., & Creighton, S. M. (2007). Requests for cosmetic genitoplasty: How should healthcare providers respond? *British Medical Journal, 334*(7603), 1090–1092.

Libby, S. (2010, July 20). Is Forever 21 glamorizing teen pregnancy? Salon.com. Retrieved August 10, 2010, from http://www.salon.com/life/broadsheet/2010/07/20/forever_21_maternity.

Liben, L. S., & Bigler, R. S. (2002). The developmental course of gender differentiation. *Monographs of the Society of Research in Child Development, 67*(2), vii–147.

Lichtenberg, I. (2011, February 27). Child rape in South Africa persists unabated. *Monsters and Critics News.* Retrieved April 30, 2011, from http://www.monstersandcritics.com/news/africa/features/article_1622267.php/Child-rape-in-South-Africa-persists-unabated-Feature.

Lie, D. (2000). Contraception update for the primary care physician. Retrieved May 17, 2001, from http://www.medscape.com/medscape/CNO/200/AAFP/AAFP-06.html.

Lie, M. L., Robson, S. C., & May, C. R. (2008). Experiences of abortion: A narrative review of qualitative studies. *BMC Health Services Research, 8,* 150.

Lilley, L. L., & Schaffer, S. (1990). Human papillomavirus: A sexually transmitted disease with carcinogenic potential. *Cancer Nursing, 13,* 366–372.

Lim, M. M., & Young, L. J. (2006). Neuropeptidergic regulation of affiliative behavior and social bonding in animals. *Hormones and Behavior, 50,* 506–517.

Limanonda, B., Chongvatana, N., Tirasawat, P., & Auwanit, W. (1993). *Summary report on the demographic and behavioral study of female commercial sex workers in Thailand.* Bangkok, Thailand: Institute of Population Studies.

Limin, M., Johnsen, N., & Hellstrom, W. J. (2010). Avanafil, a new rapid-onset phosphodiesterase 5 inhibitor for the treatment of erectile dysfunction. *Expert Opinion on Investigational Drugs, 19*(11), 1427–1437.

Lindau, S., & Gavrilova, N. (2010). Sex, health, and years of sexually active life gained due to good health: Evidence from two US population based cross sectional surveys of ageing. *British Medical Journal, 340,* c810. Retrieved from http://www.bmj.com/content/340/bmj.c810.full.pdf.

Lindberg, L. D., Jones, R., & Santelli, J. S. (2008, July). Non-coital sexual activities among adolescents. *Journal of Adolescent Health.* Retrieved May 26, 2008, from http://www.guttmacher.org/pubs/JAH_Lindberg.pdf.

Linton, K. D., & Wylie, K. R. (2010). Recent advances in the treatment of premature ejaculation. *Journal of Drug Design, Development and Therapy, 18*(4), 1–6.

Linz, D. (1989). Exposure to sexually explicit materials and attitudes toward rape: A comparison of study results. *The Journal of Sex Research, 26,* 50–84.

Linz, D., & Donnerstein, E. (1992, September 30). Research can help us explain violence and pornography. *The Chronicle of Higher Education,* B3–B4.

Lippa, R. A., & Tan, F. P. (2001). Does culture moderate the relationship between sexual orientation and gender-related personality trait? *Journal of Comparative Social Science, 35*(1), 65–87.

Lips, H. (2008). *Sex & gender: An introduction* (6th ed.). New York: McGraw-Hill.

Lipsky, S., Caetono, R., Field, C. A., & Larkin, G. (2005). Psychosocial and substance-use risk factors for intimate partner violence. *Drug & Alcohol Dependence, 78*(1), 39–47.

Lipton, L. (2003). The erotic revolution. In J. Escoffier (Ed.), *Sexual revolution* (pp. 20–30). New York: Thunder's Mouth Press.

Lisak, D., & Miller, P. (2002). Repeat rape and multiple offending among undetected rapists. *Violence and Victims, 17*(1), 73–84.

Litosseliti, L. (2006). *Gender and language: Theory and practice.* London: Arnold.

Little, A. C., Burt, D. M., & Perrett, D. I. (2006). What is good is beautiful: Face preference reflects desired personality. *Personality and Individual Differences, 41,* 1107–1118.

Littleton, H., & Henderson, C. (2009). If she is not a victim, does that mean she was not traumatized? Evaluation of predictors of PTSD symptomatology among college rape victims. *Violence Against Women, 15*(2), 148–167.

Littleton, H., Breitkopf, C., & Berenson, A. (2007). Rape scripts of low-income European American and Latina women. *Sex Roles, 56,* 509–516.

Littleton, H., Grills-Taquechel, A., & Axsom, D. (2009a). Impaired and incapacitated rape victims: Assault characteristics and post-assault experiences. *Violence and Victims, 24*(4), 439–457.

Littleton, H., Tabernik, H., Canales, E., & Backstrom, T. (2009b). Risky situation or harmless fun? A qualitative examination

of college women's bad hook-up and rape scripts. *Sex Roles, 60*(11–12), 793–805.

Liu, C. (2004). County health officials call for condoms in porn movies. *LA Times.* Retrieved November 15, 2008, from http://articles.latimes.com/2004/oct/08/local/me-porn8.

Liu, C., Xie, J., Wang, L., Zheng, Y., Ma, Z., Yang, H., Chen, X., Shi, G., Li, S., Zhao, J., et al. (2011). Immediate analgesia effect of single point acupuncture in primary dysmenorrhea: A randomized controlled trial. *Pain Medication, 12*(2), 300–307.

Liu, D. F., Jiang, H., Hong, K., Zhao, L. M., Tang, W. H., & Ma, L. L. (2010). Influence of erectile dysfunction course on its progress and efficacy of treatment with phosphodiesterase type 5 inhibitors. *Chinese Medical Journal, 123*(22), 3258–3261.

Livingston, G., & Cohn, D. (2010). The new demography of American motherhood. Pew Research Center. Retrieved July 2, 2011, from http://pewsocialtrends.org/files/2010/10/754-new-demography-of-motherhood.pdf.

Lloyd, T., Petit, M. A., Lin, H. M., & Beck, T. J. (2004). Lifestyle factors and the development of bone mass and bone strength in young women. *Journal of Pediatrics, 144*(6), 776–782.

Lock, J., & Steiner, H. (1999). Gay lesbian and bisexual youth risks for emotional, physical, and social problems: Results from a community-based survey. *Journal of American Academy of Child and Adolescent Psychiatry 38*(3), 297–305.

Locker, L., McIntosh, W., Hackney, A., Wilson, J., & Wiegand, K. (2010). The breakup of romantic relationships: Situational predictors of perception of recovery. *North American Journal of Psychology, 12*(3), 565–578.

Lockwood, S. (2008, April 7). Homeless GLBT youths often face violent life on the streets. *Columbia Spectator.* Retrieved October 2, 2008, from http://www.columbiaspectator.com/node/30281.

Lohiya, N. K., Suthar, R., Khandelwal, A., Goyal, S., Ansari, A. S., & Manivannan, B. (2010). Sperm characteristics and teratology in rats following vas deferens occlusion with RISUG and its reversal. *International Journal of Andrology, 33*(1), e198–e206.

Loke, A., & Poon, C. (2011). The health concerns and behaviours of primigravida: Comparing advanced age pregnant women with their younger counterparts. *Journal of Clinical Nursing, 20,* 1141–1150.

Lombardi, G., Del Popolo, G., Macchiarella, A., Mencarini, M., & Celso, M. (2010). Sexual rehabilitation in women with spinal cord injury: A critical review of the literature. *Spinal Cord, 48*(12), 842–849.

Lombardi, G., Macchiarella, A., Cecconi, F., & Del Popolo, G. (2009). Ten-year follow-up of sildenafil use in spinal cord-injured patients with erectile dysfunction. *Journal of Sexual Medicine, 6*(12), 3449–3457.

Lombardo, W., Cretser, G., & Roesch, S. (2001). For crying out loud—the differences persist into the '90s. *Sex Roles, 45*(7–8), 529–547.

Long, S., Ullman, S., Long, L., Mason, G., & Starzynski, L. (2007). Women's experiences of male-perpetrated sexual assault by sexual orientation. *Violence and Victims, 22,* 684–701.

Long, V. E. (2003). Contraceptive choices: New options in the U.S. market. *SIECUS Report, 31*(2), 13–18.

Longua, P. (2010). "I love you" (but I can't look you in the eyes): Explicit and implicit self-esteem predict verbal and nonverbal response to relationship threat. Chicago: Loyola University, AAT #3434370.

Lonsway, K., Cortina, L., & Magley, V. (2008). Sexual harassment mythology: Definition, conceptualization, and measurement. *Sex Roles, 58,* 599–616.

Lopez, L., Grimes, D. A., Gallo, M., & Schulz, K. (2008). Skin patch and vaginal ring versus combined oral contraceptives for contraception. *Cochrane Database Systems Review, 23,* CD003552.

LoPiccolo, J., & Lobitz, W. C. (1972). The role of masturbation in the treatment of orgasmic dysfunction. *Archives of Sexual Behavior, 2,* 163–171.

LoPiccolo, J., & Stock, W. E. (1986). Treatment of sexual dysfunction. *Journal of Consulting and Clinical Psychology, 54,* 158–167.

Lott, A. J., & Lott, B. E. (1961). Group cohesiveness, communication level, and conformity. *Journal of Abnormal & Social Psychology, 62,* 408–412.

Loucks, A. B., & Nattiv, A. (2005). The female athlete triad. *Lancet, 366,* s49–s50.

Love, E., Bhattacharya, S., Smith, N., & Bhattacharya, S. (2010). Effect of interpregnancy interval on outcomes of pregnancy after miscarriage: Retrospective analysis of hospital episode statistics in Scotland. *British Medical Journal, 341,* c3967.

Lovejoy, F. H., & Estridge, D. (Eds.). (1987). *The new child health encyclopedia.* New York: Delacorte Press.

Low, W. Y., Wong, Y. L., Zulkifli, S. W., & Tan, H. (2002). Malaysian cultural differences in knowledge, attitudes and practices related to erectile dysfunction. *International Journal of Impotence Research, 14*(6), 440–445.

Lu, W., Mueser, K., Rosenberg, S., & Jankowski, M. (2008). Correlates of adverse childhood experiences among adults with severe mood disorders. *Psychiatric Services, 59,* 1018–1026.

Lubbers, M., Jaspers, E., & Ultee, W. (2009). Primary and secondary socialization impacts on support for same-sex marriage after legalization in the Netherlands. *Journal of Family Issues, 30*(12), 1714–1745.

Lucie-Smith, E. (1991). *Sexuality in western art.* London: Thames & Hudson.

Luckenbill, D. F. (1984). Dynamics of the deviant scale. *Deviant Behavior, 5,* 337–353.

Ludermir, A., Lewis, G., Valongueiro, S., de Araujo, T., & Araya, R. (2010). Violence against women by their intimate partner during pregnancy and postnatal depression: A prospective cohort study. *Lancet, 376*(9744), 903–910.

Lue, T. (2000). Erectile dysfunction. *New England Journal of Medicine, 342*(24), 1802–1813.

Lundstrom, M., & Walsh, D. (2010, November 14). Secrecy shrouds UOP sexual attack suit. *The Sacramento Bee.* Retrieved May 1, 2011, from http://www.sacbee.com/2010/11/14/v-mobile/3183395/secrecy-shrouds-sexual-assault.html.

Lutfey, K. E., Link, C., Rosen, R., Wiegel, M., & McKinlay, J. (2008, January 11). Prevalence and correlates of sexual activity and function in women: Results from the Boston Area Community Health (BACH) survey. *Archives of Sexual Behavior.* Retrieved October 30, 2008, from http://www.springerlink.com/content/f47306253471w048/?p=efd510bd7d9a43c29bd1f1b7ca8b33b3&pi=0.

Luxenburg, J., & Klein, L. (1984). CB radio prostitution: Technology and the displacement of deviance. In Chaneles, S. (Ed.), *Gender issues, sex offences, and criminal justice: Current trends* (pp. 71–87). New York: The Haworth Press.

Maas, C. P., ter Kuile, M. M., Laan, E., Tuynman, C. C., Weyenborg, P., Trimbos, J. B., & Kenter, G. G. (2004). Objective assessment of sexual arousal in women with a history of hysterectomy. *British Journal of Obstetrics and Gynaecology, 111,* 456–462.

Maas, J. (1998). *Power sleep.* New York: HarperCollins.

Maccio, E. M. (2010). Influence of family, religion, and social conformity on client participation in sexual reorientation therapy. *Journal of Homosexuality, 57*(3), 441–458.

Maccoby, E. E. (2002). Gender and group process: A developmental perspective. *Current Directions in Psychological Science, 11*(2), 54–58.

Maccoby, E. E., Jacklin, C. N. (1987). Gender segregation in childhood. In H. W. Reese (Ed.), *Advances in child development and behavior,* (Vol. 20, pp. 239–287). San Diego, CA: Academic Press.

Macdorman, M. F., Declercq, E., & Menacker, F. (2011). Trends and characteristics of home births in the United States by race and ethnicity, 1990–2006. *Birth, 38*(1), 17–23.

MacDorman, M. F., Mathews, T. J., Martin, J. A., & Malloy, M. H. (2002). Trends and characteristics of induced labour in the U.S., 1989–1998. *Paediatric & Perinatal Epidemiology, 16*(3), 263–274.

Macdowall, W., Wellings, K., Stephenson, J., & Glasier, A. (2008). Summer nights: A review of the evidence of seasonal variations in sexual health indicators among young people. *Health Education, 108,* 40.

Mackay, J. (2000). *The Penguin atlas of human sexual behavior.* New York: Penguin.

Mackenzie, C. (2011, April 7). Personal communication.

Mackesy-Amiti, M., Fendrich, M., & Johnson, T. (2008). Substance-related problems and treatment among men who have sex with men in comparison to other men in Chicago. *Journal of Substance Abuse and Treatment.* Epub ahead of print. Retrieved September 19, 2008, from http://www.ncbi.nlm.nih.gov/pubmed/18715744.

MacKinnon, C. A. (1985, March 26). Pornography: Reality, not fantasy. *The Village Voice.*

MacKinnon, C. A. (1986). Pornography: Not a moral issue. (Special Issue: Women and the law.) *Women's Studies International Forum, 9,* 63–78.

MacKinnon, C. A. (1987). *Feminism unmodified: Discourses on life and law.* Cambridge, MA: Harvard University Press.

MacKinnon, C. A. (1993). *Only words.* Cambridge, MA: Harvard University Press.

Macklon, N., & Fauser, B. (2000). Aspects of ovarian follicle development throughout life. *Hormone Research, 52,* 161–170.

Macneil, S. (2004). It takes two: Modeling the role of sexual self-disclosure in sexual satisfaction. *Dissertation Abstracts International: Section B: The Sciences & Engineering, 65*(1-B), 481. (#0419–4217).

Madan, R. A., & Gulley, J. L. (2010). The current and emerging role of immunotherapy in prostate cancer. *Clinical Genitourinary Cancer, 8*(1), 10–16.

Madan, R. A., & Gulley, J. L. (2011). Therapeutic cancer vaccine fulfills the promise of immunotherapy in prostate cancer. *Immunotherapy, 3*(1), 27–31.

Madigan, N. (2004). Man, 86, convicted under new law against Americans who go abroad to molest minors. Retrieved November 11, 2004, from http://travel2.nytimes.com/2004/11/20/national/20predator.html?ex=1129003200&en=8275e98301fbe992&ei=5070&n=Top%2fFeatures%2fTravel%2fDestinations%2fUnited%20States%2fRegions.

Maffini, M. V., Rubin, B. S., Sonnenschein, C., & Soto, A. M. (2006). Endocrine disruptors and reproductive health: The case of bisphenol-A. *Molecular and Cellular Endocrinology, 254–255,* 179–186.

Mah, K., & Binik, Y. (2005). Are orgasms in the mind or the body? Psychosocial versus physiological correlates of orgasmic pleasure and satisfaction. *Journal of Sex & Marital Therapy, 31*(3), 187–200.

Mahabir, S., Spitz, M. R., Barrera, S. L., Dong, Y. Q., Eastham, C., & Forman, M. R. (2008). Dietary boron and hormone replacement therapy as risk factors for lung cancer in women. *American Journal of Epidemiology* (Epub). Retrieved March 18, 2008, from http://www.ncbi.nlm.nih.gov/sites/entrez.

MaHood, J., & Wenburg, A. R. (1980). *The Mosher survey.* New York: Arno.

Maines, R. (1999). *Hysteria, the vibrator, and women's sexual satisfaction.* Baltimore: The Johns Hopkins University Press.

Maisto, S. A., Carey, M. P., Carey, K. B., Gordon, C. M., Schum, J., & Lynch, K. (2004). The relationship between alcohol and individual differences variables on attitudes and behavioral skills relevant to sexual health among heterosexual young adult men. *Archives of Sexual Behavior, 33*(6), 571–584.

Makarainen, L., van Beek, A., Tuomivaara, L., Asplund, B., & Coelingh-Bennink, B. (1998). Ovarian function during the use of a single contraceptive implant: Implanon compared with Norplant. *Fertility and Sterility, 69,* 714–721.

Makrantonaki, E., Schönknecht, P., Hossini, A. M., Kaiser, E., Katsouli, M. M., Adjaye, J., Schröder, J., & Zouboulis, C. C. (2010). Skin and brain age together: The role of hormones in the ageing process. *Experimental Gerontology, 45*(10), 801–813.

Malmo, C., & Laidlaw, T. (2010). Symptoms of trauma and traumatic memory retrieval in adult survivors of childhood sexual abuse. *Journal of Trauma and Dissociation, 11*(1), 22–43.

Malone, F. D., Canick, J. A., Ball, R. H., Nyberg, D. A., Comstock, C. H., Bukowski, R., Berkowitz, R. L., Gross, S. J., Wolfe, H. M., et al. (2005). First-trimester or second-trimester screening, or both, for Down's syndrome. *The New England Journal of Medicine, 353*(19), 2001–2011.

Malone, P., & Steinbrecher, H. (2007). Medical aspects of male circumcision. *British Medical Journal, 335*(7631), 1206–1290.

Maltz, D. W., & Borker, R. A. (1982). A cultural approach to male-female communication. In J. J. Gumperz (Ed.), *Language and social identity* (pp. 196–216). New York. Cambridge University Press.

Maltz, W. (1990, December). Adult survivors of incest: How to help them overcome the trauma. *Medical Aspects of Human Sexuality, 38*–43.

Maltz, W. (2002). Treating the sexual intimacy concerns of sexual abuse survivors. *Sexual and Relationship Therapy, 17*(4), 321–327.

Maltz, W., & Boss, S. (2001). *Private thoughts: Exploring the power of women's sexual fantasies.* Novato, CA: New World Library.

Mandelbaum, J. (2010). What motivates female suicide bombers? Open Salon. Retrieved April 10, 2010, from http://open.salon.com/blog/judy_mandelbaum/2010/04/05/what_motivates_female_suicide_bombers.

Maness, D. L., Reddy, A., Harraway-Smith, C. L., Mitchell, G., & Givens, V. (2010). How best to manage dysfunctional uterine bleeding. *Journal of Family Practice, 59*(8), 449–458.

Manganiello, A., Hoga, L., Reberte, L., Miranda, C., & Rocha, C. (2011). Sexuality and quality of life of breast cancer patients post mastectomy. *European Journal of Oncology Nursing, 15*(2), 167–172.

Mannheimer, S., Friedland, G., Matts, J., Child, C., & Chesney, M. (2002). The consistency of adherence to antiretroviral therapy predicts biologic outcome for HIV-infected persons in clinical trials. *Clinical Infectious Disease, 34*(8), 1115–1121.

Manniche, L. (1987). *Sexual life in ancient Egypt.* London: KPI Ltd.

Manson, J. E. (2004, December). Your doctor is in. *Glamour,* p. 104.

Mansour, D. (2010). Nexplanon: What Implanon did next. *Journal of Family Planning and Reproductive Health Care, 36*(4), 187–189.

Mantica, A. (2005). Better test for a stealthy cancer. *Prevention, 57*(3), 48–51.

Maranghi, F., Mantovani, A., Macrì, C., Romeo, A., Eleuteri, P., Leter, G., Rescia, M., Spanò, M., & Saso, L. (2005). Long-term effects of lonidamine on mouse testes. *Contraception, 72*(4), 268–272.

Marchbanks, P. A., McDonald, J. A., Wilson, H. G., Folger S. G., Mandel M. G., Daling J. R., et al. (2002). Oral contraceptives and the risk of breast cancer. *New England Journal of Medicine, 346,* 2025–2032.

Margolis, J. (2004). *O: The intimate history of the orgasm.* New York: Grove/Atlantic Press.

Margulies, S. (2003). The psychology of prenuptial agreements. *Journal of Psychiatry & Law, 31*(4), 415–432.

Margulis, L., & Sagan, D. (1991). *Mystery dance: On the evolution of human sexuality.* New York: Summit Books.

Marinakis, G., & Nikolaou, D. (2011). What is the role of assisted reproduction technology in the management of age-related infertility? *Human Fertility, 14,* 8–15.

Marino, T. (2010). Embryology and disorders of sexual development. *Perspectives of Biological Medicine, 53*(4), 482–490.

Maritz, G. S. (2008). Nicotine and lung development. *Birth Defects Research, Part C. 84,* 45–53.

Mark, K., Wald, A., Mageret, A., Selke, S., Olin, L, Huang, M., & Corey, L. (2008). Rapidly cleared episodes of herpes simplex virus reactivation in immunocompetent adults. *Journal of Infectious Disease.* Epub ahead of print. Retrieved September 19, 2008, from http://www.ncbi.nlm.nih.gov/sites/entrez.

Markel, H. (2005). The search for effective HIV vaccines. *The New England Journal of Medicine, 353*(8), 753–757.

Marrazzo, J. (2004). Barriers to infectious disease care among lesbians. *Emerging Infectious Disease, 10,* 1974–1978.

Marrazzo, J., Cook, R., Wiesenfeld, H., Murray, P., Busse, B., Krohn, M., & Hillier, S. (2007). *Lactobacillus* capsule for the treatment of bacterial vaginosis. *Journal of Women's Health, 15,* 1053–1060.

Marrazzo, J., Koutsky L., Kiviat, N., Kuypers J., & Stine, K. (2001). Papanicolaou test screening and prevalence of genital human papillomavirus among women who have sex with women. *American Journal of Public Health, 91,* 947–952.

Marrazzo, J., Thomas, K., Fiedler, T., Ringwood, K., & Fredricks, D. (2008). Relationship of specific vaginal bacteria and bacterial vaginosis treatment failure in women who have sex with women. *Annals of Internal Medicine, 149,* 20–28.

Marrazzo, M., Thomas, K., Fiedler, T., Ringwood, K., & Fredricks, D. (2010). Risks for acquisition of bacterial vaginosis among women who report sex with women: A cohort study. *PLoS One, 5*(6), e11139.

Marshal, M. P., Friedman, M. S., Stall, R., & Thompson, A. L. (2009). Individual trajectories of substance use in lesbian, gay and bisexual youth and heterosexual youth. *Addiction, 104*(6), 974–981.

Marshall, D. S. (1971). Sexual behavior on Mangaia. In D. S. Marshall & R. C. Suggs (Eds.), *Human sexual behavior.* New York: Basic Books.

Marshall, W. L. (1979). Satiation therapy: A procedure for reducing deviant sexual arousal. *Journal of Applied Behavior Analysis, 12*(3), 377–389.

Martens, W. (2007). Optimism therapy: An adapted psychotherapeutic strategy for adult female survivors of childhood sexual abuse. *Annals of the American Psychotherapy Association, 10,* 30–38.

Martin, D., Martin, M., & Carvalho, K. (2008). Reading and learning-disabled children: Understanding the problem. *The Clearing House, 81,* 113–118.

Martin, H. P. (1991). The coming-out process for homosexuals. *Hospital and Community Psychiatry, 42,* 158–162.

Martin, J. A., Hamilton, B. E., Sutton, P. D., Ventura, S. J., Menacker, F., Kirmeyer, S., & Mathews, T. J. (2009). Births: Final data for 2006. *National Vital Statistics Reports, 57*(7), National Center for Health Statistics.

Martin, J. A., Hamilton, B. E., Sutton, P., Ventura, S., Menacker, F., Kirmeyer, S., & Munson, M. (2007, December 5). Births: Final data for 2005. *National Vital Statistics Report, 56*(6). Retrieved May 31, 2008, from http://www.cdc.gov/nchs/data/nvsr/nvsr56/nvsr56_06.pdf.

Martin, J. T., Puts, D. A., & Breedlove, S. M. (2008). Hand asymmetry in heterosexual and homosexual men and women: Relationship to 2D:4D digit ratios and other sexually dimorphic anatomical traits. *Archives of Sexual Behavior, 37*(1), 119–132.

Martin, K., & Luke, K. (2010). Gender differences in the ABC's of the birds and bees: What mothers teach young children about sexuality and reproduction, *Sex Roles, 62*(3–4), 278–291.

Martin, K., Hutson, D., Kazyak, E., & Scherrer, K. (2010). Advice when children come

out: The cultural tool kits of parents. *Journal of Family Issues, 31*(7), 960–991.

Martin, R. P., Dombrowski, S. C., Mullis, C., Wisenbaker, J., & Huttunen, M. O. (2005, July 7). Smoking during pregnancy: Association with childhood temperament, behavior, and academic performance. *Journal of Pediatric Psychology,* Epub ahead of print. Retrieved July 17, 2005, from http://www.ncbi.nlm.nih.gov/entrez/query.fcgi?cmd=Retrieve&db=pubmed&dopt=Abstract&list_uids=16002482&query_hl=23.

Martin, T. A. (2003). Power and consent: Relation to self-reported sexual assault and acquaintance rape. *Dissertation Abstracts International: Section B: The Sciences & Engineering, 64*(3-B), #0419–4217.

Martin, W. E. (2001). A wink and a smile: How men and women respond to flirting. *Psychology Today, 34*(5), 26–27.

Martinez, G., Abma, J., & Copen, C. (2010). Educating teenagers about sex in the United States. *NCHS Data Brief, 44,* 1–8.

Martinez, G. M., Chandra, A., Abma, J. C., Jones, J., & Mosher, W. D. (2006). Fertility, contraception, and fatherhood: Data on men and women from cycle 6 (2002) of the National Survey of Family Growth. *Vital Health Statistics, 23*(26). Hyattsville, MD: National Center for Health Statistics, Centers for Disease Control.

Martínez-Burgos, M., Herrero, L., Megías, D., Salvanes, R., Montoya, M. C., Cobo, A. C., & Garcia-Velasco, J. A. (2011). Vitrification versus slow freezing of oocytes: Effects on morphologic appearance, meiotic spindle configuration, and DNA damage. *Fertility and Sterility, 95*(1), 374–377.

Martinson, F. M. (1981). Eroticism in infancy and childhood. In L. L. Constantine & F. M. Martinson (Eds.), *Children and sex: New findings, new perspectives* (pp. 23–35). Boston: Little, Brown.

Maruo, T., Ohara, N., Yoshida, S., Nakabayashi, K., Sasaki, H., Xu, Q., Chen, W., & Yamada, H. (2010). Translational research with progesterone receptor modulator motivated by the use of levonorgestrel-releasing intrauterine system. *Contraception, 82*(5), 435–441.

Masho, S., & Anderson, L. (2009). Sexual assault in men: A population-based study of Virginia. *Violence and Victims, 24*(1), 98–110.

Mason, M. A., Fine, M. A., & Carcochan, S. (2001). Family law in the new millennium: For whose families? *Journal of Family Issues, 22*(7), 859–882.

Masoomi, M., Zare, J., Kahnooj, M., Mirzazadeh, A., & Sheikhvatan, M. (2010). Sex differences in potential daily triggers of the onset of acute myocardial infarction: A case-crossover analysis among an Iranian population. *Journal of Cardiovascular Medicine, 11*(10), 723–726.

Massa, G., Verlinde, F., DeSchepper, J., Thomas, M., Bourguignon, J. P, Craen, M., de Segher, F., Francois, I., Du Caju, M., Maes, M., & Heinrichs, C. (2005). Trends in age at diagnosis of Turner syndrome. *Archives of Disease in Childhood, 90*(3), 267–275.

Massart, F., & Saggese, G. (2010). Morphogenetic targets and genetics of undescended testis. *Sexual Development, 4*(6), 326–335.

Masser, B., Viki, T., & Power, C. (2006). Hostile sexism and rape proclivity amongst men. *Sex Roles, 54,* 565–574.

Masters, W. H., & Johnson, V. E. (1966). *Human sexual response.* Boston: Little, Brown.

Masters, W. H., & Johnson, V. E. (1970). *Human sexual inadequacy.* Boston: Little, Brown.

Masters, W. H., & Johnson, V. E. (1979). *Homosexuality in perspective.* Boston: Little, Brown.

Masters, W. H., Johnson, V. E., & Kolodny, R. C. (1982). *Human sexuality.* Boston: Little, Brown.

Masterton, G. (1987). *How to drive your woman wild in bed.* New York: Penguin Books.

Matek, O. (1988). Obscene phone callers. (Special issue: The sexually unusual: Guide to understanding and helping.) *Journal of Social Work and Human Sexuality, 7,* 113–130.

Mather, M., & Lavery, D. (2010). In U.S., proportion married at lowest recorded levels. Population Reference Bureau. Retrieved May 11, 2011, from http://www.prb.org/Articles/2010/usmarriagedecline.aspx.

Mathers, M., Degener, S., & Roth, S. (2011). Cryptorchidism and infertility from the perspective of interdisciplinary guidelines. *Urologe A, 50*(1), 20–25.

Mathes, E. W. (2005). Relationship between short-term sexual strategies and sexual jealousy. *Psychological Reports, 96*(1), 29–35.

Matsubara, H. (2001, June 20). Sex change no cure for torment. *Japan Times.*

Matsumoto, D. (1996). *Culture and psychology.* Pacific Grove, CA: Brooks/Cole.

Matthews, A., Dowswell, T., Haas, D. M., Doyle, M., & O'Mathúna, D. P. (2010). Interventions for nausea and vomiting in early pregnancy. *Cochrane Database Systems Review, 8*(9), CD007575.

Matthews, A. K., Tartaro, J., & Hughes, T. L. (2003). A comparative study of lesbian and heterosexual women in committed relationships. *Journal of Lesbian Studies, 7,* 101–114.

Matthews, T., & Hamilton, B. (2009, August). Delayed childbearing: More women are having their first child later in life. *NCHS Data Brief, 21,* 1–8.

Maugh, T. H. (2006, July 14). Rates of prematurity, low birth weight highest ever. *Los Angeles Times.* Retrieved from http://articles .latimes.com/2006/jul/14/science/sci-children14.

Maunder, R., & Hunter, J. (2008). Attachment relationships as determinants of physical health. *Journal of the American Academy of Psychoanalysis and Dynamic Psychiatry, 36*(1), 11–33.

Maurer, T., & Robinson, D. (2008). Effects of attire, alcohol, and gender on perceptions of date rape. *Sex Roles, 58,* 423–435.

Maxmen, J., & Ward, N. (1995). *Essential psychopathology and its treatment* (2nd ed.). New York: Norton.

Mayer, J. (2011). Gay rights in Costa Rica: Pura vida. *The Costa Rica News.* Retrieved February 20, 2011, from http:// thecostaricanews.com/gay-rights-in-costa-rica/5650.

Maynard, E., Carballo-Dieguez, A., Ventuneac, A., Exner, T., & Mayer, K. (2009). Women's experiences with anal sex: Motivations and implications for STD prevention. *Perspectives on Sexual and Reproductive Health, 41*(3), 142–149.

Mays, V. M., Yancy, A. K., Cochran, S. D., Weber, M., & Fielding, J. E. (2002). Heterogeneity of health disparities among African-American, Hispanic and Asian American women. *American Journal of Public Health, 92*(4), 632–640.

Mbah, A., Alio, A., Marty, P., Bruder, K., Wilson, R., & Salihu, H. (2011). Recurrent versus isolated pre-eclampsia and risk of feto-infant morbidity outcomes: Racial/ethnic disparity. *European Journal of Obstetrics and Gynecological and Reproductive Biology, 156*(1), 23–28.

Mbügua, K. (2006). Reasons to suggest that the endocrine research on sexual preference is a degenerating research program. *History & Philosophy of the Life Sciences, 28,* 337–358.

McAdams, M. (1996). Gender without bodies. Retrieved September 3, 2005, from http://

www.december.com/cmc/mag/1996/mar/mcadams.html

McAndrew, F. T., Bell, E. K., & Garcia, C. M. (2007). Who do we tell and whom do we tell on? Gossip as a strategy for status enhancement. *Journal of Applied Social Psychology, 37,* 1562–1577.

McBride, J. L. (2007). The family. In *The behavioral sciences and health care* (2nd ed., Section VI, #19). Ashland, OH: Hogrefe & Huber.

McCabe, M., & Wauchope, M. (2005). Behavioral characteristics of men accused of rape: Evidence for different types of rapists. *Archives of Sexual Behavior, 34,* 241–253.

McCabe, M. P. (2002). Relationship functioning among people with MS. *Journal of Sex Research, 39*(4), 302–309.

McCabe, S., Bostwick, W., Hughes, T., West, B., & Boyd, C. (2010). The relationships between discrimination and substance use disorders among lesbian, gay, and bisexual adults in the U.S. *American Journal of Public Health, 100*(10), 1946–1952.

McCall-Hosenfeld, J. S., Freund, K. M., Legault, C., Jaramillo, S. A., Cochrane, B. B., Manson, J. E., Wenger, N. K., Eaton, C. B., McNeeley, S. G., Rodriguez, B. L., & Bonds, D. (2008). Sexual satisfaction and cardiovascular disease: The Women's Health Initiative. *American Journal of Medicine, 121*(4), 295–301.

McCarthy, B. W., & Fucito, L. M. (2005). Integrating medication, realistic expectations, and therapeutic interventions in the treatment of male sexual dysfunction. *Journal of Sex and Marital Therapy, 31*(4), 319–328.

McCarthy, B. W., & Ginsberg, R. L. (2007). Second marriages: Challenges and risks. *Family Journal, 15,* 119.

McCarthy, B., & Casey, T. (2008). Love, sex, and crime: Adolescent romantic relationships and offending. *American Sociological Review, 73*(6), 944–969.

McCauley, J., Calhoun, K., & Gidycz, C. (2010). Binge drinking and rape: A prospective examination of college women with a history of previous sexual victimization. *Journal of Interpersonal Violence, 25*(9), 1655–1668.

McClintock, E. (2010). When does race matter? Race, sex, and dating at an elite university. *Journal of Marriage and Family, 72*(1), 45–73.

McConaghy, N., Hadzi-Pavlovic, D., Stevens, C., Manicavasagar, V., Buhrich, N., & Vollmer-Conna, U. (2006). Fraternal birth order and ratio of heterosexual/

homosexual feelings in women and men. *Journal of Homosexuality, 51*(4), 161–174.

McCoubrey, C. (2002, May 24). Alan P. Bell, 70, researcher of influences on homosexuality. *New York Times.* Retrieved October 12, 2010, from http://www.nytimes.com/2002/05/24/us/alan-p-bell-70-researcher-of-influences-on-homosexuality.html.

McCracken, P. (2006, August 20). Bullying women into suicide to restore honor. *San Francisco Chronicle.* Retrieved October 5, 2010, from http://www.sfgate.com/cgi-bin/article.cgi?file5/chronicle/archive/2006/08/20/INGD9KJ5U61.DTL.

McDougall, D. (2010, May 30). Cries from the beloved country. *The Sunday Times.* Retrieved April 30, 2011, from http://www .timesonline.co.uk/tol/news/world/africa/article7133312.ece.

McDowall, A., & Khan, S. (2004, November 25). The Ayatollan and the transsexual. *The Independent.* Retrieved December 20, 2010, from http://www.independent.co.uk/news/world/middle-east/the-ayatollah-and-the-transsexual-534482.html.

McDowell, B. (1986). The Dutch touch. *National Geographic, 170,* 501–525.

McEwen, G. N., Jr., & Renner, G. (2006). Validity of anogenital distance as a marker of in utero phthalate exposure. *Environmental Health Perspectives, 114*(1), A19–A20.

McFadden, D. (2011). Sexual orientation and the auditory system. *Front Neuroendocrinology.* Retrieved February 20, 2011, from http://www.ncbi.nlm.nih.gov/pubmed/21310172.

McFadden, D., Loehlin, J. C., Breedlove, S., Lippa, R. A., Manning, J. T., & Rahman, Q. (2005). A reanalysis of five studies on sexual orientation and the relative length of the 2nd and 4th fingers (the 2D:4D). *Archives of Sexual Behavior, 34,* 341–356.

McGlynn, K. A., Sakoda, L. C., Rubertone, M. V., Sesterhenn, I. A., Lyu, C., Graubard, B. I., & Erickson, R. L. (2007). Body size, dairy consumption, puberty, and risk of testicular germ cell tumors. *American Journal of Epidemiology, 165*(4), 355–363.

McGrath, R. (1991). Sex offender risk assessment and disposition planning. *International Journal of Offender Treatment and Comparative Criminology, 35*(4), 328–350.

McGuirk, E. M., & Pettijohn, T. F. (2008). Birth order and romantic relationship styles and attitudes in college students. *North American Journal of Psychology, 10,* 37–52.

McKeganey, N., & Bernard, M. (1996). *Sex work on the streets: Prostitutes and their clients.* Philadelphia: Open University Press.

McLaren, A. (1990). *A history of contraception.* Cambridge, MA: Basil Blackwell.

McLean, L. M., & Gallop, R. (2003). Implications of childhood sexual abuse for adult borderline personality disorder and complex post traumatic stress disorder. *American Journal of Psychiatry, 160*(2), 369–371.

McMahon, S. (2004). Student-athletes, rape-supportive culture, and social change. Retrieved October 16, 2005, from http://sexualassault. rutgers.edu/pdfs/ student-athletes_rape-supportive_culture_and_ social_change.pdf.

McMahon, S. (2010). Rape myth beliefs and bystander attitudes among incoming college students. *Journal of American College Health, 59*(1), 3–12.

McManus, A. J., Hunter, L., & Renan, H. (2006). Lesbian experiences and needs during childbirth: Guidance for health care providers. *Journal of Obstetrics and Gynecology in Neonatal Nursing, 35*, 13–23.

McNally, R. J., Clancy, S. A., Barrett, H. M., & Parker, H. A. (2004). Inhibiting retrieval of trauma cues in adults reporting histories of childhood sexual abuse. *Cognition and Emotion, 18*(4), 479–493.

McNally, R. J., Clancy, S. A., Barrett, H. M., & Parker, H. A. (2005). Reality monitoring in adults reporting repressed, recovered, or continuous memories of childhood sexual abuse. *Journal of Abnormal Psychology, 114*(1), 147–152.

Mead, M. (1935/1988/2001). *Sex and temperament in three primitive societies.* New York: William Morrow.

Medrano, M. A., Hatch, J. P., & Zule, W. A. (2003). Childhood trauma and adult prostitution behavior in a multiethnic heterosexual drug-using population. *American Journal of Drug and Alcohol Abuse, 29*(20), 463–486.

Medved, M. (1992). *Hollywood vs. America: Popular culture and the war on traditional values.* New York: HarperCollins.

Mehl, M. R., Vazire, S., Ramirez-Esparza, N., Slatcher, R. B., & Pennebaker, J. W. (2007). Are women really more talkative than men? *Science, 317*, 82.

Mehrabian, A. (2009). *Nonverbal communication.* Piscataway, NJ: Transaction Publishers.

Mehta, C., & Strough, J. (2010). Gender segregation and gender-typing in adolescence. *Sex Roles, 64*(3–4), 251–263.

Meier, E. (2002). Child rape in South Africa. *Pediatric Nursing, 28*(5), 532–535.

Meirik, O., Fraser, I., & d'Arcangues, C. (2003). Implantable contraceptives for women. *Human Reproduction Update, 9*(1), 49–59.

Melisko, M. E., Goldman, M., & Rugo, H. S. (2010). Amelioration of sexual adverse effects in the early breast cancer patient. *Journal of Cancer Survivorship, 4*(3), 247–255.

Meltzer, D. (2005). Complications of body piercing. *American Family Physician, 72*(10), 2029–2034.

Menacker, F., & Hamilton, B. (2010, March). Recent trends in cesarean delivery in the United States. NCHS data brief, no 35. Hyattsville, MD: National Center for Health Statistics. Retrieved from http://www.cdc.gov/nchs/data/databriefs/db35.pdf.

Ménard, K. S., Nagayama Hall, G., Phung, A., Erian Ghebrial, M., & Martin, L. (2003). Gender differences in sexual harassment and coercion in college students. *Journal of Interpersonal Violence, 18*(10), 1222–1239.

Menke, L., Sas, T., Keizer-Schrama, S., Zandwijken, G., Ridder, M., Odink, R., Jansen, M., et al. (2010). Efficacy and safety of oxandrolone in growth hormone-treated girls with Turner syndrome. *Journal of Clinical Endocrinology & Metabolism, 95*(3), 1151–1160.

Menon, R. (2008). Spontaneous preterm birth, a clinical dilemma: Etiologic, pathophysiologic and genetic heterogeneities and racial disparity. *Acta Obstetrica Gynecologic Scandinavica, 87*, 590–600.

Menzler, K., Belke, M., Wehrmann, E., Kradow, K., Lengler, U., Jansen, A., Hamer, H., Oertel, W., Rosenow, F., & Knake, S. (2011). Men and women are different: Diffusion tensor imaging reveals sexual dimorphism in the microstructure of the thalamus, corpus callosum and cingulum. *Neuroimage, 54*, 2557–2562.

Merki-Feld, G. S., & Hund, M. (2007). Clinical experience with NuvaRing in daily practice in Switzerland: Cycle control and acceptability among women of all reproductive ages. *European Journal of Contraceptive and Reproductive Health Care, 12*, 240–247.

Merki-Feld, G. S., Seeger, H., & Mueck, A. O. (2008). Comparison of the proliferative effects of ethinylestradiol on human breast cancer cells in an intermittent and a continuous dosing regime. *Hormone and Metabolic Research.* Retrieved March 18, 2008, from http://www.thieme-connect.com/ ejournals/abstract/hmr/ doi/10.1055/s-2007–1004540.

Mertz, G. (2008). Asymptomatic shedding of herpes simplex virus 1 and 2: Implications for prevention of transmission. *Journal of Infectious Diseases, 198*(8), 1098–1100.

Meschke, L. L., Bartholomae, S., & Zentall, S. R. (2000). Adolescent sexuality and parent-adolescent processes: Promoting healthy teen choices. *Family Relations, 49*(2), 143–155.

Messenger, J. C. (1993). Sex and repression in an Irish folk community. In D. N. Suggs & A. W. Miracle (Eds.), *Culture and human diversity.* Pacific Grove, CA: Brooks/Cole.

Messina, M. (2010). Soybean isoflavone exposure does not have feminizing effects on men: A critical examination of the clinical evidence. *Fertility and Sterility, 93*(7), 2095–2104.

Meston, C. M., & Worcel, M. (2002). The effects of yohimbine plus L-arginine glutamate on sexual arousal in post menopausal women with sexual arousal disorders. *Archives of Sexual Behavior, 31*(4), 323–332.

Meston, C. M., Hull, E., Levin, R., & Sipski, M. (2004). Disorders of orgasm in women. *Journal of Sexual Medicine, 1*, 66–68.

Meston, C. M., Trapnell, P. D., & Gorzalka, B. B. (1996). Ethnic and gender differences in sexuality: Variations in sexual behavior between Asian and non-Asian university students. *Archives of Sex Behavior, 25*(1), 33–71.

Metropolitan Community Churches. (2005). About us. Retrieved November 7, 2005, from http://www.mccchurch.org/AM/TextTemplate.cfm?Section=About_Us&Template=/CM/HTMLDisplay.cfm&ContentID=877.

Meyer-Bahlburg, H. F., Dolezal, C., Baker, S. W., & New, M. I. (2008). Sexual orientation in women with classical or non-classical CAH as a function of degree of prenatal androgen excess. *Archives of Sexual Behavior, 37*, 85–99.

Meyer-Bahlburg, H., Ehrhardt, A., Feldman, J., Rosen, L., Veridiano, N., & Zimmerman, I. (1985). Sexual activity level and sexual functioning in women prenatally exposed to diethylstilbestrol. *Psychosomatic Medicine, 47*(6), 497–511.

Mhloyi, M. M. (1990). Perceptions on communication and sexuality in marriage in Zimbabwe. *Women and Therapy, 10*(3), 61–73.

Mi, T., Abbasi, S., Zhang, H., Uray, K., Chunn, J., Wei, L., Molina, J., Weisbrodt, N., Kellems, R., Blackburn, M., & Xia, Y. (2008).

Excess adenosine in murine penile erectile tissues contributes to priapism via A2B adenosine receptor signaling. *Journal of Clinical Investigation, 118*(4), 1491–1501.

Michael, R. T., Gagnon, J. H., Laumann, E. O., & Kolata, G. (1994). *Sex in America.* Boston, MA: Little, Brown.

Mihalik, G. (1988). Sexuality and gender: An evolutionary perspective. *Psychiatric Annals, 18,* 40–42.

Mikulincer, M., & Shaver, P. (2005). Attachment theory and emotions in close relationships: Exploring the attachment-related dynamics of emotional reactions to relational events. *Personal Relationships, 12*(2), 149–168.

Miletski, H. (2002). *Understanding bestiality and zoophilia.* Bethesda, MD: East-West.

Miller, E., Decker, M. R., Reed, E., Raj, A., Hathaway, J. E., & Silverman, J. G. (2007). Male partner pregnancy-promoting behaviors and adolescent partner violence: Findings from a qualitative study with adolescent females. *Ambulatory Pediatrics, 7*(5), 360–366.

Miller, J. (1998). A review of sex offender legislation. *Kansas Journal of Law and Public Policy, 7,* 40–67.

Milner, J., & Robertson, K. (1990). Comparison of physical child abusers, intrafamilial sexual child abusers, and child neglecters. *Journal of Interpersonal Violence, 5,* 37–48.

Milner, J., Dopke, C., & Crouch, J. (2008). Paraphilia not otherwise specified. In D. Laws & W. O'Donohue (Eds.), *Sexual deviance: Theory, assessment and treatment* (2nd ed., pp. 384–418). New York: Guilford Press.

Mindel, A., & Sawleshwarkar, S. (2008). Condoms for sexually transmissible infection prevention: Politics versus science. *Sexual Health, 5,* 1–8.

Miner, M. H., Coleman, E., Center, B., Ross, M., & Simon Rosser, B. (2007). The compulsive sexual behavior inventory: Psychometric properties. *Archives of Sexual Behavior, 36*(4), 579–587.

Minervini, A., Ralph, D., & Pryor, J. (2006). Outcome of penile prosthesis implantation for treating erectile dysfunction: Experience with 504 procedures. *British Journal of Urology, 97,* 129–133.

Miranda, A., & Fiorello, K. (2002). The connection between social interest and the characteristics of sexual abuse perpetuated by male pedophilies. *Journal of Individual Psychology, 58,* 62–75.

Mirbagher-Ajorpaz, N., Adib-Hajbaghery, M., & Mosaebi, F. (2010). The effects of acupressure on primary dysmenorrheal: A randomized controlled trial. *Complementary Practices in Clinical Practices, 17*(1), 33–36.

Mishna, F., Newman, P., Daley, A., & Soloman, S. (2008, January 5). Bullying of lesbian and gay youth: A qualitative investigation. *British Journal of Social Work.* Retrieved October 2, 2008, from http://bjsw.oxford-journals.org/cgi/content/abstract/bcm148.

Misra, G. (2009). Decriminalising homosexuality in India. *Reproductive Health Matters, 17*(34), 20–28.

Misri, S., Kostaras, X., Fox, D., & Kostaras, D. (2000). The impact of partner support in the treatment of postpartum depression. *Canadian Journal of Psychiatry, 45*(6), 554–559.

Mitchell, K., Finkelhor, D., & Wolak, J. (2003). The exposure of youth to unwanted sexual material on the Internet: A national survey of risk, impact, and prevention. *Youth and Society, 34,* 330–358.

Mitchell, K., Finkelhor, D., & Wolak, J. (2010). Conceptualizing juvenile prostitution as child maltreatment: Findings from the National Juvenile Prostitution Study. *Child Maltreatment, 15*(1), 18–36.

Mittendorf, R., Williams, M. A., Berkey, C. S., & Cotter, P. F. (1990). The length of uncomplicated human gestation. *Obstetrics and Gynecology, 75*(6), 929–932.

Mocarelli, P., Gerthoux, P. M., Patterson, D., Milani, S., Limonta, G., Bertona, M., et al. (2008). Dioxin exposure, from infancy through puberty, produces endocrine disruption and affects human semen quality. *Environmental Health Perspectives, 116,* 70–77.

Mock, S. E., & Cornelius, S. W. (2007). Profiles of interdependence: The retirement planning of married, cohabiting, and lesbian couples. *Sex Roles, 56*(11–12), 793–800.

Modan, B., Hartge, P., Hirsh-Yechezkel, G., Chetrit A., Lubin F., Beller U., et al. (2001). Parity, oral contraceptives, and the risk of ovarian cancer among carriers and noncarriers of a BRCA1 or BRCA2 mutation. *New England Journal of Medicine, 345,* 235–240.

Moegelin, L., Nilsson, B., & Helström, L. (2010). Reproductive health in lesbian and bisexual women in Sweden. *Acta Obstet Gynecol Scand, 89*(2), 205–209.

Moen, V., & Irestedt, L. (2008). Neurological complications following central neuraxial blockades in obstetrics. *Current Opinions in Anesthesiology, 21,* 275–280.

Mofrad, S., Abdullah, R., & Uba, I. (2010). Attachment patterns and separation anxiety symptom. *Asian Social Science, 6*(11), 148–153.

Moller, N. P., Fouladi, R. T., McCarthy, C. J., & Hatch, K. D. (2003). Relationship of attachment and social support to college students' adjustment following a relationship breakup. *Journal of Counseling & Development, 81,* 354–369.

Mommers, E., Kersemaekers, J., Kepers, M., Apter, D., Behre, H., Beynon, J., et al. (2008). Male hormonal contraception: A double-blind, placebo-controlled study. *Journal of Clinical Endocrinology and Metabolism, 93,* 2572–2580.

Monasch, R., & Boerma, J. (2004). Orphanhood and childcare patterns in sub-Saharan Africa: An analysis of national survey from 40 countries. *AIDS, 18, (suppl 2),* S55-S65.

Monat-Haller, R. K. (1992). *Understanding and experiencing sexuality.* Baltimore: Brookes.

Money, J. (1955). Hermaphroditism, gender, and precocity in hyper-adrenocorticism: Psychologic findings. *Bulletin of the Johns Hopkins Hospital, 96,* 253–254.

Money, J. (1975). Ablatio penis: Normal male infant sex-reassigned as a girl. *Archives of Sexual Behavior, 4*(1), 65–71.

Money, J. (1984). Paraphilias: Phenomenology and classification. *American Journal of Psychotherapy, 38,* 164–179.

Money, J. (1986). *Venuses penuses: Sexology, sexophy, and exigency theory.* Buffalo, NY: Prometheus Books.

Money, J. (1990). Pedophilia: A specific instance of new phylism theory as applied to paraphiliac lovemaps. In J. Feierman (Ed.), *Pedophilia: Biosocial dimensions* (pp. 445–463). New York: Springer-Verlag.

Mongiat-Artus, P. (2004) Torsion of the spermatic cord and testicular annexes. *Annals of Urology, 38*(1), 25–34.

Monroe, L. M., Kinney, L., Weist, M., Dafeamekpor, D., Dantzler, J., & Reynolds, M. (2005). The experience of sexual assault: Findings from a statewide victim needs assessment. *Journal of Interpersonal Violence, 20*(7), 767–776.

Montemurro, B., & McClure, B. (2005). Changing gender norms for alcohol consumption. *Sex Roles, 52,* 279–288.

Montirosso, R., Peverelli, M., Frigerio, E., Crespi, M., & Borgatti, R. (2010). The development of dynamic facial expression recognition at different intensities in 4- to 18-year-olds. *Social Development, 19*(1), 71.

Monto, M. A. (2000). Why men seek out prostitutes. In R. Weitzer (Ed.), *Sex for sale:*

Prostitution, pornography, and the sex industry (pp. 67–83). New York: Routledge.

Monto, M. A. (2001). Prostitution and fellatio. *Journal of Sex Research, 38*(2), 140–146.

Monto, M. A., & McRee, N. (2005). A comparison of the male customers of female street prostitutes with national samples of men. *International Journal of Offender Therapy and Comparative Criminology, 49*(5), 505–529.

Mookodi, G., Ntshebe, O., & Taylor, I. (2004). Botswana. In R. T. Francoeur & R. J. Noonan (Eds.), *The Continuum International encyclopedia of sexuality* (pp. 89–97). New York/London: Continuum International.

Moor, B., Crone, E., & der Molen, M. (2010). The heartbrake of social rejection: Heart rate deceleration in response to unexpected peer rejection. *Psychological Science, 21*(9), 1326–1333.

Moore, M. (1994, October 8). Changing India: Arranged marriages persist with 90s twist. *The Washington Post.*

Moore, M. E. (2010). Communication involving long-term dating partners' sexual conversations: The connection between religious faith and sexual intimacy. *Dissertation Abstract International, 48/05.* University of Arkansas, AAT #1484652.

Morales, A. (2004). Andropause (or symptomatic late-onset hypogonadism): Facts, fiction and controversies. *Aging Male, 7*(4), 297–304.

Morales, A. M., Casillas, M., & Turbi, C. (2011). Patients' preference in the treatment of erectile dysfunction: A critical review of the literature. *International Journal of Impotence Research, 23*(1), 1–8.

Moreira, A. J. (2007). Equality for same sex couples: Brazilian courts and social inclusiveness. *Harvard Review of Latin America.* Retrieved February 20, 2011, from http://www.drclas.harvard.edu/revista/articles/view/967.

Morello, C. S., Levinson, M. S., Kraynyak, K. A., & Spector, D. H. (2011). Immunization with herpes simplex virus 2 (HSV-2) genes plus inactivated HSV-2 is highly protective against acute and recurrent HSV-2 disease. *Journal of Virology, 85*(7), 3461–3472.

Moreno, V., Bosch, F. X., Munoz, N., Meijer C. J., Shah K. V., Walboomers J. M., et al. (2002). Effect of oral contraceptives on risk of cervical cancer in women with human papillomavirus infection: The IARC multicentric case-control study. *Lancet, 359*, 1085–1092.

Moreno-Garcia, M., Fernandez-Martinez, F. J., & Miranda, E. B. (2005). Chromosomal anomalies in patients with short stature. *Pediatric International, 47*(5), 546–549.

Morgan, S. P., & Rindfuss, R. (1985). Marital disruption: Structural and temporal dimensions. *American Journal of Sociology, 90*(5), 1055–1077.

Morley, J., & Perry, H. (2000). Androgen deficiency in aging men. *Journal of Laboratory and Clinical Medicine, 135*(5), 370–378.

Morris, B. J. (2007). Why circumcision is a biomedical imperative for the 21st century. *Bioessays, 29*, 1147–1158.

Morris, R. J. (1990). Aikane: Accounts of Hawaiian same-sex relationships in the journals of Captain Cook's third voyage (1776–1780). *Journal of Homosexuality, 19*, 21–54.

Morrison, T. G. (2007). Children of homosexuals and transsexuals more apt to be homosexual: A reply to Cameron. *Journal of Biosocial Science, 39*(1), 153–156.

Morrison-Beedy, D., Carey, M. P., Cote-Arsenault, D., Seibold-Simpson, S., & Robinson, K. A. (2008). Understanding sexual abstinence in urban adolescent girls. *Journal of Obstetric, Gynecologic, and Neonatal Nursing, 37*, 185.

Morrow, K. M., & Allsworth, J. E. (2000). Sexual risk in lesbians and bisexual women. *Journal of Gay and Lesbian Medical Association, 4*(4), 159–165.

Morse, E. V., Simon, P. M., Balson, P. M., & Osofsky, H. J. (1992). Sexual behavior patterns of customers of male street prostitutes. *Archives of Sexual Behavior, 21*, 347–357.

Mortenson, S. T. (2002). Sex, communication, values, and cultural values. *Communication Reports, 15*(1), 57–71.

Mosconi, A. M., Roila, F., Gatta, G., & Theodore, C. (2005). Cancer of the penis. *Critical Reviews in Oncology/Hematology, 53*(2), 165–178.

Moser, C. (1988). Sadomasochism. Special issue: The sexually unusual: Guide to understanding and helping. *Journal of Social Work and Human Sexuality, 7*, 43–56.

Mosher, W. D., & Jones, J. (2010). Use of contraception in the United States: 1982–2008. *Vital Health Statistics, 23*(29), 1–44.

Mosher, W. D., Martinez, G. M., Chandra, A., Abma, J. C., & Wilson, S. J. (2004). Use of contraception and use of family planning services in the United States: 1982–2002. *Advance Data from Vital and Health Statistics,* no. 350. Retrieved May 27, 2008,

from http://www.cdc.gov/nchs/data/ad/ad350.pdf.

Moskowitz, C. (2008, May 16). Same sex couples common in the wild. *LiveScience.* Retrieved October 2, 2008, from http://www.livescience.com/animals/080516-gay-animals.html.

Mruk, D. D. (2008). New perspectives in non-hormonal male contraception. *Trends in Endocrinology and Metabolism, 19*(2), 57–64.

Mueck, A. O., & Seeger, H. (2008). The World Health Organization defines hormone replacement therapy as carcinogenic: Is this implausible? *Gynecological Endocrinology, 24*, 129–132.

Mueck, A. O., Seeger, H., & Rabe, T. (2010). Hormonal contraception and risk of endometrial cancer: A systematic review. *Endocrine Related Cancer, 17*(4), R263–R271.

Muehlenhard, C. L., & Cook, S. W. (1988). Men's self-reports of unwanted sexual activity. *Journal of Sex Research, 24*, 58–72.

Muehlenhard, C., & Shippee, S. (2010). Men's and women's reports of pretending orgasm. *Journal of Sex Research, 47*(6), 552–567.

Mufti, U., Ghani, K., Samman, R., Virdi, J., & Potluri, B. (2008). Anejaculation as an atypical presentation of prostate cancer: A case report. *Cases Journal, 1*, 81.

Muir, J. G. (1993, March 31). Homosexuals and the 10% fallacy. *The Wall Street Journal,* p. A14.

Mukherjee, B., & Shivakumar, T. (2007). A case of sensorineural deafness following ingestion of sildenafil. *Journal of Laryngology and Otology, 121*, 395–397.

Mulders, T. M., & Dieben, T. (2001). Use of the novel combined contraceptive vaginal ring NuvaRing® for ovulation inhibition. *Fertility and Sterility, 75*, 865–870.

Mulick, P. S., & Wright, L. W. (2002). Examining the existence of biphobia in the heterosexual and homosexual populations. *Journal of Bisexuality, 2*, 45–65.

Muller, J. E., Mittleman, M. A., Maclure, M., Sherwood, J. B., & Toffer, G. H. (1996). Triggering myocardial infarction by sexual activity. *Journal of the American Medical Association, 275*(18), 1405–1409.

Mulligan, E., & Heath, M. (2007). Seeking open minded doctors. How women who identify as bisexual, queer or lesbian seek quality health care. *Australian Family Physician, 36*, 385–480.

Mulvaney, B. M. (1994). Gender differences in communication: An intercultural experience. Paper prepared by the Department of Communication, Florida Atlantic University.

Mumba, M. (2010). A phenomenological study of how college students communicate about anal sex and its implications for health. *Dissertation Abstracts,* Ohio University, AAT #3433979.

Munk-Olsen, T., Laursen, T. M., Pedersen, C. B., Lidegaard, Ø., & Mortensen, P. B. (2011). Induced first-trimester abortion and risk of mental disorder. *New England Journal of Medicine, 364*(4), 332–339.

Munsey, C. (2009, October). Insufficient evidence to support sexual orientation change efforts. *Monitor on Psychology, 40*(9), 29.

Munson, M. (1987). How do you do it? *On Our Backs, 4*(1).

Muratori, M., Marchiani, S., Tamburrino, L., Forti, G., Luconi, M., & Baldi, E. (2011). Markers of human sperm functions in the ICSI era. *Frontiers in Bioscience, 1*(16), 1344–1363.

Murina F., Bernorio R., & Palmiotto, R. (2008). The use of amielle vaginal trainers as adjuvant in the treatment of vestibulodynia: An observational multicentric study. *Medscape Journal of Medicine, 10*(1), 23.

Murina, F., Bianco, V., Radici, G., Felice, R., & Signaroldi, M. (2010). Electrodiagnostic functional sensory evaluation of patients with generalized vulvodynia: A pilot study. *Journal of Lower Genital Tract Diseases, 14*(3), 221–224.

Murnen, S., & Kohlman, M. (2007). Athletic participation, fraternity membership, and sexual aggression among college men: A meta-analysis review. *Sex Roles, 57,* 145–157.

Murnen, S. K., Wright, C., & Kaluzny, G. (2002). If boys will be boys then girls will be victims? A meta-analytic review of the research that relates masculine ideology to sexual aggression. *Sex Roles, 46*(11–12), 359–375.

Murphy, L. (2010). Understanding the social and economic contexts surrounding women engaged in street-level prostitution. *Issues in Mental Health Nursing, 31*(12), 775–784.

Murphy, L. R. (1990). Defining the crime against nature: Sodomy in the United States appeals courts, 1810–1940. *Journal of Homosexuality, 19,* 49–66.

Murphy, W., & Page, J. (2008). Exhibitionism: Psychopathology and theory. In D. Laws & W. O'Donohue (Eds.), *Sexual deviance: Theory, assessment and treatment* (2nd ed., pp. 61–75). New York: Guilford Press.

Murray, J. (2000). Psychological profile of pedophiles and child molesters. *Journal of Psychology, 134*(2), 211–224.

Murray, K. M., Ciarrocchi, J. W., & Murray-Swank, N. A. (2007). Spirituality, religiosity, shame, and guilt as predictors of sexual attitudes and experiences. *Journal of Psychology and Theology, 35,* 222–234.

Murray, S., & Dynes, W. (1999). Latin American gays: Snow Whites and snake charmers. *The Economist, 353*(8150), 82.

Murray-Swank, N. A., Pargament, K., & Mahoney, A. (2005). At the crossroads of sexuality and spirituality: The sanctification of sex by college students. *International Journal of the Psychology of Religion, 15,* 199–219.

Musacchio, N., Hartrich, M., & Garofalo, R. (2006). Erectile dysfunction and Viagra use: What's up with college males? *Journal of Adolescent Health, 39,* 452–454.

Mustanski, B. (2001). Getting wired: Exploiting the internet for the collection of valid sexuality data. *Journal of Sex Research, 38*(4), 292–302.

Musters, A. M., Taminiau-Bloem, E. F., van den Boogaard, E., van der Veen, F., & Goddijn, M. (2011). Supportive care for women with unexplained recurrent miscarriage: Patients' perspectives. *Human Reproduction, 26,* 873–877.

Myslewski, R. (2009, September 29). UK, France mull photoshop fakery laws. *The Register.* Retrieved October 1, 2010, from http://www.theregister.co.uk/2009/09/29/photoshop_laws/.

Nacci, P. L., & Kane, T. R. (1983). The incidence of sex and sexual aggression in federal prisons. *Federal Probation, 47,* 31–36.

Nadelson, C. C., Notman, M. T., Zackson, H., & Gornick, J. (1982). A follow-up study of rape victims. *American Journal of Psychiatry, 139,* 1266–1270.

Nader, S. (2010). Infertility and pregnancy in women with polycystic ovary syndrome. *Minerva Endocrinology, 35*(4), 211–225.

Nagai, A., Hara, R., Yokoyama, T., Jo, Y., Fujii, T., & Miyaji, Y. (2008). Ejaculatory dysfunction caused by the new alpha1-blocker silodosin: A preliminary study to analyze human ejaculation using color Doppler ultrasonography. *International Journal of Urology, 15*(10), 915–918.

Nagel, B., Matsuo, H., McIntyre, K. P., & Morrison, N. (2005). Attitudes toward victims of rape: Effects of gender, race, religion, and social class. *Journal of Interpersonal Violence, 20*(6), 725–737.

Nagel, J. (2003). *Race, ethnicity and sexuality.* New York: Oxford University Press.

Nahshoni, K. (2010, July 28). US rabbis: Accept homosexuals. *Ynet news.* Retrieved February 19, 2011, from http://www.ynetnews.com/articles/0,7340,L-3926452,00.html.

Nair, V. R., & Baguley, S. (2010). Tracking down chlamydia infection in primary care. *Practitioner, 254*(1732), 24–26, 3.

Najman, J. M., Dunne, M. P., Purdie, D. M., Boyle, F. M., & Coxeter, P. D. (2005). Sexual abuse in childhood and sexual dysfunction in adulthood: An Australian population-based study. *Archives of Sexual Behavior, 34*(5), 517–526.

Namuo, C. (2010, October 8). UNH football player charged with rape. Manchester, NH: *The Union Leader,* p. A1.

Nanda, S. (2001). *Gender diversity: Crosscultural variations.* Prospect Heights, IL: Waveland Press.

Nappi, R., Albani, F., Santamaria, V., Tonani, S., Martini, E., Terreno, E., Brambilla, E., & Polatti, F. (2010). Menopause and sexual desire: The role of testosterone. *Menopause International, 16*(4), 162–168.

Narod, S. (2011). Age of diagnosis, tumor size, and survival after breast cancer: Implications for mammographic screening. *Breast Cancer Research and Treatment, 128,* 259–266.

Narod, S. A., Dube, M. P., Klijn, J., Lubinski, J., Lynch, H. T., Ghadirian, P., Provencher, D., Heimdal, K., Moller, P., Robson, M., Offit, K., Isaacs, C., Weber, B., Friedman, E., et al. (2002). Oral contraceptives and the risk of breast cancer in BRCA1 and BRCA2 mutation carriers. *Journal of National Cancer Institute, 94*(23), 1773–1779.

Narod, S. A., Sun, P., Ghadirian, P., Lynch, H., Isaacs, C., Garber, J., Weber, B., Karlan, B., Fishman, D., Rosen, B., Tung, N., & Neuhausen, S. L. (2001). Tubal ligation and risk of ovarian cancer in carriers of BRCA1 or BRCA2 mutations: A case-control study. *Lancet, 357*(9267), 843–844.

Natali, A., & Turek, P. (2011). An assessment of new sperm tests for male infertility. *Urology, 77*(5), 1027–1034.

National Cancer Institute. (2009). Human papillomavirus (HPV) vaccines. U.S. National Institutes of Health, National Cancer Institute. Retrieved April 1, 2010, from http://www.cancer.gov/cancertopics/factsheet/prevention/HPV-vaccine.

National Coalition of Anti-Violence Programs. (1998, October 6). Annual report on lesbian, gay, bisexual, and transgender domestic violence. Retrieved May 23, 2003, from http://www.hrc.org/issues/hate_crimes/antiviolence.asp.

National Student GenderBlind. (2010). 2010 Campus Equality Index: Colleges and universities with inclusive rooming policies. Retrieved November 13, 2010, from http://www.genderblind.org/wp-content/uploads/2010/07/2010CampusEqualityIndex.pdf.

National Telecommunications and Information Administration and the U.S. Department of Commerce. (1999). Falling through the Net: Defining the digital divide: A report on the telecommunications and information technology gap in America. Retrieved June 1, 2002, from http://www.ntia.doc.gov/ntiahome/fttn99/contents.html.

Nauru, T., Suleiman, M., Kiwi, A., Anther, M., Wear, S. Q., Irk, S., & Rive, J. (2008). Intra-cytoplasmic sperm injection outcome using ejaculated sperm and retrieved sperm in azoospermic men. *Urology, 5,* 106–110.

Navai, R. (2009, March 27). Women told: 'You have dishonoured your family, please kill yourself.' *The Independent.* Retrieved October 5, 2010, from http://www.independent.co.uk/news/world/europe/women-told-you-have-dishonoured-your-family-please-kill-yourself-1655373.html.

Naz, R. K. (2005). Contraceptive vaccines. *Drugs, 65,* 593–603.

Naz, R. K. (2009). Development of genetically engineered human sperm immunocontraceptives. *Journal of Reproductive Immunology, 83*(1–2), 145–150.

Naziri, D. (2007). Man's involvement in the experience of abortion and the dynamics of the couple's relationship: A clinical study. *European Journal of Contraceptive and Reproductive Health Care, 12,* 168–174.

Neal, J., & Frick-Horbury, D. (2001). The effects of parenting styles and childhood attachment patterns on intimate relationships. *Journal of Instructional Psychology, 28*(3), 178–183.

Nebehay, S. (2004). Cervical cancer epidemic in poor countries. Retrieved December 12, 2004, from http://www.reuters.co.uk/printerFriendlyPopup.jhtml?type=healthNews&storyID=7114888.

Needham, B. L., & Austin, E. L. (2010). Sexual orientation, parental support, and health during the transition to young adulthood. *Journal of Youth and Adolescence, 39*(10), 1189–1198.

Neergaard, L. (2005). Doctors are holding off on surgery for newborns of uncertain gender. Retrieved February 22, 2005, from http://www.cleveland.com/health/plain-

dealer/index.ssf?/base/news/110889699317860.xml.

Neff, C., Kurisu, T., Ndolo, T., Fox, K., & Akkina, R. (2011). A topical microbicide gel formulation of CCR5 antagonist maraviroc prevents HIV-1 vaginal transmission in humanized RAG-hu mice. *PLoS One, 6*(6). Retrieved July 27, 2011, from http://www.plosone.org/article/info%3Adoi%2F10.1371%2Fjournal.pone.0020209.

Neff, L., & Karney, B. (2005). To know you is to love you: The implications of global adoration and specific accuracy for marital relationships. *Journal of Personality & Social Psychology, 88*(3), 480–497.

Neisen, J. H. (1990). Heterosexism: Redefining homophobia for the 1990s. *Journal of Gay and Lesbian Psychotherapy, 1,* 21–35.

Nelson, A. L. (2007). Communicating with patients about extended-cycle and continuous use of oral contraceptives. *Journal of Women's Health, 16,* 463–470.

Nelson, C., Ahmed, A., Valenzuela, R., & Melhall, J. (2007). Assessment of penile vibratory stimulation as a management strategy in men with secondary retarded orgasm. *Urology, 69,* 552–555.

Nelson, H. D. (2008). Menopause. *Lancet, 372,* 760–770.

Nelson, R. (2005). Gottman's sound medical house model. Retrieved September 3, 2005, from http://www.psychpage.com/family/library/gottman.html

Németh, Z., Kun, B., & Demetrovics, Z. (2010). The involvement of gamma-hydroxybutyrate in reported sexual assaults: A systematic review. *Journal of Psychopharmacology, 24*(9), 1281–1287.

Neri, Q., Takeuchi, T., & Palermo, G. (2008). An update of assisted reproductive technologies results in the U.S. *Annals of the New York Academy of Sciences, 1127,* 41–49.

Neruda, B. (2005). Development and current status of combined spinal epidural anaesthesia [article in German]. *Anasthesiol Intensivemed Nofallmed Schmerzther, 40*(8), 4590–460.

Ness, R. B., Dodge, R. C., Edwards, R. P., Baker, J. A., & Moysich, K. B. (2011). Contraception methods, beyond oral contraceptives and tubal ligation, and risk of ovarian cancer. *Annals of Epidemiology, 21*(3), 188–196.

New, J. F. H. (1969). *The Renaissance and Reformation: A short history.* New York: Wiley.

Newcomb, M. E., & Mustanski, B. (2010). Internalized homophobia and internalizing

mental health problems: A meta-analytic review. *Clinical Psychology Review, 30*(8), 1019–1029.

Newell, M., Coovadia, H., Cortina-Borja, M., Rollins, N., Gaillard, P., & Dabis, F. (2004). Mortality of infected and uninfected infants born to HIV-infected mothers in Africa: A pooled analysis. *Lancet, 364*(9441), 1236–1243.

Newfield, E., Hart, S., Dibble, S., & Kohler, L. (2006). Female-to-male transgender quality of life. *Quality of Life Research, 15,* 1447–1457.

Newman, L., & Nyce, J. (Eds.). (1985). *Women's medicine: A cross-cultural study of indigenous fertility regulation.* New Brunswick, NJ: Rutgers University Press.

Newring, K., Wheeler, J., & Draper, C. (2008). Transvestic fetishism: Assessment and treatment. In D. Laws & W. O'Donohue (Eds.), *Sexual deviance: Theory, assessment and treatment* (2nd ed., pp. 285–304). New York: Guilford Press.

Ng, E., & Ma, J. L. (2004). Hong Kong. In R. T. Francoeur & R. J. Noonan (Eds.), *The Continuum International encyclopedia of sexuality* (pp. 489–502). New York/London: Continuum International.

Ngun, T. C., Ghahramani, N., Sanchez, F. J., Bocklandt, S., & Vilain, E. (2011). The genetics of sex differences in brain and behavior. *Frontiers in Neuroendocrinology, 32*(2), 227–246.

Nicholas, D. R. (2000). Men, masculinity and cancer. *Journal of American College Health, 49*(1), 27–33.

Nichols, M. (1990). Lesbian relationships: Implications for the study of sexuality and gender. In D. McWhiter, S. A. Sanders, & J. Reinish (Eds.), *Homosexuality/heterosexuality: Concepts of sexual orientation* (pp. 350–364). The Kinsey Institute Series. New York: Oxford University Press.

Nicolaides, K. H., Spencer, K., Avgidou, K., Faiola, S., & Falcon, O. (2005). Multicenter study of first-trimester screening for trisomy 21 in 75,821 pregnancies: Results and estimation of the potential impact of individual risk-orientated two-stage first-trimester screening. *Ultrasound Obstetrics and Gynecology, 25*(3), 221–226.

Nicoll, L. M., & Skupski, D. W. (2008). Venous air embolism after using a birth-training device. *Obstetrics and Gynecology, 111,* 489–491.

Niedzviecki, H. (2009). *The peep diaries: How we're learning to love watching ourselves and our neighbors.* San Francisco, CA: City Lights Books.

Nieman, L. K., Blocker, W., Nansel, T., Mahoney, S., Reynolds, J., Blithe, D., Wesley, R., & Armstrong, A. (2011). Efficacy and tolerability of CDB-2914 treatment for symptomatic uterine fibroids: A randomized, double-blind, placebo-controlled, phase IIb study. *Fertility and Sterility, 95*(2), 767–772.e1–2.

Nilsson, L. (1990). *A child is born.* New York: Delacorte Press, Bantam Books.

Njus, D., & Bane, C. (2009). Religious identification as a moderator of evolved sexual strategies of men and women. *Journal of Sex Research, 46*(6), 546–557.

Noland, C. M. (2010). *Sex talk: The role of communication in intimate relationships.* Portland, OR: Praeger Publishing.

Noller, P. (1993, March-June). Gender and emotional communication in marriage: Different cultures or differential social power? *Journal of Language & Social Psychology, 12*(1–2), 132–152.

Nonnemaker, J., McNeely, C., & Blum, R. (2003). Public and private domains of religiosity and adolescent health risk behaviors: Evidence from the National Longitudinal Study of Adolescent Health. *Social Science & Medicine, 57*(11), 2049–2054.

Nordling, N., Sandnabba, N., Santilla, P., & Alison, L. (2006). Differences and similarities between gay and straight individuals involved in the SM subculture. *Journal of Homosexuality, 50*(2–3), 41–67.

Nordtveit, T., Melve, K., Albrechtsen, S., & Skjaerven, R. (2008). Maternal and paternal contribution to intergenerational recurrence of breech delivery: Population based cohort study. *British Medical Journal, 336,* 843–844.

Notman, M. T. (2002). Changes in sexual orientation and object choice in midlife in women. *Psychoanalytic Inquiry, 22,* 182–195.

Nour, N. M. (2004). Female genital cutting: Clinical and cultural guidelines. *Obstetrical & Gynecological Survey, 59*(4), 272–279.

Nour, N. M. (2006). Health consequences of child marriage in Africa. *Emerging Infectious Diseases, 12*(11). Retrieved June 26, 2008, from http://www.cdc.gov/ncidod/EID/vol12no11/06–0510.htm.

Novák, A., de la Loge, C., Abetz, L., & van der Meulen, E. (2003). The combined contraceptive vaginal ring, NuvaRing: An international study of user acceptability. *Contraception, 67,* 187–194.

NuvaRing now available for Australian women. (2007, April 8). *Women's Health Law Weekly.* NewsRX. Retrieved December 19, 2008, from http://www.newsrx.com/article.php?articleID=519768

Oakes, M., Eyvazzadeh, A., Quint, E., & Smith, Y. (2008). Complete androgen insensitivity syndrome—a review. *Journal of Pediatric and Adolescent Gynecology, 21,* 305–310.

Ochsenkühn, R., Hermelink, K., Clayton, A. H., von Schönfeldt, V., Gallwas, J., Ditsch, N., Rogenhofer, N., & Kahlert, S. (2011). Menopausal status in breast cancer patients with past chemotherapy determines long-term hypoactive sexual desire disorder. *Journal of Sexual Medicine, 8*(5), 1486–1494.

O'Connell, H. E., & DeLancey, D. O. (2005). Clitoral anatomy in nulliparous, healthy, premenopausal volunteers using enhanced magnetic resonance imaging. *Journal of Urology, 173,* 2060–2063.

O'Connor, M. (2008). Reconstructing the hymen: Mutilation or restoration? *Journal of Law, Medicine, and Ethics, 16*(1), 161–175.

O'Farrell, N. (2002). Donovanosis. *Sexually Transmitted Infections, 78,* 452–457.

Ofman, U. (2004). "… And how are things sexually?": Helping patients adjust to sexual changes before, during, and after cancer treatment. *Supportive Cancer Therapy, 1,* 243–247.

Ogilvie, G., Taylor, D., Trussler, T., Marchand, R., Gilbert, M., Moniruzzaman, A., & Rekart, M. (2008). Seeking sexual partners on the Internet: A marker for risky sexual behavior in men who have sex with men. *Canadian Journal of Public Health, 99,* 185–188.

Ogletree, S. M., & Ginsburg, H. J. (2000). Kept under the hood: Neglect of the clitoris in common vernacular. *Sex Roles, 43*(11–12), 917–927.

O'Grady, R. (2001). Eradicating pedophilia toward the humanization of society. *Journal of International Affairs, 55*(1), 123–140.

O'Halloran, R. L., & Dietz, P. E. (1993). Autoerotic fatalities with power hydraulics. *Journal of Forensic Sciences, 38,* 359–364.

O'Hare, T. (2005). Risky sex and drinking contexts in freshman first offenders. *Addictive Behaviors, 30*(3), 585–588.

Ohl, D. A., Quallich, S. A., Sønksen, J., Brackett, N. L., & Lynne, C. M. (2008). Anejaculation and retrograde ejaculation. *Urology Clinics of North America, 35*(2), 211–220.

Ojanen, T., Sijtsema, J., Hawley, P., & Little, T. (2010). Intrinsic and extrinsic motivation in early adolescents' friendship development: Friendship selection, influence, and prospective friendship quality. *Journal of Adolescence, 33*(6), 837.

Okami, P. (1990). Sociopolitical biases in the contemporary scientific literature on adult human sexual behavior with children and adolescents. In J. Feierman (Ed.), *Pedophilia* (pp. 91–121). New York: Springer Verlag.

Okami, P., Olmstead, R., & Abramson, P. R. (1997). Sexual experiences in early childhood: 18-year longitudinal data from the UCLA Family Lifestyles Project. *Journal of Sex Research, 34*(4), 339–347.

Okami, P., Olmstead, R., & Abramson, P. R. (1998). Early childhood exposure to parental nudity and scenes of parental sexuality ("primal scenes"): An 18-year longitudinal study of outcome. *Archives of Sexual Behavior, 27*(4), 361–384.

Oliver, C., Beech, A., Fisher, D., & Beckett, R. (2007). A comparison of rapists and sexual murderers on demographic and selected psychometric measures. *International Journal of Offender Therapy and Comparative Criminology, 51,* 298.

Olsson, S. E., & Möller, A. (2006). Regret after sex reassignment surgery in a male-to-female transsexual: A long-term follow up. *Archives of Sexual Behavior, 35,* 501–506.

O'Neill, N., & O'Neill, G. (1972). *Open marriage: A new life style for couples.* New York: Evans.

Oner, B. (2001). Factors predicting future time orientation for romantic relationships with the opposite sex. *Journal of Psychology: Interdisciplinary & Applied, 135*(4), 430–438.

Oriel, K. A., & Schrager, S. (1999). Abnormal uterine bleeding. *American Family Physician, 60*(5), 1371–1380.

Orlandi, F., Rossi, C., Orlandi, E., Jakil, M. C., Hallahan, T. W., Macri, V. J., & Krantz, D.A. (2005). First-trimester screening for tisomy-21 using a simplified method to assess the presence or absence of the fetal nasal bone. *American Journal of Obstetrics & Gynecology, 192*(4), 1107–1111.

Ornish, D. (1999). *Love and survival: The scientific basis for the healing power of intimacy.* New York: Harper Paperbacks.

Ortigue, S., Bianchi-Demicheli, F., Patel, N., Frum, C., & Lewis, J. (2010). Neuroimaging of love: fMRI meta-analysis evidence toward new perspectives in sexual medicine. *Journal of Sexual Medicine, 7*(11), 3541–3552.

Ortiz, C. A., Freeman, J. L., Kuo, Y. F., & Goodwin, J. S. (2007). The influence of marital status on stage at diagnosis and survival of older persons with melanoma. *Journals of Gerontology, Series A: Biological Sciences and Medical Sciences, 62,* 892–898.

Oselin, S. (2010). Weighing the consequences of a deviant career: Factors leading to an exit from prostitution. *Sociological Perspectives, 53*(4), 527–549.

O'Sullivan, L., & Allgeier, E. (1998). Feigning sexual desire: Consenting to unwanted sexual activity in heterosexual dating relationships. *Journal of Sex Research, 35,* 234–243.

O'Sullivan, L. F., Udell, W., Montrose, V. A., Antoniello, P., & Hoffman, S. (2010). A cognitive analysis of college students' explanations for engaging in unprotected sexual intercourse. *Archives of Sexual Behavior, 39*(5), 1121–1131.

Oswald, R., & Clausell, E. (2005). Same-sex relationships and their dissolution. In M. Fine & J. Harvey (Eds.), *Handbook of divorce and relationship dissolution* (pp. 499–513). New York: Routledge.

Otis, M. D., & Skinner, W. F. (1996). The prevalence of victimization and its effect on mental well-being among lesbian and gay people. *Journal of Homosexuality, 30,* 93–121.

Oultram, S. (2009). All hail the new flesh: Some thoughts on scarification, children and adults. *Journal of Medical Ethics, 35*(10), 607–610.

Owen, J., & Fincham, F. (2011). Young adults' emotional reactions after hooking up encounters. *Archives of Sexual Behavior, 40*(2), 321–341.

Owen, R. (2009). Dapoxetine: A novel treatment for premature ejaculation. *Drugs Today, 45*(9), 669–678.

Ozdemir, O., Simsek, F., Ozkardes, S., Incesu, C., & Karakoc, B. (2008). The unconsummated marriage: Its frequency and clinical characteristics in a sexual dysfunction clinic. *Journal of Sex and Marital Therapy, 34,* 268–279.

Pacey, A. (2010). Environmental and lifestyle factors associated with sperm DNA damage. *Human Fertility, 13*(4), 189–193.

Pachankis, J. E., & Goldfried, M. R. (2004). Clinical issues in working with lesbian, gay, and bisexual clients. *Psychotherapy: Theory, Research, Practice, Training, 41,* 227–246.

Pacik, P. T. (2009). Botox treatment for vaginismus. *Plastic and Reconstructive Surgery, 124*(6), 455e–456e.

Padgett, V. R., Brislin-Slutz, J. A., & Neal, J. A. (1989). Pornography, erotica, and attitudes toward women: The effects of repeated exposure. *The Journal of Sex Research, 26,* 479–491.

Paek, H., Nelson, M., & Vilela, A. (2010). Examination of gender-role portrayals in television advertising across seven countries. *Sex Roles, 64,* 192–207.

Paik, A. (2010). "Hookups," dating, and relationship quality: Does the type of sexual involvement matter? *Social Science Research, 39*(5), 739–753.

Palacios, S. (2011). Hypoactive sexual desire disorder and current pharmacotherapeutic options in women. *Womens Health, 7*(1), 95–107.

Palca, J. (1991). Fetal brain signals time for birth. *Science, 253,* 1360.

Palefsky, J. (2008). Human papillomavirus and anal neoplasia. *Current HIV/AIDS Report, 5,* 78–85.

Palit, V., & Eardley, I. (2010). An update on new oral PDE5 inhibitors for the treatment of erectile dysfunction. *Nature Reviews Urology, 7*(11), 603–609.

Palomares, N., & Lee, E. (2010). Virtual gender identity: The linguistic assimilation to gendered avatars in computer-mediated communication. *Journal of Language and Social Psychology, 29*(1), 5.

Pandey, M. K., Rani, R., & Agrawal, S. (2005). An update in recurrent spontaneous abortion. *Archives of Gynecology & Obstetrics, 272*(2), 95–108.

Pandey, S., & Bhattacharyta, S. (2010). Impact of obesity on gynecology. *Women's Health, 6*(1), 107–117.

Panjari, M., Bell, R., & Davis, S. (2011). Sexual function after breast cancer. *Journal of Sexual Medicine, 8*(1), 294–302.

Papalia, D. E., Sterns, H. L., Feldman, R., & Camp, C. (2002). *Adult development and aging* (2nd ed.). Boston: McGraw-Hill.

Pappo, I., Lerner-Geva, L., Halevy, A., Olmer, L., Friedler, S., Raziel, A., et al. (2008). The possible association between IVF and breast cancer incidence. *Annals of Surgical Oncology, 15,* 1048–1055.

Pardue, A., & Arrigo, B. (2008). Power, anger, and sadistic rapists: Toward a differentiated model of offender personality. *International Journal of Offender Therapy and Comparative Criminology, 52,* 378–400.

Pardun, C. J., L'Engle, K. L., & Brown, J. D. (2005). Linking exposure to outcomes: Early adolescents' consumption of sexual content in six media. *Mass Communication & Society, 8*(2), 75–91.

"Parental involvement in minors' abortions." (2011, March 1). State policies in brief, Alan Guttmacher Institute. Retrieved March 18, 2011, from http://www.guttmacher.org/statecenter/spibs/spib_PIMA.pdf.

Park, A. J., & Paraiso, M. F. (2009). Successful use of botulinum toxin type A in the treatment of refractory postoperative dyspareunia. *Obstetrics and Gynecology, 114*(2 Pt 2), 484–487.

Parker Pope, T. (2010). *For better: The science of marriage.* Boston: Dutton.

Parker, S. E., Mai, C. T., Canfield, M. A., Rickard, R., Wang, Y., Meyer, R. E., Anderson, P., Mason, C. A., Collins, J. S., Kirby, R. S., & Correa, A. (2010). Updated national birth prevalence estimates for selected birth defects in the United States, 2004–2006. National Birth Defects Prevention Network. *Birth Defects Research: Part A, Clinical and Molecular Teratology, 88*(12), 1008–1016.

Parker, S. K., & Griffin, M. A. (2002). What is so bad about a little name calling? *Journal of Occupational Health Psychology, 7*(3), 195–210.

Parkhill, M., & Abbey, A. (2008). Does alcohol contribute to the confluence model of sexual assault perpetration? *Journal of Social and Clinical Psychology, 27,* 529–554.

Parks, K. A., & Scheidt, D. M. (2000). Male bar drinkers' perspective on female bar drinkers. *Sex Roles, 43*(11/12), 927–935.

Parrott, D., & Peterson, J. (2008). What motivates hate crimes based on sexual orientation? Mediating effects of anger on antigay aggression. *Aggressive Behavior, 34,* 306–318.

Parry, B. L. (2008). Perimenopausal depression. *American Journal of Psychiatry, 165,* 23–27.

Parsonnet, J., Hansmann, M., Delaney, M., Modern, P., Dubois, A., Wieland-Alter, W., Wissemann, K., Wild, J., Jones, M., Seymour, J., & Onderdonk, A. (2005). Prevalence of toxic shock syndrome toxin 1-producing Staphylococcus aureus and the presence of antibodies to this superantigen in menstruating women. *Journal of Clinics in Microbiology, 43*(9), 4628–4634.

Passel, J., Wang, W., & Taylor, P. (2010). Marrying out: One-in-seven new U.S. marriages is interracial or interethnic. Pew Research Center. Retrieved May 11, 2011, from http://pewresearch.org/pubs/1616/american-marriage-interracial-interethnic.

Pasterski, V., Hindmarsh, P., Geffnew, M., Brook, C., Brain, C., & Hines, M. (2007).

Increased aggression and activity level in 3- to 11-year old girls with congenital adrenal hyperplasia (CAH). *Hormones and Behavior, 52,* 368–374.

Pasterski, V. L., Brain, C., Geffner, M. E., Hindmarsh, P., Brook, C., & Hines, M. (2005). Prenatal hormones and postnatal socialization by parents as determinants of male-typical toy play in girls with congenital adrenal hyperplasia. *Child Development, 76*(1), 264–279.

Pastor, Z. (2010). G spot—Myths and realities. *Czechoslovakian Gynecology, 75*(3), 211–217.

Pasupathy, D., & Smith, G. C. (2005). The analysis of factors predicting antepartum stillbirth. *Minerva Ginecology, 57*(4), 397–410.

Patrick, K. (2007). Is infant male circumcision an abuse of the rights of the child? No. *British Medical Journal, 335*(7631), 1181.

Pattatucci, A. M. (1998). Molecular investigations into complex behavior: Lessons from sexual orientation studies. *Human Biology, 70*(2), 367–387.

Patton, G. C., & Viner, R. (2007). Pubertal transitions in health. *Lancet, 369,* 1130–1139.

Paul, B. (2009). Predicting Internet pornography use and arousal: The role of individual difference variables. *Journal of Sex Research, 46*(4), 344–357.

Paul, B., & Shim, J. (2008). Gender, sexual affect, and motivations for internet pornography use. *International Journal of Sexual Health, 20*(3), 187–199.

Paul, E., & Hayes, K. (2002). The casualties of 'casual' sex: A qualitative exploration of the phenomenonology of college students' hookups. *Journal of Social and Personal Relationships, 19,* 639–661.

Paul, J. P. (1984). The bisexual identity: An idea without social recognition. *Journal of Homosexuality, 9,* 45–63.

Paul, P. (2005). *Pornified: How pornography is transforming our lives, our relationships and our families.* New York: Times Books.

Paul, P. (2010, July 30). The un-divorced. *New York Times.* Retrieved August 6, 2010, from http://www.nytimes.com/2010/08/01/fashion/01Undivorced.html.

Pawelski, J. G., Perrin, E. C., Foy, J. M., Allen, C. E., Crawford, J. E., Del Monte, M., et al. (2006). The effects of marriage, civil union, and domestic partnership laws on the health and well-being of children. *Pediatrics, 118,* 349–364.

Payer, P. J. (1991). Sex and confession in the thirteenth century. In J. E. Salisbury (Ed.),

Sex in the Middle Ages. New York: Garland.

Pearce, A., Chuikova, T., Ramsey, A., & Galyautdinova, S. (2010). A positive psychology perspective on mate preferences in the U.S. and Russia. *Journal of Cross-Cultural Psychology, 41*(5–6), 742.

Pearson, J. C., Turner, L. H., & Todd-Mancillas, W. (1991). *Gender and communication* (2nd ed.). Dubuque, IA: William C. Brown.

Peck, S. (1978). *The road less traveled: A new psychology of love, traditional values and spiritual growth.* Oxford, England: Simon & Schuster.

Pedrera-Zamorano, J. D., Lavado-Garcia, J. M., Roncero-Martin, R., Calderon-Garcia, J. F., Rodriguez-Dominguez, T., & Canal-Macias, M. L. (2009). Effect of beer drinking on ultrasound bone mass in women. *Nutrition, 25*(10), 1057–1063.

Peele, S., & Brodsky, A. (1991). *Love and addiction.* Jersey City, NJ: Parkwest.

Peeples, E. H., & Scacco, A. M. (1982). The stress impact study technique: A method for evaluating the consequences of male-on-male sexual assault in jails, prisons, and other selected single-sex institutions. In A. M. Scacco (Ed.), *Male rape: A casebook of sexual aggressions* (pp. 241–278). New York: AMS Press.

Pelosi, M., & Pelosi, M. (2010). Breast augmentation. *Obstetrics and Gynecology Clinics of North America, 37*(4), 533–546.

Penke, L., & Asendorpf, J. B. (2008). Evidence for conditional sex differences in emotional but not in sexual jealousy at the automatic level of cognitive processing. *European Journal of Personality, 22,* 3–30.

Penna-Firme, T., Grinder, R. E., & Linhares-Barreto, M. S. (1991). Adolescent female prostitutes on the streets of Brazil: An exploratory investigation of ontological issues. *Journal of Adolescent Research, 6,* 493–504.

Peplau, L. A., & Conrad, E. (1989). Beyond nonsexist research: The perils of feminist methods in psychology. *Psychology of Women Quarterly, 13,* 381–402.

Peplau, L. A., & Fingerhut, A. (2004). The paradox of the lesbian worker. *Journal of Social Issues, 60*(4), 719–736.

Peplau, L. A., Garnets, L. D., & Spalding, L. R. (1998). A critique of Bem's "Exotic becomes erotic" theory of sexual orientation. *Psychological Review, 105*(2), 387–394.

Peralta, R. L. (2008). "Alcohol allows you to not be yourself": Toward a structured understanding of alcohol use and gender differ-

ence among gay, lesbian, and heterosexual youth. *Journal of Drug Issues, 38,* 373–400.

Perelman, M. (2007). Clinical application of CNS-acting agents in FSD. *Journal of Sexual Medicine, 4*(Suppl. 4), 280–290.

Perelman, M., & Rowland, D. (2006). Retarded ejaculation. *World Journal of Urology, 24,* 645–652.

Perilloux, C., & Buss, D. (2008). Breaking up romantic relationships: Costs experienced and coping strategies deployed. *Evolutionary Psychology, 6*(1), 164–181.

Perkins, R., & Bennett, G. (1985). *Being a prostitute: Prostitute women and prostitute men.* Boston: Allen & Unwin.

Perlman, D. (2007). The best of times, the worst of times: The place of close relationships in psychology and our daily lives. *Canadian Psychology, 48,* 7–24.

Perovic, S. V., & Djinovic, R. P. (2010). Current surgical management of severe Peyronie's disease. *Archives of Españoles Urology, 63*(9), 755–770.

Perovic, S. V., Stanojevic, D., & Djordjevic, M. (2005). Vaginoplasty in male to female transsexuals using penile skin and urethral flap. *International Journal of Transgenderism, 8,* 43–64.

Perper, T. (1985). *Sex signals: The biology of love.* Philadelphia, PA: ISI Press.

Perrigouard, C., Dreval, A., Cribier, B., & Lipsker, D. (2008). Vulvar vestibulitis syndrome: A clinicopathological study of 14 cases. *Annals of Dermatologie et de Venereologie, 135,* 367–372.

Perrin, E. C. (2002). Technical report: Coparent or second-parent adoption by same-sex parents. *Pediatrics, 109*(2), 341–345.

Perrow, C., & Guillén, M. F. (1990). *The AIDS disaster.* New Haven, CT: Yale University Press.

Peter, J., & Valkenburg, P. (2007). Adolescents' exposure to a sexualized media environment and their notions of women as sex objects. *Sex Roles, 56,* 381–395.

Peterson, H. B. (2008). Sterilization. *Obstetrics and Gynecology, 111,* 189–203.

Pew Research Center. (2010). The decline of marriage and rise of new families. Pew Research Center's Social and Demographic Trends Project. Retrieved May 12, 2011, from http://pewsocialtrends.org/files/2010/11/pew-social-trends-2010-families.pdf.

Pfaus, J., Giuliano, F., & Gelez, H. (2007). Bremelanotide: An overview of preclinical CHS effects of female sexual function. *Journal of Sexual Medicine, 4*(Suppl. 4), 269–279.

Phillips, B. (2001, December 11). Baby rapes shock South Africa. *BBC News*. Retrieved April 30, 2011, from http://news.bbc.co.uk/2/hi/africa/1703595.stm.

Phipps, M. G., Matteson, K. A., Fernandez, G., Chiaverini, L., & Weitzen, S. (2008, March 19). Characteristics of women who seek emergency contraception and family planning services. *American Journal of Obstetrics and Gynecology, 199*(2), 111 (e1–5).

Phipps, W., Saracino, M., Magaret, A., Selke, S., Remington, M., Huang, M. L., Warren, T., Casper, C., Corey, L., & Wald, A. (2011). Persistent genital herpes simplex virus-2 shedding years following the first clinical episode. *Journal of Infectious Disease, 203*(2), 180–187.

Piaget, J. (1951). *Play, dreams, and imitation in children*. New York: Norton.

Pialoux, G., Vimont, S., Moulignier, A., Buteux, M., Abraham, B., & Bonnard, P. (2008). Effect of HIV infection on the course of syphilis. *AIDS Review, 10*, 85–92.

Piccinino, L. J., & Mosher, W. D. (1998). Trends in contraceptive method use in the United States: 1982–1994. *Family Planning Perspectives, 30*, 4–10.

Pierangeli, A., Scagnolari, C., Degener, A., Bucci, M., Ciardi, A., Riva, E., et al. (2008). Type-specific human papillomavirus-DNA load in anal infection in HIV-positive men. *AIDS, 22*, 1929–1935.

Pillard, R. C. (1991). Masculinity and femininity in homosexuality: "Inversion" revisited. In J. C. Gonsiorek & J. D. Weinrich (Eds.), *Homosexuality: Research implications for public policy* (pp. 32–43). Newbury Park, CA: Sage.

Pillard, R. C. (1998). Biologic theories of homosexuality. *Journal of Gay and Lesbian Psychotherapy, 2*(4), 75–76.

Pillard, R. C., & Bailey, J. M. (1998). Human sexual orientation has a heritable component. *Human Biology, 70*(2), 347–366.

Pilver, C., Kasi, S., Desai, R., & Levy, B. (2010). Health advantage for black women: Patterns in premenstrual dysphoric disorder. *Psychological Medicine*, 1–10.

Pines, A. (2011). Male menopause: Is it a real clinical syndrome? *Climacteric, 14*(1), 15–17.

Ping, W. (2002). *Aching for beauty: Footbinding in China*. New York: Random House.

Pinheiro, A. P., Raney, T. J., Thornton, L. M., Fichter, M. M., Berrettini, W. H., Goldman, D., Halmi, K. A., Kaplan, A. S., Strober, M., Treasure, J., Woodside, D. B., Kaye, W. H., & Bulik, C. M. (2010). Sexual functioning in women with eating disorders. *International Journal of Eating Disorders, 43*(2), 123–129.

Pinheiro, A. P., Thorton, L., & Plotonicov, K. (2007). Patterns of menstrual disturbance in eating disorders. *International Journal of Eating Disorders, 40*(5), 424.

Pinkerton, J., & Stovall, D. (2010). Reproductive aging, menopause, and health outcomes. *Annals of the New York Academy of Science, 1204*, 169–178.

Pinkerton, S., Galletly, C., & Seal, D. (2007). Model-based estimates of HIV acquisition due to prison rape. *The Prison Journal, 87*(3), 295–310.

Pino, N. W., & Meier, R. F. (1999). Gender differences in rape reporting. *Sex Roles, 40*(11–12), 979–990.

Pinquart, M., Stotzka, C., & Silberreisen, R., (2008). Personality and ambivalence in decisions about becoming parents. *Social Behavior and Personality, 36*, 87–96.

Piot, P. (2000). Global AIDS epidemic: Time to turn the tide. *Science, 288*(5474), 2176–2188.

Pipitone, R., & Gallup, G. (2008). Women's voice attractiveness varies across the menstrual cycle. *Evolution and Human Behavior, 29*(4), 268–274.

Pisetsky, E. M., Chao, Y., Dierker, L. C., May, A. M., & Striegel-Moore, R. (2008). Disordered eating and substance use in high-school students: Results from the Youth Risk Behavior Surveillance System. *International Journal of Eating Disorders, 41*, 464.

Pitkin, J. (2010). Cultural issues and the menopause. *Menopause International, 16*(4), 156–161.

Pivarnik, J. M. (1998). Potential effects of maternal physical activity on birth weight: Brief review. *Med Science Sports Exercise, 30*(3), 400–406.

Planned Parenthood Federation of America. (2005). Abstinence-only "sex" education. Retrieved May 30, 2005, from http://www.plannedparenthood.org/pp2/portal/medicalinfo/teensexualhealth/fact-abstinence-education.xml.

Plante, A. F., & Kamm, M. A. (2008). Life events in patients with vulvodynia. *British Journal of Obstetrics and Gynecology, 115*, 509–514.

Plaud, J. J., Gaither, G. A., Hegstand, H. J., Rowan, L., & Devitt, M. K. (1999). Volunteer bias in human psychophysiological sexual arousal research: To whom do our research results apply? *The Journal of Sex Research, 36*, 171–179.

Plaut, A., & Kohn-Speyer, A. C. (1947). The carcinogenic action of smegma. *Science, 105*, 392.

Pleak, R. R., & Meyer-Bahlburg, H. F. (1990). Sexual behavior and AIDS knowledge of young male prostitutes in Manhattan. *Journal of Sex Research, 27*, 557–587.

Plosker, G. L. (2011). Sipuleucel-T: In metastatic castration-resistant prostate cancer. *Drugs, 71*(1), 101–108.

Pluchino, N., Bucci, F., Cela, V., Cubeddu, A., & Genazzani, A. (2011). Menopause and mental well-being: Timing of symptoms and timing of hormone treatment. *Women's Health, 7*(1), 71–80.

Plummer, K. (1989). Lesbian and gay youth in England. *Journal of Homosexuality, 17*, 195–223.

Plummer, K. (1991). Understanding childhood sexualities. *Journal of Homosexuality, 20*, 231–249.

Pogatchnik, S. (1995, November 26). Ireland legalized divorce. *Hartford Courant*, p. A1.

Poimenova, A., Markaki, E., Rahiotis, C., & Kitraki, E. (2010). Corticosterone-regulated actions in the rat brain are affected by perinatal exposure to low dose of bisphenol A. *Neuroscience, 167*(3), 741–749.

Polaris Project. (2005). Testimony of Rosa. Retrieved December 13, 2005, from http://www.humantrafficking.com/humantrafficking/features_ht3/Testimonies/testimonies_mainframe.htm.

Polek, C., & Hardie, T. (2010). Lesbian women and knowledge about human papillomavirus. *Oncology Nursing Forum, 37*(3), E191-E197.

Pollock, N. L., & Hashmall, J. M. (1991). The excuses of child molesters. *Behavioral Sciences and the Law, 9*, 53–59.

Polman, R., Kaiseler, M., & Borkoles, E. (2007). Effect of a single bout of exercise on the mood of pregnant women. *Journal of Sports Medicine and Physical Fitness, 47*, 102–111.

Pomeroy, W. B. (1982). *Dr. Kinsey and the Institute for Sex Research*. New Haven, CT: Yale University Press.

Ponseti, J., Bosinski, H., Wolff, S., Peller, M., Jansen, O., Mehdorn, H., Buchel, C., & Siebner, H. (2006). A functional endophenotype for sexual orientation in humans. *Neuroimage, 33*(3), 825–833.

Ponseti, J., Granert, O., Jansen, O., Wolff, S., Mehdorn, H., Bosinski, H., & Siebner, H. (2009). Assessment of sexual orientation using the hemodynamic brain response to visual sexual stimuli. *Journal of Sexual Medicine, 6*(6), 1628–1634.

Popovic, M. (2005). Intimacy and its relevance in human functioning. *Sexual and Relationship Therapy, 20*(1), 31–49.

Porter, R. (1982). Mixed feelings: The Enlightenment and sexuality in eighteenth-century Britain. In P.-G. Goucé (Ed.), *Sexuality in eighteenth-century Britain* (pp. 1–27). Manchester, U.K.: Manchester University Press.

Posey, C., Lowry, P., Roberts, T., & Ellis, T. (2010). Proposing the online community self-disclosure model: The case of working professionals in France and the UK who use online communities. *European Journal of Information Systems, 19*(2), 181–196.

Posner, R. A. (1993). Obsession. *The New Republic, 209,* 31–36.

Pothen, S. (1989). Divorce in Hindu society. *Journal of Comparative Family Studies, 20*(3), 377–392.

Potter, B., Gerofi, J., Pope, M., & Farley, T. (2003). Structural integrity of the polyurethane female condom after multiple cycles of disinfection, washing, drying and relubrication. *Contraception, 67*(1), 65–72.

Potterat, J. J., Rothenberg, R. B., Muth, S. Q., Darrow, W. W., & Phillips-Plummer, L. (1998). Pathways to prostitution: The chronology of sexual and drug abuse milestones. *Journal of Sex Research, 35*(4), 333–340.

Potterat, J. J., Woodhouse, D. E., Muth, J. B., & Muth, S. Q. (1990). Estimating the prevalence and career longevity of prostitute women. *Journal of Sex Research, 27,* 233–243.

Poulson, R. L., Eppler, M. A., Satterwhite, T. N., Wuensch, K. L., & Bass, L. A. (1998). Alcohol consumption, strength of religious beliefs, and risky sexual behavior in college students. *Journal of American College Health, 46*(5), 227–233.

Pouriayevali, M. H., Bamdad, T., Parsania, M., & Sari, R. (2011). Full length antigen priming enhances the CTL epitope-based DNA vaccine efficacy. *Cell Immunology, 268*(1), 4–8.

Povey, A., & Stocks, S. (2010). Epidemiology and trends in male subfertility. *Human Fertility, 13*(4), 182–188.

Pozniak, A. (2002). Pink versus blue: The things people do to choose the sex of their baby. Retrieved June 3, 2002, from http://abcnews.go.com/sections/living/DailyNews/choosingbabysex020603.html.

Predrag, S. (2005). LGBT news and views from around the world. *Lesbian News, 30*(9), 19–21.

Prentice, A. (2001). Endometriosis. *British Medical Journal, 323*(7304), 93–96.

Prentky, R. A., & Knight, R. A. (1986). Impulsivity: In the lifestyle and criminal behavior of sexual offenders. *Criminal Justice and Behavior, 13*(2), 141.

Previti, D., & Amato, P. (2004). Is infidelity a cause or a consequence of poor marital quality? *Journal of Social and Personal Relationships, 21*(2), 217–230.

Price, J. (2008). Parent-child quality time: Does birth order matter? *Journal of Human Resources, 43,* 240–265.

Price, M., Kafka, M., Commons, M., Gutheil, T., & Simpson, W. (2002). Telephone scatologia: Comorbidity with other paraphilias and paraphilia-related disorders. *International Journal of Law & Psychiatry, 25*(1), 37–49.

Prior, V., & Glaser, D. (2006). *Understanding attachment and attachment disorders: Theory, evidence and practice.* London: Jessica Kingsley.

Proto-Campise, L., Belknap, J., & Wooldredge, J. (1998). High school students' adherence to rape myths. *Violence Against Women, 4,* 308–328.

Proulx, N., Caron, S., & Logue, M. (2006). Older women/younger men: A look at the implications of age difference in marriage. *Journal of Couple & Relationship Therapy, 5*(4), 43–64.

Pryzgoda, J., & Chrisler, J. C. (2000). Definitions of gender and sex: The subtleties of meaning. *Sex Roles, 43*(7–8), 499–528.

Puente, S., & Cohen, D. (2003). Jealousy and the meaning (or nonmeaning) of violence. *Personality and Social Psychology Bulletin, 29*(4), 449–460.

Pyne, J., Asch, S., Lincourt, K., Kilbourne, A., Bowman, C., Atkinson, H., & Gifford, A. (2008). Quality indicators for depression care in HIV patients. *AIDS Care, 20,* 1075–1083.

Quadagno, D., Sly, D. F., & Harrison, D. F. (1998). Ethnic differences in sexual decisions and sexual behavior. *Archives of Sexual Behavior, 27*(1), 57–75.

Rabin, R. C. (2010a, October 9). Grown-up, but still irresponsible. *New York Times.* Retrieved October 10, 2010, from http://www.nytimes.com/2010/10/10/weekinreview/10rabin.html.

Rabin, R. C. (2010b, May 10). New spending for a wider range of sex education. *New York Times.* Retrieved January 24, 2011, from http://www.nytimes.com/2010/05/11/health/policy/11land.html.

Rabinovici, J., David, M., Fukunishi, H., Morita, Y., Gostout, B. S., & Stewart, E. A.; MRgFUS Study Group. (2010). Pregnancy outcome after magnetic resonance-guided focused ultrasound surgery (MRgFUS) for conservative treatment of uterine fibroids. *Fertility and Sterility, 93*(1), 199–209.

Rabinowitz Greenberg, S. R., Firestone, P., Bradford, J., & Greenberg, D. M. (2002). Prediction of recidivism in exhibitionists: Psychological, phallometric, and offense factors. *Sexual Abuse: Journal of Research & Treatment, 14*(4), 329–347.

Rabkin, J. (2008). HIV and depression: 2008 review and update. *Current HIV/AIDS Reports, 5,* 163–171.

Radestad, I., Olsson, A., Nissen, E., & Rubertsson, C. (2008). Tears in the vagina, perineum, spincter ani, and rectum and first sexual intercourse after childbirth: A nationwide follow up. *Birth, 35,* 98–106.

Radford, B. (2006). Predator panic. *The Skeptical Inquirer, 20,* 20–23.

Rado, S. (1949, rev. 1955). An adaptional view of sexual behavior. *Psychoanalysis of behavior: Collected papers.* New York: Grune & Stratton.

Raffaelli, M., & Green, S. (2003). Parent-adolescent communication about sex; retrospective reports by Latino college students. *Journal of Marriage and the Family, 65,* 474–481.

Rahman, Q. (2005). Fluctuating asymmetry, second to fourth finger length ratios and human sexual orientation. *Psychoneuroendocrinology, 30*(4), 382–391.

Rahman, Q., & Koerting, J. (2008). Sexual orientation-related differences in allocentric spatial memory tasks. *Hippocampus, 18,* 55–63.

Rahman, Q., & Symeonides, D. (2008). Neurodevelopmental correlates of paraphilic sexual interests in men. *Archives of Sexual Behavior, 37,* 166–171.

Rahman, Q., Newland, C., & Smyth, B. M. (2011). Sexual orientation and spatial position effects on selective forms of object location memory. *Brain Cognition, 75*(3), 217–224.

Rahnama, P., Hidarnia, A., Amin Shokravi, F., Kazemnejad, A., Ghazanfari, Z., & Montazeri, A. (2010). Withdrawal users' experiences of and attitudes to contraceptive methods: A study from Eastern district of Tehran, Iran. *BMC Public Health, 10,* 779.

Rajaraman, P., Simpson, J., Neta, G., Berrington de Gonzalez, A., Ansell, P., Linet, M. S.,

Ron, E., & Roman, E. (2011). Early life exposure to diagnostic radiation and ultrasound scans and risk of childhood cancer: Case-control study. *British Medical Journal, 342,* d472.

Ramirez, A., & Zhang, S. (2007). When online meets offline: The effect of modality switching on relational communication. *Communication Monographs, 74,* 287.

Ramjee, G., Kamali, A., & McCormack, S. (2010). The last decade of microbicide clinical trials in Africa: From hypothesis to facts. *AIDS, 24*(Suppl. 4), S40–S49.

Ramlau-Hansen, C., Thulstrup, A., Storgaard, L., Toft, G., Olsen, J., & Bonde, J. P. (2007). Is prenatal exposure to tobacco smoking a cause of poor semen quality? A follow-up study. *American Journal of Epidemiology, 165*(12), 1372–1379.

Rammouz, I., Tahiri, D., Aalouane, R., Kjiri, S., Belhous, A., Ktiouet, J., & Sekkat, F. (2008). Infanticide in the postpartum period: About a clinical case. *Encephale, 34,* 284–288.

Ramsey, F., Hill, M., & Kellam, C. (2010). Black lesbians matter: An examination of the unique experiences, perspectives, and priorities of the Black lesbian community. Retrieved February 20, 2011, from http://zunainstitute.org/2010/research/blm/blacklesbiansmatter.pdf.

Rancour-Laferriere, D. (1985). *Signs of the flesh.* New York: Mouton de Gruyter.

Rand, M. R. (2009). Criminal victimization, 2008. National Crime Victimization Survey, Bureau of Justice Statistics. *Bureau of Justice Statistics Bulletin.* Retrieved April 13, 2011, from http://bjs.ojp.usdoj.gov/content/pub/pdf/cv08.pdf.

Rankin, P. T. (1952). The measurement of the ability to understand spoken language. *Dissertation Abstracts.* University of Michigan, 1953–06117–001.

Rape, Abuse, and Incest National Network. (2011). Sexual assault statistics. Retrieved April 11, 2011, from http://www.rainn.org/get-information/statistics/frequency-of-sexual-assault.

Rapkin, A., Berman, S., Mandelkern, M., Silverman, D., Morgan, M., & London, E. (2011). Neuroimaging evidence of cerebellar involvement in premenstrual dysphoric disorder. *Biological Psychiatry, 69*(4), 374–380.

Rapkin, A. J., & Winer, S. A. (2008). The pharmacologic management of premenstrual dysphoric disorder. *Expert Opinions in Pharmacotherapy, 9,* 429–445.

Raskin, N. J., & Rogers, C. R. (1989). Person-centered therapy. In R. J. Corsini & D. Wedding (Eds.), *Current psychotherapies* (4th ed., pp. 155–196), Pacific Grove, CA: F. E. Peacock.

Rasmussen, P. R. (2005). The sadistic and masochistic prototypes. In P. R. Rasmussen (Ed.), *Personality-guided cognitive-behavioral therapy* (pp. 291–310). Washington, DC: American Psychological Association.

Raspberry, C. N. (2007). A qualitative and quantitative exploration of secondary sexual abstinence among a sample of Texas A&M University undergraduates. Texas A&M University. *Dissertation Abstracts International, Section A: Humanities and Social Sciences, 68*(6-A), 2346.

Rauer, A. J., & Volling, B. L. (2007). Differential parenting and sibling jealousy: Developmental correlates of young adults' romantic relationships. *Personal Relationships, 14,* 495–511.

Raval, A. P., Hirsch, N., Dave, K. R., Yavagal, D. R., Bramlett, H., & Saul, I. (2011). Nicotine and estrogen synergistically exacerbate cerebral ischemic injury. *Neuroscience, 181,* 216–225.

Ravert, A. A., & Martin, J. (1997). Family stress, perception of pregnancy, and age of first menarche among pregnant adolescents. *Adolescence, 32*(126), 261–269.

Ray, N. (2006). Lesbian, gay, bisexual and transgendered youth: An epidemic of homelessness. National Gay and Lesbian Task Force Policy Institute. Retrieved February 17, 2011, from http://www.thetaskforce.org/downloads/reports/reports/HomelessYouth.pdf.

Ray, N. (2007). Lesbian, gay, bisexual, and transgendered youth: An epidemic of homelessness. National Gay and Lesbian Task Force Policy Institute. Retrieved October 3, 2008, from http://www.thetaskforce.org/downloads/HomelessYouth.pdf.

Raymond, E., Stewart, F., Weaver, M., Monteith, C., & Van Der Pol, B. (2006). Impact of increased access to emergency contraceptive pills: A randomized controlled trial. *Obstetrics and Gynecology, 108,* 1098–1106.

Raymond, J. G., & Hughes, D. M. (2001). Sex trafficking of women in the United States. Retrieved November 16, 2008, from http://www.uri.edu/artsci/wms/hughes/sex_traff_us.pdf.

Read, C. M. (2010). New regimens with combined oral contraceptive pills—moving away from traditional 21/7 cycles. *European Journal of Contraceptive and Reproductive Health Care, 15*(Suppl. 2), S32–S41.

Reece, M., Herbenick, D., Sanders, S., Dodge, B., Ghassemi, A., & Fortenberry, J. (2010a). Prevalence and predictors of testicular self-exam among a nationally representative sample of men in the U.S. *International Journal of Sexual Health, 22*(1), 1–4.

Reece, M., Herbenick, D., Sanders, S., Dodge, B., Ghassemi, A., & Fortenberry, J. (2009). Prevalence and characteristics of vibrator use by men in the US.: Results from a nationally representative study. *Journal of Sexual Medicine, 6,* 1867–1874.

Reece, M., Herbenick, D., Schick, V., Sanders, S. A., Dodge, B., & Fortenberry, J. D. (2010b). Background and considerations on the National Survey of Sexual Health and Behavior (NSSHB). *Journal of Sexual Medicine, 7*(Suppl. 5), 243–245.

Reece, M., Herbenick, D., Schick, V., Sanders, S., Dodge, B., & Fortenberry, D. (2010c). Condom use rates in a national probability sample of males and females ages 14–94 in the United States. *Journal of Sexual Medicine, 7*(Suppl. 5), 266–276.

Reece, M., Herbenick, D., Schick, V., Sanders, S., Dodge, B., & Fortenberry, J. (2010d). Sexual behaviors, relationships, and perceived health among adult men in the United States: Results from a national probability sample. *Journal of Sexual Medicine, 7*(Suppl. 5), 291–304.

Reese, J. B. (2011). Coping with sexual concerns after cancer. *Current Opinions in Oncology, 23*(4), 313–321.

Reese, J. B., Keefe, F. J., Somers, T. J., & Abernethy, A. P. (2010). Coping with sexual concerns after cancer: The use of flexible coping. *Support Care Cancer, 18*(7), 785–800.

Regan, P. C. (2006). Love. In R. D. McAnulty & M. M. Burnette (Eds.), *Sex and sexuality: Sexual functions and dysfunctions* (pp. 87–113). Westport, CT: Praeger.

Regnerus, M. D., & Luchies, L. B. (2006). The parent-child relationship and opportunities for adolescents' first sex. *Journal of Family Issues, 27,* 159–183.

Rehman, U. S., & Holtzworth-Munroe, A. (2007). A cross-cultural examination of the relation of marital communication behavior to marital satisfaction. *Journal of Family Psychology, 21,* 759–763.

Reid, R., Bonomi, A., Rivara, F., Anderson, M., Fishman, P., Carrell, D., & Thompson, R.

(2008). Intimate partner violence among men: Prevalence, chronicity, and health effects. *American Journal of Preventive Medicine, 34,* 478–485.

Reid, R.; Society of Obstetricians and Gynaecologists of Canada. (2010). SOGC clinical practice guideline. No. 252, December 2010. Oral contraceptives and the risk of venous thromboembolism: An update. *Journal of Obstetrics and Gynecology, 32*(12), 1192–1204.

Reilly, D. R., Delva, N. J., & Hudson, R. W. (2000). Protocols for the use of cyproterone, medroxyprogesterone, & leuprolide in the treatment of paraphilia. *Canadian Journal of Psychiatry, 45*(6), 559–564.

Reips, U. D. (2000). The Web experiment method: Advantages, disadvantages, and solutions. In M. H. Birnbaum (Ed.), *Psychological experiments on the Internet* (pp. 89–114). San Diego, CA: Academic Press.

Reips, U. D., & Bachtiger, M. T. (2000). Are all flies drosophilae? Participant selection bias in psychological research. Unpublished manuscript.

Reis, L. O., Dias, F. G., Castro, M. O., & Ferreira, U. (2011). Male breast cancer. *Aging Male, 14*(2), 99–109.

Reiss, I. L. (1982). Trouble in paradise: The current status of sexual science. *Journal of Sex Research, 18,* 97–113.

Reiss, I. L. (1986). *Journey into sexuality: An exploratory voyage.* Englewood Cliffs, NJ: Prentice Hall.

Rellini, A. H., & Meston, C. M. (2011). Sexual self-schemas, sexual dysfunction, and the sexual responses of women with a history of childhood sexual abuse. *Archives of Sexual Behavior, 40*(2), 351–362.

Remafedi, G. (1987). Male homosexuality: The adolescent perspective. *Pediatrics, 79*(3), 326–330.

Remez, L. (2000, November/December). Oral sex among adolescents: Is it sex or is it abstinence? *Family Planning Perspectives, 32*(6), 298–304.

Rempel, J. K., & Baumgartner, B. (2003). The relationship between attitudes towards menstruation and sexual attitudes, desires, and behavior in women. *Archives of Sexual Behavior, 32*(2), 155–163.

Remsberg, K. E., Demerath, E. W., Schubert, C. M., Chumlea, C., Sun, S. S., & Siervogel, R. M. (2005). Early menarche and the development of cardiovascular disease risk factors in adolescent girls: The Fels Longitudinal Study. *Journal of Clinical Endocrinology & Metabolism,* published online ahead of print. Retrieved March 22, 2005, from http://jcem.endojournals.org/cgi/content/abstract/jc.2004–1991v1

Renaud, C. A., & Byers, E. S. (1999). Exploring the frequency, diversity, and content of university students' positive and negative sexual cognitions. *Canadian Journal of Human Sexuality, 8*(1), 17–30.

Rendas-Baum, R., Yang, M., Gricar, J., & Wallenstein, G. (2010). Cost-effectiveness analysis of treatments for premenstrual dysphoric disorder. *Applied Health Economics and Health Policy, 8*(2), 129–140.

Rensberger, B. (1994, July 25). Contraception the natural way: Herbs have played a role from ancient Greece to modern-day Appalachie. *Washington Post,* p. A3.

Renshaw, D. C. (2005). Premature ejaculation-revisted—2005. *Family Journal: Counseling & Therapy for Couples and Families, 13*(2), 150–152.

Resnick, H., Acierno, R., Kilpatrick, D. G., & Holmes, M. (2005). Description of an early intervention to prevent substance abuse and psychopathology in recent rape victims. *Behavior Modification, 29*(1), 156–188.

Resnick, M. D., Bearman, P. S., Blum, R. W., Bauman, K. E., Harris, K. M., Jones, J., et al. (1997). Protecting adolescents from harm: Findings from the National Longitudinal Study on Adolescent Health. *Journal of the American Medical Association, 278*(10), 823–832.

Rettenmaier, N., Rettenmaier, C., Wojciechowski, T., Abaid, L., Brown, J., Micha, J., & Goldstein, B. (2010). The utility and cost of routine follow-up procedures in the surveillance of ovarian and primary peritoneal carcinoma: A 16-year institutional review. *British Journal of Cancer, 103*(11), 1657–1662.

Reynaert, C., Zdanowicz, N., Janne, P., & Jacques, D. (2010). Depression and sexuality. *Psychiatria Danubina, 22*(Suppl. 1), S111-S113.

Reynolds, H. (1986). *The economics of prostitution.* Springfield, IL: Charles C. Thomas.

Reynolds, T., Vranken, G., Nueten, J. V., & Aldis, J. (2008). Down's syndrome screening: Population statistic dependency of screening performance. *Clinical Chemistry and Laboratory Medicine, 46*(5), 639–647.

Rhoades, G. K., Stanley, S. M., & Markman, H. J. (2009). The pre-engagement cohabitation effect: A replication and extension of previous findings. *Journal of Family Psychology, 23*(1), 107–111.

Rhoads, J. M., & Boekelheide, P. D. (1985). Female genital exhibitionism. *The Psychiatric Forum,* Winter, 1–6.

Riccio, R. (1992). Street crime strategies: The changing schemata of streetwalkers. *Environment and Behavior, 24,* 555–570.

Rich, A. (1983). Compulsory heterosexuality and lesbian existence. In A. Snitow, C. Stinsell, & S. Thompson (Eds.), *Powers of desire: The politics of sexuality* (pp. 177–205). New York: Monthly Review Press.

Richardson, B. A. (2002). Nonoxynol-9 as a vaginal microbicide for prevention of sexually transmitted infections. *Journal of American Medication Association, 287,* 1171–1172.

Richardson, C. T., & Nash, E. (2006). Misinformed consent: The medical accuracy of state-developed abortion counseling materials. *Guttmacher Policy Review, 9*(4). Retrieved March 18, 2011, from http://www.guttmacher.org/pubs/gpr/09/4/gpr090406.html.

Richardson, D., & Campbell, J. L. (1982). The effect of alcohol on attributions of blame for rape. *Personality and Social Psychology Bulletin, 8,* 468–476.

Richardson, D., Nalabanda, A., & Goldmeier, D. (2006). Retarded ejaculation: A review. *International Journal of STDs and AIDS, 17,* 143–150.

Richters, J., Hendry, O., & Kippax, S. (2003). When safe sex isn't safe. *Culture, Health & Sexuality, 5*(1), 37–52.

Rickert, V. I., Sanghvi, R., & Weimann, C. M. (2002). Is lack of sexual assertiveness among adolescent and young adult women a cause for concern? *Perspectives on Sexual and Reproductive Health, 34*(4), 178–183.

Rideout, V., Roberts, D. F., & Foehr, U. G. (2005). Generation M: Media in the lives of 8–18-year-olds. Retrieved November 7, 2005, from http://www.kff.org/entmedia/upload/Executive-Summary-Generation-M-Media-in-the-Lives-of-8–18-Year-olds.pdf.

Rideout, V. J., Foehr, U. G., & Roberts, D. F. (2010). *Generation M2: Media in the lives of 8- to 18-year-olds.* Menlo Park, CA: Kaiser Family Foundation.

Ridge, R. D., & Reber, J. S. (2002). "I think she's attracted to me": The effect of men's beliefs on women's behavior in a job interview scenario. *Basic and Applied Social Psychology, 24*(1), 1–14.

Rieger, G., Chivers, M. L., & Bailey, J. M. (2005). Sexual arousal patterns of gay men. *Psychological Science, 16*(8), 579–584.

Riggle, E., Rostosky, S., & Horne, S. (2010). Psychological distress, well-being, and legal recognition in same-sex couple relationships. *Journal of Family Psychology, 24*(1), 82–86.

Riggs, J. M. (2005). Impressions of mothers and fathers on the periphery of child care. *Psychology of Women Quarterly, 29*(1), 58.

Ringdahl, E., & Teague, L. (2006). Testicular torsion. *American Family Physician, 74*(10), 1739–1743.

Rio, L. M. (1991). Psychological and sociological research and the decriminalization or legalization of prostitution. *Archives of Sexual Behavior, 20,* 205–218.

Riordan, M., & Kreuz, R. (2010). Cues in computer-mediated communication: A corpus analysis. *Computers in Human Behavior, 26*(6), 1806–1817.

Rischer, C. E., & Easton, T. (1992). *Focus on Human Biology.* New York: HarperCollins.

Riskind, R., & Patterson, C. (2010). Parenting intentions and desires among childless lesbian, gay, and heterosexual individuals. *Journal of Family Psychology, 24*(1), 78–81.

Risman, B., & Schwartz, P. (1988). Sociological research on male and female homosexuality. *Annual Review of Sociology, 14,* 125–147.

Rittenhouse, C. A. (1991). The emergence of premenstrual syndrome as a social problem. *Social Problems, 38*(3), 412–425.

Rivers, I., & Noret, N. (2008). Well-being among same-sex- and opposite-sex-attracted youth at school. *School Psychology Review, 37,* 174–187.

Rivers, J., Mason, J., Silvestre, E., Gillespie, S., Mahy, M., & Monasch, R. (2008). Impact of orphanhood on underweight prevalence in sub-Saharan Africa. *Food and Nutrition Bulletin, 29*(1), 32–42.

Rizwan, S., Manning, J., & Brabin, B. J. (2007). Maternal smoking during pregnancy and possible effects of in utero testosterone: Evidence from the 2D:4D finger length ratio. *Early Human Development, 83,* 87–90.

Roan, S. (2010, August 15). Medical treatment carries possible side effect of limiting homosexuality. *Los Angeles Times.* Retrieved October 15, 2010, from http://articles.latimes.com/2010/aug/15/science/la-sci-adrenal-20100815.

Roberts, A., Austin, S., Corliss, H., Vandermorris, A., & Koenen, K. (2010). Pervasive trauma exposure among US sexual orientation minority adults and risk of post-traumatic stress disorder. *American Journal of Public Health, 100*(12), 2433–2441.

Roberts, D. F., Foehr, U. G., & Rideout, V. (2005). Generation M: Media in the lives of 8–18-year-olds. Retrieved November 3, 2005, from http://www.kff.org/entmedia/upload/Generation-M-Media-in-the-Lives-of-8-18-Year-olds-Report.pdf.

Roberts, J. E., & Oktay, K. (2005). Fertility preservation: A comprehensive approach to the young woman with cancer. *Journal of the National Cancer Institute Monograph, 34,* 57–59.

Roberts, S. (2010, September 15). Study finds wider view of family. *New York Times.* Retrieved September 15, 2010, from http://query.nytimes.com/gst/fullpage.html?res59504E7DE163AF936A2575AC0A9669D8B63.

Roberts, S., & Roiser, J. P. (2010). In the nose of the beholder: Are olfactory influences on human mate choice driven by variation in immune system genes or sex hormone levels? *Experimental Biology and Medicine, 235*(11), 1277–1281.

Roberts, S., Gosling, L., Carter, V., & Petrie, M. (2008). MHC-correlated odour preferences in humans and the use of oral contraceptives. *Proceedings of the Royal Society B, 275*(1652), 2715–2722.

Robin, G., Boitrelle, F., Marcelli, F., Colin, P., Leroy-Martin, B., Mitchell, V., Dewailly, D., & Rigot, J. M. (2010). Cryptorchidism: From physiopathology to infertility. *Gynecological Obstetrics and Fertility, 38*(10), 588–599.

Robinson, E. D., & Evans, B. G. I. (1999). Oral sex and HIV transmission. *AIDS, 16*(6), 737–738.

Robinson, J. D. (2001). The thematic content categories of lesbian and bisexual women's sexual fantasies, psychological adjustment, daydreaming variables and relationships functioning. *Dissertation Abstracts,* California School of Professional Psychology-Los Angeles, #0–493–12701–1.

Robinson, J. D., & Parks, C. W. (2003). Lesbian and bisexual women's sexual fantasies, psychological adjustment, and close relationship functioning. *Journal of Psychology & Human Sexuality 15*(4), 85–203.

Robinson, P. (1993). *Freud and his critics.* Berkeley, CA: University of California Press.

Roby, J. L., & Shaw, S. A. (2006). The African orphan crisis and international adoption. *Social Work, 51*(3), 199–210.

Rodriguez, I. (2004). Pheromone receptors in mammals. *Hormones & Behavior, 46*(3), 219–230.

Rogers, S. C. (1978). Woman's place: A critical review of anthropological theory. *Comparative Studies in Society and History, 20,* 123–162.

Roisman, G., Clausell, Holland, A., Fortuna, K., & Elieff, C. (2008). Adult romantic relationships as contexts of human development: A multimethod comparison of same-sex couples with opposite-sex dating, engaged, and married dyads. *Developmental Psychology, 44*(1), 91–101.

Rome, E. (1998). Anatomy and physiology of sexuality and reproduction. In The Boston Women's Health Collective (Eds.), *The new our bodies, ourselves* (pp. 241–258). Carmichael, CA: Touchstone Books.

Romenesko, K., & Miller, E. M. (1989). The second step in double jeopardy: Appropriating the labor of female street hustlers. (Special issue: Women and crime.) *Crime and Delinquency, 35,* 109–135.

Romer, D., Sznitman, S., DiClemente, R., Salazar, L., Vanable, P., Carey, M., Hennessy, M., Brown, L., Valois, R., Stanton, B., Fortune, T., & Juzang, I. (2009). Mass media as an HIV-prevention strategy: Using culturally sensitive messages to reduce HIV-associated sexual behavior of at-risk African American youth. *American Journal of Public Health, 99,* 2150–2159.

Romero-Daza, N., Weeks, M., & Singer, M. (2003). "Nobody gives a damn if I live or die": Violence, drugs, and street-level prostitution in inner-city Hartford, Connecticut. *Medical Anthropology, 22*(3), 233–259.

Röndahl, G., Innala, S., & Carlsson, M. (2004). Nurses' attitudes towards lesbians and gay men. *Journal of Advanced Nursing, 47,* 386–392.

Ropelato, J. (2008). Internet pornography statistics. *Top Ten Reviews.* Retrieved October 7, 2008, from http://internet-filter-review.toptenreviews.com/internet-pornography-statistics.html.

Rosa, M., & Masood, S. (In press). Cytomorphology of male breast lesions: Diagnostic pitfalls and clinical implications. *Diagnostic Cytopathology.*

Rosario, M., Schrimshaw, E., & Hunter, J. (2004). Predictors of substance use over time among gay, lesbian, and bisexual youths. An examination of three hypotheses. *Addictive Behaviors, 29*(8), 1623–1631.

Rosen, R. C., & Leiblum, S. R. (1987). Current approaches to the evaluation of sexual desire disorders. *Journal of Sex Research, 23,* 141–162.

Rosenbaum, D. E. (2005, October 30). Commissions are fine, but rarely what changes the light bulb. Retrieved November 6, 2005, from http://www.nytimes.com/2005/10/30/weekinreview/30rosenbaum.html?fta=y.

Rosenbaum, T. (2011). Addressing anxiety in vivo in physiotherapy treatment of women with severe vaginismus: A clinical approach. *Journal of Sex and Marital Therapy, 37*(2), 89–93.

Rosenblatt, P. C., Karis, T. A., & Powell, R. D. (1995). *Multiracial couples.* Thousand Oaks, CA: Sage.

Rosenthal, R., & Rosnow, R. L. (1975). *The volunteer subject.* New York: Wiley.

Rosmalen-Nooijens, K., Vergeer, C., & Lagro-Janssen, A. (2008). Bed death and other lesbian sexual problems unraveled: A qualitative study of the sexual health of lesbian women involved in a relationship. *Women & Health, 48*(3), 339–362.

Rosman, J. P., & Resnick, P. J. (1989). Sexual attraction to corpses: A psychiatric review of necrophilia. *Bulletin of the American Academy of Psychiatry and the Law, 17,* 153–163.

Ross, C. A. (2009). Psychodynamics of eating disorder behavior in sexual abuse survivors. *American Journal of Psychotherapy, 63*(3), 211–227.

Ross, L. E. (2005). Perinatal mental health in lesbian mothers: A review of potential risk and protective factors. *Women Health, 41*(3), 113–128.

Ross, L. E., Steele, L., & Epstein, R. (2006a). Lesbian and bisexual women's recommendations for improving the provision of assisted reproductive technology services. *Fertility and Sterility, 86,* 735–738.

Ross, L. E., Steele, L. S., & Epstein, R. (2006b). Service use and gaps in services for lesbian and bisexual women during donor insemination, pregnancy, and the postpartum period. *Journal of Obstetrics and Gynecology Canada, 28,* 505–511.

Ross, L. E., Steele, L., & Sapiro, B. (2005). Perceptions of predisposing and protective factors for perinatal depression in same-sex parents. *Journal of Midwifery Women's Health, 50,* 65–70.

Ross, L. E., Steele, L., Goldfinger, C., & Strike, C. (2007). Perinatal depressive symptomatology among lesbian and bisexual women. *Archives of Women's Mental Health, 10,* 1434–1816.

Rossato M., Pagano C., & Vettor R. (2008). The cannabinoid system and male reproductive functions. *Journal of Neuroendocrinology, 20*(Suppl 1), 90–93.

Rosser, B. R. (1999). Homophobia: Description, development and dynamic of gay bashing. *Journal of Sex Research, 36*(2), 211.

Rossi, A. S. (1978). The biosocial side of parenthood. *Human Nature, 1,* 72–79.

Rossi, N. E. (2010). "Coming out" stories of gay and lesbian young adults. *Journal of Homosexuality, 57*(9), 1174–1191.

Rossi, W. A. (1993). *The sex life of the foot and shoe.* Melbourne, FL: Krieger.

Rothblum, E., Balsam, K., & Solomon, S. (2008). Comparison of same-sex couples who were married in Massachusetts, had domestic partnerships in California, or had civil unions in Vermont. *Journal of Family Issues, 29*(1), 48–78.

Rothman, S. M. (1978). *Woman's proper place.* New York: Basic Books.

Roughgarden, J. (2004). A review of evolution, gender, and rape. *Ethology, 110*(1), 76.

Rowland, D., McMahon, C. G., Abdo, C., Chen, J., Jannini, E., Waldinger, M. D., & Ahn, T. Y. (2010). Disorders of orgasm and ejaculation in men. *Journal of Sexual Medicine, 7*(4 Pt 2), 1668–1686.

Rowlands, S., Sujan, M. A., & Cooke, M. (2010). A risk management approach to the design of contraceptive implants. *Journal of Family Planning and Reproductive Health Care, 36*(4), 191–195.

Roy, J. R., Chakraborty, S., & Chakraborty, T. R. (2010). Estrogen-like endocrine disrupting chemicals affecting puberty in humans—a review. *Medical Science Monitor, 15*(6), 137–145.

Ruan, F., & Lau, M. P. (2004). China. In R. T. Francoeur & R. J. Noonan (Eds.), *The Continuum International encyclopedia of sexuality* (pp. 182–209). New York/London: Continuum International.

Ruan, F. F., & Tsai, Y. M. (1988). Male homosexuality in contemporary mainland China. *Archives of Sexual Behavior, 17,* 189–199.

Rubin, B., & Soto, A. (2009). Bisphenol A: Perinatal exposure and body weight. *Molecular and Cellular Endocrinology, 302*(1–2), 55–62.

Rubin, L. (1990). *Erotic wars.* New York: Farrar, Straus, & Giroux.

Rubin, R. (2008, January 7). Answers prove elusive as C-section rate rises. *USAToday,* Retrieved October 14, 2008, from http://www.usatoday.com/news/health/2008–01–07-csections_N.htm.

Rubin, R. H. (2001). Alternative lifestyles revisited, or whatever happened to swingers, group marriages, and communes. *Journal of Family Issues, 22*(6), 711–728.

Rubin, Z. (1970). Measurement of romantic love. *Journal of Personality & Social Psychology, 16*(2), 265–273.

Rubin, Z. (1973). *Liking and loving: An invitation to social psychology.* Oxford, England: Holt, Rinehart & Winston.

Rudd, J. M., & Herzberger, S. D. (1999). Brother-sister incest, father-daughter incest: A comparison of characteristics and consequences. *Child Abuse and Neglect, 23*(9), 915–928.

Rudolph, K., Caldwell, M. & Conley, C. (2005). Need for approval and children's well-being. *Child Development, 76*(2), 309–323.

Rudy, K. (2000). Queer theory and feminism. *Women's Studies, 29*(2), 195–217.

Rue, V. M., Coleman, P. K., Rue, J. J., & Reardon, D. C. (2004). Induced abortion and traumatic stress: A preliminary comparison of American and Russian women. *Medical Science Monitor, 10*(10), SR5–SR16.

Ruffman, T., Halberstadt, J., & Murray, J. (2009). Recognition of facial, auditory, and bodily emotions in older adults. *Journals of Gerontology, 64B*(6), 696.

Ruggles, S. (2009). Reconsidering the northwest European family system: Living arrangements of the aged in comparative historical perspective. *Population and Development Review, 35*(2), 249–273.

Rugh, A. B. (1984). *Family in contemporary Egypt.* Syracuse, NY: Syracuse University Press.

Ruhl, M., Knuschke, T., Schewior, K., Glavinic, L., Neumann-Haefelin, C., Chang, D. I., Klein, M., Heinemann, F. M., Tenckhoff, H., Wiese, M., Horn, P. A., Viazov, S., Spengler, U., Roggendorf, M., Scherbaum, N., Nattermann, J., Hoffmann, D., Timm, J.; East German HCV Study Group. (2011). The CD81 T-cell response promotes evolution of hepatitis C virus nonstructural proteins. *Gastroenterology, 140*(7), 2064–2073.

Rupp, J. (2007). The photography of Joseph Rupp: Bound feet. Retrieved December 19, 2008, from http://www.josephrupp.com/.

Russell, D. E. H. (1984). *Sexual exploitation: Rape, child sexual abuse, and workplace harassment.* Beverly Hills, CA: Sage.

Russell, D. E. H., & Howell, N. (1983). The prevalence of rape in the United States revisited. *Signs: Journal of Women in Culture and Society,* 688–695.

Russell, S., Driscoll, A., & Truong, N. (2002). Adolescent same-sex romantic attractions and relationship: Implications for substance use and abuse. *American Journal of Public Health, 92*(2), 198–202.

Rust, P. C. R. (2000). *Bisexuality in the U.S.* New York: Columbia University Press.

Ryan, C., & Futterman, D. (2001). Social and developmental challenges for lesbian, gay, bisexual youth. *SIECUS Report, 29*(4), 5–18.

Ryan, C., Huebner, D., Diaz, R. M., & Sanchez, J. (2009). Family rejection as a predictor of negative health outcomes in white and Latino lesbian, gay, and bisexual young adults. *Pediatrics, 123*(1), 346–352.

Ryan, C. J., & Small, E. J. (2005). Progress in detection and treatment of prostate cancer. *Current Opinion in Oncology, 17*(3), 257–260.

Sabelli, H., Fink, P., Fawcett, J., & Tom, C. (1996). Sustained antidepressant effect of PEA replacement. *Journal of Neuropsychiatry and Clinical Neuroscience, 8*(2), 168–171.

Sable, M., Danis, F., Mauzy, D., & Gallagher, S. (2006). Barriers to reporting sexual assault for women and men: Perspectives of college students. *Journal of American College Health, 55,* 157–162.

Sabo, D. S., & Runfola, R. (1980). *Jock: Sports and male identity.* New York: Prentice Hall.

Sadovsky, R., Basson, R., Krychman, M., Morales, A., Schover, L., Wang, R., & Incrocci, L. (2010). Cancer and sexual problems. *Journal of Sexual Medicine, 7*(1 Pt 2), 349–373.

Saewyc, E. M., Bearinger, L. H., Heinz, P. A., Blum, R. W., & Resnick, M. (1998). Gender differences in health and risk behaviors among bisexual and homosexual adolescents. *Journal of Adolescent Health, 23*(2), 181–188.

Safarinejad, M. R. (2008). Evaluation of the safety and efficacy of bremelanotide, a melanocortin receptor agonist, in female subjects with arousal disorder: A double-blind placebo-controlled, fixed dose, randomized study. *Journal of Sexual Medicine, 5,* 887–897.

"Safer sex basics." (2005). Retrieved October 12, 2005, from http://sexuality.about.com/cs/safersex/a/safersexbasics.htm.

Saftlas, A., Wallis, A., Shochet, T., Harland, K., Dickey, P., & Peek-Asa, C. (2010). Prevalence of intimate partner violence among an abortion clinic population. *American Journal of Public Health, 100*(8), 1412–1415.

Sagarin, B. J., Becker, D., Guadagno, R. E., Nicastle, L. D., & Millevoi, A. (2003). Sex differences (and similarities) in jealousy. The moderating influence of infidelity experience and sexual orientation of the infidelity. *Evolution and Human Behavior, 24*(1), 17–23.

Saha, P., Majumdar, S., Pal, D., Pal, B. C., & Kabir, S. N. (2010). Evaluation of spermicidal activity of MI-saponin A. *Reproductive Science, 17*(5), 454–464.

Sakorafas, G. H. (2005). The management of women at high risk for the development of breast cancer: Risk estimation and preventative strategies. *Cancer Treatment Reviews, 29*(2), 79–89.

Salazar-Gonzalez, J. F., Salazar, M. G., Learn, G. H., Fouda, G. G., Kang, H. H., Mahlokozera, T., Wilks, A. B., Lovingood, R. V., et al. (2011). Origin and evolution of HIV-1 in breast milk determined by single-genome amplification and sequencing. *Journal of Virology, 85*(6), 2751–2763.

Saleh, F. M., & Berlin, F. (2003). Sex hormones, neurotransmitters, and psychopharmacological treatments in men with paraphilic disorders. *Journal of Child Sexual Abuse, 12,* 233–253.

Saleh, L., & Operario, D. (2009). Moving beyond "the down low": A critical analysis of terminology guiding HIV prevention efforts for African American men who have secretive sex with men. *Social Science Medicine, 68*(2), 390–395.

Salter, D., McMillan, D., Richards, M., Talbot, T., Hodges, J., Bentovim, A., et al. (2003). Development of sexually abusive behavior in sexually victimized males. *Lancet, 361*(9356), 471–476.

Salzmann, Z. (2007). *Language, culture, and society* (4th ed.). Boulder, CO: Westview Press.

Sample, I. (2010). The price of love? Losing two of your closest friends. *Guardian.* Retrieved January 17, 2011, from http://www.guardian.co.uk/science/2010/sep/15/price-love-close-friends-relationship.

Samter, W., & Burleson, B. R. (2005). The role of communication in same-sex friendships: A comparison among African Americans, Asian Americans, and European Americans. *Communication Quarterly, 53,* 265–284.

Samuel, A. S., & Naz, R. K. (2008). Isolation of human single chain variable fragment antibodies against specific sperm antigens for immunocontraceptive development. *Human Reproduction, 23*(6), 1324–1337.

Samuels, A. (2011, May 1). Reality TV trashes Black women. *Newsweek.* Retrieved May 5, 2011, from http://www.newsweek.com/2011/05/01/reality-tv-trashes-black-women.html.

Sánchez, F., & Vilain, E. (2010). Genes and brain sex differences. *Progress in Brain Research, 186,* 65–76.

Sánchez, J. M., Milam, M. R., Tomlinson, T. M., & Beardslee, M. A. (2008). Cardiac troponin I elevation after orogenital sex during pregnancy. *Obstetrics and Gynecology, 111,* 487–489.

Sanday, P. R. (1981). The socio-cultural context of rape: A cross-cultural study. *Journal of Social Issues, 37,* 5–27.

Sanders, S. A., & Reinisch, J. M. (1999). Would you say you "had sex" if . . . ? *Journal of the American Medical Association, 281*(3), 275–277.

Sandnabba, N., Santilla, P., Alison, L., & Nordling, N. (2002). Demographics, sexual behavior, family background and abuse experiences of practitioners of sadomasochistic sex: A review of recent research. *Sexual and Relationship Therapy, 17,* 39–55.

Sandnabba, N. K., & Ahlberg, C. (1999). Parents' attitudes and expectations about children's cross-gender behavior. *Sex Roles, 40*(3–4), 249–263.

Sandowski, C. L. (1989). *Sexual concerns when illness or disability strikes.* Springfield, IL: Charles C. Thomas.

Santa Ana, R. (2008, June 30). Watermelon may have Viagra-effect. *Texas A&M Agricultural Communication.* Retrieved August 31, 2008, from http://vfic.tamu.edu/Documents/News/2008/0630%20agnews%20watermelon.pdf.

Santen, R. J. (1995). The testis. In P. Felig, J. D. Baxter, & L. A. Frolman, (Eds.), *Endocrinology and metabolism* (3rd ed.). New York: McGraw-Hill.

Santilla, P., Sandnabba, N., & Nordling, N. (2000). Retrospective perceptions of family interaction in childhood as correlates of current sexual adaptation among sadomasochistic males. *Journal of Psychology and Human Sexuality, 12,* 69–87.

Santos, P., Schinemann, J., Gabarcio, J., & da Graca, G. (2005). New evidence that the MHC influences odor perception in humans: A study with 58 Southern Brazilian students. *Hormones and Behavior, 47*(4), 384–388.

Sarkisian, N., & Gerstel, N. (2008). Till marriage do us part: Adult children's relationships with their parents. *Journal of Marriage and Family, 70,* 360–377.

Sarrel, P., & Masters, W. (1982). Sexual molestation of men by women. *Archives of Sexual Behavior, 11,* 117–131.

Sartorius, A., Ruf, M., Kief, C., & Demirakca, T. (2008). Abnormal amygdala activation profile in pedophilia. *European Archives of Psychiatry and Clinical Neuroscience, 258,* 271–279.

Saslow, B., Boetes, C., Burke, W., Harms, S., Leach, M., Lehman, C., et al. (2007). American Cancer Society guidelines for breast screening with MRI as an adjunct to mammography. *CA Cancer Journal for Clinicians, 57,* 75–89.

Sassler, S., Cunningham, A., & Lichter, D. (2009). Intergenerational patterns of union formation and relationship quality. *Journal of Family Issues, 30*(6), 757–786.

Sati, N. (1998). Equivocal lifestyles. The Living Channel. Retrieved July 7, 2003, from http://www.glas.org/ahbab/Articles/arabia1.html.

Sato, S. M., Schulz, K. M., Sisk, C. L., & Wood, R. I. (2008). Adolescents and androgens, receptors and rewards. *Hormones and Behavior 53*(5), 647–658.

Saulny, S. (2010, January 30). Black? White? Asian? More young Americans choose all of the above. *New York Times.* Retrieved January 30, 2011, from http://www.nytimes.com/2011/01/30/us/30mixed.html?src5twrhp.

Sauter, D., Eisner, F., Ekman, P., & Scott, S. (2010). Cross-cultural recognition of basic emotions through nonverbal emotional vocalizations. *Proceedings of the National Academy of Sciences of the United States of America, 107*(6), 2408.

Savareux, L., Droupy, S.; les membres du comité d'andrologie de l'AFU. (2009). [Evaluation of sexual dysfunction in prostate cancer management]. *Progress in Urology, 19*(Suppl. 4), S189–S192.

Savaya, R., & Cohen, O. (2003). Divorce among Moslem Arabs living in Israel: Comparison for reasons before and after the actualization of the marriage. *Journal of Family Issues, 24*(3), 338–351.

Savic, I., & Lindström, P. (2008, June 16). PET and MRI show differences in cerebral asymmetry and functional connectivity between homo- and heterosexual subjects. *Proceedings of the National Academy of Sciences.* Retrieved October 3, 2008, from http://www.pnas.org/cgi/content/abstract/0801566105v1.

Savic, I., Berglund, H., & Lindström, P. (2005). Brain response to putative pheromones in homosexual men. *Proceedings of the National Academy of Sciences, 102,* 7356–7361.

Savic, I., Garcia-Falgueras, A., & Swaab, D. (2010). Sexual differentiation of the human brain in relation to gender identity and sexual orientation. *Progress in Brain Research, 186,* 41–62.

Savin-Williams, R. C. (2001). *"Mom, Dad. I'm gay." How families negotiate coming out.* Washington, DC: American Psychological Association.

Savin-Williams, R. C., & Diamond, L. M. (2000). Sexual identity trajectories among sexual minority youths: Gender comparisons. *Archives of Sexual Behavior, 29,* 607–627.

Savin-Williams, R. C., & Dube, E. M. (1998). Parental reactions to their child's disclosure of a gay/lesbian identity. *Family Relations, 47,* 7–13.

Savitz, L., & Rosen, L. (1988). The sexuality of prostitutes: Sexual enjoyment reported by "streetwalkers." *Journal of Sex Research, 24,* 200–208.

Sawyer, R. G., Thompson, E. E., & Chicorelli, A. M. (2002). Rape myth acceptance among intercollegiate student athletes. *American Journal of Health Studies, 18*(1), 19–25.

Sayal, K., Heron, J., Golding, J., & Emond, A. (2007). Prenatal alcohol exposure and gender differences in childhood mental health problems: A longitudinal population-based study. *Pediatrics, 119,* 426–434.

Scaravelli, G., Vigiliano, V., Mayorga, J. M., Bolli, S., De Luca, R., & D'Aloja, P. (2010). Analysis of oocyte cryopreservation in assisted reproduction: The Italian National Register data from 2005 to 2007. *Reproductive Biomedicine Online, 21*(4), 496–500.

Scarce, M. (1997). *The hidden toll of stigma and shame.* New York: De Capo Press.

Schachter, S., & Singer, J. (1962). Cognitive, social, and physiological determinants of emotional state. *Psychological Review, 69*(5), 379–399.

Schachter, S., & Singer, J. (2001). Cognitive, social, and physiological determinants of emotional state. In W. Parrott (Ed.), *Emotions in social psychology: Essential readings* (pp. 76–93). New York: Psychology Press.

Schauer, E., & Wheaton, E. (2006). Sex trafficking into the U.S.: A literature review. *Criminal Justice Review.* Retrieved May 7, 2011, from http://www.worldwideopen.org/uploads/resources/files/631/TFGLO052_Lit_Review_Trafficking_into_the_US.pdf.

Schembri, G., & Schober, P. (2011). Risk factors for chlamydial infection in chlamydia contacts: A questionnaire-based study. *Journal of Family Planning and Reproductive Health Care, 37*(1), 10–16.

Schick, V., Herbenick, D., Reece, M., Sanders, S. A., Dodge, B., Middlestadt, S. E., & Fortenberry, J. D. (2010). Sexual behaviors, condom use, and sexual health of Americans over 50: Implications for sexual health promotion for older adults. *Journal of Sexual Medicine, 7*(Suppl. 5), 315–329.

Schiffer, J. T., Abu-Raddad, L., Mark, K. E., Zhu, J., Selke, S., Koelle, D. M., Wald, A., & Corey, L. (2010). Mucosal host immune response predicts the severity and duration of herpes simplex virus-2 genital tract shedding episodes. *Proceedings of the National Academy of Sciences, 107*(44), 18973–18978.

Schiffrin, H., Edelman, A., Falkenstern, M., & Stewart, C. (2010). The associations among computer-mediated communication, relationships, and well-being. *Cyberpsychology, Behavior, and Social Networking, 13*(3), 299–306.

Schildkraut, J. M., Calingaert, B., Marchbanks, P. A., Moorman, P. G., & Rodriguez, G. C. (2002). Impact of progestin and estrogen potency in oral contraceptives on ovarian cancer risk. *Journal of the National Cancer Institute, 94,* 32–38.

Schindler, A. E. (2010). Non-contraceptive benefits of hormonal contraceptives. *Minerva Ginecol, 62*(4), 319–329.

Schlegel, R. (2007, January 17). HPV vaccine. *Washington Post.* Retrieved September 16, 2008, from http://www.washingtonpost.com/wp-dyn/content/discussion/2007/01/16/DI2007011600929.html.

Schlichter, A. (2004). Queer at last? *GLW: A Journal of Lesbian and Gay Studies, 10*(4), 543–565.

Schnarch, D. (1997). *Passionate marriage.* New York: Henry Holt.

Schneider, F., Habel, U., Kessler, C., Salloum, J. B., & Posse, S. (2000). Gender differences in regional cerebral activity during sadness. *Human Brain Mapping, 9*(4), 226–238.

Schneider, J. P. (2000a). Qualitative study of cybersex participants: Gender differences, recovery issues, and implications for therapists. *Sexual Addiction & Compulsivity, 7*(4), 249–278.

Schneider, J. P. (2000b). Effects of cybersex addiction on the family: Results of a survey. *Sexual Addiction & Compulsivity, 7*(1), 31–58.

Schneider, L., Mori, L., Lambert, P., & Wong, A. (2009). The role of gender and ethnicity in perceptions of rape and its aftereffects. *Sex Roles, 60*(5–6), 410–422.

Schneider, M. (1989). Sappho was a right-on adolescent: Growing up lesbian. *Journal of Homosexuality, 17,* 111–130.

Schover, L., & Jensen, S. B. (1988). *Sexuality and chronic illness.* New York: Guilford Press.

Schrodt, P. (2009). Family strength and satisfaction as functions of family communication environments. *Communication Quarterly, 57*(2), 171–186.

Schrodt, P., & Ledbetter, A. (2007). Communication processes that mediate family communication patterns and mental well-being: A means and covariance structures analysis of young adults from divorced and non-divorced families. *Human Communication Research, 33,* 330–356.

Schrodt, P., Ledbetter, A., Jembert, K., Larson, L., Brown, N., & Glonek, K. (2009). Family communication patterns as mediators of communication competence in the parent-child relationship. *Journal of Social and Personal Relationships, 26*(6–7), 853–874.

Schuberg, K. (2009, October 16). Despite widespread contraceptive use, 1/3 of pregnancies in France 'unplanned,' new study confirms. CBS News. Retrieved October 17, 2009, from http://www.cnsnews.com/node/55580.

Schüklenk, U., Stein, E., Kerin, J., & Byne, W. (1997). The ethics of genetic research on sexual orientation. *Hastings Center Report, 27*(4), 6–13.

Schuler, P., Vinci, D., Isosaari, R., Philipp, S., Todorovich, J., Roy, J., & Evans, R. (2008). Body-shape perceptions and body mass index of older African American and European American Women. *Journal of Cross-Cultural Gerontology, 23*(3), 255–264.

Schultheiss, D. (2008). Urogenital infections and male sexuality: Effects on ejaculation and erection. *Andrologia, 40,* 125–129.

Schultz, J. S. (2010, August 6). Divorce insurance (Yes, divorce insurance). *New York Times.* Retrieved October 12, 2010, from http://bucks.blogs.nytimes.com/2010/08/06/divorce-insurance-yes-divorce-insurance/.

Schumm, W. (2010). Children of homosexuals more apt to be homosexuals? A reply to Morrison and to Cameron based on an examination of the multiple sources of data. *Journal of Biosocial Science, 42*(6), 721–743.

Schützwohl, A. (2008). The intentional object of romantic jealousy. *Evolution and Human Behavior, 29,* 92–99.

Schwandt, H., Coresh, J., & Hindin, M. (2010). Marital status, hypertension, coronary heart disease, diabetes, and death among African American women and men: Incidence and prevalence in the atherosclerosis risk in communities study participants. *Journal of Family Issues, 31*(9), 1211–1229.

Schwartz, G., Kim, R., Kolundzija, A., Rieger, G., & Sanders, A. (2010). Biodemographic and physical correlates of sexual orientation in men. *Archives of Sexual Behavior, 39,* 93–109.

Schwartz, J. L., & Gabelnick, H. L. (2002). Current contraceptive research. *Perspectives on Sexual and Reproductive Health, 34*(6), 310–316.

Scott, J. E., & Schwalm, L. A. (1988). Rape rates and the circulation rates of adult magazines. *Journal of Sex Research, 24,* 241–250.

Scott, J. R. (2005). Episiotomy and vaginal trauma. *Obstetrics and Gynecology Clinics of North America, 32*(2), 307–321.

Scott-Sheldon, L., Carey, M., & Carey, K. (2010). Alcohol and risky sexual behavior among heavy drinking college students. *AIDS and Behavior, 14*(4), 845–853.

Scribner, R., Mason, K., Simonsen, N., Theall, K., et al. (2010). An ecological analysis of alcohol-outlet density and campus-reported violence at 32 U.S. colleges. *Journal of Studies on Alcohol and Drugs, 71*(2), 184–191.

Scully, D., & Marolla, J. (1983). *Incarcerated rapists: Exploring a sociological model.* Final Report for Department of Health and Human Services, NIMH.

Sedgh, G., Hussain, R., Bankole, A., & Singh, S. (2007a). Unmet need for contraception in developing countries: Levels and reasons for not using a method. Alan Guttmacher Institute, Occasional Report No. 37. Retrieved July 29, 2008, from http://www.guttmacher.org/pubs/2007/07/09/or37.pdf.

Seeber, B., & Barnhart, K. (2006). Suspected ectopic pregnancy. *Obstetrics and Gynecology, 107*(2 pt 1), 399–413.

Segraves, R. T. (2010). Considerations for a better definition of male orgasmic disorder in DSM V. *Journal of Sexual Medicine, 7*(2 Pt 1), 690–695.

Sehovic, N., & Smith, K. P. (2010). Risk of venous thromboembolism with drospirenone in combined oral contraceptive products. *Annals of Pharmacotherapy, 44*(5), 898–903.

Seidman, S. N. (2007). Androgens and the aging male. *Psychopharmacological Bulletin, 40,* 205–218.

Seidman, S. N., & Rieder, R. O. (1994). A review of sexual behavior in the U.S. *American Journal of Psychiatry, 151,* 330–341.

Seiffge-Krenke, I., Shulman, S., & Klesinger, N. (2001). Adolescent precursors of romantic relationships in young adulthood. *Journal of Social & Personal Relationships, 18*(3), 327–346.

Seki, K., Matsumoto, D., & Imahori, T. T. (2002). The conceptualization and expression of intimacy in Japan and the United States. *Journal of Cross Cultural Psychology, 33,* 303–319.

Seligman, L., & Hardenburg, S. A. (2000). Assessment and treatment of paraphilias. *Journal of Counseling and Development, 78*(1), 107–113.

Sell, R., Wells, J., & Wypij, D. (1995). The prevalence of homosexual behavior and attraction in the U.S., the U.K and France: Results of a national population-based sample. *Archives of Sexual Behavior, 24,* 235–249.

Seltzer, J. A. (2000). Families formed outside of marriage. *Journal of Marriage and Family, 62*(4), 1247.

Sepilian, V., & Wood, E. (2004). Ectopic pregnancy. Retrieved July 19, 2005, from http://www.emedicine.com/med/topic3212.htm.

Seppa, N. (2001). Study reveals male link to preeclampsia. *Science News, 159*(12), 181–182.

Serefoglu, E. C., Yaman, O., Cayan, S., Asci, R., Orhan, I., Usta, M. F., Ekmekcioglu, O., Kendirci, M., Semerci, B., & Kadioglu, A. (2011). Prevalence of the complaint of ejaculating prematurely and the four premature ejaculation syndromes: Results from the Turkish Society of Andrology Sexual Health Survey. *Journal of Sexual Medicine, 8*(2), 540–548.

Serino, L., Moriel, D., Rappuoli, R., & Pizza, M. (2010). Towards a vaccine against Escherichia coli-associated urinary tract infections. *Future Microbiology, 5*(3), 351–354.

Seto, M. (2008). Pedophilia: Psychopathology and theory. In D. Laws & W. O'Donohue (Eds.), *Sexual deviance: Theory, assessment and treatment* (2nd ed., pp. 164–183). New York: Guilford Press.

Seveso, M., Taverna, G., Giusti, G., Benetti, A., Maugeri, O., Piccinelli, A., & Graziotti, P. (2010). Corporoplasty by plication: Outpatient surgery for the correction of penile cancer. *Archives of Italian Urological Andrology, 82*(3), 164–166.

Sexuality Information and Education Council of the United States. (2004). Guidelines for comprehensive sexuality education (3rd ed.). Retrieved September 22, 2005, from http://www.siecus.org/pubs/guidelines/guidelines.pdf.

Sexwork.com. (1999). Thailand's long tradition of prostitution: Modern attitude shifts vs. huge economic benefits. Retrieved June 29, 2011, from http://www.sexwork.com/Thailand/traditiions.html.

Sexwork.com. (1999). The influence of Thai Buddhism on prostitution. Retrieved November 16, 2008, from http://www.sexwork.com/Thailand/buddhism.html.

Seymour, A., Murray, M., Sigmon, J., Hook, M., Edmunds, C., Gaboury, M., et al. (Eds.). (2000). Retrieved May 22, 2003, from http://www.ojp.usdoj.gov/ovc/assist/nvaa2000/academy/welcome.html.

Shackelford, T. K., & Goetz, A. T. (2007). Adaptation to sperm competition in humans. *Current Directions in Psychological Science, 16*, 47–50.

Shadiack, A., Sharma, S., Earle, D., Spana, C., & Hallam, T. (2007). Melanocortins in the treatment of male and female sexual dysfunction. *Current Topics in Medical Chemistry, 7*, 1137–1144.

Shafaat, A. (2004). Punishment for adultery in Islam: A detailed examination. Retrieved April 10, 2008, from http://www.islamicperspectives.com/Stoning4.htm.

Shafik, A. (1991). Testicular suspension: Effect on testicular function. *Andrologia, 23*(4), 297–301.

Shamloul, R. (2005). Treatment of men complaining of short penis. *Urology, 65*(6), 1183–1185.

Shamloul, R. (2010). Natural aphrodisiacs. *Journal of Sexual Medicine, 7*(1 Pt 1), 39–49.

Shapiro, J., Radecki, S., Charchian, A. S., & Josephson, V. (1999). Sexual behavior and AIDS-related knowledge among community college students in Orange County, California. *Journal of Community Health, 24*(1), 29–43.

Shapiro, S., & Dinger, J. (2010). Risk of venous thromboembolism among users of oral contraceptives: A review of two recently published studies. *Journal of Family Planning and Reproductive Health Care, 36*(1), 33–38.

Sharma, O., & Haub, C. (2008). Sex ratio at birth begins to improve in India. Population Reference Bureau. Retrieved February 24, 2011, from http://www.prb.org/Articles/2008/indiasexratio.aspx.

Sharma, R. (2001). Condom use seems to be reducing number of new HIV/AIDS cases. *British Medical Journal, 323*(7310), 417–421.

Sharp, E., & Ispa, J. (2009). Inner-city single Black mothers' gender-related childrearing expectations and goals. *Sex Roles, 60*, 656–668.

Sharpe, R. M., & Skakkebaek, N. E. (2008). Testicular dysgenesis syndrome: Mechanistic insights and potential new downstream effects. *Fertility and Sterility, 89*(Suppl. 2), e33–38.

Sharpsteen, D. J., & Kirkpatrick, L. A. (1997). Romantic jealousy and adult romantic attachment. *Journal of Personality & Social Psychology, 72*(3), 627–640.

Shaver, F. M. (2005). Sex work research: Methodological and ethical challenges. *Journal of Interpersonal Violence, 20*(3), 296–319.

Shaver, P., & Hazan, C. (1987). Being lonely, falling in love: Perspectives from attachment theory. *Journal of Social Behavior & Personality, 2*(2, Pt 2), 105–124.

Shaver, P. R., Wu, S., & Schwartz, J. C. (1992). Cross-cultural similarities and differences in emotion and its representation: A prototype approach. In M. S. Clark (Ed.), *Emotion* (pp. 175–212). Newbury Park, CA: Sage.

Sheaffer, A. T., Lange, E., & Bondy, C. A. (2008). Sexual function in women with Turner syndrome. *Journal of Women's Health, 17*, 27–33.

Shear, M. D. (2010, April 16). Obama extends hospital visitation rights to same-sex partners of gays. *The Washington Post*. Retrieved May 11, 2011, from http://www.washingtonpost.com/wp-dyn/content/article/2010/04/15/AR2010041505502.html.

Shechory, M., & Idisis, Y. (2006). Rape myths and social distance toward sex offenders and victims among therapists and students. *Sex Roles, 54*, 651–658.

Sheehan, P. (2007). Hyperemesis gravidarum—assessment and management. *Australian Family Physician, 36*, 698–701.

Sheldon, K. M. (2007). Gender differences in preferences for singles ads that proclaim extrinsic versus intrinsic values. *Sex Roles, 57*, 119–130.

Shellenbarger, S. (2008, February 14). Why some single women choose to freeze their eggs. *Wall Street Journal*, p. D1.

Shelton, J. F., Tancredi, D. J., & Hertz-Picciotto, I. (2010). Independent and dependent contributions of advanced maternal and paternal ages to autism risk. *Autism Research, 3*(1), 30–39.

Sheppard, C., & Wylie, K. R. (2001). An assessment of sexual difficulties in men after treatment for testicular cancer. *Sexual and Relationship Therapy, 16*(1), 47–58.

Sherfey, J. (1972). *The nature and evolution of female sexuality*. New York: Random House.

Sherif, B. (2004). Egypt. In R. T. Francoeur & R. J. Noonan (Eds.), *The Continuum complete international encyclopedia of sexuality* (pp. 345–358). New York/London: Continuum International.

Sherr, L., Varrall, R., Mueller, J., Richter, L., Wakhweya, A., Adato, M., Belsey, M., Chandan, U., Drimie, S., Haour-Knipe, V., Hosegood, M., Kimou, J., Madhavan, S., Mathambo, V., & Desmond, C. (2008). A systematic review on the meaning of the concept 'AIDS orphan': Confusion over definitions and implications for care. *AIDS Care, 20*(5), 527–536.

Shettles, L., & Rorvik, D. (1970). *Your baby's sex: Now you can choose*. New York: Dodd, Mead.

Sheynkin, Y., Jung, M., Yoo, P., Schulsinger, D., & Komaroff, E. (2005). Increase in scrotal temperature in laptop computer users. *Human Reproduction, 20*(2), 452–455.

Shibusawa, T. (2009). A commentary on "gender perspectives in cross-cultural couples." *Clinical Social Work Journal, 37*, 230–233.

Shields, R. (2010, May 16). South Africa's shame: The rise of child rape. *The Independent UK*. Retrieved April 20, 2011, from http://www.independent.co.uk/news/world/africa/south-africas-shame-the-rise-of-child-rape-1974578.html.

Shifren, J. L., & Avis, N. E. (2007). Surgical menopause: Effects on psychological well-being and sexuality. *Menopause, 14*, 586–591.

Shifren, J. L., Monz, B. U., Russo, P., Segreti, A., & Johannes, C. (2008). Sexual problems and distress in United States women. *Obstetrics & Gynecology, 112*, 970–978.

Shih, G., Turok, D. K., & Parker, W. J. (2011). Vasectomy: The other (better) form of sterilization. *Contraception, 83*(4), 310–315.

Shilts, R. (2000). *And the band played on: Politics, people, and the AIDS epidemic.* New York: St. Martin's Press.

Shimanaka, K. (2008, August 8). Ominous rumblings on the love hotel front. *The Tokyo Reporter.* Retrieved August 23, 2008, http://www.tokyoreporter.com/2008/08/11/ominous-rumblings-on-the-love-hotel-front.

Shoffman, M. (2006, December 11). Italian politicians attack Vatican's "anti-gay" attitude. *Pink News.* Retrieved July 4, 2008, from http://www.pinknews.co.uk/news/view.php?id=3229.

Shrewsberry, A., Weiss, A., & Ritenour, C. W. (2010). Recent advances in the medical and surgical treatment of priapism. *Current Urological Reports, 11*(6), 405–413.

Shtarkshall, R. A., & Zemach, M. (2004). Israel. In R. T. Francoeur & R. J. Noonan (Eds.), *The Continuum International encyclopedia of sexuality* (pp. 581–619). New York/London: Continuum International.

Shteynshlyuger, A., & Freyle, J. (2011). Familial testicular torsion in three consecutive generations of first-degree relatives. *Journal of Pediatric Urology, 7*, 86–91.

Shufaro, Y., & Schenker, J. G. (2010). Cryopreservation of human genetic material. *Annals of New York Academy of Science, 1205*, 220–224.

Shulman, J. L., & Horne, S. G. (2006). Guilty or not? A path model of women's sexual force fantasies. *Journal of Sex Research, 43*, 368–377.

Shulman, L. P. (2010). Gynecological management of premenstrual symptoms. *Current Pain and Headache Reports, 14*(5), 367–375.

Shulman, S., Davilla, J., & Shachar-Shapira, L. (2010). Assessing romantic competence among older adolescents. *Journal of Adolescence, 34*(3), 397–406.

Shutty, M. S., & Leadbetter, R. A. (1993). Case report: Recurrent pseduocyesis in a male patient with psychosis, intermittent hyponatremia, and polydipsia. *Psychosomatic Medicine, 55*, 146–148.

Sigal, J., Gibbs, M. S., Goodrich, C., Rashid, T., Anjum, A., Hsu, D., Perrino, C., Boratrav, H., Carson-Arenas, A., et al. (2005). Cross-cultural reactions to academic sexual harassment: Effects of individualist vs. collectivist culture and gender of participants. *Sex Roles, 52*(3–4), 201–215.

Siker, J. S. (1994). *Homosexuality in the Church: Both sides of the debate.* Louisville, KY: Westminster John Knox Press.

Silbert, M. (1998). Compounding factors in the rape of street prostitutes. In A. W. Burgess (Ed.), Rape and sexual assault II. London: Taylor & Francis.

Silverman, B., & Gross, T. (1997). Use and effectiveness of condoms during anal intercourse. *Sexually Transmitted Diseases, 24*, 11–17.

Silverman, E. K. (2004). Anthropology and circumcision. *Annual Reviews in Anthropology, 33*(1), 419–445.

Silverman, J., Decker, M., McCauley, H., Gupta, J., Miller, E., Raj, A., & Goldberg, A. (2010). Male perpetration of intimate partner violence and involvement in abortions: An abortion-related conflict. *American Journal of Public Health, 1100*(8), 1415–1417.

Silverstein, C. (1984). The ethical and moral implications of sexual classification: A commentary. *Journal of Homosexuality, 9*, 29–38.

Simforoosh, N., Tabibi, A., Khalili, S., Soltani, M., Afjehi, A., Aalami, F., & Bodoohi, H. (In press). Neonatal circumcision reduces the incidence of asymptomatic urinary tract infection: A large prospective study with long-term follow up using Plastiball. *Journal of Pediatric Urology.*

Simmons, M., & Montague, D. (2008). Penile prosthesis implantation: Past, present and future. *International Journal of Impotence Research, 20*, 437–444.

Simon, P. M., Morse, E. V., Osofsky, H. J., & Balson, P. M. (1992). Psychological characteristics of a sample of male street prostitutes. *Archives of Sexual Behavior, 21*, 33–44.

Simon, R. W. (2002). Revisiting the relationships among gender, martial status, and mental health. *American Journal of Sociology, 107*(4), 1065–1097.

Simons, M. (1996, January 26). African women in France battling polygamy. *New York Times*, p. A1.

Simons, R. L., & Whitbeck, L. B. (1991). Sexual abuse as a precursor to prostitution and victimization among adolescent and adult homeless women. *Journal of Family Issues, 12*, 361–379.

Simpson, J. L., & Lamb, D. J. (2001). Genetic effects of intracytoplasmic sperm injection. *Seminars in Reproductive Medicine, 19*(3), 239–249.

Simpson, J., Collins, W., Tran, S., & Haydon, K. (2007). Attachment and the experience and expression of emotions in romantic relationships: A developmental perspective. *Journal of Personality and Social Psychology, 92*(2), 355–367.

Simsir, A., Thorner, K., Waisman, J., & Cangiarella, J. (2001). Endometriosis in abdominal scars. *American Surgeon, 67*(10), 984–987.

Singh, A., Wong, T., & De, P. (2008). Characteristics of primary and late latent syphilis cases which were initially non-reactive with the rapid plasma regain as the screening test. *International Journal of STDs and AIDS, 19*, 464–468.

Singh, D., Vidaurri, M., Zambarano, R. J., & Dabbs, J. M. (1999). Lesbian erotic role identification: Behavioral, morphological, and hormonal correlates. *Journal of Personality and Social Psychology, 76*(6), 1035–1049.

Singh, S., Wulf, D., Hussain, Bankole, A., & Sedgh, G. (2009). *Abortion worldwide: A decade of uneven process.* New York: Guttmacher Institute.

Sipski, M., Alexander, C., & Gomez-Marin, O. (2006). Effects of level and degree of spinal cord injury on male orgasm. *Spinal Cord, 44*, 798–804.

Skinner, B. F. (1953). *Science and human behavior.* New York: Macmillan.

Skolnick, A. (1992). *The intimate environment: Exploring marriage and the family.* New York: HarperCollins.

Slater, J. (2011, April 1). Students file title IX suit against Yale. NBC Connecticut. Retrieved April 26, 2011, from http://www.nbcconnecticut.com/news/Students-File-Title-IX-Suit-Against-Yale-University-119036069.html.

Slavney, P. R. (1990). *Perpectives on hysteria.* Baltimore, MD: Johns Hopkins University Press.

Slevin, K. F. (2010). "If I had lots of money...I'd have a body makeover": Managing the aging body. *Social Forces, 88*(3), 1003–1020.

Smith, C. J., McMahon, C., & Shabsigh, R. (2005). Peyronie's disease: The epidemiology, aetiology and clinical evaluation of deformity. *British Journal of Urology International, 95*(6), 729–732.

Smith, D. K., Taylor, A., Kilmarx, P. H., Sullivan, P., Warner, L., Kamb, M., Bock, N., Kohmescher, B., & Mastro, T. D. (2010). Male circumcision in the United States for the prevention of HIV infection and other adverse health outcomes: Report from a CDC consultation. *Public Health Report, 25*(Suppl. 1), 72–82.

Smith, G. D., & Travis, L. (2011). Getting to know human papillomavirus (HPV) and the HPV vaccines. *Journal of the American Osteopathic Association, 111*(3 Suppl. 2), S29–S34.

Smith, K. T. (1971). Homophobia: A tentative personality profile. *Psychological Reports, 29,* 1091–1094.

Smith, L. E. (2010). Sexual function of the gynecologic cancer survivor. *Oncology, 24*(10 Suppl.), 41–44.

Smith, M. E. (2005). Female sexual assault: The impact on the male significant other. *Issues in the Mental Health Nursing, 26*(2), 149–167.

Smith, S. A., & Michel, Y. (2006). A pilot study on the effects of aquatic exercises on discomforts of pregnancy. *Journal of Obstetrics and Gynecological Neonatal Nursing, 35,* 315–323.

So, H. W., & Cheung, F. M. (2005). Review of Chinese sex attitudes & applicability of sex therapy for Chinese couples with sexual dysfunction. *Journal of Sex Research, 42*(2), 93–102.

Soares, C. (2010). Can depression be a menopause-associated risk? *BMC Medicine, 8,* 79.

Sobsey, D. (1994). *Violence and abuse in the lives of people with disabilities.* Baltimore, MD: Paul H. Brookes.

Society for the Advancement of Sexual Health. (2008b). *Public service announcement: Sexual addiction.* Retrieved October 2, 2008, from http://www.sash.net/.

Soley, L., & Kurzbard, G. (1986). Sex in advertising: A comparison of 1964 and 1984 magazine advertisements. *Journal of Advertising, 15,* 46–54.

Soloman, S. E., Rothblum, D., & Balsam, K. F. (2005). Money, housework, sex, and conflict: Same-sex couples in civil unions, those not in civil unions, and heterosexual married siblings. *Sex Roles, 52,* 561–575.

Sommerfeld, J. (1999). Megan's Law expands to the Internet. Retrieved March 31, 2003, from http://www.msnbc.com/news/297969.asp?cp1=1.

Song, A., & Halpern-Felsher, B. (2011). Predictive relationship between adolescent oral and vaginal sex: Results from a prospective, longitudinal study. *Archives of Pediatrics & Adolescent Medicine, 165*(3), 243–249.

Song, L. M., Gu, Y., Lu, W., Liang, X., & Chen, Z. (2006). A phase II randomized controlled trial of a novel male contraception, an intra-vas device. *International Journal of Andrology, 29,* 489–495.

Sontag, S. (1979). The double-standard of aging. In J. H. Williams (Ed.), *Psychology of women: Selected readings* (pp. 462–478). New York: W.W. Norton Publishers.

Soper, D. E. (2010). Pelvic inflammatory disease. *Obstetrics and Gynecology, 116*(2 Pt 1), 419–428.

Sorenson, S., & Brown, V. (1990). Interpersonal violence and crisis intervention on the college campus. *New Directions for Student Services, 49,* 57–66.

Sotirin, P. (2000). All they do is bitch, bitch, bitch: Political and interactional features of women's office talk. *Women and Language, 23*(2), 19.

Spence, J. T. (1984). Gender identity and its implications for the concepts of masculinity and femininity. In T. B. Sonderegger (Ed.), *Psychology and gender* (pp. 59–95). Lincoln: University of Nebraska Press.

Spolan, S. (1991, March 22). Oh, by the way. *Philadelphia City Paper,* p. 7.

Sprecher, S. (2002). Sexual satisfaction in premarital relationships: Associations with satisfaction, love, commitment and stability. *Journal of Sex Research, 39*(3), 190–196.

Sprecher, S., & Hendrick, S. (2004). Self-disclosure in intimate relationships: Associations with individual and relationship characteristics over time. *Journal of Social and Clinical Psychology, 23*(6), 857–877.

Sprecher, S., & Regan, P. (1996). College virgins: How men and women perceive their sexual status. *Journal of Sex Research, 33*(1), 3–16.

Sprecher, S., & Regan, P. (2002). Liking some things (in some people) more than others: Partner preferences in romantic relationships and friendships. *Journal of Social & Personal Relationships, 19*(4), 463–481.

Sprecher, S., & Toto-Morn, M. (2002). A study of men and women from different sides of earth to determine if men are from Mars and women are from Venus in their beliefs about love and romantic relationships. *Sex Roles, 46*(5–6), 131–147.

Sprecher, S., Cate, R., & Levin, L. (1998). Parental divorce and young adults' beliefs about love. *Journal of Divorce & Remarriage, 28*(3–4), 107–120.

Srinivasan, P., & Lee, G. R. (2004). The dowry system in Northern India: Woman's attitudes and social change. *Journal of Marriage and the Family, 66*(5), 1108–1118.

Srivastava, R., Thakar, R., & Sultan, A. (2008). Female sexual dysfunction in obstetrics and gynecology. *Obstetrics and Gynecology Survey, 63,* 527–537.

St Pierre, M., & Senn, C. (2010). External barriers to help-seeking encountered by Canadian gay and lesbian victims of intimate partner abuse: An application of the barriers model. *Violence and Victims, 25*(4), 536–551.

Stacey, D. (2008). No more periods: The safety of continuous birth control. Retrieved March 18, 2008, from http://contraception.about.com/od/prescriptionoptions/p/MissingPeriods.htm.

Stahlhut, R. W., vanWijngaarden, E., Dye, T. D., Cook, S., & Swan, S. H. (2007). Concentrations of urinary phthalate metabolites are associated with increased waist circumference and insulin resistance in adult U.S. males. *Environmental Health Perspectives, 115,* 876–882.

Stanford, E. K. (2002). Premenstrual syndrome. Retrieved July 18, 2002, from http://www.medical-library.org/journals/secure/gynecol/secure/Premenstrual%20syndromes.

Stanger, J. D., Vo, L., Yovich, J. L., & Almahbobi, G. (2010). Hypo-osmotic swelling test identifies individual spermatozoa with minimal DNA fragmentation. *Reproductive Biomedicine Online, 21*(4), 474–484.

Stark, R. (1996). *The rise of Christianity.* Princeton, NJ: Princeton University Press.

Starkman, N., & Rajani, N. (2002). The case for comprehensive sex education. *AIDS Patient Care and STDs, 16*(7), 313–318.

Starling, K. (1999). How to bring the romance back. *Ebony, 54*(4), 136–137.

Stayton, W. R. (1996). Sexual and gender identity disorders in a relational perspective. In F. W. Kaslow (Ed.), *Handbook of relational diagnosis and dysfunctional family patterns* (pp. 357–370). New York: Wiley.

Steen, S., & Schwartz, P. (1995). Communication, gender, and power: Homosexual couples as a case study. In M. A. Fitzpatrick & A. L. Vangelisti (Eds.), *Explaining family interactions* (pp. 310–343). Thousand Oaks, CA: Sage.

Steiger, H., Richardson, J., Schmitz, N., Israel, M., et al. (2010). Trait-defined eating disorder subtypes and history of childhood abuse. *International Journal of Eating Disorders, 43*(5), 428–432.

Stein, J. H., & Reiser, L. W. (1994). A study of white, middle-class adolescent boys' responses to 'semenarche'. *Journal of Youth and Adolescence, 23*(3), 373–384.

Stein, R. (2008, May 20). A debunking on teenagers and "technical virginity"; researchers find that oral sex isn't commonplace among young people who avoid intercourse. *The Washington Post*. Retrieved May 29, 2008, from http://www.guttmacher.org/media/nr/nr_euroteens.html.

Steiner, A. Z., D'Aloisio, A. A., DeRoo, L. A., Sandler, D. P., & Baird, D. D. (2010). Association of intrauterine and early-life exposures with age at menopause in the Sister Study. *American Journal of Epidemiology, 172*(2), 140–148.

Stengers, J., & Van Neck, A. (2001). *Masturbation: The history of a great terror*. New York: Palgrave/St. Martins.

Stephenson, J. M., Imrie, J., Davis, M. M., Mercer, C., Black, S., et al. (2003). Is use of antiretroviral therapy among homosexual men associated with increased risk of transmission of HIV infection? *Sexually Transmitted Diseases, 79*(1), 7–10.

Stern, B., Russell, C., & Russell, D. (2007). Hidden persuasions in soap operas: Damaged heroines and negative consumer effects. *International Journal of Advertising, 26*(1), 9–36.

Sternberg, R. J. (1985): *Beyond IQ: A triarchic theory of human intelligence*. New York: Cambridge University Press.

Sternberg, R. J. (1987). Liking versus loving: A comparative evaluation of theories. *Psychological Bulletin, 102*(3), 331–345.

Sternberg, R. J. (1998). *Cupid's arrow: The course of love through time*. New Haven, CT: Yale University Press.

Sternberg, R. J. (1999). *Love is a story*. New York: Oxford University Press.

Sternberg, S. (2006). Once-a-day drug cocktail—in one pill—wins FDA approval. *USAToday*. Retrieved October 8, 2008, from http://www.usatoday.com/news/health/2006-07-12-hiv-pill_x.htm.

Sternfeld, B., Swindle, R., Chawla, A. Long, S., & Kennedy, S. (2002). Severity of premenstrual symptoms in a health maintenance organization population. *Obstetrics & Gynecology, 99*(6), 1014–1024.

Stevenson, B., & Isen, A. (2010). Who's getting married? Education and marriage today and in the past. A briefing paper prepared for the Council on Contemporary Families, January 26, 2010. Retrieved January 29, 2011, from http://www.contemporary-families.org/images/stories/homepage/orange_border/ccf012510.pdf.

Stevenson, B., & Wolfers, J. (2007). Marriage and divorce: Changes and their driving forces. *Journal of Economic Perspectives, 21*(2), 27–52.

Stevenson, B., & Wolfers, J. (2008). Marriage and the market. Cato Institute. Retrieved January 29, 2011, from http://bpp.wharton.upenn.edu/betseys/papers/Policy%20Papers/Cato%20Unbound.pdf.

Stewart, E. A. (2001). Uterine fibroids. *Lancet, 357*(9252), 293–298.

Stewart, F., & Gabelnick, H. L. (2004). Contraceptive research and development. In R. A. Hatcher et al. (Eds.), *Contraceptive technology* (18th rev. ed., pp. 601–616). New York: Ardent Media.

Stewart, F. H., Ellertson, C., & Cates, W. (2004). Abortion. In R. A. Hatcher et al. (Eds.), *Contraceptive technology* (18th rev. ed., pp. 673–700). New York: Ardent Media.

Stewart, H. (2005). Senoritas and princesses: The quinceanera as a context for female development. *Dissertation Abstracts, 65*(7-A), 2770, #0419–4209.

Stewart, J. (1990). *The complete manual of sexual positions*. Chatsworth, CA: Media Press.

Stillwell, L. (2010). To date or not to date? Religious and racial dating choices among conservative Christians. Denton, TX: University of North Texas, AAT 3436546.

Stokes, C., & Ellison, C. (2010). Religion and attitudes toward divorce laws among U.S. adults. *Journal of Family Issues, 31*(10), 1279–1304.

Stoller, R. J. (1991). The term perversion. In G. I. Fogel & W. A. Myers (Eds.), *Perversions and near-perversions in clinical practice: New psychoanalytic perspectives* (pp. 36–58). New Haven, CT: Yale University Press.

Stoller, R. J. (1996). The gender disorders. In I. Rosen (Ed.), *Sexual deviation* (3rd ed., pp. 111–133). London: Oxford University Press.

Stoller, R. J., & Herdt, G. H. (1985). Theories of origins of male homosexuality. *Archives of General Psychiatry, 42*, 399–404.

Storgaard, L., Bonde, J. P., Ernst, E., Spano, M., Andersen, C. Y., Frydenberg, M., & Olsen, J. (2003). Does smoking during pregnancy affect sons' sperm counts? *Epidemiology, 14*(3), 278–286.

Storm, L. (2011). Nurturing touch helps mothers with postpartum depression and their infants. Interview by Deb Discenza. *Neonatal Network, 30*(1), 71–72.

Storms, M. D. (1980). Theories of sexual orientation. *Journal of Personality and Social Psychology, 38*, 783–792.

Storms, M. D. (1981). A theory of erotic orientation development. *Psychological Review, 88*, 340–353.

Stout, A. L., Grady, T. A., Steege, J. F., Blazer, D. G., George, L. K., & Melville, M. L. (1986). Premenstrual symptoms in Black and White community samples. *American Journal of Psychiatry, 143*(11), 1436–1469.

Strand, L. B., Barnett, A. G., & Tong, S. (2011). The influence of season and ambient temperature on birth outcomes: A review of the epidemiological literature. *Environmental Research, 111*, 451–462.

Strandberg, K., Peterson, M., Schaefers, M., Case, L., Pack, M., Chase, D., & Schlievert, P. (2009). Reduction in staphylococcus aureus growth and exotoxin production and in vaginal interleukin 8 levels due to glycerol monolaurate in tampons. *Clinics in Infectious Diseases, 49*(11), 1718–1717.

Strasburger, V. C. (2005). Adolescents, sex, and the media: Oooo, baby, baby—a Q&A. *Adolescent Medicine Clinics, 16*(2), 269–288.

Strasburger, V. C., & The Council on Communications and Media. (2010). Sexuality, contraception, and the media. *Pediatrics, 126*, 576–582.

Strassberg, D. S., & Lockerd, L. K. (1998). Force in women's sexual fantasies. *Archives of Sexual Behavior, 27*(4), 403–415.

Strauss, G. (2010). Sex on TV: It's increasingly uncut and unavoidable. *USA Today*. Retrieved May 3, 2011, from http://www.usatoday.com/life/television/news/2010-01-20-sexcov20_CV_N.htm#.

Strauss, L., Gamble, S., Parker, W., Cook, D., Zane, S., & Hamdan, S. (2006). Abortion surveillance—United States, 2003. *Morbidity and Mortality Weekly Report Surveillance Summaries, 55*(11), 1–32.

Strauss, L. T., Herndon, J., Chang, J., Parker, W., Bowens, S., Zane, S., & Berg, C. J. (2004, November 26). Abortion surveillance—United States, 2001. *MMWR Surveillance Summary, 53*, 1–32.

Strickler, J. (2010, December 21). More couples saying 'I do' to prenups. *Chicago Tribune*. Retrieved May 11, 2011, from http://articles.chicagotribune.com/2010-12-21/travel/sc-fam-1221-prenup-20101221_1_prenups-moss-barnett-second-marriages.

Strine, T. W., Chapman, D. P., & Ahluwalia, I. B. (2005). Menstrual-related problems and psychological distress among women in the United States. *Journal of Women's Health, 14*(4), 316–323.

Strohmaier, J., Wüst, S., Uher, R., Henigsberg, N., Mors, O., Hauser, J., Souery, D., Zobel, A., Jordan, R., Hallam, T. J., Molinoff, P., & Spana, C. (2011). Developing treatments for female sexual dysfunction. *Clinical*

Pharmacology and Therapeutics, 89(1), 137–141.

Stromsvik, N., Raheim, M., Oyen, N., Enge-bretsen, L., & Gjengedal, E. (2010). Stigmatization and male identity: Norwegian males' experience after identification as BRCA1/2 mutation carriers. *Journal of Genetic Counseling, 19*(4), 360.

Struble, C. B., Lindley, L. L., Montgomery, K., Hardin, J., & Burcin, M. (2010). Overweight and obesity in lesbian and bisexual college women. *Journal of American College Health, 59*(1), 51–56.

Struckman-Johnson, C., & Struckman-Johnson, D. (1994). Men pressured and forced into sexual experience. *Archives of Sexual Behavior, 23*, 93–115.

Struckman-Johnson, C., & Struckman-Johnson, D. (2002). Sexual coercion reported by women in three midwestern prisons. *Journal of Sex Research, 39*(3), 217–227.

Stuebe, A. M., Willett, W. C., Xue, F., & Michels, K. B. (2009). Lactation and incidence of premenopausal breast cancer. *Archives of Internal Medicine, 169*(15), 1364–1371.

Stumpe, J., & Davey, M. (2009, May 31). Abortion doctor shot to death in Kansas church. *New York Times.* Retrieved March 14, 2011, from http://www.nytimes.com/2009/06/01/us/01tiller.html.

Su, J., Berman, S., Davis, D., Weinstock, H., & Kirkcaldy, R. (2010). Congenital syphilis, US, 2003–2008. Centers for Disease Control and Prevention. *MMWR Morbidity and Mortality Weekly Report, 59*, 413–417.

Sugrue, D. P., & Whipple, B. (2001) The consensus-based classification of female sexual dysfunction: Barriers to universal acceptance. *Journal of Sex and Marital Therapy, 27*, 232.

Sulak, P. J., Kuehl, T. J., Ortiz, M., & Shull, B. L. (2002). Acceptance of altering the standard 21-day/7-day oral contraceptive regimen to delay menses and reduce hormone withdrawal symptoms. *American Journal of Obstetrics and Gynecology, 186*(6), 1142–1149.

Sulak, P. J., Scow, R. D., Preece, C., Riggs, M., & Kuehl, T. (2000). Withdrawal Symptoms in Oral Contraceptive Users. *Obstetrics & Gynecology, 95*, 261–266.

Sullivan, P. S., Drake, A. J., & Sanchez, T. H. (2007). Prevalence of treatment optimism-related risk behavior and associated factors among men who have sex with men in 11 states, 2000–2001. *AIDS Behavior, 11*(1), 123–129.

Sun, L., Huang, X., Suo, J., Fan, B., Chen, Z., Yang, W., & Li, J. (2011). Biological evaluation of a novel copper-containing composite for contraception. *Fertility and Sterility, 95*(4), 1416–1420.

Suppe, F. (1984). Classifying sexual disorders: The diagnostic and statistical manual of the American Psychiatric Association. *Journal of Homosexuality, 9,* 9–28.

Sutphin, S. T. (2010). Social exchange theory and the division of household labor in same-sex couples. *Marriage and Family Review, 46*(3), 191–209.

Svoboda, E. (2006, December 5). All the signs of pregnancy except one: A baby. Retrieved from http://www.nytimes.com/2006/12/05/health/05pseud.html.

Svoboda, E. (2011). Breaking up in hard to do. *Psychology Today, 44*(1), 64.

Swaab, D. F. (2004). Sexual differentiation of the human brain: Relevance for gender identity, transsexualism and sexual orientation. *Gynecological Endocrinology, 19*(6), 201–312.

Swaab, D. F., & Hofman, M. A. (1990). An enlarged suprachiasmatic nucleus in homosexual men. *Brain Research, 537,* 141–148.

Swami, V., & Furnham, A. (2008). *The Psychology of Physical Attraction.* New York: Routledge/Taylor & Francis Group.

Swan, S. (2006). Semen quality in fertile U.S. men in relation to geographical area and pesticide exposure. *International Journal of Andrology, 29,* 62–68.

Swanson, J. M., Dibble, S., & Chapman, L. (1999). Effects of psychoeducational interventions on sexual health risks and psychosocial adaptation in young adults with genital herpes. *Journal of Advanced Nursing, 29*(4), 840–851.

Swartz, J. (2004, March 9). Online porn often leads high-tech way. *USA Today.* Retrieved October 7, 2008, from http://www.usatoday.com/money/industries/technology/2004–03–09-onlineporn_x.htm.

Swearingen, S., & Klausner, J. D. (2005). Sildenafil use, sexual risk behavior, and risk for sexually transmitted diseases, including HIV infection. *American Journal of Medicine, 118,* 571–577.

Szymanski, D. M., Chung, Y., & Balsam, K. (2001). Psychosocial correlates of internalized homophobia in lesbians. *Measurement and Evaluation in Counseling and Development, 34*(1), 27–39.

Taft, C., Resick, P., Watkins, L., & Panuzio, J. (2009). An investigation of posttraumatic stress disorder and depressive symptom-atology among female victims of interpersonal trauma. *Journal of Family Violence, 24*(6), 407–416.

Tai, Y. C., Domchek, S., Parmigiani, G., & Chen, S. (2007). Breast cancer risk among male BRCA1 and BRCA2 mutation carriers. *Journal of the National Cancer Institute, 99,* 1811–1814.

Taioli, E., Marabelli, R., Scortichini, G., Migliorati, G., Pedotti, P., Cigliano, A., & Caporale, V. (2005). Human exposure to dioxins through diet in Italy. *Chemosphere, 61,* 1672–1676.

Tait, R. (2005, July 28). A fatwa for transsexuals. *Salon.* Retrieved December 14, 2010, from http://dir.salon.com/story/news/feature/2005/07/28/iran_transsexuals.

Talakoub, L., Munarriz, R., Hoag, L., Gioia, M., Flaherty, E., & Goldstein, I. (2002). Epidemiological characteristics of 250 women with sexual dysfunction who presented for initial evaluation. *Journal of Sex and Marital Therapy, 28* (Suppl. 1), 217–224.

Talbot, J., Baker, J., & McHale, J. (2009). Sharing the love: Prebirth adult attachment status and coparenting adjustment during early infancy. *Parenting: Science & Practice, 9*(1), 56–77.

Talwar, G. P., Vyas, H. K., Purswani, S., & Gupta, J. C. (2009). Gonadotropin-releasing hormone/human chorionic gonadotropin beta based recombinant antibodies and vaccines. *Journal of Reproductive Immunology, 83*(1–2), 158–163.

Tamiello, M., Castelli, L., Vighetti, S., Perozzo, P., Geminianib, G., & Weiskrantz, http://www.pnas.org/content/early/2009/10/02/0908994106.abstract-aff-6#aff-6 L., et al. (2009). Unseen facial and bodily expressions trigger fast emotional reactions. *Proceedings of the National Academy of Sciences of the United States of America, 106*(42), 17661.

Tan, D. H., Kaul, R., Raboud, J. M., & Walmsley, S. L. (2011). No impact of oral tenofovir disoproxil fumarate on herpes simplex virus shedding in HIV-infected adults. *AIDS, 25*(2), 207–210.

Tang, S., & Gui, G. (In press). A review of the oncologic and survival management of breast cancer in the augmented breast: Diagnostic, surgical, and surveillance challenges. *Annals of Surgical Oncology.*

Tannahill, R. (1980). *Sex in history.* New York: Stein & Day.

Tannen, D. (1990). *You just don't understand: Women and men in conversation.* New York: Ballantine Books.

Tannen, D., Kendall, S., & Gordon, C. (2007). *Family talk: Discourse and identity in four American families.* New York: Oxford University Press.

Tanveer, K. (2002, July 7). In Pakistan, gang rape as a tribal punishment. *The Hartford Courant,* A2.

Tanweer, M., Fatima, A., & Rahimnaijad, M. (2010). Yohimbine can be the new promising therapy for erectile dysfunction in type 2 diabetics. *Journal of the Pakistan Medical Association, 60*(11), 980.

Tao, G. (2008). Sexual orientation and related viral sexually transmitted disease rates among U.S. women aged 15–44 years. *American Journal of Public Health, 98,* 1007–1009.

Tarkovsky, A. (2006). Sperm taste: 10 simple tips for better tasting semen. Ezine articles. Retrieved August 10, 2008, from http://ezinearticles.com/?Sperm-Taste—-10-Simple-Tips-For-Better-Tasting-Semen&id=164106.

Tay, J. I., Moore, J., & Walker, J. J. (2000). Ectopic pregnancy. *British Medical Journal, 320*(7239), 916–920.

Taylor, H. E. (2000). Meeting the needs of lesbian and gay young adults. *The Clearing House, 73*(4), 221.

Taywaditep, K. J., Coleman, E., & Dumronggittigule, P. (2004). Thailand. In R. T. Francoeur & R. J. Noonan (Eds.), *The Continuum complete international encyclopedia of sexuality* (pp. 1021–1053). New York/London: Continuum International.

Teitelman, A. (2004). Adolescent girls' perspectives of family interactions related to menarche and sexual health. *Qualitative Health Research, 14*(9), 1292–1308.

Teles, M., Bianco, S., Brito, V., Trarbach, E., Kuohung, W., Xu, S., Seminara, S., Mendonca, B., Kaiser, U., & Latronico, A. (2008). A GPR54-activating mutation in a patient with central preconscious puberty. *New England Journal of Medicine, 358,* 709–715.

Tenore, J. L. (2000). Ectopic pregnancy. *American Family Physician, 61*(4), 1080–1088.

Tepavcevic, D., Kostic, J., Basuroski, I., Stojsavljevic, N., Pekmezovic, T., & Drulovic, J. (2008). The impact of sexual dysfunction on the quality of life measured by MSQoL-54 in patients with multiple sclerosis. *Multiple Sclerosis,* 14(8), 1131–1136.

Terada, Y., Schatten, G., Hasegawa, H., & Yaegashi, N. (2010). Essential roles of the sperm centrosome in human fertilization: Developing the therapy for fertilization failure due to sperm centrosomal dysfunc-

tion. *Tohoku Journal of Experimental Medicine, 220*(4), 247–258.

Terao, T., & Nakamura, J. (2000). Exhibitionism and low-dose trazodone treatment. *Human Psychopharmacology: Clinical & Experimental, 15*(5), 347–349.

Terry, J. (1990). Lesbians under the medical gaze: Scientists search for remarkable differences. *The Journal of Sex Research, 27,* 317–339.

Teuscher, U., & Teuscher, C. (2006). Reconsidering the double standard of aging: Effects of gender and sexual orientation on facial attractiveness ratings. *Personality and Individual Differences, 42*(4), 631–639.

Tewksbury, R. (2007). Effects of sexual assaults on men: Physical, mental and sexual consequences. *International Journal of Men's Health, 6,* 22–36.

This, P. (2008). Breast cancer and fertility: Critical review, considerations and perspectives. *Bulletin du Cancer, 95,* 17–25.

Thomas, S. L., & Ellertson, C. (2000). Nuisance or natural and healthy: Should monthly menstruation be optional for women? *Lancet, 355,* 922–924.

Thomasset, C. (1992). The nature of woman. In C. Klapisch-Zuber (Ed.), *A history of women in the West, Volume II: Silences of the Middle Ages* (pp. 43–70). Cambridge, U.K.: Belknap Press.

Thompson, A. P. (1984). Emotional and sexual components of extramarital relations. *Journal of Marriage and the Family, 46,* 35–42.

Thompson, K. M. (2009). Sibling incest: A model for group practice with adult female victims of brother-sister incest. *Journal of Family Violence, 24,* 531–537.

Thompson, P. (2008). Desperate housewives? Communication difficulties and the dynamics of marital (un)happiness. *The Economic Journal, 118*(532), 1640–1669.

Thompson, S. J. (2005). Factors associated with trauma symptoms among runaway/homeless adolescents. *Stress, Trauma and Crisis: An International Journal, 8*(2–3), 143–156.

Thomson, R., & Murachver, T. (2001). Predicting gender from electronic discourse. *British Journal of Social Psychology, 40*(2), 193–208.

Thomson, R., Finau, S., Finau, E., Ahokovi, L., & Tameifuna, S. (2007). Circumcision of Pacific boys: Tradition at the cutting edge. *Pacific Health Dialogue, 13,* 115–122.

Thorne, N., & Amrein, H. (2003). Vomeronasal organ: Pheromone recognition with a twist. *Current Biology, 13*(6), R220-R222.

Thornhill, R., & Palmer, C. T. (2000). *A natural history of rape: Biological bases of sexual coercion.* Boston: MIT Press.

Thorp, J. M., Hartmann, K. E., & Shadigian, E. (2003). Long-term physical and psychological health consequences of induced abortion: Review of the evidence. *Obstetrical and Gynecological Survey, 58*(1), 67–79.

Thorup, J., McLachlan, R., Cortes, D., Nation, T. R., Balic, A., Southwell, B. R., & Hutson, J. (2010). What is new in cryptorchidism and hypospadias—a critical review on the testicular dysgenesis hypothesis. *Pediatric Surgery, 45*(10), 2074–2086.

Tiefer, L. (1991). Historical, scientific, clinical and feminist criticisms of "the Human Sexual Response Cycle" model. *Annual Review of Sex Research, 2,* 1–23.

Tiefer, L. (1996). The medicalization of sexuality: Conceptual, normative and professional issues. *Annual Review of Sex Research, 7,* 252–282.

Tiefer, L. (2001). A new view of women's sexual problems: Why new? Why now? *Journal of Sex Research, 38*(2), 89–96.

Tiefer, L. (2002). Beyond the medical model of women's sexual problems: A campaign to resist the promotion of "female sexual dysfunction." *Sexual & Relationship Therapy, 17*(2), 127–135.

Tiefer, L. (2004). *Sex Is Not a Natural Act and Other Essays.* Boulder, CO: Westview Press.

Tiefer, L. (2006). Female sexual dysfunction: A case study of disease mongering and activist resistance. PLoS Medicine, 3(4). Retrieved June 19, 2008, from http://medicine.plosjournals.org/perlserv/?request=get-document&doi=10.1371/journal.pmed.0030178&ct=1.

Timmreck, T. C. (1990). Overcoming the loss of a love: Presenting love addiction and promoting positive emotional health. *Psychological Reports, 66*(2), 515–528.

Timur, S., & Sahin, N. (2010). The prevalence of depression symptoms and influencing factors among perimenopausal and postmenopausal women. *Menopause, 17*(3), 545–551.

Ting-Toomey, S., Gao, G., & Trubisky, P. (1991). Culture, face maintenance, and styles of handling interpersonal conflicts: A study in five cultures. *International Journal of Conflict Management, 2*(4), 275–296.

Tirabassi, R. S., Ace, C. I., Levchenko, T., Torchilin, V. P., Selin, L. K., Nie, S., Guberski, D. L., & Yang, K. (2011). A mucosal vaccination approach for herpes simplex virus type 2. *Vaccine, 29*(5), 1090–1098.

Titshaw, S. (2010). The meaning of marriage: Immigration rules and their implications for same-sex spouses in a world without DOMA. *William & Mary Journal of Women & Law, 16,* 537–611.

Tjaden, P., & Thoennes, N. (1998). *Stalking in America: Findings from the National Violence Against Women Survey.* National Institute of Justice and the Centers for Disease Control and Prevention.

Tjaden, P., & Thoennes, N. (2000). *Extent, nature, and consequences of intimate partner violence: Findings from the National Violence Against Women Survey.* Washington, DC: National Institute of Justice and the Centers for Disease Control and Prevention.

Tjepkema, M. (2008). Health care use among gay, lesbian and bisexual Canadians. *Health Reports, 19,* 53–64.

Tjioe, M., & Vissers, W. (2008). Scabies outbreaks in nursing homes for the elderly: Recognition, treatment options, and control of reinfestation. *Drugs Aging, 25*(4), 299–306.

Tobian, A. A., Gray, R. H., & Quinn, T. C. (2010). Male circumcision for the prevention of acquisition and transmission of sexually transmitted infections: The case for neonatal circumcision. *Archives of Pediatric Adolescent Medicine, 164*(1), 78–84.

Tokushige, N., Markham, R., Crossett, B., Ah, S., Nelaturi, V., Khan, A., & Fraser, I. (2011). Discovery of a novel biomarker in the urine in women with endometriosis. *Fertility and Sterility, 95*(1), 46–49.

Tom, S., Kuh, D., Guralnik, J., & Mishra, G. (2010). Self-reported sleep difficulty during the menopausal transition: Results from a prospective cohort study. *Menopause, 17*(6), 1128–1135.

Tomaso, B. (2008, July 25). After 40 years, birth control decree still divides American Catholics. *Dallas News.* Retrieved October 28, 2008, from http://religionblog.dallasnews.com/archives/2008/07/after-40-years-birth-control-d.html.

Tomassilli, J., Golub, S., Bimbi, D., & Parsons, J. (2009). Behind closed doors: An exploration of kinky sexual behaviors in urban lesbian and bisexual women. *Journal of Sex Research, 46*(5), 438–445.

Tommola, P., Unkila-Kallio, L., & Paavonen, J. (2010). Surgical treatment of vulvar vestibulitis: A review. *Acta Obstetrics and Gynecology Scandinavia, 89*(11), 1385–1395.

Toppari, J., Virtanen, H. E., Main, K. M., & Skakkebaek, N. E. (2010). Cryptorchidism and hypospadias as a sign of testicular dysgenesis syndrome (TDS): Environmental connection. *Birth Defects Research, 88*(10), 910–919.

Toto-Morn, M., & Sprecher, S. (2003). A cross-cultural comparison of mate preferences among university students: The United States vs. the People's Republic of China. *Journal of Comparative Family Studies, 34*(2), 151–170.

Tovar, J., Bazaldua, O., Vargas, L., & Reile, E. (2008). Human papillomavirus, cervical cancer, and the vaccines. *Postgraduate Medicine, 120,* 79–84.

Towne, B., Czerwinski, S. A., Demerath, E. W., Blangero, J., Roche, A. F., & Siervogel, R. M. (2005). Heritability of age at menarche in girls from the Fels Longitudinal Study. *American Journal of Physical Anthropology,* published online ahead of print. Retrieved March 22, 2005, from http://www.ncbi.nlm.nih.gov/entrez/query.fcgi?cmd=Retrieve&db=pubmed&dopt=Abstract&list_uids=15779076.

Trabert, B., Sigurdson, A. J., Sweeney, A. M., Strom, S. S., & McGlynn, K. A. (2011). Marijuana use and testicular germ cell tumors. *Cancer, 117*(4), 848–853.

Tramel, J. (2011, April 5). Cowboy to stand trial for rape charges. *McClatchy-Tribune Business News.* Retrieved April 13, 2011, from http://www.tulsaworld.com/news/article.aspx?no5subj&articleid520110405_93_B5_CUTLIN644366&.

Treas, J., & Giesen, D. (2000). Sexual infidelity among married and cohabiting Americans. *Journal of Marriage and Family, 62*(1), 48–61.

Tremble, B., Schneider, M., & Appathurai, C. (1989). Growing up gay or lesbian in a multicultural context. In G. Herdt (Ed.), *Gay and lesbian youth* (pp. 253–267). New York: Harrington Park Press.

Trends in HIV/AIDS Diagnoses. (2005, November 18). Trends in HIV/AIDS Diagnoses—33 States, 2001–2004. *Morbidity and Mortality Weekly Report, 54,* 1149–1153.

Trenholm, C., Devaney, B., Fortson, K., Quay, L., Wheeler, J., & Clark, M. (2007). Impact of four Title V, Section 510 Abstinence Education Programs. Princeton, NJ: Mathematic Policy Research. Retrieved from http://www.mathematica-mpr.com/publications/PDFs/impactabstinence.pdf.

Trivits, L. C., & Reppucci, N. D. (2002). Application of Megan's Law to juveniles. *American Psychologist, 57*(9), 690–704.

Troiden, R. R. (1989). The formation of homosexual identities. In G. Herdt (Ed.), *Gay and lesbian youth* (pp. 43–73). New York: Harrington Park Press.

Trost, J. E. (2004). Sweden. In R. T. Francoeur & R. J. Noonan (Eds.), *The Continuum International encyclopedia of sexuality* (pp. 984–994). New York/London: Continuum International.

Trotter, E. C., & Alderson, K. G. (2007). University students' definitions of having sex, sexual partner, and virginity loss: The influence of participant gender, sexual experience, and contextual factors. *Canadian Journal of Human Sexuality, 16,* 11–20.

Trudel, G., & Desjardins, G. (1992). Staff reactions toward the sexual behaviors of people living in institutional settings. *Sexuality and Disability, 10,* 173–188.

Trudel, G., Villeneuve, L., Preville, M., Boyer, R., & Frechette, V. (2010). Dyadic adjustment, sexuality and psychological distress in older couples. *Sexual and Relationship Therapy, 25*(3), 306–315.

Trumbach, R. (1990). Is there a modern sexual culture in the West, or, did England never change between 1500 and 1900? *Journal of the History of Sexuality, 1,* 206–309.

Tsai, S., Stafanick, M., & Stafford, R. (2011). Trends in menopausal hormone therapy use of US office-based physicians, 2000–2009. *Menopause, 18*(4), 385–392.

Tsivian, M., Mayes, J. M., Krupski, T. L., Mouraviev, V., Donatucci, C. F., & Polascik, T. J. (2009). Altered male physiologic function after surgery for prostate cancer: Couple perspective. *International Brazilian Journal of Urology, 35*(6), 673–682.

Tsuiji, K., Takeda, T., Li, B., Wakabayashi, A., Kondo, A., Kimura, T., & Yaegashi, N. (2011). Inhibitory effect of curcumin on uterine leiomyoma cell proliferation. *Gynecological Endocrinology, 27*(7), 512–517.

Tsui-Sui, A., Loveland-Cherry, C., & Guthrie, B. (2010). Maternal influences on Asian American-Pacific Islander adolescents' perceived maternal sexual expectations and their sexual initiation. *Journal of Family Issues, 31*(3), 381–406.

Tsunokai, G., Kposowa, A., & Adams, M. (2009). Racial preferences in internet dating: A comparison of four birth cohorts. *Western Journal of Black Studies, 33*(1), 1–16.

Tuller, E. R. (2010, December 26). Personal communication.

Turner, C. F., Ku, L., Rogers, S. M., Lindberg, L., Pleck, J., & Sonenstein, F. (1998). Adolescent sexual behavior, drug use, and violence: Increased reporting with computer survey technology. *Science, 280,* 867–873.

Turner, C. F., Villarroel, M., Chromy, J., Eggleston, E., & Rogers, S. (2005). Same-gender sex among U.S. adults. *Public Opinion Quarterly, 69,* 439–462.

Turner, W. (2000). *A genealogy of queer theory.* Philadelphia: Temple University Press.

Twiss, J., Wegner, J., Hunter, M., Kelsay, M., Rathe-Hart, M., & Salado, W. (2007). Perimenopause symptoms, quality of life, and health behaviors in users and nonusers of hormone therapy. *Journal of the American Academy of Nurse Practioners, 19,* 602–613.

Tye, M. H. (2006). Social inequality and well-being: Race-related stress, gay-related stress, self-esteem, and life satisfaction among African American gay and bisexual men. *Dissertation Abstracts International: Section B, 67*(4-B), 0419–4217.

Tzeng, O. (1992). Cognitive/comparitive judgment paradigm of love. In O. Tzeng (Ed.), *Theories of love development, maintenance, and dissolution: Octagonal cycle and differential perspectives,* pp. 133–149.

Tzortzis, V., Skriapas, K., Hadjigeorgiou, G., Mitsogiannis, I., Aggelakis, K., Gravas, S., et al. (2008). Sexual dysfunction in newly diagnosed multiple sclerosis women. *Multiple Sclerosis, 14,* 561–563.

U.S. Census Bureau. (2007, September 19). *Most people make only one trip down the aisle, but first marriages shorter, census bureau reports.* Retrieved September 20, 2007, from http://www.census.gov/Press-Release/www/releases/archives/marital_status_living_arrangements/010624.html.

U.S. Department of Justice, Bureau of Justice Statistics. (2006). Criminal victimization in the United States, 2005 statistical tables (U.S. Department of Justice Publication NCH 2152244, Table 2, Number of victimizations and victimization rates for persons age 12 and over, by type of crime and gender of victims). Washington, DC: Author.

U.S. Department of Justice, Office of Justice Programs. (2002). Rape and sexual assault: Reporting to police and medical attention, 1992–2000. Retrieved October 22, 2005, from http://www.ojp.usdoj.gov/bjs/pub/pdf/rsarp00.pdf.

U.S. Department of Justice, Office on Violence Against Women. (2008). Anonymous reporting and forensic examinations. Retrieved October 25, 2008, from http://www.ovw.usdoj.gov/docs/faq-arfe052308.pdf.

U.S. Department of State. (2005). Trafficking in persons report. Retrieved December 12, 2005, from http://www.state.gov/documents/organization/47255.pdf.

U.S. Preventive Services Task Force (USPSTF). (2005). Screening for ovarian cancer: Recommendation statement. *American Family Physician, 71*(4), 759–763.

Uecker, J., & Regnerus, M. (2010). BARE MARKET: Campus sex ratios, romantic relationships, and sexual behavior. *Sociological Quarterly, 51*(3), 408–435.

Uji, M., Shono, M., Shikai, N., & Kitamura, T. (2007). Case illustrations of negative sexual experiences among university women in Japan: Victimization disclosure and reactions of the confidant. *International Journal of Offender Therapy and Comparative Criminology, 51,* 227–242.

Ullman, S., Townsend, S., Filipas, H., & Starzynski, L. (2007). Structural models of the relations of assault severity, social support, avoidance coping, self-blame, and PTSD among sexual assault survivors. *Psychology of Women Quarterly, 31,* 23–37.

UNAIDS. (2005). AIDS Epidemic Update: December, 2005. Retrieved November 22, 2005, from http://www.unaids.org/epi2005/doc/report_pdf.html.

UNAIDS. (2008). 2008: Report on the global AIDS epidemic. UNAIDS Joint United Nations Programme on HIV/AIDS. Retrieved November 3, 2008, from http://www.unaids.org/en/KnowledgeCentre/HIVData/GlobalReport/2008/2008_Global_report.asp.

UNAIDS. (2010). Global report on the AIDS epidemic. Joint United Nations Programme on HIV/AIDS. Retrieved April 1, 2011, from http://www.unaids.org/globalreport/documents/20101123_GlobalReport_full_en.pdf.

United National Children's Fund. (2005). *Early marriage: A harmful traditional practice.* Retrieved July 16, 2008, from http://www.unicef.org/publications/files/Early_Marriage_12.lo.pdf.

United Nations Educational, Scientific, and Cultural Organization (UNESCO). (2006). UNESCO guidelines on language and content in HIV- and AIDS-related materials. Paris: Author.

United Nations Educational, Scientific, and Cultural Organization (UNESCO). (2008). Review of sex, relationships, and HIV education in the schools. UNESCO Global Advisory Group. Retrieved January 26, 2011, from http://unesdoc.unesco.org/images/0016/001629/162989e.pdf.

United Nations Educational, Scientific, and Cultural Organization (UNESCO). (2009).

International technical guidance on sexuality education: An evidence-informed approach for schools, teachers, and health educators. Retrieved May 10, 2011, from http://unesdoc.unesco.org/images/0018/001832/183281e.pdf.

Upchurch, D. M., Aneshensel, C. S., Mudgal, J., & McNeely, C. S. (2001). Sociocultural contexts of time to first sex among Hispanic adolescents. *Journal of Marriage and Family, 63*(4), 1158.

Upchurch, D. M., Levy-Storms, L., et al. (1998). Gender and ethnic differences in the timing of first sexual intercourse. *Family Planning Perspectives, 30*(3), 121–128.

Urato, A. C., & Norwitz, E. R. (2011). A guide towards pre-pregnancy management of defective implantation and placentation. *Best Practices and Research in Clinical Obstetrics and Gynecology, 25*(3), 367–387.

Usatine, R. P., & Tinitigan, R. (2010). Nongenital herpes simplex virus. *American Family Physician, 82*(9), 1075–1082.

Ussher, J., & Perz, J. (2008). Empathy, egalitarisnism and emotion work in the relationship negotiation of PMS: The experience of women in lesbian relationships. *Feminism and Psychology, 18*(1), 87–111.

Vajta, G., Rienzi, L., Cobo, A., & Yovich, J. (2010). Embryo culture: Can we perform better than nature? *Reproductive BioMedicine Online, 20*(4), 453–469.

Valdiserri, R. O. (2002). HIV/AIDS stigma: An impediment to public health. *American Journal of Public Health, 92*(3), 341–343.

Valente, S. M. (2005). Sexual abuse of boys. *Journal of Child and Adolescent Psychiatric Nursing, 18*(1), 10–16.

Valenzuela, C. Y. (2008). Prenatal maternal mnemonic effects on the human neuro-psychic sex: A new proposition from fetus-maternal tolerance-rejection. *La Revista Medica de Chile, 136*(12), 1552–1558.

Valenzuela, C. Y. (2010). Sexual orientation, handedness, sex ratio and fetomaternal tolerance-rejection. *Biological Research, 43*(3), 347–356.

van Basten, J. P., Van Driel, M. F., Hoekstra, H. J., Sleijfer, D. T., van de Wiel, H. B., Droste, J. H., et al. (1999). Objective and subjective effect of treatment for testicular cancer on sexual function. *British Journal of Urology, 84*(6), 671–678.

Van Berlo, W., & Ensink, B. (2000). Problems with sexuality after sexual assault. *Annual Review of Sex Research, 11,* 235–257.

Van Damme, L., Ramjee, G., Alary, M., Vuylsteke, B., Chandeying, V., Rees, H., et al. (2002). Effectiveness of COL-1492, a N-9 vaginal gel on HIV-transmission in female sex workers. *Lancet, 360*(9338), 971–977.

Van de Ven, P., Campbell, D., & Kippax, S. (1997). Factors associated with unprotected anal intercourse in gay men's casual partnerships in Sydney, Australia. *AIDS Care, 9*(6), 637–649.

Van den Heuvel, M., van Bragt, A., Alnabawy, A., & Kaptein, M. (2005). Comparison of ethinylestradial pharmacokinetics in three hormonal contraceptive formulation: The vaginal ring, the transdermal patch and an oral contraceptive. *Contraception, 72,* 168–174.

van Lankveld, J. J., Granot, M., Weijmar Schultz, W. C., Binik, Y. M., Wesselmann, U., Pukall, C. F., Bohm-Starke, N., & Achtrari, C. (2010). Women's sexual pain disorders. *Journal of Sexual Medicine, 7*(1 Pt 2), 615–631.

van Lankveld, J., Everaerd, W., & Grotjohann, Y. (2001). Cognitive-behavioral bibliotherapy for sexual dysfunctions in heterosexual couples: A randomized waiting-list controlled clinical trial in the Netherlands. *Journal of Sex Research, 38*(1), 51–67.

van Teijlingen, E., Reid, J., Shucksmith, J., Harris, F., Philip, K., Imamura, M., Tucker, J., & Penney, G. (2007). Embarrassment as a key emotion in young people talking about sexual health. *Sociological Research, 12*(2). Retrieved April 15, 2011, from http://www.socresonline.org.uk/12/2/van_teijlingen.html.

Van Voorhis, B. J. (2006). Outcomes from assisted reproductive technology. *Obstetrics and Gynecology, 107,* 183–200.

Vanderbilt, H. (1992). Incest: A chilling report. *Lears,* (Feb.), 49–77.

VanderLaan, D., & Vasey, P. (2008). Mate retention behavior of men and women in heterosexual and homosexual relationships. *Archives of Sexual Behavior, 37,* 572–586.

Vanfossen, B. (1996). ITROWs women and expression conference. Institute for Teaching and Research on Women, Towson University, Towson, MD. Retrieved April 15, 2003, from http://www.towson.edu/itrow.

Vardi, Y., McMahon, C., Waldinger, M., Rubio-Aurioles, E., & Rabinowitz, D. (2008). Are premature ejaculation symptoms curable? *Journal of Sexual Medicine, 5,* 1546–1551.

Vedantam, S. (2011, March 24). Pedophiles use online social networks to foil investigators. *The Washington Post,* p. A3.

Venâncio, D. P., Tufik, S., Garbuio, S. A., da Nóbrega, A. C., & de Mello, M. T. (2008). Effects of anabolic androgenic steroids on sleep patterns of individuals practicing resistance exercise. Retrieved April 6, 2008, from http://www.ncbi.nlm.nih.gov/pubmed/18043934?ordinalpos=2&itool=EntrezSystem2.PEntrez.Pubmed.Pubmed_ResultsPanel.Pubmed_RVDocSum.

Vendittelli, F., Riviere, O., Crenn-Hebert, C., Rozan, M., Maria, B., & Jacquetin, B. (2008). Is a breech presentation at term more frequent in women with a history of cesarean delivery? *American Journal of Obstetrics and Gynecology, 198,* 521.

Venkat, P., Masch, R., Ng, E., Cremer, M., Richman, S., & Arslan, A. (2008, May 23). Knowledge and beliefs about contraception in urban Latina women. *Journal of Community Health, 33*(5), 357–362.

Venkatesh, K., Biswas, J., & Kumarasamy, N. (2008). Impact of highly active antiretroviral therapy on ophthalmic manifestations in human immunodeficiency virus/acquired immune deficiency syndrome. *Indian Journal of Ophthalmology, 56*(5), 391–393.

Ventura, S. J., Abma, J. C., Mosher, W. D., & Henshaw, S. K. (2007). *Recent trends in teenage pregnancy in the United States, 1990–2002.* Hyattsville, MD: National Center for Health Statistics, Centers for Disease Control. Retrieved May 27, 2008, from http://www.cdc.gov/nchs/products/pubs/pubd/hestats/teenpreg1990–2002/teenpreg1990–2002.htm.

Ventura, S. J., Abma, J. C., Mosher, W. D., & Henshaw, S. K. (2009). Estimated pregnancy rates for the United States, 1990–2005: An update. *National Vital Statistics Reports, 58*(4), 1–14.

Verkasalo, P. K., Thomas, H. V., Appleby, P. N., Davey, G. K., & Key, T. J. (2001). Circulating levels of sex hormones and their relation to risk factors for breast cancer: A crosssectional study in 1092 pre- and postmenopausal women. *Cancer Causes and Control, 12*(1), 47–59.

Versfeld, N. J., & Dreschler, W. A. (2002). The relationship between the intelligibility of time-compressed speech and speech-in-noise in young and elderly listeners. *Journal of the Acoustical Society of America, 111,* 401–408.

Verweij, K., Shekar, S., Zietsch, B., Eaves, L., Bailey, J., Boomsma, D., & Martin, N. (2008). Genetic and environmental influences on individual differences in attitudes toward homosexuality: An Australian twin study. *Behavior Genetics, 38,* 257–265.

Vesperini, H. (2010, October 4). Rwanda working to curb population explosion. *Asia One News.* Retrieved October 5, 2010, from http://www.asiaone.com/News/AsiaOne%2BNews/World/Story/A1Story20101005-240682.html.

Vessey, M., Yeates, D., & Flynn, S. (2010). Factors affecting mortality in a large cohort study with special reference to oral contraceptive use. *Contraception, 82*(3), 221–229.

Vestal, C. (2008, May 16). California gay marriage ruling sparks new debate. *Stateline.* Retrieved from http://www.stateline.org/live/printable/story?contentId=310206.

Vetten, L., Jewkes, R., Sigsworth, R., Christofides, N., Loots, L., & Dunseith, O. (2008). "Tracking justice: The attrition of rape cases through the criminal justice system in Gauteng." Johannesburg, South Africa: Tsh-waranang Legal Advocacy Centre, the South African Medical Research Council and the Centre for the Study of Violence and Reconciliation.

Vidaurri, M., Singh, D., Zambarano, R., & Dabbs, J. (1999). Lesbian erotic role identification: Behavioral, morphological, and hormonal correlates. *Journal of Personality and Social Psychology, 76*(6), 1035–1050.

Vigano, P., Parazzini, F., Somigliana, E., & Vercellini, P. (2004). Endometriosis: Epidemiology and aetiological factors. *Best Practice & Research Clinical Obstetrics & Gynaecology, 18*(2), 177–200.

Vincke, J., & van Heeringen, K. (2002). Confidant support and the mental well-being of lesbian and gay young adults: A longitudinal analysis. *Journal of Community and Applied Social Psychology, 12,* 181–193.

Vissers, W. (2008). Scabies outbreaks in nursing homes for the elderly: Recognition, treatment options and control of reinfestation. *Drugs and Aging, 25,* 299–306.

Voigt, H. (1991). Enriching the sexual experience of couples: The Asian traditions and sexual counseling. *Journal of Sex and Marital Therapy, 17,* 214–219.

Voiland, A. (2008). More problems with plastics: Like BPA, chemical called phthalates raise some concerns. *U.S. News and World Report, 144,* 54.

Voller, E., & Long, P. (2010). Sexual assault and rape perpetration by college men: The role of the big five personality traits. *Journal of Interpersonal Violence, 25*(3), 457–480.

Von Sydow, K. (2000). Sexuality of older women: The effect of menopause, other physical and social and partner-related factors. *Arztl Fortbild Qualitatssich, 94*(3), 223–229.

Vorsanova, S., Iurov, I., Kolotii, A., Beresheva, A., Demidova, I., Kurinnaia, O., Kravets, V., Monakhov, V., Solov'ev, I., & Iurov, I. (2010). Chromosomal mosaicism in spontaneous abortions: Analysis of 650 cases. *Genetika, 46*(10), 1356–1359.

Vrabel, K., Hoffart, A., Ro, O., Martinsen, E., & Rosenvinge, J. (2010). Co-occurrence of avoidant personality disorder and child sexual abuse predicts poor outcome in long-standing eating disorder. *Journal of Abnormal Psychology, 119*(3), 623–629.

Vukovic, L. (1992, November-December). Cold sores and fever blisters. *Natural Health,* 119–120.

Waal, F. B. M. (1995). Bonobo sex and society. *Scientific American,* 82–88. Retrieved July 4, 2003, from http://songweaver.com/info/bonobos.html.

Wacker, J., Parish, S., & Macy, R. (2008). Sexual assault and women with cognitive disabilities: Codifying discrimination in the United States. *Journal of Disability Policy Studies, 19,* 86–95.

Wagner, E. (1991). Campus victims of date rape should consider civil lawsuits as alternatives to criminal charges or colleges' procedures. *The Chronicle of Higher Education,* August 7, B2.

Waite, L., Luo, Y., & Lewin A. (2008). Marital happiness and marital stability: Consequences for psychological well-being. *Social Science Research, 38*(1), 201–212.

Wakelin, A. (2003). Effects of victim gender and sexuality on attributions of blame to rape victims. *Sex Roles, 49*(9–10), 477–487.

Walch, K., Eder, R., Schindler, A., & Feichtinger, W. (2001). The effect of single-dose oxytocin application on time to ejaculation and seminal parameters in men. *Journal of Assisted Reproductive Genetics, 18,* 655–659.

Wald, A., Zeh, J., Selke, S., Warren, T., Ryncarz, A. J., Ashley, R., et al. (2000). Reactivation of genital herpes simplex virus type-2 infection in asymptomatic seropositive persons. *New England Journal of Medicine, 342*(12), 844–850.

Waldinger, M. (2005). Lifelong premature ejaculation: Definition, serotonergic neurotransmission and drug treatment. *World Journal of Urology, 23,* 102–108.

Waldinger, M. D., & Schweitzer, D. H. (2009). Persistent genital arousal disorder in 18 Dutch women: Part II. A syndrome clustered with restless legs and overactive bladder. *Journal of Sexual Medicine, 6*(2), 482–497.

Waldinger, R., & Schulz, M. (2010). What's love got to do with it? Social functioning, perceived health, and daily happiness in married octogenarians. *Psychology and Aging, 25*(2), 422–431.

Walen, S. R., & Roth, D. (1987). A cognitive approach. In J. H. Geer & W. T. O'Donahue (Eds.), *Theories of human sexuality* (pp. 335–360). New York: Plenum Press.

Walker, J., & Milton, J. (2006). Teachers' and parents' roles in the sexuality education of primary school children: A comparison of experiences in Leeds, UK and in Sydney, Australia. *Sex Education, 6*(4), 415–428.

Walker, J., Archer, J., & Davies, M. (2005). Effects of rape on men: A descriptive analysis. *Archives of Sexual Behavior, 34*(1), 69–80.

Walker, K. E. (2002). Exploitation of children and young people through prostitution. *Journal of Child Health Care, 6*(3), 182–188.

Walker-Rodriguez, A., & Hill, R. (2011). Human sex trafficking. *FBI Law Enforcement Bulletin, 80*(3), 1–9.

Wallerstein, E. (1980). *Circumcision: An American health fallacy.* New York: Springer.

Walters, J. (2005, January 2). No sex is safe sex for teens in America. Retrieved October 19, 2005, from http://observer.guardian.co.uk/international/story/0,6903,1382117,00.html.

Wampler, S. M., & Llanes, M. (2010). Common scrotal and testicular problems. *Primary Care, 37*(3), 613–626.

Wang, H., & Amato, P. R. (2000). Predictors of divorce adjustment: Stressors, resources and definitions. *Journal of Marriage and Family, 62*(3), 655–669.

Wang, M., Lv, Z., Shi, J., Hu, Y., & Xu, C. (2009a). Immunocontraceptive potential of the Ig-like domain of Izumo. *Molecular Reproduction and Development, 76*(8), 794–801.

Wang, M., Shi, J. L., Cheng, G. Y., Hu, Y. Q., & Xu, C. (2009b). The antibody against a nuclear autoantigenic sperm protein can result in reproductive failure. *Asian Journal of Andrology, 11*(2), 183–192.

Wang, S. (2007, November 15). Fertility therapies under the microscope. *Wall Street Journal,* p. D1.

Wanja, J. (2010, June 2). Young Kenyan women top contraception users. *Daily Nation.* Retrieved June 3, 2010, from http://www.nation.co.ke/News/Contraception%20high%20among%20women%20in%20mid%2020s/-/1056/930606/-/5an94h/-/.

Ward, D., Carter, T., & Perrin, D. (1994). *Social deviance: Being, behaving, and branding.* Boston: Allyn & Bacon.

Wardle, L. D. (1999). Divorce reform at the turn of the millennium: Certainties and possibilities. *Family Law Quarterly, 33,* 783–900.

Wardle, L. D. (2001). Multiply and replenish: Considering same-sex marriage in light of state interests in marital procreation. *Harvard Journal of Law and Public Policy, 24*(3), 771–815.

Warin, J. (2000). The attainment of self-consistency through gender in young children. *Sex Roles, 41,* 209–232.

Warne, G. L., Grover, S., & Zajac, J. D. (2005). Hormonal therapies for individuals with intersex conditions: Protocol for use. *Treatments in Endocrinology, 4*(1), 19–29.

Warren, J., Harvey, S., & Agnew, C. (In press). One love: Explicit monogamy agreements among heterosexual young adult couples at increased risk of sexually transmitted infections. *Journal of Sex Research,* Retrieved July 3, 2011, from http://www.ncbi.nlm.nih.gov/pubmed/21191869.

Warren, J., Harvey, S., & Henderson, J. (2010). Do depression and low self-esteem follow abortion among adolescents? Evidence from a national study. *Perspectives on Sexual and Reproductive Health, 42*(4), 230–235.

Warren, M. P., Brooks-Gunn, J., Fox, R. P., Holderness, C. C., Hyle, E. P., & Hamilton, W. G. (2002). Osteopenia in exercise-associated amenorrhea using ballet dancers as a model: A longitudinal study. *Journal of Clinical Endocrinology Metabolism, 87*(7), 3162–3168.

Watkins, J. (2003). Insolent and contemptuous carriages. Re-conceptualization of illegitimacy in colonial British America. Retrieved April 10, 2008, from http://etd.fcla.edu/SF/SFE0000137/Thesis.pdf.

Watson, C., & Calabretto, H. (2007). Comprehensive review of conventional and non-conventional methods of management of recurrent vulvovaginal candidiasis. *Australian and New Zealand Journal of Obstetrics and Gynaecology, 47*(4), 262–272.

Watson, W., Miller, R., Wax, J., Hansen, W., Yamamura, Y., & Polzin, W. (2008). Sonographic findings of trisomy 18 in the second trimester of pregnancy. *Journal of Ultrasound in Medicine, 27,* 1033–1038.

Wattleworth, R. (2011). Human papillomavirus infection and the links to penile and cervical cancer. *Journal of the American Os-*

teopathic Association, 111(3 Suppl. 2), S3–S10.

Watts, D. J. (2003). *Six degrees: The science of a connected age.* New York: Norton.

Waxman, H. (2004). Abstinence-only education. Retrieved September 17, 2005, from http://www.democrats.reform.house.gov/investigations.asp?Issue=Abstinence-Only+Education.

Wdowiak, A., Wdowiak, L., & Wiktor, H. (2007). Evaluation of the effect of using mobile phones on male fertility. *Annals of Agricultural and Environmental Medicine, 14,* 169–172.

Weatherall, A. (2002). *Gender, language and discourse.* London: Hove Routledge.

Weaver, K., Campbell, R., Mermelstein, R., & Wakschlag, L. (2008). Pregnancy smoking in context: The influence of multiple levels of stress. *Nicotine and Tobacco Research, 10,* 1065–1073.

Weaver, T. L. (2009). Impact of rape on female sexuality: Review of selected literature. *Clinics in Obstetrics and Gynecology, 52*(4), 702–711.

Weed, S. E. (2008). Marginally successful results of abstinence-only program erased by dangerous errors in curriculum. *American Journal of Health Behavior, 32,* 60–73.

Wei, E.H. (2000). Teenage fatherhood and pregnancy involvement among urban, adolescent males: Risk factors and consequences. *Dissertation Abstracts International: Section B, 61*(1-B), #0419–4217.

Weigel, D. J. (2007). Parental divorce and the types of commitment-related messages people gain from their families of origin. *Journal of Divorce and Remarriage, 47,* 15.

Weijing H., Neil, S., Kulkarni, H., Wright, E., Agan, B., Marconi, V., et al. (2008). Duffy antigen receptor for chemokines mediates trans-infection of HIV-1 from red blood cells to target cells and affects HIV-AIDS susceptibility. *Cell Host and Microbe, 4,* 52–62.

Weinberg, M. S., Williams, C. J., & Pryor, D. W. (1994). *Dual attraction: Understanding bisexuality.* New York: Oxford University Press.

Weinstock, H., Berman, S., & Cates, W. (2004). Sexually transmitted diseases among American youth: Incidence and prevalence estimates, 2000. *Perspectives in Sex and Reproductive Health, 36*(1), 6–10.

Weinstock, H., Berman, S., & Cates, W. (2004, January/February). Sexually transmitted diseases among American youth: Incidence and prevalence estimates, 2000. *Perspectives on Sexual and Reproductive Health, 36*(1), 6–10. Retrieved October 19, 2005, from http://www.guttmacher.org/pubs/journals/3600604.html.

Weisel, J. J., & King, P. E. (2007). Involvement in a conversation and attributions concerning excessive self-disclosure. *Southern Communication Journal, 72,* 345–354.

Weiss, H., Dickson, K., Agot, K., & Hankins, C. (2010). Male circumcision for HIV prevention: Current research and programmatic issues. *AIDS,* (Suppl. 4), S61–S69.

Weitzman, G. D. (1999). What psychology professionals should know about polyamory: The lifestyles and mental health concerns of polyamorous individuals. Paper presented at the 8th Annual Diversity Conference. Retrieved June 11, 2005, from http://www.polyamory.org/~joe/polypaper.htm.

Welch, L. (1992). *Complete book of sexual trivia.* New York: Citadel Press.

Wellings, K., Collumbien, M., Slaymaker, E., Singh, S., Hodges, Z., et al. (2006). Sexual behavior in context: A global perspective. *Lancet, 368,* 1706–1728.

Wellisch, M. (2010). Communicating love or fear: The role of attachment styles in pathways to giftedness. *Roeper Review, 32,* 116–126.

Welty, S. E. (2005). Critical issues with clinical research in children: The example of premature infants. *Toxicology and Applied Pharmacology,* Epub ahead of print. Retrieved July 19, 2005, from http://www.ncbi.nlm.nih.gov/entrez/query.fcgi?cmd=Retrieve&db=pubmed&dopt=Abstract&list_uids=16023161&query_hl=14.

Wespes, E., & Schulman, C. C. (2002). Male andropause: Myth, reality and treatment. *International Journal of Impotence Research, 14*(Suppl. 1), 593–598.

West, L. (1989). Philippine feminist efforts to organize against sexual victimization. *Response to the Victimization of Women and Children, 12,* 11–14.

West, S., D'Aloisio, A., Agans, R., Kalsbeek, W., Borisov, N., & Thorp, J. (2008). Prevalence of low sexual desire and hypoactive sexual desire disorder in a nationally representative sample of U.S. women. *Archives of Internal Medicine, 168,* 1441–1449.

West, S., Hatters-Friedman, S., & Knoll, S. (2010). Lessons to learn: Female educators who sexually abuse their students. *Psychiatric Times, 9–10*(27), 8–9.

Westermarck, E. (1972). *Marriage ceremonies in Morocco.* London, U.K.: Curzon Press.

Whalen, R. E., Geary, D. C., & Johnson, F. (1990). Models of sexuality. In D. P. McWhirter, S. A. Sanders, & J. M. Reinisch (Eds.), *Homosexuality/heterosexuality: Concepts of sexual orientation* (pp. 61–70). New York: Oxford University Press.

Whatley, M. A. (2005). The effect of participant sex, victim dress, and traditional attitudes on causal judgments for marital rape victims. *Journal of Family Violence, 20*(3), 191–200.

Wheeler, J., Newring, K., & Draper, C. (2008). Transvestic fetishism: Psychopathology and theory. In D. Laws & W. O'Donohue (Eds.), *Sexual deviance: Theory, assessment and treatment* (2nd ed., pp. 272–285). New York: Guilford Press.

Whelan, C. I., & Stewart, D. E. (1990). Pseudocyesis: A review and report of six cases. *International Journal of Psychiatry in Medicine, 20,* 97–108.

Whipple, B. (2000). Beyond the G spot. *Scandinavian Journal of Sexology, 3,* 35–42.

Whipple, B., & Brash-McGreer, K. (1997). Management of female sexual dysfunction. In M. L. Sipski & C. Alexander (Eds.), *Maintaining sexuality with disability and chronic illness: A practitioner's guide* (pp. 509–534). Baltimore: Aspen.

Whitam, F. L., Daskalos, C., Sobolewski, C. G., & Padilla, P. (1999). The emergence of lesbian sexuality and identity cross-culturally. *Archives of Sexual Behavior, 27*(1), 31–57.

White, S. D., & DeBlassie, R. R. (1992). Adolescent sexual behavior. *Adolescence, 27,* 183–191.

Whiteman, M. K., Hillis, S. D., Jamieson, D. J., Morrow, B., Podgornik, M. N., Brett, K. M., & Marchbanks, P. A. (2008). Inpatient hysterectomy surveillance in the United States, 2000–2004. *American Journal of Obstetrics and Gynecology, 198*(1), 34.e1–34.e7.

Whiting, B. B., & Whiting, J. W. (1975). *Children of six cultures: A psycho-cultural analysis.* Cambridge, MA: Harvard University Press.

Whiting, B., & Edwards, C. P. (1988). A cross-cultural analysis of sex differences in the behavior of children aged 3 through 11. In G. Handel (Ed.), *Childhood socialization* (pp. 281–297). New York: Aldine De Gruyter.

Whitley, R. J., & Roizman, B. (2001). Herpes simplex virus infections. *Lancet, 357*(9267), 1513–1519.

Whitmore, S. K., Zhang, X., Taylor, A. W., & Blair, J. M. (In press). Estimated number of infants born to HIV-infected women in the United States and five dependent areas, 2006. *Journal of Acquired Immune Deficiency Syndrome.*

Whittaker, P. G., Merkh, R. D., Henry-Moss, D., & Hock-Long, L. (2010). Withdrawal attitudes and experiences: A qualitative perspective among young urban adults. *Perspectives in Sex and Reproductive Health, 42*(2), 102–109.

Whitty, M. T., & Quigley, L (2008). Emotional and sexual infidelity offline and in cyberspace. *Journal of Marital and Family Therapy, 34*(4), 461–468.

Wiederman, M. W. (1999). Volunteer bias in sexuality research using college student participants. *Journal of Sex Research, 36*(1), 59–66.

Wienke, C., & Hill, G. (2008). Does the "marriage benefit" extend to partners in gay and lesbian relationships? Evidence from a random sample of sexually active adults. *Journal of Family Issues, 30*(2), 259–289.

Wiesemann, C., Ude-Koeller, S., Sinnecker, G., & Thyen, U. (2010). Ethical principles and recommendations for the medical management of differences of sex development (DSD)/intersex in children and adolescents. *European Journal of Pediatrics, 169*(6), 671–679.

Wikan, U. (1977). Man becomes woman: Transsexualism in Oman as a key to gender roles. *Man, 12,* 304–391.

Wilcox, A. J., Weinberg, C. R., & Baird, D. D. (1995). Timing of sexual intercourse in relation to ovulation. Effects on the probability of conception, survival of the pregnancy, and sex of the baby. *New England Journal of Medicine, 333*(23), 1517–1521.

Wilcox, W. B., & Nock, S. L. (2006). What's love got to do with it? Equality, equity, commitment and women's marital quality. *Social Forces, 84,* 1321–1346.

Wildemeersch, D., & Andrade, A. (2010). Review of clinical experience with the frameless LNG-IUS for contraception and treatment of heavy menstrual bleeding. *Gynecological Endocrinology, 26*(5), 383–389.

Wilkinson, D., Tholandi, M., Ramjee, G., & Rutherford, G. W. (2002). Nonoxynol-9 spermicide for prevention of vaginally acquired HIV and other sexually transmitted infections: Systematic review and meta-analysis of randomised controlled trials including more than 5000 women. *Lancet Infectious Diseases, 2,* 613–617.

Williams, A. (2010, February 5). The new math on campus. *New York Times.* Retrieved January 26, 2011, from http://www .nytimes.com/2010/02/07/fashion/ 07campus.html.

Williams, J. E., & Best, D. L. (1994). Cross-cultural views of women and men. In W. J. Lonner & R. Malpass (Eds.), *Psychology and culture.* Boston: Allyn & Bacon.

Williams, K., & Umberson, D. (2004). Marital status, marital transitions, and health: A gendered life course perspective. *Journal of Health and Social Behavior, 45,* 81–99.

Williams, W. L. (1986). *The spirit and the flesh: Sexual diversity in American Indian culture.* Boston: Beacon Press.

Williams, W. L. (1990). Book review: P. A. Jackson, Male homosexuality in Thailand: An interpretation of contemporary Thai sources. *Journal of Homosexuality, 19,* 126–138.

Wilson, C. (2005). Recurrent vulvovaginitis candidiasis: An overview of traditional and alternative therapies. *Advanced Nurse Practitioner, 13*(2), 24–29.

Wilson, C. A., & Davies, D. C. (2007). The control of sexual differentiation of the reproductive system and brain. *Reproduction, 133,* 331–359.

Wilson, E., Dalberth, B., & Koo, H. (2010). "We're the heroes!": Fathers' perspectives on their role in protecting their preteen-age children from sexual risk. *Perspectives on Sexual and Reproductive Health, 42*(2), 117–124.

Wilson, G. D. (1987). An ethological approach to sexual deviation. In G. D. Wilson (Ed.), *Variant sexuality: Research and theory* (pp. 84–115). Baltimore: Johns Hopkins University Press.

Wilson, P. (1994). Forming a partnership between parents and sexuality educators. *SIECUS Report, 22,* 1–5.

Wilson, R. F. (2008). Keeping women in business (and the family). (Washington Lee Legal Studies Paper No. 2008–34.) Retrieved December 18, 2008, from http:// ssrn.com/abstract=1115468.

Wilson, S. K., Delk, J. R., 2nd, & Billups, K. L. (2001). Treating symptoms of female sexual arousal disorder with the Eros-Clitoral Therapy Device. *Journal of Gender Specific Medicine, 4*(2), 54–58.

Wimalawansa, S. J. (2008). Nitric oxide: New evidence for novel therapeutic indications. *Expert Opinions in Pharmacotherapy, 9,* 1935–1954.

Wind, R. (2008). Perception that teens frequently substitute oral sex for intercourse a myth. [News release]. New York: Alan Guttmacher Institute. Retrieved September 2, 2008, from http://www.guttmacher. org/media/nr/2008/05/20/index.html.

Wise, L., Palmer, J., Stewart, E., & Rosenberg, L. (2005). Age-specific incidence rates for self-reported uterine leiomyomata in the Black Women's Health Study. *Obstetrics and Gynecology, 105*(3), 563–568.

Wise, L. A., Cramer, D. W., Hornstein, M. D., Ashby, R. K., & Missmer, S. A. (2011). Physical activity and semen quality among men attending an infertility clinic. *Fertility and Sterility 95*(3), 1025–1030.

Wiseman, J. (2000). *Jay Wiseman's Erotic Bondage Handbook.* Oakland, CA: Greenery Press.

Wittchen, H. U., Becker, E., Lieb, R., & Krause, P. (2002). Prevalence, incidence and stability of premenstrual dysphoric disorder in the community. *Psychological Medicine, 32*(1), 119–132.

Wittmann, D., Foley, S., & Balon, R. (2011). A biopsychosocial approach to sexual recovery after prostate cancer surgery: The role of grief and mourning. *Journal of Sex and Marital Therapy, 37*(2), 130–144.

Wojnar, D. (2007). Miscarriage experiences of lesbian couples. *Journal of Midwifery Women's Health, 52,* 479–485.

Wolak, J., Finkelhor, D., & Mitchell, K. J. (2005). Child pornography possessors arrested in Internet-related crimes: Findings from the National Juvenile Online Victimization Study. Retrieved November 7, 2005, from http://www.missingkids.com/ en_US/publications/NC144.pdf.

Wolf, M. (2005, January 3). Married without children: Finding fulfillment with no kids. *Rocky Mountain News.* Retrieved August 6, 2008, from http://www.freerepublic .com/focus/f-news/1312995/posts.

Wolf, N. (1991). *The beauty myth: How images of beauty are used against women.* New York: W. Morris.

Wolfinger, N. H. (2000). Beyond the intergenerational transmission of divorce. *Journal of Family Issues, 21,* 1061–1086.

Wolitski, R. J., Valdiserri, R. O., Denning, P. H., & Levine, W. C. (2001). Are we headed for a resurgence of the HIV epidemic among men who have sex with men? *American Journal of Public Health, 91*(6), 883–888.

Wolitzky-Taylor, K., Resnick, H., McCauley, J., Amstadter, A., et al. (2011). Is reporting of rape on the rise? A comparison of women with reported versus unreported rape experiences in the National Women's Study-Replication. *Journal of Interpersonal Violence, 26*(4), 807–832.

Wolpe, J. (1958). *Psychotherapy by reciprocal inhibition.* Stanford, CA: Stanford University Press.

Wong, E. W., & Cheng, C. Y. (2011). Impacts of environmental toxicants on male reproductive dysfunction. *Trends Pharmacological Science, 32*(5), 290–299.

Woo, J., Fine, P., & Goetzl, L. (2005). Abortion disclosure and the association with domestic violence. *Obstetrics & Gynecology, 105*(6), 1329–1334.

Wood, E., Desmarais, S., & Gugula, S. (2002). The impact of parenting experience on gender stereotyped toy play of children. *Sex Roles, 47*(1–2), 39–49.

Wood, J. (1999). Gendered lives: Communication, gender, and culture. Belmont, CA: Wadsworth.

Wood, P. (2008). What your eyes say about you. *Career World, 36,* 5–8.

Woods, N. F., Most, A., & Dery, G. K. (1982). Prevalence of perimenstrual symptoms. *American Journal of Public Health, 72*(11), 1257–1264.

Woolf, L. M. (2002). Gay and lesbian aging. *SIECUS Report, 30*(2), 16–21.

Wooltorton, E. (2006). Visual loss with erectile dysfunction medications. *Canadian Medical Association Journal, 175,* 355.

Workowski, K., & Berman, S. (2010). Sexually transmitted disease treatment guidelines, 2010. *Morbidity and Mortality Weekly Report, 59*(RR-12), 1–110.

"World Contraceptive Use 2009." (2009). New York: United Nations, Department of Economic and Social Affairs, Population Division. Retrieved from http://www.un.org/esa/population/publications/contraceptive2009/contraceptive2009.htm.

World Health Organization. (2008). *Eliminating female genital mutilation: An interagency statement.* Retrieved March 22, 2008, from http://data.unaids.org/pub/BaseDocument/2008/20080227_interagencystatement_eliminating_fgm_en.pdf.

World Professional Organization for Transgender Health. (2001). "The Harry Benjamin International Gender Dysphoria Association's Standards of Care for Gender Identity Disorders, Sixth Version." Retrieved April 17, 2011, from http://wpath.org/Documents2/socv6.pdf.

Wright, K. (1994). The sniff of legend—human pheromones. Chemical sex attractants? A sixth sense organ in the nose? What are we animals? *Discover, 15*(4), 60.

Wright, L., Mulick, P., & Kincaid, S. (2006). Fear of and discrimination against bisexu-

als, homosexuals, and individuals with AIDS. *Journal of Bisexuality, 6,* 71–84.

Wright, S. (2010). Depathologizing consensual sexual sadism, sexual masochism, transvestic fetishism, and fetishism. *Archives of Sexual Behavior, 39*(6), 1229–1230.

Wright, V. C., Chang, J., Jeng, G., & Macaluso, M. (2008). Assisted reproductive technology surveillance—United States. *Morbidity and Mortality Weekly Report, 57,* 1–23.

Wu, F., Tajar, A., Beynon, J., Pye, S., Phil, M., Silman, A., Finn, J., O'Neill, T., & Bartfai, G. (2010). Identification of late-onset hypogonadism in middle-aged and elderly men. *New England Journal of Medicine, 363,* 123–135.

Wu, M. V., & Shah, N. M. (2011). Control of masculinization of the brain and behavior. *Current Opinions in Neurobiology, 21,* 116–123.

Wu, S. C. (2010). Family planning technical services in China. *Frontiers of Medicine in China. 4*(3), 285–289.

Wuthnow, R. (1998). Islam. In *Encyclopedia of politics and religion* (pp. 383–393). Washington, DC: Congressional Quarterly Books.

Wyatt, G. (1998). *Stolen women: Reclaiming our sexuality, taking back our lives.* New York: Wiley.

Wyatt, K. (2008, May 13). Anonymous rape tests are going nationwide. *ABC News.* Retrieved October 7, 2008, from http://abcnews.go.com/Health/Story?id=4847901&page=1.

Wysoczanski, M., Rachko, M., & Bergmann, S. R. (2008, April 2). Acute myocardial-infarction in a young man using anabolic-steroids. *Angiology 59*(3), 376–378.

Xiaohe, X., & Whyte, M. (1990). Love matches and arranged marriages: A Chinese replication. *Journal of Marriage and the Family, 53*(3), 709–722.

Xu, F., Sternberg, M., Kottiri, B., McQuillan, G., Lee, F., Nahmias, A., Berman, S., & Markowitz, L. E. (2006). Trends in herpes simplex virus type 1 and type 2 seroprevalence in the U.S. *Journal of the American Medical Association, 296,* 964–973.

Yamawaki, N. (2007). Differences between Japanese and American college students in giving advice about help seeking to rape victims. *Journal of Social Psychology, 147,* 511–530.

Yamawaki, N., & Tschanz, B. T. (2005). Rape perception differences between Japanese and American college students: On the mediating influence of gender role traditionality. *Sex Roles, 52*(5–6), 379–392.

Yanagimachi, R. (2011). Problems of sperm fertility: A reproductive biologist's view. *Systems in Biological Reproductive Medicine, 57*(1–2), 102–114.

Yancey, G. (2007). Homogamy over the net: Using Internet advertisements to discover who interracially dates. *Journal of Social and Personal Relationships, 24,* 913–930.

Yang, X., & Reckelhoff, J. (2011). Estrogen, hormonal replacement therapy and cardiovascular disease. *Current Opinions in Nephrology and Hypertension, 20*(2), 133–138.

Yao, M. Z., Mahood, C., & Linz, D. (2010). Sexual priming, gender stereotyping, and likelihood to sexually harass: Examining the cognitive effects of playing a sexually-explicit video game. *Sex Roles, 62*(1), 77–88.

Yassin, A. A., & Saad, F. (2008). Testosterone and sexual dysfunction. *Journal of Andrology, 29*(6), Epub ahead of print. Retrieved October 29, 2008, from http://www.andrologyjournal.org/cgi/content/abstract/29/6/593.

Yates, P., Hucker, S., & Ingston, D. (2008). Sexual sadism: Psychopathology and theory. In D. Laws & W. O'Donohue (Eds.), *Sexual deviance: Theory, assessment and treatment* (2nd ed., pp. 213–230). New York: Guilford Press.

Yee, L. (2010). Aging and sexuality. *Australian Family Physician, 39*(10), 718–721.

Yen, H. (2011, February 3). Census: Number of multiracial Americans tops 5 million. *Houston Chronicle.* Retrieved May 11, 2011, from http://www.chron.com/disp/story.mpl/chronicle/7410810.html.

Yen, J., Chang, S., Ko, C., Yen, C., Chen, C., Yeh, Y., & Chen, C. (2010). The high-sweet-fat food craving among women with PMDD: Emotional response, implicit attitudes and rewards sensitivity. *Psychoneuroendocrinology, 35*(8), 1203–1212.

Yllo, K., & Finkelhor, D. (1985). Marital rape. In A. W. Burgess (Ed.), *Rape and sexual assault* (pp. 146–158). New York: Garland.

Yoder, V. C., Virden, T. B., & Amin, K. (2005). Internet pornography and loneliness: An association? *Sexual Addiction & Compulsivity, 12*(1), 19–44.

Yost, M. R. (2010). Development and validation of the attitudes about sadomasochism scale. *Journal of Sex Research, 47*(1), 79–91.

Young, K. A., Liu, Y., & Wang, Z. (2008, March 2). The neurobiology of social attachment: A comparative approach to behavioral, neuroanatomical, and neurochemical studies. *Comparative Biochemistry and Physiology: Toxicology and Pharmacology.* Retrieved October 3, 2008, from http://www.ncbi.nlm.nih.gov/pubmed/18417423?ordinalpos=1&itool=EntrezSystem2.PEntrez.Pubmed.Pubmed_ResultsPanel.Pubmed_RVDocSum.

Young, K. S., Griffin-Shelley, E., Cooper, A., O'Mara, J., & Buchanan, J. (2000). Online infidelity. In A. Cooper (Ed.), *Cybersex: The dark side of the force* (pp. 59–74). Philadelphia, PA: Brunner Routledge.

Young, L. J., & Wang, Z. (2004). The neurobiology of pair bonding. *Nature, 7,* 1048–1054.

Younger, J., Aron, A., Parke, S., Chatterjee, N., & Mackey, S. (2010). Viewing pictures of a romantic partner reduces experimental pain: Involvement of neural reward systems. *PLoS One, 5*(10), E13309.

Youssry, M., Ozmen, B., Zohni, K., Diedrich, K., & Al-Hasani, S. (2008). Current aspects of blastocyst cryopreservation. *Reproductive Biomedicine Online, 16,* 311–320.

Yun, R. J., & Lachman, M. E. (2006). Perceptions of aging in two cultures: Korean and American views on old age. *Journal of Cross Cultural Gerontology, 21*(1–2), 55–70.

Zacur, H. A., Hedon, B., Mansourt, D., Shangold, G. A., Fisher, A. C., & Creasy, G. W. (2002). Integrated summary of Ortho Evra contraceptive patch adhesion in varied climates and conditions. *Fertility and Sterility, 77* (2 Suppl. 2), 532–535.

Zak, A., Collins, C., & Harper, L. (1998). Self-reported control over decision-making and its relationship to intimate relationships. *Psychological Reports, 82*(2), 560–562.

Zanetti-Dallenbach, R. A., Krause, E. M., Lapaire, O., Gueth, U., Holzgreve, W., Wight, E. (2008). Impact of hormone replacement therapy on the histologic subtype of breast cancer. Epub retrieved on March 18, 2008, from http://www.ncbi.nlm.nih.gov/pubmed/18335229?ordinalpos=1&itool=EntrezSystem2.PEntrez.Pubmed.Pubmed_ResultsPanel.Pubmed_RVDocSum.

Zaslow, J. (2007, August 23). Are we teaching our kids to be fearful of men? *Wall Street Journal.* Retrieved June 10, 2008, from http://online.wsj.com/public/article/SB118782905698506010.html.

Zhang, Y., Huang, Z., Ding, L., Yan, H., Wang, M., & Zhu, S. (2010). Simultaneous determination of yohimbine, sildenafil, vardenafil and tadalafil in dietary supplements using high-performance liquid chromatography-tandem mass spectrometry. *Journal of Separation Science, 33*(14), 2109–2114.

Zhao, Y., Garcia, J., Jarow, J., & Wallach, E. (2004). Successful management of infertility due to retrograde ejaculation using assisted reproductive technologies: A report of two cases. *Archives of Andrology, 50*(6), 391–394.

Zhao, Y., Montoro, R., Igartua, K., & Thombs, B. D. (2010). Suicidal ideation and attempt among adolescents reporting "unsure" sexual identity or heterosexual identity plus same-sex attraction or behavior: Forgotten groups? *Journal of the American Academy of Child and Adolescent Psychiatry, 49*(2), 104–113.

Zieman, M., Guillebaud, J., Weisberg, E., Shangold, G., Fisher, A., & Creasy, G. (2002). Contraceptive efficacy and cycle control with the Ortho Evra transdermal system: The analysis of pooled data. *Fertility and Sterility, 77,* S13–18.

Zimmer-Gembeck, M. J., & Helfand, M. (2008). Ten years of longitudinal research on U.S. adolescent sexual behavior: Developmental correlates of sexual intercourse, and the importance of age, gender and ethnic background. *Developmental Review, 28,* 153–224.

Zimmerman, F., Christakis, D., & Meltzoff, A. (2007). Television and DVD/video viewing in children younger than 2 years. *Archives of Pediatrics and Adolescent Medicine, 161,* 473–479.

Zinaman, M. J., Clegg, E. D., Brown, C. C., O'Connor, J., & Selevan, S. G. (1996). Estimates of human fertility and pregnancy loss. *Journal of Fertility and Sterility, 65*(3), 503–509.

Zolese, G., & Blacker, C. V. R. (1992). The psychological complications of therapeutic abortion. *British Journal of Psychiatry, 160,* 742–749.

Zucker, K. J. (1990). Psychosocial and erotic development in cross-gender identified children. *Canadian Journal of Psychiatry, 35,* 487–495.

Zukov, I., Ptacek, R., Raboch, J., Domluvilova, D., Kuzelova, H., Fischer, S., & Kozelek, P. (2010). PMDD—Review of actual findings about mental disorders related to menstrual cycle and possibilities of their therapy. *Prague Medical Reports, 111*(1), 12–24.

Zurbriggen, E. L., & Yost, M. R. (2004). Power, desire, and pleasure in sexual fantasies. *Journal of Sex Research, 41*(3), 288–300.

Zverina, J. (2004). Czech Republic. In R. T. Francoeur & R. J. Noonan (Eds.), *The Continuum International encyclopedia of sexuality* (pp. 320–328). New York/London: Continuum International.

subject INDEX